Recommended by Teachers
Trusted by Toppers

AF814435

All in One®

Social Science

CBSE Class 10

Focused Theory | Practice Exercises | Sample Papers & Boards Papers

Authors
Kriti Arora
Susmita Dhar

arihant
SUCCESS AND NOTHING LESS

arihant
SUCCESS AND NOTHING LESS

ARIHANT PRAKASHAN

(School Division Series)

卐 ADMINISTRATIVE & PRODUCTION OFFICES

Regd. Office

'Ramchhaya' 4577/15, Agarwal Road, Darya Ganj, New Delhi -110002
Tele: 011- 47630600, 43518550; Fax: 011- 23280316

卐 *Head Office*

Kalindi, TP Nagar, Meerut (UP) - 250002, Tel: 0121-7156203, 7156204

卐 SALES & SUPPORT OFFICES

Agra, Ahmedabad, Bengaluru, Bareilly, Chennai, Delhi, Guwahati, Hyderabad, Jaipur, Jhansi, Kolkata, Lucknow, Nagpur & Pune.

PO No : TXT-XX-XXXXXXX-X-XX

Published By Arihant Publications (India) Ltd.

For further information about the books published by Arihant, log on to www.arihantbooks.com or e-mail at info@arihantbooks.com

Follow us on

卐 PRICE ₹ 550.00

PRODUCTION TEAM

Publishing Managers Mahendra Singh Rawat & Keshav Mohan	*Cover Designer* Salman Shaikh	*Inner Designer* Ankit Tyagi
Project Head Shivam Gupta	*Page Layouting* Sundar Bisht	*Proof Reader* Sundip

Index *cum* Study Planner

**This chapter is to be done as project work.*

One Book- Endless Features

to Help you Succeed

Chapter Intro

A quick information about the coverage of the chapter to explain students about what they are going to study.

The Rise of Nationalism in Europe

CHAPTER 1

During the 19th century, nationalism emerged as a force which brought about changes like the emergence of the nation-states in place of the different dynastic empires of Europe.

In 1848, **Frederic Sorrieu**, a French artist, visualised world made up of democratic and social republics.

1.1 The French Revolution and the Idea of Nation

The first idea of nationalism came with the French Revolution in 1789. French Revolution led to the transfer of sovereignty from the monarchy to a body of French citizens.

The various measures and practices introduced by the French revolutionaries to create a sense of collective identity amongst the French people were as follows

- New ideas like ***la patrie*** (the fatherland) and ***le citoyen*** (the citizen) promoted the idea of a united community with equal rights under a Constitution.
- Adoption of **A new French flag** replacing the former **royal.**

Complete Theory in Each Chapter

Each chapter has Complete, Easy to Understand and Simplified theory covering latest syllabus and rationalized NCERT Textbook. Theory is developed in such a way that it perfectly rectifies the complexity of NCERT Text making it suitable for all types of learners.

Try These

1. By what name is the Civil Code of 1804 of France more commonly known?
2. Which among the social and political class, was dominant in Europe in the mid 18th century?
3. The independence of which country was recognised by the Treaty of Constantinople of 1832?
4. Who was the King of Prussia?
5. In which year, the first upheaval took place in France?

Try These

To explain the application of concept Solved Examples have been given in between the theory. These examples have been solved in Step-by-Step manner, so that students can learn the problem solving process completely.

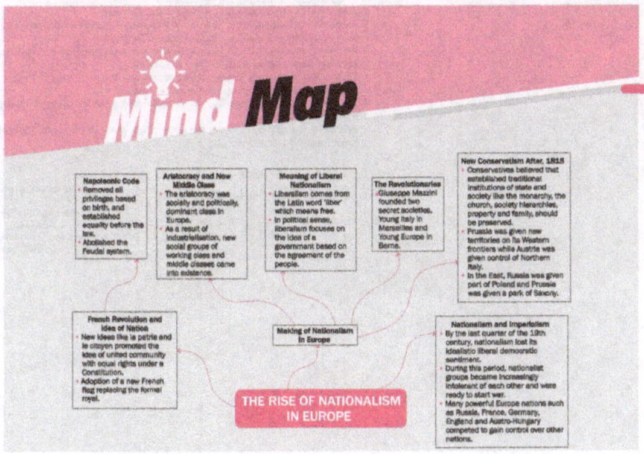

Mind Map

A quick revision visual tool for the complete chapter.

One Book- Endless Features

to Help you Succeed

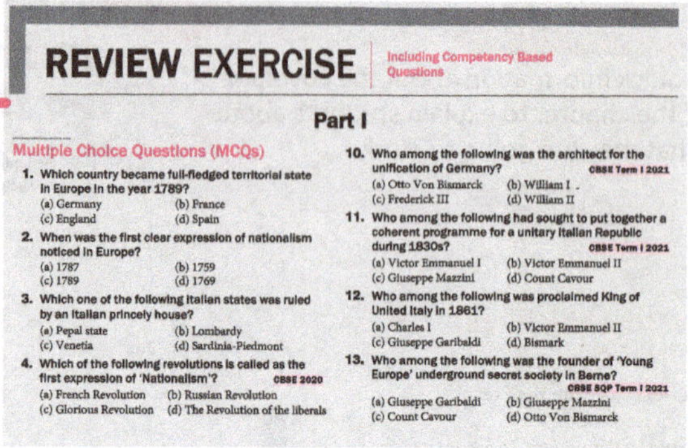

REVIEW EXERCISE

Including Competency Based Questions

Part I

Multiple Choice Questions (MCQs)

1. Which country became full-fledged territorial state in Europe in the year 1789?
(a) Germany (b) France
(c) England (d) Spain
2. When was the first clear expression of nationalism noticed in Europe?
(a) 1787 (b) 1759
(c) 1789 (d) 1769
3. Which one of the following Italian states was ruled by an Italian princely house?
(a) Papal state (b) Lombardy
(c) Venetia (d) Sardinia-Piedmont
4. Which of the following revolutions is called as the first expression of 'Nationalism'? CBSE 2020
(a) French Revolution (b) Russian Revolution
(c) Glorious Revolution (d) The Revolution of the liberals
10. Who among the following was the architect for the unification of Germany? CBSE Term I 2021
(a) Otto Von Bismarck (b) William I
(c) Frederick III (d) William II
11. Who among the following had sought to put together a coherent programme for a unitary Italian Republic during 1830s? CBSE Term I 2021
(a) Victor Emmanuel I (b) Victor Emmanuel II
(c) Giuseppe Mazzini (d) Count Cavour
12. Who among the following was proclaimed King of United Italy in 1861?
(a) Charles I (b) Victor Emmanuel II
(c) Giuseppe Garibaldi (d) Bismark
13. Who among the following was the founder of 'Young Europe' underground secret society in Berne? CBSE SQP Term I 2021
(a) Giuseppe Garibaldi (b) Giuseppe Mazzini
(c) Count Cavour (d) Otto Von Bismarck

Review Exercise

Chapter exercise having all types of questions; MCQs, Assertion-Reason, Matching, Case based, VSA, SA & LA.

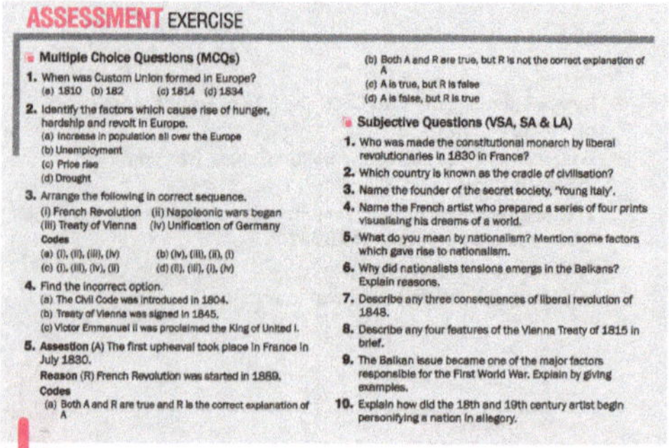

ASSESSMENT EXERCISE

Multiple Choice Questions (MCQs)

1. When was Custom Union formed in Europe?
(a) 1810 (b) 182 (c) 1814 (d) 1834
2. Identify the factors which cause rise of hunger, hardship and revolt in Europe.
(a) Increase in population all over the Europe
(b) Unemployment
(c) Price rise
(d) Drought
3. Arrange the following in correct sequence.
(i) French Revolution (ii) Napoleonic wars began
(iii) Treaty of Vienna (iv) Unification of Germany
Codes
(a) (i), (ii), (iii), (iv) (b) (iv), (iii), (ii), (i)
(c) (i), (iii), (iv), (ii) (d) (ii), (iii), (i), (iv)
4. Find the incorrect option.
(a) The Civil Code was introduced in 1804.
(b) Treaty of Vienna was signed in 1845.
(c) Victor Emmanuel II was proclaimed the King of United I.
5. Assertion (A) The first upheaval took place in France in July 1830.
Reason (R) French Revolution was started in 1889.
Codes
(a) Both A and R are true and R is the correct explanation of A
(b) Both A and R are true, but R is not the correct explanation of A
(c) A is true, but R is false
(d) A is false, but R is true

Subjective Questions (VSA, SA & LA)

1. Who was made the constitutional monarch by liberal revolutionaries in 1830 in France?
2. Which country is known as the cradle of civilisation?
3. Name the founder of the secret society, 'Young Italy'.
4. Name the French artist who prepared a series of four prints visualising his dreams of a world.
5. What do you mean by nationalism? Mention some factors which gave rise to nationalism.
6. Why did nationalists tensions emerge in the Balkans? Explain reasons.
7. Describe any three consequences of liberal revolution of 1848.
8. Describe any four features of the Vienna Treaty of 1815 in brief.
9. The Balkan issue became one of the major factors responsible for the First World War. Explain by giving examples.
10. Explain how did the 18th and 19th century artist begin personifying a nation in allegory.

Assessment Exercise

Complete Test of chapter in Exam format.

Sample Question Papers

To make students practice of examination in real sense, there are 3 Sample Question Papers at the end. All these Sample Questions Papers are exactly prepared on the latest syllabus & pattern of examination.

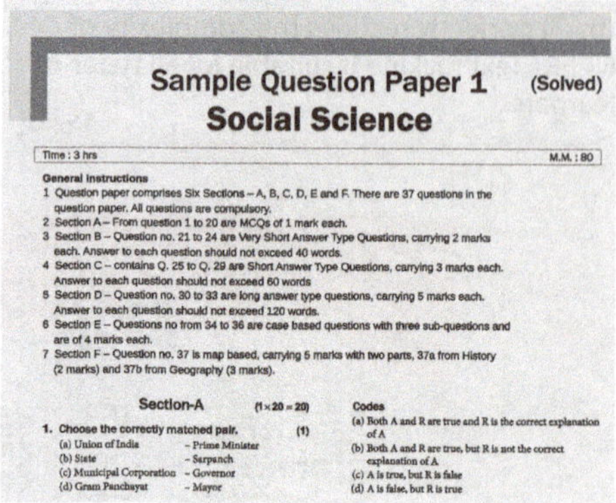

Sample Question Paper 1 (Solved)

Social Science

Time : 3 hrs M.M. : 80

General Instructions

1. Question paper comprises Six Sections – A, B, C, D, E and F. There are 37 questions in the question paper. All questions are compulsory.
2. Section A – From question 1 to 20 are MCQs of 1 mark each.
3. Section B – Question no. 21 to 24 are Very Short Answer Type Questions, carrying 2 marks each. Answer to each question should not exceed 40 words.
4. Section C – contains Q. 25 to Q. 29 are Short Answer Type Questions, carrying 3 marks each. Answer to each question should not exceed 60 words.
5. Section D – Question no. 30 to 33 are long answer type questions, carrying 5 marks each. Answer to each question should not exceed 120 words.
6. Section E – Questions no from 34 to 36 are case based questions with three sub-questions and are of 4 marks each.
7. Section F – Question no. 37 is map based, carrying 5 marks with two parts, 37a from History (2 marks) and 37b from Geography (3 marks).

Section-A (1×20 = 20)

1. Choose the correctly matched pair. (1)
(a) Union of India – Prime Minister
(b) State – Sarpanch
(c) Municipal Corporation – Governor
(d) Gram Panchayat – Mayor

Codes
(a) Both A and R are true and R is the correct explanation of A
(b) Both A and R are true, but R is not the correct explanation of A
(c) A is true, but R is false
(d) A is false, but R is true

Latest Course Structure

History (India and Contemporary World-II)			Suggestive no. of periods = 60	20 inclusive of map pointing
Section	**Chapter No.**	**Chapter Name**	**No. of Periods**	**Marks Allocated**
I Events and Processes	I	The Rise of Nationalism in Europe	17	18 + 2 map pointing*
	II	Nationalism in India	17	
II Livelihoods, Economies and Societies	III	The Making of a Global World (To be evaluated in the Board Examination • Subtopics : 1 to 1.3 Pre Modern World to Conquest, Disease and Trade)	6	
		Interdisciplinary project as part of multiple assessments (Internally assessed for 5 Marks Subtopics: 2 to 4.4 The 19th century (1815-1914) to End of Bretton Woods and the Beginning of "Globalisation.")	4	–
	IV	The Age of Industrialisation (To be assessed as part of Periodic Assessment only)	6	
III Everyday Life, Culture and Politics	V	Print Culture and the Modern World	10	*Marks as mentioned above

Geography (Contemporary India-II)		Suggestive no. of periods = 55	20 inclusive of map poining
Chapter No.	**Chapter Name**	**No. of Periods**	**Marks Allocated**
1	Resources and Development	7	17 + 3 map pointing
2	Forest and Wildlife Resources	7	
3	Water Resources	7	
4	Agriculture	10	
5	Minerals and Energy Resources	10	
6	Manufacturing Industries	10	
7	Lifelines of National Economy Only map pointing to be evaluated in the Board Examination	2	
	Interdisciplinary project as part of multiple assessments (Internally assessed for 5 Marks)	2	–

Political Science (Democratic Politics-II)			Suggestive no. of periods = 50	20
Unit No.	**Chapter No.**	**Chapter Name**	**No. of Periods**	**Marks Allocated**
I	1	Power Sharing	15	20
	2	Federalism	–	
II	3	Gender, Religion and Caste	12	
III	4	Political Parties	12	
IV	5	Outcomes of Democracy	11	

Understanding Economic Development (Economics)		Suggestive no. of periods = 50	20
Chapter No.	**Chapter Name**	**No. of Periods**	**Marks Allocated**
1	Development	12	20
2	Sectors of the Indian Economy	12	
3	Money and Credit	12	
4	Globalisation and the Indian Economy To be evaluated in the Board Examination • What is Globalisation? • Factors that have enabled Globalisation	8	
	Interdisciplinary project as part of multiple assessments (Internally assessed for 5 Marks) • Production across the countries • Chinese toys in India • World Trade Organisation • The Struggle for a Fair Globalisation	6	-
5	Consumer Rights (Project Work)		

List of Map Items

Subject	Name of the Chapter	List of areas to be Pointed on the Map
History	Nationalism in India	I. **Congress Sessions:** • 1920 Calcutta • 1920 Nagpur • 1927 Madras Session II. **3 Satyagraha Movements:** • Kheda • Champaran • Ahmedabad mill workers III. Jallianwala Bagh IV. Dandi March
Geography	Resources and Development	Identify : Major Soil Types
	Water Resources	**Locating and Lebelling:** • Salal • Bhakra Nangal • Tehri • Rana Pratap Sagar • Sardar Sarovar • Hirakud • Nagarjuna Sagar • Tungabhadra
	Agriculture	Identify: • Major areas of Rice and Wheat • Largest/ Major producer states of Sugarcane, Tea, Coffee, Rubber, Cotton and Jute
	Minerals and Energy Resources	Identify: a. Iron Ore mines • Mayurbhanj • Durg • Bailadila • Bellary • Kudremukh b. Coal Mines • Raniganj • Bokaro • Talcher • Neyveli c. Oil Fields • Digboi • Naharkatia • Mumbai High • Bassien • Kalol • Ankaleshwar
		Locate & Label : Power Plants a. Thermal • Namrup • Singrauli • Ramagundam b. Nuclear • Narora • Kakrapara • Tarapur • Kalpakkam

Subject	Name of the Chapter	List of areas to be pointed on the Map
	Manufacturing Industries	**I. Manufacturing Industries (Locating and Labelling Only)** • Cotton Textile Industries: a. Mumbai b. Indore c. Surat d. Kanpur e. Coimbatore • Iron and Steel Plants: a. Durgapur b. Bokaro c. Jamshedpur d. Bhilai e. Vijayanagara f. Salem • Software Technology Parks: a. Noida b. Gandhinagar c. Mumbai d. Pune e. Hyderabad, f. Bengaluru g. Chennai h. Thiruvananthapuram
	Lifelines of National Economy	**Locating and Labelling:** **a. Major Sea Ports** • Kandla • Mumbai • Marmagao • New Mangalore • Kochi • Tuticorin • Chennai • Visakhapatnam • Paradip • Haldia **b. International Airports** • Amritsar (Raja Sansi - Sri Guru Ram Dass jee) • Delhi (Indira Gandhi) • Mumbai (Chhatrapati Shivaji) • Chennai (Meenam Bakkam) • Kolkata (Netaji Subhash Chandra Bose) • Hyderabad (Rajiv Gandhi)

Note : Items of Locating and Labelling may also be given for Identification.

The Rise of Nationalism in Europe

CHAPTER 1

During the 19th century, nationalism emerged as a force which brought about changes like the emergence of the nation-states in place of the different dynastic empires of Europe. In 1848, **Frederic Sorrieu**, a French artist, visualised world made up of democratic and social republics.

1.1 The French Revolution and the Idea of Nation

The first idea of nationalism came with the French Revolution in 1789. French Revolution led to the transfer of sovereignty from the monarchy to a body of French citizens.

The various measures and practices introduced by the French revolutionaries to create a sense of collective identity amongst the French people were as follows

- New ideas like ***la patrie*** (the fatherland) and ***le citoyen*** (the citizen) promoted the idea of a united community with equal rights under a Constitution.
- Adoption of **a new French flag** replacing the former **royal standard.**
- Establishment of a centralised administrative system with uniform laws for all citizens.
- New hymns were composed and oaths were taken. Martyrs were remembered in the name of the nation.
- Internal custom duties and dues were abolished.
- **Estates General** was elected by the body of citizens and renamed the **National Assembly.**
- Regional dialects were discouraged. French language for speaking and writing was accepted as a common language of the country.
- Uniform system of weights and measures were adopted.
- As news of the French Revolution spread across Europe, educated middle-class citizens in many cities formed Jacobin clubs. Their campaigns opened the way for French armies to enter Holland, Belgium, Switzerland, and Italy during the 1790s. French armies carried the idea of nationalism throughout Europe.

Napoleonic Code

In 1804, Napoleon introduced the Civil Code in France which came to be known as the Napoleonic Code.

The main features of this Code were

- It removed all privileges based on birth, established equality before the law and secured the right to property.
- It simplified administrative divisions in Dutch Republic, Switzerland, Italy and Germany.
- It abolished the **Feudal system**[1] and freed peasants from **serfdom**[2] and **manorial dues**[3].
- It removed **Guild**[4] restrictions in the town areas, and improved the transport and communication systems.
- It established uniform laws, standardised weights and measures, and common national currency which facilitate the movement and exchange of goods from one region to another.

In the regions that Napoleon conquered, local citizens had mixed reactions to French rule. At first, they welcomed French armies in many places like Holland, Switzerland, and cities like Brussels, Mainz, Milan and Warsaw, seeing them as liberators.

However, this changed to anger when it became clear that the new administrative systems didn't guarantee political freedom.

1 **Feudal System** It is a system in which the people were given land and protection by the people of higher rank, and in return they had to work for them.
2 **Serfdom** It was the system under which peasants were forced to live and work under feudal lords.
3 **Manorial Dues** These refer to the fees that peasants or serfs of farmer owe to the nobles, who were their landlord.
4 **Guild System** It was an association of artisans/merchants, who oversee the practice of their craft/trade in a particular area.

The negative effects of higher taxes, censorship and compulsory military service in the French armies, seemed greater than the benefits of administrative changes.

1.2 The Making of Nationalism in Europe

In mid 18th century, there were no nation-states[5] in Europe. **Germany**, **Italy** and **Switzerland** were divided into kingdoms, duchies and cantons, whose rulers had their autonomous territories. They did not share a collective identity or a common culture. More often, they had different dialects or belonged to different ethnic community.

The **Habsburg Empire** that ruled over Austria-Hungary was a combination of many different regions and people. It included

- The Alpine regions (Tyrol, Austria (and) Sudetenland and Bohemia) where the aristocracy spoke German.
- Italian speaking provinces of Lombardy and Venetia.
- Hungary in which half of the population spoke Magyar.
- Galicia, where the aristocracy spoke Polish.
- Ordinary people like Bohemians and Slovaks in the North, Slovenes in Carniola, Croats in the South, and Roumans in Transylvania spoke a variety of language.

These differences made it hard for them to feel united politically. The only thing connecting these groups was their loyalty to the emperor.

The Aristocracy and the New Middle Class

The aristocracy was socially and politically, dominant class in Europe. The people in this group shared a similar way of living and ignored regional differences. They owned estates and property both in countryside and town houses. The powerful aristocracy in Europe primarily spoke French for diplomatic and high-society interactions.

Their families were often connected by ties of marriage. However, this influential aristocratic group constituted a small numerical portion of the population. The peasantry formed the majority of the population.

In Western and parts of Central Europe, the growth of industrial production and trade meant the growth of towns and the emergence of commercial classes, whose existence was based on production for the market.

As a result of industrialisation, the new social groups of working class population and middle classes including industrialists, businessmen and professionals came into existence. Industrialisation started in England in the mid 18th century but it reached France and Germany during 19th century.

After aristocratic privileges were removed, ideas of national unity gained popularity among the educated and liberal middle classes .

KNOWLEDGE PLUS According to **Ernest Renan**, "A nation is the culmination of a long past of endeavours, sacrifice and devotion." A nation is large scale solidarity, its existence is a daily Plebiscite.'

Meaning of Liberal Nationalism

Ideas of national unity in the early 19th century Europe were closely related to the ideology[6] of **liberalism.** The word 'liberalism' comes from the Latin word *liber*, which means free.

For the new middle classes, liberalism meant freedom for individual and equality of all before the law.

In **political sense**, liberalism focuses on the idea of a government based on the agreement of the people.

Liberalism had supported the idea of ending autocracy and clerical privileges, a constitution and a government with representatives chosen by the people in parliament. They also emphasised the importance of protecting private property.

However, political liberty did not ensure **universal suffrage** (equal voting rights). Only men who owned property had the right to vote and to get elected. Men without property and all women couldn't participate in politics.

During 19th century, women and non-propertied men organised opposition movements, demanding equal political rights.

In the **economic sphere**, liberalism meant freedom of markets and the abolition of restrictions imposed by the state on the movement of goods and capital.

Taxes were frequently based on the weight or measurement of goods, and since each region had its own system, it involved time-consuming calculations. The new commercial classes considered these changes as limitations to economic exchange and growth.

In 1834, a **Customs Union** or *Zollverein* was formed which abolished tariff barriers and reduced the number of currencies from over thirty to two. This custom union was formed at the initiative of Prussia and later joined by Germany.

5 Nation State It is a state in which the great majority shares the same culture.
6 Ideology It is a system of ideas reflecting a particular social and political vision.

A New Conservatism After, 1815

After the defeat of Napoleon in 1815, European governments were inspired by a spirit of conservatism[7]. Conservatives believed that established traditional institutions of state and society like the monarchy, the church, social hierarchies, property and the family, should be preserved.

Most conservatives did not want to return to the society before the revolution. Instead, they realised that the changes Napoleon made could modernise and strengthen traditional institutions like the monarchy. A modern army, a well-functioning government, a strong economy, and abolition of feudalism and serfdom could strengthen the autocratic monarchies in Europe.

In 1815, the representatives of the European powers like Britain, Russia, Prussia and Austria, who had collectively defeated Napoleon, met at Vienna to draw up a settlement for Europe.

The Congress was hosted by the Austrian Chancellor Duke Metternich. They drew up the **Treaty of Vienna** of 1815 with the goal to reverse many of the changes that happened in Europe during the Napoleonic Wars.

Major Points of the Treaty of Vienna

- The **Bourbon dynasty**, which had been deposed during the French Revolution, was restored to power.
- France lost the territories which it had annexed under Napoleon.
- A series of states were set up on the boundaries of France to prevent its expansion in future.
- The Kingdom of the Netherlands, which included Belgium was set up in the North and Genoa was added to Piedmont in the South.
- Prussia was given new territories on its Western frontiers, while Austria was given control of Northern Italy.
- German confederation of **39 states** that had been set up by Napoleon was not affected by the treaty.
- In the East, Russia was given part of Poland and Prussia was given a part of Saxony.

The main intention was to restore traditional monarchies that had been overthrown by Napoleon and create a new conservative order in Europe.

Characteristics of New Conservative Regimes

They were autocratic. They didn't accept criticism and tried to suppress activities challenging their authority. Censorship laws were enforced to control liberal expressions in various forms like newspapers, books and songs.

The Revolutionaries

After 1815, the fear of being suppressed led many liberal-nationalists to go underground. They created secret groups across Europe to train and share ideas among revolutionaries.

The liberal-nationalists opposed monarchial forms that had been established after the Vienna Congress and fight for liberty and freedom.

Many of these revolutionaries believed that creation of nation-states was a necessary part of this struggle for freedom.

Giuseppe Mazzini

Giuseppe Mazzini, born in 1805, was an influential Italian revolutionary and founder of secret societies like young Italy and young Europe. Exiled in 1831 for his revolutionary efforts, he sought to unify Italy into a republic. Mazzini's vision of democratic republics, opposition to monarchy, and belief in national unity posed a significant threat to conservatives across Europe.

1.3 The Age of Revolutions : 1830-1848

Liberalism and nationalism were associated with the revolution in many regions of Europe such as the Italian and German states, the provinces of Ottoman Empire[8], Ireland and Poland. These revolutions were led by liberal-nationalists belonging to educated middle class.

These revolutions in different places were as follows

- The first upheaval or disruption took place in France in July, 1830. The Bourbon kings were overthrown by liberal revolutionaries, who installed **Louis Philippe** as the constitutional monarch.
- The **July Revolution** started an uprising in Brussels, which led to Belgium separating away from the United Kingdom of the Netherlands.

---

7 Conservatism It refers to a political philosophy that stressed the importance of tradition, established institutions, customs and preferred gradual development to quick change.

8 Ottoman Empire It refers to the Turkish empire ruled by the Caliph, the spiritual and temporal head of the Muslims.

- In the early 1800s, Greeks fought for independence from the Ottoman Empire. Many people supported the Greek cause and in 1832, Greece was officially recognised as an independent nation through the **Treaty of Constantinople.**

The Romantic Imagination and National Feeling

Culture played an important role in creating the idea of the nation. Art and poetry, stories and music helped to express and shape the nationalist feelings.

Romanticism was a cultural movement that aimed to develop a specific type of nationalist feeling. Romantic artists and poets criticised the glorification of reason and science. They focussed on emotions, instincts and mystical feelings, and tried to create a sense of a shared collective heritage as a basis of a nation.

Romanticist German philosopher **Johann Gottfried Herder** (1744-1803), claimed that true German culture was to be discovered among the common people or ***das volk.***

Through collection of folklore like folk songs, folk poetry and folk dances, the spirit of the nation was popularised.

Focusing on local languages and gathering traditional stories was a way to share modern nationalist ideas with people who couldn't read, especially in Poland. Poland had been divided by powerful countries like Russia, Prussia, and Austria in the late 1700s.

Poland supported nationalist feeling through music and language. **Karol Kurpinski** celebrated the national struggle through his operas and music and transformed folk dances like the Polonaise and Mazurka into symbols of nationalism.

Language also played an important role in developing national sentiments. After Russian occupation on Poland, Polish language was forced out of schools and Russian language was imposed in place of it.

In 1831, there was a rebellion against Russian control, but it was suppressed. The clergies in Poland used Polish language for religious instruction and used it as a weapon against the Russian dominance.

Hunger, Hardship and Popular Revolt

The 1830s were the years of great economic hardship in Europe as

- The first half of the 19th century saw an enormous increase in population all over the Europe. Population from rural areas migrated to the cities to live in overcrowded slums.
- Small producers in town faced tough competition from imports of cheap machine-made goods from England due to their advanced industrialisation. This was especially in textile production, which mostly took place in homes or small workshops and was only partly automated.
- Peasants struggled under the burden of feudal dues and obligations. The rise of food prices or a year of bad harvest led to widespread poverty in the country.
- The condition of the workers in town was extreme. In 1845, weavers of Silesia village led a revolt against contractors. It was because the contractors supplied raw material to weavers and gave them orders for finished textiles but reduced their payments.

  On 4th June, a large crowd of weavers left their homes and marched to their contractor's mansion, demanding higher wages. However, they were treated badly and threatened by the contractor.

In 1848, population of Paris revolted due to food shortage and widespread unemployment. Barricades were erected and **Louis Philippe** was forced to flee.

As a result, a National Assembly proclaimed a republic and granted **suffrage**[9] to adult males above 21. It also guaranteed them the right to work. National workshops were set-up to provide employment.

1848 : The Revolution of the Liberals

In 1848, revolution led by the educated middle class led to the resignation of monarch. A republic was declared, allowing all men to vote.

In other parts of Europe like Germany, Italy, Poland and the Austro-Hungarian Empire, men and women of the liberal middle classes combined their demands for constitutionalism with national unification.

This demand was based on parliamentary principles like Constitution, freedom of press and freedom of association.

In Germany, many political groups decided to vote for an all-German National Assembly.

May Revolution

On 18th May, 1848, the elected representatives assembled in the Church of St Paul and drafted a Constitution for a German nation. According to this Constitution, the nation was to be headed by a monarchy which was under the parliament.

When the deputies offered highest position to **Friedrich Wilhelm IV** (King of Prussia) on these terms, he rejected it and joined other monarchs to oppose the elected assembly.

9 **Suffrage** It refers to the right to vote.

The parliament was dominated by the middle classes, who resisted the demands of workers and artisans due to which it consequently lost the support of its members. In the end, the assembly was forced to dissolve.

In 1848, conservative forces were able to suppress liberal movements, but could not restore the old order.

Monarchs understood that the cycle of revolutions and suppressions could only be stopped by making compromises with the liberal-nationalist revolutionaries. After 1848, the monarchies of Central and Eastern Europe introduced changes that had already taken place in Western Europe before 1815.

The changes were that serfdom and bonded labour were abolished both in the Habsburg dominions and in Russia.

Issue of Political Rights to Women

The issue of extending political rights to women was a dispute within the liberal movement, in which large numbers of women had participated actively over the years.

Women had formed their own political associations, founded newspapers and had taken part in political meetings and demonstrations.

Despite this, women were not allowed to vote during the Assembly election. When the Frankfurt Parliament met at the Church of St Paul, women were admitted only as observers.

Try These

1 **By what name is the Civil Code of 1804 of France more commonly known?**

2 **Which among the social and political class, was dominant in Europe in the mid 18th century?**

3 **The independence of which country was recognised by the Treaty of Constantinople of 1832?**

4 **Who was the King of Prussia during May Revolution?**

5 **In which year, the first upheaval took place in France?**

1.4 The Making of Germany and Italy

Unification of Germany

After 1848, nationalist sentiments were promoted by conservatives often for promoting state power and political domination over Europe. In Germany, nationalist feelings were widespread among middle-class.

In 1848, the middle class tried to unite the different regions of the German **confederation**[10] into a nation-state governed by an elected Parliament.

The attempt to build a nation with liberal ideas faced strong opposition from the monarchy, military, and the powerful landowners (known as Junkers) in Prussia. Prussia took on the leadership of the movement for this national unification.

Prussia's Chief Minister **Otto Von Bismarck**, aimed to achieve the goal of unification with the help of Prussian army and bureaucracy.

The major events that occurred at the time of unificaton of Germany were

- Three wars over seven years with Austria, Denmark and France ended in Prussian victory and completed the process of unification.
- On 18th January, 1871, an Assembly comprising the princes of the German states, representatives of the army and important Prussian ministers including the Chief Minister Otto von Bismarck, declared the new German Empire headed by **Kaiser William I** of Prussia.

The nation building process in Germany highlighted the dominance of the Prussian government. The new state Germany had a strong emphasis on modernising the currency, banking, legal and judicial systems in Germany.

Unification of Italy

During the middle of the 19th century, Italy was divided into seven states, out of which only one state, **Sardinia-Piedmont** was ruled by an **Italian Princely House.**

The North was ruled by Austrian Habsburgs, the centre was ruled by the Pope and the Southern regions were ruled by the Bourban king of Spain.

Major Events that Led to the Unification of Italy

- In 1860, the army (regular troops and armed volunteers) under Garibaldi marched into South Italy and the Kingdom of the **Two Sicilies**. They succeeded in winning the support of the local peasants in order to drive out the Spanish rulers.
- In 1861, **Victor Emmanuel II** was declared king of United Italy.

Contribution of Famous Personalities

- **Giuseppe Mazzini** During the 1830s, Giuseppe Mazzini was a revolutionary, who actively supported the Unification of the Italian states.

10 **Confederation** an organisation of smaller groups which have joined together.

An Italian revolutionary, **Giuseppe Mazzini** became a member of the secret society of the Carbonari. He was sent into exile in 1831 for attempting a revolution in Liguria.

Giuseppe Mazzini founded two secret societies, **Young Italy in Marseilles** and **Young Europe in Berne**, whose members were like-minded young men from Poland, France, Italy, and the German states. He believed that nations were intended by God to be natural units for humanity.

Mazzini argued that Italy could not continue to be a patchwork of small states and kingdoms. So, it had to be unified for liberty.

Following his model, secret societies emerged in Germany, France, Switzerland, and Poland. Metternich described Mazzini as "the most dangerous enemy of the social order."

After failed uprisings in 1831 and 1848, Sardinia-Piedmont's King Victor Emmanuel II took on the task of unifying Italy through war.

- **Count Camillo Cavour** Chief Minister Cavour led the movement to unify the regions of Italy. He was neither a revolutionary nor a democrat. Due to his efforts of forming an alliance with France, Sardinia-Piedmont succeeded in defeating Austrian Forces in 1859.
- **Giuseppe Garibaldi** He was a prominent personality in the Unification of Italy. In 1833, he met Mazzini and joined the Young Italy Movement. He participated in a republican uprising in Piedmont in 1834. In 1854, he supported Victor Emmanuel II for his effort to unify the Italian states.

  In 1860, he led the famous expedition to South Italy and the Kingdom of two Sicilies with his 'Red Shirt' army. In 1867, he led the army to Rome to fight for Papal states where a French garrison was stationed. In 1870, France withdrew its troops and Papal states were finally joined to Italy.

The Growth of Great Britain

There was no British nation before the 18th century. The primary identities of the people who inhabited the **British Isles** were ethnic[11] like English, Welsh, Scot or Irish.

However, as the English nation steadily grew in wealth, importance and power, it was able to extend its influence over the other nations of islands. In 1688, the English Parliament seized power from the monarchy.

A new 'British' nation was established through the propagation of a dominant English culture.

The symbol of the new Britain were the **British flag** (*Union Jack*), the **National Anthem** (*God Save Our Noble King*) and the **English language**. These were actively promoted and the older nations survived only as subordinate partners in this union.

Incorporation of Scotland and Ireland

The Act of Union (1707) between England and Scotland resulted in the formation of the United Kingdom of Great Britain. By this Act, Scotland was incorporated in England. Hence, the British Parliament was dominated by its English members.

Ireland was a country divided into Catholics and Protestants. The English supported the Protestants of Ireland to establish their dominance over Catholics. As a result, revolt was raised by Catholics under **Wolfe Tone** and his United Irishmen, but it was suppressed in 1748.

In 1801, Ireland was forcibly included into the United Kingdom of Britain.

1.5 Visualising the Nation

In the 18th and 19th century, artists portrayed the nation as female figures. The female form that was chosen to personify the nation did not stand for any particular woman in real life.

The female figure became an allegory[12] of the nation. In France, the female allegory was Marianne and her features were the red cap, the tricolour and the cockade, which were drawn from liberty and republic. Marianne images were marked on coins and stamps.

Germania became the allegory of the German nation. Germania was represented by a crown of Oak leaves, because German Oak stood for heroism.

1.6 Nationalism and Imperialism

By the last quarter of the 19th century, nationalism lost its idealistic liberal democratic sentiment. During this period, nationalist groups became increasingly intolerant of each other and were ready to start war.

11 Ethnic This term relates to a common racial, tribal or cultural origin or background that a community identifies with or claims.
12 Allegory It refers to a story or picture that uses symbols to convey a hidden meaning.

The Balkans was a region of geographical and ethnic differences. It comprised of modern-day Romania, Bulgaria, Albania, Greece, Macedonia, Croatia, Bosnia-Herzegovina, Slovenia, Serbia and Montenegro. Its inhabitants were broadly known as the **Slavs.**

A large part of the Balkans was under the control of the **Ottoman Empire.** The Balkans became an area of intense conflict as different Slavic nationalities struggled to define their identity and independence.

During this time, many powerful European nations such as Russia, France, Germany, England and Austro-Hungary competed to gain control over the Balkans. This led to a series of wars in the region and finally led to the First World War.

Nationalism, aligned with **imperialism**[13], led Europe to disaster in 1914. At the same time, many countries that had been colonised by European powers in the 19th century started to resist imperial rule.

Try These

1. **In which year conservative regimes were set up?**
2. **Which countries comprised the Balkan Peninsula?**
3. **Who were the inhabitants of Balkan region?**
4. **What does the crown of oak leaves worn by Germania stand for?**

TIME LINE

Covering Major Events with their Time Periods in Chronological Order

Period	Important Events
1789	The French Revolution occurred.
1797	Napoleon invaded Italy; Napoleonic Wars began.
1804	Napoleonic Code was introduced prohibiting privileges based on birth. Upheld the equality before law.
1814-15	Fall of Napoleon; the Vienna Peace Settlement
1821	Greek struggle for independence began.
1824	English poet Lord Byron died.
1831	Giuseppe Mazzini established young Italy. An armed rebellion against Russian rule took place.
1832	Greece gained independence. The Treaty of Constantinople signed.
1834	Zollverein or the Customs Union was formed in Prussia to abolish tariff barriers.
1848	Revolutions in Europe: Artisans, industrial workers and peasants revolt against economic hardships; middle classes demand Constitutions and representative governments; Italians, Germans, Magyars, Poles, Czechs, etc demanded for nation-states.
1859	Piedmont and France defeated Austria.
1861	Victor Emmanuel-II of Piedmont-Sardinia became the king of Italy.
1859-1870	Unification of Italy.
1866-1871	Unification of Germany.
1871	The Prussian King, William I was proclaimed the German emperor.
1905	Slavs nationalism gathered their force in the Habsburg and Ottoman Empires.

13 **Imperialism** It means when a country extends its power into other territories for economic and political gain.

Mind Map

THE RISE OF NATIONALISM IN EUROPE

Making of Nationalism In Europe

Napoleonic Code
- Removed all privileges based on birth, and established equality before the law.
- Abolished the Feudal system.

Aristocracy and New Middle Class
- The aristocracy was socially and politically, dominant class in Europe.
- As a result of industrialisation, new social groups of working class and middle classes came.

Meaning of Liberal Nationalism
- Liberalism comes from the Latin word 'liber' which means free.
- In political sense, liberalism focuses on the idea of a government based on the agreement of the people.

The Revolutionaries
- Giuseppe Mazzini founded two secret societies, Young Italy in Marseilles and Young Europe in Berne.

New Conservatism After, 1815
- Conservatives believed that established traditional institutions of state and society like the monarchy, the church, society hierarchies, property and family, should be preserved.
- Prussia was given new territories on its Western frontiers while Austria was given control of Northern Italy.
- In the East, Russia was given part of Poland and Prussia was given a part of Saxony.

French Revolution and Idea of Nation
- New ideas like la patrie and le citoyen promoted the idea of united community with equal rights under a Constitution.
- Adoption of a new French flag replacing the formal royal.

Nationalism and Imperialism
- By the last quarter of the 19th century, nationalism lost its idealistic, liberal, democratic sentiment.
- During this period, nationalist groups became increasingly intolerant of each other and were ready to start war.
- Many powerful European nations such as Russia, France, Germany, England and Austro-Hungary competed to gain control over other nations.

Visualising the Nation
- In the 18th and 19th century, artists portrayed the nation as female figures.
- In France, the female allegory was Marianne.

Age of Revolutions : 1830 – 1848

Romantic Imagination and National Feeling
- Romanticism was a cultural movement that aimed to develop a specific type of nationalist feeling.
- Language played an important role in developing nationalist sentiments.
- Polish language was removed from school and Russian language was

1848: The Revolution of the Liberals
- In Germany, Italy, Poland and the Austro-Hungarian Empire, men and women of the liberal middle classes combined their demands for constitutionalism with national unification.

Hunger, Hardship and Popular Revolt
- On 4th June, when weavers revolted and demanded contractor for higher wages, they were treated badly and threatened by him.
- In 1848, population of Paris revolted due to food shortage and widespread unemployment.

Making of Germany and Italy

Growth of Great Britain
- There was no British nation before the 18th century.
- The Act of Union (1707) between England and Scotland resulted in the formation of United Kingdom of Great Britain.

Contribution of Famous Personalities
- Giuseppe Mazzini
- Count Camillo de Cavour
- Giuseppe Garibaldi

Unification of Germany
- In 1848, the middle class tried to unite the different regions of the German confederation.
- Liberal initiative to nation-building faced strong opposition from the monarchy, military and the powerful landowners.
- Otto Von Bismark aimed to achieve the goal of unification with the help of Prussian army.

Unification of Italy
- During the middle of the 19th century, Italy was divided into seven states, out of which only one state, Sardinia-Piedmont was ruled by an Italian Princely House.

NCERT FOLDER

Covering Intext Questions and Exercises of NCERT

INTEXT QUESTIONS

Q.1 What way do you think this picture depicts about Utopian vision?

The dream of worldwide democratic and social republics-The pact between Nations, a print prepared by Frederic Sorrieu, in 1848.

Ans. This picture depicts a Utopian vision as the French artist Frederic Sorrieu was visualising a dream of a world made up of nations (all of them did not exit as nations at that time when these prints were made). He had showed the German people with a common flag, although actually they were a number of different states at that time. So, it is an idealistic or Utopian vision. On the Earth in foreground of the image lie the shattered remains of the symbols of **absolutist** institutions.

Q.2 Describe the cause of the 'Silesian Weavers' uprising. Comment on the viewpoint of the journalist.

Ans. The cause of the 'Silesian Weavers' uprising was due to the cheating of the weavers by the contractors.

In 1845, the weavers raised a revolt against the contractors as the contractors drastically reduced their payments.

The viewpoint of the journalist Wilhelm Wolff for this uprising was – a large crowd of weavers reached the house of the contractor and demanded higher wages. They were not treated well, so a group of the crowd entered the contractor's house forcibly and destroyed the furniture, windowpanes and plundered it.

The contractor fled with his family to a neighbouring village but did not get shelter. After 24 hours, he returned back with army and eleven weavers were shot dead.

The viewpoint of the journalist was based against the weavers and in favour of the contractor. He did not understand the misery of the weavers properly.

Q.3 Look at the picture given below. Imagine you were a citizen of Frankfurt in March 1848 and were present during the proceedings of the Parliament. How would you

(a) as a man seated in the hall of deputies, and

(b) as a woman observing from the galleries, relate to the banner of Germania hanging from the ceiling?

The Frankfurt Parliament in the Church of St Paul.

Ans. (a) As a man seated in the hall of deputies, I would relate positively to the banner of Germania, as I would feel all that it symbolised was coming true.

(b) As a woman observing from the galleries, I would consider the banner to depict the truth only partially. This is because women had participated with men equally in the struggle for constitutionalism with national unification, but they were denied suffrage rights during elections to the National Assembly. Women were only admitted to the assembly as passive citizens and observers.

Q.4 Describe the caricature. How does it represent the relationship between Bismarck and the elected deputies of Parliament? What interpretation of democratic processes is the artist trying to convey?

Caricature of Otto von Bismarck in the German Reichstag (Parliament), from Figaro, Vienna, 5th March

Ans. The caricature depicts Bismarck, Chancellor of Germany as holding a whip (signifying that he is a ruthless man ruling with an iron hand) while leading the parliament. The deputies who were elected are afraid of him and so are hiding under their tables. The caricature depicted the dominance of Bismarck over the deputies and how he hated liberalism and parliamentary assemblies.

The artist is trying to convey the democratic system in a funny way in which democracy exists only for namesake. In reality, it is one man's i.e. Bismarck's autocracy that exists in Parliament.

Q.5 The artist has portrayed Garibaldi as holding on to the base of the boot, so that the King of Sardinia-Piedmont can enter it from the top.
Look at the map of Italy once more. What statement is this caricature making?

Garibaldi helping King Victor Emmanuel II Sardinia-Piedmont to pull on boot named 'Italy'. English caricature of 1859.

Ans. The base of the boot symbolises the kingdom of the Two Sicilies, which lay in the Southernmost part of the Italian peninsula. Garibaldi had won this Kingdom and handed it over to King Victor Emmanuel II. This cartoon signifies the unification of Italy and Garibaldi's role in it.

Q.6 With the help of the chart given below, identify the attributes of Veit's Germania and interpret the symbolic meaning of the painting.

Meanings of Symbols

Attributes	Significance
Broken Chains	Being freed.
Breastplate with eagle	Symbol of the German Empire-strength.
Crown of oak leaves	Heroism.
Sword	Readiness to fight.
Olive branch around the sword	Willingness to make peace.
Black, red and gold tricolour	Flag of the liberal- nationalists in 1848, banned by the Dukes of the German states.
Rays of the rising Sun	Beginning of a new era.

In an earlier allegorical rendering of 1836, Veit had portrayed the Kaiser's crown at the place where he has now located the broken chain. Explain the significance of this change.

Ans. The symbolic meaning of the painting is that the German nation has emerged. The female figure of Germania is an allegory of the German nation. All the attributes of the German nation can be seen in the painting as given in the chart. The replacement of the Kaiser's crown with the broken chain signifies that the German nation is now free from autocratic monarchical rule.

Q.7 Describe what you see in figure below. What historical events could Hubner be referring to in this allegorical vision of the nation?

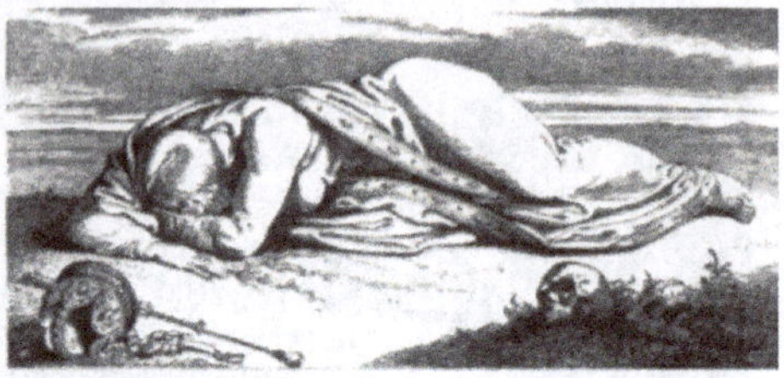

Ans. The painter depicted Germania as a fallen woman with the crown and stick thrown aside because German people's hopes to be united under one monarch (King Friedrich Wilhelm IV) were not fulfilled as he rejected their demand in 1848. The artist, Julius Hubner, depicted Germania in a miserable state due to the rejection by the king. It symbolised the loss of hope. The crown and stick are symbols of the monarchy, which have been cast aside.

EXERCISE

Q.1 What steps did the French revolutionaries take to create a sense of collective identity among French people?

Ans. The French revolutionaries took the following steps to create a sense of collective identity among the French people

- They introduced the ideas of *la patrie* (the fatherland) and *le citoyen* (the citizen), emphasising the concept of a united community enjoying equal rights under a Constitution.
- They chose a new French flag, the tricolour, to replace the royal standard.
- The Estates General was elected by the body of active citizens and renamed the National Assembly.
- In the name of the nation, new hymns were composed, oaths taken and martyrs commemorated.
- They established a centralised administrative system, which formulated uniform laws for all citizens.
- They adopted a uniform system of weights and measures.
- All internal custom duties were abolished.

- They promoted the French language, as spoken and written in Paris and discouraged regional dialects.
- They declared that it was the mission and destiny of the French nation to liberate people of Europe from despotism. It is meant that they would help other people of Europe to become nation-states like them.

Q.2 What changes did Napoleon introduce to make the administrative system more efficient in the territories ruled by him?

Or Explain any five reforms introduced by Napoleons in the regions under his control.

Ans. Napoleon introduced the following changes to make the administrative system more efficient in the areas ruled by him

- He established the Civil Code of 1804, also known as the Napoleonic Code. This ended all privileges based on birth. It established equality before law and secured the right to property.
- He simplified administrative divisions.
- He abolished the feudal system and freed peasants from serfdom and manorial dues.
- In towns, guild systems were removed.
- Transport and communication systems were improved.

Due to the above measures, peasants, artisans, businessmen and workers enjoyed a new found freedom. Businessmen and small-scale producers realised that uniform laws, a common currency and standardised weights and measures would facilitate movement and exchange of goods between regions.

Q.3 Briefly trace the process of German unification.

Or Explain the nation building process of Germany after 1848.

Or Analyse the process of German Unification. CBSE 2024

Ans. The Frankfurt Parliament, which was convened in the church of St Paul on 18th May, 1848, was the first major step towards the unification of German states. Otto von Bismarck, the Chief Minister of Prussia, carried out the process of unification with the help of the Prussian Army and bureaucracy.

The building process of Germany after 1848 include the following events

- The liberal initiatives of nation building were repressed by the monarchy and big landlords of Prussia. From then on, Prussia took the initiative to unify Germany.
- There were widespread nationalist feelings among middle-class Germans, who in 1848, tried to unite the different regions of the German confederation into a Nation-state.
- Bismarck was convinced that the unification of Germany could only be achieved by the princes, not by the common people. He wanted to achieve his aim by merging Prussia into Germany. In 1867, Bismarck became the Chancellor of the North Confederation.
- Bismarck's main objective was to unify Germany and was accomplished by three wars with Austria, Denmark and France which were fought in a brief period of seven years. These wars were ended with the victory of Prussia which helped in completing the process of German unification.
- On 18th January, 1871, in the Royal Palace of Versailles, the king of Prussia, Kaiser William I was crowned as the German Emperor. It symbolised the birth of a United Germany.

Q.4 Who were Marianne and Germania? What was the importance of way in which they were portrayed?

Ans. Marianne and Germania were the female allegories of France and German nations respectively.

Significance/Importance of portraying Female Figures

The female allegories stood as personifications of the 'Republic' and 'Liberty'. They were portrayed such that would instill a sense of nationality in the citizens of these countries.

In France, Marianne's characteristics were drawn from those of Liberty and the Republic—the red cap, the tricolour, the cockade. Statues of Marianne were erected in public squares to remind the public of national symbol of unity. Germania wears a crown of oak leaves which stands for heroism.

Q.5 Write a note on

(a) The Greek War of Independence
(b) Frankfurt Parliament
(c) The Role of Women in Nationalist Struggles
(d) Giuseppe Mazzini
(e) Count Camillo de Cavour

Ans. (a) **The Greek War of Independence** It was a successful war waged by Greek revolutionaries between 1821 to 1832 against the Ottoman Empire. Greek nationalists were influenced by the idea of liberal nationalism. They were supported by the West European countries in this war of independence.

Further, the poets and artists, who added romanticism to the Greek struggle of independence, participated in this war against the Ottoman empire. With the Treaty of Constantinople in July 1832, Greece was recognised as an independent nation.

(b) **Frankfurt Parliament** It is the name of the German National Assembly, founded during the Revolution of 1848 that tried to unite Germany in a democratic way. The assembly was attended by 831 deputies.

The members had drafted the Constitution for a new German nation. The new Constituion was rejected by Friedrich Wilhelm IV, the king of Prussia. Though the Frankfurt Parliament failed to unite Germany, it had consequences on Germany.

The Parliament also faced strong opposition from the aristocracy and military as it was dominated by the middle-class who resisted the demands of workers and artisans. As result of this, the middle-class lost their mass support. Ultimately, the monarchy and military combined together with the aristocracy and won over the liberal nationalist middle-class.

This forced the assembly to disband. Therefore, the Frankfurt Parliament is famous in history as a failure of liberalism and a victory of the monarchy.

(c) **The Role of Women in Nationalist Struggles** A large number of women had participated in liberal and national movements in European countries. They had formed their own political associations, started newspapers and taken part in political meetings and demonstrations. Universal male suffrage was adopted in the country and the women continued their fight for the voting right.

However, when the Frankfurt Parliament was convened in Church of St Paul, women were admitted only as observers to stand in the visiter's gallery.

(d) **Giuseppe Mazzini** He was an Italian revolutionary, who was born in Genoa in 1805. He was sent into exile in 1831 at the age of 24, for attempting a revolution in Liguria. He founded underground societies named 'Young Italy' in Marseilles and 'Young Europe' in Berne whose members were like minded young men from Poland, France, Italy and the German states. He believed that God had intended notions to be the natural units of mankind. He opposed monarchy and supported the vision of democratic Republic.

Following his ideas and on the model of his secret societies, more such societies were set up in Germany, France, Switzerland and Poland. Austrian Chancellor Duke Matternich once described him as 'the most dangerous enemy of our social order'.

(e) **Count Camillo de Cavour** He was the Chief Minister of Sardinia-Piedmont. He was neither a democratic nor a revolutionary. But he led the movement to unify the regions of Italy. Through tact and diplomacy, he entered into an alliance with France and succeeded in defeating Austrian forces in 1859 and thereby freed the Northern part of Italy from the Austrian Habsburg.

Q.6 Choose three examples to show the contribution of culture to the growth of nationalism in Europe.

Ans. Examples of contribution of culture to the growth of nationalism in Europe are

- The idea of a nation can be created through stories, poems and writings. Music too can help in expressing nationalist feelings or sentiments.
- Collecting and recording the different forms of folk culture was important for building a national conciousness. Being a part of the lives of the common people, folk culture enabled nationalist to carry the message of nationalism to a large and diverse audience. For example, Karol Kurpinski celebrated the national struggle through his operas and music turning Folk dances like the Polonaise and Mazurka into nationalist symbol.
- Romanticism, a cultural movement which emerged in Europe, sought to develop a particular form of nationalist sentiments or national feelings. The main aim of Romantic artists was to create a sense of a shared collective heritage and a common cultural past.
- Language also played an important role in developing the national sentiments or nationalist feeling. For example, in Poland, language began to be used as a weapon of national resistance. The wide scale use of Polish language came to be seen as a symbol of struggle against national dominance.

Q.7 Explain what is meant by the '1848 Revolution of the Liberals'. What were the political, social and economic ideas supported by the liberals?

Ans. The 1848 Revolution of the Liberals refers to a series of uprisings across Europe, driven by liberal-nationalists, especially from the educated middle class, against conservative regimes.

The political, social and economic ideas supported by the liberals were

- Politically, it emphasised the concept of government by consent, abolition of autocracy and special privileges.
- Socially, the liberals supported the abolition of discrimination based on birth.
- Economically, it stood for the abolition of trade restrictions imposed by the state.

Q.8 Through a focus on any two countries, explain how nations developed over the 19th century.

Ans. The German and Italian nation-states in the 19th century developed in the following ways

- **Political Fragmentation** Till the middle of the 19th century, the present-day states of Germany and Italy were fragmented into separate regions and kingdoms ruled by different Princely Houses.
- **Revolutionary Uprisings** 19th century Europe was characterised by both popular uprisings of the masses and revolutions led by the educated and liberal middle classes. In the case of the German people, the middle classes belonging to different German regions came together to form an all German National Assembly in 1848. However, on facing opposition from the aristocracy and military and on losing its mass support base, it was forced to disband.

In the Italian region, during the 1830s, revolutionaries like Giuseppe Mazzini tried to establish an Italian Republic. However, the revolutionary uprisings of 1831 and 1848 failed to unite Italy.

- **Unification with the help of the Army** After the failure of the revolutions, the process of unification was pursued by the aristocracy and the army in both these nations.

Germany United

Germany was united by the Prussian Chief Minister Otto von Bismarck with the help of the Prussian Army and bureaucracy. Prussia fought three wars with Austria, Denmark and France over seven years and won. It completed the process of unification. Finally, the German Empire was proclaimed in 1871.

Italy United

The Italian state of Sardinia-Piedmont played the role of uniting Italy, similar to that played by Prussia in the case of Germany. Count Camillo de Cavour (the Chief Minister of Sardinia-Piedmont) led the movement to unite the separate states of 19th century Italy with the help of the army and an alliance with France.

The regions annexed by Giuseppe Garibaldi and his Red hirts joined with the Northern regions to form a United Italy in 1861. The Papal states joined it in 1870.

Q.9 How was the history of nationalism in Britain unlike the rest of Europe?

Ans. In Britain, the development of nationalism followed a different pattern from the rest of Europe. Before the 18th century, different ethnic groups of people were there in the British Isles, such as English, Welsh, Scot and Irish. Each of these ethnic groups had its own cultural and political traditions. The British Parliament became the chief instrument to curb the power of the monarchy in 1688 through a bloodless revolution.

The Act of Union (1707) between England and Scotland formed the United Kingdom of Great Britain. With the advent of English power, the English removed the cultural, political institutions of Scotland forcefully and the Scots were banned from speaking the Gaelic language and put on their national dress.

The English with the help of the protestants suppressed the Catholics of Ireland and forcibly incorporated United Ireland with the United Kingdom in 1801. Scotland and Ireland became the subordinate partners of the United Kingdom. The symbols of the New Britain, the National Flag (Union Jack), the National Anthem (God save our Noble King) and the English language were actively promoted.

Q.10 Why did nationalist tensions emerge in the Balkans?

Ans. Nationalist tensions emerged in the Balkans because the Balkan states were aspiring for nationalism. The Balkans was a region comprising modern day Romania, Bulgaria, Albania, Greece, Macedonia, Croatia, Bosnia-Herzegovina, Slovenia, Serbia and Montenegro and their inhabitants were called Slavs.

In 19th century, the major portion of the Balkans was under the Ottoman Empire. The ideas of romantic nationalism developed in the Balkans. The rebellions nationalities in the Balkans thought that their struggle was the attempt to win back their long-lost independence.

REVIEW EXERCISE

Including Competency Based Questions

Part I

Multiple Choice Questions (MCQs)

1. Which country became full-fledged territorial state in Europe in the year 1789?

(a) Germany (b) France
(c) England (d) Spain

2. When was the first clear expression of nationalism noticed in Europe?

(a) 1787 (b) 1759
(c) 1789 (d) 1769

3. The author of 'Book of Marvels' is: CBSE 2025

(a) Marco Polo (b) Columbus
(c) Vasco da Gama (d) Alfred Crosby

4. Which of the following revolutions is called as the first expression of 'Nationalism'? CBSE 2020

(a) French Revolution (b) Russian Revolution
(c) Glorious Revolution (d) The Revolution of the liberals

5. Which type of governments were mainly driven in Europe after the defeat of Napoleon in 1815? CBSE Term I 2021

(a) Conservative (b) Liberal
(c) Federal (d) Feudal

6. Which one of the following group of countries collectively defeated Napoleon in 1815?

(a) Britain, Russia, Prussia and Austria
(b) Britain, Russia, Prussia and Australia
(c) Britain, Russia, Netherlands and Germany
(d) Britain, Luxembourg, Germany and Italy

7. **In which one of the following countries did the first liberalist-nationalist upheaval take place in July 1830?** **CBSE Term I 2021**

(a) France (b) Germany
(c) England (d) Italy

8. **Who among the following remarked "When France sneezes, the rest of Europe catches cold"?**

(a) Lord Byron (b) Metternich
(c) Johann Herder (d) Napoleon

9. **Choose the correct option from the following regarding nineteenth century "liberalism"** **CBSE 2024**

(a) Monarchy, social hierarchy and property must be maintained.
(b) The abolition of state-imposed restrictions on the movement of goods and capital.
(c) Criticised the glorification of reason and science.
(d) Not tolerating dissent and imposing censorship.

10. **Who among the following was the architect for the unification of Germany?** **CBSE Term I 2021**

(a) Otto Von Bismarck (b) William I
(c) Frederick III (d) William II

11. **Who among the following had sought to put together a coherent programme for a unitary Italian Republic during 1830s?** **CBSE Term I 2021**

(a) Victor Emmanuel I
(b) Victor Emmanuel II
(c) Giuseppe Mazzini
(d) Count Cavour

12. **Who among the following was proclaimed King of United Italy in 1861?**

(a) Charles I (b) Victor Emmanuel II
(c) Giuseppe Garibaldi (d) Bismark

13. **Who among the following was the founder of 'Young Europe' underground secret society in Berne?** **CBSE SQP Term I 2021**

(a) Giuseppe Garibaldi (b) Giuseppe Mazzini
(c) Count Cavour (d) Otto Von Bismarck

14. **Find the incorrect option.**

(a) The Napoleanic Code (Civil Code) was introduced in 1804.
(b) The 1820, were the years of great economic hardship in Europe.
(c) Count Camillo de Cavour was central figure in the Unification of Italy.
(d) In 1831, an armed rebellion against Russian rule took place.

15. **Which one of the following is not true about female allegory of France?** **CBSE 2023**

(a) She was named Marianne.
(b) She took part in the French Revolution.
(c) She was a symbol of national unity.
(d) Her image were marked on coins and stamps.

16. **During the nineteenth century, nationalism emerged as a force which brought about sweeping changes in the political and mental world of Europe. The end result of these changes led to which of the following?** **Competency Based**

(a) The strengthening of multi-national dynastic empires.
(b) The continuation of decentralised power within the modern state.
(c) The establishment of a nation-state, replacing the dynastic empires.
(d) The decline of the concept and practices of a modern state.

17. **Through a return to monarchy, Napoleon had no doubt, destroyed democracy in France, but in the administrative field he had incorporated revolutionary principles, called the Napoleonic Code, in order to make the whole system more rational and efficient.**

How did the Napoleonic Code, introduced by Napoleon, contribute to legal and social changes in the regions under French control? **Competency Based**

(a) Inequity before the law and the maintenance of birth-based privileges.
(b) Introduction of guild restrictions in towns.
(c) Abolishment of feudal systems and establishment of equality before the law.
(d) Promotion of forced recruitment into the French armies.

18. **What impact did the storming of the Bastille by the French have on Europe?** **Competency Based**

(a) People across Europe got inspired to fight against the rule of the monarch.
(b) Made monarchs from different parts of Europe abdicate from the throne.
(c) Inspired nations across Europe to colonise other countries of the world.
(d) People in Europe started to fear the French revolutionaries.

19. **Omar wanted to learn more about the Ottoman Empire.** **Competency Based**

Which of the following European countries he should visit?

(a) France (b) Austria
(c) Bulgaria (d) Switzerland

20. **Arrange the following events in chronological order and choose the correct option.** **CBSE 2024**

I. Treaty of Constantinople
II. Hamburg granted autonomy to Hungary
III. Balkan Conflict
IV. Napoleonic Civil Code

Codes

(a) IV, II, I, III (b) IV, III, II, I
(c) IV, I, II, III (d) I, IV, III, II

21. **Arrange the following regions of Italy in the order of their inclusion in the Unified Italy and choose the correct option.** CBSE 2025

I. Venetia II. Savoy Sardinia
III. Sicilies

Options
(a) I, II and III (b) II, III and I
(c) I, III and II (d) II, I and III

22. **Read the facts regarding the Revolution of the Liberals in Europe during 1848.** CBSE Term I 2021

I. Abdication of the monarch
II. Universal male suffrage had been proclaimed
III. Political rights to women were given
IV. Freedom of the press had been asked for

Codes
(a) Both I and II are correct (b) I, II and III are correct
(c) Both II and IV are correct (d) I, II and IV are correct

23. **On which of the following modern aspects did the new Germany place a strong emphasis?** CBSE Term I 2021

I. Currency II. Banking
III. Legal system IV. Demography

Codes
(a) Both I and II are correct
(b) Both II and III are correct
(c) Both III and IV are correct
(d) Both I, II and III are correct

24. **Identify the characteristics of Cavour among the following.** CBSE Term I 2021

I. He was an Italian statesman.
II. He spoke French much better than Italian
III. He was a tactful diplomat.
IV. He belonged to a royal family.

Codes
(a) Both I and II are correct (b) I, II and III are correct
(c) II, III and IV are correct (d) II, II and IV are correct

25. **What measures and practices were introduced by the French revolutionaries to foster a sense of collective identity among the French people during the French Revolution?** Competency Based

I. Promotion of regional dialects
II. Adoption of the tricolour as the new French flag
III. Abolition of the Estates General
IV. Promotion of a uniform system of weights and measures

Codes
(a) Statements II and III are correct.
(b) Statements I and IV are correct.
(c) Statements II and IV are correct.
(d) Statements I and III are correct.

26. **Consider the statements given below and choose the correct answer.** Competency Based

Statement I Nationalist feelings among middle-class Germans in 1848 aimed to establish a nation-state governed by an elected parliament.

Statement II The liberal initiative for nation-building in Germany in 1848 was suppressed by the combined forces of the monarchy, military, and junkers of Prussia.

Options
(a) Statement I is correct and Statement II is incorrect.
(b) Statement I is incorrect and Statement II is correct.
(c) Both Statements I and II are correct.
(d) Both Statements I and II are incorrect.

27. **Consider the statements given below and choose the correct answer.**

Statement I The Habsburg empire the ruled over Austria- Hungary was a patchwork of many different regions and peoples.

Statement II It only included German-speaking provinces.

Options
(a) Statement I is correct and Statement II is incorrect.
(b) Statement I is incorrect and Statement II is correct.
(c) Both Statements I and II are correct.
(d) Both Statements I and II are incorrect.

28. **Identify the personality with the help of given information.**

- He was a prominent personality in the Unification of Italy.
- In 1833, he met Mazzini and joined the Young Italy Movement.
- He participated in a republican uprising in Piedmont in 1834.
- In 1854, he supported Victor Emmanuel II for his effort to unify the Italian states.

Options
(a) Giuseppe Garibaldi (b) Giuseppe Mazzini
(c) Count Camillo Cavour (d) Napoleon Bonaparte

Answers

1. (b)	**2.** (c)	**3.** (a)	**4.** (a)	**5.** (a)
6. (a)	**7.** (a)	**8.** (b)	**9.** (b)	**10.** (a)
11. (c)	**12.** (b)	**13.** (b)	**14.** (b)	**15.** (b)
16. (c)	**17.** (c)	**18.** (a)	**19.** (c)	**20.** (c)
21. (d)	**22.** (d)	**23.** (d)	**24.** (b)	**25.** (c)
26. (b)	**27.** (a)	**28.** (a)		

Match the Following

1.

List I (Year)	List II (Events)
A. 1804	1. Greek struggle for independence began
B. 1815	2. Napoleon Wars began
C. 1797	3. Treaty of Vienna
D. 1821	4. Civil Code

Codes

	A	B	C	D		A	B	C	D
(a)	1	2	3	4	(b)	4	3	2	1
(c)	1	3	2	4	(d)	4	2	1	3

2.

List I (Year)	List II (Events)
A. 1789	1. Unification of Italy
B. 1859-70	2. Unification of Germany
C. 1866-71	3. Piedmont and France defeated Austria.
D. 1859	4. The French Revolution occurred

Codes

	A	B	C	D		A	B	C	D
(a)	4	1	2	3	(b)	3	2	1	4
(c)	4	3	2	1	(d)	1	2	3	4

Ans. 1. (b) 2. (a)

Assertion-Reason

1. Assertion (A) On Prussian initiative 'Zolleverin' Custom Union was formed.

Reason (R) It was to create unified economic territory allowing the unhindered movement of goods, people and capital. **CBSE 2024**

Codes

(a) Both A and R are true and R is the correct explanation of A
(b) Both A and R are true, but R is not the correct explanation of A
(c) A is true, but R is false
(d) A is false, but R is true

2. Assertion (A) After Russian occupation in Poland, the Russian language was imposed on its people.

Reason (R) The use of Polish soon came to be a symbol of struggle against Russian dominance. **CBSE 2021 Term I**

Codes

(a) Both A and R are true and R is the correct explanation of A
(b) Both A and R are true, but R is not the correct explanation of A
(c) A is true, but R is false
(d) A is false, but R is true

3. Assertion (A) In Britain, the formation of the nation-state was not the result of a sudden upheaval.

Reason (R) Ethnic groups of Britain extended its influence. **CBSE 2021 Term I**

Codes

(a) Both A and R are true and R is the correct explanation of A
(b) Both A and R are true, but R is not the correct explanation of A
(c) A is true, but R is false
(d) A is false, but R is true

4. Assertion (A) Eastern and Central Europe, including the territories under the Habsburg Empire, was characterised by diverse peoples with distinct languages and ethnic groups.

Reason (R) The Habsburg Empire, ruling over Austria-Hungary, was consisted of various regions and linguistic communities.

Codes

(a) Both A and R are true and R is the correct explanation of A
(b) Both A and R are true, but R is not the correct explanation of A
(c) A is true, but R is false
(d) A is false, but R is true

5. Assertion (A) Napoleon introduced administrative reforms in the territories under his control, incorporating revolutionary principles for rationalising and improving efficiency.

Reason (R) The Napoleonic Code, implemented in regions under French control, abolished privileges based on birth, established equality before the law, and secured the right to property.

Codes

(a) Both A and R are true and R is the correct explanation of A
(b) Both A and R are true, but R is not the correct explanation of A
(c) A is true, but R is false
(d) A is false, but R is true

6. Assertion (A) The Frankfurt Parliament of 1848 faced challenges in establishing a unified German nation-state, leading to its ultimate disbandment.

Reason (R) The opposition from the aristocracy and military, coupled with the erosion of social support, weakened the Frankfurt Parliament's position.

Codes

(a) Both A and R are true and R is the correct explanation of A
(b) Both A and R are true, but R is not the correct explanation of A
(c) A is true, but R is false
(d) A is false, but R is true

7. Assertion (A) Napoleon's French army brought democracy and accountability in governance across Europe by 1804.

Reason (R) Napoleon simplified administrative division, abolished the feudal system, and freed peasants from serfdom and manorial dues. **Competency Based**

Codes

(a) Both A and R are true and R is the correct explanation of A

(b) Both A and R are true, but R is not the correct explanation of A

(c) A is true, but R is false

(d) A is false, but R is true

8. Assertion (A) Many artists and poets within Europe made paintings and wrote poems to highlight the plight of Greeks under the Ottoman empire.

Reason (R) Many Europeans had sympathies for ancient Greek culture and supported the work of Greek nationalists. **Competency Based**

Codes

(a) Both A and R are true and R is the correct explanation of A

(b) Both A and R are true, but R is not the correct explanation of A

(c) A is true, but R is false

(d) A is false, but R is true

Ans. 1. (a) Both A and R are true and R is the correct explanation of A.

2. (a) Both A and R are true and R is the correct explanation of A

3. (a) Both A and R are true and R is the correct explanation of A

4. (a) Both A and R are true and R is the correct explanation of A

5. (a) Both A and R are true and R is the correct explanation of A

6. (a) Both A and R are true and R is the correct explanation of A

7. (d) A is false, but R is true

8. (a) Both A and R are true and R is the correct explanation of A

Picture Based Questions

1. Napoleon in the given picture is depicted as a postman. What do each letter falling from his bag represent? **(SQP 2024-25)**

(a) Number of wars he fought

(b) Letters he posted to the monarchs

(c) Territories lost by him

(d) Areas conquered by him

2. Given below is the painting 'Imperial Federation - Map of the World showing the extent of the British Empire in 1886'. Observe the painting and answer the question that follows. **Competency Based**

Which of the following elements depicted in the painting seem conflicting when presented together?

(a) The British soldiers and British colonies spread in both East and West.

(b) The variety of animals and costumed figures depicting countries and their people.

(c) Britannia, the personification of Britain, seated on top of the world and the words federation written at the top of the image.

(d) The words 'freedom' and 'fraternity' written at the top and Atlas, depicting human labour, holding the world upon his shoulders

3. Look at the image given below and answer the following question.

What does this caricature of Bismarck primarily suggest?

(a) Bismarck's fear of parliamentary opposition

(b) Bismarck's admiration for liberal ideologies

(c) Bismarck's authoritarian control over the parliament

(d) Bismarck's collaborative approach with the deputies

4. Look the image given below and answer the following question.

What does the symbolism of the "Portrait Garibaldi as holding on to the base of the boot" in the cartoon primarily represent?

(a) Garibaldi's attempt to establish a new kingdom.

(b) The annexation of the Northern Italian states.

(c) The unification of Italy and Garibaldi's contribution.

(d) The division of Italian territories between monarchs.

5. Look at the image given below and answer the following question.

What does the symbolism of the "Olive branch around the sword" in the image primarily represent?

(a) Symbol of the German empire – strength

(b) Readiness to fight

(c) Willingness to make peace

(d) Heroism

Ans. 1. (c) Territories lost by him

2. (c) Britannia, the personification of Britain, seated on top of the world and the words federation written at the top of the image.

3. (c) Bismarck's authoritarian control over the parliament

4. (c) The unification of Italy and Garibaldi's contribution.

5. (c) Willingness to make peace

Case Based Question

1. Read the source given below and answer the questions that follow.

Socially and politically, a landed aristocracy was the dominant class on the continent. The members of this class were united by a common way of life that cut across regional divisions. They owned estates in the countryside and also town-houses. They spoke French for purposes of diplomacy and in high society. Their families were often connected by ties of marriage. This powerful aristocracy was, however, numerically a small group. The majority of the population was made up of the peasantry. To the west, the bulk of the land was farmed by tenants and small owners, while in Eastern and Central Europe the pattern of landholding was characterised by vast estates which were cultivated by serfs.

In Western and parts of Central Europe the growth of industrial production and trade meant the growth of towns and the emergence of commercial classes whose existence was based on production for the market. Industrialisation began in England in the second half of the eighteenth century, but in France and parts of the German states it occurred only during the nineteenth century. In its wake, new social groups came into being: a working-class population, and middle classes made up of industrialists, businessmen, professionals. In Central and Eastern Europe these groups were smaller in number till late nineteenth century. It was among the educated, liberal middle classes that ideas of national unity following the abolition of aristocratic privileges gained popularity.

(i) What characterised the dominant class socially and politically during the mentioned period?

(a) Majority owning vast estates and town-houses, speaking French for diplomacy.

(b) Landed aristocracy, small but powerful, with common way of life and French-speaking.

(c) Industrialists and businessmen from the growth of towns and trade.

(d) Peasantry actively participating in industrial production.

(ii) In which regions did the landed aristocracy own vast estates and cultivate them with the help of serfs?

(a) Western Europe (b) Central Europe

(c) Northern Europe (d) None of these

(iii) During which century did industrialisation begin in England?

(a) 17th century, marking early industrial development.

(b) 18th century, significant growth in industrial production and trade.

(c) 19th century, industrialisation in France and parts of the German states.

(d) 20th century, a delayed onset of industrialisation.

(iv) Among which social classes did ideas of national unity gain popularity after abolishing aristocratic privileges?

(a) Working-class population in industrial production.

(b) Peasantry seeking political freedom.

(c) Landed aristocracy preserving traditional privileges.

(d) Educated, liberal middle classes advocating national unity.

Ans. (i) (b) Landed aristocracy, small but powerful, with common way of life and French-speaking.

(ii) (b) Central Europe, with vast estates cultivated by serfs.

(iii) (b) 18th century, significant growth in industrial production and trade.

(iv) (d) Educated, liberal middle classes advocating national unity.

Part II

Very Short Answer Type Questions

1. To which country did the artist Frederic Sorrieu belong?

Ans. Frederic Sorrieu belonged to France.

2. Name the French artist who prepared a series of four prints visualising his dream of a new world.

Ans. The French artist Frederic Sorrieu prepared a series of four prints visualising his dream of a new world.

3. Name the painting prepared by Frederic Sorrieu in 1848.

Ans. In 1848, Frederic Sorrieu prepared the painting 'The Dream of Worldwide Democratic and Social Republics–The Pact between Nations'.

4. What was the main aim of the French Revolutionaries?

Ans. The main aim of the French Revolutionaries was to liberate the people of France and also the people of Europe from despotism and establish nation-state under common people's rule.

5. Which type of government was functioning in France before the revolution of 1789?

Ans. The Monarchical type of government was functioning in France before the revolution of 1789.

6. What was a major step taken by the revolutionaries in France to centralise governance?

Ans. Introduction of uniform laws for all citizens within the territory was a major step taken by the revolutionaries in France to centralise governance.

7. When did Napoleon invade Italy?

Ans. Napoleon invaded Italy, in 1797.

8. Who implemented the Civil Code of 1804 in France?

Ans. Napoleon Bonaparte implemented the Civil Code of 1804 in France.

9. Who hosted the Congress at Vienna in 1815?

Ans. The Congress at Vienna in 1815 was hosted by the Austrian Chancellor Duke Metternich.

10. Explain the aim to form Zollverein , a Customs Union, in 1834 in Germany?

Ans. The aim to form Customs Union or Zollverein in 1834 in Germany was to strength nationalism among its member states.

11. 'During the nineteenth century, nationalism emerged as a force which brought about sweeping changes in the political and mental world of Europe'. **Competency Based**

How did nationalism affect the political and mental realms of Europe in the 19th century?

Ans. The rise of nationalism in the 19th century fundamentally changed Europe's political and intellectual landscape. It resulted in the redrawing of borders, the development of nation-states and the emergence of a collective consciousness among people, impacting their views and mindsets about identity and belonging.

12. "In Sorrieu's utopian vision, the peoples of the world are grouped as distinct nations, identified through their flags and national costume."

How does Sorrieu visually differentiate various nations in his utopian depiction? **Competency Based**

Ans. In his utopian vision, Sorrieu depicts nations with unique flags and national costumes to differentiate them. The purpose of these visual markers is to represent the distinct identities of every country, showing a diverse yet unified global population under the general subject of distinct national characteristics.

13. "The political and constitutional changes that came in the wake of the French Revolution led to the transfer of sovereignty from the monarchy to a body of French citizens."

What fundamental shift occurred regarding sovereignty after the French Revolution? **Competency Based**

Ans. The fundamental shift which occurred after the French Revolution was the monarchy surrendering authority to the French people. It established that people, rather than the monarchy, would constitute the nation and have the power to define its path and governance, marking a significant transition in the political landscape of France.

14. " The Habsburg Empire that ruled over Austria- Hungary was a patchwork of many different regions and peoples. The only tie binding these diverse groups together was a common allegiance to the emperor."

What factor provided unity among the diverse regions within the Habsburg Empire, in the absence of nation-states? **Competency Based**

Ans. The factor that provided unity among the diverse regions within the Habsburg Empire, in the absence of nation-states was their shared loyalty to the emperor as there was no collective identity or common culture binding the territories. Their political unity originated from their loyalty to a common monarch, and the absence of centralised nation-states meant that each region retained a significant degree of autonomy.

15 **"Industrialisation began in France and parts of the German states during the nineteenth century. In its wake, new social groups emerged, such as a working-class population and middle classes composed of industrialists and businessmen."**

How did industrialisation influence the emergence of new social classes? Competency Based

Ans. Industrialisation played an important role in the emergence of new social classes. The rise of industrialisation, which marked the establishment of market production, resulted in the emergence of a working-class population and middle classes. This new social class, which included industrialists, business people and professionals, was especially visible in the West and parts of Central Europe.

16. Write one key feature of constitutional monarchy.

Ans. The key feature of constitutional monarchy is that the monarch exercises authority in accordance with a written or unwritten Constitution.

17. State two characteristics of Utopian society.

Ans. The two characteristics of Utopian society were

- Everyone has equal access to resources, opportunities and benefits in the society.
- The absence of social conflicts and tensions, thus promoting a peaceful coexistence.

18. The French revolutionaries introduced the French flag as a measure to create a sense of collective identity amongst the French people.

Name two nation-states that had adopted a national flag for their respective nations by 1848. Competency Based

Ans. The two nation-states that had adopted a national flag for their respective nations by 1848 were Switzerland and United States.

19. How did the Treaty of Vienna in 1815 impact the political map of Europe? Discuss the decisions made by the Congress of Vienna and their long-term effects on European politics.

Ans. The Treaty of Vienna aimed to restore conservative order in Europe after Napoleon's defeat. It reshaped Europe's political map, restoring monarchies and creating a balance of power to prevent future revolutions.

Short Answer Type Questions

1. Why did Frederic Sorrieu present Utopian vision in his prints in 1848? Explain one reason.

Ans. Frederic Sorrieu presented Utopian vision in his prints in 1848 because of his dream of a world made up of 'democratic and social republics.' He prepared a series of four prints visualising his dream.

In one of the prints it showed that people of all ages of Europe and America marched in a long train and offered homage to the Statue of Liberty. France with his tricolour flag reached the statue.

2. How did nationalism and the idea of the nation-state emerge?

Ans. Nationalism and the idea of the nation state emerged within the culturally and regionally diverse groups of Europe. Due to industrialisation and transformation of society, there emerged a middle-class consisting of businessmen, working professionals, industrialists, labourers and working class people.
Out of these, the educated middle-class people thought of uniting the culturally compatible sections of people in Europe by abolishing the privileges enjoyed by the aristocracy. This led to nationalism and emergence of idea of the nation-state.

3. How had Napoleonic Code exported to the regions under French control? Explain with examples.

Ans. The Napoleonic Code which was also known as the Civil Code of 1804 was exported to the regions under French control in the following ways

- In the Dutch Republic, in Switzerland, in Italy and Germany, Napoleon simplified administrative divisions, abolished the feudal system and freed peasants from serfdom and manorial dues.
- In the towns, guild restriction were removed. Transport and communication systems were improved.
- The Napoleonic Code introduced uniform laws, standardised weights and measures, common national currency. These were helpful for peasants, artisans, workers, businessmen and small-scale producers. They enjoyed a new found freedom. These laws facilitated the movement and exchange of goods and capital from one region to another.

4. What were the various impact of French Revolution?

Ans. The various impacts of French Revolution were

- The revolution led to the setting up of Jacobin Clubs in different cities of Europe by students and other members of educated middle classes. It further paved the way for the French armies to moved into Holland, Belgium, Switzerland and some parts of Italy in the 1790s.
  The idea of nationalism began to be carried by French armies.
- Another impact of the revolution was the rise of Napoleon. He took several steps to reform the economy of Europe. The most important among them was the Civil Code of 1804 which brought the concept of equality of law and uniform laws.
- French Revolutionaries wanted to liberate the people of Europe from despotism.

5. Explain any four reasons how the initial enthusiasm of the people of France soon turned to hostility after Napoleon's takeover of France.

Or Explain by giving four reasons as to why the people, who earlier had welcomed Napoleon opposed him later?

Ans. Initially, the French Armies were welcomed as harbingers of liberty. But the initial enthusiasm soon turned to hostility because people gradually understood that the new administrative arrangements did not go hand in hand with political freedom.

The four factors which seemed to outweigh the advantages of the administrative changes are

- Increased taxation on people.
- Strict censorship on printing media and books.
- Forced conscription into the French armies to satisfy its imperialist ambition.
- Restriction on freedom.

6. Explain the functioning of conservative regimes established in France in 1815. **CBSE 2025**

Ans. The functioning of conservative regimes established in France in 1815 is given below

- After Napoleon's defeat in 1815, the Bourbon monarchy was restored in France under Louis XVIII. The goal was to bring back the monarchy and aristocratic privileges that had existed before the French Revolution. The conservative regime aimed to maintain the monarchy's power while ensuring that the revolutionary ideas from the French Revolution did not resurface.
- Louis XVIII issued the Constitutional Charter of 1814, which served as a compromise between the monarchy and the constitutionalists. This charter guaranteed certain civil liberties, like freedom of the press and equality before the law, and established a bicameral legislature. However, it kept the monarchy powerful and limited the power of the legislature.'
- The conservative regimes were highly concerned about the spread of revolutionary ideals. After the French Revolution and the rise of Napoleon, the conservative powers in Europe wanted to ensure that revolutionary movements did not spread further. In France, the monarchy sought to control and suppress the growth of liberal and republican ideas. They were particularly cautious about liberal nationalism, which sought more democratic and nationalist changes.

7. How did Romanticism seek to develop a particular form of nationalist sentiments during 18th century? Explain.

Or 'Romanticism, a cultural movement sought to develop a particular form of nationalist sentiment. Justify the statement with suitable arguments. **CBSE SQP 2024-25**

Ans. Romanticism referred to a cultural movement which sought to develop a particular form of national sentiment in the following ways

- Romantic artist and poets generally criticised the glorification of reason and science.
- They focussed on emotions, intuition and mystical feelings.
- Their effort was to create a sense of a shared collective heritage, a common cultural past as the basis of a nation.
- Some German romantics like Johann Gottfried Herder thought that through folk songs, folk poetry and folk dance, the true spirit of the nation could, be popularised. He claimed that true German culture was to be discovered among the common people.

8. 'The decade of 1830 had brought great economic hardship in Europe'. Support the statement with arguments. **CBSE 2024**

Ans. The decade of 1830 had brought great economic hardship or crisis in Europe in the following ways

- There was an enormous increase in population all over Europe. As a result, unemployment became a common feature in most of the countries.
- Migration of rural people to the cities further made the situation worse. Small scale producers in towns sometimes faced with stiff competition from rural areas where production was carried out mainly in homes or small workshops. These products imported from rural areas were obviously cheaper than the town-made products.
- Due to population, the demand of foods increased. It led to the rise of food prices. This increased price along with a year of bad harvests led to widespread poverty in town and whole country.

9. Describe the role of Otto Von Bismarck in the making of Germany.

Ans. The role of Bismarck in the unification of Germany was

- Under Bismarck's command, Prussia took the leadership of the movement for national unification.
- Otto Von Bismarck was the chief architect of the process of unification which was carried with the help of Prussian army and bureaucracy.
- On 18th January, 1871, Prussian ministers including the Chief Minister Otto Von Bismarck gathered in the unheated Hall of Mirrors in the Royal palace of Varsailles to proclaim the new German Empire headed by Kaiser William I of Prussia.

10. Explain the political situation of Italy before its unification.

Or Give a brief account of political fragments of Italy.

Ans. Italy had a long history of political fragmentation. This is shown in the points below

- Italians were scattered over several dynastic states as well as the multi-national Habsburg empire.

- During the middle of the 19th century, Italy was divided into seven states of which only one, Sardinia- Piedmont was ruled by an Italian Princely House.
- The North was under Austrian Habsburgs, the center was ruled by the Pope and the Southern regions were under the domination of the Bourbon kings of Spain.
- Even the Italian language had not any standard common form. It had many regional and local variations.

11. How did Britain came into existence as a nation-state? Explain?

Ans. Britain became a nation-state in the following ways

- Before the 18th century, there were different ethinic identified with its own culture and politics *viz* English, Welsh, Scot and Irish . As the English nations grew in wealth and power, its influences over other Island nation also increased.
- The English Parliament had taken the power from the monarchy in 1688. It became an instrument in building the nation-state of Britain, with England at its centre.
- United Kingdom of Britain was established through the Act of Union in 1707 between England and Scotland. Scotland eventually got suppressed by the English politically and culturally.
- Ireland was forcibly incorporated into the United Kingdom in 1801. A new British nation was emerged with the dominant English culture.

12. "Liberalism in the early-nineteenth-century advocated for economic freedom, aiming to eliminate barriers in the movement of goods and capital." Justify this statement. **Competency Based**

Ans. Early-nineteenth-century liberalism advocated economic freedom, aiming to eradicate obstacles in goods and capital movement. It is evident from following

- Liberalism emphasised free markets and the removal of state-imposed restrictions.
- Commercial classes found diverse customs duties and regional measures obstructive to economic growth.
- The call for a unified economic territory led to the creation of Zollverein in 1834, abolishing tariff barriers and reducing currencies, alongside railway development.
- Railways increased mobility, aligning economic interests with national unification and strengthening economic nationalism.

13. "The growth of revolutionary nationalism in Europe sparked a struggle for independence amongst the Greeks starting in 1821." Justify this statement. **Competency Based**

Ans. The growth of revolutionary nationalism in 19th-century Europe sparked the Greek War of Independence, starting in 1821. Greek nationalists, encouraged by sympathy from West Europeans (which was drawn by Greek cultural symbolism), led to a movement to free Greece from the Ottoman Empire's rule.

International support was further shown by individuals such as Lord Byron, who contributed to the war effort and provided money for it. This culmination resulted in the Treaty of Constantinople in 1832, recognising Greece as an independent nation, showcasing how revolutionary nationalism sparked the flames of independence movements.

14. "Mazzini believed that God had intended nations to be the natural units of mankind. So Italy could not continue to be a patchwork of small states and kingdoms."
How did Giuseppe Mazzini's vision of national unity, as a reflection of divine intent, influence his drive for Italian unification? **Competency Based**

Ans. Giuseppe Mazzini's vision for the unification of Italy was influenced by his idea that states were meant to be the natural units of humanity. According to Mazzini, Italy's fragmented structure of small states and kingdoms contradicted this divine plan.

He advocated for a unified republic, believing that such unification was fundamental to securing Italian liberty. This idea had a significant influence on Mazzini, who founded secret societies across Europe and Italy with the intention of unifying the country and spreading the model of a unified republic.

15. In 1815, representatives of the European powers– Britain, Russia, Prussia and Austria– who had collectively defeated Napoleon, met at Vienna to draw up a settlement for Europe. The main intention was to restore the monarchies that had been overthrown by Napoleon and create a new conservative order in Europe. **Competency Based**

(i) How did the Treaty of Vienna in 1815 aim to address the political fallout from Napoleon's defeat?

(ii) What was the primary objective behind the restoration of monarchies in Europe?

Ans. (i) The Treaty of Vienna in 1815 aimed to address the political fallout from Napoleon's defeat by restoring political order. It aimed to reverse the disruptions caused by the Napoleonic era, intending to bring back traditional monarchical systems, which were overthrown by Napoleon's conquests. The restoration of the Bourbon dynasty in France and the redistribution of territories were significant steps taken to reinstate the pre-Napoleonic order and establish a stable and conservative structure in Europe.

(ii) The primary objective behind restoring the monarchies in Europe after Napoleon's fall was to bring back the pre- Napoleonic order, thereby establishing a conservative political structure. This action intended to bring stability by restoring the traditional institutions of the monarchy, which had been damaged during the Napoleonic wars.

16. Oliver ran a business that spread across Germany, the Dutch Republic and Italy when the Napoleonic Code of 1804 was implemented.
What were the five key changes he might have experienced due to the Napoleonic Code of 1804? **Competency Based**

Ans. The key changes that Oliver might have experienced due to the Napoleonic Code of 1804 were

- He was able to operate his entire business in one currency because all locations used the same currency.
- He was able to carry his commodities and capital easily from one location to another due to improvement in transportation.
- He and his other business partners and consumers were all subject to the one uniform law.
- He was able to employ standardised weights and measurements across many places.
- He was no longer required to pay taxes to any aristocrat.

Long Answer Type Questions

1. "Napoleon had destroyed democracy in France but in the administrative field he had incorporated revolutionary principles in order to make the whole system more rational and efficient." Analyse the statement with arguments.

Or **How would you evaluate Napoleon as an administrator who created a more rational and efficient system? Elucidate with suitable examples.**

Ans. Napoleon implemented many significant reforms in the territories under his control. Despite his return to monarchy, which effectively destroyed democracy, his administrative changes were based on revolutionary principles aimed at improving the efficiency and fairness of governance. Napoleon made the whole system more rational in the following ways

- The Napoleonic Code of 1804 abolished privileges based on birth, ensuring that all citizens were equal before the law. The Code also secured the right to property, which encouraged economic growth by providing a sense of legal security for property owners, whether they were landowners or small-scale businessmen.
- In many of the regions he controlled, such as the Dutch Republic, Switzerland, and parts of Italy and Germany, Napoleon dismantled the feudal system, which had created social and economic inequalities. This move ended the privileges of the nobility and brought about a more egalitarian society.
- Napoleon reorganised administrative divisions, making them more efficient and easier to govern. This reduced complexity and improved governance across his empire, creating more uniformity in the way territories were managed.
- Napoleon introduced uniform laws, standardised weights and measures, and a common currency throughout the territories he controlled. This made trade and commerce more efficient, as businessmen and small-scale producers could rely on consistent regulations, reducing confusion and fostering economic exchange.
- Napoleon improved transport and communication systems, including roads and postal services, which facilitated the movement of goods, people, and information. This also helped integrate his empire economically, allowing goods and capital to flow more freely across regions.

2. How did ideas of national unity in early nineteenth century Europe allied to the ideology of liberalism? Explain. **CBSE 2020**

Or **How was liberalism allied to national unity in Europe in the early decades of the 19th century? Analyse.** **CBSE 2025**

Ans. The ideas of national unity in early nineteenth century Europe allied to the ideology of liberalism in the following ways

- For the liberal middle classes, the ideas of national unity means the abolition of aristocratic privileges. Liberalism stood for freedom for the individual and equality of all before the law.
- Liberalism emphasised the concept of government. It urged for a Constitution and representative government through Parliament. National unity can be maintained by the proper governance of the Parliament.
- In the economic sphere, liberalism is in favour of the freedom of markets and the abolition of state-imposed restrictions on the movement of goods and capital. During the nineteenth century, this was a strong demand of the middle class which was in favour of national unity.

3. Explain the term conservatism. Explain with special reference to Europe.

Ans. Conservatism is a political philosophy that stressed the importance of tradition, established institutions and customs and preferred gradual development to quick change.

After the defeat of Napoleon in 1815, European Governments were driven by conservatism. Conservatives were people who believed that established, traditional institutions of state and society like the monarchy church, social hierarchies, property and the family should be preserved. After the rule of Napoleon, the basic ideas of conservatism were changed. Most conservatives did not want to return to the society of pre-revolutionary days.

They realised the changes initiated by Napoleon strengthened the traditional institutions like the monarchy in reality. They understood that a modern army, an efficient bureaucracy, a dynamic economy, the abolition of feudalism and serfdom could strengthen the autocratic monarchies in Europe. They did not tolerate criticism and dissent and sought to curb activities that questioned the legitimacy of their government. Thus, the conservatives of that time accepted the changes which were in favour of their interests.

4. 'The Treaty of Vienna depicted the spirit of conservatism'. Substantiate the statement with key features of the treaty. **CBSE SQP 2024-25**

Ans. The Treaty of Vienna of 1815 embodied the spirit of conservatism through several key measures

- **Restoration of Monarchies** The treaty aimed to restore the monarchies that Napoleon had overthrown, including restoring the Bourbon dynasty in France. This reflected a conservative desire to return to traditional rulers and institutions.
- **Redrawing Boundaries** To prevent future French expansion, new states were created around France's borders, such as the Kingdom of the Netherlands and additions to Piedmont. This reinforced a conservative approach to maintaining stability through territorial adjustments.
- **Territorial Redistributions** Prussia and Austria gained territories to strengthen their positions, while the German Confederation of 39 states, established by Napoleon, was preserved. This upheld existing power structures and aimed to balance power conservatively across Europe.
- **Division of Poland** Russia and Prussia were granted parts of Poland, further reshaping the map in a conservative effort to maintain the influence of established powers.

Overall, the Treaty of Vienna sought to undo the revolutionary changes brought by Napoleon and restore a conservative order in Europe.

5. How did nationalism develop through culture in Europe? Explain.

Or **How did culture play an important role in creating the idea of the 'nation' in Europe? Explain with examples.** **CBSE 2024**

Or **"Culture played an important role in creating the idea of the nation in 19th century Europe". Evaluate the statement in the context of romanticism.** **CBSE 2025**

Ans. The nationalism developed through culture in Europe in the following ways

- Art, poetry, stories and music helped express and shape nationalist feelings in Europe.
- Romanticism, a cultural movement in Europe developed a particular form of nationalist sentiment. Romantic artists and poets criticised the glorification of science and reason. They tried to create a sense of a shared collective heritage as the basis of a nation. They gave importance on emotions, intuitions and mystical feelings.
- German philosopher Johann Gottfried Herder claimed that true German culture was to be discovered among the common people (*das volk*) in their folk song, folk poetry and folk dances.
- Vernacular languages and folklores strengthen the national spirit.
- In Poland, Karol Kurpinski celebrated the national struggle through opera and music.
- Allegory of Germania and Marianne developed national feelings among citizens.

6. Analyse the process of Italian Unification. **CBSE 2024**

Or **Explain the process of Unification of Italy.** **CBSE 2023**

Or **Analyse the role of Giuseppe Mazzini in the Unification of Italy.** **CBSE 2025**

Ans. The process or various stages in the Unification of Italy were as follows

- **Political Fragmentation of Italy** Italy had a long history of political fragmentation. Italy was divided into seven states during the middle of the nineteenth century. Of these seven states, only Sardinia-Piedmont was ruled by an Italian Princely House. At that time, North of Italy was under Austrian Habsburg, the centre was ruled by Pope and the Southern regions were ruled by the Bourbon kings of Spain.
- **Role of Giuseppe Mazzini** During 1830s, Giuseppe Mazzini had tried to unite Italy. He formed the secret society called Young Italy. But both the uprising in 1831 and 1848 failed. Even the ruling elites also wanted a unified Italy which would offer economic development and political dominance.
- **Role of Cavour** The Unification of Italy was a result of many wars. Chief Minister Cavour made a tactful diplomatic alliance with France, and Sardinia- Piedmont succeeded in defeating the Austrian forces in 1859.
- **Role of Garibaldi** A large number of armed volunteers under the leadership of Giuseppe Garibaldi joined the unification movement. In 1860, they marched into South Italy and the Kingdom of the Two Sicilies succeeded to drive out the Spanish rulers with the help of local people. In 1861, Victor Emmanuel II was proclaimed as king of United Italy.

7. Describe the explosive conditions prevailed in Balkans after 1871 in Europe.

Or **"The most serious source of nationalist tension in Europe after 1871 was the area called the Balkans". Evaluate the statement in context of Slavic Movement.**

Ans. The explosive conditions prevailed in Balkans after 1871 in Europe were

- The Balkans was a region of geographical and ethnic variation comprising modern-day Romania, Bulgaria, Albania, Greece, Macedonia, Croatia, Bosnia-Herzegovina, Slovenia, Serbia and Montenegro whose inhabitants were broadly known as the Slavs.

- A large part of the Balkans was under the control of the Ottoman Empire. The spread of the ideas of romantic nationalism in the Balkans together with the disintegration of the Ottoman Empire made this region very explosive.
- All through the nineteenth century the Ottoman Empire had sought to strengthen itself through modernisation and internal reforms but with very little success. One by one, its European subject nationalities broke away from its control and declared independence.
- The Balkans people based their claims for independence or political rights on nationality and used history to prove that they had once been independent but had subsequently been subjugated by foreign powers. Hence, the rebellious nationalities in the Balkans thought of their struggles as attempts to win back their long-lost independence.

8. Highlight the various measures and practices that French revolutionaries introduced to create a sense of collective identity amongst the French people. CBSE SQP 2022-23

Ans. The various measures and practices that French revolutionaries introduced to create a sense of collective identity amongst the French people were :

- The ideas of la Patrie (the fatherland) and le citoyen (the citizens) were introduced, which unified people by giving them equal rights under a Constitution.
- The French tricolour was chosen as the new flag instead of the former royal standard.
- Citizens were allowed to elect members to the Estates-General, which was renamed as the National Assembly.
- A central administrative system was put in place and it formulated uniform laws for all citizens within its territory.
- French became the common language as it was written and spoken in the capital city of Paris, and regional languages were discouraged.
- A uniform system of weights and measures was introduced and it was followed by the abolition of customs duties and dues.

9. Read the following information given below and answer the question that follows.

"Nineteenth-century liberals also stressed the inviolability of private property. Yet, equality before the law did not necessarily stand for universal suffrage. You will recall that in revolutionary France, which marked the first political experiment in liberal democracy, the right to vote and to get elected was granted exclusively to property-owning men. Men without property and all women were excluded from political rights. Only for a brief period under the Jacobins did all adult males enjoy suffrage."

How did the concept of liberalism in nineteenth-century Europe, particularly in revolutionary France, intersect with the issue of suffrage, and what were the exclusions and inclusions associated with political rights? Competency Based

Ans. The concept of liberalism in nineteenth-century Europe, particularly in revolutionary France, had a close relationship with suffrage, reflecting the ideals of individual freedom and equality before the law. However, this relationship was complex, and the issue of suffrage was combined with exclusions and inclusions in political rights.

In revolutionary France, from where liberal democracy started, the right to vote and be elected was exclusively granted to property-owning men. This meant that men without property and all women were excluded from participating in the political process and enjoying these fundamental rights. Although there was a brief period during the Jacobins' rule when all adult males had suffrage, subsequent developments, notably the Napoleonic Code, led to a reversion to limited suffrage. This exclusionary approach prompted ongoing struggles as women and non-propertied men organised opposition movements, advocating for equal political rights. The tension between liberal ideals and the constraints on suffrage emphasise the complex evolution of political thought during this transformative era.

10. Do you agree that the period of 1848 was considered as a phase of the Revolution of the Liberals in Europe? Elucidate with suitable examples. CBSE Additional SQP 2023-24

Ans. Yes, the period of 1848 was considered a phase of the Revolution of the Liberals in Europe. This period saw widespread uprisings and demands for liberal reforms across several European states.

The revolutions of 1848 were characterised by a shared desire for constitutionalism, political rights and national unification.

One well known example is the February Revolution in France, where widespread discontent led to the overthrow of the Monarchy and the establishment of the Republic on the basis of universal male suffrage.

Another example is the Frankfurt Parliament in Germany, where middle-class professionals, businessmen, and artisans came together to vote for an all-German National Assembly.

The assembly drafted a constitution for a German nation with a Constitutional monarchy. In Italy, various states experienced uprisings seeking national unification and liberal reforms. Similarly in other regions like Poland, and the Austro-Hungarian Empire, liberal middle-class individuals sought constitutionalism and national unification.

11. How would you evaluate Napoleon as an administrator who created a more rational and efficient system? Elucidate with suitable examples.

Ans. Napoleon was an administrator who created a more rational and efficient system. This statement can be justified by the following reasons

- The Civil Code of 1804 usually known as the Napoleonic Code, secured the right to property, established equality before the law and removed all privileges based on birth. The Napoleonic Code was followed by the regions under French control.
- New businessmen, artisans, peasants and workers enjoyed a new-found freedom.
- In territories under French control such as Italy, Germany, Switzerland and Dutch Republic, peasants were freed from manorial dues, peasants were freed from serfdom, feudal system was abolished, administrative divisions were simplified.
- Guild restrictions were removed in towns.
- There were improvements in communication and transport systems.
- To facilitate the movement and exchange of goods and capital from one region to another, small-scale producers of goods and businessmen began to realise that common national currency, standardised measures and weights, and uniform laws were of great help.

12. Analyse the decisions taken by the conservatives at the Congress of Vienna in the year 1815.

Ans. The decisions of the Conservatives at the Congress of Vienna in the year 1815 led to the following

- The Bourbon dynasty, (deposed during the French Revolution) was restored to power.
- France lost the territories it had annexed under Napoleon.
- A series of states were set up on the boundaries of France to prevent it from expansion in the future. E.g., kingdom of the Netherlands, which included Belgium, was set up in the North.
- Genoa was added to Piedmont in the South. Prussia was given territories on its Western frontiers. Austria was given control of Northern Italy.
- The German confederation of 39 states set up by Napoleon was left untouched in the East, Russia was given part of Poland while Prussia was given a portion of Saxony.

13. How did the Greek war of independence mobilise nationalist feelings among the educated elite across Europe? Explain **CBSE 2024**

Ans. Thre Greek war of independence mobilised nationalist feelings among the educated elite in the following ways

- Many Western Europeans had a natural sympathy for the ancient Greek Culture and other Greeks in exile supported Greek nationalists.
- The Greeks were motivated to launch their independence movement in 1821 by the rise of revolutionary nationalism in Europe. The European educated class was inspired by the outcome of the struggle and become more patriotic. Greece received assistance from the fellow Greeks living abroad.
- Poets and artists praised Greece as the cradle of European civilisation and they encouraged the public to fight against the Muslim empire.
- Lord Byron, an English poet, raised money, fought in a war and died of fever in 1824.

Case Based Questions

1. Read the sources given below and answer the questions that follow.

Source A A New Conservatism After 1815

In 1815, representatives of the European powers -Britain, Russia, Prussia and Austria-who had collectively defeated Napoleon, met at Vienna to draw up a settlement for Europe. The Congress was hosted by the Austrian Chancellor Duke Metternich. The delegates drew up the Treaty of Vienna of 1815 with the object of undoing most of the changes that had come about in Europe during the Napoleonic Wars. The Bourbon dynasty, which had been deposed.

(i) Why and where did the representatives of the European powers who had collectively defeated Napoleon meet?

Nationalists in Greece got support from other Greeks living in exile and also from many West Europeans who had sympathies for ancient Greek culture. Poets and artists lauded Greece as the cradle of European civilisation and mobilised public opinion to support its struggle against a Muslim empire. The English poet Lord Byron organised funds and later went to fight in the war, where he died of fever in 1824. Finally, the Treaty of Constantinople of 1832 recognised Greece as an independent nation.

(ii) What role did the poets and artists play in the Greek War of Independence?

Source C Hunger, Hardship and Popular Revolt

In 1848, food shortage and widespread unemployment brought the population of Paris out on the roads. Barricades were erected and Louis Philippe was forced to flee. A National Assembly proclaimed a republic and granted suffrage to adult males above 21 and guaranteed the right to work.

(iii) Why was Louis Philippe forced to flee?

Ans. (i) The Europeon powers who had collectively defeated Napoleon met at Vienna to draw up a settlement for Europe.

(ii) Poets and artists considered Greece as the cradle of European civilisation and mobilised public opinion to support their struggle against a Muslim Empire.

(iii) Louis Philippe was forced to flee because revolution started due to food shortage and wide spread unemployment.

2. Read the source given below and answer the questions that follow.

What we know today as Germany, Italy and Switzerland were divided into kingdoms, Duchies and Cantons whose ruler had their autonomous territories. Eastern and Central Europe were under autocratic monarchies within the territories of which lived diverse peoples.They did not see themselves as sharing a collective identity or a common culture. Often, they even spoke different languages and belonged to different ethnic groups. The Habsburg Empire that ruled over Austria-Hungary, for example, was a patchwork of many different regions and peoples. It included the Alpine regions-the Tyrol, Austria and the Sudetenland-as well as Bohemia, where the aristocracy was predominantly German- speaking. It also included the Italian- speaking provinces of Lombardy and Venetia.

In Hungary, half of the population spoke Magyar while the other half spoke a variety of dialects. In Galicia, the aristocracy spoke Polish. Besides these three dominant groups, there also lived within the boundaries of the empire, a mass of subject peasant peoples-Bohemians and Slovaks to the North, Slovenes in Carniola, Croasts to the South and Roumans to the East in Transylvania.

Such differences did not easily promote a sense of political unity. The only tie binding these diverse groups together was a common allegiance to the emperor.

(i) Why were Germany, Italy and Switzerland were not nation states till the mid-eighteenth century?

(ii) Were there any nations-States in Europe till the mid-eighteenth-century? How ?

(iii) Describe the Habsburg Empire.

Ans. (i) Germany, Italy and Switzerland were not nation states till the mid-eighteenth century. As they were divided into Kingdoms, Duchies and Cantons, whose rulers had their autonomous territories.

(ii) Yes, there were nation-states in Europe till the mid 18th century. Eastern and Central Europe were under autocratic monarchies within the territories of diverse peoples. They did not see themselves as sharing a collective identity or a common culture.

(iii) The Habsburg Empire ruled over Austria-Hungry was a patchwork of many different regions and peoples. It included the Alpine regions the Tyrol, Austria and the Sudetenland- as well as Bohemia. Its also included the provinces of Lombardy and Venetia.

ASSESSMENT EXERCISE

Multiple Choice Questions (MCQs)

1. When was Custom Union formed in Europe?

(a) 1810 (b) 1824 (c) 1814 (d) 1834

2. Identify the factors which cause rise of hunger, hardship and revolt in Europe.

(a) Increase in population all over the Europe

(b) Unemployment

(c) Price rise

(d) Drought

3. Arrange the following in correct sequence.

(i) French Revolution

(ii) Napoleonic wars began

(iii) Treaty of Vienna

(iv) Unification of Germany

Codes

(a) (i), (ii), (iii), (iv) (b) (iv), (iii), (ii), (i)

(c) (i), (iii), (iv), (ii) (d) (ii), (iii), (i), (iv)

4. Find the incorrect option.

(a) The Civil Code was introduced in 1804.

(b) Treaty of Vienna was signed in 1845.

(c) Victor Emmanuel II was proclaimed the King of United Italy.

(d) None of the above

5. Assertion (A) The first upheaval took place in France in July 1830.

Reason (R) French Revolution was started in 1889.

Codes

(a) Both A and R are true and R is the correct explanation of A

(b) Both A and R are true, but R is not the correct explanation of A

(c) A is true, but R is false (d) A is false, but R is true

Subjective Questions (VSA, SA & LA)

1. Who was made the constitutional monarch by liberal revolutionaries in 1830 in France?

2. Which country is known as the cradle of civilisation?

3. Name the founder of the secret society, 'Young Italy'.

4. Name the French artist who prepared a series of four prints visualising his dreams of a world.

5. What do you mean by nationalism? Mention some factors which gave rise to nationalism.

6. Why did nationalists tensions emergs in the Balkans? Explain reasons.

7. Describe any three consequences of liberal revolution of 1848.

8. Describe any four features of the Vienna Treaty of 1815 in brief.

9. The Balkan issue became one of the major factors responsible for the First World War. Explain by giving examples.

10. Explain how did the 18th and 19th century artist begin personifying a nation in allegory.

CHAPTER 2

Nationalism in India

In India, the growth of modern nationalism is connected to the anti-colonial movement. People began discovering their unity in the process of their struggle with colonialism. The Congress under the leadership of Mahatma Gandhi tried to unite each class and group together within one movement.

2.1 The First World War, Khilafat and Non-Cooperation Movement

The First World War (1914) created a new economic and political situation worldwide. India faced various problems during the war period. For example

- Defence expenditure was increased.
- Custom duties were raised and income tax was introduced.
- Prices of food grains were increased and doubled between 1913 and 1918.
- Villagers were recruited forcefully in army, which caused widespread anger.

In 1918-19 and 1920-21, crop failures in many parts of India led to severe food shortages. This was followed by an influenza epidemic. People hoped their struggles would end after the war, but things did not improve.

In such a critical situation, a new leader **Mahatma Gandhi** came to India from South Africa in January, 1915.

The Idea of Satyagraha

Gandhiji's method of movement and protest based on **truth** and **non-violence** was known as **Satyagraha.** The idea of Satyagraha emphasised on the power of truth and the need to search for truth.

As per Gandhiji, without being aggressive a Satyagrahi could win the battle through non-violence. This could be achieved by touching the conscience of the oppressor.

Mahatma Gandhi thought that following the '*dharma*' of non-violence could bring all Indians together.

In 1917, Gandhiji travelled to **Champaran** in Bihar to inspire the peasants to struggle against oppressive plantation system.

In the same year, Gandhiji also organised a Satyagraha to support the peasants in **Kheda** district of Gujarat who were suffering from shortage of food due to crop failure and a plague epidemic. The farmers in Kheda were unable to pay the tax payment and were requesting a reduction in the revenue collection.

In 1918, Gandhiji went to **Ahmedabad** to organise a Satyagraha movement amongst cotton mill workers.

The Rowlatt Act

The Rowlatt Act was passed through the **Imperial Legislative Council in 1919** but Indian members opposed the Act.

This act provided the government with significant authority to control and limit political actions and the political prisoners could be detained in prison for two years without any trial.

On 6th April, 1919 Gandhiji launched a nation wide **Satyagraha** with a *hartal* against this act.

Rallies were organised in various cities, workers went on strike in railway workshop and shops were closed down.

British government decided to take actions against nationalists because they were concerned about the popular uprising and feared that communication channels like telegraph and railways would be disrupted.

Mahatma Gandhi was not allowed to enter Delhi and local leaders were picked up from Amritsar.

On 10th April, 1919 the police in Amritsar upon fired on peaceful procession. Martial Law[1] was imposed in Amritsar and the command of the area was given to **General Dyer**.

Jallianwala Bagh Massacre

On **13th April, 1919**, a large crowd gathered in the enclosed ground of Jallianwala Bagh in Amritsar, Punjab.

Some people gathered there to protest against government's repressive measures, while some came to attend the annual **Baisakhi fair**. Many of them were unaware of the martial law that was imposed.

General Dyer blocked the exit points of the ground and gave order to open fire on the crowd. Many people were killed in this incident.

As the news spread, strikes, clashes with the police and attacks on government buildings started in many North Indian towns.

The government responded with force to end the movement by humiliating people. Satyagrahis were forced to rub their noses on the ground, crawl on the streets and do *salaam* (salute) to all sahibs.

Mahatma Gandhi called off the Satyagraha Movement when he saw spread of violence.

Khilafat Movement

The First World War had ended with the defeat of Ottoman Empire. After the First World War, rumours were spread that a peace treaty was going to be imposed on Khalifa (spiritual head of the Islamic world) of Ottoman Empire.

Gandhiji believed that by taking up the Khilafat issue, he could unite the Hindus and Muslims to launch a nationwide movement in India.

A **Khilafat Committee** was formed in Bombay in March 1919, **Muslim leaders like the Muhammad Ali** and **Shaukat Ali** brothers began discussion with Gandhiji about a united mass action on the Khilafat issue. Gandhiji saw this as an opportunity of uniting Hindus and Muslims.

The Congress passed the resolution in its **Calcutta Session** in September 1920 to start a Non-Cooperation movement in support of Khilafat as well as for Swaraj.

Need of Non-Cooperation Movement

Gandhiji in his famous book ***Hind Swaraj*** (1909) declared that British rule was established in India with the cooperation of Indians. If Indians refused to cooperate, British rule in India would collapse within a year and Swaraj would come.

Mahatma Gandhi proposed the following stages for the implementation of the Non-Cooperation as a Movement

- The movement would begin with a surrender of titles, honours and honorary posts by people.
- The movement would boycott[2] Civil Services, Army, Police, British Courts and Legislative Assemblies, School and Colleges and British goods.
- In case of government suppression, Civil Disobedience Movement would be launched.

The Non-Cooperation Movement was adopted by the Congress during the **Nagpur Conference** in December 1920 and it began under the leadership of Mahatma Gandhi.

2.2 Differing Strands within the Movement

In January 1921, the Non-Cooperation-Khilafat Movement started. Various social groups participated in the movement with their own specific aspirations.

The Movements in the Towns

- Non-Cooperation Khilafat Movement started in the cities with middle-class participation.
- Students and teachers left government-controlled school and lawyers left courts.
- Foreign goods were boycotted. The merchants and traders refused to trade in foreign goods or finance foreign trade. As a result, the production of Indian textile mills and handlooms increased.
- Liquor shops were picketed[3].
- Council elections were boycotted in most provinces except Madras where the Justice Party, representing non-Brahmans, believed that joining the council was a way for them to have some influence, which was typically reserved for Brahmans.

---

1 Martial Law Law of military government. When martial law is imposed, ordinary laws are suspended.

2 Boycott The refusal to deal and associate with people or participate in activities or buy and use things; usually a form of protest.

3 Picketed A form of demonstration or protest by which people block the entrance to a shop, factory or office.

However, this movement gradually slowed down for many reasons like expensive *Khadi* clothes were not suitable for poor people and no alternative institutions were set-up. Finally, the teachers and students had to resume their studies and jobs in government schools and lawyers joined back in government courts.

Rebellion in the Countryside

From cities, the Non-Cooperation Movement spread to the countryside.

Peasant Movement in Awadh

- In Awadh, the Peasant Movement developed under the leadership of **Baba Ramchandra** (a *Sanyasi* who had earlier been to Fiji as an **indentured labourer**[4]).
- The protest was against *talukdars* and landlords who asked peasants for very high rents and additional fees. Peasants were also forced to do ***begar***[5] and work on landlords' farms without pay. As tenants, they didn't have rights to the land and were often evicted, preventing them from gaining any ownership rights.
- This Peasant Movement demanded reduction of revenue, abolition of *begar* and social boycott of oppressive landlords.
- In many places, ***nai-dhobi bandhs*** were organised by panchayats to deny services to all landlords.
- In October, 1920, the **Oudh Kisan Sabha** was set-up. It was headed by Jawaharlal Nehru, Baba Ramchandra and a few others. Within a month, over 300 branches of this sabha had been set up in the villages around the region.
- As the peasant movement spread, the houses of *talukdars* (Indian land-holders) and merchants were attacked, bazaars were looted and grain hoards were taken over.

Tribal Movement in Andhra Pradesh

Tribal peasants interpreted the message of Mahatma Gandhi and the idea of *Swaraj*.

- In the **Gudem Hills** of Andhra Pradesh, a **militant Guerrilla Movement** spread in the early 1920 under the leadership of **Alluri Sitaram Raju**.
- In these hills, the colonial government had closed large areas, preventing people from entering for grazing and collecting resources. This angered the hill people, affecting their livelihoods and traditional rights. When the government forced them to contribute unpaid labour for road building, the hill people revolted.
- Raju convinced people to wear *'Khadi'* and give up drinking according to Gandhian ideas.
- The **Gudem rebels**[6] attacked police stations, attempted to kill British officials and carried on **Guerrilla warfare**[7] for achieving Swaraj.
- Raju was captured and executed in 1924 and gradually he became a folk hero.

Swaraj in the Plantations

For plantation workers in Assam, freedom meant the right to move in and out of their restricted area and maintaining a connection with their home village.

According to **Inland Emigration Act** of **1859**, plantation workers were not permitted to leave the tea gardens without permission.

When the news of Non-Cooperation Movement spread to the plantantion, they left their job and headed towards their home.

The plantation workers believed that in Gandhi Raj, everyone would be given land in their own village. However, they were caught by the police and brutally beaten up.

Try These

1. **Where did the Jallianwala Bagh incident take place?**
2. **Besides Gandhiji who were the main leaders of Khilafat Movement?**
3. **A Sabha was headed by Jawaharlal Nehru and Baba Ramachandra. Which Sabha was it?**
4. **Who was Alluri Sitaram Raju?**
5. **When was the Inland Emigration Act passed?**

2.3 Towards Civil Disobedience

In February 1922, Mahatma Gandhi decided to withdraw the Non-Cooperation Movement as he felt that movement was turning violent in many places and Satyagrahis needed to be properly trained before they would be ready for mass struggles.

---

4 **Indentured Labour** It refers to bonded labour where people agree to work to pay off for the debt.

5 **Begar** It refers to labour that villagers were forced to contribute without any payment.

6 **Gudem Rebels** These were people who participated in the militant Guerrilla Movement in the Gudem hills of Andhra Pradesh.

7 **Guerrilla Warfare** It refers to irregular military actions carried out by small usually independent forces.

Chauri Chaura incident was the main reason behind withdrawing the Non-Cooperation Movement.
The Chauri Chaura incident occurred in Gorakhpur district of United Province in February, 1922.

Different Views within Congress

Some leaders within Congress were tired of mass struggles and wanted to participate in the election to the provincial councils set up by the **Government of India Act of 1919**. They felt that it was important to oppose British policies within the councils.

CR Das and **Motilal Nehru** formed the **Swaraj Party** within the Congress to argue for a return to council politics whereas some younger leaders like **Jawaharlal Nehru** and **Subhash Chandra Bose** argued for more strong mass agitation and for full independence.

In this situation of internal debate and discussions, two factors shaped Indian politics towards the late 1920 that were

(i) **The first** was the effect of the worldwide economic depression.

(ii) **The second** was agricultural prices which began to fall from 1926 and collapsed after 1930.

Formation of Simon Commission

Simon Commission was constituted under **John Simon.** The main objective of **Simon Commission** was to review the functioning of the constitutional system in India and suggest changes in the system.

Indian leaders opposed the commission as there were no Indians in it. When the commission arrived in India, in 1928, it was greeted with the slogan **Go Back Simon.**

All parties including the Congress and the Muslim League participated in the demonstrations.

Demand of Purna Swaraj

In October 1929, the Viceroy, Lord Irwin announced an uncertain offer of **dominion status**[8] for India and a **Round Table Conference** to discuss a future Constitution.

In December 1929, under the Presidency of Jawaharlal Nehru, the Lahore Congress formalised the demand of Purna Swaraj or complete independence for India.

It was declared that 26th January, 1930 would be celebrated as the Independence Day.

The Salt March and the Civil Disobedience Movement

Mahatma Gandhi believed that salt was a powerful symbol that could unite the nation. On 31st January, 1930, Mahatma Gandhi sent a letter to Viceroy Irwin which claimed eleven demands. One of these eleven demands was to abolish salt tax. Irwin was not ready to talk upon the demands. Thus, Gandhiji took the decision to launch the movement.

Alongwith 78 followers, Gandhiji started Salt March from **Sabarmati Ashram** on 12th March, 1930, for **Dandi,** the coastal town of Gujarat.

On 6th April, he reached Dandi and broke the Salt Law by boiling seawater and manufacturing salt. Many people across the country broke the salt law, made their own salt and protested in front of government salt factories. This marked the **beginning of the Civil Disobedience Movement.**

As the movement spread,

- Foreign clothes were boycotted and liquor shops were picketed.
- Peasants refused to pay revenue and *chaukidari* taxes.
- Village officials resigned.
- In many places, forest people violated forest laws.

However, British government arrested all the leaders including Gandhiji.

Calling Off the Civil Disobedience Movement

During Civil Disobedience Movement, peaceful Satyagrahis were attacked, women and children were beaten and about 1,00,000 people were arrested.

When **Abdul Gaffar Khan** was arrested on April 1930, several violent incidents took place in Peshawar. In this situation, Mahatma Gandhi call off the movement and signed the Gandhi-Irwin Pact with Lord Irwin on 5th March, 1931. According to the pact, Gandhiji agreed to attend the Second Round Table Conference in London and the government agreed to release political prisoners.

Relaunching of Civil Disobedience Movement

In December 1931, Gandhiji went to London for the **Second Round Table Conference** but he returned disappointed as the British government refused to release the prisoners.

When Gandhiji came back in India, he found that Congress had been declared illegal and Abdul Ghaffar Khan and Jawaharlal Nehru were imprisoned.

8 Dominion Status It refers to semi-autonomous country within the British empire that is also called British commonwealth countries.

Mahatma Gandhi relaunched the Civil Disobedience Movement. This movement continued for a year but lost its strength by the year 1934.

Formation of Hindustan Socialists Republican Army (HSRA)

Many nationalists did not believe in non-violent method for achieving freedom.

In 1928, some nationalists like Bhagat Singh, Jatin Das and Ajoy Ghosh founded the Hindustan Socialists Republican Army (HSRA) in 1928 at a meeting in Ferozshah Kotla ground in Delhi.

In April 1929, Bhagat Singh and Batukeswar Dutta threw a bomb in the legislative assembly. Bhagat Singh was executed by the colonial government at the age of 23.

Participation in the Movement

- In the countryside, rich peasant communities like the Patidars of Gujarat and the Jats of Uttar Pradesh were supporters of the Civil Disobedience Movement.
- As producers of cash crops, they suffered from a decline in trade, low prices and inability to pay the government's taxes. They organised their communities to participate in boycott programmes. For them, the fight for Swaraj was a struggle against high revenues.
- The poor peasantry found it difficult to pay their rent to the landlords as the depression continued. They joined a variety of radical movements often led by Socialists and Communists in the hope that they would not have to pay the rent any further.
- Associations like **Indian Industrial and Commercial Congress** and **Federation of the Indian Chamber of Commerce** and industries under the leadership of **GD Birla**, **Purushottam Thakur Das**, etc supported the Civil Disobedience Movement in the hope that business restrictions would be lifted.

The Indian merchants and industrialists formed the **Indian Industrial and Commerce Congress** in 1920 and the **Federation of the Indian Chamber of Commerce and Industries** (FICCI) in 1927.

- The industrial working classes did not participate in the Civil Disobedience Movement in large numbers, except in the Nagpur region.
- Some workers joined the Civil Disobedience Movement, adopting aspects like boycotting foreign goods for their protests against low wages and bad working conditions.
- The railway workers organised strikes in 1930 and dockworkers in 1932. In 1930, tin mine workers in Chota Nagpur wore Gandhi caps for protests. However, Congress hesitated to include workers' demands, fearing it might split nationalist forces.
- An important feature of this movement was the large scale participation of women. In urban areas, women came from high-caste families. In rural areas, women came from rich peasant households. Women were inspired by Gandhiji's call and they began to see service to the nation as their sacred duty.

The Limits of Civil Disobedience

Dalits or untouchables and Muslims did not actively participated in this movement.

For a long time, the Congress had ignored the Dalits because of the fear of *Sanatanis*, the conservative high caste Hindus.

Gandhiji called Dalits **Harijan** or the **Children of God**. He believed that Swaraj would not come for hundred years if untouchability was not eliminated. He organised **Satyagraha** for them, to secure their entry into temples and access to public wells, tanks, roads and schools.

Gandhiji himself cleaned the toilets to dignify the work of *bhangi* community (the sweepers). Gandhiji urged the upper class to change their mindset regarding the untouchables.

Many Dalit leaders demanded reserved seats in educational institutions, and a separate electorate for choosing Dalit members in legislative councils. They believed that political empowerment would address social issues.

Dalit involvement in the Civil Disobedience Movement was limited, especially in Maharashtra and Nagpur where their organisation was quite strong.

Stand of Dalit Leaders

Dalit leaders wanted a different political solution to the problems of their community. **Dr BR Ambedkar** demanded reserved seats in educational institutions and a separate electorate that would choose Dalit members for Legislative Councils.

Ambedkar organised the Dalits into the **Depressed Classes Association** in 1930. His views differed with Mahatma Gandhi at the Second Round Table Conference as he demanded separate electorate for Dalits.

When the British Government admitted Ambedkar's demand, Gandhiji strongly opposed it and began a fast unto death. Gandhiji believed that separate electorate for Dalits would slow down the process of their integration into the main society.

Ambedkar ultimately accepted Gandhiji's position and as a result, **Poona Pact** of September 1932 was signed. This pact gave the depressed classes reserved seats in Provincial and Central Legislative Council, but the voting was to be done by the general electorate.

Hindu-Muslim Clash

Some of the Muslim political organisations in India rarely participated in the Civil Disobedience Movement.

After the decline of the Non-Cooperation and Khilafat Movement, a large section of Muslims felt separated from the Congress.

From the mid 1920, the Congress came to be more associated with openly Hindu religious nationalist groups like the **Hindu Mahasabha**. As a result, Hindu-Muslim communal clashes and riots occurred in various cities.

Difference between Hindu Mahasabha and Muslim League

The Congress and Muslim League made efforts to talk again for unity. In 1927, it appeared that such a unity could be possible.

The only difference in the opinion of Congress and Muslim League was based on the representation in the future assemblies that were to be elected.

The leader of the Muslim League, **Muhammad Ali Jinnah** was willing to give up the demand for separate electorate on two conditions which were as follows

(i) Muslims were assured reserved seats in the Central Assembly.

(ii) Representation would be in proportion to the population in Muslim dominated provinces (Bengal and Punjab).

In 1928, at the All Parties Conference, **MR Jayakar** of the Hindu Mahasabha strongly opposed the demands of Jinnah.

Many Muslim leaders and intellectuals feared that the culture and identity of minorities could be submerged under the domination of Hindu majority.

In 1930, **Sir Muhammad Iqbal,** the President of Muslim League demanded for separate electorates for Muslims. He thought that it would safeguard their minority's political interest. He justified the Muslim demand for i.e. the creation of a Muslim India within India.

2.4 The Sense of Collective Belonging

Nationalist movements spread when people belonging to different regions and communities began to develop a sense of collective belongingness. It is developed through the experience of united struggles.

History, fiction, folklore, songs, popular prints and symbols, all played a part in the making of nationalism in the following ways

- The identity of a nation is most often symbolised in a figure or image. This image of **Bharat Mata** was first created by **Bankim Chandra Chattopadhyay** in 1870, when he wrote **Vande Mataram** for our motherland.
- Later, this song was included in his novel *Anandamath* and widely sung by the freedom fighters. The image of Bharat Mata was first painted by **Abanindranath Tagore**.
  In the painting, Bharat Mata is shown as a calm, divine and spiritual figure, resembling an ascetic. Being devoted to this mother figure became a symbol of one's nationalism.
- Indian folk songs and folk tales sung by bard (wandering poets) played an important role for making the idea of nationalism.
- In Bengal, **Rabindranath Tagore** collected ballads nursery rhymes and songs, which led the movement for folk revival.
- In Madras, **Natesa Sastri** published a huge four-volume set of Tamil folk tales titled ***The Folklore of Southern India***.
- During the Swadeshi Movement, a **tricolour (red, green and yellow) flag** was designed in Bengal. It had eight lotuses representing eight provinces and a crescent moon representing Hindus and Muslims.
- By 1921, Gandhiji had designed the **Swaraj Flag**. It was a tricolour (red, green and white) having a spinning wheel in the centre representing the Gandhian ideal of self help.

Nationalism through Indian Ancient History

Another means of creating feeling of nationalism was explaining the meaning of history again. The nationalist writers urged the readers to take pride in India's great achievements in the past and struggle to change the miserable conditions of life under British rule.

However, unification of people involved some problems. When the past that was being glorified belonged to Hindus and the images celebrated were taken from Hindu **iconography**, the people of other communities felt left out.

2.5 Conclusion

A growing anger against the Colonial Government brought together various groups and classes of Indians into a common struggle for freedom in the first half of the 20th century.

However, different expectations of diverse groups pose a constant threat to unity. The Congress under the leadership of Mahatma Gandhi tried to divert people's sufferings into organised and united movement for independence.

Try These

1. **When and Where the demand of 'Purna Swaraj' was accepted by the Congress?**
2. **During which movement was the Indian tricolour flag first designed?**
3. **Who had first created the image of Bharat Mata?**
4. **He worked for the revival of folk culture in Madras. Identify the person.**
5. **Who wrote the novel Anandamath?**

TIME LINE

Covering Major Events with their Time Periods in Chronological Order

Period	Important Events
1915	Mahatma Gandhi returned to India from South Africa.
1917	Gandhiji travelled to Champaran to inspire peasants against the oppressive plantation system.
1917	Gandhiji organised Satyagraha in Kheda district of Gujarat.
1918	Gandhiji went to Ahmedabad to organise Satyagraha among cotton mill workers.
1918-19	Distressed Uttar Pradesh peasants organised by Baba Ramchandra.
1919	Khilafat Committee was formed in Bombay; Hartal against Rowlatt Act; Jalianwala Bagh Massacre
1920	Gandhiji convinced other leaders of the need to start a Non-Cooperation Movement in support of Khilafat as well as for Swaraj in Calcutta Congress Session.
1921	Non-Cooperation and Khilafat Movement launched.
1922	Incident of Chauri Chaura; Gandhiji withdrew Non-Cooperation Movement.
1924	Alluri Sitaram Raju arrested ending a two years armed tribal struggle.
1927	Federation of the Indian Chamber of Commerce and Industries (FICCI) was formed.
1928	The Simon Commission arrived in India. The Hindustan Socialist Republic Army (HSRA) was founded.
1929	Lord Irwin announced a vague offer of 'dominion status' for India; Lahore Congress; Congress adopted the demand for 'Purna Swaraj'.
1930	Dr BR Ambedkar established Depressed Classes Association; Gandhiji started Civil Disobedience Movement by breaking Salt Law at Dandi.
1931	Gandhiji ends Civil-Disobedience Movement; Gandhi-Irwin Pact; Second Round Table Conference.
1932	Poona pact signed between Dr Bhimrao Ambedkar and Mahatma Gandhi/Civil Disobedience Movement relaunched.

Mind Map

NATIONALISM IN INDIA

The First World War, Khilafat and Non-Cooperation Movement

The Idea of Satyagraha
- It emphasised on the power of truth and the need to search for truth.
- In 1918, Gandhiji organised Satyagraha Movement amongst Cotton mill workers in Ahmedabad.

The Rowlatt Act
- It was passed through the Imperial Legislative Council in 1919.
- The act provided the government with significant authority to control and limit political actions.

Jallianwala Bagh Massacre
Martial Law was imposed in Amritsar and the command of the area was given to General Dyer. Fire opened on the crowd gathered to celebrate Baisakhi

Khilafat Movement
Muhammad Ali and Shaukat Ali began discussing with Gandhiji about a united mass action on the Khilafat issue.

Need for Non-Cooperation
- To end the British rule in India.
- Adopted by the Congress during the Nagpur Conference in December, 1920.

Differing Strands Within The Movement

The Movements in the Towns
- Non-Cooperation Khilafat Movement was started.
- Foreign goods were boycotted.
- Liquor shops were picketed.
- Council elections were

Swaraj in the Plantations
According to Inland Emigration Act of 1859 plantation workers were not permitted to leave the tea gardens without permission.

Rebellion in the Countryside

Peasant Movement in Awadh
- It was developed under the leadership of Baba Ramchandra
- In October 1920, the Oudh Kisan Sabha was set up.

Tribal Movement in Andhra Pradesh
In the Gudem hills of Andhra Pradesh, a militant Guerilla Movement spread in the early 1920 under the leadership of Alluri Sitaram Raju.

Sense of Collective Belonging
- Nationalism spreads when people begin to believe that they are part of the same region.
- In 1870, Bankim Chandra Chattopadhyay wrote 'Vande Mataram' that was widely sung in Swadeshi Movement in Bengal.

Towards Civil Disobedience

Demand of Purna Swaraj
In October 1929, the Viceroy, Lord Irwin announced an uncertain offer of dominion status for India and a Round Table Conference to discuss a future Constitution.

Relaunching of the Civil Disobedience Movement
Gandhiji went to London for the Second Round Table Conference in December, 1931 and relaunched Civil Disobedience

Calling off the Civil Disobedience Movement
- Salt March led by Gandhiji from Sabarmati Ashram to Dandi on 12th March, 1930.
- Gandhiji broke the salt law by reaching Dandi on 6th April, 1930.
- Several violent incidents took place in Peshawar when Abdul Gaffar Khan was arrested.
- Gandhi- Irwin Pact was signed on 5th March, 1931.

Different Views within Congress
- CR Das and Motilal Nehru formed the Swaraj Party within the Congress to argue for a return to council politics.
- Jawaharlal Nehru and Subash Chandra Bose argued for strong mass agitation and for full independence.

The Limits of Civil Disobedience

Hindu-Muslim Clash
- In 1928, MR Jayakar of Hindu Mahasabha opposed the demands of Jinnah.
- Sir Muhammad Iqbal in 1930 demanded the importance of separate electorates for Muslims.

Stand of Dalit Leaders
- Ambedkar organised the leaders into the Depressed Classes Association.
- Poona Pact of September, 1932 was signed.

NCERT FOLDER

Covering Intext Questions and Exercises of NCERT

INTEXT QUESTIONS

Q.1 Source A

Mahatma Gandhi on Satyagraha

It is said of 'passive resistance' that it is the weapon of the weak, but the power which is the subject of this article can be used only by the strong. This power is not passive resistance; indeed it calls for intense activity. The movement in South Africa was not passive, but active.

'Satyagraha is not physical force. A Satyagrahi does not inflict pain on the adversary; he does not seek his destruction. In the use of Satyagraha, there is no ill-will whatever'.

'Satyagraha is pure soul force. Truth is the very substance of the soul. That is why this force is called Satyagraha. The soul is informed with knowledge. In it burns the flame of love. Non-violence is the supreme dharma'.

'It is certain that India cannot rival Britain or Europe in force of arms. The British worship the war-God and they can all of them become, as they are becoming, bearers of arms. The hundreds of millions in India can never carry arms. They have made the religion of non-violence their own'.

Read the above text carefully.

What did Mahatma Gandhi mean when he said, "Satyagraha is active resistance"?

Ans. When Gandhiji said that Satyagraha is active resistance, he meant that it requires a lot of soul force activity. It involves very great sacrifices to be made, which can be done only by strong-willed persons. It requires resistance to oppression without using any force. It emphasises the power of truth and the need to search for it.

If the cause is true, physical force is not necessary to fight the oppressor. The Satyagrahi can win the battle against the oppressor by appealing to his conscience, by persuading him to see the truth.

Q.2 If you were a peasant in Uttar Pradesh, in 1920, how would you have responded to Gandhiji's call for Swaraj? Give reasons for your response.

Ans. I would have responded positively to Gandhiji's call by refusing to pay the Zamindar's illegal demands, ask for reduction of the revenue and also ask for security of tenure. In short, I would boycott the system of Zamindari, in a non-violent manner.

The reasons for my above action are that, as a peasant, I will limit my requirement to my area of work. Swaraj would mean freedom from the atrocities caused by the Zamindars.

Q.3 Why did various classes and groups of Indians participate in the Civil Disobedience Movement?

Ans. Various classes and different social groups of Indians participated in the Civil Disobedience Movement led by Gandhiji in 1930. All of them joined this movement on account of their own needs, aspirations and limited understanding as follows

- In the rural areas, rich farmers and peasant communities such as Patidars (Gujarat) and Jats in Uttar Pradesh were very hardly hit by the trade depression and they participated in the Civil Disobedience Movement and supported the boycott programmes.
- The poor peasants also demanded that their dues of rent should be remitted.
- The business classes participated in the movement to oppose the colonial policies that restricted business activities.
- Some prominent industrialists supported the movement financially and boycott the trading of foreign goods.
- The industrial working classes except the workers in Nagpur region stayed away from this movement as big industrialists came closer to the Congress. This was the first time that the large number of women participated in the Nationalist Movement.

Q.4 Source D

In 1930, Sir Muhammad Iqbal, as President of the Muslim League, reiterated the importance of separate electorates for the Muslim as an important safeguard for their minority's political interests. His statement is supposed to have provided the intellectual justification for the Pakistan demand that came up in subsequent years.

This is what he said: 'I have no hesitation in declaring that if the principle that the Indian Muslim is entitled to full and free development on the lines of his own culture and tradition in his own Indian home lands is recognised as the basis of a permanent communal settlement, he will be ready to stake his all for the freedom of India.

The principle that each group is entitled to free development on its own lines is not inspired by any feeling of narrow communalism.

A community which is inspired by feelings of ill-will towards other communities is low and ignoble. I entertain the highest respect for the customs, laws, religions and social institutions of other communities. Nay, it is my duty according to the teachings of the Quran, even to defend their places of worship, if need be. Yet, I love the communal group which is the source of life and behaviour and which has formed me what I am by giving me its religion, its literature, its thought, its culture and thereby its whole past as a living operative factor in my present consciousness'.

'Communalism in its higher aspect, then is indispensable to the formation of a harmonious whole in a country like India. The units of Indian society are not territorial as in European countries. The principle of European democracy cannot be applied to India without recognising the fact of communal groups. The Muslim demand for the creation of a Muslim India within India is, therefore perfectly justified.

'The Hindu thinks that separate electorates are contrary to the spirit of true nationalism, because he understands the word "nation" to mean a kind of universal amalgamation in which no communal entity ought to retain its private individuality. Such a state of things, however does not exist. India is a land of racial and religious variety.

Add to this the general economic inferiority of the Muslims, their enormous debt, especially in the Punjab and their insufficient majorities in some of the provinces, as at present constituted and you will begin to see clearly the meaning of our anxiety to retain separate electorates.'

Read the Source D carefully.

Do you agree with Iqbal's idea of communalism? Can you define communalism in a different way?

Ans. No, I do not agree with Iqbal's idea of communalism. He believed that it is a quest for a community to develop on its own lines. He believed that religion is the basis on which thinking and behaviour are based. He felt that religion gives persons a common culture and literature. He believed in the concept that Hindus and Muslims should exist as separate entities in India. This line of thinking encouraged separatism and ultimately led to the partition of the country.

We understand communalism now-a-days as having a negative connotation i.e. it is understood as conflict between people of different religions, which also can lead to violence between them. It has now become politics under the guise of religious conflict for extracting favours or favourable treatment by the government.

Q.5 Look at figures A and B. Do you think these images will appeal to all castes and communities? Explain your views briefly.

Fig. A

Fig. B

Ans. Since in both pictures Bharat Mata is depicted as a Hindu Goddess, it will not have an appeal for all castes and communities. Non-Hindus will definitely not be in any way attracted to these images. Since India is a secular country with diversity in religions, a secular symbol would be better.

EXERCISE

Q.1 Explain

(a) Why the growth of nationalism in colonies is linked to an anti-colonial movement?

Or **"In India, the growth of modern nationalism was intimately connected to the anti-colonial movement." Analyse the statement.** **CBSE 2024**

Or **Explain the role of anti-colonial movement in the rise of nationalism in India.** **CBSE 2025**

(b) How the First World War helped in the growth of the National Movement in India?

(c) Why Indians were outraged by the Rowlatt Act?

Or **Why was the Rowlatt Act opposed in India? Explain.** **CBSE 2025**

(d) Why did Gandhiji decide to withdraw Non-Cooperation Movement?

Ans. (a) The growth of nationalism in the colonies is closely linked to the anti-colonial movement because, in places like India, people united in their struggle against colonial rule. The shared experience of being oppressed by colonial powers created a sense of unity across different groups. However, each group experienced colonialism in different ways and had different ideas of freedom. Leaders like Mahatma Gandhi and the Congress worked to bring these groups together in a single movement, but this unity was not achieved easily and involved conflicts.

(b) The First World War helped grow India's National Movement by causing economic and political problems. War spending led to higher taxes, raised prices, and increased hardship for people. Forced recruitment for soldiers angered rural communities. Crop failures and an influenza epidemic between

1918 and 1921 caused food shortages and millions of deaths. As life didn't improve after the war, these struggles fueled anger and strengthened the National Movement.

(c) Indians were outraged by the Rowlatt Act for the following reasons

- Rowlatt Act was introduced in 1919. This act had been hurriedly passed through the Imperial Legislative Council despite the opposition from Indian members.
- Under this Act, the police could arrest anybody and put in prison without trial for two years.
- The provisions of this Act outraged Indians and hurt their nationalist sentiments and dignity.

(d) Gandhiji decided to withdraw Non-Cooperation Movement because the movement took a violent turn at Chauri Chaura, Uttar Pradesh where the people set on fire a Police Station in which 22-23 policemen were burnt alive in 1922. Seeing the spread of violence, Gandhiji ended the movement.

Q.2 What is meant by the idea of Satyagraha?

Ans. Satyagraha is a method of agitation and protest based on truth and non-violence. It was first introduced by Mahatma Gandhi in the National Movement. The methods included passive resistance, consisting of defiance of laws, non-payment of taxes, boycott of government institutions, etc.

First, Gandhiji applied Satyagraha in 1917, in Champaran district of Bihar to help the peasants against the unjust indigo plantation owners. Then he organised Satyagraha in Kheda district of Gujarat in support of peasants in 1917 and also in Ahmedabad, in favour of cotton mill workers in 1918.

Q.3 Write a newspaper report on

(a) The Jallianwala Bagh Massacre

(b) The Simon Commission

Ans. (a) Jallianwala Bagh is situated in Amritsar (Punjab). Here as a mark of protest against the Rowlatt Act, a peaceful assembly was going on. People from many surrounding villages were participating. Some came here to attend the annual Baisakhi fair.

This garden is enclosed on three sides and has only one entrance. In order to terrorise the people, General Dyer entered the park with troops.

Without giving any warning to the people, he ordered his sepoys to fire at them. In this firing, many people were killed and many wounded.

(b) Simon Commission arrived in India, in 1928. It was greeted with black flags and slogans like 'Simon Go Back'. Both Congress and Muslim League unitedly protested against it.

This commission was boycotted by the Indian people as it did not include any Indian member in it. Also the Commission did not give any hope of 'Swaraj for the Indians'.

Q.4 List all the different social groups which joined the Non-Cooperation Movement of 1921. Then choose any three and write about their hopes and struggles to show why they joined the movement.

Ans. The Non-Cooperation and Khilafat Movement started in January 1921. Various social groups which joined the Non-Cooperation Movement were

(i) **Middle Class People in Towns** In towns, middle class people who consisted of students, teachers and lawyers responded to the clarion call of Non-Cooperation and boycott. They saw the movement as a way to freedom from the foreign rule. They boycotted foreign goods and clothes and picketed liquor shops.

(ii) **Plantation Workers** They participated in the movement with the hope that they would be free to move out of the confined space in which they had been enclosed. They hoped that Gandhi Raj was coming, and everyone would be given land in his own village.

(iii) **Peasants and Tribal People** In various places, peasants and tribals also participated in the movement. The movement was launched against the talukdars and landlords. For them 'Swaraj' meant that they would not be required to pay land dues i.e., land revenue and the land they were cultivating would be distributed among them. When the colonial government began forcing the tribal people to contribute 'begar' (free labour) for road building, they revolted.

Q.5 Discuss the Salt March to make clear why it was an effective symbol of resistance against colonialism.

Ans. Salt March was an effective symbol or tool of resistance against colonialism because all classes could identify with salt as it was an essential food item. Tax on salt and the monopoly over its manufacturing was a sign of the oppression of British rule.

Gandhiji reached Dandi on 6th April, 1930 and violated Salt law by manufacturing salt from sea water. Breaking the Salt law was an apparent defiance of British authority and was a direct challenge to British rule in India.

People were not only asked to refuse cooperation with the British, but to break the unjustified colonial laws.

Thousands of people from different parts of the country broke the Salt law, manufactured it and demonstrated in front of government salt factories.

With the spread of the movement, foreign cloth was boycotted, liquor shops were picketed, peasants refused to pay revenue, *chaukidari* taxes, village officials resigned, forest people violated forest laws by collecting wood and grazing their cattle in the forest.

In this way, Salt March inspired people from different segments of our society and became our effective tool of resistance against the colonial power.

Q.6 Imagine you are a woman participating in Civil Disobedience Movement. Explain what the experience meant to your life.

Ans. I was very happy to participate in Civil Disobedience Movement because I understood that I had to serve the nation in whatever capacity I could. I had heard Gandhiji speaking and asking us to participate in this movement. Inspired by him, I also offered Satyagraha, picketed liquor shops and shops selling foreign cloth and also courted arrest.

I felt empowered by these activities and felt that women also could help the men actively in the ultimate goal of achieving independence from the British. The experience has made me realise that women also have an important role to play in realising our freedom.

Q.7 Why did political leaders differ sharply over the question of separate electorates?

Ans. Political leaders differed sharply over the question of separate electorates because

(i) The Muslim leaders thought that their interest could only be protected in a Muslim state and in a Hindu majority state they would be at the mercy of the Hindus. They wanted reserved seats in the Central Assembly and representation in proportion to population in the Muslim-dominated provinces, viz, Bengal and Punjab. However, this was dangerous for the unity of the nation.

(ii) Dr BR Ambedkar, the leader of the depressed classes, was in favour of separate electorates for his community but Gandhiji believed that separate electorate for Dalits would slow down the process of their integration into society and create divisions in the society. Later, Ambedkar accepted Gandhiji's position and signed 'Poona Pact'.

REVIEW EXERCISE

Including Competency Based Questions

Part I

Multiple Choice Questions (MCQs)

1. In India, the growth of modern nationalism in intimately connected to the ....

(a) Western education
(b) Awarness of people
(c) Anti-colonial movement
(d) None of the above

2. According to the census of 1921, 12 to 13 million people perished in India as a result of ....

(a) Famines (b) Epidemic
(c) First World War (d) Both (a) and (b)

3. Gandhiji organised a Satyagraha to support the peasants of the Kheda district of Gujarat in ....

(a) 1915 (b) 1916 (c) 1917 (d) 1918

4. When was the Non-cooperation and Khilafat Movement begin in India?

(a) January 1919 (b) January 1921
(c) February 1920 (d) February 1922

5. Who among the following led the peasant movement in Bardoli, in 1928? CBSE 2023

(a) Baba Ramchandra (b) Jawaharlal Nehru
(c) Subhash Chandra Bose (d) Vallabhbhai Patel

6. Which province did not boycott the council election?

(a) Madras
(b) Ahmedabad
(c) Hyderabad
(d) Lucknow

7. In Awadh, peasants were led by which sanyasi who had earlier been to Fiji, as an indentured labourer?

(a) Baba Ramdev
(b) Baba Nagarjuna
(c) Baba Ramchandra
(d) Baba Parmanand

8. With the growth of nationalism, who created the image of Bharat Mata in the 20th century?

(a) Nand Lal Bose
(b) Abanindranath Tagore
(c) Rabindranath Tagore
(d) Bankim Chandra Chattopadhyay

9. Who himself took interest to revive folklore in West Bengal?

(a) Rabindranath Tagore
(b) Bankim Chandra Chatopadhyay
(c) Abanindranath Tagore
(d) All of the above

10. Find the incorrect option.

(a) Mahatma Gandhi return to India from South Africa in 1918.

(b) In 1918, Gandhiji went to Ahmedabad to organise a Satyagrahi Movement.

(c) Khilafat Movement was started in 1921.

(d) Jallianwala Bagh massacre took place on 13th April, 1919.

11. Find the incorrect option.

(a) Simon Commission was constituted under John Simon.

(b) 'Oudh Kisan Sabha' was headed by Mahatma Gandhi.

(c) In Awadh, the Peasant Movement developed under the leadership of Baba Ramchandra.

(d) In 1921, Gandhiji had designed a tricolour Swaraj Flag.

12. Identify the appropriate reason for the formation of the Swaraj Party from the option given below.

(a) It wanted members of Congress to return to Council politics.

(b) It wanted members of Congress to ask for Poorna Swaraj for Indians.

(c) It wanted members of Congress to oppose Simon Commission.

(d) It wanted members of Congress to ask Dominion State for India.

13. The Non-Cooperation-Khilafat Movement began in January, 1921. Various social groups participated in this movement, each with its own specific aspiration.

Which quote reflects the anti-imperialist sentiment that prevailed among many Indians during the Non-Cooperation Movement? Competency Based

(a) "The British Empire is a fraud and a sham. It is built on force and injustice. We must not cooperate with it in any way."

(b) "Swaraj (self-rule) is not merely political independence. It is much more than that. It is the regeneration of Indian society. It is the purification of Indian society."

(c) "We must not only boycott British goods, but we must also boycott British institutions, such as schools and courts. We must build our own institutions, based on our own principles."

(d) "Swaraj (self-rule) is my birthright, and I shall have it."

14. 'The Salt Satyagraha March, also known as the Dandi March of 1930, was a landmark event in the history of India's freedom struggle. As part of the Civil Disobedience Movement against the British rule, satyagrahis led by Gandhi marched from the Sabarmati Ashram in Ahmedabad to the coastal village of Dandi from 12th March to 5th April, 1930 and made salt from seawater, breaking the Salt Law imposed by the British.'

Source : The Economic Times

What did Mahatma Gandhi declare about the tax on salt and the government monopoly over its production during British rule?

(a) Gandhiji supported the tax on salt as a necessary source of revenue.

(b) Gandhiji believed that salt was not essential for the people.

(c) Gandhiji declared that the tax on salt revealed the most oppressive face of British rule.

(d) Gandhiji argued for the expansion of the government monopoly on salt production.

15. After the withdrawal of the Non-Cooperation Movement, two distinct approaches emerged within the Congress.

Which of the following accurately reflects these contrasting views?

(a) CR Das and Motilal Nehru advocated for boycott of all British institutions and focus on radical mass agitation.

(b) Jawaharlal Nehru and Subhash Chandra Bose supported participation in provincial councils to oppose British policies from within.

(c) Gandhi and the older Congress leadership were divided over the use of violence in the movement, eventually leading to a split.

(d) Younger leaders wanted immediate independence while the older generation preferred gradual reforms.

16. The Congress Working Committee, in its meeting, in Wardha on 14th July, 1942, passed the historic 'Quit India' resolution demanding the immediate transfer of power to Indians and Quit India.

How did the British government respond to the Quit India Movement? Competency Based

(a) They welcomed the movement and offered to negotiate with Indian leaders.

(b) They used force to suppress the movement and arrested thousands of people.

(c) They ignored the movement and allowed it to continue unhindered.

(d) They sympathised with the movement and offered to grant India independence.

17. Mahatma Gandhi relaunched the Civil Disobedience Movement, for over a year, the movement continued, but by 1934 it lost its momentum.

Which of the following events prompted Mahatma Gandhi to relaunch the Civil Disobedience Movement?

(a) The release of political prisoners following the Round Table Conference.

(b) The breakdown of negotiations at the Round Table Conference and the subsequent repression by the British government.

(c) The growing support for the Congress and its policies.

(d) The failure of the British government to implement the recommendations of the Simon Commission.

18. Identify the correct option that describes the movement given below.
The movement broke colonial laws and also refused cooperation with the British. **CBSE Additional SQP 2023-24**

(a) Rowlatt Satyagraha Movement
(b) Civil Disobedience Movement
(c) Non-Cooperation Movement
(d) Quit India Movement

19. How was the Rowlatt Act of 1919 perceived in terms of fundamental rights and civil liberties by Indians? **CBSE Additional SQP 2023-24**

(a) It was viewed as a regressive legislation in favour of the majority Indians.
(b) It was considered as severely curtailing the right to personal liberty.
(c) It was seen as a necessary measure to prevent communal tensions.
(d) It was regarded as a safeguard for protecting British soldiers.

20. Why did nationalists in late-nineteenth-century India focus on recording and preserving folklore? **CBSE SQP 2024-25**

(a) To create new forms of artistic expression that reflected modern India.
(b) To restore a sense of pride in traditional culture and national identity.
(c) To use folklore as a tool for economic development and modernisation.
(d) To promote a uniform culture that could be adopted across all Indian regions.

21. Arrange the following events of Indian National Movement in chronological order and choose the correct option. **CBSE 2024**

I. Formation of Swaraj Party
II. Lahore session of the Indian National Congress
III. Gandhi–Irwin Pact
IV. Formation of Depressed Class Association

Options

(a) II, III, I, IV (b) I, II, IV, III
(c) I, III, IV, IV (d) IV, III, II, I

22. Arrange the following events in chronological order and choose the correct option. **CBSE 2024**

I. Formation of Khilafat Committee in Bombay
II. Jallianwala Bagh Massacre
III. Bardoli Satyagraha
IV. Withdrawal of Non-Cooperation Movement

Codes

(a) I, II, III, IV (b) II, I, IV, III
(c) I, II, IV, III (d) III, IV, II, I

23. Arrange the following events in chronological order and choose the correct option. **CBSE 2024**

I. Establishment of Depressed Classes Association
II. Gandhi-Irwin Pact
III. Formation of the Federation of Indian Chambers of Commerce and Industry (FICCI)
IV. Second Round Table Conference in London.

Codes

(a) I, II, III, IV (b) II, I, III, IV
(c) III, I, II, IV (d) IV, I, II, III

24. Arrange the following events in the correct chronological order leading upto the Civil Disobedience Movement. **CBSE SQP 2024-25**

I. Boycott of the Simon Commission.
II. Poorna Swaraj resolution passed.
III. Letter with 11 demands sent to Viceroy Irwin.
IV. Salt March.

Codes

(a) IV, III, II, I (b) II, I, III, IV
(c) I, IV, III, II (d) I, II, III, IV

25. Arrange the following historical events in chronological order and choose the correct option. **CBSE 2025**

I. Second Round Table Conference
II. Simon Commission arrives in India
III. Beginning of Dandi March
IV. Incident of Chauri-Chaura

Options

(a) I, II, III and IV (b) IV, II, III and I
(c) IV, II, I and III (d) I, II, IV and III

26. What is correct in context of Jallianwala Bagh Massacre?

I. Being from outside the city, all villagers were aware of the martial law that had been imposed.
II. Only men to protest against the government's new repressive measures.
III. On 13th April, the infamous Jallianwalla Bagh incident took place.
IV. On that day a large crowd gathered in the enclosed ground of Jallianwalla Bagh.

Codes

(a) Only I (b) III and IV (c) I and II (d) Only II

27. After arriving in India, Mahatma Gandhi successfully organised satyagraha movements in various places. Choose from the appropriate statements among the following options

I. In 1917, he travelled to Champaran in Bihar to inspire the peasants to struggle against the oppressive plantation system.
II. In 1917, he organised a satyagraha to support the peasants of the Kheda district of Gujarat.
III. Affected by crop failure and a plague epidemic, the peasants of Kheda could not pay the revenue, and were demanding that revenue collection be relaxed.
IV. In 1918, Mahatma Gandhi went to Ahmedabad to organise a satyagraha movement amongst cotton mill workers.

Options
(a) Statements I and II are appropriate.
(b) Statements I, II and III are appropriate.
(c) All the statements are appropriate.
(d) Only statement iv is appropriate.

28. **Consider the statements given below and choose the correct answer.** **Competency Based**

Statement I In his famous book Hind Swaraj (1909) Mahatma Gandhi declared that British rule was established in India with the cooperation of Indians, and had survived only because of this cooperation.

Statement II Gandhiji proposed that the Non-Cooperation Movement should unfold in stages.

Codes
(a) Statement I is correct and II is incorrect
(b) Statement I is incorrect and II is correct
(c) Both I and II are incorrect
(d) Both I and II are correct

29. **Identify the movement with the help of given information.**
(i) The movement was launched to attain 'Purna Swaraj' or complete Independence.
(ii) It was launched in 1930 by Gandhiji.
(iii) The movement was aimed at breaking certain laws like the Salt Laws.
(iv) The movement was started from Sabarmati Ashram to Dandi.

Options
(a) Non-Cooperation Movement
(b) Civil Disobedience Movement
(c) Khilafat Movement
(d) Quit India Movement

30. **Identify the correct option that describes the act given below.** **CBSE Additional SQP 2023-24**
(i) The act was passed by was Imperial Legislative Council.
(ii) It gave power to the government to repress political activities.
(iii) It empowered the government to detain political prisoners without trial.

Options
(a) Rowlatt Act
(b) Vernacular Press Act
(c) Government of India Act
(d) Inland Emigration Act

Answers

1. (c)	**2.** (d)	**3.** (c)	**4.** (b)	**5.** (d)
6. (a)	**7.** (c)	**8.** (d)	**9.** (a)	**10.** (a)
11. (b)	**12.** (a)	**13.** (a)	**14.** (c)	**15.** (d)
16. (b)	**17.** (b)	**18.** (b)	**19.** (b)	**20.** (b)
21. (b)	**22.** (c)	**23.** (c)	**24.** (d)	**25.** (b)
26. (b)	**27.** (c)	**28.** (d)	**29.** (b)	**30.** (a)

Match the Following

1.

List I (Year)	**List II** (Events)
A. 1921	1. Non-Cooperation Movement
B. 1917	2. Khilafat Committee was formed
C. 1919	3. Chauri-Chaura incident
D. 1922	4. Gandhi travelled to Champaran

Codes

	A	B	C	D		A	B	C	D
(a)	1	4	2	3	(b)	1	2	3	4
(c)	4	3	2	1	(d)	3	4	1	2

2.

List I (Year)	**List II** (Events)
A. 1919	1. Jallianwala Bagh Massacre
B. 1924	2. Alluri Sitaram Raju was executed
C. 1931	3. Second Round Table Conference
D. 1930	4. Salt March

Codes

	A	B	C	D		A	B	C	D
(a)	1	2	3	4	(b)	4	3	2	1
(c)	4	3	1	2	(d)	3	4	2	1

Ans. 1. (a) 2. (a)

Assertion-Reason

1. **Assertion** (A) In 1918, Gandhiji went to Ahmedabad to organise a Satyagraha Movement amongst cotton mill workers.

Reason (R) After arriving in India, Gandhiji successfully organised Satyagraha Movement in various places.

Codes
(a) Both A and R are true and R is the correct explantionof A
(b) Both A and R are true, but R is not the correct explanation of A
(c) A is true, but R is false
(d) A is false, but R is true

2. **Assertion** (A) The Chauri-Chaura incident occurred at Chauri-Chaura in Gorakhpur district of United Province in February, 1922.

Reason (R) Large number of people participated in Non-Cooperation Movement.

Codes
(a) Both A and R are true and R is the correct explantion of A
(b) Both A and R are true, but R is not the correct explanation of A
(c) A is true, but R is false
(d) A is false, but R is true

3. Assertion (A) Mahatma Gandhi believed that dharma of non-violence could not unite all Indians.

Reason (R) Without seeking vengeance or being aggressive, a satyagrahi could win the battle through non-violence.

Codes

(a) Both A and R are true and R is the correct explanation of A
(b) Both A and R are true, but R is not the correct explanation of A
(c) A is true, but R is false
(d) A is false, but R is true

4. Assertion (A) On 13th April the infamous Jallianwalla Bagh incident took place.

Reason (R) Dyer entered the area, blocked the exit points and opened fire on the crowd, killing hundreds.

Codes

(a) Both A and R are true and R is the correct explanation of A
(b) Both A and R are true, but R is not the correct explanation of A
(c) A is true, but R is false
(d) A is false, but R is true

5. Assertion (A) The Non-Cooperation Movement was a unanimous decision within the Congress.

Reason (R) Many Congress members were concerned about the potential for violence and the boycott of council elections.

Codes

(a) Both A and R are true and R is the correct explanation of A
(b) Both A and R are true, but R is not the correct explanation of A
(c) A is true, but R is false
(d) A is false, but R is true

6. Assertion (A) The Simon Commission's arrival in India sparked widespread protests and demonstrations.

Reason (R) All major political parties, including the Congress and the Muslim League, opposed the commission due to its lack of Indian representation.

Codes

(a) Both A and R are true and R is the correct explanation of A
(b) Both A and R are true, but R is not the correct explanation of A
(c) A is true, but R is false
(d) A is false, but R is true

7. Assertion (A) The Non-Cooperation Movement had a significant impact on the minds of Indians.

Reason (R) The movement led to a boycott of foreign goods, which in turn boosted the production of Indian textile mills and handlooms.

Codes

(a) Both A and R are true and R is the correct explanation of A
(b) Both A and R are true, but R is not the correct explanation of A
(c) A is true, but R is false
(d) A is false, but R is true

Ans. 1. (a) Both A and R are true and R is the correct explanation of A
2. (b) Both A and R are true, but R is not the correct explanation of A
3. (d) A is false, but R is true
4. (a) Both A and R are true and R is the correct explanation of A
5. (d) A is false, but R is true
6. (a) Both A and R are true and R is the correct explanation of A
7. (a) Both A and R are true and R is the correct explanation of A

Picture Based Questions

1. The given picture depict which among the following events during British rule?

(a) Boycott of Foreign Cloth
(b) The Dandi March
(c) Khilafat Movement
(d) Kisan Sabha

2. Three famous personalities in the picture given below are Mahatma Gandhi, Jawaharlal Nehru and ....

(a) Maulana Azad (b) BR Ambedkar
(c) Muhammad Ali Jinnah (d) Shaukat Ali

3. This picture of Bharat Mata as given below is drawn by

(a) Rabindranath Tagore (b) Abanindranath Tagore
(c) Ravi Varma (d) Amrita Shergil

Ans. 1. (b) The Dandi March 2. (a) Maulana Azad
3. (b) Abanindranath Tagore

Case Based Question

1. Read the given passage and answer the questions that follows.

The failure of the Cripps Mission and the effects of World War II created widespread discontentment in India. This led Gandhiji to launch a movement calling for complete withdrawal of the British from India. The Congress Working Committee, in its meeting, in Wardha on 14th July, 1942, passed the historic 'Quit India' resolution demanding the immediate transfer of power to Indians and Quit India.

On 8th August, 1942 in Bombay, the All India Congress Committee endorsed the resolution which called for a non-violent mass struggle on the widest possible scale throughout the country. It was on this occasion that Gandhiji delivered the famous 'Do or Die' speech.

The call for 'Quit India' almost brought the state machinery to a standstill in large parts of the country as people voluntarily threw themselves into the thick of the movement. People observed hartals, demonstrations and processions were accompanied by national songs and slogans. The movement was truly a mass movement which brought into its ambit thousands of ordinary people, namely students, workers and peasants. The British responded with much force, yet it took more than a year to suppress the movement.

(i) Which event triggered the Quit India Movement?
(a) The success of the Cripps Mission.
(b) The failure of the Cripps Mission and the effects of World War II.
(c) The appointment of Lord Linlithgow as the Viceroy of India.
(d) The outbreak of the Quit India Movement.

(ii) What are some of the ongoing challenges in studying and understanding the Quit India Movement?
(a) Access to limited historical records and documents.
(b) Bias in various interpretations and narratives.
(c) Balancing the role of individual leaders and mass participation.
(d) All of the above

(iii) The British response to the Quit India Movement included
(a) Targeting specific leaders for negotiation.
(b) Utilising mass arrests and detentions.
(c) Implementing censorship and media control.
(d) All of the above

(iv) The Quit India Movement resolution was passed in a tense atmosphere, with the imminent threat of
(a) Japanese invasion
(b) World War II escalation
(c) Internal party disagreements
(d) British Government crackdown

Ans. (i) (b) The failure of the Cripps Mission and the effects of World War II.
(ii) (d) All of the above
(iii) (d) All of the above
(iv) (d) British Government crackdown

Part II

Very Short Answer Type Questions

1. Mention the views of Mahatma Gandhi on Satyagraha. CBSE Term II 2022

Ans. The views of Mahatma Gandhi on Satyagraha were

- Gandhi's method on movement and protest based on the truth and non-violence.
- As per Gandhiji, without being aggressive, a satyagrahi could win the battle through non-violence.

2. In which city Mahatma Gandhi launched Satyagraha in 1918?

Ans. Gandhiji launched Satyagraha in 1918 at Ahmedabad amongst cotton mill workers.

3. When was Rowlatt Act passed?

Ans. The Rowlatt Act was passed in 1919.

4. When did the Non-Cooperation and Khilafat Movement begin?

Ans. In January 1921, the Non-Cooperation and Khilafat Movement began.

5. How did the Non-Cooperation Movement unfold in the cities and towns of India? CBSE SQP Term II 2021

Ans. The Non-cooperation Movement unfolded in the cities and towns of India in the following manner

- There was a large-scale participation of the middle-class people living in the cities and towns.
- As the Non-cooperation began, thousands of students boycotted and left the government-controlled schools and colleges. Similarly, teachers also resigned from their positions and lawyers to gave up their legal practices.

6. Why was the Inland Emigration Act of 1859 troublesome for plantation workers? CBSE 2020

Ans. Under the Inland Emigration Act of 1859, plantation workers were not permitted to leave the tea gardens without permission, so it was troublesome for plantation workers.

7. What was the reason for calling off the Non-Cooperation Movement?

Ans. Due to Chauri-Chaura violent incident, Gandhiji called off the Non-Cooperation Movement in 1922.

8. Who announced a vague offer of 'Dominion status' for India in 1929?

Ans. Viceroy Lord Irwin announced a vague offer of 'Dominion status' for India in 1929.

9. How many miles were covered in Gandhiji's Salt March?

Ans. 240 miles were covered in Gandhiji's Salt March.

10. The resolution of Purna Swaraj was adopted at which Congress Session?

Ans. In Lahore, the resolution of Purna Swaraj was adopted in 1929.

11. Dr BR Ambedkar, who organised the dalits into the Depressed Classes Association in 1930, clashed with Mahatma Gandhi at the Second Round Table Conference by demanding separate electorates for dalits. Competency Based

(i) What was the primary objective of Dr BR Ambedkar in organising the Dalits into the Depressed Classes Association in 1930?

(ii) Why did Dr BR Ambedkar and Mahatma Gandhi clash at the Second Round Table Conference?

Ans. (i) The primary objective of Dr BR Ambedkar in organising the Dalits into the Depressed Classes Association in 1930 was to mobilise the Dalits and fight for their rights. He aimed to uplift the Dalits, who were socially and economically marginalised, and ensure that they received equal treatment and opportunities.

(ii) Dr BR Ambedkar and Mahatma Gandhi clashed at the Second Round Table Conference over the issue of separate electorates for Dalits.

12. Chauri Chaura — whose name derives from that of two villages — is a town in Gorakhpur district, about halfway between Gorakhpur and Deoria. It has a small railway station, which initially put Chauri Chaura on the map. The town was the scene of a violent incident with far-reaching consequences during the freedom struggle a century ago.

Source : The Indian Express Competency Based

(i) When and where did the Chauri Chaura incident occur?

(ii) What was the main cause of the incident?

Ans. (i) The Chauri Chaura incident occurred on 4th February, 1922, in Chauri Chaura village, Gorakhpur district, United Provinces (present-day Uttar Pradesh) in India.

(ii) The main cause of the incident was a clash between a large group of protesters participating in the Non-Cooperation Movement and local police officials.

13. On 13th April, 1919, the Baisakhi Day, a meeting of freedom fighters was scheduled at Jallianwalla bagh to protest against the Rowlatt Act. Competency Based

Source : Times of India

(i) When and where did the Jallianwala Bagh massacre occur?

(ii) Who was responsible for the massacre?

Ans. (i) The Jallianwala Bagh massacre occured on 13th April, 1919, in Jallianwala Bagh, an enclosed public garden in Amritsar, Punjab, India.

(ii) British troops commander Brigadier General Dyer was responsible for the massacre.

14. Mahatma Gandhi found in salt a powerful symbol that could unite the nation. On 31st January, 1930, he sent a letter to Viceroy Irwin stating eleven demands. Where and when did the Salt March take place? Competency Based

Ans. The Salt March took place on 12th March, 1930, in Sabarmati Ashram, Ahmedabad and culminated in Dandi, Gujarat, on 6th April, 1930.

15. During the Non-Cooperation Movement, thousands of workers defied the authorities, left the plantations and headed home. They believed that Gandhi Raj was coming.
What was the historical significance of the Non-Cooperation Movement?

Ans. The Non-Cooperation Movement was a pivotal event in the Indian independence movement as it demonstrated the power of non-violent resistance and laid the groundwork for future struggles against British rule. The movement also helped to shape the ideology and strategies of the Indian National Congress.

Short Answer Type Questions

1. What was the impact of the First World War on India?

Or How was the social and political situation of India affected by the First World War? Explain. CBSE SQP 2022-23

Ans. The First World War deeply affected India though it was under the British rule at that time.

The impacts of the First World War on India were as follows

- The British Government raised taxes, custom duties and income taxes in India to finance the war expenditures.
- Villagers and farmers were forcefully recruited in the British army.
- There was a rise in prices of food and other essential things.

2. What was the Rowlatt Act? How did it affect the National Movement?

Or What was Rowlatt Act? How did the Indians show their disapproval towards this Act?

Ans. Rowlatt Act was an oppressive act introduced by the British Government in 1919. It gave the Government enormous powers to repress, political activities and allowed detention of political person without trial for two years.

The Rowlatt Act affected the National Movement in the following ways

- Rallies were organised in various cities, workers went on strike in railway workshops and shops were closed down.
- British administration suppressed the nationalists. As a result, local leaders were picked up from Amritsar and Mahatma Gandhi was barred from entering Delhi.

3. How did Indians react to the Jallianwala Bagh massacre ? Explain. CBSE 2025

Ans. Indians reacted to the Jallianwala Bagh massacre with shock, anger, and grief. The brutal killing of unarmed protesters by British forces sparked widespread resentment against British rule. It led to protests, demonstrations, and calls for a stronger independence movement.

The incident galvanised the Indian freedom struggle, with leaders like Mahatma Gandhi urging for non-cooperation with the British government, and it increased nationalist sentiments across the country.

4. Explain any three effects of the Non-Cooperation Movement on the Indian economy. CBSE 2023

Or Analyse the economic impacts of the Non-Cooperation Movement. CBSE 2024

Ans. The effects of Non-Cooperation Movement on the economic front were

- Foreign goods were boycotted, liquor shops were picketed and foreign clothes were burnt hugely.
- The import of foreign clothes halved between 1921 and 1922, its value dropping from 102 crore to 57 crore rupees.
- In many areas, traders and merchants refused to trade in foreign goods and sometimes even they refused to finance foreign trade.
- As the boycott movement spread, people used only Indian clothes and began to discard foreign clothes. As a result, production of Indian textile mills and handloom went up largely.

5. Why did Non-Cooperation Movement gradually slow down in cities? Explain two reasons.

Ans. The Non-Cooperation Movement in the cities gradually slowed down for various reasons

(i) Khadi cloth was often more expensive than mass produced mill cloth and poor people could not afford to buy it. Thus, boycott of foreign goods could not continue for long.

(ii) Similarly, the boycott of British institutions posed a problem. No alternative institutions were set-up in their place. So, the students, teachers lawyers and other professionals finally had to resume their studies and jobs in government institutions like schools, colleges, courts, etc.

6. Describe the spread of Non-Cooperation Movement in the countryside.

Ans. The Non-Cooperation Movement spread to the countryside in the following ways

- In Awadh, the Peasant Movement developed under the leadership of Baba Ramchandra (a Sanyasi who had earlier been a Fiji as an indentured labourer).
- This Peasant Movement demanded reduction of revenue, abolition of begar and social boycott of oppressive landlords.

- In many places, nai-dhobi bandhs were organised by panchayats to deny services to all landlords.
- In October, 1920 the Oudh Kisan Sabha was set-up. It was headed by Jawaharlal Nehru, Baba Ramchandra and a few others. Within a month, over 300 branches of this sabha had been set up in the villages around the region.
- As the peasant movement spread, the houses of *talukdars* (Indian land-holders) and merchants were attacked, bazaars were looted and grain hoards were taken over.

7. Describe any three major problems faced by the peasants of Awadh in the days of Non-Cooperation Movement.

Ans. In the days of Non-Cooperation Movement, the peasants of Awadh faced a lot of problems. These were

- Talukdars and landlords demanded very high rents and a variety of other taxes from the peasants.
- Peasants had to do *begar* (labour without any payment).
- The peasants had no security of tenure, they were evicted regularly so that they could not acquire right over the leased land.

Thus, the peasant movement in Awadh demanded reduction of revenue, abolition of begar and social boycott of oppressive landlords.

8. "Tribal peasants interpreted the message of Mahatma Gandhi and the idea of swaraj in another way and participated in the Non-Cooperation Movement differently." Justify the statement. **CBSE SQP Term II 2021**

Or **"Tribal peasants interpreted the message of Mahatma Gandhi and the idea of 'Swaraj in yet another way." Explain the statement in the context of Non-cooperation Movement.** **CBSE 2025**

Ans. The tribal peasants interpreted the message of Mahatma Gandhi and the idea of Swaraj in different manner and participated in the Non-Cooperation Movement differently. For example, in the Gudem Hills of Andhra Pradesh, a militant guerrilla movement spread in the early 1920s. It is not a form of struggle that the Congress could approve. They were against the colonial rule and policies because it affected their livelihood as well as their traditional rights were also denied.

The leader of the guerilla movement, Alluri Sitaram Raju talked about the greatness of Mahatma Gandhi and said he was inspired by the Non-Cooperation Movement and Swaraj. He persuaded people to wear khadi and give up drinking. But at the same time, he asserted that India could be liberated only by the use of force, not non-violence. The Gudem rebels attacked police stations, attempted to kill British officials and carried on guerrilla warfare for achieving Swaraj.

9. Why was Non-Cooperation Movement started in 1920? Why did Gandhiji call off the movement in 1922?

Ans. Non-Cooperation movement was started by Gandhiji in 1920, for the following reasons

- Gandhiji saw this as opportunity to unite Muslims and Hindus.
- He wanted a solution on Khilafat issue.
- The most important objective was the attainment of Swaraj.

Gandhiji called off Non-Cooperation Movement in 1922, due to the following reasons

- The movement became violent at Chauri-Chaura (Gorakhpur) where a peaceful demonstration in a bazar turned into a violent clash in which more than 20 policemen were killed.
- Gandhiji felt that the Satyagrahis needed to be properly trained before they would be ready for mass struggle.

10. Explain the effects of 'world wide economic depression' on India, towards late 1920s.

Ans. The effects of worldwide depression on India were as follows

- India's trade was affected, exports decreased as international prices crashed.
- Agricultural prices fell due to which farmers could not sell their produce and the British government continued to take high taxes.
- The economic instability and colonial rule provided an opportunity to Mahatma Gandhi to launch the Civil Disobedience Movement in 1930.

11. Explain the reason for the Lahore Session of the Congress in 1929 to be called the historical session.

Or **Mention the main contents of Indian National Congress in December 1929 held under the leadership of Jawaharlal Nehru.**

Ans. The Lahore session of the Congress in 1929 is considered historical because of the following reasons

- In the Lahore Session-December 1929, under the presidency of Jawaharlal Nehru, the Lahore Congress formalised the demand of 'Purna Swaraj' or full independence for India.
- This session declared that 26th January, 1930, would be celebrated as Independence Day, with people pledging to struggle for complete independence.
- It was after this session that Gandhiji sought to devise ways to relate the idea of independence with the daily issues of the people to make the struggle more relatable.

12. Why did Gandhiji launch the Civil Disobedience Movement? Explain any three reasons.

Ans. The main reasons behind launching the Civil Disobedience Movement are

- Mahatma Gandhi sent a letter on 31st January, 1930 to Viceroy Irwin stating eleven demands. Some of these were of general interest, others were specific demands of different classes. However, Viceroy Irwin refused the demands.
- Gandhiji believed that the tax on salt and the Government monopoly over salt production was the most oppressive measure taken by the British Government. This law had to be removed. Thus, he broke the salt law by manufacturing salt by boiling water in Dandi and urged the people to refuse cooperation with the British. The Salt March marked the beginning of the Civil Disobedience Movement.

13. Why did Mahatma Gandhi find in 'salt' a powerful symbol that could unite the nation? Explain.

Ans. Mahatma Gandhi found in salt a powerful symbol that could unite the nation because

- Salt is consumed by everyone and is regarded as one of the most essential items of food. By levying tax on salt and establishing monopoly over its production, the communal power revealed the most oppressive face of them.
- Gandhiji thought if any movement could be arranged against this oppression which affected people from all strata, it could unite the nation. He believed 'salt' had this power. So, he gave an ultimatum to the British Government, but Irwin was not willing to negotiate.
- Gandhiji started his famous Salt March with his trusted 78 followers from the Sabarmati ashram towards Dandi, the coastal town of Gujarat. This marked the beginning of the Civil Disobedience Movement all over India.

In this way, 'salt' inspired the nation to rebel against the British.

14. Mention three reasons for which the rich peasant communities took active participation in the Civil Disobedience Movement.

Ans. Three reasons for which the rich peasant communities took active participation in the Civil Disobedience Movement are

(i) Being producers of commercial crops, they were hit very hard by the trade depression and falling prices.

(ii) As their cash income disappeared, they found it impossible to pay the government's revenue demand.

(iii) The government refused to reduce the revenue demand. This led to widespread resentment among the rich peasants and they enthusiastically supported the movement.

15. Analyse the role of merchants and the industrialists in the Civil Disobedience Movement.

Ans. Indian merchants and industrialists made huge profits during the First World War.

The following points analyse the role of merchants and the industrialists in the Civil Disobedience Movement

- They became powerful in the society and wanted to expand their business. So, they started opposing colonial policies that restricted their business.
- They wanted protection against imports of foreign goods and a rupee-sterling foreign exchange ratio that would discourage imports.
- The industrialists criticised colonial control over the Indian economy and supported the Civil Disobedience Movement at its first stage.
- They gave financial assistance and refused to buy or sell imported goods.
- Most industrialists thought 'Swaraj' as a time when colonial restriction did not exist on business world. As a result trade and business would flourish without constraints.

16. Mention the efforts of Gandhiji to get Harijans their rights.

Ans. The efforts of Gandhiji for Harijans were

- Gandhiji organised Satyagraha to secure the entry of the untouchables into temples and access to public wells, tanks, roads and schools.
- Gandhi himself cleaned toilets to dignify the work of the bhangi (the sweepers) and persuaded the upper caste to change their heart and give up the sin of untouchability.
- Gandhiji signed Poona Pact (September 1932) with Dr Ambedkar. It gave the depressed classes reserved seats in Provincial and Central Legislative Councils, but they were to be voted in by the General Electorate.

17. "Not all social groups were moved by the abstract concept of Swaraj." Support the statement in the light of Civil Disobedience Movement of 1930s.

Competency Based

Ans. In April 1930, Gandhiji launched the Civil Disobedience Movement. But all social groups were not moved by the abstract concept of Swaraj or full independence. One such social group was the 'dalit'. Dalit or oppressed were the 'untouchable' class of our society.

Many dalit leaders, specially Dr BR Ambedkar were keen on a different political solution to the problems of the community. They believed political empowerment would only resolve the problems of their social disability. They demanded reserved seats in educational institutions and separate electorate in the legislative councils.

Thus, Dalit participation in the Civil Disobedience Movement was limited particularly in Maharashtra and Nagpur region where the organisation of dalit was quite strong.

18. Explain the role of Ambedkar in uplifting the dalits or the depressed classes.

Ans. The role of Ambedker in uplifting the dalit or the depressed classes was as follows

- Dr BR Ambedkar joined active polities in 1930 and organised the Depressed Classes Association to uplift the dalits.
- He demanded separate electorates for dalits and reservation of seats in educational institutions for them.
- He signed the Poona Pact that gave reserved seats to the depressed classes in provincial and Central Legislative Councils.

19. What type of flag was designed during the 'Swaraj Movement' in Bengal? Explain its main features.

Or **Who designed the Swaraj flag? What were the features of this flag? How was it used as a symbol of defiance?**

Ans. At the time of Swadeshi or Swaraj Movement, a tricolour flag was designed in Bengal. Its features were

- It had eight lotuses representing eight provinces of British India and a crescent moon representing Hindu-Muslim community.
- It was a tricolour (red, green and yellow) flag. While Gandhiji had designed a Swaraj flag in 1921, which was a tricolour (red, green, white) with a spinning wheel in the centre.

Symbol of Defiance

It represented Gandhian ideal of self-help. Carrying the flag and holding it aloft during procession or marches, became a symbol of defiance.

20. Disucss the most likely events which led to the launch of the Non-Cooperation Movement.

Build the answer around these points **Competency Based**

- **The idea of Satyagraha**
- **The Rowlatt Act**
- **Jallianwala Bagh Massacre**

Ans. The Non-Cooperation Movement's launch was fueled by three key events

(i) **The Rowlatt Act** This harsh law authorised the British to detain individuals without trial, sparking widespread outrage and igniting the flames of nationalism.

(ii) **The Jallianwala Bagh Massacre** In April 1919, British troops opened fire on a peaceful gathering of unarmed civilians in Jallianwala Bagh, Amritsar, killing hundreds. This evil act became a symbol of British brutality and solidified the movement's resolve.

(iii) **Gandhi's Leadership** Mahatma Gandhi, a staunch advocate for non-violent resistance, emerged as the movement's leader. His call for Satyagraha, a philosophy of non-violent protest, related with millions who were barred from freedom under British rule.

Long Answer Type Questions

1. Explain four points about Gandhiji's Satyagraha.

Or **Gandhiji's idea of Satyagraha emphasised the power of truth and the need to search for truth. In the light of this statement assess the contribution of Gandhiji towards Satyagraha.**

Ans. After arriving in India, in 1915, Gandhiji successfully organised Satyagraha (which he had applied in South Africa), in various parts of India.

The idea of Satyagraha consists of

(i) The idea of Satyagraha emphasised the power of truth and the need to search for truth.

(ii) This idea suggested that if the cause was true and if the struggle was against injustice, then physical force was not necessary to fight the oppressor. Without being aggressive, the Satyagrahi could win the battle.

(iii) One can win the oppressor even by appealing to the conscience. Oppressor should be made to see the truth.

(iv) By this struggle, truth was bound to triumph (victory) ultimately. Gandhiji believed that this dharma of non-violence could unite all Indians.

2. Who launched the Khilafat Movement? Why was the movement launched?

Or **What were the circumstances which led to the Khilafat and the Non-Cooperation Movement?**

Ans. The Khilafat Movement was a united struggle launched by Muhammad Ali and Shaukat Ali. It was launched because Gandhiji saw this as an opportunity to bring Muslims under the umbrella of a unified National Movement.

The circumstances which led to the launch of Khilafat and Non-Cooperation Movements were :

(i) The Khilafat Movement (1919-1924), was a pan-Islamic, political protest campaign launched by Muslims in British India to influence the British Government and to protect the Ottoman Empire during the aftermath of First World War.

(ii) There was a fear that the power of the spiritual head of the Islamic world (Khalifa) would be curtailed.

(iii) To defend his power, a Khilafat Committee was formed in Bombay, in 1919. The Khilafat leaders put pressure upon the British Government to give better treatment to Turkey.

3. Why did Mahatma Gandhi launch the 'Non-Cooperation Movement'? How did this movement unite the country? Explain.

Ans. Gandhiji launched the Non-Cooperation Movement in 1920 for the following reasons :

- Gandhiji saw this as an opportunity to bring Muslims under the umbrella of a unified National Movement.

- Gandhiji thought that through the Non-Cooperation Movement, British rule in India would collapse within a year and Swaraj would come.

Thus, at the Congress Session in Nagpur, in December 1920, the Non-Cooperation programme was finalised and Gandhiji launched the Non-Cooperation Movement. This movement united the country in the following ways

- The Non-Cooperation Movement spread from the cities to the countryside. Different sections of our society interpreted this movement differently. The name of Gandhiji was invoked to sanction all actions and aspirations.
- In Awadh, peasants under the leadership of Baba Ram Chandra revolted against the talukdars and the landlords who demanded very high rent and different taxes from them.
- The peasant demanded reduction of revenue, abolition of begar and social boycott of oppressive landlords.
- In Gudem hills of Andhra Pradesh, Alluri Sitaram Raju inspired by Gandhiji's ideals came to lead them and the Gudem rebels attacked police stations and carried on guerrilla warfare for achieving Swaraj.

4. How did the 'Non-Cooperation Movement' spread in cities across the country? Explain its effects on the economic front.

Ans. The Non-Cooperation-Khilafat Movement was started by the Congress party in January 1921. Initially, this movement started with middle class participation in the cities.

Thousands of students, teachers and lawyers gave up their institutions and profession and joined the movement.

This movement began in different cities across the country. The Non-Cooperation Movement dramatically affected the economy of British India.

The economic effects of Non-Cooperation Movement were as follows

(i) As foreign goods and foreign clothes were boycotted, the import of foreign clothes halved between 1921 and 1922 and its value dropped from 102 crore to 57 crore rupees.

(ii) In many places, merchants and traders refused to trade in foreign goods or invest in foreign trade.

(iii) As people discarded imported clothes and started to use Indian clothes, production of Indian textile mills and handlooms went up. In this way, the Non-Cooperation Movement helped to boost the Indian economy.

5. How did plantation workers in Assam had their own understanding of Mahatma Gandhi and the notion of Swaraj? Explain.

Ans. The plantation workers in Assam had understood the notion of Swaraj in the following ways

- For plantation workers in Assam, freedom meant the right to move freely in and out of the confined space in which they were enclosed.
- Under the Inland Emigration Act of 1859, plantation workers were not permitted to leave the Tea Gardens without permission.
- Swaraj for them meant retaining a link the village from which they had come.
- When they heard of the Non-Cooperation Movement thousands of workers refused to obey their authorities, left the plantations and headed home.
- They believed that Gandhi Raj was coming and everyone would be given land in their own village.

6. 'The Civil Disobedience Movement was different from the Non-Cooperation Movement.' Support the statement with examples. Competency Based

Ans. The Civil Disobedience Movement was different from the Non-Cooperation Movement. The main differences between these two movements are

Civil Disobedience Movement	Non-Cooperation Movement
Civil Disobedience Movement was launched in 1930.	The Non-Cooperation Movement was launched in 1921 by Gandhiji.
The Civil Disobedience Movement was first supported by the Industrialists like GD Birla, Purshottamdas Thakur.	The Non-Cooperation Movement started with middle class participation.
The growing proximity of the Congress party and Hindu Mahasabha prevented the Muslims to participate in Civil Disobedience Movement.	Due to Khalifa issues, Muslim community participated in Non-Cooperation on a large scale.
The Civil Disobedience Movement was withdrawn in 1931, when Gandhi signed 'Gandhi-Irwin' pact.	The Non-Cooperation Movement was withdrawn by Gandhiji due to violent incident at Chauri Chaura.
Large scale participation of women is one of the most significant features of the Civil Disobedience Movement.	In Non-Cooperation Movement, women did not participate on a large scale.

7. Why did Mahatma Gandhi started the Civil Disobedience Movement? How did this movement unite the country? Explan.

Ans. Gandhiji launched the Civil Disobedience Movement because Lord Irwin ignored Gandhi's eleven demands including the abolition of the Salt tax. Gandhiji's 'Salt March' marked the beginning of the Civil Disobedience Movement all over India. Thousands of people in different parts of the country broke the salt law by manufacturing salt and giving demonstrations in front of government salt factories.

The Civil Disobedience Movement came into force in various parts of the country and united different groups in the country in the following ways

- With the spread of the movement, foreign cloths were boycotted and liquor shops were picketed. Peasants refused to pay revenue and *chaukidari* taxes. Village officials resigned from their post. Forest people violated forest laws.
- In the countryside, rich peasant communities *viz,* Patidars of Gujarat and the Jats of Uttar Pradesh became the supporters of the Civil Disobedience Movement.
- The poorer peasantry, often led by the socialist and the communist, joined a variety of radical movements for the remission of their unpaid rent to the landlords.
- Industrialists led by Purshottamdas Thakurdas and GD Birla supported the Civil Disobedience Movement. Moreover railway workers, dock workers, mine workers from Chota Nagpur and large number of women from all over India participated in the Civil Disobedience Movement.

8. Explain the role of women in the Civil Disobedience Movement.

***Or* When did the women of India see service to the nation as a sacred duty?**

Ans. An important feature of the Civil Disobedience Movement was the large-scale participation of women. The role of women in the movement is discussed below

- Women played a significant role in the Civil Disobedience Movement by joining Gandhiji's Salt March, participating in protest marches, and picketing foreign cloth and liquor shops.
- In urban areas, women were mainly from high-caste families, while in rural areas, they came from wealthy peasant households.
- Many women were inspired by Gandhiji's call and began to view serving the nation as a sacred duty.
- Despite their active participation, women's roles were still seen as primarily focused on home and family, with Gandhiji emphasising the importance of women being good mothers and wives.
- The Congress was reluctant to allow women to hold leadership positions and valued their symbolic presence more than actual authority.

But all these participation were symbolic as women did not hold any position of authority for a long time.

9. "Dalit participation was limited in the Civil Disobedience Movement". Examine the statement.

Ans. Dalit participation was limited in the Civil Disobedience Movement. It can understood through following points

- Dalits or untouchables belong to the lower strata of our society. The Congress party ignored the Dalits for fear of offending the conservative high caste Hindus, i.e. Sanatanis. Gandhiji first realised that Swaraj would not come for a hundred years if untouchability was not eliminated. But many Dalit leaders believed in a different political solution to the problem of their community.
- Dalits thought that only political empowerment would resolve their problem of social disabilities.
- They began organising themselves, demanding reserve seats in educational institutions and a separate electorate that would choose their Dalit members for Legislative Councils.
- Dr Ambedkar demanded separate electorates for Dalits which was denied by Gandhiji.
- Dalit movement continued to be apprehensive of the Congress led national movement and their participation was limited.

Thus, it can be concluded that Dalit participation was limited in the Civil Disobedience Movement.

10. There were variety of cultural processes through which Indian captured people's imagination." Explain the statement with examples. **CBSE 2024, Competency Based**

***Or* "History and fiction, folklore and songs, popular prints and symbols all played a part in the making of nationalism in India". Support the statement.** **Competency Based**

***Or* The ideas of nationalism developed through a movement to revive Indian folklore. Explain the statement in the context of the national movement.** **CBSE 2025**

Ans. There were a variety of cultural processes through which nationalism spread in people. History and fiction, folklore and songs, popular prints and symbols played a significant role in making of nationalism in the following ways

- Nationalist historians urged the readers to take pride in India's great achievements in the past and inspired them to struggle to change their miserable condition under British rule. Novels like 'Anandamath' written by Bankim Chandra Chattopadhayay inspired the revolutionaries in our country.
- Ideas of nationalism also developed through a movement to revive Indian folklore. In late 19th century, Indian, nationalists, like Rabindranath Tagore and Natesa Sastri collected folk tales, folk songs, ballads, nursery rhymes, myths.
  They wanted to give a true picture of traditional culture that had damaged by colonisers. Because folklore was the most trust worthy manifestation of people's real thoughts and characteristics.
- In the 20th century, with the growth of nationalism, the identity of India came to be visually associated with the image of Bharat Mata.
  Abanindranath Tagore and many more artists painted Bharat Mata and the devotion to this mother figure came to be seen as evidence of one's nationalism.

Further, Gandhiji designed the Swaraj flag (red, green, white). Carrying this flag, holding it aloft during marches became a symbol of defiance.

11. "Nationalism spreads when people begin to believe that they are all part of the same nation". Justify the statement.

Or **Explain the major factors which promoted the sense of nationalism in the Indians?**

Ans. The spreading of nationalism took place due to following factors

- **United Struggle** Different religious groups and communities unitedly struggled against the British rule.
- **Cultural Processes** Unity spread through various cultural processes like history, folklore, songs and symbols that helped in spread of nationalism.
- **Common Identity** The painting of 'Bharat Mata' was commonly identified as motherland and inspired the people equally.
- **Revival of Indian Folklore** Reviving the folklore through folk songs, legends helped in promoting traditional culture and restore a sense of pride in the past history and culture.
- **Role of the Leaders** Leaders like Mahatma Gandhi, Jawaharlal Nehru aroused the feelings of nationalism through their motivational speeches and political activities.

Thus, it can be concluded that nationalism spread, when people began to believe that they were all part of the same nation.

12. 'Mahatma Gandhi decided to withdraw the Non-Cooperation Movement as he felt that the movement is turning violent in many places and satyagrahi needed to be properly trained before they would be ready for mass struggles.'

Justify the statements with relevant points referring to Indian National Movement.

Ans. Gandhi's decision to withdraw the Non-Cooperation Movement in 1922 reflected his commitment to non-violent resistance.

He observed that the movement has turned into violence in several places, specifically the Chauri Chaura incident where protestors set a police station on fire. His core principle of Satyagraha, caused him to believe the movement was losing its direction.

The movement, in its initial stage, had not adequately prepared participants for the challenges of non-violent resistance. Gandhi recognised the need for rigorous training to instill discipline and control, preventing future violence. Gandhi believed in a long-term, non-violent struggle for independence. He viewed the withdrawal as a strategic retreat, allowing time for reflection, internal reorganisation and development of a more sustainable and disciplined approach.

The withdrawal aimed to maintain public trust and support. The withdrawal served as a valuable learning experience for the Indian National Movement. It allowed leaders to identify weaknesses, refine strategies and prepare for future campaigns, ultimately contributing to the movement's long-term success.

In conclusion, Gandhi's decision to withdraw the Non-Cooperation Movement was not a sign of defeat, but a strategic move to preserve the movement's core principles, protect lives, and ensure its long-term success.

13. Simon Commission, group appointed in November 1927 by the British Conservative government under Stanley Baldwin to report on the working of the Indian constitution established by the Government of India Act of 1919. The commission consisted of seven members—four Conservatives, two Labourites and one Liberal—under the joint chairmanship of the distinguished Liberal lawyer, Sir John Simon and Clement Attlee, the future Prime Minister. Its composition met with a storm of criticism in India because Indians were excluded. The commission was boycotted by the Indian National Congress and most other Indian political parties. It, nevertheless, published a two-volume report, mainly the work of Simon.

Source: Britanica

Analyse the Simon commission in terms of its impact - negative and /or positive on the development of Indian National Movement. **Competency Based**

Ans. The Simon Commission was established in 1927 to assess constitutional reforms in India. It had a significant impact on the development of the Indian National Movement, generating both negative and positive consequences as follows

- **Negative Impacts** There was no Indian representation in the commission which angered Indians. This disregard for Indian participation strengthened the demand for self-rule and fueled nationalist sentiments. The commission faced widespread boycotts and protests across India. This united diverse factions of the independence movement under a common banner of opposition to British rule.
- **Positive Impact** The commission's presence helped in greater collaboration and unity amongst diverse factions within the national movement. This facilitated a more unified approach towards achieving independence. The commission's recommendations, though ultimately rejected, forced the Indian National Congress to frame a clear vision for India's future Constitution. This led to the creation of the Nehru Report, which solidified their political agenda and provided a concrete roadmap for self-governance.

  The commission's activities and the Indian response attracted international attention. This garnered sympathy for the Indian cause and raised the profile of the independence movement on the global stage.

Case Based Questions

1. Read the source given below and answer the questions that follow. **CBSE Additional SQP 2023-24**

Mahatma Gandhi's letter was, in a way, an ultimatum. If the demands were not fulfilled by 11th March, the letter stated, the Congress would launch a civil disobedience campaign. Irwin was unwilling to negotiate. So, Mahatma Gandhi started his famous salt march accompanied by 78 of his trusted volunteers. The march was over 240 miles, from Gandhiji's ashram in Sabarmati to the Gujarati Coastal Town of Dandi. The volunteers walked for 24 days, about 10 miles a day. Thousands came to hear Mahatma Gandhi wherever he stopped and he told them what he meant by Swaraj and urged them to peacefully defy the British. On 6th April he reached Dandi and ceremonially violated the law, manufacturing salt by boiling sea water.

(i) What did Gandhiji's letter to Lord Irwin state?

(ii) Why did Gandhiji march to Dandi?

(iii) Gandhiji chose to defy salt tax in the civil disobedience movement. Substantiate the statement giving reasons.

Ans. (i) Gandhiji's letter to Lord Irwin stated that if the demands of the Indian National Congress were not fulfilled by 11th March, the Congress would launch a Civil Disobedience Campaign.

(ii) Gandhiji marched to Dandi as a part of the Civil Disobedience Campaign against the British salt laws. The march was a non-violent protest against the British monopoly on the production and sale of salt.

(iii) Gandhiji chose to defy the salt tax in the civil disobedience movement for several reasons. Firstly, the salt tax affected almost every Indian, making it a unifying issue for the movement. Secondly, making salt from sea water was a simple act that any Indian could perform, thereby enabling widespread participation in the movement. Lastly, by choosing a non-violent method of protest, Gandhiji aimed to demonstrate the unjust nature of British rule and the power of peaceful resistance.

2. Read the source given below and answer the questions that follow. **CBSE SQP 2023-24**

It is said of "passive resistance" that it is the weapon of the weak, but the power which is the subject of this article can be used only by the strong. This power is not passive resistance; indeed, it calls for intense activity. The movement in South Africa was not passive but active 'Satyagraha is not physical force'. A satyagrahi does not inflict pain on the adversary; he does not seek his destruction in the use of satyagraha, there is no ill will whatever. 'Satyagraha is pure soul force'. Truth is the very substance of the soul. That is why this force is called satyagraha. The soul is informed with knowledge. In it burns the flame of love. Non-violence is the supreme dharma...' It is certain that India cannot rival Britain or Europe in force of arms. The British worship the war God and they can all of them become, as they are becoming, bearers of arms. The hundreds of millions in India can never carry arms. They have made the religion of non-violence their own.

In his famous book Hind Swaraj (1909) Mahatma Gandhi declared that British rule was established in India, with the cooperation of Indians and had survived only because of this cooperation. If Indians refused to cooperate, British rule will collapse within a year.

(i) Gandhiji said, "passive resistance is not the weapon of the weak". Why?

Or Why did Gandhiji say "Satyagraha is pure soul force"? Explain by giving two arguments.

(ii) What according to Mahatma Gandhi is the best weapon to use to collapse British rule in India?

Ans. (i) Gandhiji said, 'passive resistance is not the weapon of the weak because it calls for intense activity with a lot of inner strength'.

Or Gandhiji referred to 'Satyagraha' as 'pure soul force' because

- It is a non-violent way of resisting injustice, relying on truth and inner strength.
- It emphasises that the power to resist comes from one's spirit and conviction, rather than physical force.

(ii) Mahatma Gandhi in his book 'Hind Swaraj' declared that through non-cooperation (Satyagraha) only British rule could be collapsed in India as they could build their empire only with the cooperation of Indians.

3. Read the source given below and answer the questions that follow **CBSE 2020**

The Movement in the Towns

The movement started with middle-class participation in the cities. Thousands of students left government-controlled schools and colleges, headmasters and teachers resigned and lawyers gave up their legal practices. The council elections were boycotted in most provinces except Madras, where the Justice Party, the party of the non-Brahmans, felt-that entering the council was one way of gaining some power-something that usually only Brahmans had access to.

The effects of non-cooperation on the economic front were more dramatic. Foreign goods were boycotted, liquor shops picketed and foreign cloth burnt in huge bonfires. The import of foreign cloth halved between 1921 and 1922, its value dropping from ₹ 102 crore to ₹ 57 crore. In many places merchants and traders refused to trade in foreign goods or finance foreign trade. As the boycott movement spread and people began discarding imported clothes and wearing only Indian ones, production of Indian textile mills and handlooms went up.

(i) Explain the role of 'Justice Party' in boycotting of Council elections.

(ii) How was the effects of 'non-cooperation on the economic front' dramatic?

(iii) Explain the effect of 'Boycott' movement on 'foreign textile trade.'

Ans. (i) The council elections were boycotted in most provinces but, it was not boycotted in Madras. In Madras, the 'Justice Party', the party of the non-Brahmans was powerful. They felt that entering the council was one way of gaining power which was enjoyed by the Brahmans only, so they did not oppose council election.

(ii) The effects of Non-Cooperation Movement were dramatic on economic front as foreign goods were boycotted, foreign clothes were burnt and foreign trade and financing foreign trade was refused.

(iii) With the spread of Boycott movement, people began discarding foreign clothes and started wearing only Indian ones. As a result, production of Indian textile mills and handlooms went up.

4. Read the source given below and answer the questions that follow. **CBSE Term II 2022**

The Independence Day Pledge, 26th January, 1930

'We believe that it is the inalienable right of the Indian people, as of any other people, to have freedom and to enjoy the fruits of their toil and have the necessities of life, so that they may have full opportunities of growth. We believe also that if any government deprives a people of these rights and oppresses them, the people have a further right to alter it or to abolish it.

The British Government in India has not only deprived the Indian people of their freedom but has based itself on the exploitation of the masses and has ruined India economically, politically, culturally and spiritually. We believe, therefore, that India must sever the British connection and attain Purna Swaraj or Complete Independence.

(i) Why was freedom considered an inalienable right of the Indian people?

(ii) Why was Purna Swaraj considered essential by the people of India?

(iii) Explain the significance of the Lahore Session of Congress (1930).

Or **(i) Why was Swaraj considered as an inalienable right of India?** **CBSE 2025**

(ii) Which type of government is supported in the source? **CBSE 2025**

(iii) Explain any two effects of British rule in India. **CBSE 2025**

Ans. (i) It was the inalienable right of the Indian people to have freedom and to enjoy the fruits of their hard labour and have the necessities of life, so that they might have full opportunities of growth.

(ii) Purna Swaraj has a deep significance in the history of India's struggle for attaining complete freedom. It was the starting point of an extensive political movement against the British Raj (colonial rule).

(iii) The Lahore Session of Congress (1930) was very significant because in this session, the prominent party Indian National Congress, took the resolution of Purna Swaraj or complete independence. In this, the Indian tricolour flag was hoisted by Pandit Jawaharlal Nehru on the banks of the Ravi river.

Or (i) Swaraj was considered an inalienable right of Indians because it was sbelieved that all people have the fundamental right to freedom. Under British rule Indians were deprived of this right. Therefore, they had the right to abolish British rule and attain Purna Swaraj.

(ii) The source supports a democratic government based on self-rule, where the people have the right to freedom, economic well-being and opportunities for growth.

(iii) Two effects of British rule in India are

- **Economic exploitiation** The British government in India exploited the Indian masses, leading to economic ruin. The British colonial policies drained India's wealth, resulting in poverty.
- **Cultural and spiritual decline** British rule negatively impacted India's cultural and spiritual life, undermining traditional practices.

5. Read the source given below and answer the questions that follow.

Emboldened with his success, Gandhiji in 1919 decided to launch a nationwide Satyagraha against the proposed Rowlatt Act (1919). This Act had been hurriedly passed through the Imperial Legislative Council despite the united opposition of the Indian members. It gave the government enormous powers to repress political activities and allowed detention of political prisoners without trial for two years. Mahatma Gandhi wanted non-violent civil disobedience against such unjust laws, which would start with a hartal on 6th April. **CBSE SQP 2024-25**

(i) Why did the British introduce the Rowlatt Act?

(ii) Examine the affect of this Act on Indians?

(iii) How did Mahatma Gandhi respond to the Rowlatt Act? Provide one reason for his reaction.

Ans. (i) The British introduced the Rowlatt Act in 1919 to suppress the revolutionary activities and movements where Indian revolutionaries were using different methods to challenge British rule.

(ii) The Rowlatt Act had a profound affect on Indians. This act was seen as an oppressive measure. This sparked widespread mass protests in the country. It played a significant role in widening the nationalist movement in India.

(iii) Gandhiji criticised the Rowlatt Act as an oppressive and unfair law that violated the civil rights of the citizens. He wanted non-violent civil disobedience against such unjust laws. Gandhiji emphasised peaceful protests and civil disobedience movement against the act, encouraging citizens to refuse to comply with the unfair provisions of the law.

Map Based Questions

1. Mark and locate the following on the given map of India.

(i) A place where the Congress Session was held in 1920. **CBSE 2025**

Or **Indian National Congress session at this place in 1920.** **CBSE SQP 2022-23, CBSE 2024, CBSE SQP 2024-25**

(ii) A place where the Congress Session was held in 1927. **CBSE 2025**

Ans. (i) 1920-Calcutta, Nagpur (ii) 1927-Madras

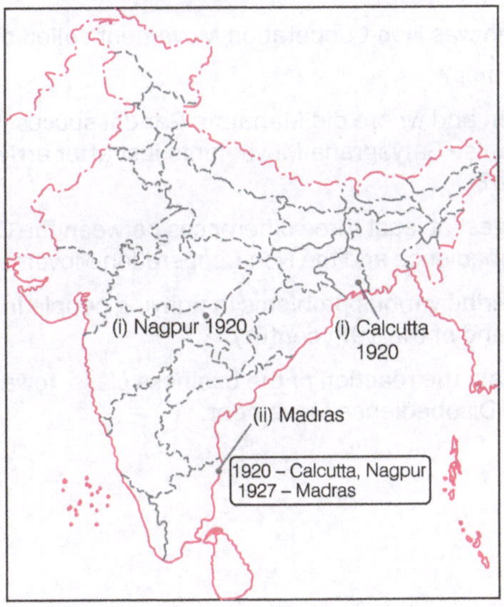

2. Mark and locate the following in given map of India.

(i) Jallianwala Bagh incident **CBSE 2024**

(ii) The place where Gandhiji started Dandi March **CBSE 2025**

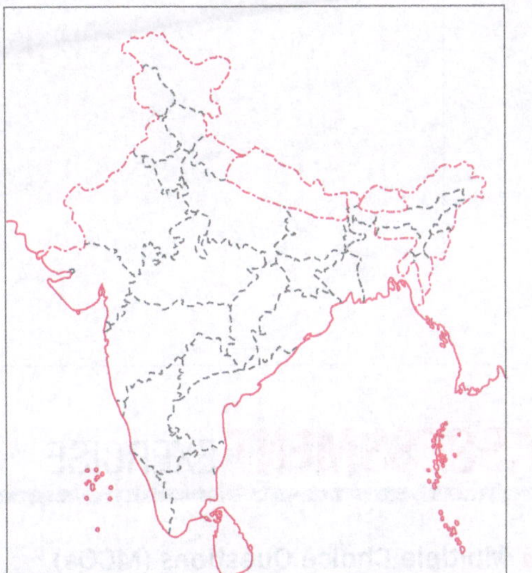

Ans. (i) Amritsar 1919-(Punjab). (ii) Dandi (Gujarat)

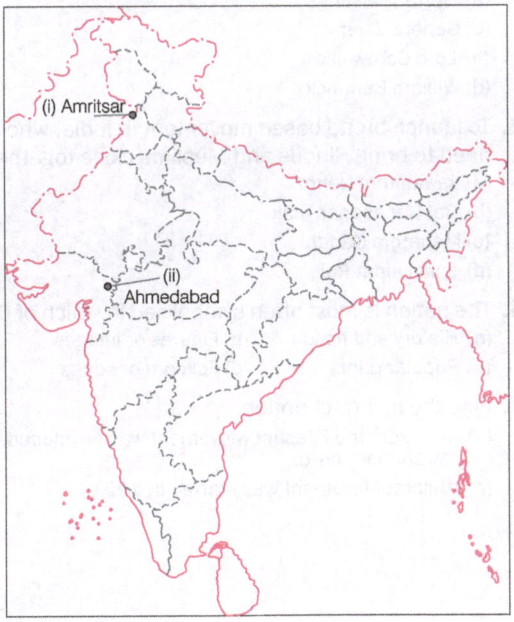

3. **Mark and locate the following in given map of India.**

(i) Movement of Indigo planters

(ii) Peasant Satyagraha

Or The place where the peasant Satyagraha took place **CBSE SQP 2024-25**

(iii) Cotton mill workers Satyagraha **CBSE 2025**

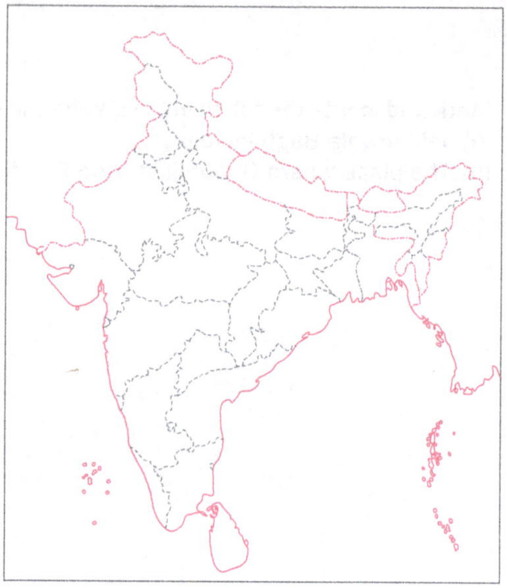

Ans. (i) Champaran (ii) Kheda

(iii) Ahmedabad

ASSESSMENT EXERCISE

Multiple Choice Questions (MCQs)

1. Who was responsible for the infamous Jallianwalla Bagh incidence on 13th April, 1919 at Amritsar?

(a) Warren Hastings

(b) General Dyer

(c) Lord Cornwallis

(d) William Bentinck

2. To launch broad based movement in India, who felt the need to bring Hindus and Muslims close together?

(a) Jawaharlal Nehru

(b) Bal Gangadhar Tilak

(c) Mahatma Gandhi

(d) Lala Lajpat Rai

3. The nation is most often symbolised in which of the forms?

(a) History and fiction (b) Figures or images

(c) Popular prints (d) Folklore or songs

4. Find the incorrect option.

(a) In Awadh, the Peasant Movement was developed under Pt Jawaharlal Nehru.

(b) Khilafat Movement was started in 1921.

(c) Ambedkar organised the Dalit into the Depressed Classes Association in 1930.

(d) In 1921, Gandhiji had designed a tricolour Swaraj Flag.

Subjective Questions (VSA, SA & LA)

1. Why was the Kheda Satyagraha launched by Gandhiji?

2. Why was the Simon Commission boycotted?

3. When was Non-Cooperation Movement called off by Gandhiji?

4. When and where did Mahatma Gandhi successfully organise Satyagraha Movements just after arriving in India?

5. Suggest at least three differences between the Civil Disobedience and the Non-Cooperation Movement.

6. Describe various problems in unifying people in India by the end of the 19th century.

7. Explain the reaction of the business class towards the Civil Disobedience Movement.

CHAPTER 3

The Making of a Global World

Globalisation is an economic system, which is hardly 50 years old but the making of the global world has a long history. To understand the phenomena of globalisation, it is required to understand the history of trade, migration, people's search for work, the movement of capital, etc.

3.1 The Pre-Modern World

Human societies have steadily become more interlinked throughout the history. From ancient times, travellers, traders, priests and pilgrims travelled vast distances for various reasons, like

- to gain knowledge
- for more opportunities
- for religious or spiritual fulfilment
- to escape from ill-treatment

They carry with themselves goods, money, ideas, skills, values, inventions and even germs and diseases.

An active coastal trade linked the Indus Valley Civilisations with West Asia in the early 3,000 BC.

For more than a millennia, *Cowries* (sea shells) were used as a form of currency from the Maldives to China and East Africa. By the 13th century, a strong link was established between the countries.

Silk Routes Link the World

Silk routes[1] have existed since the Christian era and flourished till the 15th century. The silk routes are good examples of pre-modern trade and cultural links.

Historians have identified various silk routes, both over land and by sea, connecting extensive regions across Asia and establishing links between Asia, Europe and Northern Africa.

Chinese pottery, Indian and South-East Asian textiles and spices all followed the same route. In exchange, Europe sent precious metals like gold and silver to Asia.

The Buddhist preachers, Christian missionaries and later on, Muslim preachers travelled along these routes.

Food Travels : New Crops Introduced

Traders and travellers introduced new crops to the land they visited. Foods like potatoes, soya, groundnuts, maize, tomatoes, chillies, sweet potatoes were introduced in Europe and Asia after Americas was discovered by **Christopher Columbus**.

Noodles travelled West from China and became spaghetti. Europe's poor began to eat better and live longer after the introduction of potatoes.

Arab traders took pasta to Sicily, an island in Italy. Ireland's poor peasants depended on the potatoes and when the Irish potato famine occurred in the mid 1840s, many people died of starvation in Ireland.

Conquest, Disease and Trade

The pre-modern world shrank after European sailors found a sea route to Asia and America in the 16th century.

Precious metal, mainly silver found in the mines of Peru and Mexico enhanced Europe's wealth and financed its trade with Asia. Many expeditions were taken in search of **El Dorado**, the fabled city of gold in South America.

The Spanish and Portuguese were the first Europeans to conquer America in mid-16th century.

The conquest of America was possible through the deadly disease smallpox that the Spanish conquerors carried on their person. America's original inhabitants had no immunity against these diseases.

1 **Silk Route** The route taken by traders to carry silk cargoes from China to the West.

Before the 19th century, many people in Europe faced poverty and hunger. Cities were crowded with people and diseases were widespread. Thus, many Europeans moved to America. By the eighteenth century, plantations[2] worked by African slaves were growing cotton and sugar for European markets.

India and China until 18th century were among the world's richest countries and the main centres of Asian trade. However, with Indian's colonisation and China's restriction of overseas contacts, Europe emerged as the centre of world trade.

3.2 The 19th Century (1815-1914)

In the 19th century, economic, political, social, cultural and technological factors interacted in complex ways. It changed the society and reshaped its external relations.

Economists identify three types of movement or flows within international economic exchanges

(i) The flow of trade in goods (especially cloth and wheat).

(ii) The flow of labour due to migration of people in search of employment.

(iii) The movement of capital for short-term or long-term investments over long distances.

All these flows affected people's lives significantly.

A World Economy Takes Shape

In the late 18th century, industrialisation and population growth had increased the demand for foodgrains in Britain. This situation resulted in the increase in prices of foodgrain.

Due to the pressure from the landowners, the government restricted the import of corn. These laws were commonly known as **Corn Laws**.

After the introduction of the Corn Laws, food prices became exorbitant[3].

Industrialists and people living in towns were unhappy with high food prices. They forced the British Government to abolish the Corn Laws.

After the abolition of the Corn Laws, food could be imported into Britain at much cheaper rates than before.

British agriculture was unable to compete with imports. Vast areas of land were now left uncultivated and thousands of people lost their livelihood. They came to the cities in search of works or migrated overseas.

Effects of Abolition of Corn Laws

- As food prices fell, consumption in Britain increased.
- From the mid-19th century, faster industrial growth in Britain led to higher incomes and more demand for food.
- Around the world in Eastern Europe, Russia, America and Australia, land was cleared to cultivate more foodgrains to meet the increasing demand of Britain.
- Railways were needed to link the agricultural regions to the ports. New harbours had to be built and old ones were expanded to ship the new cargoes.
- Increasing number of workers needed more homes and settlements as they began settling.
- Food was transported using specially built railways and ships. The ships were mostly operated by workers from Southern Europe, Asia, Africa and the Caribbean, who were paid lower wages.
- Capital flowed from financial centres such as London.
- By the 1890, a **global agricultural economy** had developed.
- Food came from thousands of miles away by railways or ships.
- The abolition of corn laws also affected India as some change occured in West Punjab. The British rulers transformed semi-desert wastes into a fertile agricultural land by developing irrigation system for growing wheat and cotton for export. The areas irrigated by the new canals, known as the **Canal Colonies**, were populated by peasants from different regions of Punjab.

Regional commodities developed so fast that between 1820 and 1914, world trade had multiplied 25 to 40 times. About 60% of this trade comprised primary products i.e., agricultural products like wheat and cotton, and minerals like coal.

Role of Technology

Technology or new inventions like **railways, steamships** and the **telegraph** had a great impact on the transformation of 19th century world.

2 Plantation Estate for cultivation of cash crops like tea, coffee, cotton, tobacco, sugarcane, etc.

3 Exorbitant Going far beyond what is fair, reasonable; to high, expensive, etc.

Faster railways, lighter wagons and larger ships helped to move food more cheaply and quickly from far away farms in America, Australia or New Zealand to final markets of Europe.

Till the 1870s, animals were shipped live from America to Europe and then slaughtered when they arrived there. Live animals took up a lot of space in ship and many animals also died in voyage, fell ill and became unfit to eat.

Meat was a costly luxury that the poor in Europe could not afford. The development of **refrigerated ships** greatly helped to transport the perishable food items over long distances. Frozen meat was exported from America, Australia, New Zealand to different European countries.

The role of technology in meat transportation decreased the price of meat in European market and the cost of shipping. Meat (sometimes butter and egg) became a daily diet for the poor. This better living conditions created social peace within the country and support for imperialism in the colonies.

Colonialism in the Late 19th Century

Trade flourished and markets expanded in the late 19th century. The European conquest in 19th century led to many painful economic, social and ecological changes in the colonised countries.

In many parts of the world, expansion of trade led to loss of freedoms and livelihood. Britain, France, Germany, Belgium and later USA became colonial powers.

Rinderpest or the Cattle Plague

In the late 19th century, Europeans were attracted to Africa to establish plantations and mines to produce crops and minerals for export to Europe.

A shortage of labour willing to work for wages became a challenge for Europeans in Africa. Thus, employers imposed heavy taxes, forcing people to work for wages on plantations and mines.

Inheritance laws were changed, displacing peasants from land and forcing them into the labour market.

In 1890s, a fast-spreading disease of cattle plague or **Rinderpest** affected a large number of cattle in Africa, which impacted people's livelihoods and the local economy.

Rinderpest arrived in Africa in the late 1880s. It was carried by infected cattle imported from British Asia. It killed 90% of the cattle, leading to a significant loss of livelihoods for Africans.

Planters, mine owners and colonial governments monopolised the remaining cattle resources, to strengthen their power and to force Africans into the labour market.

Indentured Labour Migration from India

In the 19th century, many Indian and Chinese indentured labourers went to work on plantations, in mines and in different construction projects around the world.

Indentured labourers[4] in India were hired through contracts that assured them return travel to India after working for five years on their employer's plantation.

Most Indian indentured workers came from the present-day regions of Eastern Uttar Pradesh, Bihar, Central India and Tamil Nadu.

In mid-19th century, these regions of India experienced many social changes like decline of cottage industries, increased land rents and clearance of lands for mines and plantations.

All these forced the poors to migrate in search of work, as they failed to pay their rents and became deeply indebted.

The main **destinations** of Indian indentured migrants were the **Caribbean Islands**, mainly Trinidad, Guyana and Surinam, Mauritius and Fiji.

Tamil migrants went to Ceylon and Malaya. Some indentured workers were recruited in Assam's tea plantations.

Recruitment of indentured labourers was done by agents engaged by employers and paid a small commission.

Many migrants accepted work in the hope of escaping poverty or oppression in their home villages.

In some cases, migrants were not informed about the long sea distance that they had to travel. Occasionally, agents even forcibly captured less willing migrants.

19th century indenture has been described as a **new system of slavery**. Although, living and working conditions were harsh, workers discovered their own ways of surviving.

They developed new forms of festivals and other forms of entertainment by combining their different cultural forms.

4 **Indentured Labour** A bonded labourer under contract to work for an employer for a specific amount of time, to pay-off his passage to a new country or home.

Some of the examples of cultural fusion are

- In Trinidad, the Muharram procession turned into the lively **Hosay**[5] carnival, bringing together people from all backgrounds.
- **Rastafarianism**, made famous by Bob Marley, has ties to Indian migrants in the Carribean.
- **Chutney music** in Trinidad and Guyana is an other example of different cultures mixing.

Descendants of Indentured Labourers and its Abolition

Many indentured labourers permanently settled in the countries where they had gone after their contracts ended. So, there are large communities of people of Indian descent in these countries.

For example, Nobel Prize winner writer like **VS Naipaul**, some famous West Indies cricketers like **Shivnarine Chanderpaul** and **Ramnaresh Sarwan** are descended from indentured labourers from India.

From the 1900s, India's nationalist leaders started criticising the indentured labour migration system as harsh and inhumane. The system of indentured labour was abolished in 1921.

Indian Entrepreneurs Abroad

Indian bankers were amongst the many groups of bankers and traders, who financed export agriculture in Central and South-East Asia, using either their own funds or those borrowed from European Banks. **Shikaripuri Shroffs, Nattukottai Chettiars** were some famous Indian bankers.

Indian traders and moneylenders also followed European colonisers into Africa. Hyderabadi Sindhi traders developed flourishing trades at busy ports worldwide. They usually sold local and imported curios (rare objects) to tourists.

Indian Trade, Colonialism and the Global System

Fine cottons from India were exported all over the Europe. With industrialisation, British cotton manufacturers began to expand.

The industrialists pressurised the government to restrict cotton imports from India and protect local industries. Due to this, the flow of fine Indian cotton in Britain began to decline.

The British Government introduced high tariffs[6] on import of cotton cloth.

From the early 19th century, British manufacturers also began to seek overseas markets for their cloth. As a result, the Indian textile industry was adversely affected.

Indian textile faced stiff competition in other international markets. Consequently, India's share in international cotton textiles exports declined from 30% in 1800 to 3% in 1870.

As the exports of manufactures declined rapidly, export of raw materials increased equally fast. Between 1812 to 1871, the share of raw cotton exports increased from 5% to 35%.

British forced the farmers of India to produce indigo. Indigo that was used for dyeing cloth was exported to Britain.

Opium grown (from the 1820) in India was exported to China. The money earned through opium sale was used by Britain to finance its tea and other imports from China.

Trade Relationship Between India and Britain

Over the 19th century, the British manufactures were available in large numbers in the Indian market. Export of foodgrains and raw material from India to Britain and the rest of the world increased.

The value of British exports to India was much higher than the value of British imports from India. Thus, Britain had a **trade surplus** with India and it used this surplus to balance its trade deficits with other countries.

This trade surplus of Britain helped to pay the home charges which included private remittances[7] of British officials and traders, interest payments on external debt and pensions of British officials in India.

Try These

1. **A route linked Asia with Europe and Northern Africa. Identify the route.**
2. **Which crop made a difference between life and death in Europe in mid 1840s?**
3. **What is 'El Dorado' in South America famous for?**
4. **Name the Europeans who first conquered America in the mid-16th century.**
5. **Who were the two famous Indian Bankers in the 19th century?**

3.3 The Inter-War Economy

The First World War (1914-18) was mainly fought in Europe but it had impact on whole world.

The First World War was fought between two power blocs. On one side were the **Allies** – Britain, France, Russia (later

5 **Hosay** A riotous carnival in Trinidad when workers of all races and religions join to celebrate.
6 **Tariff** Tax imposed on a country's imports from the rest of the world. Tariffs are levied at the point of entry i.e. at the border or the airport.
7 **Remittance** It refers to an amount of money that is sent as a payment for something.

joined by the US) and on the opposite side were the **Central Powers** –Germany, Austria-Hungary and Ottoman Turkey.

World's leading industrial nations joined the war and used the power of modern industry to cause maximum destruction to their enemies.

The First World War was the first modern industrial war. For the first time, modern weapons like machine guns, tanks, aircraft, chemical weapons, etc. were used on a massive scale.

Impacts of the First World War

- During the war, 9 million were dead and 20 million were injured.
- Household incomes also declined due to the death or injury of the earning members of the family and women had to take the jobs.
- The war caused the disruption of economic connections among some of the world's major economic powers, as they were now engaged in conflict against each other to pay for them.
- Britain borrowed large sums of money from US banks as well as the US public. This made the USA an international creditor from an international debtor.

Post-War Recovery

The post-war recovery was difficult. After the war, Britain found it difficult to recapture its earlier position of dominance in the Indian market and to compete with Japan internationally.

Britain faced an economic crisis and was burdened with huge external debts. The war initially sparked economic growth, marked by a significant rise in demand, production, and employment.

However, after the war ended, production decreased and unemployment increased. At the same time, the government reduced war expenditures to match them with earnings in time of peace. This led to many British workers being out of work in 1921.

The wheat exports from Eastern Europe were disrupted during the war, as a result wheat production in Canada, America and Australia expanded.

After the war, production in Eastern Europe revived and created a **glut**[8] in wheat output. Grain prices fell, rural incomes declined and farmers fell deeper into debt.

Rise of Mass Production and Consumption

After a short period of economic trouble, the US economy resumed its strength in the early 1920s. During that period, mass production became a characteristic feature of industrial production in USA.

Car manufacturer **Henry Ford** adapted the **assembly line method** of a Chicago slaughter house to his new car plant in Detroit. He realised that this method would allow a faster and cheaper way of producing vehicles.

This assembly line method forced the worker to repeat a single task mechanically and continuously which is dictated by the conveyor belt.

As a result, Henry Ford's cars came-off the assembly line at three-minute intervals. The **T-Model Ford** was the **world's first mass-produced car.**

Ford paid high wages to the workers to do **monotonous**[9] tasks, but recovered this cost through faster production. Car production in the US increased from 2 million in 1919 to more than 5 million in 1929.

Mass production lowered cost and prices of engineered goods like refrigerators, washing machines, radios, gramophone players, etc.

The housing and consumer increase created prosperity in US. Investments in housing and goods led to more jobs and higher incomes, which increased demand and further boosted employment and income. In 1923, US started lending money to other countries and become largest lender abroad.

The Great Depression

The Great Depression began around 1929 and lasted till the mid-1930s.

During this period, most of the countries of the world experienced **catastrophic**[10] declines in production, employment, income and trade. The agricultural sector, in general was the worst affected.

This happened because the prices of agricultural goods decreased and stayed low for a longer time than the prices of industrial goods.

Factors Responsible for Depression

- Agricultural overproduction remained a problem. This decreased the prices of agricultural products. Farmers tried to expand production by bringing a larger volume

8 **Glut** It refers to supply of something in excess.
9 **Monotonous** It refers to something which is boring because it is always the same.
10 **Catastrophic** It refers to a terrible disaster.

of produce to the market to maintain their overall income. But, this further decreased the prices of agricultural products in the market.

- In the mid-1920s, many countries financed their investment through the loans they got from the USA. American capitalists stopped all loans to European countries. In Europe, this led to the failure of some major banks and collapse of currencies like Sterling.

Impacts of the Depression

- The US was severely affected by the depression, as the banks had cut domestic lending and called back loans.
- Farms could not sell their harvests, households were ruined and businesses collapsed.
- The US banking system collapsed because the banks were unable to recover investments, collect loans and repay depositors.
- The US attempted to protect its economy in the depression by doubling the import duties, which hit the world trade badly.

India and the Great Depression

As a result of the Great Depression, India's export and imports declined to half (50 per cent) and prices of primary products like wheat and jute fell sharply between 1928 and 1934.

During this period, India became an exporter of precious metals, especially gold. It promoted global economic recovery and helped to speed up Britain's recovery but did not help the Indian peasants to improve their conditions.

Peasants suffered more than urban dwellers as agricultural prices fell, but the colonial government did not reduce taxes. Jute producers in Bengal faced a drop of over 60% in the price of raw jute with the collapse of exports of gunny bags. This pushed the peasants further into poverty.

Across India, peasants condition became worst. People having fixed income faced less problem due to the price fall.

In 1931, Mahatma Gandhi launched the Civil Disobedience Movement as a result of depression.

3.4 Rebuilding a World Economy : The Post-War Era

The Second World War resulted in immense devastation in human and economic terms. It broke out after two decades of the First World War (1939-45).

It was fought between the **Axis Powers** (Nazi Germany, Japan and Italy) and the **Allies** (Britain, France, Soviet Union and USA).

At least 60 million (about 3 per cent of the world's 1939 population) people were killed and millions were injured in this war.

Vast parts of Europe and Asia were devastated and several cities were destroyed by the war, therefore reconstruction became long and difficult task.

Two crucial influences shaped post-war reconstruction

(i) The **US** emerged as the world's dominant political, economic and military power in the Western world.

(ii) **Soviet Union** became a super power. It defeated Nazi Germany. It transformed itself from an agricultural country into a world power.

Post-War Settlement and the Bretton Woods Institutions

From inter-war economic experiences, two key lessons were drawn by the economists and politicians. These were

(i) The first lesson was that an industrial society based on mass production needed mass consumption. Mass consumption needed high and stable income. Stable income required steady and full employment, for which government should take necessary steps to minimise fluctuations of price, output and employment.

(ii) The second lesson was related to a country's economic links with other countries. The target of full employment could be achieved only if government had the power to control flows of goods, capital and labour.

The post-war international economic system was supported by the United Nations Monetary and Financial Conference held in July, 1944 at Bretton Woods in New Hampshire, USA.

Establishment of IMF and World Bank

The Bretton Woods Conference established the **International Monetary Fund** (IMF) to deal with external surpluses and deficits of its member nations.

The **International Bank for Reconstruction** and **Development**, also known as **World Bank**, was set up to finance post-war reconstruction.

The IMF and World Bank are referred as the Bretton Woods Institutions or **Bretton Woods twins**. They started financial operations in 1947. The decision making in these institutions were mostly controlled by the Western Industrial powers.

The International Monetary System is the system linking national currencies and monetary system. Under this system, the national currencies followed the fixed exchange rates[11] and were fixed to the US dollar. The US has an effective right of veto over key IMF and World Bank decisions.

KNOWLEDGE PLUS The post-war international economic system is also commonly referred to as the Bretton Woods system.

The Early Post-War Years

The Bretton Woods System inaugurated an era of stable growth of trade and income for the Western industrial nations and Japan.

World trade grew annually at over 8% between 1950-1970 and incomes at nearly 5%. The unemployment rate of this period was averaged less than 5% in most industrial countries.

Developing countries invested vast amounts of capital, and imported industrial plant and equipment featuring modern technology.

Decolonisation and Independence

When the Second World War ended, many countries were still under European colonial rule.

Over the next two decades, most colonies in Asia and Africa became free and emerged as independent nations. However, independence did not bring freedom from poverty or a lack of resources to these countries. Their economies and societies suffered a lot by long periods of colonial rule.

The IMF and the World Bank were designed to meet the financial needs of the industrial countries. However, as Europe and Japan rapidly rebuilt their economies, they were less dependent on the IMF and the World Bank.

Therefore, from the late 1950s, the Bretton Woods Institutions began to shift their attention more towards developing countries.

Condition of Developing Nations

Newly independent countries were trying to lift their population out of poverty. But even after many years of decolonisation, former colonial powers still control important resources like minerals and lands in their old colonies.

Most developing countries did not benefit from fast growth like the Western economies in the 1950s and 1960s. Thus, they organised themselves as a group, the **Group of 77** (or G-77) countries to demand a **New International Economic Order** (NIEO).

By the NIEO, they meant a system that would give them

- real control over their natural resources.
- more development assistance,
- fairer prices for raw materials
- better access for their manufactured goods in developed countries' markets.

End of Bretton Woods and the Beginning of 'Globalisation'

From the 1960s, the rising cost of US's overseas involvements weakened its finances and competitive strength. The US dollar could not maintain its value in relation to gold.

This eventually led to the collapse of the system of **fixed exchange rates** and the introduction of a system of **floating exchange rates.**

Change in International Financial System

From the mid-1970s, the international financial system changed. The developing countries were forced to borrow from Western commercial banks and private lending institutions.

This change led to periodic debt crises, lower incomes and increased poverty in the industrial world especially in Africa and Latin America.

From the late 1970s, MNCs also began to shift production operations to low-wage Asian countries.

New Economic Policy of China

After the revolution in 1949, China had been cut-off from the post-war world economy. But new economic policies in China and the collapse of the Soviet Union and Soviet-style communism in Eastern Europe, brought many countries back in the world economy.

11 **Exchange Rates** They link national currencies for purposes of international trade. There are broadly two kinds of exchange rates : fixed exchange rate and floating exchange rate.

Wages were comparatively low in countries like China. Thus, they became attractive destinations for investment by Foreign MNCs, competing to capture world markets.

In the last two decades, countries like China, India and Brazil have achieved rapid economic development.

Try These

1. **Which institutions were known as Bretton Woods Twins?**
2. **When did MNC's develop worldwide?**
3. **Name the country from which Britain borrowed large sums of money during the First World War.**
4. **Which organisation was formed by the former colonies to demand a New International Economic Order (NIEO)?**

TIME LINE

Covering Major Events with their Time Periods in Chronological Order

Period	Important Events
3000 BCE	An active coastal trade linked the Indus Valley Civilisation with West Asia.
15th century CE	Existence of silk routes.
Mid-16th century	Portuguese and Spanish conquest and colonisation of America was decisively under way.
1845-1849	Potato Famine in Ireland.
Late 1880s	Rinderpest arrived in Africa.
1885	European powers meet in Berlin to divide-up Africa between themselves.
1890s	Global agricultural economy takes shape. Rinderpest had a disastrous impact on livelihoods of the African people and the local economy. South Africa contributed over 20 per cent of the world gold production.
1914-1918	The First World War.
1921	Indentured labour abolished.
1929-1935	The Great Depression.
1931	Mahatma Gandhi launched the Civil Disobedience Movement at the height of the Great Depression.
1939-1945	The Second World War.
1947	International Monetary Fund (IMF) and World Bank commence financial operations.
1949	The Chinese Communist Revolution which was the culmination of the Chinese Communist Party's drive to power.

Mind Map

THE MAKING OF A GLOBAL WORLD

Pre-modern World

Silk Routes Link the World
- Historians linked Asia, Europe and North America.
- Chinese Pottery, Indian and South-East Asian textiles, spices, gold and silver all followed the same route.

Food Travels
- New crops introduced, e.g. Potatoes
- Soya, groundnut, maize, etc, were introduced in Asia and Europe after discovery of America by Christopher Columbus.

Conquest, Disease and Trade
- The conquest of America was possible through the deadly disease smallpox.
- With India's colonialisation and China's restriction of overseas contacts, Europe emerged as the centre of world trade.

Rebuilding and World Economy

Post-War Settlement and Bretton Woods Institutions
- The Bretton Woods Conference established the International Monetary Fund.
- The International Bank for Recontruction and Development known as the World Bank was setup to finance post war reconstruction.

The Early Post-War Years
The Bretton Woods System inaugurated an era of stable growth of trade and income for the Western industrial nations and Japan.

Decolonisation and Independence
- Most developing countries did not benefit from fast growth like the Western economies in the 1950s and 1960s.
- These countries grouped themselves as Group of 77 countries to demand a New International Economic Order.

Beginning of Globalisation
System of fixed exchange rates collapsed and a system of floating exchange rates was introduced.

The Nineteenth Century

A World Economy Takes Shape

Abolition of Corn Laws
- Corn laws were imposed to restrict the import of corn.
- Food prices fell.
- By the 1890, a global agricultural economy had developed.

Role of Technology
- Railways
- Steamships
- Telegraphs

Colonialism in the Late 19th Century
- Trade flourished and markets expanded.
- Expansion of trade led to loss of freedoms and livelihoods.

The Cattle Plague
- In 1890s, this affected a large number of cattles in Africa.
- It led to loss of livelihoods in Africa.

Migration of Indentured labour from India
- Indian labourers went to work on plantations around the world.
- They were hired under contracts which promised return travel to India after five years.

Inter War Economy

Post-War Recovery
- Britain faced difficulty in dominating Indian market.
- Britain faced economic crisis.

Rise of Mass Production and Consumption
- Henry Ford adapted the assembly line method.
- The T-Model Ford was the world's first mass produced car.

Great Depression
- Began around 1929 and lasted till mid-1930s.
- Most of the countries of the world faced catastrophic declines in production, trade, employment and income.

Impacts
- US Banking System collapsed.
- Farmer could not sell their harvests.

Responsible factors
- Agriculture overproduction
- American capitalist stopped all loans to European countries

Impact of First World War
- Millions were dead and injured.
- War caused some of the world's biggest economic powers to stop doing business with others.

NCERT FOLDER

Covering Intext Questions and Exercises of NCERT

INTEXT QUESTIONS

Q.1 Explain what we mean when we say that the world 'shrank' in the 1500s.

Ans. When we say that the world shrank in the 1500s, we mean that

- Europeans discovered the sea route to Asia and trade activities increased between Asia and Europe.
- The American continent was discovered only when the sea route through the Atlantic Ocean to America was found.

Due to the above reasons, there was increased interaction among the people living in various continents of the world, thus causing the world to 'shrink' in metaphorical terms.

Q.2 Who profits from jute cultivation according to the jute growers' lament? Explain.

Ans. According to the jute growers' lament, only the traders and moneylenders profited from jute cultivation, not the growers. Peasants of Bengal cultivated raw jute which was processed in factories for export in the form of gunny bags.

They grew raw jute hoping that a better time would come and there would be increase in exports. But this did not happen as gunny exports collapsed due to the depression. Due to excess in the local market, the price of raw jute crashed by more than 60 per cent and so, they fell into heavy debt.

Thus, only the traders and moneylenders profited from jute cultivation, not the farmers.

Q.3 Briefly summarise the two lessons learnt by economists and politicians from the inter-war economic experience.

Ans. Two lessons learnt by economists and politicians from the inter-war economic experience were

(i) An industrial society based on large production is unsustainable without consumption on a large scale. For this, high and stable incomes through full employment are necessary.

(ii) Economic links of a country should be maintained with other countries. The target of full employment could be achieved only if the governments has power to control the flow of capital, labour and goods. The government should take appropriate steps to achieve the goal.

EXERCISE

Q.1 Give two examples of different types of global exchange which took place before the 17th century, choosing one example from Asia and one from the Americas.

Ans. Two examples of different types of global exchange were

(i) Before the 17th century, China exported silk and pottery to Europe in exchange for gold and silver from Europe. This trade was carried out using the traditional 'silk route'.

(ii) Many common food items like potatoes, soya, groundnuts, maize, tomatoes, chillies and sweet potatoes were introduced into Europe from America, after it was discovered by Christopher Columbus at the end of the 15th century.

Q.2 Explain how the global transfer of disease in the pre-modern world helped in the colonisation of the Americas.

Ans. The global transfer of disease in the pre-modern world led to the colonisation of the Americas in the following ways

- The Portuguese and the Spanish had a strong army. But the most powerful weapon of the Spanish conquerors was not a military weapon, but the germs like smallpox, that they brought with them.
- As Americans were isolated earlier, the original inhabitants had no immunity against the germs and viruses present in Europe.
- The diseases once introduced, spread very fast. The diseases, like smallpox affected whole communities that were paving the way for the conquest of the colonisers.
- The germs were more dangerous as compared to guns and firearms because guns could be bought or captured, but there was no way to escape from these diseases.

Q.3 Give two examples from history to show the impact of technology on food availability.

Ans. Two examples of impact of technology on food availability

- The technique of cold storage and use of refrigerated ships boosted the export of perishable foods over long distances. Meat exported from America, Australia and New Zealand could be sent to Europe where meat was not available easily or cheaply.

- Faster railways, larger ships and lighter wagons enabled cheaper and quicker movement of perishable foodstuffs from far away farms to their final markets. Now the poor in Europe could add meat (even butter and egg) to their daily diet.

Q.4 What is meant by Bretton Woods Agreement?

Ans. The Bretton Woods Agreement was an agreement to preserve global economic stability and full employment in the industrialised world. The Bretton Woods Conference was held in July of 1944 at Bretton Woods in New Hampshire, USA.

Under the Bretton Woods Agreement, the International Monetary Fund (IMF) and the International Bank for Reconstruction and Development (IBRD), popularly known as the World Bank were established.

The IMF and the World Bank are referred to as the Bretton Woods Institutions or Bretton Woods twins. The decisions in these institutions were mostly controlled by Western powers.

Q.5 Write a note to explain the effect of the following

(a) The British Government's decision to abolish the Corn Laws.
(b) The coming of rinderpest to Africa.
(c) The death of men of working age in Europe because of the World War.
(d) The Great Depression on the Indian economy.
(e) The decision of MNCs to relocate production to Asian countries.

Ans. (a) The effect of the British Governments decision to abolish the Corn Laws was that, food could be imported into Britain at a lower cost than it could be produced locally. Due to this, farmers did not grow corn, leaving the land uncultivated. This resulted in unemployment on a large scale and the people started migrating to the cities or overseas, looking for work.

(b) The coming of rinderpest to Africa caused a loss of livelihood for countless Africans. Rinderpest was a cattle plague spread by Asian cattle taken to Africa to feed the Italian soldiers by the European colonisers. The disease infected the African cattle, which spread like 'forest fire'. Rinderpest killed 90 per cent of the cattle. This virtually destroyed the African economic system based on cattle and land. Africans, who worked rearing cattle, were unemployed and forced to earn their livelihood by working in mines and on plantations set-up by the Europeans.

Using this situation to their advantage, colonising nations successfully monopolised cattle resources. By this, they strengthen their power and forced Africans into the labour market.

(c) The death of most men of working age in Europe due to the World War reduced the workforce of able-bodied people with fewer members in the family. Thus, household incomes declined after the war.

(d) The Great Depression immediately affected Indian trade in agricultural goods. Indian exports and imports nearly halved between 1928-1934. As international prices crashed, prices in India also plunged. Wheat prices fell in India by 50 per cent and prices of raw jute crashed by 60 per cent. Peasants and farmers were worst hit.

The colonial government refused to reduce revenue demands in spite of this. The jute producers of Bengal faced a severe loss. The depression less affected urban land- owners and salaried people, who had fixed income.

(e) The decision of MNCs to relocate production to Asian countries led to increased world trade and capital flows. These are as follows :

- The low cost structure of these economies enabled mass production at a much lower cost.
- It led to a stimulation of world trade and capital flow.
- It benefitted the Asian countries by increase of employment and a quick economic transformation.

Q.6 Explain the three types of movements or flows within international economic exchange. Find one example of each type of flow which involved India and Indians, and write a short account of it.

Ans. The three types of movements or flows in international economic exchange are

(i) **Flow of Trade** This refers to trade in goods like wheat, cotton, etc.

Historically, fine cotton cloth was produced in India by weavers and exported to European countries. But when the industrial revolution started in Europe and the European countries imposed tariff barriers, the export of textiles dropped drastically. In fact, India started exporting raw cotton and importing mill-made cloth from England.

(ii) **Flow of Labour** This refers to migration of people in search of employment.

During the 19th century, a large number of Indian labourers migrated to Africa, the West Indies and other countries.

They migrated to work on plantations, in mines, in railway and road construction projects set-up by the Europeans. These Indians settled in the countries where they had gone after their contracts ended and now their descendants are found in these countries.

(iii) **Flow of Capital** This refers to movement of capital over long distances for short-term and long-term investments.

Groups of Indian financers, traders like the Shroffs, Chettiars, etc financed agriculture and plantations in various Asian and African countries. They used their own funds or those borrowed from European banks.

Q.7 Explain the causes of the Great Depression.

Ans. The causes of the Great Depression were

- **Conditions Created by War** The Great Depression was the result of war. There was an immense industrial expansion due to the increased demand of goods supplied to the army, during the period of the First World War. After the war, the demand for these goods suddenly dropped. So, there was no demand in many industries. There was also a large fall in the agricultural prices due to reduced demand.
- **Over Production in Agriculture** It was another major factor responsible for the depression. This was made worse by falling agricultural prices.

  As prices fell and agricultural incomes declined, the farmers tried to increase the production. They tried to bring a larger volume of produce to the market to maintain their overall income. This act pushed down the prices of farm produce further.
- **Shortage of Loans** In the mid-1920s, many countries financed their investments through loans from the USA.

  While it was often very easy to raise loans in the USA during the boom period, lenders in the USA panicked at the first sign of trouble. Countries that depended crucially on US loans, now faced an acute crisis.
- **Collapse of Banking System** With the fall in prices and the prospect of a depression i.e. banks in the USA slashed domestic lending and some stopped bank loans, thousands of banks went bankrupt and were forced to close down. Factories closed, leading to unemployment, which further aggravated the crises. The US banking system collapsed.
- **Large-scale Unemployment** Farmers could not sell their harvests, which led to businesses collapse. As a result, large scale unemployment occurred.

Q.8 Explain what is referred to as the G-77, countries. In what ways can G-77 be seen as a reaction to the activities of the Bretton Woods twins?

Ans. The G-77 is a coalition of developing nations designed to promote its members collective, economic interest.

The G-77 countries have demanded a New International Economic Order (NIEO) in which they have a real control over their natural resources.

By NIEO, they got more development assistance and fairer prices for raw materials and better access to the markets in developed countries for their manufactured goods.

G-77 was seen as a reaction to the activities of the Bretton Woods twins. The Bretton Woods twins, IMF and World Bank were mainly set-up to favour the developed nations. As a result, most developing countries could not benefit from the fast growth that the Western economics experienced in the 1950s and 1960s. So, they organised themselves as a group–the group of 77 or G-77, to demand a new economic order. They also wanted a better opportunity for their manufactured goods in the markets of developed nations.

REVIEW EXERCISE

Including Competency Based Questions

Part I

Multiple Choice Questions (MCQs)

1. What was the form of currency used for more than a millennia ago?

(a) Cowdi or cowries (b) Rupaya
(c) Paisa (d) Rupees

2. Which country introduced 'Corn Laws' to restrict the import of corn?

(a) France (b) Germany
(c) Britain (d) Spain

3. Who later joined the Allies during the First World War?

(a) Britain (b) France (c) Russia (d) USA

4. In the 17th century the city El Dorado in South America became famous as which one of the following? CBSE 2025

(a) City of Diversity (b) City of Gold
(c) Small pox City (d) Trading City

5. Choose the correct option to fill in the blank.

.... from India and South-East Asia travelled through 'Silk Route' to other parts of the wo CBSE 2024

(a) Gold and Silver ornaments
(b) Clothes and Spices
(c) Grain and Pulses
(d) Iron and other metals

6. Which one of the following religions emerged from Eastern India and spread in several directions through intersecting points on the 'Silk Routes'? CBSE 2024

(a) Hinduism
(b) Christianity
(c) Buddhism
(d) Jainism

7. Find the incorrect option.

(a) The system of indentured labour was abolished in 1921.
(b) The Bretton Woods conference was established in 1950.
(c) By the 1890, a global agricultural economy had developed.
(d) The World War I was the first Modern Industrial War.

8. Food offers many examples of long-distance cultural exchange. Traders and travellers introduced new crops to the lands they travelled. Even 'ready' foodstuff in distant parts of the world might share common origins.

Which foods were introduced in Europe and Asia after Christopher Columbus discovered America? Competency Based

(a) Potatoes and soya
(b) Groundnuts and tomatoes
(c) Both (a) and (b)
(d) None of these

9. The IMF and World Bank are referred as the Bretton Woods Institution or Bretton Woods Twins. The IMF and the World Bank were designed to meet the financial needs of the industrial countries.

Why the Bretton Woods Institutions were established? Choose the correct option from the following. Competency Based

(a) To promote the International trade
(b) To reconstruct the economies damaged during the Second World War
(c) To improve the adverse balance of payment situation of the non-member countries
(d) All of the above

10. The First World War had led to an economic boom, that is, to a large increase in demand, production and employment. When the war boom ended, production contracted and unemployment increased.

During the First World War, women in Europe stepped into jobs which earlier men were expected to do. What was the reason? Competency Based

(a) Because men went to battle.
(b) Because men went to other countries in search of jobs.
(c) Because of liberalisation of women in society.
(d) Because menfolk decided to take charge of the household work.

11. Which of the following statements is/are correct regarding the role of technology in the nineteenth-century world? Competency Based

(a) Technology advancements were solely responsible for the transformation of the nineteenth century world.
(b) The nineteenth century world transformation occurred Independently of technological advancements.
(c) Technology played a significant role, alongside larger social, political and economic factors, in the transformation of the nineteenth-century world.
(c) Larger social, political and economic factors were negligible compared to the impact of technological advancements in the nineteenth-century world transformation.

12. First World War was the first modern industrial war. It saw the use of machine guns, tanks, aircraft, chemical weapons, etc on a massive scale. These were all increasingly products of modern large scale industry.

Identify the aim of the post-war international economic system.

(a) To ensure economic stability of underdeveloped countries.
(b) To promote good health for the people of the world.
(c) Promotion of education worldwide.
(d) To preserve economic stability and full employment in the industrial world.

13. Globalisation means the assimilation of economics and societies through the flow of information, ideas, technologies, goods, services, capital, finance and people. The real meaning of Globalisation in a broad sense is connectivity in all aspects of human life.

The term "Globalisation" refers to Competency Based

(a) The process of creating a global government.
(b) The process of increasing inter-connectedness of the world's economies.
(c) The process of spreading a particular culture around the world.
(d) The process of establishing world peace.

14. Which goods from the American continent enhanced Europe's wealth and financed its trade with Asia after its discovery in the 16th century?

(a) Food products
(b) Cash crops
(c) Precious metals, particularly silver
(d) Pottery and arts

15. Choose the correct option regarding the Axis powers in the Second World War. CBSE 2024

(a) Germany, Italy and China
(b) Britain, France and Germany
(c) Germany, France and Italy
(d) Germany, Japan and Italy

16. **In the late 19th century, Europeans were attracted to Africa due to its vast resources of land and minerals. Europeans came to Africa hoping to establish plantations and mines to produce crops and minerals for export to Europe but there was an unexpected problem – a shortage of labour willing to work for wages.**

Give the correct reason for decline of household income in Europe after the First World War **Competency Based**

(a) People' stopped going to work, as they were scared of the war situation.
(b) Death and injuries had reduced the number of able bodied work force.
(c) Home governments had imposed heavier taxes.
(d) People could not go to work because they got busy with reorganisation of their households.

17. **Arrange the following in the correct sequence.**

I. Existence of Silk Route
II. Potato Famine in Ireland.
III. Rinderpest arrived in Africa
IV. The First World War

Codes

(a) III, IV, I, II (b) I, IV, III, II
(c) III, I, II, IV (d) I, II, III, IV

18. **'Buddhism emerged from Eastern India and spread in several directions'.**

Read the following reasons for its spread and choose the correct option. **CBSE 2024**

I. Due to cultural exchange
II. Due to silk route
III. Due to trade and travellers
IV. Due to European efforts

Options

(a) Only I, II and IV are correct.
(b) Only II, III and IV are correct.
(c) Only I, II and III are correct.
(d) Only I, III and IV are correct.

19. **Identify the effect of spreading disease in cattle in 19th centuries. Choose from the appropriate statements among the following options.** **Competency Based**

I. European colonisers forced Africans into the labour market, strengthen their power, subdue and conquer Africa.
III. Europeans imposed heavy taxes which could be paid only by working in mines and plantations.
III. Scarce cattle resources were monopolised by colonial governments, mine owners and planters.
IV. To displace peasants from their lands, inheritance laws were changed.

Options

(a) Statements I and II are appropriate
(b) Statements I, II and III are appropriate
(c) All the statements are appropriate
(d) Only statement IV is appropriate

20. **Read the following reasons of migration of people from Europe to America till the 19th century and choose the correct option.** **CBSE 2025**

I. Poverty and hunger
II. Slaves for sale
III. Wide spread of diseases
IV. Religious conflicts and persecution

Options

(a) Only I, II and III are correct.
(b) Only II, III and IV are correct.
(c) Only I, III and IV are correct.
(d) Only I, II and IV are correct.

21. **Consider the statements given below and choose the correct answer.** **Competency Based**

Statement I In 19th century, technological advances were often the result of larger social, political and economic factors.

Statement II Colonisation stimulated new investments and improvements in transport faster railways, lighter wagons and larger ships helped move food more cheaply and quickly from faraway farms to final market.

Options

(a) Statement I is correct and II is incorrect
(b) Statement I is incorrect and II is correct
(c) Both I and II are incorrect
(d) Both I and II are correct

Answers

1. (a)	2. (c)	3. (d)	4. (b)	5. (b)
6. (c)	7. (b)	8. (c)	9. (b)	10. (a)
11. (c)	12. (d)	13. (b)	14. (c)	15. (d)
16. (b)	17. (d)	18. (c)	19. (c)	20. (c)
21. (d)				

Match the Following

1.

	List I (Year)		List II (Events)
A.	1914-18	1.	The First War
B.	1921	2.	Indentured labour abolished
C.	1929-35	3.	The Great Depression
D.	1939-45	4.	Second World War

Codes

	A	B	C	D		A	B	C	D
(a)	1	2	3	4	(b)	4	3	2	1
(c)	2	3	1	4	(d)	2	3	4	1

Ans. (a)

Assertion-Reason

1. **Assertion** (A) The silk routes were regarded as the most important route linking the distant parts of the world.
Reason (R) Routes were existed even before the Christian Era and flourished till the 15th century.
Codes
(a) Both A and R are true and R is the correct explanation of A
(b) Both A and R are true, but R is not the correct explanation of A
(c) A is true, but R is false
(d) A is false, but R is true

2. **Assertion** (A) After the Corn Laws were scrapped, food could be imported into Britain more cheaply than it could be produced in the country.
Reason (R) Technology had a great impact on the transformation of 19th century world such as railways, steamship and telegraph.
Codes
(a) Both A and R are true and R is the correct explanation of A
(b) Both A and R are true, but R is not the correct explanation of A
(c) A is true, but R is false
(d) A is false, but R is true

3. **Assertion** (A) To deal with external surpluses and deficits a conference was held in July, 1944 at Bretton Woods in New Hampshire, USA.
Reason (R) The world wide spread of MNCs was a notable feature in the 1950s and 1960s as US business expanded worldwide.
Codes
(a) Both A and R are true and R is the correct explanation of A
(b) Both A and R are true, but R is not the correct explanation of A
(c) A is true, but R is false
(d) A is false, but R is true

4. **Assertion** (A) Discovery of America resulted in transformation of trade, life and abundance of wealth for Europeans.
Reason (R) The Americas had vast lands, minerals, silver and gold which enhanced European trade.
Codes
(a) Both A and R are true and R is the correct explanation of A
(b) Both A and R are true, but R is not the correct explanation of A
(c) A is true, but R is false
(d) A is false, but R is true

5. **Assertion** (A) India played a crucial role in the late 19th century world economy.
Reason (R) Britain was using trade surplus with India to balance its trade deficit with other countries.
Codes
(a) Both A and R are true and R is the correct explanation of A
(b) Both A and R are true, but R is not the correct explanation of A
(c) A is true, but R is false
(d) A is false, but R is true

Ans. 1. (a) Both A and R are true and R is the correct explanation of A
2. (b) Both A and R are true, but R is not the correct explanation of A
3. (b) Both A and R are true, but R is not the correct explanation of A
4. (a) Both A and R are true and R is the correct explanation of A
5. (a) Both A and R are true and R is the correct explanation of A

Picture Based Questions

1. **The given picture represents which of the following?**

(a) East India Company House, London
(b) The Smithfield Club
(c) Mt. Washington Hotel
(d) East India Company Surat

2. **Which of the following aspects best signifies this image during World War I?**

(a) Indian indentured labours
(b) Workers in a ammunition factory
(c) Diggers at work (South Africa)
(d) Irish emigrants

Ans. 1. (a) East India Company, London
2. (b) Workers in a ammunition factory

Case Based Question

1. Read the source given below and answer the questions that follow.

Rinderpest arrived in Africa in the late 1880s. It was carried by infected cattle imported from British Asia to feed the Italian soldiers invading Eritrea in East Africa. Entering Africa in the East, rinderpest moved West 'like a forest fire', reaching Africa's Atlantic coast in 1892. It reached the Cape (Africa's southernmost tip) five years later. Along the way, rinderpest killed 90 per cent of the cattle. The loss of cattle destroyed African livelihoods. Planters, mine owners and colonial governments now successfully monopolised what scarce cattle resources remained, to strengthen their power and to force Africans into the labour market.

(i) What was one significant impact of rinderpest on African societies in the late 19th century?

(a) Increased availability of consumer goods.
(b) Destruction of livelihoods dependent on cattle.
(c) Expansion of agricultural practices.
(d) Decrease in European interest in African resources.

(ii) How did European colonisers exploit the scarcity of cattle following the rinderpest outbreak?

(a) By offering free land to African communities
(b) By encouraging self-sufficiency in local economies.
(c) By monopolising remaining cattle resources to strengthen control.
(d) By implementing policies to protect indigenous agricultural practices.

(iii) What measures were taken by employers to address the shortage of labour willing to work for wages in Africa during the late 19th century?

(a) Providing incentives for workers to remain on their own land.
(b) Imposing heavy taxes to force labour participation in plantations and mines.
(c) Implementing universal basic income for all citizens.
(d) Encouraging migration to urban areas for employment opportunities.

(iv) How did the introduction of rinderpest affect the power dynamics between African communities and European colonisers?

(a) It led to increased cooperation and collaboration between the two groups.
(b) It strengthened the autonomy of African communities.
(c) It enabled European colonisers to monopolise scarce resources and further exert control.
(d) It resulted in the complete withdrawal of European influence from Africa.

Ans. (i) (b) Destruction of livelihoods dependent on cattle.
(ii) (c) By monopolising remaining cattle resources to strengthen control.
(iii) (b) Imposing heavy taxes to force labour participation in plantations and mines.
(iv) (c) It enabled European colonisers to monopolise scarce resources and further exert control.

Part II

Very Short Answer Type Questions

1. Explain the word El Dorado.

Ans. El Dorado was the fabled city of South America. In 17th century, Europe legends spread about South America's fabled wealth, so many expeditions set-off in search of El Dorado.

2. Which was the most powerful weapon used by the Spanish to conquer America?

Ans. Smallpox was the most powerful weapon used by the Spanish to conquer America.

3. Why did smallpox kill a large number of native Americans?

Ans. Smallpox killed a large number of native Americans because of their long isolation, they had no immunity against this disease.

4. Where did the big European powers meet in 1885 for dividing Africa?

Ans. In 1885, the big European powers met in Berlin to complete the carving up of Africa between them.

5. How the 19th century 'indentured labour' has often been described?

Ans. The 19th century 'indentured labour' has often been described as 'new system of slavery'.

6. Indian indentured workers came from which regions of India?

Ans. Most Indian indentured workers came from Eastern Uttar Pradesh, Bihar, Central India and dry districts of Tamil Nadu.

7. Name a Noble Prize winning writer who is a descendant of indentured labour from India.

Ans. VS Naipaul is a Nobel Prize winning writer who is a descendant of indentured labour from India.

8. In 1820s, India was the single largest exporter of which commodity?

Ans. India was the single largest exporter of opium in 1820s.

9. Give the names of nations which constituted the two power blocs during the First World War.

Ans. The Nations which constituted the two power blocs during the First World War are- Britain, France and Russia, US (Allies) and Germany, Austria-Hungary and Ottomon Empire (Central powers).

10. Which group of countries were known as the 'Central Powers' in Europe?

Ans. Germany, Austria-Hungary and Ottoman Turkey were the countries known as the 'Central Powers' in Europe.

11. Which countries were considered as Axis Powers during the Second World War?

Ans. Nazi Germany, Japan and Italy were considered as Axis Powers during the Second World War.

12. How was the Indian subcontinent crucial for the trade network during the sixteenth century? Explain. CBSE 2024

Ans. In the 16th century, the Indian subcontinent was vital for trade because of its key location along the Indian ocean. It acted as a central hub where trade routes met, allowing the exchange of goods, people and ideas. This region played a crucial role in connecting different parts of Asia, making it a vital point in the complex trade networks of that era.

13. How did our foods facilitate cultural exchanges between distant countries? Explain with any two examples. CBSE 2024

Ans. Food has played an important role in facilitating cultural exchanges between distant countries. This can be justified by the following examples

- Tradeers and travellers introduced new crops to the regions they travelled.
- Pasta was brought to Sicily by Arab traders, while noodles travelled West from China to become spaghetti.

14. Globalisation has altered the way we live and earn a livelihood. Consequently, trade and travel have been recognised as significant determinants of the spread of disease.

What led to globalisation? Competency Based

Ans. Trade, migration of people in search of work, the movement of capital, etc led to Globalisation.

15. In the 19th century, hundreds of thousands of Indian and Chinese labourers went to work on plantations, in mines and in road and railway construction projects around the world. Competency Based

(i) What does the flow of labour mean?

Ans. The flow of labour mean the migration of people in search of employment.

(ii) What do you mean by indentured labour?

Ans. Indentured labour is a bonded labour under contract to work for an employer for a specific amount of time.

Short Answer Type Questions

1. The silk routes are a good example of trade and cultural link between distant parts of the world. Explain with examples. Competency Based

Or **How did silk routes link the world? Explain with three examples.**

Or **'The silk routes are a good example of vibrant pre-modern trade and cultural links between distant parts of the world'. Substantiate the statement with illustrations.** SQP 2024-25

Ans. Silk routes existed before the Christain era and flourished till the 15th century.

The significance of silk routes was as follows

- The silk routes are good examples of pre-modern trade and cultural links between the distant parts of the world, *i.e.* linking Asia with Europe and North Africa.
- Along the silk routes, the silk cargoes from China, Indian spices and textiles, gold and silver from Europe were carried to different parts of the world.
- The Buddhist preachers, Christian missionaries and later on, Muslim preachers travelled along these routes.
- These routes proved to be a great source of trade and cultural links between distant parts of the world.

Thus, it can be concluded that silk routes are a good example of trade and cultural link between distant parts of the world.

2. What were the effects of the British Government's decision to abolish the Corn Laws?

Or **Explain the impacts of scrapping of the Corn Laws.**

Ans. Under the pressure from industrialists and urban dwellers, the British Government abolished the Corn Laws. The effects of abolishing corn laws were

- Food could be imported into Britain more cheaply than it would be produced within the country.
- British agriculture was unable to compete with imports. Vast areas of lands were left uncultivated and people started migrating to cities or other countries in search of work.
- As food prices fell, consumption in Britain rose. Faster industrial growth in Britain also led to higher incomes and therefore, more food imports.
- Around the world in Eastern Europe, Russia, America, Australia, lands were cleared and food production expanded to meet the British demand.

3. What were canal colonies? Why were they built?

Ans. Canal colonies were the areas irrigated by the new canals.

The British government built these new canals for the following reasons

- They built a network of irrigation canals in West Punjab to transform semi-desert land into a fertile agricultural lands.
- The Britishers wanted to export wheat and cotton. So people from other parts of Punjab were called and settled to grow wheat and cotton canal colonies.

4. Explain three reasons for the attraction of Europeans to Africa.

Ans. The three reasons for the attraction of European to Africa were

(i) Africa had abundant land and was rich in mineral resources. Its population was relatively small.

(ii) The Europeans were hoping to establish plantations and mines in Africa to produce crops and minerals for export to Europe.

(iii) In Africa, industrial revolution did not take place. Africans were militarily weak and backward. Europeans thought that they could easily capture the country and use its resource and people for their own profit.

5. Who were indentured labourers? How were they recruited? Explain condition of the indentured labourers who went to work in different parts of the world.

***Or* Write a short note on indentured labourers.**

Ans. Indentured labourers were bonded labourers under contract to work for an employer for a specific amount of time, to pay-off their passage to a new country or home.

Recruitment of indentured labourers was done by agents engaged by employers and were paid a small commission.

The conditions of the indentured labourers in different parts of the world was very pathetic. It can be described as

- They were subjected to harsh, inhuman and unsympathetic conditions.
- If they were unwilling to migrate, they were abducted by agents.
- If they were caught while escaping, they faced severe punishment.
- They had very few legal rights.
- Deductions were made from their wages if the work was found unsatisfactory.

6. Mention any three circumstances that compelled Indians and Chinese to work as indenture labour in plantation and mines.

Ans. In the 19th century, many Indians and Chinese labourers went to work on plantations, in mines and in different construction projects as indentured labour around the world.

The circumstances that compelled them to work as indentured labour were

(i) Decline of cottage industry.

(ii) Increase in land rents.

(iii) Unemployment, poverty and indebtedness.

Due to these reasons, poor were forced to migrate in search of work. The prospective migrants were tempted by the false promises of the agents and became indentured labourers.

7. Explain the impact of the First World War on Britain's economy.

Ans. The impact of First World War on Britain's economy were as follows

- Britain which was a leading economy of the world before the First World War faced a prolonged crisis. While Britain was pre-occupied with war, industries had developed in Japan and India. After the war, Britain found it difficult to recapture its earlier position.
- Britain had borrowed huge amount of money from the USA for its war time expenditure, thus at the end of the war, Britain was burdened with huge external debt.
- After the war, production in Britain declined which led to huge job losses. In 1921, one in every five British workers was out of work. Anxiety and uncertainty about work became an enduring part of the post-war time.

8. How did housing and consumer boom lead to prosperity in the US?

Ans. The housing and consumer boom in the 1920s created the basis of prosperity in the US. It happened in the following ways

- Large investments in housing and household goods seemed to create a cycle of higher employment and incomes. This led to rising consumption demand, more investment and again more employment and incomes.
- In 1923, the US resumed exporting capital to the rest of the world and became the largest overseas lender.
- US imports and capital exports boosted European recovery and world trade and also it enhanced the income growth over the next six years.

9. How did Bretton Woods inaugurated an era of unprecedented growth in trade?

Ans. Bretton Woods inaugurated an era of unprecedented growth in trade in the following ways

- The Bretton Woods Conference established the International Monetary Fund (IMF) to deal with external surplus and deficits of its member nations.
- The conference also established the International Bank for Reconstruction and Development (known as World Bank) to finance post-war reconstruction. The IMF and World Bank were referred as the Bretton Woods Institutions or the twins of the Bretton Woods.

- Both these institutions commenced financial operations in 1947.
- Decision making in these institutions was controlled by the Western industrial powers.

10. Why did Group 77 countries demand a New International Economic Order? Explain.

Ans. Group 77 countries demanded a New International Economic Order (NIEO) because

- They wanted to revise the International Economic System in favour of the developing countries.
- They wanted a system that would give them a real control over their natural resources.
- They wanted to set-up a system under which they could get a fairer price for raw materials and better access for their manufactured goods in the developed countries' market.

11. 'The global transfer of diseases became instrumental in colonisation of Africa and South America'. Explain the statement. **Competency Based**

Ans. This statement states the fact that the European conquest of colonies in Africa and South America was not just a result of superior, modern, sophisticated firepower. It was because of the germs such as those of smallpox that they carried with them.

Smallpox in particular proved to be a fatal disease. Once, it reached the continent, it started spreading deep into the continent. It killed and destroyed a large portion of the community and paved the way for conquest. Thus, the global transfer of disease became instrumental in colonisation of Africa and South America.

12. Explain how the First World War was so horrible war like none other.

Ans. The First World War was so horrible war like none other before. Two main characteristics of this war were

(i) To fight the war, millions of soldiers had to be recruited from around the world and moved to the frontlines on large ships and trains.

(ii) The scale of death and destruction was devastating, 9 million people were died and 20 million were injured, which was not possible without the use of industrial arms.

13. A good place to start is the changing pattern of food production and consumption in industrial Europe. Traditionally, countries liked to be self-sufficient in food. But in 19th century Britain, self-sufficiency in food meant lower living standards and social conflict. Why was this so? **Competency Based**

Build the answer around these point

- **Corn Laws**
- **Import and export**
- **Demand and supply**

Ans. In the context of the changing pattern of food production and consumption in industrial Europe, particularly in 19th century Britain, several factors contributed to the conflict between self-sufficiency in food and living standards as follows

- **Corn Laws** The Corn Laws in Britain imposed tariffs and restrictions on imported grains, particularly corn (wheat). These laws were implemented to protect domestic agriculture by keeping grain prices high. However, this policy made imported food expensive and constrained the supply of cheaper grains from overseas markets.
- **Import and Export Dynamics** The Corn Laws' ban on imported grains made it harder for Britain's growing urban population to find affordable food. It was because they had to pay more for needs like food, the working class's living conditions were worsened by this situation.
- **Imbalance between Supply and Demand** The industrial revolution caused a sharp rise in urbanisation and a large increase in the number of people living in cities. This raised the need for food, but the import prohibition limited the amount of reasonably priced grains available, leading to food shortages and price increases.

14. Read the statements given below regarding trade in 19th century. **Competency Based**

Statement 1 (S1) Trade flourished and markets expanded in the late 19th century. But this was not only a period of expanding trade and increased prosperity.

Statement 2 (S2) The expansion of trade and a closer relationship with the world economy also meant a loss of freedoms and livelihoods.

Explain what is the relationship between expanding trade and increased prosperity.

Ans. The relationship between expanding trade and increased prosperity during the late 19th century is complex, as evident from the two statements provided.

Statement 1 (S1) highlights the positive aspects of the period, emphasising the flourishing trade and expanded markets. Expanding trade usually leads to increased economic activity, greater access to goods, wider markets for products and potentially higher profits. This expansion in trade contributed to economic growth, stimulated industrialisation and facilitated the exchange of goods on a global scale.

On the other hand, Statement 2 (S2) clarifies the adverse effects linked to trade growth. It led to important changes that had a negative impact on some groups. Greater competition for regional industries and customary livelihoods resulted from the economy's growing integration with the global economy.

Long Answer Type Questions

1. (a) What were the Corn Laws?
(b) Why was the Corn Laws abolished?
(c) What was the result of the abolishing of Corn Laws?

Ans. (a) The laws allowing the government to restrict the import of corn were commonly known as the Corn Laws. From the late 18th century, the demand for foodgrains increased in Britain due to population growth.

As urban areas expanded due to industrialisation, the demand for agricultural products went up, pushing up foodgrain prices. Under pressure from landed groups, the government also restricted the import of corn.

(b) Industrialists and urban dwellers were unhappy with high food prices. As a result, they forced the British Government to abolish the Corn Laws.

(c) The abolishing of Corn Laws brought following results

(i) After the Corn Laws were abolished, food could be imported into Britain more cheaply than it could be produced within the country.

(ii) British agriculture was unstable to compete with imports.

(iii) Vast areas of land were now left uncultivated and thousands of men and women were thrown out of work. They migrated to the cities or other countries in search of work.

(iv) As the food prices fell, consumption in Britain rose. From the mid-19th century, faster industrial growth in Britain also led to higher incomes and therefore, more food imports.

2. How did Europeans try to recruit and retain labour? Explain any two methods.

Ans. The European employers found it difficult to recruit labour in Africa because historically Africa had abundant land and a relatively small population. For centuries, land and livestock sustained African livelihoods and people had no need to work for a wage.

In late 19th century Africa, there were few consumer goods, so there was little reason to work for a wage. Europeans were attracted to Africa due to its vast resources of land and mineral. They came to Africa hoping to establish plantations and mines to produce crops and minerals for export to Europe. But there was an acute problem of shortage of labour.

The Europeans then used some methods to recruit and retain labour. These were

(i) Heavy taxes were imposed which could be paid only by working for wages on plantations and mines.

(ii) Inheritance laws were changed so that peasants were displaced from lands. Only one member of a family was allowed to inherit land, as a result of which the others were pushed into labour markets.

(iii) Mine workers were confined to compounds and not allowed to move freely.

(iv) Cattle disease rinderpest was introduced which destroyed their dependence on livestock for sustenance.

3. Write any three factors responsible for indentured labour migration from India.

Ans. In the 19th century, a large number of Indian labourers went to work on plantations, in mines and in road and railway construction projects around the world. The following factors were responsible for indentured labour migration from India

(i) In India, indentured labourers were hired under contracts. They promised with return travel to India. The agents provide them false information about the nature of work, living and working conditions. Hoping for a better future, the workers migrated in other countries.

(ii) Most Indian indentured workers came from the present-day regions of Uttar Pradesh, Bihar, Central India and the dry districts of Tamil Nadu. In these regions, cottage industries declined, land rents rose, lands were cleared for mines and plantations. All these factors forced the poor to migrate in search of work.

(iii) Many indentured labourers agreed to take up work hoping to escape poverty or oppression in their home villages. Labourers were largely required in other countries and the scope of employment forced the workers to migrate.

4. What led to the decline of textile exports from India in the 19th century? Explain in three points.

Ans. The following factors led to the decline of textile exports from India in 19th century

(i) The British Government introduced high tariffs on import of cotton cloth. Indian textile industry faced stiff competition and export of cotton textiles began to decline.

From the early 19th century, British manufacturers also began to seek overseas markets for their cloth. As a result, the Indian textile industry was adversely affected.

(ii) Indian textile industry faced stiff competition in other international markets. A steady decline of Indian cotton textile was seen from some 30 per cent around 1800 to 15 per cent by 1815.

By the 1870s, this proportion had dropped to below 3 per cent. While exports of manufacturers decline rapidly, exports of raw materials increased. Between 1812 and 1871, the share of raw cotton increased from 5 per cent to 35 per cent.

(iii) British forced the farmers of India to produce indigo and opium instead of textile. Indigo used for dyeing cloth was exported to Britain.

Opium grown (from the 1820) in India was exported to China and with the money earned through opium sale, Britain financed its tea and other imports from China.

5. Explain any five consequences of the Great Depression of 1929 on Indian economy.

Or **Explain the effects of the Great Depression of 1929 on the Indian economy.**

Or **When did the Great Depression begin? Explain its impact on the world.**

Ans. The Great Depression began around 1929. During this period, most parts of the world experienced dangerous declines in production employment, income and trade. In the 19th century, colonial India had become an exporter of agricultural goods and importer of manufactures.

The Great Depression immediately affected Indian trade in the following ways :

(i) India's exports and imports nearly halved between 1928 and 1934. As international prices crashed, prices in India also plunged.

(ii) Peasants and farmers suffered more than urban dwellers. Agricultural prices fell sharply, but the colonial government refused to reduce revenue demands.

(iii) Peasants producing for the world market were the worst hit. As gunny exports collapsed, the price of raw jute crashed more than 60 per cent.

(iv) Jute producers fell deeper and deeper into debt.

(v) The Great Depression had a political impact. It paved the way for Gandhiji to launch the Civil Disobedience Movement in India.

6. Until the 19th century, poverty and hunger were common in Europe. Cities were crowded and deadly disease were wide spread .Religious conflicts were common and religious dissenters were persecuted. Thousands therefore fled Europe for America. Here by the 18th century, plantations worked by slaves captured in Africa were growing cotton and sugar for European markets.

Why the year 1929 known as the Great Depression? Explain the main factors responsible for the Great Depression. **Competency Based**

Ans. The year of 1929 came to be known as the Great Depression because during this period most parts of the world experienced large decline in production, employment, income and trade.

The Great Depression was caused by several factors such as

- Many countries financed their investments through loans from the US. In the early 1920s, the economy of the US was strong. But the over production in industrial and agricultural sector led to the depression.
- There was a sudden growth in the purchase of refrigerators, washing machines, radios, gramophone players, etc through hire-purchase. With the fall in prices and the prospect of depression, US banks slashed domestic lending and called back loans.
- Farms could not sell their harvests, households were ruined and business collapsed. The consumerist prosperity of 1920s disappeared.
- Faced with falling incomes, many households could not repay what they had borrowed. They even were forced to give up their homes, cars and other consumer durables.
- US banking system collapsed.

7. Describe the role of technology in transformation of the world in the 19th century.

Ans. Technology has played an important role in transformation the world economy in the 19th century in the following ways

- Technology can be regarded as the primary source in economic development. The railways, steamships, the telegraph were important inventions in the 19th century.
- The technological advances were the result of larger social, political and economic factors. For example, colonisation stimulated new investment and improvements in transport system.
- Faster railways, lighter wagon and large refrigerated ships helped move food more cheaply and quickly from America, Australia or New Zealand to final markets in different European countries.
- The reduced shipping costs lowered meat prices in Europe. The poor in Europe could consume a more varied diet which included meat, butter and eggs.
- Better living condition in Europe promoted social peace within the country and people started to support the policies of imperialism.

Case Based Questions

1. Read the given sources and answer the following questions.

Source A Decolonisation and Independence

At the same time, most developing countries did not benefit from the fast growth the Western economies experienced in the 1950s and 1960s. Therefore, they organised themselves as a group i.e. the Group of 77 (or G-77) to demand a New International Economic Order (NIEO).

By the NIEO they meant a system' that would give them real control over their natural resources, more development assistance, fairer prices for raw materials and better access for their manufactured goods in developed countries' markets.

(i) Why did most developing countries organise themselves into the Group of 77 during 1960s?

Source B Indentured labour Migration from India

Recruitment was done by agents engaged by employers and paid a small commission. Many migrants agreed to take up work hoping to escape poverty or oppression in their home villages. Agents also tempted the prospective migrants by providing false information about final destinations, modes of travel, the nature of the work and living and working conditions. Often migrants were not even told that they were to embark on a long sea voyage. Sometimes agents even forcibly abducted less willing migrants.

(ii) How were the indentured workers exploited by the recruiting agents?

Sources C The Great Depression

The Great Depression began around 1929 and lasted till the mid-1930s. During this period, most parts of the world experienced catastrophic declines in production, employment, incomes and trade. The exact timing and impact of the depression varied across countries.

But in general, agricultural regions and communities were the worst affected. This was because the fall in agricultural prices was greater and more prolonged than that in the prices of industrial goods.

(iii) During the Great Depression, why was the agricultural sector worst affected?

Ans. (i) Most developing countries organise themselves into the Group of 77 during 1960s because they did not benefit from the fast economic growth experienced in 1950s and 1960s.

(ii) The recruiting agents provided indentured workers false information about final destination, modes of travel, the nature of work and living and working conditions. Sometimes agent even forcibly abducted less willing workers. In this way, recruiting agents exploited indentured workers.

(iii) During the Great Depression, the agricultural sector was worst affected because the fall in the agricultural prices was greater and more prolonged than the price of industrial goods.

2. Read the extract and answer the questions that follows

The Bretton Woods conference established the International Monetary Fund (IMF) to deal with external surpluses and deficits of its member nations. The International Bank for Reconstruction and Development (popularly known as the World Bank) was set up to finance post-war reconstruction: The IMF and the World. Bank are referred to as the Bretton Woods institutions or sometimes the Bretton Woods twins. The post-war international economic system is also often described as the Bretton Woods system. The IMF and the World Bank commenced financial operations in 1947.

Decision-making in these institutions is controlled by the Western industrial powers. The US has an effective right of veto over key IMF and World Bank decisions.

The international monetary system is the system linking national currencies and monetary system. The Bretton Woods system was based on fixed exchange rates. In this system, national currencies, for example, the Indian rupee, were pegged to the dollar at a fixed exchange rate. The dollar itself was anchored to gold at a fixed price of $35 per ounce of gold.

(i) Why the International Monetary Fund (IMF) was set-up?

(ii) What was the Bretton Woods system?

(iii) What decision was taken at Bretton Woods in New Hampshire, USA?

Ans. (i) The IMF was set-up to promote International Monetary Cooperation.

(ii) The Bretton Woods System was based on fixed exchange rates. In this system, national currencies viz. the Indian rupees were pegged to the dollar at a fixed exchange rate.

The dollar itself was anchored to gold at a fixed price of $ 35 per ounce of gold.

(iii) In Bretton Woods Conference, New Hampshire USA, decision were taken for establishing World Bank and International Monetary Fund (IMF) to preserve Global economical stability and full employment in the industrial world.

These institutions would also deal with surplus and deficit of member nations and finance post war reconstruction.

ASSESSMENT EXERCISE

Multiple Choice Questions (MCQs)

1. Which of our common foods were not known to our ancestors until about 5 centuries ago?
(a) Sweet potatoes and potatoes
(b) Groundnut and maize
(c) Soya, chillies and tomatoes
(d) All of the above

2. Where animals are not slaughtered for food at the starting point?
(a) America
(b) Australia
(c) New Zealand
(d) Europe

3. Which among the following appropriate statement associated with IMF?
(a) The Bretton Woods Conference established the IMF.
(b) It was held in May 1945.
(c) The IMF and the World Bank commenced financial operation in 1948.
(d) The conference was held at Bretton Woods in New Hampshire, UK.

4. Find the incorrect option.
(a) The Great Depression began around 1939 and lasted till the mid 1980s.
(b) The system of indentured labour was abolished in 1921.
(c) Rinderpest arrived in Africa in late 1880s.
(d) The First World War fought in 1914-18.

Subjective Questions (VSA, SA & LA)

1. Name the countries where 'Chutney music' is popular.
2. When did the Great Depression begin?
3. What do you mean by G-77?
4. What was the impact of technology on food availability?
5. The G-77 group of nations demand a New International Economic Order. Why?
6. What is rinderpest? Who brought it to Africa? How did rinderpest help the Europeans to conquer Africa?
7. Analyse the effects of the First World War on the world economy.
8. Give three examples to show that the world changed with the discovery of new sea routes of America.

CHAPTER 4

The Age of Industrialisation

Industrialisation is often linked with the growth of factories. Industrial production refers to factory production and industrial workers refers to factory workers. However, before the widespread establishment of factories in England and Europe, significant industrial production for an international market existed. This was not based on factories. This early stage is called **proto-industrialisation**.

4.1 Before the Industrial Revolution

In the 17th and 18th centuries, merchants from European towns moved to the villages. They provided money to peasants and artisans, encouraging them to produce for the international market.

World trade expansion and colonial acquisitions increased the demand for goods. But merchants could not increase production due to powerful urban crafts and trade guilds.

Guilds controlled production, regulated competition and prices, and restricted entry into the trade. Rulers granted guilds monopoly rights to trade and produce specific products. Thus, it was difficult for the new merchants to set up businesses in towns and they moved to the villages.

In rural areas, poor peasants and artisans started working for merchants. People with small plots of land couldn't find enough work for everyone in their families. When merchants offered money advances to make things for them, these families happily accepted.

Proto-Industrialisation System

The proto-industrial system was a network of commercial exchange. It was controlled by the merchants.

A merchant clothier in England first purchased wool from a wool stapler[1] and supplied it to the spinners. The thread that was spun was taken in different stages of production to weavers, fullers[2] and then to dyers.

The finished products passed through several stages and reached the market of London. Gradually, London came to be known as a **finishing centre**.

At each stage of production, 20-25 members were employed by each merchants. The goods were produced by a vast number of producers working within their family farms, instead of factories.

The Coming Up of the Factory

The earliest factories in England came up by the 1730s. However, the number of factories multiplied in the late 18th century. **Cotton textile** was the main industry at that time.

In 1760, Britain imported 2.5 million pounds of raw cotton for its industry. By 1787, this increased to 22 million pounds due to changes in production processes.

A series of inventions in the 18th century increased the efficacy[3] of each step of the production process which included carding[4], **twisting**, **spinning** and **rolling**. They improved the amount each worker could produce, allowing for the production of stronger threads and yarn.

Richard Arkwright is credited to create the cotton mill. Within the mill, all the processes were carried out at one place.

In the 19th century, factory system increased largely in England.

The Pace of Industrial Change

Cotton and metal became the most dynamic industries in Britain. Cotton was the leading sector in the first phase of industrialisation upto the 1840s, followed by iron and steel industry.

Railway expansion in England from the 1840s and later in colonies from the 1860s increased demand for iron and steel.

---

1 Stapler A person who 'staples' or sorts wool according to its fibre.

2 Fuller A person who 'fulls' i.e. gathers cloth by pleating.

3 Efficacy The power to produce a desired result or effect.

4 Carding The process in which fibres, such as cotton or wool, are prepared prior to spinning.

By 1873, Britain was exporting iron and steel twice the value of its cotton exports.

The new machinery and industries could not easily displace traditional industries. At the end of 19th century, less than 20 per cent of the total workforce was employed in technologically advanced industrial sectors.

Textile was a dynamic sector, but a large portion of the output was not produced within factories. Most of the textiles were primarily produced within domestic units.

Ordinary and small innovations were seen in non-mechanised sectors like food processing, building, furniture making, production of implements, pottery, glasswork and tanning.

The technological changes occurred slowly. They did not spread largely across the country. Merchants and industrialists were cautious about using new expensive technology.

James Watt improved the steam engine produced by Newcomen and patented the new engine in 1781.

Mathew Boulton manufactured the new model of steam engine but it was not easily accepted by the industrialists. At the beginning of the 19th century, there were only 321 steam engines all over the England.

4.2 Hand Labour and Steam Power

In Britain, there was no shortage of human labour. Poor peasants and **vagrants**[5] moved to the cities in search of jobs so workers were available at low wages.

In many industries, the demand for labour was seasonal. For example, gas works and breweries, book binding and printing, ship repairing, etc needed seasonal labour.

A range of products could be produced only with hand labour. These required human skill, instead of mechanical technology.

In Victorian Britain, the upper classes preferred handmade products, seeing them as a symbol of refinement and class. These items were well-made and designed, while machine made goods were mainly for export to the colonies.

Life of the Workers

- The possibility of getting a job depended on existing networks of friendship and relations.
- Many job seekers had to wait for weeks, spending nights under bridges. Some stayed in night shelters that were set up by private individuals.
- After the busy season was over, labourers looked for even odd jobs which were difficult to find till the mid-19th century.
- The wages increased during the Napoleonic War but this increase was balanced by an increase in prices of commodities.
- The income of workers depended on the number of days of their work along with the wage rate.
- About 10 per cent of the urban population was extremely poor till the mid-19th century.
- In 1830s, unemployment rose to between 35% to 75% in different regions.
- The fear of unemployment made workers unfriendly to the introduction of new technology.
- When the **Spinning Jenny**[6] was introduced in the woollen industry, women who survived on hand spinning began opposing new machines.
- After the 1840s, building activities like construction of railways, roads, railway lines, etc. increased in the cities which needed large-scale employment.
- The number of labourers employed in the transport industry doubled in the 1840s which again doubled in the next 30 years.

4.3 Industrialisation in the Colonies

British colonies like India industrialised with the development of factories, industries and non-mechanised sector.

The Age of Indian Textiles

Silk and cotton products of India dominated the international market before the age of machine industries.

Armenian and Persian merchants took the goods from Punjab to Afghanistan, Eastern Persia and Central Asia.

Surat, Masulipatnam and Hooghly were the most important ports, which were used for trade. Many Indian merchants and bankers were involved in financing production, carrying goods and supplying to exporters.

5 **Vagrants** It refers to a person who has no home or job, especially one who begs.

6 **Spinning Jenny** This machine was devised by James Hargreaves in 1764, which speeded up the spinning process and reduced labour demand. By turning one single wheel, a worker could set in motion a number of spindles and spin several threads at the same time.

By the 1750s, with the arrival of the European companies, the Indians started losing their control over the trade.

The European companies were gaining power by securing a variety of concessions from local courts. Some of the companies got monopoly rights to trade.

All this resulted in a decline of the old ports like Surat and Hooghly, and emergence of new ports like Bombay and Calcutta. This change was an indication of the growth of new colonial power.

Situation of Weavers

In 1760s, the Indian fine textiles were in great demand in Europe. So, the East India Company was keen on expanding textile exports from India.

In 1760s and 1770s, the East India Company faced problems in getting a regular supply of goods for export. This is because it faced competition from the French, Dutch, Portuguese and local traders.

After the Company established its political power, it developed a system of management and control. By this system, it started to eliminate its competitors and tried to assert a monopoly over right to trade.

The company did it through a series of steps as follows

- The Company tried to remove the current traders and brokers involved in the cloth trade and establish direct control over the weavers.
- They assigned a paid servant known as the *gomasthas* to manage weavers, procure materials, and inspect the cloth's quality.
- Company weavers were restricted from engaging with other buyers. This was done through the system of advances.

  After receiving an order, weavers were provided loans to buy the necessary raw materials. As the loans increased, and the demand for high-quality textiles grew, weavers willingly accepted the advances, hoping for higher earnings and dedicating all their time to weaving.

However, conflicts emerged in many weaving villages between weavers and gomasthas.

Condition of Weavers

The new *gomasthas* were outsiders with no long-term social links with the village.

They displayed arrogance, entering villages with sepoys and peons, and penalised weavers for supply delays, resorting to beating and flogging[7].

Weavers lost the ability to negotiate prices and sell to various buyers. The Company's offered prices were extremely low, and the loans they had accepted tied them to the Company.

In several locations in Carnatic and Bengal, weavers left their villages and migrated. In other regions, weavers with village traders, rebelled against the Company and its representatives.

Gradually, numerous weavers started rejecting loans, closing down their workshops and taking to agricultural labour. As the 19th century began, cotton weavers faced new challenges.

Manchester Comes to India

In 1811-12, the share of cotton textile industry was 33 per cent of India's export and by 1850-51, it was just 3 per cent. In the 19th century, textile industries in England developed.

The industrialists pressurised the government to impose import duties on cotton textiles, so that Manchester goods could sell in Britain without facing any competition.

At the same time, industrialists persuaded the East India Company to sell British manufactures in Indian markets. By 1850s, cotton goods made up more than 31% of India's imports and by the 1870s, this increased to over 50%.

Indian weavers faced following two problems at that time

(i) Indian export market collapsed. The local market was filled with Manchester goods (goods imported from Britain). These imported cotton goods produced by machines were so cheap that Indian weavers could not easily compete with them.

(iii) As cotton exports from India increased due to the civil war in USA, weavers in India did not get sufficient and good quality cotton and they were forced to buy raw cotton from Britain at higher prices.

Try These

1. **Which city came to be known as the finishing centre?**
2. **Who were the competitors of the East India Company in textile industry in 18th century?**
3. **Which products in India dominated the international market before the age of machine industries?**
4. **What was the task of paid servant known as gomasthas?**
5. **What was the response of industrial groups in England to the development of the cotton industries?**

7 **Flogging** It is the act of hitting hard with a whip or stick as punishment.

4.4 Factories Come Up

Cotton and jute mills were the first to be established in India. The **first cotton mill** was set up in 1854 in **Bombay** and the **first jute mill** was set up in 1855 in **Bengal**.

In North India, **Elgin Mill** was started in Kanpur in 1860s and a year later, first cotton mill was set-up in Ahmedabad.

By 1874, the **first spinning and weaving mill** of Madras began production. Most of these industries were set-up by Indian entrepreneurs.

The Early Entrepreneurs

From the late 18th century, the British in India began exporting opium to China and took tea from China to England. Many Indian businessmen were involved in this trade.

Some famous industrialists were Dwarkanath Tagore, Dinshaw Petit, Jamsetjee Nusserwanjee Tata, Shiv Narayan Birla (Grandfather of GD Birla), Seth Hukumchand, etc.

Dwarkanath Tagore set up six joint stock companies in the 1830s and 1840s. **JN Tata** set up first iron and steel works in India at Jamshedpur in 1912.

Seth Hukumchand set up the first Indian jute mill in Calcutta in 1917.

As colonial power gained control over Indian trade, the scope of business for Indian merchants became limited in the following ways

- Indian merchants were not allowed to trade with Europe in manufactured goods.
- Indian merchants were allowed to export only raw materials and foodgrains like cotton, opium, wheat and indigo which were required by the British.
- European Managing Agencies controlled a large sector of Indian industries till the First World War. Some of them were Bird Heiglers & Co. Andrew Yule and Jardine Skinner & Co. These agencies gathered capital, established joint-stock companies, and managed them.
- In most cases, Indian financiers provided the capital while the European Agencies made all investment and business decision.
- The European merchant-industrialists had exclusive chambers of commerce that Indian businessmen were not allowed to join.

Demand for Workers and their Condition

With the expansion of factories, the demand for workers increased. Peasants and artisans who found no work in the village went to the industrial centres in search of work. Many workers travelled distant places in the hope of work in the mills. For example, from the United Provinces, they even went to work in Bombay or Calcutta.

The problems faced by workers were

- They did not get jobs easily.
- Number of workers were more as compared to jobs.
- Entry to the mills was restricted.
- Industrialists employed a **jobber** to get new recruits. Jobber was an old and trusted worker. Jobber got people from his village, ensured them jobs, helped them settle in the city and provided them money in times of crisis.
- The jobber became a person with some authority and power. He controlled the lives of workers and demanded money and gift for his favour.

4.5 The Peculiarities of Industrial Growth

The European Managing Agencies, which controlled industrial production in India, focused on certain kinds of products.

They established tea and coffee plantations and invested in mining, indigo and jute. Most of these were products required primarily for export trade and not for sale in India.

In the late 19th century, Indian businessmen establishing industries avoided direct competition with goods from Manchester in the Indian market.

By the 20th century, a series of changes affected the pattern of industrialisation as follows

- As swadeshi movement became stronger, the nationalist leaders urged the people to boycott foreign cloth. Industrial groups came together to protect their shared interests, urging the government to increase tariff protection and provide additional concessions.
- From 1906, India began shifting from yarn to cloth production, as India's yarn export to China declined because produce from Chinese and Japanese mills flooded Chinese market. Cotton piece-goods production in India doubled from 1900-1912.
- New factories were set up during the First World War to supply war needs and Indian industrial production increased.
- After the war, Manchester could never capture its old position in the Indian market. The economy of Britain collapsed, as Manchester was unable to modernise and compete with the US, Germany and Japan.

Predomination of Small-Scale Industries

Large industries were mainly located in Bengal and Bombay and formed only a small segment of the economy.

Over the rest of the country, small-scale production continued to predominate. **Handicrafts** production actually expanded in the 20th century by adopting new technology like looms with a fly shuttle[8].

Amongst weavers, some produced coarse cloth while others wove finer qualities. The coarse cloth was purchased by the poor. Its demand fluctuated due to bad harvests or famines.

Even if weavers and other craftspeople expanded production throughout the 20th century, they had to work for long hours. Often, entire households, including women and children, had to contribute at different stages of the production process.

The finer varieties were bought by the rich. Famines did not affect the sale of fine varieties such as Baluchari and Banarasi saris. Mills could not copy the intricate[9] designs of the weavers.

4.6 Market for Goods

Advertisement, labelling and calendars were used to popularise products by both British and Indian manufactures.

Advertisement through newspapers, TV, street walls, magazines and hoardings were used by the producers to expand their market.

Advertisement makes products appear desirable and necessary. It played a very significant role from the very beginning of the industrial age, for developing a new consumer culture.

When Manchester industrialists began selling cloth in India, they put labels on the cloth bundles 'MADE IN MANCHESTER'. Sometimes, the images of Indian Gods, Goddesses (e.g. Krishna, Saraswati) were also used on these labels.

The label was needed to make the place of manufacture and the name of the company familiar to the buyer. The image of Indian gods and goddesses were imprinted on goods for making a foreign product familiar to the Indian people.

By the late 19th century, manufacturers were printing calendars to popularise their products as calendars were used even by people who could not read.

Besides, the images of Gods, figures of important persons, emperors and nawabs were used in advertisements and calendars.

Advertisements sometimes became a medium of the nationalist message of Swadeshi which guaranteed the quality of the product.

Conclusion

The age of industries has meant major technological changes, growth of factories and the making of a new industrial labour force. Small-scale production and hand technology also played key role in the industrial landscape.

Try These

1. **Dwarkanath Tagore set up six .... in the 1830s and 1840s.**
2. **The first cotton mill was set up in ....**
3. **Name some famous Indian industrialists of 19th century.**
4. **Name the Indian Gods and Goddesses which were generally used by the foreign manufacturers.**

TIME LINE | Covering Major Events with their Time Periods in Chronological Order

Period	Important Events
17th and 18th century	Age of proto-industrialisation.
1730s	Earliest factories started in England.
1764	James Hargreaves invents the Spinning Jenny.
1781	James Watt patents the steam engine.
1854	First cotton mill is set up in Bombay.
1855	First jute mill comes up in Bengal.
1856	First cotton mill in India started production in Bombay.
1874	First spinning and weaving mill of Madras starts production.
1912	JN Tata set up the first iron and steel works of India in Jamshedpur.
1917	First jute mill owned by an Indian set up in Calcutta.

8 **Fly Shuttle** It is a mechanical device used for weaving, moved by means of ropes and pullies. It is used by weavers to operate large looms.

9 **Intricate** It is the thing which is very complicated and detailed.

Mind Map

THE AGE OF INDUSTRIALISATION

Before the Industrial Revolution

Proto-Industrialisation System
- It was a network of commercial exchange.
- London came to be known as finishing centre.

The Coming Up of the Factory
- Earliest factories in England came up by the 1730s.
- Cotton Textile was the main industry at that time.
- Richard Arkwright is credited to create the Cotton Mill.

The Pace of Industrial Change
- Railway expansion in England and later in colonies increased demand for iron and steel.
- James Watt improved the steam engine produced by Newcomen and patented the new engine in 1781.
- Mathew Boulton manufactured the new model of steam engine but it was not easily accepted by the industrialists.

Life of the Workers
- About 10% of the urban population was extremely poor till the mid-19th century.
- The number of labourers employed in the transport industry doubled in the 1840s which again doubled in the next 30 years.

Hand Labour and Steam Power
Handmade products were preferred by the aristocrats and the bourgeoisie.

Industrialisation in the Colonies

The Age of Indian Textiles
- Silk and cotton products of India dominated the international market before the age of machine industries.
- Surat, Hooghly and Masulipatnam were the most important ports, which were used for trade.

Manchester Comes to India
- Indian export market collapsed.
- The local market was filled with Manchester goods.
- Indian weavers were forced to buy raw cotton from Britain at higher prices.

Situation of Weavers
- East India Company appointed a paid servant known as the Gomastha.
- Company weavers were restricted from engaging with other buyers by the system of advances.

Market for Goods
- Advertisement, labelling and calenders were used to popularise products by both British and Indian manufacturers.
- Advertisement through newspapers, TV, street walls and hoardings were used by the producers to expand their market.
- By the late 19th century, manufacturers were printing calendars to popularise their products as calendars were used even by people who could not read.

The Peculiarities of Industrial Growth
- As Swadeshi Movement became stronger, the nationalist leaders urged the people to boycott foreign cloth.
- From 1906, India began shifting from yarn to cloth production when India's yarn export to China declined.
- New factories were setup during the war to supply war needs and Indian industrial production increased.

Factories Come Up
- The first Cotton Mill was setup in 1854 in Bombay and the first Jute Mill was setup in 1855 in Bengal.
- Elgin Mill was started in Kanpur in 1860s and a year later, first Cotton Mill was setup in Ahmedabad.

The Early Entrepreneurs
- Dwarkanath Tagore setup six joint stock companies in the 1830s and 1840s.
- J N Tata setup first iron and still works in India at Jamshedpur in 1912.
- Seth Hukumchand setup the first Indian Jute Mill in Calcutta in 1917.

Demand for Workers and their Condition
- Getting job was not easy.
- Number of workers were more as compared to jobs.
- Entry to the mills was restricted.

NCERT FOLDER

Covering Intext Questions and Exercises of NCERT

INTEXT QUESTION

Q.1 Look at the three pictures given below and Source B. Explain why many workers were opposed to the use of the Spinning Jenny?

• Picture I

• Picture II

• Picture III

SOURCE B

A magistrate reported in 1790 about an incident when he was called in to protect a manufacturer's property from being attacked by workers:

'From the depredations of a lawless Banditti of colliers and their wives, for the wives had lost their work to spinning engines ... they advanced at first with much insolence, avowing their intention of cutting to pieces the machine lately introduced in the woollen manufacture; which they suppose, if generally adopted, will lessen the demand for manual labour. The women became clamorous. The men were more open to conviction and after some expostulation were induced to desist from their purpose and return peaceably home.' JL Hammond and B Hammond, The Skilled Labourer 1760-1832, quoted in Maxine Berg, The Age of Manufactures.

Ans. The picture I shows that each member of the family is involved in the production of yarn. It is also clear from the picture that one wheel is moving only one spindle. In the 19th century, spinning was a source of alternative income for the poor peasants.

Many of them had small plots of land which could not provide work for all members of the family. Proto-industrial production gave employment to each member of the family. In picture II, a cotton mill glowing with electricity in the twilight is seen. This shows positive impact of industrialisation.

The machine shown in the picture III is called a Spinning Jenny, which was devised by James Hargreaves in 1764.

Many workers were opposed to the use of spinning jenny because

- Its one wheel could operate several spindles at a time. As a result, it created unemployment in the labour class and so they opposed it.
- Spinning Jenny was introduced in woollen industry. Women who survived on hand spinning opposed the introduction of this new machine.

EXERCISE

Q.1 Explain the following

(a) In the 17th century, merchants from towns in Europe began employing peasants and artisans within the villages.

(b) Women workers in Britain attacked the Spinning Jenny.

(c) The port of Surat declined by the end of the 18th century.

(d) The East India Company appointed *gomasthas* to supervise weavers in India.

Ans. (a) World trade expanded at very fast rate during the 17th century. The trade and commerce guild controlled the market, raw materials, employees and also the production of goods in the towns.

This created problems for merchants who wanted to increase production by employing extra men. Therefore, they started employing peasants and artisans who lived in village.

(b) Women workers in Britain attacked the spinning Jenny because it speeded up the spinning process in woollen industry and reduced the demand for labour. By the use of this machine, a single worker could turn a number of spindles and spin several threads at a time.

This caused a valid fear of unemployment among women working in the woollen industry. Till date they had survived on hand spinning, but it was placed in danger by the introduction new machine.

(c) The port of Surat declined by the end of the 18th contury due to the growing power of European companies engaged in trade with India. The European companies were gaining power by securing a variety of concessions as well as monopoly rights to trade from the local courts.

This led to a decline of the old ports of Surat and Hooghly from where local merchants operated. Exports slowed and local banks went bankrupt.

(d) The East India Company appointed the paid servants called gomasthas.

They were appointed because of the following reasons

- To eliminate the existing traders and brokers connected with the cloth trade and establish a more direct control over the weavers.
- To supervise weavers collect supplies and examine the quality of cloth.
- To prevent the company weavers from the dealing with other buyers. Those who took loans had to hand over the cloth they produced to the gamasthas.

Q.2 Write true or false against each statement.

(a) At the end of the 19th century, 80 per cent of the total workforce in Europe was employed in the technologically advanced industrial sector.

(b) The international market for textiles was dominated by India till the 18th century.

(c) The American Civil War resulted in the reduction of cotton exports from India.

(d) The introduction of the fly shuttle enabled the handloom workers to improve their productivity.

Ans. (a) False (b) True (c) False (d) True

Q.3 Explain what is meant by proto- industrialisation?

or **Explain the conditions in 18th century English countryside that created conditions for proto-industrialisation.**

or **What is meant by proto-industrialisation? How did it affect the life of the people?**

Ans. The early phase of industrialisation in which large-scale production was carried out for international market demands at decentralise units but not at factories is called proto-industrialisation.

It affected the life of 18th century English countryside in the following ways

- In the urban areas, guilds were set up which produced a variety of things before the introduction of machines.
- In the rural areas, the merchants had set up their own production units where most of the work was done by the workers manually. Many workers even produced in their family-farms. By working for the merchants, they could continue to cultivate their small plots. Income from proto-industrial production supplemented their income.

Q.4 Imagine that you have been asked to write an article for an encyclopedia on Britain and the history of cotton. Write your piece using information from the entire chapter.

Ans. Before the age of industrialisation, silk and finer quality cotton goods of India dominated the international market in textiles. Armenian and Persian merchants along with Indian merchants were involved in trading of textiles.

During the industrialisation, the European countries gradually gained powers in trading. The history of cotton can be understood from the points given below

- The use of steam power played a very significant role in running cotton mills. Production of textiles increased in a very short time and with less manual labour. At the beginning of the 19th century, there were near about 321 steam engines in England and out of them 80 were used in cotton textile mills.
- The East India Company appointed *gomasthas*, paid servants of the company to supervise weavers, collect supplies and inspect the quality of textiles. Gomasthas were the link between the East India Company and the weavers.
- The Indian weavers could not compete with the imported cotton goods and so by the beginning of the 19th century export of textile declined. Cheap and durable textiles from Manchester (England) started flooding Indian markets. Cotton weavers of India had to face two problems simultaneously, the export market collapsed and the local market shrank.
- In the 1860s, weavers faced a new problem of insufficient supply of raw cotton from USA due to the American Civil War. The price of raw cotton increased rapidly due to the big demand of raw cotton export from India. Weavers found themselves unable to pay for it.
- After the First World War, Manchester could never capture again its old position in the Indian market. Britain could not match with the USA, Germany and Japan in reference of modernisation and competition. As a result, production of cotton collapsed and export of cotton textiles from England fell down badly.

Q.5 Why did some industrialists in 19th century Europe prefer hand labour over machines?

Ans. Some industrialists in 19th century Europe preferred hand labour over machines because

- In many industries, the demand for labour was seasonal.
- Labour was available at low wages at that period of time.
- Machines were costly, ineffective, difficult to repair and required huge capital investments.
- Market demands of a variety of designs and colour and specific type could not be fulfilled by machine made clothes. Intricate designs and colours could be done by human skills only.
- In Victorian Britain, the upper classes *viz*, the aristocrats and the bourgeoisie preferred things produced by hand only.

Q.6 Why did the industrial production in India increased during the First World War?

or **Why did the Indian industrial growth suddenly shoot up in the years of the First World War? Describe any three reasons.**

Ans. Indian industrial growth suddenly increased during the First World War due to the following reasons

- With the decline of imports suddenly, Indian mills had a vast domestic market to supply their products.
- As the war continued, Indian factories were called upon to supply war needs also, such as jute bags, cloth for uniforms of soldiers, tents, leather boots, etc and many other items.
- New factories were set up and old ones organised multiple shifts. Many new workers were employed and everyone was made to work for longer hours during the war years.

Q.7 How did the East India Company procure regular supplies of cotton and silk textiles from Indian weavers?

Ans. After establishing political power, the East India Company successfully procured regular supplies of cotton and silk textiles from Indian weavers *via* a series of actions. These actions were aimed at eliminating competition from other colonial powers, controlling costs and ensuring regular supplies of cotton and silk goods for Britain.

Firstly, it appointed gomasthas or paid servants to supervise weavers, collect supplies and examine textile quality. Secondly, it disallowed Company weavers from dealing with other buyers. This was ascertained by a system of giving advances to the weavers for procuring raw materials. Those who took these loans could not sell their cloth to anyone but the gomasthas.

REVIEW EXERCISE

Including Competency Based Questions

Part I

Multiple Choice Questions (MCQs)

1. Name the country which is considered to be the first industrial nation of the world.

(a) France (b) Germany (c) Britain (d) Italy

2. Which among the following city was known as a finishing centre of the cloth at the time of proto-industrialisation?

(a) London (b) Berlin (c) Paris (d) Rome

3. In the first phase of industrialisation, which was/were the most dynamic industries in Britain?

(a) Metals (b) Coal
(c) Cotton (d) Both (a) and (c)

4. Identify the companie(s) which gradually gained power in the 1750s after the decline of Indian merchant's trade capacity.

(a) Chinese companies (b) Russian companies
(c) English companies (d) European companies

5. Which among the following two ports grew after the European companies gained power in trade?

(a) Surat and Hoogly (b) Madras and Masulipatnam
(c) Bombay and Calcutta (d) Kandla and Visakhapatnam

6. Which one of the following is not an European managing agency who controlled large sector of Indian industries during the First World War?

(a) Bird Heiglers and Company (b) Andrew Yule
(c) Jardine Skinner (d) East India Company

7. Which image of a God was most commonly used to popularise baby products?

(a) Ram (b) Shiva
(c) Krishna (d) Hanuman

8. Industralisation began in which one of the following European countries in the second half of the eighteenth century? CBSE Term I 2021

(a) Germany (b) France (c) Italy (d) England

9. Consider the following statements and choose the appropriate statement associated with emergence of mills.

(a) The earliest factories in England came up by the end of 1830s.
(b) Iron industries was the main industry at that time.
(c) The most dynamic industries in England were cotton and metals.
(d) James Watt is credited to create the cotton mills.

10. Find the incorrect option.

(a) Earliest factories started in England in 1730.
(b) James Watt patented the Steam Engine in 1781
(c) In 1855, first Jute mill came up in Punjab.
(d) First jute mill owned by an Indian set up in Calcutta.

11. Find the incorrect option.

(a) Richard Arkwright is credited to create the cotton mill.
(b) The most dynamic industries in Britain were cotton and metals.
(c) Seth Hukumchand set up the first Indian jute mill in Calcutta in 1917.
(d) In 1903, London underground railway starts operation.

12. The Industrial Revolution, which began in Britain in the mid-18th century, transformed the world of manufacturing and ushered in an era of mass production.

How did the import of raw cotton from foreign markets impact the British textile industry? Competency Based

(a) It stimulated the industry's growth and expansion
(b) It reduced the cost of raw materials and increased profits
(c) It led to the development of new textile manufacturing techniques
(d) All of the above

13. After the war, Manchester could never recapture its old position in the Indian market. Unable to modernise and compete with the US, Germany and Japan, the economy of Britain crumbled after the war.

Which of the following events led to the collapse of the British economy post World War I? Competency Based

(a) Native industrialists of British colonies failed to establish their industries.
(b) British cotton cloth exports fell drastically.
(c) Britain modernised its economy well.
(d) None of the above

14. In the 17th and 18th centuries, George, a merchant moved to towns in Europe supplying money to peasants and artisans in rural area, persuading them to produce for an international market.

Accordingly, which development happened in the world because of George movement in the 17th and 18th centuries? Competency Based

(a) The expansion of world trade and the acquisition of colonies in different parts of the world.
(b) The expansion of cotton work in the world.
(c) Merchants production started growing within towns.
(d) All of the above

15. Mr. X started a new business of hair products. He wanted to advertise his product why? Competency Based

(a) It makes products more valuable.
(b) It makes products appear desirable and necessary.
(c) It will help in making new more products.
(d) It will look good

16. The Industrial Revolution transformed Britain from an agricultural society to an industrial powerhouse. Machines became increasingly important in manufacturing, leading to increased productivity and lower costs. However, hand labour remained essential for many industries, particularly those producing goods with intricate designs and specific shapes.

How did hand labour impact the status of artisans and craftsmen in mid-19th-Century Britain? Competency Based

(a) Hand labour made them respected members of their communities.
(b) Hand labour elevated them to a higher social status.
(c) Hand labour was seen as outdated and unimportant.
(d) Hand labour was seen as a necessary but unskilled trade.

17. Arrange the following in the correct sequence.

I. First spinning and weaving mill of Madras began production.
II. First Jute mill comes up in Bengal.
III. James Watt patents the Steam engine.
IV. Earliest factories start in England.

Codes

(a) IV, III, II, I (b) I, II, III, IV
(c) III, IV, I, II (d) IV, III, I, II

18. Which of the following statements accurately describes the perception of handmade products in Victorian Britain?

I. They were associated with craftsmanship, individuality, and attention to detail.
II. They were seen as mass-produced and inferior to machine-made goods.
III. They were considered affordable and accessible to all social classes.
IV. They were primarily exported to colonies and not valued in Britain.

Codes

(a) Only I (b) Only III
(c) Only IV (d) Both I and II

19. Consider the statements given below and choose the correct answer Competency Based

Statement I Ahmedabad on the Gujarat coast connected India to the Gulf and Red Sea Ports. India traded by sea routes in pre-colonial times.

Statement II Before the age of machine industries, silk and cotton goods from India dominated the international market in textiles.

Options

(a) Statement I is correct and statement II is incorrect
(b) Statement I is incorrect and statement II is correct
(c) Statement I and II are incorrect
(d) Statement I and II are correct

20. Identify the reason as to why Indian weavers of cotton industries has to face a new problem in 1860s. Choose from the appropriate statements among the following options.

I. They could not get sufficient supply of raw cotton of good quality.

II. The buyers of cotton were not giving any money to the sellers.

III. They had to pay double tax of lands.

IV. The buyers of cotton from different parts of the world receiving cotton from the other country.

Options

(a) Statements I and II are appropriate.
(b) Statements I, II and III are appropriate.
(c) All the statements are appropriate.
(d) Only statement I is appropriate.

21. Consider the statements given below and choose the correct answer

Statement I Before establishing political power in Bengal and Carnatic in the 1760s and 1770s, the East India Company had found it difficult to ensure a regular supply of goods for export.

Statement II East India Company established political power, it could assert a monopoly right to trade.

Options

(a) Statement I is correct and statement II is incorrect
(b) Statement I is incorrect and statement II is correct
(c) Statement I and II are incorrect
(d) Both statment I and II are correct

Answers

1. (c)	**2.** (a)	**3.** (d)	**4.** (d)	**5.** (c)
6. (d)	**7.** (c)	**8.** (d)	**9.** (c)	**10.** (c)
11. (d)	**12.** (d)	**13.** (b)	**14.** (a)	**15.** (b)
16. (a)	**17.** (a)	**18.** (a)	**19.** (b)	**20.** (d)
21. (d)				

Match the Following

1.

List I (Year)	**List II** (Events)
A. 1730	1. Earliest factories starts in England.
B. 1781	2. James Watt patents the Steam Engine.
C. 1860	3. Elgin Mill started in Kanpur.
D. 1855	4. First Jute mill came up in Bengal.

Codes

	A	B	C	D		A	B	C	D
(a)	1	2	3	4	(b)	3	2	4	1
(c)	4	3	1	2	(d)	4	2	3	1

Ans. (a)

Assertion-Reason

1. Assertion (A) The period of industrialisation before the first factories came up in Europe is termed as proto-industrialisation.

Reason (R) This period was marked by merchants from towns getting products made in villages.

Codes

(a) Both A and R are true and R is the correct explanation of A
(b) Both A and R are true, but R is not the correct explanation of A
(c) A is true, but R is false
(d) A is false, but R is true

2. Assertion (A) The establishment of cotton mills in India marked the beginning of the industrial revolution in the country.

Reason (R) The first cotton mill in Bombay was set up in 1854 and it began production two years later.

Codes

(a) Both A and R are true and R is the correct explanation of A
(b) Both A and R are true, but R is not the correct explanation of A
(c) A is true, but R is false
(d) A is false, but R is true

3. Assertion (A) The Manchester industrialists' practice of labelling their cloth bundles was a strategic marketing move.

Reason (R) The labels served to identify the place of manufacture and the name of the company, establishing brand recognition and fostering trust among Indian buyers.

Codes

(a) Both A and R are true and R is the correct explanation of A
(b) Both A and R are true but R is not the correct explanation ofA
(c) A is true, but R is false
(d) A is false, but R is true

Ans. 1. (a) Both A and R are true and R is the correct explanation of A

2. (b) Both A and R are true, but R is not the correct explanation of A

3. (a) Both A and R are true and R is the correct explanation of A

Picture Based Questions

1. Which of the following aspects best signifies this image during 1874?

(a) Houseless and hungry
(b) Workers in iron works
(c) People on the move in search of work
(d) Railway workers in England

2. What is the main power source used to drive the spindles in the factory shown in the image below?

(a) Diesel
(b) Steam power
(c) Coal
(d) Electricity

Ans. 1. (a) Houseless and hungry
2. (b) Steam power

Case Based Question

1. Read the source given below and answer the following questions.

Before establishing political power in Bengal and Carnatic in the 1760s and 1770s, the East India Company had found it difficult to ensure a regular supply of goods for export. The French, Dutch, Portuguese as well as the local traders competed in the market to secure woven cloth. So the weaver and supply merchants could bargain and try selling the produce to the best buyer. In their letters back to London, Company officials continuously complained of difficulties of supply and the high prices. However, once the East India Company established political power, it could assert a monopoly right to trade. It proceeded to develop a system of management and control that would eliminate competition, control costs, and ensure regular supplies of cotton and silk goods.

(i) What was the main reason for the East India Company's difficulty in securing a regular supply of goods for export?

(a) Limited production capacity in India.
(b) Unfavourable weather conditions.
(c) Competition from other European traders and local merchants.
(d) Lack of efficient transportation infrastructure

(ii) How did the French, Dutch and Portuguese contribute to the difficulties faced by the East India Company?

(a) They imposed high tariffs on Indian goods.
(b) They offered higher prices to weavers and suppliers.
(c) They disrupted trade routes and transportation networks.
(d) They collaborated with local rulers to oppose the Company.

(iii) What were the potential negative consequences of the East India Company's monopoly on trade?

(a) Increased prices for consumers
(b) Exploitation of weavers and artisans
(c) Stagnation and decline of traditional industries
(d) All of the above

(iv) What were some of the long-term impacts of the East India Company's rule on India?

(a) Modernisation of the economy and infrastructure
(b) Development of a strong national identity
(c) Exploitation of resources and poverty
(d) Increased political instability and unrest

Ans. (i) (c) Competition from other European traders and local merchants.
(ii) (b) They offered higher prices to weavers and suppliers.
(iii) (d) All of the above
(iv) (c) Exploitation of resources and poverty

Part II

Very Short Answer Type Questions

1. What were trade guilds?

Ans. Trade guilds were associations of producers that trained craft people, maintained control over production, regulated competition and prices and restricted the entry of new people into the trade.

2. Why did the British merchants engage farmers from the countryside to produce textile for the market?

Ans. The British merchant engaged farmers from the countryside to produce textile for the market. This is because in towns, urban crafts and trade guilds were powerful and they regulated competition and prices and restricted the entry of new people into the trade.

3. Name some industries where labour demand was seasonal.

Ans. Industries like gas works, wine breweries, book- binding, printing and ship-repairing were some industries where labour demand was seasonal.

4. When was Spinning Jenny devised and by whom?

Ans. Spinning Jenny was devised by James Hargreaves in 1764.

5. To which ports did Surat on the Gujarat coast connect India?

Ans. Surat on the Gujarat coast connected India to the Gulf and Red Sea port.

6. Who were Koshtis?

Ans. Koshtis were a community of weavers.

7. When and where JN Tata set up the first iron and steel works in India?

Ans. JN Tata set up the first iron and steel works in India at Jamshedpur in 1912.

8. Name two materials which were exported to England from India.

Ans. Cotton and jute were exported to England from India.

9. At which place was the first spinning and weaving mill began production in 1874?

Ans. The first spinning and weaving mill began production in Madras in 1874.

10. How did the Indian weavers and merchants resist colonial control?

Ans. Indian weavers and merchants resisted colonial control by adopting following strategies

- They demanded tarrif protection to safeguards their interests.
- They created their own space and worked towards expanding the market for their produce.

11. Name some European Managing Agencies who controlled a large sector of Indian industries.

Ans. Some European Managing Agencies who controlled a large sector of Indian industries were Bird Heiglers & Co., Andrew Yule and Jardine Skinner & Co.

12. What technological change helped in improving production of Indian industry during the 20th century?

Ans. The introduction of fly shuttle (a mechanical device used for weaving) during the second decade of the 20th century helped in improving production of Indian handloom industry.

13. What are advantages of advertisement?

Ans. The advantages of advertisement are

- They make products appear desirable and necessary.
- They try to shape up the minds of people and create new needs in them.

14. Why did the British manufacturers print calendars for popularising their products in the late 19th century?

Ans. British manufacturers printed calendars for popularising their products in the late 19th century because calendars were used even by people who could not read.

15. What was the role of jobbers in the mill hiring process, according to Vasant Parkar? Explain.

Ans. The role of jobbers was to receive money from workers to get their sons work in the mill. Jobbers acted as intermediaries between mill workers and the mills themselves facilitating the hiring process in exchange for bribes from the workers.

16. There is a sizeable body of literature that seeks to explain India's poor industrial track record. Reasons identified include resource constraints, oppressive regulations and a general lack of skilled labour due to....... **Competency Based**

Source (edited) : Livemint

(i) What are the factors that affected India's industrial growth, according to the text?

(ii) What was the Swadeshi Movement and how did it impact industrialisation in India?

Ans. (i) Resource limitations, harsh regulations, and a shortage of skilled labour are the factors that affected in India's industrial growth. These factors increase costs, limit efficiency, and discourage investment.

(ii) The Swadeshi Movement was a campaign that encouraged the use of Indian-made goods and the boycott of foreign products, particularly British textiles. The boycott of foreign cloth led to demand for Indian textiles, creating opportunities for domestic textile mills and encouraging the expansion of the industry.

Short Answer Type Questions

1. Explain the meaning of the term 'Industrial Revolution'.

Ans. The term 'Industrial Revolution' stands for those developments and inventions which revolutionised the technique and organisation of production in the later half of the 18th century. This Industrial Revolution replaced the previous domestic system of production by the new factory system.

In place of manual and animal power, new machines and steam power were used for producing things. This revolution replaced cottage industries by factories, hand labour by machine work and craftsmen and artists by capitalists and factory owners.

2. How did factory production begin in England?

Ans. The early factories were established in England by the 1730s. The number of factories increased dramatically in the late 18th century. During this period, the production of cotton flourished. It was followed by the rapid establishment and expansion of the iron and steel industry.

The driving force of industrialisation were the inventions and technological changes of the 18th century. These innovations increased the efficiency at each stage of production and enhanced the output produced per worker, especially in the case of cotton and other textile industry.

Richard Arkwright laid the foundation of the factory system by creating the cotton mill. The spinning Jenny and other devices were invented to speed up textile production. This allowed more careful supervision over the production process, proper check over quality and regulation of labour force employed.

Thus in the late 19th century, factories increasingly became an intimate part of Britain.

3. Describe the conditions of workers in Europe after the Industrial Revolution.

Ans. The conditions of workers in Europe after the Industrial Revolution were as follows

- In most of the industries, the demand for labour was seasonal. The actual possibility of getting a job depended on existing networks of friendship and relations.
- The workers were getting very low wages.
- Factories employed large number of women. With technological development, women gradually lost their industrial jobs.
- Most of the workers were living in slums. Factory or workshop owners did not house the migrant workers.

4. Explain how were Indian merchants and bankers involved in the export trade in the early 18th century.

Ans. The Indian merchants and bankers were involved in the export trade in early 18th century in the following ways

- They were financing production, carrying goods and supplying exporters.
- The supply merchants linked the port towns to the inland regions.
- They gave advances to the weavers, procured the woven cloth from weaving villages and carried the supply to the ports.
- At the port, the big shippers and export merchants had brokers who negotiated the price and bought goods from the supply merchants operating inland.

5. "Indian trade had played a crucial role in the late 19th century world economy." Analyse the statement. **Competency Based**

Ans. Indian trade had played a crucial role in the late 19th century world economy. The following points analysed this statement

- Britain had a trade surplus with India, which means a situation under which the value of exports is more than the imports. Britain used this surplus to balance its trade deficit with other countries.
- Britain's trade surplus in India also helped to pay the 'home charges' that included private remittances by British officials and traders, interest payments on India's external debts and pensions of the British officials in India.
- India remained a major supplier of raw cotton to Britain which was required to feed the cotton textile industry of Britain.
- Many indentured workers came from Bihar, Uttar Pradesh, Central India. They migrated to other countries to work in mines and plantations.
- India become a major market for the final goods especially cotton textile.

6. Describe the role of early entrepreneurs of India in the development of industries. **Competency Based**

Ans. The role of early entrepreneurs of India in the development of industries can be explained in the following ways

- From the late 18th century, the British in India began exporting opium to China and took tea from China to England. Many Indian businessmen were involved in this trade.
- In the 19th century, many cotton mills, jute mills, spinning and weaving mills were set up and most of these were set up by Indian entrepreneurs.
- In Bengal, Dwarkanath Tagore, in Bombay Dinshaw Petit and Jamsetjee Nusservanjee Tata built huge industrial empire by accumulating their initial wealth partly from exports to China and partly from raw cotton exports to England.
- In Tata set up the first iron and steel works in India in 1912. Other businessmen like Seth Hukumchand set up the first Indian jute mill in Calcutta in 1917.

- Some merchants from Madras traded with Burma and some others traded with the Middle East and East Africa.
- Some entrepreneurs operated within India, carrying goods from one place to another, banking money, transferring funds between cities and financing other traders. When opportunities of investment were opened up, many factories were set up.

7. How did many Indian entrepreneurs survive despite of tight economic controls imposed by the British Government?

Ans. As British control over Indian trade tightened, Indian merchants had less room to operate. But many Indian entrepreneurs survived by adopting the following ways

- Some merchants traded with Burma, Middle East and East Africa and accumulated capital through other trade networks.
- Some merchants operated within India, carrying goods from one place to another, banking money, transferring funds between cities and financing traders.
- When opportunities of investment in industries opened up, many Indian entrepreneurs set up their own factories.

8. Explain the role of European Managing Agencies in India.

Ans. The role of European Managing Agencies in India was

- European Managing Agencies (e.g. Bird Heiglers and Co., Andrew Yule, Jardine Skinner and Co.) dominated industrial production in India. They were interested in certain kinds of products which could be exported.
- By acquiring land at cheap rates from the colonial government, they established tea and coffee plantations.
- They invested money in mining, indigo and jute. These products were not for sale in India. Most of these products were used for export trade.
- Till the First World War, these agencies controlled a large sector of Indian industries.
- These agencies mobilised capital, set up joint stock companies and managed them.

9. Mention any three restrictions imposed by the British Government upon the Indian merchants in the 19th century.

Ans. As the British Government established political power, it imposed a few restrictions upon Indian merchants to trade in India. These restrictions were

(i) The British Government developed a system of management and control that would eliminate competition and restrict the space within which Indian merchants could function.

(ii) Indian merchants were not allowed to trade with Europe in manufactured goods.

(iii) Indian merchants had to export mostly raw materials like raw cotton, opium, wheat and indigo required by the British. They were also gradually thrown out of the shipping business.

10. What was the role of a Jobber?
***Or* State any three functions of a Jobber.**

Ans. Jobbers were people employed by industrialists to recruit the right people from among the job seekers. Very often the Jobber was an old and trusted worker.

The following were the functions of a Jobber

- He got people from his village and ensured them jobs.
- He helped people to settle them in the city.
- He provided money in times of crisis. Jobbers became persons with some authority and power.

11. Describe any four impacts of Manchester imports on the cotton weavers of India.
***Or* How did the cotton weavers in India suffer due to Manchester import?**

Ans. The bad impacts of Manchester imports on the cotton weavers of India were

(i) Export market of cotton weavers collapsed and local market shrank.

(ii) Cotton clothes made up of machine were so cheap, that Indian weavers could not easily compete with them.

(iii) As American Civil War broke out and cotton supplies from the US were cut off, Indian weavers could not get sufficient supply of raw cotton.

(iv) Raw cotton exports from India increased, so Indian weavers could not get enough raw cotton and were forced to buy raw cotton at very high price.

12. Why did industrial production in India increase during the First World War?
***Or* Explain the impact of the First World War on industrial production in India.**

Ans. Industrial production in India increased during the First World War due to the following reasons

- British industries were busy with war production to meet the needs of the army. British imports into India declined.
- It was a good opportunity for Indian industries to fill in empty markets with their own products. Suddenly, Indian industries had a vast home market to supply.
- As the war continued, Indian factories were called upon to supply war needs like-jute bags, cloth or army uniform, tents and leather boots, etc.
- The increased demand for a variety of products led to the setting up of new factories. Production was also increased by the old industries.
- Many new workers were employed and forced to work more hours.

13. Highlight the position of weavers who produced coarse cloth in 20th century.

Ans. Weavers who produced coarse cloth in 20th century lived difficult lives. Amongst weavers, some produced coarse cloth while others wove finer qualities.

The position of weavers who produced only coarse cloth can be explained in the following ways

- The coarse cloth was purchased by the poor. Its demand fluctuated violently.
- During bad harvests and famines, when the rural poor had little food and no cash income, they could not afford to buy cloth.

14. How did Indian businessmen benefit from their participation in the China trade? **Competency Based**

Build answer around these points

- Many Indians became junior players in this trade.
- Setting up six joint-stock.
- Dwarkanath Tagore, a successful China trader, turned to industry.

Ans. Indian businessmen benefit from their participation in china trade because, the British in India began exporting opium to China and took tea from China to England.

Many Indians became junior players in this trade, providing finance, procuring supplies, and shipping consignments. Having earned through trade, some of these businessmen had visions of developing industrial enterprises in India.

In Bengal, Dwarkanath Tagore made his fortune in the China trade before he turned to industrial investment, setting up six joint-stock companies in the 1830s and 1840s.

Tagore's enterprises sank along with those of others in the wider business crises of the 1840s, but later in the 19th century many of the China traders became successful industrialists.

15. Read the statements given below regarding expansion of World Trade

Statement 1 (S1) The guilds controlled the production and restricted the entry of new merchants in the trade.

Statement 2 (S2) World trade expanded at a very fast rate during the 17th and 18th century.

Explain these statements S1 and S2 reflected in the Expansion of world trade. **Competency Based**

Ans. Statement 1 reflects the restrictive practices of guilds that controlled production and entry into trade.

In the pre-modern era, guilds were associations of skilled craftsmen or merchants that often controlled the production of goods and services. These guilds regulated various aspects of trade, including restricting the entry of new merchants. This control was a form of protectionism, aiming to maintain the quality of products and limit competition within the guild.

Statement 2 highlights the historical reality of rapid global trade expansion during the 17th and 18th centuries.

The 17th and 18th centuries marked a period of significant global trade expansion, often referred to as the Age of Mercantilism. European powers, particularly colonial powers, established vast trading networks. This expansion was driven by factors such as exploration, colonisation, and the establishment of overseas colonies, leading to increased intercontinental trade in goods like spices, textiles and precious metals.

Long Answer Type Questions

1. In what ways the proto-industrial production helped the poor farmers in countryside?

Ans. In the 17th and 18th centuries with the expansion of world trade and acquisition of colonies, the demand for goods expanded. But the merchants could not set up business in towns due to the strict restriction imposed by guilds. So the merchants turned to the countryside.

This helped the poor farmers in the countryside in the following ways

- The peasants and cottagers looked for alternative ways for their survival.
- Many had small land holdings, which couldn't provide work for all the members.
- When merchants came around and offered money to produce goods for them, peasants eagerly accepted.
- By working for the merchants, they could remain in the countryside and also could cultivate their own small plots of land. They also made full use of their family labour.

In this way, proto-industrial production supplemented the shrinking income of the poor peasants and raised their standard of living.

2. "The abundance of labour in the market affected the lives of workers." Explain it in the context of 19th century, Britain.

Or How did the abundance of labour in the market affect the lives of the workers in the 19th century, Europe? Explain with examples.

Ans. The abundance of labour in the market affected the lives of workers in the following ways

- When the news of possible jobs spread to the countryside, many came to the cities. However, the possibility of getting job was dependent on friends and acquaintances. Many job-seekers had to wait for weeks, spending nights under the bridges or in night shelters.
- Seasonality of work in many industries meant prolonged period without work. After the busy season was over, the poor were unemployed again.

- The income of the workers did not depend on the wage rate alone. There were long periods of unemployment. The number of days of work determined the average income of workers.
- The fear of unemployment made workers hostile to the new technology. When Spinning Jenny was introduced in the woollen industry, they began attacking the new machine.

3. Examine the causes of clashes between weavers and *gomasthas* in many weaving villages.

Ans. The East India Company appointed paid servants called *gomasthas* to supervise weavers. They used to collect supplies and examine the quality of cloth. The causes of clashes between the weavers and the gomasthas were

- The gomasthas gave loans to the weavers to purchase the raw material for their production. Those who took loans had to hand over the product timely to the gomasthas. They had no option to sell their products to other traders.
- Often the price given by the gomasthas (dictated by the company) was miserably low and the loans the weavers had accepted tied them to company.
- Weavers along with village traders revolted and opposed the company officials and sometimes migrated to other villages.
- The gomasthas had no social connection to the village. They marched into villages with sepoys and peons and punished the weavers. Thus, clashes between the weavers and gomasthas became very common.

4. Why did the export of Indian textile decline at the beginning of the 19th century? Explain any three reasons. CBSE 2020

Or **Describe any three problems faced by the Indian cotton weavers in the 19th century.**

Ans. By the end of the 19th century, Indian textile industry started to decline due to the following reasons

(i) **East India Company Gained Power** Once the East India Company established political power, it asserted a monopoly right to trade. It proceeded to develop a system of management and control that would eliminate competition, control costs and ensure regular supplies of cotton and silk goods.

(ii) **Growth of Cotton Industries in England** As cotton industries developed in England, industrial group became worried about the imports from other countries.

They pressurised the government to impose import duties on cotton textile, so that Manchester goods could easily sell in Britain without facing any competition from outside.

Further the industrialists persuaded the East India Company to sell British products forcefully in Indian market.

(iii) **The Result of Two Edge Policy** To sell British products in India the East India Company followed a two edged policy, i.e. no taxes on imports but high taxes on exports. Due to this policy, local Indian market shrank and flooded with cheap Manchester machine made products.

(iv) **Shortage of Raw Material** Due to the American Civil War, cotton supplies from the US cut off and Britain turned to India for cotton supplies. As raw cotton exports from India increased, Indian weavers faced the problem due to the shortage of raw materials for textile industry.

5. By the first decade of the 20th century, a series of changes affected the pattern of industrialisation in India. Explain.

Ans. By the first decade of the 20th century, a series of changes affected the pattern of industrialisation in India.

These are explained in the following points

(i) **Effect of Swadeshi and Boycott Movement** After the partition of Bengal, Swadeshi Movement was developed. It had both positive and negative sides. On the positive side, nationalists urged people to use only swadeshi goods and on the negative side they mobilised people to boycott foreign goods.

This movement had an immense effect on economy. There was an increase in the demand of Indian goods, specially clothes.

(ii) **Aim of Industrial Groups** Industrial groups organised themselves to protect their collective interests. They pressurised the government to increase tariff protection and grant other concessions.

(iii) **Decline of Exports to China** From 1906, the export of Indian yarn to China declined as produce from Chinese and Japanese mills flooded the Chinese markets. Thus, industrialist in India began shifting from yarn to cloth production. Cotton goods production in India doubled between 1900 and 1912.

(iv) **Result of First World War** Till the First World War, industrial growth was slow. British mills became busy with war production, thus Manchester imports to India declined. Suddenly, Indian mills got a vast home market to supply. As the war prolonged, Indian factories had to supply different war needs. This led to set up new factories and multiple shifts for the old factories.

Indian industry developed immensely at that period. After the war, Manchester could not recapture its old position in Indian market.

6. 'We find that from the very beginning of the industrial age, advertisements played a vital role in expanding the markets for products.' Explain the statement in the context of pre-independence period of our country.

Ans. From the very beginning of the industrial age, advertisements played a vital role in expanding the markets for products. The role of advertisement was as follows

- The Manchester industrialists began selling their cloth in India by putting labels on the cloth bundles. When buyers saw such labels on the cloth like 'Made In Manchester', they felt confident about buying the cloth.
- The manufacturers also used images of Indian Gods, Goddesses and important personalities on these labels. These images helped to make the foreign products familiar to Indian people.
- In the late 19th century, the British manufacturers used calendars to popularise their products. Unlike newspapers and magazines, calendars were being used even by illiterate people.
- Indian manufacturers even advertised the nationalist message which was clear and specific. For example, 'if you care for the nation then buy products that Indians produce'. Advertisement became a medium of the message of Swadeshi.

7. Read the information about industry grow and answer the question that follows.

While factory industries grew steadily after the war, large industries formed only a small segment of the economy. Most of them about 67 percent in 1911 – were located in Bengal and Bombay. Over the rest of the country, small-scale production continued to predominate. Only a small proportion of the total industrial labour force worked in registered factories: 5 per cent in 1911 and 10 per cent in 1931. The rest worked in small workshops and household units, often located in alleys and bylanes, invisible to the passer-by.

Explain the distribution of large industries in India after the war, focusing on the regional concentration. Competency Based

Ans. After the war, the growth of factory industries in India was steady, yet large industries constituted a minor segment of the economy.

In 1911, approximately 67% of these large industries were concentrated in Bengal and Bombay, indicating a regional imbalance. The majority of the country witnessed the prevalence of small-scale production, maintaining a decentralised industrial landscape.

Despite the growth, only a small proportion of the industrial labor force, 5% in 1911 and 10% in 1931, worked in registered factories.

The others worked in small workshops and home-based units, often hidden in alleys and bylanes, indicating the dominance of decentralised, small-scale production practices. This regional concentration and the prevalence of small-scale units had significant implications for India's industrial development, shaping the economic landscape in diverse ways.

Case Based Questions

1. Read the sources given below and answer the questions that follow.

Source A Hand Labour and Steam Power

In Victorian Britain, the upper classes-the aristocrats and the bourgeoisie-preferred things produced by hand. Handmade products came to symbolise refinement and class.

They were better finished, individually produced and carefully designed. Machine-made goods were for export to the colonies.

(i) Evaluate the preference of handmade products by the aristocrats and bourgeoisie in England.

Source B Life of the Workers

The abundance of labour in the market affected the lives of workers. As news of possible jobs travelled to the countryside, handreds tramped to the cities. The actual possibility of getting a job depended on existing networks of friendship and kin relations. If you had a relative or a friend in a factory, you were more likely to get a job quickly. But not everyone had social connections. Many job-seekers had to wait weeks, spending nights under brigdes or in night.

(ii) Why the life of workers affected?

Source C Manchester comes to India

Cotton weavers in India thus faced two problems at the same time: their export market collapsed and the local market shrank, being glutted with Manchester imports. Produced by machines at lower costs, the imported cotton goods were so cheap that weavers could not easily compets with them. By the 1850s, reports from most weaving regions of India narrated stories of decline and desolation.

(iii) To what extent the problems were faced by cotton weavers in India?

Ans. (i) The upper class-the aristocrats and the bourgeoisie preferred things produced by hand because it symbolised refinement and class. They were better finished, designed and individually produced.

(ii) The life of workers affected because of the abundance of labour in the market.

(iii) The problems faced by the Indian weavers were
- Their export market collapsed.
- The local market shrank due to the low cost machine made British products.

2. Read the source given below and answer the questions that follow. **CBSE SQP 2022-23**

Will Thorne is one of those who went in search of seasonal work, loading bricks and doing odd jobs. He describes how job-seekers walked to London in search of work.

'I had always wanted to go to London and my desire was stimulated by letters from an old workmate who was now working at the Old Kent Road Gas Works. I finally decided to go in November, 1881. With two friends I started out to walk the journey, filled with the hope that we would be able to obtain employment, when we get there, with the kind assistance of my friend we had little money when we started, not enough to pay for our food and lodgings each night until we arrived in London. Some days we walked as much as twenty miles and other days less. Our money was gone at the end of the third day. For two nights we slept out once under a haystack and once in an old farm shed.

On arrival in London we tried to find my friend but were unsuccessful. Our money was gone, so there was nothing for us to do but to walk around until late at night, and then try to find some place to sleep. We found an old building and slept in it that night. The next day, Sunday, late in the afternoon, we got to the Old Kent Gas Works and applied for work. To my great surprise, the man we had been looking for was working at the time. He spoke to the foreman and I was given a job.'

Quoted in Raphael Samuel, 'Comers and Goers', in H.J. Dyos and Michael Wolff, eds, The Victorian City: Images and Realities, 1973.

(i) Analyse the major factor which led London become an attractive place for the job seekers.

(ii) Analyse the reason for the appointment of Will Thorne by the Old Kent Gas Works.

(iii) Examine the preference of hand labour over machines by the industrialists of the Victorian Britain.

Ans. (i) London became an attractive place for the job seekers due to the industrial revolution and availability of job opportunities in factories.

(ii) The reason for the appointment of 'Will Thorne' by the Old Kent Gas Works was that it was the seasonal industry and it was in need of low wage workers.

(iii) The preference of hand labour over machines by the industrialists of the Victorian Britain was due to following reasons
- Machines needed huge capital investments.
- Machines were costly, ineffective and difficult to repair, and labour was available at low wages.

3. Read the source given below and answer the questions that follow. **CBSE 2023**

The first cotton mill in Bombay came up in 1854 and it went into production two years later. By 1862, four mills were at work with 94,000 spindles and 2,150 looms. Around the same time jute mills came up in Bengal, the first being set up in 1855 and another one seven years later, in 1862. In North India, the Elgin Mill was started in Kanpur in the 1860 and a years later the first cotton mill of Ahmedabad was set up.

By 1874, the first spinning and weaving mill of Madras began production.

(i) When was the first cotton mill set up in India?

(ii) Name any two early industrialists of India.

(iii) How did many Indian entrepreneurs survive despite tight economic control imposed by the British Government ? Explain.

Ans. (i) The first cotton mill in Bombay came up in 1854 and it went into production two years later.

(ii) The two early industrialists of India were Dwarkanath Tagore and Jamsetji Tata.

(iii) As British control over Indian trade tightened, the Indian merchants found it difficult to operate. But many Indian entrepreneurs survived by adopting the following ways
- Many Indians became junior players (small traders) in the trade with China by providing finance, procuring supplies and shopping consignments.
- Some merchants operated within India, carrying goods from one place to another, banking money, transferring funds between cities and financing traders.

ASSESSMENT EXERCISE

Multiple Choice Questions (MCQs)

1. Who set up six joint-stock companies in Bengal in the 1830s and 1840s?
   (a) Dwarkanath Tagore
   (b) JN Tata
   (c) Jamsetjee Jeejeebhoy
   (d) RD Tata

2. In the year 1931, which of the following locations has highest concentration of large scale industries in India?
   (a) Madras
   (b) Punjab
   (c) Bombay
   (d) Bengal

3. Find the incorrect option.
   (a) During the World War I, local industries captured the home market.
   (b) The first cotton mill was set up in 1854 in Bombay.
   (c) First Jute mill was set up in 1856 in, Surat.
   (d) Iron and Steel works were set up in Jamshedpur in 1912.

4. **Assertion** (A) Machine-made goods were standardised and could not match the high quality finish of hand-made goods.

   Reason (R) The people from the upper classes preferred things produced by hand.

   Codes
   (a) Both A and R are true and R is the correct explanation of A
   (b) Both A and R are true, but R is not the correct explanation of A
   (c) A is true, but R is false
   (d) A is false, but R is true

Subjective Questions (VSA, SA & LA)

1. What was Spinning Jenny?
2. Who established six joint-stock companies in India during 1830-40?
3. How did the Indian and British manufacturers try to expand their market?
4. What was trade guild? Explain.
5. The First World War created dramatically a new situation for Indian industries. Analyse how this happened by giving three situations.
6. Why did the poor peasants and artisans in the countryside begin to work for the merchants from the towns?
7. Explain giving four reasons why the industrialists of Europe preferred hand labour over machines during the 19th century.
8. The Indian cotton export market collapsed and the local market shrank in the beginning of the 19th century. Why?

Print Culture and the Modern World

CHAPTER 5

The evidence of printed material can be found everywhere like in journals, magazines, newspapers, books, theatre programmes, calendars, diaries, advertisements, cinema posters, etc. Print itself has a history which has shaped our contemporary world. The coming of print had a great impact on social life and change in culture.

5.1 The First Printed Books

The earliest kind of print technology was developed in **China**, **Japan** and **Korea**. It was a system of hand printing.

Print in China

From AD 594 onwards, books in China were printed by rubbing paper against the inked surface of wood blocks.

The traditional Chinese 'Accordion Book' was folded and stitched at the side because both sides of the thin, porous[1] sheet could not be printed. The skilled craftsmen could copy the beauty of calligraphy[2] with remarkable accuracy.

For a long time, the Imperial State in China was the major producer of printed material. China had a huge bureaucratic system, which recruited its personnel through Civil Service examinations. So, the vast number of text books were printed in China under the sponsorship of the Imperial State.

By the 17th century, the use of print expanded in China due to growing urban culture.

The diversification of print brought the following changes

- The new readers preferred fictional narratives, poetry, autobiographies, anthologies of literary master pieces, romantic plays, etc.
- Rich women began to read and many women began publishing their poetry and plays.
- Wives of scholar officials published their writings and courtesans wrote about their lives.
- Western printing techniques and mechanical presses were imported to China in the late 19th century as Western powers established their outposts settlements in China.
- **Shanghai** became the **hub of the new print culture,** providing books to the Western-style schools.
- There was now a gradual shift from hand printing to mechanical printing.

Print in Japan

Buddhist missionaries from China introduced hand- printing technology into Japan around AD 768-770.

The oldest Japanese book is the Buddhist ***Diamond Sutra*** printed in 868 AD. Pictures were printed on textiles, playing cards and paper money.

In medieval Japan, poets' and prose writers' works were regularly published and books were cheap and abundant. Printing of visual material led to interesting publishing practices.

Libraries and bookstores had various types of hand printed books on diverse topics like women, musical instruments, calculations, tea ceremony, flower arrangements, etiquette, cooking and famous places.

Kitagawa Utamaro: A Japanese Artist

Kitagawa Utamaro, born in Edo in 1753, was famous for his contributions to an art form called ***Ukiyo*** (pictures of the floating world) or depiction of ordinary human experiences, especially urban ones.

His works influenced artists like Manet, Monet and Van Gogh. Publishers like Tsutaya Juzabura asked artists and skilled wood block carvers to reproduce these prints. The original drawing would be destroyed in this process and only prints would survive.

1 **Porous** It means having small holes that allow air or liquid to pass through.

2 **Calligraphy** It is the art of beautiful and stylised writing.

5.2 Print Comes to Europe

Chinese paper reached Europe via silk route which was used for the trade of silk and spices. In 1295, **Marco Polo** returned to Italy and brought the technology of **wood block printing** from China.

Italians began producing books with woodblocks. Luxury editions were still hand written on very expensive **vellum**[3] which were made for nobles.

As demand for books increased, booksellers started exporting them globally and organising book fairs. **Manuscripts**[4] production was organised to meet the demand. **Scribes**[5] who were earlier employed by wealthy patrons, were now employed by booksellers, with over 50 scribes working for one bookseller.

Production of hand written manuscripts was increased by book sellers but it could not fulfil the increasing demand. Copying was costly, slow and difficult. Manuscripts were fragile, hard to handle and not easy to read so, their circulation was limited.

Wood block printing became more popular with the growing demands for books. By the early 15th century, woodblocks were used in Europe to print textiles, playing cards and religious pictures with simple and brief texts.

There was a great need for quicker and cheaper reproduction of texts which could be possible with the invention of new print technology.

Jikji of Korea

The Jikji of Korea is among the oldest existing books printed with movable metal type. It is related to **Zen Buddhism.** The first volume of this book is unavailable, but the second volume is kept in the National Library of France.

Gutenberg and the Printing Press

Gutenberg was the son of a German merchant. He developed the **first printing press in the 1430s.**

His knowledge for the olive press provided the model for new printing press and moulds were used for casting the metal types for the letters of the alphabet. By 1448, Gutenberg perfected the system.

The **first book printed by Gutenberg was Bible.** It took three years to print 180 copies. The Gutenberg press could print 250 sheets on one side per hour. The printed books at first were closely resembled the written manuscripts in appearance and layouts.

Printing presses were set up in most countries of Europe in between 1450 to 1550. This shift from hand printing to mechanical printing led to the print revolution. Books could now be produced much faster than before.

5.3 The Print Revolution and its Impact

The print revolution was not just a new way of producing books. It transformed the lives of people by changing their knowledge and relationship with institutions and authorities.

A New Reading Public

With the printing press, a new reading public emerged, as printing had reduced the cost of books.

There was a large number of people who could not read, but could enjoy listening to books being read out. The rates of literacy in most European countries were very low till the 20th century.

To increase the reach of printed books among those who could not read, printers began publishing popular **ballads**[6] and folk tales with lots of pictures. These were then sung and recited at gatherings in villages and in **taverns**[7] in towns.

Religious Debates and the Fear of Print

Innovation of printing created the possibility of wide circulation of ideas and introduced a new world of debate and discussion.

It was feared that if there was no control over what was printed and read, then rebellious ideas might spread. If that happened, the authority of 'valuable' literature would be destroyed. This anxiety was expressed by the religious authorities, monarchs, writers and artists.

In 1517, **Martin Luther** wrote '**Ninety Five Theses**' criticising many of the practices and rituals of the Roman Catholic Church. His writings were immediately reproduced in vast numbers and read widely. It led to the beginning of the **Protestant Reformation**[8].

3 **Vellum** It refers to a parchment made from the skin of animals.
4 **Manuscript** It refers to book or document written by hand, author's original copy handwritten or typed, not printed.
5 **Scribes** These refer to skilled people who copy manuscripts or handwriters of ancient and medieval periods before the invention of printing.
6 **Ballad** It refers to a historical account or folk tale in verse, poem or song usually sung or recited.
7 **Taverns** These refer to places where people gathered to drink alcohol, to be served food and to meet friends and exchange news.
8 **Protestant Reformation** It was a 16th century movement to reform the Catholic Church dominated by Rome. Martin Luther was one of the main Protestant reformers. Several traditions of anti-Catholic Christianity developed out of the movement.

Print and Dissent

Print and popular religious literature encouraged many distinctive individual interpretations of faith even among little-educated working people.

In the 16th century, **Menocchio** (a miller in Italy), reinterpreted the message of the Bible which made the Roman Catholic Church angry.

When the Roman Church started its investigation to repress **heretical**[9] ideas, Menocchio was executed. After that, the Roman Church imposed severe controls over publishers and book-sellers and began to maintain an Index of Prohibited Books from 1558.

5.4 The Reading Mania

During the 17th and 18th centuries, the literacy rates increased in most parts of Europe. Churches of different **denominations**[10] set up schools in villages, carrying literacy to peasants and artisans.

Introduction of New Forms of Literature

By the end of 18th century, people wanted books to read and printers produced books in large numbers.

New forms of popular literature appeared in print, that target new audiences. Pedlars roamed around villages, carrying little books for sale. The new forms of literature were as follows

- There were **almanacs**[11] or ritual calendars, along with ballads and folktales.
- In England, penny **chapbooks**[12] were sold for a penny, so that even the poor could buy them.
- In France, the **Biliotheque Bleue** were sold. They were low priced books printed on poor quality paper and bounded in cheap blue covers.
- The discoveries of scientists like **Isaac Newton** and the writings of thinkers like **Thomas Paine**, **Voltaire** and **Jean Jacques Rousseau** were widely printed and read. Thus, their ideas about science, reason and rationality become part of popular literature.

Power of Books

In the mid-18th century, many people believed that books could change the world, free society from **despotism**[13] and tyranny and make a society which would be ruled by reason and intellect.

Louise-Sebastien Mercier, a novelist in 18th century France, declared that the printing press is the most powerful engine of progress.

Print Culture and French Revolution

Many historians argued that print culture created the conditions for French Revolution.

Three types of arguments have been usually put forward

(i) **First** Print popularised the ideas of the enlightened thinkers. Their writings provided a critical commentary on tradition, superstition and despotism.

(ii) **Second** Print created a new culture of dialogue and debate. All values, norms and institutions were re-evaluated and discussed by public.

(iii) **Third** By the 1780s, literature, especially cartoon and **caricatures**[14] began to mock the royalty and criticise their morality.

Print helped the spread of ideas of great thinkers and also their monarchical and church propaganda.

Try These

1. **Which city became the hub of the new print culture in late 19th century?**
2. **Who introduced the hand printing technology in Japan?**
3. **In Europe, Gutenberg first developed the printing press in which year?**
4. **Name the books in France that were low priced, printed on poor quality paper and bounded in cheap blue covers.**
5. **Who declared that the printing press is the most powerful engine of progress and public opinion?**

5.5 The 19th Century

The 19th century saw increase in mass literacy in Europe, bringing a large number of new readers among children, women and workers.

Children, Women and Workers

As primary education became compulsory from the late 19th century, children became an important category of readers. The **Grimm Brothers** in Germany compiled traditional folk tales collected from peasants and published them in 1812.

The children's press was set up in France in 1857 which published fairy tales and folk tales for children.

9 **Heretical** It refers to beliefs which do not follow the accepted teachings of the Church. In medieval times, heresy was seen as a threat to the right of the church to decide on what should be believed and what should not. Heretical beliefs were severely punished.

10 **Denominations** These refer to sub groups within a religion.

11 **Almanac** It refers to an annual calendar that gives astronomical data, information about movement of the Sun, Moon, eclipses, etc.

12 **Chapbook** It refers to a small pamphlet or pocket book containing tales, ballads sold by pedlars.

13 **Despotism** It refers to a system of governance in which absolute power is exercised by an individual, unregulated by legal and constitutional checks.

14 **Caricature** It refers to a picture, description or imitation of a person or thing in order to create comic effect.

Anything that was considered unsuitable for children or would appear vulgar to the elites, was not included in the published version.

Women became important as readers as well as writers. Penny magazines for women were manuals about proper behaviour and house-keeping.

Some of the best-known women novelists were **Jane Austen**, **George Eliot** and the **Bronte sisters**.

In the late 19th century, lending libraries in England became instruments for educating white-collar workers, artisans and lower-middle class people.

After the working day was shortened from the mid-19th century, workers had some time for self-improvement and self-expression. They wrote many political tracts and autobiographies.

Further Innovations in Printing

By the mid-19th century, Richard M Hoe of New York had perfected the power-driven **cylindrical press** which could print 8000 sheets per hour. It was particularly useful for printing newspapers.

In the late 19th century, the **offset press** was developed which could print upto six colours at a time.

In 20th century, **electrically operated presses** began printing operations. Methods of feeding paper improved, the quality of plates became better, and automatic paper reels and photoelectric controls of the colour register were introduced.

Strategies to Sell Books

Some new strategies to sell books were incorporated in 19th century. Periodicals serialised important novels, shaping a new style of writing. In the 1920s, popular works in England were sold in the **Shilling Series**. The book jacket was also introduced in the 20th century. During the Great Depression in the 1930s, publishers released cheap paperback editions to boost sales.

5.6 India and the World of Print

Before the age of print in India, ideas and information were in written form.

Manuscripts Before the Age of Print

India had a very rich and ancient tradition of hand written manuscripts in Sanskrit, Arabic and Persian as well as in various vernacular languages[15]. These manuscripts were copied on palm leaves or on handmade paper.

Manuscripts were highly expensive and got damaged easily. They had to be handled carefully and were not widely used in everyday life.

Print Comes to India

The **first printing press came to Goa** with the **Portuguese missionaries** in the mid–16th century.

Jesuit priests learnt Konkani and printed several books. About 50 books had been printed in Konkani and Kanara languages by 1674.

In 1579, Catholic priests printed the **first Tamil book** at Cochin and the **first Malayalam book** was printed in 1713.

By 1710, Dutch Protestant missionaries had printed 32 Tamil books.

The English East India Company began to import presses from the late 17th century in India.

From 1780, ***Bengal Gazette*** a weekly English magazine was edited by **James Augustus Hickey**.

James published a lot of gossip about the company's senior officials, so the Governor General Warren Hastings persecuted him.

By the end of the 18th century, Indians began to publish Indian newspapers. The **first Indian newspaper** was the weekly newspaper **Bengal Gazette**, brought out by **Gangadhar Bhattacharya** who was close to Raja Rammohun Roy.

5.7 Religious Reform and Public Debates

From the early 19th century, the religious debates were carried out in public and in print. Printed tracts and newspapers spread the new ideas and shaped the nature of the debate.

The first printed edition of the ***Ramcharitmanas* of Tulsidas** (a 16th century text) was published in 1810 from Calcutta.

19th century was a time of intense controversies between social and religious reformers and Hindu Orthodoxy people over matters of widow persecution, monotheism[16], Brahmanical priesthood and idol worship.

Raja Rammohun Roy published the ***Sambad Kaumudi*** in 1821 and the Hindu Orthodoxy commissioned the ***Samachar Chandrika*** to oppose his views.

15 Vernacular languages The languages spoken in a particular area or by a particular group, especially one that is not the official or written language.

16 Monotheism It refers to the doctrine or belief that there is only one God.

From 1822, two Persian newspapers were published, ***Jam-i-Jahan Nama*** and ***Shamsul Akhbar***. Gujarati newpaper the ***Bombay Samachar*** was also published in the same year.

In North India, *Ulama*, who feared that colonial rulers would change Muslim personal laws, published Persian and Urdu translations of holy scriptures and printed religious newspaper.

The Deoband Seminary[17] was founded in 1867 which published thousands of *fatwas*[18] telling the Muslims how to conduct their everyday life and explained the meanings of Islamic doctrines.

From the 1880s, the **Naval Kishore Press** at Lucknow and **Shri Venkateshwar Press** in Bombay published various religious texts in vernaculars. It encouraged discussion and debates among different religions.

5.8 New Forms of Publication

Printing created need for new kinds of writings. The novel which had developed in Europe met this need. It aquired different Indian forms and styles.

Besides novels, other new literary forms like lyrics, short stories and essays about social and political matters also entered the world of reading.

By the end of the 19th century, a new visual culture was taking shape. Painters like **Raja Ravi Varma** produced images for mass circulation.

Even poor could easily buy the calendars and cheap prints for the decoration of his house and office. These prints began shaping popular ideas about modernity and tradition, religion and politics and society and culture.

By the 1870s, caricatures and cartoons were being published in journals and newspapers, commenting on social and political issues. Some caricatures mocked western taste, while some expressed the fear of social change.

Women and Print

Liberal husbands and fathers began educating their women folk at home and sent them to schools.

After the mid-19th century, women's schools were set up in the cities and towns. Many journals began carrying the writings of women and explained why women should be educated.

Many women contributed to print culture. Prominent among them were

- **Rashsundari Debi** In East Bengal, Rashsundari Debi, a young married girl in a very orthodox family, learnt to read in the secrecy of her kitchen. She wrote her autobiography[19] ***Amar Jiban*** which was published in 1876 in Bengali language.
- **Kailashbashini Debi** Bengali women Kailashbashini Debi highlighted the experiences of women i.e. how they were imprisoned at home, kept in ignorance, forced to do hard domestic work and treated unjustly.
- **Tarabai Shinde and Pandita Ramabai** In the 1880s, women writers like Tarabai Shinde and Pandita Ramabai both from Maharashtra, wrote about the miserable lives of upper caste Hindu women, especially widows.
- **Begum Rokeya Sakhawat Hossein** In 1926, famous educationist and literary figure, Begum Rokeya Sakhawat Hossein disapproved men for withholding education from women in the name of religion.

Print culture and Women Education

Urdu, Tamil, Bengali and Marathi print culture had developed early, while Hindi printing began from 1870s.

In the early 20th century, many journals edited by women, discussed about women's education, widowhood, widow remarriage, significance of national movement, etc.

In Punjab, **Ram Chaddha** published the fast-selling '*Istri Dharm Vichar*' to teach women how to be obedient wives. The Khalsa Tract Society published cheap booklets with a similar message.

In Bengal, **Battala** was an area in central Calcutta. It published various types of popular books including novels and religious scriptures.

These books were very cheap and illustrated with woodcuts and coloured lithographs (inscriptions) and popular among housewives.

Print and the Poor People

In 19th century, in towns of Madras, cheap small books were brought to markets and sold at crossroads, so that the poor people could purchase them.

17 Deoband Seminary It refers to a school for training muslims to aware about the code of conduct to be followed in their everyday lives and explained the meaning of Islamic doctrines.

18 Fatwa It refers to a ruling on a point of Islamic law given by a recognised authority.

19 Autobiography It refers to the story of one's own life written by the author himself or herself.

Public libraries were set up from the early 20th century, most of which were located in cities and towns and some libraries were set up in prosperous villages.

From the late 19th century, issues of caste discrimination began to be written in many printed tracts and essays.

The social reformers like **Jyotiba Phule** wrote about the injustices of the caste system in his book ***Gulamgiri*** (1871).

In 20th century, **BR Ambedkar** and **EV Ramaswamy Naicker** wrote about casteism which was read by people all over India.

Kashibaba, a Kanpur millworker, wrote and published '*Chhote Aur Bade Ka Sawal*' in 1938, which suggested the links between caste and class exploitation.

Another Kanpur mill worker, **Sudarshan Chakr** wrote poems and published in a collection called '*Sacchi Kavitayan*'.

By the 1930s, Bangalore cotton mill workers set up libraries to educate themselves. These were sponsored by social reformers who tried to restrict excessive drinking among them, to bring literacy and to promote the message of nationalism.

5.9 Print and Censorship

Before 1798, the colonial state was not too concerned with censorship. By the 1820s, the Calcutta Supreme Court passed certain regulations to control press freedom.

In 1835, responding to petitions from newspapers editors, Governor-General Bentinck agreed to revise press laws.

Thomas Macaulay, a liberal colonial official, formulated new rules that restored the earlier freedoms.

After the revolt of 1857, the attitude to freedom of the press changed. As vernacular newspapers became dominantly nationalist, the Colonial government began debating measures of strict control.

In 1878, the **Vernacular Press Act** was passed which provided the government with extensive rights to censor reports and editorials in the vernacular press.

Despite repressive measures, many nationalist newspapers grew in all parts of India. They reported colonial misrule and encouraged nationalist activities. This in turn led to a renewed cycle of persecution and protests.

Balgangadhar Tilak wrote about the Punjab revolutionaries who were deported (expelled) in 1907, in his newspaper **Kesari**. This led to his imprisonment in 1908 that provoked widespread protests all over India.

Try These

1. **Where was children's press set up and when?**
2. **In which year did the first Malayalam book print?**
3. **Who was the editor of English weekly magazine 'Bengal Gazette'?**
4. **Name the Governor-General who agreed to revise press laws.**
5. **On which law, the Vernacular Press Act of 1878 was based?**

TIME LINE | Covering Major Events with their Time Periods in Chronological Order

Printing in the World

Period	Important Events
AD 594 onwards	Printing done in China by rubbing paper against the inked surface of woodblocks.
768-770	Buddhist missionaries from China introduced hand printing technology into Japan.
11th century	Paper reached Europe from China via silk route.
1295	Marco Polo brought woodblock printing technology to Europe from China.
1430	Gutenberg developed the first known printing press.
1448	Gutenberg perfected the system of the printing press.
1508	Erasmus, a Latin scholar and a catholic reformer expressed concern about printing in his work Adages.
1517	Martin Luther wrote 'Ninety Five Theses'
1558	The Roman Church begins maintaining an Index of Prohibited Books.
1812	Fairy Tales printed by the Grimm Brothers.
1857	A press devoted to literature for children alone set up in France.

Printing in India

Period	Important Events
Mid-16th century	The printing press came to Goa in India with Portuguese missionaries.
1579	The first Tamil book printed in Cochin.
1674	About 50 books printed in Konkani and Kanara languages.
1710	Dutch Protestant missionaries print 32 Tamil texts, mostly translations.
1713	The first Malayalam book was printed.
1780	Weekly magazine 'Bengal Gazette' started its publication.
1810	First printed edition of Ramcharitmanas of Tulsidas came out in Calcutta.
1820s	Calcutta Supreme Court passed regulations to control press freedom.
1821-22	Many newspapers in various languages started its publication.
1867	The Deoband Seminary founded and published thousands of fatwas.
1870	Hindi printing began seriously.
1871	Jyotiba Phule wrote about the injustices of the caste system in his book 'Gulamgiri'.
1877	'The Statesman' newspaper was founded.
1878	Vernacular Press Act passed.
1907	Tilak wrote about Punjab revolutionaries sympathetically in his newspaper 'Kesari'.
1930	Bangalore cotton mill workers set-up libraries to educate themselves.
1942	At the time of Quit India Movement, about 90 newspapers were suppressed.

Mind Map

PRINT CULTURE AND THE MODERN WORLD

The First Printed Books

Print in China

- From AD 594 onwards, books in China were printed by rubbing paper against the inked surface of wood blocks.

Print in Japan

- Buddhist missionaries from China introduced hand printing technology into Japan around 768-770 AD.
- The oldest Japanese book is the Buddhist Diamond Sutra printed in 868 AD .

Print Comes to Europe

- In 1295, Marco Polo returned to Italy and brought the technology of wood block printing from China.
- By the early 15th century, wood blocks were used in Europe to print textiles, playing cards and religious pictures, with simple and brief texts.

Gutenberg and the Printing Press

- Gutenberg was the son of a merchant. He developed the first printing press in the 1430s.
- The first book printed by Gutenberg was the Bible.
- The Gutenberg Press could print 250 sheets on one side per hour.

New Forms of Publication

- New visual culture developed
- Number of printing presses increased.
- Cheap prints, paintings and calendars were easily available.

The Reading Mania

New Form of Literature

- There were almanacs or ritual calendars along with ballads and folktales.
- In England, penny chapbooks were sold by pedlars called chapmen.
- In France, the Biliotheque Bleue were low priced books printed on poor quality paper and bounded in cheap blue covers.

Printing Culture and French Revolution

- Print popularised the idea of the enlightened thinkers.
- Print created a new culture of dialogue and debate.
- By the 1780s, there was a flow of literature, especially cartoon and caricatures that mocked or insulted the royalty and criticised their morality.

The Print Revolution and Its Impact

Religious Debates and the Fear of Print

In 1517, Martin Luther wrote 'Ninety Five Theses' criticising many of the practices and rituals of the Roman Catholic Church

Print and Dissent

In 16th Century, Menocchio reinterpreted the message of Bible which made the Roman Catholic Church angry.

New Reading Public

- There was a large number of people who could not read but could enjoy listening to books being read out.
- Printers began publishing popular ballads and folk tales with lots of pictures which were sung and recited at gatherings in villages and in taverns in towns.

India and the World of Print

Print Comes to India

- The first printing press came to Goa with the Portuguese missionaries in the mid-16th century.
- Jesuit priests learnt Konkani and printed several books.
- About 50 books had been printed in Konkani and Kanara languages in 1674.

Manuscripts Before Printing

India had a very rich and ancient tradition of hand written manuscripts in Sanskrit, Arabic and Persian as well as in various vernacular languages.

Print and Censorship

- By the 1820s, the Calcutta Supreme Court passed certain regulations to control press freedom.
- In 1878, the Vernacular Press Act was passed.

Religious Reforms and Public Debates

- The first printed edition of the Ramcharitmanas of Tulsidas was published in 1810 from Calcutta.
- Rammohun Roy published the Sambad Kaumudi in 1821.

The Nineteenth Century

Children, Women and Workers

- The Grimm Brothers in Germany compiled traditional folk tales collected from peasants and compiled them in 1812.
- The Children's Press was setup in France in 1857, which published fairy tales and folk tales for children.
- Some of the best women novelists were Jane Austen, George Eliot and Bronte sisters.

Further Innovations in Printing

- By the mid-19th century, Richard M Hoe of New York had perfected the power driven cylindrical press, which could print 8000 sheets per hour.
- In the late 19th century, the offset press was developed, which printed six colours at once.
- In 20th century, electrically operated presses began printing.

NCERT FOLDER

Covering Intext Questions and Exercises of NCERT

INTEXT QUESTIONS

Q.1 Write briefly why some people feared that the development of print could lead to the growth of dissenting ideas.

Ans. People feared that the development of print could lead to the growth of dissenting ideas because print and popular literature encouraged many distinctive interpretations of religious faith and ideas.

For example, Menocchio, a miller in Italy, gave a new interpretation of the Bible and formulated a view of God and Creation which made the Roman Catholic Church angry. As a result, he was executed when the Roman Church began its inquisition to repress heretical ideas.

Troubled by such incident, the Roman Catholic Church imposed severe controls over publishers and book-sellers and began to maintain an Index of Prohibited Books from 1558.

Q.2 Why do some historians think that print culture created the basis for the French Revolution?

Ans. Some historians think that print culture created the basis for the French Revolution because

- Print popularised the ideas of the enlightened thinkers. The writings of Voltaire and Rousseau were read widely. Their writings provided a critical commentary on tradition, superstition and despotism.
  They argued that everything be judged through the application of reason and rationality.
  As these writers attacked the despotic rulers and the authority of the Church, the readers saw the world through new eyes that were questioning, critical and rational.
- Print created a new culture of dialogue and debate in which all institutions, norms and values were discussed and re-evaluated.
- By the 1780s, a lot of literature was published criticising and insulting the royalty. The underground circulation of such literature increased hostile sentiments against the monarchy.

Q.3 What impact do the following advertisements have on the public mind? Do you think everyone reacts to printed material in the same way?

Ans. These advertisements tried to attract the people to believe in their product, ideas, discoveries, writings and belief. People felt connected with the product because of the advertisement.

No, not everyone reacts to the printed material in the same way. Some people finds it practical, funny and significant while others may perceive it unnecessary.

Q.4 Look at the pictures 19, 20 and 21 (Page 125-126) of your NCERT Textbook carefully and answer the following questions

(a) What comment are the artists making on the social changes taking place in society?

(b) What changes in society were taking place to provoke this reaction?

(c) Do you agree with the artist's view?

Ans. (a) The artists are very carefully noticing the social change and are trying to describe it in their creations. The artist is trying to show the deteriorating family relations, where a husband is totally dominated by his wife. He is cruel towards his mother and is shown dragging her like an animal by the noose.

(b) In Fig. 20, the image depicts that the man was playing Veena and the woman was smoking hookah. The artists are anxious about the changes in the behaviour and activities of the society which was not showing positive signs for the future.

In Fig. 21, the Sahib holds a liquor bottle in his hand while the Memsahib plays the violin.

The picture depicted the declining family values and the breakdown of traditional family roles caused different reactions.

(c) The artists are correct to show the real conditions of the society but these are cases related to few of the many chosen families. These examples does not depict the overall culture, tradition, lifestyles and view of the society. Artists have successfully depicted the problems of the progressing society though.

EXERCISE

Q.1 Give reasons for the following.

(a) Woodblock print only came to Europe after 1295.

(b) Martin Luther was in favour of print and spoke out in praise of it.

(c) The Roman Catholic Church began keeping an Index of Prohibited Books from the mid-16th century.

(d) **Gandhi said the fight for Swaraj is a fight for liberty of speech, liberty of the press and freedom of association.**

Ans. (a) Woodblock print only came to Europe after 1295 as Italian traveller, Marco Polo brought this knowledge from China when he returned to Europe in 1295.

(b) Martin Luther was in favour of printing and spokeout in praise of it because it was printing press through which he got a chance to criticise many of the corrupt practices of the Catholic Church. In 1517, Martin Luther, wrote 'Ninety Five Theses' and pasted a printed copy of this on the church door in Wittenberg. Very soon, thousand of copies of Luther's Theses were printed, spreading his ideas among people.

(c) In 1558, the Roman Church decided to maintain an Index of Prohibited Book as print and popular literature encouraged many distinctive interpretations of religious faiths and ideas.

For example, in the 16th century, Menocchio, a miller in Italy, began to read books available readily in his locality. He gave a new interpretation of the Bible and formulated a view of God and Creation which made the Roman Catholic Church angry. As a result, Menocchio was executed when the Roman Catholic Church began its inquisition to repress the heretical ideas.

(d) Mahatma Gandhi said these words in 1922 during the Non-cooperation Movement (1920-22) because according to him, without the liberty of speech, the liberty of press and freedom of association, no nation can even survive. If the country was to get free from foreign domination, then these liberties were quite important.

If there is no liberty of speech, liberty of press and freedom of association, then there is no nationalism. Nationalism requires these three pre-requisites for its survival.

Q.2 Write short notes on

(a) The Gutenberg press

(b) Erasmus's idea of the printed book

(c) The Vernacular Press Act

Ans. (a) **The Gutenberg Press** It was the first printing press of Europe. It was invented by Johann Gutenberg of Strasbourg. He used knowledge and experience in operating olive and wine presses to develop printing press.

The olive press provided him the model for the printing press and he used moulds for casting metal types for letters of the alphabet. He invented the printing press around the year 1448.

(b) **Erasmus's Idea of the Printed Book** Erasmus was a Latin scholar. He was not happy with printing of books because he was afraid that this would lead to circulation of books with rebellious ideas.

He felt that although a few books may give useful information, the majority of books may be just useless or give stupid, scandalous or irreligious ideas which may lead to provoke rebellion. According to him, such books devalue the valuable books.

(c) **The Vernacular Press Act** It was passed in 1878 by the British Government in India. This Act provided the government with extensive rights to censor reports and editorials in the vernacular press. If a vernacular paper published any seditious material, it was banned and its printing machinery was seized. This was a complete violation of the freedom of expression.

Q.3 What did the spread of print culture in 19th century India mean to

(a) Women (b) The poor (c) Reformers

Or **How did printing technology affect the lives of Indian women? Analyse** **CBSE 2025**

Or **How did the advent of print culture affect the poor people in India? Explain.** **CBSE 2025**

Ans. (a) **Women** The spread of print culture in the 19th century India benefited Indian women through learning and education. Reading habits improved among them.

With increase in literacy, women took great interest in reading and writing. Many journals started emphasising the importance of women's education. Many magazines and books were specially published for women. The print culture gave the women some amount of freedom to read and develop their own views on various issues, especially those related to women.

Women novelists such as Jane Austen and Bronte sisters in Europe and Kailashbashini Debi, Tarabai Shinde and Pandita Ramabai in India presented the new type of woman; a woman with the power to think and with the ability to act with determination.

(b) **The Poor** The poor people benefited from the spread of print culture as books were available at a low price. As the literacy rate improved in Europe as well as in India, printed material, especially for entertainment, began to reach even the poor.

In England, Penny Magazines were carried by pedlars and sold for a penny, so that even poor people could buy them. Those who could not read, could listen to the stories and folklore. These could be read out to them by others.

Books could be hired on a nominal fee from some book owners. Even in India, very cheap small books were brought to market in 19th century Madras and small towns, allowing poor people to have an access to print culture.

Public libraries were set up in the early 20th century where poor people could visit and borrow books. Gradually, even poor people began to read religious stories, books with simple instructions or stories and folklore.

(c) **Reformers** Reformers used newspapers, journals and books to highlight the social evils prevailing in society. Raja Rammohun Roy published the '*Sambad Kaumudi*' to highlight the plight of widows. This newspaper actively campaigned for the abolition of Sati.

In the 1880s, Tarabai Shinde and Pandita Ramabai wrote with passionate anger about the miserable lives of the upper-caste Hindu women, especially the widows.

Jyotiba Phule wrote about the poor condition of the 'low caste people.' In his book '*Gulamgiri*' (1871), he wrote about the injustices of the caste system.

In the 20th century, BR Ambedkar also wrote powerfully against the caste system. He also wrote against untouchability. EV Ramaswamy Naicker, also known as Periyar, wrote about the caste system prevailing in Madras.

Q.4 Why did some people in 18th century Europe think that print culture would bring enlightenment and end despotism?

Ans. Some people in the 18th century thought that print culture would bring enlightenment and end despotism due to following reasons

- **Spreading of New Ideas** After the coming of print culture, the ideas of scientists and philosophers became more accessible to the common people. Ancient and medieval scientific texts were compiled and published.
- **Books as Medium of Progress** By the 18th century, books became a medium of spreading progress and enlightenment which could change society and the world. It was also believed that the books could liberate society from despotism and tyranny.
- **Writings of Scholars** The writings of thinkers such as Jean Jacques Rousseau, Thomas Paine and Voltaire were also widely printed and gained popularity. Thus, their ideas about science, rationality and reasoning found their way into popular literature.
- **Scientific Discoveries** Maps and more accurate scientific diagrams were widely printed when scientists like Isaac Newton began to publish their discoveries. They could influence a much wider circle of scientifically-minded readers.
- **Ideas of Enlightened Thinkers** Print popularised the ideas of the enlightened thinkers like Martin Luther who attacked the authority of the church and the despotic powers of the state.
- **A New Culture of Dialogue and Debate** The printing press was believed to be the most powerful engine of progress and public opinion. Many historians have argued that print culture created the conditions for the end of despotism in France through the French Revolution.

Q.5 Why did some people fear the effect of easily available printed books? Choose one example from Europe and one from India.

Ans. Some people especially those from upper and powerful classes, feared the effect of easily-available printed books because not everyone welcomed printed books and those who did, also had fear about them. Many were of the opinion that printed words and the wider circulation of books, would have a negative impact on people's minds.

They feared that if there was no control over what was printed and read, then rebellious and irreligious thoughts might gain importance. There was also fear in the minds of scholars that the authority of 'valuable' literature would be destroyed. The new print medium was criticised by religious authorities and monarchs, as well as by writers and artists.

Example from Europe

In Europe, Martin Luther was a German monk, priest, professor and a church reformer. He wrote 'Ninety Five Theses' in 1517 and openly criticised many of the practices and rituals of the Roman Catholic Church. A printed copy of this was pasted on a church door in Wittenberg. It challenged the church to debate his ideas. Luther's writings were immediately copied in vast numbers and read widely. This led to a division within the church and led to the beginning of the Protestant Reformation.

Example from India

In India, the British Government favoured censorship of the press and passed a law to hinder free circulation of newspapers and journals. Vernacular Press Act, 1878 provided the government with extensive rights to censor reports and editorials.

Q.6 What were the effects of the spread of print culture for the poor people in the 19th century in India?

Ans. The effects of the spread of print culture on poor people in 19th century India were as follows

- The literacy rate improved in India. Printed material, especially for entertainment, began to reach even the poor in the 19th century. Publishers started producing small and cheap books for the poor. These books were sold at crossroads. Public libraries were setup by Christian missionaries and rich people.
- Enlightening essays and articles were written against caste discrimination and its inherent injustices. These were read by people across the country.

- On the encouragement and support of social reformers, overworked factory workers set up libraries for self-education. Some of them even published their own works, like Kashibaba published *Chhote Aur Bade Ka Sawal.*

Q.7 Explain how print culture assisted the growth of nationalism in India.

Ans. Print not only stimulated the publication of conflicting opinions amongst communities but it also connected communities and people in different parts of India.

Following factors assisted the growth of nationalism in India throughout print culture

- **New Ideas and Debates** There were many persons who criticised the existing practices and campaigned for reforms, while some of others countered the arguments of the reformers. These debates were carried out openly in public and in print. Printed tracts and newspapers not only spread the new ideas, but they also shaped the nature of the debate. For example, Jyotiba Phule wrote about the injustice of the caste system in his Gulamgiri. A Kanpur mill worker published a collection called Sacchi Kavitayan. These were sponsored by the social reformers who not only tried to bring literacy but also propogate the message of nationalism.
- **Print and Newspapers** Despite repressive measures, nationalist newspapers grew in numbers in all parts of India. They reported on colonial misrule and encouraged nationalist activities. When Punjab revolutionaries were deported in 1907, Balgangadhar Tilak wrote with great sympathy about them in his 'Kesari.'
- **Connecting Various Communities** Print not only stimulated the publication of conflicting opinions amongst communities, but also connected communities and people living in different parts of India. Newspapers conveyed news from one place to another, creating a pan-Indian identity.

REVIEW EXERCISE

Including Competency Based Questions

Part I

Multiple Choice Questions (MCQs)

1. Which of the following countries had the earliest kind of print technology?

(a) China (b) Korea (c) Japan (d) All of these

2. Which of the following cities became the hub of the Western style-school culture printing?

(a) Berlin (b) Shanghai (c) Paris (d) Tokyo

3. In which of the following years, Buddhist missionaries from China introduced hand-printing technology?

(a) 758-760 AD (b) 772-774 AD
(c) 768-770 AD (d) 776-778 AD

4. Which of the following books is the oldest Japanese book, printed in 868 AD containing six sheets of text and woodcut illustrations?

(a) Diamond Sutra (b) Harshcharita
(c) Brihatsutra (d) Mrichkatika

5. ....was the first book, printed by Gutenberg.

(a) Chapbooks (b) Amar Jivan
(c) Bible (d) Aimanac

6. The Jikji of Korea, one the world's oldest books contained the essential features of

(a) Judaism (b) Hinduism
(c) Jainism (d) Zen Buddhism

7. At which of the following places, a children's press was set up in 1857?

(a) England (b) Spain (c) France (d) China

8. At which of the following places in India, first printing press was established?

(a) Bombay (b) Madras
(c) Calcutta (d) Goa

9. Why was reading of manuscript not easy in India? Choose the appropriate reason from the following options. CBSE 2020

(a) Manuscripts were highly cheap.
(b) Manuscripts were widely spread out.
(c) Manuscripts were written in English and Hindi.
(d) Manuscripts were fragile.

10. Who among the following published 'Sambad Kaumudi'? CBSE 2024

(a) Rashsundari Debi (b) Tarabai Shinde
(c) Raja Rammohun Roy (d) Ram Chaddha

11. Find the incorrect option.

(a) Martin Luther wrote 'Ninety Five Theses
(b) The first Tamil Book printed in Cochin
(c) In 1870, Hindi Printing began seriously
(d) Fairy Tales printed by the Bronte sisters

12. **In the hundred years between 1450 and 1550, printing presses were set up in most countries of Europe. Printers from Germany travelled to other countries, seeking work and helping start new presses. As the number of printing presses grew, book production boomed.**

What was the primary reason for the boom in book production? **Competency Based**

(a) Increased demand for reading materials
(b) Advancement in printing technology
(c) Improved paper quality
(d) Government subsidies for printing

13. **The novel, a literary firm which had developed in Europe, ideally catered to this need. It soon acquired distinctively Indian forms and styles. For readers, it opened up new worlds of experience, and gave a vivid sense of the diversity of human lives.**

What effect did printing have on the desire for new kinds of writing? **Competency Based**

(a) It increased the need for religious texts.
(b) It fueled a demand for personal stories and experiences.
(c) It led to a decline in traditional forms of literature.
(d) It had no significant impact on reading preferences.

14. **Assume you are doing research on 15th century print culture. Which of the following would be the most significant advantage for your research?** **CBSE 2025**

(a) Easier access to rare manuscripts
(b) Reduced need for libraries
(c) Increase in the ability to copy text by hand
(d) Increased speed and accuracy of print

15. **In North India, the ulama were deeply anxious about the collapse of Muslim dynasties. They feared that colonial rulers would encourage conversion, change the Muslim personal laws. To counter this, they used cheap lithographic presses, published Persian and Urdu translations of holy scriptures, and printed religious newspapers and tracts.**

What can we infer about the relationship between the ulama and the colonial rulers? **Competency Based**

(a) They were allies in promoting modernisation and reform.
(b) They maintained a neutral stance towards the colonial government.
(c) They were distrustful and apprehensive of colonial policies.
(d) They were actively involved in supporting the colonial administration.

16. **In 1878, the Vernacular Press Act was passed, modelled on the Irish Press Laws. It provided the government with extensive rights to censor reports and editorials in the vernacular press.**

What was the primary purpose of the Vernacular Press Act?

(a) To promote education in english language
(b) To regulate the press
(c) To support the vernacular languages
(d) To give more freedom to press

17. **After the mid-19th century, women's schools were set up in the cities and towns. Shivani, a 30 year old journalist began carrying the writings of women and explained why women should be educated.**

Accordingly, which development happened in India because of Shivani's contribution in writings?

(a) Women literacy rates suddenly increased.
(b) Specific changes in societal perception towards women's education.
(c) Men literacy rates decreased.
(d) She became inspiration for other women to become journalist.

18. **Sometimes, the government found it hard to find candidates for editorship of loyalist papers. When Sanders, editor of the Statesman that had been founded in 1877, was approached, he asked rudely how much he would be paid for suffering the loss of freedom. The Friend of India refused a government subsidy, fearing that this would force it to be obedient to government commands.**

What did Sanders, editor of the Statesman, do when approached by the government?

(a) He immediately accepted the offer to edit a loyalist paper.
(b) He demanded an exorbitant salary for the position.
(c) He refused the offer, expressing his disapproval of government censorship.
(d) He requested more information about the specific duties and responsibilities.

19. **Arrange the following in sequence.**

I. Martin Luther 'Ninety Five Theses'
II. The first Tamil Book Printed
III. The first Malayalam book was printed
IV. Vernacular Press Act was passed.

Codes

(a) IV, III, II, I
(b) I, IV, III, II
(c) I, II, III, IV
(d) III, II, IV, I

20. **Arrange the following in chronological order.**

I. Print culture created the conditions for the French Revolution.
II. Martin Luther's writing led to beginning of the Protestant Reformation.
III. Menocchio re-interpreted the message of the Bible
IV. Johannes Gutenberg invented Printing Press.

Codes **CBSE SQP 2022-23**

(a) IV, III, II, I
(b) I, IV, III, II
(c) I, II, III, IV
(d) IV, II, III, I

21. Choose the correctly matched pair.

(a) Buddhist Missionaries Introduced hand printing technology	_	Japan
(b) First Printing Press came in India	_	Bombay
(c) Marco Polo brought woodblock printing	_	America
(d) First printed edition of Ramcharitmanas	_	Uttar Pradesh

22. Identify the magazine with the help of given features. **Competency Based**

(i) It was the first English-language newspaper published on the Indian subcontinent.

(ii) It was founded in Calcutta, capital of British India.

(iii) The magazine was edited by Augustus Hickey.

(iv) The magazine was started in 1780.

Options

(a) Bengal Gazette (b) Sambad Kaumudi

(c) Rast Goftar (d) Hindu Patriot

23. Identify the reason as to why manuscripts could not be read easily. Choose from the appropriate statements among the following options.

I. It was written in different language.

II. The scripts were not clear

III. Scripts were written in different styles.

IV. Most of the Manuscripts were damage.

Codes

(a) Statements I and II are appropriate.

(b) Statements I, II and III are appropriate.

(c) All the statements are appropriate.

(d) Only statement III is appropriate.

24. Identify the reason as to why was Balgangadhar Tilak imprisoned in 1908. Choose from the appropriate statements among the following options:

I. He wrote about Punjab revolutionaries who were deported in 1907, in his newspaper 'Kesari'.

II. Spreading disaffection towards the British the Raj.

III. Fought for Indian independence against British rule.

IV. He started writing against about British rule in his writing.

Options

(a) Only statement I is appropriate.

(b) Statements I, II and III are appropriate.

(c) All the statements are appropriate.

(d) Statements I and II are appropriate.

25. Which of the following statements accurately describes about the "Fatwa" in the Muslim term?

I. Fatwa defined as an act, object, or conduct over which the individual has freedom of choice.

II. In the Quran, the word Fatwa is variously used to mean arbitration, judgement, authority, or God's will.

III. It refers, in simple terms, to an edict or ruling by a recognised religious authority on a point of other laws.

IV. A legal pronouncement on Islamic law usually given by a mufti (legal scholar) to clarify issues on which the law is uncertain.

Codes

(a) Only IV (b) Only II (c) Both II and IV (d) Both I and II

26. Consider the statements given below and choose the correct answer.

I. Western printing techniques and mechanical press were imported in the late 19th century as Western powers established their outposts in China.

II. Beijing became the hub of the new print culture, catering to Western-style schools. **CBSE SQP 2023-24**

Codes

(a) Only I (b) Only II

(c) Both I and II are incorrect

(d) Both I and II are correct

27. Which of the following statements are correct about the "Manuscripts"?

I. Manuscripts were written in Sanskrit, Arabic, Persian, as well as in various vernacular languages.

II. Manuscripts were copied on palm leaves or on handmade paper.

III. Manuscripts continued to be produced even after the introduction of print.

IV. Script was written in only one style.

Codes

(a) Only I (b) Only II

(c) Both II and IV (d) I, II and III

28. Consider the statements given below and choose the correct answer. **Competency Based**

Statement I With the onset of the Great Depression in the 1930s, publishers feared a decline in book purchases. To sustain buying, they brought out cheap paperback editions.

Statement II In the 1920s in England, popular works were sold in cheap series, called the Shilling Series.

Options

(a) Statement I is correct and II is incorrect

(b) Statement I is incorrect and II is correct

(c) Both I and II are incorrect

(d) Both I and II are correct

29. **Consider the statements given below and choose the correct answer**

Statement I With the setting up of a decreasing number of printing presses, visual images could be easily reproduced in multiple copies.

Statement II Printing created an appetite for new kinds of writing. As more and more people could now read, they wanted to see their own lives, experiences, emotions and relationships reflected in what they read.

Options
(a) Statement I is correct and II is incorrect
(b) Statement I is incorrect and II is correct
(c) Both I and II are incorrect
(d) Both I and II are correct

30. **Consider the statements given below and choose the correct answer**

Statement I From 1780, James Augustus Hickey began to edit the Bengal Gazette, a weekly magazine that described itself as 'a commercial paper open to all, but influenced by none.'

Statement II Hickey also published a lot of gossip about the Company's senior officials in India.

Options **CBSE Additional SQP 2023-24**
(a) Statement I is correct II is incorrect.
(b) Statement I is incorrect and II is correct
(c) Both I and II are incorrect
(d) Both I and II are correct

31. **Consider the statements given below and choose the correct answer**

Statement I By the 1870s, caricatures and cartoons were being published in Indian journals and newspapers, commenting on social and political issues.

Statement II Some caricatures praised the educated Indians fascination with Western tastes and clothes, while others were looking forward to social change.

Options **CBSE SQP 2024-25**
(a) Statement I is correct II is incorrect.
(b) Statement I is incorrect and II is correct
(c) Both I and II are incorrect
(d) Both I and II are correct

Answers

1. (d)	**2.** (b)	**3.** (c)	**4.** (a)	**5.** (c)
6. (d)	**7.** (c)	**8.** (d)	**9.** (d)	**10.** (c)
11. (d)	**12.** (b)	**13.** (b)	**14.** (d)	**15.** (c)
16. (b)	**17.** (b)	**18.** (c)	**19.** (c)	**20.** (d)
21. (a)	**22.** (a)	**23.** (d)	**24.** (a)	**25.** (a)
26. (a)	**27.** (d)	**28.** (d)	**29.** (b)	**30.** (d)
31. (a)				

Match the Following

1.

List-I (Publication)	**List-II** (Authors)
A. Bengal Gazette	1. Tulsidas
B. Kesari	2. James August Hickey
C. Ramcharitmanas	3. Ram Mohan Roy
D Sambad Kaumudi	4. Bal Gangadhar Tilak

Codes **CBSE 2025**

	A	B	C	D		A	B	C	D
(a)	1	2	3	4	(b)	2	3	4	1
(c)	2	4	1	3	(d)	4	1	2	3

Ans. (b)

Assertion-Reason

1. **Assertion** (A) By the 17th century, the use of print diversified in China because of a blooming urban culture.

Reason (R) The imperial state in China was the major producers of printed materials.

Codes
(a) Both A and R are true and R is the correct explanation of A
(b) Both A and R are true, but R is not the correct explanation of A
(c) A is true, but R is false
(d) A is false, but R is true

2. **Assertion** (A) After the mid of 19th century women's schools were set up in the cities and towns.

Reason (R) Many journals begans carrying the writings of women and explained why women should be educated.

Codes
(a) Both A and R are true and R is the correct explanation of A
(b) Both A and R are true, but R is not the correct explanation of A
(c) A is true, but R is false
(d) A is false, but R is true

3. **Assertion** (A) During World Wars, the Indian press faced severe restrictions under various laws.

Reason (R) The Defence of India Rules, the Sedition Committee Report, and the Defence of India Act imposed censorship and penalties on newspapers, leading to closures and suppression.

Codes
(a) Both A and R are true and R is the correct explanation of A
(b) Both A and R are true, but R is not the correct explanation of A
(c) A is true, but R is false
(d) A is false, but R is true

4. **Assertion** (A) The Vernacular Press Act of 1878 limited the freedom of expression in the vernacular press.

Reason (R) The Act granted the government broad censorship powers, allowing them to suppress any content deemed 'seditious,' with potential seizure of printing presses and confiscation of machinery.

Codes

(a) Both A and R are true and R is the correct explanation of A

(b) Both A and R are true, but R is not the correct explanation of A

(c) A is true, but R is false

(d) A is false, but R is true

5. **Assertion** (A) The distribution, application, and preservation of knowledge were fundamentally altered with the invention of printing.

Reason (R) Printing enabled intellectuals to produce, comment on, and evaluate texts which spread as ideas across Europe. **CBSE Additional SQP 2023-24**

Codes

(a) Both A and R are true and R is the correct explanation of A

(b) Both A and R are true, but R is not the correct explanation of A

(c) A is true, but R is false

(d) A is false, but R is true

Ans. 1. (b) Both A and R are true, but R is not the correct explanation of A

2. (b) Both A and R are true, but R is not the correct explanation of A

3. (b) Both A and R are true, but R is not the correct explanation of A

4. (d) A is false, but R is true

5. (a) Both A and R are true and R is the correct explanation of A

Picture Based Question

1. **Identify the picture.**

(a) Portrait of Rabindranath Tagore

(b) Portrait of Raja Rammohan Roy

(c) Portrait of J Gutenberg

(d) Portrait of Balgangadhar Tilak

Ans. 1. (c) Portrait of J Gutenberg

Case Based Question

1. **Read the source given below and answer the following questions.**

From the late nineteenth century, issues of caste discrimination began to be written about in many printed tracts and essays. Jyotiba Phule, the Maratha pioneer of 'low caste' protest movements, wrote about the injustices of the caste system in his Gulamgiri (1871).

In the 20th century, BR Ambedkar in Maharashtra and EV Ramaswamy Naicker in Madras, better known as Periyar, wrote powerfully on caste and their writings were read by people all over India. Local protest movements and sects also created a lot of popular journals and tracts criticising ancient scriptures and envisioning a new and just future. Workers in factories were too overworked and lacked the education to write much about their experiences. But Kashibaba, a Kanpur millworker, wrote and published Chhote Aur Bade Ka Sawal in 1938 to show the links between caste and class exploitation. The poems of another Kanpur millworker, who wrote under the name of Sudarshan Chakr between 1935 and 1955, were brought together and published in a collection called Sacchi Kavitayan.

(i) What was the primary reason why factory workers did not write much about their experiences?

(a) Lack of interest

(b) Fear of repercussions

(c) Overwork and lack of education

(d) Unawareness of social issues

(ii) What is the main focus of Kashibaba's book "Chhote Aur Bade Ka Sawal"?

(a) Critique of ancient scriptures

(b) The link between caste and class exploitation

(c) The struggles of factory workers

(d) A vision for a new future

(iii) What was the impact of the writings of individuals like BR Ambedkar and EV Ramaswamy Naicker?

(a) The immediate abolition of the caste system.

(b) Increased awareness and public debate about caste issues.

(c) The formation of a unified movement against caste discrimination.

(d) The creation of separate political parties for different castes.

(iv) How did local protest movements contribute to the fight against caste discrimination?

(a) By organising boycotts and strikes

(b) By publishing journals and tracts

(c) By providing legal aid to victims of caste violence

(d) By lobbying the government for reform

Ans. (i) (c) Overwork and lack of education

(ii) (b) The link between caste and class exploitation

(iii) (b) Increased awareness and public debate about caste issues.

(iv) (b) By publishing journals and tracts

Part II

Very Short Answer Type Questions

1. When was print technology introduced in Japan?

Ans. Print technology was introduced in Japan around 768-770 AD by Buddhist missionaries from China.

2. What do you mean by Edo?

Ans. Edo was the earlier name of Tokyo.

3. Who is known for his contribution to an art form called Ukiyo?

Ans. Kitagawa Utamaro is known for his contribution to an art form called Ukiyo.

4. In Europe, who was the developer of first printing press?

Ans. Johann Gutenberg developed the first printing press in Europe.

5. Why was Gutenberg's press too slow as compared to present press technology?

Ans. Gutenberg's press was too slow as it used hand printing method, but, present press technology follows mechanical printing method.

6. How many theses did Martin Luther write?

Ans. Martin Luther wrote Ninety Five theses criticising many of the practices and rituals of the Roman Catholic Church.

7. What was the basic objective of selling penny chapbooks in England?

Ans. The basic objective of selling penny chapbooks in England was that even the poor could purchase it.

8. What were penny magazines?

Ans. Penny magazines were especially meant for women and these were manuals teaching proper behaviour and house-keeping.

9. On what material were the manuscripts written in ancient India?

Ans. In ancient India, manuscripts were written on palm leaves or on handmade paper.

10. Name the first weekly paper published in India.

or **Who started to edit the Bengal Gazette weekly in 1780 ?**

Ans. Bengal Gazette, edited by James Augustus Hickey, was the first weekly paper published in India.

11. Name two Persian newspapers which began to be published in India in the early 19th century.

Ans. Jam-i-Jahan Nama and Shamsul Akhbar were the two Persian newspapers which published in India from 1822.

12. Name a Gujarati newspaper published in 1822.

Ans. In 1822, the 'Bombay Samachar', a Gujarati newspaper made its appearance.

13. Name the autobiography of Rashsundari Debi.

Ans. 'Amar Jiban' was the autobiography written by Rashsundari Debi. It was published in 1876.

14. Who published the fast-selling 'Istri Dharm Vichar' to teach women how to be obedient wives?

Ans. Ram Chaddha published the fast-selling 'Istri Dharm Vichar' to teach women how to be obedient wives.

Short Answer Type Questions

1. What was an 'accordion book'? Describe any two features of hand printing in China.

Ans. 'Accordion book' was the traditional book of China. It was folded and stitched at the side. This book was hand printed.

Two features of hand printing in China are

(i) Books in China were printed by rubbing paper against the inked surface of woodblocks.

(ii) Skilled craftsmen duplicated with remarkable accuracy, the beauty of calligraphy in hand printing.

2. By the 17th century, as urban culture bloomed in China, the uses of print diversifield? Explain the statement by giving suitable examples. CBSE SQP 2024-25

Ans. As urban culture flourished, the uses of print diversified. Print was not only limited to scholar officials, merchants also used print in their daily lives to acquire trade information. Reading increasingly became a leisure activity. The new readership preferred fictional narratives, poetry, autobiographies, anthologies of literacy masterpieces, and romantic plays. Rich women began to read, and many woman began publishing their poetry and plays.

3. Who was Marco Polo? What was his contribution to print culture?

Ans. Marco Polo was a great explorer of Italy who stayed for many years in China. The main contribution of Marco Polo was that he introduced woodblock printing in Italy.

Marco Polo returned back to Italy in 1295, after many years of explorations in China. The earliest kind of woodblock printing technology was developed in China. Marco Polo brought this knowledge with him in Italy.

As a result, Italians began producing books with woodblocks and soon this technology spread to other parts of Europe.

4. How did the ideas of scientists and philosophers become more accessible to common people after the beginning of print revolution in Europe?

Ans. After the beginning of print revolution, the ideas of scientists and philosophers became more accessible to the common people in the following ways

- Ancient and medieval scientific texts were compiled and published.
- Different types of maps and scientific diagrams were widely printed.
- Scientists like, Isaac Newton began to publish their discoveries, which could easily influence a large number of scientifically minded readers.
- The writings of great thinkers like Thomas Paine, Voltaire, Rousseau were widely printed and read.

All these made the minds of common people more reasonable and rational.

5. Who was Martin Luther? What was his contribution to the Protestant Reformation?

Or How did Martin Luther's writings bring reforms in religious field? Explain.

Ans. Martin Luther was a German monk, priest and professor of theology.

His contribution to the protestant reformation was

- He wrote 'Ninety Five Theses' criticising many of the practices and rituals of the Roman Catholic Church.
- Luther taught that salvation is not earned by good deeds but received only as a free gift of God's grace through faith in Jesus Christ as redeemer from sin.
- A National Church was established by him in Germany and prayers began to be held in German language. It led to the beginning of the Reformation Movement in Europe.

6. How did books create new culture of reading? Explain with three examples.

or How had the printing press created a new culture of reading in Europe? Explain with example.

Ans. Printing press and books created a new culture of reading habits in the following ways

(i) Earlier reading was restricted to the aristocrats and nobels only. Common people heard sacred texts read out, ballads recited and folk tales narrated. Now books reached a large section of people, so 'reading public' increased instead of 'hearing public'.

(ii) Printers began publishing popular ballads and folk tales with beautiful illustrations. These could be sung or recited at large gatherings.

(iii) With the expansion of printing technology, the distance between oral and reading cultures decreased thus the hearing public and reading public became intermingled.

7. What restrictions were imposed by the Vernacular Press Act on the Indian Press? Explain.

Or In what ways the Vernacular Press Act of 1878 was a repressive step by the government? Explain.

Or Why was the Vernacular Press Act passed in 1878? **CBSE 2020**

Ans. The 'Vernacular Press Act' was passed in 1878 under the viceroy Lord Lytton to control the Vernacular papers.

The act empowered the government to impose restrictions on the press in the following ways

- This Act provided the government with extensive rights to censor reports and editorials in the vernacular press.
- The Act controlled the printing and circulation of seditious material, specifically which were against the British Government in India.
- The Act gave powers to the government to track the Vernacular newspapers.

8. Why did the production of handwritten manuscripts not satisfy the demand for books?

Or What is manuscript? Write any three shortcomings of manuscript?

Ans. The production of handwritten manuscripts could not satisfy the ever increasing demand for books due to the following shortcomings

Three shortcomings of manuscript are

(i) Manuscripts were fragile, awkward to handle and could not be carried around or read easily.

(ii) Copying was an expensive, laborious and time consuming task.

(iii) Their circulation remained limited. This could not satisfy the increasing demand for books.

9. Examine the role of missionaries in the growth of press in India.

Ans. The missionaries played a very significant role in the growth of press in India, in the following ways

- Portuguese missionaries in the mid-16th century introduced the printing press first in Goa.
- Jesuit priests learnt Konkani and printed several tracts. By 1674, about 50 books had been printed in the Konkani and in Kanara languages.
- Catholic priests printed the first Tamil book in 1579 at Cochin and the first Malayalam book in 1713.
- By 1710, Dutch Protestant missionaries also had printed 32 Tamil texts, many of these were translations of older books.

10. Write about the different innovations in the printing technology during the 19th century.

Or Mention any three innovations which improved the printing technology after the 17th century.

Or Explain any five innovations in print technology in Europe that took place after the 18th century.

Or Analyse the significant changes in printing technology during 19th century in the world. CBSE 2025

Ans. Through the 19th century, there was a series of new innovations in printing technology. They were

(i) By the mid of 19th century, Richard M Hoe of New York had perfected the power-driven cylindrical press. It was capable of printing 8000 sheets per hour which was specially useful for printing newspapers.

(ii) In the late 19th century, the offset press was developed which could print upto six colours at a time.

(iii) From the beginning of the 20th century, electrically operated presses accelerated printing operations.

(iv) Some other improvements were developed e.g. methods of feeding paper improved, the quality of plates became better, automatic paper reels and photoelectric controls of the colour register were introduced.

(v) The 19th century periodicals serialised important novels, which gave birth to a particular way of writing novels.

11. Mention any three characteristic features of the printed books in the late 17th century.

Ans. The three characteristic features of printed books were

(i) In these books, borders were illuminated by hand with foliage and other different patterns. Illustrations in these books were painted.

(ii) In the books printed for the rich, some spaces were kept blank for the decoration.

Each purchaser had the right to select the design and decide the particular painting school that would do the decoration.

(iii) The printed books and literature could stimulate many distinctive individual interpretations of faith even among less educated working people.

12. Read the statements given below regarding expansion of world trade.

Statement 1 (S1) In 1295, Marco Polo, a great explorer, returned to Italy after many years of exploration in China.

Statement 2 (S2) Production of handwritten manuscripts was also organised in new ways to meet the expanded demand.

Explain, how these statements are reflecting in print culture. Competency Based

Ans. Statements 1 and 2 are reflecting in print culture because Marco Polo was spreading knowledge and the importance of organised manuscript production. Marco Polo was a great explorer from Italy. While returning from China in 1295 he brought the technology of woodblock printing along with him. Marco Polo served as an important medium for the transfer of knowledge between East and West.

The introduction of woodblock printing marked the beginning of the new era in communication and information sharing, paving the way for future technological advancements such as the printing press.

Production of handwritten manuscripts was also organised in new ways to meet the expanded demand. With the increasing demand for books, especially religious texts, universities, monasteries, and scriptoria became bustling centers of manuscript production. Manuscripts were copied by scribes, often monks, who dedicated their lives to this laborious task.

13. How did printing technology evolve during the 19th century? Competency Based

Build answer around these points

- **Made out of metal**
- **8,000 sheets per hour**
- **Printing newspapers**

Ans. Printing technology evolved during the 19th century in the following ways

- In the late 18th century, the press came to be made out of metal. Through the 19th century, there were a series of further innovations in printing technology. This was capable of printing 8,000 sheets per hour. This press was particularly useful for printing newspapers.
- In the late 19th century, the offset press was developed which could print up to six colours at a time.
- From the turn of the 20th century, electrically operated presses accelerated printing operations.

Long Answer Type Questions

1. Explain the different stages of development of printing technology in China.

Ans. China was one of the countries where the earliest kind of print technology was developed.

The different stages of development of printing technology in China are

- From AD 594 onwards, books in China were printed by rubbing paper against the inked surface of woodblocks. These papers were also invented in China. The imperial state of China was the major producer of printed material for a very longtime.
  At that time, China possessed a huge bureaucratic system which recruited its personnel through Civil Service examination. From the 16th century, the number of candidates for the examination increased, so the number of books also increased.

- By the 17th century, urban culture developed in China and merchants, rich women, wives of scholar-officials not only started reading different books like, fictions, poetry, autobiographies, anthologies of literary masterpieces, romantic plays, they also began to write.
- In the late 19th century, Shanghai became the hub of the new print culture by importing Western printing techniques and mechanical presses. From hand printing, there was a gradual shift to mechanical printing in China.

2. "How did easy access to books develop a new culture of reading during the 18th century?" Analyse. **CBSE 2025**

Ans. Easy access to books played a crucial role in developing a new culture of reading during the 18th century. This period saw significant changes in the way books were produced and distributed, which helped to democratise knowledge and foster a new reading culture.

Factors contributing to the development of the reading culture are as follows

- **Printing Revolution** The invention of the printing press in the 15th century and its spread in the 18th century made books more affordable and widely available.
- **Rise of Public Libraries and Bookshops** In the 18th century, public libraries and bookshops began to emerge in European cities. These spaces allowed people from different social backgrounds, including the middle class, to access books and engage with literature and ideas.
- **Growth of Literature in Vernacular Languages** In addition to classical languages like Latin, books began to be printed in vernacular languages, making literature and knowledge more accessible to a wider audience.
- **New Ideas and Enlightenment** The 18th century was also the period of the Enlightenment, where there was a surge of intellectual and philosophical ideas about democracy, rights, science and society. Books and pamphlets containing these ideas spread quickly, encouraging the culture of reading and the exchange of new ideas.
- **Increased Literacy and Social Change** As more people learned to read, literacy rates rose, leading to an educated middle class that engaged in discussions and contributed to social and political transformations.

3. "Printing press played a major role in shaping the Indian society of the 19th century". Support the statement with examples.

Or **How did the print initiate public debates and affect the religious and social reforms? Explain.**

Or **Analyse any three impacts of print culture on the religious reform movement of 16th century.**

Ans. Printing press played a major role in shaping the Indian society of the 19th century. The impacts of print culture on the Indian society and religion were

- From the early 19th century, there were intense debates around religious issues. Different groups in colonial society offered a new interpretation of the beliefs of different religions.
- Newspaper spread the new ideas and also shaped the nature of the debate. New contradictory ideas were emerged and a wider public could participate in these discussions and expressed their views.
- In the early 19th century, an intense controversy between social and religious reformers and the Hindu orthodox section emerged. They angered about Brahmanical priesthood and idolatry, widow immolation, monotheism etc. Raja Rammohun Roy published '*Sambad Kaumudi*' and wrote about the social evils at that time.

  The Hindu orthodoxy commissioned the '*Samachar Chandrika*' to oppose his opinions. At that time, two Persian newspapers '*Jam-i-Jahan Nama*' and '*Shamsul Akhbar*', a Gujarati newspaper, the 'Bombay Samachar' were also published.
- In North India, the ulama used cheap lithographic presses to print religious newspapers and published Persian and Urdu translations of holy scriptures. They feared that colonial rule would change their personal laws. Urdu print helped them to battle against this fear.

Thus, print connected communities and people in different parts of India helped to develop their own views.

4. 'By the end of the 19th century, a new visual culture was taking shape'. Explain.

Ans. By the end of the 19th century, a new visual culture was taking shape with the setting-up of an increasing number of printing press in the following ways

- Painters like Raja Ravi Varma produced images for mass circulation. During his lifetime, Varma is most remembered for his paintings of sari-clad women portrayed as graceful. His paintings were a fusion of Indian traditions with the techniques of European academic art.
- Cheap prints and calendars were easily available in the markets which could be bought by poor people to decorate walls of their homes. These prints began shaping popular ideas about modernity and tradition, religion, politics, society and culture.
- Innovations made colour prints more beautiful. By the 1870's, cartoons and caricatures were being published in newspapers and *journals*. These caricatures had a great effect on people's minds.

5. Read the information about New Print Technology and answer the question that follows.

Gutenberg printed about 180 copies, of which no more than 50 have survived. They were not just products of new technology. The text was printed in the new Gutenberg press with metal type, but the borders were carefully designed, painted and illuminated by hand by artists.

What made the copies of Gutenberg's Bible unique, besides being products of new technology? How it reflected the preferences of the elites of that time? Competency Based

Ans. The uniqueness of Gutenberg's Bible copies extended because of the innovative printing technology. Each copy was distinct because of the meticulous handwork involved in their production.

Artists carefully designed, painted, and illuminated the borders, ensuring that no two copies were exactly the same. Even seemingly similar copies revealed differences upon close inspection. The manual addition of color to highlight holy words further enhanced the individuality of each page, making every copy a unique and personalised piece of craftsmanship.

The preferences of the elites during Gutenberg's time were intricately reflected in the unique features of the printed copies. Elites highly valued owning items that were exclusive and rare. The fact that no two copies were exactly the same, even when they appeared similar, appealed to their desire for uniqueness. Each elite could claim ownership of a Bible that was distinctly their own. Elites appreciated the artistic craftsmanship, aligning with their taste for finely crafted and aesthetically pleasing possessions.

6. In the 17th century, as urban culture bloomed in China, the uses of print diversified. Print was no longer used just by scholar officials. Merchants used print in their everyday life, as they collected trade information.
Reading increasingly became a leisure activity.

Why did Shanghai in China become a significant hub for the new print culture, and how did it cater to Western-style schools? Competency Based

Ans. Shanghai became a significant hub for the new print culture because it was influenced by a combination of Western impact, educational developments, economic significance, technological progress, and a changing cultural landscape that embraced a diverse readership.

With the coming of Western powers and establishing outposts in China during the late nineteenth century, Shanghai experienced a notable Western influence. This influence extended to various aspects of culture, including technology and education. Shanghai's status as a major commercial and economic center made it an ideal location for the development of the print industry.

Shanghai's catering to Western-style schools involved not only the adoption of Western printing technology but also the adaptation of content and formats to align with the educational needs and preferences of these institutions. By catering to Western-style schools, Shanghai became a center where traditional Chinese literary forms coexisted and integrated with Western literary styles and educational practices.

Case Based Questions

1. Read the source given below and answer the questions that follow.

New forms of popular literature appeared in print, targeting new audiences. Booksellers employed pedlars who roamed around villages, carrying little books for sale.

There were almanacs or ritual calendars, along with ballads and folktales. But other forms of reading matters, largely for entertainment, began to reach ordinary readers as well. In England, penny chapbooks were carried by petty pedlars known as chapmen, and sold for a penny, so that even the poor could buy them.

In France, were the 'Biliotheque Bleue', which were low-priced small books printed on poor quality paper, and bound in cheap blue covers.

Then there were the romances, printed on four to six pages, and the more substantial 'histories' printed on four to six pages and the more substantial 'histories' which were stories about the past. Books were of various sizes, serving many different purposes and interests.

(i) What were chapbooks?

(ii) How Biliotheque Bleue was different from chapbooks?

(iii) What were the new forms of literature introduced in Europe to attract the new readers?

Ans. (i) Chapbooks were the pocket size books that were sold by travelling pedlars called chapmen.

(ii) 'Biliotheque Bleue' were low priced small books printed in France. There were printed on poor quality paper and bound in cheap blue covers.

On the other hand chapbooks were pocket size book, published in England. These became popular from the time of the 16th century print revolution.

(iii) Some new forms of literature introduced in Europe to attract the new readers were
- Almanacs along with ballads and Folktales.
- In England, chapbooks were carried by petty peddlers and sold for penny.
- Biliotheque Bleues were low priced books sold in France.

2. Read the following source and answer the questions that follow. CBSE 2024

Why Newspapers ?

Krishnaji Trimbuck Ranade inhabitant of Poona intends to publish a Newspaper in the Marathi language with a view of affording useful information on every topic of local interest. It wil be open for free discussion on subjects of general utility, scientific investigation and the speculations connected with the antiquities, statistics, curiosities, history and geography of the country and of the Deccan especially the patronage and support of all interested in the diffusion of knowledge and welfare of the people is earnestly solicited.'

Bombay Telegraph and Courier, 6th January, 1849

'The task of the native newspapers and political associations is identical to the role of the opposition in the House of Commons in Parliament in England. That is of critically examining government policy to suggest improvements, by removing those parts that will not be to the benefit of the people and also by ensuring speedy implementation.

These associations ought to carefully study the particular issues, gather diverse relevant information on the nation as well as on what are the possible and desirable improvements, and this will surely earn it considerable influence.'

Native Opinion, 3rd April, 1870

(i) Analyse the primary objective proposed by Ranade for publishing Marathi language newspaper.

(ii) Why did the Bombay Telegraph emphasise the role of newspaper in promoting welfare of Deccan region?

(iii) What were the key responsibilities attributed to native newspapers ? Mention any two.

Ans. (i) The primary objective proposed by Ranade for publishing Marathi language newspapers was to provide useful information on every topic of local interest.

(ii) The Bombay Telegraph emphasised the role of newspapers in promoting welfare of the Deccan region as it performed tasks similar to the role of opposition. It critically examined government policy to suggest improvements and also ensured speedy implementation.

(iii) The key responsibilities attributed to native newspapers were

- To critically examine government policy to suggest improvements, by removing those parts that will not be benefit the people,
- To ensure speedy implementation.

ASSESSMENT EXERCISE

Multiple Choice Questions (MCQs)

1. When was Marco Polo, a great explorer, returned to Italy after many years of exploration in China?
(a) 1280 AD (b) 1290 AD (c) 1285 AD (d) 1295 AD

2. Which of the following, a Latin scholar and Catholic reformers, who criticised the excesses of Catholicism but kept his distance from Martin Luther?
(a) George Eliot (b) JV Schdey
(c) Erasmus (d) James Lackington

3. In which of the following years, two Persian newspapers *viz* Jam-i-Jahan Nama and Shamsul Akhbar were published?
(a) 1822 AD (b) 1830 AD (c) 1825 AD (d) 1835 AD

4. Consider the following statements and choose the appropriate statements associated with India and the world of print.
(a) The English East India Company began to import presses from the late 18th century in India.
(b) About 100 books had been printed in Konkani and Konera languages in 1674.
(c) Manuscripts were highly expensive and got damaged easily.
(d) 'Bengal Gazette' brought out by Balgangadhar Tilak in 1780.

Subjective Questions (VSA, SA & LA)

1. What is the name of the oldest printed book of Japan?

2. Who was Menocchio?

3. 'Cartoons and caricatures played a significant role in french revolution'. Evaluate.

4. Describe in brief how the print revolution affected the lifestyles of people.

5. Who was Johann Gutenberg? How did he come to innovate the printing press?

6. Describe the progress of print in Japan.

7. Analyse how did 'print' opened the possibility of thinking differently?

8. Explain how print culture affected women in 19th century in India.

9. How did a new reading culture bloom in China?

10. Print culture affected the reformers. Explain how?

CHAPTER 1

Resources and Development

The concept of resource and development focuses on the geographical distribution, utilisation and management of natural resources as well as the impact of human activities on the environment.

It explores the dynamic relationship between humans and their environment, emphasising the role of natural resources in shaping economic, social and cultural landscape.

1.1 Resources and their Classification

Everything available in our environment that can be used to satisfy our needs, is technologically accessible, economically achievable and culturally acceptable can be termed as 'resource'.

There is a relationship between nature, technology and institutions, in the process of transformation of things available in the environment. Human beings themselves are essential components of resources. They transform material available in the environment into resources and use them.

The resources can be classified in the following ways

(i) On the basis of origin – **biotic** and **abiotic**

(ii) On the basis of exhaustibility – **renewable** and **non-renewable**

(iii) On the basis of ownership – **individual, community,** national and **international**

(iv) On the basis of status of development – **potential, developed stock** and **reserves**

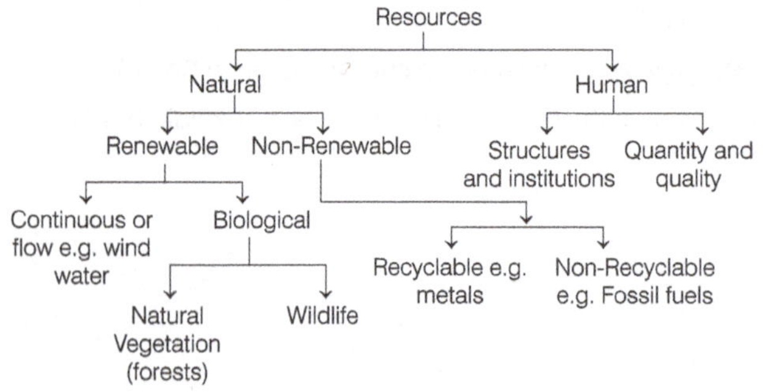

Development of Resources

Resources are essential for human survival as well as for maintaining the quality of life.

However, human beings used them indiscriminately/randomly and this has led to following major problems

- Resources are depleted for satisfying the greed of few individuals.
- The accumulation of resources in few hands divided the society into rich and poor.
- Over utilisation of resources led to the global ecological crisis, e.g. global warming, ozone layer depletion, environmental pollution and land degradation.

Thus, resource planning (equal distribution of resources) and sustainable development are essential for sustainable existence of all forms of life.

Sustainable development means development should take place without damaging the environment and development in the present should not compromise with the needs of the future generations.

Rio De Janeiro Earth Summit, 1992

The **first International Earth Summit** was held in **Rio De Janeiro in June 1992.** The summit addressed the problems of environmental protection and socio-economic development.

More than 100 heads of states signed the Declaration on Global Climatic Change and Biological Diversity. They also adopted **Global Forest Principles** and **Agenda 21** for achieving sustainable development in the 21st century.

Agenda 21 aims at achieving global sustainable development. It aims to resist environmental damage, poverty and disease, through global co-operation, mutual needs and shared responsibilities. It also aims that every local government should draw its own local Agenda 21.

Resource Planning in India

Resource planning refers to the strategy adopted for judicious use of the available resources.

In India, it is very important because some regions are rich in resources while some are deficient. There is shortage of vital resources in some areas while some areas are self-sufficient in resources. For example,

- States like **Jharkhand**, **Chhattisgarh** and **Madhya Pradesh** are rich in coal and minerals deposits.
- **Arunachal Pradesh** has abundant water resources, but lacks in infrastructure development.
- **Rajasthan** is enriched with wind and solar energy, but lacks water resources.
- The cold desert[1] of **Ladakh** lacks natural resources, although it has a rich cultural heritage.

Process of Resource Planning in India

The resource planning is necessary to balance equal resources distribution at the national, state, regional and local levels.

The complex process of resource planning in India is divided into **three** stages. They are as follows

(i) Identification and inventory of resources across the regions of the country. This involves surveying, mapping, qualitative and quantitative estimation and measurement of the resources.

(ii) Planning for resource development using appropriate skill, technology and institutional set-up.

(iii) Matching the resource development plans with overall national development plans.

India followed the policy of resource planning from the very first **Five Year Plan** rightly after the Independence. Resources can contribute to the development only with proper technological development and institutional change. India has experienced this in the different phases of colonisation[2].

Thus, in India, development does not only involve the availability of resources, but also the technology, quality of human resources and the historical experiences of the people.

Conservation of Resources

Resource conservation at various levels is important due to irrational consumption and over-utilisation of resources.

Gandhiji viewed that there are enough resources for everybody's need but not for anybody's greed. He was against mass production and wanted to replace it with production by the masses.

Concern for resource conservation has been raised at the following events

- At the international level, resource conservation was advocated for the first time in 1968 at club of Rome.
- In 1974, Schumacher in his book **Small is Beautiful**, accepted Gandhian philosophy of resource conservation.
- In 1987, the Brundtland Commission[3] **Report**, mentioned the necessity of resources conservation at global level. It also introduced the concept of 'Sustainable Development' which was later published in a book titled **Our Common Future.**

Try These

1. **Where was the first international Earth summit held in 1992?**
2. **What does agenda 21 aim to achieve at global level?**
3. **Name a state that is backward inspite of having abundant water resources.**
4. **The concept of sustainable development was introduced in Brundtland Commission Report. Name the book in which it was published.**

1.2 Land Resources

Land is a very important natural resource as it supports natural vegetation, wildlife, human life, economic activities, transport and communication systems. However, land is limited so, it needs to be used with careful planning.

India's geographical area comprises of a variety of relief features like mountains, plateaus, plains and islands. They are distributed as follows

- About 43 per cent plain land area support agriculture and industry activities.
- About 27 per cent of the plateau region which is the source of minerals, fossil fuels and forests.
- Mountains cover 30 per cent area which provide perennial river water and sites for tourism and ecological aspects.

1 Cold Desert It refers to a snow covered place in higher latitudes (temperate or polar) and higher altitudes (mountain tops etc) which are characterised with scanty annual precipitation and very little vegetation.

2 Colonisation It is the political practice of acquiring indigenous people's land of a country and exploit them.

3 Brundtland Commission It was formally known as World Commission on Environment and Development (WCED) constituted to look into the matter of sustainable development by UN. Gro Harlem Brundtland was its first Chairman.

Land Utilisation

In India, land resources are used for the following purpose

(i) Forests

(ii) Land not available for cultivation
  (a) Barren and waste land
  (b) Land put to non-agricultural uses, e.g., buildings, roads, factories, etc.

(iii) Other uncultivated land (excluding fallow land)
  (a) Permanent pastures and grazing land
  (b) Land under miscellaneous tree crops and groves (not included in net sown area)
  (c) Culturable waste land (left uncultivated for more than 5 agricultural years)

(iv) Fallow lands
  (a) **Current fallow** Land left uncultivated for one or less than one agricultural year.
  (b) **Other than Current Fallow** Land not cultivated for the past 1 to 5 agricultural years.

(v) **Net Sown Area** The physical extent of land on which crops are harvested.
Gross Cropped Area The area sown more than once in an agricultural year plus the net sown area.

Land Use Pattern in India

The total geographical area of India is 3.28 million sq km but the land use data is available only for 93 per cent of total area. It is because land use reporting of North-Eastern states except Assam and some part of Jammu and Kashmir occupied by Pakistan and China has not been surveyed.

The use of land is determined by the following factors

(i) **Physical Factors** These include climate, soil type, topography, etc.

(ii) **Human Factors** These include population density, cultural, traditions, technological capability, etc.

Some facts related to land use pattern in India are as follows

- As per the National Forest Policy[4] of 1952, area under forests is far less than 33 per cent, which is necessary for maintenance of the ecological balance.
- The land under permanent pastures has decreased.
- Most of the other than current fallow land are of poor quality or cost of cultivation of such land is very high. These lands are cultivated once or twice in about two to three years. If these are included in the net sown area, then NSA becomes 54 per cent.
- The pattern of **Net Sown Area** varies widely between different states. It is over 80 per cent in Punjab and Haryana due to intensive agricultural facilities. It is less than 10 per cent in Arunachal Pradesh, Manipur, Mizoram and Andaman and Nicobar Islands.

Some land is considered as 'waste land,' like rocky, arid, or desert areas and the land that are used for non-agricultural purposes like – settlements, roads, railways, industry, etc.

Land Degradation

The continuous use of land over a long period of time without conserving and managing it, has resulted in land degradation.

95% of basic needs like food, shelter and clothing are obtained from land. However, human activities have degraded lands and also increased the rate of damage to lands caused by natural forces.

Some of the causes of land degradation are as follows

- Deforestation, overgrazing and expansion of mining and quarrying operations. For example, deforestation due to mining in states like Jharkhand, Chhattisgarh, Madhya Pradesh and Odisha. Overgrazing is the main reason for land degradation in states like Gujarat, Rajasthan, Madhya Pradesh and Maharashtra.
- Over irrigation in the states of Punjab, Haryana and Western Uttar Pradesh, which led to water logging leading increase in salinity and alkalinity in the soil.
- Mineral processing, e.g. grinding of limestone for cement industry and calcite and soapstone for ceramic industry generate large amounts of dust in the atmosphere. When this dust is settled down on the land, it slowdown water infiltration into the soil.
- Industrial effluents are major source of land and water pollution in many parts of the country.

Conservation Measures

- Afforestation and proper management of grazing lands.
- Discharge and disposal of industrial wastes after treatment.
- Control over mining activities.
- Planting of shelter belts[5] of trees.
- Control on overgrazing.
- Stabilisation of sand dunes by growing thorny bushes in arid areas.
- Proper management of waste lands.

---

4 National Forest Policy It is a policy implemented by the Indian Government for preservation, development and sustainable use of forest resource.

5 Shelter Belts It refers to planting rows of trees to prevent soil erosion.

Try These

1. What percentage of land in India is put for agricultural uses?
2. 33% area should be under forest cover to maintain ecological balance. This statement is given in which policy?
3. Name two states where land degradation is caused by overgrazing.
4. What is the best way of land conservation in the arid areas?

1.3 Soil as a Resource

Soil is the most important renewable natural resource. It takes millions of years to form soil upto a few centimeters in depth. Soil is a living system and supports different types of living organisms. The important factors in the soil formation are relief, parent rock or bed rock, climate, vegetation and forms of life and time. Forces of nature such as change in temperature, actions of running water, wind and glaciers, activities of decomposers, etc. also contribute to soil formation. Soil consists of both **inorganic** and **organic materials** (i.e. humus).

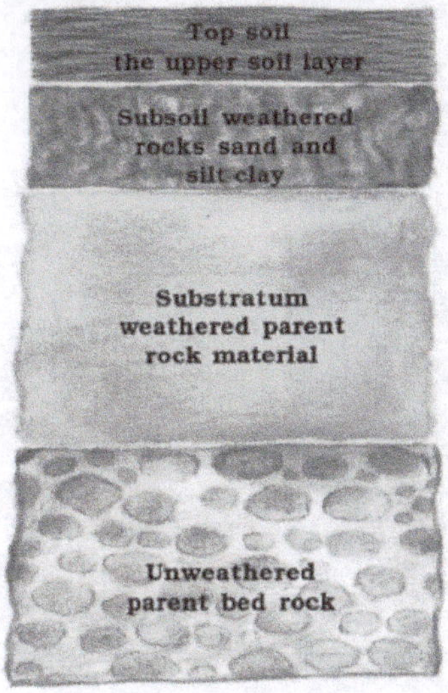

• Soil Profile

Classification of Soils

Soils in India are classified on the basis of chemical and physical properties like colour, thickness, texture, age, etc. Different type of soils are as follows

Alluvial Soils

It is the most widespread and important soil in India, which has been deposited by three important Himalayan river systems i.e. the **Indus**, the **Ganges** and the **Brahmaputra**.

The regions of alluvial soil are intensively cultivated and densely populated due to its high fertility.

Some features of alluvial soil are given below

- It is made up of sand, silt and clay and contains adequate proportion of potash, phosphoric acid and lime.
- The particles of this soil is bigger towards the river valleys and this soil is coarse in upper reaches of valley.
- On the basis of age, it can be categorised as **Bangar** (old alluvial) and **Khadar** (new alluvial). Bangar soil has high concentration of kankar nodules, but Khadar soil has fine particles and is more fertile.
- It is suitable for growing paddy, wheat, sugarcane and other cereal and pulse crops.
- Alluvial soil in the drier areas is more alkaline and need proper treatment and irrigation to be productive.
- It is more common in the **piedmont plains**[6] that are at the foothills such as **Duars, Chos** and **Terai.**
- It is mostly found in river valleys of the **Northern Plains** (Indus, Ganga, Brahmaputra), parts of Gujarat and Rajasthan and in Eastern coastal plains, especially in the deltas of Peninsular rivers (Mahanadi, Godavari, Krishna, Kaveri).

Black Soils

It is also known as **black cotton soil** or **regur soil**. The factors that are important for the formation of black soil are climatic condition along with parent rock material.

Some features of black soil are given below

- It is found in the **Deccan trap**[7] (Basalt) region and is made up of **lava flows.**
- It is made up of extremely fine i.e. clayey material and suitable for growing cotton.
- It is rich in nutrients like calcium carbonate, magnesium carbonate, potash and lime, but is poor in phosphoric content.
- It develops deep cracks during the hot summer, which helps in **aeration**[8] of the soil. It becomes sticky (due to their capacity to hold moisture retention) when wet and becomes difficult to be tilled.
- It covers the plateau areas of Saurashtra, Maharashtra, Malwa, Madhya Pradesh, Chhattisgarh and also lies along the valleys of the Godavari and Krishna rivers.

6 **Piedmont Plains** It is a flat or gently sloping area at the base of mountain, formed by the soil and debris carried by rivers and streams.
7 **Deccan Trap** It is a large igneous area located on the deccan plateau of West central India. It contains black soil.
8 **Aeration** It is the process by which air is circulated through, mixed with or dissolved in a liquid or substance.

Red and Yellow Soils

Red soil develops in low rainfall areas of the Deccan plateau (Eastern and Southern parts).

It is **red in colour** due to diffusion of iron particles in **crystalline** and metamorphic rocks[9]. It turns **yellow** when it occurs in a hydrated form.

Red and yellow soils are found in parts of Odisha, Chhattisgarh, Southern parts of Middle Ganga Plain and along the piedmont zone of the Western Ghats.

Laterite Soil

The word laterite has been derived from the Latin word **later** which means **brick.** Laterite soil develops in tropical and sub-tropical climate with alternative wet and dry season.

Some features of laterite soil are given below

- It is formed in areas of heavy rainfall resulting in intense leaching[10].
- It supports deciduous, evergeen forests as it is rich in humus. However, at some places it is poor in humus due to semi-arid environment and sparse vegetation.
- It is prone to erosion and degradation due to its position on the landscape.
- It is more acidic with pH < 6.0 and deficient in plant nutrients.
- It is found mostly in Southern states, Western Ghats region of Maharashtra, Odisha, some parts of West Bengal and North-East regions.
- In hilly areas of Karnataka, Kerala and Tamil Nadu, tea and coffee is grown in this soil, after adopting appropriate soil conservation techniques.
- Red laterite soil is found in Kerala, Tamil Nadu and Andhra Pradesh and it is suitable for growing cashew nuts.

Arid Soil

It is found in dry areas. In some areas, the salt content is very high and common salt is obtained by evaporating of water.

Some features of arid soil are given below

- It ranges from red to brown in colour, sandy in texture and saline in nature.
- It lacks **humus** and **moisture** due to dry climate, high temperature and faster rate of evaporation.
- **Kankar** are found in the lower horizons of this soil. It is due to increasing calcium content downwards, which restrict the infiltration of water.
- It can be useful for cultivation only with suitable irrigation methods as in case of Western Rajasthan.

Forest Soil

It is found in hilly and mountainous areas where sufficient rain forests are available.

Some features of forest or mountain soils are given below

- It varies in texture from **loamy** and **silty** in valley sides to coarse grained in the upper slopes.
- In the snow covered area of Himalayas , it is acidic with low humus content due to denudation[11].
- It is fertile in lower parts of valleys particularly on the river terraces and **alluvial fans**.

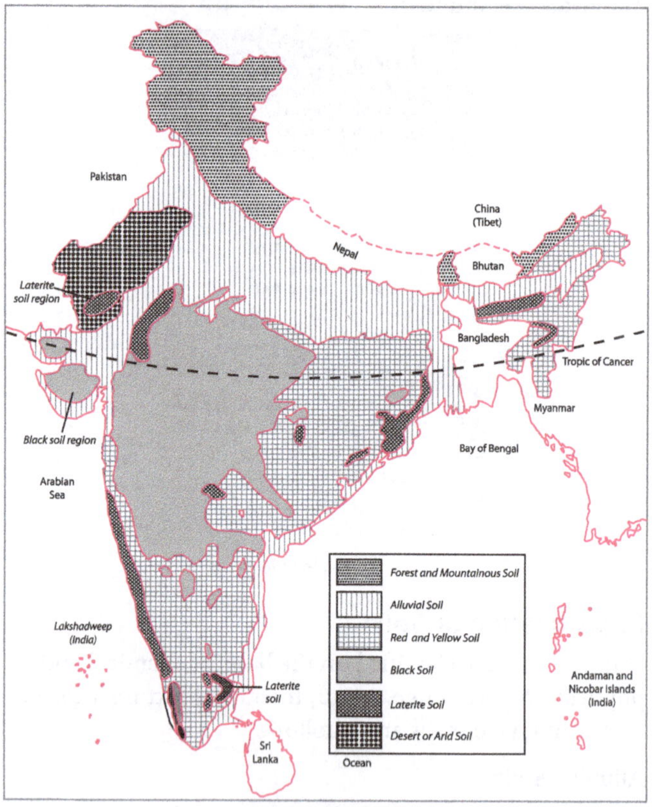

• India : Major Soil Types

9 Metamorphic rocks Rocks formed from the change in physical and chemical characteristics of existing rocks.

10 Leaching It refers to process of draining away of the plant nutrients from the soil due to excess rainfall.

11 Denudation It refers to geological process in which moving water, ice, wind and waves erodes the Earth's surface.

Soil Erosion

Soil erosion is the removing of the soil cover and later washing down of top soil.

The process of soil formation and erosion go on simultaneously and generally there is a balance between the two process. However, this balance is disturbed due to natural and human cases.

Natural causes included natural forces like wind, glacier and water. **Human causes** include human activities like deforestation, overgrazing, construction and mining.

Types of Soil Erosion

- **Gully Erosion** Running water creates deep channels in clayey soils, forming gullies which makes land unfit for cultivation and is known as **bad land**. In the Chambal basin, these gullies are known as **ravines**.
- **Sheet Erosion** When water flows as a sheet over large areas down a slope and washed away the top soil, it is known as sheet erosion.
- **Wind Erosion** When wind blows the loose soil from flat or sloping land, it is known as wind erosion.
- **Defective Farming Methods** Soil erosion is also caused by defective farming method. For example, ploughing in wrong way i.e. up and down slopes, can lead to channel formation and quick water flow, causing soil erosion.

Soil Conservation

- **Contour Ploughing** It involves ploughing along contour lines to slow down water flow on slopes.
- **Terrace Cultivation** In this method, steps are cut on slopes to make terraces which helps restrict soil erosion. Well-developed terrace farming is observed in the Western and Central Himalayas.
- **Strip Cropping** In this method, large fields can be divided into strips. The strips of grass are left to grow between the crops. This breaks the force of wind.
- **Shelter Belts** In this method, a line of trees is planted to create shelter along the edge of fields. This prevents the spread of sand dunes and stabilises the desert areas of Western India.

Try These

1. **Tea and coffee grown well in this soil after proper soil conservation, as it is more acidic in nature. Identify the soil type.**
2. **What restricts the infiltration of water in desert soil due to deposition of calcium content?**
3. **Name methods of preventing soil erosion by wind.**
4. **Which method can prevent soil erosion in non-slope areas or plains?**

Mind Map

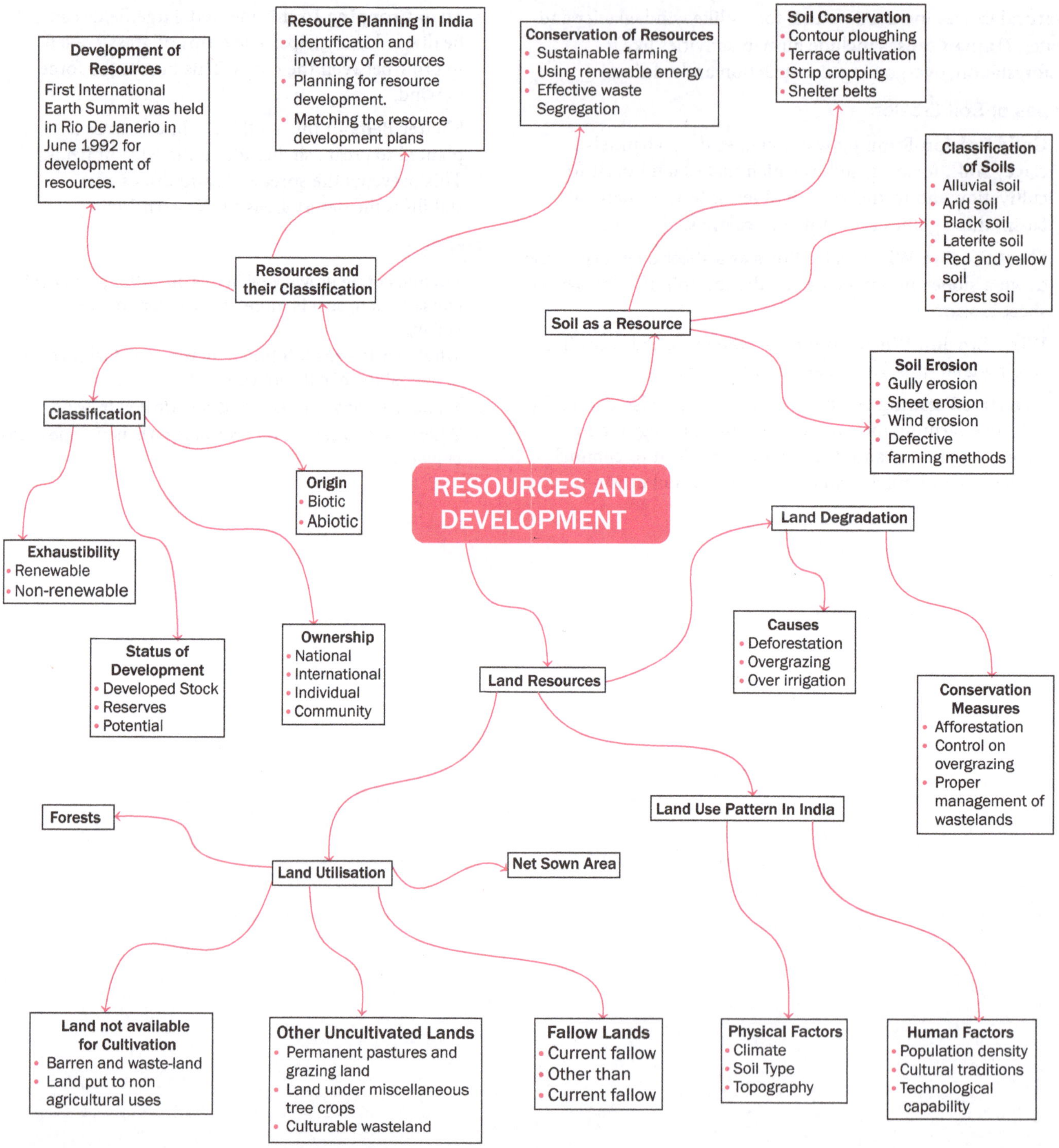
RESOURCES AND DEVELOPMENT
Resources and their Classification
Development of Resources
First International Earth Summit was held in Rio De Janerio in June 1992 for development of resources.
Resource Planning in India
• Identification and inventory of resources
• Planning for resource development.
• Matching the resource development plans
Conservation of Resources
• Sustainable farming
• Using renewable energy
• Effective waste Segregation
Classification
Origin
• Biotic
• Abiotic
Exhaustibility
• Renewable
• Non-renewable
Status of Development
• Developed Stock
• Reserves
• Potential
Ownership
• National
• International
• Individual
• Community
Soil as a Resource
Soil Conservation
• Contour ploughing
• Terrace cultivation
• Strip cropping
• Shelter belts
Classification of Soils
• Alluvial soil
• Arid soil
• Black soil
• Laterite soil
• Red and yellow soil
• Forest soil
Soil Erosion
• Gully erosion
• Sheet erosion
• Wind erosion
• Defective farming methods
Land Resources
Land Degradation
Causes
• Deforestation
• Overgrazing
• Over irrigation
Conservation Measures
• Afforestation
• Control on overgrazing
• Proper management of wastelands
Land Use Pattern In India
Physical Factors
• Climate
• Soil Type
• Topography
Human Factors
• Population density
• Cultural traditions
• Technological capability
Land Utilisation
Forests
Net Sown Area
Land not available for Cultivation
• Barren and waste-land
• Land put to non agricultural uses
Other Uncultivated Lands
• Permanent pastures and grazing land
• Land under miscellaneous tree crops
• Culturable wasteland
Fallow Lands
• Current fallow
• Other than
• Current fallow

NCERT FOLDER

Covering Intext Questions and Exercises of NCERT

INTEXT QUESTIONS

Q.1 Can you identify and name the various items used in making life comfortable in our villages and towns? List the items and name the material used in their making.

Ans. Various items that contribute to the comfort of life in villages and towns include furniture (wood, metal), clothing (cotton, silk, wool), utensils (steel, copper, aluminium), housing materials (brick, wood, concrete), transportation vehicles (steel, rubber), and electronic devices (plastic, metal). These items help create a comfortable and functional living environment in both towns and villages.

Q.2 Prepare a list of stock and reserve, resources that you are familiar with from your local area.

Ans. In my local area, we have various stock and reserve resources. The stock resources include fertile agricultural land used for cultivation, freshwater from nearby rivers and minerals like limestone. Additionally, the reserve resources consist of dense forests that serve as a habitat for diverse flora and fauna, ensuring environmental balance and supporting local biodiversity.

Q.3 Imagine, if the oil supply gets exhausted one day, how would this affect our life style?

Ans. If the oil supply gets exhausted, our lifestyle would undergo significant changes as follows

- Transportation, heavily reliant on fossil fuels, would be disrupted, impacting daily commuting.
- Industries, agriculture and electricity generation would be affected, leading to shortages.
- Everyday products, from plastics to electronics, may become scarce.
- Transitioning to alternative energy sources and sustainable practices would become imperative for a balanced and resilient lifestyle.

Q.4 What resources are being developed in your surroundings by the community/village panchayats/ward level communities with the help of community participation?

Ans. In most parts of India, community/village panchayats or ward-level communities actively participate in developing resources like community parks, waste management systems and local sanitation initiatives. These efforts involve planting trees, organizing cleanliness drives and creating awareness campaigns. By fostering community participation, these initiatives contribute to the overall well-being and cleanliness of the neighborhood, enhancing the quality of life for residents.

Q.5 Find out reasons for the low proportion of net sown area in these states (Arunachal Pradesh, Mizoram and Manipur and Andaman and Nicobar Islands).

Ans. The low proportion of net sown area in states like Arunachal Pradesh, Mizoram, Manipur and Andaman and Nicobar Islands can be attributed to factors such as hilly terrain, dense forests, and the presence of large uncultivable areas. These states may face geographical constraints, making a significant portion of the land unsuitable for agriculture, limiting the extent of net sown area.

EXERCISE

Q.1 Multiple Choice Questions

(i) Which one of the following is the main cause of land degradation in Punjab?

(a) Intensive cultivation (b) Deforestation
(c) Over irrigation (d) Overgrazing

(ii) In which one of the following states is terrace cultivation practiced?

(a) Punjab (b) Plains of Uttar Pradesh
(c) Haryana (d) Uttarakhand

(iii) In which of the following states black soil is predominantly found?

(a) Jammu and Kashmir (b) Maharashtra
(c) Rajasthan (d) Jharkhand

Ans. (i) (c) (ii) (d) (iii) (b)

Q.2 Answer the following questions in about 30 words.

(i) Name three states having black soil and the crop which is mainly grown in it. CBSE 2014

(ii) What type of soil is found in the river deltas of the Eastern coast? Give three main features of this type of soil.

(iii) What steps can be taken to control soil erosion in the hilly areas? CBSE 2015

Ans. (i) The three states having black soil are Madhya Pradesh, Chhattisgarh and Maharashtra. Cotton crops is mainly grown in black soil.

(ii) Alluvial soil is found in the river deltas of the Eastern coast. Three main features of this type of soil are
   (a) It is very fertile.
   (b) It contains adequate proportion of potash, phosphoric acid and lime.
   (c) It is more alkaline in the drier areas.

(iii) Following steps can be taken to control soil erosion in the hilly areas
   (a) **Afforestation** This is done by planting trees.
   (b) **Terrace farming** In this methods, steps are cut on slopes to make terraces which help restrict soil erosion.
   (c) **Contour ploughing** In this method, ploughing is done along contour lines to slow down water flow on slopes.

Q.3 Answer the following questions in about 120 words.

(i) Explain land use pattern in India and why has the land under forest not increased much since 1960-61?

(ii) How have technical and economic development led to more consumption of resources?

Ans. (i) Land resources in India are primarily divided into agricultural land, forest land, land meant for pasture and grazing, land for other non-agricultural use (such as housing, roads and industry) and waste land (rocky, arid and desert areas).

According to recent data available (2014-15), the percentage of Net Sown Area (NSA) in India is about 45.5% of the total reporting area 23.3% is covered by forests and 3.38% is used for grazing. The rest is waste land with traces of miscellaneous cultivation.

Land under forest has increased by only about 5 per cent since 1960-61 due to following reasons

- Improper use of forest land has degraded the available land area and made conservation of forests difficult.
- Human activities such as deforestation, mining and quarrying have contributed to the slow growth rate of forests.

(ii) The technical and economic development have led to more consumption of resources in the following ways

- Technological development has led to industrialisation which has increased the use of natural resources.
- Technological development has shifted the subsistence agriculture to commercial agriculture and this has led to the over-utilisation of soil.
- Technological development has also improved the process of mining, which cause more extraction of minerals.
- Economic development has led to increasing urbanisation and modernisation which demand more resources.

REVIEW EXERCISE

Including Competency Based Questions

Part I

Multiple Choice Questions (MCQs)

1. Which of the following is essential for sustainable existence of all forms of life?

(a) Resource planning (b) Resource modification
(c) Resource extraction (d) Resource generation

2. Area sown more than once in an agricultural year plus net sown area is known as

(a) Fallow lands (b) Gross cropped area
(c) Cropped area (d) Grazing land

3. In which one of the following states is overgrazing the main reason for land degradation? CBSE Term I 2021

(a) Maharashtra
(b) Punjab
(c) Haryana
(d) Uttar Pradesh

4. Identify the soil which ranges from red to brown in colour and saline in nature. CBSE Term I 2021

(a) Red soil (b) Laterite soil
(c) Arid soil (d) Alluvial soil

5. Which of the following is not an important factor in the formation of soil?

(a) Running water
(b) Chemical reactions
(c) Atmospheric pressure
(d) Change in temperature

6. Deforestation due to mining has caused severe land degradation in which one of the following states? CBSE Term I 2021

(a) Odisha (b) Tamil Nadu
(c) Kerala (d) Gujarat

7. Which among the following is not a problem of resource development? CBSE Term I 2021

(a) Depletion of resources for satisfying the greed of few individuals.
(b) Accumulation of resources in few hands.
(c) Indiscriminate exploitation of resources.
(d) An equitable distribution of resources.

8. Mention the main reason for land degradation in states like Jharkhand, Chhattisgarh and Odisha. CBSE 2023

(a) Over-grazing (b) Mining
(c) Over irrigation (d) Mineral processing

9. The piece of land left uncultivated for the past 1 to 5 agricultural years is called .... CBSE SQP Term I 2021

(a) Barren land (b) Forest land
(c) Grazing land (d) Fallow land

10. Historically, colonising countries took advantage of India's rich resources to gain supremacy.

Why was India not able to resist the exploitation of its resources?

(a) Due to lack of use for products derived from natural resources.
(b) Due to the colonising countries superior technology.
(c) Due to lack of awareness about India's resources.
(d) Due to over-utilisation of resources.

11. 'Raman, a resident from Himachal Pradesh regularly takes his 25 cows for grazing. Apart from him, other villagers also take their cows for the same place'.

Which of the following will most likely lead to in the above place in near future? Competency Based

(a) Increase in the fertility of the soil
(b) Lowering of the level of groundwater
(c) Degradation of the land
(d) Earthquake

12. "There has been massive soil erosion in the Western Ghats region over the last 30 years which is likely to accelerate future disasters, warns a new study led by researchers from the Indian Institute of Technology (IIT), Bombay. Of all states covered by the mountain range, Tamil Nadu has shown the highest rate of soil loss followed by Gujarat and Maharashtra."

Source : News 18

Gully erosion of soils happens due to which of the following environmental agents? Competency Based

(a) Wind (b) Snow
(c) Water (d) Insects

13. 'An X cement industry grinds limestone and a ceramic industry named T processes calcite and limestone.'

Which of the following will likely be caused by huge dust generated by these industries? Competency Based

(a) The dust will cover almost all buildings of the city.
(b) The dust will drastically damage the crops.
(c) The dust will cause pneumonia and silicosis to around 85% of the population.
(d) The dust will settle down on land and retard the process of infiltration of water into the soil.

14. "An equitable distribution of resources gas become essential for a sustained quality of life and global peace. If the present trend of resource depletion by a few individuals and countries continues, the future of our planet is in danger."

Accordingly, which of the following quotes best reflects the essence of the above statement? Competency Based

(a) "If conservation of natural resources goes wrong, nothing else will go right."
(b) "There is enough for everybody's need and not for anybody's greed."
(c) "You must be the change you wish to see in the world."
(d) "The best way to find yourself is to lose yourself in the service of others."

15. 'Most of the alluvial soil found in India is formed from the silt deposited by the Indo-Gangetic-Brahmaputra rivers.'

Which of the following regions contains the parent rock that forms this silt?

(a) Himalayas (b) Northern plains
(c) Gangetic delta (d) Eastern coastal plains

16. Which of the following actions should be taken by the government to reduce land degradation?

(a) Setting up three new quarries for the mining of limestone near the capital city.
(b) Granting permissions for cement factories near farmlands.
(c) Converting forest areas to greenhouse horticulture.
(d) Creating separate grazing zones for livestock.

17. Why do you think that resources are essential ?

(a) Because it allows humans to fullfill its ambitions and makes them dominant among other life forms on Earth.
(b) Because resources are vital for human survival as well as for maintaining quality of life.
(c) Because resources are mandatory for the growth and success of human beings.
(d) Because resources make Earth a beautiful place for living and provides a delightful ambience for human beings.

18. The inequitable distribution of access to resources has disrupted world peace by dividing society into

(a) The owners and tenants
(b) The environmentalists and the exploiters
(c) Resource-rich regions and resource-poor regions
(d) The climate change believers and climate change deniers

19. Resource planning is a widely accepted strategy for the judicious use of resources that is essential for sustainable existence.

Which of the following examples does not represents resource planning?

(a) Surveying, mapping, qualitative and quantitative estimation and measurement of the resources by the government.
(b) Evolving a planning structure endowed with appropriate technology, skill and institutional set-up for implementing resource development plans by the national government.
(c) Providing excessive resources of all kinds to every individual of a country by the government.
(d) Matching the resource development plans with overall national development plans by the government.

20. Satyaprakash is a 32 years old farmer from a village in Western Rajasthan. His land has arid soil due to which the kankar layer formations in the bottom horizons restrict the infiltration of water.

Accordingly, which of the following actions would be the most crucial to make his land cultivable? **Competency Based**

(a) Increasing the calcium carbonate content of the soil.
(b) Providing proper irrigation to the soil.
(c) Increased tillage on the land.
(d) Growing leguminous crops on the land.

21. Arrange the following in the correct sequence.

(i) Brundtland Commission Report
(ii) National Forest Policy of India
(iii) Resource Conservation at the Club of Rome
(iv) Rio De Janeiro Earth Summit

Codes

(a) III, I, II, IV
(b) I, IV, II, III
(c) IV, II, I, III
(d) II, III, I, IV

22. A farmer named Z is planning to do farming on a land that has slope. He choses to apply contour ploughing as **Competency Based**

I. Ploughing along the contour lines can decelerate the flow of water.
II. Contour ploughing helps to restrict soil erosion.
III. Contour ploughing increases the fertility of land by around 50 per cent.
IV. Contour ploughing is easy as compared to other methods.

Codes

(a) Only I (b) I and II
(c) I and III (d) II and IV

23. Which of the following statements accurately describes 'Khadar'?

I. It is one of the classification of alluvial soil.
II. Khadar is the old alluvial.
III. Khadar soil has less kanker nodules than the bangar.
IV. Khadar is less fertile than bangar.

Codes

(a) I and II (b) I, II and III
(c) I and III (d) I , II , III and IV

24. 'M gave his friend clues about a type of soil that suits for growing cotton'. Which of the following clues provided by 'M' would be most useful in identifying the ideal type of soil? **Competency Based**

I. It is well-known for its capacity to hold moisture.
II. It turns yellow when it is hydrated.
III. It is rich in kankar and bhangar nodules.
IV. It is a well-drained loamy soil.

Codes

(a) Only I (c) I and II (b) I and III (d) Only IV

25. Consider the statements given below and choose the correct option.

Statement I Planting rows of big trees in large fields is known as strip farming.

Statement II The shelter belts have contributed significantly to the stabilisation of sand dunes and in stabilising the desert in Western India.

Codes

(a) Statement I is correct and statement II is incorrect
(b) Statement I is incorrect and statement II is correct
(c) Both statements I and II are incorrect
(d) Both statements I and II are correct

26. Identify the reasons as to why the Rio de Janeiro Earth Summit was organised. Choose from the appropriate statements among the following options.

I. To address the urgent problems of environmental protection at the global level.
II. To address the financial problems that needs actions at the international level.
III. To address the urgent issues of socio-economic development at the global level.
IV. To warn the industrialised nations about the indiscriminate pollution caused by them.

Codes

(a) Statements I and II are appropriate
(b) Statements I, II and III are appropriate
(c) All the statements except the statement IV are appropriate
(d) Statements I and III are appropriate

Answers

1. (a)	2. (b)	3. (a)	4. (c)	5. (a)
6. (a)	7. (d)	8. (d)	9. (d)	10. (b)
11. (c)	12. (c)	13. (d)	14. (b)	15. (a)
16. (d)	17. (b)	18. (c)	19. (c)	20. (b)
21. (d)	22. (b)	23. (c)	24. (a)	25. (b)
26. (d)				

Match the Following

1

	List I		List II
A.	Laterite soil	1.	High moisture retention
B.	Black soil	2.	Intensively cultivated
C.	Alluvial soil	3.	Source of salt
D.	Arid soil	4.	Problem of leaching

Codes

	A	B	C	D		A	B	C	D
(a)	1	1	2	3	(b)	2	1	3	4
(c)	4	1	2	3	(d)	1	4	3	2

Ans. (c)

Assertion-Reason

1. Assertion (A) The lower horizon of the arid soil is occupied by kankar.

Reason (R) It is because of the increasing calcium content downwards in arid soil.

Codes

(a) Both A and R are true but R is not the correct explanation of A
(b) Both A and R are true and R is the correct explanation of A
(c) Both A and R are incorrect
(d) A is correct but R is incorrect

2. Assertion (A) Soil formation and erosion go hand in hand but sometimes this balance is disrupted by human activities.

Reason (R) The formation of soil takes millions of years while soil erosion takes much less time.

Codes

(a) Both A and R are true but R is not the correct explanation of A
(b) Both A and R are true and R is the correct explanation of A
(c) Both A and R are incorrect
(d) A is correct but R is incorrect

3. Assertion (A) The availability of resources is not the only necessary condition for the development of any region.

Reason (R) Not only availability of resources but corresponding change in technology is also necessary for development of any region.

Codes

(a) Both A and R are true but R is not the correct explanation of A
(b) Both A and R are true and R is the correct explanation of A
(c) Both A and R are incorrect
(d) A is correct but R is incorrect

4. Assertion (A) Resource planning is a complex process in India.

Reason (R) Resource planning involves planning structure, identification and inventory of resource across the regions.

Codes

(a) Both A and R are true but R is not the correct explanation of A
(b) Both A and R are true and R is the correct explanation of A
(c) Both A and R are incorrect
(d) A is correct but R is incorrect

5. Assertion (A) Arid soil is unsuitable for cultivation.

Reason (R) Arid soil is generally sandy in texture and saline in nature. The Kankar layer in the bottom restricts the infiltration of water.

Codes

(a) Both A and R are true but R is not the correct explanation of A
(b) Both A and R are true and R is the correct explanation of A
(c) Both A and R are incorrect
(d) A is correct but R is incorrect

6. Assertion (A) Controlling on mining activities controls land degradation.

Reason (R) In states like Gujarat, Rajasthan, Madhya Pradesh, deforestation has occurred due to overgrazing and minings.

Codes

(a) Both A and R are true but R is not the correct explanation of A.
(b) Both A and R are true and R is the correct explanation of A
(c) Both A and R are incorrect
(d) A is correct but R is incorrect.

7. Assertion (A) Running water cuts through the clayey soils and makes deep channels as gullies. This restricts the cultivation of crops.

Reason (R) Terrace cultivation does not restrict erosion.

Codes

(a) Both A and R are true but R is not the correct explanation of A
(b) Both A and R are true and R is the correct explanation of A
(c) Both A and R are incorrect
(d) A is correct but R is incorrect

Ans. 1. (b) Both A and R are true and R is the correct explanation of A
2. (b) Both A and R are true and R is the correct explanation of A
3. (a) Both A and R are true but R is not the correct explanation of A
4. (b) Both A and R are true and R is the correct explanation of A
5. (b) Both A and R are true and R is the correct explanation of A
6. (d) A is correct but R is incorrect.
7. (d) A is correct but R is incorrect

Picture Based Question

1. Which type of erosion is depicted in the picture given below?

(a) Sheet erosion (b) Glacial erosion
(c) Gully erosion (d) Wind erosion

Ans. (c) Gully erosion

Case Based Question

1. Read the source given below and answer the questions that follow.

At the international level, the Club of Rome advocated resource conservation for the first time in a more systematic way in 1968. Subsequently, in 1974, Gandhian philosophy was once again presented by Schumacher in his book 'Small is Beautiful'. The seminal contribution with respect to resource conservation at the global level was made by the Brundtland Commission Report, 1987. This report introduced the concept of 'Sustainable Development' and advocated it as a means for resource conservation, which was subsequently published in a book entitled 'Our Common Future'. Another significant contribution was made at the Earth Summit at Rio de Janeiro, Brazil in 1992.

(i) Which of the following initiatives talked about resource conservation?
(a) Brundtland Commission Report
(b) UNEP Report
(c) Club of Rome
(d) Both (a) and (c)

(ii) Which of the following statements correctly describes Mahatma Gandhi's view on resource conservation?
(a) Greedy and selfless individuals are cause of resource depletion.
(b) He was in favour of mass production.
(c) The exploitative nature of modern technology is the root cause for resource depletion at the global level.
(d) He was against production by masses.

(iii) The sustainable development concept as put forward by the Brundtland Commission means
(a) Less economic development and more moral development.
(b) Development in present should not compromise with the needs of the future generations.
(c) Both economic development and environmental development to the level of threshold limit of the earth.
(d) The development which is in sync with the carrying capacity of the environment.

(iv) Which of the following initiatives was adopted during Rio de Janeiro Summit in 1992?
(a) Agenda 21
(b) Declaration on global climate change and biological diversity
(c) Both (a) and (b)
(d) None of the above

Ans. (i) (d) Both (a) and (c)
(ii) (c) The exploitative nature of modern technology is the root cause for resource depletion at the global level.
(iii) (c) Both economic development and environmental development to the level of threshold limit of the earth.
(iv) (c) Both (a) and (b)

Part II

Very Short Answer Type Questions

1. The development of resources depend on which two factors?

Ans. The development of resources depends on technology and quality of human resource.

2. State any one reason for overuse of resources. CBSE 2015

Ans. Rapid increase in population is the reason for overuse of resources.

3. Define sustainable development.

Ans. Sustainable development is defined as the development should take place without damaging the environment and development in the present should not compromise with the needs of the future generations.

4. Suggest any two ways for the conservation of resources. **CBSE 2024**

Ans. Two ways for the conservation of resources are

(i) Judicious use of limited energy resources

(ii) Use of public transport

5. In which Five Year Plan, resource planning was introduced in India?

Ans. Resource planning was introduced in the First Five Year Plan in India after independence.

6. Why only 93 per cent of the total geographical area is measured for land use pattern in India?

Ans. Only 93% of the total geographical area is measured for land use pattern in India because most of the North-East states except Assam is inaccessible and some parts of Jammu and Kashmir is occupied by Pakistan and China, that accounts to about 7 per cent of the total area.

7. How are mining activities responsible for land degradation in Jharkhand? **CBSE 2019**

Ans. Jharkhand is a mineral rich state where mining activities are done at large scale. When excavation work is completed, the mining sites represent deep scars and evidences of over burdening which lead to land degradation.

8. How is overgrazing responsible for land degradation in Gujarat?

Ans. Gujarat is one of the fastest growing states in India and has a large number of livestock. Thus, overgrazing by this large livestock leads to land degradation.

9. Why soil in some parts is red and yellow in colour?

Ans. The soil that develops on crystalline and metamorphic rocks have iron diffused in it, which makes the soil red. It turns yellow when the diffusion of iron occurs in hydrated form.

10. Which type of soil is most suitable for growing the crop of cashew nut? **CBSE 2019**

Ans. Red laterite soil is most suitable for growing the crop of cashew nuts.

11. Which soil is well-known for its capacity to hold moisture?

Ans. Black soil or regur soil in deccan plateau in India is well-known for its capacity to hold moisture.

12. Which type of soil is found in the piedmont zone of Western Ghats?

Ans. Red and yellow soil is found in the piedmont zone/ foothill of Western Ghats.

13. Which type of soil in India is most widespread and important? **CBSE 2019**

Ans. Alluvial soil is the most wide spread and important soil in India. The entire Northern plains are made of alluvial soil.

14. How is over irrigation responsible for land degradation in Punjab? **CBSE 2019**

Ans. Over irrigation is responsible for land degradation in Punjab, which led to water logging leading to increases the salinity and alkalinity in the soil.

15. How is cement industry responsible for land degradation? **CBSE 2019**

Ans. Cement industry is responsible for land degradation. When grinding of limestone to make cement, is done, then this process generates huge quantity of dust in the atmosphere. After some times when this dust settles down on the land, this reduces the infiltration capacity of land and water does not reach to the soil. It ultimately leads land degradation.

16. Mr. Palani is from Tamil Nadu, wishes to cultivate either tea or wheat.

Which one of the crops out of the two can he cultivate in his state? Substantiate your answer with any two reasons. **Competency Based**

Ans. Mr. Palani can cultivate tea in his state Tamil Nadu. Tea is more suitable in his state than wheat due to the following reasons

(i) Laterite soil is found in Tamil Nadu which is very useful for growing tea, after adopting appropriate soil conservation techniques.

(ii) Laterite soil lacks nutrient due to leaching which is required by wheat crops.

17. 'Madhya Pradesh has nearly 18 lakh hectares of ravines with steep but shallow gullies. This area is mainly along the banks of the river Chambal and its tributaries.'

Source : India TV

Define the phenomenon responsible for the formation of ravines and gullies. **Competency Based**

Ans. The denudation of the soil cover and it's subsequent washing down is described as soil erosion. It is responsible for the formation of gullies and ravines.

18. Aaron gave his friends three clues about a type of soil.

- **It is found in Maharashtra, the largest producer of cotton in India.**
- **During summers, the soil exhibits self-aeration capacity.**
- **It is rich in nutrients.**

What soil is being referred to by Aaron? **Competency Based**

Ans. From the above descriptions, it is known that black soil is being referred to by Aaron as this type of soil is mainly found in Maharashtra.

Short Answer Type Questions

1. Explain the role of human beings in resource development. **CBSE 2011, 10**

Ans. Human beings are also a resource and are the dynamic factor in resource development. By technological advancement, humans have developed ways to make the natural resources more useful and economically beneficial.

For example, extracting metals from minerals and making different things from metals. Humans have added value to the natural resource. Thus, the interaction of humans with nature is essential to develop natural resources.

2. "Sustainability of development is a new area of knowledge". Do you agree? Justify your answer. **CBSE 2015**

Ans. No, we do not agree with the statement because sustainable development is not a new area of knowledge.

This had been the main concern of leaders, philosophers and thinkers in the past. Gandhiji was also very apt in voicing his concern about resource conservation.

However, the term 'sustainable development' is recently originated by the Brundtland Commission Report, 1987 for this purpose.

3. "India is rich in certain types of resources, but deficient in some other resources." Do you agree with the statement? Support your answer with examples.

Ans. Yes, I agree with the statement that in India, there are regions which are rich in certain types of resources, but some are deficient in other resources. There are some regions which can be considered self-sufficient in terms of the availability of resources, while some regions have acute shortage of vital resources.

Some examples are as follows

- States like Jharkhand, Chhattisgarh and Madhya Pradesh are rich in coal and minerals deposits.
- Arunachal Pradesh has abundant water resources, but lacks in infrastructure development.
- Rajasthan is well endowed with wind and solar energy, but lacks water resources.
- The cold desert of Ladakh lacks natural resources, although it has a rich cultural heritage.

4. What are the main advantages of India's land under a variety of relief features? **CBSE 2011**

Or **"India has land under a variety of relief features." Justify the statement with three examples.** **CBSE 2019**

Ans. India has land under a variety of relief features. 30 per cent of its area is covered by mountain, 27 per cent is covered by plateaus and 43 per cent is covered by plains, all of these have specific advantages to be utilised.

The main advantages of India's land with variety of relief features are

- Mountains are source to many streams and rivers, some of them are perennial. These regions have very high potential for hydro-electricity productions, etc and are also good tourism destinations.
- Plateaus are mostly laden (heavily loaded) with minerals, fossil fuels and forest, etc so they are economically very useful.
- Plains are most important land resource for human beings. These are fertile and most of the food crops, etc are grown here. They are also useful for the development of factories, roads, etc.

5. Why is resource planning essential? Give some examples which explain its need.

Or **Describe the importance of judicious use of resources.** **CBSE 2020**

Ans. Resource planning is essential as resources are limited and unevenly distributed over the country. Planning will help in reducing wastage as well as taking care of the requirements of future generations.
For example,

- An example of uneven distribution is Arunachal Pradesh, which has abundance of water resources, but lacks in infrastructural development to utilise the water resources.
- Irrational consumption and over utilisation of resources leads to socio-economic and environmental problems like in Punjab, water logging has increased salinity and alkalinity in the soil.

6. "Resource planning is a complex process." Justify the statement with arguments. **CBSE 2019**

Or **Explain the various stages of resource planning and its need in India.** **CBSE 2025**

Ans. It is true that resource planning is a complex process. It can be proved through the following arguments

(i) Resource planning involves identification and taking stock of the resources. It is very difficult to estimate the quantity and quality of each resource of a country.

(ii) Resource planning involves using appropriate technology and skill to utilise the resources.
It becomes difficult to match the available technology that can be used to utilise the resources fully.

(iii) Matching the resource development plans to the overall national development plans for the betterment of the country, its people and maintaining the environmental balance at the same time is a complex process.

7. What problems have been caused by human beings using resources indiscriminately? Explain in brief.

Or What are the negative effects of human activities on resources?

Or Explain any two problems of the global ecology arising due to indiscriminate use of resources. **CBSE 2025**

Ans. Human beings have used resources indiscriminately, leading to the following major problems

- Excessive use of resources have depleted their stock throughout the world.
- Resources have accumulated in a few hands, which in turn has divided the society into two segments i.e. 'haves' and 'have nots' or rich and poor.
- Exploitation of resources has led to the global ecological crisis e.g. global warming, ozone layer depletion, environmental pollution and land degradation.

8. Which is the main cause of land degradation in Gujarat, Rajasthan and Madhya Pradesh? How can it be checked? **CBSE 2012**

Or Explain any two measures to solve the problem of land degradation. **CBSE 2025**

Ans. Gujarat, Rajasthan and Madhya Pradesh are semi-arid regions with patches of vast grasslands. These states have large number of cattle population which are left open to graze on the grasslands. Large-scale overgrazing has caused severe land degradation in these states.

Different measures may be taken to check such problems as follows

- Afforestation and proper management of grazing lands.
- Control on overgrazing by limiting certain areas for grazing only.

9. Give three main features of the soil found in the river deltas of the Indian coast.

Or Describe any three main features of alluvial soil found in India. **CBSE 2019**

Ans. The three main features of the soil found in the river deltas of the Indian coast (alluvial soil) are

(i) It is more common in the piedmont plains or plains at the foothills such as Duars, Chos and Terai.

(ii) It is also known as transported soil, as the soil has been transported by the rivers to its current location.

(iii) It can also be described on the basis of age. The older alluvial soil, further away from the rivers is known as bangar, whereas the newer soil near the rivers is known as khadar.

10. Describe any three main features of black soil found in India. **CBSE 2019**

Or Discuss the nature and distribution of black soil in India.

Or Give the characteristics of the soil used for growing cotton. List the areas in India where this soil is found.

Or Write any three characteristics of black soil. **CBSE 2015, CBSE 2025**

Ans. The characteristics of black soil used for growing cotton are

(i) It is made up of fine clayey material with a high moisture retention capacity.

(ii) It is rich in soil nutrients like calcium carbonate, magnesium carbonate, potash and lime, but poor in phosphoric content.

(iii) It develops deep crack during hot weather which helping in proper aeration of the soil.

(iv) This is found in the plateau areas of Maharashtra, Gujarat, Madhya Pradesh and Chhattisgarh, as well as in the Godavari and Krishna valleys.

11. Describe any three main characteristics of arid soil of India. **CBSE 2010**

Ans. The three main characteristics of arid soil of India are

(i) It ranges from red to brown in colour, sandy in texture and saline in nature.

(ii) It lacks humus and moisture due to dry climate, high temperature and faster rate of evaporation.

(iii) Kankars are found in the lower horizon of this soil. It is due to increasing calcium content downwards, which restricts infiltration of water.

12. Mention any two human activities which are responsible for the process of soil erosion. Explain the two types of soil erosion mostly observed in India. **CBSE 2012**

Ans. Human activities responsible for soil erosion are deforestation, mining activities and excessive use of fertiliser.

The two types of soil erosion seen mostly in India are

(i) **Gully Erosion** Gullies cut the clayey soils into deep creeps and the land becomes unfit for cultivation and popularly known as bad lands.

(ii) **Sheet Erosion** It washes away top soils over large areas and productivity is mostly decreased.

13. Distinguish between red soil and laterite soil stating any three points of distinction.

Ans. The differences between red soil and laterite soil are as follows

Red Soil	Laterite Soil
Red soil develops on crystalline igneous rocks in areas of low rainfall.	Laterite soil develops in areas with high temperature and heavy rainfall.
It formed due to weathering.	It formed due to leaching
Red soil is found in parts of Odisha and Chhattisgarh, southern parts of the middle of Ganga plain and along the piedmont zone of the Western Ghats.	Laterite soil is mainly found in Karnataka, Kerala and the hilly areas of Odisha and Assam.

14. Give two reasons why the future generation may not have sufficient resources as compared to the present generations.

Ans. The future generation may not have sufficient resources as compared to the present generation due to the following reasons

(i) Human activities like deforestation, expansion of agriculture, mining, etc result in land degradation. This makes the land unfit for use in future.

(ii) Excessive use of fossil fuels like coal, petrol deplete the stock of resources. As these are limited in nature, they may not be left for the future generations.

15. Compare the diagrams given and find out land use category which had the highest increase during the period 1960-61 to 2014-15 and the category which had the highest decrease during the period. Give one major reason for each.

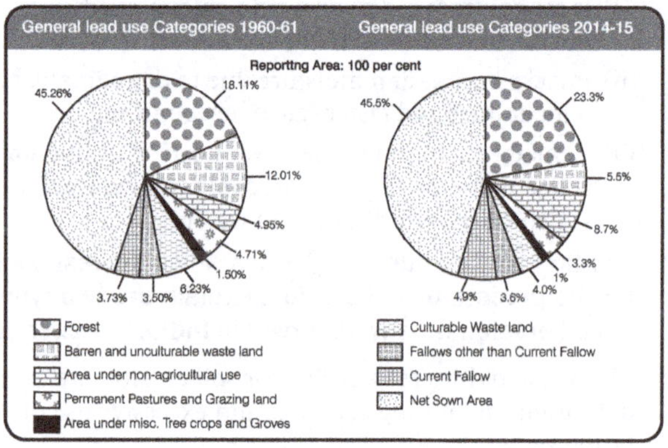

Ans. The highest increase was in forest cover i.e. from 18.11% in 1960-61 to 23.3% in 2014-15.

This increase is due to government efforts made in the field of conservation of environment by demarking the forest areas. Still, it is below the outline of 33% set in National Forest Policy, 1952.

The highest decrease was in barren and unculturable wasteland i.e. from 18.11% to 5.5%. It is due to rise in area under non-agricultural uses. Massive urbanisation, development of roads, railways and other uses have brought waste land into area under non-agricultural uses.

16. 'A drought-induced water shortage can have far-reaching consequences, affecting agricultural productivity, the availability of food resources, industrial activities, and livelihoods, thereby significantly impacting human well-being.' **Competency Based**

(i) What does the above statement represent about the relationship between different resources?

(ii) How does such a situation represents lack of resource planning?

Ans. (i) The above statement represent that different resources are interlinked with each other. If there is any change in one resource it can led to changes in other resources as well. These changes can be harmful for survival of human beings.

(ii) Such a situation represents lack of resource planning because it shows failure to reduce the impacts of a drought induced water shortage. Proper resource planning would involve measures such as water conservation strategies and investment in alternative water resources.

17. It's surely our responsibility to do everything within our power to create a planet home not just for us, but for all life on Earth.

(i) What is meant by the above quote? Explain in two points.

(ii) How does this quote align with sustainable development?

Ans. (i) The above quote means that it is our responsibility to conserve Earth's resources. We must conserve resources not just for humans but for all species.

(ii) This quote talks about creating a planet that does not compromise the needs of life on Earth. This is based on the concept of sustainable development, which refers to development without harming the environment and in a way that does not compromise the needs of future generations.

18. Radha once visited a desert town in Rajasthan where she saw that people are struggling hard to get drinking water and water for other purposes is also scarce. She realised that in her city people waste a huge quantity of water. She decided to raise awareness in her city related to conservation of resources such as water. Examine the major problems caused by indiscriminate use of resources. **Competency Based**

Ans. Human beings have used resources indiscriminately, leading to the following major problems

(i) Excessive use of resources have depleted their stock throughout the world.

(ii) Resources have accumulated in a few hands, which in turn has divided society into two segments i.e. 'haves' and 'have nots' or rich and poor.

(iii) Indiscriminate use of resources has also led to soil layer depletion, environmental pollution and land degradation.

19. Read the statements given below regarding soil erosion.

Statement I Gullies cut the clayey soil into deep creeps and the land becomes unfit for cultivation and popularly known as bad lands.

Statement II Sheet erosion washes away top soils over large areas and productivity is mostly decreased.

Explain the methods through which the soil erosion due to above causes can be minimised.

Ans. The soil erosion can be minimised through the following methods/techniques

(i) **Terrace farming and contour ploughing** Farming along the hill slopes by cutting it into terraces or along the contour lines helps in soil conservation.

(ii) **Shelter belt** Planting rows of trees along the edges of fields helps in checking soil erosion through wind.

(iii) **Strip cropping** Dividing the field into strips and letting grass grow between the crops breaks the force of the wind thereby checking soil erosion.

Long Answer Type Questions

1. Discuss the purpose of Rio de Janeiro Earth Summit and Agenda 21.

Or **What was the purpose of the Earth Summit held in Rio de Janeiro, Brazil in 1992? What are the main provisions of Agenda 21 signed at this Summit?**

Ans. The purpose of Rio de Janeiro Earth Summit and Agenda 21 were as follows

Rio de Janeiro Earth Summit

- It was held in June 1992, to address urgent issues related to environmental protection and socio-economic development at the global level.
- More than 100 heads of states convened to discuss and find solutions to pressing problems. During the summit, the leaders signed the Declaration on Global Climatic Change and Biological Diversity.
- Additionally, the Rio Convention endorsed the global Forest Principles and adopted Agenda 21.

Agenda 21

- It is the declaration signed by world leaders in 1992 at the United Nations Conference on Environment and Development (UNCED)in Rio de Janeiro, Brazil.
- The primary aim of Agenda 21 is to achieve global sustainable development by addressing environmental damage, poverty and disease through global cooperation on common interests, mutual needs and shared responsibilities.
- It encourages every local government to develop its own local Agenda 21, emphasising a decentralised approach to sustainable development.

2. A research based institution wants to study the properties of alluvial soils that makes it most successful soil type in India for agriculture purpose. What features of the alluvial soil should be included in the above research ? Explain.

Or **Trace the features of alluvial soil with reference to its formation, area, classification and containing minerals.** **CBSE 2015**

Or **Explain the main features of alluvial soil.** **CBSE 2025**

Ans. The important features of the alluvial soil that should be studied for the above research are

- **Formation** Alluvial soil is made-up of silt, sand and clay. It is deposited by three important Himalayan river systems the Indus, the Ganga and the Brahmaputra. It is bigger and coarser in the upper reaches of the river and becomes finer as the river flows down.
- **Distribution/Area** Alluvial soil is prevalent in the river valleys of the Northern plains (Indus, Ganga, Brahmaputra), strips in Gujarat and Rajasthan, as well as in the Eastern coastal plains in the deltas of rivers of the Peninsular plateau (Mahanadi, Krishna, Kaveri).
- **Classification** According to their age, alluvial soils can be classified as (Bangar) old alluvial and Khadar (new alluvial). Khadar has higher concentration of kankar and contains more fine particles than Bangar.
- **Nutrients/Minerals** Alluvial soil is rich in nutrients like potash, phosphoric acid and lime, which is suitable for growing paddy, wheat, sugarcane and other cereal and pulses crops.

3. List the main types of soil found in India, identify which of these is most widespread. Describe the characteristics of this type of soil.

Ans. The main types of soil found in India are listed below

(i) Alluvial (ii) Black
(iii) Red and Yellow (iv) Laterite
(v) Arid (vi) Forest

Soil and their characteristics are listed below

Alluvial Soils

- This is the most widely spread and important soil.
- These soils are very fertile.
- Mostly these soils contain adequate proportion of potash, phosphoric acid and lime.

Black Soils

- These soils has capacity to hold moisture.
- These soils are rich in soil nutrients, such as calcium carbonate, magnesium, potash and lime.
- The black soils are made up of extremely fine i.e. clayey material.

Red and Yellow Soils

- These soils develop a reddish colour due to diffusion of iron in crystalline and metamorphic rocks.
- They look yellow when they occur in a hydrated form.

Laterite Soil

- Laterite soils are mostly deep to very deep, acidic ($pH < 6.0$) generally deficient in plant nutrients.
- In deciduous and evergreen forests, laterite soil is rich in humus, but under sparse vegetation and in semi-arid environment, it is generally poor in humus.

- They are prone to erosion and degradation due to their position on the landscape.

Arid Soils

- In some areas, the salt content is very high and common salt is obtained by evaporating the water.
- These soil has lacks of humus and moisture.

Forest Soils

- The soils texture varies according to the mountain environment where they are formed.
- They are loamy and silty in valley sides and coarse grained in the upper slopes.
- In the snow covered areas of Himalayas, these soils experience denudation and are acidic with low humus content.

4. In Mahatma Gandhi's opinion, sustainable development is economic development based on ecological principles like environmental harmony, economic efficiency, resource (including energy) conservation, local self-reliance, and equity with social justice.
Source : The Statesman
Analyse the need for conservation of resources in the light of Gandhiji's view. **Competency Based**

Ans. According to Gandhiji, 'there is enough for everybody's need and not for anybody's greed'. He blamed the greedy and selfish individuals and exploitative nature of modern technology as the root cause for resource depletion at the global level.

Irrational consumption and overutilisation of resources has led to the socio-economic and environmental problems of shortages and pollution.

As resources are vital for any developmental activity, resource conservation at various levels is important to overcome these problems. If resources are used up at the same/lower rate as they are generated or formed, they will be available for use by future generations.

5. 'Human activities have contributed significantly in land degradation.' Justify the statement with three examples. **CBSE 2019**

Or **'Human activities have not only brought about degradation of land but have also aggravated the pace of natural forces to cause damage to land.' Justify the statement with the relevant points.**

Ans. The human activities are responsible for land degradation in India in the following ways

(i) Deforestation due to mining activities in Jharkhand, Chhattisgarh, Madhya Pradesh and Odisha have caused severe land degradation. Mining sites are abandoned after excavation work is completed, leaving deep scars.

(ii) Mineral processing like grinding of limestone for cement industry as well as calcite and soapstone for ceramic industry generate huge quantities of dust which falls down on land. This retards the process of infiltration of water into the soil.

(iii) Effluents as waste from industries have become a major source of land and water pollution in many parts of the country.

(iv) Over irrigation in Punjab, Haryana and Western Uttar Pradesh is responsible for land degradation due to waterlogging, leading to increase in salinity.

6. (i) Give two examples of resource conservation practices in our daily lives that make way for sustainable development.

(ii) 'We need sustainable development because resource exploitation is leading to inequality.' Explain the inequity of resources in two points.

(iii) Name international summit that discussed sustainable development as a goal.

Ans. (i) Examples of resource conservation practices in our daily lives that make way for sustainable development are as follows

(ii) We need sustainable development because resource exploitation is leading to inequality. The inequity of resources can be understood from the following two points

(a) Accumulation of resources in the hands of a few

(b) Division of society into segments i.e. haves and have nots or rich and poor.

(iii) The international summit that discussed sustainable development as a goal as follows

(i) Rio de Janeiro Earth Summit 1992

(ii) Johannesburg Summit 2002

(iii) The Kyoto Protocol 1997

(iv) Millennium Summit and Sustainable Development Conference 2000

(v) New York and the New Sustainable Development Goals 2015

7. (a) Analyse the measures adopted to prevent soil erosion.

(b) "There are many ways to solve the problems of land degradation." Substantiate the statement with illustrations.

Ans. (a) The measures adopted to prevent soil erosion are

- Ploughing along the contour lines can slow down the flow of water down the slopes. This is called contour ploughing.
- Steps can be cut out on the slopes making terraces. Terrace cultivation restricts erosion. Western and central Himalayas have well developed terrace farming.
- Large fields can be divided into strips. Strips of grass are left to grow between the crops. This breaks up the force of the wind. This method is known as strip cropping.

- Planting lines of trees to create shelter also works in a similar way. Rows of such trees are called shelter belts. These shelter belts have contributed significantly to the stabilisation of sand dunes and in stabilising the desert in western India.

(b) To solve the problem of land degradation, the following methods of conservation can be employed
- Afforestation and proper management of grazing lands.
- Discharge and disposal of industrial wastes after treatment.
- Control over mining activities.
- Planting of shelter belts of trees in arid areas.
- Control on overgrazing.
- Stabilisation of sand dunes by growing thorny bushes.
- Proper management of waste lands.

Case Based Questions

1. Read the sources given below and answer the questions that follow.

Source A Soil Erosion and Soil Conservation

Large fields can be divided into strips. Strips of grass are left to grow between the crops. This breaks up the force of wind. This method is known as strip cropping. Planting lines of trees to create shelter also works in a similar way. Rows of such trees are called shelter belts. These shelter belts have contributed significantly to the stabilisation of sand dunes and in stabilising the desert in Western India.

(i) Evaluate the effectiveness of shelter belts in stabilisation of sand dunes.

Source B Land use pattern in India

The pattern of net sown area varies greatly from one state to another. It is over 80 per cent of the total area in Punjab and Haryana and less than 10 per cent in Arunachal Pradesh, Mizoram, Manipur and Andaman and Nicobar Islands.

(ii) Give one reason for so much variation in net sown area in India.

Source C Resource planning in India

The history of colonisation reveals that rich resources in colonies were the main attractions for the foreign invaders. It was primarily the higher level of technological development of the colonising countries that helped them to exploit resources of other regions and establish their supremacy over the colonies. Therefore, resources can contribute to development only when they are accompanied by appropriate technological development and institutional changes. India has experienced all this in different phases of colonisation.

(iii) What led the imperial powers to exploit the rich resources of the colonies?

Ans. (i) In shelter belts, rows of trees are planted at the edge of farm lands. This breaks up the force of wind thereby reducing the spreading of sand dunes.

(ii) There is so much variation in net sown area in India due to the presence of different types of landforms i.e. mountains, plateaus and plains.

(iii) Their high level of technological development led to the exploitation of rich resources of the colonies.

2. Read the source given below and answer the questions that follow.

Planning is the widely accepted strategy for judicious use of resources. It has importance in a country like India, which has enormous diversity in the availability of resources. There are regions which are rich in certain types of resources, but are deficient in some other resources. There are some regions which can be considered self sufficient in terms of the availability of resources and there are some regions which have acute shortage of some vital resources. For example, the states of Jharkhand, Chhattisgarh and Madhya Pradesh are rich in minerals and coal deposits. Arunachal Pradesh has abundance of water resources, but lacks in infrastructural development.

(i) How judicious use of resources can be done by planning?

(ii) Why planning is necessary in India?

(iii) State two examples of resource availability in India.

Ans. (i) Judicious use of resources can be done by planning as it involves identification and quantification of resources and by knowing the exact quantity of resources, ways can be developed to use them properly.

(ii) Planning is necessary in India due to two reasons as follows

(a) There are regions which are rich in certain types of resources, but are deficient in some other resources.

(b) There are some regions which can be considered self-sufficient in terms of the availability of resources and there are some regions which have acute shortage of some vital resources.

(iii) Example of resource availability in India are
- The states of Jharkhand, Chhattisgarh and Madhya Pradesh are rich in minerals and coal deposits.
- Arunachal Pradesh has abundance of water resources.

Map Based Question

1 **On the physical outline map of India given below, identify the soil types of India.** **CBSE 2015**

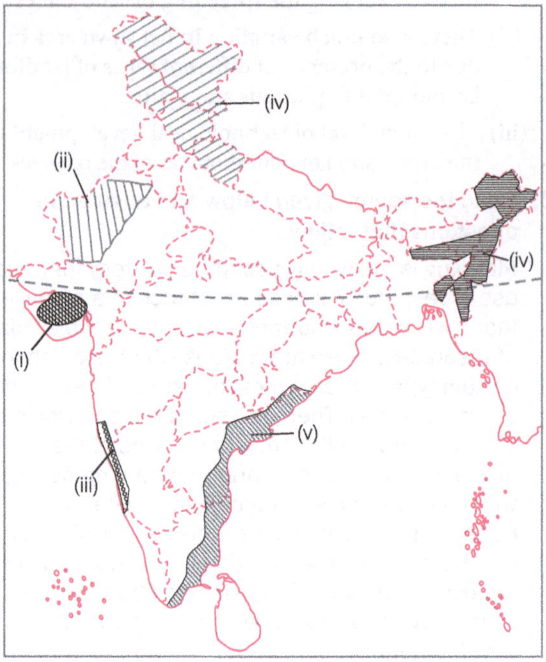

Ans. (i) Black soil (ii) Arid soil
(iii) Laterite soil (iv) Forest and Mountainous soil
(v) Alluvial soil (vi) Red and yellow soil

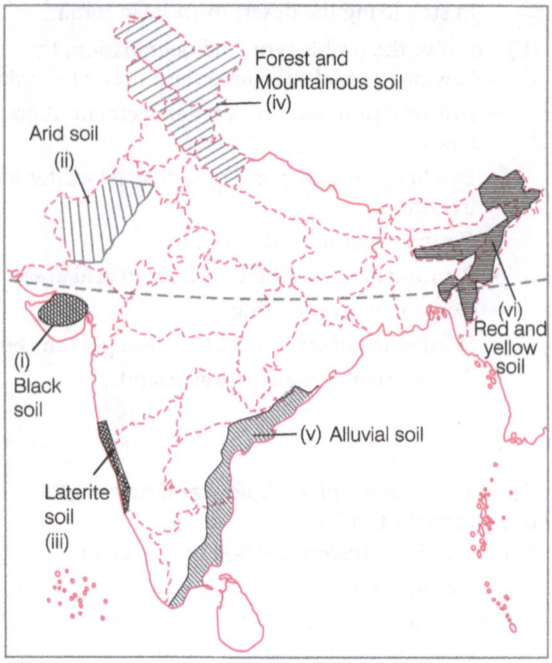

ASSESSMENT EXERCISE

Multiple Choice Questions (MCQs)

1. Who among the following said these words "There is enough for everybody's need and not for anybody's greed"?
(a) Pt Jawaharlal Nehru (b) Indira Gandhi
(c) Mahatma Gandhi (d) Sardar Patel

2. Which of the following physical factor influencing land use?
(a) Population density (b) Technological capability
(c) Topography (d) Culture and traditions

3. How long does it take for soil to form up to a few centimeters in depth?
(a) Thousands of years (b) Millions of years
(c) Hundreds of years (d) Two million years

4. What makes alluvial soil highly fertile?
(a) High acidity levels (b) Insufficient potash content
(c) Adequate proportion of potash, phosphoric acid and time
(d) Low fertility due to excessive irrigation

5. Some areas of .... occupied by Pakistan and China have not been surveyed for land use.
(a) Jammu and Kashmir (b) Himachal Pradesh
(c) Punjab (d) All of these

Subjective Questions (VSA, SA & LA)

1. Write down different methods of checking soil erosion.

2. Overgrazing may cause land degradation. Give example of some states affected by this.

3. Differentiate fallow land from other fallow land.

4. What is the comparative change in barren and waste land pattern in India between 1960-61 and 2014-15?

5. Differentiate between Net Sown Area and cultivable land.

6. Distinguish between khadar and bangar soils.

7. How is red soil different from laterite soil?

8. Why is it important to have a planned strategy for the development of resources in India?

9. Mention any four characteristics of forest soils.

10. How does land get degraded due to human activities?

11. Discuss the basis on which soils are classified in India.

CHAPTER 2

Forest and Wildlife Resources

The Earth has huge biodiversity as it is shared by both human being along with other living organisms, starting from micro-organism, bacteria, plants and animals. Humans alongwith all living organisms inclusively form a complex web of ecological systems, where forests play a key role as primary producers on which other living beings depend.

2.1 Flora and Fauna in India

In India, varieties of flora (plants) and fauna (animals) are found. Thus, it is one of the world's richest countries in terms of biological diversity. However, they are under threat mainly due to insensitivity towards environment.

Biodiversity or **biological diversity** refers to rich wildlife and plant (cultivated) species which are diverse or varied in form and function but are close integrated in a system through interdependencies.

2.2 Conservation of Forest and Wildlife in India

Conservation became essential due to rapid decline of wildlife population and forestry. It preserves the ecological diversity[1] and our life support systems like water, air and soil.

It also preserves the genetic diversity of plants and animals for better growth of species and breeding. For example, maintenance of aquatic biodiversity is necessary for fisheries.

Wildlife Protection Act

In the 1960 and 1970s, conservationists demanded a national wildlife protection programme. The Wildlife Protection Act, was implemented in 1972.

This act consisted of various provisions for protecting habitats of wildlife. Under this Act, an all India list of protected species was published.

The main objective of the programme was protecting the remaining population of certain endangered species by banning hunting and restricting trade in wildlife.

Later, the Central and many State Governments have established many national parks and wildlife sanctuaries to protect biodiversity.

The Central Government has announced several projects for protecting threatened species. These include tiger, one-horned rhinoceros, the Kashmir stag or hangul, three types of crocodiles (freshwater crocodile, salt water crocodile and Gharial), Asiatic lion and others.

Most recently, the Indian elephant, black buck, (Chinkara), the great Indian bustard (godawan) and snow leopard have been given (partial or full) legal protection against hunting, poaching and illegal trade throughout India.

In the notification of Wildlife Act of 1980 and 1986, many insects including butterflies, moths, beetles and a dragonfly have been added to the list of protected species.

In 1991, plants were also added to the list for the first time, starting with six species.

1 Ecological Diversity The structural abundance of flora and fauna in response to the landscape and physical forces active on its part of land is collectively called ecological diversity.

Project Tiger

Tiger is an important wildlife species. In 1973, Project Tiger was launched due to a major decrease in tiger population to 1,827 from an estimated 55,000.

The major threats to tiger population include poaching for trade, habitat loss, prey species depletion, human population growth, etc.

The trade of tiger skins and bones for traditional medicines, especially in Asian countries resulted in the near extinction of tiger population

India and **Nepal** contribute about two-thirds of the world's remaining tiger population, making them prime targets for poaching and illegal trading.

Tiger conservation is an effort to save endangered species and preserving **biotypes**[2] of large and significant ecosystems.

Tiger reserves in India include Corbett National Park (Uttarakhand), Sunderbans National Park (West Bengal), Bandhavgarh National Park (Madhya Pradesh), Sariska Wildlife Sanctuary (Rajasthan), Manas Tiger Reserve (Assam) and Periyar Tiger Reserve (Kerala).

2.3 Types and Distribution of Forest and Wildlife Resources

In India, much of its forest and wildlife resources are either owned or managed by the government through the Forest Department or other government departments.

The forests are classified under three categories as follows

(i) Reserved Forests

- These forests are owned by the government and all the human activities like collection of timber, grazing of cattle, etc. are not allowed in these forests.
- They are regarded as the most valuable forests in terms of conservation of forest and wildlife resources. They constitute about more than half of the total forest land in India.
- Jammu and Kashmir, Andhra Pradesh, Uttarakhand, Kerala, Tamil Nadu, West Bengal and Maharashtra have large percentages of reserved forests.

(ii) Protected Forests

- These forests are also owned by the government but the local people are allowed here to collect fuel wood and grazing their cattle without causing serious damage to the forests.
- They constitute about one-third of the total forest area in India as declared by Forest Department.
- This forest land are protected from any further depletion.
- Haryana, Odisha, Punjab, Bihar, Himachal Pradesh, and Rajasthan have extensive protected forests.

(iii) Unclassed Forests

- These are other forests and wastelands belonging to private individuals, government and communities.
- North-Eastern states and parts of Gujarat have high percentage of unclassed forests managed by local communities.

Permanent Forest Estates

Reserved forests and protected forests are collectively called **permanent forest estates**. These forests are maintained for producing timber and other forest products and for protective reasons.

Madhya Pradesh has **maximum forest cover** under permanent forests constituting 75 per cent of its total forest cover.

2.4 Community and Conservation

In India, forests are also home to many traditional communities. In some areas of India, local communities along with government officials are struggling to conserve these habitats, as only this will secure their long term livelihood. For example,

- In the **Sariska Tiger Reserve in Rajasthan**, villagers have fought against the mining by refering to the Wildlife Protection Act.
- The inhabitants of five villages in Alwar district of Rajasthan have declared 1200 hectares of forest land as the Bhairodev Dakav **Sonchuri**[3] (sanctuary). They have declared their own set of rules and regulations which do not allow hunting and are protecting the wildlife against any outside encroachments.
- The famous **Chipko Movement** was conducted in the Himalayas. It has successfully resisted deforestation as well as shown the community afforestation by the native people at a large scale.

---

2 **Biotype** It is a specific type of habitat where particular plants and animals thrive together.

3 **Sonchuri** It refers to an area where wild birds or animals are protected and encouraged to breed. It is a local word for sanctuary.

- Attempts to revive the traditional conservation methods or developing new methods of ecological farming are widespread.

  For instance, farmers and citizens groups like the **Beej Bachao Andolan** in Tehri and **Navdanya** have shown that it is possible and economically viable to produce adequate diversified crops without the use of artificial chemicals.

Joint Forest Management (JFM)

In India, joint forest management involves the local communities in managing and restoring the degraded forests.

The programme has been officially established since 1988 when the state of **Odisha** passed the **first resolution** for JFM.

Under this programme, local (village) institutions are formed that under take protection activities mostly on the degraded forest land managed by the forest department.

In return, the members of these communities are allowed to get benefits like non-timber forest produce and also share in the timber harvested by successful protection.

Measures to Conserve

- To protect forest and wildlife resources, the local communities have to be involved in some kind of natural resource management.
- The government should adopt only those economic or developmental-friendly and economically rewarding.

Sacred Groves : A Wealth of Diverse and Rare Species

There is an old tribal belief that all creations of nature have to be protected. This belief preserved several virgin forests that are called Sacred Groves (the forests of God and Goddesses). Any interference in these forests is banned by the local people. For example,

- The Mundas and Santhals of Chota Nagpur region worship **mahua** *(Bassia latifolia)* and **kadamba** (*Anthocephalus cadamba*) trees.
- The tribals of Odisha and Bihar worship the **tamarind** (*Tamarindus indica*) and **mango** (*Mangifera indica*) trees during weddings.
- **Peepal** and **banyan trees** are also considered sacred.
  In India, sacred qualities are also connected with springs, mountains, plants and animals. For example, in and around Bishnoi village in Rajasthan, herds of blackbuck, (*chinkara*), nilgai and peacocks are an integral part of the community and are protected.

Try These

1. **Under which Act, an all India list of protected species was published?**
2. **Name the state that his maximum forest cover under permanent forests.**
3. **A newly initiated programme, first started in Odisha, includes local community in protection and management of forests. What is that programme?**
4. **Which movements shows that the varieties of crops production can possible without using artificial chemicals?**

Mind Map

FORESTS AND WILDLIFE RESOURCES

Flora and Fauna in India
- Varieties of Flora and Fauna are found in India.
- India is one of the richest countries in terms of biological diversities.

Conservation of Forest and Wildlife in India
- The Wildlife Protection Act implemented in 1972.
- Protect the remaining population of certain endangered species.
- For example, Tiger, one-horned rhinoceros, asiatic lion and others.

Types and Distribution of Forest and Wildlife Resources

Reserved Forests
- Owned by Government.
- Human activities like collection of timber, grazing of cattle, etc are not allowed.
- Andhra Pradesh, Jammu and Kashmir, Uttarakhand, Kerala, Tamil Nadu, West Bengal and Maharashtra.

Protected Forests
- Owned by Government.
- Local people are allowed to collect fuel wood and grazing cattle.
- Haryana, Odisha, Bihar, Himachal Pradesh and Rajasthan.

Unclassed Forests
- Forests and wastelands belonging to private individuals, government and communities.
- North- Eastern states and parts of Gujarat.

Community and Conservation

Community Contribution
- Joint Forest Management Chipko Movement
- Beej Bachao Andolan

Conservation Methods

The government should adopt economic or developmental friendly and economically rewarding methods.

NCERT FOLDER

Covering Intext Questions and Exercises of NCERT

INTEXT QUESTION

Q.1 Write a short essay on any practices which you may have observed and practised in your everyday lives that conserve and protect the environment around you.

Ans. Everyday life practices to conserve and protect the environment include

- Reducing plastic usage by carrying a reusable water bottle and bag.
- Turning off lights and electronics devices when not needed, as it helps in save energy.
- Planting trees and using public transport contribute to cleaner air.
- These small actions, when done collectively, make a positive impact on conserving and safeguarding our environment.

EXERCISE

Q.1 Multiple Choice Questions.

(i) Which of the following conservation strategies do not directly involve community participation?

(a) Joint Forest Management
(b) Beej Bachao Andolan
(c) Chipko Movement
(d) Demarcation of Wildlife Sanctuaries

Ans. (d) Demarcation of Wildlife Sanctuaries

Q.2 Match the following.

List I	List II
A. Reserved forests	1. Forests are regarded as most valuable as far as the conservation of forests and wildlife resources.
B. Protected forests	2. Forest lands are protected from any further depletion.
C. Unclassed forests	3. Other forests and wastelands belonging to both government and private individuals and communities.

Codes

	A	B	C		A	B	C
(a)	2	3	1	(b)	1	2	3
(c)	3	2	1	(d)	1	3	2

Ans. (b)

Q.3 Answer the following question in about 30 words.

(i) What is biodiversity ? Why is biodiversity important for human lives?

Ans. Biodiversity refers to rich flora and wildlife. Here, species which are diverse or varied form and functions but are close integrated and interconnected in a system through interdependencies.

Biodiversity is important for human lives because the human being, alongwith the biodiversity, form a complex web of ecological systems in which we are only a part and are dependent on this system for our own existence.

(ii) How have human activities affected the depletion of flora and fauna? Explain.

Ans. The human activities have affected the depletion of flora and fauna in the following ways

- **Agricultural Expansion** Clearing large areas for farming has led to the destruction of natural habitats, reducing the space available for flora and fauna.
- **Mining Activities** Extracting resources from the Earth often involves removing vegetation and disrupting ecosystems, causing harm to various plant and animal species.
- **Rapid Urbanisation** As cities expand, natural habitats are replaced by buildings and infrastructure, displacing many species and disrupting their ecosystems.
- **Large-Scale Development Projects** Mega projects like dams and highways can fragment habitats, making it difficult for plants and animals to move freely, affecting their breeding and survival.

Q.4 Answer the following questions in about 120 words.

(i) Describe how communities have conserved and protected forests and wildlife in India?

Ans. Communities have conserved and protected forests and wildlife in India in the following ways

- The Chipko Movement which was conducted in the Himalayas, has successfully resisted deforestation in several areas. It showed community afforestation with indigenous species to be successful.
- The Beej Bachao Andolan in Tehri district of Uttarakhand conserved local seed diversity and forests, while defending small farmers and promoting traditional agriculture and knowledge systems.

- In the Sariska Wildlife Sanctuary in Rajasthan, villagers have fought against mining activities taking place nearby by citing the Wildlife Protection Act.

(ii) Write a note on good practices towards conserving forest and wildlife.

Ans. Conservation of forests involves various positive practices. These practices are as follows

- People worship trees and animals, recognising their importance in nature. They use plants and animals in religious ceremonies, creating a harmonious relationship with the environment.
- Laws with penalties discourage the killing of animals, promoting their preservation.
- Community initiatives like Vanmahotsav raise awareness, educating people about the significance of wildlife. These practices collectively contribute to the protection of forests and biodiversity, ensuring a sustainable and balanced coexistence between humans and the natural world.

REVIEW EXERCISE

Including Competency Based Questions

Part I

Multiple Choice Questions (MCQs)

1. When was Indian Wildlife (Protection) Act implemented? CBSE 2023

(a) 1972 (b) 1978 (c) 1980 (d) 1985

2. Which is the first project for Wildlife Conservation in India?

(a) Project Elephant (b) Project Tiger
(c) Project Crocodile (d) None of these

3. Mr. Y has to write a short essay on wildlife protection in India. He also mentioned the India Wildlife Protection Act , 1972 in his essay. Why ? Competency Based

(a) It has various provisions for protecting habitats of wild species.
(b) This act contains the names of some rare animals which has not been mentioned anywhere in the world.
(c) Under this act, an All India list of protected species was also published.
(d) Both (a) and (c)

4. Which among the following species has been granted full or partial legal protection against hunting and trade in India? Competency Based

(a) Indian elephant (b) Black buck
(c) Snow leopard (d) All of these

5. 'Sariska Tiger Reserve' is located in which one of the following states? CBSE 2025

(a) Madhya Pradesh (b) Rajasthan
(c) Uttar Pradesh (d) Maharashtra

6. Which of the following national park is/are the site dedicated to preservation of one-horned rhinoceros?

(a) Bandhavgarh National Park
(b) Buxa Wildlife Reserve
(c) Kaziranga National Park
(d) All of the above

7. Which of the following is an example of the conservation of biological diversity? Competency Based

(a) An NGO working for the rehabilitation of people affected by Sardar Sarovar dam.
(b) An online advertisement spreading awareness about organic products.
(c) A self help group working for the protection of local varieties of seeds in the village.
(d) None of the above

8. We humans along with all living organisms form a complex web of ecological system in which we are only a part and very much dependent on this system for our own existence. Competency Based

Accordingly, which of the following quotes best reflects the linkage of humans with the forest conservation.

(a) 'What we are doing in the forests is a mirror reflection of what we are doing to ourselves'.
(b) 'The forests are the 'lungs' of our land, purifying the air and giving fresh strength to our people'.
(c) 'I love the forest. It is the place where you hear yourself better.'
(d) 'To forget how to dig the Earth and to tend the soil is to forget ourselves.'

9. In India, communities have been involved in conservation of forest and wildlife in India. Conservation in the background of rapid decline in wildlife population and forestry has become essential. Why do we need to conserve our forests and wildlife? Choose the most probable option.

(a) Conservation ensures that people will lead a good life.
(b) Conservation preserves the ecological diversity and our life support systems.
(c) Conservation instills confidence in the citizens of a country.
(d) Conservation provides livelihood to the people.

10. Why do you think the Indian government has classified the forests into various categories?

(a) Because it is difficult to manage, control and regulate the forests without such classification.
(b) Because such a classification is mandatory in every country which are a part of United Nations.
(c) Because such a classification has been adopted by so many countries around the world.
(d) Because such a classification is very important for a developing country like India.

11. Which state of India has the maximum area under permanent forest? **CBSE 2025**

(a) Haryana (b) Himachal Pradesh
(c) Punjab (d) Madhya Pradesh

12. Find the incorrect option regarding Joint Forest Management Programme.

(a) Odisha passed the first resolution for Joint Forest Management.
(b) This programme was initiated in the year 1988.
(c) It is a combined effort of local community with local committees.
(d) Members are entitled to cash benefits from the forests.

13. Akriti, a resident of a village in Andhra Pradesh is involved in joint forest management programme along with other villagers. They undertook protection activities on degraded forest lands which has resulted in increase in the forest cover in her village.

Which of the following reflects the lessons that can be learnt from the above example? **Competency Based**

(a) Joint forest management is the only solution left to protect forests.
(b) Only women from villages can find success in conservation of biodiversity.
(c) Local communities everywhere have to be involved in some kind of natural resource management.
(d) Decision making does not needs the involvement of local communities.

14. Arrange the following in chronological order and choose the correct codes from the options given below.

I. Tigers declared extinct from India
II. Project tiger started
III. Indian Wildlife Protection Act implemented
IV. Initiation of JFM

Codes

(a) III, II, I, IV (b) IV, III, II, I
(c) I, III, II, IV (d) III, II, IV, I

15. Which of the following options represent potential measures that can be taken to mitigate the threats posed on the tiger population and biodiversity?

I. Banning hunting, giving legal protection to their habitats and restricting trade in wildlife.
II. Prohibiting the visit of public into forest area.
III. Establishing wildlife sanctuaries and national parks.
IV. Converting forests into reserved and protected forests.

Codes

(a) I and II (b) II, III and IV
(c) Only II (d) I, III and IV

16. Which of the following statements is/are correct regarding the community and conservation in India?

I. Villagers in Sariska reserve in Rajasthan have fought against mining citing the wildlife protection act.
II. Bhairodev Dakav 'Sonchuri' have been declared in Madhya Pradesh.
III. Beej Bachao Andolan was carried out in Chamoli district of Uttarakhand.
IV. Chipko Movement in the Himalayas has been successful in resisting deforestation in several areas.

Codes

(a) Only I (b) I and III
(c) I and IV (d) II and III

17. Identify the reason as to why a government would like to collaborate with the tribals for the conservation of forest resources.

Choose the appropriate statements among the following options.

I. Tribals follow nature worship and believe that all creations of nature have to be protected.
II. Tribals have been involved in preserving several tracts of pristine forests in the form of sacred groves.
III. Tribals have better body structure and body built which they can use in working for the conservation works.
IV. Tribals are better at taking decisions related to conservation of forest resources as they have been provided training of some advanced techniques.

Options

(a) I and II (b) I, II and III
(c) Only IV (d) All of these

18. Consider the statements given below and choose the correct answer.

Statement I Certain societies worship a particular tree which they have preserved from time immemorial.

Statement II The Mundas and the Santhal of Chota Nagpur region worship tamarind (Tamarindus indica) and mango (Mangifera indica) trees.

Options

(a) Statement I is correct and statement II is incorrect
(b) Statement I is incorrect and statement II is correct
(c) Both statements I and II are incorrect
(d) Both statements I and II are correct

19. **Consider the statements given below and choose the correct answer.**

Statement I In and around Bishnoi villages in Rajasthan, herds of blackbuck, (chinkara), nilgai and peacocks can be seen as an integral part of the community and nobody harms them.

Statement II The tribals of Mundas and the Santhal of Chota Nagpur region worship mahua (*Bassia latifolia*) and kadamba (*Anthocaphalus cadamba*) trees.

Options

(a) Statement I is correct and statement II is incorrect
(b) Statement I is incorrect and statement II is correct
(c) Both statements I and II are incorrect
(d) Both statements I and II are correct

20. **Which of the following statements is/are correct regarding Beej Bachao Andolan and Navdanya in India?**

I. These movements were involved in the protection of biodiversity.
II. These movements were led by farmers and citizen's groups.
III. These movements have shown that adequate levels of diversified crop production without the use of synthetic chemicals are possible.
IV. These movements were a part of the larger Chipko Movement.

Options

(a) Only I (b) Only II
(c) I, II and IV (d) I, II and III

21. **Consider the following statements about unclassed forests.**

I. Unclassed forests are mostly managed by both private communities and the government.
II. All human activities are allowed in these forests.
III. North-Eastern states and parts of Gujarat have mostly unclassed forests.

Which of the following statements are correct?

(a) I and II (b) II and III
(c) I and III (d) All of these

22. **Consider the following statements about reserved forests.**

I. Reserved forests are owned by the government and all the human activities are not allowed in these forests.
II. These forests are regarded as the most valuable forests in terms of conservation of forests and wildlife.
III. These forests constitute about more than half of the total forest land in India.

Which of the following statements are correct?

(a) I and II (b) II and III
(c) I and III (d) All of these

Answers

1. (a)	**2.** (b)	**3.** (d)	**4.** (d)	**5.** (b)
6. (c)	**7.** (c)	**8.** (a)	**9.** (b)	**10.** (a)
11. (d)	**12.** (d)	**13.** (c)	**14.** (c)	**15.** (d)
16. (c)	**17.** (a)	**18.** (a)	**19.** (d)	**20.** (d)
21. (d)	**22.** (d)			

Match the Following

1.

	List I		List II
A.	Reserved forests	1.	North-Eastern states
B.	Protected forests	2.	Andhra Pradesh
C.	Unclassed forests	3.	Haryana

Codes

	A	B	C		A	B	C
(a)	1	2	3	(b)	3	2	1
(c)	1	3	2	(d)	2	3	1

Ans. (d)

Assertion-Reason

1. **Assertion** (A) Tiger population has reduced rapidly in India from 55,000 to just 1827 in 1973.

Reason (R) Increase in demand of traditional medicines in Asian countries led to large scale poaching of tigers.

Codes

(a) Both A and R are true but R is not the correct explanation of A
(b) Both A and R are true and R is the correct explanation of A
(c) Both A and R are incorrect
(d) A is correct, but R is incorrect

2. **Assertion** (A) Neglecting our environment has led to the destruction and extinction of many species of animals and plant life.

Reason (R) Decreasing forest cover area is a major reason of destruction of species.

Codes

(a) Both A and R are true but R is not the correct explanation of A
(b) Both A and R are true and R is the correct explanation of A
(c) Both A and R are incorrect
(d) A is correct, but R is incorrect

3. **Assertion** (A) Depletion of forests causes a lot of threat to environment.

Reason (R) Forests are vital for the quality of life and environment.

Codes

(a) Both A and R are true but R is not the correct explanation of A
(b) Both A and R are true and R is the correct explanation of A
(c) Both A and R are incorrect
(d) A is correct, but R is incorrect

4. Assertion (A) Wildlife sanctuaries and National parks are critical for the conservation of endangered species.

Reason (R) These protected areas provide a safe habitat for animals, free from human disturbances like poaching and habitat destruction.

Codes

(a) Both A and R are true but R is not the correct explanation of A

(b) Both A and R are true and R is the correct explanation of A

(c) Both A and R are incorrect

(d) A is correct, but R is incorrect

5. Assertion (A) Destruction of forests and wildlife resulted into the loss of cultural diversity.

Reason (R) The conservation of forests and wildlife is essential to provide a better quality of life.

Codes

(a) Both A and R are true but R is not the correct explanation of A

(b) Both A and R are true and R is the correct explanation of A

(c) Both A and R are incorrect

(d) A is correct, but R is incorrect

6. Assertion (A) Wildlife protection laws in India are crucial for conserving endangered species.

Reason (R) These laws helped in reducing illegal hunting and habitat destruction.

Codes

(a) Both A and R are true but R is not the correct explanation of A

(b) Both A and R are true and R is the correct explanation of A

(c) Both A and R are incorrect

(d) A is correct, but R is incorrect

7. Assertion (A) Community involvement in natural resource management is crucial for both environmental protection and sustainable development.

Reason (R) Local communities play a vital role in the conservation of habitats and biodiversity, as seen in examples like the Chipko movement and community afforestation.

Codes

(a) Both A and R are true but R is not the correct explanation of A

(b) Both A and R are dtrue and R is the correct explanation of A

(c) Both A and R are incorrect

(d) A is correct, but R is incorrect

Ans. 1. (b) Both A and R are true and R is the correct explanation of A

2. (a) Both A and R are true, but R is not the correct explanation of A

3. (b) Both A and R are true and R is the correct explanation of A

4. (b) Both A and R are true and R is the correct explanation of A

5. (a) Both A and R are true, but R is not the correct explanation of A

6. (b) Both A and R are true and R is the correct explanation of A

7. (b) Both A and R are true and R is the correct explanation of A

Picture Based Questions

1. Observe the newspaper cutting given below showing decrease in the population of wildlife species.

Ghariál on the brink

Bird deaths blamed on dirty Yamuna

Indian government provides legal protection to several animal species in India. However the population of many of the species have been declining rapidly.

Accordingly, which of the following is/are the most probable reasons for the above problem?

(a) Degradation of water and land resources

(b) Destruction of the habitats of wildlife species

(c) Pollution caused by human beings

(d) All of the above

2. Given below is the picture showing the tribal women of Odisha making baskets and other items with bamboo and other plant based materials.

Which of the following is/are an example(s) of other occupations or works done by the tribal communities in India ?

(a) Tribal girls using bamboo saplings in a nursery at Mukhali near silent valley.

(b) Tribal women selling minor forest produce.

(c) Leaf litter collection by women folk.

(d) All of the above

Ans. 1. (d) All of the above

2. (b) Tribal women selling minor forest produce.

Case Based Question

1. **Read the passage given below and answer the questions that follow.**

If you look around, you will be able to find that there are some animals and plants which are unique in your area. In fact, India is one of the world's richest countries in terms of its vast array of biological diversity. This is possibly twice or thrice the number yet to be discovered. You have already studied in detail about the extent and variety of forest and wildlife resources in India. You may have realised the importance of these resources in our daily life. These diverse flora and fauna are so well integrated in our daily life that we take these for granted. But, lately, they are under great stress mainy due to insensitivity to our environment.

(i) Which of the following is included under biological diversity ?

(a) Wildlife (b) Humans
(c) Cultivated species (d) All of these

(ii) What is suggested about the number of species in India?

(a) The number is limited and unlikely to grow.
(b) The number is twice or thrice the current known species yet to be discovered.
(c) There are no more species to be discovered.
(d) India has fewer species than expected.

(iii) Why the biological diversity today is under great stress? Choose the most appropriate options.

(a) Because of the success of drought resistant variety of plants.
(b) Because of their linkage in a food web.
(c) Because of the introduction of invasive species.
(d) Because of indiscriminate and exploitative human activities.

(iv) Conservation strategies should involve the conservation of

(a) Ecological and genetic diversity only
(b) Genetic diversity, ecological diversity and all the life support systems.
(c) Genetic diversity and all the life support systems only
(d) Ecological diversity and all the life support systems only.

Ans. (i) (d) All of these

(ii) (b) The number is twice or thrice the current known species yet to be discovered.

(iii) (d) Because of indiscriminate and exploitative human activities.

(iv) (b) Genetic diversity, ecological diversity and all the life support systems.

Part II

Very Short Answer Type Questions

1. **Briefly differentiate a national park and a wildlife sanctuary.**

Ans. The difference between a national park and a wildlife santuary is that national park has well defined boundary and human interference is restricted and regulations are strict, whereas wildlife sanctuary have no defined boundary and limited human activities are permitted in it.

2. **In which year a few plants were added to the protected species list in India?**

Ans. In the year 1991, plants were added to the protected species list for the first time in India, starting with six-species.

3. **A famous site in Madhya Pradesh was dedicated to protection of tigers through Project Tiger. Which site was it?**

Ans. Bandhavgarh National Park in Madhya Pradesh was dedicated to protection of tigers through Project Tiger.

4. **Name some wild animals who are given legal protection in India.**

Ans. Tiger, one-horned rhinoceros, Kashmir stag, some crocodiles, Asiatic lion, Indian elephant, blackbuck, the great Indian bustard and snow leopard, etc. are some wildlife who are given legal protection in India.

5. **What is the impact of Beej Bachao Andolan?**

Ans. The impact of Beej Bachao Andolan is that it has shown that it is economically viable to produce significant levels of diverse crop production without the use of artificial chemicals.

6. **State the main effect of Chipko Movement in India.**

Ans. This movement has successfully resisted deforestation in several areas of the Himalayas and also shows the community afforestation by the native people at a large scale.

7. **Do you think, Indian society lacks knowledge of conservation of nature?**

Ans. No, Indian society has traditional methods of conservation of nature and culturally adopted with suitability.

Indian method of nature conservation rely on prevention rather than modern methods of remedy.

8. **Compare the eco-sensitiveness of tribes and modern urbanised man.**

Ans. Tribes are much eco-sensitive. The tribes worship and protect forest and ecology whereas modern people exploit the forests and ecology insensitively for their commercial purposes.

9. What percentage of total forest area is under permanent forest in Madhya Pradesh?

Ans. In Madhya Pradesh about 75% of total forest area is under permanent Forest.

10. What does the example of the 'Bhairodev Dakav Sonchuri' in Rajasthan illustrate?

Ans. The example of 'Bhairodev Dakav Sonchuri' in Rajasthan illustrates the concept of community level initiative. Inhabitants declared 1200 hectares of forest, implementing self imposed rules that banned hunting and protected wildlife from external threats. This shows effective local conservation efforts.

11. What are the different types of forest categories in India?

Ans. In India, different types of forest categories include Reserved Forests (valued for conservation), Protected Forests (protected from further depletion) and Unclassed Forests (including government and private lands).

12. What is the key lesson learned from environmental dynamics in India?

Ans. The key lesson learned from environmental dynamics in India is that local communities must be involved in natural resource management. It highlights the importance of considering people-centric, environmentally friendly and economically rewarding activities.

13. On 9th March, Mohammad Arif, a 35-years-old man from Mandkha, Uttar Pradesh, was booked under the Wildlife Protection Act, 1972, for 'illegally' keeping and nursing an injured Sarus crane (Grus Antigone) he found in his village.

What are the protections provided under the Wildlife Protection Act, 1972? **Competency Based**

Ans. The Indian Wildlife (Protection)Act was implemented in 1972. This act consisted of various provisions for protecting habitats. Under this act, an all India list of protected species was also published. The main objective of this programme was protecting the remaining population of certain endangered species by banning hunting and restricting trade in wildlife.

14. Aman conducted a research on people's involvement in the conservation efforts with the government. His research shows that the project where local people were involved has a higher success rate than projects implemented by government alone.

What can be inferred from the findings of this research?

Ans. This research shows that local communities have to be involved in the conservation of resources. Those economic and developmental activities have to be accepted that are people centric, environment-friendly and economically rewarding.

15. Sonam, a class 10th student visited a tribal village in Meghalaya and found that the tribal living there play a role in the conservation of nature through their own traditional practices.

How the traditional methods of conservation are placed in India?

Ans. The traditional methods of conservation are placed in India in the form of traditional methods of conserving nature and its creations. Sacred qualities are often ascribed to springs, mountain peaks, plants and animals which are closely protected. We find troops of macaques and langurs around many temples. They are fed daily and treated as a part of temple devotees.

Short Answer Type Questions

1. How humans are dependent on the ecological system for their existence?

Ans. Humans are dependent on the ecological system for their existence in the following ways

This can be understood through the following points

- Humans breathe air, drink water and grow crops in soil which are the non-living components of the ecological system.
- The living components like plants, animals and micro-organisms recreate the quality of the air humans breathe, the water humans drink and the soil that produces humans food. Without these elements human beings cannot survive.
- Human beings are dependent on both living and non-living components for their ecological existence.

2. What are the different conservation methods adopted in India?

Or **Explain any three methods of forest conservation adopted by the Government of India after independence.**

Or **What efforts are made to protect forest and wildlife in India?**

Ans. Methods of conservation adopted in India are

(i) The Government of India has implemented the Indian Wildlife (Protection) Act in 1972 for conservation of wildlife and forests.

(ii) The government has classified forests into three categories such as reserved forests, protected forests and unclassed forests. Out of these forests two categories, the 'reserved' and the 'protected' forests have been restricted for use.

(iii) The government has started Joint Forest Management (JFM) programmes involving local communities in management and restoration of degraded forests.

(iv) The Central and many State Governments have established many national parks and wildlife sanctuaries to protect forest and wildlife of India.

3. Write the important features of Joint Forest Management (JFM) Programme.

***Or* Describe any three features of Joint Forest Management.**

Ans. Joint Forest Management (JFM) programmes have been launched by various State Governments. The first state to start this programme was Odisha in 1988.

The important features of JFM programme are

(i) In India, Joint Forest Management (JFM) programme has been proved to be a good example for involving local communities in the management and restoration of degraded forests.

(ii) The major purpose of the JFM is to protect the forests from encroachments, grazing, theft and fire and also to improve the forests in accordance with an approved Joint Forest Management Plan.

(iii) JFM depends on the formation of local (village) institutions that undertake protection activities mostly on the degraded forest land managed by the forest department.

4. What has been the contribution of the Indian Wildlife Protection Act in protecting animal habitats in India?

Ans. The contribution of Indian Wildlife Protection Act, 1972 can be seen through the following points

- Under this act, an all India list of protected species was published. The act banned hunting of certain endangered species.
- It also gave legal protection to their habitats and restricting trade in wildlife.
- The Central and many State Governments have established many national parks and wildlife sanctuaries to protect forest and wildlife of India.
- Central Government has also announced several projects for protecting specific animals, which were gravely threatened. These include the tiger, the one-horned rhinoceros, the Kashmir stag or hangul, three types of crocodiles-freshwater crocodile, saltwater crocodile and the Gharial, the Asiatic lion and others.
- Most recently, the Indian elephant, blackbuck (chinkara) the great Indian bastard (godawan) and the snow leopard, etc have been given full or partial legal protection against hunting and trade throughout India.

5. Mr. Y from America visits India and finds that one patch of forests was completely prohibited for all kinds of activities while in other some of the activities were allowed. He asks an Indian citizen about this difference. What do you think the Indian person would have said about the above difference. Also mention four points of differences between these two kinds of forests. Competency Based

Ans. The Indian citizens must have explained to Mr. Y from America that forests in India have been divided into three classes out of which reserved forests are completely prohibited from any activities while protected forests allow certain activities.

Four points of differences between a reserved and a protected forests are as follows

Reserved Forests	Protected Forests
In reserved forests, right to all activities like hunting, grazing, etc are banned unless specific orders are issued by the government.	In protected areas, right to do activities like hunting and grazing, etc are sometimes given to communities living on the fringes of the forests and depend on forests for their livelihood.
Reserve forests enjoy a higher degree of protection and may be upgraded to the status of wildlife sanctuary and national parks.	The protected forests do not face such possibility.
More than half of the total forest land has been declared as reserved forests.	Only one-third of the total forest area is under protected forests.
Madhya Pradesh, Jammu and Kashmir, Andhra Pradesh, Uttarakhand, Kerala, Tamil Nadu, West Bengal and Maharashtra have large percentages of reserved forests of their total forest area.	Bihar, Odisha, Haryana, Punjab, Himachal Pradesh and Rajasthan have their large area under protected forests.

6. 'Tiger is one of the key wildlife species in the faunal web. In 1973, the authorities realised that the tiger population had dwindled to 1,827 from an estimated 55,000 at the turn of the century.' Competency Based

(i) What are the major threats to tiger population?

(ii) Mention the names of some of the tiger reserves in India.

Ans. (i) The major threats to tiger population are numerous, such as poaching for trade, shrinking habitat, depletion of prey base species, growing human population, etc. The trade of tiger skins and the use of their bones in traditional medicines, especially in the Asian countries left the tiger population on the verge of extinction.

(ii) Some of the tiger reserves of India are Corbett National Park in Uttarakhand, Sunderbans National Park in West Bengal, Bandhavgarh National Park in Madhya Pradesh, Sariska Wildlife Sanctuary in Rajasthan, Manas Tiger Reserve in Assam and Periyar Tiger Reserve in Kerala.

7. Read the statements given below regarding the biological diversity.

Statement 1 Biodiversity involves integration of diverse wildlife and cultivated species in a system through multiple network of dependencies.

Statement 2 We share this planet with millions of other living beings.

Explain what relationship the above statements - S1 and S2 reflects among different living organisms.

Competency Based

Ans. The above statements shows that humans share this planet with millions of other living beings, starting from micro-organisms and bacteria, lichens to banyan trees, elephants and blue whales. This entire habitat that we live in has immense biodiversity. We humans along with all living organisms form a complex web of ecological system in which we are only a part and very much dependent on this system for our own existence.

For example, the plants, animals and micro-organisms re-create the quality of the air we breathe, the water we drink and the soil that produces our food without which we cannot survive.

Long Answer Type Questions

1 Why is conservation of forests and wildlife necessary? In what way have conservation projects changed in recent years?

Ans. Conservation of forests and wildlife is necessary for maintenance of the ecological balance. If this is disturbed, it can cause long-term damage to the environment and ecology, thus threatening even human existence. We should implement biodiversity conservation practices to maintain biodiversity and to prevent future generations from suffering due to our negligence at present.

Earlier the conservation projects concentrated on particular components of biodiversity. For example, Project Tiger was started to conserve the tiger population in India. However, in recent years more intensive search for different conservation measures focusing on preservation of biodiversity as a whole have started. Revisions in the list of protected species of the Wildlife Act in recent years have included insects, moths, butterflies and even plants for preservation.

2. A think tank has been approached by the government to research on whether the tribal are responsible for destroying forest for their use or they are most eco-sensitive and protect nature better.

Discuss the points that can be given by the think tank regarding both the views in its research report.

Competency Based

Ans. Points that can be given by the think tank in its research report are as follows

(i) **Tribals are responsible for destroying forest** Tribal people rely on forest products for their survival i.e. food, wood, fuel wood, medicines, etc but they use them in sustainable manner. Only incidence of deforestation is slash and burn agriculture practiced by many tribals which deplete forests.

(ii) **Tribals are Eco-sensitive** When Tribals abandon the land, after some years trees again grow. The tribals are nature lovers. They worship trees, consider wildlife as God or other sacred elements and protect the nature with traditional methods. Tribals do not destroy the ecology knowingly and not exploit the nature for commercial purpose extensively as the modern men do.

3. "Our Gods are everywhere. We see more in nature than others," said Maranda, as he led the men back to their homes.

But the government does not legally acknowledge their faith — a fact that is increasingly becoming a rallying point for change for some of the 5 million or so indigenous tribes people in the country who follow Sarna Dharma. They say formal recognition would help preserve their culture and history in the wake of the slow erosion of Indigenous tribes people's rights in India.

Source : The Wire

Analyse why different traditional communities are involved in conserving their own natural habitats in India.

Competency Based

Ans. The different traditional communities are involved in conserving their own natural habitats in India because nature worship is an age old tribal belief based on the belief that all creations of nature have to be protected in pure form called sacred groves. This can be analysed through the following points

- Certain societies reserve a particular tree which they have preserved from time immemorial.
- The Mundas and the Santhals of Chota Nagpur region worship and protect mahua (*Bassia latifolia*) and kadamba (*Anthocaphalus cadamba*) trees.
- Tribals of Odisha and Bihar worship the tamarind (*Tamarindus indica*) and mango (*Mangifera indica*) trees during wedding and protect them.
- In and around Bishnoi villages in Rajasthan, herds of blackbuck (*chinkara*), nilgai and peacocks are protected. Monkeys and langoor are fed in many temples.

Case Based Questions

1. Read the sources given below and answer the questions.

Sacred Groves - A Wealth of Diverse and Rare Species

Nature worship is an age old tribal belief based on the premise that all creations of nature have to be protected. Such beliefs have preserved several virgin forests in pristine form called Sacred Groves (the forests of God and Goddesses). These patches of forest or parts of large forests have been left untouched by the local people and any interference with them is banned.

Certain societies revere a particular tree which they have preserved from time immemorial. The Mundas and the Santhal Chota Nagpur region worship mahua (*Barria lafifolia*) and Kadamba (*Anthocaphalus cadamba*) trees and the tribals of Odisha and Bihar worship the tamarind (*Tamarindus Indica*) and mango (*mangifera indica*) trees during weddings. To many of us peepal and banyan trees are considered sacred. Indian society comprises several cultures, each with its own set of traditional methods of conserving nature and its creations.Sacred qualities are often ascribed to springs, mountain peaks, plants and animals which are closely protected. You will find troops of macaques and langurs around many temples. They are fed daily and treated as a part of temple devotees. In and around Bishnoi villages in Rajasthan, herds of blackbuck, (chinkara), nilgai and peacocks can be seen as an integral part of the community and nobody harms them.

(i) How does sacred groves relate to the belief in nature worship?

(ii) **How do communities incorporate trees into their cultural practices? Explain with example.**

(iii) **Explain the cultural values that contribute to the coexistence of nature.**

Ans. (i) Nature worship is an age-old tribal belief based on the premise that all creations of nature have to be protected. Such beliefs have preserved several virgin forests in pristine form called sacred groves.

(ii) Certain communities revere a particular tree which they preserved from time immemorial, and thus incorporated trees into their cultural practices. For example, the Mundas and Santhals of Chota Nagpur region worship Mahua and Kadamba trees.

(iii) There are several cultural values that contribute to the coexistence of nature. These are

- The cultures have their own set of traditional methods of conserving nature and its creations. Sacred qualities are often ascribed to springs, mountain peaks, plants and animals which are closely protected.
- We find troops of macaques and langurs around many temples. They are fed daily and treated as a part of temple devotees.

2. Read the source given below and answer the questions that follow.

The trade of tiger skins and the use of their bones in traditional medicines, especially in the Asian countries left the tiger population on the verge of extinction.

Since India and Nepal provide habitat to about two-thirds of the surviving tiger population in the world, these two nations became prime targets for poaching and illegal trading.

'Project Tiger', one of the well-publicised wildlife campaigns in the world, was launched in 1973. Tiger conservation has been viewed not only as an effort to save an endangered species, but with equal importance as a means of preserving biotypes of sizeable magnitude.

Corbett National Park in Uttarakhand, Sunderbans National Park in West bengal, Bandhavgarh National Park in Madhya Pradesh, Sariska Wildlife Sanctuary in Rajasthan, Manas Tiger Reserve in Assam and Periyar Tiger Reserve in Kerala are some of the tiger reserves of India.

(i) **Why India and Nepal became prime targets for poaching?**

(ii) **In your views why tiger was chosen to be protected under a project?**

(iii) **Why is tiger conservation considered important beyond saving an endangered species?**

Ans. (i) India and Nepal were prime targets of poaching because these two countries provide habitat to about two-thirds of the surviving tiger population of the world.

(ii) The population of tigers was on the verge of extinction. There was a trend of hunting and poaching of tigers for trade. Hunters traded tiger skins and used their bones in traditional medicines. These activities minimised the population of this species.

Besides, it is the national animal of India and is considered India's pride. Therefore, it was chosen as an animal to be protected under a project.

(iii) Tiger conservation is considered important beyond saving an endangered species as it give equal importance for preserving biotype at a large scale.

ASSESSMENT EXERCISE

Multiple Choice Questions (MCQs)

1. In which year was Project Tiger launched?

(a) 1973 (b) 1983

(c) 1993 (d) 1963

2. Which state in India has the largest area under permanent forests cover?

(a) Uttar Pradesh (b) Madhya Pradesh

(c) Assam (d) Meghalaya

3. Match the following.

List I	List II
A. Corbett National Park	1. Madhya Pradesh
B. Sunderbans National Park	2. West Bengal
C. Bandhavgarh National Park	3. Assam
D. Manas Tiger Reserve	4. Uttarakhand

Codes

	A	B	C	D		A	B	C	D
(a)	4	2	1	3	(b)	1	2	3	4
(c)	4	3	2	1	(d)	2	1	3	4

Subjective Questions (VSA, SA & LA)

1. Mention the community in India which is famous for protecting the black buck.

2. What was the aim of Chipko Movement?

3. How are conservation projects evolved in India and what is their current focus?

4. Analyse the government's strategy to conserve biodiversity in India.

5. 'Consumption pattern is also a reason for ecological damage'. Justify with example.

6. Explain how communities have taken measures for conservation of forests in India.

CHAPTER 3

Water Resources

Water is a precious resource which is necessary for life. Three-fourth of the Earth's surface is covered with water, but there is only a small amount of fresh water that can be used.

Fresh water is mainly obtained from surface run off and ground water. It is continually being renewed and recharged through **hydrological cycle**[1], ensuring that water is a renewable resource. It is predicted that by 2025, nearly two billion people will live in absolute water scarcity.

3.1 Water Scarcity and its Causes

The shortage of water as compared to its demand is known as **water scarcity**.

The causes of water scarcity are as follows

- Water scarcity is caused due to low rainfall and variations in seasonal and annual precipitation. This type of situation creates drought like conditions in the country.
- In most of the cases, water scarcity occurs due to **over-exploitation**, excessive use and unequal access to water among different social groups.
- Another major factor for water scarcity is the increased demand for water for domestic use and producing food by large population.
- Agriculture is also a cause of water scarcity as it requires huge water for irrigation for producing higher food grains, especially in dry-season agriculture.
- Intensive industrialisation and urbanisation in post-independent India has put pressure on freshwater resources. Industries need power to run them which comes from hydroelectric power.
- Many housing colonies have their own ground water pumping devices to meet the needs of the people. This leads to over exploitation of water.

Government of India has accorded highest priority to improve the quality of life and enhance ease of living of people especially those living in rural areas by announcing the **Jal Jeevan Mission** (JJM).

The goal of JJM is to enable every rural household get assured supply of potable piped water at a service level of 55 lts. per capita per day regularly.

Atal Bhujal Yojana

- The scheme is being implemented in 8220 water stressed gram panchayats in Gujarat, Haryana, Karnataka, Madhya Pradesh, Maharashtra, Rajasthan and Uttar Pradesh. These states account for 37% of total water stressed region of India.
- Key aspects of Atal Jal is to bring in behavioural changes in the community from the prevailing attitude of consumption and smart water management.

Need for Water Conservation and Management

- To safeguard people from health hazards caused by drinking toxic water.
- To ensure food security.
- To ensure continuation of our livelihoods and productive activities.
- To prevent degradation of our natural ecosystems.

1 Hydrological Cycle This is the cycle in which water circulates from the land to the sky and back again. It is also known as the 'Water Cycle'.

3.2 Multi-Purpose River Projects

Hydraulic structures have been constructed from ancient times. A hydraulic structure is a system to channelise the natural flow of water.

These hydraulic structures include dams built of stone rubble (broken stone), reservoirs or lakes, embankments and canals for irrigation.

The hydraulic structures built in Ancient India were as follows

- In the **1st century BC, Sringaverapura** near Allahabad had water harvesting system for channelling the flood waters of the river Ganga.
- During the time of **Chandragupta Maurya**, dams, lakes and irrigation systems were extensively built.
- Evidences of irrigation works have also been found in Kalinga (Odisha), Nagarjunakonda (Andhra Pradesh), Bennur (Karnataka) and Kolhapur (Maharashtra).
- In the **11th century**, one of the **largest artificial lakes** of that time i.e. **Bhopal lake** was built.
- In the **14th century**, tank in **Hauz Khas**, Delhi was constructed by **Iltutmish** for supplying water to Siri Fort area.
- In the modern India, the tradition of constructing hydraulic structures is continued by building dams.

Dams were originally built to regulate river and collect rainwater, which was used to irrigate agricultural fields. Today, dams are built for many purposes like electricity generation, water supply for domestic and industrial uses, flood control, recreation, inland navigation and fish breeding. Thus, they are now referred to as **multi-purpose projects**.

Multipurpose river projects were launched after Independence and were believed to lead the nation to development and progress.

First Prime Minister, **Pt Jawaharlal Nehru**, proclaimed multi-purpose river projects as **The Temples of Modern India**. This was because they combine development of agriculture and the village economy with rapid industrialisation and growth of the urban economy.

Dams

A dam is a barrier across flowing water that obstructs, directs or slows down the flow, often creating a reservoir or a lake. Dams refers to the reservoir rather than the structure.

Most dams have a section called a **spillway or weir** through which the river water flow continuously. Dams are classified according to structure, intended purpose or height as follows

- On the basis of structure and the materials used, dams are classified as **timber dams, embankment dams** or **masonry dams** with several sub-types.
- According to the height, dams can be categorised as large dams and major dams or low dams, medium height dams and high dams.
- Sardar Sarovar dam has been built over the Narmada River in Gujarat. This is one of the largest water resource projects of India covering four states i.e. Maharashtra, Madhya Pradesh, Gujarat and Rajasthan.
- 75% of the command area would meet the requirement of water in drought-prone and desert areas of Gujarat and Rajasthan.

Negative Impacts of Multi-purpose Projects

- **Effect on Soil Fertility** The reservoirs that are created on the flood plains submerge the existing vegetation and soil leading to its decomposition over a period of time.
- **Impact on Aquatic Life** Dams break up rivers making it difficult for aquatic fauna like fishes to migrate especially for **spawning** (release or deposit eggs).
- **Change in Cropping Pattern** Dams have helped in improving irrigation facilities. However, irrigation has changed the cropping pattern in many regions with farmers shifting to water intensive and commercial crops. This has great ecological consequences like salinisation of soil.
- **Excessive Sedimentation at the Bottom of the Reservoir** Regulating and damming of rivers affect their natural flow. This causes poor sediment flow and excessive collection of sediments at the bottom of the reservoir.

Further, this results in rocky **stream beds**[2] and poorer habitat for aquatic animals.

- **Inter-State Water Disputes** These disputes are also becoming common over sharing the costs and benefits of multi-purpose projects. For example, Krishna-Godavari water dispute between Karnataka, Maharashtra and Andhra Pradesh government.

Pradhan Mantri Krishi Sinchai Yojana

Objectives of the schemes are :

- To enhance the physical access of water on the farm.
- To expand cultivable area under assured irrigation.
- To improve on-farm water use efficiency to reduce wastage and increase availability both in duration and extent.
- To introduce sustainable water conservation practices, etc.

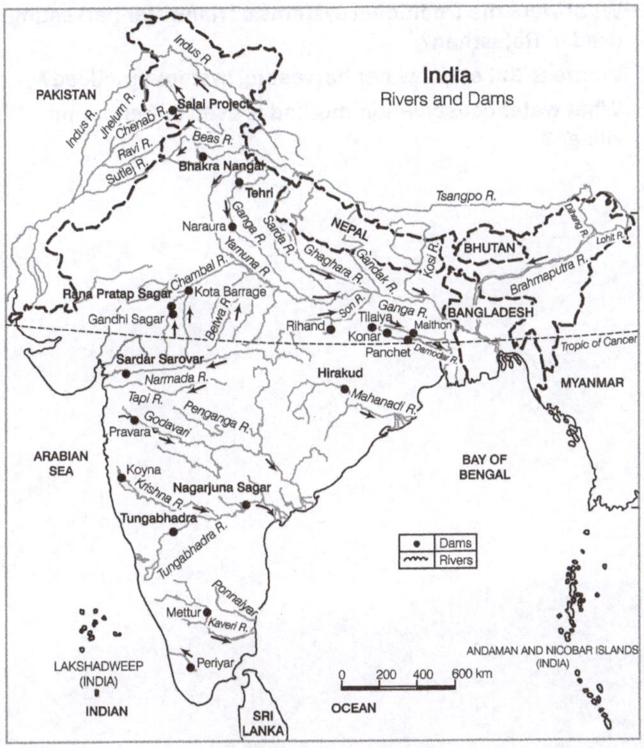

- Major Rivers and Dams

Try These

1. What % of the Earth's surface is covered with water?
2. According to Citizen's Fifth Report CSE 1999, which two rivers are far from being pure?
3. Which ruler in ancient India had extensively built dams, lakes and irrigation system?
4. What percentage of energy requirement is fulfilled by hydroelectricity in India?
5. Name a Multi-purpose project on which river has created inter-state dispute.

3.3 Rainwater Harvesting

Rainwater harvesting is the collection and storage of rainwater for reuse. In ancient India, people developed many techniques to harvest rainwater, ground water river water, and flood water which are as follows

- **Guls or Kuls** In hilly and mountainous regions, people built diversion channels like 'guls' or 'kuls'. *For example*, in Western Himalayas guls or kuls are built for agriculture.
- **Khadins and Johads** In arid and semi-arid regions, agricultural fields were converted into rainfed storage structures. This allowed the rain water to stand and moisten the soil. For example, Khadins in Jaisalmer and Johads in other parts of Rajasthan.
- **Inundation Channels** In the flood plains of Bengal, people developed **inundation channels**[3] to irrigate their fields.
- **Bamboo Drip Irrigation System** This system is in practice for 200 years in Meghalaya. In this system, water from streams and springs in the hills get transported to agricultural fields by using bamboo as pipes.

  About 15-20 liters of water enters the bamboo pipe system gets transported over hundreds of meters and finally reduces to 20-80 drops per minute at the site of the plant.
- **Rooftop Rainwater Harvesting** It is mainly practised to store drinking water, particularly in Rajasthan. It is also practiced in Gendathur village in Mysuru, Karnataka and towns and villages of the Thar.

2 **Stream bed** It refers to the channel of the river in which the water flows.
3 **Inundation channel** It is a channel that is connected to a large river so that the flood water in the rivers flows in it.

- **Tankas** or underground tanks are built for storing water insides the main house or the courtyard. The tanks could be as large as a big room.
  Tankas were connected to the sloping roofs of the houses through a pipe. Rain falling on the rooftops would travel down the pipe and was stored in these underground tankas. This is mainly practised in the semi-arid and arid regions of Rajasthan, particularly in Bikaner, Phalodi and Barmer.

  This rainwater, which is commonly referred as **palar pani** can be used during dry periods (summers) when other sources are dried up. The first spell of rain was usually not collected as this would clean the roofs and pipes. Many houses constructed underground rooms adjoining the 'tanka' to avoid the summer heat as it would keep the room cool.

Rooftop Rainwater Harvesting in Shillong and Karnataka

Rooftop rainwater harvesting is the most common practice in Shillong, Meghalaya. **Cherapunjee** and **Mawsynram**, situated at a distance of 55 km from Shillong, receive the **highest rainfall** in the world, but still the state capital Shillong faces acute shortage of water. Therefore, nearly every household in the city has a rooftop rainwater harvesting structure. Nearly 15-25 per cent of the total water requirement of the household comes from rooftop water harvesting.

Gendathur is a backward village in Mysuru, Karnataka which receives an annual precipitation of 1000 mm. Every house has installed rooftop rain water harvesting system and can collect and use about 50000 litres of water annually.

KNOWLEDGE PLUS In Western Rajasthan, the practice of rooftop rainwater harvesting is on decline. It is because the plenty of water is available due to Indira Gandhi Canal. **Tamil Nadu** is the **first state** in India which has made rooftop rainwater harvesting structure compulsory to all the houses across the state and punish the defaulters.

Try These

1. **Sabarmati basin is located in which state?**
2. **What were the traditional systems of rainwater harvesting used in Rajasthan?**
3. **Where is Gul or Kul water harvesting system practiced?**
4. **What water conservation method is used in Gendathur village?**

Mind Map

WATER RESOURCES

Water Scarcity and its Causes

Need for Water Conservation and Management
- Safeguard people from health hazards by drinking toxic water.
- Ensure food security.
- Prevent degradation of our natural ecosystems.
- Ensure continuation of our livelihoods and production activities.

Causes
- Low rainfall
- Over-exploitation of water
- Intensive industrialisation and urbanisation
- Water pollution
- Agriculture

Rainwater Harvesting

Techniques
- Guls or Kuls
- Khadins and Johads
- Inundation Channels
- Bamboo Drip Irrigation System
- Rooftop Rainwater Harvesting
- Tankas

Multi-Purpose River Projects

Negative Impacts
- Effect on soil fertility
- Impact on aquatic life.
- Change in cropping pattern
- Excessive sedimentation at the bottom of the reservoir
- Inter-state water disputes

Hydraulic Structures
- Water Harvesting System in Sringaverapura
- Dams, lakes and irrigation systems built extensively during the time of Chandragupta Maurya.
- Tank in Hauz Khas, Delhi in 14th Century.
- Largest artificial lake, Bhopal lake in 11th Century.
- Hydraulic structures built in modern India for development of agriculture and industrialisation and growth of urban economy.

NCERT FOLDER

Covering Intext Questions and Exercises of NCERT

EXERCISES

Q.1 Multiple choice questions

(i) Based on the information given below classify each of the situations as 'suffering from water scarcity' or 'not suffering from water scarcity.'

(a) Region with high annual rainfall.

(b) Region having high annual rainfall and large population.

(c) Region having high annual rainfall but water is highly polluted.

(d) Region having low rainfall and low population.

Ans.

Suffering from water scarcity	Not suffering from water scarcity
(b) Region having high annual rainfall and large population.	(a) Region with high annual rainfall.
(c) Region having high annual rainfall but water is highly polluted.	
(d) Region having low rainfall and low population.	

(ii) Which one of the following statements is not an argument in favour of multi-purpose river projects?

(a) Multi-purpose projects bring water to those areas which suffer from water scarcity.

(b) Multi-purpose projects by regulating water flow helps to control floods.

(c) Multi-purpose projects lead to large- scale displacements and loss of livelihood.

(d) Multi-purpose projects generate electricity for our industries and our homes.

Ans. (c) Multi-purpose projects lead to large-scale displacements and loss of livelihood.

(iii) Here are some false statements. Identify the mistakes and rewrite them correctly.

(a) Multiplying urban centres with large and dense populations and urban lifestyles have helped in proper utilisation of water resources.

(b) Regulating and damming of rivers does not affect the river's natural flow and its sediment flow.

(c) Today in Rajasthan, the practice of rooftop rainwater harvesting has gained popularity despite high water availability due to the Indira Gandhi Canal.

Ans. (a) Multiplying urban centres with a large and dense populations and urban lifestyles have not only added to water and energy requirements, but have further aggravated the problem.

(b) Regulating and damming of rivers affect their natural flow causing poor sediment flow and excessive sedimentation at the bottom of the reservoir. It result in rockier stream beds and poorer habitats for the rivers' aquatic life.

(c) Today, in Western Rajasthan, the practice of rooftop rainwater harvesting is on the decline as plenty of water is available due to the perennial Rajasthan canal, though some houses still maintain the tanks since they do not like the taste of tap water.

Q.2 Answer the following questions in about 30 words.

(i) Explain how water becomes a renewable resource.

Ans. Water becomes a renewable resource through the hydrological cycle. Freshwater is mainly obtained from the surface runoff and groundwater is continually being renewed and recharged through the hydrological cycle.

(ii) What is water scarcity and what are its main causes?

Ans. The shortage of water as compared to its demand is known as water scarcity.

The main causes of water scarcity are as follows

- **Growing Population** A large population means more water requirement for cooking, washing and bathing.
- **Industrialisation** The increasing number of industries put pressure on the existing freshwater resources. Industries are heavy users of water.
- **Commercialisation of Agriculture** Commercial crops need more water and other inputs. Means of irrigation like tubewells and canals are responsible for the falling groundwater levels.

(iii) Compare the advantages and disadvantages of multi-purpose river projects.

Ans. The various advantages and disadvantages of multi-purpose river projects can be compared as given below

Advantages

- Irrigation of crops
- Electricity generation
- Water supply for industrial and domestic purposes
- Flood control

- Inland navigation
- Fish breeding

Disadvantages

- Effect on soil fertility
- Impact on aquatic life
- Change in cropping pattern
- Excessive sedimentation at the bottom of the reservoir
- Excessive use of water
- Increasing social crop

Q.3 Answer the following questions in about 120 words.

(i) Discuss how rainwater harvesting in semi-arid regions of Rajasthan is carried out.

Ans. Rainwater harvesting in semi-arid regions of Rajasthan is carried out in the following ways

- In arid and semi-arid regions of Rajasthan, agricultural fields were converted into rainfed storage structures that allowed the rain water to stand and moister the soil like the Khadins in Jaisalmer and Johads in other parts of Rajasthan.
- Rooftop rainwater harvesting was commonly practiced to store drinking water in semi-arid and arid regions of Rajasthan, particularly in Bikaner, Phalodi, Barmer and across the towns and villages of the Thar desert.
- Every house in these regions had underground tanks or tankas to store the water for drinking purposes.
- These tankas are large and deep tanks which were built inside the courtyard. They were linked to the sloping roofs of the houses through a pipe. Rainwater falling on the rooftops would run down through the pipe and collect in the underground tankas.
- The collected rainwater was stored in the underground tankas providing drinking water till the next seasons. When all other sources have dried up, these tankas were beneficial to beat the summer heat as they kept the room cool.

(*ii*) Describe how modern adaptations of traditional rainwater harvesting methods are being carried out to conserve and store water.

Ans. Modern adaptations of traditional rainwater harvesting methods which are being carried out to conserve and store water are as follows

- 'Rooftop rainwater harvesting' is practiced in semi-arid areas of Rajasthan to store drinking water.
- In the semi-arid and arid regions of Rajasthan, particularly in Bikaner, Phalodi, Barmer and across the towns and villages of the Thar desert, almost all the houses traditionally had underground tanks or tankas for storing drinking water.
- In hills and mountainous regions, people build diversion channels to collect rainwater, spring water and store in circular tanks.
- In arid and semi-arid regions, agricultural fields were converted into rainfed storage structures that allowed the water to stand and moisten the soil like the 'Khadins' in Jaisalmer and the 'Johads' in other parts of Rajasthan.
- In the flood plains of Bengal, people developed inundation channels to irrigate their fields.
- Bamboo drip irrigation system is also being used for water from streams and springs in the hills get transported to agricultural fields by using bamboo as pipes.

REVIEW EXERCISE

Including Competency Based Questions

Part I

Multiple Choice Questions (MCQs)

1. Which one of the following factors is mainly responsible for declining water level in India? CBSE Term I 2021

(a) Irrigation (b) Industrialisation
(c) Urbanisation (d) Over-utilisation

2. Ankur, a resident from Rajasthan, decided to install a submersible water pump in his house, capable of extracting groundwater from depths of 250-300 m. This practice of installing similar pumps is becoming increasingly popular across the state.

Which of the following will this growing practice most likely lead to in the near future? CBSE Additional SQP 2023-24

(a) Decline in the groundwater quality
(b) Reduced monsoon water resources
(c) Increased number of waterborne diseases
(d) Water scarcity resulting from excessive utilisation

3. Which place in India has an artificial lake to conserve water that dates back to 11th century?

(a) Delhi (b) Bhopal
(c) Bennur (d) Kolhapur

4. Who among the following proclaimed the dam as the 'Temples of Modern India'?

(a) Mahatma Gandhi (b) Jawaharlal Nehru
(c) Moti Lal Nehru (d) Lal Bahadur Shastri

5. Apart from flood control and irrigation, what are the other uses of multi-purpose projects?

(a) Recreation (b) Fish breeding
(c) Inland navigation (d) All of these

6. The Hirakud dam is built on which of the following rivers?

(a) Satluj (b) Beas
(c) Mahanadi (d) Krishna

7. Choose the correct option regarding major states involved in the Krishna - Godavari issue. CBSE 2025

(a) Karnataka, Kerala and Tamil Nadu
(b) Maharashtra, Karnataka and Andhra Pradesh
(c) Gujarat, Maharashtra and Madhya Pradesh
(d) Jharkhand, Andhra Pradesh and Odisha

8. Which among the following regions of India experience low rainfall and is drought prone?

(a) Rajasthan (b) Gujarat (c) Bihar (d) Telangana

9. In which part of India, rooftop rainwater harvesting is declining?

(a) Western Rajasthan
(b) Eastern Kerala
(c) Eastern Rajasthan
(d) Tamil Nadu

10. Rainwater harvesting involves developing wide ranging techniques to harvest rainwater, groundwater, river water and flood water in keeping with the local ecological conditions and their water needs.

Which of the following examples does not represent rainwater harvesting?

(a) A farmer built diversion channel in Western Himalayas called 'guls' or 'kuls' for agriculture.
(b) Farmers of Jaisalmer converted their fields into Khadins.
(c) Government gave subsidy to farmers for the installation of solar water pumps.
(d) An NGO donated 25 lakh rupees in a village at Barmer district for the construction of underground tankas.

11. Which of the following places gets the highest rainfall in the world?

(a) Mawsynram (b) Aizawl
(c) Shillong (d) Cherrapunji

12. Which one of the following is the irrigation system in Meghalaya? CBSE 2024

(a) To irrigation land only during rainy season.
(b) To use large volumes of water.
(c) To remove water from soil for irrigation.
(d) To use bamboo drip irrigation system.

13. Akash, a farmer from Madhya Pradesh has recently installed new water pump in his farm. Since then he is focusing more on water intensive and commercial crops.

Following him several farmers of this region has adopted the same practice.

Accordingly, which of the following will be the most likely consequence generated in this region due to this shift in cropping pattern? Competency Based

(a) Sharp increase in crop production
(b) Guaranteed production of high quality crops
(c) Infestation of pests in the crops
(d) Salinisation of the soil

14. Arrange the following in correct sequence regarding rainwater harvesting process.

I. Pipes are connected to underground tanks.
II. Rocks and sand in the tanks filter the rainwater.
III. Rainwater from rooftops is collected using pipes.
IV. Clean water is then available for drinking purposes.

Codes

(a) III, I, II, IV
(b) IV, I, III, II
(c) II, I, III, IV
(d) I, III, II, IV

15. In a debate competition at a school two groups of students had an issue over whether water is a renewable resource or a non-renewable resource. The teacher resolved the situation by telling them that the water is a renewable resource because **Competency Based**

I. Three-fourth of Earth is covered with water.
II. Large amount of fresh water is stored as Groundwater.
III. There is existence of a hydrological cycle on the Earth.
IV. It is available everywhere on Earth.

Codes

(a) Only I
(b) III and IV
(c) Only III
(d) I, II, III and IV

16. Which of the following statements is/are correct regarding 'water scarcity'?

I. Water scarcity is also due to human factors.
II. Availability of sources of water varies over space and time.
III. Water availability affects food production adversely.
IV. Irrigated agriculture is preferred over dry season agriculture to conserve water.

Codes

(a) Only I
(b) Only II
(c) I, II, III and IV
(d) I, II and III

17. Which of the following statements are true regarding Atal Bhujal Yojana (ABY)?

I. It is being implemented in 8220 gram panchayats of eight states
II. The selected states accounts for 37% of total number of water stressed blocks in India.
III. One of the key aspect of scheme is to bring behavioural change in community.
IV. One of the goal is to provide piped drinking water.

Codes

(a) I and II
(b) II and III
(c) II and IV
(d) I, II and IV

18. Identify the reasons as to why rainwater harvesting system should be promoted in a country. Choose the appropriate statement(s) among the following options. **Competency Based**

I. Rainwater harvesting can provide solution to the problems associated with the multi-purpose river projects.
II. Rainwater harvesting system is environmentally sustainable.
III. Rainwater harvesting system is socio-economically viable.
IV. Rainwater harvesting system is very useful for those regions which are drought prone.

Codes

(a) Statement I and II are appropriate
(b) Statements II, III and IV are appropriate
(c) All the statements are appropriate
(d) Only statement IV is appropriate

19. Consider the following statements and choose the correct option. **Competency Based**

Statement I Telangana is the first state in India which has made rooftop rainwater harvesting structure compulsory to all the houses across the state.

Statement II In Tamil Nadu, there are legal provisions to punish the defaulters who do not install rooftop rainwater harvesting structure.

Codes

(a) Statement I is correct and II is incorrect
(b) Statement I is incorrect and II is correct
(c) Both I and II are incorrect
(d) Both I and II are correct

Answers

1. (d)	**2.** (d)	**3.** (b)	**4.** (b)	**5.** (d)
6. (c)	**7.** (b)	**8.** (a)	**9.** (a)	**10.** (c)
11. (a)	**12.** (d)	**13.** (d)	**14.** (a)	**15.** (c)
16. (d)	**17.** (c)	**18.** (c)	**19.** (b)	

Match the Following

1.

List I (Dam)		List II (River)	
A.	Hirakud	1.	Chambal
B.	Gandhi Sagar	2.	Krishna
C.	Nagarjuna Sagar	3.	Kaveri
D.	Mettur	4.	Mahanadi

Codes

	A	B	C	D		A	B	C	D
(a)	4	1	1	2	(b)	1	2	4	3
(c)	4	1	2	3	(d)	1	2	3	4

Ans. 1. (c)

Assertion-Reason

1. Assertion (A) The availability of water resources varies over space and time.

Reason (R) Availability of water resources helps in storing water.

Codes

(a) Both A and R are true, but R is not the correct explanation of A
(b) Both A and R are true and R is the correct explanation of A
(c) Both A and R are incorrect
(d) A is correct, but R is incorrect

2. Assertion (A) Dams are referred to as multi-purpose projects.

Reason (R) Dams are built for irrigation, electricity generation, water supply for domestic and industrial use, flood control, recreation and fish breeding.

Codes

(a) Both A and R are true, but R is not the correct explanation of A
(b) Both A and R are true and R is the correct explanation of A
(c) Both A and R are incorrect
(d) A is correct, but R is incorrect

3. Assertion (A) Irrigation is considered to be the major source of agriculture.

Reason (R) Dams are well-known for their capacity to hold water for agriculture.

Codes

(a) Both A and R are true, but R is not the correct explanation of A
(b) Both A and R are true and R is the correct explanation of A
(c) Both A and R are incorrect
(d) A is correct, but R is incorrect

4. Assertion (A) The Practice of rainwater harvesting is encouraged to recharge groundwater levels.

Reason (R) Rainwater harvesting helps in storing water, particularly in regions experiencing water scarcity.

Codes

(a) Both A and R are true, but R is not the correct explanation of A
(b) Both A and R are true and R is the correct explanation of A
(c) Both A and R are incorrect
(d) A is correct, but R is incorrect

5. Assertion (A) Sophisticated hydraulic structures like Sringaverapura were build in 19th century to fulfill water needs for industrial purposes.

Reason (R) Sringaverapura near Allahabad had sophisticated water harvesting system channelling the flood water of the river Ganga.

Codes

(a) Both A and R are true, but R is not the correct explanation of A
(b) Both A and R are true and R is the correct explanation of A
(c) Both A and R are incorrect
(d) A is correct, but R is incorrect

Ans. 1. (a) Both A and R are true, but R is not the correct explanation of A
2. (b) Both A and R are true and R is the correct explanation of A
3. (a) Both A and R are true, but R is not the correct explanation of A
4. (b) Both A and R are true and R is the correct explanation of A
5. (d) A is correct, but R is incorrect

Picture Based Questions

1. Identify the techniques of water conservation shown in the picture.

(a) Rainwater harvesting
(b) Hydraulic structures
(c) Plant vegetation
(d) None of the above

2. Which technique of water conservation is shown below?

(a) Zero Net Deforestation
(b) Rainwater Harvesting
(c) Bamboo Drip Irrigation System
(d) None of the above

3. Observe the map given below showing the distribution of major rivers and dams across India.

Sardar Sarovar dam has been built over the Narmada river in Gujarat and it is one of the largest water resource projects of India.

Accordingly, which of the following states of India have been covered by this project?

(a) Gujarat, Maharashtra and Rajasthan
(b) Gujarat, Rajasthan , Madhya Pradesh and Maharashtra
(c) Gujarat, Rajasthan, Andhra Pradesh and Maharashtra
(d) Gujarat, Rajasthan, Uttar Pradesh and Madhya Pradesh

Ans. 1. (a) Rainwater harvesting
2. (c) Bamboo Drip Irrigation System
3. (b) Gujarat, Rajasthan , Madhya Pradesh and Maharashtra

Case Based Question

1 Read the passage given below and answer the questions that follow.

Archaeological and historical records show that from ancient times we have been constructing sophisticated hydraulic structures like dams built of stone rubble, reservoirs or lakes, embankments and canals for irrigation. Not surprisingly, we have continued this tradition in modern India by building dams in most of our river basins.

Dams were traditionally built to impound rivers and rainwater that could be used later to irrigate agricultural fields. Today, dams are built not just for irrigation but for electricity generation, water supply for domestic and industrial uses, flood control, recreation, inland navigation and fish breeding. Hence, dams are now referred to as multi-purpose projects where the many uses of the impounded water are integrated with one another.

(i) Which of the following places near Allahabad had sophisticated water harvesting system channelling the flood water of river Ganga in 1st century BC?

(a) Dwarasamudra (b) Sringaverapura
(c) Srikalahasti (d) Sringeri

(ii) Which of the following projects have been built over the Mahanadi river?

(a) Hirakud project
(b) Bhakra-Nangal project
(c) Sardar Sarovar project
(d) Krishnaganga project

(iii) In which of the following areas the multi-purpose river projects can be utilised?

(a) Water conservation
(b) Flood control
(c) Hydel power generation
(d) All of these

Ans. (i) (b) Sringaverapura
(ii) (a) Hirakud project
(iii) (d) All of these

Part II

Very Short Answer Type Questions

1. What are the sources of freshwater on the Earth?

Ans. Precipitation, surface runoff that goes into the rivers and groundwater are the sources of freshwater on the Earth.

2. What is the most important benefit of 'hydrological cycle'?

Ans. Hydrological cycle is important as it renewed and recharged the fresh water which is quite essential for sustenance of life.

3. What will be the consequences, if the fresh water is not conserved now?

Ans. If freshwater is not conserved now, then in near future all the living beings will suffer from water shortage and food crisis.

4. Why are multi-purpose projects considered important for agriculture?

Ans. Multi-purpose projects are important for agricultre because they provide irrigation water and help in enchancing agricultural productivity.

5. What are popularly termed as 'The Temples of Modern India'?

Ans. Multi-purpose projects are popularly known as 'The Temples of Modern India'.

6. Name the hydraulic structure that obstructs the flowing water and regulates the flow for constructive purpose.

Ans. The hydraulic structure that obstructs the flowing water and regulates the flow for constructive purpose is dam.

7. Give an example where ancient large hydraulic structure was built.

Ans. An example where ancient large hydraulic structure was in Sringaverapura near Allahabad' in North India (in 1st century BC). It had sophisticated water harvesting system to control flood water of the river Ganga.

8. What is the importance of Hirakud project?

Ans. Hirakud Dam project is important for irrigation, flood management and power production. It is essential for agriculture and generating electricity.

9. Name some hydroelectric projects on Damodar river basin.

Ans. Some major hydroelectric projects on Damodar river are Damodar Tilaya, Konar, Maithon and Panchet.

10. 'The combination of climate change and population growth poses a serious threat to India's water scarcity and without adequate measures to address these challenges.......'.

Source Business standard

How a large population poses threat to water scarcity? **Competency Based**

Ans. A large population poses threat to water scarcity due to excessive use and unequal access to water among different social groups, and the increased demand for water for domestic use and producing food by large population.

11. Arun performed a web search for 'water scarce regions' and found that there exists some areas where water is sufficiently available to meet the needs of the people but it still suffers from water scarcity. How this situation can arise? **Competency Based**

Ans. The situation where water is sufficiently available to meet the needs of the people but still suffers from water scarcity can arise due to pollution caused by domestic and industrial wastes, as well as chemicals, pesticides and fertilisers used in agriculture.

In such cases, even though these may be an abundance of water, its quality is not good, making it hazardous for human use. The pollution can lead the water scarcity issues despite the presence of enough water supply.

Short Answer Type Questions

1. "Water scarcity may be an outcome of large and growing population in India." Analyse the statement.

Ans. Water scarcity may be an outcome of large and growing population in India. It can be analysed through the following points

(i) Post-independent India witnessed intensive industrialisation and urbanisation. This situation increased water demand.

(ii) The increasing demand of water by the growing population leads to the over-exploitation of water resources for various purposes. For example, for drinking, domestic uses, agriculture, electricity generation and so on.

(iii) Increasing urban centres with large and dense populations and urban lifestyles have not only added to water and energy requirements but have further aggravated the problem of water scarcity.

2. Multi-purpose projects, launched after Independence with their integrated water resources management approach, were thought of as the vehicle that would lead the nation to development and progress, overcoming the handicap of its colonial past.

Why do you think that multi-purpose projects were given such importance? Substantiate your answer by giving any four reasons. **Competency Based**

Ans. The reasons for launching multi-purpose river projects in India after independence and giving them importance, are as follows

(i) Electricity generation is one of the objectives of multi-purpose projects. India generates approximately 22 per cent of its energy needs through these projects.

(ii) They control floods by storing excess water in their reservoirs.

(iii) During the dry season, the stored water in these projects can be used to irrigate the fields.

(iv) Trees are systematically planted around reservoirs in these projects which help in preserving the natural eco-system as well as wildlife.

3. Multi-purpose projects are 'Temples of Modern India'. Justify.

Or **Why are multi-purpose projects considered as the 'Temples of Modern India'?**

Ans. Multi-purpose river projects are 'Temples of Modern India' due to the following reasons

- They were considered to bring development in agriculture and the village economy with rapid industrialisation and growth in the urban economy.
- The dams were an important symbol of these projects and consequently of the modernisation of India. That is why, Nehru called dams as the 'Temples of Modern India'.
- The multi-purpose projects controls flood as well as useful in irrigation, electricity generation, fish breeding, etc.

4. Do you think multi-purpose projects have failed to achieve the purpose for which they were built? Justify your answer.

Ans. Yes, multi-purpose projects have failed to achieve their purpose. The following reasons supports the statement :

- The multi-purpose projects were constructed to control floods, but due to excessive sedimentation at the bottom of the reservoir, these cause floods in nearby areas.
- These projects have displaced local population leading to mass protests, agitations and movements.
- They also cause destruction of the environment, as forest land have to be cleared around the rivers to construct huge reservoirs.

5. Identify any three hydraulic structures as part of water management programmes initiated in ancient India along with the period when they were built.

Or **Highlight any three hydraulic structures as a part of water management programmes initiated in ancient India?**

Ans. The three hydraulic structures that were built in ancient India as a part of water management are as follows

- In the 1st century BC, Sringaverapura near Allahabad had water harvesting system channelling the flood water of the river Ganga.
- During the reign of Chandragupta Maurya, dams, lakes and irrigation systems were extensively built.
- In the period of 11th century, Bhopal lake, one of the largest artificial lakes was built.
- In the 14th century, the tank in Hauz Khas, Delhi was built by Iltutmish for supplying water to Siri Fort area.

6. Give two reasons why is rainwater harvesting important in India. Name two states which practise rainwater harvesting in India.

Or **Analyse the importance of rainwater harvesting.**

Ans. Importance of rainwater harvesting can be analysed through the following points

(i) With the help of rainwater harvesting techniques groundwater can be recharged and its level can be increased.

(ii) The water harvested can be conserved and used during the dry season. Thus, the water demand of growing population can be met.

Two states practising rainwater harvesting in India are Rajasthan and Gujarat.

7. "Traditional harvesting system is a useful system to conserve and store water". Highlight the importance of this system with two examples.

Ans. Traditional harvesting system is a useful system to conserve and store water. The two examples that highlight the importance of traditional harvesting system are as follows

(i) In hilly areas like Himachal Pradesh, the system of using diversion channels called 'guls' and 'kuls'. These are used for storing water for irrigation.

(ii) In Meghalaya, the bamboo pipe drip irrigation system is used. It is used to irrigate crops.

8. Aadarsh visits a village in Western Uttar Pradesh and listens to the conversation of two people who were discussing about the water scarcity problem in the area during the dry season. Aadarsh notices that this area receives sufficient amount of rainfall but still faces water scarcity due to underutilisation of the rainwater.

How can this problem be solved? Explain. Competency Based

Ans. This problem can be solved by installing a rooftop rainwater harvesting system.

The procedure or working of rooftop rainwater is a typical method. The rainwater falling on the roof is collected through a PVC pipe and filtered using sand and bricks. Then, it is collected in the sump for immediate use.

Excess water from the sump is transferred to a well, which recharges the groundwater. Any further requirement of water can be taken from the well. Sometimes, a hand pump is attached to the pipe that connects the sump. With the use of hand pump, the collected rain water can then be drain out and used.

9. 'India's rivers, especially the smaller ones, have all turned into toxic streams. And even the big ones like the Ganga and Yamuna are far from being pure.' Competency Based

(i) What are the reasons behind the above situations of our rivers?

Ans. The rivers in India are continuously being polluted due to population growth, agricultural modernisation, urbanisation and industrialisation. All these factors have become enormous and growing day by day leading to pressure on our rivers and thus resulting into pollution. This situation makes the entire life stands threatened.

(ii) What is the need of the hour in the above situation?

Ans. The need of the hour is to conserve and manage our water resources, to safeguard ourselves from health hazards, to ensure food security, continuation of our livelihoods and productive activities and also to prevent degradation of our natural ecosystems. Over exploitation and mismanagement of water resources will impoverish this resource and cause ecological crisis that may have profound impact on our lives.

Long Answer Type Questions

1. 'True, the availability of water resources varies over space and time, mainly due to the variations in seasonal and annual precipitation, but water scarcity in most cases is caused by over-exploitation, excessive use and unequal access to water among different social groups.'

Justify the statement by giving five relevant points regarding the factors responsible for water scarcity in India. Competency Based

Ans. Following are the five important factors responsible for the water scarcity in India

(i) Water scarcity is an outcome of large and growing population and consequent greater demands for water and unequal access to it.

(ii) To facilitate higher foodgrain production, water resources are being over-exploited to expand irrigated areas and dry season agriculture.

(iii) Industries apart from being heavy users of water, also require power to run them. Much of this energy comes from hydroelectric power.

(iv) Increasing urban centres with large and dense populations and urban life styles have not only added to water and energy requirements but have further aggravated the problems.

(v) Much of water is polluted due to domestic and industrial wastes, chemicals, pesticides and fertilisers used in agriculture. Thus, making it unfit for human use.

2. India is one of the world's biggest crop producers and more than half of its 1.3 billion people rely on agriculture for their livelihoods. But the groundwater that makes up 40% of the country's water supply has been steadily depleting for years. The study,

published Wednesday in the journal Science Advances, found that overuse of groundwater could cause winter harvests in some regions of the country to fall up to two thirds by 2025.

Source : CNN

Analyse as to why groundwater is a highly overused resource ?

Ans. Now-a-days, groundwater is highly overused because of several reasons as follows

- Groundwater is a fresh water source and used for drinking purpose. It is over-exploited in urban areas for domestic purposes and drinking purpose.
- Groundwater is also over-exploited for irrigation purpose especially in Green Revolution areas of Punjab-Haryana-Western Uttar Pradesh region. Intensive agricultural practices intensify over-exploitation of groundwater.
- In urban areas, housing societies draw out ground water with the use of electric pumps to fulfill their water needs. In this way, ground water is used up rapidly.
- After the toxication and pollution of many rivers and lakes, groundwater becomes the only source of fresh water used directly without treatment. For all these reasons, groundwater is highly exploited.

Case Based Questions

1. Read the source given below and answer the questions that follows. **CBSE Additional SQP 2023-24**

Given the abundance and renewability of water, it is difficult to imagine that we may suffer from water scarcity. The moment we speak of water shortages; we immediately associate it with regions having low rainfall or those that are drought prone.

We instantaneously visualise the deserts of Rajasthan and women balancing many 'matkas' (earthen pots) used for collecting and storing water and travelling long distances to get water. True, the availability of water resources varies over space and time, mainly due to the variations in seasonal and annual precipitation, but water scarcity in most cases is caused by over-exploitation, excessive use and unequal access to water among different social groups.

(i) How do women collect water in Rajasthan?

Ans. Women in Rajasthan travel to long distances carrying earthen pots balanced on their heads to collect water.

(ii) How is water scarcity in most areas caused?

Ans. Water scarcity in most areas caused by human activities such as over-exploitation, excessive use and unequal access to water among different social groups.

(iii) Do you think rainwater harvesting can help? Give reasons to justify your answer.

Ans. Yes, I think rainwater harvesting can help in this situation because of the following reasons

- Rainwater can be harvested under a variety of conditions.
- It is an easy and simple process, and requires less cost.
- Providing piped water supply to every region is sometimes not feasible. In this case rainwater harvesting is a good option.

2. Read the source given below and answer the questions that follow. **CBSE SQP 2023-24**

Maharashtra is a state located in Western India, with a population of over 110-million people. The state is home to several large cities, including Mumbai, and has a significant agricultural sector. However, the state is facing a severe water crisis, with its water resources coming under increasing pressure due to climate change, industrialisation and urbanisation.

The main challenges faced by water resource management in Maharashtra are

Overexploitation of groundwater Maharashtra is one of the most groundwater-stressed states in India, with the demand for water exceeding the supply. Overexploitation of groundwater for agriculture and urban use has led to a decline in water levels, which has severe implications for the sustainability of water resources.

Pollution of surface water Industrialisation and urbanisation have led to the pollution of surface water bodies such as rivers and lakes. The pollution has led to water quality degradation, which poses risks to human health and the environment.

Inefficient irrigation practices The agricultural sector is the largest user of water in Maharashtra, accounting for around 80% of total water use. However, traditional irrigation practices such as flood irrigation are inefficient and lead to the wastage of water.

(i) Mention any two reasons for the water crisis faced by the state Maharashtra.

Ans. Two reasons for facing a water crisis in Maharashtra are overexploitation of groundwater and pollution of surface water bodies due to industrialisation and urbanisation.

(ii) Despite being the second highest rainfall-receiving state of the country, Maharashtra still faces water crisis. Substantiate this statement in 40 words.

Ans. Despite receiving the second-highest rainfall in the country, traditional irrigation practices like flood irrigation leading to water shortages in Maharashtra. This is because flood irrigation involves excessive water use, and the water gets lost due to runoff, leading to less water available for other uses.

(iii) Propose any one solution to mitigate the water crisis faced by Maharashtra state.

Ans. To mitigate the water crisis in Maharashtra, one solution could be to promote the adoption of more efficient irrigation practices, such as drip irrigation and sprinkler systems, that use less water and are more targeted in their delivery.

3. Read the source given below and answer the questions that follow.

In ancient India, along with the sophisticated hydraulic structures, there existed an extraordinary tradition of water-harvesting system. People had an in-depth knowledge of rainfall regimes and soil types and developed wide ranging techniques to harvest groundwater, rainwater, river water and flood water in keeping with the local ecological conditions and their water needs. In hilly and mountainous regions, people built diversion channels like the kuls and guls of Western Himalayas for agriculture. Rooftop rainwater harvesting was very commonly practised to store drinking water, particularly in Rajasthan.

(i) Mention any two methods of traditional water-harvesting used in India.

(ii) How do people of Rajasthan utilise rainwater?

(iii) Explain any two benefits of rainwater harvesting.

Ans. (i) The two methods of rainwater harvesting used in India are

(a) **Guls and Kuls** People built guls and kuls in hilly and mountainous regions to divert water. They are mainly used for agriculture in the Western Himalayas.

(b) **Khadins and Johads** In arid and semi-arid regions of Rajasthan, agricultural fields were converted into rain fed storage structures. This allowed the rain water to stand and moisten the soil.

(ii) The people of the semi-arid regions of Rajasthan have traditionally constructed tanks (Tankas) for storing drinking water. They are big and are a part of the well-developed rooftop rainwater harvesting system.

The tanks are constructed inside the main house or the courtyard, and are connected to the sloping roofs of the houses through a pipe. The rain falling on the rooftop would travels down the pipe and is stored in the tanks.

(iii) Following are the benefits of rainwater harvesting

(a) It improves the access to drinking and irrigation water.

(b) It increases groundwater recharge and reduce storm water discharges.

Map Based Questions

1. **On the outline map of India given below, locate and label the following dams.** **CBSE SQP 2022-23**
   (i) Hirakud dam (ii) Tungabhadra dam
   (iii) Bhakra Nangal dam (iv) Salal dam
   (v) Tehri dam
   (vi) Sardar Sarovar dam

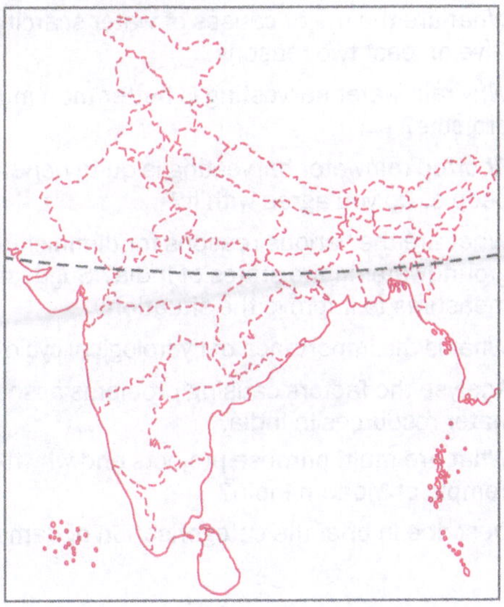

Ans.

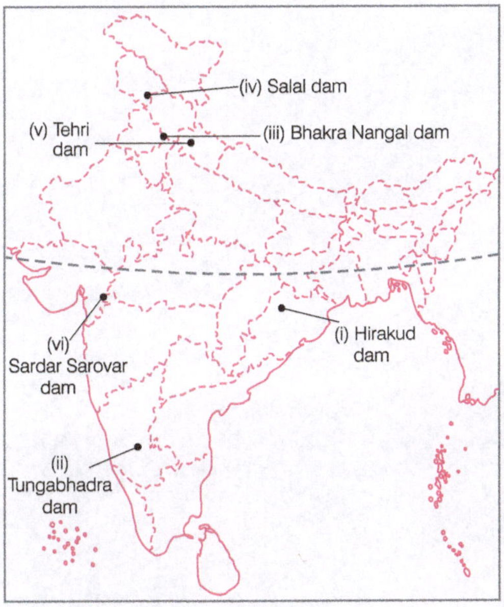

2. **On the outline map of India given below, mark and label the following.**
   (i) Rana Pratap Sagar dam
   (ii) Nagarjuna Sagar dam

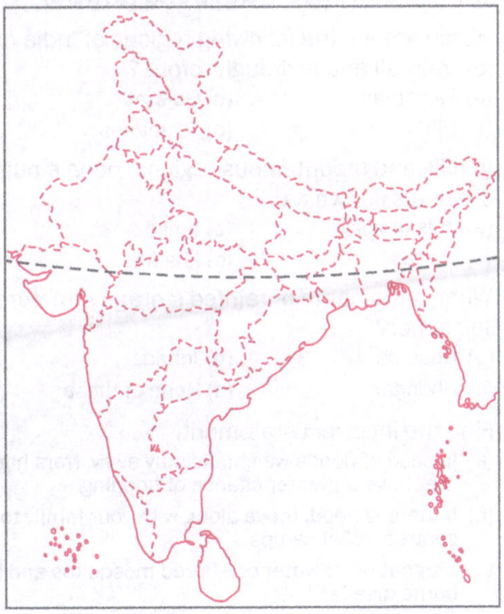

Ans.

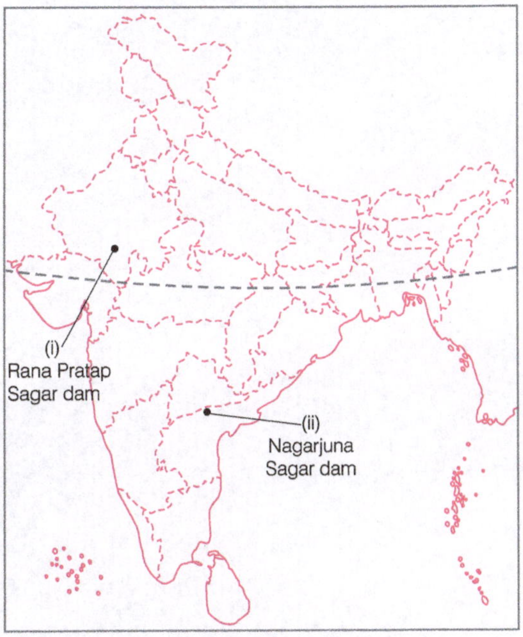

ASSESSMENT EXERCISE

Multiple Choice Questions (MCQs)

1. Which among the following regions of India experience low rainfall and is drought prone?
(a) Rajasthan (b) Gujarat
(c) Bihar (d) Telangana

2. In hills and mountainous regions, people built diversion channels known as
(a) guls or kuls (b) tanks
(c) johads (d) khadins

3. What is the name of rainfed storage structure in Jaisalmer?
(a) Khadins (b) Johads
(c) Bhangan (d) None of these

4. Find the incorrect statement.
(a) In case of floods we should stay away, from higher areas as they have a greater chance of flooding.
(b) If there is flood, move along with your family to evacuation centres, relief camps.
(c) Stagnation of water can breed mosquitos and lead to water borne diseases.
(d) Use bleaching powder and lime to disinfect the surroundings.

Subjective Questions (VSA, SA and LA)

1. What is fresh water? What is its availability on the Earth?

2. Jal Jeevan Mission is initiated to provide water to every household. Mention any other objective of the mission.

3. What are the major causes of water scarcity in India? Give at least two reasons.

4. Why rain water harvesting is better than multi-purpose projects?

5. Rooftop rainwater harvesting is quite beneficial for urban people. Do you agree with it?

6. What are the various reasons for diminishing levels of groundwater in the states of India? Suggest some measures to improve the situation.

7. What is the importance of hydrological cycle on the Earth?

8. Analyse the factors causing problems associated with water resources in India.

9. What are multi-purpose projects and why they are called Temple of Modern India?

10. Describe in brief the categorisation of dams in India.

Agriculture

CHAPTER 4

In India two-third of the population is engaged in agricultural activities. Agriculture is a **primary activity**[1] It produces food for our consumption and provides raw materials for various industries. Besides this, some agricultural products like tea, coffee, spices, etc are also exported.

4.1 Types of Farming

On the basis of the characteristics of physical environment, land productivity, technological advancement and socio-cultural practices, there are various types of farming in India. They are as follows

Primitive Subsistence Farming

This type of farming is practiced on small pieces of land with the help of old tools like hoe, dao, digging sticks, and using the family or community labour.

This farming depends upon rainfall, natural fertility of soil and suitability of other environmental conditions. It is also called **slash and burn agriculture.**

In this type of agriculture, farmers clear a patch (part) of land by burning it and produce crops from it. When the soil fertility decreases, farmers shift and clear a new patch of land for cultivation. This allows the nature to restore the fertility of the soil.

The production in this type of farming is done only for self-consumption.

In this type of farming, land productivity is low as the farmer does not use fertilisers or other modern inputs. It is known by different names in India and the world.

Other Names of Primitive Subsistence Farming

Name	State/Region	Country
Dipa	Bastar district of Chhattisgarh and Andaman and Nicobar Islands	India
Pamlou	Manipur	India
Jhumming	North-Eastern states (Assam, Meghalaya, Mizoram and Nagaland)	India
Bewar or Dahiya	Madhya Pradesh	India
Podu or Penda	Andhra Pradesh	India
Pama Dabi or Koman or Bringa	Odisha	India
Kumari	Western Ghats	India
Valre or Waltre	South-Eastern Rajasthan	India
Khil	Himalayan belt	India
Kuruwa	Jharkhand	India
Milpa	–	Mexico and Central America
Conuco	–	Venezuela
Roca	–	Brazil
Masole	–	Central Africa
Ladang	–	Indonesia
Ray	–	Vietnam

Intensive Subsistence Farming

This type of farming in India is practiced in areas where there is high population pressure on land. It is a labour intensive farming. Farmers use heavy biochemical inputs, intensive irrigation to obtain higher production.

There is enormous pressure on agricultural land, because the **right of inheritance**, which divides the land, has led to smaller landholdings. Since farmers have no other source of livelihood, they continue to take maximum output from the limited land.

1 Primary Activity These activities include economic activities that involve the direct use of natural resources from the Earth, such as land, water, vegetation, building materials and minerals.

Commercial Farming

This type of farming is practiced on large land holdings and use high levels of modern inputs, such as **High Yielding Variety** (HYV) **seeds**, good irrigation facilities, chemical fertilisers, insecticides, pesticides, etc.

The degree of commercialisation of farming varies from one area to another, depending on climatic conditions, irrigation facilities and other factors. For example, rice is a commercial crop in Haryana and Punjab but in Odisha, it is a subsistence crop.

Plantation is also a type of commercial farming. In this type, only a single crop is grown on a large area using capital intensive inputs and migrant labourers.

A good network of transport and communication which connects plantation areas, processing industries and markets are required to develop plantations.

Important plantation crops are tea in Assam and North Bengal and coffee in Karnataka. Some other crops are rubber, banana, sugarcane, etc.

Try These

1. **Which are the two states where commercial farming is practiced?**
2. **In which type of farming primitive tools are used?**
3. **Name the farming method in which a patch of land is cleared and burned for cultivation.**
4. **Identify the country in which slash and burn agriculture is called Roca.**

4.2 Cropping Pattern

It refers to environmental differences (such as climate, topography, soil type, etc) that give rise to different cropping seasons.

India has three cropping seasons i.e. **rabi, kharif and zaid.**

Rabi Crops

These are sown in winter from (October to December) and harvested in summer from April to June.

Some of the important crops cultivated in this season are wheat, barley, peas, gram and mustard. These crops are grown mainly in the regions of Punjab, Haryana, Himachal Pradesh, Jammu and Kashmir, Uttarakhand and Uttar Pradesh.

Availability of rainfall during winter months due to the Western temperate cyclones helps in the production of these crops.

The Green Revolution[2] in Punjab, Haryana, Western Uttar Pradesh and parts of Rajasthan has led to the growth of rabi crop in these regions.

Kharif Crops

These crops are sown during the onset of monsoon (May-July) and harvested in September-October. Major kharif crops are paddy (rice), maize, jowar, bajra, tur (arhar), moong, urad, cotton, jute, groundnut and soybean.

Major areas where rice is cultivated are Assam, West Bengal, coastal regions of Odisha, Andhra Pradesh, Telangana, Tamil Nadu, Kerala, Maharashtra (Konkan Coast), Uttar Pradesh, Bihar, Punjab and Haryana.

In Assam, West Bengal and Odisha, three crops of paddy are grown in a year namely ***Aus, Aman*** and ***Boro.***

Zaid Crops

These crops are sown between Rabi and Kharif seasons (March-June). Some of the crops produced during this season are watermelon, muskmelon, cucumber, vegetables and fodder crops.

Major Crops

Many varieties of food and non-food crops are grown in various regions of the country depending upon the different cultivation practices, soil type and climatic conditions. Some major crops of India are given below

Grains and Leguminous Crops

Rice, wheat, millets and maize are important grains grown in India. Pulses are the leguminous crops.

- **Rice** It is the main food crop of a majority of the people in India. It requires high temperature (above 25°C) and high humidity.

  It is grown in areas of heavy rainfall (above 100 cm) like the plains of North and North-Eastern India, coastal areas and the deltaic regions.

  In areas with less rainfall like in Punjab, Haryana, Western Uttar Pradesh and parts of Rajasthan, it is grown with proper irrigation through canals and tube wells. India is the second largest producer of rice in the world after China.

2 Green Revolution It refers to a significant increase in agricultural productivity resulting from the introduction of High Yielding Variety (HYV) of seeds, the use of chemical fertilisers and pesticides, and improved management techniques.

- **Wheat** It is the second most important cereal crop in India. It is the main food crop in North and North-Western part of the country. It requires a cool growing season and bright sunshine at the time of ripening. It requires 50-70 cm of annual rainfall during the growing season.

  The two important wheat growing zones in the country are the Ganga-Satluj plains in the North-West and the black soil region of the Deccan.

- **Millets** Jowar, bajra and ragi are the important millets grown in India. These are also known as **coarse grains** and have very high nutritional value.

  Jowar is the third most important food crop with respect to area and production. It is a rain-fed crop mostly grown in the moist areas. Major jowar producing states are Maharashtra, Karnataka, Andhra Pradesh and Madhya Pradesh.

  Bajra (Pearl Millet) contains iron, folate, vitamins. It grows well on sandy soils and shallow black soil. Major bajra producing states are Rajasthan, Uttar Pradesh, Maharashtra, Gujarat and Haryana.

  Ragi (Finger Millet) is rich in iron, calcium, other micro-nutrients and roughage. It grows well in dry regions on red, black, sandy, loamy and shallow black soils. Major ragi producing states are Karnataka, Tamil Nadu, Himachal Pradesh, Uttarakhand, Sikkim, Jharkhand and Arunachal Pradesh.

- **Maize** It is used both as food and fodder. It is a kharif crop and requires temperature between 21°C to 27°C and grows well in old alluvial soil. In some states it is also grown as rabi crop.

  The use of modern inputs such as HYV seeds, fertilisers and irrigation have increased the production of maize. Major maize producing states are Karnataka, Madhya Pradesh, Uttar Pradesh, Bihar, Andhra Pradesh and Telangana.

- **Pulses** India is the **largest producer** and **consumer** of pulses in the world. Pulses are an important source of protein in a vegetarian diet. Pulses need less moisture (water) and can survive in dry conditions.
  Pulses are leguminous crops[3] which help to fix nitrogen from air and restore soil fertility (except arhar). They are mostly grown in rotation with other crops.

  Major pulses that are grown in India are tur (arhar), urad, moong, masur, peas and gram. Major pulse producing states in India are Madhya Pradesh, Rajasthan, Maharashtra, Uttar Pradesh and Karnataka.

Food Crops Other than Grains

- **Sugarcane** It is a tropical as well as sub-tropical crop that requires almost a year to grow. It grows well in hot and humid climate. It requires temperature between 21°C to 27°C and annual rainfall between 75 cm-100 cm. Irrigation is required in the regions of low rainfall. It can be grown on a variety of soils. Manual labour from sowing to harvesting is required for sugarcane. India is the 2nd largest producer of sugarcane after Brazil.

  Sugarcane is the main source of sugar, gur (jaggery), khandsari and molasses[4].

  The major sugarcane producing states are Uttar Pradesh, Maharashtra, Karnataka, Tamil Nadu, Andhra Pradesh, Telangana, Bihar, Punjab and Haryana.

- **Oil seeds** Many varieties of oil seeds are grown on about 12% cropped area of the country. In 2018, India was the 2nd largest producer of groundnut after China. The major oil seeds produced are groundnut, mustard, coconut, sesamum (til), soyabean, castor seeds, cotton seeds, linseed and sunflower.

  The oilseeds are used as a cooking medium and as raw material in the production of soap, cosmetics and ointments.

  Groundnut is the major oil seed produce and is a kharif crop. In 2019-20 **Gujarat** was the **largest producer** of groundnut followed by Rajasthan and Tamil Nadu.
  Linseed and mustard are rabi crops and castor is both a rabi and kharif crop. Sesamum is a kharif crop in North India and a rabi crop in South India.

- **Tea** It is a beverage crop that was introduced in India by the British. Today, most of the tea plantations are owned by Indians. India was the second largest producer of tea after China (2018).

  The tea plant requires a tropical and sub-tropical climate with deep and fertile soil, which is rich in humus[5] and organic matter.

---

3 Leguminous Crops It refers to crops that have nodules in their roots that contain nitrogen-fixing bacteria. It includes peas, beans and lentils.

4 Molasses It is thick dark syrup received after refining sugarcane and is used in flavouring foods.

5 Humus It refers to the topmost layer of soil surface containing organic matter that increases the fertility of the soil.

Tea bushes require warm and moist frost free climate throughout the year. Frequent showers evenly distributed over the years ensure growth of tender leaves.

Tea cultivation is an example of plantation agriculture. It is a labour-intensive industry which requires abundant, cheap and skilled labour. The plucked leaves are processed within the tea gardens to maintain their freshness.

Major tea producing states are Assam, hills of Darjeeling and Jalpaiguri district, West Bengal, Tamil Nadu and Kerala. Apart from these, Himachal Pradesh, Uttarakhand, Meghalaya, Andhra Pradesh and Tripura are also tea producing states.

- **Coffee** Indian coffee is known in the world for its good quality. The **Arabica** variety, initially brought from Yemen, is produced in India. It has great demand all over the world. Its cultivation was introduced in India on the **Baba Budan hills.** It is limited to the Nilgiri in Karnataka, Kerala and Tamil Nadu.

Horticulture Crops

These include the cultivation of both fruits and vegetables. In 2018, India was the second largest producer of fruits and vegetables in the world after China.
Important vegetable produced in India are pea, cauliflower, onion, cabbage, tomato, brinjal and potato.

Most of the fruits are plantation crops. India produces both tropical as well as temperate fruits.

Fruit Producing Regions of India

Fruit	Areas
Mango	Maharashtra, Andhra Pradesh, Telangana, Uttar Pradesh and West Bengal
Orange	Nagpur and Cherrapunjee (Meghalaya)
Banana	Kerala, Mizoram, Maharashtra, Tamil Nadu and Karnataka.
Pineapple	Meghalaya
Grapes	Andhra Pradesh, Telangana and Maharashtra
Lichi and Guava	Uttar Pradesh and Bihar
Apple, Pear, Apricot and Walnut	Jammu and Kashmir and Himachal Pradesh

Non-Food Crops

- **Rubber** It is an equatorial crop[6], but it is also grown in tropical and sub-tropical areas under special conditions. It requires moist and humid climate with rainfall of more than 200 cm and temperature above 25°C. It is an important industrial raw material. It is mainly grown in Kerala, Tamil Nadu, Karnataka and Andaman and Nicobar islands and Garo hills of Meghalaya.
- **Fibre Crops** Cotton, jute, hemp and natural silk are the four major fibre crops grown in India.
The first three are plant products while silk is obtained from cocoons of the silkworms which fed on green leaves specially mulberry. Rearing of silkworms for the production of silk fibre is known as **sericulture.**
- **Cotton** It is one of the major raw materials for cotton textile industry. In 2017, India was the second biggest producer of cotton, after China. It grows well in dry regions of the black soil of Deccan plateau.

  It requires high temperature, light rainfall or irrigation,
  210 frost-free days and bright sunshine for its growth. It is a kharif crop and requires 6 to 8 months to mature.

  Major cotton producing states are Maharashtra, Gujarat, Madhya Pradesh, Karnataka, Andhra Pradesh, Telangana, Tamil Nadu, Punjab, Haryana and Uttar Pradesh.
- **Jute** It is known as the **golden fibre.** It grows well on well-drained fertile soils in the flood plains because soils are renewed every year in these plains.

  It requires high temperature during the growing period. It is used in making gunny bags, mats, ropes, yarn, carpets and other artefacts. West Bengal, Bihar, Assam, Odisha and Meghalaya are the major producer of Jute.

Try These

1. Rabi crops are majorly grown in which month?
2. Give one example of leguminous crops.
3. The crop is one of the major food crops in India and mostly rainfed. Name the crop.
4. Which crop provides raw material for jaggery and molasses?
5. Apart from cooking, what are the other uses of oilseeds?

6 Equatorial Crop These refer to the crops grown in the equatorial region which remains hot and humid throughout the year.

4.3 Technological and Institutional Reforms

Sustained uses of land without proper techno-institutional changes have slowed down the pace of agricultural development.

Most of the farmers still depend on monsoon to carry out agricultural activities. Thus, technical and institutional reforms are required in agriculture, which provides livelihood for more than 60% of its population.

The Government of India in 1960s–70s introduced agricultural reforms to improve Indian agriculture like **Green revolution** and **White** revolution[7] (operation flood). But this led to concentration of development only in a few selected areas.

Major institutional reforms were introduced in India from the First Five Year Plan. Their focus was **land reforms** that include collectivisation[8], consolidation of land holdings (*Chakbandi*), abolition of zamindari, etc. The laws of land reforms were enacted but lacked in their implementation.

Thus, a comprehensive **Land Development Programme** (LDP), was introduced during 1980s and 1990s. This programme included both institutional and technical reforms.

Some of the reforms introduced after this programme are

- **Kisan Credit Card** (KCC) scheme for giving easy and cheap loans to small farmers and **Personal Accident Insurance Scheme** (PAIS) for Kisan Credit Card (KCC) holders were introduced.
- Special weather bulletins and agricultural programmes for farmers were introduced through radio and television channels.
- Government announces Minimum Support Price[9] (MSP), remunerative and procurement prices[10] to check the exploitation of farmers by middlemen.
- Some other important reforms were
  - provision for crop insurance against drought, flood, cyclone, fire and disease.
  - establishment of grameen banks, cooperative societies and banks for providing loan facilities to the farmers at lower rates of interest.

Bhoodan-Gramdan

This movement was initiated by **Vinoba Bhave**, who followed the ideals of Mahatma Gandhi.

It was started when poor landless villagers in Andhra Pradesh demanded some land for their economic well-being. It is also known as the **Blood-less Revolution**

Under this movement, **Sri Ram Chandra Reddy** offered 80 acre land to be distributed among 80 landless villagers. This act was known as **Bhoodan** (donation of land).

Later, some zamindars offered to distribute some villages among the landless. This was known as **Gramdan** (donation of villages).

Under this movement, some landowners also chose to provide some part of their land to the poor farmers due to the fear of the **Land Ceiling Act**.

7 White Revolution Also called 'Operation Flood', this revolution aimed at increasing the production of milk by setting up milk processing centres, milk cooperatives, good transport system. India is the largest producer of milk.

8 Collectivisation This means small farms would be gathered together into one large farm so that farmers can work collectively. It was first started in USSR and promoted in India during the period of Green Revolution.

9 Minimum Support Price It is the minimum price set by the government for certain Kharif and Rabi crops to protect farmers sharp drop in prices.

10 Procurement Price It refers to the price at which government obtains agricultural produce from farmers to maintain the buffer stock.

Mind Map

AGRICULTURE

Types of Farming

Intensive Subsistence Farming
- It is a labour intensive farming.
- Practiced in areas where there is high population pressure on land.

Commercial Farming
- It involves capital intensive inputs and migrant labourers.
- Practiced on large land holdings using HYV seeds.

Primitive Subsistence Farming
- Also called slash and burn agriculture.
- Practiced on small pieces of land.

Technological and Institutional Reforms

Technological Reforms
- Green Revolution
- White Revolution

Institutional Reforms
- Land reforms
- Land development programme
- Kisan Credit Card
- Personal accident
- Insurance scheme

Major Crops

Grains and Leguminous Crops
- Rice
- Wheat
- Millets
- Maize
- Pulses

Non- food Crops
- Rubber
- Fibre crops
- Cotton
- Jute

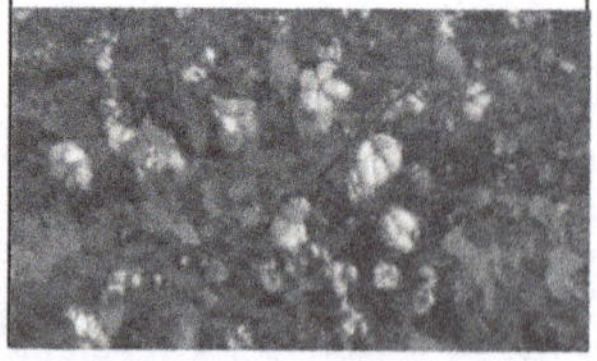

Food Crops other than Grains
- Sugarcane
- Oilseeds
- Tea
- Coffee

Horticulture Crops
- Pea
- Cauliflower
- Onion
- Cabbage
- Tomato
- Brinjal

Cropping Pattern

Kharif
- Sown during the onset of monsoon and harvested in September-October.
- Grown in Odisha, Tamil Nadu, Andhra Pradesh, Uttar Pradesh, Maharashtra, Bihar, Punjab and Haryana.
- For Example, Rice, maize, jowar bajra, moong, urad, cotton, jute, soyabean and groundnut.

Zaid
- Sown between Rabi and Kharif seasons.
- For Example, Watermelon, muskmelon, cucumber, vegetables and fodder foods.

Rabi
- Sown in winter and harvested in summer.
- Grown in Punjab, Himachal Pradesh, Haryana, Jammu and Kashmir, Uttar Pradesh and Uttarakhand.
- For Example, Wheat, barley, peas, gram and mustard.

NCERT FOLDER

Covering Intext Questions and Exercises of NCERT

INTEXT QUESTIONS

Q.1 Can you name some industries based on agricultural raw material?

Ans. Some industries based on agricultural raw material include the following

(i) **Cotton Textiles Industry** Raw material used in this industry is cotton fibre from the plant.

(ii) **Jute Sacks Industry** Raw material used in this industry is jute fibre from the jute plant.

(iii) **Tea/Coffee Processing Industry** Tea leaves and coffee beans are required as raw materials in this industry.

Q.2 Can you enlist some crops which are grown in primitive subsistence farming?

Ans. Crops which are grown in primitive subsistence farming includes cereals like bajra and rice as well as vegetables/fruit crops.

Q.3 Can you name some of the states of India where intensive subsistence farming is practiced?

Ans. Some of the states of India in which intensive subsistence farming is practiced are Madhya Pradesh, Chhattisgarh, Assam and other North-Eastern states, Andhra Pradesh and Odisha.

Q.4 Can you give some more examples of crops which may be commercial in one region and may provide subsistence in another region.

Ans. Wheat is an example of crop which may be commercial in one region and may provide subsistence in another region.

Q.5 List the items which are made of rubber and are used by us.

Ans. Some items made of rubber and used by us are

(i) Automobile tyres and tubes

(ii) Conveyor or belts used in industries

(iii) Insulating mats (iv) Footwears

(v) Toys (vi) Gloves

(vii) Erasers (viii) Balls

(ix) Tools and equipment

EXERCISE

Q.1 Multiple Choice Questions.

(i) Which one of the following describes a system of agriculture where a single crop is grown on a large area?

(a) Shifting Agriculture (b) Plantation Agriculture

(c) Horticulture (d) Intensive Agriculture

Ans. (b) Plantation Agriculture

(ii) Which one of the following is a rabi crop?

(a) Rice (b) Millets

(c) Gram (d) Cotton

Ans. (c) Gram

(iii) Which one of the following is a leguminous crop?

(a) Pulses (b) Millets

(c) Jowar (d) Sesamum

Ans. (a) Pulses

Q.2 Answer the following questions in 30 words.

(i) Name one important beverage crop and specify the geographical conditions required for its growth.

(ii) Name one staple crop of India and the regions where it is produced.

(iii) Enlist the various institutional reform programmes introduced by the government in the interest of farmers.

Ans. (i) Tea is one of the important beverage crops. The geographical conditions required for tea cultivation are

- It grows well in tropical and sub-tropical climate with deep and fertile well-drained soil which is rich in humus and organic matter.
- Tea bushes require warm and moist frost free climate throughout the year. Frequent rainfall evenly distributed over the years ensure growth of tender leaves.

(ii) Rice is the staple crop of India. It is produced in the areas of heavy rainfall like the North and North-Eastern parts and coastal areas and deltaic regions. With the help of irrigation, through canals and tubewells, rice is also grown in areas of less rainfall. For example, Punjab, Haryana, Western Uttar Pradesh and parts of Rajasthan.

(iii) The following institutional programmes have been introduced by the government in the interest of the farmers

- The Kisan Credit Card (KCC), Personal Accident Insurance Scheme (PAIS), etc have been launched by the government. A comprehensive Land Development Programme (LDP) has also been launched.

- The government is investing in rural infrastructure to link the rural market with the international market.
- Special weather bulletins and agricultural programmes for farmers were introduced through radio and television channels.

Q.3 Answer the following questions in about 120 words.

(i) Suggest the initiative taken by the government to ensure the increase in agricultural production.

(ii) Describe the geographical conditions required for the growth of rice.

Ans. (i) Government has initiated many institutional and technological reforms for increasing production and productivity in agriculture sector. Among technological reforms, major initiatives are

- Promotion of Green Revolution, White Revolution, etc.
- Introduction of High Yielding Variety (HYV) seeds, chemical fertilisers, pesticides, etc.
- Practice of drip irrigation or other irrigation techniques for better production.
- Power supply for irrigation, etc.

Among institutional reforms, major initiatives are

- Land reform including collectivisation, consolidation of land holdings, etc.
- Financial assistance to farmers like subsidies, insurance against crop failure and personal harm, Kisan Credit Card (KCC), Personal Accident Insurance Scheme (PAIS) and so on.
- Establishment of advanced research institutions for further progress, *i.e.*, Indian Council of Agricultural Research (ICAR), agricultural universities, meteorological research unit, agriculture specific satellite launch, etc.
- Minimum Support Price for buying of surplus crops in protection from market exploitation.

(ii) The geographical conditions required for the growth of rice are

- It requires high temperature above 25°C and high humidity.
- It needs a lot rainfall, *i.e.* more than 100 cm. It can grow in areas with less rainfall, but with proper irrigation through canals and tube wells..
- Rice can grow in a variety of soils including silts, loams and gravels. But it is grown best in alluvial soil with a sub-soil of impervious clay.

REVIEW EXERCISE

Including Competency Based Questions

Part I

Multiple Choice Questions (MCQs)

1. Which of the following methods have been changed depending upon the characteristics of physical environment, technological know-how and socio-cultural practice?

(a) Industrial activity
(b) Irrigation Pattern
(c) Cultivation
(d) None of these

2. 'Primitive subsistence farming is the practice of doing agriculture on small patches of land with the help of primitive tools.'

Which of the following examples represents the primitive subsistence farming ? Competency Based

(a) Rina uses water from a nearby tube well to irrigate her farmland.
(b) Suresh has bought HYV seeds for his land.
(c) Mrityunjay grows his crops without any chemical inputs and depends on rainfall for irrigation.
(d) Radha puts high dose of biochemical inputs to grow her wheat crop.

3. Logan, a 18 years old boy belongs to a tribal community that lives on agriculture. His family is continuously doing cultivation on the same patch of land for past three years without the use of any chemical fertilisers.

Which of the following will this practice most likely lead to in the near future? Competency Based

(a) Reduction in the forest cover
(b) Decrease in the quality of seeds
(c) Decrease in the soil fertility
(d) Destruction of the habitat of local organisms

4. Which type of agriculture practice is famous in North-Eastern states like Assam, Meghalaya, Mizoram and Nagaland?

(a) Jhumming cultivation
(b) Plantation
(c) Commercial farming
(d) Subsistence farming

5. Radheyshyam is a agricultural farmer who has a certain area of agricultural land under him. Upon his old age, he divides his land into four pieces among his sons. His sons did the same on their old age and the same practice continues.

Which of the following will this practice most likely lead to in the near future? **Competency Based**

(a) Enormous pressure on the agricultural land.

(b) Abandon of agriculture profession by later generations.

(c) Increase in productivity of the land due to better management because of its small size.

(d) Buying of the agricultural land by an industrialist for setting up an industry.

6. In an area located in the Western region of India, farmers mostly grow water intensive crops such as rice. However, the government is worried about the decreasing groundwater level of the area and discourages the farmers from growing water intensive crops.

What is the best resolution to this situation ?

(a) Government should start the work of constructing more canals and water bodies in the state.

(b) Government should make it mandatory for all the people of the area to install rooftop rainwater harvesting system.

(c) The farmers should leave this area and move to other region of the country which has enough water resources.

(d) The farmers should be encouraged to grow less water consuming crops by increasing the MSP on these crops.

7. Why do you think rabi crops are grown in the winter months?

(a) Winter season prevents these crops from sunlight which is harmful for the crops.

(b) Because of the availability of fog during winter months which aids their growth.

(c) Because of the availability of precipitation during winter months due to Western cyclones which helps in the success of these crops.

(d) Because of the minimum presence of insects and pests in the winter season which helps these crops to grow.

8. Important crops like paddy, maize, jowar, bajra, etc are grown during which of the following seasons?

(a) Spring (b) Summer

(c) Monsoon (d) Winter

9. Imagine you are travelling from Delhi to Chandigarh to attend a wedding, by road in January. Which of the following crops will you notice prominently in the fields during the journey? **CBSE 2025**

(a) Paddy (b) Maize

(c) Wheat (d) Jowar

10. What is the minimum temperature required for the cultivation of rice?

(a) Below 15°C (b) Between 25-30°C

(c) Above 30°C (d) Above 25°C

11. Sericulture is the rearing of silk worms for the production of silk.

During sericulture , the silkworms are fed on the leaves of which of the following trees?

(a) Blueberry (b) Strawberry

(c) Mulberry (d) Jackfruit

12. Rama, a 35 years old lady whose husband has started doing farming activities that her husband did to support her kids. However, she regularly faces problems with various expenses related to agriculture and household needs.

Accordingly, which of the following can be the most crucial for improving her well-being? **Competency Based**

(a) Giving her knowledge about minimum support price.

(b) Providing her with the Kisan Credit Card.

(c) Encouraging her to avail crop insurance scheme.

(d) Making her open a bank account in a nearby bank.

13. Choose the correctly matched pair. **CBSE 2023**

(a) Primitive subsistence farming	–	Practiced on large patches of land
(b) Intensive subsistence farming	–	Single crop production farming
(c) Commercial farming	–	Use of higher doses of modern inputs
(d) Plantation farming	–	Practiced on small patches of land

14. Find the incorrect match.

(a) Sugarcane – Tropical as well as sub-tropical crop

(b) Cotton – In 2015, India was largest producer

(c) Pulses – India is the largest producer

(d) Ragi – Rich in iron and calcium

15. Ravi says that he grows a crop that is edible and used in cooking mediums. He also says that the crop is used as a raw material in the production of soap, cosmetics and ointments.

Which of the following crops is grown by Ravi?

(a) Sugarcane (b) Rice

(c) Jute (d) Oilseeds

16. 'According to data from the state government, Mizoram has an area of around 21,08,700 hectares, of which 18,899 hectares are under Jhum cultivation. Moreover, 60,681 families practice Jhum cultivation throughout the state. Local government officials, however, conceded that Jhum farming is a significant problem.'

Source : LIFEGATE Daily

Which of the following problems is being possibly indicated above?

(a) When many people practice jhum cultivation on a large scale, it could lead to destruction of forests.
(b) Jhum cultivation is a major problem that has caused loss of socialties among tribal families.
(c) Jhum cultivation does not enable the tribal people to make contact with outside world.
(d) Jhum farming deteriorates the natural quality of land.

17. Consider the following statements about millets.

I. Bajra, wheat, ragi are rainfed crops.
II. Millets can grow easily in varied conditions.
III. They provide plenty of micro-nutrients.

Which of the following statements are correct?

(a) I and II (b) II and III
(c) I and III (d) All of these

18. Which of the following statements accurately describes "intensive subsistence farming"?

I. This type of farming is practiced in areas of high population pressure on land.
II. It is a labour intensive farming.
III. The crop is mainly grown for market purpose.
IV. Coffee, sugarcane and banana, etc are the prominent crops grown.

Codes

(a) Only I (b) Only IV (c) I and III (d) I and II

19. Mr. Y wants to grow rice crop. He choose the kharif season for this crop as which requires. Competency Based

I. low temperature
II. high humidity
III. rainfall below 100cm
IV. temperature above 25°C

Codes

(a) Only I (b) Only II
(c) IV and III (d) III and II

20. Identify the reasons as to why nowadays several international organisations are promoting the cultivation and consumption of millets. Choose from the appropriate statements among the following options.

I. Millets are very high in nutritional value.
II. These crops hardly needs any irrigation.
III. These crops can easily grow in dry conditions.
IV. They are an attractive food choice for youths.

Codes

(a) Statements I and IV are appropriate
(b) Statements I, II and III are appropriate
(c) All the statements are appropriate
(d) Only statement I is appropriate

21. Which of the following statements accurately describes the sugarcane crop?

I. It is a tropical as well as sub-tropical crop.
II. It grows well in hot and humid climate.
III. It requires an annual rainfall between 75 cm and 100 cm.
IV. It can be grown on a variety of soils.

Options

(a) Only II and I
(b) Only III
(c) I, II, III and IV
(d) II, III and IV

22. Consider the following statements and choose the correct option.

Statement I Maize is a kharif crop which requires temperature between 21°C to 27°C.

Statement II In some states like Bihar, maize is grown in rabi season also.

Options

(a) Statement I is correct and II is incorrect
(b) Statement I is incorrect and II is correct
(c) Both I and II statements are incorrect
(d) Both I and II statements are correct

23. Read the following informations and identify the crop.

- It is the staple food crop of majority of people in India.
- India is the second largest producer of this crop.
- It is a Kharif crop.
- It requires high humidity with 100 cm of annual rainfall. **CBSE 2024**

Options

(a) Ragi (b) Bajra
(c) Wheat (d) Rice

24. Identify the crop with the help of given information. **CBSE SQP 2022-23**

- It is a crop which is used both as food and fodder.
- It is a kharif crop which requires temperature between 21°C to 27 °C.
- It grows well in old alluvial soil.
- Use of modern inputs have contributed to the increasing production of this crop.

Options

(a) Maize (b) Millets (c) Wheat (d) Jowar

Answers

1. (c)	2. (c)	3. (c)	4. (a)	5. (a)
6. (d)	7. (c)	8. (c)	9. (c)	10. (d)
11. (c)	12. (b)	13. (c)	14. (b)	15. (d)
16. (a)	17. (d)	18. (d)	19. (c)	20. (b)
21. (c)	22. (d)	23. (d)	24. (a)	

Match the Following.

1.

	List I		List II
A.	Wheat	1.	Both Rabi and Kharif
B.	Jowar	2.	Rabi
C.	Muskmelon	3.	Kharif
D.	Pulses	4.	Zaid

Codes

	A	B	C	D		A	B	C	D
(a)	2	4	3	1	(b)	2	3	4	1
(c)	1	2	3	4	(d)	1	4	3	2

Ans. (b)

Assertion-Reason

1. Assertion (A) Change in cropping pattern from cereals to high value crops is seen beneficial for Indian economy.

Reason (R) India can follow the way of successful economies by exporting farm products and importing cereals.

Codes

(a) Both A and R are true and R is the correct explanation of A

(b) Both A and R are true, but R is not the correct explanation of A

(c) A is true, but R is false

(d) A is false, but R is true

2. Assertion (A) Indian farmers should diversify their cropping pattern from cereals to high value crops.

Reason (R) This will increase income and reduce environmental degradation simultaneously.

Codes **CBSE 2021 Term I**

(a) Both A and R are true and R is the correct explanation of A

(b) Both A and R are true, but R is not the correct explanation of A

(c) A is true, but R is false

(d) A is false, but R is true

3. Assertion (A) Agriculture is not an old economic activity.

Reason (R) Farming varies from subsistence to commercial type.

Codes

(a) Both A and R are true and R is the correct explanation of A

(b) Both A and R are true, but R is not the correct explanation of A

(c) A is true, but R is false

(d) A is false, but R is true

4. Assertion (A) Plantation has an interface of agriculture and industry.

Reason (R) Plantation is a type of commercial farming, a single crop is grown on a large area.

Codes

(a) Both A and R are true and R is the correct explanation of A

(b) Both A and R are true, but R is not the correct explanation of A

(c) A is true, but R is false

(d) A is false, but R is true

5. Assertion (A) Crops are grown depending upon the variations in soil, climate and cultivation practices.

Reason (R) Crops are also grown according to availability of water.

Codes

(a) Both A and R are true and R is the correct explanation of A

(b) Both A and R are true, but R is not the correct explanation of A

(c) A is true, but R is false

(d) A is false, but R is true

6. Assertion (A) Tea cultivation, is a labour-intensive industry.

Reason (R) Cultivation can be done throughout the year. Tea bushes require warm and moist frost- free climate.

Codes

(a) Both A and R are true and R is the correct explanation of A

(b) Both A and R are true, but R is not the correct explanation of A

(c) A is true, but R is false

(d) A is false, but R is true

Ans. 1. (a) Both A and R are true and R is the correct explanation of A

2. (a) Both A and R are true and R is the correct explanation of A

3. (d) A is false, but R is true

4. (a) Both A and R are true and R is the correct explanation of A

5. (b) Both A and R are true, but R is not the correct explanation of A

6. (b) Both A and R are true, but R is not the correct explanation of A

Picture Based Questions

1. Identify the type of agriculture shown in the given picture.

(a) Primitive agriculture (b) Intensive agriculture
(c) Jhuming agriculture (d) Commercial agriculture

Ans. 1. (d) Commercial agriculture

Case Based Question

1. Read the passage given below and answer the following questions. CBSE Term I 2021

The 'slash and burn' agriculture is known as 'Milpa' in Mexico and Central America, 'Conuco' in Venezuela, 'Roca' in Brazil, 'Masole' in Central Africa, 'Ladang' in Indonesia, 'Ray' in Vietnam. In India, this primitive form of cultivation is called 'Bewar' or 'Dahiya' in Madhya Pradesh, 'Podu' or 'Penda' in Andhra Pradesh, 'Pama Dabi' or 'Koman' or 'Bringa' in Odisha, 'Kumari' in Western Ghats, 'Valre' or 'Waltre' in South-Eastern Rajasthan, 'Khil' in the Himalayan belt, 'Kuruwa' in Jharkhand, and 'Jhumming' in the North-Eastern region.

(i) How is primitive subsistence agriculture related with Jhumming?
(a) It is based on shifting cultivation.
(b) It is intensive in nature.
(c) It is based on plantation cultivation.
(d) It depends upon cash crop.

(ii) Why do farmers shift and clear a fresh patch of land for cultivation in 'slash and burn' agriculture?
(a) To promote culture
(b) To reduce soil erosion
(c) To allow nature to replenish soil fertility
(d) To practice crop diversification

(iii) What happens when the soil fertility decreases in the slash and burn agriculture?
(a) Farmers use chemical fertilisers
(b) Farmers abandon the land
(c) Farmers practice crop rotation
(d) Farmers implement terrace farming

(iv) Identify the major problem of Jhumming cultivation.
(a) Single crop dominance (b) Modern inputs
(c) High cost (d) Low production

Ans. (i) (a) It is based on shifting cultivation.
(ii) (c) To allow nature to replenish soil fertility
(iii) (b) Farmers abandon the land
(iv) (d) Low production

Part II

Very Short Answer Type Questions

1. Name the major factors which significantly influence the method of cultivation in India.

Ans. The major factors which significantly influence the method of cultivation in India are physical environment, land productivity, technological advancement and socio-cultural practices.

2. What are coarse grains?

Ans. Jowar, bajra and ragi are the important millets grown in India. These are also known as coarse grains.

3. What is the position of India in sugarcane production in the world? CBSE 2015

Ans. India is the second largest producer of sugarcane in the world after Brazil.

4. What is commercial farming? CBSE 2015

Ans. Commercial farming is a type of farming which is practice on a large scale and aims to provide raw materials for industries and exports.

5. What term does describe the system of agriculture where a single crop is grown on a large area? CBSE 2016

Ans. The system of agriculture where a single crop is grown on a large area is plantation agriculture.

6. Mention two factors that are important for the growth of plantations.

Ans. The two factors that are important for the growth of plantations are well-developed system of transport and communication which connects plantation areas, processing industries and markets.

7. Akash performed a web search to know about the commercial farming in India. He noticed that most of the processing units and transport facilities are set up in the vicinity of the plantation crop growing areas.
What is the reason behind the location of such facilities? Competency Based

Ans. The processing units and transport facilities are set up in the vicinity of the crop growing areas because the commercial farming or plantation is mainly done for the market. Well developed network of transport and communication facility allows the connecting of plantation areas. Processing industries and markets plays an important role in the development of plantations.

8. Categorise the following as Kharif and Rabi crops. **CBSE 2019**

(i) Wheat (ii) Maize
(iii) Barley (iv) Peas
(v) Bajra (vi) Tur (Arhar)

Ans. The **Kharif** crops are maize, bajra, tur
The **Rabi** crops are wheat, barley, peas

9. Categorise the following as Rabi and Zaid crops. **CBSE 2019**

(i) Wheat (ii) Watermelon
(iii) Fodder (iv) Mustard
(v) Cucumber (vi) Peas

Ans. The **Rabi** crops are wheat, mustard, peas
The **Zaid** crops are watermelon, fodder, cucumber

10. What is zaid season in India?

Ans. Zaid season is an agricultural season during summer months in between rabi and kharif season.

11. What is the sowing period of kharif crops?

Ans. Kharif crops are sown at the beginning of the monsoon in the months of June and July.

12. A strengthening El Nino is causing drought in India, leading to a 35% decrease in rainfall in August and a 9% deficiency in the monsoon season. This could impact yields of important crops, such as soybean, cotton and pulses, which are produced in central Indian states. **Competency Based**

Source : Hindustan Times

(i) What kind of crops are grown with the onset of monsoon season in India?

Ans. Kharif crops are grown with the onset of monsoon season in India.

(ii) Are pulses a kharif crop?

Ans. Some of the pulses are kharif crop while some are rabi crop.

13. Harshit was once reading about tea cultivation in India in a magazine and he was amazed to know that most of the tea gardens are located in North-Eastern regions of the country.

What can be inferred about the climatic requirements of the tea crop from this information? **Competency Based**

Ans. It can be inferred that tea plant grows well in tropical and sub-tropical climates endowed with deep and fertile well-drained soil which is rich in humus and organic matter. Tea bushes require warm and moist frost-free climate through the year.

14. 'Recent rains have hit farmers from Buldhana district who grow tur, a major crop in Vidarbha after cotton and soybean. The rain may prove to be a blessing in disguise for the rabi crop.

Source (edited) : The Times of India

(i) What kind of crop is tur according to season of sowing?

Ans. Tur or arhar is a Kharif crop.

(ii) Why the rain may prove to be a blessing in disguise for the rabi crop?

Ans. The rain has proved to be a blessing in disguise for the rabi crops because availability of precipitation during winter months due to the Western temperate cyclones helps in the success of these crops. But tur crop are destroyed due to rains because it does not need rain during harvesting period.

Short Answer Type Questions

1. What are salient features of slash and burn agriculture?

Ans. Salient features of slash and burn agriculture are as follows

- This type of farming is carried out by tribal communities in India. A patch of land is cleared and burned for cultivation for a few years.
- This farming depends upon rainfall, natural fertility of soil and suitability of other environmental conditions.
- In this farming, land productivity is quite low as farmers does not use fertiliser and other modern inputs.

2. 'This type of farming is still practiced in few pockets of India. Primitive subsistence agriculture is practiced on small patches of land with the help of primitive tools like hoe, dao and digging sticks, and family/ community labour. This type of farming depends upon monsoon, natural fertility of the soil and suitability of other environmental conditions to the crops grown.' **Competency Based**

(i) What does the above statement tells about the people that practice this type of farming?

Ans. From the above description it can be said that the people who practice this type of farming belong to some tribal or indigenous groups who still rely on natural processess for their survival. These groups clears a patch of forest by burning it then do agriculture on that land and after few years they leave this place and clears another land. In this way the previous land replenishes its fertility without any chemical input.

(ii) Why is subsistence agriculture still practiced in certain parts of the country? Give three reasons.

Ans. Reasons due to which subsistence agriculture is still practiced are

(i) Patch of land are divided and small, so large scale farming cannot be done.

(ii) Large number of family members in rural areas depend on agriculture which makes it necessary to grow crops for self consumption.

(iii) Some farmers do not have the resources to buy better inputs like fertilisers, pesticides, irrigation, facilities and other modern means.

3. Write three points of difference between primitive subsistence farming and intensive subsistence farming.

Or Explain any three features of intensive subsistence farming. CBSE 2025

Ans. Three points of difference between primitive subsistence farming and intensive subsistence farming are as follows

Primitive Subsistence Farming	Intensive Subsistence Farming
This type of farming is practice on very small patches of land.	This type of farming is practiced in areas where there is high population pressure on land.
In this type of farming, primitive tools like hoe, digging sticks are used for cultivation.	In this type of farming, modern agricultural inputs like chemical fertilisers, HYV seeds, machines are used wherever suitable.
This agriculture is dependent on rainfall and natural fertility of the soil.	In this type of farming, means of irrigation like tubewells, canals are used. Soil fertility is also increased by the use of fertilisers.

4. Over the past few years , the commercial farming is becoming more popular among the farmers as compared to the subsistence farming. What do you think are the reasons for the gain in popularity of the commercial farming? Explain by providing any four characteristics of commercial farming in India. CBSE 2011

Ans. Major characteristics of commercial farming in India are as follows

(i) Commercial farming is crop selective and aims to provide raw materials for industries.

(ii) It is practice for selling the agricultural products in the market or for exports.

(iii) It requires intensive use of modern inputs like High Yielding Variety (HYV) seeds, chemical fertilisers, insecticides, pesticides, etc to increase productivity.

(iv) Commercial farming generates development activities in transport, connectivity and processing industries.

5. Analyse Kharif and Rabi crops through different parameters.

Or Highlight any three differences between Kharif cropping season and Rabi cropping season. CBSE 2019

Or Describe any three main features of 'Rabi crop season'. CBSE 2019

Or Describe any three main features of 'Kharif crop season.' CBSE 2019

Ans. Differences between or main features of Rabi and Kharif cropping season are as follows

Basis	Rabi Cropping Season	Kharif Cropping Season
Sowing period	Rabi cropping season starts in winter months, i.e. October to December.	Kharif cropping season starts on the onset of Monsoon i.e. May to July.
Harvesting period	Rabi season ends in spring or at the start of summer i.e. April to June.	Kharif cropping season ends in September to October.
Water requirement	Crops of this season need less irrigation as compared to Kharif crops.	Crops of this season need high rainfall or better irrigation sources.
Regions	These crops are grown Northern and North-Western parts of the country.	These crops are grown almost every part of the country.
Crops grown	Important crops of this season are wheat, barley, peas, gram and mustard.	Important crops of this season are paddy, maize, jowar, bajra, cotton, jute and groundnut.

6. Explain any three features of Plantation Agriculture. CBSE 2025

Ans. Three features of plantation agriculture are

(i) **Monoculture** Plantation agriculture involves the cultivation of a single crop over a large area. Common crops include tea, coffee, rubber and sugarcane, which are grown for commercial purposes.

(ii) **Large-Scale Farming** Plantation agriculture is typically carried out on large estates or plantations. These estates are often owned by private individuals or companies and involve significant investments in infrastructure and labour.

(iii) **Labour-Intensive** Plantation agriculture requires a large amount of labour, particularly for activities like planting, maintaining, and harvesting crops. It often depends on both skilled and unskilled labourers, with many workers employed seasonally.

7. Hari owns a farm in Uttar Pradesh, he wishes to cultivate either jute or sugarcane. He shall cultivate which crop out of these two keeping in mind the conditions required for their growth? Explain. CBSE 2013

Ans. Hari will cultivate sugarcane in his farmland in Uttar Pradesh as it is more suitable for that crop.

Sugarcane is a plantation crop. The conditions required for the cultivation of sugarcane are as follows

- It is a tropical as well as sub-tropical crop that requires temperature between 21°C to 27°C and annual rainfall between 75-100 cm.
- It grows well in fertile, well-drained soil and hot and humid type of climate.
- It is an annual crop and needs manual labour from sowing to harvesting.

8. Name any four oilseeds produced in India. What is their economic importance? CBSE 2015

Or Name any four oilseeds produced in India. Explain the importance of oilseeds in our day to day life. CBSE 2012

Or Which oilseeds are produced in India? Explain their economic importance.

Ans. Oilseeds produced in India are groundnut, mustard, coconut, sesamum (til), soybean, castor seeds, cotton seeds, linseed and sunflower.

Economic importance of oilseeds are as follows

- Oilseeds are used as a cooking medium.
- Oilseeds are used as raw material in the production of soap, cosmetics and ointments.
- After extraction of oil from oilseeds, a byproduct is remained. This is known as oil cake. This oil cake is used as fertilisers and also for cattle fuel.

9. Write a short note on horticulture in India. Mention the states that are famous for the production of oranges and apricots.

Ans. The cultivation of fruits and vegetables is known as horticulture. India ranked second after China (2018) in the production of fruits and vegetables in the world. It produces both tropical as well as temperate fruits. Fruits are grown in orchards and plantation.

Some of the important fruits produced in India are mango, banana, orange, pineapple, grape, apple, apricot, walnut, litchi and guava. India produces around 13% of the world's vegetables. Some of the important vegetables produced in large quantities in India are peas, cauliflower, onion, cabbage, tomato, brinjal and potato. States that are famous for the production of oranges are Maharashtra (Nagpur), Meghalaya (Cherrapunji) and the production of apricot are Himachal Pradesh, Jammu and Kashmir.

10. Discuss the most significant impact of Bhoodan Andolan in the agricultural sector in India.

Ans. Bhoodan Movement was initiated by Vinoba Bhave to solve the problem of landless labourers, he undertook a padyatra (Journey on Foot). The most significant impacts of Bhoodan Andolan in agriculture sector are as follows

- Rich landlords offered their lands and villages to landless agricultural laboures.
- It also significantly increased the agricultural production as the labours became owner of their land and could cultivate on it.
- This movement is also known as blood-less revolution because it helped to bring about revolution in the agricultural sector of the country without any war, agitation or struggle.

Long Answer Type Questions

1. What are the difference between subsistence agriculture and commercial agriculture?

Or Describe any five features of commercial farming. CBSE 2019

Or Mention any three features of commercial farming. CBSE 2025

Ans. Differences between subsistence farming and commercial farming are as follows

Basis	Subsistence Farming	Commercial Farming
Purpose	This farming practice is done mainly for self consumption or local consumption.	This farming practice is done mainly for the commercial or market purpose.
Land holding	In this type of farming, landholding is smaller than 2 hectares.	In this type of farming, landholding is larger than 2 hectares.
Crops grown	Important crops grown under this cultivation are food grains and vegetables.	Important crops grown under this cultivation are cash crop (i.e. cotton, rubber, sugarcane, etc) and cereals.
Irrigation method	This type of farming is mainly dependent on rainfall and primitive methods.	This type of farming is mainly based on modern irrigation methods. For example, tubewells and canals
Fertilisers used	This farming is based on manure and natural fertility of soil.	This farming is based on chemical fertilisers.

2. In agriculture, there are four – what economists would call – "factors of production": land, water, labour and energy. Farmers use these factors or inputs to produce crops. For a given level of technology, the output produced by them is largely determined by the quantity of inputs used.

Source : The Indian Express

Analyse the features of the agriculture sector in India in terms of its types, cropping seasons and level of technology. **Competency Based**

Ans. Some major features of agriculture in India are as follows

- In India, agriculture is a primary activity. It provides foodgrain as well as raw material for various industries.
- Three types of farming are found namely primitive subsistence farming in hilly and forested areas, intensive subsistence farming in highly populated areas and commercial farming on a large scale.
- Indian agriculture has three cropping seasons i.e., rabi, kharif and zaid.
- Agriculture provides boost to other services like transport and communication, etc.
- Today, Indian agriculture is becoming modernised due to improved technological and institutional reforms.

3. Name the two most important staple food crops of India. Name the states where they are produced. Write the geographical conditions required for their growth.

Or **Give an account of rice cultivation in India, under the following heads**

(a) Climatic condition (b) Soil requirement

(c) Two major rice producing states **CBSE 2013**

Or **Describe the geographical conditions required for the growth of wheat in India.** **CBSE 2014**

Or **Explain the climatic conditions for the production of rice. Name any two major rice producing states in India.** **CBSE 2015**

Ans. The most important staple food crops of India are rice and wheat.

The geographical conditions for the production of rice and wheat are tabulated below

Geographical Conditions	Rice	Wheat
Soil	It required clay or clay loam (good water retention capacity)	It required well-drained fertile soil, heavy textured soil with lime, clayey loamy soil or black soil
Temperature	Above 25°C	10°-15°C during growth and 25°-28°C at the time of ripening.
Rainfall	Above 100 cm	50-75 cm
Cropping season	Kharif season	Rabi season
States where crops grown	West Bengal Andhra Pradesh, Uttar Pradesh, Punjab and Odisha	Ganga-Satluj plains of Uttar Pradesh, Punjab, Haryana, Rajasthan and Deccan region of Madhya Pradesh

4. Name the two major beverage crops grown in India. Describe their growing areas. **CBSE 2019**

Ans. The two major beverage crops grown in India are tea and coffee.

Tea

Tea plants grow well in tropical and sub-tropical climates. In these types of climates, deep and fertile, well-drained soil is available which is rich in humus and organic matter.

Tea bushes requires warm, moist and frost-free climate throughout the year. Another specific requirement is the availability of abundant, cheap and skilled labour force.

All these conditions are available in North-Eastern states of India. So, tea plantation is mainly concentrated in Assam, Darjeeling and Jalpaiguri districts of West Bengal, Meghalaya, Tripura.

Coffee

Coffee production in India is mainly practiced in the hilly parts of South-Western India, especially in Nilgiri hills regions of Karnataka, Kerala and Tamil Nadu.

It is due to the presence of favourable climatic conditions and soil type. Coffee was first introduced in Baba Budan hills in Nilgiri region and the practice of coffee plantation is still carried by the farmers in the region.

5. A group of reasearch students has been given to the task of studying any two fibre crops in India. The groups choose to study cotton and jute.

Discuss the key information that the group should consider while formulating the report of the above research.

Ans. Cotton and jute are the two major fibre crops grown in India. India is believed to be the original home of cotton. Cotton is one of the major raw materials for cotton textile industry.

The conditions for the growth of cotton are

- It grows well in drier parts of the black cotton soil of the Deccan Plateau.
- It requires high temperature, light rainfall or irrigation, 210 frost-free days and bright sunshine for its growth.
- It is a kharif crop and required 6 to 8 months to mature.

Major cotton producing states are Maharashtra, Gujarat, Madhya Pradesh, Karnataka, Andhra Pradesh, Telangana, Tamil Nadu, Punjab, Haryana and Uttar Pradesh.

Jute is known as the 'golden fibre'. It is very strong and due to its roughness it is used for make gunny bags, mats, ropes and other artefacts.

The condition for the growth of jute are

- It grows well on well-drained fertile soil in the flood plains where soils are renewed every year.
- It requires high temperature during the time of growth.
  Major jute producing states are West Bengal, Bihar, Assam, Odisha and Meghalaya.

6. Mr. D wants to start a new jute manufacturing plant. He also want to buy land for growing jute for this manufacturing plant.
What geographical conditions he should look for while buying and land and what are the different uses of jute he should keep in mind while designing various products in his manufacturing plant? **Competency Based**

Ans. Jute is called golden fibre for its colour and high cash value in India. The geographical conditions required for jute are

- It grows well on well-drained fertile soil in the flood plain where soil is renewed every year.
- It requires high temperature during the time of growth. So hot and humid climate is required.

The uses of jute are

- Jute is used in making gunny bags, carpets, ropes, yarn and other artefacts.
- Its stem is used for fuel in rural belt.
- After refining and proper treatment, it can be used for clothes.
- It is used to replace polythene bags in India to promote pollution free environment.

7. Explain the technological and institutional reforms taken by the government in the interest of farmers.

Ans. Technological and Institutional Reforms taken by the government in the interest of farmers are as follows

- **Technological Reforms** The Government of India in 1960s–70s introduced agricultural reforms to improve Indian agriculture like Green Revolution and White Revolution (Operation Flood).
- **Institutional Reforms** Major institutional reforms were introduced in India from the First Five Year Plan. Their focus was land reforms that include collectivisation, consolidation of land holdings (Chakbandi), development of cooperative societies, abolition of zamindari, etc.
  As right of inheritance divide the land holdings to very small units that reduce productivity, so land reform was the main focus in institutional reforms.
- **Land Development Programme** (LDP) A comprehensive Land Development Programme (LDP), was introduced during 1980s and 1990s. This programme included both institutional and technical reforms.

Case Based Questions

1. Read the following sources and answer the questions that follow.

Source A Pulses

Pulses need less moisture and survive even in dry conditions. Beings leguminous crops, all these crops except arhar help in restoring soil fertility by fixing nitrogen from the air. Therefore, these are mostly grown in rotation with other crops.

(i) Find out the importance of pulses in agricultural pattern in India.

Source B Plantation

In this type of farming, a single crop is grown on a large area. The plantation has an interface of agriculture and industry. Plantations cover large tracts of land, using capital intensive inputs, with the help of migrant labourers. All the produce is used as raw material in respective industries.

(ii) Briefly explain how plantation is an interface of agriculture and industry.

Source C Jhumming

She loves the surroundings and wants to stay here as long as she can, but this little girl has no idea about the declining fertility of the soil and her family's search for a fresh patch of land in the next season.

(iii) What technique will be used by the little girl's family to acquire a fresh patch of land?

Ans. (i) Pulses are mostly grown in rotation with other crops, and they fix nitrogen from air with soil and restore the soil fertility.

(ii) Plantation is an interface of agriculture and industry as plantation is an agricultural activity that produces raw material for various industries like tea, sugarcane, etc.

(iii) The technique of jhumming or slash and burn agriculture will be used here. Farmers will burn the plant cover on a patch of land to clear it and will do cultivation there.

2. Read the following source given below and answer the questions that follow.

Through the 'right of inheritance' leading to the division of land among successive generations has rendered land-holding size uneconomical, the farmers continue to take maximum output from the limited land in the absence of alternative source of livelihood. Thus, there is enormous pressure on agricultural land.

The main characteristic of Commercial farming is the use of higher doses of modern inputs. e.g. High Yielding Variety (HYV) seeds, chemical fertilisers, insecticides and pesticides in order to obtain higher productivity. The degree of commercialisation of agriculture varies from one region to another. For example, rice is a commercial crop in Haryana and Punjab, but in Odisha, it is a subsistence crop.

(i) How do farmers continue to take maximum output from limited land?

(ii) Why rice is considered a subsistence crop in Odisha?

(iii) Which two states of India produce rice commercially?

Ans. (i) To take maximum output from limited land farmers buy agricultural inputs like fertilisers, pesticides, HYV seeds and provide irrigation facilities.

(ii) Rice is considered a subsistence crop in Odisha because it is grown on small patches of land with very little agricultural inputs. Productivity is also less.

(iii) Punjab and Haryana are the two states which produce rice commercially.

Map Based Questions

1. Some features are marked on the map of India given below. Identify them with the help of the following information and write their correct names on the lines marked on the map.

(i) A major wheat producing state

(ii) A major producer of jute

(iii) The state which is the major producer of coffee

(iv) A major rice producing state

(v) A major sugarcane producer in the South

(vi) A major rubber producing state

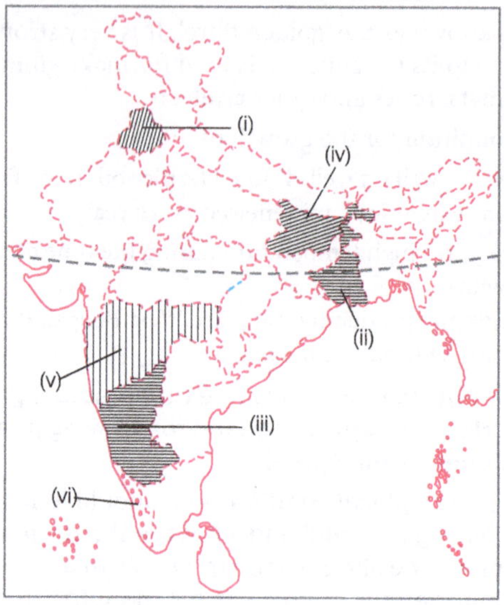

Ans.

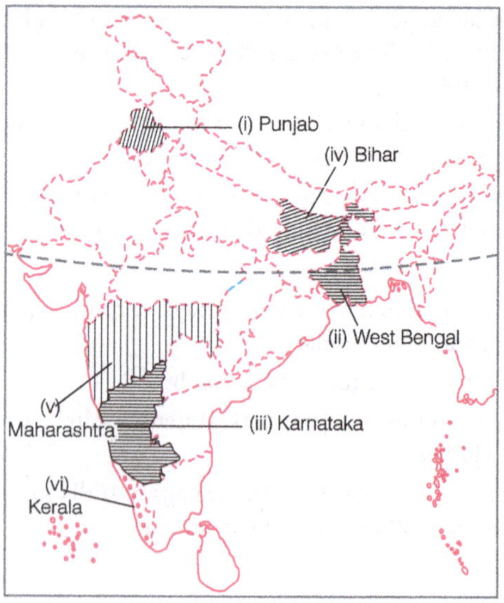

2. Identify the major producing areas of the crops marked on the map with the help of information given below.

(i) Sugarcane plantation (ii) Coffee plantation

(iii) Tea cultivation (iv) Rubber cultivation

(v) Cotton cultivation (vi) Wheat Cultivation

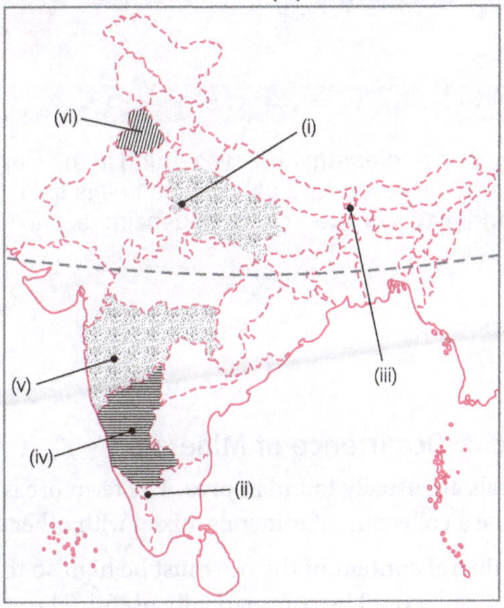

Ans.

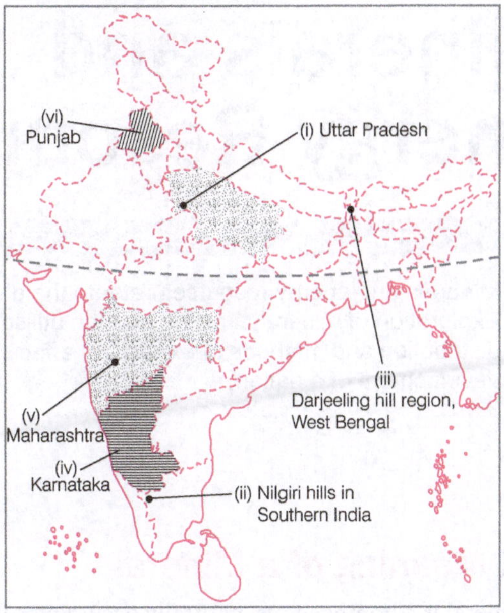

ASSESSMENT EXERCISE

Multiple Choice Questions (MCQs)

1. Which type of agriculture practice is famous in the North-Eastern states like Assam, Meghalaya, Mizoram and Nagaland?

(a) Jhumming

(b) Slash and burn farming

(c) Commercial farming

(d) Subsistence farming

2. Which of the following is the staple food crop of a majority of the people in India?

(a) Jowar (b) Bajra

(c) Wheat (d) Rice

3. Which industry in Manchester and Liverpool flourished due to a product exported from India?

(a) Cotton (b) Jute

(c) Steel (d) Wheat

4. Find the incorrect option.

(a) Agriculture was the main cause of Champaran Movement in 1917.

(b) Condition of marginal and small farmers is not good in India.

(c) Green Revolution is also called packaged technology.

(d) Genetic engineering cannot be adopted in India due to varied topography.

Subjective Questions (VSA, SA & LA)

1. Name two industries based on agricultural raw material.

2. Give two reasons for variation of degree of commercialisation of agriculture from region to region.

3. Give two examples of zaid crops.

4. Why organic farming is much in demand today?

5. Briefly discuss the cultivation of oil seeds in India.

6. Discuss the technological innovations which improved farming in India.

7. Give the reason for which intensive subsistence farming still flourish in India.

8. Give a brief discussion on pulses cultivation in India.

9. What are the regions in the Western part of India where rice is cultivated? Why is it cultivated in these regions?

10. Describe horticulture as important activity in India.

11. Discuss the challenges that agricultural sector faces in India.

Minerals and Energy Resources

CHAPTER 5

Minerals and energy resources refer to the diverse wealth of minerals and energy reserves found in the Earth's crust. Exploration of minerals, mining and the utilisation of different energy resources are all included in this field. The distribution and methods of extraction, effects the environment and play a crucial role in influencing economy and development of a nation.

5.1 Meaning of a Mineral

A mineral is a homogenous, naturally occurring substance having a defined internal structure. Rocks are the combinations of homogenous substances called minerals. Some rocks consist of single mineral, for e.g. limestone, while most of them consist of several minerals in different quantity.

The formation of minerals depend upon physical and chemical conditions which results in a wide range of colours, hardness, crystal forms, lustre and density of a particular mineral.

Minerals are found in different forms in nature, ranging from the hardest diamond to the softest talc.

Importance of Minerals

- Minerals are important in our daily lives, forming everything from a small pin to large buildings.
- Minerals help in building machinery, roads and transportation like planes buses, trains and cars. Even our food contains important minerals.
- People have always depended on minerals for their livelihood, decoration, festivities, religious and ceremonial.
- Geographers study minerals in Earth's crust to understand landforms. They focus on mineral distribution and economic activities. Geologists on the other hand, study mineral formation, their age and composition (physical and chemical).
- Life processes require minerals to work normally. We intake only 0.3 percent of minerals as nutrients, but they are so important that we will not be able to consume other 9.7 percent of food without them.

Mode of Occurrence of Minerals

Minerals are usually found in **ores**. The term ore is used to describe a collection of minerals mixed with other elements.

The mineral content of the ore must be high so that its **extraction**[1] would be commercially useful. The structure in which minerals are found determines how easy or difficult it is for mining them.

Mineral generally occur in the following forms

- **Veins and Lodes** In **igneous** and **metamorphic** rocks, minerals can be found in cracks or faults. Small faults are called veins, and big cracks or faults are called lodes. They are formed when minerals in liquid or gaseous form moves upwards towards the Earth's surface, cools down and becomes solid. Metals like tin, lead and copper are obtained from veins and lodes.
- **Beds or Layers** In **sedimentary** rocks, minerals are formed in the form of beds or layers due to deposition, accumulation and concentration in horizontal layers of the rock. Coal, some forms of iron ore, gypsum, potash salt and sodium salt are found in these beds or layers.

  Some sedimentary minerals like potash, salt gypsum, and sodium salt are formed due to evaporation, particularly in dry areas.
- **By Decomposition of Surface Rocks** When decomposition of surface rocks and the removal of soluble parts takes place, it leaves a residual mass of weathered material containing mineral ores. Bauxite is formed by the decomposition of surface rocks.
- **Alluvial Deposits** Some minerals are found as alluvial deposits in sands of valley floors and at the base of hills. These deposits are known as **placer deposits**.

1 **Extraction** It refers to the process of taking our minerals from rocks under Earth's Surface.

These minerals are not corroded (rusted) by water, e.g. gold, silver, platinum and tin.

- **In Ocean Waters** Many minerals like common salt, magnesium and bromine are obtained from ocean waters. Manganese nodules are found in ocean beds.

KNOWLEDGE PLUS Most of the minerals in India are nationalised and their mining extraction is possible only after obtaining permission from the government. However, in most of the tribal areas of the North-East India, minerals are owned by individuals or communities.

Distribution of Minerals in India

India has rich and varied mineral resources, but these resources are unevenly distributed. In India, there large variations are found in occurrence of minerals.

It is because of the differences in the geological structure, processes and time involved in the formation of minerals.

The distribution of minerals in India is discussed below

- **Peninsular Plateau** It contain most of the reserves of coal, metallic minerals, mica, non-ferrous mineral and non-metallic minerals.
- **Gujarat and Assam** Sedimentary rocks on the Western and Eastern side of the Peninsula in Gujarat and Assam have most of the petroleum deposits.
- **Rajasthan** The rock systems of the peninsula in Rajasthan has many reserves of non-ferrous minerals[2].
- **Northern Plains** There is very little or no minerals of economic value in vast alluvial plains of the North India.

The amount of mineral in the ore, case of extraction and its closeness to the market are the factors that makes the reserve economically viable. When these factors are fulfilled, then mineral deposit or reserve turns into a **mine**.

Rat Hole Mining

It is a type of mining that is done by digging long narrow tunnels to reach the coal deposits under the ground.

The practice of rat hole mining is declared illegal by National Green Tribunal.

In Meghalaya, there are large deposits of coal, iron ore, limestone and dolomite, etc. Rate hole mining is practiced in regions of **Jowai** and **Cherapunjee** of Meghalaya.

5.2 Classification of Minerals

Minerals are mainly classified as metallic, non-metallic and energy minerals.

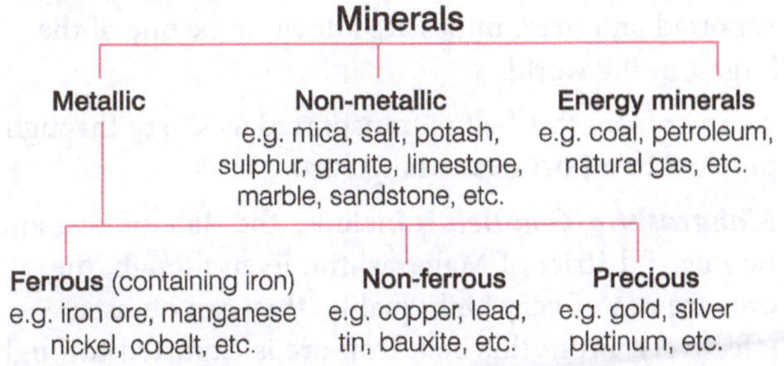

Metallic Minerals

Minerals containing metals are called metallic minerals, like gold, silver, tungsten, etc. They are of two types

(i) Ferrous Minerals

Metallic minerals having iron content are called ferrous minerals. These minerals account for about three-fourth of the total value of the production of metallic minerals.

Some of the ferrous minerals are discussed below

- **Iron Ore** It is the basic mineral and the backbone of industrial development. India has huge amount of good quality iron ore.

  The finest iron ore is **magnetite**. It has a very high iron content upto 70%. Magnetite has excellent magnetic qualities, which are valuable in the electrical industry. **Haematite** ore has an iron content upto 50-60%. It is the most important industrial iron ore in terms of the quantity used.

  In 2018-19, almost 97% of the iron ore is obtained from Odisha, Chhattisgarh, Karnataka and Jharkhand.

  The major iron ore belts in India are

  Odisha-Jharkhand Belt In Odisha, high grade haematite ore is found in Badampahar mines in the Mayurbhanj and Kendujhar districts.

  In the adjoining Singbhum district of Jharkhand, haematite iron ore is mined in Gua and Noamundi.

  Durg-Bastar-Chandrapur Belt It lies in Chhattisgarh and Maharashtra. 14 deposits of very high grade haematites are found in the famous **Bailadila range** of hills in the Bastar district of Chhattisgarh.

  The super high grade haematite iron has the best physical properties needed for making steel. Iron ore from these mines is exported to Japan and South Korea through Vishakhapatnam port.

2 Non-Ferrous minerals Minerals that do not contain iron content are called non-ferrous minerals.

Ballari-Chitradurga-Chikkamagaluru-Tumakuru Belt This belt in Karnataka has large reserves of iron ore. The Kudremukh mines are located in the Western Ghats of Karnataka. All the iron produced in these mines are exported and these mines are known to be one of the largest in the world.

The ore from this belt is transported as slurry through a pipeline to a port near Mangaluru.

Maharashtra-Goa Belt It includes the state of Goa and Ratnagiri district of Maharashtra. Even though, the ores are not of very high quality, they can be used effectively. From this belt, iron ore is exported through Marmagao port.

KNOWLEDGE PLUS The Bailadila hills looks like the hump of ox. Rudre, the highest peak in the Western Ghats of Karnataka resembles the face of a horse.

- **Manganese** It is a metallic element used in manufacturing of steel and ferro-manganese alloys. Nearly 10 kg of manganese is used to manufacture one tonne of steel.
  It is also used in manufacturing insecticides, bleaching powder and paints.

(ii) Non-Ferrous Minerals

Minerals that do not contain iron content are called non-ferrous minerals. The reserves and production of non-ferrous minerals in India is not sufficient.

These minerals include copper, lead, zinc, bauxite, gold, etc which are essential for various industries like metallurgical, engineering and electrical industries.

The distribution of non-ferrous minerals i.e. copper and bauxite is discussed below

- **Copper** It is an important mineral due to its excellent electrical conductivity. It is used in manufacturing of electrical cables and in electronics and chemical industries. India lacks in the reserve and production of copper. The leading producers of copper in India are **Khetri mines** in **Rajasthan**, **Balaghat** mines in **Madhya Pradesh** and **Singhbhum** district of **Jharkhand**.
- **Bauxite** Bauxite ore is used for obtaining aluminium. It is formed by decomposition of a wide variety of rocks rich in aluminium silicates.
  Bauxite is a clay-like substance from which alumina is extracted and later alumina is developed into aluminium.
  Aluminium is known for its strength, lightness and good conductivity. It is widely used in manufacturing of utensils, electrical goods, etc.
  Amarkantak plateau, Maikal hills and the **plateau region of Bilaspur-Katni** are the main regions of bauxite deposits in Madhya Pradesh.
  Odisha was the largest bauxite producing state in India in 2016-17. **Panchpatmali** deposits in Koraput district are the most-important centres of bauxite deposits in Odisha.

Non-Metallic Minerals

These minerals do not contain any metal substances in them, e.g mica, limestone, etc.

Mica

It is used in electrical and electronics industries due to its di-electric strength, low power loss factor, insulating properties and resistance to high voltage.

Mica occurs in the form of plates or leaves, which can be split into thin sheets. Mica can be clear, black, green, red, yellow or brown.

Its deposits are mainly found in the Northern edge of the Chota Nagpur plateau. **Koderma-Gaya-Hazaribagh belt** of Jharkhand is the leading producer of mica. Other mica producing regions are Ajmer (Rajasthan) and Nellore (Andhra Pradesh).

Limestone

It is a **rock mineral** found in sedimentary rocks. It is composed of calcium carbonates or calcium and magnesium carbonates.

Limestone is used for smelting iron ore in blast furnaces of steel plants and is the basic raw material for manufacturing of cement. **Rajasthan** has the largest share in limestone production in India i.e. 20%, in 2018-19.

Hazards of Mining

Mining is a hazardous industry in the following ways

- It has a risk to life due to collapse of roofs, overflow of water, and fire.
- Dumping of waste and slurry leads to land degradation, soil erosion, and increases the stream and river pollution.
- Mining causes respiratory diseases and pulmonary disorder to miners.

Thus, strict laws are needed to prevent it from becoming a **killer industry**.

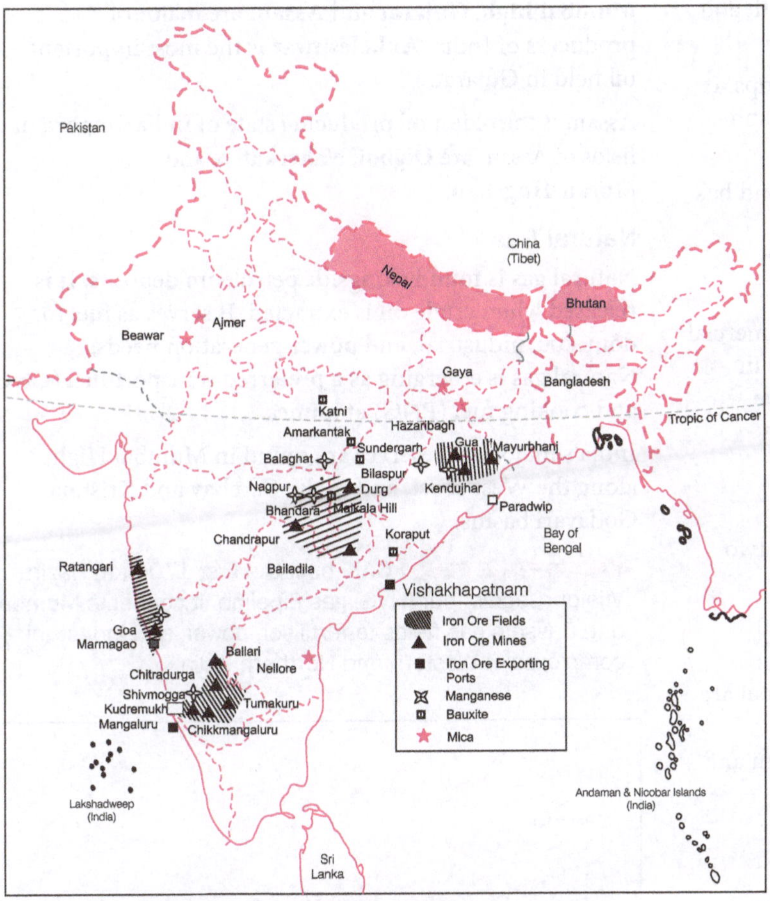

• India: Distribution of Iron ore, Manganese, Bauxite and Mica

5.3 Conservation of Minerals

Mineral resources are finite (exhaustible) and non-renewable. The rate at which the minerals are being used is much faster than the rate at which they can naturally renew or replace. So, there is need to conserve our mineral resources and use it judiciously in the following ways

- Mineral resources should be used in planned and sustainable manner.
- Technologies should be developed to use lower grade ores at lower costs.
- Metals should be recycled and alternative materials like scrap metal should be used so that minerals can be conserved.

Try These

1. **Name one hard and one soft mineral.**
2. **Coal is found in beds or layers of which rocks?**
3. **List two chief mica producing regions in India.**
4. **Name a metal that can be easily recycled.**

5.4 Energy Resources

Energy is essential for various activities, including cooking, heating, lighting, and powering industries. It can be derived from sources such as petroleum, natural gas, electricity, and uranium.

Energy resources can be classified as **conventional** or **non-conventional sources.**

Non-conventional sources of energy include wind power, solar energy, tidal energy, geothermal energy, atomic energy and biogas energy. They are freely available, usually inexhaustible and renewable.

Firewood and cattle dung cake are two most common energy in rural India, from which 70% of energy requirements are fulfilled.

However, the use of these two sources is becoming difficult because of the decreasing forest area and use of dung cake is discouraged as it uses manure, which is essential for agriculture.

Conventional Sources of Energy

Conventional sources include firewood, cattle dung cake, coal and petroleum, natural gas and electricity (both hydel and thermal). Some of these are discussed below

Coal

It is the most abundantly available fossil fuel in India. It fulfills a great amount of energy needs of the country. India is highly dependent on coal for meeting its commercial energy needs.

Coal is a **bulky material** (of large size for its weight), which loses weight on use as it is reduced to ash. Thus, heavy industries and thermal power stations are located on or near the coalfields.

Coal is formed by the compression of plant materials over millions of years.

Coal is formed by the compression of plant material over millions of years. The degree and compression creates various types of coals.

Depending on the degrees of compression, the depth and time of burial, there are following varieties of coal

- **Peat** It is formed by decaying of plants in swamps. It has a low carbon content, low heating capacity and high moisture content.
- **Lignite** It is a low grade brown coal. It is soft and has high moisture content. It is used for electricity generation. The important lignite reserves are in Neyveli in Tamil Nadu.
- **Bituminous** It is the most popular coal in commercial use. High grade bituminous coal is ideal for use in metallurgy (metal industries). It has special value for smelting iron in blast furnaces. It is found in greater depths.
- **Anthracite** It is the highest quality hard coal.

In India, coal occurs in rock series of the following two main geological ages

(i) **Gondwana Coal** This coal was formed over 200 million years ago. This type of coal is used in metallurgy. The major sources of Gondwana coal are located in the **Damodar valley** (West Bengal-Jharkhand). In this belt, Jharia, Raniganj and Bokaro are important coal fields.

Coal deposits are also present in the Godavari, Mahanadi, Son and Wardha valleys.

(ii) **Tertiary Coal** This coal was formed 55 million years ago. This type of coal is found in the North-Eastern states of Meghalaya, Assam, Arunachal Pradesh and Nagaland.

Petroleum

It is also known as **mineral oil** and **liquid gold**. It is the second highest energy source (after refining into various products like furnace oil, diesel, petrol, kerosene, etc) used in India after coal. It is used as a fuel.

Petroleum refineries provide raw materials for synthetic textile, fertiliser and chemical due to which these act as **nodal industry**.

Natural occurrence of petroleum in India is associated with **anticlines**[3] and **fault traps** of tertiary rocks.

In folding anticline or dome regions, oil is trapped in the crest (top portion) of the upfold (layered rocks).

Oil flows through a **porous**[4] layer of limestone or sandstone. Non-porous layers prevent the oil from sinking or rising.

Mumbai high, **Gujarat** and **Assam** are major oil producers of India. **Ankeleshwar** is the most important oil field in Gujarat.

Assam is the oldest oil producing state of India. Important oil fields of Assam are **Digboi**, **Naharkatiya** and **Moran-Hugrijan**.

Natural Gas

Natural gas is found alongside petroleum deposits. It is released when crude oil is extracted. It serves as fuel for domestic, industrial, and power generation needs. Natural gas is emerging as a preferred transport fuel (CNG) and cooking fuel (PNG) at homes.

India's major gas reserves are found in Mumbai High, along the West coast, and in the Cambay and Krishna Godavari basins.

KNOWLEDGE PLUS **GAIL** built the first 1700 km Hazira-Vijaipur Jagdishpur (HVG) gas pipeline. It connects Mumbai and Bassein gas fields to fertiliser, power, and industrial complexes in Western and Northern India.

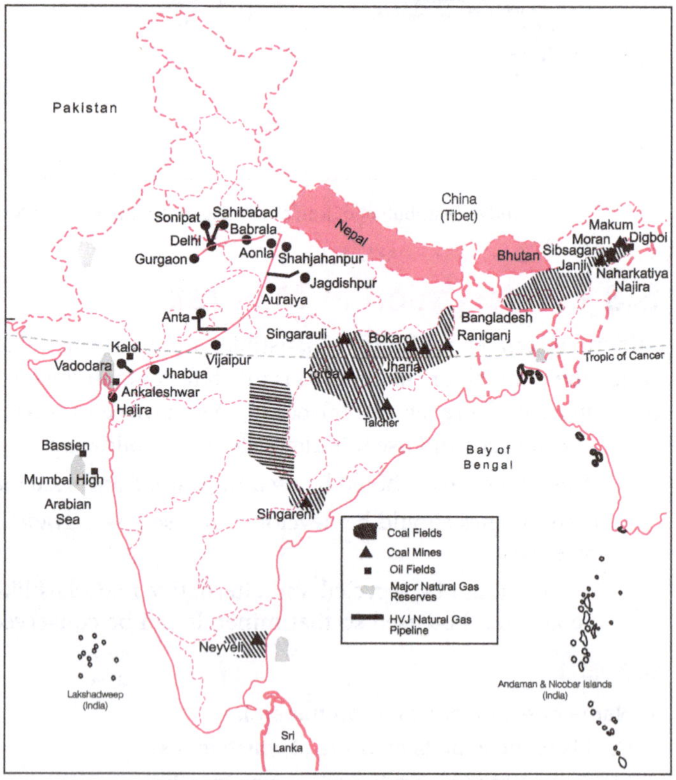

• Conventional Energy Resources

3 **Anticlines** A formation of rocks raised up by folding into a broad arch so that the strata slopes downwards on both sides from a common centre.

4 **Porous** It means having small holes that allow air or liquid to pass through.

Electricity

It has a wide range of application in today's world. The per capita consumption of electricity in a place is considered as an index of development. There are two ways through which electricity is generated. These are

(i) By burning fossil fuels[5] (coal, petroleum, natural gas etc) that supplies energy to drive turbines and produce thermal power. Thermal power stations use non-renewable fossil fuels for generating electricity.

(ii) By running water which drives hydro turbines to generate hydro power. Hydro electricity is generated by fast flowing water. India has various multi-purpose projects, like Bhakra Nangal, Damodar valley, the Kopili Hydel Project, etc.

Non-Conventional Sources of Energy

Non-conventional sources of energy are environment friendly and sustainable ways to generate electricity without depleting Earth's resources, e.g. solar, wind and thermal energy.

Some of these sources are discussed below

Nuclear or Atomic Energy

It is generated by changing the structure of atoms that releases heat and energy, which is used to generate electric power.

Uranium and **thorium** found in Aravalli ranges of Rajasthan and Jharkhand are used for generating nuclear or atomic energy. Thorium is also found in monazite sands of Kerala.

Solar Energy

India is a tropical country. It has enormous possibilities of using solar energy. **Photovoltaic technology** converts sunlight directly into electricity.

It is fast emerging as a fuel source in rural and remote places. It will reduce the dependence of rural households on fire wood and dung cakes, which can then be used as manure in agriculture.

Wind Power

India has great potential of wind power. The **largest wind form cluster** is located in Tamil Nadu from Nagarcoil to Madurai.

Apart from these, Andhra Pradesh, Karnataka, Gujarat, Kerala, Maharashtra and Lakshadweep have important wind farms.

Nagarcoil and Jaisalmer (Rajasthan) are very famous for effective use of wind energy in India.

Biogas

It is generated by the decomposition of organic matter like shrubs, farm waste, animal and human wastes.

It has higher thermal efficiency than kerosene, dung cake and charcoal. It provides improved quality of manure. It also prevents loss of trees and manure due to burning of fuel wood and cow-dung cakes.

Biogas plants are set up by municipal, cooperatives and also by individuals. Biogas plants are also known as **Gobar gas plants** in rural India.

Tidal Energy

It is the energy generated by movement of oceanic tides, which can be used to generate electricity.

To produce electricity, floodgate dams are built across inlets. The water enters into the inlet during high tide and gets trapped when the gates are closed.

When the tide falls outside the floodgate, the water retained inside the gate flows back to the sea through a pipe that carries it through a power generating turbine.

In India, the Gulf of Khambhat, the Gulf of Kutch in Gujarat on the Western coast and Gangetic delta in Sunderban regions of West Bengal provide ideal conditions for utilising tidal energy.

Geo-thermal Energy

It refers to the heat and electricity produced by using the heat from the interior of the Earth. Geothermal energy exists because the Earth grows hotter with increase in depth.

The areas where geothermal gradient is high, high temperatures are also found at shallow depths. Groundwater present in these areas absorb heat from the rocks, becomes hot and rises as steam. This steam is used to drive turbines for the generation of electricity.

Parvati valley near Manikarn in Himachal Pradesh and **Puga valley** in Ladakh are two experimental projects to produce geothermal energy.

5 Fossil Fuels These refer to fuels formed by the decomposition of organic matter in the earth's crust or seabed.

5.5 Conservation of Energy Resources

Energy is a basic requirement for economic development. Energy sector of national economy needs inputs of energy. Thus, consumption of energy in all forms has been rising continuously all over the country.

For sustainable methods of energy development, promotion of energy conservation by avoiding wastage and increased use of renewable energy sources are required. Presently India is one of the least energy efficient countries of the world.

Some of the ways of conserving energy are

- Using public transport systems instead of individual vehicles.
- Switching off electrical appliances when not in use.
- Using power-saving devices.
- Using non-conventional sources of energy.

Try These

1. **Where is the most useful variety of coal found in India?**
2. **In which region largest amount of natural gas is produced in India?**
3. **Name the minerals used to generate atomic power.**
4. **Where is geothermal energy project located in India?**

Mind Map

MINERALS AND ENERGY RESOURCES

Distribution
- Peninsular plateau
- Gujarat and Assam
- Rajasthan
- Northern Plains

Mode of Occurrence
- Veins and lodes in igneous and metamorphic rocks.
- Beds or layers in sedimentary rocks.
- Decomposition of surface rocks.
- Alluvial deposits

Conservation of Minerals
- Should be used in planned and sustainable manner.
- Lower-grade ores should be used at lower costs
- Metals should be recycled and scrap metals should be used.

Conservation of Energy Resources
- Using public transport instead of individual vehicles.
- Switching off electric appliances when not in use.
- Using power saving devices of energy.
- Using non-conventional sources of energy.

Importance
- In building roads, machinery and transportation like planes and cars.
- People depend on minerals for decoration, livelihood, etc.
- Geographers study minerals to understand landforms.

Energy Resources

Conventional Sources
- Coal
- Petroleum
- Natural Gas

Non-Conventional Sources
- Nuclear or Atomic Energy
- Solar Energy
- Wind Power
- Biogas
- Tidal Energy
- Geothermal Energy

Classification of Minerals

Rock Minerals
- Limestone is a rock mineral.
- It is used for smelting iron-ore in blast furnaces and raw material for cement manufacturing.
- Rajasthan has the largest share of limestone in India.

Non-Metallic Minerals
- Mica is a non-metallic mineral.
- It is used in electrical and electronics industries.
- Koderma-Gaya-Hazaribagh belt of Jharkhand is the leading producer of mica.

Metallic Minerals

Ferrous Minerals
Have iron content

Non-ferrous Minerals
Do not contain iron content

Iron Ore
- Finest form is magnetite.
- Found in
  - Odisha-Jharkhand Belt.
  - Durg-Bastar-Chandrapur Belt
  - Maharashtra-Goa Belt

Manganese
- Used in manufacturing of steel and ferro-manganese alloys.
- Used in manufacturing of insecticides, bleaching powder and paints

Copper
- Found in
  - Khetri mines in Rajasthan
  - Balaghat mines in Madhya Pradesh.
  - Singhbhum district in jharkhand

Bauxite
- Found in
  - Amarkantak Plateau
  - Maikal Hills
  - Plateau region of Bilaspur-Katni.
  - Panchpatmali in Odisha

NCERT FOLDER

Covering Intext Questions and Exercises of NCERT

INTEXT QUESTIONS

Q.1 Find out where these minerals (silica, limestone, aluminium oxide, fluorite, rutile, ilmenite, anatase, mica, petroleum) are found.

Ans. (i) **Silica** These are commonly found in Gujarat, Rajasthan, Andhra Pradesh, West Bengal and Tamil Nadu.

(ii) **Limestone** These are commonly found in Madhya Pradesh, Rajasthan and Andhra Pradesh.

(iii) **Aluminium Oxide** (Alumina/Bauxite) These are found in Madhya Pradesh, Chhattisgarh and Odisha.

(iv) **Fluorite** These are found in Nasik and Jalgaon areas of Maharashtra.

(v) **Rutile, Ilmenite, Anatase** These are found in Kerala and Tamil Nadu.

(vi) **Mica** These are found in Koderma and Hazaribagh areas of Jharkhand, Gaya in Bihar and in Rajasthan.

(vii) **Petroleum** These are found in Assam, offshore Maharashtra and Rajasthan.

Q.2 What is the difference between an open pit mine, a quarry and an underground mine with shafts?

Ans. The differences between an open pit mine, a quarry and an underground mine with shafts are

Open Pit Mine	Quarry	Underground Mine with Shafts
Minerals are extracted from a pit dug in the ground.	Minerals are extracted from a shallow pit dug in the ground.	Minerals are extracted through deep shafts dug in the ground.
It is used where commercially useful minerals are found near the surface.	It is used for extracting building materials like dimension stone.	It is used where the mineral occurs as veins in hard rock deep below the surface of the Earth.
Minerals are extracted by using Earth moving machinery.	Minerals are extracted by using Earth moving machinery.	Minerals are extracted by using elevators that can carry minerals, extraction equipment as well as persons into the area where the mineral is available.

Q.3 Superimpose the maps showing distribution of iron ore, manganese, coal and iron and steel industry. Do you see any correlation? Why?

Ans. Yes, there is a correlation among these minerals. The iron and steel industries are located in the same regions of India where the iron ore, coal and manganese mines are located.

As coal and manganese are required as inputs to the iron and steel industry, their availability in the same region saves the transportation costs as well as provide ease of availability.

So, it is profitable to locate these industries in the regions where these minerals are available.

Q.4 Study the maps to explain why Chota Nagpur is a storehouse of minerals.

Ans. Chota Nagpur plateau is considered as a storehouse of minerals due to the following reasons

- Iron ore is found in abundance and about 40% of iron ore in India is found in this area.
- Over 50% of manganese in India is found in this region.
- Almost 60% of copper in India is found here.
- Almost 60% of bauxite in India is found here.
- The region is also rich in coal.

Q.5 Have you ever wondered about the efforts the miners make in making life comfortable for you? What are the impacts of mining on the health of the miners and the environment?

Ans. Yes, miners are very hardworking and do very risky jobs in order to make our life comfortable. They provide raw materials to the manufacturing industries which turn them into finished goods.

The impacts of mining on the health of miners are

- The dust and noxious fumes inhaled by miners make them vulnerable to pulmonary diseases.
- The risk of collapsing mine roofs, inundation and fires in coal mines are a constant threat to miners.
  The impacts of mining on the environment are that the water sources in the region get contaminated due to mining, and dumping of waste and slurry lead to degradation of land, soil and increase stream and river pollution.

Q.6 Make a list of items where substitutes are being used instead of minerals. Where are these substitutes obtained from?

Ans. Substitutes are being used instead of mineral products as given below

Substitute	Mineral Product	Item in which used
Chemicals of plastics family	Steel (from iron ore), Aluminium	Furniture, vehicle parts
Artificial jewellery made from plastics	Gold and silver	Jewellery

The majority of these substitutes are obtained from petroleum after it is suitably processed in a refinery.

EXERCISE

Q.1 Multiple choice questions.

(i) Which one of the following minerals is formed by decomposition of rocks, leaving a residual mass of weathered material?

(a) Coal (b) Bauxite
(c) Gold (d) Zinc

(ii) Koderma, in Jharkhand is the leading producer of which one of the following minerals?

(a) Bauxite (b) Mica
(c) Iron ore (d) Copper

(iii) Minerals are deposited and accumulated in the stratas of which of the following rocks?

(a) Sedimentary rocks
(b) Metamorphic rocks
(c) Igneous rocks
(d) None of these

(iv) Which one of the following minerals is contained in the Monazite sand?

(a) Oil (b) Uranium
(c) Thorium (d) Coal

Ans. (i) (b) Bauxite (ii) (b) Mica
(iii) (a) Sedimentary rocks (iv) (c) Thorium

Q.2 Answer the following questions in about 30 words.

(a) Distinguish between the following in not more than 30 words.

(i) Ferrous and non-ferrous minerals

(ii) Conventional and non-conventional sources of energy

(b) What is a mineral?

(c) How are minerals formed in igneous and metamorphic rocks? **CBSE 2011**

(d) Why do we need to conserve mineral resources?

Ans. (a)

(i) The differences between ferrous and non-ferrous minerals are

Ferrous Minerals	Non-ferrous Minerals
The minerals which contain iron ore are known as ferrous minerals.	The minerals which do not contain iron ore are known as non-ferrous minerals.
These are helpful in the development of metallurgical industries.	These minerals play an important role in engineering and electrical industries.
Iron ore, chromite, cobalt, etc are the examples of ferrous minerals.	Copper, zinc, lead and aluminium are the examples of non-ferrous minerals.

(ii) The differences between conventional and non-conventional sources of energy are

Conventional Sources of Energy	Non-conventional Sources of Energy
They have been used since a long time.	These are of recent origin and have not been commonly used.
They are non-renewable and exhaustible sources of energy.	They are renewable sources of energy.
These source of energy include firewood, fuel, coal, petroleum, etc	These source of energy include wind, tidal energy, solar energy, etc.
These sources pollute the environment.	These sources are pollution free sources.

(b) A mineral is a homogenous, naturally occurring substance, having a definite chemical composition and comprising of one or more elements.

(c) Minerals are formed in igneous and metamorphic rocks. When liquid molten material and gaseous form moves upwards towards the Earth's surface, cools down and becomes solid.

(d) We need to conserve mineral resources because

- Minerals are non-renewable sources of energy. Minerals take million years to be formed and our consumption rate is very fast as compared to the replenishment rate of minerals.
- Minerals are needed for economic growth and industrialisation.
- Minerals are unevenly distributed. Thus, to maintain equal distribution of these resources, minerals need to be conserved.

Q.3 Answer the following questions in about 120 words.

(a) Describe the distribution of coal in India.

(b) Why do you think that solar energy has a bright future in India?

Ans. (a) In India, coal is the most abundantly available fossil fuel. It is found in a variety of forms depending on the degress of compression, the depth and time of burial. As per these basis, coal deposits are found mainly of two geological ages. These are

(i) **Gondwana Coal Deposits** These coal deposits were formed over 200 million years ago. This type of coal deposits are used in metallurgy which are high in quality.

These are located in Damodar Valley (West Bengal-Jharkhand). Jharia, Raniganj and Bokaro are important coal deposit fields. Besides, the Godavari, Mahanadi, Son and Wardha Valleys also contain such coal deposits.

(ii) **Tertiary Coal Deposits** These coal deposits were formed 55 million years ago. This type of coal deposits are found in the North-Eastern states of Meghalaya, Assam, Arunachal Pradesh and Nagaland. This coal is of lower quality than the Gondwana coal.

(b) Solar energy has a bright future in India due to the following reasons

(i) Solar energy is an inexhaustible source of energy that is produced from sunlight. India is a tropical country thus, there is enough scope for the development of solar energy.

(ii) Many parts (regions) of the country receive at least 300 days of sunlight annually so, it becomes possible to generate 20 MW solar energy per square kilometer in such areas.

(iii) It is easy to establish solar plants in urban and rural areas.

(iv) Solar plants in rural areas, will reduce the dependence of rural households on fire wood and cow dung cakes, which can then be used as manure in agriculture.

REVIEW EXERCISE

Including Competency Based Questions

Part I

Multiple Choice Questions (MCQs)

1. Which of the following minerals is/are obtained from ocean waters?

(a) Common salt (b) Bromine
(c) Magnesium (d) All of these

2. Sangita and her husband belongs to mizo-tribe in the North-East region of India. They live in an area that is rich in mineral resources. They both are involved in rat-hole mining along with other individuals of the community.

Accordingly, which of the following steps would be most crucial in this situation? Competency Based

(a) Government should immediately stop them from rat hole mining as it is declared illegal by national green tribunal.
(b) Government should make some provisions to make rat hole mining easy for them.
(c) Government should give monetary help to the people belonging to this community to prevent them from this practice.
(d) Government should give them awareness about the other methods of mining.

3. Which of the following is the basic mineral and the backbone of industrial development?

(a) Zinc ore (b) Iron ore (c) Manganese ore (d) Silver ore

4. Which is the finest iron ore with a very high content of iron?

(a) Magnetite (b) Haematite
(c) Lignite (d) None of these

5. The Badampahar mine in Mayurbhanj and Kendujhar district is situated in which of the following Indian state?

(a) Karnataka (b) Odisha
(c) Chhattisgarh (d) Jharkhand

6. Iron ore is exported to Japan and South Korea through which port?

(a) Chennai (b) Visakhapatnam
(c) Haldia (d) Mangaluru

7. Why do you think that mining is a risky activity?

(a) Because it can result in death of the miner.
(b) Because people are engaged in bloodshed over mining related issues.
(c) Because mining has impact on the health of the miners and environment.
(d) Because it is done underground.

8. Large reserves of natural gas have been discovered in which place in India?

(a) Arabian Sea
(b) Andaman and Nicobar Islands
(c) Krishna Godavari Basin
(d) Gulf of Mannar

9. Non-conventional sources of energy are renewable form of energy that is continuously produced in nature and is limitless.

Which of the following examples represents the non-conventional sources of energy? Competency Based

(a) Production of thermal energy
(b) Use of natural gas
(c) A biogas plant set up at municipal level
(d) A petroleum station

10. Which type of sand in Kerala is rich in thorium?

(a) Monazite sands (b) Gypsum sands
(c) Silica sands (d) Black sands

11. Where is the largest wind farm cluster located in India?

(a) Andhra Pradesh (b) Kerala
(c) Karnataka (d) Tamil Nadu

12. In India, the Gulf of Khambhat, the Gulf of Kuchchh and the Gangetic delta provide ideal condition for utilising which energy?

(a) Tidal energy
(b) Wind energy
(c) Solar energy
(d) Non-conventional energy

13. Which of the following is true for geothermal energy?

(a) Experimental projects for geothermal energy are set up in Puga Valley, Ladakh.
(b) Aravalli ranges of Rajasthan have small reserves of geothermal energy.
(c) It develops in regions where there is low temperature.
(d) Geothermal energy is a good source for exhaustible conventional fuels.

14. Choose the correct option. **CBSE 2020**

(a) Chandrapur thermal power plant – Odisha
(b) Mayurbhanj iron ore mines – Amarkantak
(c) Kalol oil fields – Gujarat
(d) Bauxite producer – Jharkhand

15. 'India's Energy Transition: Challenges and Opportunities for a Sustainable Future'

India is a crucial player in the global clean energy transition, given its status as the third-largest energy consumer in the world as of 2022. As the need to accelerate this transition becomes urgent in the face of rising climate catastrophes, India is taking prompt action to address its high carbon emissions and environmental challenges.

Source : The Times of India

Should India shift to sustainable sources of energy ?

(a) Yes, because sustainable sources are cheaper and can contribute to economic growth of a country.
(b) No, because conventional sources can be used in a way that minimises pollution.
(c) Yes, because clean energy transition requires developing sustainable alternatives.
(d) No, because India is already working for conservation of forest resources which in turn balances its environmental emissions.

16. Arrange the following manganese producing states from highest to lowest production.

I. Odisha II. Madhya Pradesh
III. Karnataka IV. Andhra Pradesh

Codes

(a) II, I, III, IV (b) I, II, III, IV
(c) III, II, I, IV (d) II, III, IV, I

17. Consider the following statements about bauxite.

I. Bauxite is a clay-like substance from which alumina is extracted.
II. Jharkhand is largest bauxite producer of India
III. Bellari-Chitradurga belt is famous for bauxite reserves in India.

Which of the following statements is/are correct?

(a) Only I (b) II and III
(c) I and III (d) All of these

18. Which of the following statements accurately describes the 'petroleum' ?

I. It is the most abundantly available energy resource
II. Lignite is a type of petroleum reserves.
III. It provides lubricants for machinery.
IV. It is also found in fault traps between porous and non-porous rocks.

Codes

(a) Only III (b) II and IV
(c) I and II (d) III and IV

19. Mr. Z lives in a village where women use cow dung cakes and firewood to cook food. He decided to install a small biogas plant in his farm because

I. It provides most efficient use of cattle dung in the form of energy.
II. Farm waste can be used for the production of biogas.
III. It improves the quality of manure.
IV. It does not cause pollution nor have any bad effect on health of women.

Codes

(a) Only I (b) II and III
(c) III and IV (d) All of these

20. Read the characteristics given in the box and identify the type of coal from the option given below. **CBSE 2025**

- **This is low grade brown coal.**
- **The principal reserves are in Neyveli in Tamil Nadu.**
- **It is soft with high moisture content.**

Options

(a) Pit Coal (b) Anthracite Coal
(c) Lignite Coal (d) Bituminous Coal

21. **Consider the following statements and choose the correct option.**

Statement I Mineral is a heterogeneous, naturally occurring substance.

Statement II Minerals have a definable internal structure.

Options

(a) Statement I is correct and statement II is incorrect.
(b) Statement I is incorrect and statement II is correct
(c) Both statements I and II are incorrect
(d) Both statements I and II are correct

22. **Consider the following statements and choose the correct option.**

Statement I Majority of rocks contains several minerals however some rocks may contain single mineral only.

Statement II Rocks are combinations of minerals.

Options

(a) Statement I is correct and statement II is incorrect.
(b) Statement I is incorrect and statement II is correct
(c) Both I and statements II are incorrect
(d) Both I and statements II are correct

Answers

1. (d)	**2.** (a)	**3.** (b)	**4.** (a)	**5.** (b)
6. (b)	**7.** (c)	**8.** (c)	**9.** (c)	**10.** (a)
11. (d)	**12.** (a)	**13.** (a)	**14.** (c)	**15.** (c)
16. (a)	**17.** (a)	**18.** (d)	**19.** (d)	**20.** (c)
21. (b)	**22.** (d)			

Match the Following

1.

List I (Minerals)	List II (Examples)
A. Iron ore	1. Gaya
B. Mica	2. Singrauli
C. Bauxite	3. Chandrapur
D. Coal	4. Maikala

Codes

	A	B	C	D		A	B	C	D
(a)	3	1	4	2	(b)	3	1	2	4
(c)	2	3	1	4	(d)	2	3	4	1

Ans. (a)

Assertion-Reason

1. **Assertion** (A) Minerals are an indispensable part of our lives. **CBSE 2025**

Reason (R) All living things need minerals.

Codes

(a) Both A and R are true and R is the correct explanation of A
(b) Both A and R are true, but R is not the correct explanation of A
(c) A is true, but R is false
(d) A is false, but R is true

2. **Assertion** (A) Uses of iron brought a radical change in human life.

Reason (R) Different kinds of tools were invented by using minerals.

Codes

(a) Both A and R are true and R is the correct explanation of A
(b) Both A and R are true, but R is not the correct explanation of A
(c) A is true, but R is false
(d) A is false, but R is true

3. **Assertion** (A) Mica is a non-metallic mineral.

Reason (R) Mica mineral is the basic raw material for cement industry

Codes

(a) Both A and R are true and R is the correct explanation of A
(b) Both A and R are true, but R is not the correct explanation of A
(c) A is true, but R is false
(d) A is false, but R is true

4. **Assertion** (A) Geological processes of mineral formation is slow.

Reason (R) Minerals resources are consumed way quickly than they are formed.

Codes

(a) Both A and R are true and R is the correct explanation of A
(b) Both A and R are true, but R is not the correct explanation of A
(c) A is true, but R is false
(d) A is false, but R is true

5. **Assertion** (A) Thermal power stations are located on or near the coalfields.

Reason (R) Coal is a bulky material, which loses weight on use as it is reduced to ash. Hence, heavy industries and thermal power stations are located on or near the coalfields.

Codes

(a) Both A and R are true and R is the correct explanation of A
(b) Both A and R are true, but R is not the correct explanation of A
(c) A is true, but R is false
(d) A is false, but R is true

6. **Assertion** (A) Natural gas is referred as an environment friendly fuel.
Reason (R) Natural gas contains low carbon dioxide emissions.
Codes
(a) Both A and R are true and R is the correct explanation of A
(b) Both A and R are true, but R is not the correct explanation of A
(c) A is true, but R is false
(d) A is false, but R is true

7. **Assertion** (A) Increased use of fossil fuels creates a healthy environment.
Reason (R) Fossil fuels such as coal, oil and gas are non-replenishable and non-renewable.
Codes
(a) Both A and R are true and R is the correct explanation of A
(b) Both A and R are true, but R is not the correct explanation of A
(c) A is true, but R is false
(d) A is false, but R is true

8. **Assertion** (A) Conservation of energy resources is essential.
Reason (R) Energy is a basic requirement for economic development.
Codes
(a) Both A and R are true and R is the correct explanation of A
(b) Both A and R are true, but R is not the correct explanation of A
(c) A is true, but R is false
(d) A is false, but R is true

Ans. 1. (a) Both A and R are true and R is the correct explanation of A
2. (a) Both A and R are true and R is the correct explanation of A
3. (c) A is true, but R is false
4. (b) Both A and R are true, but R is not the correct explanation of A
5. (a) Both A and R are true and R is the correct explanation of A
6. (a) Both A and R are true and R is the correct explanation of A
7. (d) A is false, but R is true
8. (a) Both A and R are true and R is the correct explanation of A

Picture Based Questions

1. **What work do the following picture show?**

(a) Construction work in progress
(b) Mining
(c) Trapping of nuclear energy
(d) Conservation of minerals

2. **The given picture shows the development of which source of energy?**

(a) Biogas
(b) Geo-thermal energy
(c) Solar energy
(d) Nuclear energy

Ans. 1. (b) Mining 2. (a) Biogas

Case Based Question

1. **Read the following passage and answer the questions that follow.**

India is fortunate to have fairly rich and varied mineral resources. However, these are unevenly distributed. Broadly speaking, peninsular rocks contain most of the reserves of coal, metallic minerals, mica and many other non-metallic minerals. Sedimentary rocks on the Western and Eastern flanks of the peninsula, in Gujarat and Assam have most of the petroleum deposits. Rajasthan with the rock systems of the peninsula, has reserves of many non-ferrous minerals.

The vast alluvial plains of North India are almost devoid of economic minerals. These variations exist largely because of the differences in the geological structure, processes and time involved in the formation of minerals.

(i) **Which of the following places in Peninsular India is famous for iron ore mines?**
(a) Nellore (b) Ballari (c) Katni (d) Hazaribagh

(ii) **Which kind of fuel is obtained from sedimentary deposits?**
(a) Petroleum (b) Natural gas
(c) Bauxite (d) Both (a) and (b)

(iii) **Which of the following is not a non-ferrous mineral?**
(a) Bauxite (b) Manganese (c) Copper (d) Zinc

(iv) **What can be the reason behind non-availability of any economic minerals in Northern plains?**
(a) Because this region is formed due to deposits of numerous rivers.
(b) Because this region is formed due to lava flow.
(c) Because this region is located along Himalayan fault line.
(d) All of the above

Ans. (i) (b) Ballari
(ii) (d) Both (a) and (b)
(iii) (b) Manganese
(iv) (a) Because this region is formed due to deposits of numerous rivers.

Part II

Very Short Answer Type Questions

1. What is the general interest of geologists towards minerals?

Ans. A geologist is mainly interested in the formation of minerals, their age and physical and chemical composition.

2. Veins and lodes are found in which kind of rocks? Also, name some minerals found in them.

Or

Which type of minerals are mainly obtained from veins and lodes? **CBSE 2017**

Ans. Veins and lodes are found in igneous and metamorphic rocks.
Some minerals found in veins and lodes are tin, zinc, lead and copper.

3. What do you understand by placer deposits? What are the properties of minerals that are found in placer deposits?

Ans. Some minerals may occur as alluvial deposits in sands of valley floors and the base of hills. These deposits are called placer deposits.
These minerals are not corroded by water.

4. Give a list of minerals found in placer deposits.

Ans. Gold, silver, tin and platinum are important minerals found in placer deposits.

5. 'Rat-hole mining has been declared as illegal and has recommended that these activities should be stopped forthwith.'
Discuss what is meant by rat-hole mining and where it is practiced. **Competency Based**

Ans. Rat hole mining is a type of mining that is done by digging long narrow tunnels to reach the coal deposits under the ground. It is practiced in regions of Jowai and Cherapunjee.

6. Name the regions containing the highest and the lowest amounts of mineral deposits in India.

Ans. Regions having the highest amount of mineral deposit is the peninsular plateau and the lowest amount of mineral deposits is the Northern Plains.

7. What factors affect the economic viability of a reserve?

Ans. The concentration of mineral in the ore, the ease of extraction and closeness to the market play an important role in affecting the economic viability of a reserve.

8. Suggest any two ways for the conservation of minerals. **CBSE 2025**

Ans. Two ways for the conservation of minerals are

(i) **Recycling of Metals** Recycling helps in reducing the need for extracting new minerals from the Earth. By reusing metals such as aluminum, copper and iron, we can conserve the minerals used in their production.

(ii) **Using Alternative Resources** Instead of relying solely on non-renewable mineral resources, we can look for alternatives. For example, the use of renewable energy sources like solar and wind power.

9. What is the significance of the Kudremukh mines?

Ans. The Kudremukh mines are located in the Western Ghats of Karnataka. All the iron produced in these mines are exported and these are known to be one of the largest in the world.

10. Why mica is used in electrical and electronics industry?

Ans. Mica is used in electrical and electronics industries due to its excellent di-electric strength, low power loss factor and insulating properties and resistance to high voltage.

11. How bauxite is formed in rocks?

Ans. The formation process of bauxite involves the decomposition of surface rocks and leaving a residual mass of weathered material containing ores of bauxite.

12. "Coal is, and would, remain an important part of India's energy needs," said foreign secretary Vinay Mohan Kwatra hours before Prime Minister Narendra Modi headed to Dubai for the Conference of the Parties (CoP) to the UN Framework Convention on Climate Change (UNFCCC).

Source (edited) : The Wire

(i) Why is so much importance attached to the coal in India?

Ans. In India so much importance is attached to the coal as it provides a substantial part of the nation's energy needs. It is used for power generation, to supply energy to industry as well as for domestic needs.

(ii) In which series of rock does the coal occurs?

Ans. In India, coal occurs in rock series of two main geological ages, namely Gondwana, a little over 200 million years in age and in tertiary deposits which are only about 55 million years old.

13. Tanu performed a web search to about the petroleum reserves in India. She found that there are few reserves of petroleum in India which are mostly located along the coast in Mumbai High and Gujarat or in North-East in Assam.

Mention the reasons behind location of petroleum reserves in the above areas. **Competency Based**

Ans. Most of the petroleum occurrences in India are associated with anticlines and fault traps in the rock formations of the tertiary age. In regions of folding, anticlines or domes, it occurs where oil is trapped in the crest of the upfold. These conditions are present in India in Mumbai high, Gujarat and Assam and thus, reserves of petroleum are mostly located in these areas.

14. 'We need to expand our nuclear energy and then we can have round-the-clock green energy. Then we will reduce coal (based power).

Source : The Indian Express

Why it is desirable to expand our nuclear energy? **Competency Based**

Ans. It is desirable to expand our nuclear energy capacity because it is a renewable form of energy. This energy can contribute to reduction in air pollution due to a great extent.

15. Why is the conservation of conventional sources of energy significant? Explain any two reasons. **CBSE 2025**

Ans. Conservation of conventional sources of energy is significant for the following two reasons

(i) **Finite Nature of Resources** Conventional sources of energy, such as coal, oil and natural gas, are non-renewable and limited. Conservation is essential to ensure their availability for future generations.

(ii) **Environmental Impact** The use of conventional energy sources often leads to environmental degradation, such as air pollution and climate change. By conserving these resources and using them more efficiently, we can reduce the harmful impact on the environment.

16. Wind energy received in abundance in Western Rajasthan and Gujarat has not been so far utilised and developed to the maximum. It falls in which category of resources? **CBSE 2019**

Ans. Wind energy falls in the category of potential resources.

Short Answer Type Questions

1. What are minerals? Give two examples. Also name any two carrier rocks of minerals. **CBSE 2012**

Ans. A homogeneous naturally occurring substance that has a definable internal structure is known as mineral. Minerals are important resources which are very useful for the national economy.

The two examples of minerals are coal and iron-ore.

Two carrier rocks of minerals are igneous and metamorphic rocks.

2. Explain any three types of formations in which minerals occur.

Ans. The three main types of formations in which minerals occur are

(i) **Veins and Lodes** Smaller faults are called veins, and bigh cracks or faults are called lodes. In igneous and metamorphic rocks, minerals may occur in cracks, faults or joints.

(ii) **Beds or Layers** In sedimentary rocks, minerals occur in the form of bed or layers due to deposition, accumulation and concentration in horizontal layers of the rock.

(iii) **Placer Deposits** Some minerals occur as alluvial deposits in sands of valley floors and at the base of hills. These deposits are known as placer deposits.

3. India is fairly rich in mineral resources, however its distribution is uneven. Comment.

Ans. India is fairly rich in mineral resources, however its distribution is uneven. For example,

- Gujarat and Assam have petroleum deposits as oil is found in sedimentary rocks on the Western and Eastern flanks of the peninsula. But rest of India does not have any oil deposit.
- Minerals deposits are mostly available in the peninsular plateau region of Chota Nagpur and rock systems of Rajasthan.
- The vast alluvial plains of the North India, mountainous regions and coastal plains do not have any mineral deposits.

4. Discuss the factors that most likely determine the economic viability of a reserve. CBSE 2014

Ans. The three factors that determine the economic viability of a reserve are as follows

(i) The quality and quantity of mineral concentration in the ore. For example, magnetite is regarded better than haematite as it has more concentration of iron.

(ii) The cost of extraction. If the cost of extraction is high than mining is not profitable.

(iii) Location of mines near the industries.

5. How is Durg-Bastar-Chandrapur belt important for India?

Ans. The Durg-Bastar-Chandrapur belt is important for India in the following ways

- Very high grade haematites are found in the Bailadila range of hills in the Bastar district of Chhattisgarh.
- This range of hills comprises of 14 deposits of super high grade haematite iron ore.
- It has the best physical properties needed for making steel.
- Iron ore from these mines is also exported to Japan and South Korea through Visakhapatnam port.

6. Which state is the largest producer of manganese in India? Mention any four uses of manganese. CBSE 2013

Or **Which is the largest producer of manganese in India? Mention two uses of manganese.** CBSE 2017

Ans. Odisha is the largest producer of manganese in India.

Uses of manganese are as follows

(i) It is used in the manufacturing of steel and ferro-manganese alloy.

(ii) It is used in the manufacturing of bleaching powder.

(iii) It is used in insecticides, paint industries and manufacturing of batteries.

(iv) It is used in manufacturing of steel. Nearly 10 kg of manganese is required to manufacture one tonne of steel.

7. Explain the formation of bauxite and name the metal obtained from it. CBSE 2014

Ans. Bauxite is formed by the decomposition of a wide variety of rocks that are rich in aluminium silicates. Intense weathering of the surface rocks helps in their decomposition, thus forming bauxite deposits. The metal obtained from bauxite is aluminium. Alumina occurs in a clay-like formation within the bauxite deposits from which aluminium is obtained.

8. Name the non-metallic mineral which can split easily into thin sheets. Mention its uses. CBSE 2014

Ans. Mica is the non-metallic mineral which can be split easily into thin sheets as it occurs in the form of plates or leaves of different colours. Uses of mica are as follows

- It is used in paints as a pigment extender. It also helps to brighten the tone of coloured pigments.
- It is used in electrical and electronic industry due to its di-electric strength, insulating properties and resistance to high voltage.
- It is used in making toothpaste and cosmetics due to its shiny and glittery appearance.

9. What is the importance of energy resources? Give two examples each of conventional and non-conventional sources of energy.

Ans. Energy resources are important as they are needed to cook, to provide light and heat, for agricultural activities, propel vehicles and to drive machinery in industries. Thus, the sustainable development of energy resources is vital for all human activities.

The two examples of conventional sources of energy are coal and petroleum.

The two examples of non-conventional sources of energy are solar energy and wind energy.

10. "Energy is an indispensable requirement in our modern lives." Explain the statement with three examples.

Ans. It is true that energy is an indispensable requirement in our modern lives. It can be understood through the following examples

(i) Every sector of the national economy requires energy. For example, agriculture, industry, transport, commercial and domestic needs require inputs of energy.

(ii) Implementation of economic development plans necessarily require increasing amounts of energy to remain operational.

(iii) Energy is required for all domestic activities like cooking, lighting and heating and even air-conditioning (cooling).

11. Read the statements given below regarding coal reserves in India.

Statement 1 (S1) Coal provides a substantial part of India's energy needs.

Statement 2 (S2) India is highly dependent on coal for meeting its commercial energy requirements.

Explain what does the statements – S1 and S2 indicate by giving supporting arguments.

Ans. It is true that coal provides a substantial part of India's energy needs. India is highly dependent on coal for meeting its commercial energy requirement.

It can be supported from the following arguments

- The majority of electricity generation plants in India are based on burning of coal for generating steam to power turbines.
- Many industries use coal in the blast furnaces for generating heat for their various operations.
- Coal is an important constituent in steel production, alumina refineries, and in chemical and pharmaceutical industries.

12. State the importance of petroleum as an energy resource. Mention any four oil fields of India.

Ans. The importance of petroleum as an energy resource can be seen through the following points

- Petroleum or mineral oil is the second highest energy source in India after coal.
- It provides fuel for heating and lighting, lubricants for machinery and raw materials for a number of manufacturing industries.
- It is a fuel used in all the automobiles.

The four major oil fields of India are

(i) Mumbai High
(ii) Ankleshwar and Kalol in Gujarat
(iii) Digboi, Naharkatiya and Moran in Assam
(iv) Rajasthan, Mangala, district Barmer

13. What is natural gas? What is its advantage? Name one region of India where its reserves are found.

Or **"Natural gas is an important source of energy." Support the statement.** **CBSE 2017**

Ans. Natural gas is an important source of energy. It is an important clean energy resource found in association with or without petroleum. It is also used as an industrial raw material in the petrochemical industry.

The advantages of natural gas are

- It is an environment friendly fuel.
- It generates low carbon dioxide emission during use.
- It is increasingly replacing pollution causing fuels.

The large reserves of natural gas have been found in the Krishna-Godavari basin.

14. How naturally occurring gas is different from biogas?

Ans. The naturally occurring gas is different from biogas in the following ways

Natural Gas	Biogas
It is a mixture of hydro-carbons and occur frequently with petroleum in the rocks of the Earth's crust.	It is formed by the decomposition of animal, plant and farm wastes with the help of 'micro organisms in the presence of water'.
It occurs naturally.	It undergoes a process of formation under controlled man-made conditions.
It is non-renewable.	It is renewable.
It is used as a raw material in the petrochemical.	It is used as a fuel and for lighting purposes.
It is mainly used in urban areas.	It is mainly used in the rural areas.

15. Crude oil reserves are limited all over the world. If people continue to extract it at the present rate, the reserves would last only 35-40 years more. Explain any three ways to solve this problem. **CBSE 2019**

Ans. Crude oil reserves are limited all over the world. If people continue to extract it at the present rate, the reserves would last only 30-40 years more.

For energy conservation we can take the following steps

(i) We have to adopt a cautious approach for the judicious use of our limited energy resources.
(ii) We can use public transport systems instead of individual vehicles.
(iii) We can switch off electricity when not in use, using power saving devices. We can use non-conventional energy like solar energy, wind power, biogas, etc instead of using petroleum.

16. Mr. Y, a renewable energy expert visits a village where two group of people were discussing and debating about development of energy resources in the country. One group was in favour of Hydroelectricity while the other one was with thermal electricity. How can Mr. Y solve this confusion? **Competency Based**

Ans. Mr. Y can solve this confusion by providing them the differences between the two forms of energy and then let them decide which one is better.

The two main ways of generating electricity are by running water (hydro electricity) and by burning fuels (thermal electricity).

The difference between hydro electricity and thermal electricity are as follows

Hydro Electricity	Thermal Electricity
It is generated from fast flowing water falling on turbines.	It is generated from petroleum, coal and natural gas.
Its source is perennial or inexhaustible i.e. water.	Its sources are exhaustible or non-renewable sources i.e. coal and petroleum.
It does not cause pollution.	The burning of coal and oil cause a lot of pollution.

17. Why India has the potential to develop wind energy? Which places in India are sources of wind energy?

Ans. India has the potential to develop wind energy as India has a long coastline in which there is scope of developing wind energy. The areas along the coastline are windy and wind mills can be established there.

The places in India having source of wind energy or wind mills are

- Wind farm cluster located in Tamil Nadu from Nagarcoil to Madurai.
- Wind farms in Gujarat, Kerala, Maharashtra, Lakshadweep and Andhra Pradesh.
- Wind farm in Jaisalmer.

18. What is tidal energy? Which regions in India provide ideal conditions for utilising tidal energy?

Ans. Tidel energy is the electrical energy that can be generated through the oceanic tides to generate electricity. This can be done by building flood gate dams in areas that get submerged during high tides.

During high tide when the water flows inside the dam, the gates are closed. After the high tide, the water retained by the flood gate falls back to the sea via a pipe that carries it through a power generating turbine.

The regions in India that provide ideal conditions for utilising tidal energy are the Gulf of Khambhat, the Gulf of Kuchchh and Gangetic delta in Sunderban.

19. What is geo-thermal energy? Which regions in India show potential of developing this energy?

Ans. Geo-thermal energy is the internal heat of the Earth that can be used to generate electricity. This happens when there is high concentration of Earth's energy at one place leading to high temperatures in that region such as hot springs in mountain areas.

In India, the Parvati Valley near Manikaran in Himachal Pradesh and Puga Valley in Ladakh have potential of developing this energy resource.

20. What are the uses of limestone? Mention names of two states of India which are major producers of limestone.

Ans. The uses of limestone are as follows

- It is used in cement industry as the raw material of cement.
- It is used for smelting iron ore in the blast furnaces of steel plants.

Rajasthan (largest producer) Madhya Pradesh, Andhra Pradesh and Karnataka are important states which are major producers of limestone.

21. 'The total volume of workable mineral deposits is an insignificant fraction i.e. one per cent of the Earth's crust. We are rapidly consuming mineral resources that required million of years to be created and concentrated.' Competency Based

(i) What does the above statement means to say about the creation of mineral resources?

Ans. The above statement indicates that geological processes of mineral formation are so slow that the rates of replenishment are infinitely small in comparison to the present rates of consumption. Mineral resources are, therefore, finite and non-renewable. Continued extraction of ores leads to increasing costs as mineral extraction comes from greater depths along with decrease in quality.

(ii) What needs to be done in order to solve the problem indicated in the above statement?

Ans. A concerted effort has to be made in order to use our mineral resources in a planned and sustainable manner. Improved technologies need to be constantly evolved to allow use of low grade ores at low costs. Recycling of metals, using scrap metals and other substitutes are steps in conserving our mineral resources for the future.

Long Answer Type Questions

1. "Minerals are an indispensable part of our lives." Justify this statement with suitable examples. CBSE 2016

Ans. It is true that minerals are an indispensable part of our lives. This can be understood through the following examples

- Almost everything that we use in our daily life, from a tiny pin to a towering building or a big ship, all are made from minerals.
- The railway lines and the paving of the roads, machinery, implements and tools too are made from minerals.
- Minerals form the basis of all industries.
- Our food contains various minerals that are essential for our body. They are absorbed by the body. In conclusion, we can say that in all stages of development, human beings have used minerals for their livelihood, decoration, festivities, religious and ceremonial rites.

2. Differentiate between metallic and non- metallic minerals with examples. CBSE 2013

Ans. Differences between metallic and non-metallic minerals are as follows

Metallic minerals	Non-metallic minerals
Minerals containing metals are called metallic minerals.	Minerals which do not contain metals are called non-metallic minerals.
These minerals are malleable and ductile.	These minerals are non-malleable and non-ductile.
These minerals are generally associated with igneous and metamorphic rocks.	These minerals are mostly associated with sedimentary rocks.
Metallic minerals show lusture.	Non-metallic minerals do not show lusture.
Iron-one, manganese, copper, tin, etc are the examples of metallic minerals.	Gypsum, potash, salt, etc are examples of non-metallic minerals.

3. A think tank has been given the task to identify the major sources of energy in rural areas and suggest solutions to solve the problem that exists.

Discuss the key problems posed by these sources of energy in rural areas that the think tank should consider while giving suggestions. Also specify the major suggestions that can be given. Competency Based

Ans. Firewood and cattle dung cake are the major sources of energy in rural household of India.

Major problems faced due to these sources are

- Using cow dung is discouraged because it consumes most valuable manure which could be used in agriculture.
- Use of firewood as fuel is becoming difficult due to decreasing forest area.

The major suggestions to solve these problems are

- Awareness must be developed in the rural areas regarding the non-conventional sources of energy like solar energy, wind energy, biogas, etc. It will minimise the dependence of rural households on firewood and dung cakes, which in turn will contribute to environmental conservation and adequate supply of manure in agriculture.
- Government should take initiatives in setting up the biogas plants in rural areas.

4. Union Power and New and Renewable Energy Minister R K Singh on Tuesday said India will not compromise on meeting growing energy demands of the Indian economy, but will develop generation capacity with responsibility. He mentioned that we were nine years ahead in achieving the Nationally Determined Contributions (NDC) target of having 40 per cent of installed power capacity from non-fossil-fuel sources by 2030.

Source (edited) : Business Standard

Analyse why there is pressing need to use non-conventional energy resources in the scenario of growing energy consumption in the country. **Competency Based**

Ans. There is a growing need for increasing the use of non-conventional energy resources due to the following reasons

- The conventional or non-renewable sources of energy are depleting very fast and we are dependent on imports of petroleum and natural gas to meet our needs.
- Renewable energy sources do not cause environmental pollution with their use and so, to preserve our environment, we must change over to use more of such sources.
- Non-conventional or renewable sources of energy are very economical in use as compared to conventional sources. Thus, to save expenses, we should use renewable energy sources.

5. "Consumption of energy in all forms has been rising all over the country. There is an urgent need to develop a sustainable path of energy development and energy saving." Suggest and explain any three measures to solve this burning problem. **CBSE 2016**

Ans. It is justified that the consumption of energy in all forms has been rising all over the country.

To take care of this concern various measures that need to be adopted are as follows

(i) We need to increase the use of renewable energy resources like solar, wind power, biogas, tidal energy and geothermal energy. This will decrease the dependence on non-renewable sources.

(ii) We have to adopt a cautious approach for judicious use of our limited energy resources. For example, as a concerned citizen, we can use public transport system in place of individual vehicle.

(iii) Another measure that needs to be adopted is promotion of energy conservation, e.g. switching off electrical devices when not in use, using power saving devices.

6. Which is the most abundantly available fossil fuel in India? Assess the important characteristics of its different forms. **CBSE 2015**

Ans. Coal is the most abundantly available fossil fuel in India. The important characteristics of fossil fuel in different forms are as follows

(i) **Peat**

- It is formed by decaying of plants in swamps.
- It is burnt as fuel or applied to the soil to improve the texture or raise its water-retaining property.

(ii) **Lignite**

- It has 60-70% carbon and has lowest heat content per kg. It is soft and brown in colour, and having high moisture content.
- It is used for electricity generation

(iii) **Bituminous**

- It has 75-90% carbon content, dense sedimentary rock, usually black in colour and has medium heat content per kg.
- It is used for commercial purpose especially ideal for smelting iron in blast furnaces.
- It is also used as making coke.

(iv) **Anthracite**

- It is a good quality hard coal. It is used in the metal smelting and fabrication industries.
- It has more than 90% carbon content per kg and its heating content per kg is highest.
- It is also used in residential and commercial space heating.

7. A village in a remote area in Uttar Pradesh is dealing with energy access problems. However, this village produces a large amount of cow dung waste. How can the biogas produced from this cow dung solve the energy problems in the rural areas? **CBSE 2015**

Ans. Biogas can solve the energy problem in the rural areas in the following ways

- It produces gas having higher thermal efficiency than charcoal and kerosene.

- It provides a way for optimum utilisation of animal and plant wastes.
- It produces enriched organic manure that can supplement or even replace chemical fertilisers.
- It burns smoothly and does not leave much residue behind.
- It is easy to produce and store.

Some suggestions to improve the biogas energy production in rural areas are given below

- Government should provide monetary assistance to people in the rural areas to set-up biogas plants.
- Awareness must be created for using this alternative sources of energy.

8. Nuclear energy is expected to play an increasingly important role in India when there is a great stress on shifting to non-conventional and green sources of energy'. Justify the statements with relevant points referring to India. CBSE 2016

Ans. Nuclear energy is expected to play an increasingly important role in India due to the following reasons

- India has limited reserves of coal and petroleum. Nuclear energy minerals like Thorium is found in plenty in India. Hence, nuclear energy can compensate for deficiency of fossil fuels.
- Nuclear power stations can be established easily and conveniently in those areas where other sources are not available.
- Nuclear power releases tremendous amounts of energy. India can utilise this energy for peaceful purposes such as generation of electricity that can be used to run machines in industries.
- Nuclear energy is a non-conventional source of energy. After the initial expenses, it becomes very economical.

9. Why is conservation of mineral resources essential? Explain any three methods to conserve them. CBSE 2016

Or **Explain the importance of conservation of minerals. Highlight any three measures to conserve them.** CBSE 2015

Ans. Conservation of mineral resources are essential due to the following reasons

- Minerals are required in many industries. So it is important to use them carefully as it is needed everywhere.
- Minerals are already in limited quantities and they are non-renewable resources. Their reserves are fast depleting.
- Lot of economic developmental plans have been possible due to the presence of certain minerals. So to continue those developmental plans and projects, judicious use of minerals is needed.

The three methods to conserve the minerals are

(i) Better and improved technology should be used to reduce wastage of minerals during extraction.

(ii) Minerals and metals made out of those minerals should be recycled wherever possible.

(iii) Scrap metals and substitutes of metals should be used wherever possible.

10. "There is a pressing need for using renewable energy sources in India." Justify the statement. CBSE 2017

Ans. There is a growing need for increasing the use of renewable energy sources due to the following reasons

(i) The conventional or non-renewable sources of energy are depleting very fast and we are dependent on imports of petroleum and natural gas to meet our needs.

(ii) Renewable energy sources do not cause environmental pollution with their use and so, to preserve our environment, we must change over to use more of such sources.

(iii) Non-conventional or renewable sources of energy are very economical in use as compared to conventional sources. Thus, to save expenses, we should use renewable energy sources.

11. Analyse the impact of mining activities on the local environment and the health of the surrounding communities. CBSE SQP 2023-24

Ans. The impact of mining activities on the local environment and the health of the surrounding communities are

- The dust and noxious fumes inhaled by miners make them vulnerable to pulmonary diseases.
- The risk of collapsing mine roofs, inundation and fires in coal mines are a constant threat to miners.
- Mining usually has a negative impact on the environment with the production of a lot of waste. Disruption to the local flora and fauna, and contamination of local water sources.
- It could require the removal of massive amounts of topsoil, leading to erosion, loss of habitat and pollution.

12. "Non conventional resources are the best option to conserve the natural resources." Substantiate this statement with examples. CBSE SQP 2023-24

Ans. Non-conventional resources are the best option to conserve the natural resources and are also known as renewable sources of energy. Examples of non-conventional sources of energy include solar energy, bio energy, tidal energy, wind energy, geo-thermal energy, natural gas, etc.

Importance of non-conventional resources are as follows

- They are inexhaustible and renewable.
- They are also considered as clean sources of energy.
- Optimal use of resources of energy minimises environmental impact and non-conventional resources produce minimum secondary waste compared to use conventional sources.

- Rising prices of oil and gas and their potential shortages have raised uncertainties about the security of energy supply in future, which in turn has serious repercussions on the growth of the national economy.
- Natural gas is considered an environmentally friendly fuel because of low carbon dioxide emissions.
- It does not cause air pollution or environmental degradation.

Thus, it is the fuel for present century. Renewable energy resources technologies provide an excellent opportunity for mitigation of greenhouse gas emission and reducing global warming through substituting conventional energy sources.

Case Based Questions

1. Read the sources given below and answer the questions that follow.

Source A Biogas

Shrubs, farm waste, animal and human waste are used to produce biogas for domestic consumption in rural areas. Decomposition of organic matter yields gas, which has higher thermal efficiency in comparison to kerosene, dung cake and charcoal.

(i) To what extent do you think biogas is better than dung cake for fuel?

Source B Solar Energy

India is a tropical country. It has enormous possibilities of tapping solar energy. Photovoltaic technology converts sunlight directly into electricity. Solar energy is fast becoming popular in rural and remote areas.

(ii) Why solar energy has more potential to be developed as major fuel in rural areas?

Source C Wind Energy

India has great potential of wind power. The largest wind farm cluster is located in Tamil Nadu from Nagarcoil to Madurai. Apart from these, Andhra Pradesh, Karnataka, Gujarat, Kerala, Maharashtra and Lakshadweep have important wind farms.

(iii) What similarity or trait can be seen in the places idealy suited for setting up wind farm?

Ans. (i) Biogas is much better than dung cakes as it produces no smoke and has more thermal efficiency.

(ii) There is more potential of developing solar energy in rural areas as there are relatively more open spaces. This will reduce the dependence on firewood and dung cakes fuel.

(iii) The similarities identified are that the areas should be close to sea where there is lot of potential for blowing of wind or other windy areas.

2. Read the following source given below and answer the questions that follow.

Decaying plants in swamps produce peat which has a low carbon and high moisture content and low heating capacity. Lignite is low grade brown coal, which is soft with high moisture content. The principal lignite reserves are in Neyveli in Tamil Nadu and are used for generation of electricity. Coal that has been buried deep and subjected to increased temperatures is bituminous coal. It is the most popular coal in commercial use.

Metallurgical coal is high grade bituminous coal which has a special value for smelting iron in blast furnaces. Anthracite is the highest quality hard coal.

In India, coal occurs in rock series of two main geological ages, namely Gondwana, a little over 200 million years in age and in tertiary deposits which are only about 55 million years old. The major resources of Gondwana coal, which are metallurgical coal, are located in Damodar valley (West Bengal, Jharkhand). Jharia, Raniganj, Bokaro are important coalfields. The Godavari, Mahanadi, Son and Wardha valleys also contain coal deposits. Tertiary coals occur in the North-Eastern states of Meghalya, Assam, Arunachal Pradesh and Nagaland.

(i) Which reserves are important for lignite in India?

(ii) In what extent do you agree that bituminous coal is metallurgical coal? State its one property.

(iii) Why is coal associated with geological ages? State where it is found?

Ans. (i) Neyveli reserves in Tamil Nadu are important lignite reserves in India. These are used for generation of electricity.

(ii) Bituminous coal is a high grade coal and thus, is a metallurgical coal. This type of coal has a special value for smelting iron in blast furnaces.

It is buried deep under the Earth's surface and is subjected to increased temperature. It makes special value for smelting iron-ore in blast furnaces.

(iii) Coal is associated with geological ages because coal is formed due to compression of plant material and takes million of years to come into existence.

In India, coal occurs in rock series of two main geological ages, namely Gondwana rock series which is a little over 200 million years in age and in tertiary deposits rock series which are only about 55 million years old. Gondwana coal deposits are found in Damodar valley (West Bengal, Jharkhand), Jharia, Raniganj, Bokaro, coalfields. The Godavari, Mahanadi, Son and Wardha valleys also contain coal deposits. Tertiary coal deposits are found in the North-Eastern states of Meghalaya, Assam, Arunachal Pradesh and Nagaland.

Map Based Questions

1. On the given political map of India, identify and label the following features with appropriate symbols.

(i) Iron ore mine in Chhattisgarh

(ii) An oil field in Assam

(iii) A major oil field of India located in Arabian Sea. **CBSE 2025**

(iv) An oil field in Gujarat

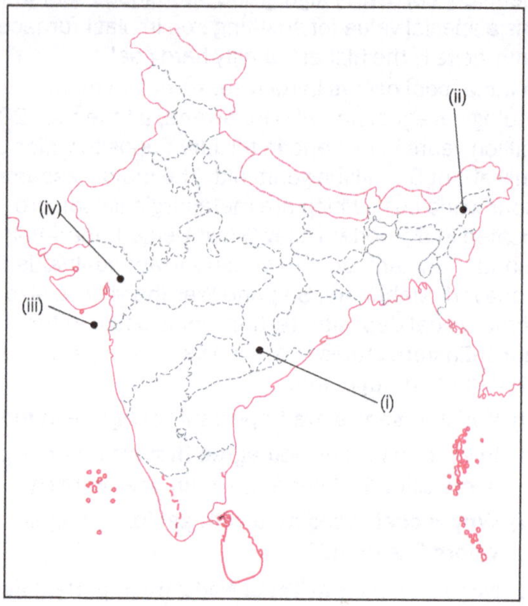

Ans.

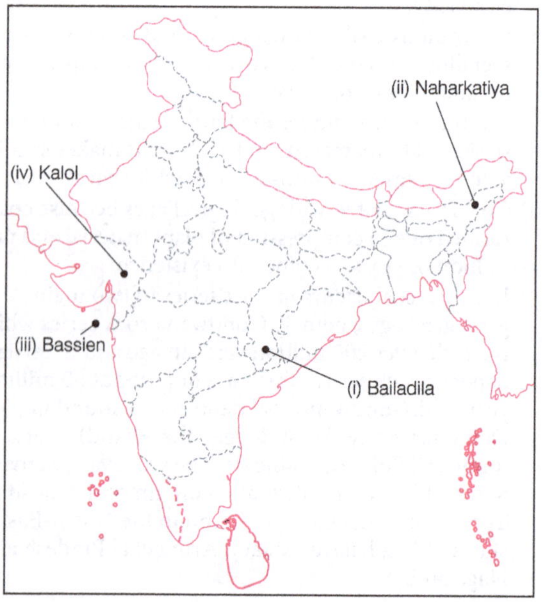

2. On the given political map of India, identify the features and name the following.

(i) An oil field in Assam

(ii) Coal mine in Jharkhand

(iii) An oil field in Gujarat

(iv) An iron ore mine in Karnataka

(v) An iron ore mine in Chhattisgarh

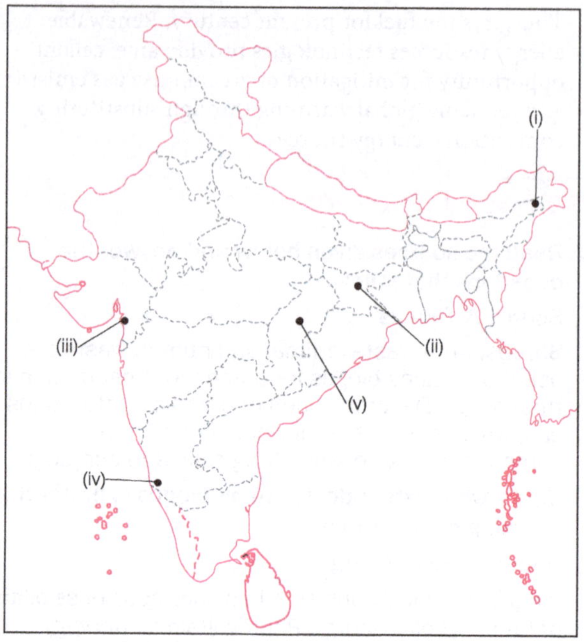

Ans.

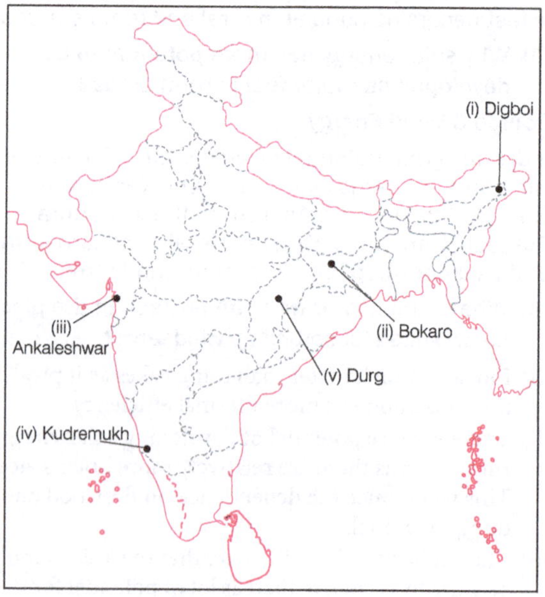

3. Identify the features on the given map of India.

(i) Iron ore mine
(ii) Oil field
(iii) Coal mine
(iv) Iron ore mine in Odisha
(v) Coal mine

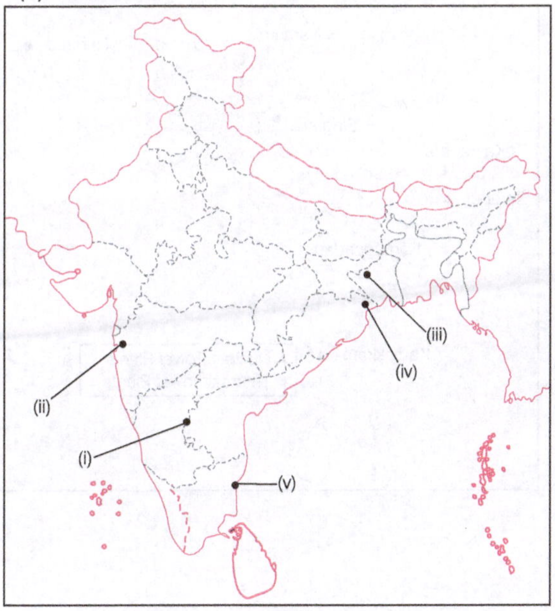

Ans.

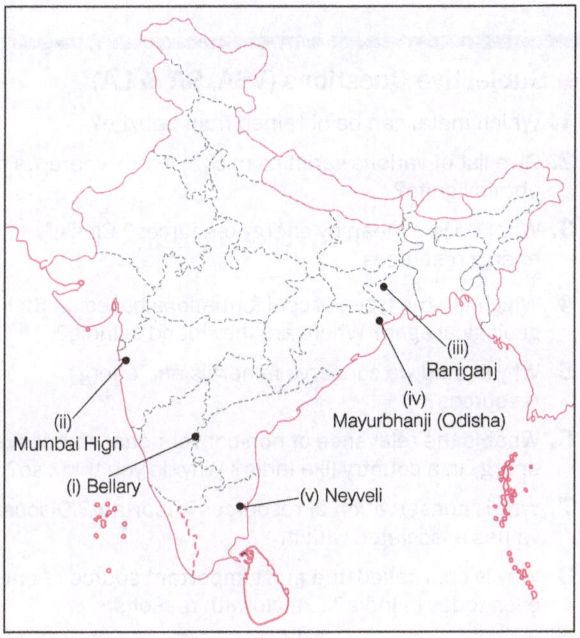

4. Identify the features marked on the given political map of India.

(i) Coal mines in Odisha
(ii) Iron ore mine in Chhattisgarh
(iii) offshore oil field
(iv) Oil field in Gujarat
(v) Oil field in Assam

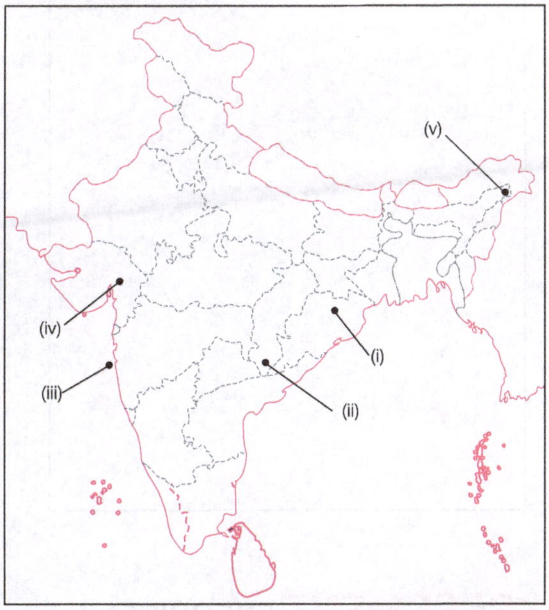

Ans.

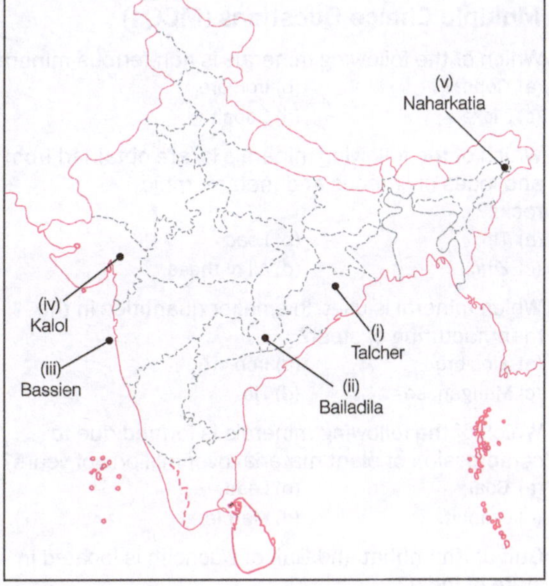

5. Locate the following nuclear and thermal power plants on the map of India.

(i) Nuclear Power plants — Naraura, Kakrapara, Tarapur, Kalpakkam.

(ii) Thermal Power plants— Namrup, Ramagundam, Singrauli.

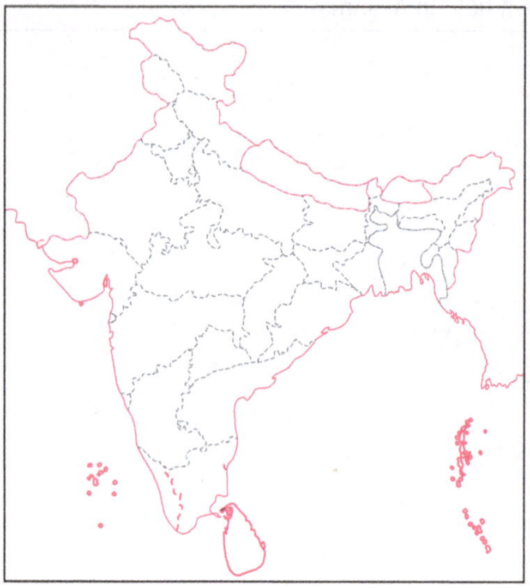

Ans.

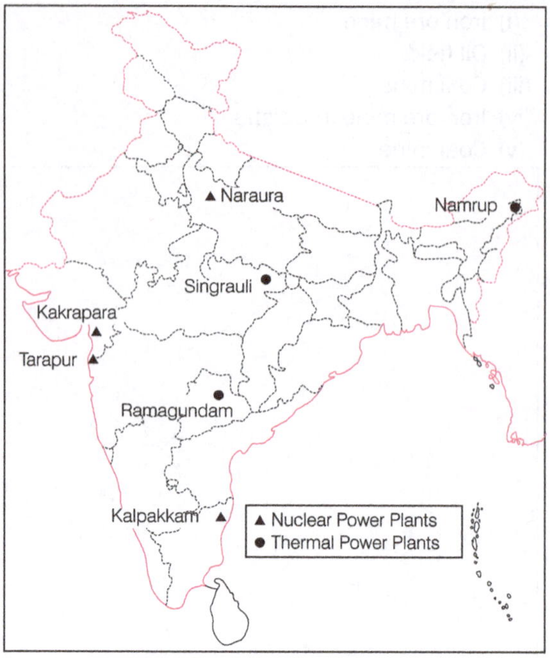

ASSESSMENT EXERCISE

Multiple Choice Questions (MCQs)

1. Which of the following minerals is non-ferrous mineral?

(a) Copper (b) Iron ore
(c) Nicke (d) Cobalt

2. Which of the following minerals is/are obtained from veins and lodes of igneous and metamorphic rocks?

(a) Tin (b) Lead
(c) Zinc (d) All of these

3. Which mineral is used in smaller quantities in the manufacturing of steel?

(a) Zinc ore (b) Iron ore
(c) Manganese (d) Tin

4. Which of the following minerals is formed due to compression of plant material over millions of years?

(a) Coal (b) Lead
(c) Graphite (d) Marble

5. Gulf of Khambhat and Gulf of Kuchchh is located in which state of India?

(a) Andhra Pradesh (b) Kerala
(c) Karnataka (d) Gujarat

Subjective Questions (VSA, SA & LA)

1. Which metal can be obtained from bauxite?

2. Give list of various varieties of coal. From where we can obtain lignite?

3. What do you mean by energy resources? Classify energy resources.

4. Which are the types of coal formations based on their geological ages? Where are they found in India?

5. Why should we conserve minerals and energy resources?

6. What is the relevance of non-conventional sources of energy in a country like India? Why do you think so?

7. Why is conservation of resources important? Discuss values associated with it.

8. Why is coal called the most important source of energy even today in India? Explain with reasons.

9. Explain the development of non-conventional sources of energy in India.

10. Examine tidal energy and geo-thermal energy as sources of energy for the future.

CHAPTER 6

Manufacturing Industries

Production of goods in large quantities by converting raw materials to more valuable products is called **manufacturing**.
Manufacturing industries are known as secondary activities, as these industries manufacture primary material (like cotton fibre) into finished goods (like textiles). The economic strength of a country is measured by the development of manufacturing industries.

6.1 Importance of Manufacturing

Manufacturing sector is considered as the backbone of economic development because

- Manufacturing industries help in modernising agriculture, which forms an important part of our economy.
- Manufacturing also reduces the heavy dependence of people on agricultural income by providing them jobs in secondary and tertiary sectors.
- Industrial development helps in removal of unemployment and poverty as it creates jobs and more income. It also aims at reducing regional differences by establishing industries in tribal and backward areas.
- Export of manufactured goods increase trade and commerce, and brings foreign exchange.
- Countries that transform their raw material into a wide variety of value finished goods of higher value are prosperous. Thus, India's prosperity lies in increasing and diversifying its manufacturing industries.

Agriculture and Industries

Agriculture and industries depend upon each other. For example, agro-industries in India have encouraged agriculture by increasing its productivity and making the production process more efficient.

The industries depend on agriculture for their raw materials. On the other hand, farmers depend on industries for products like fertilisers, irrigation pumps, PVC pipes, tractors, machines and tools, for increasing agricultural productivity.

6.2 Classification of Industries

Industries are classified on the basis of the following criteria

(i) On the basis of source of raw material used

- **Agro-Based Industries** Cotton, woolen, silk, jute, textile, rubber, tea, sugar, edible oil.
- **Mineral Based Industries** Iron and steel, cement, aluminium, petrochemicals and machine tools.

(ii) On the basis of their role

- **Basic or Key Industries** They supply their raw materials that are used to manufacture other goods. For example, iron and steel, aluminium smelting, etc.
- **Consumer Industries** They produce goods for direct use by consumers. For example, sugar, toothpaste, paper, sewing machines, fans, etc.

(iii) On the basis of capital investment

- Small scale industry is the industry in which a maximum investment of one crore is allowed.

(iv) On the basis of ownership

- **Public Sector Industries** These are owned and operated by government agencies, e.g., SAIL (Steel Authority of India), BHEL (Bharat Heavy Electrical Limited), etc.
- **Private Sector Industries** These are owned and operated by individuals or group of individuals, e.g., TISCO, Bajaj, Dabur industries, etc.
- **Joint Sector Industries** These are jointly run by government and industrialists. OIL (Oil India Ltd) is jointly owned by public and private sector.

- **Cooperative Sector Industries** These are owned and operated by the producers or suppliers of raw materials, workers or both. They pool the resources and share the profits or losses accordingly. For example, sugar industry in Maharashtra, and coir industry in Kerala.

(v) On the basis of bulk and raw material and finished goods
- Heavy industries such as iron and steel.
- Light industries such as electrical goods industries (which use light raw materials).

6.3 Agro-Based Industries

Industries that are based on agricultural raw materials belong to this category. Some of these industries are discussed below

Textile Industry

This industry contributes significantly to industrial production, employment generation and foreign exchange earnings. It is the only industry in the country that is self-reliant and complete in the value chain. It means everything, from raw material to the highest value added products, is done in India.

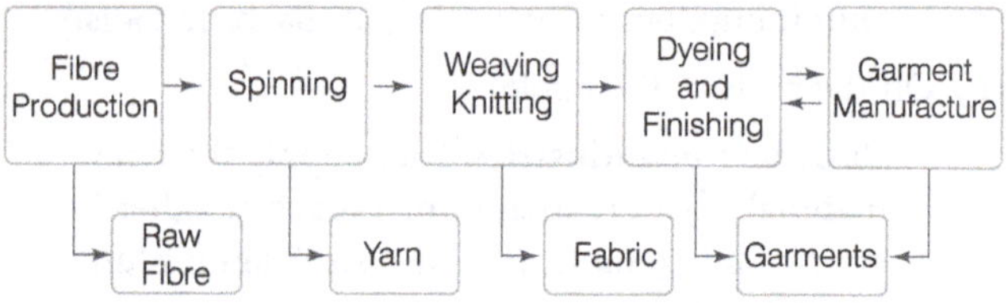

• Value Addition in the Textile Industry

Cotton Textiles

In ancient India, cotton textiles were produced with hand spinning and handloom weaving techniques. After 18th century, machines called **power-looms** started being used.

The traditional industries faced problems during the colonial (British) times because English machine made cloth was cheaper.

Earlier, cotton textiles were largely located in Gujarat and Maharashtra, due to the availability of cotton market, transport facilities, moist climate, labour, etc.

This industry is closely related to agriculture and provide living to many people like cotton boll pluckers and workers in weaving, spinning, dyeing, etc. It also supports other industries like packaging materials, engineering works and chemicals and dyes.

Spinning is mainly done in Tamil Nadu, Maharashtra and Gujarat. However, weaving is done in different places, allowing for inclusion of traditional skills and designs of weaving in cotton, silk, zari, embroidery, etc.

India has world class production in spinning but weaving supplies low quality of fabric as it cannot use much of the high quality yarn produced in the country.

Weaving is done by powerloom, handloom and in mills. The handspun khadi provides large scale employment to weavers in their homes.

> **KNOWLEDGE PLUS** The **first cotton textile mill** was set-up in Mumbai in 1854.
> During world wars India was colony of British. Due to demand for cloth in UK, they gave boost to development of cotton textile industry in India.

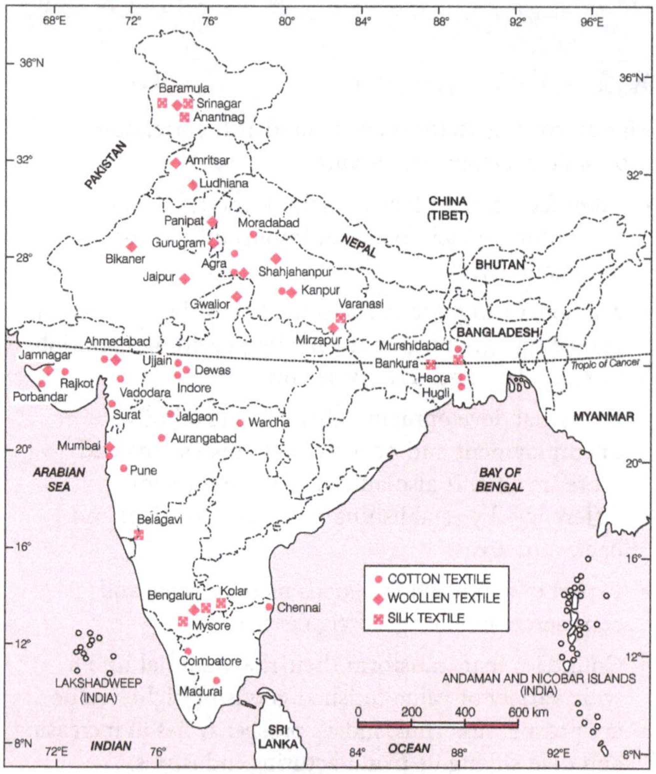

• Textile Industries

Jute Textiles

India is the largest producer of raw jute and jute goods.

It occupies second place in the jute export after Bangladesh. Jute industry is located along the Hugli river in West Bengal. The first jute mill was set-up near **Kolkata** in 1855 at **Rishra**. After partition in 1947 only three-fourth of jute producing area left with India, while other went to Bangladesh.

The factors responsible for the location of jute mills in Hugli basin are

- Closeness of the jute producing areas reduces the cost of transportation.
- Inexpensive water transport and good network of railways, roadways for easy movement of raw material to the mills.
- Abundant water supply from nearby river for processing raw jute.
- Cheap labour from West Bengal and adjoining stated that are Bihar, Odisha and Uttar Pradesh.
- Kolkata is a large urban centre that provides banking, insurance and port facilities for export of jute goods.

Sugar Industry

India occupies second position in the world in sugar production and first in the production of ***gur*** and ***khandsari***.

Sugar industry uses bulky raw materials and loses its sucrose (sugar) content during transportation. This industry is seasonal in nature, thus it is ideally suitable for cooperative sector.

Sugar mills are located in Uttar Pradesh, Bihar, Maharashtra, Tamil Nadu, etc. 60% mills are located in Bihar and Uttar Pradesh.

In recent years, more mills are being setup in the Southern and Western states, especially in Maharashtra. This is because the cane produced here has a higher sucrose content and the cooler climate ensures a longer crushing season.

Try These

1. **Manufacturing industries are known as which activities?**
2. **Name the primary material which is used to produce textile.**
3. **Which is the only self-reliant industry in India?**
4. **What are agro-based industries?**

6.4 Mineral Based Industries

Industries that use minerals and metals as raw materials are called mineral based industries. Some of these industries are discussed below

Iron and Steel Industry

It is a basic industry as heavy, medium and light industries depend on it for their machinery. It is also considered heavy industry as raw material used and finished goods produced in it are both heavy and bulky involving heavy transportation costs.

Steel is required to manufacture a variety of engineering goods, defence, medical and consumer goods. Production and consumption of steel is considered as an indicator of country's development. Iron ore, coking coal and limestone are required in the ratio of approximately 4 : 2 : 1 to produce steel. Some quantities of manganese are also required to harden the steel.

Factors which are responsible for the location of iron and steel industry are low cost of iron ore, closeness to high grade raw materials, cheap labour and great growth potential in the market.

Iron and steel industries are mainly concentrated in the Chhotanagpur plateau region.

Aluminium Smelting

It is the second most important metallurgical industry in India. Bauxite is the basic raw material for this industry which is a very bulky, dark reddish coloured rock.

Aluminium is light, resistant to **corrosion**[1], a good conductor of heat, **malleable**[2] and becomes strong when it is mixed with other metals. It is used to manufacture aircraft, utensils and wires.

Aluminium has gained popularity as an alternative substitute of steel, copper, zinc and lead in different industries.

Regular supply of electricity and availability of raw material are two important factors for the location of aluminum industry.

In India, aluminium smelting plants are located in Odisha, West Bengal, Kerala, Uttar Pradesh, Chhattisgarh, Maharashtra and Tamil Nadu.

Chemical Industries

In India, the chemical industry is fast growing and expanding in nature. It comprises both large and small scale manufacturing units.

Chemical industry has two sectors as follows

(i) **Organic Sector** It produces organic chemicals. These chemicals include petrochemicals. Petrochemicals are used for manufacturing of synthetic fibres, synthetic rubber, plastics, dye-stuffs, drugs and pharmaceuticals.

Organic chemical plants are located near oil refineries or petrochemical plants.

1 **Crrosion** It is a process by which a metal surface is attached by a certain substance such as air or water.

2 **Melleable** If refers to the property of a material by which it can be beaten to form thin sheets.

(ii) **Inorganic Sector** It produces inorganic chemicals. These chemicals include sulphuric acid (used to manufacture fertilisers, synthetic fibres, plastics, adhesives, paints, dyes stuffs), nitric acid, alkalies, soda ash (used to make glass, soaps and detergents paper) and caustic soda. These chemical plants are located all over the country.

The chemical industry itself is a large consumer. Basic chemicals go through some processing to produce other chemicals that are used in industries, agriculture or directly for consumer markets.

Fertiliser Industry

It produces a number of different fertilisers which include nitrogenous fertilisers (mainly urea), phosphatic fertilisers and Diammonium Phosphate (DAP).

It also produces complex fertilisers which have a combination of nitrogen (N), phosphate (P), and potash (K). India imports potash from other countries because it does not have any reserves of commercially usable potash or potassium compounds in any form.

The **Green Revolution** provided a boost to this industry in the country. Gujarat, Tamil Nadu, Uttar Pradesh, Punjab and Kerala contribute towards half of the fertiliser production. Other important producers are Andhra Pradesh, Odisha, Rajasthan, Bihar, Maharashtra, Assam, West Bengal, Goa, Delhi, Madhya Pradesh and Karnataka.

Cement Industry

Cement industry requires bulky and heavy raw materials such as limestone, silica and gypsum. Coal and electric power along with rail transportation are other important requirements in this industry.

Cement is the basic requirement for construction activities like building houses, factories, bridges, roads, airports, dams and other commercial establishments.

Cement plants are mainly located in Gujarat because it has suitable access to market in the Gulf countries.

The first cement plant was set up in Chennai in 1904.

Automobile Industry

It provides quick transportation vehicles for goods and passengers. In India, there are centers for manufacture of trucks, buses, cars, motor cycles, scooters, three-wheelers and multi-utility vehicles.

This industry is mainly located around Gurugram, Mumbai, Pune, Chennai, Kolkata, Lucknow, Indore, Hyderabad, Jamshedpur, Delhi and Bengaluru.

Information Technology (IT) and Electronics Industry

The electronics industry covers wide ranging products from transistor sets to televisions, telephones, cellphones, telephone exchanges, radars, computers and other equipments required by the telecommunication and computer industry.

Bengaluru has emerged as the **electronic capital of India.** Other important centres for electronic goods are Noida, Mumbai, Chennai, Hyderabad, Pune, Delhi, Kolkata, Lucknow and Coimbatore. The major factor for the success of IT industry in India is the continuous growth in the software and hardware. IT industry has contributed majorly in employment generation.

6.5 Industrial Pollution and Environmental Degradation

Industries have contributed greater to India's economic growth and development but the pollution caused by them have caused environmental degradation.

Industries are responsible for four types of pollution i.e. air, water, land and noise. They are discussed below

Air Pollution

It is caused by the presence of high amounts of sulphur dioxide, carbon monoxide, air borne **particulate matter**[3] like dust, sprays mist and smoke.

Smoke is released by chemical and paper factories, brick klins, refineries and **smelting**[4] plants, and burning of fossil fuels in big and small factories. Toxic gas leaks are very dangerous with long-term effects.

Air pollution adversely affects human health, animals, plants, buildings and the atmosphere as a whole.

Water Pollution

It is caused when organic and inorganic industrial wastes are discharged into rivers.

Textile and dyeing, petroleum refineries, tanneries and electroplating industries are the main industries causing water pollution.

Fly ash, phospho-gypsum, and iron and steel slags are major solid wastes in India.

3 **Particulate Matter** Solid or liquid matter that remains dispersed in gas or liquid emissions and creates pollution.

4 **Smelting** Metal extraction process from an ore.

Thermal Pollution

It occurs when hot water from factories and thermal plants is drained into rivers and ponds before cooling.

Wastes from nuclear power plants, nuclear and weapon production factories can cause cancer, birth defects and miscarriages.

Soil Pollution

Soil becomes polluted when harmful chemicals, industrial waste, glass, packaging salts and garbage are dumped into the soil. Chemicals get absorbed in the soil, making the soil useless.

NTPC

National Thermal Power Corporation (NTPC) is a major power providing corporation in India. It has ISO certification 14001 for developing Environment Management Systems.

The main task of NTPC is to set-up power plants by conserving the natural environment and resources like air, water, oil gas, coal and other fuels. This is possible through

- Optimum utilisation of equipments, adopting latest techniques and upgrading old equipment wherever possible.
- Minimising waste generation in thermal power plants by adopting ash utilisation techniques.
- Development of green belts by afforestation to maintain ecological balance.
- Reducing environmental pollution through ash pond management, ash water recycling system and liquid waste management.
- Installing facilities for ecological monitoring, review and online database management in all the power stations.

Noise Pollution

Noise from industrial and construction activities, machinery, generators, saws and pneumatic and electric drills, etc contribute to noise pollution.

Noise pollution results in hearing problems, increased heart rate, blood pressure and physiological effects such as stress and irritation.

Control of Environmental Degradation

The wastewater released by industries, pollutes 8 times the quantity of freshwater.

Some suggestions to minimise the industrial pollution of freshwater are as follows

- Minimising water usage by reusing and recycling waste water in two or more stages.
- Rainwater harvesting to meet water requirements.
- Treating hot water and industrial wastes before releasing them in rivers and ponds.

This treatment can be done in three phases

(i) **Primary treatment** by mechanical means which involve **screening**,[5] grinding, **flocculation**[6] and sedimentation.

(ii) **Secondary treatment** by biological processes such as planting trees, rain water harvesting.

(iii) **Tertiary treatment** by chemical, physical and biological processes which involve recycling of waste water.

General measures to minimise environmental pollution are

- Overdrawing of groundwater reserves by industries needs to be regulated legally.
- Generators and other machinery should be fitted with silencers and other noise absorbing materials to reduce their sound.
- Particulate matter (tiny air particles) can be reduced by installing smoke stacks to factories with electrostatic **precipitators**[7], **fabric filters**[8], **scrubbers**[9] and **inertial separators**[10].
- Use of oil or gas instead of coal to reduce smoke emission from factories.
- Redesigning of machinery to increase their efficiency in using energy.
- Promoting sustainable development by integrating economic development with environmental concerns.

Try These

1. **Name the two sectors of chemical industry.**
2. **Name the major solid wastes in India.**
3. **What are the major sources of water pollution?**
4. **What are software technology parks?**

---

5 **Screening** It is a method to trap solid (large objects) from the waste water.
6 **Flocculation** It is a process by which individual particles of clay combine into dot like mass.
7 **Electrostatic Precipitator** It is an air pollution control device for removing fine solid particles from emitted smoke.
8 **Fabric Filter** It is an air pollution control device that removes particulates out of air by using woven or felted fabric as a filter medium.
9 **Scrubber** It is a pollution control device which uses liquid spray to wash out particulate matter and neutralises gaseous pollutants.
10 **Inertial Separator** It is a device that uses centrifugal force to separate waste particles.

Mind Map

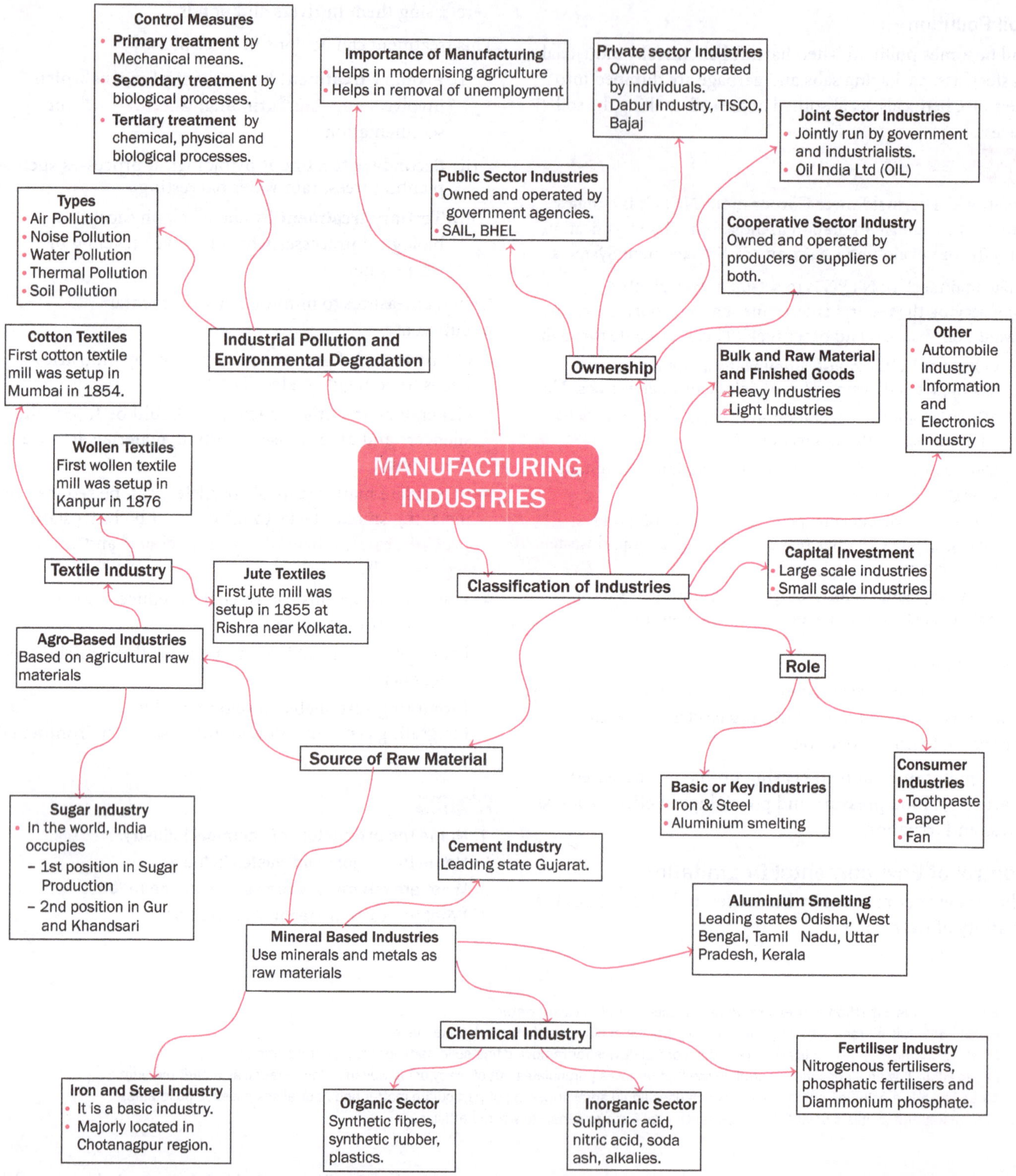

MANUFACTURING INDUSTRIES
Industrial Pollution and Environmental Degradation
Types
• Air Pollution
• Noise Pollution
• Water Pollution
• Thermal Pollution
• Soil Pollution
Control Measures
• Primary treatment by Mechanical means.
• Secondary treatment by biological processes.
• Tertiary treatment by chemical, physical and biological processes.
Importance of Manufacturing
• Helps in modernising agriculture
• Helps in removal of unemployment
Ownership
Public Sector Industries
• Owned and operated by government agencies.
• SAIL, BHEL
Private sector Industries
• Owned and operated by individuals.
• Dabur Industry, TISCO, Bajaj
Joint Sector Industries
• Jointly run by government and industrialists.
• Oil India Ltd (OIL)
Cooperative Sector Industry
Owned and operated by producers or suppliers or both.
Classification of Industries
Bulk and Raw Material and Finished Goods
Heavy Industries
Light Industries
Other
• Automobile Industry
• Information and Electronics Industry
Capital Investment
• Large scale industries
• Small scale industries
Role
Basic or Key Industries
• Iron & Steel
• Aluminium smelting
Consumer Industries
• Toothpaste
• Paper
• Fan
Source of Raw Material
Agro-Based Industries
Based on agricultural raw materials
Textile Industry
Cotton Textiles
First cotton textile mill was setup in Mumbai in 1854.
Wollen Textiles
First wollen textile mill was setup in Kanpur in 1876
Jute Textiles
First jute mill was setup in 1855 at Rishra near Kolkata.
Sugar Industry
• In the world, India occupies
– 1st position in Sugar Production
– 2nd position in Gur and Khandsari
Mineral Based Industries
Use minerals and metals as raw materials
Cement Industry
Leading state Gujarat.
Aluminium Smelting
Leading states Odisha, West Bengal, Tamil Nadu, Uttar Pradesh, Kerala
Iron and Steel Industry
• It is a basic industry.
• Majorly located in Chotanagpur region.
Chemical Industry
Organic Sector
Synthetic fibres, synthetic rubber, plastics.
Inorganic Sector
Sulphuric acid, nitric acid, soda ash, alkalies.
Fertiliser Industry
Nitrogenous fertilisers, phosphatic fertilisers and Diammonium phosphate.

NCERT FOLDER

Covering Intext Questions and Exercises of NCERT

INTEXT QUESTIONS

Q.1 Why did Mahatma Gandhi lay emphasis on spinning yarn and weaving khadi?

Ans. Mahatma Gandhi laid emphasis on spinning yarn and weaving khadi due to the following reasons

(i) To boycott foreign made cloth as a means of protest.

(ii) To develop a sense of nationalism among the people.

(iii) To give employment to a large number of people who were unemployed.

(iv) To promote cloth making as a cottage industry.

Q.2 Why is it important for our country to keep the mill sector loomage lower than powerloom and handloom?

Ans. It is important for our country to keep the mill sector loomage lower than powerloom and handloom because it will increase the employment in the rural areas, where powerloom and handloom work is located. This will lead to more prosperity in rural areas, thus, reducing the migration of villagers to towns and cities.

Q.3 Where would it be economically viable to set up the cement manufacturing units?

Ans. It would be economically viable to set-up the cement manufacturing units near the areas where raw materials like silica limestone are found, to reduce the cost of transportation of these materials.

Regular availability of electrical power and availability of rail transport are also main factors which are taken into consideration while deciding the location of a cement manufacturing plant.

EXERCISE

Q.1 Multiple Choice Questions.

(i) Which one of the following industries uses limestone as a raw material?

(a) Aluminium (b) Cement
(c) Plastic (d) Automobile

(ii) Which one of the following industries uses bauxite as a raw material?

(a) Aluminium Smelting (b) Cement
(c) Paper (d) Steel

Ans. (i) (b), (ii) (a)

Q.2 Answer the following briefly in not more than 30 words.

(i) What is manufacturing?

Ans. Manufacturing is the production of goods in large quantities after processing raw materials into ready-to-use, more valuable products.

The economic strength of the country is measured by the development of manufacturing industries.

(ii) What are basic industries? Give an example.

Ans. Basic industries are industries that supply their products as raw materials to other industries for manufacturing other goods.

An example of a basic industry is the iron and steel industry. Their products are used by different industries like machinary, infrastructure, etc.

Q.3 Write the answers of the following questions in 120 words.

(i) How do industries pollute the environment?

(ii) Discuss the steps to be taken to minimise environmental degradation by industry.

Ans. (i) Industries pollute the environment by polluting air, water and land. They also cause environmental pollution by noise pollution.

These are discussed below

- **Thermal Pollution** This pollution occurs when hot water from factories and thermal plants is drained into rivers and ponds before cooling. It badly affects the aquatic life.
- **Air Pollution** Industries cause air pollution by the emission of gases from industrial complexes and power generation units. Leakage of poisonous gases and chemicals and smoke from chemical industries also lead to air pollution.
- **Water Pollution** It is caused when industrial effluents both organic and inorganic are discharged into rivers or other water bodies.

  Industries like paper, pulp, chemical, textile and dyeing, petroleum refineries, tanneries and electroplating industries discharge detergents acids, salts and heavy metals like lead and mercury, pesticides, fertilisers, synthetic chemicals with carbon, plastic and rubber, etc into water bodies.
- **Noise Pollution** Undesirable noise pollution from industries like construction, running of generators to generate power, electrical drills, etc is responsible for disturbing our environment.

(ii) The steps to be taken to minimise environmental degradation by industry are as follows
- Minimise the use of water for processing by reusing/recycling it in successive stages.
- Harvesting rainwater to meet water requirements.
- Treating effluents before releasing them in water bodies. This can be done by
  - Primary treatment by mechanical means (i.e screening grinding, flocculation and sedimentation)
  - Secondary treatment by biological processes. Such as planting trees, rain water harvesting.
  - Tertiary treatment by chemical, physical and biological processes like recycling of waste water in sewage treatment plants.
- Overdrawing of groundwater reserves by industries needs to be regulated legally.
- Generators and other machinery should be fitted with silencers and other noise absorbing materials to reduce their sound. Redesigning of machinery to increase their efficiency in using energy.
- Particulate matter in the air can be reduced by fitting smoke stacks to factories with electrostatic precipitators, fabric filters, scrubbers and inertial separators.
- Use of oil or gas instead of coal to reduce smoke emission from factories.
- Promote sustainable development by integrating economic development goals with environmental construction.

ACTIVITY

Q.4 Give one word for each of the following with regard to industry. The number of letters in each word are hinted in brackets.

(i)	Used to drive machinery	(5) P ....
(ii)	People who work in a factory	(6) W ....
(iii)	Where the product is sold	(6) M ....
(iv)	A person who sells goods	(8) R ....
(v)	Thing produced	(7) P ....
(vi)	To make or produce	(11) M ....
(vii)	Land, water and air degraded	(9) P ....

Ans. (i) Power (ii) Worker (iii) Market (iv) Retailer (v) Product (vi) Manufacture (vii) Pollution

REVIEW EXERCISE

Including Competency Based Questions

Part I

Multiple Choice Questions (MCQs)

1. Which of the following is transformed into a wide variety of furnished goods of higher value?

(a) Manufactured goods (b) Raw material
(c) Industrial goods (d) All of these

2. Which of the following activities employs people in the manufacturing of primary materials into finished goods?

(a) Secondary activities (b) Primary activities
(c) Tertiary activities (d) None of these

3. Which of following occurs after the increase in industrial activities?

(a) Urbanisation (b) Rural expansion
(c) Development (Loss of labour) (d) All of these

4. Basic or key industry are those which supply their products as raw materials to manufacture other goods. Which of the following examples does not represents Key industry?

(a) Iron and steel industry
(b) Paper industry
(c) Copper smelting industry
(d) Aluminium smelting industry

5. Which of the following is the correct order of steps involved in garment manufacturing?

(a) Spinning, fibre production, dyeing ,weaving
(b) Weaving, spinning, fibre production, dyeing
(c) Fibre production, spinning, weaving, dyeing
(d) Spinning , dyeing , fibre production, weaving

6. Why do you think that handspun khadi should be encouraged in India?

(a) Because handspun khadi is always better in quality than machine made clothes.
(b) Because it looks more elegant than a machine made cloth.
(c) Because it signifies emphasis on India's culture.
(d) Because it provides large scale employment to weavers in their homes as a cottage industry.

7. **Manya, a 27 years old women lives in West Bengal and was involved in a factory producing Jute. Recently, this jute industry was closed without any compensation to the employees. This region has seen the closure of many Jute industries.**

Accordingly, which of the following actions by government would be the most crucial for saving these jute industries and associated workers in the long term? **Competency Based**

(a) Giving money as grant to the industries and also for compensating workers.

(b) Formulating policies and taking steps to increase the consumption of Jute in the country.

(c) Helping the workers to find alternate employment opportunities.

(d) Opening of jute industries in other areas of the country.

8. **'The manufacturing industry is a significant contributor to global air pollution, with industrial emissions releasing hazardous waste fumes that pose serious risks to both human health and the environment.**

Should India close such industries as they cause environmental pollution? **Competency Based**

(a) Yes, because such pollution will deteriorate environmental quality in the long run.

(b) No, because these industries are important for growth of India and we cannot afford to lose this growth.

(c) Yes, because other green industries are sufficient for the growth of our country.

(d) No, because these industries are important for developing country like India but steps should be taken to regulate the pollution cause by them legally.

9. **Which among the following crop is known as 'Golden Fibre'?** **CBSE 2025**

(a) Cotton (b) Wool

(c) Jute (d) Silk

10. **Which of the following adversely affects human health, animals, plants, building and the atmosphere as a whole?**

(a) Noise pollution (b) Thermal pollution

(c) Air pollution (d) Water pollution

11. **Paper, pulp, chemical, textile and dyeing, petroleum refineries and tanneries are agents of causing which type of pollution?**

(a) Air pollution (b) Water pollution

(c) Noise pollution (d) None of these

12. **Harish, a resident of a village in Bihar works in an industry outside his village in a remote town. The noise emitted from the equipment and other processes in the industry exceeds the normal acceptable level of sound. All the workers in the industry is continuously exposed to the noise.**

Which of the following will this most likely lead to in the near future? **Competency Based**

(a) Ban on the industry by the government.

(b) Strike by the workers over the issue of noise.

(c) Hearing impairment, stress and anger issues in workers.

(d) Compensation provided by the industry to the workers.

13. **Mr Z is the owner of a paper and pulp industry in a remote area in Kanpur. His industry draws a large amount of groundwater. People in nearby areas have experienced that water level have gone down in the area. They are protesting against this industry.**

What is the best resolution to this conflict?

(a) Closure order for this industry by the authorities.

(b) Asking the industry to shift it's operations somewhere else.

(c) Strict regulations for the industry to use a specific amount of groundwater only and obtain rest of the amount from rainwater harvesting, reuse and recycling.

(d) Asking the industry to invest in afforestation activities all over this region to maximize rainwater infiltration.

14. **Which of the following is/are not a public sector industry?**

I. BHEL II. TISCO

III. SAIL IV. Bajaj Auto Ltd.

Options

(a) Only IV (b) II and III

(c) II, III and IV (d) IV and II

15. **Which of the following is used as raw materials for cement industry?**

I. Coal II. Silica

III. Limestone IV. Gypsum

Options

(a) I, II and III (b) II and IV

(c) II, III and IV (d) Only I

16. **Identify the reasons as to why most jute mills are mainly located along the banks of the Hooghly river. Choose from the appropriate statements among the following options.**

I. Proximity to jute producing areas.

II. Inexpensive water transport.

III. Good network of railways, roadways and waterways to facilitate movement of raw materials to mills.

IV. Easy availability of cheap labour from West Bengal, Bihar, Odisha, etc.

Codes

(a) Statements I and II are appropriate

(b) Statements I, II and III are appropriate

(c) All the statements are appropriate

(d) Only statement IV is appropriate

17. **Which of the following statements is accurate about the 'sugar industry' in India?**

I. The raw material used in this industry is light.

II. Fifty percent of the sugar mills are located in Uttar Pradesh and Bihar.

III. Cane produced in Southern areas has a lower sucrose content than in Northern areas.

IV. Sugar industry is seasonal in nature.

Codes

(a) Only I (b) Only III

(c) Only IV (d) Both I and II

18. **Mr. Y is planning to shift his sugar industry to Maharasthra. He took this decision because** **Competency Based**

I. cooler climate ensures a longer crushing season.

II. cooperatives are more successful in these states.

III. cane produced here has a lower sucrose content which is good for health.

IV. these regions have low population density and more areas for agricultural production.

Codes

(a) Only I (b) III and IV

(c) I and II (d) Only II

19. **Consider the statements given below and choose the correct answer.**

Statement I Production and consumption of steel is often regarded as the index of a country's development.

Statement II In steel production, manganese is also required.

Options

(a) Statement I is correct and II is incorrect

(b) Statement I is incorrect and II is correct

(c) Both I and II are incorrect

(d) Both I and II are correct

20. **Consider the statements given below and choose the correct answer.**

Statement I Aluminium is a good conductor of heat.

Statement II Aluminium is easily prone to corrosion.

Options

(a) Statement I is correct and II is incorrect

(b) Statement I is incorrect and II is correct

(c) Both I and II are incorrect

(d) Both I and II are correct

21. **Consider the following statements about textile industry**

I. There is value addition at every stage.

II. Value addition increases cost at each stage.

III. From fibre production to garment manufactures, many stages are involved.

Which of the following is/are true?

(a) I and II (b) II and III

(c) I and III (d) All of these

Answers

1. (b)	**2.** (a)	**3.** (a)	**4.** (b)	**5.** (c)
6. (d)	**7.** (b)	**8.** (d)	**9.** (c)	**10.** (c)
11. (b)	**12.** (c)	**13.** (c)	**14.** (d)	**15.** (c)
16. (c)	**17.** (c)	**18.** (c)	**19.** (d)	**20.** (a)
21. (d)				

Match the Following

1.

List I	List II
A. Aluminium smelting	1. Manufacturing of synthetic fibres
B. Chemical industry	2. Manufacturing of multi-utility vehicles
C. Automobile industry	3. Manufacturing of aircraft
D. Fertiliser industry	4. Manufacturing of Diammonium phosphate

Codes

	A	B	C	D		A	B	C	D
(a)	3	1	2	4	(b)	1	4	2	3
(c)	2	4	3	1	(d)	3	4	2	1

Ans. (a)

Assertion-Reason

1. **Assertion** (A) India imports Potash from other countries.

Reason (R) India does not have any of commercially usable potash or potassium compounds in any form.

Codes

(a) Both A and R are true and R is the correct explanation of A

(b) Both A and R are true, but R is not the correct explanation of A

(c) A is true, but R is false

(d) A is false, but R is true

2. **Assertion** (A) India has world class production in spinning.

Reason (R) Weaving is done by handloom, power loom, and in mills.

Codes

(a) Both A and R are true and R is the correct explanation of A

(b) Both A and R are true, but R is not the correct explanation of A

(c) A is true, but R is false

(d) A is false, but R is true

3. Assertion (A) Aluminium is light, resistant to corrosion, and is a good conductor of heat.

Reason (R) Aluminium smelting is the second most important metallurgical industry in India.

Codes

(a) Both A and R are true and R is the correct explanation of A

(b) Both A and R are true, but R is not the correct explanation of A

(c) A is true, but R is false

(d) A is false, but R is true

4. Assertion (A) Goods for direct use by consumers are produced by the Consumer industries.

Reason (R) Consumer industries are agro-based.

Codes

(a) Both A and R are true and R is the correct explanation of A

(b) Both A and R are true, but R is not the correct explanation of A

(c) A is true, but R is false

(d) A is false, but R is true

5. Assertion (A) India has vast reserves of the non-coking coal.

Reason (R) India is well endowed with nearly all the raw materials necessary for iron and steel industry.

Codes

(a) Both A and R are true and R is the correct explanation of A

(b) Both A and R are true, but R is not the correct explanation of A

(c) A is true, but R is false

(d) A is false, but R is true

Ans. 1. (a) Both A and R are true and R is the correct explanation of A

2. (b) Both A and R are true, but R is not the correct explanation of A

3. (b) Both A and R are true, but R is not the correct explanation of A

4. (b) Both A and R are true, but R is not the correct explanation of A

5. (d) A is false, but R is true

Case Based Question

1. Read the passage given below and answer the questions that follow .

Production of goods in large quantities after processing from raw materials to more valuable products is called manufacturing. Paper is manufactured from wood, sugar from sugarcane, iron and steel from iron ore and aluminium from bauxite. Some types of clothes are manufactured from yarn which itself is an industrial product.

People employed in the secondary activities manufacture the primary materials into finished goods. The workers employed in steel factories,car, breweries, textile industries, bakeries, etc. fall into this category. Some people are employed in providing services.

The economic strength of a country is measured by the development of manufacturing industries.

(i) Which of the following is true with respect to manufacturing?

(a) It helps in modernising agriculture.

(b) Industrial development does not contribute in eradication of poverty and unemployment.

(c) Industrial development has no relation with bringing of foreign exchange in a country.

(d) Prosperity and industrial development has no connection to each other.

(ii) A cloth manufacturing industry falls under which of the following categories?

(a) Key industry

(b) Agro-based industry

(c) Mineral based industry

(d) None of the above

(iii) Which of the following actions is required in manufacturing sector for contributing in a country's prosperity?

(a) Employability

(b) Enhancing reach

(c) Diversification

(d) Increasing competition

(iv) How can industrial development bring down regional disparity? Choose the correct option.

(a) By manufacturing seasonal items.

(b) By establishing industries in tribal areas.

(c) By giving more employment through. advertisement in local newspapers.

(d) By using money earned from industrial activities for the development of backward areas.

Ans. (i) (a) It helps in modernising agriculture.

(ii) (b) Agro-based industry

(iii) (c) Diversification

(iv) (b) By establishing industries in tribal areas.

Part II

Very Short Answer Type Questions

1. How agriculture and industries depend upon each other?

Ans Agriculture and industries depend upon each other as many industries like sugar, textile, etc depend upon agricultural products.

On the other hand, many industrial products like fertilisers, irrigation pumps, PVC pipes, tractors, machines and tools help in increasing agricultural productivity.

2. How industrialisation depend upon urbanisation?

Ans Industrialisation depend upon urbanisation as industries are located around the cities where the market of industrial goods and services like banking, insurance, transport, labour, consultants and financial services are available.

3. Since independence India has focused on the growth of its industrial sector. What was the philosophy behind public sector industries and joint ventures in India?

Ans. The main philosophy behind public sector industries and joint sector ventures in India was that industrial development is a precondition for eradication of unemployment and poverty from our country. It was also aimed at bringing down regional disparities by establishing industries in tribal and backward areas.

4. 'India has assumed a key position in the worldwide sugar economy, emerging as the foremost sugar producer since 2021-22, surpassing Brazil.......'
Discuss the sugar industry in India in the light of the above statement. Competency Based

Ans. India occupies the first place in the production of *gur* and *khandsari*. The raw material used in this industry is bulky, and in haulage its sucrose content reduces. The mills are located in Uttar Pradesh, Bihar, Maharashtra, Karnataka, Tamil Nadu, Andhra Pradesh, Gujarat, Punjab, Haryana and Madhya Pradesh.

5. What is mineral based industry? Give one example of such industry.

Ans. Mineral based industries are the industry which uses minerals as raw material, e.g. oil refinery.

6. What factors are responsible for location of aluminium smelting industry?

Ans The factors responsible for location of aluminium smelting industry are

- Regular supply of electricity.
- Availability of raw material at minimum cost.

7. Give examples of some places where automobile industries are located.

Ans Automobile industries are located around Gurugram, Mumbai, Pune, Chennai, Kolkata, Lucknow, Indore, Hyderabad, Jamshedpur, Delhi and Bengaluru.

8. How do thermal pollution occurs?

Ans Thermal pollution occurs when hot water from factories and thermal plants is drained into rivers and ponds before cooling.

9. What is the main aim of NTPC?

Ans The main aim of NTPC is to set up power plants by conserving the natural environment and resources like air, water, oil, gas, coal and other fuels.

10. How the particulate matter in the air can be reduced?

Ans The particulate matter in the air can be reduced by fitting smoke stacks to factories with eletrostatic precipitators, fabric filters, scrubbers and inertial separators.

11. Study the given flow chart and answer the questions that follow. CBSE Term II 2022

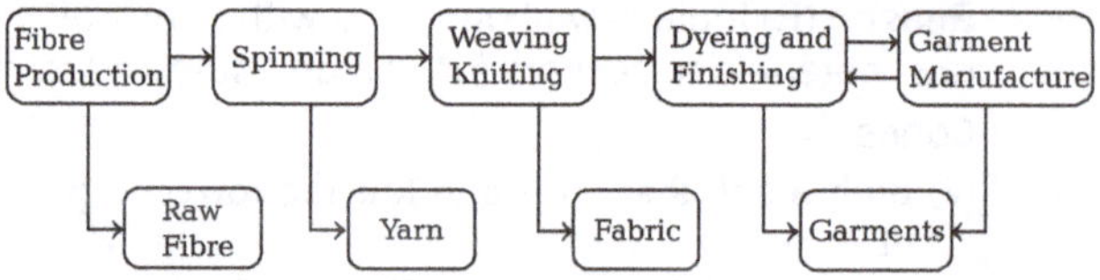

(i) Which is the basic material required for garment manufacturing ?

(ii) Give one example of value addition in the textile industry.

Ans. (i) Raw fibre is the basic material required for garment manufacturing.

(ii) Dyeing is one of the value addition in textile industry.

12. Arun read in a magazine that manufacturing industries are becoming important in the economy. He found that manufacturing industry not only does manufacturing functions but also helps agriculture sector. How the industrial sector influences agriculture sector? Competency Based

Ans. Industrial sector influences the agriculture sector by introducing new technology for better farming. This includes tools, machines and fertilisers to boost the production in agriculture sector.

13. 'The Kakatiya Mega Textile Park would facilitate the production of items across the textiles value chain ranging from spinning, weaving, knitting, processing and readymade garments...'

(i) Where are the spinning and weaving centres in India located?

(ii) Which other industries is the spinning and weaving industry related to?

Ans. (i) The spinning centres in India are located in Maharashtra, Gujarat and Tamil Nadu. However, weaving is distributed almost all over the country to incorporate regional and traditional skills.

(ii) Spinning and weaving industry is related to industries of chemicals and dyes, packaging materials and engineering works.

14. In the early years , the cotton textile industry was concentrated in Maharashtra and Gujarat. Discuss the factors that contributed to this concentration.

Ans. In the early years, the cotton textile industry was concentrated in the cotton growing belt of Maharashtra and Gujarat. Availability of raw cotton, market, transport including accessible port facilities, labour, moist climate, etc. contributed towards this concentration.

Short Answer Type Questions

1. What is manufacturing? How does manufacturing lead to value addition of the raw material? Explain with the help of examples. **CBSE 2013**

Ans. Manufacturing is the process of production of goods in large quantities by processing of raw materials to more valuable products.

Manufacturing leads to value addition of the raw material. People employed in the secondary activities manufacture the primary materials into finished goods. These finished goods are more useful, hence more in value.

For example, paper is manufactured from wood, sugar from sugarcane, iron and steel from iron ore, aluminium from bauxite, etc. Thus, raw materials are transformed into a wide variety of finished goods of higher value.

2. Classify industries on the basis of ownership with examples.

Ans. Classification of the industries on the basis of ownership is as follows

(i) **Public Sector** These industries are owned and operated by government agencies.Examples- SAIL, BHEL, ONGC, etc.

(ii) **Private Sector** These industries are owned and operated by individuals or a group of individuals. Examples- TISCO, Reliance, Mahindra, etc.

(iii) **Joint Sector** These industries are jointly owned by the government and individuals or a group of individuals.Examples- Oil India Limited.

(iv) **Cooperative Sector** These industries are owned and operated by the producers or suppliers of raw materials, workers or both. Examples-AMUL milk cooperative, Maharashtra sugar industries.

3. "Agriculture and industries complement each other. Justify the statement. **CBSE 2025**

Or **Describe the role of industries in the development of agriculture.** **CBSE 2019**

Or **"Agriculture and industry move hand in hand." Explain.** **CBSE 2013, 12**

Ans. Agriculture and industry are not exclusive of each other. They move hand in hand.

The role of industries in the development of agriculture can be seen through the following points

(i) The agro-based industries have given a major boost to agriculture by raising productivity of those crops which are used as raw material in industries.

(ii) The agro-based industries provide industrial products such as fertilisers, insecticides, irrigation pumps, PVC pipes, machines and tools, etc to the farmers to increase agriculture productivity.

(iii) The industrial sector provides employment to the excess labour (labours who are actually disguised unemployed) in the agriculture sector.

Thus, development of manufacturing industry has not only helped agriculturists in increasing their production but also made production process very efficient.

4. "Agriculture gives boost to the industrial sector". Justify the statement with any three relevant points. **CBSE SQP 2023-24**

Ans. Agriculture gives boost to the industrial sector in the following ways

(i) **Raw Material Supply** Agriculture is a significant source of raw materials for various industries, such as food processing, textiles and paper. For instance, the cotton industry relies heavily on the production of cotton from agricultural fields.

(ii) **Market Expansion** Agriculture provides a vast market for industrial products. For example, the use of agricultural machinery such as tractors, tillers and harvesters creates a demand for industrial goods, including steel, plastics and rubber.

(iii) **Employment Generation** Agriculture is a labour intensive sector that generates employment opportunities for a significant population in India.

5. Suraj and Gautam hails from same village. They together went to a city for employment. While Suraj got work in a textile industry, Gautam was hired in a steel industry.

How two of them can differentiate their industries? **Competency Based**

Ans. The two of them can differentiate between these two industries in following ways

Textile industry	Steel industry
Textile industry is an agro-based industry.	Steel industry is a mineral based industry.
Textile industry is the only industry in the country which is self-reliant and complete in the value chain.	This industry serves as the basic industry since all the other industries depend on it for their machinery.
Process in a textile industry includes fibre production, spinning, weaving, dyeing, etc.	Steel industry involves melting of iron ore with other materials in a blast furnace, conversion of raw material into pig iron, rolling, pressing, casting and forging of the metal and finally the steel making.

6. Read the statements given below regarding spinning and weaving in India.

Statement 1 (S1) Spinning is centralised while weaving is highly decentralised.

Statement 2 (S2) India has world class production in spinning but weaving supplies low quality of fabric.

Explain what trend do these statements 1 and 2 reflect in the textile sector in India. **Competency Based**

Ans. These statements reflects that while spinning continues to be centralised in Maharashtra, Gujarat and Tamil Nadu, weaving is highly decentralised to provide scope for incorporating traditional skills and designs of weaving in cotton, silk, zari, embroidery, etc.

India has world class production in spinning, but weaving supplies low quality of fabric as it cannot use much of the high quality yarn produced in the country. Weaving is done by handloom, powerloom and in mills.

7. Why is the Jute industry mainly concentrated in Hugli basin?

Ans. The Jute industry is mainly concentrated in the Hugli basin due to its closeness to jute-producing areas, affordable water transport along the Hugli river, well-connected railways, roads and waterways for easy movement of raw materials, ample water for jute processing, cheap labour from West Bengal, Bihar , Odisha and Uttar Pradesh and Kolkata provides urban facilities like banking, insurance and ports for jute goods export.

8. What are mineral based industries? Give four examples. **CBSE 2013**

Ans. Mineral based industries are the industries that use minerals and metals as raw materials

Four examples of mineral based industries are as follows

(i) **Aluminium Smelting** This industry manufacture aircraft, utensils and wires.

(ii) **Chemical Industry** It contributes approximately 3 per cent of India's GDP.

(iii) **Fertiliser Industry** It is centered around the production of nitrogenous, phosphatic, ammonium phosphate and complex fertiliser.

(iv) **Automobile Industry** This industry provides quick transportation vehicles for goods and passengers.

9. Iron and steel is a heavy industry because all the raw materials as well as finished goods are heavy and bulky entailing heavy transportation costs. Iron ore, coking coal and limestone are required in the ratio of approximately 4: 2: 1.

In your opinion where should the iron and steel industry ideally be located? Which region in India has maximum concentration of iron and steel industry and why? **Competency Based**

Ans. Iron and steel industry should ideally be located in areas where there is an efficient transport network for their distribution to the markets and consumers.

Chota Nagpur plateau region has the maximum concentration of iron and steel industries. It is largely, because of the relative advantages this region has for the development of this industry. These include, low cost of iron ore, high grade raw materials in proximity, cheap labour and vast growth potential in the home market.

10. The Chemical industry in India is fast growing and diversifying. It comprises both large and small scale manufacturing units. Rapid growth has been recorded in both inorganic and organic sectors. **Competency Based**

(i) Discuss the inorganic and organic chemicals in the chemical industry.

(ii) Who is the largest consumer of the chemical industry products?

Ans. (i) Inorganic chemicals include sulphuric acid (used to manufacture fertilisers, synthetic fibres, plastics, adhesives, paints, dyes stuffs), nitric acid, alkalies, soda ash (used to make glass, soaps and detergents, paper) and caustic soda.

Organic chemicals include petrochemicals, which are used for manufacturing of synthetic fibers, synthetic rubber, plastics, dye-stuffs, drugs and pharmaceuticals. Organic chemical plants are located near oil refineries.

(ii) The chemical industry is its own largest consumer. Basic chemicals undergo processing to further produce other chemicals that are used for industrial application, agriculture or directly for consumer markets.

11. Mention any two factors that have contributed to a healthy growth of the automobile industry in India. Name two centres where this industry is located.

Ans. Two factors contributing to healthy growth of the automobile sector are

(i) Liberalisation provided boost to the growth of the automobile industry in India.
With the introduction of new and contemporary models of automobiles in the country, the demand for these vehicles increased at a faster pace.

(ii) With the introduction of new technology in this sector, Indian industries are now capable to compete with the global technologies by way of Foreign Direct Investment (FDI).

Two major centres where this industry is located are Gurugram and Indore.

12. Explain any three factors responsible for air pollution. **CBSE 2025**

Ans. Three factors responsible for air pollution are

(i) **Industrial Emissions** Industries release a variety of pollutants such as sulfur dioxide (SO_2), nitrogen oxides (NOx), and particulate matter into the atmosphere. These emissions result from the burning of fossil fuels and industrial processes, contributing significantly to air pollution.

(ii) **Vehicle Exhaust** The increasing number of vehicles on the road leads to higher emissions of harmful gases, such as carbon monoxide (CO), nitrogen oxides (NO_2), and particulate matter. These pollutants are harmful to human health and contribute to the formation of smog and respiratory diseases.

(iii) **Burning of Fossil Fuels** The widespread use of coal, oil, and natural gas for energy production, heating, and transportation releases large amounts of carbon dioxide (CO_2), carbon monoxide (CO), and other harmful gases into the air, leading to air pollution and contributing to global warming.

13. Explain any five measures to control industrial pollution in India. **CBSE 2013**

Or Suggest any three steps to minimise environmental degradation caused by industrial development in India. **CBSE 2017, CBSE 2016**

Ans. Five measures or steps to control or minimise industrial pollution in India are as follows

(i) Particulate matter in the air can be reduced by fitting smoke stacks to factories with electrostatic precipitators, fabric filters, scrubbers and inertial separators.

(ii) Smoke can be reduced by using oil or gas instead of coal in factories.

(iii) Updated machinery and equipment should be used that makes less noise and generators fitted with silencers should be used.

(iv) Pollution check certificates should be made compulsory.

(v) Machineries used in the industries can be redesigned to increase energy efficiency and reduce noise. Noise absorbing material may also be used.

14. Suggest some measures to minimise the environment degradation by industries in India. **CBSE 2012**

Ans. Some Suggestion of measures to minimise the environment degradation by industries are as follows

(i) Minimising use of water for processing by reusing and recycling it in two or more successive stages.

(ii) Harvesting rainwater to meet water requirements.

(iii) Treating hot water and effluents before releasing them in rivers and ponds.

(iv) Particulate matter in the air can be reduced by fitting smokestacks to factories with electrostatic precipitators, fabric filters, scrubbers and inertial separators.

(v) Smoke can be reduced by using oil or gas instead of coal in factories.

(vi) Machinery and equipment can be used and generators should be fitted with silencers.

(vii) All machinery can be redesigned to increase energy efficiency and reduce noise.

15. Discuss the most likely impact of industries in India operated without any regulation on their activities. Build the answer around these points

- Pollution
- Depletion of groundwater
- Sustainable development

Ans. If industries in India operates without any regulation on their activities the following impacts would be observed

- **Environmental Pollution** Industries contribute significantly to increase in pollution of land, water, air, noise and resulting in degradation of environment. They cause air, water, land and noise pollution.
- **Groundwater depletion** Overdrawing of ground water reserves by industry where there is a threat to groundwater resources can pose a serious problem.
- **Sustainable development** The challenge of sustainable development requires integration of economic development with environmental concerns which is not possible if industries are unregulated.

Long Answer Questions

1. The Co-operative sector stands poised to play a pivotal role in propelling India to become one of the world's top economies, according to Defence Minister Rajnath Singh.
Source : Financial Express
Discuss the types of industries on the basis of ownership in India.

Ans. On the basis of ownership, industries can be classified as
- **Public Sector** These industries are owned and operated by the government agencies.
- **Private Sector** These industries are owned and operated by private entrepreneurs, e.g. TISCO, Bajaj Auto Ltd., Reliance Industries, Dabur Industries, etc.
- **Joint Sector** These industries are jointly run by the state and individual or a group of individuals. Oil India Ltd. (OIL) is jointly owned by public and private sectors.
- **Cooperative Sector** These industries are owned and operated by the producers or suppliers of raw materials, workers or both. They pool in the resources and share the profits or losses proportionately such as the sugar industry in Maharashtra, the coir industry in Kerala.

2. A person X living in India wants to increase his income. However , the only products that he has access to is from the agricultural sector.
Discuss how the agro-based industry can help him increase his income as well as contribute to India's economic growth. **Competency Based**

Ans. The role that the agro-based industries have played in the growth of Indian economy as well as the potential role that it can play in increasing the income of a person X are as follows
- The agro-based industries in India have given a major boost to agriculture by raising its productivity as they obtain their raw material from agriculture.
- Development and competitiveness of industries has not only assisted agriculturists in increasing their production but also made the production processes very efficient.
- The farmers are heading for commercial farming to produce high value crops for industries. This may in turn help to improve the economic status of the farmers.
- These agro-based industries, by creating demand, support the growth of many other industries e.g., packaging materials and engineering works etc.

3. Explain the role of industries in increasing water pollution and suggest any three measures to reduce water pollution. **CBSE 2025**

Ans. Role of industries in increasing water pollution is as follows
- **Discharge of Industrial Waste** Industries often discharge untreated or inadequately treated waste into rivers, lakes, or other water bodies.
- **Chemical Contamination** Many industries, such as chemical factories, textile mills and paper mills, use harmful chemicals in their processes.
- **Effluents and Sewage** In addition to industrial waste, the sewage generated from industrial activities also contributes significantly to water pollution.

Measures to reduce water pollution are as follows
- **Treatment of Industrial Wastewater** Industries should install proper wastewater treatment plants to treat and filter out harmful chemicals and contaminants before discharging water into natural water bodies.
- **Strict Regulations and Enforcement** Government should enforce stricter regulations to ensure industries follow proper disposal guidelines for waste.
- **Promotion of Eco-friendly Technologies** Encouraging the use of green technologies and cleaner production methods can help reduce the generation of harmful waste.

4. The Chemical industry in India is fast growing and diversifying. It comprises both large and small scale manufacturing units. Rapid growth has been recorded in both inorganic and organic sectors.
Why chemical industry is known as its own largest consumer? Explain any three characteristics of the chemical industry of India.

Ans. Chemical industries are known as its own largest consumers as basic chemicals undergo processing to further produce other chemicals that are used for industrial application, agriculture or directly for consumer markets.

Three characteristics of the chemical industries of India are
- Chemical industries in India are fast growing and diversifying.
- It contains both large scale and small scale manufacturing units.
- Inorganic chemical industry is more widespread while organic chemical industry is located near oil refineries or petro-chemical plants.

5. 'India does not have any reserves of commercially usable potash or potassium compounds in any form.'
Apart from Potash what other compounds are produced in a fertiliser industry. Also discuss the spread of the fertilisers industry in India.

Ans. Apart from Potassium compounds, the fertiliser industry is centered around the production of nitrogenous fertilisers (mainly urea), phosphatic fertilisers and Diammonium phosphate (DAP) and complex fertilisers which have a combination of Nitrogen (N), Phosphate (P) and Potash (K). The third, i.e. potash is entirely imported as the country does not have any reserves of commercially usable potash or potassium compounds in any form.

After the Green Revolution, the fertiliser industry expanded to several other parts of the country. The spread of this industry is mainly in Gujarat, Tamil Nadu, Uttar Pradesh, Punjab and Kerala contribute towards half of the fertiliser production. Other significant producers are Andhra Pradesh, Odisha. Rajasthan, Bihar, Maharashtra, Assam, West Bengal, Goa, Delhi, Madhya Pradesh and Karnataka.

6. "Electronic industry has revolutionised the life of the masses and the country's economy." Justify the statement with relevant points referring to India. **Competency Based**

Ans. Electronic industry has revolutionised the life of the people and the country's economy in the following ways

- It produces a wide range of products from transistor sets to televisions and computers for the masses.
- It has helped us set up telephone exchanges, telephones, cellular telecom, radios and many other equipments which have application in space technology, aviation, defence, meteorological departments, etc.
- It has generated employment for a large number of people particularly in cities such as Mumbai, Delhi, Hyderabad, Pune , Chennai, Kolkata, Lucknow, Coimbatore, etc.
- This industry has been a major foreign exchange earner because of its fast growing Business Process Outsourcing (BPO) Sector.
- The continuing growth in the hardware and software is the key to the success of IT industry in India.

7. Explain the pro-active approach by the National Thermal Power Corporation (NTPC) for preserving the natural environment and resources. **CBSE 2015**

Or **What does NTPC refer to? List out two ways through which NTPC has contributed towards the preservation of natural environment.**

Ans. NTPC stands for National Thermal Power Corporation. NTPC has adopted a pro-active approach to preserve the natural environment and resources around the thermal power plants it sets-up.

To ensure minimum pollution of the environment near these plants, the measures it adopts while setting-up these plants are

- Using the latest techniques and upgrading existing equipment to minimise generation of polluting by-products.
- Maximising the utilisation of ash generated so that the waste generated is reduced.
- Establishing green belts and forests to maintain an ecological balance around the power plants being set-up.
- Setting-up ash pond management, ash water recycling and liquid waste management systems in the plants to reduce environmental pollution.
- Monitoring, reviewing and managing the databases online for all the power plants set-up.

Case Based Questions

1. Read the sources given below and answer the questions that follow.

Source A Importance of Manufacturing

Manufacturing industries not only help in modernising agriculture, which forms the backbone of our economy, they also reduce the heavy dependence of people on agricultural income by providing them jobs in secondary and tertiary sectors.

(i) To what extent do you agree that manufacturing industries are important for people? State only one reason.

Source B Industrialisation and Urbanisation

The textile industry occupies unique position in the Indian economy, because it contributes significantly to industrial production, employment generation and foreign exchange earnings. It is the only industry in the country, which is self-reliant and complete in the value chain i.e., from raw material to the highest value added products.

(ii) The textile industry is the only industry which is self reliant and complete in the value-chain? Justify.

Source C Thermal Pollution

Thermal pollution of water occurs when hot water from factories and thermal plants is drained into rivers and ponds before cooling.

Wastes from nuclear power plants, nuclear and weapon production facilities cause cancer, birth defects and miscarriages.

(iii) Is, thermal is related to temperature. How industries can cause thermal pollution?

Ans. (i) It is true that manufacturing industries are important for people because these industries create jobs for people and reduce heavy dependence of people on agricultural income.

(ii) The textile industry is the only industry which is self reliant and complete in the value-chain because

- It contributes significantly to industrial production.
- It employs largest number of people after agriculture.

(iii) Yes thermal is related to temperature. The industries cause thermal pollution when hot water from factories and thermal plants is drained into river and ponds before cooling.

2. Read the source given below and answer the questions that follow. **CBSE Term II 2022**

National Thermal Power Corporation (NTPC) shows the way

NTPC is a major power providing corporation in India. It has ISO certification for EMS (Environment Management System) 14001. The corporation has a proactive approach for preserving the natural environment and resources like water, oil, gas and fuels in places where it is setting up power plants. This has been possible through

- Optimum utilisation of equipment adopting latest techniques and upgrading existing equipment.
- Minimising waste generation by maximising ash utilisation.
- Providing green belts for nurturing ecological balance and addressing the question of special purpose vehicles for afforestation.
- Reducing environmental pollution through ash pond management, ash water recycling system and liquid waste management.
- Ecological monitoring, reviews and online database management for all its power stations.

(i) Define the term 'sustainable development'.

(ii) What is the idea behind ISO certification?

(iii) Examine the proactive approach of National Thermal Power Corporation (NTPC).

Ans. (i) Sustainable development means development that meets the needs of the present without compromising the ability of future generations to meet their own needs.

(ii) ISO (International Organisation for Standardisation) is an independent, non-governmental, international organisation that develops standards to ensure the quality, safety, and efficiency of products, services and systems.

(iii) National Thermal Power Corporation (NTPC) has taken great measures for preservation of the environment. It has an ISO certification of EMS 14001. The cooperation has a proactive approach for preserving the natural environment and resources like water, oil, gas and fuels in a places where it is setting up power plants.

Map Based Questions

1. On the given political map of India, mark and label the following features with appropriate symbols.

(i) Bokaro Steel Plant. **CBSE 2019**

(ii) Mumbai Cotton Textile Industry

(iii) Salem Iron and Steel Plant **CBSE 2019**

(iv) Indore Cotton Textile Industry

(v) Leading state in production of Jute **CBSE 2025**

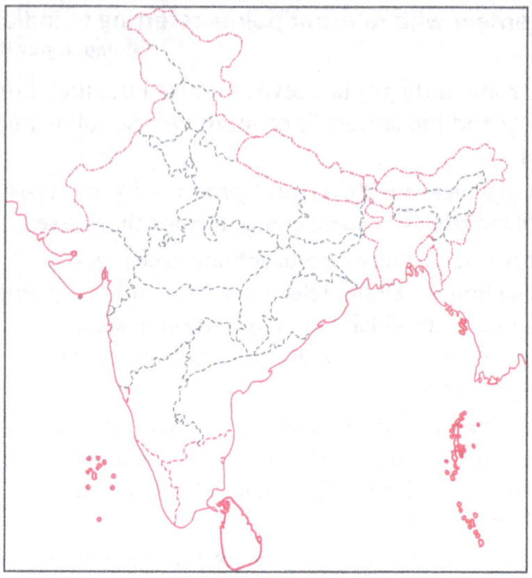

Ans.

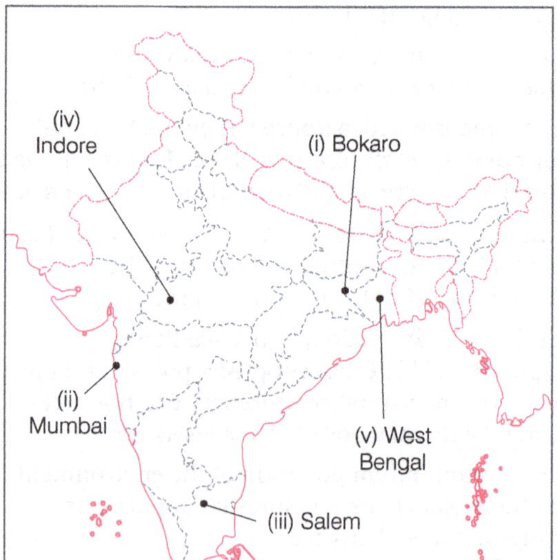

2. **On the given political map of India, locate and label the following features with appropriate symbols.** **CBSE 2015**

(i) Surat Cotton Textile Industry

(ii) Iron and steel plant located in Jharkhand **CBSE 2025**

(iii) Gandhinagar Software Technology Park **CBSE 2019**

(iv) Noida Software Technology Park **CBSE 2024**

(v) Coimbatore Cotton Textile Industry

(vi) Bengaluru Software Technology Park

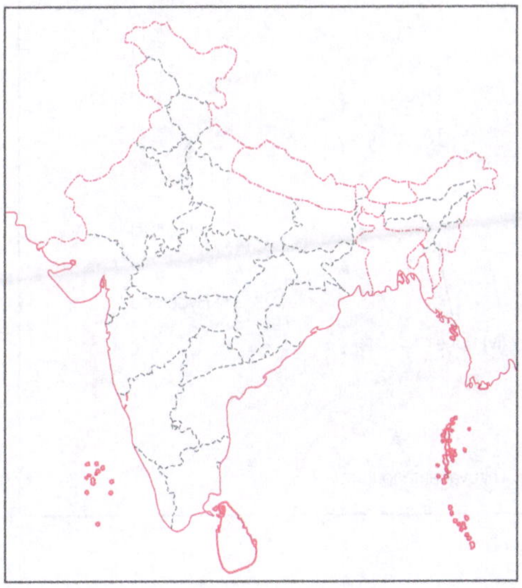

Ans.

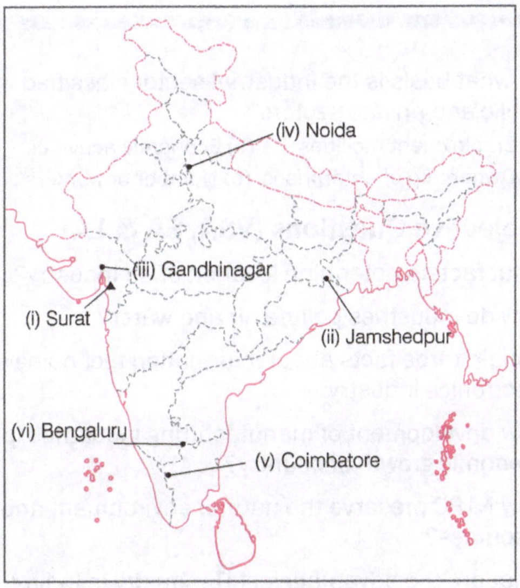

3. **On the following political map of India, locate, mark and label the following with appropriate symbols.**

(i) Mumbai– Software Technology Park

(ii) Kanpur–Cotton Textile Industry **CBSE 2011**

(iii) Bhilai–Iron and Steel Plant **CBSE 2012, 16**

(iv) Chennai Software Technology Park **CBSE 2019**

(v) Vijaynagara Iron and Steel Plant **CBSE 2019**

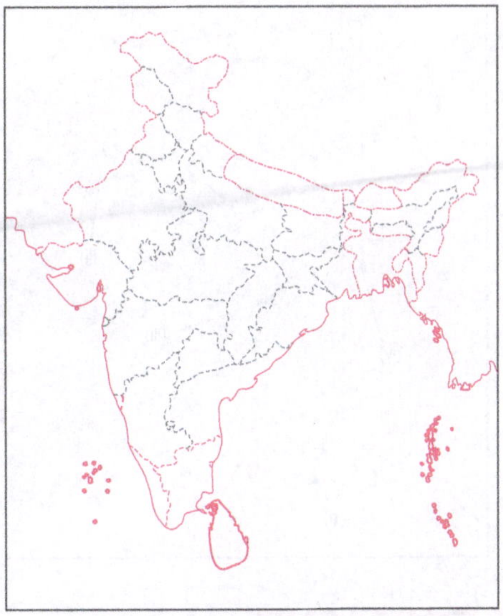

Ans.

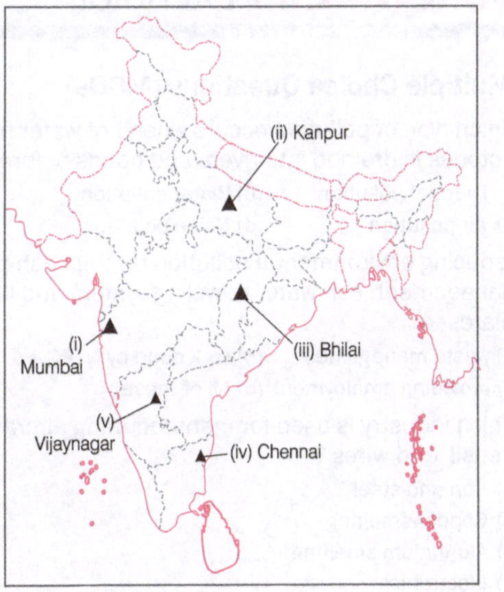

4. On the given political map of India, locate and label the following features.

(i) Thiruvananthapuram Park

(ii) Durgapur Iron and Steel Plant

(iii) Hyderabad Software Technology Park **CBSE 2019**

(iv) Pune Software Technology Park

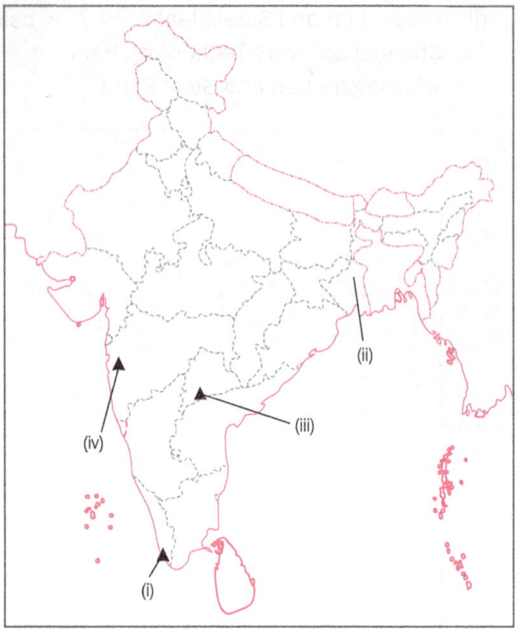

Ans.

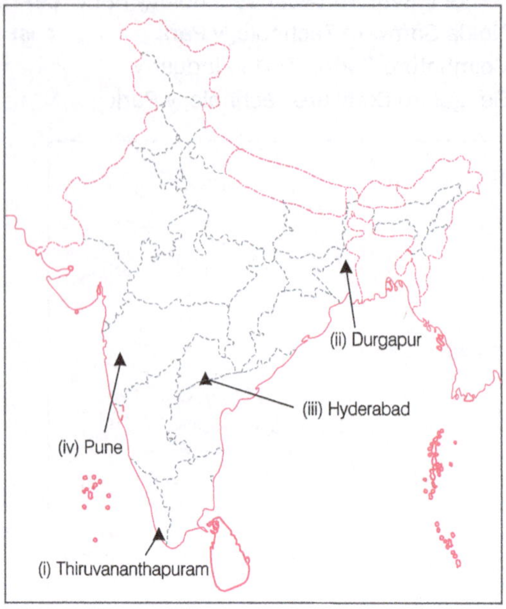

ASSESSMENT EXERCISE

Multiple Choice Questions (MCQs)

1. Which type of pollution occurs when hot water from factories is drained into rivers and ponds before cooling?

(a) Thermal pollution (b) Water pollution
(c) Air pollution (d) Noise pollution

2. Reducing environmental pollution through ash pond management, ash water recycling system and liquid relates to

(a) waste management (b)work done by NTPC
(c) providing employment (d) All of these

3. Which industry is used for manufacturing aircrafts , utensil and wires ?

(a) Iron and steel
(b) Copper smelting
(c) Aluminium smelting
(d) Electronics

4. Apart from Bengaluru, which cities are mentioned as important centres for electronic goods?

(a) Lucknow and Coimbatore
(b) Kolkata and Chennai
(c) Pune and Mumbai
(d) Delhi and Hyderabad

5. On what basis is the industrial sector classified into public and private sectors?

(a) Employment facilities (b) Economic activities
(c) Ownership of enterprises (d) Number of workers

Subjective Questions (VSA, SA & LA)

1. What factors determine location of an industry?

2. How do industries pollute air and water?

3. Explain three facts about information technology and electronics industry.

4. How development of manufacturing industries led to economic growth of country?

5. How NTPC preserve the natural environment and resources?

6. What are the advantages of IT industry in India?

7. How does the manufacturing industry helps other sectors of the economy?

8. What is the negative impact of industries?

9. Why is economic strength of a country measured by the development of manufacturing industries?

CHAPTER 7

Lifelines of National Economy

The modern means of transport and communication serve as lifelines of our nation and its modern economy. The modes of transportation and communication like railways, airways, waterways, newspapers, radio, television, cinema, internet, etc are contributing to India's socio-economic progress by linking India with the world.

For a long time, transport and trade were limited. But with the development of Science and Technology, the influence of trade and transport expanded.

World can now be considered as a large village, because of the effective means of transportation. Transport has been able to achieve this with the help of developed means of communication. Thus, transport and communication depend each other.

7.1 Transport

The movement of goods and services from supply locations to demand locations is termed as transportation. The efficient means of transportation is a necessary condition for fast development of a country.

Traders are people who make the goods available to consumers through transportation. The speed of country's development depends on the production of goods and services, and how easily they can be transported.

There are different means of transport through which movement of goods and services is done over three important domains of the Earth i.e. land, water and air.

The means of transport can be categorised as follows

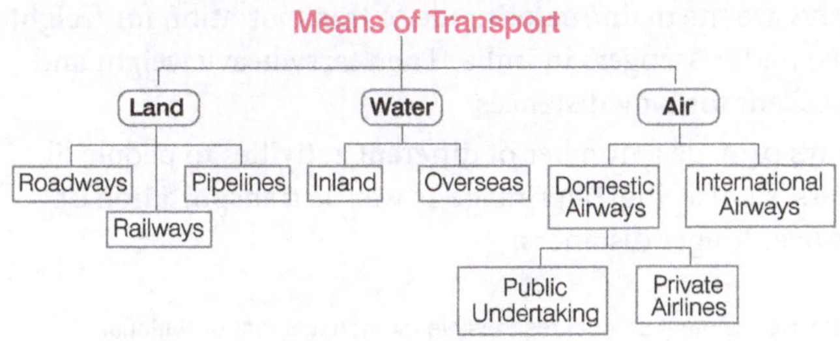

Roadways

India has the second largest road networks in the world which is about 62.16 lakh km (2020-21).

In India, roads came before railways. They are better than railways because they are easier and cheaper to build and maintain.

Road transport is growing in importance as compared to railways because of the following reasons

- Construction cost of roads is much lower than that of railway lines.
- Roads can be built in uneven surfaces like hills and mountains.
- They can be built over higher slopes and can traverse (cross) mountains such as the Himalayas.
- Road transport is economical in transportation of few persons and relatively smaller amount of goods over short distances.
- It also provides door-to-door service, thus, the cost of loading and unloading is much lower.
- It links other modes of transport like between railway stations, air and sea ports.

Classification of Roads on the Basis of Capacity

In India, roads are classified in six classes according to their capacity as given below

(i) **Golden Quadrilateral Super Highways** This is an important road development project which has been launched by the Government of India. In this project, these are **six lane super highways** which connect Delhi-Kolkata-Chennai-Mumbai and Delhi.

They have the following corridors

- **North-South corridors** linking Srinagar (Jammu and Kashmir) and Kanniyakumari (Tamil Nadu).
- **East-West corridors** linking Silchar (Assam) and Porbander (Gujarat).

The major objective of these super highways is to save time and reduce distance between the mega cities in India.

National Highway Authority of India (NHAI)[1] is the regulatory body which implements these highway projects.

(ii) **National Highways** They link extreme parts of the country. National Highways are the main road systems and are constructed and maintained by the **Central Public Works Department** (CPWD) under NHAI's supervision.

India has a number of National Highways which connect the North-South and East-West parts of the country.

KNOWLEDGE PLUS The **National Highway No-1** is a historical highway which is known as **Sher Shah Suri Marg**. This highway connects Delhi and Amritsar.

(iii) **State Highways** These are roads linking a state capital with its district headquarters.

(iv) **District Roads** These roads connect the district headquarters with other places of the district.

(v) **Other Roads** Rural roads, which link rural areas and villages with towns, are classified under this category. These are constructed under **Pradhan Mantri Grameen Sadak Yojana** (PMGSY). Under this scheme, special provisions have been made to link every village to a major town in the country by an all season road.

(vi) **Border Roads** These roads are constructed in border areas of the country. They are maintained by **Border Roads Organisation** (BRO) which was established in 1960.

The objective of this organisation is to develop roads of strategic importance in the Northern and North-Eastern border areas.

Border roads have improved accessibility in areas of difficult geography and have helped in the economic development of these areas.

KNOWLEDGE PLUS The **world's longest highway tunnel, Atal Tunnel** (9.02 km), has been built by Border Roads Organisation. It connects Manali to Lahaul-Spiti valley. It is built in the Pir Panjal range of Himalayas at an altitude of 3000 metres from the Mean Sea Level (MSL).

Classification of Roads on the Basis of Material Used

Roads can be classified on the basis of the material used into **metalled** and **unmetalled** roads.

- Metalled roads may be made of cement, concrete or even bitumen of coal. These are all weather roads.
- Unmetalled or unpaved roads are not accessible during rainy season.

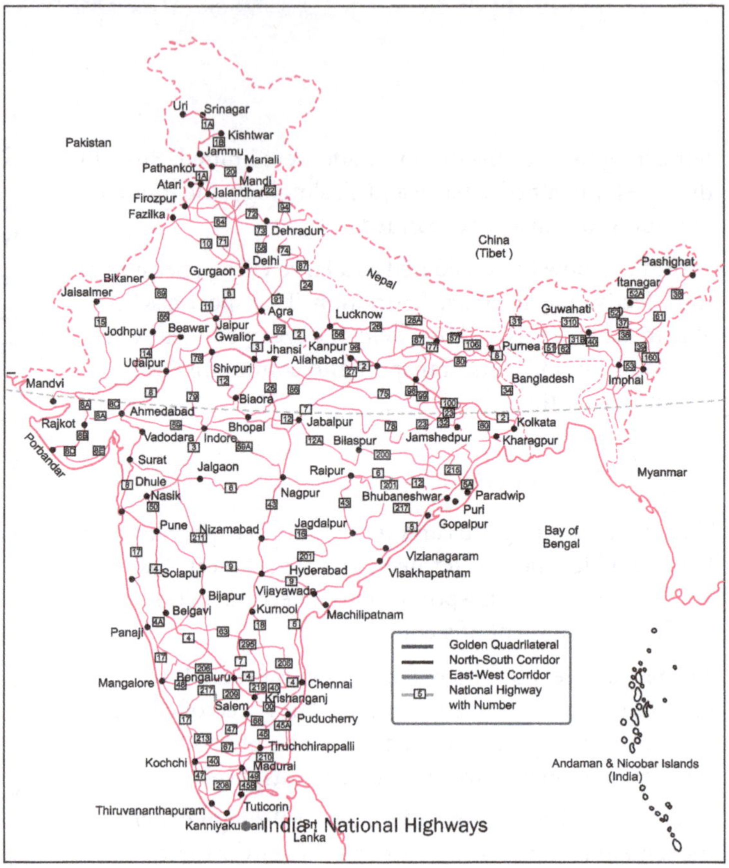

India: National Highways

Railways

Railways are the main/major mode of transportation for freight (goods) and passengers in India. They carry heavy weight and are excellent for long distances.

Railways provide a number of different activities to people like business, sightseeing, pilgrimage as well as transportation of goods over longer distances.

1 National Highways Authority of India (NHAI) It is an autonomous agency of the Government of India responsible for management of National Highways in India.

Railways bind the economic life of the country and help industries and agriculture to grow faster.

Indian Railways is the **largest public sector undertaking** in the country. It is reorganised into 17 railway zones. The first train started from **Mumbai to Thane** in 1853, covering a distance of 34 km.

Rail Gauge

The Indian Railway network runs on three gauge operations extending over 67,956 km. These include **broad gauge** (63,950 km) with width of 1.676 m, **metre gauge** (2,402 km) with width of 1 m and **narrow gauge** with width between 0.762 and 0.610 m.

Railway network in the country is dependent on the geographic, economic and administrative factors. The Northern plains are best suited for the growth of railway network in our country, since they have levelled land, high population density and rich agricultural resources.

Challenges for Indian Railways

- It is difficult to lay railway lines in the hilly regions of peninsular India. In these regions railways tracts are laid through low hills, gaps[2] or tunnels.
- The Himalayan mountainous regions are unfavourable for the construction of railway lines, due to high relief, sparse population and lack of economic opportunities.
- There is problem in constructing bridges over a large number of river due to their wide river beds[3].
- It is difficult to lay railway lines on the sandy plain of Western Rajasthan, swamps of Gujarat, forested tracks of Madhya Pradesh, Chhattisgarh, Odisha and Jharkhand.
- There are problems of sinking of railway tracks. For example, Sahyadri or Western Ghats has faced a number of problems such as sinking of track in some stretches and landslides.
- The initial costs of laying the tracks are very high.

Apart from these challenges, some problems that Indian Railways have to face are

- Many passengers travel without tickets.
- Theft and damaging of railway property has not yet stopped completely.
- People stop train by pulling the chain unnecessarily that causes heavy damage to the railway.

Try These

1. Which organisation is responsible for implementation of the Golden Quadrilateral Highways Project?
2. National Highway-1 (NH-1) connects which two regions?
3. Border Roads Organisation (BRO) was established in which year?
4. Into how many zones is Indian Railway divided?

Pipelines

Pipelines are used for transporting crude oil, petroleum products, natural gas and solids like iron ore when converted into slurry[4]. Earlier, it was used to transport water to industries and cities. India's overall gas pipeline infrastructure has expanded from 1700-18500 km of cross-country pipelines.

Some of the benefits of pipelines are

- The far inland locations of refineries like Barauni, Mathura, Panipat are approachable through pipelines.
- Initial cost of laying pipelines is high (especially for underground pipelines), but subsequent running costs are minimal.
- Pipelines control trans-shipment losses or delays.

Important pipeline transportation networks in India are

- **Pipeline from Oil Fields in Upper Assam to Kanpur (Uttar Pradesh) *via* Guwahati, Barauni and Allahabad** It has branches from Barauni to Haldia, via Rajbandh, Rajbandh to Maurigram and Guwahati to Siliguri.
- **Pipeline from Salaya in Gujarat to Jalandhar in Punjab, *via* Viramgam, Mathura, Delhi and Sonipat** It has branches to connect Koyali (near Vadodara, Gujarat) Chakshu and other places.
- **Hazira-Vijaipur-Jagdishpur (HVJ) Pipeline** It is 17,000 km long first cross country gas pipeline which connects Mumbai High and Bassein gas fields with various fertiliser, power and industrial complexes in Western and Northern India.

Waterways

Waterways are the cheapest means of transport. It is fuel-efficient, environment-friendly and suitable for carrying heavy and bulky goods.

India has inland navigation waterways of about 14,500 km in length out of which 5,685 km are navigable by mechanised boats.

---

2 **Pass or Gap** It is a gap or break, in high, rugged terrain such as a mountain ridge.

3 **River beds** It is a channel in which river flows.

4 **Slurry** It is a thin mixture of semi-solid with liquid, especially water and any of several finely crushed substances, such as cement, clay or mineral ore particles.

The following waterways are declared as the National Waterways by Government of India

National Waterways	Description
NW - 1	Allahabad to Haldia on the Ganga river system with length of 1,620 km.
NW - 2	Sadiya to Dhubri on the Brahmaputra river with length of 891 km.
NW - 3	West-Coast canal in Kerala, (Kottapuram-Komman, Udyogamandal and Champakkara canals) with length of 205 km.
NW - 4	Parts of Krishna and Godavari rivers along with Kakinada-Puducherry stretch of canals with length of 1,078 km.
NW - 5	Parts of Brahmani river along with Matai river, delta channels of Mahanadi and Brahmani rivers and East coast canal with length of 588 km.

There are some other inland waterways on which substantial transportation takes place. These are Mandavi, Zuari and Cumberjua, Sunderbans, Barak and backwaters of Kerala.

KNOWLEDGE PLUS India's trade with foreign countries is done through ports which are located on the coast. 95% of India's trade (68% in value) is carried through sea.

Major Sea Ports

With a long coastline of about 7516.6 km, India has 12 major and 200 notified intermediate/minor ports.

Some prominent sea ports of India are discussed below

- **Kandla** It is located in the Gulf of Kuchchh. It was the **first port** which was developed soon after independence, when the Karachi port went to Pakistan due to partition.

  It was developed to ease the volume of trade on the Mumbai port. It is also known as the **Deendayal port**. It is a **tidal port**[5]. It handles exports[6] and imports[7] of granary and industrial belt stretching across the states of Jammu and Kashmir, Himachal Pradesh, Punjab, Haryana, Rajasthan and Gujarat.
- **Mumbai** It is the **biggest port in India** with **natural harbour**[8]. **Jawaharlal Nehru** port was developed to decrease pressure on Mumbai port.
- **Marmagao** (Goa) It is the leading iron ore exporting port in India. This port account for about 50% of India's iron ore export.
- **New Mangalore** It is located in Karnataka. It caters to export of iron-ore from Kudremukh mines.
- **Kochchi** It is the extreme South-Western port located at the entrance of a **lagoon**[9] with a natural harbour.
- **Tuticorin** It is located in Tamil Nadu. It is the extreme South-Eastern port with a natural harbour and hinterland[10]. It handles a large variety of cargoes to neighbouring countries like Sri Lanka, Maldives, etc and coastal regions of India.
- **Chennai** It is the **oldest artificial port** ranking next to Mumbai in terms of cargo and volume of trade.
- **Visakhapatnam** It is the **deepest landlocked** and well protected port for exporting mainly iron-ore.
- **Paradwip** It is located in Odisha and specialises to export of iron-ore.
- **Kolkata** It is a tidal port and inland riverine port[11]. It serves as a very large and rich hinterland of Ganga-Brahmaputra basin.
- **Haldia** It was developed to relieve pressure on the Kolkata port.

Airways

The air travel is the fastest, most comfortable and prestigious mode of transport. It can cover very difficult terrains like high mountains, vast deserts, dense forests and long oceanic stretches. Air travel has made access easier.

Pawanhans Helicopters Limited provides helicopter services to Oil and Natural Gas Corporation (ONGC) to inaccessible areas and difficult terrains like the North-Eastern states and the interior parts of Jammu and Kashmir, Himachal Pradesh and Uttarakhand.

UDAN (Ude Desh ka Aam Nagrik)

- It is first scheme that boost regional aviation market.
- Regional connectivity scheme (RCS)-UDAN was adopted by the Ministry of Aviation.

5 Tidal Port It refers to the port in which the level of water within port varies with the change of water levels in oceans.
6 Export When goods are sent to another country it is called export.
7 Import When goods come from another country be sold in India, it is called import.
8 Natural Harbour It is a landform where a part of a body of water is protected and deep enough to furnish anchorage for ships.
9 Lagoon It is a shallow body of water separated from a larger body of water by a narrow landform.
10 Hinterland Remote areas of a country away from the coast or the banks of major rivers.
11 Riverine Port A place on a waterway with facilities for loading and unloading ships.

- It reduced the cost of regional tickets.
- The main objectives is to encourage airlines to operate flights on regional and remote routes.

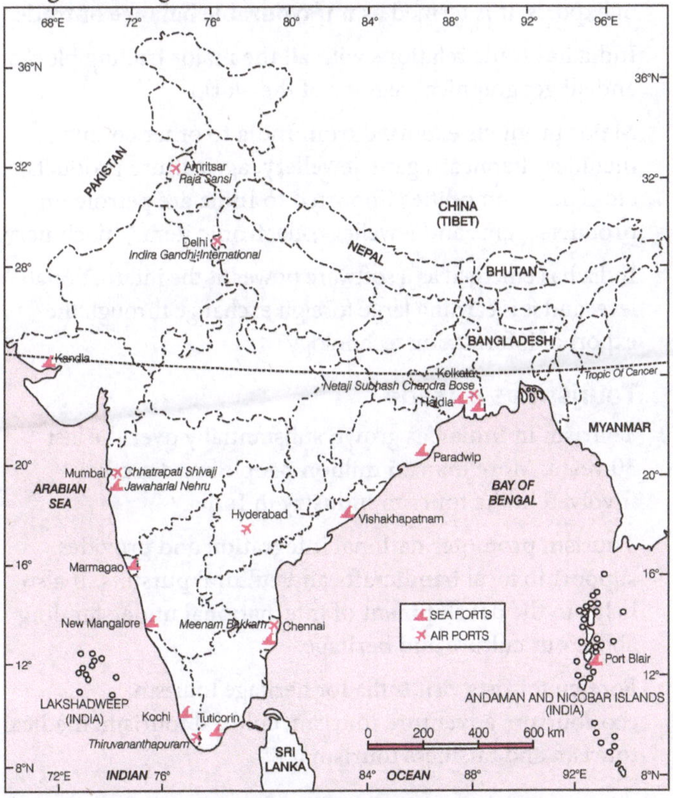

- Major Ports and Some International Airports

Try These

1. Name any one refinery which became viable due to pipelines.
2. What is the length of National Waterway No-1?
3. Name any one inland waterway other than national waterways.
4. After independence Karachi port became a part of which country?

7.2 Communication

It is an act of exchanging information. **Personal communication** and **mass communication** including television, radio, press, films, etc are the major means of communication in the country.

Personal Communication

It is a process of transferring or transmitting message between two people. Postal network and telecom network are examples of personal communication.

These are discussed below.

- **Postal Network** The Indian Postal Network is the largest in the world. It handles parcels as well as personal written communications.

  Mails in India are categorised *viz,* **first-class mail** and **second-class mail.**

  Post cards and envelopes are considered as **first-class mail.** These mails are airlifted (send by airways) between stations covering both land and air.

  Second-class mail includes book packets, registered newspapers and periodicals. These mails are carried by surface mails, covering land and water transport.

  Mail Channels allow quick delivery of mails in large cities. Six mail channels have been introduced i.e. Rajdhani Channel, Metro Channel, Green Channel, Business Channel, Bulk Mail Channel and Periodic Channel.

- **Telecom Networks** India has **one of the largest telecom networks** in Asia. The government has made special provision to extend 24 hours **Subscriber Trunk Dialling** (STD) facility to every village in the country. This has been done to improve telephonic communications from the grassroot to the higher level. More than two-thirds of the villages in India, excluding urban places have already been covered with STD telephone facility.

There is a same rate of STD facilities all over India. It has been made possible by combining the development in space technology with communication technology.

Digital India

It is a programme to prepare India for a knowledge based transformation.

The focus of Digital India Programme is on being transformative to realise IT (Indian Talent) + IT (Information Technology) = IT (India Tomorrow), and is on making technology central to enabling change.

Mass Communication

It is a process of transferring or transmitting a message to a large group of people. It provides entertainment and creates awareness among people about various national programmes and policies. It includes radio, television, newspapers, magazines, books and films. Some of these are discussed below

- **Radio and Television All India Radio** (Akashwani) broadcasts a variety of programmes in national, regional and local languages for various categories of people.
- **Doordarshan, the national television channel of India** is one of the largest land networks in the world. It broadcasts a variety of programmes from

entertainment, educational to sports, etc for people of different age groups.

- **Newspapers and Periodicals** In India, a large number of periodicals and newspapers are published annually. They are of different types depending upon their regularity.

  Newspaper are published in 100 languages and dialects. The largest number of newspapers published in the country are in Hindi, followed by English and Urdu.

- **Films** India is the **largest producer of feature films** in the world. It produces short films, video feature films and video short films. The **Central Board of Film Certification** is the authority to certify both Indian and foreign films.

7.3 International Trade

The exchange of goods among people, states and countries is referred to as **trade**. Trade between two countries is called international trade.

The market is a place where such exchanges take place. The international trade may take place through sea, air or land routes.

Local trade is carried in cities, towns and villages and state level trade is carried between two or more states.

International trade is very essential and no country can survive without it. Economic growth of a country can be measured through its advancement of international trade.

Components of Trade

Export and **import** are the components of trade. The **balance of trade** is the difference between export and import of a country.

When the value of export is greater than the value of imports, it is called a **favourable balance of trade.** On the other hand, if the value of imports is more than the value of exports, it is termed as **unfavourable balance of trade.**

India has trade relations with all the major trading blocks and all geographical regions of the world.

Major products exported from India to other countries includes chemicals, gem, jewellery, agriculture products, etc. The commodities imported to India are petroleum products, gems and jewellery, electronic items, machinery.

India has emerged as a software power at the international level and it is earning large foreign exchange through the export of information technology.

Tourism as a Trade

Tourism in India has grown substantially over the last 30 years. More than 15 million people are directly involved in the tourism industry in India.

Tourism promotes national integration and provides support to local handicrafts and cultural pursuits. It also helps in the development of international understanding about our culture and heritage.

Foreign tourists visit India for heritage tourism, eco-tourism, adventure tourism, cultural tourism, medical tourism and business tourism.

Try These

1. Which is a new way of transportation system?
2. Which is the cheapest means of transport?
3. What is the full form of STD?
4. Name the authority that certifies films in India.

Mind Map

LIFELINES OF NATIONAL ECONOMY

Transport

Airways
- Fastest mode of Transport.
- Covers all geographic barriers.

Waterways
- Cheapest mode of transport.
- India's coastline is about 7516.6 km.
- Used for International trade.

Pipelines
- Used for transporting crude oil.
- Pipeline from oil fields in Upper Assam to Kanpur.
- Pipeline from Salaya in Gujarat to Jalandhar.
- Hazira-Vijaipur-Jagdishpur (HVJ) pipeline.

Railways
- Largest public sector undertaking.
- First train started from Mumbai to Thane in 1853.

Roadways
India has second largest road network.

Based on Basis of Material used
- Metalled Roads
- Unmetalled Roads

Based on basis of Capacity
- Golden Quadrilateral
- National Highways
- District Roads
- Border Roads
- Super Highway
- State Highways
- Other Roads

International Trade

Components of Trade
- Export
- Import

Tourism as a Trade
Promotes national integration and provides support to local handicrafts and local pursuits

Communication

Personal Communication

Postal Network
- First Class Mail
- Second Class

Telecom Network
Subscriber Trunk Dialing (STD)

Mass Communication
- Radio and Television, e.g. All India Radio and Doordarshan.
- Newspapers and Periodicals
- Films

NCERT FOLDER

Covering Intext Questions and Exercises of NCERT

EXERCISE

Q.1 Multiple choice questions.

(i) Which two of the following extreme locations are connected by the East-West corridor?

(a) Mumbai and Nagpur (b) Silchar and Porbandar
(c) Mumbai and Kolkata (d) Nagpur and Siligudi

(ii) Which mode of transportation reduces trans-shipment losses and delays?

(a) Railways (b) Roadways
(c) Pipeline (d) Waterways

(iii) Which one of the following states is not connected with the HVJ pipeline?

(a) Madhya Pradesh (b) Maharashtra
(c) Gujarat (d) Uttar Pradesh

(iv) Which one of the following ports is the deepest land-locked and well-protected port along the East coast? CBSE 2020

(a) Chennai (b) Paradwip
(c) Tuticorin (d) Visakhapatnam

(v) Which one of the following is the most important mode of transportation in India?

(a) Pipeline (b) Railways
(c) Roadways (d) Airways

(vi) Which one of the following terms is used to describe trade between two or more countries?

(a) Internal trade (b) International trade
(c) External trade (d) Local trade

Ans. (i) (b), (ii) (c), (iii) (b), (iv) (d), (v) (b), (vi) (b)

Q.2 Answer the following questions in about 30 words.

(i) State any three merits of roadways.

Ans. Three merits of roadways are

(a) They provide us door-to-door service.
(b) It is easier to construct roads at low cost as compared to railway lines.
(c) They provide a feeder service to link other means of transportation.

(ii) Where and why is rail transport the most convenient means of transportation?

Ans. Rail transport is the most convenient means of transportation in the Northern Plains because

(a) Construction of railway lines in the plains is easy due to the gentle slope of the land.
(b) The Northern Plains are densely populated, which enables the maximum number of people to utilise this means of transport.
(c) Railways are the principle mode of transportation for freight (goods) and passengers in India. They carry heavy weight and are excellent for long distance.

(iii) What is the significance of the border roads?

Ans. The significance of border roads can be seen through the following points

- They have improved accessibility in areas of difficult terrain.
- They have helped in the economic development of these areas.
- They have made the movement of defence forces easy.

(iv) What is meant by trade? What is the difference between international and local trade?

Ans. Trade refers to the exchange of goods among people, states and countries.

The differences between international trade and local trade are

International Trade	Local Trade
International trade is carried out between two or more countries.	Local trade is carried out within a country between states or between cities, towns and villages in the same state.
Foreign currency is required for this type of trade.	National currency is required for this type of trade.

Q.3 Answer the following questions in about 120 words.

(i) Why are the means of transportation and communication called the lifelines of a nation and its economy?

(ii) Write a note on the changing nature of the international trade in the last fifteen years.

Ans. (i) The means of transportation and communication are called the lifelines of a nation and its economy because

- An efficient and well-developed system of transport is essential for proper utilisation of the available natural resources.
- A well-developed system of transportation like roadways and railways maintain the movement of persons and goods to different regions of the country.
- The means of communication help in sending and receiving messages, thus, playing a vital role in the running of the country efficiently.

- Railways provide a number of different activities to people like business, sightseeing, pilgrimage as well as transportation of goods over longer distances.
- Pipelines are used for transporting crude oil, petroleum products and natural gas to refineries, factories and big thermal power plants.
- Waterways are cheapest means of transport. These are most suitable for carrying heavy and bulky goods.
- Air transport provides fastest service even in those areas which are inaccessible by other means of transport.

(ii) The changing nature of the international trade in the last fifteen years can be seen through the following points

- Exchange of commodities and goods in foreign trade has increased due to exchange of information and knowledge.
- The exchange of information and knowledge has also improved trade relations of India with the rest of the world.
- Due to its advanced software knowledge and excellence in the field of information technology, India has emerged as a software power at the international level and it is earning a large amount of foreign exchange through the export of information technology.
- India has trade relations with all the major trading blocks and all geographical regions of the world.
- India has become a major exporter of a number of commodities. For example, agriculture and allied products, gems and jewellery, chemicals and related products and so on.
- Tourism industry has also emerged as a big industry in India. It helps in the development of international understanding about our culture and heritage.

REVIEW EXERCISE

Including Competency Based Questions

Part I

Multiple Choice Questions (MCQs)

1. Why do you think that means of transport should be well-developed in a country?

(a) Because the movement of goods and services from their supply locations to demand locations necessitates the need for transport.

(b) Because transport facilities ensures the political success of a country.

(c) Because without transport facilities, the country faces political instability however transport facility end this instability.

(d) Because transport facilities allows people to mix with each other and this relieves their mental pressure and loneliness.

2. Arunali lives in a remote area in Arunachal Pradesh which is at present inaccessible due to its terrain. Arunali along with the other members of her family struggles hard to travel to other parts of the country. Accordingly, which of the following transport facilities would be the most suitable to improve the connectivity of the area for the villagers? **Competency Based**

(a) Railways (b) Roadways

(c) Waterways (d) Airways

3. Which of the following corridors links Srinagar and Kanniyakumari?

(a) North-South corridor (b) East-West corridor

(c) North-East corridor (d) South-West corridor

4. Find the incorrect option.

(a) National Highways link extreme parts of India.

(b) National Highways are the main road system.

(c) National Highways are laid and maintained by the State Public Works Department.

(d) National Highways No-1 connects Delhi and Amritsar.

5. 'There has been a huge increase in the number of national highway projects, power plants and hotels in the Himachal Pradesh and indiscriminate construction has its impact on environment. The number of landslides has increased wildly following the construction of Chandigarh-Shimla Expressway, Kiratpur-Manali project and other national highways and dozens of people have also lost their lives in these incidents.'
Should the construction of such roads and other development projects be reconsidered in such areas?

(a) Yes, alternative methods to increase the connectivity should be explored in areas with high risk taking into account the environmental sustainability.

(b) No, connectivity to each and every corner of the country is the foremost action to achieve the goal of economic growth.
(c) Yes, the goal of protecting environment is the only goal which should be prioritised.
(d) No, the benefits of such projects outweigh some of these type of incidents.

6. Which of the following national highway is called Sher-Shah Suri Marg?
(a) National Highway-5 (b) National Highway-7
(c) National Highway-1 (d) National Highway-9

7. Metalled roads are
(a) unpaved roads (b) seasonal roads
(c) dry season roads (d) all weather roads

8. Gas pipelines from Hazira in Gujarat connects Jagdishpur in which of the following states?
(a) Madhya Pradesh (b) Uttar Pradesh
(c) Bihar (d) Himachal Pradesh

9. Which of the following was the first port developed soon after independence to use the volume of trade on the Mumbai port?
(a) Kandla (b) Karachi
(c) Kochchi (d) Vizag

10. Find the odd one out. **CBSE 2025**
(a) Hindustan Computers Limited
(b) Hindustan Unilever
(c) Bharti Airtel Limited
(d) Indian Postal Service

11. Harish, a resident from a village in Jharkhand went to a city for higher education. When he returned after 5 years, he saw that there is still no means of communication in his village. He decided to install a common telephone connection in his village.
Which of the following will this step most likely lead to in the near future? **Competency Based**
(a) All the village people will become literate.
(b) Most of the villagers will become modernised.
(c) People of the village will be more well connected with the outside world.
(d) People of the village will get goods and services at a cheaper price.

12. Mass communication provides entertainment and creates awareness among people about various national programmes and policies.
Which of the following examples is not representing mass communication?
(a) An information about a government scheme on radio.
(b) A company shares an important information about the market statistics in an e-mail.
(c) Information about the global economic recession in a national newspaper.
(d) Broadcast of a programme related to female menstrual health on a TV show.

13. Six mail channels have been introduced recently. They ware called Rajdhani Channel, Metro Channel, Green Channel, Business Channel, Bulk Mail Channel and Periodical Channel.
What is the purpose of the six recently introduced mail channels, such as Rajdhani Channel and Business Channel? **Competency Based**
(a) To facilitate surface mail transportation.
(b) To prioritise delivery of registered newspapers and periodicals.
(c) To enhance quick mail delivery in large towns and cities.
(d) To improve the efficiency of book packets delivery.

14. Which of the following promotes national integration and provides support to local handicrafts and cultural pursuits?
(a) Tourism
(b) Sports
(c) Services
(d) National Heritages

15. Identify the port with the help of given information.
- The port is located in Gulf of Kuchchh.
- It is one of India's major ports on the West coast.
- It is the largest port of India by volume of cargo handled.

Codes
(a) Kandla Port (b) Mumbai Port
(c) Marmagao Port (d) Kochchi Port

16. Identify the reasons as to why road transport is more important than a rail transport. Choose the appropriate statements among the following options
I. Construction of roads is cheaper than rails.
II. Roads can be built in undulating topography.
III. Road can negotiate higher gradients of slopes.
IV. Road transport is economical to carry few persons over longer distances.

Codes
(a) Statements I and II are appropriate.
(b) Statements I, II and III are appropriate.
(c) All the statements are appropriate.
(d) Only statement IV is appropriate.

17. Consider the following statements and choose the correct option.
Statement I Railways are the principal mode of transportation for freight and passengers in India.
Statement II The Indian railways is the largest public sector undertaking in the country.
Codes
(a) Statement I is correct and statement II is incorrect
(b) Statement I is incorrect and statement II is correct
(c) Both statements I and II are incorrect
(d) Both statements I and II are correct

18. Consider the following statements about Golden Quadrilateral Super Highways and choose the correct option.

I. Golden Quadrilateral Super Highways are a major road development project.
II. These highways link Delhi-Kolkata-Chennai-Mumbai and Delhi.
III. East-West and North-South corridors are part of this project.

Codes

(a) Only I (b) I and II (c) II and III (d) All of these

19. Mr D belongs to a middle class family. He took his family on a tour in train. Why? Competency Based

I. It is cheap and affordable.
II. It is a suitable options for sightseeing in India.
III. He can travel even without spending money on tickets.
IV. He is provided free food in a train.

Codes

(a) Only I (b) III and IV (c) I and II (d) Only II

20. Which of the following statements accurately describes the 'pipeline transport network'?

I. Pipeline transport is the recent mode of transport developed.
II. This mode of transport was never used in the past.
III. Pipelines are used for transporting crude oil only.
IV. Solids cannot be transported through a pipeline in any form.

Codes

(a) Only I (b) Only III
(c) Only IV (d) Both I and II

21. Arrange the following National Waterways as per their total length in India (in decreasing order).

I. NW-1 II. NW-2 III. NW-3 IV. NW-4

Codes

(a) I, II, III, IV (b) II, III, IV, I
(c) I, IV, II, III (d) II, IV, I, III

Answers

1. (a)	2. (d)	3. (a)	4. (c)	5. (a)
6. (c)	7. (d)	8. (b)	9. (a)	10. (b)
11. (c)	12. (b)	13. (c)	14. (a)	15. (a)
16. (b)	17. (d)	18. (d)	19. (c)	20. (a)
21. (a)				

Match the Following

1.

List I	List II
A. National Highways	1. Central Public Works Department
B. Other Rural Roads	2. Pradhan Mantri Grameen Sadak Yojana
C. Border Roads	3. Border Roads Organisation

Codes

	A	B	C		A	B	C
(a)	1	2	3	(b)	1	3	2
(c)	3	2	1	(d)	3	1	2

Ans. (a)

Assertion-Reason

1. Assertion (A) International trade is very essential and no country can survive without it.
Reason (R) Resources are space bound and no country is self-sufficient in every kind of resources.

Codes

(a) Both A and R are true and R is the correct explanation of A
(b) Both A and R are true, but R is not the correct explanation of A
(c) A is true, but R is false
(d) A is false, but R is true

2. Assertion (A) Roadways have an edge over railways.
Reason (R) Roadways can be built and maintained easily even in undulating topography.

Codes

(a) Both A and R are true and R is the correct explanation of A
(b) Both A and R are true, but R is not the correct explanation of A
(c) A is true, but R is false
(d) A is false, but R is true

3. Assertion (A) Communication is an unessential requirement of human life.
Reason (R) Communication between people creates awareness.

Codes

(a) Both A and R are true and R is the correct explanation of A
(b) Both A and R are true, but R is not the correct explanation of A
(c) A is true, but R is false
(d) A is false, but R is true

4. Assertion (A) Cost of laying pipelines is less but the running costs are more.
Reason (R) Pipelines facilitates an easy transportation of goods.

Codes

(a) Both A and R are true and R is the correct explanation of A
(b) Both A and R are true, but R is not the correct explanation of A
(c) A is true, but R is false
(d) A is false, but R is true

5 **Assertion** (A) Tourism promotes national integration.
Reason (R) Millions of people are directly engaged in tourism industry.

Codes

(a) Both A and R are true and R is the correct explanation of A
(b) Both A and R are true, but R is not the correct explanation of A
(c) A is true, but R is false
(d) A is false, but R is true

Ans. 1. (a) Both A and R are true and R is the correct explanation of A
2. (a) Both A and R are true and R is the correct explanation of A
3. (d) A is false, but R is true
4. (d) A is false, but R is true
5. (b) Both A and R are true, but R is not the correct explanation of A

Picture Based Question

1. Given below is the picture of a cargo ship carrying goods. Observe the picture and answer the question that follows.

Why are ships the best option for transporting heavy and bulky goods?

(a) They have more space for keeping these items.
(b) They are cheaper, fuel efficient and environment friendly.
(c) Although it is expensive , this is still the fastest mode of transport.
(d) Waterways can be developed anywhere in the world and ships are easy to manufacture.

Ans. (b) They are cheaper, fuel efficient and environment friendly.

Case Based Question

1. Read the following passage and answer the questions that follow.

The exchange of goods among people, states and countries is referred to as trade. The market is the place where such exchanges take place. Trade between two countries is called international trade. It may take place through sea, air or land routes. While local trade is carried in cities, towns and villages, state level trade is carried between two or more states. Advancement of international trade of a country is an index to its economic prosperity. It is, therefore, considered the economic barometer for a country. As the resources are space bound, no country can survive without international trade. Export and import are the components of trade.

(i) Which of the following correctly signifies balance of trade of a country?

(a) Balance of trade = Import - Export
(b) Balance of trade = Import × Export
(c) Balance of trade = Import / Export
(d) Balance of trade = Import - Export / 100

(ii) Favourable balance of trade occurs in which of the following situations?

(a) When the value of exports is equal to the value of imports.
(b) When the value of imports exceeds to that of export.
(c) When the value of exports exceeds the value of imports.
(d) When the number of exported items is more than the number of imported items.

(iii) Which of the following items is/are exported from India to other countries?

(a) Gems and Jewellery (b) Chemicals
(c) Agricultural products (d) All of these

(iv) India has emerged as a software power by exporting which of the following?

(a) Machines (b) Computers
(c) Information Technology (d) Electronic items

Ans. (i) (a) Balance of trade = Import - Export
(ii) (c) When the value of exports exceeds the value of imports.
(iii) (d) All of these
(iv) (c) Information Technology

Part II

Very Short Answer Type Questions

1. Analyse the contribution of fast transport in globalisation. CBSE 2019

Ans. Fast transportation network helps to provide boost to the globalisation process. Fast means of transport save time and provide quick delivery of goods from source regions to the market place. For eg. ships, railways, airways and pipelines.

2. What are Super Highways?

Ans. Super highways are four to six lane highways that allow fast movement of traffic.

3. National Highways are constructed and maintained by which department?

Ans. National highways are constructed and maintained by Central Public Works Department (CPWD).

4. How state highways are different from district roads?

Ans. State Highways are different from district roads as they link a state capital with its district headquaters, while district roads connect district headquarters with other places of the district.

5. Which agency maintains the roads connecting villages to district headquarters?

Ans. Zila Parishad of the district maintains the district roads.

6. What is the importance of Konkan railways?

Ans. Konkan railways are important as it connects the important industrial and economic regions of South-West India.

7. Name the major mode of transportation for freight and passengers in India.

Ans. Railways are the major mode of transportation for freight and passengers in India.

8. Name the factors which are responsible for distribution pattern of railways network in the country.

Ans. The distribution pattern of railway network is influenced by geographical, economic and administrative factors.

9. Why Himalayan region is unfavourable for construction of railway line?

Ans. The Himalayan region is unfavourable for construction of railway line due to high relief, less population and lack of economic opportunities.

10. 'The India-Bangladesh Friendship Pipeline (IBFP) is a joint effort to transport high-speed diesel from the Numaligarh Refinery Limited in Assam, India to 16 districts in Northern Bangladesh......' Competency Based

Source : Mint

(i) What is the advantage of pipelines over other transportation means?

(ii) What other products can be transported through pipelines apart from petroleum?

Ans. (i) Use of pipelines reduces trans-shipment loss and delays which is most significant advantage of pipelines over other transportation means.

(ii) Apart from petroleum, other products such as natural gas from oil and fertiliser can also be transported through pipelines. Solids can also be transported through a pipeline when converted into slurry.

11. Name any two national waterways in India.

Ans. The two national waterways in India are

(i) **NW-1** It is the Ganga river stretch between Allahabad and Haldia.

(ii) **NW-2** It is the Brahmaputra river stretch between Sadiya and Dhubri.

12. National Waterway-1 is navigable between which places? CBSE 2014

Ans. National Waterway-1 is navigable between Allahabad and Haldia.

13. Name some inland waterways apart from national waterways on which transportation takes place.

Ans. Inland waterways on which transportation takes place includes Mandavi, Zuari, Cumberjua, Sunderbans, Barak and backwaters of Kerala.

14. What is Tidal port? Give example of one such port.

Ans. Tidal port is the port in which the level of water within port varies with the change of water levels in oceans, e.g. Kandla port.

15. Which port is the biggest with a spacious natural and well-sheltered harbour? CBSE 2013

Ans. Mumbai port is the biggest with a spacious natural and well-sheltered harbour.

16. Which port exports more than half of the total iron ore of the country?

Ans. Marmagao port exports more than half of the total iron ore export of the country.

17. Which port on South-Eastern coast has a natural harbour and hinterland?

Ans. Tuticorin port has a natural harbour and hinterland.

18. Which is the oldest artificial sea port of India? CBSE 2020

Ans. Chennai is the oldest artificial sea port of India.

19. Name any four ports on East Coast of India. CBSE 2014

Ans. The four ports on East Coast of India are Chennai, Visakhapatnam, Paradwip and Kolkata port.

20. Mention the role of Pawanhans helicopters in India.

Ans. Pawanhans helicopters provide transportation to inaccessible areas, difficult terrains like the North-Eastern states and the interior parts of Jammu and Kashmir, Himachal Pradesh and Uttarakhand.

Short Answer Type Questions

1. What has necessitated the need for transport? Is it right to say that efficient means of transport are pre-requisites for fast development? Justify.

Or "Efficient means of transport are pre-requisites for fast development of the country." Support the statement with examples. CBSE 2020

Ans. The need for transport has been necessitated due to the need for movement of goods and services from their supply locations to demand locations or market.

Efficient means of transport are pre-requisite for fast development because more development of goods and services are not enough. The goods need to be transported from one place to another in proper time for their distribution and consumption. This requires efficient means of transport.

2 Discuss the most likely impact of means of transport and communication in the growth of industries in India. Build the answer around these points. Competency Based

- **Transport facilities**
- **Communication lines**
- **Regional development**

Ans. The ways by which means of transport and communication help the growth of industries in India are

- Transport facilities are required to transport raw materials from their source region to industrial locations. Final products from industries also require transport facilities for their transportation to market.
- Communication lines supply required information about various industries.
- Means of transport and communication also help in reduction of regional imbalances resulting in balanced regional development.

3 "Transport routes are called the basic arteries of our economy." Support this statement with relevant examples.

Ans. Transport routes are called basic arteries of our economy because of the following reasons

- Dense network of transport is important for the economic development of a region or a country.
- Roads and railways are like arteries that connect areas of production with that of consumption. For example, agricultural farms are connected to agro-based industries and markets.
- Roads and railways also help in industrial development by assemblage of raw materials and distribution of finished goods.

4. "Road transport in India is not competitive but complementary to railways." Justify the statement by giving four points. CBSE 2015

Or India has second largest road networks in the world, aggregating to about 62.16 lakh km (2020-21). In India, roadways have preceded railways. However, it is also true that road transport in India is not competitive but complementary to railways. How can you justify this statement? Substantiate your answer by giving any four reasons. Competency Based

Ans. Road transport in India is not competitive but complementary to railways. This can be justified through the following points

(i) Road transport is suitable for short distances. On the other hand, rail transport is more suitable for long distances.

(ii) Bulky and non-perishable goods are transported by railways over long distances and longer time. On the other hand, perishable goods can be transported by roads in shorter time.

(iii) Railways can stop only at specific destinations where loading/unloading facilities should be available, but vehicles on the road can be loaded or unloaded virtually anywhere.

(iv) Road transportation increases the reach of railways by providing the final links, i.e. giving door-to-door service.

5. (i) Why are metalled roads better than unmetalled roads?

(ii) What is the role of border roads and national highways in transportation?

Or Explain the importance of 'Border Roads' for India. CBSE 2017

Ans. (i) Metalled roads are better than unmetalled roads because they have a waterproof coating on their upper surface, this makes them usable in all seasons. On the other hand, unmetalled roads are difficult to use in the rainy season, as their upper surface becomes uneven due to absorption of rain water.

(ii) The role of border roads are as follows

- They have improved accessibility in areas of difficult terrain.
- These roads help in the economic development of the border areas of the country.

The role of national highways are as follows

- National Highways link important parts of the country like state capitals and commercial centres.
- They enable fast and efficient movement of goods in areas connected to them.

6. Describe some of the major improvements made by Indian Railways in its functioning since independence.

Or Explain the improvements made by the Indian Railways in its functioning. CBSE 2012

Ans. Some major improvements made by Indian Railways in its functioning since independence are

- Electrification of railway lines to reduce burden on fossil fuels and to increase speed.

- Introduction of computerised reservation system for convenience of passengers.
- Conversion of metre gauge lines to broad gauge to ensure higher speed and carrying capacity.
- Construction of new railway lines to improve the connectivity in the country.
- Replacing steam engines, which cause heavy pollution, by diesel and electric engines.

7. Explain any two merits and two demerits of pipelines transport.

Ans. The two merits of pipelines transport are

(i) The running costs of pipeline transport are minimal.

(ii) Pipelines are highly efficient in transporting liquids such as crude oil, petroleum products and gases (natural gas).

The two demerits of pipelines transport are

(i) Initial costs of laying pipelines are very high, particularly oil and gas pipelines which have to be laid underground.

(ii) Leakage in pipes or damage to the pipeline might pollute soil and ground water, damaging the environment.

8 Explain the importance of pipelines as a means of transportation in India. **CBSE 2023**

Ans. The importance of pipelines as a means of transportation in India are

- Pipelines are used for transporting crude oil, petroleum products, natural gas, solids like iron ore when converted into slurry.
- The far inland locations of refineries like Barauni, Mathura and Panipat and gas based fertilisers plants could be thought of only because of pipelines.
- Pipelines control trans-shipment losses or delays.

9. Explain any four characteristics of Kandla sea port. **CBSE 2012, 10**

Ans. The four characteristics of Kandla sea port are

(i) It was the first port developed soon after independence. When the Karachi port went to Pakistan due to partition.

(ii) It was developed to reduce the volume of trade on Mumbai port.

(iii) It is a tidal port.

(iv) It handles exports and imports of highly productive granary and industrialised belts including Jammu and Kashmir, Himachal Pradesh, Punjab, Haryana, Rajasthan and Gujarat.

10. "Airways is the most preferred mode of transport in North-Eastern states of India." Give three reasons to prove this preference. **CBSE 2017**

Or **Why is air transport more popular in the North-Eastern part of the country? Give three reasons.**

Ans. Air transport is the most preferred mode of transport in the North-Eastern states in India due to the following reasons

(i) Big and wide rivers are present in the North-Eastern states, due to which rail or road bridges over them are difficult and costly to construct.

(ii) This area has dissected relief features, preventing durable construction of rail and road links.

(iii) Dense forests in this region create many difficulties in construction of railway lines and roads.

11. Explain any four merits and two demerits of air transport. **CBSE 2016, 2012**

Ans. The four merits of air transport are

(i) Air transport is the fastest, most comfortable and prestigious mode of transport.

(ii) It can cover very difficult terrains with great ease.

(iii) It makes access to far-flung and remote or otherwise inaccessible areas easier and quicker.

(iv) It provides transport services to offshore oil and gas exploration activities.

The two demerits of air transport are

(i) Air transport is a very costly means of transportation.

(ii) Places that does not have airports or helipads are not covered by it.

12. Explain the importance of 'Radio and Television' as an effective means of mass communication in India.

Ans. The importance of 'Radio and Television' can be understood from the following points

- These media provide news to people throughout the country including rural areas.
- People are also made aware of the programmes and policies of the government.
- They provide educational programmes that can be understood even by the illiterate people.
- The media also gives information involving various natural and man-made disasters. It helps in broadcasting early warnings.

13. Mention any four features of the telecom network of India.

Ans. The four features of telecom network are

(i) India has one of the largest telecom networks in Asia.

(ii) More than two-thirds of the villages in India, excluding urban places have already been covered with Subscriber Trunk Dialing (STD).

(iii) This facility is to be extended 24 hours in every village of the country.

(iv) There is a uniform rate of STD facilities all over India.

14. What is Balance of Trade? In which situations is it favourable and unfavourable? CBSE 2013

Ans. The Balance of Trade of a country is the difference between its total export and import in a year.

In following situations, Balance of trade is favourable and unfavourable

(i) When the value of export is greater than the value of imports, it is called a favourable balance of trade.

(ii) On the other hand, if the value of imports is more than the value of exports, it is termed as unfavourable balance of trade.

15. 'Tourism in India has grown' substantially over the last three decades. More than 15 million people are directly engaged in the tourism industry. There is a vast potential for development of tourism in all parts of the country. '

(i) What does the above statement reflect about the significance of tourism in India.

(ii) Discuss the scope of the development of tourism in India.

Ans. (i) The significance of tourism as a trade in India is stated in the points below

- Tourism promotes national integration.
- Tourism provides support to cultural activities and develops international understanding about cultural heritage.

(ii) India has a vast scope for the development of tourism because of its diverse geographical, cultural and physiographic features. A variety of tourism can be developed in India. Foreign tourists visit India for heritage tourism, eco tourism, adventure tourism, cultural tourism , medical tourism and business tourism. There is a vast potential for development of tourism in all parts of the country. Efforts are being made to promote different types of tourism for this upcoming industry.

Long Answer Type Questions

1. "Roadways still have an edge over the railways in India. "Support the statement with examples. CBSE 2017, 2019

or **A country X is a developing and middle income country with a large and diverse geographical area. It wants to increase the connectivity in its country. How can pursuing development of Roadways over railways help this country achieve this objective?** Competency Based

Ans. Roadways have an edge over the railways in India in the following ways

- Construction cost of roads is much lower than railway lines.
- Roads can be constructed easily in hilly terrains and undulating topography than railways.
- Roadways act as a feeder to other modes of transport, as they provide a link between railway stations, air and sea ports.
- Road transport is economical in transportation of few persons and relatively smaller amount of goods over short distances.
- Road transport provides door-to-door service thus, the cost of loading and unloading is much lower.

2. Classify the roads according to their capacity and describe the role of each. CBSE 2012

Ans. In India, roads are classified in six lanes according to their capacity as given below

(i) **Golden Quadrilateral Super Highways** This super highway links India's four largest metropolitan cities, i.e. Delhi-Kolkata- Chennai-Mumbai and Delhi.

North-South and East-West corridor are part of this highway. These highways reduce time and distance between mega cities.

(ii) **National Highways** These are the main road systems that link extreme parts of the country.

(iii) **State Highways** These roads link a state capital with its district headquaters. These are constructed and maintained by State Public Works Department.

(iv) **District Roads** These roads connect the district headquaters with other places of the district.

(v) **Rural Roads** These roads, also known as other roads, link rural areas and villages with towns.

(vi) **Border Roads** These roads are constructed along the international border of India by Border Road Organisation. It has improved accessibility in areas of difficult terrain.

3. "The distribution pattern of the railway network in India has been mainly influenced by physiographic and economic factors." Support the statement with suitable examples." CBSE 2017

Or **How do physiographic and economic factors influence the distribution pattern of the railway network in our country? Explain with examples.**

Or **Analyse the physiographic and economic factors that have influenced the distribution pattern of the railway network in our country.** CBSE 2015

Ans. Following are some physiographic factors that affect the distribution of railways network in our country

- The Northern Plains with their vast levelled land, high population density and rich agricultural resources provided the most favourable condition for growth of railways, although crossing wide rivers posed some obstacles.
- In the hilly terrain of the peninsular region, railway tracks were laid through low hills, gaps or tunnels.

- The Himalayan mountain regions are unfavourable for the construction of railway lines due to high relief, undulating terrain and low traffic.
- It is difficult to lay railway tracks in the sandy plains of Western Rajasthan, swamps of Gujarat and forested areas of states in Central India. e.g. Madhya Pradesh, Chhattisgarh, Odisha and Jharkhand.

Given below are some economic factors that affect the distribution patten of railways network in our country

- State funding plays a vital role in the development of railways across the nations.
- The state with flexible laws supports the growth of railways.
- The places that are highly industrialised attract the development of railways.

4. Explain any five importance of railways as a means of transport. **CBSE 2019**

Ans. The five importance of Indian railways as a means of transport are described below

(i) Railways are considered as the principal mode of transportation for freight and passengers in India.

(ii) Railways help to conduct various activities, like, business, sightseeing, pilgrimage, transportation of goods over long distances, etc.

(iii) Railways bind the economic life of our country by accelerating the development of the industry and agriculture.

(iv) The Indian railways have a huge network, connecting almost every corner of our country.

(v) The Indian railways is the largest public sector undertaking in the country which is the biggest employer in India.

5. Classify any five ports of India according to their types and main purpose.

Ans. The five ports of India according to their types and main purpose are given below

(i) Chennai Port (Tamil Nadu)

- **Type of Port** It is one of the oldest artificial ports in India.
- **Purpose** Trade and cargo

(ii) Haldia Port (West Bengal)

- **Type of Port** It is a subsidiary port of Kolkata port.
- **Purpose** It was developed to relieve pressure on Kolkata port.

(iii) Jawaharlal Nehru Port (Maharashtra)

- **Type of Port** It is specialised in handling container shipments.
- **Purpose** Made for decongesting Mumbai port and serve as a hub for the region.

(iv) Kandla Port (Gujarat)

- **Type of Port** It is a tidal port.
- **Purpose** Developed after independence to ease the volume of trade on Mumbai port.

(v) Kochchi Port (Kerala)

- **Type of Port** It is a natural port located at the entrance of a lagoon.
- **Purpose** Specialised in handling container shipments.

6. What is the difference between personal communication and mass communication? State any two points of importance of mass communication.

Ans. The differences between personal communication and mass communication are

Personal Communication	Mass Communication
Personal communication is a process of transferring or transmitting message between two people.	Mass communication is a process of transferring or transmitting a message to a large group of people.
This can be a verbal or telephonic conversation, a letter, an e-mail or an SMS.	Usually the 'media' is called the means of mass communication, which includes newspapers, television and radio channels, internet, etc.

The importance of mass communication can be seen through the following points

(i) Mass communication provides entertainment and information to people at their homes efficiently and quickly.

(ii) It creates awareness among people about various national programmes and policies.

7. Describe any five points of importance of mass communication. **CBSE 2013**

Or **Write any three importance of means of mass communication.** **CBSE 2013**

Ans. The importance of mass communication are

(i) Mass communication is required to spread the flow of information upto the grassroot level. Therefore, government has made special provision to extend 24 hours STD facility to every village in the country.

(ii) All India Radio (Akashwani) broadcasts a variety of programmes in national, regional and local languages for various categories of people spread over different parts of the country.

(iii) Doordarshan broadcasts a variety of programmes for entertainment, educational programmes to sports, etc for people of different age groups.

(iv) India publishes a large number of newspapers and periodicals annually for providing information.

(v) India is the largest producer of feature films in the world. It produces short films, video feature films and video short films for entertainment.

8. "International trade is considered the economic barometer of a country." Justify the statement with arguments. **CBSE 2019**

Ans. International trade is considered the economic barometer of a country. This statement can be justified through the following arguments

- As the resources are limited, no country can survive without international trade.
- Goods or resources possessed by one country are required by other and vice-versa. These differences create conditions for international trade.
- Foreign trade has helped India to improve its productivity of manufactured goods. International trade contributes to India's economic growth, raising income levels of people.
- In recent years, exchange of information and knowledge has benefitted in greater exchange of goods across states and countries.
- India has emerged as a software giant at the international level and it is earning large foreign exchange through the export of information technology.

9. Read the information given below regarding Delhi-Dehradun Expressway and answer the question that follows. **CBSE Additional SQP 2023-24**

The Delhi-Dehradun Expressway is all set to open to the public by the end of 2023. It would reduce the travel time between the two cities from 6 to 2 hours. The 210 km long expressway will start from North-East Delhi and pass through Baghpat, Shamli, Muzaffarnagar, Saharanpur and Dehradun. The last 20km stretch will pass through the eco-sensitive zone of Rajaji National Park, where Asia's longest elevated wildlife corridor of six-lanes and 12 km will be constructed that includes the 340 m Dat Kaali tunnel. The 340 m long tunnel near Dat Kaali temple, Dehradun will help reduce the impact on wildlife and multiple animal passes have been provided in the Ganeshpur-Dehradun section for avoiding animal-vehicle collisions.

Analyse the development of the Delhi-Dehradun Expressway in terms of its impact - negative and/ positive - on economic growth and environment. Suggest some measures to deal with negative impacts of the project.

Ans. The impact of the Delhi-Dehradun Expressway on economic growth, the environment and the goal of sustainable development are as follows

Economic Growth

- It will reduce travel time which will boost trade and tourism and can lead to greater investment in the valley.
- The construction itself will lead to the generation of employment opportunities.

Environment and Sustainable Development

- Passage of this expressway through an eco-sensitive zone will lead to loss of flora and fauna in the region.
- Increased vehicular emissions will lead to increased pollution.
- Following measures can be taken to deal with negative impacts of the projects.
- Wildlife corridors can be build to protect habitat for animals.
- Adopting green construction methods could solve the problem of pollution.
- By ensuring more greenry of habitat to wildlife Delhi-Dehradun Expressway plays a key role in achieving the goal of sustainable development.

10. As per Britannica Dictionary, when the world is seen as a community in which people are connected by computers, television, etc., and all depend on one another, the world becomes a 'global village'.

Accordingly, elaborate on the role of air transport in making the world a 'global village'. **CBSE Additional SQP 2023-24**

Ans. Global village is a term used for the world seen as a community in which people are connected through computers, television, etc., and all depend on one another. The role of air transport in making the world a 'global village' are as follows

- **Accessibility** Air transport has significantly improved accessibility to distant locations, making it a convenient mode of travel in cases where other means of transportation are impractical.
- **Facilitating International Trade** Supply chains have been revolutionised by the quick movement of cargo by air, enabling companies to easily access international markets. Now, time sensitive shipments, high-value commodities and perishable goods can all be delivered quickly, which has boosted global trade.
- **Advancing Business and Diplomacy** Face-to-face meetings, conferences and negotiations between individuals and representatives from different nations are now more feasible, fostering collaboration and cooperation.
- **Boosting Tourism** People from different countries can now explore new destinations, experience diverse cultures, and build connections with individuals from around the world.

Case Based Questions

1. Read the source given below and answer the questions that follow.

India has trade relations with all the major trading blocks and all geographical regions of the world. The commodities exported from India to other countries include gems and jewellery, chemicals and related products, agriculture and allied products, etc. The commodities imported to India include petroleum crude and products, gems and jewellery, chemicals and related products, base metals, electronic items, machinery, agriculture and allied products. India has emerged as a software giant at the international level and it is earning large foreign exchange through the export of Information Technology.

(i) What are the key sectors contributing to India's foreign exchange earnings?

Ans. The sectors contributing to India's foreign exchange earnings are information technology, gems and jewellery, chemicals, and agriculture-and allied products.

(ii) How has India established itself internationally in terms of the software industry?

Ans. India has emerged as a software giant at the international level, earning significant foreign exchange through the export of information technology.

(iii) What are some of the major commodities that India imports?

Ans. Some of the major commodities that India imports are petroleum crude and products, gems and jewellery, chemicals, base metals, electronic items, machinery and agriculture and allied products.

2. Read the sources given below and answer the questions that follow.

Source A Golden Quadrilateral Super Highways

The government has launched a major road development project linking Delhi–Kolkata–Chennai–Mumbai and Delhi by six-lane Super Highways. The North–South corridors linking Srinagar (Jammu and Kashmir) and Kanniyakumari (Tamil Nadu), and East-West Corridor connecting Silchar (Assam) and Porbander (Gujarat) are part of this project. The major objective of these Super Highways is to reduce the time and distance between the mega cities of India. These highway projects are being implemented by the National Highway Authority of India (NHAI).

(i) To what extent do you agree that Golden Quadrilateral Super Highways are important for our country? Give only one aspect.

Source B National Highways

National Highways link extreme parts of the country. These are the main road systems and are laid and maintained by the Central Public Works Department (CPWD). A number of major National Highways run in North-South and East-West directions. The historical Sher-Shah Suri Marg is called National Highway No. 1, between Delhi and Amritsar.

(ii) To what extent do you agree that India needs a number of National Highways? Give only one reason.

Source C State Highways

Roads linking a state capital with different district headquarters are known as State Highways. These roads are constructed and maintained by the State Public Works Department (PWD) in state and union territories.

(iii) Evaluate the importance of the State Highways.

Ans. (i) I agree with that Golden Quadrilateral Super Highways are important for our country because these highways reduce time and distance between mega cities of India.

(ii) I agree with that India needs a number of National Highways because India is a vast country and National Highways link extreme parts of the country with each other.

(iii) The importance of the State highways are as follows

- State Highways are constructed within a state which provide better connectivity of roads and places.
- These highways link a state capital with different district headquarters.

3. Read the source given below and answer the questions that follow. **CBSE Term II 2022**

Lifelines of National Economy

For a long time, trade and transport were restricted to a limited space. With the development in Science and Technology, the area of influence of trade and transport expanded far and wide. Today, the world has been converted into a large village with the help of efficient and fast moving transport. Transport has been able to achieve this with the help of equally developed communication system. Therefore, transport, communication and trade are complementary to each other.

Today, India is well-linked with the rest of the world despite its vast size, diversity and linguistic and socio-cultural plurality. Railways, airways, waterways, newspapers, radio, television, cinema and internet, etc. have been contributing to its socio-economic progress in many ways. The trades from local to international levels have added to the vitality of its economy. It has enriched our life and added substantially to growing amenities and facilities for the comforts of life.

(i) How is science an important factor in the development of transport ?

(ii) How has transport integrated socio-cultural plurality? Explain.

(iii) Analyse the significance of communication for a nation.

Ans. (i) Science and technology are an important factors in the development of transport as these technologies suit the needs of developing countries where reduced consumption, cheaper energy and cheaper transport techniques are important.

(ii) Transportation has integrated societies and various cultures. In ancient times, silk route was the main transportation channel. It connected China and other East Asian countries with Europe. Through silk route not only goods but also culture, arts and knowledge was shared or exchanged. People from different nations met at the silk road and tried to understand each other's language and culture.

(iii) Communication has a major role to play in the nation building. It has brought all regions in a nation close and all nations in the world closer. Without a well-developed communication infrastructure, no nation can assume an important position on the globe.

4. Read the source given below and answer the questions that follow. **CBSE SQP Term II 2021**

Ever since humans appeared on the earth, they have used different means of communication. But, the pace of change, has been rapid in modern times. Long distance communication is far easier without physical movement of the communicator or receiver. Personal communication and mass communication including television, radio, press, films, etc. are the major means of communication in the country. The Indian postal network is the largest in the world. It handles parcels as well as personal written communications. Cards and envelopes are considered first-class mail and are airlifted between stations covering both land and air. The second-class mail includes book packets, registered newspapers and periodicals.

They are carried by surface mail, covering land and water transport. To facilitate quick delivery of mails in large towns and cities, six mail channels have been introduced recently. They are called Rajdhani Channel, Metro Channel, Green Channel, Business Channel, Bulk Mail Channel and Periodical Channel.

(i) Examine the role of the Indian postal network.

(ii) Differentiate between mass communication and personal communication.

(iii) Analyse the significance of communication for a nation.

Ans. (i) The role of the Indian postal network is that it has helped the country to engage in communication and social-economic development. It provides various facilities like speed post, business post, registered post, ordinary post.

(ii) Mass Communication is the medium which provides entertainment as well as creates awareness among the masses. It includes radio, television, newspapers, magazines, books, films, etc whereas personal communication is between person to person.

(iii) The significance of communication for a nation are

- Various means of communication have connected the world closer.
- Communication is the source of entertainment and knowledge.

Map Based Questions

1. On the given political map of India, locate and label the following.

(i) Chennai (Meenam Bakkam) International Airport.

(ii) Tuticorin port **CBSE 2019**

(iii) Kolkata International Airport (Netaji Subhash Chandra Bose)

(iv) Mumbai (Chhatrapati Shivaji) International Airport.

(v) Marmagao port

Ans.

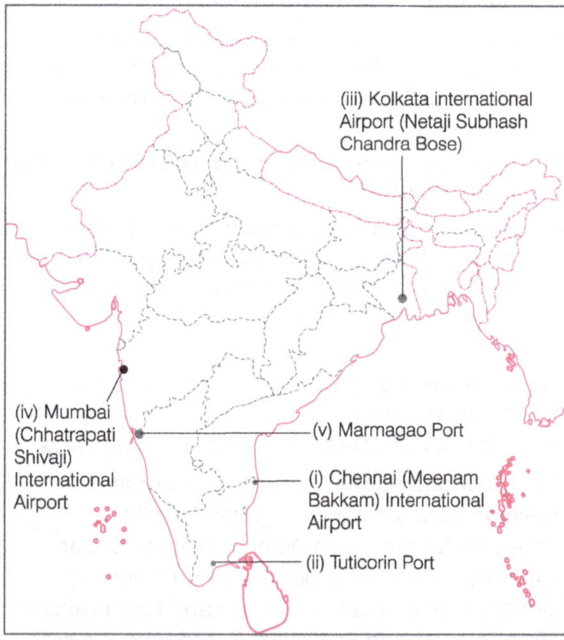

2. On the political map of India, locate, mark and label the following with appropriate symbols.

(i) Rajiv Gandhi International Airport

(ii) Visakhapatnam port

(iii) Indira Gandhi International Airport

(iv) Chennai port

(v) Raja Sansi International Airport/Sri Guru Ram Das Jee International Airport. **CBSE 2025, 2019, 2018**

Ans.

3. On the political map of India, locate and label the following features with appropriate symbols.

(i) Kandla Seaport **CBSE 2025, 2019**

(ii) Mumbai Seaport

(iii) New Mangalore Seaport

(iv) Kochchi Seaport **CBSE SQP 2022-23, CBSE 2019**

(v) Paradwip **CBSE 2019**

(vi) Haldia Seaport **CBSE 2024**

Ans.

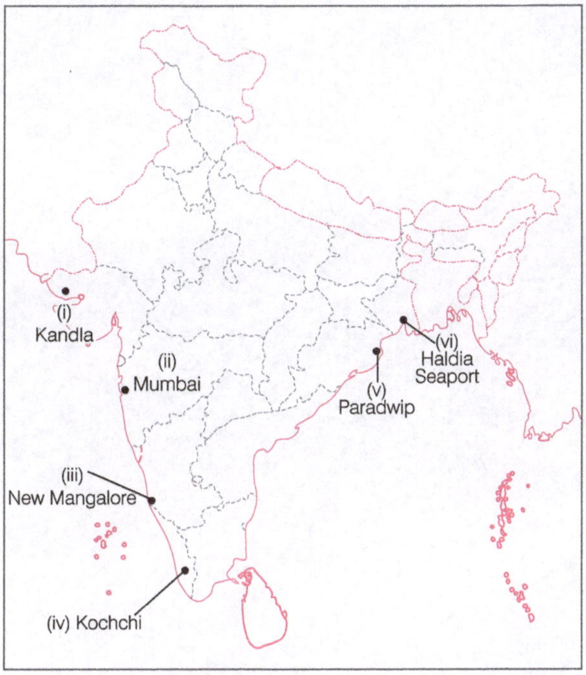

4. Find out the current railway zones and their headquarters. Also locate the headquarters of railway zones on the map of India. **NCERT**

Ans. As of March 2024, there are 19 railway zones in India. These were

SN	Name of Railway Zone	Headquarters
1.	Central Railway	Mumbai
2.	Eastern Railway	Kolkata
3.	Northern Railway	New Delhi
4.	North-Eastern Railway	Gorakhpur
5.	North-East Frontier Railway	Guwahati
6.	Southern Railway	Chennai
7.	South Central Railway	Secunderabad
8.	South-Eastern Railway	Kolkata
9.	Western Railway	Mumbai
10.	East-Central Railway	Hajipur
11.	East Coast Railway	Bhubaneswar
12.	North-Central Railway	Allahabad (Prayagraj)
13.	North-Western Railway	Jaipur
14.	South-East Central Railway	Bilaspur
15.	South-Western Railway	Hubballi
16.	West-Central Railway	Jabalpur
17.	Konkan Railway	Navi Mumbai
18.	South Coast Railway	Visakhapatnam
19.	Metro Railway	Kolkata

ASSESSMENT EXERCISE

Multiple Choice Questions (MCQs)

1. Which of the following is the largest public sector undertaking in the country?
(a) Airways (b) Roadways
(c) Waterways (d) Railways

2. The trade between two countries is called
(a) International trade
(b) National trade
(c) Community trade
(d) None of the above

3. What type of trade is carried in cities, towns and villages?
(a) State level trade
(b) Local trade
(c) District level trade
(d) None of the above

4. Which organisation among the following built the world's longest highway tunnel 'Atal-Tunnel'?
(a) BSF (Border Security Force)
(b) BRO (Border Road Organisation)
(c) Indian Army
(d) NHAI (National Highways Anthority of India)

5. In which year the first train steamed off from Mumbai to Thane?
(a) 1850 (b) 1853 (c) 1863 (d) 1873

Subjective Questions (VSA, SA & LA)

1. Which is the Northernmost terminal of North-South Corridor?

2. How will you define riverine port?

3. What is the length of coast line of India?

4. Which is the riverine port on the Eastern coast of India?

5. Where are railways developed in hilly areas and why? Trace their history in the colonial period.

6. Why are border roads important for us?

7. Explain why road transport still needs to be developed in India. What are the priority areas?

8. What is the importance of railway transport? Describe any three major problems faced by Indian railways.

9. Describe any four features of Indian tourism as a trade.

10. What is the importance of waterways in India?

CHAPTER 1

Power Sharing

Power sharing among the three organs of the government viz., **Legislature, Executive** and **Judiciary** is very important for the proper functioning of the democracy. In this chapter, the forms of power sharing in Belgium and Sri Lanka, the needs of power sharing and how to handle power sharing in democracies have been discussed.

1.1 Belgium

Belgium is a small country in Europe. It is smaller in area than the state of Haryana. It has borders with the Netherlands, France, Germany and Luxembourg.

Belgium's **Ethnic**[1] composition is very complicated. Out of the total population of the country, 59% live in the **Flemish**[2] region and speak Dutch language. Other 40% people live in the Wallonia region and speak French. The remaining 1 % of the Beligans speak German.

The capital city of Belgium is **Brussels**, where 80% people speak French, while 20% people speak Dutch language.

The minority French speaking community was relatively rich and powerful in Belgium. This was disliked by the Dutch-speaking community as they got the benefit of economic development and education much later.

This led to tensions between Dutch and French-speaking communities during the 1950s and 1960s. The tension was more serious in Brussels as the Dutch-speaking people were a majority in the country, but a minority in the capital.

Accommodation in Belgium

The Belgian leaders recognised the existence of regional differences and cultural diversities in the country. Thus, they amended the Constitution of Belgium four times between 1970 and 1993. The arrangement that they created was very innovative and different from other countries in the world.

Some of the elements of the Belgian model are given below

- The Constitution recommended that the number of Dutch and French-speaking ministers shall be equal in the Central Government. Some special laws are require to support the majority of members from each linguistic group. Thus, no single community can make decisions **unilaterally**[3].
- The State Governments are not subordinate (inferior) to the Central Government. Many powers of the Central Government have been given to the State Governments of the regions of French-speaking community and the Dutch-speaking community of the country.
- Brussels has a separate government, in which both the Dutch and French-speaking communities have equal representation. The French-speaking people accepted equal representation in Brussels because the Dutch-speaking community has accepted equal representation in the Central Government.
- A third kind of government i.e. the community government is elected by people belonging to one language community such as Dutch, French and German, no matter in which part of the country they live. The government has the power regarding cultural education and language related matters.

Belgium model was very complicated, even for the people living in Belgium, but it helped to avoid the conflict between the major communities and a possible division of the country on linguistic basis. Thus, Brussels was chosen as the headquarters of European Union when it was was formed.

1 **Ethnic** It refers to a social division based on shared culture.
2 **Flemish** It is the Dutch-speaking Northern region of Belgium.
3 **Unilaterally** It means decisions taken without the agreement of other people.

1.2 Sri Lanka

Sri Lanka is an island nation in the Indian ocean. It is just a few kilometres off the Southern coast of Tamil Nadu.

Sri Lanka has a diverse population of about 2 crore people with 74% Sinhala speakers and 18% Tamil speakers.

Most of Sinhala speaking people are Buddhists, while most of the Tamils are Hindus or Muslims. There are about 7% Christian, who are both Tamil and Sinhala.

There are two subgroups among Tamils as follows

(i) **Sri Lankan Tamils** They are the Tamil natives of Sri Lanka. They constitute 13% of the population and are concentrated in the North and East of Sri Lanka.

(ii) **Indian Tamils** They are rest of the Tamils other than Sri Lankan Tamils whose forefathers came from India as plantation workers during colonial periods.

Majoritarianism in Sri Lanka

Majoritarianism refers to a belief that the majority community should be able to rule a country in any way it wants, by disregarding the wishes and needs of the minority.

When Sri Lanka became independent in 1948, the leaders of the Sinhala community established dominance over government by their majority. As a result, the government adopted a series of majoritarian measures to establish Sinhala supremacy. These were

- In 1956, an Act was passed to recognise Sinhala as the only official language, disregarding the Tamil language.
- The government implemented policies that gave preference to Sinhala applicants per university positions and government jobs.
- A new Constitution specified that the state shall protect and promote Buddhism.

All these government measures gradually increased the feeling of isolation among Sri Lankan Tamils. They felt that no major political parties, led by the Buddhist Sinhala leaders, were sensitive to their language and culture.

They felt that the Constitution and government policies denied their equal political rights, discriminated against them in getting jobs and other opportunities, and ignored their interests.

As a result, the relation between the Sinhala and Tamil communities became tensed over time.

Struggles of Sri Lankan Tamils

The Sri Lankan Tamils launched parties and struggles for the recognition of Tamil as an official language.

They demanded regional autonomy and equality of opportunity in securing education and jobs, but their demand was repeatedly denied.

By the 1980s, several political organisations were formed demanding an independent **Tamil Eelam** (state) in Northern and Eastern parts of Sri Lanka.

The conflict between the two communities soon turned into a **Civil War**[4]. As a result, many people of both the communities were killed. Many families were forced to leave the country as refugees and many people lost their livelihood.

It also caused great impact on the social, cultural and economic life of the country. This Civil War ended in 2009.

Conclusion Derived from the Cases of Belgium and Sri Lanka

Belgium and Sri Lanka both the countries are democracies, but they deal with the question of power sharing differently.

In Belgium, the leaders have realised that the unity of the country is possible only by respecting the feelings and interests of different communities and regions.

On the other hand, Sri Lanka shows us that if a majority community wants to force its dominance over others and refuses to share power, it can weaken the unity of the country.

Try These

1. **Which minority community is relatively rich and powerful in Belgium?**
2. **What type of government prevails in Belgium?**
3. **In which region does the Dutch constitute as a majority and minority?**
4. **This city was chosen as headquarters of European Union. Identify the city.**
5. **Name two sub-groups of Tamils residing in Sri Lanka.**

4 **Civil War** It refers to a violent conflict between opposing groups within a country that becomes so intense that it appears like a war.

1.3 Desirability of Power Sharing

There are two sets of reasons which reflect that the need of power sharing is desirable.

Prudential Reasons

The **prudential**[5] reasons emphasises that power sharing will bring out better outcomes. Power sharing is good because it helps to reduce the possibility of conflict between social groups. It is a good way to ensure the stability of political order, since social conflict mostly leads to violence and political instability.

The **tyranny**[6] of the majority is not only oppressive for the minority community, but sometimes it also creates problem for the majority class itself.

Moral Reasons

The moral reasons emphasises that the act of power sharing is valuable.

Power sharing is the very spirit of democracy. A democratic rule involves sharing power with those affected by its application and who have to live with its effects.

In a democracy people have the right to be consulted on how they should be governed.

Thus, a legitimate government is one where citizens become a part of the system through participation.

1.4 Forms of Power Sharing

In a democracy, people are the source of all political power. People rule themselves through institutions of self-government.

In a good democratic government, due importance is given to diverse groups that exist in a society. Everyone has a role in the shaping of public policies. So, in a democracy, political power should be distributed among as many citizens as possible.

In modern democracies, power sharing arrangements can take many forms. Some of the most common arrangements among these are

Horizontal Distribution of Power

Power is shared among different organs of government, such as the Legislature, Executive and Judiciary.

This arrangement is called **horizontal distribution of power** because it allows different organs of government, placed at the same level, to exercise different powers.

Such a separation of power ensures that none of the organs can exercise unlimited powers and each organ checks the others. This results in a balance of power among various institutions. This arrangement is called a system of **checks and balances.**

For example, the judges are appointed by the Executive, but they can check the functioning of Executive or laws made by the Legislatures.

Federal or Vertical Division of Power

Power can be shared among governments at different levels i.e. a general government for the entire country and governments at the provincial or regional level.

Such a general government for the entire country is usually called **Federal Government.** In India, it is referred to as the **Central** or **Union Government**.

The governments at the provincial or regional level are called by different names in different countries. In India we call them state governments.

There are many countries, where there are no provincial or State Governments.

However in countries like India, there are different levels of government and the constitution clearly lays down the powers of different levels of government. This arrangement is called **federal division of power**.

This principle is also followed at lower levels of government like the Municipality and Panchayat. This arrangement is also found in Belgium. It is also known as **vertical division of power** as the power involves higher and lower levels of government.

Power Sharing among Social Groups

Power may also be shared among different social groups such as the religious and linguistic groups. **Community Government** in Belgium is a good example of this arrangement.

In some countries, there are constitutional and legal arrangements by which socially weaker sections and women are represented in the legislatures and administration. This method is used to give minority communities a fair share in power.

---

5 **Prudential** Based on prudence, or on careful calculation of gains and losses. Prudential decisions are usually contrasted with decisions based purely on moral considerations.

6 **Tyranny** It refers to oppressive or cruel rule by use of power or excessive control.

Power Sharing among Political Parties, Pressure Groups and Movements

Power sharing arrangements can also be seen in the way political parties, pressure groups and movements control or influence those in power.

In a democracy, the citizens must have freedom to choose among various contenders (competitors who stand in elections) of different political parties for power.

In modern democracies, this often takes form of competition among different parties. Such competition ensures that power does not remain in one hand.

In the long-run, power is shared among different political parties that represent different ideologies[7] and social groups.

Sometimes, this kind of sharing can be direct, when two or more parties form an alliance to contest elections. If their alliance is elected, they form a **Coalition Government** and thus, share power.

In a democracy, there are different interest groups like traders, businessmen, industrialists, farmers and industrial workers. They also have a share in governmental power through participation in governmental committees or influencing the decision-making process.

Try These

1. **What is the arrangement called when power is divided among different level of government?**
2. **In which country we find vertical division of power?**
3. **Community government is found in this country. Identify the country.**
4. **Which government method is used to give minorities a fair share in power?**
5. **Which system of power sharing is also called system of checks and balances?**

7 **Ideologies** It means a set of opinions or beliefs of a group or an individual.

Mind Map

Struggles of Sri Lanka
- The Sri Lankan Tamils launched parties and struggles for the recognition of Tamil as an official language.
- By 1980s, several political organisations were formed, demanding an independent Tamil Eelam in Northern and Eastern parts of Sri Lanka.

Majoritarianism in Sri Lanka
- An act passed in 1956, recognised Sinhala as the only official language.
- A new Constitution specified that the state shall protect and promote Buddhism.

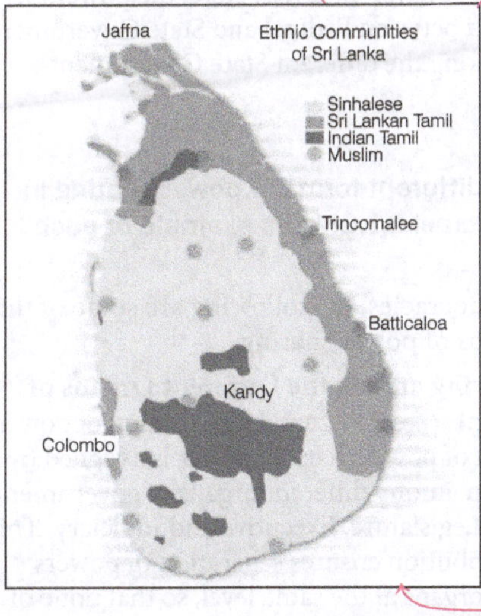

POWER SHARING

Desirability of Power Sharing

Prudential Reasons
- Emphasises that power sharing will bring out better outcomes.
- The tyranny of the majority is oppressive for minor community and creates problem for the majority class.

Moral Reasons
- Emphasises that the act of power sharing is valuable.
- A legitimate government is one where citizens become a part of the system through participation.

Belgium
The capital city of Belgium is Brussels, where 80% people speak French, while 20% speak Dutch language.

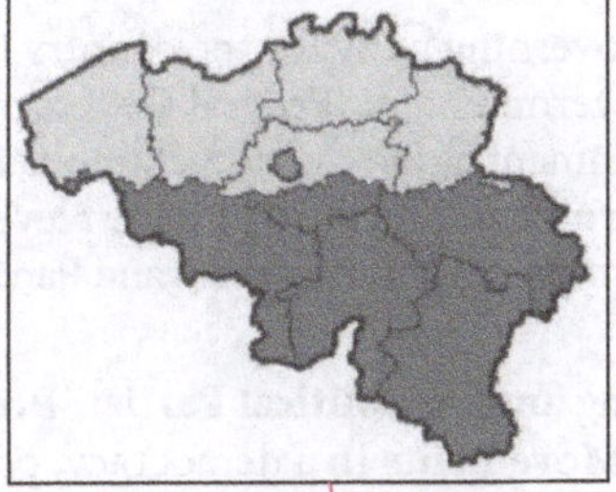

Accommodation in Belgium
- The Constitution recommended that the number of Dutch and French speaking ministers shall be equal in the Central Government.
- The State Governments are not inferior to the Central Government.

Forms of Power Sharing

Horizontal Distribution of Power
Power is shared among different organs of the government.

Federal or Vertical Division of Power
Power can be shared among the governments at different levels.

Power Sharing among Social Groups
Power is shared among different social groups such as the religious and linguistic groups.

Power Sharing among Political Parties and Pressure Groups
Power is shared among different political parties that represent different ideologies and social groups.

NCERT FOLDER

Covering Intext Questions and Exercises of NCERT

INTEXT QUESTIONS

Q.1 Sharing of power makes people more powerful. Give reasons.

Ans. Power sharing make people more powerful because of the following reasons

- Power sharing helps to reduce the possibility of conflict between different social groups.
- Power sharing helps to ensure the stability of political order.
- The absence of power sharing results into imposition of will by majority community over other. In the short run, it appears attractive, but in the long-run, it undermines the unity of the nation.
- Power sharing is the spirit of democracy. People have a right to be consulted on how they are to be governed.

Q.2 Here are some examples of power sharing. Which of the four types of power sharing do these represent? Who is sharing power with whom?

(i) The Bombay High Court ordered the Maharashtra State Government to immediately take action and improve living conditions for the 2,000-odd children at seven children's homes in Mumbai.

(ii) The Government of Ontario state in Canada has agreed to a land claim settlement with the aboriginal community.

The Minister responsible for Native Affairs announced that the government will work with aboriginal people in a spirit of mutual respect and cooperation.

(iii) Russia's two influential political parties, the Union of Right Forces and the Liberal Yabloko Movement, agreed to unite their organisations into a strong right-wing coalition. They propose to have a common list of candidates in the next Parliamentary elections.

(iv) The Finance Ministers of various states in Nigeria got together and demanded that the Federal Government declare its sources of income. They also wanted to know the formula by which the revenue is distributed to various State Governments.

Ans. (i) This is an example of power sharing among different organs of the government. Here, the power is shared between the Judiciary and the Executive.

(ii) This is an example of power sharing among different social groups. Here, the power is shared between the aboriginals and other social groups.

(iii) This is an example of power sharing arrangement between political parties, pressure groups and different organisations.

(iv) This is an example of power sharing among the government at different levels. Here, the power is being shared between Federal and State Governments and also among the different State Governments.

EXERCISE

Q.3 What are the different forms of power sharing in modern democracies? Give an example of each of these.

Ans. In modern democracies, the following are some of the important forms of power sharing

(i) **Power Sharing among the Different Organs of Government** (i.e. Horizontal distribution of power) In this form of power sharing, power is assigned by the Constitution among different organs of government such as the Legislature, Executive and Judiciary. This type of distribution ensures separation of powers among the organs at the same level, so that none of the organs can exercise unlimited power. Each organ puts a check on the others in order to maintain balance of power under the system of checks and balances.

(ii) **Power Sharing among Governments at Different Levels** (i.e. Vertical distribution of power sharing) In this form of power sharing, power is shared at the different levels of government.

The overall governing body for the country is known as 'Union Government' or 'Federal Government' and the government at the Constituent units is known as State Government. The third or lowest level is Local Government, e.g. Municipalities and Panchayats in India.

(iii) **Power Sharing among Political Parties, Pressure Groups and Movements** In a democracy, power is shared among different political parties that represent different ideologies and social groups. Sometimes, this kind of sharing can be direct, when two or more parties form an alliance to contest elections. If their alliance is elected, they form a Coalition Government and thus share power. An example is the NDA government in India, which is a Coalition government.

In a democracy, various pressure groups and movements have an indirect share in government power, either through participation in government committees or bringing influence on the decision-making process.

(iv) **Power Sharing Among Different Social Groups** In a democracy, especially, in multi-ethnic society, power is also shared among social groups such as religious and linguistic groups. 'Community government' in Belgium is a good example of this arrangement.

Q.4 State one prudential reason and one moral reason for power sharing with an example from the Indian context.

Or **Explain the two main reasons why power sharing is important in a democracy.**

Ans. The prudential reason for power sharing helps to reduce the possibility of conflict between social groups. An example is the reservation of constituencies for SC, ST and other minorities in India. In this way, the power sharing tries to reduce the possibility of conflicts.

Moral reason for power sharing is based on moral considerations. An example of power sharing for a moral reason is decentralisation of powers in India through formation of local, state and central governments operating at different levels. Here power is morally shared between different governments.

Q.5 After reading this chapter, three students drew different conclusions. Which of these do you agree with and why? Give your reasons in about 50 words.

(i) **Thommam** Power sharing is necessary only in societies which have religious, linguistic or ethnic divisions.

(ii) **Mathayi** Power sharing is suited only for big countries that have regional divisions.

(iii) **Ouseph** Every society needs some form of power sharing, even if it is small or does not have social divisions.

Ans. We agree with Ouseph because every society needs power sharing, even if it is small or does not have social divisions. A democratic system of government ensures that the citizens acquire a stake in the system by active participation. It prevents conflict between different groups in society while promoting belongingness. It helps to maintain a balance of power among various institutions and helps check how this power is exercised.

People will be more satisfied when they have a say in the functioning and decision-making process in the system. Power sharing is an essential element of a democratic form of Government.

Q.6 The Mayor of Merchtem, a town near Brussels in Belgium, has defended a ban on speaking French in the town's schools. He said that the ban would help all Non-Dutch speakers integrate in this Flemish town. Do you think that this measure is in keeping with the spirit of Belgium's power sharing arrangements? Give your reasons in about 50 words.

Ans. No, the measure taken by the Mayor of Merchtem is not in keeping with the spirit of Belgium's power sharing arrangements.

As 59% of the population in the Flemish region speak Dutch language, the ban on speaking French in the town's schools would prevent French and Dutch speakers to mix with each other. It would also create feelings of distrust and suspicion. The ban ignores regional differences and cultural diversities.

It is against the spirit of accommodating every linguistic group and creating the right environment for everyone to live. In fact, it makes the ground for a civic problems and a possible division of the community on linguistic lines.

Q.7 Read the following passage and pick out any one of the prudential reasons for power sharing offered in this.

We need to give more power to the Panchayats to realise the dream of Mahatma Gandhi and the hopes of the makers of our Constitution. Panchayati Raj establishes true democracy. It restores power to the only place where power belongs in a democracy– in the hands of the people. Giving power to Panchayats is also a way to reduce corruption and increase administrative efficiency. When people participate in the planning and implementation of developmental schemes, they would naturally exercise greater control over these schemes.

This would eliminate the corrupt middlemen. Thus, Panchayati Raj will strengthen the foundations of our democracy.

Ans. The prudential reason which is cited in the passage is that giving power to Panchayats is also a way to reduce corruption and increase administrative efficiency.

Q.8 Different arguments are usually put fourth in favour of and against power sharing. Identify those which are in favour of power sharing and select the answer using the codes given below. Power sharing

I. reduces conflict among different communities
II. decreases the possibility of arbitrariness
III. delays decision-making process
IV. accommodates diversities
V. increases instability and divisiveness
VI. promotes people's participation in government
VII. undermines the unity of a country

Codes

(a) I, II, IV, VI (b) I, III, V, VI
(c) I, II, IV, VII (d) II, III, IV, VII

Ans. (a) I, II, IV, VI

Q.9 Consider the following statements about power sharing arrangements in Belgium and Sri Lanka.

I. In Belgium, the Dutch-speaking majority people tried to impose their domination on the minority French-speaking community.

II. In Sri Lanka, the policies of the government sought to ensure the dominance of the Sinhala-speaking majority.

III. The Tamils in Sri Lanka demanded a federal arrangement of power sharing to protect their culture, language and equality of opportunity in education and jobs.

IV. The transformation of Belgium from unitary government to a federal one prevented a possible division of the country on linguistic lines.

Which of the statements given above are correct?

(a) I, II, III and IV (b) I, II and IV
(c) III and IV (d) II, III and IV

Ans. (d) II, III and IV

Q.10 Match List I (Forms of power sharing) with List II (Forms of government) and select the correct answer using the codes given below the lists.

List I	List II
A. Power shared among different organs of government	1. Community Government
B. Power shared among governments at different levels	2. Separation of powers
C. Power shared by different social groups	3. Coalition Government
D. Power shared by two or more political parties	4. Federal Government

Codes

	A	B	C	D		A	B	C	D
(a)	4	1	2	3	(b)	2	3	4	1
(c)	2	4	1	3	(d)	3	4	1	2

Ans. (c)

Q.11 Consider the following two statements on power sharing and select the answer using the codes given below.

I. Power sharing is good for democracy.

II. It helps to reduce the possibility of conflict between social groups.

Which of these statements is/are true and false?

(a) I is true, but II is false (b) Both I and II are true
(c) Both I and II are false (d) I is false, but II is true

Ans. (b) Both I and II are true

REVIEW EXERCISE

Including Competency Based Questions

Part I

Multiple Choice Questions (MCQs)

1. Which one of the following countries does not share its boundary with Belgium?

(a) France (b) Netherlands
(c) Sweden (d) Luxembourg

2. Which of the following is the capital city of Belgium?

(a) Bruges (b) Brussels (c) Ghent (d) Antwerp

3. Which of the following was the primary objective of Belgium to separate government in Brussels? CBSE 2024

(a) Promoting cultural events
(b) Managing international relations
(c) Enforcing legal laws
(d) Ensuring linguistic accomadation

4. Belgium solved its problem of majoritarianism by strengthening which of the following types of government?

(a) Unitary (b) Presidential
(c) Federal (d) Parliamentary

5. Which one of the following elements is not included in the Belgium model? CBSE Term I 2021

(a) Dutch and French speaking ministers shall be equal in the government.
(b) Many powers of the Central government have been given to State governments.
(c) Brussels has a separate government in which both the communities have equal representation.
(d) There is a community government which has special powers of administration.

6. Identify the primary objective of power sharing arrangements in Belgium from the following options. CBSE 2024

(a) Establishing a unitary form of government.
(b) Centralised political control of government.
(c) Establishing cultural and educational matters of Dutch.
(d) Accommodating linguistic and regional interest.

7. Sri Lanka is an island nation, just a few kilometres from the Southern coast of

(a) Goa (b) Kerala (c) Tamil Nadu (d) Lakshadweep

8. Which one of the following is a major caste group of Sri Lanka? CBSE 2020

(a) Christian and Tamil (b) Buddhist and Hindu
(c) Sinhali and Tamil (d) Sinhali and Christian

9. Which one of the following religions was protected and fostered by Sri Lanka in their Constitution?

(a) Christianity (b) Hinduism CBSE SQP 2022-23
(c) Buddhism (d) Islam

10. Which one of the following ethnic communities is in majority in Sri Lanka? CBSE Term I 2021

(a) Sri Lankan Tamils (b) Indian Tamils
(c) Muslims (d) Sinhalese

11. Which one of the following languages was declared as the official language of Sri Lanka by an Act passed in 1956? CBSE 2023

(a) Tamil (b) Sinhala (c) Hindi (d) English

12. Which one of the following countries adopted majoritarianism in their Constitution?

(a) Nepal (b) India
(c) Sri Lanka (d) Bangladesh

13. Find the incorrect option.

(a) Sri Lanka emerged as an independent country in 1958.
(b) Belgium has a population of a little over one crore, about half of the population of Haryana.
(c) Power sharing is a good way to ensure the stability of political order.
(d) In 1956, an Act was passed to recognise Sinhala as the only official language, thus disregarding Tamil.

14. Find the incorrect option.

(a) In Sri Lanka Tamil has two sub-groups, i.e. Srilankan Tamils and Indian Tamils.
(b) Most of the Sinhala speaking people are Hindus in Sri Lanka.
(c) There are 7% Christians in Sri Lanka.
(d) Sinhala was recognised as only official language in Sri Lanka.

15. Identify 'Horizontal power sharing' arrangements among the following in modern democ CBSE Term I 2021

(a) Different organs of government.
(b) Governments at different levels.
(c) Different social groups.
(d) Different parties, pressure groups and movements.

16. Although judges are appointed by executives, they can check functioning of executive. Executives are responsible to Parliament. Such kind of arrangement is called Competency Based

(a) Federal system
(b) System of checks and balances
(c) Presidential form of government
(d) Judicial system

17. Which of the following is not correct about prudential reason for power sharing?

(a) It helps to reduce the possibility of social conflict.
(b) It ensures stability of political order.
(c) In the short run, it is an attractive and good option but in the long-run, it undermines the unity of the ration.
(d) It will bring out better outcomes.

18. "In 2021, Myanmar Army, Tatmadaw, deposed democratically elected government in Myanmar ruled by National League for democracy."

Source : The Hindu Competency Based

What kind of impacts is possible as a outcome of such actions with respect to power sharing?

(a) Democracy will be enriched and power sharing will be ensured.
(b) It will ensure power sharing in the country.
(c) It will hamper power sharing as power has been snatched by army forcefully and concentrated into the Tatmadaw
(d) There will be no any kind of impact with respect to power sharing and democracy.

19. Arrange the following events in chronological order.

I. Sri Lanka got independence
II. End of Civil War in Sri Lanka
III. Demand of Tamil Eelam (State)
IV. Recognition of Sinhala as official language of Sri Lanka

Options

(a) I, II, III, IV (b) II, IV, I, III
(c) I, IV, III, II (d) IV, III, I, II

20. Read the following statements about power sharing arrangement Belgium and choose the correct option. CBSE 2024

I. Brussels has a separate government with equal representation.
II. Dutch and French speaking ministers are equal in Central Government.
III. Community Government is elected by people belonging to one language.
IV. Series of majoritarian measures adopted in Belgium.

Options

(a) I, II and IV (b) II, III and IV
(c) II, III and IV (d) I, II and III

21. Read the following measures and choose the correct option

Belgium took some measures to solve its problem.

I. Formation of community government.
II. Following majoritarian policy.
III. By providing equal representation of language groups.
IV. By providing additional powers to local governments.

Options

(a) Only I, II and III are correct.
(b) Only I, III and IV are correct.
(c) Only I, II and IV are correct.
(d) Only II, III and IV are correct.

22. Consider the following statements and choose the correct option. Competency Based

Statement I Majoritarianism is a belief, according to which a country should be ruled by Army.

Statement II Majoritarianism is a belief according to which majority community should be able to rule as per their will.

Options

(a) Statement I is correct and statement II is incorrect.
(b) Statement I is incorrect and statement II is correct.
(c) Both statements I and II are incorrect.
(d) Both statements I and II are correct.

23. Which of the following statements is/are correct about power sharing?

I. Power sharing is the spirit of democracy.
II. Horizontal power sharing is the only form of power sharing.
III. Power sharing is not good for a democratic rule.

Codes

(a) Only I (b) I and II (c) I and III (d) II and III

24. Identify the reasons, why power sharing is desirable in country like India.

I. India has got diversity with respect to language, religion-caste and gender.
II. India wants to be like Belgium.
III. People of India want Hindi to be declared as the official language of the country.
IV. Several minority groups live in India. To ensure their basic development, power sharing is desirable.

Options

(a) Only I (b) Only II (c) II and III (d) I and IV

25. Consider the following statements and choose the correct option.

Statement I Sri Lanka got independence in 1948. After getting Independence, a democratically elected government adopted on set of majoritarian policies in the country.

Statement II In 1908, Sri Lanka recognised Tamil as the only official language.

Options

(a) Statement I is correct and statement II is incorrect
(b) Statement I is incorrect and statement II is correct
(c) Both statements I and II are incorrect
(d) Both statements I and II are correct

26. Why do you think power is shared among different organs of government i.e. Executive, Legislature and Judiciary called horizontal distribution of power? What does it result in? CBSE Additional SQP 2023-24

(a) Because it allows different organs of government placed at the same level to exercise different powers. This results in a balance of power among various institutions.
(b) Because it allows different organs of government placed at the same level to exercise different powers. This results in an imbalance of power among various instituions.
(c) Because it allows different organs of government placed at the same level to exercise the same powers. This results in a balance of power among various institutions.
(d) Because it does not allow different organs of government placed at the same level to exercise different powers. This results in a balance of power among various institutions.

27. Which of the following statements accurately describes a "community government"? CBSE Additional SQP 2023-24

I. 'Community government' is elected by people belonging to one language community-Dutch, French and German-speaking-no matter where they live.
II. This government has the power regarding cultural, educational and language-related issues.
III. This government has the power regarding economical, educational and language-related issues.
IV. 'Community government' is elected by people belonging to one language community-Dutch, Spanish and German-speaking-no matter where they live.

Options

(a) Only I (b) Only III (c) Only IV (d) Both I and II

28. Which of the following statements accurately distinguishes between majoritarianism and power sharing? CBSE Additional SQP 2023-24

(a) Majoritarianism emphasises the dominance of the majority community, while power sharing emphasises the sharing of power among different groups.
(b) Majoritarianism emphasises the need for consensus building, while power sharing emphasises the exclusion of minority groups.

(c) Majoritarianism emphasises the importance of accommodating minority interests, while power sharing emphasises the need for majority rule.

(d) Majoritarianism emphasises the need for peaceful resolution of conflicts, while power sharing emphasises the use of force to impose the majority's will.

Answers

1. (c)	**2.** (b)	**3.** (d)	**4.** (c)	**5.** (d)
6. (d)	**7.** (c)	**8.** (c)	**9.** (c)	**10.** (d)
11. (b)	**12.** (c)	**13.** (a)	**14.** (b)	**15.** (a)
16. (b)	**17.** (c)	**18.** (c)	**19.** (c)	**20.** (d)
21. (b)	**22.** (b)	**23.** (a)	**24.** (d)	**25.** (a)
26. (a)	**27.** (d)	**28.** (a)		

Match the Following

1.

List I		List II	
A.	Sri Lanka got independence	1.	1956
B.	Act which declared Sinhala as the official language	2.	2009
C.	Civil war ended in Sri Lanka	3.	1948

Codes

	A	B	C		A	B	C
(a)	2	1	3	(b)	3	1	2
(c)	2	3	1	(d)	1	2	3

Ans. (b)

Assertion-Reason

1. Assertion (A) In Belgium, there is mutually acceptable arrangement for sharing power.

Reason (R) The leaders realised that the unity of the country is possible only by respecting the feelings and interests of different communities and regions.

Codes

(a) Both A and R are true and R is the correct explanation of A

(b) Both A and R are true, but R is not the correct explanation of A

(c) A is true, but R is false

(d) A is false, but R is true

2. Assertion (A) Power sharing is desirable.

Reason (R) Power sharing helps to reduce the possibility of conflicts between social groups.

Codes **CBSE Additional SQP 2023-24**

(a) Both A and R are true and R is the correct explanation of A

(b) Both A and R are true, but R is not the correct explanation of A

(c) A is true, but R is false

(d) A is false, but R is true

3. Assertion (A) Power sharing can help to prevent conflict in society. **CBSE Additional SQP 2023-24**

Reason (R) Power sharing ensures that different social groups are included in decision-making processes, reducing marginalisation and fostering inclusivity.

Codes

(a) Both A and R are true and R is the correct explanation of A

(b) Both A and R are true, but R is not the correct explanation of A

(c) A is true, but R is false

(d) A is false, but R is true

4. Assertion (A) Community government is elected by people belonging to one language community.

Reason (R) This government has the power regarding cultural, educational and language-related issue.

Codes

(a) Both A and R are true and R is the correct explanation of A

(b) Both A and R are true, but R is not the correct explanation of A

(c) A is true, but R is false

(d) A is false, but R is true

5. Assertion (A) There was civil war in Sri Lanka.

Reason (R) An Act was passed in 1956 to secure dominance of Sinhala community on the government.

Options **CBSE 2025**

(a) Both A and R are correct and R is the correct explanation of A.

(b) Both A and R are correct, but R is not the correct explanation of A.

(c) A is correct, but R is incorrect.

(d) A is incorrect, but R is correct.

6. Assertion (A) Division of power is good for democratic systems.

Reason (R) It helps to reduce the possibility of conflict between social groups. **CBSE 2024**

Codes

(a) Both A and R are true and R is the correct explanation of A.

(b) Both Both A and R are true and R is not the correct explanation of A.

(c) A is true, but R is false.

(d) A is false, but R is true.

Ans. 1. (a) Both A and R are true and R is the correct explanation of A

2. (a) Both A and R are true and R is the correct explanation of A

3. (a) Both A and R are true and R is the correct explanation of A

4. (a) Both A and R are true and R is the correct explanation of A

5. (b) Both A and R are true but R is not the correct explanation of A

6. (a) Both A and R are true and R is the correct explanation of A.

Picture Based Questions

1.

In 2005 election, in Germany, no party get clear majority to form government. Two major parties namely the "Christian Democratic Union" and "Social Democratic Party" came together to form government. They are historically rivals to each other.

What does the above picture depicts?

(a) Both parties are running government in the same direction.
(b) Government run by parties having different and opposite views and opinions.
(c) Government is being run very peacefully.
(d) Government is functioning with double strength.

2. Which among the following conclusions about democracy can be drawn from this cartoon?

(a) Democracy is like a horse-cart
(b) Concentration of power in few hands
(c) Putin and Bush are good friends
(d) None of the above

Ans. 1. (b) Government run by parties having different and opposite views and opinions.

2. (b) Concentration of power in few hands

Case Based Question

1. Read the passage given below and answer the questions that follow.

In India, we call them state governments. This system is not followed in all countries. There are many countries where there are no provincial or state governments. But in those countries like ours, where there are different levels of government, the Constitution clearly lays down the powers of different levels of government.

This is what they did in Belgium, but was refused in Sri Lanka. This is called federal division of power. The same principle can be extended to levels of government lower than the State government, such as the municipality and panchayat. Let us call division of powers involving higher and lower levels of government vertical division of power.

(i) What is the fundamental principle of democracy?

(a) Power belongs to a select few individuals
(b) People are the ultimate source of political power
(c) Power should be concentrated in the executive branch
(d) Power is determined by economic status

(ii) In a good democratic government, what is emphasised regarding diverse groups and views in society?

(a) Exclusion of diverse groups
(b) Disregard for different opinions
(c) Due respect and consideration for diverse groups and views
(d) Repression of dissenting voices

(iii) What is the basic principle of democracy concerning political power?

(a) Centralised decision-making
(b) Exclusion of public opinion
(c) Elitist governance
(d) Decentralised power-sharing

(iv) What is the implication of everyone having a voice in shaping public policies in a democracy?

(a) Limited participation in decision-making
(b) Concentration of power in the hands of a few
(c) Broad distribution of political power
(d) Exclusion of diverse perspectives

Ans (i) (b) People are the ultimate source of political power

(ii) (c) Due respect and consideration for diverse groups and views

(iii) (d) Decentralised power-sharing

(iv) (c) Broad distribution of political power

Part II

Very Short Answer Type Questions

1. Name any two countries with which Belgium has borders.

Ans. Belgium has borders with France and Luxembourg.

2. Which minority community is relatively rich and powerful in Belgium?

Ans. The French minority community is relatively rich and powerful in Belgium.

3. State any one step taken in Belgium to rule out the problem of regional differences and cultural diversities. **CBSE 2020**

Ans. Belgium introduced community government to rule out the problem of regional difference and cultural diversities. Community government is elected by all the people irrespective of their spoken languages.

4. Who elects the Community Government in Belgium?

Ans. People belonging to one particular language community like Dutch, French or German elect the Community Government in Belgium.

5. Which city was chosen as its headquarters when the European Union was formed?

Ans. When the European Union was formed, Brussels was chosen as its headquarters.

6. What was the name of the state proposed by the Sri Lankan Tamil?

Ans. The name of the state proposed by the Sri Lankan Tamil was Tamil Eelam.

7. Which major social group constituted the largest share in population of Sri Lanka?

Ans. Sinhalese constituted the largest share in population of Sri Lanka.

8. Name the two major ethnic communities of Sri Lanka.

Ans. The major ethnic communities of Sri Lanka are Sinhalese and Sri Lankan Tamils.

9. Which country do 'Indian Tamils' belong to?

Ans. 'Indian Tamils' belong to Sri Lanka.

10. In which year, did Sri Lanka achieve its independence?

Ans. Sri Lanka achieved its independence in 1948.

11. Why did the Sri Lankan Tamils feel alienated?

Ans. The Sri Lankan Tamil felt alienated due to discriminatory policies favouring the Sinhala majority.

12. Explain the meaning of majoritarianism as practiced in Sri Lanka.

Ans. Majoritarianism as practiced in Sri Lanka means a belief that the majority community should be able to rule a country in whichever way it wants, by disregarding the wishes and needs of the minority.

13. Why is power sharing desirable?

Ans. Power sharing is desirable because it helps to reduce the possibility of conflict between social groups. Therefore, it is strongly desired in a democracy.

14. Virat Iyer visited Sri Lanka in 1980s, where he witnessed social conflict among different communities. What was that conflict and what was its ultimate consequence? **Competency Based**

Ans. In 1956, Sri Lanka declared Sinhalese as the official language that set the majoritarianism in the country. This created conflict between Tamil and Sinhala speakers. The ultimate consequence of this linguistic conflict was civil war in Sri Lanka that ended in 2009.

Short Answer Type Questions

1. Describe the ethnic composition of Belgium.

Or **What is the complex ethnic composition of Belgium in terms of the percentage each language spoken there?**

Ans. The ethnic composition of Belgium is very complex. It is stated in the following points

- It has two main communities speaking Dutch and French languages. Of the country's total population, 59% lives in the Flemish region and speaks Dutch language.
- 40% people of Belgium live in the Wallonia region and speak French. Remaining 1% speak German.
- In the capital city Brussels, 80% people speak French while 20% are Dutch-speaking.
- The minority French-speaking people are more rich and powerful than the Dutch-speaking people.

2. Describe the tension that existed between the Dutch and the French-speaking people in Belgium.

Ans. In Belgium, the tension existed between the Dutch and French speaking people in the following ways

- The minority French-speaking community was relatively rich and powerful. This made the Dutch-speaking community angry who got the benefit of economic development and education much later.
- The social disparity between Dutch-speaking and French-speaking communities during the 1950s and 1960s led to tensions between them.
- The tension between the two communities was more acute in Brussels, the capital of Belgium, as the Dutch-speaking people constituted a majority in the country, but a minority in Brussels.

3. Describe the ethnic composition of Sri Lanka.

Ans. The ethnic composition of Sri Lanka can be described in the following ways

- The major social groups in Sri Lanka are the Sinhala speakers (74%) and the Tamil speakers (18%).
- Among Tamils there are two sub-groups. Sri Lankan Tamils or the Tamil natives of Sri Lanka (13%) and Indian Tamils (5%) whose forefather came from India as plantation workers during colonial period.
- Most of the Sinhala speakers are Buddhists. Most of the Tamils are either Hindus or Muslims.
- Christians are about 7%, who are both Tamil and Sinhala.

4. Highlight any three measures adopted by the Belgian Government to accommodate regional and cultural diversities.

Or Explain any three elements of Belgian model of accommodation.

Ans. To accommodate diverse regional and cultural diversities, Belgian Government adopted the following measures

(i) Constitution prescribes that the number of Dutch and French-speaking ministers shall be equal in the Central Government.

(ii) Many powers of the Central Government have been given to State Governments of the two regions of the country.

(iii) Brussels, the capital of Belgium, has a separate government in which both the communities have equal representation.

5. Power sharing is the very spirit of democracy. Support the statement by giving suitable arguments.

Ans. Power sharing is the very spirit of democracy because of the following reasons

- **Ensures Representation of All** In a democracy, power sharing allows diverse groups, such as different regions, communities, or social groups, to have a voice in governance.
- **Promotes Inclusivity and Fairness** When power is shared, it ensures that all citizens, regardless of their background or status, are included in the decision-making process.
- **Strengthens Legitimacy** A legitimate government is one where citizens are actively involved in decisions that affect their lives. Power sharing through participation makes people feel that they have a stake in the system, which strengthens the government's authority and legitimacy.

6. What were the Majoritarian measures taken in Sri Lanka to establish Sinhala supremacy?

Ans. Majoritarian measures taken in Sri Lanka to establish Sinhala Supremacy were

- In 1956, an Act was passed which recognised Sinhala as the only official language, thus disregarding Tamil language.
- Preferences were given to Sinhala applicants for university positions and government jobs, etc.
- The State aimed to promote Buddhism according to new Constitution. Sri Lankan Tamil felt that none of the major political parties led by Buddhist Sinhala leaders were sensitive to their language and culture.

7. Differentiate between horizontal and vertical division of powers.

Or How is horizontal power sharing different from vertical? Explain. CBSE 2024

Ans. The differences between horizontal and vertical divisions of powers are

Horizontal Division of Power	Vertical Division of Power
In this division of power sharing arrangement, power is shared among different organs of government such as Legislature, Executive and Judiciary.	In this division of power sharing arrangement, power is shared among governments at different levels like Union, State and local levels.
In this division, different organs of government exercise different powers. It is a concept of separation of power.	In this division, Constitution clearly lays down the power of the different levels of government.
It specifies the concept of checks and balances in order to check the unlimited powers of the different organs.	In this division, there is no concept of checks and balances because powers are clearly divided among higher and lower level.

8 Compare the situation of Belgium and Sri Lanka considering their location, size and cultural aspects.

Ans. The differences between Belgium and Sri Lanka considering their location, size and cultural aspects are

	Belgium	Sri Lanka
Location	Belgium is a small country in Europe which has borders with France, the Netherlands, Germany and Luxembourg.	Sri Lanka is an island nation, which is located at a few kilometres off the Southern coast of Tamil Nadu.
Size	It has a population of a little over one crore, about half the population of Haryana.	It has about two crore people, about the same as in Haryana.
Culture	In Belgium, the minority (40%) French speaking community was relatively rich and powerful, but the minority Dutch speaking (59%) community got the benefit of economic development and education.	In Sri Lanka, 74% are Sinhala speakers and 18% are Tamil speakers.

9. Evaluate the power sharing system in India.

Ans. Power sharing system in India can be described in the following ways

- In India power is shared among different organs of government, such as legislature, executive and judiciary. This separation of power ensures that none of the organs can exercise unlimited power.
- In India, power is shared among Union Government and State Government. Our constitution clearly lays down the powers of different levels of government. Under the State Government power is divided into municipality and panchayat.
- In India, there are reserved constituencies for both women and socially weaker sections, both in parliament and in assemblies.
- In India, different political parties, pressure group and movements control and influence the government.

10. Describe power sharing and its significance. How it is performed in India? Give example of power sharing in world context.

Ans. Distribution of power among various organs and at different level of government is called power sharing. The significance of power sharing can be explained through the following points

- Power sharing helps in resolving disputes in the societies by distributing power to various section.
- It helps in development of regional areas by giving them autonomy in various aspects such as economic, politics, administrative, etc.
- Power sharing helps in achieving aspiration of marginalised section by giving them voice.

Power sharing in India is performed in the following ways.

- **Vertical Power Sharing** It refers to power sharing among governments at different level such as Central government, State government and local government.
- **Horizontal Power Sharing** It refers to power sharing among different organs of the government such as Parliament, Executive and Judiciary.

Long Answer Type Questions

1. Describe any three demands of the Sri Lankan Tamils. How did they struggle for their demands?

Ans. The three demands of Sri Lankan Tamils were

(i) Recognition of Tamil as an official language

(ii) Provision of regional autonomy

(iii) Equality of opportunity in securing education and jobs

Sri Lankan Tamils struggle for their demands in the following ways

- They formed several political organisations to demand an independent Tamil Eelam (state) in Northern and Eastern parts of Sri Lanka.
- Sri Lankan Tamils launched several organisations to fight for their rights.
- When the demands were denied repeatedly, they took to violent means that started Civil War.

2. The law enacted in 1958 and other constitutional provisions led to major conflict between the two communities in Sri Lanka. Support the statement.

Ans. The statement that the law enacted in 1956 and other constitutional provisions led to major conflict between the two communities in Sri Lanka can be supported by the following

- **Sinhala as the official language** (1956 Act) In 1956, the Sinhala only Act was passed, making Sinhala the sole official language of Sri Lanka. This law marginalised the Tamil-speaking population, especially in the Northern and Eastern regions of the country, where Tamils were the majority. The Tamils felt discriminated against, as it restricted their access to government services, education, and employment, leading to tensions between the Sinhala and Tamil communities.
- **Constitutional provisions favoring the majority** The Sri Lankan constitution and other provisions favoured the Sinhala-speaking majority, which further alienated the Tamil minority. The Tamils, who had historically been in power and had distinct cultural and linguistic identity, felt sidelined by policies that promoted the dominance of the Sinhala community in government and other areas of public life.
- **Impact on ethnic relations** These discriminatory laws and provisions deepened the rift between the Sinhala and Tamil communities. The Tamils demanded equal rights and recognition of their language and culture, but the government's policies led to increased ethnic tensions. This eventually led to violent conflicts and civil unrest, with demands for Tamil autonomy and even a separate Tamil Eelam (nation).

3. Compare the ways in which the Belgium and the Sri Lankans have dealt with cultural diversity.

Ans. Belgium dealt with cultural diversity in the following ways

- Number of Dutch and French-speaking ministers were to be equal in the Central Government.
- Many powers of the Central Government were given to State Governments.
- The capital, Brussels has a separate government in which both the communities have equal representation.

- Community Government is elected by people belonging to one language community which deals with cultural, educational and language related issues.

On the other hand, Sri Lanka dealt with cultural diversity in the following ways

- Preferential policy was adopted that favoured Sinhala application for university position and government jobs.
- The state followed a policy of majoritarianism by protecting and fostering Buddhism.

4. "Both Belgium and Sri Lanka are democracies but they follow different systems of power sharing." Support the statement by giving three points of differences.

Ans. It is true that both Belgium and Sri Lanka are democracies but they follow different systems of power sharing. Belgium is a small country in Western Europe with complex ethnic composition. Of the country's total population, 59 per cent speak Dutch language. Another 40 per cent speak French. Remaining 1 per cent speak German.

Sri Lanka is an island nation in Indian Ocean where the major social groups are Sinhala speakers and the Tamil speakers.

The following three points of differences support the statement

(i) The Belgium Constitution provides that the number of Dutch and French-speaking ministers shall be equal in the Central Government. On the other hand, leaders of the Sinhala community in Sri Lanka dominated the governance and refused to power sharing of any kind.

(ii) In Belgium, the leaders have realised that the unity of the country is possible only by respecting the feelings of others. Thus, many powers of the Central Government of Belgium have been given to the State Government. On the other hand, in Sri Lanka, the democratically elected government adopted a series of Majoritarian measures to establish Sinhala supremacy thus ignoring the rights of minorities.

(iii) In Belgium, there is no discrimination between religions. On the other hand, Sri Lanka followed a path of racial and religious discrimination.

Case Based Questions

1. Read the source given below and answer the questions that follow. **CBSE 2024**

Panchayati Raj

"We need to give more power to the panchayats to realise the dream of Mahatma Gandhi and the hopes of the makers of our Constitution, Panchayati Raj establishes true democracy. It restores power to the only place where power belongs in a democracy - in the hands of the people. Giving power to Panchayats is also a way to reduce corruption and increase administrative efficiency. When people participate in the planning and implementation of developmental schemes, they would naturally exercise greater control over these schemes. This would eliminate the corrupt middlemen. Thus, Panchayati Raj will strengthen the foundations of our democracy."

(i) How does giving power to Panchayats relate to the vision of Mahatma Gandhi ?

(ii) Explain the primary objective of giving power to the Panchayats.

(iii) How does the establishment of Panchayati Raj contribute to democracy? Explain.

Ans. (i) According to Mahatma Gandhi, true democracy will be established when Panchayats are given the real power. This would restore power to the only place where power belongs in a democracy i.e. in the hands of the people.

(ii) The primary objective of giving power to the Panchayats is to increase participation of the people and give them real power.

(iii) The establishment of Panchayati Raj contributed to democracy by increasing people's participation in the planning and implementation of developmental schemes, thus giving them greater control over these schemes.It is also a way to reduce corruption and increase administrative efficiency.

2. Read the source given below and answer the questions that follow. **CBSE SQP 2022-23**

Power sharing arrangements can also be seen in the way political parties, pressure groups and movements control or influence those in power. In a democracy, the citizens must have freedom to choose among various contenders for power.

In contemporary democracies, this takes the form of competition among different parties.

Such competition ensures that power does not remain in one hand. In the long run, power is shared among different political parties that represent different ideologies and social groups. Sometimes this kind of sharing can be direct, when two or more parties form an alliance to contest elections. If their alliance is elected, they form a coalition government and thus share power. In a democracy, we find interest groups such as those of traders, businessmen, industrialists, farmers and industrial workers.

They also will have share in governmental power, either through participation in governmental committees or bringing influence on the decision-making process.

(i) **"Power sharing is an essential component of democracy." Give one example to prove the statement.**

(ii) **How is alliance of political party build an example of power sharing?**

(iii) **How political parties, pressure groups and movements help in controlling or influencing those who are in power?**

Ans. (i) Power sharing is an essential component of democracy because it helps in reducing the possibility of conflict between the social groups.

(ii) Two or more political parties form an alliance to contest elections or to form a government is called as sharing of power Alliance could be between regional and national parties which is an example of power sharing.

(iii) Political parties, pressure groups and movements help in controlling or influencing those who are in power by freedom of choice which entails competition among the different parties. Such competition ensures that power does not remain in one hand, but is shared among different political parties representing different ideologies and social groups.

3. Read the source given below and answer the questions that follow. **CBSE 2023**

Belgium is a small country in Europe, smaller in area than the state of Haryana. It has borders with France, the Netherlands, Germany and Luxembourg. It has a population of a little over one crore about half the population of Haryana. The ethnic composition of this small country is very complex. Of the country's total population 59 per cent live in the Flemish region and speak Dutch language. Another 41 per cent people live in the Wallonia region and speak French. Remaining one per cent of the Belgians speak German. In the capital city Brussels, 80 per cent of the people speak French while 20 per cent are Dutch-speaking.

(i) **Explain the ethnic composition of Belgium.**

(ii) **Explain the term ethnic.**

(iii) **How did the Belgium Government solve their ethnic problem? Explain.**

Ans (i) The ethnic composition of Belgium is complex 59% speak Dutch language, 40% speak French and remaining 1% speak German.

(ii) The term 'ethnic' implies a social division based on the shared culture. People belonging to the same ethnic group believe in their common descent because of the similarities of physical type or of culture or both. They do not need always to have the same religion or nationality.

(iii) The Belgium Government solve their ethnic problem in the following ways

- The Constitution states that the number of Dutch and French speaking ministers shall be equal in the Central Government. Thus, no single community can make decisions as per their own will.
- Brussels, the capital of Belgium, has a separate government in which both the communities have equal representation.

ASSESSMENT EXERCISE

Multiple Choice Questions (MCQs)

1. Majoritarianism was followed in which of the following countries?

(a) Belgium (b) Sri Lanka
(c) Russia (d) India

2. Which of the following was not a provision of the Act of 1956 passed in Sri Lanka?

(a) Buddhism was protected by the state.
(b) The only recognised official language was Sinhala.
(c) Sinhalas were favoured for government jobs.
(d) The provinces were given autonomy.

3. Which of the following language is not spoken in Belgium?

(a) Dutch (b) French
(c) Spanish (d) German

Subjective Questions (VSA, SA & LA)

1. What is a Civil War?

2. What is the percentage of Christian population in Sri Lanka?

3. How does a good democratic government ensure that everyone has a voice in the shaping of public polices?

4. What is the difference between prudential and moral reasons for power sharing?

5. What do you understand by the term power sharing? Explain.

6. Is Flemish language used in Belgium as a separate language? Why or why not?

7. What were the two main causes of resentment in Belgium in 1960? How was the conflict solved?

8. Why is power sharing desirable? Give any three prudential reasons.

9. Explain the importance of 'Democracy' in details.

10. What impact would lack of 'power sharing' have on the country?

11. What arrangements were worked out by the Belgium leaders in order to accommodate regional differences and cultural diversities?

CHAPTER 2

Federalism

Federalism is a system of government in which the power is divided between two or more levels of government. The Indian Constitution establishes a federal system with some unitary features. It is called as **quasi-federal system**, as it contains elements of both federal and unitary system.

2.1 Federalism

Federalism is a system of government in which the power is divided between a central authority and various constituent units of the country. A federation has two levels of government

(i) Government for the entire country that is usually responsible for a few subjects of common national interest.

(ii) Government at the level of provinces or states that look after day-to-day administration of their state.

Both these levels of governments enjoy their power independent of each other.

Key Features of Federalism

- There are two or more levels or tiers of government.
- Different tiers of government rule over same citizens but have their own jurisdiction[1] regarding legislation, taxation and administration.
- The jurisdiction of each level of government are mentioned in the Constitution. So, the **existence** and **authority** of each tier of government is constitutionally guaranteed.
- The changes in the fundamental provisions of the Constitution require the consent of both the levels of government.
- Courts have power to interpret the Constitution and the power of different levels of government. Thus, Supreme Court plays the role of an umpire if disputes arise between different levels of government in the exercise of their respective powers.
- Sources of revenue for each level of government are clearly mentioned to ensure its financial autonomy.
- The federal system has **dual objectives** *i.e.*, to safeguard and promote unity of the country it also accommodates regional diversity. An ideal federal system of government has both aspects mutual trust and agreement to live together.

Balance of Power between Central and State Government

The exact balance of power between the Central and the State Government varies from one federation to another.

Federations are formed in two ways

(i) **Coming Together Federations** In this type, states come together on their own to form a bigger unit and they have equal power and are equally strong *vis-a-vis* the Federal Government.

They come together to maintain sovereignty[2], identity and increase their security. USA, Switzerland and Australia are examples of coming together federations.

(ii) **Holding Together Federations** In this type, a large country decides to divide its power between the constituent states and the National Government.

India, Spain and Belgium are examples of holding together federations.

In this category, the Central Government has more powers than the State Government. The different units of the federations have unequal powers and some units are granted special powers.

1 Jurisdiction It refers to an area over which someone has legal authority. The area may be defined in terms of geographical boundaries or in terms of certain kinds of subjects.

2 Sovereignty It refers to the authority of a state to govern itself.

Federal System vs Unitary System

In a federal system, the Central Government cannot pass the order to the State Government to do something. The State Government has powers of its own for which it is not answerable to the Central Government.

Under the unitary system, either there is only one level of government or the sub-units are subordinate to the Central Government. The Central Government can pass an order to the provincial[3] or local governments. Both the federal and unitary system are separately answerable to the people.

2.2 India as a Federal Country

India had emerged as an independent nation after the partition. Soon after independence, several Princely States became the part of the country.

The Constitution declared India as a Union of States. The Indian Union is based on the principles of federalism, although the Constitution did not use the word federation.

The Constitution originally provided a two-tier system[4] of government which is as follows

(i) The Union Government or Central Government

(ii) The State Government

Later, a **third tier** of federalism was added in the Constitution in the form of Panchayats and Municipalities. The Constitution clearly provided a three-fold distribution of legislative powers between the Union Government and the State Government. It contains three lists

(i) **Union List** It includes **subjects of national importance** like defence, foreign affairs, banking, communications and currency as we need uniform policies on these matters throughout the country. The Union Government alone can make laws relating to the subjects mentioned in the Union list.

(ii) **State List** It contains **subjects of state and local importance** like police, trade, commerce, agriculture and irrigation. The State Government alone can make laws relating to the subjects mentioned in the State list.

(iii) **Concurrent List** It includes **subjects of common interest** to both the Union and the State Government like education, forest, trade unions, marriage, adoption and succession.

Both the Union and the State Government can make laws on these subjects. If their laws conflict with each other, the law made by the Union Government will prevail.

The subjects that do not fall in any of the three lists are known as **residuary subjects**. For example, computer software that came up after the Constitution was made. Union Government has the power to legislate on these subjects.

Special Provisions for States and Union Territories

In India, state like Assam, Nagaland, Arunachal Pradesh and Mizoram have special powers because of their unique history and culture.

Article 371 of the Indian Constitution give these states extra powers to protect the rights and culture of the indegenous people of these states.

For example, they can make their own rules about who can buy land or work for State Government. Similar special provisions also exists for some other states of India as well.

There are some units of the Indian Union which enjoy very little power. These are areas which are too small to become an independent state and could not be merged with any of the existing states. These areas, like Chandigarh, Lakshadweep, Delhi, are called **Union Territories**.

These territories do not have the powers of a state. The Central Government has special powers in administering these **areas**.

Power Sharing Between Union and State Government

The basic structure of the Constitution allows for power sharing between Union and State Government. The Parliament alone cannot make changes to this power sharing arrangement.

For any change, it has to be first passed by both the Houses of Parliament with at least two-third majority. Then, it has to be approved by the legislatures of at least half of the total states.

The judiciary plays an important role in supervising the implementation of Constitutional provisions and procedures.

In case of any dispute regarding the division of powers, the High Courts and the Supreme Court make a decision.

Both Union and State Governments have the power to raise resources by levying taxes in order to carry on the government and the responsibilities assigned to each of them.

---

3 **Provincial** It refers to a region connected with the parts of a country away from the capital city.

4 **Tier System** It is the system which signifies levels of government. It may be two levels (two-tiers) and three levels (three-tiers).

Try These

1. In federalism, different tiers of government have their own jurisdiction. Mention one area regarding which they have their own jurisdiction.
2. Name one subject of Concurrent list.
3. Which level of Government in India has the power to legislate on the residuary subjects?
4. What are areas called that are too small to become independent states and could not be merged with existing states?

2.3 Practise of Federalism in India

Constitutional provisions are necessary for the success of federalism, but these are not sufficient.

The real success of federalism in India can be attributed to the nature of democratic politics in our country.

To follow the true spirit of federalism, respect for diversity and desire for living together in harmony should become shared ideals in our country.

Linguistic States

The creation of linguistic states[5] was the first and a major test for democratic politics in our country.

In 1947, the boundaries of several old states were changed in order to create new states. This was done to ensure that the people who spoke the same language lived in the same state.

Some states were not created on the basis of language. They were recognised by differences based on culture, ethnicity and geography. These include states like **Nagaland, Uttarakhand** and **Jharkhand**.

Some national leaders resisted the demand of new states on the basis of language as they thought this would lead to the disintegration of the country. But later, the formation of linguistic states actually made the country more united and administration became easier.

Language Policy

The second test for the Indian federation is the language policy. The Indian Constitution did not give the status of national language to any of the languages.

Hindi was identified as the **official language** but it is mother tongue of only 40 per cent of Indians. The Central Government has not imposed Hindi on states where people speak a different language.

Besides Hindi, there are 21 other languages recognised as Scheduled Languages[6] by the Indian Constitution. In an examination conducted by Central Government, candidates may take the examination in any of these languages.

States too have their own official languages. The maximum work of the government takes place in the official language of that concerned state.

The use of English as official language was proposed to be stopped in 1965. However, many non-Hindi speaking states fear that this was the attempt to impose Hindi on them. So, they demanded to continue the use of English. In Tamil Nadu, this movement took a violent form.

So, Central Government withdrew the proposal and agreed to continue the use of English alongwith Hindi for official purposes.

Linguistic Diversity of India

Census of India, 2011 recorded more than 1300 distinct languages which people mentioned as their mother tongue. These languages were grouped together under some major languages, e.g. languages like Bhojpuri, Magadhi, Bundelkhandi, Chhattisgarhi, Rajasthani and many others were grouped together under 'Hindi'.

Even after this grouping, the Census found 121 major languages. Out of these, 22 languages are now included in the Eighth Schedule of the Indian Constitution and are therefore called **Scheduled Languages**. Others are called **Non-Scheduled Languages**

Scheduled Languages of India

Language	Proportion of Speakers (%)	Language	Proportion of Speakers (%)
Assamese	1.26	Manipuri	0.15
Bengali	8.03	Marathi	6.86
Bodo	0.12	Nepali	0.24
Dogri	0.21	Odia	3.10
Gujarati	4.58	Punjabi	2.74
Hindi	43.63	Sanskrit	N
Kannada	3.61	Santhali	0.61
Kashmiri	0.56	Sindhi	0.23
Konkani	0.19	Tamil	5.70
Maithili	1.12	Telugu	6.70
Malayalam	2.88	Urdu	4.19

Source : *http://www.censusindia.gov.in*

5 Linguistic States These are the states created on the basis of the languages people spoke.
6 Scheduled Languages 22 languages included in the Eighth Schedule of the Indian Constitution.

Centre-State Relations

Restructuring the Centre-State relations has also strengthened federalism in practice.

Indian Constitution has demarcated the powers of the Union and State Governments, but it depends to a large extent on how the ruling parties and leaders follow these arrangements.

The state government did not exercise their rights as **autonomous federal units**[7] when the same party ruled both at the centre and the states. But when different parties ruled centre and the states, the centre tried to undermine the power of the states.

In the past, many times, the Central Government misused the Constitution to dismiss the State Governments that were ruled by rival parties. This undermined the spirit of federalism.

The above scenario has changed after 1990. This was the beginning of the era of **Coalition Governments**[8] at the centre. Since no single party got a clear majority in the Lok Sabha, the major national parties had to enter into an alliance with many parties including several regional parties, to form a government at the centre. It led to a new culture of power sharing and respect for the autonomy of State Governments.

The culture was supported by a major judgement of the Supreme Court that made it difficult for the Central Government to dismiss state government without any reasons.

2.4 Decentralisation in India

India is a vast country and cannot be run only through a two-tier system. The states in India are as large as independent countries of Europe.

Federal power sharing in India needs another tier of government, below that of the State Governments, because some states like Uttar Pradesh, Maharashtra have huge population and they are internally very diverse.

Thus, there is a need for power sharing within each state. When power is taken away from Central and State Government and given to local government, it is called **decentralisation.**

The basic idea behind decentralisation is that there are a large number of problems and issues which are best settled at the local level.

Local Government

The idea of decentralisation led to the formation of third-tier of government. It is called local government. This local government includes **Panchayats** in villages and **Municipalities** in urban areas.

Local government allows the people to be directly involved in decision-making and promote democratic participation.

Elections to the local government were not held regularly and local governments did not have any power or resource of their own.

In 1992, a major step towards decentralisation was taken. The constitution was amended to make the third-tier of democracy more powerful and effective. The provisions made in the constitution for effective local government are

- It is constitutionally mandatory to hold regular elections to local government bodies.
- Seats are reserved in the elected bodies and the executive heads of these institutions for the **Scheduled Castes** (SCs), **Scheduled Tribes** (STs) and **Other Backward Classes** (OBCs).
- At least one-third of all positions are reserved for women.
- The **State Election Commission** (SEC) has been created in each state to conduct Panchayat and Municipal elections.
- The state governments are required to share some powers and revenue with local government bodies. The nature of sharing varies from state to state.

Panchayati Raj System

In India, rural local government is popularly known as **Panchayati Raj**. Each village or a group of villages in some states has a **Gram Panchayat**. This is a council consisting of several ward members called a **Panch** and a **President** (*Sarpanch*).

The members of Panchayat are directly elected by the adult population of that ward or village. Panchayat works under the supervision of **Gram Sabha.**

Gram Sabha meets at least twice or thrice in a year to approve annual budget and review the performance of the Gram Panchayat.

A few Gram Panchayats are grouped together to form a **Panchayat Samiti**[9] or block or mandal. The members of Panchayat Samiti are elected by all the Panchayat members in that area.

---

7 **Autonomous Federal Unit** An area that has a certain degree of self governance.

8 **Coalition Government** A government formed by the coming together of two or more political parties. Usually, partners in a coalition form a political alliance and adopt a common programme.

9 **Panchayat Samiti** It is a local government body at the *tehsil* or *taluka* level in India, which is a link between Gram Panchayat and Zilla Parishad.

All the Panchayat Samitis in a district together constitute the Zilla (district) Parishad. Most of the members of Zilla Parishad are either elected members of the Lok Sabha, MLAs of that district or some other officials at district level bodies. The **Chairperson** of Zilla Parishad is its political head.

Municipalities

Local government bodies for urban areas are known as Municipalities. In big cities they are known as Municipal Corporation. Both Municipalities and Municipal Corporations are controlled by elected bodies consisting of people's representatives.

The Chairperson of a Municipality is the political head of that Municipality. The political head of Municipal Corporation is the **Mayor**.

An Experiment in Brazil

A city called **Porto Alegre** in Brazil has carried out an extraordinary experiment in combining decentralisation with participative democracy.

The city has set up a parallel organisation operating alongside the Municipal Council, enabling local inhabitants to take real decisions for their city.

The city is divided into many sectors or wards. Each sector has a meeting (like that of the Gram Sabha) in which anyone living in that area can participate.

Constitutional Status of Local Government

The constitutional status of local government has helped to strengthen democracy in our country. It also increased women's representation and role in our democracy. However, there are many difficulties such as

- Elections are held regularly here but Gram Sabhas are not held regularly.
- Most state governments have not transferred significant powers to the local government and have not given adequate resources to them. Thus, we have still not achieved the ideal of self-government.

Try These

1. **Which incident was regarded as a major test for democratic politics in our country after independence?**
2. **How many scheduled languages are recognised in India?**
3. **Which language is identified as the official language of India?**
4. **How many seats are reserved for women in Local Government?**
5. **What constitutes the Zilla Parishad in a district?**
6. **Porto Alegre is a city of which country?**

Mind Map

FEDERALISM

Meaning of Federalism
A system of government in which the power is divided between a Central authority and various constituent units of the country.

Key Features of Federalism
- Two or more tiers of government.
- The jurisdiction of each level of Government is mentioned in the Constitution.

Types of Federations
- Coming together Federations
- Holding together Federations

Federal System vs Unitary System
- In Federal System, the Central Government cannot pass the order to the State Government to do something.
- Under the Unitary System, either there is only one level of the Government or the sub-units are subordinate to the Central Government.

Practice of Federalism in India

Centre-State Relations
Reconstructing the Centre-State relations is a way in which federalism has been strengthened.

Linguistic States
The creation of linguistic states was the first and a for democratic politics in our country.

Language Policy
Indian has no official language.

Decentralisation in India

Local Government
The idea of decentralisation led to the formation of third-tier of Government called Local Government.

Panchayati Raj System
Rural local government is known as Panchayati Raj.

Municipalities
Local government bodies for urban areas are known as Municipalities.

India as a Federal Country

Three Lists of the Constitution
- Union list includes subjects of national importance like defence, banking, communications and currency.
- State list contains subjects of the state and local importance like trade commerce, agriculture and irrigation.
- Concurrent list includes subjects of common interest to both the Union and State Government like forest, trade, education, marriage and adoption.

Power Sharing between Union and State Government
- The Parliament alone cannot make changes to this power sharing arrangement.
- The judiciary plays an important role in supervising the implementation of constitutional provisions and procedure.

Special Provisions for States and Union Territories
- Article 371 of the Indian Constitution gives Assam, Nagaland, Arunachal Pradesh and Mizoram extra power to protect the rights and culture of the indigenous people of these states.
- Chandigarh, Lakshadweep and Delhi are called Union Territories.

NCERT FOLDER

Covering Intext Questions and Exercises of NCERT

INTEXT QUESTIONS

Q.1 Read the given article carefully and answer the given question

Some Nepalese citizens were discussing the proposals on the adoption of federalism in their new Constitution. This is what some of them said

Khag Raj I don't like federalism. It would lead to reservation of seats for different caste groups as in India.

Sarita Ours is not a very big country. We don't need federalism.

Babu Lal I am hopeful that the Terai areas will get more autonomy if they get their own State Government.

Ram Ganesh I like federalism because it will mean that powers that were earlier enjoyed by the king will now be exercised by our elected representatives.

If you were participating in this conversation what would be your response to each of these?

Which of these reflect a wrong understanding of what federalism is? What makes India a federal country?

Ans. In this conversation, what Babu Lal and Ram Ganesh said are quite reasonable, but I do not support what Khag Raj and Sarita said.

My response to Khag Raj is that federalism is not only about providing reservation of seats to different caste group. Federal system has dual objectives to safeguard and promote unity of the country and also to accommodate regional diversity. These two aspects are equally important for federalism.

My response to Sarita is that generally federation is better form of government for big countries. When country is very diverse in terms of ethnicity, religion, caste, etc., it is better to adopt federal system of government, rather than unitary system, as federalism respects diversity.

The following features make India a federal country.

- There are three tiers of government in our country which has its own jurisdiction, in specific matters given by our Constitution. Each tier maintains its constitutionally guaranteed power.
- The success of federalism in India is not only because our Constitution has made it a federal country.
- The real success can be found in the nature of democratic politics in our country. Every political party in India respect the diversity of our country and try to maintain it.

Q.2 Answer the following questions.

(i) Pokharan, the place where India conducted its nuclear tests, lies in Rajasthan. Suppose the Government of Rajasthan was opposed to the Central Government's nuclear policy, could it prevent the Government of India from conducting the nuclear tests?

(ii) Suppose the Government of Sikkim plans to introduce new textbooks in its schools. But, the Union Government does not like the style and content of the new textbooks. In that case, does the State Government need to take permission from the Union Government before these textbooks can be launched?

(iii) Suppose the Chief Ministers of Andhra Pradesh, Chhattisgarh and Odisha have different policies on how their state police should respond to the naxalites. Can the Prime Minister of India intervene and pass an order that all the Chief Ministers will have to obey?

Ans. (i) Rajasthan Government cannot prevent the Central Government from conducting the nuclear test. Our Constitution has clearly provided distribution of legislative powers between Union Government and the State Government.

Formation of nuclear policy is a matter of national importance and it comes under Union list, in which only Union can take decision. So, despite its opposition of Central Governments nuclear policy, Government of Rajasthan cannot prevent it.

(ii) In our Constitution, education comes under Concurrent list that for which both the Union and State can make laws. So, Sikkim Government has within its right to launch a new textbook whether it is liked by the Central Government or not. Sikkim Government does not need prior permission of Union Government. But if there is any controversy regarding the content of the book which can affect our national interest, then the Union Government can intervene.

(iii) In our Constitution, police matter comes under State list and police has the responsibility to maintain law and order in the state.

So, Chief Ministers of Andhra Pradesh, Chhattisgarh and Odisha have full rights to manage the law and order situation in their states in response to naxalism.

Prime Minister of India or Union Government cannot force the state to obey his order on police matter. But both Union and State Government cannot ignore the problems of naxalism which is present in almost 10 states.

So, it will be better that different State Governments along with Union Governments come together and form a common policy to deal with this problem.

Q.3 Answer the following questions

(i) Has your village or town remained under the same state since independence? If not, what was the name of the earlier state?

(ii) Can you identify three state names in 1947 that have changed later?

(iii) Identify any three states which have been carved out of a bigger state.

Ans. Suggested Answer

(i) Yes, my village or town remained under the same state since independence.

(ii) The three states are Madhya Pradesh which was earlier called Central Provinces, Punjab which was earlier part of North-West Province, and Rajasthan which was earlier called Rajputana.

(iii) The three states that have been carved out from bigger states are Jharkhand from Bihar, Chhattisgarh from Madhya Pradesh and Uttarakhand from Uttar Pradesh.

Q.4 What do these newspaper clippings have to say about efforts of decentralisation in India?

Ans. These newspaper clippings are all related to Panchayats. All the seats in a Panchayat shall be filled by persons chosen by direct election from territorial constituencies in the Panchayat area. Panchayats are meant for the decentralisation of power.

The clippings show that a huge number of women are elected to Panchayats and justice had been made easily accessible to villagers.

These also reflect that Panchayats get direct funding from the Central Government but State Government oppose it.

EXERCISE

Q.1 Locate the following states on a blank outline political map of India–Manipur, Sikkim, Chhattisgarh and Goa.

Ans.

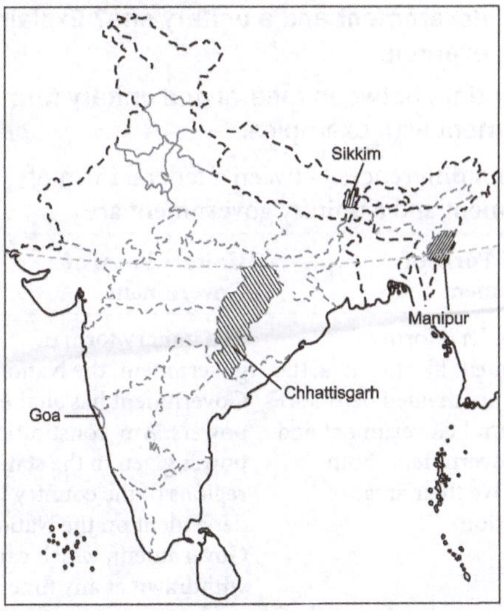

Q.2 Identify and shade three federal countries (other than India) on a blank outline political map of the world.

Ans. (i) Brazil (ii) South Africa (iii) Russia

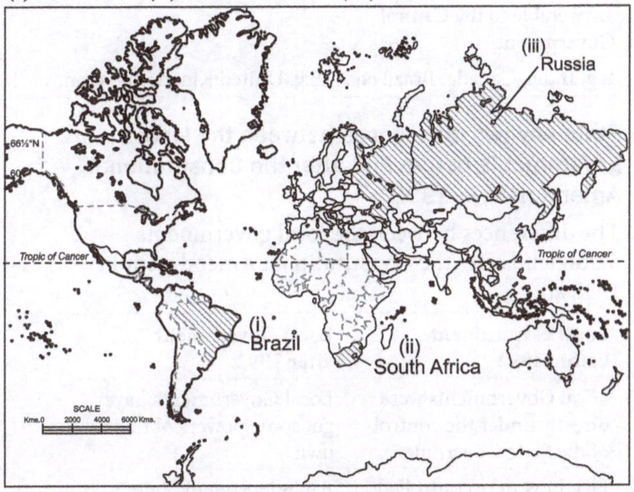

Q.3 Point out one feature in the practice of federalism in India that is similar to and one feature that is different from that of Belgium.

Ans. One similar feature of federalism between India and Belgium is that both are holding together federations, where the Central Government tends to be more powerful *vis-a-vis* the states or regions.

One different feature of federalism between India and Belgium is that in Belgium, there are three kinds of government i.e. government at the centre, government at the state level and the community government. The community government has powers regarding cultural, educational and language related issues.

But in India, the third kind of government is not a Community Government. It is the local self-government (Municipalities or Panchayats).

Q.4 What is the main difference between a federal form of government and a unitary one? Explain with an example.

Or **Differentiate between federal and unitary form of government with examples.** **CBSE 2025**

Ans. The main differences between a federal form of government and a unitary government are

Federal Form of Government	Unitary Form of Government
In the federal form of government like in India, the powers are divided between the Central Government and State Government. Both levels have their areas of jurisdiction.	In a unitary form of government, the National Government has all the powers. Any constitutional power given to the states or regions of the country is dependent on the National Government, which can be withdrawn at any time. Sri Lanka is one such example.
In a federal system, a State Government has powers of its own for which it is not answerable to the Central Government.	In a unitary system, the State Government does not have power of its own.
E.g. India, Canada, Brazil etc.	E.g. United Kingdom, Japan.

Q.5 State any two differences between the local governments before and after the Constitutional Amendment in 1992.

Ans. The differences between the local governments before and after the Constitutional Amendment in 1992 are

Local Government before 1992	Local Government after 1992
Local Governments were directly under the control of the State Government.	Local Governments have got some powers of their own.
Elections were controlled by the State Governments.	An independent State Election Commission (SEC) is responsible to conduct the elections.

Q.6 Fill in the Blanks.

Since, the United States is a .... type of federation, all the constituent states have equal powers and states are .... *vis-a-vis* the Federal Government. But India is a .... type of federation and some states have more powers than others. In India, the .... Government has more powers.

Ans. (i) coming together (ii) stronger

(iii) holding together (iv) Central

Q.7 Here are three reactions to the language policy followed in India.

Give an argument and an example to support any of these positions.

Sangeeta The policy of accommodation has strengthened national unity.

Arman Language based states have divided us by making everyone conscious of their language.

Harish This policy has only helped to consolidate the dominance of English over all other languages.

Ans. The position held by Sangeeta is the correct one. In reality, the policy of accommodation has strengthened national unity.

An example is the case of the English language. According to the Constitution, the use of English for official purposes was to stop in 1965. Many non-Hindi speaking states demanded that the use of English should continue.

The Central Government agreed to continue the use of English along with Hindi for official purposes.

Q.8 The distinguishing feature of a Federal Government is

(a) National Government gives some powers to the provincial Government.

(b) Power is distributed among the Legislature, Executive and Judiciary.

(c) Elected officials exercise supreme power in the government.

(d) Governmental power is divided between different levels of government.

Ans. (d) Governmental power is divided between different levels of government.

Q.9 A few subjects in various lists of the Indian Constitution are given here. Group them under the Union, State and Concurrent lists as provided in the table below.

(a) Defence (b) Police

(c) Agriculture (d) Education

(e) Banking (f) Forests

(g) Communications (h) Trade

(i) Marriages

Union List	Defence, Banking, Communications
State List	Police, Agriculture
Concurrent List	

Ans.

Union List	Defence, Banking, Communications
State List	Police, Agriculture, Trade
Concurrent List	Forests, Education, Marriages

Q.10 **Examine the following pairs that give the level of government in India and the powers of the government at that level to make laws on the subjects mentioned against each. Which of the following pairs is not correctly matched?**

(a) State Government – State List
(b) Central Government – Union List
(c) Central and State Governments – Concurrent List
(d) Local Government – Residuary Powers

Ans. (d) Local Government – Residuary Powers

Q.11 **Match the List I with List II and select the correct answer using the codes given below the lists.**

List I		List II	
A.	Union of India	1.	Prime Minister
B.	State	2.	Sarpanch
C.	Municipal Corporation	3.	Governor
D.	Gram Panchayat	4.	Mayor

Codes

	A	B	C	D		A	B	C	D
(a)	4	1	2	3	(b)	1	3	4	2
(c)	1	4	2	3	(d)	3	4	1	2

Ans. (b)

Q.12 **Consider the following statements.**

A. In a federation, the power of the Federal and Provincial governments are clearly demarcated.
B. India is a federation because the powers of the Union and State Governments are specified in the Constitution and they have exclusive jurisdiction on their respective subjects.
C. Sri Lanka is a federation because the country is divided into provinces.
D. India is no longer a federation because some powers of the states have been devolved to the Local Government bodies.

Which of the statements given above are correct?

(a) A, B and C (b) A, C and D
(c) A and B (d) B and C

Ans. (c) A and B

REVIEW EXERCISE

Including Competency Based Questions

Part I

Multiple Choice Questions (MCQs)

1. Which type of government does the Belgium have?
(a) Federal (b) Communist
(c) Unitary (d) Central

2. Which countries follow the unitary system of government?
(a) Belgium, Spain and India
(b) USA, Japan and Belgium
(c) Saudi Arabia, China and Sri Lanka
(d) France, Germany and India

3. A system of government in which power is divided between a central authority and various constituent unit of the country is called
(a) Federalism (b) Communalism
(c) Socialism (d) Democracy

4. Which country is an example of coming together federation?
(a) Belgium (b) USA
(c) Sri Lanka (d) India

5. In Unitary form of government,
(a) all the power is divided between the centre/union and the state provincial government.
(b) all the power is with the citizens.
(c) State Government has all the powers.
(d) power is concentrated with the Central Government.

6. Identify the correct feature of Unitary form of government from the following options. CBSE Term I 2021
(a) There are two or more levels of government.
(b) Different tiers of government govern the same citizens.
(c) Each tier of government has its own jurisdiction.
(d) The sub-units are sub-ordinate to the Central Government.

7. Which one of the following countries is the example of 'Holding together federation'? CBSE Term I 2021
(a) Australia (b) India (c) USA (d) Switzerland

8. Which one of the following subjects is included in the Union list? CBSE Term I 2021
(a) Communication (b) Trade
(c) Commerce (d) Irrigation

9. Which one of the following subjects is included in the State list? CBSE Term I 2021

(a) Banking (b) Business
(c) Currency (d) Communication

10. In which one of the following institution in India was a system of reservation for women made by amending the Constitution in 1992? CBSE 2024

(a) LokSabha
(b) RajyaSabha
(c) Legislative Council
(d) Panchayat

11. Which of the following is responsible for resolving disputes between Centre and States? CBSE 2024

(a) Finance Commission of India
(b) Supreme Court of India
(c) President of India
(d) Prime Minister of India

12. Choose the most appropriate option regarding the division of legislative rights in India. CBSE 2024

Subject List in Indian Constitution		Subjects
(a) Union List	–	Defence and Commerce
(b) State List	–	Police and Agriculture
(c) Concurrent List	–	Forest and Communication
(d) Residuary Subjects	–	Computer Software and Trade

13. Choose the correct option related to Union list. CBSE 2025

(a) Police, Foreign affairs, Agriculture
(b) Trade, Irrigation, Marriage
(c) Education, Commerce, Banking
(d) Currency, Communication, Defence

14. The creation of linguistic states was the first and a major test for democratic politics in our country. Many old states have vanished and many new states have been created. Areas, boundaries and names of the states have been changed.

Which of the following statements related to the four reactions to the language policy followed in India is true? Competency Based

(a) Language based states have divided us by making everyone conscious of their language.
(b) The policy of accommodation has strengthened national unity.
(c) The language policy has only helped to consolidate the dominance of English over all other language.
(d) It has created conflict of ideologies.

15. The states such as Assam, Nagaland, Arunachal Pradesh and Mizoram enjoy special powers under certain provisions of the Constitution of India. What is the context under which they do get these provisions? Competency Based

(a) Trade and commerce purposes
(b) Defense purposes
(c) Protection of land rights of indigenous people
(d) Special provisions for agricultural purposes

16. Mr X is appearing in an examination conducted for the recruitment to Central Government positions. In how many languages as mentioned in the Eighth schedule can he opt to take the exam? Competency Based

(a) 21 (b) 22
(c) 24 (d) 25

17. Which of the following is a definite indicator of the successful implementation of Federalism in India? CBSE Additional SQP 2023-24

(a) Courts have the power to interpret the Constitution and the powers of different levels of Government.
(b) The authority of each tier of Government is not constitutionally guaranteed.
(c) A system of Government which didn't have mutual trust and agreement to live together.
(d) Both (b) and (c)

18. In Indian states, different communities are engaged in conflict over the issue of language. The tensions further lead to a demand from communities for a national language to be made from their region only.

What is the best resolution to this situation?

(a) Delaying the demand of providing status of national language to a regional language.
(b) Indian Constitution must provide the status of national language to any of the languages.
(c) Indian Constitution must not give the status of national language to any of the languages.
(d) A foreign language like English must be given the status of a national language.

19. Consider the statements given below and choose the correct answer.

Statement I All the Panchayat Samities or Mandals in a district together constitute the Zilla Parishad. Most members of the Zilla Parishad are elected.

Statement II Members of Lok Sabha and MLA of that district and some other officials of the other District Level bodies are also its members.

Options

(a) Statement I is correct and II is incorrect.
(b) Statement I is incorrect and II is correct.
(c) Both I and II are incorrect.
(d) Both I and II are correct.

20. What happens when laws regarding Concurrent List are in conflict between the Union and State Government? Identify the appropriate reason.

(a) If their laws conflict with each other, then the law made by the President of India will prevail.
(b) If their laws conflict with each other, then the law made by the Union Government will prevail.
(c) If their laws conflict with each other, then the law made by the state government will prevail.
(d) If their laws conflict with each other, then the law made by the local governments will prevail.

21. Identify the system of Indian Government from the given information. **Competency Based**

- In this system, powers are divided between the National Government and the Regional Governments.
- In this both Centre and State Government enjoy their power independent of each other.
- System of Government in which the power is divided between a central authority and various constituent units of the country.

Options

(a) Federal system
(b) Unitary System
(c) Parliamentary system
(d) None of the above

22. Arrange in sequence according to the occurrence of the events

(i) States on the basis of language created.
(ii) Rise of regional political parties leading to coalitions.
(iii) India's journey as a democracy begins.
(iv) Central Government agrees to continue the use of English.

Codes

(a) (iii), (ii), (i), (iv)
(b) (iii), (i), (iv), (ii)
(c) (i), (iii), (iv), (ii)
(d) (iv), (i), (iii), (ii)

23. Identify the correct statement/s about the theory of federalism in the Indian Constitution. **CBSE SQP Term I 2021**

(i) The Constitution declared India as a Union of States.
(ii) Sharing of power between the Union Government and the State Governments is basic to the structure of the Constitution.
(iii) It is easy to make changes to this power sharing arrangement.
(iv) The Parliament can on its own change this arrangement.

Codes

(a) (i) and (ii)
(b) (ii) and (iii)
(c) (i) and (iii)
(d) (ii) and (iv)

24. Read the following statements regarding the creation of States on the basis of language in India and choose the correct options.

I. Formation of states on the basis of language made the country more united and stronger.
II. Formation of states on the basis of language made administration easier.
III. Formation of states on the basis of language has weakened the federal structure.
IV. Formation of states on the basis of language led to the development of Indian languages.

Options

(a) Only I, II and III are correct.
(b) Only II, III and IV are correct.
(c) Only I, II and IV are correct.
(d) Only I, III and IV are correct.

25. Which of the following statements accurately describes decentralisation of powers in India?

I. It helps to address several problems and issues at the local level itself.
II. It is autocratic in nature.
III. It has made the third tier of democracy more powerful and effective.
IV. It has deteriorated the functioning of democratic governments.

Codes

(a) Only I
(b) Only II
(c) Both I and III
(d) Only IV

26. Identify the primary reason responsible for the success of federalism in India. Choose from the appropriate statements among the following options

I. Constitutional provisions are the only one necessary for the success of federalism.
II. The real success of federalism in India can be attributed to the nature of democratic politics in our country.
III. India follows the true spirit of federalism.
IV. The formation of linguistic states made India more united and administration became easier.

Codes

(a) Statements II and IV are appropriate.
(b) Statements I, II and III are appropriate.
(c) All the statements are appropriate.
(d) Only statement IV is appropriate.

Answers

1. (a)	**2.** (c)	**3.** (a)	**4.** (b)	**5.** (d)
6. (d)	**7.** (b)	**8.** (a)	**9.** (b)	**10.** (d)
11. (b)	**12.** (b)	**13.** (d)	**14.** (b)	**15.** (c)
16. (b)	**17.** (a)	**18.** (c)	**19.** (d)	**20.** (b)
21. (a)	**22.** (b)	**23.** (a)	**24.** (c)	**25.** (c)
26. (a)				

Match the Following

1.

	List I		List II
A.	Maithili	1.	Meghalaya
B.	Bodo	2.	Jammu and Kashmir
C.	Dogri	3.	Bihar

Codes

	A	B	C		A	B	C
(a)	1	2	3	(b)	3	1	2
(c)	2	1	3	(d)	1	3	2

2.

	List I (Subject List in the Indian Constitution)		List II (Subject)
A.	Union List	1.	Trade Union
B.	State List	2.	Banking
C.	Concurrent List	3.	Police
D.	Residuary List	4.	Computer software

Codes **CBSE 2024**

	A	B	C	D		A	B	C	D
(a)	4	1	3	2	(b)	2	3	1	4
(c)	1	2	4	3	(d)	3	4	2	1

3.

	List I (List)		List II (Jurisdiction)
A.	Union List subjects	1.	State Governments alone make laws on it.
B.	State List subjects	2.	For uniformity Government legislates on it.
C.	Concurrent List subjects	3.	Subjects under jurisdiction of Centre and State Governments.
D.	Residuary subjects	4.	Central Government legislates on new subjects.

Codes **CBSE 2024**

	A	B	C	D		A	B	C	D
(a)	1	2	3	4	(b)	3	4	1	2
(c)	4	3	2	1	(d)	2	1	3	4

Ans. 1. (b) 2. (b) 3. (d)

Assertion-Reason

1. **Assertion** (A) Municipalities are set up in towns.

Reason (R) In a Municipal Corporation, chairperson is known as the Mayor.

Codes

(a) Both A and R are true and R is the correct explanation of of A
(b) Both A and R are true, but R is not the correct explanation of A
(c) A is true, but R is false
(d) A is false, but R is true

2. **Assertion** (A) Power from Central and State Governments is given to Local Government and it is known as decentralisation.

Reason (R) Large number of problems and issues are best settled at the local level and it is the basic idea behind decentralisation.

Codes

(a) Both A and R are true and R is the correct explanation of of A
(b) Both A and R are true, but R is not the correct explanation of A
(c) A is true, but R is false
(d) A is false, but R is true

3. **Assertion** (A) Besides Hindi there are 21 other languages recognised as scheduled languages by the constitution.

Reason (R) Restructuring the center-state relations is one more way in which federalism has been strengthened in practice.

Codes

(a) Both A and R are true and R is the correct explanation of A
(b) Both A and R are true, but R is not the correct explanation of A
(c) A is true, but R is false
(d) A is false, but R is true

4. **Assertion** (A) Both the Union as well as the State Governments can make laws on the subjects mentioned in Concurrent list.

Reason (R) According to our constitution the State Government has the power to legislate on these residuary subjects.

Codes

(a) Both A and R are true and R is the correct explanation of A
(b) Both A and R are true, but R is not the correct explanation of A
(c) A is true, but R is false
(d) A is false, but R is true

5. **Assertion** (A) The Central Government has not imposed Hindi on states where people speak a different language.

Reason (R) According to the constitution, the use of English for official purposes was to stop in 1965.

Codes

(a) Both A and R are true and R is the correct explanation of A
(b) Both A and R are true, but R is not the correct explanation of A
(c) A is true, but R is false
(d) A is false, but R is true

6. **Assertion** (A) Courts play a key role in interpreting the Constitution and the power of different levels of Government.

   Reason (R) The Supreme Court plays the role of an umpire if disputes arise between different levels of Government in the exercise of their respective powers.

   Codes

   (a) Both A and R are true and R is the correct explanation of A
   (b) Both A and R are true, but R is not the correct explanation of A
   (c) A is true, but R is false
   (d) A is false, but R is true

Ans. 1. (b) Both A and R are true, but R is not the correct explanation of A

2. (a) Both A and R are true, and R is the correct explanation of A

3. (b) Both A and R are true, but R is not the correct explanation of A

4. (c) A is true, but R is false

5. (b) Both A and R are true, but R is not the correct explanation of A

6. (a) Both A and R are true and R is the correct explanation of A

Picture Based Question

1 Given below is the cartoon representing Indian Prime Minister Atal Bihari Vajpayee.

What does the chair made up of bombs represent in the picture?

(a) A coalition government can explode or break at any point due to conflicts.
(b) It shows support of many smaller parties to a large party.
(c) It shows fear of smaller parties gaining power at the Union level.
(d) It shows the victory of a charismatic leader over the non-charismatic.

Ans. (a) A coalition government can explode or break at any point due to conflicts.

Case Based Question

1 Read the source given below and answer the questions that follows

Under the unitary system, either there is only one level of Government, or the sub-units are subordinate to the Central Government. The Central Government can pass on orders to the provincial or the Local Government. But in a federal system, the central Government cannot order the State Government to do something.

State Government has powers of its own for which it is not answerable to the Central Government. Both these Governments are separately answerable to the people.

(i) Which of the following is incorrect regarding Unitary Government?

(a) There is either only one Government or the sub-units are subordinate to the Central Government.
(b) The Central Government can pass on orders to the Provincial Government.
(c) A State Government is conservable to Central Government.
(d) The powers of State Governments are guaranteed by the Constitution.

(ii) Which of the following aspect shows the unitary features of the Indian Union?

(a) Formation of new states
(b) Distinction between the judiciaries
(c) Union level government is less powerful
(d) Both (a) and (b)

(iii) What are the basic objectives/goals of a federal system?

(a) To safeguard and promote unity of the country.
(b) To accommodate regional diversity.
(c) To share power among different communities.
(d) Both (a) and (b)

(iv) Can the fundamental provisions of the constitution be unilaterally changed by one level of government in federalism?

(a) Yes, it can be changed
(b) No, it can't be changed
(c) May be in special provisions
(d) Both (a) and (c)

Ans. (i) (d) The powers of State Governments are guaranteed by the Constitution.

(ii) (a) Formation of new states

(iii) (d) Both (a) and (b)

(iv) (b) No, it can't be changed

Part II

Very Short Answer Type Questions

1. What are the basic objectives of a federal system?

Ans. The basic objectives of a federal system are to safeguard and promote unity of the country and to accommodate regional diversity.

2. Is India a 'coming together federation'?

Ans. No, India is not a 'coming together federation'. It is a kind of 'holding together federation'.

3. Name two countries, besides India, which are federations.

Ans. The USA and Switzerland have federal system of Government.

4. What do you mean by 'holding together federation'?

Ans. It is a federation where a large country decides to divide the powers between the Central Government and the State Governments e.g. India.

5. Write name of any two countries which are the examples of 'holding together federations'.

Ans. India, Spain and Belgium are examples of holding together federations.

6. Whose laws prevail if there is conflict between the State Government and Central Government on the subjects of the Concurrent List?

Ans. The laws made by the Union Government prevail if there is conflict between State Government and Central Government on the subjects of the Concurrent List.

7. Examine the role of the Constitution in the Federal System of India in two points. CBSE 2024

Ans. The role of the Constitution in the federal system of India is

(i) The Constitution establishes mechanisms such as the Supreme Court and the Finance Commission, to resolve disputes between the centre and the states.

(ii) The Constitution provides a three-fold distribution of legislative powers between the Union Government and the State Governments.

8. Examine the role of the Supreme Court in the Federal System of India in two points. CBSE 2024

Ans. The role of the Supreme Court in the federal system of India is

- The Supreme Court plays an important role in overseeing the implementation of constitutional provisions and procedures. It makes a decision in case of dispute about the division of powers.
- Supreme Court has the power to interpret the Constitution and the powers of different levels of government.

9. Why was the need for decentralisation recognised in the Indian Constitution? Explain. CBSE 2024

Ans. The Indian Constitution recognised the need of decentralisation because it aims to address problems and issues more effectively at the local level. The people have better knowledge and ideas. By decentralisation, people directly participate in decision-making for efficient management.

10. Mr. X is a student who speaks language A. He protested with some students to include language A in the 8th schedule. What benefit will Mr. X get if his demand is accepted? Competency Based

Ans. If demand of Mr. X is accepted to include language A as a schedule language, then he can opt language A for the exams conducted for the Central Government positions.

11. Distinguish between unitary and federal systems of government.

Ans. **Unitary System** Under this system, either there is only one level of Government, or the sub-units are subordinate to the Central Government.

Federal System In this system, the State Government has powers of its own for which it is not answerable to the Central Government.

12. Panchayats in villages and municipalities in urban areas were set up in all the States. But these were directly under the control of State Governments. Elections to these Local Governments were not held regularly. Competency Based

(i) Which independent institution was created to conduct Panchayat and Municipal elections in each state?

(ii) Who is the political head of the Municipal Corporation?

Ans. (i) The State Election Commission was created as an independent institution to conduct Panchayat and Municipal Elections in each state.

(ii) Mayor is the political head of the Municipal Corporation.

Short Answer Type Questions

1. How have the centre-state relations been restructured to strengthen federalism?

Ans. Restructuring the centre-state relation is a way in which federalism has been strengthen in practice.
The way in which constitutional arrangements share power and work in reality depends to a large extent on how the ruling parties and their leaders follow this arrangement. For a long time, in India, the same party ruled both at the centre and in most of the states.

Here states did not exercise their autonomous power. When the ruling party at the centre and the states are different, the centre tried to dominate the state. After 1990, the era of coalition government began in India. This resulted in a new culture of power sharing between the states and the centre.

The Supreme Court authorised the autonomy of the State Government and made it difficult for the Central Government to dismiss State Government in an arbitrary manner. Thus, federal power sharing became more effective than it was before.

2. What is the meaning of decentralisation? Explain any four provisions that have been made towards decentralisation in India after the Constitutional Amendment in 1992.

Ans. When power is taken away from Central and State Governments and given to Local Government, it is called decentralisation.

The provisions that have been made towards decentralisation in India after the amendment of Constitution in 1992 are

(i) It is constitutionally mandatory to hold regular elections to Government bodies.

(ii) Seats are reserved for the Scheduled Castes (SCs), Scheduled Tribes (STs) and Other Backward Classes (OBCs).

(iii) At least one-third of all positions are reserved for women.

(iv) The State Election Commission (SEC) has been created in each state to conduct Panchayat and Municipal election.

3. Name any two subjects that are included in concurrent list. How are laws made on these subjects? **CBSE 2019**

Ans. Two subjects included in Concurrent list are education and forest.

The laws on these subjects can be made by both the Union Government i.e. Government at the Center and the State Governments. Subjects on the Concurrent list are of common interest to both (union and state) so anyone can make laws on it.

If in case, the laws conflict with each other, then the law made by Union Government will prevail. Other subjects included in the Concurrent list are trade unions, marriage, adoption, succession etc.

4. Which features of Panchayati Raj do you like the most and why?

Ans. Solving the local problems effectively and participation of people in decision-making are the two important features of Panchayati Raj system which I like the most.

This can be explained in the following ways

- Panchayati Raj is a system of governance in which Gram Panchayats are the basic unit of administration. Gram Panchayat is a council consisting of several ward members known as *Panchs* and a President or *Sarpanch*. They are directly elected by all the adult population living in that ward or village. So, this feature of Gram Panchayat is very significant.
- People in a particular village elect their own representatives who are very much familiar with the local issues. Thus, they can solve the problem of people easily and effectively. So, I like this feature of Panchayati Raj in our country.

5. What is Gram Sabha? Describe any four functions of a Gram Sabha.

Ans. Gram Sabha includes all the adult citizen voters of the village. It is empowered to support the Gram Panchayat body.

The four functions of Gram Sabha are

(i) It elects the members of the Gram Panchayat.

(ii) It supervises the work of the Gram Panchayat.

(iii) It approves the annual budget of the Panchayat.

(iv) It reviews the performance of the Gram Panchayat.

6. Describe any three features of 'Unitary Government'. **CBSE 2020**

Ans. The three features of Unitary Government are

(i) In unitary system, all powers are centralised in the hands of the Central Government and only centre is the reservoir of all state powers.

(ii) The laws of unitary system, unlike federation, are uniform because laws are made only by a single Central Government for the whole state.

(iii) It may become despotic when the rulers are not faithful as there is no check upon the exercise of these unlimited powers.

7. Mention the dual objectives of the federal system.

Ans. The dual objectives of federal system are

(i) To safeguard and promote unity of the country and at the same time accommodate regional diversity.

Different tiers of Government are made that govern the same citizens, but each tier has its own jurisdiction in respect of legislation, taxation and administration. Thus, federal system respects regional diversity and in this way protects the unity of the country.

(ii) An ideal federal system has mutual trust and agreement to live together. Governments at different levels should trust that each would abide by its part of the agreement.

8. "Federal form of government is in direct contrast to the Unitary form of government." Explain the statement. CBSE 2024

Ans. Federal form of government is in direct contrast to the Unitary form of government because in unitary form of government, either there is only one level of government or the sub-units are subordinate to the central government. The central government can pass on orders to the provincial or the local government.

But in a federal system, the central government cannot order the state government to do something. State government has powers of its own for which it is not answerable to the central government.

9. "Political power cannot be divided". Analyse suitable arguments against the statement. CBSE 2025

Ans. The argument against the statement 'Political power cannot be divided' is based on the principles of democracy and governance. In democratic systems, power is often divided among different branches of government to prevent any single entity from becoming too powerful.

This division is essential for maintaining checks and balances, ensuring that power is exercised responsibly and that citizens' rights are protected. Furthermore, the separation of powers allows for a more equitable distribution of authority, fostering accountability and transparency in governance.

10. In Panchayati Raj System, one-third of the seats have been reserved for women. Do you feel that the same should be done for State Legislature and the Parliament? Support your answer with arguments. Competency Based

Ans. In Panchayati Raj System, one-third of the seats are reserved for the women. This reservation should also be done for State Legislature and Parliament. But, the Women Reservation Bill is a pending bill in India which proposes to amend the Constitution of India to reserve 33 per cent of all seats in the Lok Sabha and in all State Legislative Assembly for women.

This bill should be passed for the following reasons

- To increase women participation in politics and society.
- To increase opportunity and respect for women.

11. "The exact balance of power between the Central and the State Government varies from one federation to another." Substantiate the statement with suitable examples. Competency Based

Ans. The exact balance of power depends on the historical context in which the federation was formed. There are two kinds of routes through which federations have been formed

(i) The first route involves independent States coming together on their own to form a bigger unit. This type of 'coming together' federations include the USA, Switzerland and Australia. In these federations, all the constituent states usually have equal power and are strong *vis-a-vis* the Federal Government.

(ii) Another route is where a large country decides to divide its power between the constituent States and the National Government. India, Spain and Belgium are examples of this kind of 'holding together' federations. Here, the Central Government tends to be more powerful *vis-a-vis* the States.

12. Discuss the most likely impact if India operated without a federal system. Competency Based

Build the answer around these points

- Regional autonomy
- Effectiveness in governance
- Decision-making process

Ans. The most likely impacts that can be visible if India operated without a federal system is discussed below

(i) **Regional Autonomy** The Regional Governments would have little or no power to make decisions. Regional aspirations may be suppressed.

(ii) **Effectiveness in Governance** Local issues may not receive adequate attention, resulting in a disconnect between grassroots reality and governance.

(iii) **Decision-making Process** The decision-making process might become undemocratic and less inclusive. It is likely to neglect regional aspirations.

Long Answer Type Questions

1. Explain any four/five key features of federalism which have been incorporated in the Indian Constitution.

Or Mention any five main features which make India a federal country.

Or Describe any three characteristics of the Indian federal system. CBSE 2024

Ans. Five main features of Indian Constitution, which make India a federal country are given below

(i) Administration of subjects which are of national importance and require uniformity in administration are given in the hands of the Central Government, while subjects of the local importance or day-to-day administration are given to the states.

(ii) Both Centre and State Governments enjoy their power independent of each other. Such a system exists in India, USA etc.

(iii) The fundamental provisions of the Constitution cannot be unilaterally changed by one level of government. Such changes require the consent of both the levels of Government.

(iv) The federal system has dual objectives i.e. to safeguard and promote unity of the country, while at the same time accommodate regional diversity.

(v) Sources of revenue for each level of Government are clearly specified to ensure its financial autonomy.

2. How are the powers divided between the states and the centre?

Or Describe the division of powers divided between State and Central Governments in India.

Or How are the legislative powers distributed between the Union Government and the State Government by the Constitution? Explain with example.

Ans. The division of power between the Central and State Governments is done in a three fold distribution of legislative powers between the Union Government and the State Government. There are three lists *i.e.* Union list, State list and Concurrent list. These are discussed below

(i) **Union List** It includes subjects of national importance, e.g. defence of the country, foreign affairs, banking, communication and currency. The Central Government alone can make decisions on these matters. The aim of including these matters in Union List is to ensure uniformity in the policy of these areas throughout the country.

(ii) **State List** It includes subjects of state and local importance such as police, trade, commerce, agriculture and irrigation. The State Government alone can make laws and decisions on these areas.

(iii) **Concurrent List** It includes those subjects which are of common interest to both the Central as well as State Governments. It includes matters like education, forests, marriage and trade unions. Both the State and Central Government can make decision on these matters.

3. Why has federalism succeeded in India? Which policies adopted by India have ensured this success?

Or 'The real success of federalism in India can be attributed to the nature of democratic politics in our country.' Explain the statement. Competency Based

Ans. The policies adopted by Indian Government which have ensured the success of federalism in India are as follows

(i) **Centre-State Relations** Federalism has been strengthened by restructuring of centre-state relations.

(ii) **Decentralisation** In India, power has been decentralised to the Local Government. The Local Government includes panchayats and municipalities.

(iii) **Linguistic States** The policy of creating linguistic states has also strengthened federalism. Despite of division, this policy united the nation.

(iv) **Language Policy** Indian federation did not gave status of national language to any language. This ultimately has strengthened federalism.

4. "The creation of a linguistic state was the first and major test for democratic politics in our country." Justify the statement. Competency Based

Ans. The creation of a linguistic state was the first and major test for democratic politics in our country. This can be justified in the following ways

- In 1947, the boundaries of several old states were changed in order to create new states. It was done according to the language that people speak. But many national leaders feared that the formation of state according to language would lead to the disintegration of the country.
- In our country, some states were created not on the basis of language but on the basis of culture, ethnicity and geography. These include Nagaland, Uttarakhand and Jharkhand.
- Linguistic states has made the country more united. It has helped to maintain our federal structure.
- Linguistic states made administration easier for the local people. People feel comfortable to work in their mother tongue. It fulfils their expectations from democracy.

5. Read the following excerpt about the Centre-State relations in India and answer the question that follows. Competency Based

In the coalition era of Indian politics, though the regional parties have acquired prominence in the centre as well as in their respective states this has led to increase in bargaining power of some state which are in power at the centre over those who are not. This has emerged as constant tension between the union and the states.

Source : inflibnet.ac.in

Critically analyse the centre-state relations prior to 1990 and after.

Ans. Before 1990, Centre-State relations in India were not very balanced. The same political party often ruled both at the Centre and in most States. When opposition parties formed State governments, the Central government sometimes misused its power to dismiss them. This weakened federalism and made States dependent on the Centre.

After 1990, the rise of regional parties and coalition governments changed this. No single party had full control at the Centre, so regional parties gained more influence. The Supreme Court also made it harder for the Centre to dismiss State governments unfairly. This created a better balance of power and strengthened federalism, allowing States to function more independently while still being part of the Union.

Case Based Questions

1. Read the source given below and answer the questions that follows.

Source A need of third tier of Government

States in India are as large as many independent countries of Europe. In terms of population, Uttar Pradesh is bigger than Russia, Maharashtra is about as big as Germany. Many of these states are internally very diverse. There is thus a need for power sharing within these States.

Federal power sharing in India needs another tier of government, below that of the State Governments.

(i) Evaluate the need of third tier Government in India.

Source B Decentralisation in India

The need for decentralisation was recognised in our constitution. Since then, there have been several attempts to decentralise power to the level of villages and towns. Panchayats in villages and municipalities in urban areas were set up in all the states. But these were directly under the control of State Governments. Elections to these Local Governments were not held regularly.

Local Governments did not have any power or resource of their own. Thus, there was very little decentralisation in effective terms.

(ii) To what extent do you think that decentralisation is applied in India?

Source C Steps towards decentralisation

A major step towards decentralisation was taken in 1992. The constitution was amended to make the third tier of democracy more powerful and effective. Now, it is constitutionally mandatory to hold regular elections to Local Government bodies. Seats are reserved in the elected bodies and the executive heads of these institutions for the Scheduled Castes, Scheduled Tribes and Other Backward Classes. At least one-third of all positions are reserved for women.

(iii) To what extent constitution amendment made the third tier of democracy more effective and powerful? Explain it by giving examples.

Ans. (i) Indian states are very large and diverse in nature. To administer the states properly only Central and State Government are not enough. Another tier of government below the State Government is needed to solve the local problems and issues. Thus, third-tier of Government is needed in India.

(ii) Our constitution has recognised the need for decentralisation. Union, state and a third-tier of Government i.e. 'Local Self-Government' below the State Government. However, it is not applied properly as Local Government do not have any power or resources of their own. They are under the direct control of State Governments. Therefore, decentralisation is not applied properly in India.

(iii) To make the third tier of democracy more effective and powerful, our constitution was amended several times. First of all, law was made for regular elections of Local Government bodies, Seats were reserved for Scheduled Castes, Scheduled Tribes, Other Backward Classes and one third of all positions for women.

2 Read the source given below and answer the questions that follows

A second test for Indian federation is the language policy. Our constitution did not give the status of national language to any one language.

Hindi was identified as the official language. But Hindi is the mother tongue of only about 40 per cent of Indians.

Therefore, there were many safeguards to protect other languages. Besides Hindi, there are 21 other languages recognised as Scheduled Languages by the Constitution. A candidate in an examination conducted for the Central Government positions may opt to take the examination in any of these languages. States too have their own official languages. Much of the government work takes place in the official language of the concerned state.

Unlike Sri Lanka, the leaders of our country adopted a very cautious attitude in spreading the use of Hindi.

According to the Constitution, the use of English for official purposes was to stop in 1965. However, many non-Hindi speaking states demanded that the use of English continue. In Tamil Nadu, this movement took a violent form. The Central Government responded by agreeing to continue the use of English along with Hindi for official purposes. Many critics think that this solution favoured the English speaking elite. Promotion of Hindi continues to be the official policy of the Government of India. Promotion does not mean that the Central Government can impose Hindi on states where people speak a different language. The flexibility shown by Indian political leaders helped our country avoid the kind of situation that Sri Lanka finds itself in.

(i) Why our constitution did not give the status of national language to any one language.

(ii) Infer the importance of continuing English as the official language of India.

(iii) How our country differs from Sri Lanka in respect of language?

Ans. (i) There are many major languages in India. Only 40 per cent people speak in Hindi. It is improper to give the status of national language to any particular language. Thus, our constitution did not give the status of national language to any one language.

(ii) According to the Constitution, the use of English for official purposes was to stop in 1965. But many non-Hindi speaking states demanded to continue English as an official language along with Hindi. Some states, specially states in South India, like Tamil Nadu revolted violently against the removal of English. Thus, Central Government took the decision to continue English as official languages.

(iii) Sri Lanka declared Sinhala as the only official language. In our country there is no national language. Hindi and English are official languages. There are 22 scheduled languages along with Hindi. Promotion of Hindi continues to be official policy of the government. Promotion does not mean to impose Hindi on non-Hindi speaking states. The flexibility in our languages policy differ from the policy taken by Sri Lanka.

ASSESSMENT EXERCISE

Multiple Choice Questions (MCQs)

1. Which one of the following languages is included in the Eighth Schedule in Indian Constitution?

(a) Hariyanavi (b) Rajasthani
(c) Garhwali (d) Odia

2. Much of the official work done in the states is in which of the following languages?

(a) Hindi
(b) English
(c) Both (a) and (b)
(d) Official language of the concerned state

3. Which government have the power to raise resources by levying taxes for carrying out government functions and assigned responsibilities?

(a) Only the State Government
(b) Only the Union Government
(c) Local Government
(d) Both (a) and (b)

4. What role do High Courts and the Supreme Court play in the resolution of disputes regarding the division of power?

(a) Legislative decision-making
(b) Judicial decision-making
(c) Executive decision-making
(d) All of these

Subjective Questions (VSA, SA & LA)

1. The state government has announced panchayat elections. Which body will conduct these elections? How many seats will be reserved?

2. Some anti-social elements use social media platforms to spread fake news. Which level of government can make law to address this problem? Give reason.

3. Explain the differences between a federal form of government and a unitary one.

4. Explain how federal power sharing in India has become more effective than in early years after the Constitution came into force.

5. 'Most federations that are formed by 'holding together' do not give equal power to its constituent units.' Analyse the statement in the context of India.

6. What experiment did take place in Brazil in decentralisation?

7. How is federalism practised in India?

8. 'The exact balance of power between the central and the state government varies from one federation to another.' Do you agree with this statement? Justify your opinion.

9. 'If the federal experiment has succeeded in India, it is not merely because of the clearly laid out constitutional provisions.' Substantiate the statement with examples.

Gender, Religion and Caste

CHAPTER 3

Every person has a right to an equal voice in a democracy. However, gender, religion and caste, all causes division in India. Women continue to face discrimination in the workplace, in school and in politics. Religion has the power to create conflict and communalism.

Furthermore, despite constitutional protection, the caste system still affects opportunities and causes restrictions. To understand the fundamentals of Indian politics, one has to understand these differences and the struggle for equality.

3.1 Gender and Politics

Gender is a form of social division which is present everywhere, but is rarely given importance in the study of politics. Gender division tends to be understood as natural and unchangeable.

Gender is not based on biological difference but on social expectations and stereotypes[1]

Public/Private Division of Labour

In gender division, unequal roles are assigned by the society to men and women. In many families, boys and girls are taught that women's main job is to take care of the house and children. This creates a **sexual division of labour**, where women do all household work, while men work outside.

When women's work becomes paid jobs, men take up these works as a profession. On the other hand, a women often work outside too but their work is not valued and recognised.

The result of the division of labour is that women's role in public life (especially in politics) is very less in most societies.

In the past, only men could vote or contest elections. Women around the world fought for equal rights, demanding for their right to vote and better opportunities in education and careers. Some even wanted equality in personal and family life. These movements are called **feminist movements**. Political **expression of demands** helped in improving women's role in the society.

Now, it is found that many women are working as scientists, doctors, engineers, lawyers, managers, college and university teachers. Earlier, these jobs were not considered suitable for women.

In Scandinavian countries, such as in Sweden, Norway and Finland, the participation of women in public life is very high.

Women's Status in India

In India, women still lag behind men despite some improvements since independence. India is still a male dominated, patriarchal[2] society. Women in India are facing discrimination in various ways as follows

- **Literacy Rate** The literacy rate among women is only 54% as compared to men, which is 76%.

  In schools and colleges, dropout rate among girls is very high mainly because parents prefer to spend their resources for their boys' education.
- **Unpaid Works** The proportion of women among the highly paid and valued jobs, is still very small. On an average, Indian woman works one hour more than an average man, but remains unpaid for work done at home.
- **Difference in Wages** The Equal Remuneration Act, 1976 provides that equal wages should be paid to equal work. Inspite of this act, women workers are paid less than men, even when both do exactly the same work.

1 Stereotype It refers to fixed image or idea of a particular type of person or thing.

2 Patriarchal It is a social system where men hold more power and authority than women.

- **Child Sex Ratio** In many parts of India, parents prefer sons and find ways to have the girl child aborted before she is born. This sex-selective abortion have led to a decline in child sex ratio (number of girls per thousand boys).

  India has a low child sex ratio i.e. 919 girl children per 1000 boys (Census 2011). In some states of the country the ratio has fallen below 850 or even 800.
- **Domestic Violence** In India, various kinds of harassment, exploitation and violence are common against women.

  In urban areas, violence against women has increased in recent years. Women are not safe even in their own home from domestic violence.

Women's Political Representation

In India, the proportion of women in the Legislature has been very low. The percentage of elected women members in Lok Sabha has reached 14.36% of its total strength for the first time in 2019.

Women's share in State Assemblies is less than 5%. In this respect, India is at the bottom group of nations in the world and even behind the averages for several developing countries of Africa and Latin America. Even when a woman becomes Chief Minister or Prime Minister, cabinets are largely dominated by male.

India has reserved **one-third** of seats for women in local government bodies, i.e. panchayats and municipalities. Women's organisations and activists have been demanding a similar reservation of at least one-third of seats in the Lok Sabha and State Assemblies for women.

In response to this demand, the Nari Shakti Vandan Adhiniyam (Women's Reservation Act, 2023) was passed. This law reserves 33% seats for women in Lok Sabha, State Legislative Assemblies and Delhi Assembly.

3.2 Religion, Communalism and Politics

Many countries including India have followers of different religions in their population. Unlike gender differences, religious differences are often expressed in the field of politics.

There are various examples which involve relation between religion and politics such as

- Gandhiji believed that politics must be guided by ethics drawn from religion. By this, he did not mean any particular religion, but moral values of all religions.
- Human rights groups are demanding special steps to protect religious minorities, as most of the victims of communal riots in our country are people from religious minorities.
- Women's movement demanded that government should change the family laws[3] of all religions which discriminate against women.

Everyone should be able to express their needs, interests and demands as a member of a religious community. This can happen if ideas, ideals and values taken from different religions play an effective role in politics. The political acts are not wrong as long as they treat every religion equally.

Communalism

It is a situation when a particular community tries to promote its own interests at the cost of other communities.

This problem becomes more critical in the following conditions

- Religion in politics is expressed in exclusive and partial/partisan terms.
- One religion and its followers are considered stronger than another.
- Beliefs of one religion are presented as superior to those of other religions.
- The demands of one religious group are formed in opposition to another.
- State power is used to establish domination of one religious group over the others.

This manner of using religion in politics is communal politics. Communal politics is based on the idea that religion is the principal basis of a social community.

Communalism involves thinking about the following

- The followers of a particular religion must belong to one community.
- The fundamental interests of the followers of particular religion are the same.
- Any difference in the followers of particular religion is irrelevant for community life.
- The people who follow different religions cannot belong to the same social community.
- People of different religions might have some things in common, but these are not very important. Their main interests are usually different, which can lead to disagreements.

3 Family laws These refer to the laws that deal with family related matters such as marriage, divorce, adoption, inheritance etc.

In its extreme form, communalism leads to the belief that people belonging to different religions cannot live as equal citizens within one nation.

Either, one of them has to dominate the other groups or they have to form different nations. There are many voices inside every community and all of them have the right to be heard.

Forms of Communalism in Politics

- The most common form of communalism is in everyday beliefs. This involves religious prejudices, stereotypes of religious communities and beliefs in the superiority of one's religion over other religions.
- A communal mind often wants to dominate one's own religious community. Majority community, adopts the majoritarian dominance and for minority, they have a desire to form a separate political unit.
- Political mobilisation on religious lines is another frequent form of communalism. This involves the use of sacred symbols, religious leaders, emotional appeal and also fear in order to bring the followers of one religion together in the political arena. In electoral politics, it appeals to the interests or emotions of voters of one religion in preference to others.
- Sometimes, communalism takes its worst form in communal violence, riots and massacre. For example, India and Pakistan suffered some of the worst communal riots at the time of partition. The post-independence period has also seen large scale communal violence.

Secular State

Secular state is a state which has no official religion of its own. The secular state provides religious equality and equal status to all religions.

The makers of our Constitution were about with the challenge of communalism. Thus, they adopted the model of secular state. The provisions related to secular state in the Constitution are

- There is no official religion for the Indian states, i.e. unlike in **Sri Lanka** (Buddhism), **Pakistan** (Islam) and **England** (Christianity). Indian Constitution does not give a special status to any religion.
- All individuals and communities have the freedom to profess, practise and propagate any religion or not to follow any religion.
- The Constitution prohibits discrimination on grounds of religion.
- It allows the state to intervene in the matters of religion in order to ensure equality within religious communities, e.g. it bans untouchability.

Try These

1. **How does the perception of unpaid domestic work contribute to gender inequality?**
2. **In which group of countries, the participation of women in public life is very high?**
3. **Name the model of state adopted by Constitution-makers of India.**
4. **Suggest one aspect of life that is covered by family laws.**
5. **Communal politics is based on the idea that .... is the principal basis of a social community.**

3.3 Caste and Politics

Social divisions in politics has both positive and the negative aspects.

Caste Inequalities

All societies in India have some kind of social inequality and some form of division of labour. Caste system is an extreme form of this. In the caste system, hereditary occupational division was approved by tradition.

In this system, all the members of the same caste group lived as one social community and all had to practice the same rituals.

People had to opt similar occupations and marry within the caste group. They were also not allowed to eat with other caste members.

Caste system was based on exclusion and discrimination against the **outcaste groups**.

Contribution of Reformers in Removal of Caste Inequalities

The most important aspect of the caste inequality is untouchability. Thus, social reformers like **Jotiba Phule**, **Mahatma Gandhi**, **Dr Bhim Rao Ambedkar** and **Periyar Ramaswami Naicker** advocated and worked for removal of caste inequalities in society.

Castes and caste system in modern India have undergone great changes due to the efforts of social reformers and other socio-economic changes due to the efforts of social reformers and other socio-economic changes.

With economic growth, the spread of cities, better education, more job opportunities and weaker control of landlords in villages, the old caste system is losing its importance.

The Indian Constitution prohibits caste discrimination and lays down the policies to correct caste injustices. However, caste still exists in modern India. Many people still marry within their own caste. Untouchability has not completely ended, despite laws against it. Caste is continued to be linked with economic status.

Social and Religious Diversity in India

The census of India records the religion of each and every Indian after every ten years. Since independence, the total population of each community has increased substantially but their proportion in the country's population has remain more or less the same.

In terms of percentage, the population of the Hindus, Jains and Christians has declined marginally since 1961.

Some important aspects are

- In 2011, the population of the Hindus (79.8%), Jains (0.4%) and Christians (2.3%) has declined marginally since 1961.
- The proportion of Muslim (14.2%), Sikh (1.7%) and Buddhist (0.7%) population has increased slightly.
- According to **Sachar Committee Report**, the proportion of Muslims is expected to go up about 3 to 4 per cent in the next 50 years. The population balance of different religious communities is not likely to change largely.
- The census of India count two social groups i.e. Scheduled Castes[4] and Scheduled Tribes. Both these groups includes hundreds of castes or tribes whose names are listed in an official schedule.
- In 2011, the Scheduled Castes were 16.6% and the Scheduled Tribes[5] were 8.6% of the country's population.

Caste in Politics

Caste plays a role in Indian politics in various ways such as

- During elections, political parties carefully choose candidates based on the caste composition of the voters to ensure support. Parties try to include representatives from different castes and tribes.
- Some parties are associated with specific castes and favour them.
- Universal Adult Franchise and the principle of one-person-one-vote has forced political leaders to mobilise and secure political support.

Caste appeals are made during elections, but elections are not only about caste which can be seen in the following points

- No parliamentary constituency has a single caste majority, requiring candidates to gain support from multiple communities.
- No party wins the vote of all the voters of a caste or community. When it is considered that a caste is a 'vote bank' of one party, it usually means that a large proportion of the voters from that caste vote for the party.
- Political parties often nominate candidates from dominant castes in specific areas. This leads to some voters having more than one candidate from their caste while many voters have no candidate from their caste.
- The ruling party often loses elections because people from different castes and communities do not always have the same political references.

Apart from caste, other factors are also important in politics like

- People often prefer political parties over caste.
- Economic conditions can vary within the same caste.
- Rich and poor individuals from the same caste often vote differently.
- People's assessment of the performance of the government and the popularity rating of the leaders are often decisive in elections.

Caste Inequality

Caste is an important source of economic inequality because it regulates access to resources of various kinds.

According to the National Sample Survey carried out in the year 1999, caste continues to be very strongly linked to economic status in many important ways. The results of the survey show that

- The average economic status (measured by criteria like monthly consumption expenditure) of caste groups still follows the old hierarchy i.e. the 'upper' castes are best, the Dalits and Adivasis are worst off and the OBCs are in between.
- Every caste has some poor members but the proportion of people living below the official poverty line is much higher for the lowest castes and much lower for the upper castes, with the OBCs in between.
- Every caste has some members who are rich, the upper castes are more among the rich while the lower castes are very much less in this group.

4 Scheduled Castes (SCs) or Dalits It includes those castes who were once considered 'outcaste' in the Hindu social system (faced exclusion and untouchability).

5 Scheduled Tribes (STs) or Adivasi It includes those communities that led a scheduled life in hills and forest and not interact with rest society.

Politics in Caste

There is not a one-way relation between caste and politics. Politics also influences the caste system and caste identities by bringing them into the political ground.

Thus, it is not politics that gets caste-ridden, it is the caste that gets politicised. It takes several forms as follows

- Each caste group tries to become bigger by incorporating within it other sub-castes.
- Various caste groups are required to enter into an alliance with other castes or communities.
- New kinds of caste groups like **backward** and **forward** caste groups have come up in the political field.

Thus, caste plays different kinds of roles in politics. Sometimes it helps disadvantaged groups like Dalits and OBCs to demand their share of power and giving them access in decision making.

Several political and non-political groups have fought to end discrimination to seek more dignity, more access to land, resources and opportunities.

However, too much focus on caste can produce negative result as well. As in the case of religion, if politics revolves only around caste, it is not good for a democracy.

It can divert attention from important issues like poverty, development and corruption. In some cases, caste division leads to tensions, conflicts and even violence.

Try These

1. **Name the system based on the exclusion and discrimination.**
2. **Suggest one reformer who worked to remove untouchability.**
3. **Define the term OBC.**
4. **Name the old notion of casteism which is breaking down nowadays.**
5. **Which communities have gained better access to decision making through caste politics?**

Mind Map

GENDER, RELIGION AND CASTE

Gender and Politics

Women's Status In India
Women's status in India is characterised by
- Literacy rate (54%)
- Unpaid work
- Difference in wages
- Child sex ratio
- Domestic violence

Women's Political Representation
- The percentage of elected women members in Lok Sabha reached 14.36% of its total strength in 2019.
- Women's share in the state assemblies is less than 5%.
- India has reserved one-third of seats for women in local government bodies.

Public/Private Division of Labour
- Sexual division of labour, where women do all household work, while men work outside.
- Political expressions of demands helped in improving women's role in the society.

Religion, Communalism and Politics

Communalism

Ideas
- Followers of a particular religion must belong to one community.
- Fundamental interests of the followers of particular religion are the same.

Problems
- Religion in politics is expressed in exclusive and partial terms.
- One religion and its followers are considered stronger than another.

Forms of Communalism in Politics
- People of different religions communities of against one another.
- Use of sacred symbols, religious leaders, emotional appeal and also fear in order to bring the followers of one religion together in the political area.

Secular State
- No official religio for the Indian states.
- The Constitution prohibits discrimination on grounds of religion.
- All individuals and communities have the freedom to profess, practice and propagate any religion or not to follow any religion.

Caste And Politics

Caste In Politics
- During elections, political parties choose candidates based on the caste composition of the voters to ensure support.
- Some parties are associated with specific castes and favour them.

Caste Inequalities
- In the caste system, all the members of the same caste group lived as one social community and all had to practice the same rituals.
- Caste system was based on exclusion and discrimination of the outcaste groups.

Politics in Caste
- Each caste group tries to become bigger by incorporating within it other subcastes.
- Backward and forward caste groups have come up in the political field.

NCERT FOLDER

Covering Intext Questions and Exercises of NCERT

INTEXT QUESTIONS

Q.1 If casteism and communalism are bad, what makes feminism a good thing? Why don't we oppose all those who divided the society on any lines-caste, religion or gender?

Ans. Casteism and communalism are bad as they usually divide the society and enhance inequality. These two are major challenges to our democracy. Our Constitution makers were aware of these challenges. That is why they chose the model of a secular state.

On the other hand, feminism is a good thing as it believes in equal rights and opportunities for men and women. It is a collection of movements and ideologies aimed at defining, establishing and defending equal political, economical and social rights for women. Feminism do not promote the equal rights particularly for one single community or caste of women but for women of all religions.

The Constitution of India also prohibited any caste-based discrimination and laid the foundations of policies to reverse the injustices due to casteism. So, we must oppose casteism and communalism, but not feminism.

Q.2 "I am not religious, why should I bother about communalism and secularism"? Comment on this statement.

Ans. If we are not religious, it means we don't believe in God, i.e. there are no deities. Communalism is a social phenomena which is based on the idea that religion is the principal basis of social community.

It believes that people who follow different religions cannot belong to the same social community. Sometimes it takes its ugliest form in communal violence, riots and massacre. So, communalism needs to be resolved.

Secularism means, there is no state religion. State should respect all religions. India does not have an official state religion.

So, whether I am religious or not, I must be secular and should not favour or discriminate against any religion. This attitude only can maintain a healthy atmosphere in our country.

Q.3 "I often crack jokes about people from one religion, does that make me communal?" Comment on this statement?

Ans. We should not make jokes about people of any religion. We should also keep in the mind that if a person of other religion cracks a joke about our religion it should not be encouraged.

Religion means a belief or the worship of God or the supernatural. The faith is very much based on personal and community grounds. Religion is a very sensitive issue. This may result communal tension in the society and we will be responsible for it. So, we should not make fun of other religion.

EXERCISE

Q.1 Mention different aspects of life in which women are discriminated or disadvantaged in India.

Ans. Women, in our country, are discriminated in the following aspects

(i) **Literacy Rate** The literacy rate among women is only 54% as compared to men with 76% among. Similarly, a few number of girl students go for higher studies because parents prefer to spend their resources for their boys education than spending equally on their daughters.

(ii) **Unpaid Work** The proportion of women among the highly paid and valued jobs is still very small. Though on an average, Indian women work one hour more than men everyday, most of them are not paid equally and therefore, their work is often not valued.

(iii) **Sex Ratio** In many parts of India, parents prefer to have sons and find ways to have the girl child aborted before she is born. This has led to a decline in the child sex ratio (the number of girl children per thousand boys) in the country.

(iv) **Domestic Violence** There are reports of various kinds of harassment, exploitation and violence against women. Both urban as well as rural areas have become unsafe for women. They are not safe even within their own homes from beating and other forms of domestic violence.

Q.2 State different forms of communal politics with one example of each.

Ans. Communalism can take several forms in politics like

- The most common expression of communalism is of communal superiority in our everyday beliefs. For example, militant religious groups.
- Sometimes, communalism takes its worst form in riots. India and Pakistan suffered some of the worst communal riots at the time of partition.

- A communal mind often leads to a quest for political dominance of one's own religious community. For example, separatists and political parties in Jammu and Kashmir.
- Political mobilisation based on religion is another form of communalism. This involves the use of sacred symbols, religious leaders, emotional appeal to bring the followers of one religion together in political areas. For example in India, politicians are trying to influence voters exploiting their religious sentiments from the two largest religious communities in the country.

Q.3 State how caste inequalities are still continuing in India.

Ans. Caste inequalities are still continuing in India in the following ways

- Every caste group has its own exclusive occupation that will be passed from generation to generation.
- Marriages are still performed mainly in the same caste. Intercaste marriage is not rare, but not welcomed by all.
- People from different castes usually do not interact with each other and untouchability is still present in some parts of the country.
- The upper caste people who got good education under the old caste system got top job positions. The castes that did not receive education lagged behind in getting the top job positions.
- The upper castes became economically better than the people from the lower castes due to education.

Q.4 State two reasons to say that caste alone cannot determine election results in India.

Ans. The two reasons which show that caste alone cannot determine election results in India are

(i) No party wins the votes of all the voters of a caste or community. When people say, the caste is a 'vote bank' of one party, it usually means that a large proportion of voters from that caste vote for that party.

(ii) No parliamentary constituency in the country has a clear majority of one single caste. So, every candidate and party needs to win the confidence of more than one caste and community to win elections.

Q.5 What is the status of women's representation in India's legislative bodies?

Ans. In India, the women's participation in the political area is very low. The women's strength in the Lok Sabha is 14.36%. Their share in State Assemblies is less than 5%.
The share of women legislators in India is behind those of several developing countries of Latin America and Africa.

In the panchayats and municipalities, it is legally binding to fill one-third of the seats by women candidates. This has resulted in 10 lakh elected women representatives in rural bodies which is more than urban local bodies.

Q.6 Mention any two constitutional provisions that make India a secular state.

Or **Suggest any two measures to promote secularism as mentioned in the Indian Constitution** **CBSE 2025**

Ans. A state that has no official religion and grants equal status to all religions is called a secular state. The Constitution of India ensures secularism through the following provisions (any two)

(i) There is no official language for India.

(ii) Unlike the status of Buddhism in Sri Lanka, that of Islam in Pakistan and Christianity in England, our Constitution does not give any special status to any religion.

(iii) Under the Right to Freedom of Religion, our Constitution provides to all citizens freedom to profess, practise and propagate any religion or not to follow any.

(iv) The Constitution prohibits discrimination on grounds of religion.

(v) The Constitution allows the state to intervene in the matters of religion in order to ensure equality within religious communities.

Q.7 When we speak of gender divisions, we usually refer to

(a) Biological difference between men and women.
(b) Unequal roles assigned by the society to men and women.
(c) Unequal child sex ratio.
(d) Absence of voting rights for women in democracies.

Ans. (b) Unequal roles assigned by the society to men and women.

Q.8 In India, seats are reserved for women in the

(a) Lok Sabha
(b) State Legislative Assemblies
(c) Cabinets
(d) Panchayati Raj Bodies

Ans. (*d*) Panchayati Raj Bodies

Q.9 Consider the following statements on the meaning of communal politics. Communal politics is based on the belief that

A. One religion is superior to that of others.
B. People belonging to different religions can live happily together as equal citizens.
C. Followers of a particular religion constitute one community.
D. State power cannot be used to establish the domination of one religious group over others.

Which of the statement(s) is/are correct?

(a) A, B, C and D (b) A, B and D
(c) A and C (d) B and D

Ans. (c) A and C

Q.10 Which among the following statements about India's Constitution is wrong?

(a) It prohibits discrimination on grounds of religion.
(b) It gives official status to one religion.
(c) It provides to all individuals freedom to profess any religion.
(d) It ensures equality of citizens within religious communities.

Ans. (b) It gives official status to one religion.

Q.11 Social divisions based on ...... are peculiar to India.

Ans. caste

Q.12 Match List I with List II and select the correct answer using the codes given below the lists.

List I	List II
A. A person who believes in equal rights and opportunities for women and men	1. Communalist
B. A person who says that religion is the principal basis of community	2. Feminist
C. A person who thinks that caste is the principal basis of community	3. Secularist
D. A person who does not discriminate others on the basis of religious beliefs	4. Casteist

Codes

	A	B	C	D		A	B	C	D
(a)	2	3	1	4	(b)	2	1	4	3
(c)	4	3	1	2	(d)	3	1	2	4

Ans. (b)

REVIEW EXERCISE

Including Competency Based Questions

Part I

Multiple Choice Questions (MCQs)

1. The participation of women in public life is very high in

(a) Sweden (b) Norway
(c) Finland (d) All of these

2. Which among the following is not a threat to Indian democracy?

(a) Low gender ratio (b) Caste system
(c) Communalism (d) None of these

3. The hierarchical unequal roles assigned to men and women by the society is known as

(a) sex ratio (b) equal wages ratio
(c) gender division (d) male ratio

4. "Religion can never be separated from politics" is said by

(a) BR Ambedkar (b) GK Gokhale
(c) Mahatma Gandhi (d) Swami Vivekananda

5. Name some prominent leaders of our country who worked for the elimination of caste system in India.

(a) Jyotiba Phule (b) Dr BR Ambedkar
(c) Mahatma Gandhi (d) All of the above

6. Communal politics is based on the idea of

(a) caste is the basis of social community.
(b) religion and caste are the basis of social community.
(c) religion is the basis of social community.
(d) None of the above

7. Which social division is unique to India?

(a) Economic division (b) Caste division
(c) Racial division (d) Religious division

8. Which term refers to the guilt from one occupation to another, breaking traditional caste-based jobs?

(a) Urbanisation (b) Occupational nobility
(c) Social hierarchy (d) Caste rigidity

9. Heredity, rituals, birth are the basis of

(a) economic system (b) caste system
(c) racial division (d) class system

10. Which Indian leader played a key role in drafting the constitution and advocating for the rights of scheduled castes?

(a) Periyar Ramaswami Naiker
(b) BR Ambedkar
(c) Joyotiba Phule
(d) Sardar Patel

11. Which factor does not weaken the caste inequalities?

(a) Urbanisation (b) Literacy growth
(c) Education (d) Politics

12. Which one of the following statements is not true ? CBSE 2023

(a) The Constitution prohibits discrimination on the grounds of religion.
(b) The Constitution allows us to practice, profess and propagate any religion or not to follow any.

(c) The Constitution of India allows the state to intervene in the matters of religion in order to ensure equality within religious communities.

(d) As per the Constitution, religion can never be separated from politics.

13. Which one of the following statements best describes women empowerment? **CBSE 2024**

(a) Encouraging men to take leadership roles.

(b) Promoting superiority of women over men.

(c) Ensuring equal opportunities and rights for women.

(d) Limiting the rights of men in all spheres.

14. Women in different parts of the world organised and protested for equal rights. These protests demanded enhancing the political and legal status of women and improving their educational and career opportunities. **Competency Based**

What is the best outcome of the political expression of gender division?

(a) It has provided superior status to women in the society.

(b) It has helped to improve women's role in public life.

(c) It has increased the exploitation of women in many sectors.

(d) It has reduced women's role in public life.

15. Women and girls represent half of the world's population and therefore also half of its potential. But gender inequality persists everywhere and stagnates social progress. On average, women in the labour market still earn 23 per cent less than men globally and women spend about three times as many hours in unpaid domestic and care work as men.

Source: un.org

Which of the following is an example of the sexual divison of labour?

(a) Men and women equally participating in household chores

(b) Women being expected to do all domestic work without pay.

(c) Men and women sharing leadership roles in politics

(d) Women being given equal opportunities in workplaces.

16. India has several political parties that have been formed on caste lines. These parties often cater to the interests of specific castes and aim to represent the political and social concerns of these castes. Examples include the Bahujan Samaj Party (BSP), which represents Dalits and other lower castes, and the Samajwadi Party (SP), which represents Yadavs and other backward castes in the state of Uttar Pradesh. **Competency Based**

Source : Mint

Which among the following is true regarding communal politics?

(a) It is based on the idea that religion is the principal basis of a social community.

(b) Beliefs of one religion are presented as superior to those of other religions.

(c) State power is used to establish the domination of one religious' group over the rest.

(d) All of the above

17. Identify the ideology of the society from the given information.

(i) It leads to communal violence, riots and massacre which disturb the very foundation of democracy.

(ii) It also leads to the belief that people belonging to different religions cannot live as equal, citizens within the nation.

(iii) It makes hindrances in the functioning of our democracy.

(iv) A situation when a particular community tries to promote its own interests at the cost of other communities.

Options

(a) Secularism (b) Communalism

(c) Idealism (d) Feminism

18. Which of the following statements suggest that it is not politics that gets caste-ridden, it is the caste that gets politicised? Identify. **Competency Based**

I. When governments are formed, political parties take care that representatives of different castes find a place in it.

II. Each caste incorporates neighbouring castes which were earlier excluded.

III. Various caste groups enter coalition with other castes.

IV. Political parties and candidates in elections make appeals to caste sentiments.

Codes

(a) Statements I and II are appropriate.

(b) Statements II and III are appropriate.

(c) Statements IV is correct.

(d) All the statements are appropriate.

19. Caste alone cannot determine elections in India. Identify the appropriate reasons from the given options.

I. No party wins the votes of all the voters of a caste or community.

II. Some political parties are known to favor some castes and are seen as their representatives.

III. No parliamentary consistency in the country has a clear majority of one single caste.

IV. Mobilising and securing political support has brought new consciousness among the lower castes.

Options

(a) Statements I and III are appropriate.
(b) Statements I and IV are appropriate.
(c) Statements II and III are appropriate.
(d) Statements II and IV are appropriate.

20. Consider the statements given below and choose the correct answer. Competency Based

Statement I Political mobilisation on religious lines is one of the frequent forms of communalism.

Statement II In electoral politics, it appeals to the interests or emotions of voters of one religion in preference to others.

Options

(a) Statement I is correct and statement II is incorrect.
(b) Statement I is incorrect and Statement II is correct.
(c) Both statements I and II are incorrect.
(d) Both statements I and II are correct.

21. Consider the statements given below and choose the correct answer.

Statement I In the caste system, hereditary occupational division was sanctioned by rituals.

Statement II Caste system was based on exclusion and discrimination of the outcaste groups.

Options

(a) Statement I is correct, and statement II is incorrect
(b) Statement I is incorrect, and statement II is correct
(c) Both statements I and II are incorrect.
(d) Both statements I and II are correct.

Answers

1. (d)	**2.** (a)	**3.** (c)	**4.** (c)	**5.** (d)
6. (c)	**7.** (b)	**8.** (b)	**9.** (b)	**10.** (b)
11. (d)	**12.** (d)	**13.** (c)	**14.** (b)	**15.** (b)
16. (d)	**17.** (b)	**18.** (b)	**19.** (a)	**20.** (d)
21. (d)				

Match the Following

1.

	List I		List II
A.	A system that values men more and gives them power over women	1	Urbanisation
B.	Law that deals with marriage and divorce	2	Occupational Mobility
C.	New generation takes up occupations other than their ancestors	3	Family Law
D.	Shift of population from rural areas to urban areas	4	Patriarchy

Codes

	A	B	C	D		A	B	C	D
(a)	4	3	2	1	(b)	4	2	3	1
(c)	3	4	2	1	(d)	2	4	1	3

Ans. (a)

Assertion-Reason

1. Assertion (A) Idea of Secularism constitutes one of the foundations of our country.

Reason (R) The Constitution prohibits discrimination on grounds of religion.

Codes

(a) Both A and R are true and R is the correct explanation of A
(b) Both A and R are true, but R is not the correct explanation of A
(c) A is true, but R is false
(d) A is false, but R is true

2. Assertion (A) There is no official religion for the Indian state for maintaining its democratic status.

Reason (R) Communalism is one of the major challenges to democracy in our country.

Codes

(a) Both A and R are true and R is the correct explanation of A
(b) Both A and R are true, but R is not the correct explanation of A
(c) A is true, but R is false
(d) A is false, but R is true

3. Assertion (A) Sex-selective abortion led to a decline of sex-ratio in India.

Reason (R) Desire for a male child makes Indian families abort a girl child.

Codes

(a) Both A and R are true and R is the correct explanation of A
(b) Both A and R are true, but R is not the correct explanation of A
(c) A is true, but R is false
(d) A is false, but R is true

4. Assertion (A) Universal Adult Franchise gives the Right to Vote for every citizen.

Reason (R) The Right to Vote should be given to the people of upper caste and class for taking wise decisions.

Codes

(a) Both A and R are true and R is the correct explanation of A
(b) Both A and R are true, but R is not the correct explanation of A
(c) A is true, but R is false
(d) A is false, but R is true

5. **Assertion** (A) Sometimes a caste group becomes a vote bank for a party.

Reason (R) Selecting the candidate from the same caste helps in ensuring better governance.

Codes

(a) Both A and R are true and R is the correct explanation of A

(b) Both A and R are true, but R is not the correct explanation of A

(c) A is true, but R is false

(d) A is false, but R is true

6. **Assertion** (A) Communalism is based on the idea that religion is the principal basis of social community.

Reason (R) Caste should be kept away from politics.

Codes

(a) Both A and R are true and R is the correct explanation of A

(b) Both A and R are true, but R is not the correct explanation of A

(c) A is true, but R is false

(d) A is false, but R is true

7. **Assertion** (A) The Equal Remuneration Act, 1976 provides that equal wages should be paid for equal work.

Reason (R) Women are physically weak, so they are righteously paid less than men.

Codes

(a) Both A and R are true and R is the correct explanation of A

(b) Both A and R are true, but R is not the correct explanation of A

(c) A is true, but R is false

(d) A is false, but R is true

Ans. 1. (b) Both A and R are true, but R is not the correct explanation of A

2. (a) Both A and R are true and R is the correct explanation of A

3. (b) Both A and R are true, but R is not the correct explanation of A

4. (c) A is true, but R is false

5. (c) A is true, but R is false

6. (b) Both A and R are true, but R is not the correct explanation of A

7. (c) A is true, but R is false

Picture Based Questions

1. **What does the given picture indicates?**

(a) Power of Parliament

(b) Passing of Women's Reservation Bill

(c) Women's Representation in Parliament

(d) Rejection of Women's Reservation Bill

2. **Given below is a cartoon created by Neelabh Banerjee, the renowned Indian cartoonist, illustrator and comics artist.** **CBSE Additional SQP 2023-24**

What is the cartoon trying to depict?

(a) The sexual division of labour in India.

(b) Natural and unchangeable gender divisions.

(c) Income generating activities done by women in rural India.

(d) The ability of men to contribute equally to domestic work as women.

3. **Given below is a cartoon that represents political leaders.**

Identify which statement highlights the meaning of vote bank politics here.

(a) It is the practice of dictating a caste-based group.

(b) It is a practice of creating and maintaining vote banks through divisive policies.

(c) It is considered useful for representative democracy.

(d) It is a practice that didn't create tensions among different castes.

Ans. 1. (b) Passing of Women's Reservation Bill

2. (a) The sexual division of labour in India.

3. (b) It is a practice of creating and maintaining vote banks through divisive policies.

Case Based Question

1. Read the source given below and answer the questions that follow.

Boys and girls are brought up to believe that the main responsibility of women is housework and bringing tup children. This is reflected in a sexual division of labour in most families, women do all work inside the home such as cooking, cleaning, washing clothes, tailoring, looking after children, etc., and men do all the work outside the home. It is not that men cannot do houswork; they simply think that it is for women to attend to these things. When these jobs are paid for, men are ready to take up these works. Most tailors or cooks in hotels are men. Similarly, it is not that women do not work outside their home. In villages, women fetch water, collect fuel and work in the fields. In urban areas, poor women work as domestic helper in middle class homes, while middle class women work in offices. In fact, the majority of women do some sort of paid work in addition to domestic labour.

(i) What is gender division primarily based on?

(a) Biological differences

(b) Social expectations and stereotypes

(c) Economic factors

(d) Educational background

(ii) According to the source, why do men typically refrain from doing housework?

(a) Lack of skills (b) Cultural beliefs

(c) Physical limitations (d) Unavailability of time

(iii) What is highlighted as a consequence of the traditional division of labour mentioned in the source?

(a) Increased economic productivity

(b) Minimal participation of women in public life

(c) Enhanced household harmony

(d) Greater opportunities for men in politics

(iv) What is the main focus of the gender issue raised in the society ?

(a) Workplace equality (b) Equal pay

(c) Equal rights for women

(d) Educational opportunities

Ans. (i) (b) Social expectations and stereotypes

(ii) (b) Cultural beliefs

(iii) (b) Minimal participation of women in public life

(iv) (c) Equal rights for women

Part II

Very Short Answer Type Questions

1. Why the literacy rate among women in India is low in comparison to their counterparts?

Ans. In India, parents prefer to spend their resources for their sons education. So, the literacy rate among women in India is lower than men.

2. Explain the term 'Feminist Movement'.

Ans. A Feminist Movement is a movement aimed at equality in personal and family life for men and women.

3. "Role of women is gradually enhancing in the politics of the country." Examine the statement. CBSE 2024

Ans. The role of women is gradually enhancing in the politics of the country. This can be seen from the reservation for women in Panchayati Raj institutions. It was implemented under the 73rd Amendment Act. It ensures a minimum of one-third seats for women in local bodies. The purpose is to encourage women's active participation and empowerment in governance.

4. Suggest any two measures to remove gender inequality

Ans. Two measures to remove gender inequality are

(i) Strengthening laws and increasing public awareness to prevent sex-selective abortions.

(ii) Ensuring timely justice for victims and expand support services to empower women.

5. State the significance of the 'Equal Wages Act.'

Ans. The act signifies that equal wages should be paid for equal work done by men and women.

6. Why is women's work often undervalued in society?

Ans. Women's work, especially household chores and caregiving, is unpaid and considered a natural duty rather than labour. Even when women participate in income-generating activities, their contributions are often overlooked, leading to lower wages, fewer opportunities, and a lack of recognition in the workforce.

7. How does patriarchy affect women's participation in politics?

Ans. Patriarchy gives men more power and authority, limiting women's role in public life. Women face social restrictions, lower literacy rates, and economic dependence, which hinder their political participation. Although legal reforms promote gender equality, women's representation in legislatures remains significantly lower than men's.

8. What is the significance of the Women's Reservation Act, 2023?

Ans. The Women's Reservation Act, 2023 reserves 33% of seats for women in the Lok Sabha, State Assemblies, and the Delhi Assembly. It aims to increase women's political participation, ensure gender equality in governance, and address the underrepresentation of women in decision-making roles.

9. Suggest any two measures to ensure participation of women in public life. CBSE 2025

Ans. Two measures to ensure the participation of women in public life are

(i) **Equal Rights in Political Participation** The Constitution of India grants women the right to vote and contest elections, ensuring their active participation in the political process.

(ii) **Reservation in Local Bodies** The Indian Constitution provides for the reservation of seats for women in local government bodies like Panchayats and Municipalities.

10. Suggest any two measures to increase the number of women in legislatures of India. CBSE 2025

Ans. Two measures to increase the number of women in legislatures in India are as follows

(i) **Reservation of Seats** Reserve 33% of seats in the Lok Sabha and State Assemblies for women, ensuring greater political representation.

(ii) **Encourage Political Participation** Provide training, support, and opportunities for women to participate in politics and take leadership roles.

11. Suggest any one way to protect women from domestic oppression. CBSE 2020

Ans. One way to protect women from domestic oppression is to raise awareness and explain their rights so that they can protect themselves.

12. What do you understand by a secular state?

Ans. A secular state is a state which is not based on any religion and does not discriminate between citizens on the basis of religion.

13. How can we define a person who does not discriminate others on the basis of religious belief?

Ans. The person who does not discriminate others on the basis of religious belief is known as secular.

14. How is the caste of a person determined in India?

Ans. The caste of a person is determined by the caste of the family in which he is born.

15. Name two leaders of our country who worked for the establishment of a casteless society.

Ans. Mahatma Gandhi and Dr BR Ambedkar worked for the establishment of a casteless society.

16. Shruti performed a web search for 'Teacher' and found that 80% of the images had women, while a search for 'Pilot' mainly showed men. Discuss how these web search results reflect societal perceptions and the sexual division of labour. Explain with an example. CBSE Additional SQP 2023-24

Ans. The web search results reflect the over-representation of women as teachers and men as pilots indicates traditional notions of job roles. The role of teaching is considered a caregiving job suitable for women while the pilot is regarded as a physically and mentally demanding job ideal for men.

17. 'Due to the efforts of social reformers and other socio-economic changes, castes and caste system in modern India have undergone great changes.'

(i) Name any four social reformers who advocated and worked to establish a society in which caste inequalities are absent.

(ii) Suggest any two ways to break caste hierarchy within the Indian society. Competency Based

Ans. (i) The four social reformers are Jyotiba Phule, Mahatma Gandhi, Dr. BR Ambedkar and Periyar Ramaswami who advocated and worked to establish a society in which caste inequalities are absent.

(ii) Two ways to break the caste hierarchy system within the Indian society are spread of education and urbanisation.

Short Answer Type Questions

1. What is sexual division of labour? Discuss.

Ans. Sexual division of labour means that work is divided between males and females according to their gender. While assigning or dividing the work, the capability of a person is not considered and only the gender is taken into consideration.

Generally, all the household unpaid work is assigned to the females and males are supposed to go out for work and earn money for the family. It is not that men cannot do housework, but they think that it is for women to do such work.

2. Suggest any two measures to integrate the people belonging to different ethnic groups in a society.

Ans. The measures to integrate the people belonging to different ethnic groups in a society are (any two)

(i) Everyone, including political leaders, social reformers and general people, should discourage casteism and work for socio-economic and political harmony.

(ii) The political and regional political parties based on caste should be removed.

(iii) The name and aim of educational institutions referring to castes should be given up.

3. Describe any five features of the caste system in India.

Ans. The five features of the caste system in India are

(i) It was a hierarchical occupational division of the society.

(ii) Caste system is both hierarchical and segmented.

(iii) Most important aspect of caste system is 'untouchability'.

(iv) In caste system, the members of the same caste group formed a social community that followed similar occupation, married within the caste and did not mix with other castes.

(v) In caste system, the people belonging to higher castes started treating others as belonging to lower castes and then started the practice of untouchability.

4. Mention the problem of 'Casteism' in Indian politics. **CBSE 2020**

Or **How can caste take several forms in politics? Explain with examples.**

Ans. Caste can take various forms in Indian politics in the following ways

(i) When parties choose candidates in elections, they keep in mind the caste composition of the electorate and nominate candidates from same castes so as to get necessary support to win elections. A candidate from a particular minority community became candidate from the constituency which is mostly inhibited by that particular minority. For example, BSP won election with the support of Dalit.

(ii) During the campaigning, political parties and candidates make appeals to people to give their votes on the basis of caste. Some political parties are known to favour some castes and are seen as their representatives.

(iii) When governments are formed, political party takes care that representatives of different castes and tribes get a place in the ministry. For example, Droupadi Murmu, the first tribal women President of India.

5. Besides caste, which other factors do matter in electoral politics? Explain.

Ans. Besides caste, there are other factors which do matter in electoral politics. These are

(i) The voters have strong attachment to political parties which is often stronger than their attachment to their caste or community.

(ii) People within the same community have different interests depending on their economic status. Rich and poor, men and women from the same caste often vote very differently.

(iii) People's own assessment of the performance of the government *vis-a-vis* the performance of the candidate for the development of his own constituency are often decisive factors in elections.

6. "Secularism is not an ideology of some political parties or persons, but it is one of the foundations of our country." Examine the statement.

Ans. It is true that secularism is not an ideology of some political parties or persons, but it is one of the foundations of our countury.

This statement can be examined by the following points

(i) There is no official religion for the Indian state. Unlike the status of Buddhism in Sri Lanka, Islam in Pakistan and Christianity in England, our Constitution does not give a special status to any religion.

(ii) The Constitution provides to all individuals and communities freedom to prefers, practice and propagate any religion or not to follow any.

(iii) The Constitution allows the state to intervene in the matters of religion in order to ensure equality within religious communities. For example, it bans untouchability.

7. Read the statements given below regarding Communal politics. **Competency Based**

Statement I Communal politics is based on the idea that religion is the principal basis of a social community.

Statement II A communal mind often wants to dominate one's own religious community.

How can communalism pose a great threat or hindrance to the Indian democracy? Justify with relevant viewpoints that do reflect these statements I and II.

Ans. Communalism can pose a great threat to the Indian democracy in the following ways

- Communalism leads to the belief that people belonging to different religions cannot live as equal citizens within one nation. Either one of them must dominate the rest or they must form a different nation.
- It further believes that any attempt to gather all followers of one religion in a context other than religion is bound to suppress many voices within the community.

8. 'In India, women still lag behind men despite some improvements which have been made since independence. India is still a male dominated, patriarchal society. Women in India are facing discrimination in many ways.' **Competency Based**

(i) Could you think of some reasons why women's representation is so low in India?

(ii) In what way proper representation of women in legislature can solve the problem of gender-based discrimination?

Ans. (i) The reasons for low level of women participation in politics are
- Low literacy rate among the women as well as lack of political motivation.
- It is not considered a good profession for women to join politics.
- Political parties in India didn't provide tickets to women candidates to fight election from a particular area.

(ii) The proper representation of women in legislature can solve the problem of gender based discrimination in the following ways
- It will bring in more women-friendly laws.
- It will bring better policing that will help in greater security for women and better law enforcement.

9. "Caste has not still disappeared from contemporary India". Discuss the statement with the most likely suitable arguments.

Build the answer around these points **Competency Based**
- **Untouchability**
- **Access to Education**
- **Economic status**

Ans. Yes, it is true that caste has not still disappeared from contemporary India. Some of the suitable arguments related to this are as follows
- Despite constitutional safeguards, untouchability still persists in our society.
- A substantial number of low caste individuals continue having lack of access to education.
- Caste and economic status continue to be associated with each other.
- Most individuals get married inside their tribe or caste.

Long Answer Type Questions

1. "Women still lag behind men in India despite some improvements since independence' Analyse the statement."

Or **"In India, women still lag behind men despite some improvement since Independence." Support the statement with examples.** **CBSE 2020**

Ans. In India women still lag behind men despite some improvements since independence.

This can be analysed in the following ways
- As India is still dominated by patriarchal society, gender discrimination is prevalent at present. For example, women's role in public life is very less.
- Parents prefer to spend money for boy's education, thus dropout among girl child is high in schools.
- Girls perform as well as boys in school, but the literacy rate among women is only 54 per cent compared with 76 per cent among men.
- The proportion of women among the highly paid and valued jobs is still very little. Much of her work is not paid and therefore not valued.
- In almost all areas of work, women are paid less than the men, even when both works exactly the same.
- Women still face harassment, exploitation and violence in our society.

2. How does gender discrimination impact a country's development, and why is it important to recognise women's work in economic growth?

Ans. Gender discrimination negatively impacts a country's development by limiting women's participation in education, employment, and decision-making. When half the population is denied equal opportunities, economic growth slows, and social progress is hindered.

Women's work, especially household and caregiving tasks, remains unpaid and unrecognised, reducing their financial independence. Recognising women's contributions is crucial because their participation in the workforce boosts productivity, reduces poverty, and strengthens the economy. A country that values and empowers women benefits from higher literacy rates, better healthcare, and overall economic stability, leading to sustainable development and a more inclusive society.

3. "Communalism is harmful for the nation". Explain. **CBSE 2023**

What is communalism? How is communalism a hindrance in the functioning of our democracy? Explain.

Ans. Communalism means the followers of a particular religion must belong to one community and their fundamental interests are the same.

People of different religions cannot belong to the same community and their interests are bound to be different and involve a conflict.

Communalism leads to the belief that people belonging to different religions cannot live as equal citizens within one nation.

Communalism is harmful or makes hindrances in the functioning of our democracy in the following ways
- Communalism involves religious prejudices, stereotypes of religious communities and beliefs in the superiority of one's religion over other religions. These are not desirable in democracy.
- Communalism leads to the majoritarian dominance of majority community and desire to form separate political unit by minority community which is dangerous for democracy.
- Communalism involves the use of sacred symbols, religious leaders, emotional appeal to the voters of one religion in preference to others which leads to political mobilisation on religions lines. This cannot be afforded by democracy.

- Sometimes communalism leads to communal violence, riots and massacre which disturbs the foundation of democracy.

4. Explain the role of caste in Indian politics.

Ans. The role of caste in Indian politics is as follows
- Castes are ranked in hierarchical order, which determines the behaviour of one member of society over another.
- Caste plays a very important role in election. Political parties select their candidates on the basis of caste composition in the constituency.
- The voting in elections and mobilisation of political support from top to bottom moves on the basis of caste.
- Caste is an important factor for influencing the selection of candidates in elections, appointment of ministers, transfer and posting of public officials, etc.
- Caste functions as a pressure group in politics. Political bargaining is also done on caste lines.

5. Define the term secularism. Explain any four features of secularism in India.

Ans. Secularism refers to the separation of religion from the state. It means that the state should not discriminate among its citizens on the basis of religion. It should neither encourage nor discourage the followers of any religion. In India, the features of secularism are

(i) There is no official religion for the Indian states, *i.e.* unlike Sri Lanka (Buddhism), Pakistan (Islam) and England (Christianity).

(ii) All individuals and communities have the freedom to profess, practice and propagate any religion or not to follow any religion.

(iii) It prohibits discrimination on grounds of religion.

(iv) It allows the state to intervene in the matters of religion in order to ensure equality within religious communities, *viz.* it bans untouchability.

6. How far is it correct to say that it is not politics that gets caste ridden, but it is the caste that gets politicised? Explain.

Ans. It is correct to say that it is not politics that gets caste ridden, but it is the caste that gets politicised as caste can take various forms in politics in the following ways

(i) Each caste group tries to become bigger by incorporating within its neighbouring castes or sub-castes which were earlier excluded from it.

(ii) Various caste groups are required to enter a coalition with other castes or communities and thus enter a dialogue and negotiation.

(iii) New kinds of caste groups have come up in the political arena like 'backward' and 'forward' caste groups.

(iv) Caste plays different kinds of roles in politics. In some cases, politics gives many disadvantaged communities the opportunity to demand their share of power.

(v) Politics has helped people from OBC and Dalit castes to gain better access to decision-making.

(vi) But sometimes exclusive attention to caste can produce negative results like tensions, conflicts and violence in our society.

7. 'Caste inequalities are still prevalent in India'. Examine the statement. **Competency Based**

Ans. Caste inequalities are still prevalent in India. This statement can be explained in the following ways

(i) In India, hereditary occupational division was sanctioned by rituals. Members of the same caste group form a social community. Often they maintain same or similar occupation.

(ii) In India, most of the marriages are is held in same caste group. Intercaste marriage is not accepted by all.

(iii) Sometimes people do not eat with members from other caste groups.

(iv) Untouchability has not ended completely, although it is prohibited by our Constitution. Discrimination against the 'outcaste group' is still prevalent in our society.

8. Read the following excerpt about the relationship between caste and politics in India and answer the question that follows. **Competency Based**

Caste acts as a dividing and cohesive force in Indian politics. It provides a basis for the emergence of several interest groups in the Indian political system each of which competes with all other groups in the struggle for power. In the rural Indian context, the caste was a mobilisation of the communication channel, representation, and leadership and a link between the electoral process and the political process.

Source : troindia.in

The focus on caste and politics can sometimes give the impression that elections are all about caste and nothing else. Do you agree? Justify.

Ans. No, I don't agree with the given statement because of the following reasons
- No parliamentary constituency in the country has a clear majority of one single caste. So, every candidate and party need to win the confidence of more than one caste and community to win the elections.
- No party wins the votes of all the voters of a caste or community. When people say that a caste is a vote bank of one party then it means that a large proportion of the voters from the caste vote for the party.

- Many political parties may put up the candidates from the same caste. Some voters have more than one candidate from their caste while many voters may have no candidates from their caste.
- The ruling party MP or MLA frequently lose elections in our country. It would not have been possible if all castes or communities restricted their political preferences.

Case Based Questions

1. Read the following sources and answer the questions that follow.

Source A Women's Main Problem

There are reports of various kinds of harassment, exploitation and violence against women. Urban areas have become particularly unsafe for women.

They are not safe even within their own home from beating, harassment and, other forms of domestic violence. All this is well known yet issues related to women's well being or otherwise are not given adequate attentlon.

This has led many feminists and women's movements to the conclusion that unless women control power, their problems will not get adequate attention. One way to ensure this is to have more women as elected representatives.

(i) Evaluate the position of women in our society.

Source B Women's Representation in Government

In India, the proportion of women in legislature has been very low. For example, the percentage of elected women members in Lok Sabha has touched 14.36 per cent of its total strength for the first time in 2019. Their share in the state assemblies is less than 5 per cent. In this respect, India is among the bottom group of nations in the world. India is behind the averages for several developing countries of Africa and Latin America. In the government, Cabinets are largely all-male, even when a woman becomes the Chief Minister or the Prime Minister. One way to solve this problem is to make it legally binding to have a fair proportion of women in the elected bodies. This is what the Panchayati Raj has done in India. One-third of seats in local government bodies in Panchayats and Municipalities are now reserved for women. Now there are more than 10 lakh elected women representatives in rural and urban local bodies.

(ii) To what extent the government of India can do justice for empowering women through involving them in administration?

Source C Social Divisions Become a Political Issue

Women, organisation and activists have been demanding a similar reservation of atleast one-third of seats in the Lok Sabha and State Assemblies for women. A bill with this proposal has been pending before the Parliament for more than a decade. In 2023, Nari Shakti Vandan Adhiniyam (Womens' Reservation Act, 2023) was passed which will give 33 percent reservation of seats for women in Lok Sabha, State Legislative Assemblies and also Delhi Assembly.

Gender division is an example that some form of social division needs to be expressed in politics. This also shows that disadvantaged groups do benefit when social divisions become a political issue.

(iii) To what extent social divisions can be rectified in our society?

Ans. (i) In our society, women face challenges like harassment and violence, which often go unnoticed. Feminists argue that increasing women's representation in decision-making roles is essential to address these issues and promote gender equality in leadership.

(ii) The Government of India can empower women by increasing their representation in legislative bodies through measures like reserving seats, implementing gender quotas, and offering training. Raising awareness and encouraging political parties to support women candidates can also help, alongside expanding initiatives like Panchayati Raj for greater gender equality in governance.

(iii) The Women's Reservation Act of 2023 addresses gender inequality by reserving 33% of seats in the Lok Sabha, State Assemblies, and Delhi Assembly for women. This political reform acknowledges the need for social divisions to be represented in decision-making, helping disadvantaged groups like women gain more opportunities and power, fostering a more equitable society.

2. Read the passage given below and answer the questions that follow.

Communalism becomes more acute when religion is expressed in politics in exclusive and partisan terms, when one religion and its followers are pitted against another. This happens when beliefs of one religion are presented as superior to those of other religions, when the demands of one religious group are formed in opposition to another and when state power is used to establish domination of one religious group over the rest. This manner of using religion in politics is communal politics.

Communal politics is based on the idea that religion is the principal basis of social community. Communalism involves thinking along the following lines. The followers of a particular religion must belong to one community. Their fundamental interests are the same. Any difference that they may have is irrelevant or trivial for community life. It also follows that people who follow different religions cannot belong to the same social community. If the followers of different, religion have some commonalities these are superficial and immaterial. Their interests are bound to be different and involve a conflict. In its extreme form communalism leads to the belief that people belonging to different religions cannot live as equal citizens within one nation. Either, one of them has to dominate the rest or they have to form different nations.

This belief is fundamentally flawed. People of one religion do not have the same interests and aspirations in every context. Everyone has several other roles, positions and identities. There are many voices inside every community. All these voices have a right to be heard.

Therefore any attempt to bring all followers of one religion together in context other than religion is bound to suppress many voices within that community.

(i) When does communalism happen in our society?

(ii) Infer what will happen if the followers of different religions have some commonalities?

(iii) How does communal politics suppress many voices within same community?

Ans. (i) When state power is used to establish domination of one religious group over the rest of the groups and the demands of one religious group are formed in opposition to another, communalism happens at that time.

(ii) If the followers of different religions have some commonalities then these will be superficial and immaterial from the stand point of communalism. Their interests should be different according to the believers of communal politics.

(iii) Communal politics suppress many voices within same communities as people of same religion do not have the same interests and aspirations. They have different views and identities. Thus any attempt to bring all followers of same religion together is to suppress many voices within same community.

ASSESSMENT EXERCISE

Multiple Choice Type Questions (MCQs)

1. What is a formation in which all caste groups are placed from highest to lowest known as?
(a) Caste hierarchy (b) Pyramid
(c) Caste discrimination (d) Caste formation

2. In which group of countries is the participation of women in public life is the highest?
(a) England, Germany and France
(b) Sri Lanka, Yugoslavia and Holland
(c) Saudi Arabia, India and Pakistan
(d) Sweden, Norway and Finland

3. How did the women around the world respond to the gender issue in politics?
(a) They withdrew from public affairs.
(b) They organised and agitated for equals rights.
(c) They focus on domestic responsibilities.
(d) None of the above

4. Match the following.

List I (2011 Census)	List II (% of the country's population)
A. Muslims	1. 8.6
B. Christians	2. 2.3
C. Scheduled Tribes	3. 14.2

Codes

	A	B	C		A	B	C
(a)	3	2	1	(b)	2	1	3
(c)	1	2	3	(d)	1	3	2

Subjective Questions (VSA, SA & LA)

1. What do you mean by stereotype?

2. In which country, the very participation of women in public life is very low?

3. 'In India women's political representation is very low'. Justify.

4. Why is it necessary to have 'secularism' in India?

5. Do the 'caste' and 'vote bank' factors completely control the election in India?

6. What is expected from the women at home?

7. How did newly developed political consciousness help to improve the status of women in India?

8. Suggest any three steps to improve the women's participation in politics.

9. Mention any positive role of caste in politics.

10. In what ways does politics influence caste system?

Political Parties

CHAPTER 4

Political parties are one of the most visible institutions in a democracy. For the ordinary citizens, democracy is equal to political parties. It is important to know the nature and working of political parties. The dynamics of political parties influence the policy **making process**, the selection of leaders and the overall direction of a nation.

4.1 Meaning of Political Parties

A political party is a group of people who come together to contest elections and hold power in the government.

All political parties have some policies and programmes for the society with a view to promote the collective good. They try to convince people that their policies are better than others. They seek to implement their policies by winning popular support through elections.

Political parties reflect fundamental political divisions in a society. All the parties favour certain part of the society and thus they involve **partisanship**[1].

A political party is recognised by its policies and its interests. It has the following three components

(i) The leaders (ii) The active members

(iii) The followers

Functions

- **Contest Elections** Candidates are recommended by political parties to contest elections. They select their candidates in different ways. These candidates may be chosen by the top party leaders like in India, or by members and supporters of the party like in USA.
- **Formulate Policies and Programmes** Parties put forward their policies and programmes and voters can choose from them. A party reduces several opinions into a few essential points that it supports. A government is expected to base its policies on ideology of the ruling party.
- **Making Laws** Political parties play a major role in making laws for the country. In the legislature, laws are passed after a debate.
- **Form and Run Government** Political parties form and run governments. The big decisions regarding the policies are taken by political executive that come from the political parties. Parties recruit leaders, train them and make them ministers.
- **Role of Opposition** Parties that lose election, play the role of **opposition**[2] to the party in power. They criticise government for their wrong policies and mobilise opposition to the government.
- **Shape Public Opinion** Parties shape public opinion by raising and highlighting issues. Parties have large number of members and activists spread all over the country.

  Many of the pressure groups are extensions of political parties. Sometimes parties also launch movements for the resolution of the problems faced by the people.
- **Access to Government and Schemes** Political parties provide people access to government machinery and welfare schemes. It is easy for the public to approach their local party leader than a government officer. The local party leader has to listen to people's need and demands, otherwise people can reject them in the next elections.

1 **Partisanship** A tendency to take a side and inability to take a balanced view on an issue. A person who is strongly committed to a party, group or action is called partisan.

2 **Opposition** The political party or a group of parties that is a part of the Legislature, but not a part of the government, is known as opposition. They criticise and check the activities of the government.

4.2 Need or Necessity of Political Parties

Political parties are needed because they perform a variety of functions. Modern democracies cannot exist without political parties.

The rise of political parties is directly linked to the emergence of representative democracies. As societies became large and complex, they needed some agency to gather different views on various issues and to present these to the government.

Society needs a mechanism to support or restrain the government, make policies, justify or oppose them. Political parties fulfil these needs of every representative government.

Political parties are found in almost all countries of the world, whether big or small, old or new, developed or developing.

In non-party based election like in panchayat election, parties do not contest formally, but the village gets split into more than one faction and each of these puts up a panels of its candidates. The political parties exactly works in this way.

Without parties, following situations may occur

- Every candidate in the elections will be independent. No one will be able to make any promises to the people about any major policy changes.
- The government may be formed, but its utility will remain uncertain. Elected representatives will be answerable to their constituency for what they do in the locality. However, no one will be responsible for how the country will be run.

Try These

1. **Name the three components of a political party.**
2. **What role do political parties play in shaping government policies?**
3. **What do you understand by the term opposition?**
4. **In which elections, parties do not contest formally?**

4.3 Systems of Political Parties

The different countries around the world choose different party systems. Party system in any country evolves over a long time depending on the nature of society, its social and regional division, history of politics and its system of election.

Each country develops a party system that is influenced by special circumstances.

Broadly, political party system can be divided into following three categories

(i) **One-Party System** In this party system, only one party is allowed to control and run the government. For example, **China** has one-party system.
This system is not a good option for democracy because the democracy must allow at least two parties to compete in election and provide a fair chance to come in power.

(ii) **Two-Party System** In this party system, two parties have a serious chance to win majority and form the government. The power usually changes between two main parties. The **United States of America** and **United Kingdom** are the examples of two-party system.

(iii) **Multi-Party System** In this party system, several parties compete for power and more than two parties have a chance of coming to power, either on their own strength or in alliance with others. For Example, India has a multi-party system. This is because the social and geographical diversity of such a large country cannot be managed easily by two or three parties.

When several parties in a multi-party system come together for the purpose of contesting and winning, it is called **alliance** or **front**. Some examples of alliances are the National Democratic Alliance (NDA) and the United Progressive Alliance (UPA) in India.
The multi-party system leads to political instability but it allows a variety of interests and opinions to enjoy political representation.

Popular Participation in Political Parties

Political parties are becoming unpopular among people, which can be inferred from the following sample surveys

- Political parties do not enjoy much trust among the people in South Asia, and it is one of the least trusted institutions all over the world.
- The level of participation in the activities of political parties is fairly high.
- The proportion of the members of some political party is higher in India than many advanced countries like Canada, Japan, Spain and South Korea.
- Over the last three decades, the proportion of members of political party in India has increased steadily.

4.4 Types of Political Parties

Democracies that follow a federal system all over the world tend to have two kinds of political parties

(i) **State Parties** Parties that are present in only one of the federal units.

(ii) **National Parties** Parties that are present in several or all units of the federation.

In India, there are both national and state parties.
Every party in the country has to register with the **Election Commission.**

The commission treats all parties equally, but it offers some special facilities to large and established parties. These parties are given a unique symbol. Only the official candidates of that party can use that election symbol.

Parties that get this privilege and some other special facilities are 'recognised' by the Election Commission and these are called **recognised political parties.**

National Parties

A party that secures at least 6% of the total votes in Lok Sabha elections or Assembly elections in four states and wins at least 4 seats in the Lok Sabha, is recognised as a National Party.

There were six recognised national parties in India in 2023. These are discussed below

(i) **Indian National Congress** (INC) It is one of the oldest parties of the world founded in 1885. It is popularly known as the Congress Party. It supports secularism and welfare of weaker sections and minorities.

(ii) **Communist Party of India-Marxist** (CPI-M) It was founded in 1964. It believes in Marxism-Leninism. It supports socialism, secularism and democracy and opposes imperialism and communalism. It enjoys strong support in West Bengal, Tripura and Kerala.

(iii) **Bharatiya Janata Party** (BJP) It was founded in 1980, by reviving the old Bharatiya Jana Sangh formed by Syama Prasad Mukherjee in 1951.

The aim of the party is to build a strong and modern India by drawing inspiration from India's ancient culture and values, and Deendayal Upadhyay's ideas of integral humanism and *Antyodaya*.

Cultural nationalism (Hindutva) is an important element in its belief of Indian nationhood and politics. It emerged as the largest party in 2019 Lok sabha elections.

(iv) **Bahujan Samaj Party** (BSP) It was founded in 1984, under the leadership of Kanshi Ram.
It seeks to represent and secure power for the Bahujan Samaj which includes the Dalits, Adivasis, OBCs and religious minorities. It draws inspiration from the ideas and teachings of Sahu Maharaj, Mahatma Phule, Periyar Ramaswami Naicker and Babasaheb Ambedkar.
It has its main base in Uttar Pradesh and substantial presence in Madhya Pradesh, Chhattisgarh, Uttarakhand, Delhi and Punjab.

(v) **Aam Aadmi Party** (AAP) It was founded on 26th November, 2012 by Arvind Kejriwal during Anti-corruption movement against the Indian Government led by Indian National Congress. The party's election symbol is a 'Broom'. The party was founded on the idea of accountability, clean administration, transparency and good governance.

(vi) **National People's Party** (NPP) It was formed in July 2013 under the leadership of P.A Sangma. NPP is the first political party from North-East India to have attained the status of a national party. The core philosophy of the party is education and employment to all as well as empowerment of all sections of the society. It formed government in Meghalaya and has presence in many of North Eastern States.

Note* *The Election Commission of India withdrew the national party status of NCP, AITC and CPI. The National People's Party (NPP) and Aam Aadmi Party accorded the status of national party.*

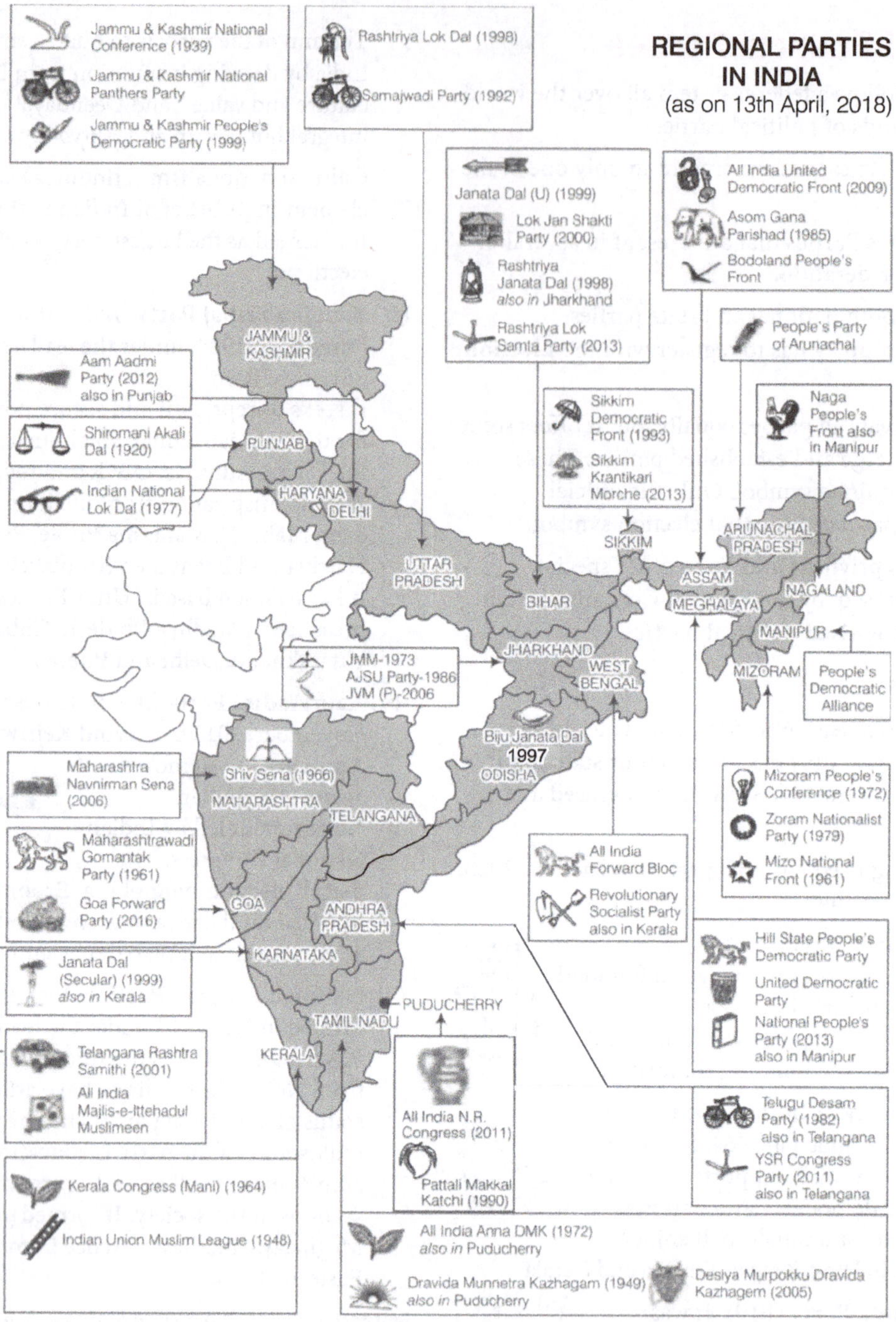

State Parties

A party that secures at least 6% of the total votes in an election to the Legislative Assembly of a state and wins at least two seats, is recognised as a State party. These are commonly referred to as **regional parties**.

Some of the regional parties are all India parties have succeeded only in some states.

Parties like the **Samajwadi Party,** and **Rashtriya Janata Dal** have national level political organisation with units in several states.

Some of the regional parties like **Biju Janata Dal, Sikkim Democratic Front** and **Mizo National Front** and Telangana Rashtra Samithi are conscious about their state identity.

Status of State Parties

Over the last three decades, the number and strength of state parties has expanded. This has made the Parliament of India politically more and more diverse.

Until 2014, no national party was able to secure on its own a majority in Lok Sabha. As a result, the national parties form alliances with state parties.

Since 1996, nearly every state party has got an opportunity to be a part of one or the other national level Coalition Government. This has contributed to the strengthening of federalism and democracy in our country.

Try These

1. **Give an example of country having two-party system.**
2. **In which Indian state does the Bahujan Samaj Party (BSP) have its main base?**
3. **In order to become a National party, what per cent of votes are required by a party in the Lok Sabha election?**
4. **Name one regional party which have National level organisation.**

4.5 Challenges to Political Parties

Popular dissatisfaction and criticism has focussed on four problem areas in the working of political parties.

Political parties need to face and overcome these problems or challenges to remain effective in democracy.

These challenges are

(i) Lack of Internal Democracy within Parties

In most of the political parties, the power is concentrated in the hands of one or few leaders at the top. Parties do not keep membership registers, do not hold organisational meetings and do not conduct internal elections regularly.

Ordinary members of the party do not get sufficient information about what happens inside the party. They do not have the connections needed to influence the decision.

As a result, the leaders assume greater power to make decisions in the name of the party.

Only one or few leaders exercise supreme power in the party and those who disagree with them find it difficult to continue in the party.

The personal loyalty of the leader become more important than loyalty towards party principles and policies.

(ii) Dynastic Succession

The top positions in many political parties are generally controlled by members of one family. This is unfair to other members of the party.

Leaders on the top have unfair chance of favouring their families and friends. This is also bad for democracy, since people who do not have adequate experience or popular support, occupy positions of power.

This tendency is present in all over the world, including some older democracies.

(iii) Money and Muscle Power

There is an increasing role of rich people and big companies in democratic politics.

As the parties are focussed only on winning elections, they tend to use shortcuts to win elections. They tend to nominate those candidates who have or can raise lots of money. Rich people and companies who give funds to the parties tend to have influence on the policies and decisions of the party. In some cases, parties support criminals who can win elections.

(iv) Meaningful Choice to the Voters

Parties do not offer a meaningful choice to the voters. In recent years, there has been a decline in the ideological difference among parties in most part of the world. In order to offer meaningful choice, parties must be significantly different.

For example, the difference between the Labour Party and the Conservative Party in Britain is very little. They agree more on fundamental aspects but differ only in the way they frame and implement the policies.

In India, the differences among all the major parties on the economic policies have reduced. Those who want really different policies have no option available to them.

Sometimes people cannot even elect very different leaders as the same set of leaders keep shifting from one party to another.

4.6 Reforms for Political Parties

Political parties need to be reformed to face the challenges. Recent efforts and suggestions in our country to reform the political parties and their leaders are as follows

- **Anti-Defection Law** According to this law, if any MLAs or MPs changes the party after the election, he or she will lose the seat in legislature.

  This was done because many elected representatives were involved in **defection**[3] in order to become ministers or for cash rewards.

3 **Defection** It means when someone leaves or switches from one party to another.

- **Details of Property and Criminal Cases** To reduce the influence of money and criminals, the Supreme Court passed an order. Now, it is compulsory for every candidate who contest elections to file an **Affidavit**[4] giving details of his property and criminal cases pending against him. However, there is no system to check if the information given by the candidate is true or not.
- **File an Income Tax Return** The Election Commission passed an order making it necessary for political parties to hold their organisational elections and file their income tax returns. The parties have started doing so, but sometimes, it is only formality.

Besides these suggestions, many other suggestions are often made to reform political parties. These are as follows

- A law should be made to regulate the internal affairs of political parties. It should be made compulsory for political parties to
  - maintain a register of its members
  - follow its own Constitution
  - have an independent authority
  - act as a judge in case of party disputes
  - hold open elections to the highest posts.
- It should be made mandatory for political parties to give a minimum number of tickets (about one-third) to women candidates. Similarly, there should be a quota for women in the decision-making bodies of the party.
- There should be state funding of elections. The government should give parties money to support their election expenses. This support could be given in kind, like petrol, paper, telephone, etc. Or it could be given in cash on the basis of votes secured by the party.

People can put pressure on political parties through petitions, publicity and agitations. Ordinary citizens, pressure groups and movements, and the media can play an important role in this.

Political parties can be improved if people who want to improve them, join political parties. The quality of democracy can be improve by the public participation. If ordinary citizens do not take part in politics, then reforming politics is impossible.

Try These

1. **What do you mean by the term defection?**
2. **Which document is mandatory to submit by the candidate who contest elections?**
3. **Is it necessary for a political party to file an income tax return?**
4. **Is dynastic succession seen in India?**

4 **Affidavit** It refers to a signed document submitted to an officer, where a person makes a sworn (promised to tell the truth) statement regarding her personal information.

Mind Map

POLITICAL PARTIES

Meaning
A group of people who come together to contest elections and hold power in the government.

Functions
- Contest elections
- Formulate policies and programmes
- Making laws
- Form and run the government
- Role of opposition
- Shape public opinion
- Access to the government and schemes

Need or Necessity of Political Parties
Without political parties, following situations may occur
- Every candidate in the elections will be independent.
- The government may be formed but its utility will remain uncertain.

Recent Reforms and Suggestions
- Anti-defection law
- Details of property and criminal cases
- File an income tax return

Other Suggestions
Law to regulate internal affairs of political parties
- Maintain a register of its members.
- Follow its own Constitution.
- Have an independent authority.
- Act as a case judge in case of party disputes.
- Hold open elections to the highest posts.

Reforms for Political Parties

Challenge to Political Parties
- Lack of Internal Democracy with in parties.
- Dynastic succession
- Money and muscle power
- Meaningful choice to the voters

Systems of Political Parties

Two Party System
Two parties have a serious chance to win majority and form the government, e.g.USA and UK

Multi Party System
Several parties compete for power and more than two parties have a chance of coming to power, either on their own strength or in alliance with others, e.g. NDA and UPA in India.

One Party System
- Only One party is allowed to control and run the government , e.g. China

Types of Political Parties

National Parties
- A party that secures at least 6% of the total votes in Lok Sabha elections or Assembly elections in four states and wins at least four seats in the Lok Sabha.
- The national parties in India are
  - Indian National Congress
  - Communist Party of India - Marxist
  - Bharatiya Janata Party
  - Bahujan Samaj Party
  - Aam Aadmi Party
  - National People's Party

State Parties
- A party that secures at least 6% of the total votes in an election to the Legislative Assembly of a state and wins at least two seats.
- The state parties in India include
  - Samajwadi Party
  - Rashtriya Janata Dal
  - Biju Janata Dal
  - Sikkim Democratic Front
  - Mizo National Front
  - Telangana Rashtra Samithi

NCERT FOLDER

Covering Intext Questions and Exercises of NCERT

EXERCISE

Q.1 State the various functions that political parties perform in a democracy.

Or **Describe any five functions of political party.** **CBSE 2020**

Or **Describe any three functions of political parties.** **CBSE 2024**

Ans. Political parties perform various functions in a democracy like

(i) They contest elections.

(ii) Parties put forward their policies and programmes for voters to choose from them.

(iii) Political parties play an important role in the law making process.

(iv) Political parties form and run governments.

(v) Political parties, which are unable to secure majority and form the government, play the role of opposition to the party in power.

(vi) They shape public opinion.

Q.2 What are the various challenges faced by political parties?

Ans. Various challenges faced by political parties are

(i) The parties are lackin internal democracy, which keeps many prospective leaders deprived of their rights.

(ii) There have been dynastic successions in many political parties. This often deprives the parties of appropriate leadership.

(iii) The parties sometimes involve in the use of money and muscle power for winning elections. This slow down development is against the spirit of democracy.

(iv) Different political parties do not have significant ideological differences among them. So, there is a lack of meaningful choice before the voters.

Q.3 Suggest some reforms to strengthen parties so that they perform their functions well.

Ans. Some suggestions to reform political parties are

(i) Anti-Defection Law which prevents elected MLAs and MPs from changing parties. At the same time, this law has made any dissent even more difficult.

(ii) It is mandatory for every candidate to give details of his property and criminal cases pending against him.

(iii) Political parties should maintain a register of its members and have periodic elections for its office bearers.

(iv) Political parties should have one-third seats reserved for women.

(v) The government should give money to the parties to support their election expenses.

(vi) People should put pressure on political parties through petitions, publicity and agitations.

Q.4 What is a political party?

Or **Explain the meaning of political party.**

Ans. A political party is a group of people who come together to contest elections and hold power in the government. It has three components, *viz*, the leaders, the active members and the followers.

Q.5 What are the characteristics of a political party?

Ans. The characteristics of a political party are

(i) They reflect fundamental political division in a society.

(ii) Parties are a part of society and thus involve partisanship.

(iii) They seek to implement policies and programmes of their agenda by winning popular support through election.

(iv) They are formed to promote the collective good through policies and programmes.

Q.6 A group of people who come together to contest elections and hold power in the government is called a ....

Ans. political party

Q.7 Match the following.

List I	List II
A. Congress Party	1. National Democratic Alliance
B. Bharatiya Janata Party	2. State Party
C. Communist Party of India (Marxist)	3. United Progressive Alliance
D. Telugu Desam Party	4. Left Front

Codes

	A	B	C	D		A	B	C	D
(a)	3	1	2	4	(b)	3	4	1	2
(c)	3	1	4	2	(d)	4	3	1	2

Ans. (c)

Q.8 Who among the following is the founder of the Bahujan Samaj Party?

(a) Kanshi Ram (b) Sahu Maharaj
(c) BR Ambedkar (d) Jyotiba Phule

Ans. (a) Kanshi Ram

Q.9 What is the guiding philosophy of the Bharatiya Janata Party?

(a) Bahujan Samaj (b) Revolutionary democracry
(c) Integral humanism (d) Modernity

Ans. (c) Integral humanism

Q.10 Consider the following statements on parties.

A. Political parties do not enjoy much trust among the people.
B. Parties are often rocked by scandals involving top party leaders.
C. Parties are not necessary to run governments.

Which of the statements given above are correct?

(a) A, B and C (b) A and B
(c) B and C (d) A and C

Ans. (b) A and B

Q.11 Read the following passage and answer the questions given below.

Muhammad Yunus is a famous Economist of Bangladesh. He received several International honours for his efforts to promote economic and social development for the benefit of the poor. He and the Grameen Bank that he started jointly, received the Nobel Peace Prize for the year 2006.

In February 2007, he decided to launch a political party and contest in the parliamentary elections. His objective was to foster proper leadership, good governance and build a new Bangladesh. He felt that only a political party different from the traditional ones would bring about new political culture.

His party would be democratic from the grassroots level. The launching of the new party, called Nagarik Shakti (Citizens' Power), has caused a stir among the Bangladeshis. While many welcomed his decision, some did not like it.

"Now I think Bangladesh will have a chance to choose between good and bad and eventually have a good government," said Shahedul Islam, a government official. "That government, we hope, would not only keep itself away from corruption but also make fighting corruption and black money a top priority." But leaders of traditional political parties who dominated the country's politics for decades were apprehensive. "There was no debate (over him) winning the Nobel, but politics is different—very challenging and often controversial," said a senior leader of the Bangladesh Nationalist Party. Some others were highly critical. They asked why he was rushing into politics. "Is he being planted in politics by mentors from outside the country," asked one political observer.

(a) Do you think Yunus made a right decision to float a new political party?
(b) Do you agree with the statements and fears expressed by various people?
(c) How do you want this new party organised to make it different from other parties?
(d) If you were the one to begin this political party, how would you defend it?

Ans. (a) Yes, I think Yunus made a right decision to float a new political party.

(b) I agree with the statement of a government official, Shahedul Islam that the launch of this new party may change the political culture of the country. But I do not agree with the view points of a senior leader of the Bangladesh Nationalist Party. He expressed his fear about the capability of Muhammad Yunus in the field of politics.

(c) I think, people like Muhammad Yunus when established a political party, it should be democratic from very grassroots level. This party should fight against corruption and the problem of black money in the country which dominated the country, as Yunus is a respected personality with a great vision.

(d) If I were one of them to begin this political party, I would try to develop direct interaction with the people living in the countryside and in towns. Regular meetings of the party members, seminars, workshops, etc. would have been adopted to win the confidence of the people. I would bring about a totally new political culture, more democratic and more transparent.

REVIEW EXERCISE

Including Competency Based Questions

Part I

Multiple Choice Questions (MCQs)

1. Which is the essential element of a political party?
(a) Organisation
(b) National interest
(c) Fundamental principles
(d) All of the above

2. Which is not a function of political party?
(a) To contest election
(b) Faith in violent methods
(c) Political education to the people
(d) Form public opinion

3. Under which system, only one-party is allowed to function?
(a) Single-party system
(b) Bi-party system
(c) Multi-party system
(d) None of the above

4. Which of the following is a regional party?
(a) Bharatiya Janata Party (BJP)
(b) Bahujan Samaj Party (BSP)
(c) Dravida Munnetra Kazhagam (DMK)
(d) Communist Party of India (Marxist) CPI (M)

5. Political parties can be reformed by
(a) reducing the role of muscle power
(b) reducing the role of money
(c) state funding of election
(d) All of the above

6. Name the political party that ruled continuously in West Bengal for 34 years.
(a) Indian National Congress
(b) Samajwadi Party
(c) Communist Party of India. (Marxist)
(d) Rashtriya Janata Dal Party

7. Lack of internal democracy is the challenge faced by
(a) national party (b) regional party
(c) political party (d) None of these

8. Which one among the following pairs is correctly matched? CBSE SQP 2022-23

(a) Bharatiya Janata Party	–	National Democratic Alliance
(b) Congress Party	–	Left Front
(c) Communist Party of India	–	Regional Party
(d) Mizo National Front	–	United Progressive Alliance

9. Which of the following is the primary factor, which contributed to the emergence of multiple political parties at the same level in India?
(a) A federal political system CBSE Additional SQP 2023-24
(b) Varied economic conditions
(c) Linguistic and regional diversity
(d) Low levels of literacy and political awareness

10. Choose the correct option related to the regional political parties of India: CBSE 2025

Party Election	Symbol	State
A. Rashtriya Lok Dal	Mashal	Uttar Pradesh
B. Telugu Desam	Cycle	Andhra Pradesh
C. Telangana Rashtra Samiti	Kite	Telangana
D. Shiromani Akali Dal	Chasma	Punjab

11. In a representative democracy, which of the following best describes the role of elected representatives? CBSE Additional SQP 2023-24
(a) They have absolute power and authority to make decisions without consulting the public.
(b) They are accountable to the public and make decisions on behalf of their constituents.
(c) They act as mere figureheads with no real power or influence in the government.
(d) They serve lifetime appointments and cannot be removed from the office.

12. It was founded in 1964. It believes in Marxism-Leninism. It supports socialism, secularism and democracy and opposes imperialism and communalism. It enjoys strong support in West Bengal, Tripura and Kerala. Identify the political party.
(a) Bahujan Samaj Party (BSP)
(b) Communist Party of India (CPI)
(c) Communist Party of India-Marxist (CPI-M)
(d) Indian National Congress (INC)

13. How do political parties ensure accountability to the public? Choose the most suitable option from the following. CBSE 2024
(a) Through Press Conferences
(b) Through Social Media Campaigns
(c) Through encouraging Partisanship
(d) Through Elections and Voter Support

14. **Which of the following are the main components of a political party?** **CBSE 2025**

Choose the correct option

I. Leaders
II. Active members
III. Followers
IV. Pressure groups

Options

(a) Only I, II and III are correct.
(b) Only II, III and IV are correct.
(c) Only I, III and IV are correct.
(d) Only I, II and IV are correct.

15. **Consider the statements given below and choose the correct answer.**

Statement I China has one-party system, where only one party is allowed to control and run the government. This is a good option for democracy.

Statement II India has a multi-party system; the government is formed by various parties coming together in a coalition.

Codes

(a) Statement I is correct and II is incorrect.
(b) Statement I is incorrect and II is correct.
(c) Both I and II statements are incorrect.
(d) Both I and II statements are correct.

16. **Consider the statements given below and choose the correct answer.**

Statement I Indian National Congress Party was founded in 1947.

Statement II The law states that if any MLA or MP changes parties, he or she will lose the seat in the legislature.

Codes

(a) Statements I and II are correct
(b) Statements I and II are incorrect
(c) Statement I is correct.
(d) Statement II is correct.

Answers

1. (d) **2.** (b) **3.** (a) **4.** (c) **5.** (d)
6. (c) **7.** (c) **8.** (a) **9.** (c) **10.** (b)
11. (b) **12.** (c) **13.** (d) **14.** (a) **15.** (b)
16. (d)

Match the Following

1.

List I	List II
A. All India Forward Bloc	1. Meghalaya
B. Samajwadi Party	2. West Bengal
C. National People's Party	3. Uttar Pradesh

Codes

	A	B	C		A	B	C
(a)	2	3	1	(b)	3	2	1
(c)	2	1	3	(d)	1	2	3

2.

List I	List II
A. Rashtriya Lok Samta Party	1. Karnataka
B. Janata Dal (Secular)	2. Bihar
C. Bodoland People's Front	3. Assam

Codes

	A	B	C		A	B	C
(a)	2	3	1	(b)	1	2	3
(c)	2	1	3	(d)	3	1	2

3.

List I	List II
A. Indian National Congress	1. 1964
B. Communist Party of India-Marxist	2. 1980
C. Bharatiya Janata Party	3. 1885

Codes

	A	B	C		A	B	C
(a)	1	3	2	(b)	2	3	1
(c)	3	1	2	(d)	3	2	1

Ans. 1. (a) 2. (c) 3. (c)

Assertion-Reason

1. **Assertion** (A) India has a multi-party system.

Reason (R) It is because of the social and geographical diversities in India.

Codes

(a) Both A and R are true and R is the correct explanation of A
(b) Both A and R are true, but R is not the correct explanation of A
(c) A is true, but R is false
(d) A is false, but R is true

2. **Assertion** (A) Political parties do not enjoy much trust among the people in South Asia.

Reason (R) Political parties are one of the least trusted institutions all over the world.

Codes

(a) Both A and R are true and R is the correct explanation of A
(b) Both A and R are true, but R is not the correct explanation of A
(c) A is true, but R is false
(d) A is false, but R is true

3. **Assertion** (A) It is often said that political parties are facing a crisis. **CBSE Additional SQP 2023-24**
Reason (R) They are very unpopular, and the citizens are indifferent to political parties.
Codes
(a) Both A and R are true and R is the correct explanation of A
(b) Both A and R are true, but R is not the correct explanation of A
(c) A is true, but R is false
(d) A is false, but R is true

4. **Assertion** (A) Those parties which are recognised as national parties can only contest elections for the Union level.
Reason (R) Recognition of a political party as a national party is accorded by the Election Commission.
Codes
(a) Both A and R are true and R is the correct explanation of A
(b) Both A and R are true, but R is not the correct explanation of A
(c) A is true, but R is false
(d) A is false, but R is true

5. **Assertion** (A) The Constitution was amended to prevent elected MLA's and MP's from changing parties.
Reason (R) It is mandatory for political parties to give one-third tickets to women.
Codes
(a) Both A and R are true and R is the correct explanation of A.
(b) Both A and R are true, but R is not the correct explanation of A.
(c) A is true, but R is false.
(d) A is false, but R is true.

6. **Assertion** (A) Political parties are easily one of the most visible institutions in a democracy.
Reason (R) For most ordinary citizens, democracy is equal to political parties.
Codes
(a) Both A and R are true and R is the correct explanation of A
(b) Both A and R are true, but R is not the correct explanation of A
(c) A is true, but R is false
(d) A is false, but R is true.

7. **Assertion** (A) Every party in the country must register with the Election Commission.
Reason (R) While the commission treats all parties equally, it offers some special facilities to large and established parties.
Codes
(a) Both A and R are true and R is the correct explanation of A
(b) Both A and R are true, but R is not the correct explanation of A
(c) A is true, but R is false
(d) A is false, but R is true

8. **Assertion** (A) Parties put forward different policies and programmes and the voters choose from them.
Reason (R) Each of us has similar opinions and views on what policies are suitable for society.
Codes
(a) Both A and R are true and R is the correct explanation of A
(b) Both A and R are true, but R is not the correct explanation of A
(c) A is true, but R is false
(d) A is false, but R is true

Ans. 1. (a) Both A and R are true and R is the correct explanation of A
2. (b) Both A and R are true, but R is not the correct explanation of A
3. (a) Both A and R are true and R is the correct explanation of A
4. (d) A is false, but R is true
5. (c) A is true, but R is false
6. (a) Both A and R are true and R is the correct explanation of A
7. (a) Both A and R are true and R is the correct explanation of A
8. (c) A is true, but R is false

Picture Based Questions

1. **This cartoon drawn during the Presidency of George Bush in USA suggests that**

(a) Two party system is ignored.
(b) Republican Party is the only party.
(c) Corporate American dictates all majors institutions of the country.
(d) Republican Party faces many problems.

2. Given below is a cartoon created by RK Laxman, the renowned Indian cartoonist and comics artist.

What is the cartoon trying to depict?

(a) Politicians are only active when there are elections.

(b) Politicians are following a certain code of conduct.

(c) Politicians are keeping an eye on the citizens.

(d) Politicians are using the media as a puppet to serve their interests.

Ans. 1. (c) Corporate American dictates all majors institutions of the country.

2. (a) Politicians are only active when there are elections.

Case Based Question

1. Read the information and answer the following questions.

The rise of political parties is directly linked to the emergence of representative democracies. As we have seen, large societies need representative democracy. As societies became large and complex, they also needed some agency to gather different views on various issues and to present these to the government. They needed some ways to bring various representatives together so that a responsible government could be formed. They needed a mechanism to support or restrain the government, make policies, justify or oppose them. Political parties fulfill these needs that every representative government has. We can say that parties are a necessary condition for a democracy.

(i) Which of the following statements best describes Representative Democracy?

(a) It is not a common form of democracy in modern times.

(b) It involves direct participation.

(c) It involves indirect participation by elected representatives.

(d) It was the most prevalent form of democracy in the colonial era.

(ii) Why does a large society need representative democracies? With reference to the above context, infer the appropriate option.

(a) To form an ideal form of government.

(b) To gather public opinions.

(c) To resolve issues of minority communities.

(d) To form a responsible government.

(iii) Consider the following statements about political parties and choose the correct option.

I. Political parties help the government to make policies.

II. Political parties are a necessary condition for a democracy.

III. Political parties justify or oppose the representative governments.

Codes

(a) Only I

(b) Both I and II

(c) Both II and III

(d) All of the above

(iv) Why can't modern democracies exist without political parties? Identify the reason/s from the given options.

(a) Loss of accountability towards people.

(b) State responsibility will lead to national integration.

(c) As the utility of government will remain uncertain in nature.

(d) Both (a) and (c)

Ans. (i) (c) It involves indirect participation by elected representatives.

(ii) (d) To form a responsible government.

(iii) (d) All of these

(iv) (d) Both (a) and (c)

Part II

Very Short Answer Type Questions

1. Which is the most visible institutions in a democracy?

Ans. Political parties are one of the most visible institutions in a democracy to promote collective good for the society.

2. Define Partisanship.

Ans. Partisanship is a tendency to take a side and inability to take a balanced view on an issue.

3. What is a ruling party?

Ans. The political party that runs government is a ruling party.

4. What is opposition?

Ans. The political party that is part of Legislature but not a part of the government is called opposition.

5. What do you mean by One-party system?

Ans. A system under which only one political party is allowed to function in the country is called one-party system.

6. Examine the possible consequences on the basic rights of party members within political organisations' that lack internal democracy. CBSE Additional SQP 2023-24

Ans. The possible consequences on the basic rights of party members within political organisations that lack internal democracy could be the following

- The party workers may face restrictions on raising their opinions, ideas, or concerns within the party structure.
- Not every party worker would get an equal chance to climb up the success ladder.

7. In a hypothetical democratic nation with a population that is religiously homogenous, should there still be multiple political parties? Justify your stance in about 40 words.

Ans. Yes, it is possible that despite being a religiously homogenous population, there are chances of having multiple political parties due to several reasons such as

- Multiple political parties help to represent diverse political perspectives.
- It helps in policy formation and to avoid authoritarianism in democracy.

8. Political Parties have lakhs of members and activists spread all over the country. Many of the pressure groups are the extensions of political parties among different sections of society. Parties sometimes also launch movements. Competency Based

(i) Why do political parties sometimes launch movements?

Ans. Political Parties sometimes launch movements for the resolution of problems faced by the people.

(ii) Why do people usually reject some political parties in the next elections?

Ans. If some political parties are not responsive to people's needs and demands, then people usually reject the parties in the next elections.

9. Riya conducted a survey to find out about the views of people about the political parties in her college. As per that survey, people expressed their dissatisfaction with the failure of political parties to perform their functions well.
How do state or regional political parties contribute to strengthening federalism and democracy in India? Competency Based

Ans. State and regional political parties contribute in strengthening federalism and democracy in India in the following ways

- They provide a variety of choices for people as each of them has different agendas and focus on different issue.
- They provide a platform for different pressure and social groups, and communities to put forward their demands.

10. Which country has one-party system?

Ans. Socialist (or Communist) country like China, has one-party system.

11. What is a two-party system?

Ans. When two major parties exist in a country and the power generally changes between them (as in USA and England), the system is known as the two-party system.

12. What do you mean by multi-party system?

Ans. When more than two political parties exist and are functioning in a country like India, the system is known as multi-party system.

13. If all the decisions of a political party are made by a single family and all other members are neglected, what challenge is being faced by that party?

Ans. If all the decisions of a political party are made by a single family and all other members are neglected, then the party faces the problem of dynastic politics.

14. Differentiate between one-party and two-party system. CBSE SQP Term II 2021

Ans. The differences between one-party and two-party system are

One-Party System	Two-Party System
It is defined as those countries where only one party is allowed to control and run the government.	It is defined as those countries where only two parties contest elections.
An example of one-party system is China where only Communist Party is allowed to rule.	Examples of countries with two-party system are United States of America and United Kingdom.

Short Answer Type Questions

1. What is the role of the opposition party in a democracy?

Ans. The opposition party plays a very important role in a democracy as

(i) It acts as guardian of civil liberties, ensuring that fundamental rights and freedom are protected.

(ii) Opposition parties participate in Parliamentary or legislatives debates, contributing to the formulation and amendment of laws.

(iii) It keeps a check on the working of the ruling party.

(iv) It puts different views in the Parliament and criticise the government for its failures or wrong policies.

2. State any two advantages of the multi-party system. In what way is an alliance different from a coalition government?

Ans. The advantages of multi-party system are

(i) This system allows a variety of interests and opinions to enjoy political representation.

(ii) Under this system, the choice of the voter is not limited to two candidates only. It gives a voter enough scope to make intelligent choice.

Alliance is different from coalition as when several parties join hands for the purpose of contesting elections, it is called an alliance or a front, e.g. the National Democratic Alliance. On the other hand, when no single party gets a majority in the election and the government is formed by two or more parties coming together, it is referred to as a coalition government.

3. Give any two merits and demerits of one-party system.

Ans. Merits of one party system are

(i) **Strong and Stable Government** Since there is no opposition party, government is strong and cannot be removed or voted out of power.

(ii) **Less Expensive** Since there is only one party and one candidate of the party, not much money is spent on the election.

Demerits of one-party system are

(i) **Undemocratic** With power concentrated in one-party, there can be a lack of accountability and transparency in government.

(ii) **No Choice** In one-party system, voters have limited options. They can't chose or differentiate between good or bad candidates.

4. Explain merits and demerits of multi-party system.

Ans. Merits of the multi-party system are

(i) Multi-party system allows a variety of interests and opinions to enjoy political representation.

(ii) In this system, people have an opportunity to make a choice between several candidates.

Demerits of the multi-party system are

(i) This system often appears very messy.

(ii) This system sometimes leads to political instability.

5. Write a short note on Bahujan Samaj Party (BSP).

Ans. Bahujan Samaj Party (BSP) was founded by Kanshi Ram in 1984.

It seeks to represent Bahujan Samaj, which includes Scheduled Castes (SCs), Scheduled Tribes (STs), OBCs and religious minorities.

It gets inspiration from the ideas and teachings of Sahu Maharaj, Mahatma Phule, Periyar Ramaswami Naicker and BR Ambedkar.

It stands for the cause of securing the interests and welfare of the dalits and oppressed people. It has its main base in Uttar Pradesh and substantial presence in neighbouring states like Madhya Pradesh, Chhattisgarh, Uttarakhand, Delhi and Punjab. After Kanshi Ram, Mayawati became the leader and formed government in Uttar Pradesh.

6. When was the Communist Party of India (Marxist) formed? Mention the ideologies of the party.

Ans. The Communist Party of India (Marxist) was formed in 1964.

The ideologies of Communist Party of India (Marxist) are

- The party believes in Marxism-Leninism. It supports socialism, secularism and democracy and opposes imperialism and communalism.
- The party accepts democratic elections as a useful and helpful means for securing the objective of socio-economic justice in India.
- The party is critical of the new economic policies that allow free flow of foreign capital and goods into the country.

7. What is meant by Regional political party? State the conditions required to be recognised as a regional political party.

Ans. Regional political party exists, operates and functions at the regional level. It gives prominence to regional issues, specific problems of the region and it has influence only on the people of that region. It lays more stress on regional culture identity, which it wants to preserve and promote.

Conditions required to be recognised as a regional political party are

- It should have polled at least 6% valid votes in an election to the Legislative Assembly.
- It had won at least 2 seats in Legislative Assembly elections.

8. Describe any three broad guidelines for devising ways and means for political reforms in India.

Ans. The three broad guidelines for devising ways and means for political reforms in India are

(i) A law should be made to regulate the internal affairs of political parties. Political parties should maintain a register of its members, hold open elections, follow its own Constitution, etc.

(ii) Political parties can be monitored by ordinary citizens, pressure groups, media, etc. Pressure on political parties can be done through petitions, publicity and agitation.

(iii) The quality of democracy depends on the degree of public participation. It is difficult to reform politics if ordinary citizens do not directly participate in politics and simply criticise it from outside.

9. What is meant by 'Defection' in democracy? Explain.

Ans. Defection in democracy is a political phenomena. It means moving of a person from one party to another party for some personal benefit. It happens when a legislature, after having been elected from a particular party leaves it and joins in other party.

Anti-Defection Law was formulated to prevent elected MLA's and MP's from changing parties. Now the law states that if any MLA or MP changes parties, he or she will lose seat in the legislature. The new law has brought percentage of defection down and has made dissent even more difficult.

10. What is the difference between National and Regional party? **CBSE 2020**

Ans. The differences between National and Regional Party are

National Party	Regional Party
It influences the whole country.	It's influence is limited and region-based.
It takes National as well as International issues.	It is interested in promoting regional/state interest only.
It has to secure at least 6% of the total votes in the Lok Sabha elections or Assembly elections in 4 states and win at least 4 seats in the Lok Sabha.	It has to secure at least 6% of the total votes in an election to the Legislative Assembly of a state and win at least 2 seats in the State Assembly.

11. "There is a decline in the ideological differences among parties in most parties of the world has been seen". What kind of challenge is being referred to with reference to a political party? Enumerate the features of this challenge. **Competency Based**

Ans. The kind of challenge being referred to here is the lack of meaningful choices for the voters.

Some of the features of this challenge are as follows

- In most regions of the world, ideological distinctions between parties have been decreasing in recent years. They agree on core issues but disagree on how policies should be expressed and implemented.
- Those who choose other policies have little choice.
- People are sometimes unable to elect extremely different leaders because the same collection of leaders continues shifting from one party to another.

12. Discuss the most likely functions performed by the ruling and opposition parties in India. **Competency Based**

Build the answer around these points

- Law making
- Criticise government policies

Ans. Functions performed by the ruling parties in India are as follows

- They play a significant role in law making for the country.
- They form the government and govern the country.
- They recruit and train leaders who are capable of handling different ministries.

Functions performed by the Opposition parties in India are as follows

- They oppose the government by voicing different views.
- They criticise government policies if the government is unable to address people's issues.

Long Answer Type Questions

1. Explain any five major functions of the political parties. **CBSE 2023**

Or Describe the role of political parties in Indian democracy.

Or Describe the role of political parties in India. **CBSE SQP 2022-23**

Ans. Political parties perform a series of functions in our democracy. These are

(i) Parties contest elections. By winning the election, political party can form the government. Sometimes more than two parties form coalition and form the government.

(ii) Parties put forward different policies and programmes and the voters choose from them.

(iii) Parties play a decisive role in making laws for our country by making debate and passing law for people.

(iv) Parties form and run government by recruiting leaders, train them and make them ministers to run the government.

(v) Parties shape public opinion by raising and highlighting important issues.

(vi) Those parties that lose in the elections play the role of opposition to the parties in power by criticising government for its failures or wrong policies.

(vii) Parties provide people access to government machinery and welfare schemes implemented by governments. Parties have to be responsive to people's needs and demands otherwise people can reject those parties in the next elections.

2. What is meant by a political party? Describe the three components of a political party.

Ans. A political party is a group of people who come together to contest elections and hold power in the government. Political parties always formulates some policies and programmes for the society with a view to promote the collective good. Every political party wants to persuade people and tries to win the support of people.
Three components of a political party are

(i) **The Leaders** Every political party has some prominent leaders who formulate policies and programmes of the party and choose candidates for contesting elections.

(ii) **The Active Members** They are involved in different committees of the party and participate directly in their activity.

(iii) **The Followers** They believe in the party's ideology and support the party by casting their votes in favour of the party at the time of election.

3. Name the national political party which gets inspiration from India's ancient culture and values. Mention four features of that party. **CBSE Term II 2022**

Ans. Bharatiya Janata Party (BJP) gets inspiration from India's ancient culture and values.
The main features of this party are

(i) Cultural nationalism or Hindutva is an important element in BJP's conception of Indian nationhood and politics.

(ii) It wants full territorial and political integration of Jammu and Kashmir with India.

(iii) The aim of the party is to build a strong and modern India by drawing inspiration from India's ancient culture and values.

(iv) It supports the ideas of 'Swadeshi' which encourages the use and promotion of domestically produced goods and services.

4. Why has India adopted a multi-party system? Explain. **CBSE Term II 2022**

Or **Why did India adopt the multi-party system? Explain with suitable arguments.** **CBSE 2025**

Ans. India adopted multi-party system for the following reasons

- India being a vast and diverse country, the multi-party system was needed to accommodate the vast population.
- The social and geographical diversity of India could not be represented by two or three parties.
- The multi-party system in India evolved over a long time, depending on the nature of society, its social, regional division, its history of politics and its system of elections.
- Multi-party system ensures a healthy competition between different parties and prevents dictatorship of a single party. Indian Constitution declares India as a democratic country. Multi-party system fulfils this criteria and provides chance for proper growth of the nation.

5. Explain in four different manners that political parties are still in the grip of some serious challenges.

Ans. The political parties are still in the grip of some serious challenges which are

(i) The first challenge is lack of democracy within parties. All over the world, there is a tendency in political parties towards the concentration of powers in one or few leaders at the top. Parties do not keep membership registers, do not hold organisational meetings and do not conduct internal elections regularly.

(ii) The second challenge is dynastic succession where the top positions of a party are always enjoyed by members of one particular family.
This trend is harmful for other members of the party as well as for democracy.

(iii) The third challenge is about the growing role of money and muscle power in parties which is specially observed during elections. Rich people and companies who give funds to the parties always have a say on the policies and decisions of the party.

(iv) The fourth challenge is that very often parties do not seem to offer a meaningful choice to the voters. In our country, the difference among all the major parties on the economic policies have reduced. Sometimes, the same set of leaders keep shifting from one party to another, thus people have no option available to them.

6. "Political parties are rightly called the government in disguise." Justify the statement with reference to democratic politics by four arguments. **Competency Based**

Ans. Political parties are rightly called the government in disguise. The four arguments to justify the statement are

(i) In most democracies, elections are fought among the candidates put up by political parties. The party which wins the majority, forms the government.
In a parliamentary system, the leader of the party in power becomes the Prime Minister and he appoints the other ministers.

(ii) In a democracy, a large number of similar opinions have to be grouped together to provide a direction in which policies can be formulated by the government.

Political party reduces a vast multitude of opinions into a few basic positions and if it is ruling party, government accepts the line taken by it.

(iii) Political parties raise and highlight issues. Often they shape public opinion. There are always some socio-economic and political issues at the domestic and international level. Political parties always try to solve the issues.

(iv) The parties which play the role of opposition in the government always criticise government for its wrong policies. Opposition parties mobilise opposition to the government.

7. "The political parties are necessary for democracy." Justify the statement. Competency Based

Or What is the necessity of a political party for a democracy?

Or Explain, how the rise of political parties are directly linked to the emergence of representative democracies. CBSE Term II 2022

Or Can you imagine a modern democratic country without political parties? Justify your answer giving relevant points. CBSE Additional SQP 2023-24

Or Explain the importance of political parties in a democracy. CBSE 2025

Ans. Modern democracies cannot exist without political parties. They are necessary due to the following reasons

- The rise of political parties is directly linked to the emergence of representatives democracies.
- As societies became large and complex, they need some agency to gather different views on various issues and present these to the government.
- Every candidate in the elections will be independent. No one will be able to make any promises to the people about any major policy changes.
- The government may be formed, but its utility will remain ever uncertain. Elected representatives will be accountable to their constituency for what they do in the locality. But no one will be responsible for how the country will be run.
- Society needs a mechanism to support or restrain the government, make policies, justify or oppose them. Political parties fulfil these needs of every representative government.

8. "Lack of internal democracy is a challenge to efficient functioning of Indian political parties." Justify the statement. Competency Based

Ans. Lack of internal democracy is a challenge to the efficient functioning of political parties in the following ways

(i) All over the world, there is a tendency in political parties towards the concentration of power in one or few leaders at the top.

(ii) Parties do not keep membership registers, do not hold organisational meetings and do not conduct internal elections regularly.

(iii) Ordinary members of the party do not get sufficient information on what happens inside the party. They do not have the means or the connection needed to influence the decisions.

As a result, the leaders assume greater power to make decision in the name of the party.

(iv) Since one or few leaders exercise the power in the party, those who disagree with the leadership find it difficult to continue in the party.

9. Identify and list the symbols of the following political parties with their states.

(i) Shiromani Akali Dal (ii) Samajwadi Party

(iii) AIADMK

(iv) All India Trinamool Congress

(v) Rashtriya Janata Dal

Ans.

Party	Place	Symbol
Shiromani Akali Dal	Punjab	Balanced Scales or Weighing balance
Samajwadi Party	Uttar Pradesh	Bicycle
AIADMK	Tamil Nadu	Two Leaves
All India Forward Bloc	West Bengal	Lion
Rashtriya Janata Dal	Bihar	Lantern

10. 'The Multi-party system often appears very messy and leads to political instability. At the same time, this system allows a variety of interests and opinions to enjoy political representation.' Justify the statements with relevant points referring to India and stating the reason for her evolution into this system. CBSE Additional SQP 2023-24, Competency Based

Ans. In a democracy, several parties compete for power. When more than two parties have a reasonable chance of coming to power either on their own strength or in alliance with others, we call it a multi-party system. Thus, in India, we have a multi-party system.

In multi-party system, the government is formed by various parties coming together in a coalition. The multi-party system often appears very messy and leads to political instability. At the same time, this system allows a variety of interests and opinions to enjoy political representation.

When several parties in a multi-party system join hands for the purpose of contesting elections and winning power, it is called an alliance or a front. For instance, in India, there were three such major alliances in 2004 parliamentary elections that are the National Democratic Alliance, the United Progressive Alliance and the Left Front. India has evolved a multi-party system because the social and geographical diversity in such a large country is not easily absorbed by two or even three parties. No system is ideal for all countries and all situations.

11. Parties shape public opinion. They raise and highlight issues. Parties have lakhs of members and activists spread all over the country. Many of the pressure groups are the extensions of political parties among different sections of society. Parties sometimes also launch movements for the resolution of problems faced by people. Often opinions in society crystallise on the lines parties take.

Suggest any five ways that helps to reform the political parties in India. **Competency Based**

Ans. Some of the suggestions that may help to reform the political parties in India are

- A law should be made to regulate the internal affairs of political parties. It should be made compulsory for political parties to
  - maintain a register of its members
  - follow its own Constitution
  - have an independent authority
  - act as a judge in case of party disputes
  - hold open elections to the highest posts.
- It should be made mandatory for political parties to give a minimum number of tickets (about one-third) to women candidates. Similarly, there should be a quota for women in the decision-making bodies of the party.
- There should be state funding of elections. The government should give parties money to support their election expenses. This support could be given in kind, like petrol, paper, telephone, etc or it could be given in cash on the basis of votes secured by the party.
- People can put pressure on political parties through petitions, publicity and agitations. Ordinary citizens, pressure groups and movements, and the media can play an important role in this.
- Political parties can be improved if people who want to improve political parties join them. The quality of democracy can be improve by the public participation. If ordinary citizens do not take part in politics, then reforming politics is impossible.

Case Based Questions

1. Read the following source and answer the questions that follow: **CBSE 2025**

The Need for Political Parties

As we have seen, large societies need representative democracy. As societies became large and complex, they also needed some agency to gather different views on various issues and to present these to the government. They needed some ways, to bring various representatives together so that a responsible government could be formed. They needed a mechanism to support or restrain the government, make policies, justify or oppose them. Political parties fulfil these needs that every representative government has. We can say that parties are a necessary condition for a democracy.

(i) Explain the meaning of 'representative democracy'.

(ii) How do political parties shape public opinion?

(iii) Why are political parties considered a necessary condition for a democracy? Explain.

Ans. (i) Representative democracy is a system of government where citizens elect representatives to make decisions and laws on their behalf, rather than participating directly. Elected officials are accountable to the people and are chosen through regular elections.

(ii) Political parties shape public opinion by gathering different views on various issues and presenting them to the government. They mobilise support, engage the public, and provide a platform for discussing and debating issues. Through their actions, campaigns, and positions, political parties influence how the public perceives and reacts to policies, thus shaping public opinion in a democracy.

(iii) Political parties are considered a necessary condition for a democracy because they gather and represent different views on various issues. In large and complex societies, political parties help bring representatives together to form a responsible government, ensuring diverse opinions are considered in decision-making. They also provide a mechanism to support or restrain the government, make policies, and either justify or oppose them. Through these functions, political parties play a crucial role in organising and facilitating democratic governance.

2. Read the source given below and answer the questions that follow.

The recent efforts and suggestions in our country to reform political parties and its leaders

The Constitution was amended to prevent elected MLAs and MPs from changing parties. This was done because many elected representatives were indulging in Defection in order to become ministers or for cash rewards. Now the law says that if any MLA or MP changes parties, he or she will lose the seat in the Legislature.

This new law has helped bring defection down. At the same time this has made any dissent even more difficult. MPs and MLAs have to accept whatever the party leaders decide. The Supreme Court passed an order to reduce the influence of money and criminals. Now, it is mandatory for every candidate who contests elections to file an Affidavit giving details of his property and criminal cases pending against him.

It should be made mandatory for political parties to give a minimum number of tickets, about one-third, to women candiates. Similarly, there should be a quota for women in the decision making bodies of the party.

There should be state funding of elections. The government should give parties money to support their election expenses. This support could be given in kind : petrol, paper, telephone, etc. Or it could be given in cash on the basis of the votes secured by the party in the last election.

(i) What is Defection?

(ii) Infer the importance of an Affidavit given by the candidate during contesting election.

(iii) How does the position of women changed due to the reforms made for political parties?

Ans. (i) Defection in politics means moving of a elected person from one party to another party.

(ii) Due to the Supreme's Court order candidate has to give the details of his property and criminal case report through an Affidavit. It helps the public to decide the suitable candidate to elect.

(iii) Many suggestions are made to reform political parties. Among these one of the most important reforms is to give at least one-third number of tickets to women candidate. This helps women to participate in direct politics and they can raise their voice for their own demands.

ASSESSMENT EXERCISE

Multiple Choice Questions (MCQs)

1. Which one of the following facilities does the Election Commission offer to a recognised political party?

(a) Election funds (b) Election symbol
(c) Party name (d) Manifesto

2. In which form of the government, rulers are always elected by people?

(a) In democracy (b) In federalism
(c) In monarchical system (d) None of these

3. What information is mandatory for election candidates to file according to Supreme Court order?

(a) Educational qualifications
(b) Health details
(c) Property details and criminal cases
(d) Family background

4. In which year Communist Party of India was founded?

(a) 1930 (b) 1925
(c) 1948 (d) 1964

Subjective Questions (VSA, SA & LA)

1. Where political parties have to register themselves?

2. What is the function of a political party?

3. Explain different forms of party system in brief.

4. Why are symbols allotted to political parties in India? Explain the reasons.

5. How will you define a regional political party?

6. What is an alternative political formation?

7. What measures have been taken to curb problem of defection?

8. What is the guiding philosophy of Communist Party of India (Marxist)?

9. What is meant by lack of internal democracy within parties? Explain.

10. 'Political parties are necessary condition for a democracy'. Analyse the statement with example.

CHAPTER 5

Outcomes of Democracy

A number of outcomes can be expected from democracy. The expected and actual outcomes of democracy can be assessed in various aspects like quality of government, economic well being, inequality, social differences, and finally by freedom and dignity.

5.1 Assessment of Democracy's Outcomes

Democracy has been considered a better form of government than other alternatives because it

- promotes equality among citizens
- enhances the dignity of an individual
- improves the quality of decision-making
- provides a method to resolve conflicts
- allows scope to correct mistakes.

Most of the people support democracy against other alternatives such as rule by a monarch or military or religious leaders. However, many people are not satisfied with the democracy in practice. Thus, democracy is seen to be good in principle, but not in its practice.

For the assessment of outcomes of democracy, it is to be recognised that democracy is just a form of government. It can only create conditions for achieving something. The citizens have to take advantage of those conditions and achieve those goals.

Political Outcomes

The political outcomes of democracy are to produce accountable, responsive and legitimate government.

Accountable and Responsible Government

In a democracy people have the right to choose their rulers and people have a control over them. Therefore, the most basic outcome of democracy is to produce an accountable government to the citizens which is responsive to their needs and expectations.

It is expected that democratic government develops mechanisms for citizens to hold the government accountable.

Democracy is based on the idea of deliberation and negotiation. So, it takes more time to follow procedures before reaching a decision, due to which its decisions are more acceptable to the people and are more effective. Democracies are concerned about majorities and public opinion.

Legitimate Government

Democratic government is a legitimate government as it is people's own government. The people have right to elect their own representative. Thus, there is an immense support for the idea of democracy all over the world.

Democracy ensures that the decision making is based on norms and procedures. The citizens have the right and means to examine the process of decision making. This is known as **transparency**.

On the basis of political outcomes, democracy can be measured by practices and institutions such as regular free and fair election, open public debate on major policies and legislations and citizens' right to information about the government and its functioning.

Democracy on the Basis of Political Outcomes

On the basis of political outcomes, democracies show a mixed record as

- Democracies have had greater success in setting up regular and free elections and in setting up conditions for open public debate.

  However, most democracies fail to make elections completely fair and subjective every decision to public debate.
- Democratic governments do not have a very good record when it comes to sharing information with citizens. However, they are better than any non-democratic government in this aspect.
- In a democracy, a government is expected to be attentive to the needs and demands of the people and largely free of corruption.

However, democracies often frustrate the needs of the people and often ignore the demands of a majority of its population. It is also not free from corruption. At the same time, non-democracies are also not free from corruption and are less sensitive to the people.

Economic Outcomes

Economic growth and development, reduction of poverty and inequality are the prominent economic outcomes of democracy.

Economic Growth and Development

It is expected from a democratic government that it should bring economic growth and development. However, many democracies of the world are unable to fulfil this expectation. It is because of population size, global situation, cooperation from other countries, economic priorities, etc.

For example, the rate of economic growth among the dictatorships countries was slightly higher in between 1950 to 2000, than the democratic countries. However, the difference in the rates of economic development between less developed countries with dictatorships and democracies is negligible.

Thus, democracy does not guarantee economic development, but it is still preferred because it has several other positive outcomes.

Reduction of Inequality and Poverty

Democracy is expected to reduce economic inequalities. It is based on political equality and all individuals have equal right to choose their representative. However, there are growing economic inequalities among the individuals.

A small number of wealthy people enjoy maximum share of wealth and incomes. As a result of this, their share in total income of the country is increasing and the income of poor is declining.

Sometimes the poor find it difficult to meet their basic needs of life, such as food, clothing, house, education and health. Poor constitute a large proportion of voters, but still the democratic governments are not concerned to improve their conditions.

The situation is much worse in some countries. In Bangladesh, more than half of its population lives in poverty. People of several poor countries are dependent on the rich countries even for food supplies.

Social Outcomes

The social outcomes of a democracy are accommodating social diversity, and providing dignity and freedom to the citizens.

Accommodation of Social Diversity

Democracy is expected to produce harmonious social life. It usually develop a procedure to accommodate various social divisions. This reduces the possibility of social tensions becoming violent.

No society can fully and permanently resolve conflicts among different groups. However, democracy is best to handle social differences, divisions and conflicts. On the other hand, non-democratic government often ignore or suppress internal social differences.

A democracy must fulfill the following two conditions in order to achieve this outcome

(i) It is necessary to understand that democracy is not simply rule by majority opinion.

The majority always needs to protect the interest of the minority, thus the government's function is to represent general interest.

(ii) It is also necessary that rule by majority does not become rule by majority community in terms of religion or race or linguistic group, etc.

Rule by majority means that in case of every decision or in case of every election, different persons and groups may and can form a majority.

Thus, democracy is recognised only when every citizen has a chance of being in majority at some point of time. If someone is not in majority on the basis of birth, then the democratic rule discontinues to be accommodative for that person or group.

Dignity and Freedom of the Citizens

Democracy is much superior to any other form of government in promoting dignity and freedom of the individual.

Every individual wants to receive respect from other human beings. Sometimes conflict arises among individuals as they feel that they are not treated with due respect.

The passion for respect and freedom are the basis of democracy. Democracies throughout the world have recognised and achieved this (respect and freedom) in various degrees.

Most of the societies across the world were historically male dominated societies. The long struggles by women have created some sensitivity today that respect and equal treatment of women are necessary for democratic societies. In spite of this, the women are not always treated with respect.

However, it becomes easier for women to organise a struggle for dignity and freedom after the recognition of the principal of individual freedom and dignity.

Democracy in India has supported the claims of the disadvantaged and discriminated castes for equal status and equal opportunity.

However, the cases of caste- based inequalities and cruelties are still present. Thus, it is the recognition that makes ordinary citizens to value their democratic rights.

Try These

1. **What is the most basic outcome of democracy?**
2. **Which type of government does not have transparency?**
3. **Name the government where all laws of the countries are equally applicable to its all citizen.**
4. **Is democracy able to give the equal treatment to women?**
5. **Democracy transforms people from the status of a ...... into that of a citizen.**

Conclusion

The most distinctive feature about democracy is that, its examination never ends. As people get some benefits, they ask for more and want to make democracy even better. Thus, people always come up with more expectations and many complaints. It shows that people have developed awareness and the ability to expect.

The people's expression of dissatisfaction with the functioning of democracy represent the success of democracy, and transforms people from the status of a subject into that of a citizen.

Mind Map

OUTCOMES OF DEMOCRACY

Economics Outcomes

Economic Growth and Development

It is expected from a democratic government that it should bring economic growth and development.

Reduction of Inequality and Poverty

- Democracy is expected to reduce economic inequalities.
- People of several poor countries are dependent on the rich countries even for food supplies.

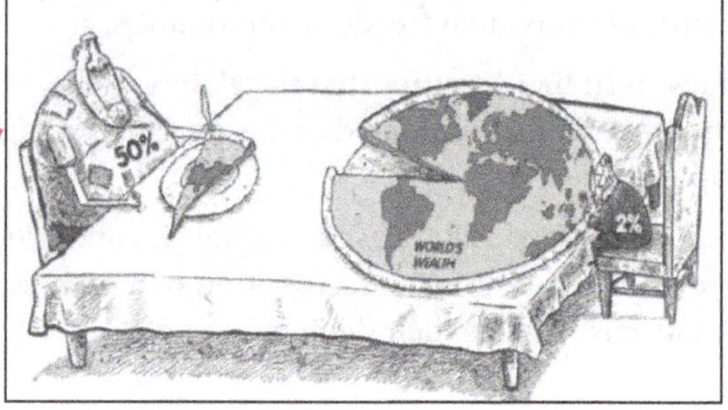

Political Outcomes

Accountable, Responsive and Legitimate Government

- In a democracy, people have the right to choose their rulers and people have a control over them.
- Democratic government develops mechanisms for citizens to hold the government accountable.
- Democracy is based on the idea of deliberation and negotiation.

Social Outcomes

Dignity and Freedom of the Citizens

- Democracies throughout the world have recognised and achieved respect and freedom in various degrees.
- Democracy in India has supported the claims of the advantaged and discriminated for equal status and equal opportunity.

Accommodation of Social Diversity

- Democracy is expected to produce harmonious social life.
- Democracy is best to handle social differences, divisions and conflicts. On the other hand, non-democratic government often ignore or suppress internal social differences.

NCERT FOLDER

Covering Intext Questions and Exercises of NCERT

EXERCISE

Q.1 How does democracy produce an accountable, responsive and legitimate government?

Or "Democracies produce an accountable, responsive and legitimate governments." Support the statement with suitable examples.

Or "Democracy is an accountable, responsible and legitimate government." Explain the statement. **CBSE 2024**

Ans. Democracy produces an accountable, responsive and legitimate government in the following ways

Accountable Government Democracy produces an accountable government as the people have the right to choose their representatives through the electoral process. These elected representatives form the government and participate in the decision-making process on behalf of the people. This is known as transparency. If these elected representatives do not work in a proper way, people have a chance to not elect them in next election.

Responsive Government Democracy produces a responsive government. As democratic government is elected by the people, it is people's own government. It promotes the formation of public opinion and take care of the needs and expectation of the people.

Legitimate Government Further, democratic government is a legitimate government because regular election after a fixed time is its key feature. It may be slow, less efficient but it is the people's own legitimate government.

Q.2 What are the conditions under which democracies accommodate social diversities?

Ans. Democracy is considered to be the most suitable form of government to accommodate these diversities as it aims at giving equal rights and opportunities to all the citizens irrespective of caste, religion, colour, sex, race, etc.

Q.3 Give arguments to support or oppose the following assertions.

(a) Industrialised countries can afford democracy but the poor need dictatorship to become rich.

(b) Democracy cannot reduce inequality of incomes between different citizens.

(c) Government in poor countries should spend less on poverty reduction, health, education and spend more on industries and infrastructure.

(d) In democracy, all citizens have one vote, which means that there is absence of any domination and conflict.

Ans. (a) This statement is incorrect. If we compare democracy and dictatorship regimes between 1950 to 2000, we find countries under dictatorship to be more economically advanced. But, if we compare between less developed countries, the difference is negligible. For example, India being a third world nation, now becomes one of the fast growing economies of the world.

On the other hand, Zimbabwe which was a fairly prosperous nation, has run into huge international debt with the progression of Robert Mugabe's rule. Thus, it is not always proper to say that the poor need dictatorship to become rich.

(b) This statement is incorrect. Democracy reduces the inequality of incomes between citizens. For example, the Minimum Wages Act, enacted by the Indian Government have helped in increasing the per capita income of the country. Thereby, making its citizens more prosperous and reducing inequality in incomes of citizens.

(c) This statement is not correct as the government in poor countries should maintain a balance between investment on poverty, food, clothing, health, education and in industries and infrastructure. A country needs to spend on all the sectors maintaining a balance, so that every sector helps the other sector to grow.

(d) This statement is not correct. In democracy, every citizen has one vote, political parties cannot avoid any social group. The political parties have to formulate policies which will benefit all the groups. But all these do not mean that conflicts are totally absent in a democracy. They can happen if the demands of one social group are against the demands of the other social group.

Democracy only avoids the possibility of such conflicts by giving everyone equal rights and freedom in the society.

Q.4 Identify the challenges to democracy in the following descriptions. Also suggest policy/institutional mechanism to deepen democracy in the given situations.

(a) Following a High Court directive a temple in Odisha that had separate entry doors for dalits and non-dalits allowed entry for all from the same door.

(b) A large number of farmers are committing suicide in different states of India.

(c) Following allegation of killing of three civilians in Gandwara in a fake encounter by Jammu and Kashmir police, an enquiry has been ordered.

Ans. (a) **Challenge Involved** Challenges of social inequality and untouchability.

Suggestion To check this challenge, a law has been passed to declare untouchability a legal offence.

Efforts have been made to promote social equality. Central Government has directed the State Government not to practice untouchability in any form. If anyone tries to do so, he will be punished under the law of Untouchability Offence Act, 1955.

(b) **Challenge Involved** Challenges of poverty and economic inequalities.

Suggestion To look into grievance of the poor farmers, loan should be provided to them at low rates of interest, that could be easily returned.

For this purpose, cooperative societies should come forward to help the poor farmers. Crop Insurance Policy should be implemented for any eventuality of crop failure.

(c) **Challenge Involved** Challenge to preserve the people trust in government agencies, like the police.

Suggestion To check such challenges in a democratic government, the law should be amended. So that, the police do not take law and order in their hands and should have a reasonable behaviour towards the civilians.

Q.5 In the context of democracies, which of the following ideas is correct.
Democracies have successfully eliminated

(a) conflicts among people
(b) economic inequalities among people
(c) differences of opinion about how marginalised sections are to be treated
(d) the idea of political inequality

Ans. (d) the idea of political inequality

Q.6 In the context of assessing democracy, which among the following is odd one out. Democracies need to ensure

(a) free and fair elections
(b) dignity of the individual
(c) majority rule
(d) equal treatment before law

Ans. (c) majority rule

Q.7 Studies on political and social inequalities in democracy show that

(a) democracy and development go together
(b) inequalities exist in democracies
(c) inequalities do not exist under dictatorship
(d) dictatorship is better than democracy

Ans. (b) inequalities exist in democracies

Q8 Read the passage given below and answer the question that follows.

Nannu is a daily wage earner. He lives in Welcome Mazdoor Colony, a slum habitation in East Delhi. He lost his ration card and applied for a duplicate one in January 2004. He made several rounds to the local Food and Civil Supplies Office for the next 3 months.

But the clerks and officials would not even look at him, leave alone do his job or bother to tell him status of his application. Ultimately, he filed an application under the Right to Information Act asking for the daily progress made on his application, names of the officials, who were supposed to act on his application and what action would be taken against these officials for their inaction.

Within a week of filing application under the Right to Information Act, he was visited by an inspector from the Food Department, who informed him that the card had been made and he could collect it from the office.

When Nannu went to collect his card next day, he was given a very warm treatment by the Food and Supply Officer (FSO), who is the Head of a Circle. The FSO offered him tea and requested him to withdraw his application under the Right to Information, since his work had already been done.

What does Nannu's example show? What impact did Nannu's action have on officials? Ask your parents their experiences when they approach government official to attend to their problems.

Ans. Nannu's example shows the importance of the Right to Information Act.

Nannu made several rounds to the local Food and Civil Supplies Office for a new ration card. But the clerks and officials did not listen to him. When he filed an application under the Right to Information Act, it created a great impact.

Within a week, an official from Food Department visited his house to inform that the card had been made and he could collect it in any working day.

On the next day, when he went to collect the card, he was warmly received by the Food and Supply Officer (FSO). Nannu was requested to withdraw his application under RTI, since he has received his ration card.

My parents had mixed experiences about the government officials when they approached for their problems. Some officers took prompt actions and were very helpful. But in some cases, they faced difficult situation where the officials were very reluctant to do the needful.

REVIEW EXERCISE

Including Competency Based Questions

Part I

Multiple Choice Questions (MCQs)

1. Rule of Law is the feature of which form of government?
(a) Dictatorship (b) Democracy
(c) Monarchy (d) All of these

2. The record of democracies is not impressive because
(a) it often frustrates the needs of the people
(b) it often ignores the demands of a majority of its population
(c) Both (a) and (b)
(d) None of the above

3. Which one the following is not true about a democratic government? **CBSE 2023**
(a) Democratic government is a legitimate government.
(b) Democratic government is a responsive government.
(c) Democratic government is the people's own government.
(d) It does not allow room to correct mistakes.

4. No deliberation and negotiation for taking decisions is part of
(a) Democratic government
(b) Federal government
(c) Parliamentry government
(d) Non-democratic government

5. Democracy has failed on which grounds?
(a) Corruption (b) Economic inequality
(c) Literacy rate (d) All of these

6. Democracy can lead to
(a) accommodation of social differences
(b) secular society
(c) harmonious social life
(d) All of the above

7. Least expectation from democracy is that
(a) it cannot accommodate various social life.
(b) it should produce a harmonious social life.
(c) it develops procedure to conduct competition.
(d) it reduces the possibility of violent tensions.

8. Democracy attain people happiness by
(a) government function to represent general view
(b) equal distribution of resources
(c) better governance
(d) All of the above

9. Why is the democratic government regarded as a better choice?
(a) It promotes equality among citizen
(b) It ensures economic development
(c) It provides a method to resolve conflict
(d) Both (a) and (c)

10. Which of the following is a definite indicator of the successful implementation of democratic governance? **CBSE Additional SQP 2022-24**
(a) Free economy dictated by the market forces.
(b) Provision of basic amenities to the citizens.
(c) Establishment of central financial institutions.
(d) Establishment of institutions to protect people's rights.

11. Which of the following statements is not true about Democracy? **CBSE Additional SQP 2022-24**
(a) People wish to be ruled by representatives elected by them.
(b) It is free from corruption.
(c) It is expected to produce good governments.
(d) Is guarantees the rights of citizens.

12. How is democracy better than other forms of Government? Choose the most appropriate option. **CBSE 2025**
(a) It enhances the dignity of individuals.
(b) It promotes equality among elites.
(c) It promotes tendency of private ownership only.
(d) It increases the individualism.

13. Our interest in and fascination for democracy often pushes us into taking a position that democracy can address all socio-economic and political problems. If some of our expectations are not met, we start blaming the idea of democracy. Or we start doubting if we are living in a democracy.
To measure democracies on expected outcomes, which of the following practices and institutions would one look for? **Competency Based**
(a) Regular, free and fair elections
(b) Open public debate on major policies
(c) Citizen's right to information about the government.
(d) All of the above

14. **The most distinctive feature about democracy is that its examination never ends. As people get some benefits, they ask for more and want to make democracy even better.**

Which of the following has been successfully eliminated by the democracies?

(a) Conflicts among people
(b) Economic Inequalities
(c) Idea of Political Inequality
(d) Difference of opinion on how marginalised communities are to be treated.

15. **Country X has adopted democracy after a prolonged struggle. Which of the following outcomes can the citizens of this country definitely expect due to this change?** **Competency Based**

(a) Rules and laws are to be made according to the needs of the majority groups.
(b) Decrease in poverty within society.
(c) Rise in the national income due to sharp economic growth.
(d) More accountability on the part of the government.

16. **Consider the statements given below and choose the correct answer.**

Statement I Democracy remains only as long as every citizen has a chance of being in majority at some point of time.

Statement II If someone is barred from being in majority based on birth, then the democratic rule ceases to be accommodative for that person or group.

Options

(a) Statement I is correct, but statement II is incorrect
(b) Statement I is incorrect, but statement II is correct
(c) Both statements I and II are incorrect
(d) Both statements I and II are correct

17. **Consider the statements given below and choose the correct answer.**

Statement I Transparency is considered missing in a non-democratic government.

Statement II In reality, democratic governments also do not have a very good level of transparency with their citizens.

Options

(a) Statement I is correct, but statement II is incorrect
(b) Statement I is incorrect, but statement II is correct
(c) Both statements I and II are incorrect
(d) Both statements I and II are correct

18. **Read the following statements regarding democracy and choose the correct option.** **CBSE 2024**

I. Promotes equality among citizens
II. Government by few individuals
III. Protection of human rights
IV. Ensures checks and balance system

Options

(a) I, II and III (b) II, III and IV
(c) I, III and IV (d) I, II and IV

19. **Which of the following statements accurately describes the correct meaning of 'Equal treatment of women' which is a necessary ingredient of a democratic society?**

I. Women are always treated with respect.
II. It is now easier for women to legally wage struggle for their rights.
III. Most societies across the world are now increasingly women dominated.
IV. Women are now treated as equals in the political arena.

Codes

(a) Only I (b) Both I and III (c) Only II (d) Only IV

Answers

1. (b)	**2.** (c)	**3.** (d)	**4.** (d)	**5.** (d)
6. (d)	**7.** (a)	**8.** (d)	**9.** (d)	**10.** (d)
11. (b)	**12.** (a)	**13.** (d)	**14.** (d)	**15.** (d)
16. (d)	**17.** (d)	**18.** (c)	**19.** (c)	

Match the Following

1.

List I	List II
A. Democracy is preferable	1. Pakistan
B. Sometime dictatorship exists	2. Brazil
C. High degree of economic inequality	3. India

Codes

	A	B	C		A	B	C
(a)	3	1	2	(b)	2	1	3
(c)	3	2	1	(d)	1	3	2

Ans. (a)

Assertion-Reason

1. **Assertion** (A) Democracy transforms people from the status of a subject into that of a citizen.

Reason (R) Most individuals believe that their vote makes a difference to the way the government runs and to their own self-interest.

Codes

(a) Both A and R are true and R is the correct explanation of A

(b) Both A and R are true, but R is not the correct explanation of A

(c) A is true, but R is false

(d) A is false, but R is true

2. Assertion (A) Democratic Governments do not have a very good record when it comes to sharing information with the citizens.

Reason (R) Democratic Regimes are much better than non-democratic regimes.

Codes

(a) Both A and R are true and R is the correct explanation of A

(b) Both A and R are true, but R is not the correct explanation of A

(c) A is true, but R is false

(d) A is false, but R is true

3. Assertion (A) Democracy ensures that decision making will be based on norms and procedures.

Reason (R) A citizen in a democracy who wants to know if a decision was taken through correct procedures can find this out easily.

Codes

(a) Both A and R are true and R is the correct explanation of A

(b) Both A and R are true but R is not the correct explanation of A

(c) A is true, but R is false

(d) A is false, but R is true

4. Assertion (A) Dictatorship is a better form of government as compared to Democracy.

Reason (R) Dictatorship has a slightly higher rate of economic growth.

Codes

(a) Both A and R are true, and R is the correct explanation of A

(b) Both A and R are true, but R is not the correct explanation of A

(c) A is true, but R is false

(d) A is false, but R is true

Ans. 1. (a) Both A and R are true and R is the correct explanation of A

2. (d) A is false, but R is true

3. (b) Both A and R are true, but R is not the correct explanation of A.

4. (d) A is false, but R is true

Picture Based Questions

1. Which of the following conclusions can be drawn from the following picture?

(a) It is reasonable to expect democracies to reduce economic disparities.

(b) In democracy, all citizens have a share in wealth and lead a better life.

(c) Democracy leads to a just distribution of goods and opportunities.

(d) Democracies do not appear to be very successful in reducing economic inequalities.

2. Given below is a cartoon depicting RK Laxman, a famous cartoonist.

Which of the following options best signifies this cartoon?

(a) Demand for a separate state from Democratic Government.

(b) The Democratic Government is facing territorial issues with the bordering states.

(c) The Democratic Government is coping with multiple pressures through accommodation.

(d) Democratic governments accept demands based on separate states.

Ans. 1. (d) Democracies do not appear to be very successful in reducing economic inequalities.

2. (c) The Democratic Government is coping with multiple pressures through accommodation.

Case Based Question

1. Read the source given below and answer the questions that follow.

If you consider all democracies and dictatorships for the fifty years between 1950 and 2000, dictatorships have a slightly higher rate of economic growth. The inability of democracy to achieve higher economic development worries us. But this alone cannot be reason to reject democracy. The difference in the rates of economic development between less developed countries with dictatorships and democracies is negligible.

(i) How can the poor get a voice for a better share in a nation? Choose the correct option.

(a) When they will be given representation.
(b) When they will be provided with adequate resources.
(c) When they will be given a chance to participate in the decision-making process.
(d) Both (a) and (c)

(ii) On which of the following factors the economic growth of a country depends? Identify from the given options.

(a) Territory of the country
(b) Cooperation among various nations
(c) Size of country's population
(d) Global scenario

(iii) Why should the gains of economic growth be evenly distributed? Identify the reason.

(a) To make an economically even society.
(b) To promote the idea of social justice.
(c) To reduce inequality in society.
(d) None of the above

(iv) What can poor countries do to receive a greater share of the world's wealth?

(a) They should take initiatives to strengthen their internal democracy.
(b) They should get united to fight for the cause.
(c) They should exploit their own available natural resources.
(d) Both (a) and (b)

Ans. (i) (d) Both (a) and (c)
(ii) (b) Cooperation among various nations
(iii) (a) To make an economically even society.
(iv) (d) Both (a) and (b)

Part II

Very Short Answer Type Questions

1. Which form of government is found in most of the countries in the world?

Ans. Democratic form of government is found in most of the countries in the world.

2. Why there is an overwhelming support for the idea of democracy all over the world?

Ans. A democratic government is people's own government, so there is an overwhelming support for the idea of democracy all over the world.

3. What does a legitimate government mean?

Ans. A legitimate government means a legally chosen government.

4. What type of government is attentive to the needs and expectations of the people'?

Ans. A responsive government is attentive to the needs and expectations of the people.

5. To whom a democratic government is responsible?

Ans. A democratic government is responsible to the people as the representatives of the democratic government are elected by the people.

6. Which idea has successfully eliminated by democracy?

Ans. The idea of political inequality has successfully eliminated by democracy.

7. Which system can reduce the possibility of tension and conflict among different groups of society?

Ans. Democratic system can do so because it can easily resolve social differences, diversions and conflicts as it has evolved by the mechanism to negotiate differences.

8. On what ground is a dictatorship form of government better than a democracy?

Ans. A dictatorship is often considered better than a democracy in terms of quick decision-making. efficiency and stability.

9. Suggest the factors which contribute to the economic development of a country.

Ans. Population size, global situation, cooperation from other countries and economic priorities adopted by the country are the important factors which contribute to the economic development of a country.

10. The idea of deliberation and negotiation in a democracy leads to what?

Ans. The idea of deliberation and negotiation in a democracy leads to some delay in decision-making.

11. The fact that people are complaining is itself a testimony to the success of democracy: it shows that people have developed awareness and the ability to expect and to look critically at power holders and the high and the mighty. Competency Based

(i) How do individuals show their participation in democracy?

Ans. Individuals show their participation in democracy through voting in the process of formation of government as well as by showing a public expression of dissatisfaction.

(ii) Through which means in a democracy, a citizen has a right to examine the process of decision-making?

Ans. Transparency is a means in a democracy through which a citizen has a right to examine the process of decision-making.

12. Imagine a form of government that may take decisions very fast, but it may take decisions that are not accepted by the people and may, therefore, face problems. On the other hand, another follow procedures, and its decisions are more effective and acceptable to the people. Which form of government is better for a diverse country?

Ans. The second form of government in the case given above is better for a diverse country that follows procedures and its decisions are more effective and acceptable to people. This form of government is called democracy.

Short Answer Type Questions

1. When is democracy considered successful? Explain.

Ans. The democracy is considered successful in the following conditions

- When the rulers are elected by the people and take all major decision in favour of all people.
- When elections offer a free choice and opportunity to the people.
- When choice available to all the people is based on political equality.

2. List the various aspects and qualifications which help in giving a clear definition of democracy.

Ans. The various aspects and qualifications which help in giving a clear definition of democracy are

- The rulers elected by the people must take all the major decisions.
- Elections must offer a choice and fair opportunity to the people to change the existing rulers.
- Choice and opportunity should be available to all on equal basis.

3. List out some of the merits of democracy.

Ans. Democracy is considered to be the best form of government.

The merits of democracy are

- It safeguards the social, economic and political interests of the individuals.
- It assures equality in all social, political and economic rights of the citizens.
- It improves the quality of decision making as decisions are taken by following a procedure.

4. "There is an overwhelming support for the idea of democracy all over the world." Support the statement.

Ans. There is an overwhelming support for the idea of democracy all over the world due to the following reasons

- Democracy can address all socio-economic and political problems.
- In democracy, there are regular and free election, and there is always a scope for open public debate.
- Democracy is a people's own government where rulers are elected by the people. People wish to be ruled by the representatives elected by them.

(*iv*) Democracy is a legitimate government.

5. "Non-democratic rulers can be very quick and efficient in decision-making and implementation." Do you think with this feature, non-democratic government is better than democratic government? Explain.

Ans. Non-democratic government is not better than democratic government, although it can take quick decision. It can be explained in the following ways

- A democratic government can take more time to take a decision as compared to other forms of government. The non-democratic governments can take decisions quickly. But there is a possibility that it is not accepted by all, as no procedure has been followed here.
- In democracy 'transparency' is very necessary. Here, the citizens has the rights to know the process of decision-making. This factor would often be missing from a non-democratic government, where decisions are made without public consultation or accountability, leading to a lake of transparency and potential misuse of power.

6. "Democratic government is a legitimate government." Explain.

Ans. Legitimate government is a government under which law and action of the government are revealed to the people and government function in a transparent manner.

Following features of a democratic government make it a legitimate government

- The laws are applicable to all the citizen whether rich or poor.

- In a democracy, there is a political equality i.e. every vote counts equally.
- People have the right to challenge the government policies and actions. If the people are not satisfied with the working of the government they have the right to change it.

7. "Democracies have had greater success in setting regular free and fair elections." Analyse the statement. **Competency Based**

Ans. This statement can be explained in the following ways

- Every democracy holds elections and it has different political parties. A democracy guarantees the voting right to its citizens.
- Every one has the right to elect their leader and has the control over the rulers.
- In democracy whenever possible and necessary citizens participate in decision making that affects them.
- Democracy should practice regular, free and fair election. This differentiates democracy from other form of governments.

8. "That democratic system of government is considered good in which maximum number of citizens are made stakeholders in political power". Explain the statement with suitable arguments. **CBSE 2025**

Ans. Suitable arguments for the above statement are as follows

- **Ensures Representation** When more citizens are stakeholders, diverse interests are represented, making policies more inclusive and reflective of society's needs.
- **Promoting Accountability** Shared political power ensures that leaders are accountable to the people, reducing corruption and abuse of power.
- **Increased Legitimacy** Broad participation in decision-making boosts the legitimacy of the government, making it more accepted and fair to the public.

9. Discuss the most likely ways in which a democracy ensures accountable, responsive and legitimate government.

Build the answer around these points.

- **Right to information**
- **Work according to needs and expectations of people**
- **Government elected by the people**

Ans. Some of the ways in which a democracy ensures accountable, responsive and legitimate form of government are discussed below

- A democratic government develops different mechanisms for citizens to take part in the decision-making process. To apply this free and fair elections, open debates on major policies, legislation, and the right to information are there in good democracies. Therefore, democracies are known as accountable governments.
- Democracy is a responsive form of government. It is responsive to the needs and expectations of the citizens. It makes policies for the welfare of the citizens.
- A democratic government is a legitimate government. It is elected by the people and people wish to be ruled by the representatives elected by them.

Long Answer Type Questions

1. Democratic system is better than other systems. Explain the statement with appropriate arguments. **CBSE 2025**

Or **'Democratic system is better than any other form of government'. Support the statement with examples.** **CBSE 2020**

Or **"Democracy is a better form of government than any other alternative." Analyse the statement.** **CBSE Term II 2022**

Or **How is Democracy better than any other form of government? Explain with examples.** **CBSE 2024**

Ans. Democracy is a better form of government when compared with any other form of government because of the following reasons

- Democracy promotes equality among citizens. Every citizen of the country has equal rights before the law. All individuals have equal rights in electing their representatives.
- Democracy enhances the dignity of the individual. By giving its citizens equal rights, it enhances dignity and freedom of the individual. Democracy gives equal treatment and respect to women, disadvantaged and discriminated castes in our society.
- Democracy improves the quality of decision-making. As there is open debate in major issues in democracy thus, quality of decisions is improved.
- Democracy provides a method to resolve conflicts. Democracy reduces the possibility of social tension which leads to peaceful social life. It allows room to correct mistakes.
- Democracy is a legitimate government. Democracy gets the popular support of the people by regular, free and fair elections.

2. Explain any five values of democracy. CBSE 2025

Ans. The five values of democracy are as follows

(i) **Equality** Democracy ensures that all citizens, regardless of their caste, creed, religion, or gender, are treated equally before the law. This value of equality is fundamental in ensuring that no one is discriminated against and everyone has the same rights and opportunities in society.

(ii) **Freedom** In a democracy, individuals are granted freedom of expression, speech, assembly, and association. Citizens have the right to express their opinions, form associations, and participate freely in political processes, without fear of oppression.

(iii) **Justice** A democratic system strives to provide justice to all its citizens by ensuring that laws are applied fairly, and individuals have access to justice through courts and legal mechanisms. It promotes both social and economic justice by addressing inequalities and upholding human rights.

(iv) **Dignity of the Individual** Democracy emphasises the dignity of every individual. It protects the rights and freedoms of individuals, ensuring that their personal dignity and autonomy are respected by others and the state. This includes the right to live without fear or discrimination.

(v) **Majority Rule with Minority Rights** While democracy is based on the rule of the majority, it also protects the rights of minorities. It ensures that the majority's decisions do not infringe on the basic rights of minority groups, thus maintaining a balance between the will of the majority and the protection of minority interests.

3. 'One distinct feature of democracy is that its scrutiny never ends'. Explain the statement with appropriate arguments. CBSE 2025

Ans. In a democracy, scrutiny of the government and its policies never stops. The explanation of the above statements with arguments is as follows

- **Elections and Public Participation** In a democracy, elections are held regularly, providing citizens with the opportunity to assess the performance of their representatives and hold them accountable. People have the power to vote for new representatives if the current ones fail to meet expectations. This cycle of periodic elections ensures that scrutiny of the government is continuous.
- **Freedom of Expression** Democracy allows citizens, media, and civil society to freely express their opinions, criticize policies, and raise issues. This creates an environment where the government's actions are always under public scrutiny. Criticism and debates ensure that decisions are not made in isolation but are subjected to public discussion and reflection.
- **Role of Institutions** In a democracy, there are independent institutions like the judiciary, media, and election commissions that continuously scrutinise government actions. For example, the judiciary can review laws, while the media plays a key role in highlighting issues of public concern, ensuring the government remains answerable.
- **Civil Rights and Activism** Civil society organisations and activists play a crucial role in monitoring government policies and advocating for the rights of citizens. The presence of a vigilant public ensures that governments cannot take unchecked actions, as they are always being observed and evaluated.

4. "Democracy often frustrate the needs of the people and often ignore the demands of a majority of its population." What are the demerits of democracy?

Ans. Following are the demerits of democracy

- **Unstable Government** Lots of political parties are allowed to criticise the government and its policies. Sometimes, it leads to the downfall of the ruling party and re-elections in the country. This gives instability to the government.
- **Slow and Inefficient Government** The most common demerit of democracy is that it is slow in its functioning. The decision-making process involves long debates and deliberations in the Parliament. This takes a lot of time before the decisions are actually taken.
- **Incompetence** Democracy gives every individual the right to voice his concern. As a result, everybody focusses on his personal interests and not the collective interests. This sometimes leads to incompetent and wrong selections of the candidates in the government.
- **Role of Money in a Democracy** Money plays an important role in democracy at the time of the elections. A lot of money is needed to organise demonstrations, public meetings and speeches. Those candidates are chosen in the elections, who can raise lot of money for the party.

5. "Democracy stands much superior to any other form of government in promoting dignity and freedom of the individual." Support the statement by giving three suitable points.

Ans. In our society, every individual wants to receive respect from fellow beings. In this respect, democratic form of government stands much superior to any other form of government in promoting dignity and freedom of the individual in the following ways

- Often conflict arises among individuals because some feel that they are not treated with equal respect in comparison to others. It is very common in non-democratic countries. But in democracy, respect and freedom are the basis of it. Democracy throughout the world has recognised this atleast in principle.

- Most societies were historically male dominating. The status of women was not satisfactory. After long struggles by women, democracy throughout the world has recognised equal treatment and respect to women at least in principles. In democracy, it becomes easier for women to wage a struggle against what is now unacceptable legally and morally for them.
- Democracy in India has strengthened the claims of the disadvantaged and discriminated castes for equal status and opportunity, which is not possible in any non-democratic country.

6. "In actual life, democracies do not appear to be very successful in reducing economic inequalities." Explain the statement giving an example. **Competency Based**

Ans. In actual life, democracies do not appear to be very successful in reducing economic inequalities.

This can be justified in the following ways

- The democracy does not guarantee economic development. In most of the democracies, a small number of ultra-rich enjoy a highly disproportionate share of wealth and income. For example, Countries like South Africa and Brazil, the top 20% people take away more than 60 % of the national income. Unfortunately, those who are at the bottom of the society have a very little share (less than 3 %) to depend upon.
- In India, the elected government looks reluctant to take necessary steps for the upliftment of the large section of poor in our society.
- In Bangladesh, more than half of its population lives in poverty. People in several poor countries are now dependent on the rich countries even for food supplies.

7. How do we assess democracy's outcomes? Explain. **CBSE 2024**

Or Explain any five bases for assessing the outcomes of democracy. **CBSE 2025**

Ans. Assessing democracy's outcomes involves evaluating whether it fulfills the expectations associated with democratic governance. This assessment can be done through following criteria

- **Promotion of Equality** Evaluate the extent to which democracy promotes equality among citizens, both in terms of political rights and socio-economic opportunities. This involves examining indicators such as income distribution, social mobility and access to education and healthcare.
- **Enhancement of Individual Dignity** Assess whether democracy upholds the dignity of individuals by safeguarding their fundamental rights and freedoms. This includes evaluating the protection of civil liberties, freedom of expression and the rule of law.
- **Quality of Decision-making** Evaluate the effectiveness and transparency of decision-making processes within democratic institutions. This involves assessing the extent to which decisions are made through open debate, public participation and adherence to democratic norms and principles.
- **Conflict Resolution** Examine democracy's ability to peacefully resolve conflicts and manage societal tensions through democratic means, such as dialogue, negotiation and compromise.
- **Capacity for Course Correction** Assess whether democracy provides mechanisms for accountability and responsiveness to address mistakes and address societal challenges.

8. Democracy's ability to generate its own support is itself an outcome that cannot be ignored.' Support the statement with examples. **CBSE SQP Term II 2021**

Ans Some features of democracy that makes it generate support for itself are as follows

- Such a form of Government is for the people, by the people, to the people. It is based on people's consent as people have the right to choose their rulers. It allows for the participation of the people in the political process as it is people's own government.
- It ensures that decision making is based on norms and procedures as per the law.
- It provides every citizen with the right and means to examine the process of decision making. For example, the Right to Information in India ensures all citizens to have an access to information regarding the functions of the government departments.
- Democracy as a form of government is accountable, legitimate and transparent governments. It has the ability to handle differences, conflicts and decisions in the diverse society.
- It is based on the idea of deliberation and negotiation thus it leads to delay in the implementation process which further promotes effective decisions that are acceptable to the common people.

9. Expectations from democracy also function as the criteria for judging any democratic country. What is most distinctive about democracy is that its examination never gets over. As democracy passes one test, it produces another test. As people get some benefits from democracy, they ask for more and want to make democracy even better.

State the areas where democracy has failed to serve people's expectations. Discuss. **Competency Based**

Ans. The areas where democracy has failed to serve people's expectations are as follows

- It is fair to assume that democracy will lead to development if it is expected to create effective governance. Numerous democracies, according to some evidence, fell short of this expectation. The incapacity of democracy to attain greater economic development represents one of the obstacles to be addressed.

- A democracy is a people's government. As a result, it should lessen economic inequality. However, the harsh reality is that, even in nations with strong economies, income is not dispersed so that everyone can benefit and live better lives.
- Additionally, democracy has not been successful in reducing poverty. A much disproportionate percentage of wealth and income is enjoyed by a smaller number of ultra-rich individuals. There is nothing that the underclass can rely on. There has been a decrease in income.
- Democracies frequently fail to meet the demands of their citizens and disregard the wishes of majority of them.

Case Based Questions

1. Read the sources given below and answer the questions that follow.

Source A Democracy is Accountable

There are some things that democracy must provide. In a democracy, we are most concerned with ensuring that people will have the right to choose their rulers and people will have control over the rulers. Whenever possible and necessary, citizens should be able to participate in decision making, that affects them all. Therefore, the most basic outcome of democracy should be that it produces a government that is accountable to the citizens, and responsive to the needs and expectations of the citizens.

(i) Evaluate the effectiveness of accountability of democracy.

Source B Transparency in Democracy

Let us think in terms of costs. Imagine a government that may take decisions very fast. But it may take decisions that are not accepted by the people and may therefore face problems. In contrast, the democratic government will take more time to follow procedures before arriving at a decision. But because it has followed procedures, its decisions may be both more acceptable to the people and more effective.

So, a citizen who wants to know if a decision was taken through the correct procedures can find this out. She has the right and the means to examine the process of decision making. This is known as transparency. This factor is often missing from a non-democratic government. Therefore, when we are trying to find out the outcomes of democracy, it is right to expect democracy to produce a government that follows procedures and is accountable to the people.

(ii) To what extent citizen has the right to examine decision making process in a democracy. Give reasons.

Source C Democracy is Better than non-Democracy

Democracies have had greater success in setting up regular and free elections and in setting up conditions for open public debate. But most democracies fall short of elections that provide a fair chance to everyone and in subjecting every decision to public debate.

Democratic governments do not have a very good record when it comes to sharing information with citizens. All one can say in favour of democratic regimes is that they are much better than any non-democratic regime in these respects.

(iii) To what extent democracy is better than non-democracy?

Ans. (i) In democracy people have the right to choose their rulers and have control over them. In this way, citizen are able to participate in decision making procedure. Thus, democracy produces a government that is accountable to its citizen.

(ii) In democracy, citizen has the rights and means to examine the process of decision making and it is known as transparency. This is not available in non-democratic state.

In democracy government develops mechanism for citizens to take part in decision making when it is possible. To this extent democracy is transparent.

(iii) Democracy is better than the non-democratic government, because in democracy people get free and fair elections through which they apply their rights to choose their leaders.

2. Read the source given below and answer the questions that follow.

Perhaps more than development, it is reasonable to expect democracies to reduce economic disparities. Even when a country achieves economic growth, will wealth be distributed in such a way that all citizens of the country will have a share and lead a better life? Is economic growth in democracies accompanied by increased inequalities among the people? Or do democracies lead to a just distribution of goods and opportunities?

Democracies are based on political equality. All individuals have equal weight in electing representatives. Parallel to the process of bringing individuals into the political arena on an equal footing, we find growing economic inequalities. A small number of ultra-rich enjoy a highly disproportionate share of wealth and incomes. Not only that, their share in the total income of the country has been increasing. Those at the bottom of the society have very little to depend upon.

Their incomes have been declining. Sometimes they find it difficult to meet their basic needs of life, such as food, clothing, house, education and health.

(i) Why it is expected that democracy will reduce the economic disparities?

(ii) Infer the reason of inability of democracy to achieve higher economic development.

(iii) Why do some poor countries depend on the rich countries ?

Ans. (i) Democracy is a rule of majority and it is based on political equality. Thus, it is expected that it will reduce the economic disparity among its citizens.

(ii) Economic development of a country depends on several factors like country's population size, global situation, economic priorities, cooperation from other countries etc, Democracy can not control all these factors. In reality, democracy is not successful to control the economic disparity between ultra-rich and the poor sections of people. Thus, democracy is unable to achieve higher economic development.

(iii) As democratically elected government`is not interested to remove the disparity between the rich and poor in the society, people in poor countries depends on the grants of rich countries. Sometimes the poor find it difficult to meet their basic needs, like, food, clothing, house, etc. Thus, poor people in some countries are even dependent on the rich countries for food supplies.

ASSESSMENT EXERCISE

Multiple Choice Questions (MCQs)

1. What is the most basic outcome of democracy?
(a) Significant decision-making
(b) Answerability to the citizens
(c) Powerful, repressive governance
(d) None of the above

2. Which feature of democracy is common in most countries of the world?
(a) They have a formal constitution.
(b) They hold elections regularly.
(c) They guarantee the rights of citizens.
(d) All of the above

3. On which of the following factors does economic development of a country depend?
(a) Cooperation from other countries
(b) The number of rich citizens in the country
(c) Political priorities adopted by the country
(d) All of the above

4. The frequent stories of .... remind us that no system is entirely without shortcomings, even democracies. Identify the issue being referred to from the options given
(a) poverty (b) black marketing
(c) terrorism (d) corruption

5. Match the following.

	List I		List II
A.	Democracy in Brazil	1.	Strengthened the claims of disadvantaged and discriminated
B.	Democracy in India	2.	Economic disparity is very high
C.	Deomcracy in Bangladesh	3.	More than half of its population lives in poverty

Codes

	A	B	C
(a)	1	2	3
(b)	2	1	3
(c)	2	3	1
(d)	1	3	2

Subjective Questions (VSA, SA & LA)

1. What do you understand by good democracy?

2. In which form of government, higher rate of economic growth is usually found in?

3. Explain the relationship between democracy and development.

4. How can we measure democracy on the basis of its expected outcomes?

5. What are the issues in which democracies have failed?

6. Examine the political outcomes of democracy.

7. A democracy usually develop a procedure to accommodate various social divisions. What are the necessary conditions in order to achieve this outcome?

8. How do democratic governments ensure transparency? Explain any three points.

9. "No society can fully and permanently resolve conflicts among different groups. However, democracy is best to handle social differences, divisions and conflicts". Justify the statement.

10. What are the factors which are responsible for the economic development of the country? Does democracy provide guarantee of economic development?

CHAPTER 1

Development

Everyone has his own aspirations or desires about how he want to lead his life. When people generate ideas to achieve these goals or desires and to improve their present condition, then development takes place.

1.1 Meaning of Development

Development means all round improvement in aspects such as freedom, income, economic equality, security, life with dignity and good standard of living. Development is also known as progress.

Different People and Different Goals

People have different goals due to which development is sometimes different and conflicting. For example, industrialists want big dams for their electricity requirement. However, dams displace local community, so local people prefer small check dams or tanks for irrigation.

This shows the following two aspects of development

(i) Different persons can have different developmental goals.

(ii) Development for one may not be development for another. It may even be harmful for the other.

Income and Other Goals

Income is considered as the most important component of development as it can be used to buy **material goods**[1] and services.

Apart from income, people also seek non-material things like equal treatment, freedom, security and respect of others. Thus, the quality of our life depends on both material things and non-material things.

For development, people look at a mix of goals and these developmental goals include both better income and other important things in life.

1.2 National Development

As the individuals have different goals, their belief of national development is also likely to be different. Their goals can also be conflicting.

National development means thinking about the following

- Whether all the ideas taken are equally important
- Whether the decisions taken are fair and just for all
- Whether there is a better way of doing things
- Whether the idea benefit a large number of people or only a small group.

1.3 Comparison of Different Countries or States

'For comparing countries, their income is considered to be one of the most important factors. Countries with higher incomes are more developed economically than others with lower incomes.

This is because more income means that people have more of the things they need, such as food, shelter and healthcare.

Total Income of the country is the income of all the residents of the country.

However, this is not a useful measure as countries have different populations and comparing total income will not state the average amount earned by a person.

Thus, **average income** is calculated by dividing total income of country (GDP) by its total population. It is also called **Per Capita Income** (PCI).

1 **Material Goods** These are items that consumers can purchase, sell or trade.

In World Development Reports, the World Bank use the criteria of Per Capita Income to classify the countries in the following ways

(i) Countries with PCI of US $ 49,300 per annum and above in 2019 are termed as **high income** or **rich countries**. These countries, excluding middle Eastern countries, are generally called **Developed countries.**

(ii) Countries with PCI of US $ 2500 or less are termed as **low income countries.** In 2019, India's per capita income was only about US $ 6700 per annum and it was classified as a low middle income country.

1.4 Income and Other Criteria

Apart from average income, other factors should also be considered for measuring the development of a nation or a region. These factors are

- **Infant Mortality Rate** (IMR) It indicates the number of children that die before the age of 1 year as a proportion of 1000 live children born in that particular year.
- **Literacy Rate** It measures the proportion of literate population aged 7 years or above.
- **Net Attendance Ratio** It is the total number of children of age group 14 and 15 years attending school, as a percentage of total number of children in the same age group.

Thus, money cannot buy all the goods and services that are needed to live well. So, income is not an adequate indicator of material goods and services that the people are able to use.

Try These

1. **What is the reason of people having contrasting and conflicting development?**
2. **Identify the term that is used to describe the overall economic production of a country.**
3. **As per World Development Report, name a country that is ranked as low middle income country.**
4. **Mention the names of the factors used for measuring the development of a nation or a region.**

1.5 Public Facilities

Money alone cannot buy everything needed for a good life. For example, it can't buy clean air or safe medicines unless you live in a place that already has these things. It also can't protect you from diseases unless everyone works together to prevent them.

Public facilities are provided by the government for collective benefit of the society.

States where adequate public facilities are provided, have more progress. For example, Kerala has low **Infant Mortality Rate** due to good basic health and educational facilities.

Similarly, in states where there is good **Public Distribution System**[2] (PDS), the health and nutritional status of people is better.

Body Mass Index (BMI)

Body Mass Index (BMI) is an international standard used to determine whether an adult person is **undernourished**[3] or not.

When the weight of a person is divided by the square of his/her height, we get a number which is called BMI.

BMI = Weight in kg/height in metres ^{2}

For example, if a girl student is 14 years and 8 month old and the BMI is 15.2, then she is undernourished. Similarly, if the BMI of a boy aged 15 years and 6 months is 28, then he is overweight.

The BMI is an important way to understand the level of nutrition a person takes.

Human Development Report

The United Nations Development Programme (UNDP) releases the Human Development Index (HDI) for 189 countries each year in its Human Development Report. The HDI is the best method to measure development.

The report compares countries based on three criterias namely

- Living standard **(Per Capita Income)**
- Health status **(Life Expectancy**[4]**)**
- Educational levels of the people (Literacy rate and years of schooling).

2 Public Distribution System (PDS) It is a food security system established by the Government of India to provide essential items at subsidised rate, e.g. rice, wheat, sugar, kerosene.

3 Undernourished It refers to a person who does not get proper nutrition as per his body weight and height.

4 Life Expectancy It refers to the number of years a person can expect to live.

India occupied 132nd rank in HDI 2021 (India ranks 134 in HDI 2023-2024). The Human Development Index (HDI) considers public health, education, poverty level, inequality and environmental aspects to measure human development.

Sri Lanka, a small neighbouring country, is ahead of India in many aspects, despite India being much larger. Nepal and Bangladesh have lower per capita income than India but perform better in life expectancy. The Human Development Report focuses on people, health and well-being, showing that true development is about improving the lives of citizens.

Sustainability of Development

Every country including India wants to become a developed country. However, the present type, and levels, of development are not sustainable.

Non-renewable resources are those that get exhausted after a few years of use. These resources can not be replenished and there is a fixed stock only. Renewable resources are replenised by nature but these are overused. For example, groundwater which is used more than what is replenished by rain. Some examples that show overuse of resources are

- **Groundwater in India** In India, nearly one-third of the country is overusing its ground water reserves. It is particularly found in agriculturally prosperous regions of Punjab, Western Uttar Pradesh, hard rock plateau areas of Central and South India.
- **Exhaustion of Natural Resources** According to World Energy Review, June 2018, the total reserves of the crude oil stock in the world is going to last just for 50 years as countries are fast using up the oil reserves.

Thus, the whole world is facing environmental degradation sustainable development[5] is the way through which this degradation can be prevent.

Environmental problems affect everyone, no matter where they live.

Try These

1. **Name an international standard to understand the level of nutrition a person takes.**
2. **Name all the criterias based on which the Human Development Report compares different countries.**
3. **Identify the term that refers to reducing the use of natural resources with the aim to save for the future.**
4. **Which states or regions are fast depleting their groundwater reserves?**

5 **Sustainable Development** It is the development that meet the needs of the present without compromising the ability of future generations to meet their own needs.

Mind Map

DEVELOPMENT

Meaning of Development

Different People and Different Goals
- Different people can have different developmental goals.
- Development for one may not be development for another. It may even be harmful for the other.

Income and Other Goals
It is considered as the most important component of development because it can be used to buy material goods and services.

National Development
- It means thinking about the following
  - Whether all the ideas are taken equally important.
  - Whether the decisions taken are just and fair for all.
  - Whether there is a better way of doing things.
  - Whether the idea benefits a large number of people or only a small group.

Sustainability of Development

Renewable Resources
These are replenished by nature but are overused.

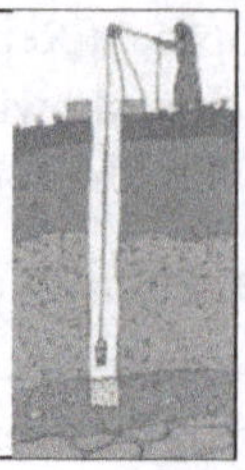

Non-Renewable Resources
These cannot be replenished by nature and there is a fixed stock only.

Comparison of Different Countries or States

High Income Countries
Countries with Per Capita Income of US $ 49300 per annum and above.

Low Income Countries
Countries with Per Capita Income of US $ 2500 per annum or less.

Income and Other Criteria
- Infant Mortality Rate
- Literacy Rate
- Net Attendance Ratio

Human Development Report
- It is the best method to measure development
- It compares countries on the basis of educational levels of the people, their health status and per capita income.

Public Facilities

Public Facilities Provided by the government for collective benefit of the society.

NCERT FOLDER

Covering Intext Questions and Exercises of NCERT

INTEXT QUESTIONS

Q.1 Developmental Goals of Different Categories of Persons

Category of Person	Developmental Goals / Aspirations
Landless rural labourers	More days of work and better wages; local school is able to provide quality education for their children; there is no social discrimination and they too can become leaders in the village.
Prosperous farmers from Punjab	Assured a high family income through higher support prices for their crops and through hardworking and cheap labourers; they should be able to settle their children abroad.
Farmers who depend only on rain for growing crops	
A rural woman from a land owning family	
Urban unemployed youth	
A boy from a rich urban family	
A girl from a rich urban family	She gets as much freedom as her brother and is able to decide what she want to do in life. She is able to pursue her studies abroad.
An *adivasi* from Narmada valley	

Ans.

Category of Person	Developmental Goals/Aspirations
Farmers who depend only on rain for growing crops	Tubewells to be dug and canals to be made for irrigation of crops; higher support prices for crops; availability of hardworking and cheap labour; better education facilities for their children.
A rural woman from a land owning family	Education of her children in English medium schools; more earning from the land by giving it on rent.
Urban unemployed youth	More opportunity of jobs; a permanent white collar job; having a self-owned home to live in.
A boy from a rich urban family	Should be allowed to decide his career or whether to go into business; pursue higher studies abroad; have his own car and house to live in.
An *adivasi* from Narmada valley	No social discrimination; school education for children; all year round employment for self; Public Distribution System PDS ration shop in village.

Q.2 Why do different persons have different notions of development? Which of the following explanations is more important and why?

(*a*) Because people are different.

(*b*) Because life situations of persons are different.

Ans. Different persons have different notions of development because life situations of people are different. Development goals of a person from a rich urban family will be surely different from a farmer in rural area. It is because their situations, lifestyle and status are very different from each other.

A goal of a person is something, which is entirely dependent on his or her present life situation. Over a period of time, if the situation changes, automatically goals of a person will also change. Hence, (b) is the more important explanation of the given question.

Q.3 Do the following two statements mean the same? Justify your answer.

(*a*) People have different developmental goals.

(*b*) People have conflicting developmental goals.

Ans. Yes, these two statements mean almost the same, as different persons could have different as well as conflicting developmental goals.

For instance, to get electricity, industrialists want more dams to be made. But this may submerge the land and disrupt the lives of people, who are displaced such as tribals. Hence, in that case development goals are different and even conflicting.

Q.4 Give some examples where factors other than income are important aspects of our lives.

Ans. Some examples where factors other than income are important aspect of our lives are as follows

- People also seek things like equal treatment, freedom, security and respect.

- Women need safe and secure environment to take up a variety of jobs or to run a business.
- People also need political rights.
- People seek a pollution-free environment.

Q.5 Explain some of the important ideas of the section (income and other goals) in your own words.

Ans. The section is based on the income and the goals of the people. Here, besides seeking more income, people also have non material needs like equal treatment, freedom, respect and security. The factor on which life depends, is money or income, but the quality of our life depends on various non-material needs. Together it gives a quality of life.

Q.6 Look at the picture given below. What should be the developmental goals for such an area?

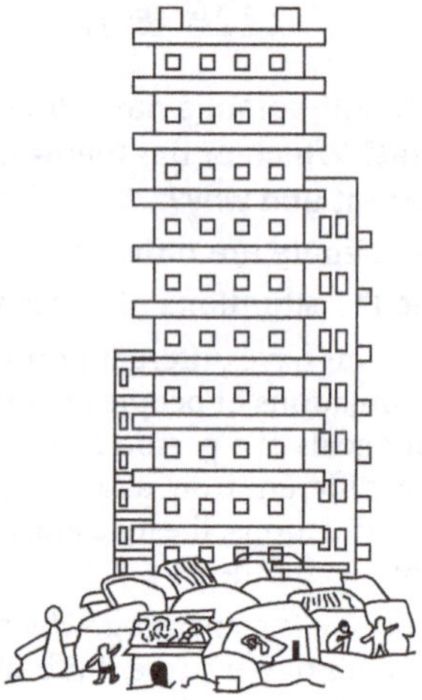

Ans. The developmental goals for the area such as shown in the picture varies in two aspects. One aspect should be that of people residing in flats and second aspect would be the perspective of slum dwellers or people residing in small hut.

For people residing in flats of multistorey building, the developmental goals would be proper space and playground for their children, security, better schooling facilities, parking space, aesthetic locality, etc. While slum dwellers would be expecting proper houses, availability of basic necessary services like electricity, water and sanitation.

Ideal way for development of locality would be a mix of developmental goals benefiting both communities without curtailing rights and interest of any community.

Q.7 Read this newspaper report and answer the questions that follow

A vessel dumped 500 tonnes of liquid toxic wastes into open-air dumps in a city and in the surrounding sea. This happened in a city called Abidjan in Ivory Coast, a country in Africa. The fumes from the highly toxic waste caused nausea, skin rashes, fainting, diarrhoea, etc. After a month, seven persons were dead, twenty in hospital and twenty-six thousand treated for symptoms of poisoning.

A multinational company dealing in petroleum and metals has contracted a local company of the Ivory Coast to dispose the toxic waste from its ship.

(i) Who are the people who benefitted and who did not?

(ii) What should be the developmental goal for this country?

Ans. (i) People who dumped the toxic waste have benefitted in getting rid of the wastes, while the people of Abidjan in Ivory Coast were not benefitted.

(ii) Pollution free environment should be developmental goal for this country.

Q.8 What can be some of the developmental goals for your village, town or locality?

Ans. Sanitation, security, better education, healthcare facilities, etc are developmental goals for our locality.

Q.9 Give three examples where an average is used for comparing situations.

Ans. Three examples where an average is used for comparing situations are

(i) Average income of two countries.

(ii) Average speed of two vehicles over a distance

(iii) Average height of the students in two different classes of a school.

Q.10 Why do you think average income is an important criterion for development? Explain.

Ans. Average income is an important criterion because it tells us what a person is likely to earn and also gives idea about the standard of living. Prosperity of a country depends not only on its income but also on the number of people who would share it. In case, the number of people is large, the average income will be less. This is the case in India.

Q.11 Besides size of per capita income, what other property of income is important in comparing two or more societies?

Ans. Besides the size of per capita income, the distribution of income is important in comparing two or more societies. If a society has higher Per Capita Income but much of its income is concentrated within a small group, then it cannot reflect the development of the society. Similarly, when a society has comparatively less Per Capita Income but is evenly distributed, then it reflects inclusiveness and real development.

Q.12 Suppose records show that the average income in a country has been increasing over a period of time. From this, can we conclude that all sections of the economy have become better? Illustrate your answer with an example.

Ans. No, it cannot be concluded that all sections of the economy have become better. Average income do not shows how well the income is distributed.

There may be greater concentration of income with higher income groups and poor income groups may be earning very little as is the case in India.

Q.13 Write a paragraph on your notion of what should India do or achieve, to become a developed country.

Ans. To become a developed country, India should encourage its industrial sector to create more jobs in industries. Modernisation of agriculture is necessary to raise crop production. At the same time, more employment opportunities should be created to raise the per capita income. Improvement in health and education is also important to ensure a better quality of life for the people.

Q.14 Look at data in Tables 1.3 and 1.4 in NCERT Text book. Is Haryana ahead of Kerala in literacy rate, etc. as it is in per capita income?

Ans. Haryana is not ahead of Kerala in literacy rate as it is in per capita income. Infant Mortality Rate in Kerala is also lower than Haryana.

Q.15 Think of other examples where collective provision of goods is cheaper than individual provision?

Ans. Examples where collective provision of goods is cheaper than individual provision are manufacturing units where large scale production takes place and mining.

Q.16 Does availability of good health and educational facilities depend only on amount of money spent by the government on these facilities? What other factors could be relevant?

Ans. No, good health and educational facilities does not depend only on amount of money spent by the government on these facilities. It is community participation or public cooperation that are relevant in fulfilling these demands.

Q.17 In Tamil Nadu, 90 per cent of the people living in rural areas use a ration shop, whereas in West Bengal only 35% per cent of rural people did so. Where would people did better off and why?

Ans. People are better off in Tamil Nadu because the ration shops are properly functioning and provide basic public assistance to rural people.

EXERCISE

Q.1 Development of a country can generally be determined by

(a) its per capita income (b) its average literacy level
(c) health status of its people (d) All of these

Ans. (d) All of the above

Q.2 Which of the following neighbouring countries of India has better performance in terms of human development than India?

(a) Bangladesh (b) Sri Lanka
(c) Nepal (d) Pakistan

Ans. (b) Sri Lanka

Q.3 Assume there are four families in a country. The average per capita income of these families is ₹ 5,000. If the income of three families is ₹ 4,000, ₹ 7,000 and ₹ 3,000 respectively, what is the income of the fourth family?

(a) ₹ 7,500 (b) ₹ 3,000 (c) ₹ 2,000 (d) ₹ 6,000

Ans. (d) Total income of four families $= 5{,}000 \times 4 =$ ₹20,000

Total income of three families

$= 4{,}000 + 7{,}000 + 3{,}000 =$ ₹14000

Income of the fourth family

$= 20{,}000 - 14{,}000 =$ ₹ 6,000

Q.4 What is the main criterion used by World Bank in classifying different countries? What are the limitations of this criterion, if any?

Ans. The World Bank uses the criterion of per capita income for classifying countries. For example, countries with per capita income of US $ 2500 or less were classified as low income countries. Countries with per capita income US $ 49,300 per annum and above in 2019 are classified as high income countries.

The limitations of the criterion are

- Other important factors including literacy rate, infant mortality rate, healthcare are ignored while classifying the countries.
- Information about the unequal distribution of income is not mentioned by the World Bank.
- The economy of the country cannot determine the development of the country.

Q.5 In what respects is the criterion used by the UNDP for measuring development different from the one used by the World Bank? **CBSE 2015, 11**

Ans. The World Bank uses only one criterion, the Per Capita Income but the UNDP uses many criteria which include Per Capita Income, health status (meaning Life Expectancy at birth) and education (which include Literacy Rate and Gross Enrollment Ratio in schools).

Q.6 Why do we use average? Are there any limitations to their use? Illustrate with your own examples related to development.

Ans. Averages are used for comparisons because they present a large amount of data into a single value in a better way than total. Average expresses the central value but total indicates absolute value. In comparisons of countries, average income, indicates the income, a person is likely to earn but total income shows the income of the entire country.

Limitations of Average Income

Average value has its limitations as it avoids/neglects inequality. So, the real situation of improvement is not reflected. While averages are useful for comparison, they also hide disparities.

Illustration Related to Development

Consider two countries-A and B. It is assumed that there are five citizens each.

In country A, the income earned by its 5 citizens are ₹ 9500, ₹ 10,500, ₹ 9800, ₹ 10200 and ₹ 10000.

In country B, the income earned by its 5 citizens are ₹ 500, ₹ 500, ₹ 500, ₹ 500 and ₹ 48,000.

Average income of both the countries is ₹ 10,000 but it can be clearly seen that income is not equally divided in country B. Only one person is rich while rest of the 4 are poor.

Therefore, average income do not tells how the income is distributed.

Q.7 Kerala, with lower per capita income has a better human development ranking than Haryana. Hence, the per capita income is not a useful criterion at all and should not be used to compare states. Do you agree? Discuss.

Ans. No, I do not agree that per capita income should not be used to compare states. However, other factors like Infant Mortality Rate, Literacy Rate and Net Attendance Ratio should be used to measure overall human development.

Q.8 Find out the present sources of energy used by the people in India. What could be the possibilities fifty years from now?

Ans. Present sources of energy used by people in India are coal, cow dung, kerosene oil, petroleum, natural gas, LPG, electricity, etc.

Fifty years from now, there is a possibility that people will be making more use of non-conventional sources of energy, nuclear energy, wind energy, hydro-energy, etc.

Q.9 Why is the issue of sustainability important for development?

Or **Why is sustainability important for development? Explain.** **CBSE 2020**

Ans. The issue of sustainability is important for development because if the natural resources are not used carefully, they may not be available for future generations.

Currently, reckless exploitation of non-renewable natural resources is going on. Since, the stock of natural resources like oil and minerals is limited, development should not take place at the cost of these scarce natural resources, as they are not renewable in the near future.

Q.10 "The Earth has enough resources to meet the needs of all but not enough to satisfy the greed of even one person".

How is this statement relevant to the discussion of development? Discuss.

Ans. This statement implies that human beings are overusing the natural resources of the Earth in the name of development. Earth provides enough resources to meet the needs of all, but human beings have become very greedy as they resort to activities like deforestation, using unsustainable fuelwood and fodder extraction, shifting cultivation, encroachment into forest lands, indiscriminate use of agro-chemicals, extraction of groundwater in excess of recharge capacity, etc.

Q.11 List a few examples of environmental degradation that you may have observed around you.

Ans. Some examples of environmental degradation that have been observed are

- Soil erosion
- Water pollution by use of chemical fertilisers and pesticides
- Groundwater depletion
- Air pollution and noise pollution by vehicles and factories
- Felling of trees
- Garbage dumps

Q.12 For each of the items given in table, find out which country is at the top and which is at the bottom.

Some Data Regarding India and its Neighbours for 2021

Country	Gross National Income (GNI) per capita (2017 PPP $)	Life Expectancy at Birth	Mean Years of Schooling of People Aged 25+ yrs and above	HDI Rank in the World (2021-22)
Sri Lanka	12578	76.4	10.8	73
India	6590	67.2	6.7	132
Myanmar	3851	65.7	6.4	149
Pakistan	4624	66.1	4.5	161
Nepal	3877	68.4	5.1	143
Bangladesh	5472	72.4	7.4	129

Ans.

Data	Top (Country)	Bottom (Country)
(a) Per Capita Income	Sri Lanka	Myanmar
(b) Life Expectancy at Birth	Sri Lanka	Pakistan
(c) HDI Rank in the World	Sri Lanka	Pakistan

Q.13 The following table shows the proportion of adults (15-49 years) whose BMI is below normal (BMI < 18.5 kg/m²) in India. It is based on a survey of various states for the year 2019-21. Look at the table and answer the following questions.

State	Male (%)	Female (%)
Kerala	8.5	10
Karnataka	17	21
Madhya Pradesh	28	28
All States	**20**	**23**

Source : National Family Health Survey 5, 2019-21

(i) Compare the nutritional level of people in Kerala and Madhya Pradesh.

(ii) Can you guess why around one fifth of people in the country are undernourished even though it is argued that there is enough food in the country? Describe in your own words.

Ans. (i) Kerala has less percentage of people who are undernourished as compared to Madhya Pradesh.

(ii) There is enough food in the country but still one fifth of the people in the country are undernourished because of the following reasons

- There is a lack of educational and health facilities in many parts of the country. So, many people remain backward and poor, and they are unable to get nutritious food.
- In most of the states, the Public Distribution System (PDS) does not function properly and the poor people cannot get food items at cheap rates so they remain undernourished.

REVIEW EXERCISE

Including Competency Based Questions

Part I

Multiple Choice Questions (MCQs)

1. If industrialists want more dams then why do local people resist it?

(a) They will be displaced.
(b) Their lands will be submerged.
(c) There will be no source of earning for them.
(d) All of the above

2. Per capita income is criterion for development of which one of the following? CBSE 2025

(a) United Nations Development Programme
(b) World Health Organisation
(c) World Trade Organisation (d) World Bank

3. Which of the following is a key indicator used to measure a country's development? CBSE 2024

(a) Primary Production (b) Secondary Production
(c) Gross Domestic Product (d) Net Domestic Product

4. The literacy rate is highest in Kerala while the Infant Mortality Rate is highest in Bihar.
In relation to this information which statement is true? Competency Based

(a) Most of the people in Kerala and Bihar have good living conditions.
(b) Both Bihar and Kerala lack basic necessities of life.
(c) The standard of living in Kerala is better than Bihar.
(d) The standard of living in Bihar is better than Kerala.

5. Suppose there are four families in your locality, the average per capita income of whom is ₹ 10,000. If the income of three families is ₹ 6,000, ₹ 8,000 and ₹ 14,000 respectively, what would be the income of the fourth family? CBSE Term I 2021

(a) ₹ 5,000 (b) ₹ 10,000
(c) ₹ 12,000 (d) ₹ 15,000

6. The total number of children attending school as a percentage of total number of children in the same age group is called

(a) net attendance ratio (b) literacy rate
(c) gross enrollment ratio (d) level of education

7. The Human Development Report (HDR) published by UNDP compares countries based on literacy rate, health status and ....

(a) National income
(b) Per capita income
(c) Both (a) and (b)
(d) None of the above

8. Sarah, an environmental researcher from a coastal region, has been studying the impact of urbanisation on the local ecosystem. She noticed a significant rise in construction activities along the coastline, leading to the destruction of mangrove forests and the natural habitat of several species of fish and birds.

Which of the following consequences is most likely to occur as a result of the described development in the coastal region? **Competency Based**

(a) Decline in marine biodiversity and disruption of the local ecosystem.
(b) Increased employment opportunities for the local community.
(c) Enhanced recreational activities and tourism influx in the area.
(d) Improved infrastructure leading to better living conditions for residents.

9. Lalita, a 35-year-old woman living in a rural area, desires to enhance her family's well-being. She cultivates a small plot of land but faces challenges due to erratic rainfall affecting her agricultural yield. Her children walk several miles to reach the nearest school, which lacks adequate facilities.

Which of the following development goals would be most essential to address Lalita's and her community's challenges? **Competency Based**

(a) Implementing sustainable water resource management techniques in the village.
(b) Constructing better roads for easier access to schools and markets.
(c) Providing advanced agricultural technology and training for better yield.
(d) Establishing healthcare centers to improve sanitation and tackle diseases.

10. "A developing country is facing a dilemma concerning its development strategies and the utilisation of natural resources. The country's economic growth heavily relies on industries that consume vast amounts of non-renewable resources."

Should the government prioritise immediate economic growth over adopting sustainable practices to ensure the availability of resources for future generations? **Competency Based**

(a) Yes, rapid economic growth is crucial for addressing immediate social needs and uplifting the standard of living, outweighing concerns about resource depletion.
(b) No, sustainable development should be the priority, as it ensures the long-term availability of resources and protects the environment, ultimately benefitting future generations.
(c) Yes, economic growth should be balanced with sustainable practices, but immediate needs take precedence over potential future resource scarcity.
(d) No, there should be a focus on alternative development models that prioritise renewable resources, balancing economic growth with environmental sustainability for the long term.

11. Which of the following scenarios best illustrates the concept of conflicting developmental goals?

(a) A government initiative aiming to build large-scale industrial zones in an economically backward region, promising significant employment opportunities but risking the displacement of local indigenous communities and ecological disruption.
(b) An urban area experiencing rapid economic growth due to the establishment of various multinational corporations, leading to increased income levels for the majority of the population but causing a rise in pollution and health issues.
(c) A rural community implementing a project to construct small-scale dams to meet local electricity demands, despite potential environmental impact on nearby wildlife and agricultural lands.
(d) A nation focusing solely on improving its Gross Domestic Product (GDP) without considering the disparities in healthcare access and education among different regions and social groups.

12. Which of the following statements best reflects the multifaceted nature of development, considering the dilemma faced by the government in the pursuit of economic growth while ensuring sustainability and inclusive progress? **Competency Based**

(a) "Development solely focused on economic growth may lead to environmental degradation and social disparities, compromising the well-being of future generations."
(b) "Prioritising economic growth is the only viable way for a low middle-income country to achieve immediate prosperity, overlooking short-term challenges for long-term gains."
(c) "Environmental sustainability should be the primary concern for any nation, even if it means sacrificing economic growth and developmental goals in the short term."
(d) "Balancing economic growth with environmental sustainability and social equity is essential for holistic and sustainable development, ensuring the well-being of current and future generations."

13. Why is the Human Development Index (HDI) considered an effective measure for comparing development among different countries?

(a) HDI solely focuses on per capita income as the primary factor for development comparison.
(b) HDI considers only the literacy rate and life expectancy to compare countries' development.
(c) HDI compares countries based on three key criteria: per capita income, life expectancy, and mean years of schooling.
(d) HDI emphasises environmental factors as the sole basis for assessing a country's level of development.

14. **Dividing the total income of country with its population, we get**

I. Per Capita Income II. National Income

III. Average Income IV. Total Income

Codes

(a) Only III (b) I and III

(c) III and IV (d) None of these

15. **Consider the following statements about exhaustion of natural resources.**

I. Crude oil resources would last only 50 years more.

II. Oil extraction is undertaken by Middle East region at a very fast pace.

III. Non-conventional fuel sources should be encouraged that reduces use of crude oil.

Which of the above statements gives an idea of sustainable development?

(a) Only II (b) I and II

(c) Only I (d) Only III

16. **Consider the following statements.**

Statement I Development solely relies on high income as its primary goal.

Statement II Human Development Index (HDI) is an effective measure to evaluate a country's development.

Statement III Conflicting developmental goals among individuals indicate varied perspectives and priorities.

Which of the statements align with the complexities and nuances of development goals?

(a) Statements I and II are appropriate.

(b) Statements II and III are appropriate.

(c) All the statements are appropriate.

(d) Only statement III is appropriate.

Answers

1. (d)	2. (d)	3. (c)	4. (c)	5. (c)
6. (a)	7. (b)	8. (a)	9. (b)	10. (d)
11. (a)	12. (d)	13. (c)	14. (b)	15. (d)
16. (b)				

Match the Following

1.

List I	List II
A. Per Capita Income	1. Total Income
B. National Income	2. Human Development Index
C. Body Mass Index	3. Average Income
D. Decent Standard of Living	4. Proper Nutrition

Codes

	A	B	C	D		A	B	C	D
(a)	4	1	3	2	(b)	3	2	4	1
(c)	1	4	3	2	(d)	3	1	4	2

Ans. (d)

Assertion-Reason

1. **Assertion** (A) Since the second half of the twentieth century, scientists have been warning that the type and levels of development are not sustainable.

Reason (R) In the name of development, natural resources are exploited at a fast rate leading to their depletion.

Codes

(a) Both A and R are true and R is the correct explanation of A

(b) Both A and R are true, but R is not the correct explanation of A

(c) A is true, but R is false

(d) A is false, but R is true

2. **Assertion** (A) In Tamil Nadu, around 90 percent of the people living in rural areas avail the opportunity of ration shops but in West Bengal only 35 per cent people do so.

Reason (R) Availability of good health and educational facilities to a large extent depend on public facilities and ration shops is one of them.

Codes

(a) Both A and R are true and R is the correct explanation of A

(b) Both A and R are true, but R is not the correct explanation of A

(c) A is true, but R is false

(d) A is false, but R is true

3. **Assertion** (A) Kerala has low infant mortality rate.

Reason (R) Kerala has adequate provision of basic health and education facilities. **CBSE Term I 2021**

Codes

(a) Both A and R are true and R is the correct explanation of A

(b) Both A and R are true, but R is not the correct explanation of A

(c) A is true, but R is false

(d) A is false, but R is true

4. **Assertion** (A) Different individuals having diverse developmental goals can lead to conflicting notions of development.

Reason (R) Development varies according to personal aspirations, leading to contrasting perspectives on what constitutes progress and well-being.

Codes

(a) Both A and R are true and R is the correct explanation of A

(b) Both A and R are true, but R is not the correct explanation of A

(c) A is true, but R is false

(d) A is false, but R is true

5. Assertion (A) Per Capita Income alone does serve as an accurate measure to evaluate the holistic development of a nation.

Reason (R) Other factors such as literacy rates, healthcare facilities, and social indicators significantly influence a country's overall development.

Codes

(a) Both A and R are true and R is the correct explanation of A
(b) Both A and R are true, but R is not the correct explanation of A
(c) A is true, but R is false
(d) A is false, but R is true

6. Assertion (A) Human Development Index (HDI) offers a less comprehensive understanding of a Nation's development compared to solely relying on per capita income.

Reason (R) HDI includes various aspects like education, health, income, poverty levels and environmental conditions for a holistic assessment.

Codes

(a) Both A and R are true and R is the correct explanation of A
(b) Both A and R are true, but R is not the correct explanation of A
(c) A is true, but R is false
(d) A is false, but R is true

Ans. 1. (a) Both A and R are true and R is the correct explanation of A
2. (b) Both A and R are true, but R is not the correct explanation of A
3. (a) Both A and R are true and R is the correct explanation of A
4. (a) Both A and R are true and R is the correct explanation of A
5. (d) A is false, but R is true
6. (d) A is false, but R is true

Data Based Questions

1. Read the given data in the table and find out the average monthly income of country A. Choose the correct option. **CBSE 2023**

Monthly Income of Citizens of Two Countries (in Rupees)

	I	II	III	IV	V	Average Income
Country A	10500	9800	9500	10000	10500	?
Country B	6000	6000	6000	6000	50000	

Codes

(a) 9500 (b) 10000
(c) 10500 (d) 10060

2. Read the given data and find out children of which state has attained maximum elementary school education. **CBSE SQP 2022-23**

State	Per Capita Income For 2018-19 (in ₹)	Infant Mortality Rate per 1,000 live births (2018)	Literacy Rate % 2017-18	Net Attendance Ratio (per 100 persons) secondary state (age 14 and 15 years) 2017-18
Haryana	2,36,147	30	82	61
Kerala	2,04,105	7	94	83
Bihar	40,982	32	62	43

Sources : *Economic Survey 2020-21, P.A 157, National Sample Survey Organisation (Report No. 585), National Statistical Office, Government of India.*

(a) Haryana (b) Bihar
(c) Haryana and Kerala (d) Kerala

3. Refer the given data and find out how much percentage of females were not literate in the age group 10-14 years?

Category	Male	Female
Literacy rate for rural population	76%	54%
Literacy rate for rural children in age group 10-14 years	90%	87%
Percentage of rural children aged 10-14 attending school	85%	82%

(a) 23% (b) 32%
(c) 13% (d) 10%

4. Read the data given in the table and find out the difference between the crude oil reserves of Middle East and USA.

Region/Country	Reserves (2017) (Thousand Million Barrels)	Number of Years Reserves will last
Middle East	808	70
United States of America	50	10.5
World	1697	50.2

(a) 785 Thousand Million Barrels
(b) 758 Thousand Million Barrels
(c) 748 Thousand Million Barrels
(d) 768 Thousand Million Barrels

5. Study the table given below carefully and answer the questions that follows. **CBSE 2024**

Country	Gross National Income (GNI) Per Capita (2011 PPP $)	HDI Rank in the World (2018)
A	12,707	73
B	6,681	130
C	4,961	148
D	5,005	154
E	3,457	143
F	4,976	134

Which of the following country has high Human Development Index Rank in the world ?

(a) Country 'A'
(b) Country 'C'
(c) Country 'D'
(d) Country 'E'

Ans. 1. (d) 10060
2. (d) Kerala
3. (c) 13%
4. (b) 758 Thousand Million Barrels
5. (a) Country 'A'

Picture Based Questions

1. Observe the following image. This image is best suitable for which given problem?

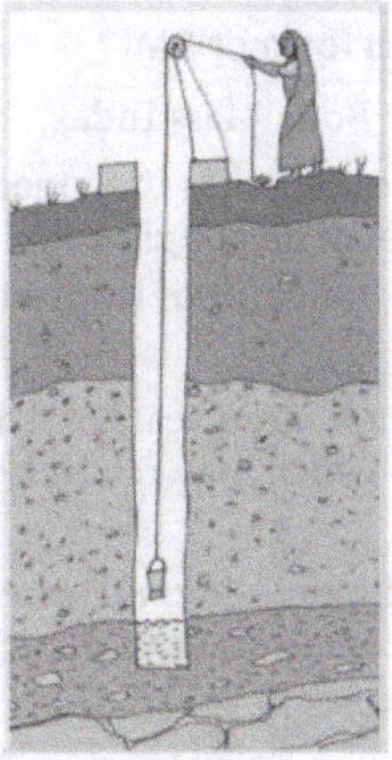

(a) Scarcity of water in region
(b) Regional crop methods
(c) Water pollution
(d) Increase population

2. The image shows a busy street scene with multiple modes of transportation. Which of the following statements is most likely true about the economic development of this place?

(a) The place has a high level of economic development because it has a variety of transport options and a large population.
(b) The place has a low level of economic development because it has a lot of traffic congestion and pollution from the vehicles.
(c) The place has a moderate level of economic development because it has some modern infrastructure and services, but also some challenges and inequalities.
(d) The place has no relation to economic development because the modes of transportation and the population size are irrelevant factors.

Ans. 1. (a) Scarcity of water in region
2. (c) The place has a moderate level of economic development because it has some modern infrastructure and services, but also some challenges and inequalities.

Case Based Question

1. Read the given passage and answer the questions that follows.

Groundwater is an example of renewable resources. These resources are replenished by nature as in the case of crops and plants. However, even these resources may be overused. For example, in the case of groundwater, if we use more than what is being replenished by rain then we would be overusing this resource. Non-renewable resources are those which will get exhausted after a few years of use. We have a fixed stock on Earth which cannot be replenished. We do discover new resources that we did not know of earlier. New sources in this way add to the stock. However, over time, even this will get exhausted.

(i) Which of the following best defines renewable resources?

(a) Resources that are limited and cannot be replenished.

(b) Resources that are replenished by nature.

(c) Resources such as fossil fuels that can be easily replaced.

(d) Resources that have a fixed stock and cannot be used sustainably.

(ii) What distinguishes non-renewable resources from renewable ones?

(a) Non-renewable resources cannot be overused.

(b) Renewable resources get exhausted quickly.

(c) Non-renewable resources have a fixed stock and can't be replenished.

(d) Renewable resources are discovered over time.

(iii) If a resource is overused beyond what nature replenishes, it falls under which category?

(a) Renewable resource (b) Non-renewable resource

(c) Sustainable resource (d) Excessive resource

(iv) How do new sources contribute to the stock of resources?

(a) They lead to the depletion of existing resources.

(b) They replenish non-renewable resources.

(c) They add to the stock of non-renewable resources.

(d) They aid in the sustainability of renewable resources.

Ans. (i) (b) Resources that are replenished by nature

(ii) (c) Non-renewable resources have a fixed stock and can't be replenished

(iii) (a) Renewable resource

(iv) (c) They add to the stock of non-renewable resources.

Part II

Very Short Answer Type Questions

1. Why do people look at a mix of goals for development?

Ans. People look at a mix of goals for development because apart from income they want respect, dignity, safety, security, pollution free environment, etc.

2. Can you imagine one developmental goal of a landless rural labour? **CBSE 2019**

Ans. More days of work and better wages are the developmental goals of a landless rural labour.

3. Write any one aspiration that a prosperous farmer from Punjab may possess for his development. **CBSE 2019**

Ans. A prosperous farmer from Punjab may want to hire more work force in his farm to produce more and earn more profit.

4. State the difference between literacy rate and attendance ratio.

Ans. Literacy rate is the proportion of literate persons in the age group of 7 or above. On the other hand, attendance ratio is the proportion of children of a specific age group attending school to the total number of children in the same group.

5. Give one major reason for which children, particularly girls are not able to achieve secondary level schooling.

Ans. Children, particularly girls are not able to achieve secondary level schooling because of the absence of proper resosurces and facilities and most importantly wide spread discrimination against the female.

6. Write one example of inequality in urban areas.

Ans. High rise building and shopping malls at the centre and slums, old colonies in the outskirts or around the high rise buildings are the best example of urban inequality.

7. Why less number of girls in the age group 10-14 years attend school in rural areas than boys.

Ans. Less number of girls in the age group 10-14 years attend school in rural areas than boys because of community negligence and also rural people do not give importance to the girls education.

8. Your friend is 150 cm tall and have weight of 40 kg. Find out his BMI and comment on his report.

Ans. My friend's BMI $= \frac{40}{1.50 \times 1.50} = 17.77 < 18.5$

He is underweight, as his BMI is less than 18.5.

9. What is the full form of BMI? **CBSE 2015**

Ans. BMI stands for Body Mass Index.

10. Name one criterion other than income which may reflect the level of development.

Or **Write any one indicator of Human Development Index.** **CBSE 2015**

Ans. Level of education mean years of schooling is an other criterion which may reflect levels of development.

11. How does the United Nations Development Program's (UNDP's) developmental criterion differ from the World Bank? Explain. **CBSE 2024**

Ans. The United Nations Development Programme's (UNDP's) development criterion differ from the World Bank because the World Bank classifies countries based on per capita income, focussing on economic indicators. Whereas, the UNDP employs a broader approach, considering income, education and health indices in its Human Development Index. It provides a comprehensive perspective on a country's well-being.

12. How many countries are included in HDI ranking? CBSE 2015

Ans. There are 189 countries for which HDI is calculated in Human Development Report.

13. What proportion of the country is over using their groundwater reserves?

Ans. About one-third of the country is over using their groundwater reserves.

14. State any two goals of development other than income. CBSE 2018

Ans. Two goals of development other than income are

(i) Equal treatment

(ii) Improvement in standard of living

15. "The provision of public facilities contributes significantly to a region's progress. Kerala, with its robust healthcare and education, shows promising indicators compared to Bihar."

What aspects of development do the variations in healthcare and education between Kerala and Bihar reflect? Competency Based

Ans. The variations in healthcare and education between Kerala and Bihar reflect that development should not be solely assessed based on income. Basic facilities like healthcare and education play a crucial role in determining the quality of life and overall development.

Short Answer Type Questions

1. Mention any four characteristics of Development. CBSE 2014, 13

Ans. The characteristics of development are

- Development is linked with the desire to improve the present condition.
- Development involves thinking about the questions and about the ways in which we can work towards achieving our desired goals.
- There can be different development goals for different people.
- Development for one may not be development for others.

2. Why income is not an adequate indicator of material goods and services that citizens are able to use? Explain with example.

Ans. Income is not an adequate indicator of material goods and services that citizens are able to use because the quality of life also depends on non-material things like equal treatment, freedom, security, respect of others, etc.

Also, money cannot buy all the goods and services that a person needs to live a fulfilled life.

For example, a person may be earning high income, but if he is not getting job security and adequate time for family then the person is not able to get the feeling of security and freedom. So, income is not an adequate indicator.

3. Developmental goals are differing goals also. Explain with an example. CBSE 2014

Ans. Development goals are differing goals because different people have different situations in life due to which their goals are different.

For example, development goals of a girl from a rich urban family will be surely different from a farmer in Rajasthan. It is because their situations, lifestyle and status are very different from each other.

The goal of a person is something, which is entirely dependent on his or her present life situation. Over a period of time, if the situation changes, automatically goals of a person will also change. Hence, developmental goals are differing goals also.

4. Although average are useful for comparing countries, they also hide disparities? Explain the meaning of this statement. Support the statement with suitable arguements. CBSE 2019

Or **Why is Per Capita Income not an adequate indicator of economic development of a country?** CBSE 2012

Ans. Average or Per Capita Income is useful for comparing countries, but they also hide disparities. They do not give the true picture of a country due to the following reasons

- They do not tell us how equally or evenly income is distributed.
- They do not give information regarding the human development index such as Literacy Rate, Infant Morality Rate, etc.
- They do not give us any information regarding the non-materialistic goods and services such as equality, freedom, respect, dignity.

5. Define 'Gross Domestic Product' and explain its importance. CBSE 2025

Ans. GDP (Gross Domestic Product) is the total value of all goods and services produced within a country's borders during a specific period, usually a year or a quarter. It is used to measure the economic performance of a country.

Importance of GDP is discussed below

- GDP serves as a key indicator of a country's economic health. A growing GDP typically indicates a thriving economy, while a declining GDP may signal an economic downturn.
- GDP allows comparisons between different countries' economic performances. It helps policymakers and researchers analyse and compare the relative prosperity of nations.
- Governments and central banks use GDP data to formulate economic policies, such as fiscal and monetary measures, to stabilise or grow the economy.

6. Why countries of the Middle-East are not called developed in spite of high Per Capita Income?

Ans. The countries of the Middle-East may have very high Per Capita Income due to revenues from selling crude oil, but they are otherwise not developed (except Israel). It is because their literacy rate, life expectancy at birth and other similar parameters do not match with the criteria necessary to become developed country.

The probable reason is that they have become rich nations recently due to sharp increase in the price of oil, but their society has not developed accordingly. Most of the wealth is accumulated by few people, so the society has widespread inequality.

7. Deepa, an 11 year old girl helps her parents in farming throughout the day. She is sick and thin. On the other hand, Geeta, living in Kerala goes to school daily and eat mid day meals there. In the evening, she helps her parents in farming. What does this show? Competency Based

Ans. This shows that Deepa lives in that part of rural India where the literacy level is low. She neither goes to school nor takes proper nutrition. She is not healthy.

On the other hand, Geeta lives in that part of rural India which is prosperous such as the state of Kerala. She goes to school and eats mid day meals that fulfills her nutritional needs. She is healthy also. It also shows that the public facilities like free school nearby, provision of meals in the school for the children is provided by the State Government.

This means that in the long run, Geeta will lead a better life than Deepa.

8. 'Money cannot buy all the goods and services that one needs to live well'. Explain. CBSE 2014

Ans. Money cannot buy all the goods and services that one needs to live well because

- Apart from money, the infrastructure and facility like health and education is required to live well.
- Money cannot fulfill non material needs like friendship, love, care, freedom, job security, good working atmosphere etc.
- Public facilities like clean environment, protection from infectious diseases can not be bought by money alone.

9. Sunita, a 25 year old woman lives in a village. Her height is 1.45m and weight is 36 kg, while Nisha of the same age and height weights 48 kg. What can be said about their nutritional condition? Competency Based

Ans. It can be said that Nisha's nutritional condition is much better than Sunita.

Nisha is taking proper nutrition due to which her weight is normal but Sunita is underweight. This is known by finding out the BMI.

$$\text{Sunita's BMI} = \frac{36}{1.45 \times 1.45} = 17.12$$

$$\text{Nisha's BMI} = \frac{48}{1.45 \times 1.45} = 22.82$$

Sunita's BMI is 17.12 which is less than 18.5, hence she is not healthy. Nisha's BMI is 22.82 which is in between 18.5 and 25, so she is healthy and hence, taking proper nutrition.

10. Explain any four different indicators of economic development of different nations/states.

Or **What is Human Development. Explain its indicators.** CBSE 2020

Ans. Human Development is the process of enlarging people's choices as well as raising the level of well being so that they can lead a purposeful and a creative life.

The four indicators of human development are

(i) **Per Capita Income** This is the total income of country divided by its total population.

(ii) **Life Expectancy at Birth** This is the number of years, a new born child is expected to live at the prevailing conditions.

(iii) **Literacy Rate** This is the total percentage of the population of an area at a particular time aged 7 years or above, who can read and write with understanding atleast one language.

(iv) **Net Attendance Ratio** It is the total number of children enrolled in or attending primary school, as a percentage of total number of children of primary school age.

11. What are the major attributes of development considered by UNDP in making the Human Development Report? Explain the importance of each of these attributes.

Or **Explain any three criteria used by Human Development Report to classify various countries.** CBSE 2015

Ans. The major attributes/criteria in making the Human Development Report are

- People with more per capita income can buy nutritious food, get better health care facilities and give proper education to their children. Therefore, per capita income is the major attribute of considering development.
- **Educational Levels of the People** Educated people will be able to get better jobs and higher earnings due to their higher education status.
- **Health Status** Health will be good and longevity will increase when people will be able to afford better healthcare facilities. Infant mortality will also reduce due to better healthcare, resulting in further increase in life expectancy at birth.

12. How is the issue of subtainability important for development? Explain with examples. CBSE 2018

Ans. The issue of sustainability is important for development due to following reasons

- There is a limited stock of natural resources if they are not used judiciously then there will be nothing left for future generations.
- Without sustainable development, an ecological disbalance may be created leading to destruction of the environment.
- Without sustainable development, ecological disbalance may also lead to environmental pollution which is very big deal to handle. For example, air and water pollution are rising due to industrial wastes.

13. What does sustainability of development mean? How can sustainable development be achieved? CBSE 2014

Ans. Sustainablity of development means that development should take place without damaging the environment, and development in the present should not compromise with the needs of the future generations. Here, the natural resources should be used in such a way that environmental balance is also maintained.

Sustainable development can be achieved in the following ways

- By scientific and proper use of the resources.
- By finding out ways to stop environmental pollution.
- By developing renewable source of energy like water, wind and solar energy.

14. Consider the following statements about Development and its multidimensional aspects

Statement 1 (S1) Development encompasses diverse goals such as freedom, economic equality, security, and a decent standard of living.

Statement 2 (S2) Different individuals might have conflicting development objectives, leading to contrasting perspectives on progress.

Discuss the implications of these statements in the context of policy formulation and societal progress, highlighting the challenges associated with aligning divergent developmental goals. Competency Based

Ans. The given statements reflect the complexity of development, encompassing varied aspirations and conflicting objectives.

Statement 1 emphasises the multifaceted nature of development, including economic, social, and personal dimensions. Statement 2 acknowledges the divergence in individual developmental aspirations, potentially causing conflicts in policy formulation and societal progress.

Aligning these distinct goals poses challenges, necessitating inclusive policies addressing diverse needs for comprehensive societal advancement. Balancing conflicting aspirations becomes crucial in policy design to achieve inclusive and sustainable development for all segments of society.

Long Answer Type Questions

1. Give examples to prove that there are other important developmental goals than income.

Ans. Besides income, the developmental goals of various categories of people are different from person to person. Some examples of developmental goals other than income are

- For rich farmer, development means higher support price for crops, cheap labour and subsidised inputs.
- For landless rural labourer, development means more days of work, schools for their children and no social discrimination.
- For adivasi, development means no social discrimination, year round employment, school education for children and ration shops in his village.
- For urban youth, development means opportunity for higher education, availability of an office job and own house.
- For urban girl from rich family, development means freedom to choose her profession or being able to pursue her higher studies abroad.

2. With the help of an example, show how two groups may have different notions of development.

Or What may be development for one, may not be development for another. Explain the statement with suitable examples.

Or The development goals of different categories of people may differ. Evaluate the statement. CBSE 2025

Ans. Two groups may have different notions of development. For example, In Saurashtra region of Gujarat the local community's notion of development on the case of construction of a dam was that the areas in which they live will be submerged and there will be greater environmental degradation.

However, the government's notion of development in this case would be that by raising the height of the dam they would be able to provide more water to the people of Saurashtra region of Gujarat, which always suffers from water scarcity. In addition, more electricity would be generated with this measure, which would benefit all the people living in that area.

3. Explain any four public facilities.

Or What do you mean by public facilities? Why are they important? Name two public facilities available in India. CBSE 2011

Or Examine the importance of public facilities for development. CBSE 2025

Ans. Public facilities are the facilities provided by the government either free of cost or at very low price for the welfare of the people like schools, health centres, public transport, etc. The importance of these facilities is to make it available to everyone for use so that the standard of living improves.

The major public facilities are as follows

- **Basic Education** Government provides school and other educational facilities like chair, books, etc. to be used by the public. But its use and performance is depended on collective response and community cooperation.
- **Basic Health Facilities** Government provides hospitals, vaccine programmes to maintain basic quality of life.
- **Law and Order Facility/Security** It is the duty of the government to ensure law and order and provide security in order to maintain peace in the country.
- **Provide for Public Distribution System** Government opens PDS shops or ration shops through which it supplies basic food items like rice, wheat, pulses, etc. at very low price/subsidised rate to the lower income group or poor people.

4. "Consequences of environmental degradation do not respect national or state boundaries". Justify the statement. CBSE 2025, 2015, 2012

Ans. It is true that the consequences of environmental degradation is now a global issue and discussed all over the world. They are not restricted to the nation or state boundary. The consequences are felt in the surrounding states, nations and also globally. For example,

- Air pollution through massive thermal power plant and other sources, in India causes pollution in Bhutan, Nepal, etc.
- Our neighbours also experience increase in asthma and other lung diseases. Acid rain, climate change, etc. are some issues which are transcontinental in consequences.
- Deforestation in Brazil has caused disturbance in rainfall pattern throughout South America.
- Land degradation and dam burst like conditions in China affect India and Bangladesh as it brings massive siltation and flood consequences.

Therefore environmental degradation is a major issue and its consequences are felt worldwide.

5. Discuss the significance of the Human Development Index (HDI) in measuring a nation's progress and elucidate how it surpasses the limitations of assessing development solely based on economic indicators like per capita income. Competency Based

Ans. The Human Development Index (HDI) is a crucial tool because it offers a broader view of a country's progress beyond just economic wealth. Unlike solely relying on income or money, HDI takes into account various important factors that contribute to people's well-being. It considers things like how long people live, how educated they are, and their standard of living.

For example, a country might have a high income, but if its citizens lack access to healthcare or education, the HDI will reflect these shortcomings. HDI serves as a more comprehensive measure, providing insights into the overall quality of life within a nation.

By incorporating multiple dimensions such as health, education, and income, the HDI enables a more nuanced assessment of a country's development. It showcases whether a nation is genuinely enhancing the lives of its citizens, offering a more realistic depiction beyond monetary wealth.

Therefore, HDI acts as a valuable indicator, highlighting areas for improvement and emphasising the importance of holistic development for a nation's population.

6. Mr. Y, an entrepreneur, is considering establishing a manufacturing unit in his hometown. He aims to create job opportunities and contribute to the local economy.

Describe how the Human Development Index (HDI) can guide Mr. Y in evaluating the developmental aspects of his region for sustainable growth. Elaborate on the factors he should consider beyond per capita income to ensure holistic development in his community. Competency Based

Ans. Mr. Y's consideration to establish a manufacturing unit requires a comprehensive understanding of his region's developmental facets for sustainable growth. The Human Development Index (HDI) offers a holistic evaluation beyond just per capita income. He should weigh factors like life expectancy, education levels, and overall living standards to assess the community's well-being.

By focusing on education and healthcare access for employees, he can elevate the region's human capital. Implementing eco-friendly practices and renewable energy sources within his venture ensures sustainability.

Moreover, investing in community infrastructure like healthcare and education positively impacts overall development.

In summary, Mr Y should use the HDI's multifaceted approach, emphasizing human well-being, education, environmental consciousness, and equitable economic growth to ensure a balanced and sustainable trajectory for his entrepreneurial venture and the region at large.

Case Based Questions

1. Read the source given below and answer the questions that follow.

Human Development Report, once it is realised that even though the level of income is important, yet it is an inadequate measure of the level of development, we begin to think of other criterion. There could be a long list of such criterion but then it would not be so useful.

What we need is a small number of the most important things. Health and education indicators, such as the ones we used in comparison of Kerala and Punjab, are among them. Over the past decade or so, health and education indicators have come to be widely used along with income as a measure of development. For instance, Human Development Report published by UNDP compares countries based on the educational levels of the people, their health status and per capita income. It would be interesting to look at certain relevant data regarding India and its neighbours from Human Development Report 2006. **(SQP 2024-25)**

(i) **On what basis the UNDP compares countries on human development?**

(ii) **Explain human development briefly.**

(iii) **Mention other aspects that should be considered in measuring human development.**

Ans. (i) The Human Development Report, published by UNDP, compares countries based on education levels, health status and income per person.

(ii) Human development means improving people's choices and opportunities, including education, healthcare, income and empowerment. It also includes having a good physical environment and enjoying economic, political, and social freedom.

(iii) Other important aspects of human development include life expectancy and access to public facilities like water, sanitation, roads, and electricity.

2. Read the passage given below and answer the questions that follow.

However, for comparison between countries, total income is not such an useful measure. Since, countries have different populations, comparing total income will not tell us what an average person is likely to earn. Hence, we compare the average income which is the total income of the country divided by its total population. The average income is also called Per Capita Income.

In World Development Reports, brought out by the World Bank, this criterion is used in classifying countries. Countries with Per Capita Income of US $ 12,056 per annum and above in 2017, are called rich countries and those with per capita income of US $ 955 or less are called low-income-countries.

India comes in the category of low middle income countries because its Per Capita Income in 2017 was just US $ 1820 per annum. The rich countries, excluding countries of Middle East and certain other small countries, are generally called developed countries.

(i) **What aspects of a country are not included in calculating total income?**

(ii) **Discuss the importance of classifying countries by the World Bank.**

(iii) **Do you agree on World Development Report to categorise India as a low middle income country?**

Ans. (i) The total income calculates only the sum total of income earned but it do not consider the total number of population into which that income is divided.

(ii) Classification of countries by the World Bank is a way to know how many countries fall in rich, middle and low income groups. With this information, the World Bank terms the countries as developed or developing. This classification can be used by the countries to know about their economic condition in the world.

(iii) Yes, World Development Report on categorising India as low middle income country is correct because India's per capita income is much lower than the income of developed countries like US. At the same time, the per capita income of India is higher than low income countries. Therefore India's category as a low middle income country is correct.

ASSESSMENT EXERCISE

Multiple Choice Questions (MCQs)

1. According to the World Bank, which one of the following criteria is the basis for measuring the development of a country?
   (a) Per Capita Income
   (b) Literacy Rate
   (c) Gross Enrollment Ratio
   (d) Life Expectancy
2. The development goal of a girl in a village will be ....
   (a) to study in a foreign country
   (b) to be free to choose her career
   (c) to be given equal opportunities like boys
   (d) All of the above
3. Average Income is also called as
   (a) National Income (b) Per Capita Income
   (c) Total Income (d) None of these

Subjective Questions (VSA, SA and LA)

1. What do you understand by the term life expectancy?
2. Name the state in India having very low Infant Mortality Rate.
3. If the Body Mass Index is more than 25, then what would be the person considered?
4. Write one limitation of average income of a country.
5. Evaluate the public facilities needed for the development of the country?
6. 'We have not inherited the world from four forefathers–We have borrowed it from our children'. Explain the significance of sustainable development for human being.
7. Explain two reasons for the need of environment friendly economic growth and one suggestion to achieve it.
8. Describe the important aspects of our lives other than income.
9. Analyse the implications of having high HDI for a country.

Sectors of the Indian Economy

CHAPTER 2

Economic activities are those activities that are related to the generation of goods and services to gain profit. Every economy has three different sectors based on the nature of the work it performs i.e. **Primary sector**, **Secondary sector** and the **Tertiary sector**.

In the Indian economy, there are two different types of economic activities. These are **organised** which are governed by rules made by the government, and **unorganised** which are not regulated by the government.

2.1 Sectors of Economic Activities

In an economy, people are associated with different economic activities. Some of these activities produce goods and others produce services. These activities are classified into various groups which are known as sectors. The major sectors of economic activities are

(i) **Primary Sector** This sector includes the activities in which goods are produced by exploiting natural resources.

Cotton, milk, minerals and ores are natural products as they are obtained from nature.

Since most of the natural products are obtained from agriculture, dairy, fishing, forestry, etc it is also called **agricultural and related sector.**

(ii) **Secondary Sector** This sector includes the activities in which natural products are changed into other forms through manufacturing. It is the next step after primary sector. The product is not produced by nature but has to be made and therefore, some process of manufacturing is essential. This may take place in a factory, workshop or at home. For example, yarn and cloth weaving from cotton fibre, sugar or *gur* from sugarcane, etc.

Since this sector is associated with different kinds of industries, it is also called **industrial sector.**

(iii) **Tertiary Sector** This sector includes the activities that help in the development of primary and secondary sectors. These activities do not produce goods, but they provide or generate services that support the production process, e.g. transport, storage, communication, banking, etc. Since this sector generate services rather than goods, it is also called **service sector.**

This sector also includes some essential services that may not directly help in production of goods. They are provided by professionals, e.g. doctors, lawyers, teachers, barbers, etc and information technology such as **software industry**[1], internet cafe, ATM booths, **call centres**[2], etc.

2.2 Comparing the Three Sectors

Primary, Secondary and Tertiary sectors are compared on the basis of people working in them and amount of goods and services produced.

The goods and services are of two types as follows

(i) **Final Goods and Services** These goods and services are directly consumed by the consumers and are not meant for further production or processing. These goods are included while calculating total production.

(ii) **Intermediate Goods and Services** These goods and services are used for further production or processing of final goods and services. These are not included in calculation of total production as their value is already included in final goods.

For example, a farmer sells wheat to a flour mill at ₹ 8 per kg. Flour mill grinds the wheat and sells to biscuit company for ₹ 10 per kg. Biscuit company adds sugar and oil to flour to make 4 packet of biscuit and sells to consumers at ₹ 60 (15 per pack).

In this example, biscuit is the final good and flour, sugar oil, service of flour mill are intermediate goods.

---

1 **Software Industries** These refer to industries that provide, develop and maintain computer operating systems.

2 **Call Centres** These are offices that provide the customer services functions.

The value of final goods and services produced in each sector during a particular year provides the total production of the sector for that year.

The sum of the value of all final goods and services produced in all the three sectors in a particular year is called the **Gross Domestic Product** (GDP). It shows the total production in the country.

The task of estimating the GDP in India is undertaken by the Central Government Ministry. This ministry, along with government departments from all Indian states and union territories, collects data on goods and services, and their prices to estimate GDP.

Historical Change in Sectors

Primary sector was most important sector in initial stages of development. With new methods of farming, more food was produced.

As new manufacturing methods emerged and factories expanded, people started working in industries and secondary sector gained importance.

Further, there is a shift from secondary to tertiary sector in developed countries. The tertiary sector has become the most important in terms of production and employment.

Try These

1. **This sector uses natural resources. Identify the sector.**
2. **What is the other name of secondary sector?**
3. **Who collects the data for GDP?**
4. **Which sector has grown in importance now a days?**

2.3 Rising Importance of the Tertiary Sector in Production

In 1973-74, primary sector was the largest producing sector in India but by 2013-14, tertiary sector became the largest producing sector.

The reasons for this are

- In a developing country, the government has to take responsibility for providing basic services such as hospitals, educational institutions, post and telegraph services, police stations, courts, transport, banks, etc.
- The development of agriculture and industry leads to the development of services such as transport, trade, storage. The demand for these services increases with the development of primary and secondary sectors.
- With the increase in income levels, certain sections of people start demanding many more services like tourism, shopping, private hospitals, private schools, etc.
- Certain new services such as those based on information and communication technology have become important and essential. The production of these services has been rising rapidly.

However, not all of the service sector is growing equally. There are a limited number of services that employ highly skilled and educated workers. This part of service sector is growing.

A very large number of workers are engaged in services such as small shopkeepers, repair persons, transport persons, etc. These people hardly manage to earn a living. This part of service sector is not growing.

2.4 Employment of People in Different Sectors

In, India there has been a change in the share of the three sectors in GDP, but a similar shift has not taken place in employment. This is because enough jobs were not created in the secondary and tertiary sectors.

More than half of working population are engaged in primary activities, mainly agriculture. Therefore, more people work than actually needed, and everyone work less than their capacity and also earns less. This is called **underemployment**.

In agriculture sector everyone does some work but no one is fully employed. This is the situation of underemployment, where people appear to be working but they work less than their potential.

This kind of underemployment is hidden in contrast to someone where it is clearly visible that a person has no job and unemployed. It is also called **disguised unemployment**.

Underemployment also occurs in other sectors and mainly in service sectors of urban areas.

2.5 Creating More Employment

It is essential to generate more employment opportunities and reduce unemployment in agricultural sector. This can be done by the following ways

- **Focus on Bank Credit** Banks can provide loan to small farmers for buying seeds, fertilisers, equipments, pumpsets, constructing wells for irrigation. This enable them to grow two or more crops thereby increasing their earnings.
- **Generating Employment** Creating employment by constructing dams and canals, making or betterment of rural roads, developing storage facilities, etc.

- **Focus on Small Scale Industries** Setting up industries in semi-rural areas where a large number of people may be employed. For example, rice mill, dal mill, honey collection centres, cold storage, food processing industries, etc.
- **Improvement in Education, Health and Tourism** Creating jobs in health and education sector by opening more dispensaries and schools in rural areas alongwith encouraging tourism. According to **NITI Aayog**[3], education sector has potential of generating 20 lakh jobs and tourism sector has potential of generating more than 35 lakh jobs.

MGNREGA 2005

Mahatma Gandhi National Rural Employment Guarantee Act (MGNREGA) was formulated in 2005.
The main features of this act are

- The scheme guarantees 100 days of wage employment in a year to those who are able to, and are in need of work in rural areas.
- The Central Government in India made this law to implement the Right to Work in about 625 districts of India. If the government fails in its duty to provide employment, it will give unemployment allowances to the people.

2.6 Division of Sectors as Organised and Unorganised

On the basis of the working conditions or how people are employed, economic activities are divided into organised and unorganised.

Organised Sector

It covers those **enterprises**[4] or places of work where terms of employment are regular and therefore, people have assured work.

They are registered by the government and follow the rules and regulations such as Factories Act, Minimum Wages Act, Payment of Gratuity Act, Shop and Establishment Act, etc. It is called organised because it has some formal procedures and processes.

The workers have job security in the organised sector. They have to work for a fixed number of hours and if they work more, they have to be paid overtime by the employer.

The workers also get benefit like provident fund, paid leaves, gratuity, medical benefits, etc.

The management in this sector ensures good working condition like clean drinking water and a safe working environment. The workers also get pensions after their retirement.

Unorganised Sector

This sector is characterised by small and scattered units which are unregistered and do not follow governmental rules and regulations.

Workers in this sector get lower wages and are not given facilities like paid holidays or paid leave due to sickness, etc. Working conditions are poor and there is no job security, so employment is irregular.

This sector consists of a large number of self-employed individuals who do small jobs. These include street vendors, repair workers and farmers.

Protection of Workers in Unorganised Sector

Many people in the unorganised sector are often exploited, paid less, and have irregular jobs. Thus, there is a need for protection of workers.

They can be protected in following ways

- In rural areas, farmers can be supported through adequate facility for timely delivery of seeds, agricultural inputs, credit, storage and marketing outlets.
- In urban areas, the small scale industries can be protected by government's support for procuring raw materials and marketing of output.

Majority of workers are from scheduled castes, tribes and backward communities. They face social discrimination. Protection and support to the unorganised sector is thus necessary for both economic and social development.

2.7 Sectors in Terms of Ownership

The economic activities can also be classified on the basis of ownership i.e. who owns the assets and who is responsible for delivery of services. On the basis of ownership, there are two sectors of the economy as follows

(i) **Public Sector** In this sector, government owns most of the assets and provides all the services, e.g. Indian Railways or Post Office.

---

3 **NITI Aayog** National Institution for Transforming India was formed on 1st January, 2015. It aims to foster India's economic development concerning transforming India.

4 **Enterprise** It refers to a business activity or an economic organisation.

(ii) **Private Sector** In this sector, ownership of assets and delivery of services is in the hands of individuals or private companies, e.g. Reliance Industries Limited (RIL), TISCO, etc activities in the private sector are aimed at earning profits.

2.8 Role of Public/Government Sector

- Government provides facilities which the private sector will not provide at a reasonable cost.
- Examples are construction of roads, bridges, railways, harbours, generating electricity, providing irrigation through dams, etc. Governments have to undertake heavy spending and ensure that these facilities are available for everyone.
- The government has to support the private sector so that they can continue their production or business. For example, selling electricity at the cost of generation may increase the costs of production of goods in many industries.
- Government here steps in by producing and supplying electricity at rates which these industries can afford. Government pays a part of the cost.
- The Government in India buys wheat and rice from farmers at a 'fair price'. It stores this in its godowns and sells at a lower price to consumers through ration shops. In this way, the government supports both farmers and consumers.
- Providing health and education facilities activities are the primary responsibility of the government.
- Running proper schools and providing quality education, particularly elementary education, is the duty of the government.
- Government needs to pay attention to aspects of human development such as availability of safe drinking water, housing facilities for the poor, food and nutrition.
- It is the duty of the government to take care of the poorest and most ignored regions of the country through increased spending in such areas.

Try These

1. **Which act is also known as Right to Work?**
2. **Under which sector (organised/unorganised) would you put a labourer who is working under a contractor?**
3. **Which sector is more concerned about people's welfare than making profits?**

Mind Map

SECTORS OF THE INDIAN ECONOMY

Types of Economic Activities

Primary Sector
- Includes the activities in which goods are produced by exploiting natural resources.
- Also called as agricultural and related sector.

Secondary Sector
- Includes the activities in which natural products are changed into other forms through manufacturing.
- Also called as industrial sector.

Tertiary Sector
- Includes the activities that help in the development of primary and secondary sectors.
- Also called as service sector.

Importance Of Tertiary Sector
- Development of trade and transport.
- Increase in income levels.
- Employ highly skilled and educated workers.

Employment Generation

Employment can be generated by the following :
- Focus on bank credit.
- Focus on small scale industries.
- Improvement in health, education and tourism.
- The Central Government in India made a law implementing Right to Work. It is called Mahatma Gandhi National Rural Employment Guarantee Act, 2005 (MGNREGA 2005).
- Under MGNREGA Act, all the people in the rural areas are guaranteed 100 days of employment in a year by the government.

Comparing the Three Sectors
- The value of final goods and services produced in each sector during a particular year provides the total production of the sector for that year.
- The sum of production in the three sectors gives what is called Gross Domestic Product (GDP) of a country.

Types of Goods and Services

Final Goods
Directly consumed by the consumers and are not meant for further production.

Intermediate Goods
Used for further production or processing of final goods and services.

Division of Sectors on Different Basis

Organised and Unorganised
- Organised sector covers those enterprises or places of work where terms of employment are regular.
- Unorganised sector is characterised by small and scattered units which are unregistered and do not follow governmental rules and regulations.

Based on Ownership
- In Public Sector, government owns most of the assets and provides all the services, e.g. Post Office or Indian Railways.
- In Private Sector, ownership of assets and delivery of services is in the hands of private companies or individuals, e.g. RIL.

NCERT FOLDER

Covering Intext Questions and Exercises of NCERT

INTEXT QUESTIONS

Q.1 Complete the table to show how sectors are dependent on each other.

Examples of Economic Activities

Example	What does this Show
1. Imagine what would happen if farmers refuse to sell sugarcane to a particular sugar mill. The mill will have to shut down.	This is an example of the Secondary or Industrial sector being dependent on the Primary.
2. Imagine what would happen to cotton cultivation if companies decide not to buy from the Indian market and import all cotton they need from other countries. Indian cotton cultivation will become less profitable and the farmers may even go bankrupt, if they cannot quickly switch to other crops. Cotton prices will fall.	
3. Farmers buy many goods such as tractors, pumpsets, electricity, pesticides and fertilisers. Imagine what would happen if the price of fertilisers or pumpsets go up. Cost of cultivation of the farmers will rise and their profits will be reduced.	
4. People working in industrial and service sector need food. Imagine what would happen if there is a strike by transporters and lorries refuse to take vegetables, milk, etc from rural areas. Food will become scarce in urban areas, whereas farmers will be unable to sell their products.	

Ans. 2. This is an example of primary sector, which is dependent on secondary sector.

3. This is an example of interdependence of both the primary sector i.e. agriculture being dependent on the products of secondary sector i.e. industry and secondary sector is dependent on primary to sell their products.

4. This is an example of interdependence of all the three sectors. Farmers will be unable to sell their farm products. Industrial and service sector will face food scarcity.

Q.2 Explain the differences between Primary, Secondary and Tertiary sectors using examples other than those mentioned in the text.

Ans.

Primary Sector	Secondary Sector	Tertiary Sector
This sector of the economy involves conversion of natural resources into primary products. Thus, this sector is directly associated with nature.	It include those activities in which natural products are changed into other forms through manufacturing.	The activities that help in the development of primary and secondary sectors are covered in tertiary sector.
For example, agriculture, forestry, mining	For example, manufacturing units, small scale units, large firms	For example, banking, communication and trade

Q.3 Classify the following list of occupations under Primary, Secondary and Tertiary sectors.

- Tailor
- Basket weaver
- Flower cultivator
- Milk vendor
- Fisherman
- Priest
- Courier
- Worker in match factory
- Moneylender
- Gardener
- Potter
- Bee-keeper
- Astronaut
- Call centre employee

Ans. **Primary sector** Flower cultivator, Fisherman, Gardener, Bee keeper

Secondary sector Basket weaver, Worker in match factory, Potter

Tertiary sector Tailor, Milk vendor, Priest, Courier, Moneylender, Astronaut, Call centre employee

Q.4 What does the history of developed countries indicate about the shifts that have taken place between sectors?

Ans. The history of developed countries indicate that the shifts have taken place from primary to secondary and then to tertiary sector. Initially, primary sector was the main economic activity. Due to improved methods of farming, productivity of agriculture sector increased and therefore, people started taking up other occupations like trading, transport, army etc.

Then, the secondary sector became the most important sector for production and employment, over a long period of time. This was a shift from primary to secondary sector as a result of industrialisation.

In developed countries, a further shift from secondary sector to tertiary sector has been observed in past decades. Major portion of the working population is now engaged in service sector.

Q.5 Correct and arrange the important aspects for calculating GDP from this jumble.

To count goods and services, we add the numbers that are produced. We count all those that were produced in the last five years. Since we shouldn't leave out anything, we add up all these goods and services.

***Or* How is GDP calculated?** **CBSE 2020**

Ans. Count the value of all final goods and services produced in an year to calculate GDP.

Q.6 Choose the correct answer.

Underemployment occurs when people ....

(a) do not want to work

(b) are working in a lazy manner

(c) are working less than what they are capable of doing

(d) are not paid for their work

Ans. (c) are working less than what they are capable of doing

Q.7 Compare and contrast the changes in India with the pattern that was observed for developed countries. What kind of changes between sectors were desired but did not happen in India?

Ans. In case of developed countries the evolution of the economy happened on the most logical pattern. Growth in the primary sector was followed by a growth in the secondary sector. After that, the growth of the tertiary sector followed. The employment generation also kept pace with related changes in different sectors.

The case of India is somewhat different. The growth of the primary sector was not followed by the growth of secondary sector, rather it was the tertiary sector which took the lead. But employment generation in either the secondary or tertiary sector cold not keep pace.

Still a large number of people depend on the primary sector for employment compared with the other two sectors.

Q.8 Why should we be worried about underemployment?

Ans. We should worry about underemployment as the earning capacity of a person is reduced, resulting in a poor standard of living. Ultimately, this can lead to poverty.

Q.9 How do you think MGNREGA 2005 is associated with 'Right to Work'?

Ans. MGNREGA 2005 was implemented with the objective to provide atleast 100 days employment to people living below poverty line. If the government fails in its duty to provide employment then it will give unemployment allowances to the people. In both cases, people are assured of allowances therefore the act is associated with 'Right to Work'.

Q.10 How would income and employment increase if farmers were provided with irrigation and marketing facilities?

Ans. If irrigation facilities are provided, then farmers can produce two or more crops, in their land besides their primary crops. It will not only settle the disguised unemployment in the sector, but will also create new employment opportunities because of scope for growth.

Market facilitation will boost the motivation in farming sector. Farmers now can sell their products in the market and will be motivated to produce more for more earning. It will also engage the extra workers i.e. disguised underemployed workers in marketing and give them opportunity for full employment.

Marketing is a part of tertiary sector, it has inter-dependency on primary sector. Market facility will induce diversification in agricultural activities and provide scope for industries to be set-up in semi-rural areas and generate employment.

Q.11 In what ways can employment be increased in urban areas?

***Or* Suggest any one way to create employment in urban areas.** **CBSE 2020**

Ans. Employment can be increased in urban areas in the following ways

(i) Invest in basic industries which provide mass employment.

(ii) Improve local and inter-city transportation, so that more people can be employed to work in the transportation industry.

(iii) Give incentives for industry in urban areas to increase their capacity.

Q.12 Look at the following examples. Which of these are unorganised sector activities?

(a) A teacher taking classes in a school

(b) A headload worker carrying a bag of cement on his back in a market

(c) A farmer irrigating her field

(d) A doctor in a hospital treating a patient

(e) A daily wage labourer working under a contractor

(f) A factory worker going to work in a big factory

(g) A handloom weaver working in her house

Ans. Unorganised activities are

(b) A headload worker carrying a bag of cement on his back in a market

(c) A farmer irrigating his/her field

(e) A daily wage labourer working under a contractor

(g) A handloom weaver working in his/her house.

Q.13 How would you distinguish between organised and unorganised sectors? Explain in your own words.

Ans. The organised sector refers to businesses or industries that follow formal rules, have legal recognition and provide employees with benefits like fixed wages, insurance, and job security. They are regulated by government laws and taxes.

On the other hand, the unorganised sector includes small businesses, informal workers or casual labour where rules are not strictly followed and workers often lack benefits and job security. This sector operates more flexibly but also faces challenges like low wages and unstable working conditions.

EXERCISE

Q.1 Fill in the blanks using the correct option given in the bracket.

(a) Employment in the service sector ...... increased to the same extent as production. (has/has not)

Ans. has not

(b) Workers in the .... sector do not produce goods. (tertiary/agricultural)

Ans. tertiary

(c) Most of the workers in the .... sector enjoy job security. (organised/unorganised)

Ans. organised

(d) A .... proportion of labourers in India are working in the unorganised sector. (large/small)

Ans. large

(e) Cotton is a ...... product and cloth is a ...... product. (natural/man-made, manufactured/artificial)

Ans. natural, manufactured

(f) The activities in primary, secondary and tertiary sectors are .... (independent / interdependent)

Ans. interdependent

Q.2 Choose the most appropriate answer.

(i) The sectors are classified into public and private on the basis of

(a) employment conditions
(b) the nature of economic activity
(c) ownership of enterprises
(d) number of workers employed in the enterprises

Ans. (c) ownership of enterprises

(ii) Production of a commodity, mostly through the natural process, is an activity in .... sector.

(a) Primary (b) Secondary
(c) Tertiary (d) Information technology

Ans. (a) Primary

(iii) GDP is the total value of .... produced during a particular year.

(a) all goods and services
(b) all final goods and services
(c) all intermediate goods and services
(d) all intermediate and final goods and services

Ans. (b) all final goods and services

(iv) In terms of GDP, the share of tertiary sector in 2013-14 is between .... per cent.

(a) 20 to 30
(b) 30 to 40
(c) 50 to 60
(d) 60 to 70

Ans. (c) 50 to 60

Q.3 Match the following.

Problems Faced by Farming Sector	Some Possible Measures
1. Unirrigated land	(a) Setting up agro- based mills
2. Low prices for crops	(b) Co-operative marketing societies
3. Debt burden	(c) Procurement of foodgrains by government
4. No job in the off season	(d) Construction of canals by the government
5. Compelled to sell their grains to the local traders soon after harvest	(e) Banks to provide credit with low interest

Ans. 1. (d), 2. (c), 3. (e), 4. (a), 5. (b)

Q.4 Find the odd one out and say why.

(a) Tourist guide, dhobi, tailor, potter

Ans. Tourist guide is the odd one, as his job may come under organised sector but other workers definitely come under unorganised sector.

(b) Teacher, doctor, vegetable vendor, lawyer

Ans. Vegetable vendor is the odd one, because he is often unskilled while the others are well qualified professionals.

(c) Postman, cobbler, soldier, police constable

Ans. Cobbler is the odd one, because he works in the unorganised sector.

(d) MTNL, Indian Railways, Air India, Sahara Airlines, All India Radio.

Ans. Sahara Airlines is the odd one because it comes under the private sector.

Q.5 A research scholar looked at the working people in the city of Surat and found the following.

Place of Work	Nature of Employment	Percentage of Working People
In offices and factories registered with the government	Organised	15
Own shops, office, clinics in marketplaces with formal license		15
People working on the street, construction workers, domestic workers		20
Working in small workshops usually not registered with the government		

Complete the table. What is the percentage of workers in the unorganised sector in this city?

Ans.

Place of Work	Nature of Employment	Percentage of Working People
In offices and factories registered with the government	Organised	15
Own shops, office, clinics in marketplaces with formal license	Organised	15
People working on the street, construction workers, domestic workers	Unorganised	20
Working in small workshops usually not registered with the government	Unorganised	50

70% of workers are employed in the unorganised sectors in this city.

Q.6 Do you think the classification of economic activities into primary, secondary and tertiary is useful? Explain how.

Ans. The classification of economic activities into primary, secondary and tertiary is useful on account of the information it provides on how and where the people of a country are employed.

Also, this helps in understanding as to which sector of economic activity contributes how much to country's GDP and per capita income.

It tells the economic planners as to which sector requires development and how much. From the analysis, new ways of development could be devised. Like, if the Tertiary sector is developing much faster than the Primary sector, it implies that more measures should be taken to increase productivity in agriculture.

Q.7 For each of the sectors that we came across in this chapter, why should one focus on employment and GDP? Could there be other issues which should be examined? Discuss.

Ans. For each of the sectors mentioned, we have focused mainly on employment and GDP. This is because growth in GDP and employment are common goals of Five Year Plans and they also determine the size of a country's economy. A focus on employment and GDP helps us to calculate and monitor important factors like per capita income, productivity, changes in employment rate and contribution to GDP by the three sectors of economy and thus, take necessary steps required for the improvement of the country's economy as a whole.

Yes, the other issues which should be examined are

- Balanced regional development
- Equality in income and wealth among the people of the country
- Eradicate poverty
- Modernisation of technology
- Self-reliance of the country
- Achievement of surplus food production in the country.

Q.8 Make a long list of all kinds of work that you find adults around you doing for a living. In what way can you classify them? Explain your choice.

Ans. Some examples of work people do and their classification are given below

S. No.	Nature of Work	Nature of Activity	Sector
1.	Bank Clerk	Tertiary	Organised
2.	Freelance cartoonist	Tertiary	Unorganised
3.	Construction worker	Secondary	Unorganised
4.	Doctor in AIIMS	Tertiary	Organised
5.	DTC bus driver	Tertiary	Organised
6.	Farmer	Primary	Unorganised
7.	Guest house receptionist	Tertiary	Unorganised
8.	Mine worker	Primary	Organised
9.	Own tailoring shop	Tertiary	Unorganised
10.	Public sector factory supervisor	Secondary	Organised

We classify them according to the nature of activity and whether they are working in organised or unorganised sector. This is useful on account of the information, it provides on how and where the people are employed.

Q.9 How is tertiary sector different from other sectors? Illustrate with a few examples.

Ans. The tertiary sector is different from the other two sectors because the other sectors produce goods, but this sector does not produce goods by itself. Instead, the Tertiary sector activities help in the development of the Primary and Secondary sectors.

The activities of tertiary sector are an aid to provide support for the production process, e.g. transport, communication, storage, banking, insurance, trade activities, etc. For this reason, this sector is also known as service sector.

Q.10 What do you understand by disguised unemployment? Give one example each from urban and rural areas.

Ans. Disguised unemployment occurs when more people are employed for the same work than actually required. When some of them are removed, the output will not reduce.

For example, In a rural area, the family of a small farmer works throughout the year on his field, even though all of them are not required all the time.

In an urban areas, all members of a family work in a shop owned by them, even though all may not be required for the whole day.

In these cases, if 2-3 members do not work in the farm or shop, then production will not decrease.

Q.11 Distinguish between open unemployment and disguised unemployment.

Ans.

Open Unemployment	Disguised Unemployment
It is an unemployment situation where one does not have a job and is clearly visible as unemployed.	It is an underemployment situation where people seem to be working but all of them work less than their capacity.
For example, an engineer not able to find a job.	For example, a family working on a small agricultural field.

Q.12 "Tertiary sector is not playing any significant role in the development of Indian economy." Do you agree? Give reasons in support of your answer.

Ans. No, I do not agree that tertiary sector is not playing any significant role in the development of Indian economy.

The reasons are as follows

(i) In terms of GDP, this sector emerged as the largest producing sector in India in 2013-14, surpassing the Primary and Secondary sectors.

(ii) In terms of employment also, the rate of growth of employment in Tertiary sector has increased. It was 15% during 1972-73 and 27% in 2011-12. The IT sector is providing jobs to educated people.

Q.13 Service sector in India employs two different kinds of people. Who are these?

Ans. The service sector in India employs the following two different kinds of people

(i) Highly skilled and educated people in public and private sector and other organised sector.

(ii) Less skilled and less educated people in unorganised sector or self-employment activities.

Q.14 Workers are exploited in the unorganised sector. Do you agree with this view? Give reasons in support of your answer.

Ans. Yes, workers are exploited in the unorganised sector because

- There are no fixed number of working hours. The workers normally work 10-12 hours without being paid overtime.
- They do not get other allowances apart from the daily wages.
- Government rules and regulations to protect the labourers are not followed in their case.
- There is no job security. They can be asked to leave the job at any time.
- Workers are poorly paid. The workers in this sector are generally illiterate and unskilled. So, they are not in a position to bargain or secure good wages.
- Being poor and without any other better option, they can be easily made to accept lower wages.

Q.15 How are the activities in the economy classified on the basis of employment conditions?

Ans. Economic activities are classified into two types on the basis of employment conditions

(i) **Organised Sector** The organised sector includes those enterprises or places of work where the terms of employment are regular and therefore, people have assured work. They are registered by the government and have to follow its rules and regulations which are given in various laws such as the Factories Act, Minimum Wages Act, Payment of Gratuity Act, Shops Act, etc. Some examples are Reliance Industries Limited, Tata Motors, etc.

(ii) **Unorganised Sector** The unorganised sector includes enterprises that are not registered by the government. The unorganised sector is characterised by small and scattered units, which do not follow proper rules for employment or give any leaves or other benefits. Some examples are casual workers in construction, shops, garages, etc.

Q.16 Compare the employment conditions prevailing in the organised and unorganised sectors.

Or **Explain five differences between organised and unorganised sector.** **CBSE 2019**

Or **Distinguish the service conditions of organised sector with that of unorganised sector.** **CBSE 2018**

Or **Explain the difference between organised and unorganised sectors of economy with example.** **CBSE 2025**

Ans. Comparison of organised and unorganised sector are as follows

Basis	Organised Sector	Unorganised Sector
Job security	In organised sector workers have job security	In unorganised sector workers do not have any job security. There jobs can be terminated anytime.
Rules and regulations	The organised sector follows all the rules and regulations and they are registered.	Unorganised sector do not follow any rules and regulations as they are not registered.
Wages	Workers in organised sector are paid regularly	Workers in unorganised sector are not paid regularly.
Other benefits	Organised sector pays other benefits like medical leaves, provident funds, paid leaves apart from wages.	Unorganised sector do not pay anything other than salary.
Number of hours	There are fixed number of hours in organised sector.	In unorganised sector the number of hours increases or decreases as per the work.

Q.17 Explain the objectives of implementing the MGNREGA, 2005.

Or **Write any two points about MGNREGA, 2005.**

Ans. The objectives of implementing the MGNREGA 2005 are

(i) This act targets the poor people of rural areas who suffer from poverty.

(ii) To provide livelihood to the people below the poverty line, this scheme guarantees 100 days of wage employment in a year to those who are able to, and are in need of work in rural areas.

(iii) In case government fails to provide employment then people below poverty line are entitled to allowances.

Q.18 Using examples from your area, compare and contrast that activities and functions of private and public sectors.

Or **Differentiate between the public and the private sector.** **CBSE 2019**

Or **How is public sector different from private sector?**

Or **Explain the difference between public and private sector of Indian economy with example.** **CBSE 2025**

Ans. Differences between public sector and private sector are

Public Sector	Private Sector
The main aim of this sector is public welfare.	The main aim of this sector is to earn maximum profit.
It is controlled and managed by the government.	It is controlled and managed by an individual or a group of individuals.
This sector provides basic facilities like education, health, food and security to the people, e.g. the Indian Railways, the Post Office.	This sector provides consumer goods to the people, e.g. the Reliance, Industries Limited (RIL), TISCO.

Q.19 Discuss and fill the following table giving one example each from your area.

	Well Managed Organisation	Badly Managed Organisation
Public Sector		
Private Sector		

Ans.

Sector	Well Managed Organisation	Badly Managed Organisation
Public Sector	Railways gives employment, develop infrastructure.	Sugar mills are poorly managed and earning loses.
Private Sector	Tata Iron and Steel Company take good care of their employees.	Flipkart earning loses. Infosys reducing the number of employees.

Q.20 Give few examples of public sector activities and explain why the government has taken them up.

Ans. Some examples of public sector activities are

(i) **Railways** The government has taken this up for the following reasons

- Only the government can invest large sums of money on a public project with long gestation period.
- To ensure and provide transportation at cheap rates in the entire country.

(ii) **Electric Power Generation by NTPC** The government has taken this up to provide electricity at a reasonable rate to consumers.

(iii) **AIIMS** To provide quality health services at a reasonable rate was the main purpose of the government to start this, besides medical education to future doctors as well as research facilities.

Q.21 Explain how public sector contributes to the economic development of a nation. **CBSE 2019**

Or **Explain any three points of importance of public sector in our society.** **CBSE 2019**

Ans. The public sector contributes to the economic development of a nation in the following ways

(i) **Improving Infrastructure** Economic development depends upon the creation of basic infrastructure such as power, transportation, communication, irrigation, education, etc. Public sector enterprises can arrange the large investment necessary for economy.

(ii) **Export Promotion** A large number of public enterprises have been set-up to promote India's export.

(iii) **Reduction in Regional Disparities** The government sets up industries in underdeveloped regions to reduce and overcome regional disparities in development.

Q.22 The workers in the unorganised sector need protection on the issues–wages, safety and health. Explain with examples.

Or **How can the workers of unorganised sector be protected?** **CBSE 2019**

Ans. The workers in the unorganised sector need protection on the following issues

(i) **Wages** They are low and not regular. There is no provision for overtime, paid leave, etc. Minimum wages rules should be implemented strictly.

(ii) **Safety** Construction workers can get injured while working and they need to work under safe conditions. There should be a check on the working conditions along with the provision of insurance.

(iii) **Health** Long working hours and unhygienic working environment affect the health of the workers adversely. Health insurance along with a fixed number of working hours should be made mandatory.

Q.23 A study in Ahmedabad found that out of 15,00,000 workers in the city, 11,00,000 worked in the unorganised sector. The total income of the city in this year (1997–1998) was ₹ 60,000 million. Out of this, ₹ 32,000 million was generated in the organised sector.

Present this data as a table. What kind of ways should be thought for generating more employment in the city?

Ans. Table showing study of employment and income in Ahmedabad is as follows

Sector	Workers Employed	Income Generated
Organised	4,00,000	₹32,000 million
Unorganised	11,00,000	₹28,000 million
Total	15,00,000	₹60,000 million

The ways of generating more employment are

- To set-up industries that process vegetables and agricultural produce like potato, rice, wheat, fruits, etc. which can be sold in outside market.
- To promote and locate industries and services in outskirts of the city where a large number of people can get employment.

Q.24 The following table gives the GDP in rupees (crores) by the three sectors

Year	Primary	Secondary	Tertiary
2000	52,000	48,500	1,33,500
2013	8,00,500	10,74,000	38,68,000

(i) Calculate the share of the three sectors in GDP for 2000 and 2013.

(ii) Show the data as a bar diagram similar to graph 2 in the chapter.

(iii) What conclusions can we draw from the bar graph?

Ans. (i) Share of sectors in GDP for 2000

Total GDP of three sectors

$$= (52{,}000 + 48{,}500 + 1{,}33{,}500) = ₹\,2{,}34{,}000 \text{ crore}$$

$$\text{Share of Primary sector} = \frac{52{,}000}{2{,}34{,}000} \times 100 = 22.22\%$$

$$\text{Share of Secondary sector} = \frac{48{,}500}{2{,}34{,}000} \times 100 = 20.72\%$$

$$\text{Share of Tertiary sector} = \frac{1{,}33{,}500}{2{,}34{,}000} \times 100 = 57\%$$

Share of sectors in GDP for 2013

Total GDP of three sectors

$$= ₹\,(8{,}00{,}500 + 10{,}74{,}000 + 38{,}68{,}000)$$

$$= ₹\,57{,}42{,}500 \text{ crore}$$

$$\text{Share of Primary sector} = \frac{8{,}00{,}500}{57{,}42{,}500} \times 100 = 13.93\%$$

$$\text{Share of Secondary sector} = \frac{10{,}74{,}000}{57{,}42{,}500} \times 100 = 18.70\%$$

$$\text{Share of Tertiary sector} = \frac{38{,}68{,}000}{57{,}42{,}500} \times 100 = 67.35\%$$

(ii) Above data as a bar diagram

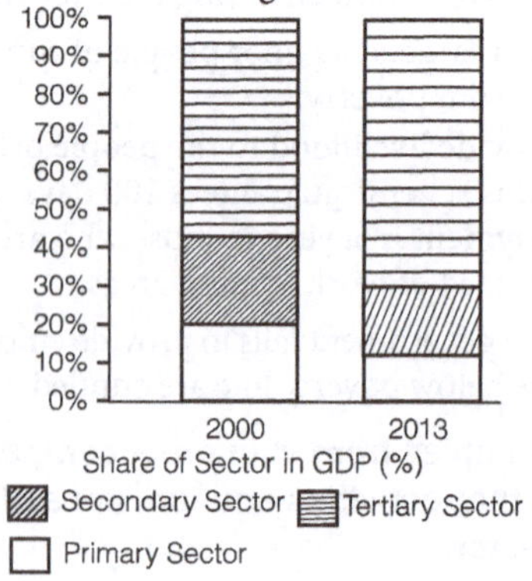

(iii) Conclusions drawn from the bar diagram are

- Share of Primary sector in GDP has decreased.
- Share of Secondary sector in GDP also decreased.
- Share of the Tertiary sector in GDP has increased.

REVIEW EXERCISE

Including Competency Based Questions

Part I

Multiple Choice Questions (MCQs)

1. All economic activities that directly involve conversion of natural resources are classified under

(a) Secondary sector
(b) Primary sector
(c) Tertiary sector
(d) Government sector

2. In Indian Economy, the three sectors (Primary, Secondary and Tertiary) are interdependent. However, the share of employment in the primary sector remains high. Most appropriate explanation for this could be. **(SQP 2024-25)**

(i) Government policies preferentially treat the primary sector.
(ii) Indian economy is largely agrarian and majority of population is dependent on agriculture.
(iii) Inadequate service sector jobs force people to continue working in primary sectors.
(iv) Primary sector provides raw material for the secondary and tertiary sector.

Choose the correct option

(a) Only (i) and (ii) are true
(b) Only (ii) and (iii) are true
(c) Only (iii) and (iv) are true
(d) All are true

3. Primary, Secondary and Tertiary sectors are divided in which one of the following basis? **CBSE 2024**

(a) Nature of employment (b) Nature of activities
(c) Nature of ownership (d) Nature of income

4. 'X' lives in a town. He cultivates flowers along with animal husbandry. The work of 'X' will fall under which sector of the economy? **CBSE 2025**

(a) Primary (b) Secondary
(c) Tertiary (d) Quaternary

5. At the initial stages of development, which one of the following sectors was the most important of economic activity? **CBSE Term I 2021**

(a) Primary (b) Secondary
(c) Tertiary (d) Quaternary

6. Activities in which natural products are changed into other forms come under which one of the following sectors? **CBSE Term I 2021**

(a) Primary (b) Secondary
(c) Tertiary (d) Quaternary

7. The products received by exploiting natural resources come under which one of the following sectors? **CBSE Term I 2021**

(a) Quaternary (b) Tertiary
(c) Secondary (d) Primary

8. The goods that are used as raw materials for further production are known by which name?

(a) Final goods (b) Consumer goods
(c) Material goods (d) Intermediate goods

9. The sum total of production of all goods and services in the three sectors are combinedly called as

(a) NDP (b) NI
(c) GNI (d) GDP

10. 'A' is a worker in a garment export industry of Jaipur. He gets facilities like health insurance, provident fund, medical leave, etc. **CBSE 2023**

In which one of the following sectors is 'A' working?

(a) Primary sector (b) Tertiary sector
(c) Organised sector (d) Unorganised sector

11. Find the incorrect option.

(a) Public Sector–Labour working under contractor
(b) Tertiary sector – Owner of a play school
(c) Unoganised sector –5 people working in a local dhaba
(d) Private sector – A company producing electric equipment

12. Which of the following provisions have been made under the Mahatma Gandhi National Rural Employment Guarantee Act-2005? **CBSE 2025**

(a) Government ensures 100 days of employment for all residents.
(b) Government ensures 200 days of employment for all rural residents.
(c) Government provides grains in exchange of work in rural areas.
(d) Government provides unemployment allowance to the beneficiaries in case of failure to provide employment.

13. **"The Challenge of Underemployment and Sectoral Evolution in India"**

In a recent study conducted by the Central Government Ministry, it was revealed that despite the surge in the tertiary sector's dominance, underemployment remains a significant issue across various sectors of the Indian economy.

Source: Economic Times

Given this scenario, should the government introduce targeted policies to address underemployment in specific sectors? **Competency Based**

(a) Yes, focusing on the primary sector by enhancing agricultural productivity and creating opportunities for small-scale industries in rural areas can mitigate underemployment.

(b) Yes, the government should prioritise schemes like MGNREGA 2005 to guarantee minimum days of wage employment to rural households, thereby curbing underemployment.

(c) No, the evolution of the tertiary sector indicates a natural progression in economic growth, and addressing underemployment might disrupt this trajectory.

(d) No, underemployment is a temporary phase and does not warrant immediate intervention as long as the GDP continues to rise.

14. **What is the rationale behind the classification of economic activities into various sectors, such as primary, secondary, and tertiary, based on their nature and operations?** **Competency Based**

(a) It helps in creating distinctions between various economic activities and ensures each sector focuses on a specific type of production.

(b) It helps us sort activities into groups, making it easier to understand their roles in the economy and how they rely on each other.

(c) It limits the growth of certain sectors, focusing primarily on the development of others.

(d) It encourages competition among sectors, resulting in a disparity in the distribution of resources and services.

15. **If there is a disruption by transporters and lorries refuse to transport vegetables, milk, etc. from rural areas to urban areas, food will become scarce in urban areas, whereas farmers will be unable to sell their products.** **CBSE SQP 2023-24**

Which of the following sectors will be affected due to this situation stated above?

(a) Primary and Secondary

(b) Secondary and Tertiary

(c) Tertiary, Primary and Secondary

(d) Tertiary and Primary.

16. **The table given below highlights the percentage of workers in the three sectors of the economy in India. The data for the year 2023 has actual figures while the data for 2040 is hypothetical based on the published figures of the year 2023. Any of the three hypothetical scenarios could be possible in the year 2040.**

Study the table carefully and answer the questions that follow **CBSE Additional SQP 2023-24**

Year	Primary	Secondary	Tertiary
2023 (Source : Statista)	44%	25%	31%
2023 (Hypothetical Scenario : 1)	20%	45%	35%
2040 (Hypothetical Scenario : 2)	60%	20%	20%
2040 (Hypothetical Scenario : 3)	15%	40%	45%

Based on the information given in the table, which of the following statements is likely to be correct?

(a) In scenarios 1 and 2, the secondary sector will need the least workers.

(b) In scenario 2, India will become a major services-based economy.

(c) The primary sector in scenario 2 will be the highest contributor to the GDP of the country.

(d) In scenarios 1 and 3, maximum employment opportunities will be created in the secondary sector.

17. **A flower cultivator grows tulips, reaps a good crop and sells it to a trader. The trader exports the tulips and earns huge profit. This increased the GDP but the farmer is still not able to earn well. Why?**

(a) Most of the profit is taken by trader.

(b) Farmer is underemployed or disguised employed.

(c) Farmers, traders, exporters work in unorganised sector.

(d) All of the above

18. **Hari, son of a farmer, after studying from Agricultural University, has become a research scientist and undertakes work for developing hybrid oil seeds. Analyse the information to know the sector in which he has shifted from past to present.**

(a) From tertiary to primary (b) From secondary to primary

(c) From primary to tertiary (d) From primary to secondary

19. **Arrange in sequence.**

I. Making of Khoya

II. Buying of sweets during Diwali

III. Extraction of milk

IV. Displaying sweets in showcase

Codes

(a) IV, I, III, II (b) III, I, IV, II

(c) I, II, IV, III (d) II, III, I, IV

20. **Consider the following statements about GDP of a country.**

(i) Purchase of sugarcane in the making of sugar.
(ii) Value of silk fabrics for sale in the market.
(iii) Final value of bakery items.

Which of the following statements should be added to find out GDP?

(a) Only (i) and (ii) (b) Only (i) and (iii)
(c) Only (ii) and (iii) (d) None as all are intermediate goods

21. **Fill in the blank.** **CBSE SQP 2022-23**

Sector	Criteria Used
Primary, Secondary and Tertiary	Nature of Economic Activity
Organised and Unorganised	?

Codes

(a) Nature of Employment Activities
(b) Nature of Social Activities
(c) Nature of Production Activities
(d) Nature of Political Activities

22. **Mrs X, a rural farmer experiencing declining productivity, seeks financial aid to enhance her agricultural activities. Opting for a bank loan, she aims for affordable funds at lower interest rates without risking her property or falling into a debt trap. Her choice prioritises favorable repayment terms and interest-free periods during the loan tenure.**

Which of the following statements best aligns with Mrs. X's reasons for choosing a bank loan to improve her agricultural activities?

(i) Accessibility to funds at lower interest rates compared to other sources.
(ii) Freedom from falling into a debt trap due to favorable repayment terms.
(iii) Avoidance of being coerced to sell her property to secure the loan.
(iv) No interest payment requirements during the repayment period. **Competency Based**

Codes

(a) Only (i) (b) (iii) and (iv)
(c) (i) and (ii) (d) Only (ii)

23. **Consider the statements given below and choose the correct answer.**

Statement I The Gross Domestic Product (GDP) is the sum of the value of final goods and services produced in only the primary sector of an economy.

Statement II The tertiary sector has replaced the secondary sector as the largest producing sector in most countries. **Competency Based**

Options

(a) Statement I is correct and statement II is incorrect.
(b) Statement I is incorrect and statement II is correct.
(c) Both statements I and II are incorrect.
(d) Both statements I and II are correct.

24. **Identify the sector of economy with the help of given information.**

- It covers activities in which primary goods are used to produce some other commodity.
- This sector mainly includes services such as manufacturing, construction, gas, water electricity supply, etc.
- It produces more than half of the total country's output.
- The employees of this sector are less than half of the working population.

Options

(a) Primary sector (b) Secondary sector
(c) Tertiary sector (d) None of these

Answers

1. (b)	**2.** (b)	**3.** (b)	**4.** (a)	**5.** (a)
6. (b)	**7.** (d)	**8.** (d)	**9.** (d)	**10.** (c)
11. (a)	**12.** (d)	**13.** (b)	**14.** (b)	**15.** (c)
16. (c)	**17.** (d)	**18.** (c)	**19.** (b)	**20.** (c)
21. (a)	**22.** (c)	**23.** (c)	**24.** (b)	

Match the Following

1.

List I	List II
A. Selling Woollen Garments	1. Private Sector
B. Rearing of Sheep	2. Secondary Sector
C. Raymond Coats	3. Tertiary Sector
D. Preparing Woollen fibres	4. Primary Sector

Codes

	A	B	C	D		A	B	C	D
(a)	3	4	1	2	(b)	1	3	2	4
(c)	1	2	3	4	(d)	1	4	3	2

Ans. 1. (a)

Assertion-Reason

1. **Assertion** (A) Repair persons and daily wage earners are not very productive in tertiary sector.

Reason (R) Repair persons and daily wage earners are unskilled, therefore they are mostly unemployed on a short-term basis.

Codes

(a) Both A and R are true and R is the correct explanation of A
(b) Both A and R are true, but R is not the correct explanation of A
(c) A is true, but R is false
(d) A is false, but R is true

2. **Assertion** (A) The tertiary sector has become the dominant sector in India's economy.

Reason (R) The rise in demand for basic services and the development in primary and secondary sectors have contributed to the growth of the service sector.

Codes

(a) Both A and R are true and R is the correct explanation of A
(b) Both A and R are true, but R is not the correct explanation of A
(c) A is true, but R is false
(d) A is false, but R is true

3. Assertion (A) The organised sector in India ensures better working conditions and job security for its workers.
Reason (R) Enterprises in the organised sector do not follow government regulations and provide benefits like paid holidays, medical leaves and a safe working environment.

Codes

(a) Both A and R are true and R is the correct explanation of A
(b) Both A and R are true, but R is not the correct explanation of A
(c) A is true, but R is false
(d) A is false, but R is true

4. Assertion (A) The primary sector was initially the least important sector in the country's development.
Reason (R) With advancements in farming methods, there was increased food production.

Codes

(a) Both A and R are true and R is the correct explanation of A
(b) Both A and R are true, but R is not the correct explanation of A
(c) A is true, but R is false
(d) A is false, but R is true

5. Assertion (A) The Mahatma Gandhi National Rural Employment Guarantee Act (MGNREGA) aimed to provide employment opportunities in rural areas.
Reason (R) The Act guarantees a certain number of days of wage employment to households in rural regions and issues job cards for this purpose.

Codes

(a) Both A and R are true and R is the correct explanation of A
(b) Both A and R are true, but R is not the correct explanation of A
(c) A is true, but R is false
(d) A is false, but R is true

Ans. 1. (a) Both A and R are true and R is the correct explanation of A
2. (a) Both A and R are true and R is the correct explanation of A
3. (c) A is true, but R is false
4. (d) A is false, but R is true
5. (a) Both A and R are true and R is the correct explanation of A

Picture Based Questions

1. Look at the picture carefully and state the sector in which this economic activity may belong to be undertaken.

(a) Unorganised Sector (b) Primary Sector
(c) Both (a) and (b) (d) Neither (a) nor (b)

2. The person in this picture seems to be which of the following.

(a) Daily wage earner-Unorganised sector
(b) Skilled professional-Unorganised sector
(c) Skilled craftsmen-Organised sector
(d) Shopkeeper-Unorganised sector

3. Which of the following is an example of a service that belongs to the tertiary sector of the Indian economy?

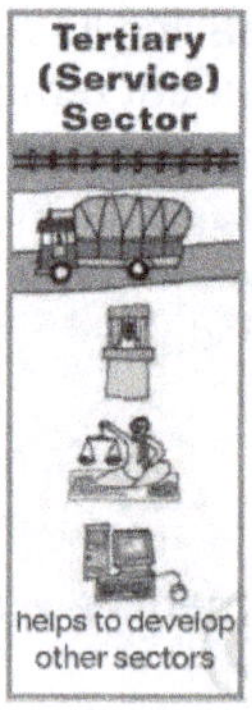

(a) Farming (b) Manufacturing
(c) Banking (d) Mining

Ans. 1. (c) Both (a) and (b)
2. (a) Daily wage earner-Unorganised sector
3. (c) Banking

Case Based Question

1. In any country several services such as hospitals, educational institutions, post and telegraph services, police stations, courts, village administrative offices, municipal corporations, defence, transport, banks, insurance companies, etc. are required. These can be considered as basic services. In a developing country the government has to take responsibility for the provision of these services. the development of agriculture and industry leads to the development of services such as transport, trade, storage and the like, as we have already seen. Greater the development of the primary and secondary sectors, more would be the demand for such services.

(i) In a developing country, which entities are typically considered as basic services that the government is responsible for providing?

(a) Entertainment hubs and shopping malls
(b) Manufacturing industries and technology firms
(c) Hospitals, educational institutions, police stations and post services
(d) Agriculture and mining sectors

(ii) What leads to the expansion of services such as transport, trade, and storage in a country?

(a) Decrease in demand for primary and secondary sector goods
(b) Technological advancements in agriculture
(c) Development in agriculture and industry
(d) Government regulations on service sectors

(iii) Which sectors' growth triggers a higher demand for services like transport, storage, and trade?

(a) Tertiary sector only
(b) Primary and secondary sectors
(c) Only the primary sector
(d) Secondary sector only

(iv) In a developing nation, what does the government's responsibility involve regarding the provision of services?

(a) Solely developing technology and innovation
(b) Ensuring profitability of private sectors
(c) Providing basic services like healthcare, education, security, and communication
(d) Managing natural resources for industries

Ans. (i) (c) Hospitals, educational institutions, police stations, and post services
(ii) (c) Development in agriculture and industry
(iii) (b) Primary and secondary sectors
(iv) (c) Providing basic services like healthcare, education, security, and communication.

Part II

Very Short Answer Type Questions

1. What is secondary sector? CBSE 2016

Ans. The secondary sector includes activities in which natural products are changed into other useful forms through machines.

2. Why is the primary sector also called the agricultural and allied sector? CBSE 2014

Ans. Since most of the natural products are obtained from agriculture, dairy, fishing, forestry, etc, so it is called agricultural and allied sector.

3. What do you mean by tertiary sector?

Ans. The sector in which services are produced rather than goods is called Tertiary sector. Tertiary sector helps in the development of Primary and Secondary sectors.

4. Name the sector of economy that does not produce any good.

Ans. Tertiary sector does not produce any good. It provides services.

5. Do you think Primary sector is linked with tertiary sector? Give one example to justify it.

Ans. Yes, the primary sector is linked with the tertiary sector. The primary sector involves activities like farming, mining, and fishing, which provide raw materials. These raw materials are then processed or sold in the tertiary sector, which involves services like transportation, retail, and finance.

For example, farmers grow crops, which are then transported and sold by retailers in stores. This shows how both sectors are connected, with the primary sector supplying goods and the tertiary sector handling the services related to these goods.

6. Distinguish between primary and secondary sectors. CBSE 2019

Ans. Primary sector involves activities that utilises Earth's resources directly like agriculture, forestry, fishing. But secondary sector involves activities that manufactures, construct or processes like cotton textile industry.

7. Distinguish between secondary and tertiary sector. CBSE 2019

Ans. Secondary sector refers to the manufacturing of various goods but tertiary sector refers to providing services like transport, communication, etc.

8. What are final goods?

Ans. Final goods are directly consumed by the consumers and are not meant for further production or processing.

9. **Give brief idea about GDP.**

Or **What do you understand by GDP of a country?** CBSE 2015

Ans. GDP is the calculation of total production in a country/ state within a time period, normally a year. It is the calculation of values of all final goods and services within a year.

10. **What type of goods and services are included for calculation of GDP in India?**

Ans. All final goods and services are included for calculation of GDP in India.

11. **In which sector are the terms of employment regular?** CBSE 2016

Ans. The terms of employment are regular in organised sector.

12. **Denote the situation in which more persons are employed in a job than optimally required.**

Ans. This is a situation of disguised unemployment.

13. **Give one suggestion to neutralise disguised unemployment in agricultural sector.**

Ans. Promotion of bee keeping, pisciculture, forestry like allied activities can provide regular employment to neutralise disguised unemployment.

14. **Give one example of tertiary activity of unorganised sector of economy.**

Or **State any two activities which do not come under the primary sector.** CBSE 2015, 2014

Ans. Micro transportation like auto, truck, etc are examples of tertiary activity and do not come under primary sector.

15. **How does public sector help in the development of a country?** CBSE 2016

Ans. Public sector helps in improving the infrastructure by developing transport, power, irrigation facilities, etc.

16. **"Government introduces reforms to boost organised sector benefits, improve unorganised sector conditions".** Competency Based

Source: Economics Times

Identify the sector of economic activities associated with extraction and direct use of natural resources.

Ans. The sector primarily linked with the extraction and immediate utilisation of natural resources is the primary sector.

Short Answer Type Questions

1. **Mr.Y from a city in India visits a rural area and finds five people working in a small agricultural farm. More than two people are not required to work in the farm and removing the other three will not affect production. How can one solve this problem of underemployment in rural areas? Explain.** CBSE 2024-25

Ans. Disguised unemployment happens when more people are working than necessary. The extra workers should find other jobs to boost family income. This problem of underemployment in rural areas can be solved through the following

- The government can invest in better transport and storage for crops, or improve rural roads for mini-trucks.
- Setting up industries like dal mills or cold storage can help farmers store and sell produce when prices are high.
- In forested areas, starting honey collection centers or processing local produce can create jobs and increase income.

2. **All the three sectors of economy are interdependent. Explain their interdependence taking iron ore as an example.** CBSE 2015

Ans. It is correct that all the three sectors are highly interdependent. Raw materials are produced in Primary sector and processed into finished items in Secondary sector. Assistance is provided by Tertiary sector to these two activities. For example, iron ore is extracted in mining which is a primary activity, then it is transported to industries for making pig-iron and steel in iron and steel plant, which is a secondary activity. Transportation and finance services are provided to these two sectors by tertiary sector.

3. **Study the data given in the table and answer the questions that follow.** CBSE 2015

Workers in Different Sectors (in Million)

Sector	Organised	Unorganised	Total
Primary	2	240	242
Secondary	9	54	63
Tertiary	17	76	93
Total	28	370	398

(i) **Which is the most important sector which provides most jobs to people?**

(ii) **What is the number of people engaged in the unorganised sector?**

(iii) **Why this unorganised sector is more important?**

Ans. (i) Unorganised sector is the most important sector which provides most jobs to people.

(ii) 370 million people are engaged in the unorganised sector.

(iii) Unorganised sector is important as it provides employment to a large number of people.

4. **Evaluate the contribution of the tertiary sector in Gross Domestic Product (GDP) in India.** CBSE 2025

Ans. Contribution of the tertiary sector to GDP in India is discussed below

- **Largest Contributor** The tertiary sector (also known as the service sector) is the largest contributor to India's

GDP. It includes industries such as transportation, communication, banking, education, health services, tourism, and information technology (IT).

- **Growth in Services** Over the years, the service sector in India has grown rapidly. It has become the dominant sector, contributing more than 50% of the total GDP, reflecting a shift from an agrarian-based economy to a service-oriented one.
- **Employment Generation** The tertiary sector also provides significant employment opportunities, particularly in sectors like IT, tourism, retail, and financial services. This has helped reduce unemployment and underemployment in the country.

5. Suggest any three ways to create more employment opportunities in urban areas.

or Highlight any three ways to increase employment in India. CBSE 2019

Ans. Creating more employment opportunities in urban areas can be accomplished by the following means

(i) **Strengthening the Information Technology Sector** This involves opening of more call centres, cyber cafes and software development units.

(ii) **Strengthening the Tourism Sector** By opening more hotels, restaurants, amusement parks and similar other tourism destinations, demand for employment in this sector will increase.

(iii) **Improving Infrastructure** Opening more schools, hospitals and providing transportation facilities will generate greater employment in urban areas.

6. Why does disguised unemployment not help to enhance the productivity of the country? CBSE 2015

***or* Disguised unemployment destroys the productive assets of a country. Comment.**

Ans. Disguised unemployment does not help to enhance the productivity of the country because more number of people work than actually needed, which reduces the income earned by the people. More than half of the workers in the country are working in the Primary sector, mainly in agriculture, producing only a quarter of the GDP.

In contrast to this, the Secondary and Tertiary sectors produce three-fourth of the produce, whereas they employ less than half of the people.

If we move a few people out from agricultural sector, production will not be affected. These people are disguised unemployed and are not productive assets for country.

7. Describe the role played by Mahatma Gandhi National Rural Employment Guarantee Act (MGNREGA) in improving the employment situation in India. CBSE 2016

Ans. Mahatma Gandhi National Rural Employment Guarantee Act (MGNREGA) provides guaranteed 100 days of employment per year to those who are able to, and are in need of work in the rural areas. It has now been extended to villages in over 625 districts.

Thus, it provides employment to rural people in the activities specified under the scheme and has helped in reducing the number of unemployed population in India.

8. "Workers are exploited in unorganised sector in India". Support the statement with suitable examples. CBSE 2016

Ans. Workers are exploited in unorganised sector in India. The following examples support the statement

- **Low Salary** Generally workers are given low wages as compared to organised sectors.
- **Long Working Hours** In most construction sites, labourers have to work for a time spread over 10-12 hours in a day.
- **Temporary Jobs** There are no permanent jobs and employees can be asked any time to leave.
- **No Facilities and Benefits** Many construction companies do not provide adequate security at worksite due to which workers face risk of working in unsafe environment.

9. Sunil and Raman did their graduation from the same college. Sunil got employed in an unorganised sector and was not satisfied whereas Raman got employed in an organised sector and was happy and satisfied. Identify three reasons for Sunil's dissatisfaction as compared to Raman. SQP 2024-25

Ans. Sunil's dissatisfaction compared to Raman's happiness is the result of several key differences between the organised and unorganised sectors as follows

- **Job Security and Benefits** Raman's organised sector job offers stability, paid leave, overtime and medical benefits. On the other hand, Sunil's unorganised sector job lacks these, often being low-paid and unstable.
- **Working Conditions** Raman enjoys fixed hours and safe conditions with amenities like drinking water. Sunil faces poor working conditions and minimal facilities.
- **Employment Stability** Raman's job provides stable employment with legal protections. Sunil's job is insecure, with no guarantee of continuous work and easy dismissal.

10. How far is it correct to say that several services which cannot be provided by private sector can be provided by the public sector? Explain. CBSE 2016

Ans. It is correct that several services which cannot be provided by private sector can be provided by the public sector. It is due to following reasons

- Only the government can invest large sums of money on projects with a long gestation period such as the railways.

- Only the public sector provides quality health services at economical rates, as it works for the welfare of the people, e.g. AIIMS.
- Public sector provide electricity at a lower cost rate to protect and encourage the small scale industries, e.g. NTPC. Private sector cannot provide electricity at reasonable rate.

11. Examine the role of public sector in the development and well-being of a country. CBSE 2024

Ans. Role of public/government sectors in the development and well-being of a country is as follows

- Developing infrastructure which is done by developing, communication, heavy industries, building bridges, roads and railways, dams, generating electricity.
- Encouraging private sector to open industries and generate employment.
- Provides health care facilities and education in backward and rural areas especially elementary education.

12. Consider the following statements regarding the sectors of economic activities in India.

Statement 1 (S1) The tertiary sector in India has witnessed a significant increase in its contribution to the Gross Domestic Product (GDP) over the last few decades.

Statement 2 (S2) Despite the growth in its GDP contribution, the Tertiary sector has not proportionally increased employment opportunities at the same pace.

Explain the trends reflected in statements 1 and 2 concerning the Tertiary sector's role in India's economy. Competency Based

Ans. Statement 1 highlights the substantial growth of the Tertiary sector in India, depicting its increased contribution to the GDP. Conversely, statement 2 points out a discrepancy wherein this growth in the tertiary sector hasn't corresponded to an equivalent surge in employment opportunities.

Despite its economic significance, the tertiary sector's failure to generate adequate jobs suggests a mismatch between its contribution to GDP and employment generation, posing a challenge for balanced economic development in India.

13. Which sector, organised or unorganised, is preferable for employment? Explain. CBSE Additional SQP 2023-24

Ans. The preference between organised and unorganised sectors for employment varies based on factors like job security, benefits and regulations. Organised sectors typically offer more stability, regulated work conditions, benefits like health insurance and legal protections.

In contrast, the unorganised sector lacks formal structures, stability, and often involves lower wages and minimal job security.

Depending on individual priorities, the organised sector may be preferable due to its stability and benefits, while the unorganised sector might offer flexibility but lacks formal protections and stability.

14. A worker in an urban area, who was working in a small factory, was not paid his wages properly, he was forced to work extra hours under poor working conditions, there was no job security, recently he lost his job and was found selling electrical items in a pushcart.

Analyse the role of the government in protecting the workers working in an unorganised sector. CBSE Additional SQP 2023-24

Ans. The government plays a crucial role in safeguarding workers in the unorganised sector. It must enforce labour laws to ensure fair wages, reasonable working hours and proper working conditions. Job security measures and social security nets should be in place to support workers during unemployment.

Creating awareness, implementing schemes and establishing mechanisms to address grievances are imperative. Government initiatives like labour welfare boards, skill development programmes and ensuring adherence to minimum wage laws are pivotal for protecting workers' rights in the unorganised sector.

15. Compare Tables 'A' and 'B' and answer the question given below.

Table-A

Share of Sectors in GDP in %			
Year	Tertiary	Secondary	Primary
1973-74	50	10	40
2013-14	68	21	11

Table-B

Share of Sectors in Employment in %			
Year	Tertiary	Secondary	Primary
1977-78	18	11	71
2017-18	31	25	44

A remarkable fact about India is that while there has been a change in the share of the three sectors in GDP, a similar shift has not taken place in employment. Why didn't a similar shift out of primary sector happen in case of employment? Substantiate your answer. CBSE Additional SQP 2023-24

Ans. Substantial shift in employment in primary sector hasn't happened because of the following reasons

- **Insufficient job creation in the secondary and tertiary sectors** The primary reason for the limited shift in employment from the Primary sector is the failure to generate an adequate number of jobs in the Secondary (industrial) and Tertiary (service) sectors. The growth of industrial output and service sector production has been significant, but the corresponding increase in employment opportunities has been comparatively lower.

- **Underemployment in the agricultural sector** The Primary sector, particularly agriculture, suffers from underemployment, with more people engaged in farming than necessary. Even if a few individuals are moved out of agriculture, it does not significantly affect the production. This indicates that workers in the agricultural sector are not fully utilised, leading to a lower productivity level.

Long Answer Type Questions

1. What is the significance of secondary sector in Indian economy? **CBSE 2011**

Ans. The significance of secondary sector in Indian economy is as follows

- Secondary sector involves the industrial production. Industrial activities increase the GDP of India.
- Secondary sector creates massive employment of various scales. It also induces service sector like transport, market, etc to flourish.
- Secondary sector has a great contribution for the sustainance and growth of other sectors.
- It produces instruments and appliances that directly help primary sector for better production.
- Secondary sector absorbs excess labour from the primary sector and reduces disguised unemployment.

2. Distinguish between Primary sector and Secondary sector by stating four points of distinction.

Ans. The differences between Primary and Secondary sector are

Primary Sector	Secondary Sector
It includes economic activities involving extraction and production of natural resources.	It processes natural resources.
It provides raw materials to the secondary sector.	It converts raw materials provided by primary activities into finished or semi-finished goods.
Most of the activities are not dependent on secondary sector.	It is dependent on the primary sector for supply of raw materials.
Greater dependence on this sector indicates an underdeveloped economy.	A shift of economic activities from Primary to Secondary sectors indicates a developing economy.
For example, agriculture, mining and forestry.	For example, manufacturing and construction.

3. What is Gross Domestic Product (GDP)? How do we count the various goods and services for calculating GDP? Explain with examples. **CBSE 2019**

Ans. Gross Domestic Product (GDP) is the total sum of the value of all final goods and services of all the sectors of the economy of a country produced during a year. The counting of the various goods and services for calculating GDP can be understood by the following example.

Wheat and flour are intermediate goods used for making final products like bread and biscuits. Intermediate products should not be counted in GDP. Biscuits and breads are the final products prepared using flour and other ingredients like sugar, salt, oil, etc.

Only the final products are reaching the actual consumer. The value of the intermediate products are already counted in the final products and if this is again counted, it will lead to double counting, causing an error in the estimation of GDP.

4. Which sector has emerged as the largest producing sector in the Indian economy in the last decade? Give reasons.

Or **Explain any five reasons for service sector growth in India.** **CBSE 2014**

Or **Highlight any five reasons for the importance of tertiary sector in India.** **CBSE 2019**

Or **Why the importance of the tertiary sector in production is rising rapidly?** **CBSE 2015**

Or **Why is the tertiary sector becoming more important in India? Explain** **CBSE 2020**

Ans. The Tertiary sector has emerged as the largest producing sector in the Indian economy in the last decade because

(i) Demand for tertiary sector activities like transport, storage and trade has increased substantially with the development of the Primary and Secondary sectors.

(ii) Increasing requirement of information, communication and technology has created lot of jobs.

(iii) With increase in the income levels of the people, demand for tourism, shopping, education and other services has increased.

(iv) Liberalisation of the financial environment has boosted faster growth in financial services.

(v) Basic services of education and healthcare require a large number of people to be engaged in tertiary sector activities.

5. Describe the historical changes that have taken place in the sectors of the economy in the developed countries. **CBSE 2012**

Or **"When a country develops, the contribution of Primary sector declines and that of Secondary and Tertiary sectors increases." Analyse the statement.** **CBSE 2012**

Or **Explain how a shift has taken place between sectors in developed countries?** **CBSE 2011**

Or **"Primary sector was the most important sector of economic activity at initial stages of development." Evaluate the statement.** **CBSE 2020**

Ans. The history of developed countries reveals a general pattern of development in their economic structure.

First, primary sectors predominantly contributed to GDP and held most of the employment. Then when agricultural activities increased, there was need for industrialisation and gradually industrial sectors dominated the economy.

Much of the workers shifted to industrial sector, but agriculture productivity did not hamper as industrial sector produced farm equipments, fertilisers, etc that increased the productivity. After a hundred years, service sector increased and most of the workers shifted to service sector. Now, service sector contributes maximum to the share of economy.

The service sector has now become the most important sector in terms of total production and employment generation without disturbing the production and productivity of other two sectors.

So, it is seen that the economic structure had been shifting from primary to secondary and finally to tertiary sector in developed countries. Similarly, almost all the developing countries are following the same path but may be in a different pace.

6. **How can employment be increased in both rural and urban areas? Explain.** **CBSE 2012**

Or **Unemployment is a major problem in a country like India. Suggest various ways for generating employment opportunities both in rural and urban areas.** **CBSE 2012**

Or **What steps should be taken to create more employment? Explain.** **CBSE 2011**

Ans. Unemployment is a major problem in India and it is prevalent in both rural and urban areas. Underemployment is also visible as disguised unemployment in agricultural sector in rural areas and as unorganised service sector in urban areas. These issues need to be addressed properly.

The steps that can be taken to increase employment are

- Education and health sector can create massive employment in urban as well as rural areas.
- Vocational training also creates massive employment so these sector should be encouraged.
- Allied activities like horticulture, pisciculture should be promoted which will create employment in rural areas.
- Promotion of small scale industries will also create employment.
- Cheap credit for setting up new businesses can create employment in both rural and urban areas.
- Social safety programmes like MGNREGA, NRLM (National Rural Livelihood Mission), etc generate massive employment in rural and urban areas respectively so they should be encouraged.

7. **Suggest any five ways to provide more employment opportunities in rural areas.**

Or **How can more employment be created in agriculture sector alone?** **CBSE 2019**

Ans. The following measures can be taken to increase employment in rural areas

(i) Improve irrigation facilities, so that farmers harvest two or three crops in a year. Thus, more people can be employed.

(ii) More dams should be built on rivers, so that more water can be provided to small farmers to increase the number of crops grown annually.

(iii) Provide better roads and improve transportation and storage, which will benefit small farmers and many people will be employed in these sectors.

(iv) Alternative employment such as honey collection centres and vegetable and fruit processing units should be set-up.

(v) More cottage industries should be promoted in rural areas with loans and marketing support to boost employment.

8. **What is organised sector? Mention any four advantages of working in the organised sector.**

Or **What is an organised sector? Elaborate the working conditions of the organised sector in India.** **CBSE 2015**

Or **Highlight any five benefits of the organised sector.** **CBSE 2019**

Or **Why is organised sector preferred by the employees? Explain.** **CBSE 2020**

Ans. Organised sector included all enterprises which are either registered or under the purview of any of the relevant government rule, like Factory Act.

People enjoy working in the organised sector, as there is a proper and systematic way to get the work done from the employees.

Advantages of working in the organised sector are

(i) Workers enjoy security of employment. They cannot be removed from employment without proper intimation.

(ii) The workers work only for a fixed number of hours. If they work more, they have to be paid overtime wages by the employer.

(iii) Many benefits are given to the workers like leave, payment during holidays, provident fund, gratuity, medical benefits, etc.

(iv) Under the laws, the management of the enterprise has to ensure facilities like drinking water and a safe working environment.

Cased Based Questions

1. Read the sources given below and answer the questions that follow.

Source A Creating More Employment

A study conducted by the erstwhile Planning Commission (now known as NITI Aayog) estimates that nearly 20 lakh jobs can be created in the education sector alone. Similarly, if we are to improve the health situation, we need many more doctors, nurses, health workers, etc to work in rural areas.

(i) To what extent do you agree that there is more scope of job creation in tertiary sector?

Source B Where are most of the people employed.

Opening a cold storage could give an opportunity for farmers to store their products like potatoes and onions and sell them when the price is good. In villages near forest areas, we can start honey collection centres where farmers can come and sell wild honey. It is also possible to set up industries that process vegetables and agricultural produce like potato, sweet potato, rice, wheat, tomato, fruits, which can be sold in outside markets.

(ii) The ideas suggested above will tackle which problem prevalent in the primary sector in India?

Source C MGNREGA, 2005

The Central government in India made a law implementing the Right to Work in about 625 districts of India. It is called Mahatma Gandhi National Rural Employment Guarantee Act 2005 (MGNREGA, 2005). Under MGNREGA 2005, all those who are able to, and are in need of work in rural areas are guaranteed 100 days of employment in a year by the government.

(iii) Do you agree that implementation of Right to Work through MGNREGA, 2005, is a good initiative to generate employment?

Ans. (i) The tertiary sector has certainly more scope of job creation due to its labour-intensive nature, increasing demand for services, higher productivity levels, technological advancement and globalisation.

(ii) The ideas suggested above will tackle the problem of disguised unemployment or underemployment, which is so prevalent in India. By opening cold storage, honey collection centres and food processing industries in semi-rural areas, more employment can be generated.

(iii) Yes, it is a good initiative to generate employment. Right to Work is formulated to provide work to people in 625 districts of India and for that MGNREGA, 2005 is implemented. People in rural areas are guaranteed 100 days of employment under it.

2. Read the source given below and answer the questions that follow.

Another way of classifying economic activities into sectors could be on the basis of who owns assets and is responsible for the delivery of services. In the public sector, the government owns most of the assets and provides all the services. In the private sector, ownership of assets and delivery of services is in the hands of private individuals or companies.

Railways or post office is an example of the public sector whereas companies like Tata Iron and Steel Company Limited (TISCO) or Reliance Industries Limited (RIL) are privately owned. Activities in the private sector are guided by the motive to earn profits. To get such services we have to pay money to these individuals and companies.

The purpose of the public sector is not just to earn profits. Governments raise money through taxes and other ways to meet expenses on the services rendered by it. Modern day governments spend on a whole range of activities. There are several things needed by the society as a whole but which the private sector will not provide at a reasonable cost.

(i) The bifurcation into public and private sector is on what basis?

(ii) State one reason each as to why railways and post office is counted in public sector.

(iii) State two reasons why public sector is needed in a country like India.

Ans. (i) The bifurcation into public and private sector is based on who owns the assets and is responsible for delivery of services.

(ii) Railways are counted in the public sector because they are owned and operated by the government which provides essential transportation services to the public at affordable rates.

The post office is also part of the public sector because it is government-owned service. It is responsible for providing postal services at affordable prices and ensures communication and delivery services across the country, especially in remote areas.

(iii) Public sector is needed in India due to

- Public sector spends in different activities that are needed by the society which private sector cannot provide.
- Private sector will not provide services at reasonable price, so public sector is needed.

ASSESSMENT EXERCISE

Multiple Choice Questions (MCQs)

1. Which one of the following occupations is associated with the primary sector?
(a) Doctor
(b) Gardener
(c) Teacher
(d) Priest

2. Which of the following is the correct meaning of the organised sector?
(a) Terms of employment are regular.
(b) It is outside the control of the government.
(c) Jobs are irregular.
(d) Salaries are low.

3. Which one of the following activities does not belong to the primary sector?
(a) Growing crops
(b) Producing milk for sale
(c) Weaving Khadi cloth
(d) Extracting coal from mines

4. What is the primary function of the tertiary sector in an economy?
(a) Producing tangible goods
(b) Providing essential services
(c) Extracting raw materials
(d) Manufacturing finished products

Subjective Questions (VSA, SA & LA)

1. What has the National Rural Employment Guarantee Act, 2005 assured?

2. Give two examples of secondary sector activities in India.

3. What are intermediate goods?

4. Explain in brief what is Gross Domestic Product (GDP). Which department carries out the task of measuring the GDP in India?

5. Which sector i.e. primary, secondary or tertiary comprises largest proportion of unorganised workers? Why?

6. Underemployment is more prevalent in primary sector. Substantiate this statement with examples.

7. The workers in the unorganised sector need protection on the issues of wages, safety and health. Explain.

8. How can we tackle the problem of unemployment in semi-urban areas?

9. 'Agricultural sector in India employs the largest number of people but its contribution to national income is lowest'. Analyse the statement.

10. 'Economic activities though are grouped into three different categories but they are highly interdependent. Justify the statement.

CHAPTER 3

Money and Credit

Money is used as a medium of exchange. In earlier times, the method of barter exchange was followed. In this, both parties have to agree to sell and buy each other's commodities. Money overcomes all the limitations that existed in the barter system of exchange. In modern days, money has different forms as currency, plastic money, cheques, etc. Banks regulate the money supply in the economy by providing loan or credit. Credit can be of two forms : **formal** and **informal**.

3.1 Money as a Medium of Exchange

Money is used for several transactions. It acts as an intermediate in the exchange process, thus it is called a **medium of exchange.**

Transactions are made in money because a person holding money can easily exchange it for any commodity or service that he or she might want. Thus, everyone prefers to receive payments in money.

Barter System of Exchange

Before the use of money, people followed barter system of exchange. In this system, goods are directly exchanged without use of money between two or more people.

In this system, both parties have to agree to sell and buy each others commodities. This is called **double coincidence of wants.**

3.2 Modern Forms of Money

Before the introduction of coins, a variety of objects like grains and cattle were used as money. Later, the use of metallic coins of gold, silver, copper, etc started.

Modern forms of money include currency (paper notes and coins) and deposits with banks. The modern forms of money are closely linked to the working of the modern banking system.

Currency

It is accepted as a medium of exchange because it is authorised by the government of the country. The modern currency has no use of its own except as a medium of exchange.

In India, Reserve Bank of India[1] issue currency notes on behalf of the Central Government. As per Indian law, no other individual or organisation is allowed to issue currency.

Indian law recognises use of rupee as a medium of exchange that must be accepted for transactions in the country. Hence, the rupee is widely accepted as a **medium of exchange.**

Deposits with Banks

It refers to the amount of money that people keep in their bank accounts.

People deposit their extra money in banks by opening a bank account in their name. The money in bank account are deposits with banks.

Banks accept the deposits and also pay an interest on the deposits. People can also withdraw the money when they require. Thus, deposit with banks are called **Demand Deposits** as they can be withdrawn on demand. Since demand deposits are accepted widely as a means of payment, along with currency, they constitute money in the modern economy.

Cheque Facility

Cheque is basically a paper instructing the bank to pay a specific amount from the person's account to the person in whose name the cheque has been issued. Payments can be made with the use of cheque instead of cash.

1 Reserve Bank of India (RBI) The RBI or Central Bank of India, founded in 1935, which maintains the national currency, the rupee and the nation's currency reserves. Its primary function is to regulate the issuing of bank notes.

Loan Activities of Banks

The banks keep only a small portion of deposits (in India, it is 15%) as cash with themselves. This is kept for those depositors who wish to withdraw money from their accounts. The major portion of the deposits are given as loans by the banks. There is a huge demand for loans for various economic activities.

When banks give loans, they charge higher **rate of interest**[2] than the rate of interest paid on deposits. The difference between what is charged from borrowers and what is paid to depositors is their main source of income.

In this way, banks act as mediator between those who have surplus funds (the **depositors**) and those who are in need of funds (the **borrowers**[3]).

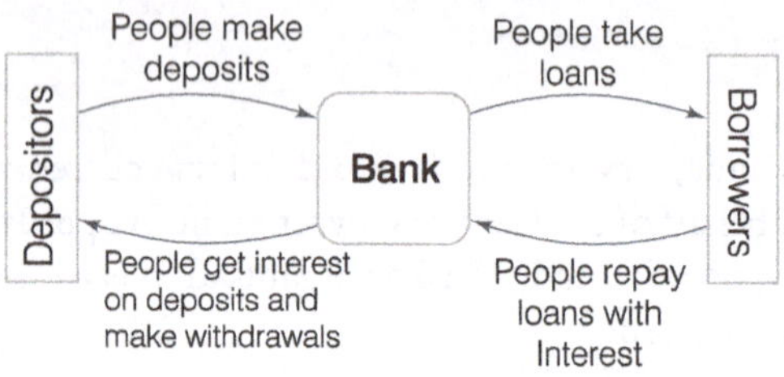

Try These

1. **Which system of exchange was used before the introduction of money?**
2. **Currency consists of which two things?**
3. **What are deposits with banks called?**
4. **Who acts as a mediator between the depositors and the borrowers?**

3.3 Different Credit Situations

Credit or loan refers to an agreement in which the lender supplies money, goods or services to borrower with the promise of future payment.

A large number of transactions in our day-to-day activities involve credit in some form or the other.

Credit can lead to two different situations, which are as follows

(i) Credit plays a **positive role** when it is obtained to meet the working capital needs of production. This credit helps the creditors to meet the ongoing expenses of production, complete production on time, and thereby increase their earnings. In this situation, credit helps to increase earnings and therefore, the condition of a person is better than before.

(ii) Credit plays a **negative role** by pushing the borrower into a situation from which recovery is difficult. Farmers often rely on crop loans for the agricultural season, and repay the loan after harvest but repayment depend on the income from farming. Crop failures can delay loan repayment. In this situation, credit pushes the person into a debt-trap.

Whether credit would be useful or not depends on the risks in the situation and whether there is some support, in case of loss.

3.4 Terms of Credit

It is a set of conditions under which a loan is given. It may include method of payment, rate of interest, duration of credit and other related conditions like, collateral, documentation requirement and the mode of repayment.

The terms of credit may vary according to the situation of the lender and the borrower.

Every loan agreement specifies an interest rate which the borrower must pay to the lender along with the repayment of the principal. In addition, lenders may demand **collateral** (security) against loans.

Collateral is an asset that the borrower owns and uses this as a guarantee to a lender until the loan is repaid.

If the borrower fails to repay the loan, the lender has the right to sell the asset or collateral to obtain payment.

Some examples of collateral security used for borrowing are land titles, deposits with banks, livestock, etc.

Variety of Credit Arrangements

- **Loan from Moneylenders** Small farmers borrow money from the village moneylender at high rate of interest. Due to high interest rate, they fell in debt-trap.
- **Loan from Traders** Farmers get loans from agricultural traders at a lower rate of interest. But the traders also get the promise of the farmers to sell their crops to him only. In this way, trader ensures that the money is repaid besides making profit. He buys crop from farmers at low price and sell it later, when price is high.
- **Loan from Banks** Some farmers take loan for cultivation from banks, at very low interest rate and at easy repayment terms. Banks also provide other facilities to such borrowers.
- **Loan from Employers** Landless agricultural labourers and workers depend on their employers for loan. The workers work for landowners in order to repay the loan.

2 **Rate of Interest** It refers to the proportion of amount charged on the principal amount taken by the borrower.
3 **Borrower** It refers to an individual, organisation or company that is taking funds, materials or services on credit/loans.

- **Loan from Cooperatives or Cooperative Societies** This is the major source of cheap credit in rural areas. Loans to member of cooperative societies can be provided for the purchase of agricultural implements, cultivation and agricultural trade, fisheries, construction of houses and other expenses.

3.5 Formal Sector Credit in India

The various types of loans can be grouped as **formal sector loans** and **informal sector loans**.

Formal Sector

The formal sector comprises banks and cooperative societies.

It provides loans comparatively at a lower rate of interest and collateral security is required to obtain loans.

This sector is mainly supervised by the **RBI** (Reserve Bank of India). The role of RBI in the formal sector is as follows

- The RBI (Reserve Bank of India) ensures that the banks give loans not just to profit-making businesses and traders, but also to small cultivators, small scale industries, small borrowers, etc.
- The banks have to submit information periodically to the RBI on how much they are lending, to whom and at what interest rate they are lending to borrowers, etc.
- The RBI monitors that banks in actually maintaining cash balance out of the deposits they receive.

Informal Sector

The informal sector may consist of moneylenders, friends and relatives, traders, landowners, large farmers, etc.

This sector charges higher interest rates on the loans that are given as there is no organisation to supervise this sector.

People who might wish to start an enterprise by borrowing from the informal sector may not do so because of the high cost of borrowing.

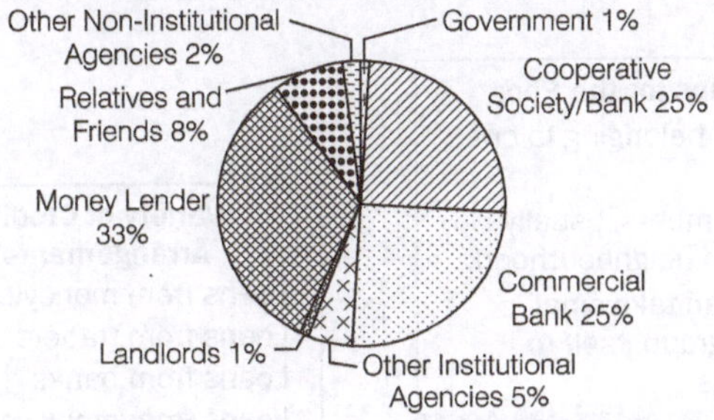

- Sources of credit per ₹ 1000 of Rural Households in India in 2012

Higher cost of borrowing means a larger part of the earnings of the borrowers is used to repay the loans. Hence, borrowers have less income left for themselves.

This sector could lead to increasing debt and debt trap.

Banks and cooperatives should increase lending which would lead to higher incomes, and many people could then borrow cheaply for a variety of needs.

They could grow crops, do business, set-up small scale industries, new industries or trade in goods. Thus, cheap and affordable credit is crucial for the country's development.

3.6 Self Help Groups (SHGs) for the Poor

Self Help Groups are groups of people usually belonging to one neighbourhood. They meet and save money regularly as per their ability.

An SHG has 15-20 members who can take small loans from the group itself to meet their needs. The group charges interest less than moneylenders on these loans.

After one or two years, if the group is regular in savings, it becomes eligible for availing loan from the bank. Loan is sanctioned in the name of group and is meant to create self-employment opportunities for the members.

Most of the important decisions regarding the saving and loan activities are taken by the group members. The group decides regarding the loans to be granted.

The group is responsible for the repayment of the loan and any case of non-repayment of loan by any one member is taken seriously by other members in the group. Due to this feature, banks provide loan to poor women when organised in SHG, even without collateral.

The SHGs help women to become financially self-reliant. Its regular meetings provide a platform for women to discuss and act on a variety of social issues such as health, nutrition, domestic violence, etc.

SHGs are the building blocks of organisation of the rural poor.

KNOWLEDGE PLUS Grameen Bank of Bangladesh was founded by Professor Muhammad Yunus, the recipient of 2006 Nobel Prize for Peace. It was started as a small project in the 1970s. It provided small credit on reasonable terms and conditions to many poor people with different occupations.

Try These

1. **Negative impact of credit can lead to which condition?**
2. **Who supervises formal sector credit in India?**
3. **Usually how many members make an SHG?**
4. **He was the founder of the Grameen Bank of Bangladesh. Identify the person.**

Mind Map

MONEY AND CREDIT

Loan Activities of Banks
- Banks act as mediators between the depositors and the borrowers.
- Banks keep a small proportion of deposits as cash with themselves, and use the major proportion of the deposits to extend loans.

Different Credit Situations

Positive Role
Credit plays a positive role when it is obtained to meet the working capital needs of production.

Negative Role
Credit plays a negative role by pushing the borrower into a situation from which recovery is difficult.

Credit Sectors in India

Formal Sector
- Comprises banks and cooperative societies.
- Provides loans at a lower rate of interest.
- Collateral security is required to obtain loans.

Informal Sector
- Consists of moneylenders, friends and relatives, traders, landowners, etc.
- Provides loans at a higher rate of interest.

Modern Forms of Money

Deposits with Banks
Amount of money that people keep in their bank accounts.

Currency
- Modern forms of currency includes paper notes and coins. It is authorised by the government of the country.
- In India, Reserve Bank of India issues currency notes on behalf of the central government.

Money as a Medium of Exchange
Money is used for several transactions. It acts as an intermediate called as medium of exchange.

Self-Help Groups for the Poor
- Group of people belonging to one neighbourhood.
- It has 15-20 members, usually belonging to one neighbourhood.
- The members can take small loans from the group itself to meet their needs.

Terms of Credit

Terms Related to Credit
- Method of payment
- Rate of Interest
- Duration of Credit
  Collateral

Variety of Credit Arrangements
- Loans from moneylenders
- Loans from traders
- Loans from banks
- Loans from employers
- Loans from cooperatives or cooperative societies

NCERT FOLDER

Covering Intext Questions and Exercises of NCERT

INTEXT QUESTIONS

Q.1 How does the use of money make it easier to exchange things?

Ans. The use of money makes it easier to exchange things in the following ways

(i) It is accepted as a medium of exchange.

(ii) It serves as a unit of value.

(iii) It solves the problem of double coincidence of wants.

Q.2 Can you think of some examples of goods and services being exchanged or wages being paid through Barter system?

Ans. Barter system of exchange is referred to as the method where goods are exchanged for goods.

Some of the examples of barter exchange are as follows

1. The worker working in the field of farmers gets wheat in return as his/her wage.
2. In a few government schemes, labourers are paid not in cash but in kind. For example, 5 kg of wheat per day of work.

Q.3 Consider the following information.

A shoe manufacturer, M Salim has to make a payment to the leather supplier and writes a cheque for a specific amount. This means that the shoe manufacturer instructs his bank to pay this amount to the leather supplier. The leather supplier takes this cheque and deposits it in his own account in the bank. The money is transferred from one bank account to another bank account in a couple of days. The transaction is complete without any payment of cash.

Now answer the following questions.

(a) M Salim wants to withdraw ₹ 20,000 in cash for making payments. How would he write a cheque to withdraw money?

(b) Tick the correct answer. After the transaction between Salim and Prem,

(i) Salim's balance in his bank account increases and Prem's balance increases.

(ii) Salim's balance in his bank account decreases and Prem's balance increases.

(iii) Salim's balance in his bank account increases and Prem's balance decreases.

Ans. (a) M Salim would write a cheque in the following way

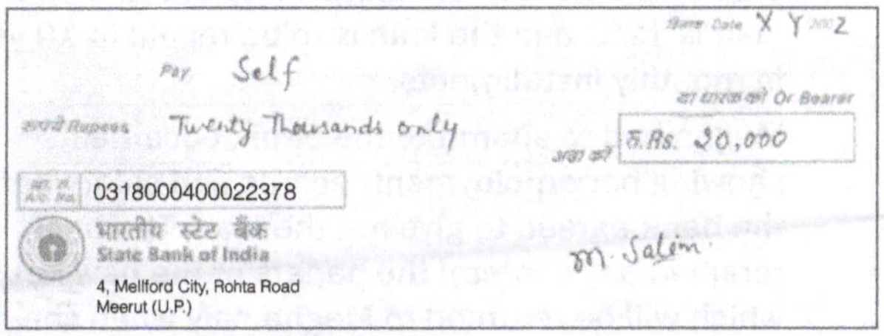
Date X Y 2022
Pay Self
Or Bearer
Rupees Twenty Thousands only
Rs. 20,000
0318000400022378
भारतीय स्टेट बैंक
State Bank of India
4, Mellford City, Rohta Road
Meerut (U.P.)
M. Salim

(b) (ii)

Q.4 Why are demand deposits considered as money?

Ans. Demand deposits are considered as money, because they can be withdrawn when required and the money withdrawn can be used for making payments.

Q.5 Fill the following table.

	Salim	Swapna
Why did they need credit?		
What was the risk?		
What was the outcome?		

Ans.

	Salim	Swapna
Why did they need credit?	To meet the working capital needs.	To meet the expenses of cultivation.
What was the risk?	No or little unknown risk.	Risk of crop failure.
What was the outcome?	Supplied the orders, earned profits and repaid the loans.	Crop failed; found herself in the debt trap.

Q.6 Suppose Salim continues to get orders from traders. What would be his position after six years?

Ans. If Salim continues to get orders from traders for the next six years, he can use the profits from the sales of shoes to finance his future business. Then, he will not have to borrow money from any source of credit.

Q.7 What are the reasons that make Swapna's situation so risky? Discuss factors - pesticides, role of money lenders, climate.

Ans. The reasons for Swapna's situation being risky are

(i) Failure of crop due to either poor rainfall or attack on the crop by pests will reduce Swapna's earning drastically. Here adding pesticides will reduce or eliminate the attack by pests and good rainfall will eliminate the risk due to climate.

(ii) Another risk is the loan taken from moneylenders. They charge high interest rates and may also take away part of Swapna's land if she is not able to repay the loan. This will reduce her earning propects in the future also.

Q.8 A House Loan

Megha has taken a loan of ₹ 5 lakh from the bank to purchase a house. The annual interest rate on the loan is 12% and the loan is to be repaid in 10 years in monthly installments.

Megha had to submit to the bank, documents showing her employment records and salary before the bank agreed to give her the loan. The bank retained as collateral the papers of the new house, which will be returned to Megha only when she repays the entire loan with interest.

Fill the following details of Megha's housing loan.

(a) Loan amount (In Rupees)	
(b) Duration of loan	
(c) Documents required	
(d) Interest rate	
(e) Mode of repayment	
(f) Collateral	

Ans. Details of Megha's loans are filled below

(a)	Loan amount (In Rupees)	5 lakhs
(b)	Duration of loan	10 years
(c)	Documents required	Salary slips, employment records
(d)	Interest rate	12 % per annum
(e)	Mode of repayment	Monthly installment in cash/ by cheque
(f)	Collateral	Papers of the new house

Q.9 Why do lenders ask for collateral while lending?

Ans. Lenders ask for collateral while lending because if payment of interest and repayment of the principal are not made on time, the lenders can sell the collateral assest and recover their money.

Q.10 Given that a large number of people in our country are poor, does it in any way affect their capacity to borrow?

Ans. Large number of poor people in a country does not effect their capacity to borrow. Poor have low capacity to borrow since they have no collateral to offer. They cannot get any credit from formal sources of credit like banks and cooperatives. They mostly take loans from informal sources of credit like moneylenders, friends, relatives, etc.

Q.11 Fill in the blanks choosing the correct option from the brackets.

While taking a loan, borrowers look for easy terms of credit. This means ...... (low/high) interest rate, ... (easy/tough) conditions for repayment, ... (less/ more) collateral and documentation requirements.

Ans. low, easy, less.

Q.12 List the various sources of credit in Sonpur.

Ans. Various sources of credit in village Sonpur are

(i) Village moneylender
(ii) Traders
(iii) Landowner as moneylender
(iv) Commercial banks
(v) Krishak cooperative society

Q.13 Compare the terms of credit for the small farmer, the medium farmer and the landless agricultural worker in Sonpur.

Ans. (i) Terms of credit for small farmer are

- The rate of interest is high.
- The farmer has to sell crops to traders at low prices as repayment of loan.

(ii) Terms of credit for medium farmer are

- The farmer can take loan from bank or from cooperative who charge very low rate of interest.
- Loan can be paid back in the next three years.

(iii) Landless agricultural workers in Sonpur are

- Borrower has no means to repay the loan in cash. So, he pledges to repay loans by working for the landowner.
- The rate of interest is high.

Q.14 Why will Arun have a higher income from cultivation compared to Shyamal?

Ans. Arun will have a higher income from cultivation compared to shyamal because of their different credit source. Arun got a loan from the commercial bank at a rate of interest 8.5% per annum, while Shyamal got loan from a village moneylender at an interest rate of 5% per month (i.e., 60% per annum).

Q.15 Can everyone in Sonpur get credit at a cheap rate? Who are the people who can?

Ans. Everyone cannot get credit at a cheap rate. Only the following people are able to get it

- who have some collateral.
- who have organised themselves into cooperative society.
- who can fulfill the bank's documentation requirements.

Arun has the capacity to pay bank loans as compared to Shyamal and gets a fresh loan in next three years. Like Shyamal he is not bound to sell his produce to the moneylenders who give a low price. He can sell his produce at market rates.

Q.16 What are the differences between formal and informal sources of credit?

Ans. The differences between formal sources and informal sources of credit are

Points of Difference	Formal Sources of Credit	Informal Sources of Credit
Borrower's capacity	Richer people have assets which can be pledged as collateral.	Poorer people does not have assets which can be pledged.
Rate of interest	Reasonably low	Very high
Sources	Banks and cooperative societies.	Traders, moneylenders, landowners, etc.
Action on default of payment	Collateral can be sold to recover the loan.	Borrowers can be made to work without pay or made to part with land owned by them.

Q.17 Why should credit at reasonable rates be available for all?

Ans. Credit at reasonable rates should be available for all, so that the poor people can benefit from the cheaper loan rates.

Q.18 Should there be a supervisor, such as the Reserve Bank of India, that looks into the loan activities of informal lenders? Why would its task be quite difficult?

Ans. Yes, there should be a supervisor for checking the loan activities of informal lenders.

Its task would be quite difficult because informal sector constitutes large number of people who may have other businesses of their own, besides lending. It is not possible to register them.

Q.19 Why do you think that the share of formal sector credit is higher for the richer households compared to the poorer households?

Ans. The share of the formal sector credit is higher for the richer households because the richer households are in a better position to provide collateral and other necessary documents which are required by the banks and cooperatives.

Richer households have means to exert pressure on banks and cooperatives to sanction loans. These households have greater capacity to repay the loans as compared to the poor households.

EXERCISE

Q.1 In situations with high risks, credit might create further problems for the borrower. Explain.

Ans. Yes, it is true that in situations of high risk, taking credit may increase the problem. Borrower may not be able to pay back the credit taken and loose whatever he has, to repay the loan back.

For example, a small farmer has taken a loan to meet cultivation expenses. In case, the crop fails, he will not be able to repay the loan and may have to sell part of his land for repaying the loan.

Q.2 How does money solve the problem of double coincidence of wants? Explain with an example of your own.

Ans. In double coincidence of wants, goods are directly exchanged by taking each other's goods. Using money as a medium of exchange, eliminates the double coincidence of wants by providing the crucial intermediate step of exchange i.e. money.

For example, it is not necessary for a shoemaker to look for a rice farmer who will buy shoes made by him and at the same time, sell rice to him. All he has to do is to find a buyer for his shoes, who will pay him money for them. With this money, he can purchase rice or any other commodity available in the market.

Q.3 How do banks mediate between those who have surplus money and those who need money?

Ans. People having surplus money deposit it in their banks. In this way, banks have large amount of deposit money. Banks then hold a small portion of deposits and the major portion of deposits is given as loans to those people who need to borrow. Here depositors and borrowers do not know each other but banks extend the deposits as loans.

In this way, banks act as a mediators between those who have surplus money and those who need it.

Q.4 Look at a ₹ 10 note. What is written on top? Can you explain this statement?

Ans. The following words are written on the top of a ₹ 10 note

Reserve Bank of India

Guaranteed by the Central Government

I promise to pay the bearer the sum of

Ten Rupees *Governor*

These words state that ₹ 10 note is acceptable as a medium of exchange because this is authorised by government of the country.

In India, the Reserve Bank of India issues currency notes on behalf of the Central Government. As per Indian law, no other individual or organisation is allowed to issue currency.

Q.5 Why do we need to expand formal sources of credit in India?

Ans. The reasons for expanding formal sources of credit in India are

- High cost of borrowing leads to a major share of earnings going into payment of interest on the loan so formal source of credit is needed.
- Sometimes the higher interest rate leads to the requirement to pay more than the earnings, thus falling into a debt-trap. To eliminate this, formal sources are needed.
- Borrowers falling into debt-traps discourage more people from borrowing, which ultimately reduces development of the country.
- Formal sources of lending to more borrowers will lead to higher incomes and many people could then borrow cheaply for a variety of needs like growing crops, set-up business or small-scale industries.

Q.6 What is the basic idea behind the SHGs for the poor? Explain in your own words.

Or **Explain the role of Self Help Groups in the rural economy.** **CBSE 2020**

Ans. The basic idea behind the formation of SHGs is to create self-employment for the poor, particularly rural poor women. The SHGs help poor borrowers to overcome the problem of lack of collateral.

They can get timely loans for a variety of purposes at a reasonable interest rate in the name of the SHG, of which they are members. The SHGs are thus the building blocks of organisation of the rural poor.

Q.7 What are the reasons why the banks might not be willing to lend to certain borrowers?

Ans. The banks may not lend to certain borrowers due to the following reasons

- Banks require some necessary documents and collateral as security against loans, some persons do not meet these requirements.
- The borrowers who did not repay their previous loans, the banks do not lend them further.
- The banks may not be willing to lend loans to those entrepreneurs who are going to invest in their business with high risks.
- One of the main objectives of a bank is to earn more profits. They would thus be unwilling to provide money to individuals from whom repayment is uncertain.

Q.8 In what ways does the Reserve Bank of India supervise the functioning of banks? Why is this necessary? **CBSE 2019**

Or **Which government body supervises the functioning of formal sources of loans in India? Explain.** **CBSE 2012**

Or **Explain the functions of the Reserve Bank of India.** **CBSE 2017**

Ans. The Reserve Bank of India supervises the functioning of banks in the following ways

- The Reserve Bank of India checks that the banks actually maintain a minimum cash balance out of the deposits they receive.
- The banks have to periodically submit information to the Reserve Bank of India on how much they are lending, to whom, at what interest rate, etc.
- The Reserve Bank of India ensures that the banks give loans not just to big businesses and traders, but also to small cultivators and borrowers.

This supervision is necessary to ensure that small businesses also grow. Further, this monitoring ensures that banks do not loan more money than they are supposed to, as such an action can create a crisis situation.

Q.9 Analyse the role of credit for development.

Or **Describe the importance of formal sources of credit in the economic development.** **CBSE 2019**

Or **Explain the role of credit for economic development.** **CBSE 2020**

Ans. Credit plays following role in economic development

- Credit availability at cheaper rates of interest encourages the business or firms to borrow more.
- Borrowing more money will lead to the growth of business or increase in production in the economy.
- For cultivators, credit is needed for improving agricultural practices. If they get a loan at cheaper rates, they would be able to generate self employment for themselves.

So, credit supply is the key factor for economic development and plays a vital role.

Q.10 Manav needs a loan to set-up a small business. On what basis will Manav decide whether to borrow from the bank or the moneylender? Discuss.

Ans. Manav will decide whether to borrow from a bank or moneylender on the basis of the following loan terms

- The collateral and documentation required, which he should be able to make available.
- The rate of interest to be charged from him.
- The mode of repayment, its periodicity, in cash / kind, etc.
- The penalty in case of default in repayment.

Q.11 In India, about 80% of farmers are small farmers, who need credit for cultivation.

(a) Why might banks be unwilling to lend to small farmers?

(b) What are the other sources from which the small farmers can borrow?

(c) Explain with an example how the terms of credit can be unfavourable for the small farmer.

(d) **Suggest some ways by which small farmers can get cheap credit.**

Ans. (a) Banks might be unwilling to lend to small farmers because they don't have collateral to deposit in the bank. Some of these farmers are not in the position of paying loan; due to their already existing loan.

(b) Small farmers can take loans from cooperatives, SHGs (if they are members) or informal sector credit sources like moneylenders, traders, relatives, friends, etc.

(c) An example of unfavourable terms of credit is given below

Shiva is a small farmer who borrows money at the rate of 4% per month (i.e. 48% per annum) from a local moneylender to grow his crop. This is a very high rate of interest.

If the crop fails due to a severe drought then Shiva has to sell part of his land to repay the loan. Thus, his condition becomes worse than before.

(d) Small farmers can get cheap credit from sources like grameen banks, agricultural cooperatives, SHGs, etc.

Q.12 Fill in the blanks.

(a) Majority of the credit needs of the .... households are met from informal sources.

(b) ...... costs of borrowing increase the debt-burden.

(c) .... issues currency notes on behalf of the Central Government.

(d) Banks charge a higher interest rate on loans than what they offer on ....

(e) .... is an asset that the borrower owns and uses as a guarantee until the loan is repaid to the lender.

Ans. (a) poor

(b) High

(c) Reserve Bank of India

(d) Bank deposits

(e) Collateral

Q.13 Choose the most appropriate answer.

(a) In a SHGs most of the decisions regarding savings and loan activities are taken by

(i) bank
(ii) members
(iii) non-government organisation

(b) Formal sources of credit do not include

(i) banks (ii) cooperatives
(iii) employers

Ans. (a) (ii), (b) (iii)

REVIEW EXERCISE

Including Competency Based Questions

Part I

Multiple Choice Questions (MCQs)

1. A system where goods were exchanged without using money is better known as

(a) goods system (b) exchange system
(c) barter system (d) no-money system

2. The problem of similar wants made exchange difficult, so a new medium of exchange was developed known as

(a) capital (b) cost (c) rent (d) money

3. What is the most important function of money?

(a) Used in banking transactions (b) Payment of loans
(c) Medium of exchange (d) Stock market exchange

4. Modern forms of money include which of the following?

(a) Currency notes and coins
(b) Cowrie shells and stones
(c) Gold and silver coins
(d) Grains and cattle

5. Raghav has surplus money so he opens a bank account and deposits in it. Whenever he needs money, he can go to his bank and withdraw from there. This kind of deposit with the banks are known as Competency Based

(a) demand deposit (b) term deposit
(c) fixed deposit (d) surplus deposit

6. A person can withdraw money by issuing a cheque. What is a cheque?

(a) Loan taken by the bank.
(b) Loan taken by the depositor from the bank.
(c) Paper instructing the bank to pay a specific amount.
(d) Paper specially valid to withdraw money only from account holder's account.

7. Which one of the following banks in India controls the issuance of currency and regulates the credit system in the country? CBSE 2024

(a) Punjab National Bank (b) Indian Bank
(c) Reserve Bank of India (d) State Bank of India

8. Mr. X has taken credit to make candles during the festive season. Choose the correct options that defines the importance of credit from the given options. SQP 2024-25

(i) It plays a vital and positive role in meeting his target and accelerating his income.

(ii) The credit helps him to meet the ongoing expenses of production.

(iii) The credit helps him complete the production on time.

(iv) It helps him in exercising restraint and get into the habit of taking more credit.

Options

(a) Only (iv) (b) (iii) and (iv)
(c) (i), (ii) and (iii) (d) Only (ii)

9. Which of the following groups in urban India depend on informal sources to meet their credit needs? CBSE 2025

(a) Poor households
(b) Households with few assets
(c) Both poor households and households with few assets
(d) Both well-off households and households with few assets

10. Aruna, a young entrepreneur from a rural village, aspires to start her own tailoring business. She envisions creating employment opportunities for women in her community by providing them with sewing machines and training. Aruna plans to seek financial assistance to initiate her venture and has been contemplating different sources of credit.

Considering her aspirations and the information provided, which credit source might be most suitable for Aruna's entrepreneurial endeavor? Competency Based

(a) Loan from traders with a promise to sell her products exclusively to them.
(b) Formal sector credit from banks or cooperatives at a lower interest rate.
(c) Borrowing from moneylenders within her village.
(d) Self Help Groups (SHGs) to access loans with reduced interest rates.

11. In a country, the financial landscape is supported by various credit sources and systems, affecting individuals and their economic decisions.

What best describes the importance of formal sector credit? Competency Based

(a) Formal sector credit involves higher interest rates and is often unregulated.
(b) It requires collateral and provides loans at comparatively lower interest rates.
(c) It necessitates only a promise of future payment without any security.
(d) It mainly comprises moneylenders and friends as lending institutions.

12. Rahul has a sack of cotton but he is in need of wheat and Anush has a sack of wheat and is in need of cotton. Under this situation, both will be able to exchange their goods. In case of absence of such coincidence of wants, they may not exchange their goods.

Which one of the following would be the best option that describes the mutual exchange of goods and eliminate the exchange of goods?

Codes CBSE Additional SQP 2023-24

(a) Double coincidence of want, Exchanging commodity for commodity.
(b) Double Coincidence of want, Credit on Commodity
(c) Double coincidence of want, Loan on commodity.
(d) Double coincidence of want, Money

13. Select which among the following cannot be purchased through money. Choose the correct option. CBSE 2023

I. Full protection from infectious diseases
II. A pollution-free atmosphere
III. High quality education
IV. A luxury home

Codes

(a) I and III (b) III and IV
(c) I and IV (d) I and II

14. Rama is a farmer. She needs loan for agriculture work. Which of the following sources of loan will be beneficial for Rama? Choose the most appropriate option. CBSE 2025

I. Bank
II. Agricultural Trader
III. Self-Help Group
IV. Government

Options

(a) Only I, III and IV are correct.
(b) Only I, II and III are correct.
(c) Only II, III and IV are correct.
(d) Only I, II and IV are correct.

15. Which of the following statements accurately describes the role of 'Collateral' in the loan system? Competency Based

I. It is a security against loans and is used as a guarantee to a lender until the loan is repaid.
II. Collateral is not required by lenders as it increases the risk involved in loaning money.
III. Collateral is a term used to describe the process of credit given by moneylenders.
IV. Collateral is solely an agreement between borrowers and lenders without any legal backing.

Codes

(a) Only I (b) Only II
(c) Both I and III (d) Only IV

16. Mr. X is contemplating borrowing money for his agricultural business. Which of the following factors highlights the benefits of obtaining a loan from a formal banking institution? **Competency Based**

I. Lower interest rates compared to other informal sources.

II. A potential risk of being trapped in a debt trap.

III. Requirement of surrendering property as collateral.

IV. No interest charges on the loan.

Codes

(a) Only I (b) III and IV

(c) I and II (d) Only II

17. Identify the reason as to why countries often resort to the use of currency as a medium of exchange instead of the barter system. Choose from the appropriate statements among the following options.

I. Currency eliminates the need for double coincidence of wants, unlike the barter system, facilitating smoother transactions.

II. Currency allows for a more standardised measure of value and divisibility compared to goods traded in the barter system.

III. Barter systems limit the scope of trade, while currency promotes trade across a wider spectrum.

IV. Currency helps in reducing the risk and uncertainty involved in the valuation of goods traded, unlike the barter system.

Options

(a) Statements I, II, and III are appropriate.

(b) Statements I, II, and IV are appropriate.

(c) All the statements are appropriate.

(d) Only statement iii is appropriate.

18. Consider the statements given below and choose the correct answer. **Competency Based**

Statement I In the context of modern banking systems, banks act as intermediaries between individuals with surplus funds (depositors) and those in need of funds (borrowers).

Statement II Formal sector credit sources, supervised by the Reserve Bank of India (RBI), offer loans at higher interest rates and do not require collateral security.

Codes

(a) Statement I is correct and statement II is incorrect.

(b) Statement I is incorrect and statement II is correct.

(c) Both statements I and II are incorrect.

(d) Both statements I and II are correct.

19. Ram and Shyam are small farmers who have taken loans of ₹ 20,000 from different parties. Ram has taken credit at 1.5% per month interest from a trader while Shyam has taken credit at 8% per annum from a cooperative. Analyse the loan information given above, considering one of the following correct option.

(a) Shyam is better because he receives more interest.

(b) Ram is better as he does no paper work.

(c) Shyam is worse off as he pays more interest.

(d) Ram is worse off as he pays more interest.

20. Sunita owns a small flower shop near a temple. She wants to expand her shop by keeping exotic flowers and flower bouquetts. To whom she should approach for a very short term credit?

(a) Moneylenders as they provide short term credit.

(b) Banks as they charge low interest

(c) Cooperatives as they do not require collateral as a land, house, live-stock, etc.

(d) All of the above

21. Sunil works in a private company while Anil works as a daily wage earner. Both want a credit of ₹ 30000/-. The bank is more likely to give credit to whom?

(a) Sunil as he has regular employment

(b) Anil as he is more needy

(c) Neither Sunil nor Anil

(d) Both Sunil and Anil

22. Read the information given below and select the correct option. **CBSE SQP 2022-23**

Rohan has taken a loan of ₹ 5 lakhs from the bank to purchase a house on 12% rate of interest. He has to submit papers of new house and salary record to the bank. What is this process called as?

(a) Interest Rate (b) Collateral

(c) Principal Amount (d) Installments

Answers

1. (c)	**2.** (d)	**3.** (c)	**4.** (a)	**5.** (a)
6. (c)	**7.** (c)	**8.** (c)	**9.** (c)	**10.** (d)
11. (b)	**12.** (a)	**13.** (d)	**14.** (a)	**15.** (a)
16. (a)	**17.** (a)	**18.** (a)	**19.** (d)	**20.** (c)
21. (a)	**22.** (b)			

Match the Following

1.

List I	List II
A. Interest on loan	1. 10.5%, 5 years, cold storage, salary slip
B. Mode of re-payment	2. Papers of shop
C. Terms of credit	3. Monthly installment in cheque
D. Collateral	4. 3% per month

Codes

	A	B	C	D
(a)	3	2	4	1
(b)	4	3	1	2
(c)	2	4	3	1
(d)	1	2	4	3

Ans. (b)

Picture Based Questions

1. Look at the picture below and select the correct option which describes it properly.

(a) Banks link depositors to borrowers.
(b) Banks are useful in keeping surplus cash.
(c) Banks are mediator between depositors and borrowers.
(d) Banks are very important for the economy.

Ans. 1. (a) Banks link depositors to borrowers.

Assertion-Reason

1. Assertion (A) When Borrowers borrow from informal sources, then they fall into debt traps.
Reason (R) Formal sector institution need to lend more to the borrowers in order to prevent them from falling into debt traps.

Codes
(a) Both A and R are true and R is the correct explanation of A
(b) Both A and R are true, but R is not the correct explanation of A
(c) A is true, but R is false
(d) A is false, but R is true

2. Assertion (A) Banks are responsible to act as links between depositors and borrowers by accepting deposits and providing loans, charging higher interest rates on loans than the interest paid on deposits.
Reason (R) Banks keep a small portion of deposits as cash and lend the rest to borrowers, earning income through the interest charged on loans.

Codes
(a) Both A and R are true and R is the correct explanation of A
(b) Both A and R are true, but R is not the correct explanation of A
(c) A is true, but R is false
(d) A is false, but R is true

3. Assertion (A) Rupees is accepted as medium of exchange in India. **CBSE 2025**
Reason (R) The World Bank legalises the use of rupee as a medium of payment in India.

Options
(a) Both A and R are correct and R is the correct explanation of A
(b) Both A and R are correct, but R is not the correct explanation of A
(c) A is correct, but R is incorrect
(d) A is incorrect, but R is correct.

4. Assertion (A) Self-Help Groups (SHGs) facilitate financial independence among rural poor communities by offering loans at lower interest rates compared to moneylenders.
Reason (R) SHGs promote regular savings and group-based lending, which encourages self-employment opportunities and reduces dependency on low-interest informal loans.

Codes
(a) Both A and R are true and R is the correct explanation of A
(b) Both A and R are true, but R is not the correct explanation of A
(c) A is true, but R is false
(d) A is false, but R is true

Ans. 1. (b) Both A and R are true, but R is not the correct explanation of A
2. (a) Both A and R are true, but R is not the correct explanation of A
3. (c) A is correct, but R is incorrect.
4. (a) Both A and R are true and R is the correct explanation of A

Case Based Question

1. Read the following source and answer the questions that follow. **CBSE Term II 2022**

Every loan agreement specifies an interest rate which the borrower must pay to the lender along with the repayment of the principal. In addition, lenders may demand collateral (security) against loans. Collateral is an asset that the borrower owns (such as land, building, vehicle, livestocks, deposits with banks) and uses this as a guarantee to a lender until the loan is repaid. If the borrower fails to repay the loan, the lender has the right to sell the asset or collateral to obtain payment. Property such as land titles, deposits with banks, livestock are some common examples of collateral used for borrowing.

(i) What does credit, in the context of loans, involve?
(a) Immediate payment for goods or services.
(b) Borrower supplying money to the lender.
(c) Lender supplying money, goods or services with a promise of future payment.
(d) Exchange of goods without any payment.

(ii) How is credit defined in day-to-day transactions?
(a) A one-time payment for services.
(b) An agreement where the borrower supplies goods to the lender.
(c) An agreement where the lender provides money in exchange for future payment.
(d) A process of bartering goods for immediate services.

(iii) Why is modern currency widely accepted as a medium of exchange, despite lacking intrinsic value?

(a) Because it is made of precious metals like gold, silver and copper.

(b) Because it is use in everyday transactions.

(c) Because it is authorised by the government and accepted as a medium of payment.

(d) Because it has inherent value similar to grain and cattle.

(iv) If a borrower fails to repay a loan, what right does the lender have according to the collateral provided?

(a) The lender can increase the interest rate.

(b) The lender can repossess and sell the collateral to obtain payment.

(c) The lender can extend the loan term.

(d) The lender can deny any future loans to the borrower.

Ans. (i) (c) Lender supplying money, goods, or services with a promise of future payment

(ii) (c) An agreement where the lender provides money, goods, or services in exchange for future payment.

(iii) (c) Because it is authorised by the government and accepted as a medium of payment.

(iv) (b) The lender can repossess and sell the collateral to obtain payment.

Part II

Very Short Answer Type Questions

1. Are gold seals a modern form of money or an ancient form of money?

Ans. Gold seals were used in ancient times as money.

2. How does money acts as a medium of exchange? CBSE 2019

Ans. Money acts as a medium of exchange as it acts as intermediate in the exchange process and transactions.

3. What do you mean by 'Barter system'?

***or* What is the meaning of 'Barter system'?**

Ans. Barter system was a system of exchange where goods were exchanged without use of money between two or more people. Under this system, people exchanged commodities for commodities to satisfy their wants.

4. What do you mean by double coincidence of wants?

Ans. Double coincidence of wants means both parties agree to buy and sell each other's commodities respectively.

5. What are the modern forms of money? CBSE 2014, 11

Ans. Modern forms of money include currency (paper notes and coins) and deposits with banks.

6. What is the reason for accepting paper notes as a medium of exchange in India? CBSE 2013

Ans. The reason for accepting paper notes as medium of exchange in India is that paper notes are authorised by the Government of India.

7. Which agency has the sole right to print currency notes on behalf of Government of India?

Ans. Reserve Bank of India (RBI) has the sole right to print currency notes on behalf of Government of India.

8. What is demand deposit?

Ans. A deposit with a bank that can be withdrawn whenever the depositor wants to do so is known as a demand deposit.

9. What is a cheque?

Ans. Cheque is basically a paper instructing the bank to pay a specific amount from the person's account to the person in whose name the cheque has been issued.

10. State the role of Reserve Bank of India. CBSE SQP Term II 2021

Ans. The role of Reserve Bank of India is that it supervises the functioning of formal sources of credit from banks and cooperative societies. It monitors the banks in maintaining cash balance.

11. Why payments made in rupees cannot be refused in India? CBSE 2016

Ans. Payments made in rupees cannot be refused because the Indian law legalises the use of rupee as a medium of payment.

12. What do you mean by the term collateral? CBSE 2017

Ans. Collateral is an asset that the borrower owns and uses this as a guarantee to a lender until the loan is repaid.

13. Samantha owns a small business and seeks financial aid. She's unsure about approaching formal or informal credit sources. Mention the difference between formal and informal sector credit. Competency Based

Ans. Formal sector credit involves banks and cooperatives offering lower interest rates with collateral requirements. On the other hand, informal sector credit lacks regulation, charging higher rates.

14. Read the following source and answer the questions that follow. CBSE Term II 2022

A House Loan

Megha has taken a loan of ₹ 5 lakhs from the bank to purchase a house. The annual interest rate on the loan is 12 per cent and the loan is to be repaid in 10 years in monthly installments. Megha had to submit to the bank, documents showing ther employment records and salary before the bank agreed to give her the loan. The bank retained as collateral the papers of the new house, which will be returned to Megha only when she repays the entire loan with interest.

(i) From which source of credit Megha has taken loan?

(ii) Explain the terms of credit given in the source.

(iii) What did the bank retain as collateral from Megha to give her the House Loan?

Ans. (i) Megha has taken loan from formal source.

(ii) Terms of credit given in the source are salary slip, employment record, interest rate, mode of payment and new house paper.

(iii) The bank retained the papers of the new house as collateral.

Short Answer Type Questions

1. How is money used as a medium of exchange? Explain with examples. **CBSE 2013**

Ans. Following examples justify the use of money as a medium of exchange

- In day-to-day transactions, goods are being bought and sold with the use of money.
- A person holding money can easily exchange it for any commodity or services.
- Use of money has made it easier to exchange services such as the service of a doctor, teacher, etc.

2. Why is modern currency accepted as a medium of exchange without any use of its own? Find out the reason. **CBSE 2015**

Ans. Modern currency is accepted as money because it is backed by the trust and authority of the government. Though it has no intrinsic value (like gold or silver), people accept it because they believe it will be accepted by others in exchange for goods and services. This trust is established through government regulations.

The currency is considered legal tender which means it must be accepted for payments. The stability and authority of the government ensure that the currency retains its value in the economy

3. Which type of deposits with the banks are called demand deposits? State some important features of demand deposits. **CBSE 2012**

Or **Why are the deposits in bank called demand deposits? What are the benefits of such deposits?** **CBSE 2010**

Ans. The deposits in the bank accounts that can be withdrawn on demand, are called demand deposits.

Some important features of demand deposits are

- Demand deposits are accepted widely as a means of payment by way of a cheque along with currency.
- Demand deposits are closely linked to the working of the modern banking system. Such deposits earn an amount as interest.
- Demand deposits can be withdrawn from the bank whenever it is required.

4. Credit can play a negative role. Justify the statement. **CBSE 2019, 16**

Or **Explain the term debt-trap. Why is it more rampant in rural areas? Give two reasons.**

Or **"Credit sometimes pushes the borrower into a situation from which recovery is very painful. 'Support the statement with examples.** **CBSE 2020**

Or **Analyse the situation in which credit pushes the borrower into a situation from which recovery is painful.** **CBSE Term II 2022**

Ans. Credit play a negative role when it results in formation of a circle or a trap known as debt-trap. Debt-trap is a situation in which a person after taking a loan is not able to pay back the loan and takes a fresh loan. The recovery from this situation is painful.

It is more common in rural areas because

(i) Farmers repay the loan after harvest but repayment depend on the income from farming. Crop failures can delay loan repayment. In this situation, credit pushes the person into a debt-trap.

(ii) Rural borrowers normally depend on informal sources of credit who charge a high rate of interest. This repayment of larger amounts may sometimes be larger than their income.

5. "Deposits with the banks are beneficial to the depositors as well as to the nation." Examine the statement.

Ans. The deposits with the banks are beneficial to the depositors in the following ways

- There is safety of the surplus money.
- Interest can be earned on the surplus money.
- Payment can be made easily through cheques.

Benefits of bank deposits to the nation are

- Availability of cheap loans as large part of these deposits are given as loans.
- Boost the industry and agriculture by providing cheap loans.

6. "Loans from banks always help to raise people's earning capacity." Justify this statement using suitable examples.

Ans. Loans from banks always help to raise people's earning capacity. For example,

- People can purchase machinery and equipment with a loan to start productive activities in manufacturing.
- With a loan, people can purchase raw materials for processing into finished products, thus increasing their earning capacity.
- With the loans, people can set training or learn some kind of skill which helps them in the future to increase their earning.

7. "Whether credit would be useful or not, it depends on the situation." Give two different examples in support of this statement.

Ans. Whether credit would be useful or not, it depends on the situation. For example,

(i) A manufacturer taking credit for supplying goods in the festival season usually has low risk, as the products are most likely to be sold completely which will raise his income.

(ii) A small farmer taking credit for crops has larger risks in case of crop failure. His only support in case of loss is the land, which he has to sell. So, this will make him poor.

(iii) In some cases, if the borrower is able to get some amount as advance payment, then the risks are lessened.

8. Why is cheap and affordable credit important for the country's development? Explain any three reasons.

***Or* Describe the importance of formal sources of credit in the economic development.** **CBSE 2019**

Ans. Cheap and affordable credit is important for a country's development because

- If credit is cheap then more lending will take place. This means people will invest in agriculture, business, small industries, etc.
- More investment will mean employment for the people which means poor people will get jobs.
- Cheap and affordable credit will allow the poor people to get rid of moneylenders and come out of debt trap.

9. Why do most of the rural households still remain dependent on the informal sources of credit? Explain. **CBSE SQP 2021 Term II**

Ans. Most of the rural households still remain dependent on the informal sources of credit due to the following reasons

- There is limited availability of banks in rural areas which increases dependence on informal sources of credit as they are easily available in rural areas.
- Bank loans require proper documentation and collateral which is rarely available with poor households.
- Rural people lack collateral that prevents them from getting bank loans. As the banks are formal sources of credit which requires a collateral for loans.

10. Explain any three reasons for the banks and cooperative societies to increase their lending facilities in rural areas.

***or* Why is it necessary for the banks and cooperative societies to increase their lending facilities in rural areas? Explain.** **CBSE 2019, 2017, 2015**

Ans. Banks and cooperatives are needed to increase their lending facilities in rural areas due to the following reasons

- People in rural areas take credit from moneylenders and traders who charge very high rate of interest.
- Rural people are exploited by using unfair means, thus leading them to debt traps.
- Formal sources of credit could provide cheap and affordable credit in rural areas without any undue exploitation.

11. Seema wants to open a small flower shop near the village temple for which she needs ₹ 35000. Briefly explain which is the best credit source for her and why? **Competency Based**

Ans. The best credit source for Seema is to go to SHGs.

The reasons are as follows

(i) The Self Help Groups are organisations of the rural poor people specially women. They provide small loans on reasonable rates.

(ii) SHGs do not require collateral and documentation.

(iii) SHGs also take up social issues related to women so if Seema becomes a member of SHGs, then she will not only get financial assistance but also support of other women members.

12. Mr S, a farmer in a rural area, wants to expand his agricultural operations but lacks the necessary funds. Explain how Mr S can access credit sources from both formal and informal sectors to support his agricultural expansion. Discuss the advantages and disadvantages of these credit sources for his farming activities. **Competency Based**

Ans. Mr S can access credit from both formal and informal sources.

If Mr S borrows from the bank he will face the following

- **Advantages** Low interest rates; structured repayment plans.
- **Disadvantages** Complicated paperwork; strict eligibility criteria.

If Mr S borrows from the informal sector he will face the following

- **Advantages** Quick access to loans; less paperwork.
- **Disadvantages** Limited funds available and high interest rates.

13. Over the years, the evolution of credit systems has significantly impacted economic transactions. Explain the transition from barter systems to modern banking and credit facilities. **Competency Based**

Ans. The shift from barter to modern credit mechanisms marks a crucial progression in economic systems.

(i) The advent of money as a medium of exchange resolved the issue of 'double coincidence of wants', facilitating smoother transactions.

(ii) The emergence of currency further streamlined trade by providing a standardised medium.

(iii) The development of formal banking institutions expanded access to credit, aiding economic growth.

These milestones revolutionised economic exchanges, enabling greater efficiency and accessibility in transactions.

Long Answer Type Questions

1. How do banks play an important role in the economy of India? Explain. CBSE 2017

Or "Banks plays an important role in economic development of the country. Support the statement with examples. CBSE 2020

Ans. Banks play an important role in the economy of India in the following ways

(i) **Provide Deposits** Bank accept the deposits and also pay an amount as interest on the deposits. In this way, people's money is safe with the banks and it earns an amount as interest. People also have the provision to withdraw the money as and when they require. Since the deposits in the bank account can be withdrawn on demand, these deposits are called demand deposits.

(ii) **Provide Loans** Banks keep only a small portion of their deposits as cash with themselves. Banks use the major portion of the deposits to give loans. There is a huge demand for loans for various economic activities. Banks make use of the deposits to meet the loan requirements of the people.

In this way, banks provide credit to set up industries and in agriculture. This generates more employment and raises income thereby bringing economic development.

2. Which government body supervises the functioning of formal sources of loans in India? Explain its functioning.

Or How does Reserve Bank of India play crucial role in controlling the formal sector loans? Explain. CBSE 2012

Or Describe the functions of the Reserve Bank of India. CBSE 2019

Or Describe the significiance of the Reserve Bank of India. CBSE 2020

or Explain the significance of the Reserve Bank of India in the Indian economy. CBSE SQP 2022-23

Ans. The Reserve Bank of India supervises the functioning of formal sources of loans in India.

Functions of Reserve Bank of India are as follows

- The Reserve Bank of India monitors that the banks actually maintain the cash balance and do not give all the deposits as loans.
- The Reserve Bank of India ensures that the banks give loans not just to profit-making businesses and rich traders, but also to small cultivators, small scale industries, small borrowers, etc.
- The banks have to submit information periodically to the Reserve Bank of India on how much they are lending, to whom, etc.
- The rate of interest charged on loans given by the banks is decided by the Reserve bank.
- In this way, the RBI keeps a check on all the activities of banks and checks the flow of credit also.

3. What is a collateral ? Why is it a main reason to prevent the poor getting a loan from banks? Explain. CBSE 2023

Ans. Collateral is an asset that the borrower owns and use this as a guarantee to a lender until the loan is repaid.

It is a main reason to prevent the poor getting a loan from banks as the formal sector loan providers offer loans only if the person taking the loan has a property or an asset in the form of collateral.

But, unfortunately, the poor section of society has no property to be kept as collateral. As a result, the poor section of society prefers to take loans from the informal sector even after knowing that they charge more interest.

4. How can the formal sector loans be made beneficial for poor farmers and workers? Explain. CBSE 2024, 2016

Ans. The formal sector loans can be beneficial for poor farmers and workers in the following ways

- The formal sector like banks and cooperatives should lend more to poor people and workers, particularly in rural areas.
- The formal sector should provide cheap and affordable credit to the poor people so that repayment is easy.
- Formal sector should work out other ways of arranging collateral from the poor people.
- By providing linkage between Self Help Groups and banks, formal sector of credit can be increased.
- There should be more number of cooperatives and banks in rural areas and people should be made aware of their presence.

5. Miss X wants to start a savoury food store in her village. She wants to supplement her income to raise the standard of living of her family. How do you think, Self-Help Groups can help, support your answer with reasons? CBSE SQP 2024-25

Ans. Self Help Groups (SHGs) can help the poor in becoming self-reliant in the following ways

- **Access to Loans** SHGs enable members to get loans from banks at low interest rates.
- **No Collateral Required** Loans from SHGs do not require collateral, making them easier to access.
- **Focus on Rural Women** SHGs are designed to help rural women become economically independent through self-employment.
- **Business Growth** SHGs assist in starting and expanding businesses, which improves living standards.
- **Skill Development** SHGs offer training programme to develop skills needed for successful businesses.
- **Social Empowerment** SHGs provide a platform for women to connect, share experiences and support each other, empowering them to be active in their communities.

6. What is the idea behind the formation of Self Help Groups (SHGs)? Explain the functioning of the SHGs. CBSE 2016, 2015

Ans. Self Help Groups are small groups that usually consist of people sharing a common local area and a common type of work or financial condition. The idea behind its formation is to encourage people to do savings and there by increase their opportunities for earnings.

The functioning of the SHGs is as follows

- SHGs typically consist of 15-20 members and each member is required to save their resources.
- The SHGs are constituted to provide loans to its members at a reasonable rate.
- After a year or two and with regular savings, the group is eligible to take loans from banks.
- SHGs seek loans from banks for its member collectively and meet the needs of buying assets, machinery, raw materials, construction or repair.
- SHGs also meet regularly to discuss and act on various social issues like dowry, domestic violence, child marriage, health, nutrition, etc.

7. Money by providing the crucial intermediate step eliminates the need for double coincidence of wants. Justify the statement highlighting the significance of the modern form of money in India. CBSE SQP 2024-25

Ans. The significance of the modern forms of money in India are as follows

- With money, you can buy what you need without having to barter goods. Money serves as a medium of exchange, making transactions easier.
- Modern money comes in the form of paper notes and coins, which are different from the old forms like gold or silver. Today's currency has no intrinsic value but is widely accepted because it is issued and regulated by the government.
- In India, the Reserve Bank of India issues currency on behalf of the central government. Only this institution is allowed to produce money, and according to the law, everyone must accept rupees for transactions. This legal backing ensures that the rupee is universally accepted as a medium of exchange.

Case Based Questions

1. Read the following source and answer the questions that follow : CBSE 2025

Loans from Co-operatives

Besides banks, the other major source of cheap credit in rural areas are the co-operative societies. Members of a co-operative pool their resources for co-operation in certain areas. There are several types of co-operatives possible such as farmers co-operatives, weavers co-operatives, industrial workers co-operatives etc. Krishak Co-operative functions in a village not very far away from Sonpur. It has 2300 farmers as members. It accepta deposits from its members.

With these deposits as collateral, the co-operative has obtained a large loan from the bank. These funds are used to provide loans-to members. Once these loans are repaid, another round of lending can take place. Krishak Co-operative provides loans for the purchase of agriculture equipments, loans for cultivation and agricultural trade, fishery loans, loans for constructions of houses and for variety of other expenses.

(i) Which sector includes credit facilities offered by co-operative societies?

(ii) How do Self-Help Groups access external funding?

(iii) Explain the functioning of co-operative societies.

Ans. (i) The formal sector includes credit facilities offered by cooperative societies.

(ii) Self-Help Groups (SHGs) access external funding primarily through bank linkage. Once they establish a good savings and repayment record, SHGs can receive loans from banks at concessional rates. They may also benefit from government schemes and support from microfinance institutions or NGOs that provide financial assistance to rural communities.

(iii) Cooperative societies function by pooling the resources of their members to offer financial services and support. Members, such as farmers or workers, contribute money or deposits to the cooperative society. The cooperative uses these deposits as collateral to secure larger loans from banks or other financial institutions.

The funds obtained are then lent out to members at low-interest rates for various purposes, such as purchasing agricultural tools, cultivating crops, or building houses. Once the loans are repaid, the funds are used for another round of lending, continuing the cycle of support for the community.

2. Read the passage given below and answer the questions that follow.

In India, the Reserve Bank of India issues currency notes on behalf of the Central Government. As per Indian Law, no other individual or organisation is allowed to issue currency. Moreover, the law legalises the use of rupee as a medium of payment that cannot be refused in setting transactions in India.

No individual in India can legally refuse a payment made in rupees. Hence, the rupee is widely accepted as a medium of exchange.

The other form in which people hold money is as deposits with banks. At a point of time, people need only some currency for their day-to-day needs. For instance, workers who receive their salaries at the end of each month have extra cash at the beginning of the month.

What do people do with this extra cash? They deposit it with the banks by opening a bank account in their name. Banks accept the deposits and also pay an amount as interest on the deposits.

In this way people's money is safe with the banks and it earns an amount as interest. People also have the provision to withdraw the money as and when they require. Since the deposits in the bank accounts can be withdrawn on demand, these deposits are called demand deposits.

(i) Why is there a need to legalise rupee as a medium of exchange?

(ii) Mention two uses of opening a bank account by the people.

(iii) How demand deposits are useful for the banks as well as for the people?

Ans. (i) There is a need to legalise rupee as a medium of exchange so that all payments can be made and no one can refuse rupee in settling of transactions.

(ii) Two uses of opening a bank account
- To deposit surplus cash into the bank account.
- To earn interest given by the banks on deposits.

(iii) For the banks, demand deposits provide an opportunity to extend them as loans. For the people, demand deposits are like near money that can be easily withdrawn from the bank. In this way, demand deposits are useful for the banks as well as for the people.

ASSESSMENT EXERCISE

Multiple Choice Questions (MCQs)

1. Which of the following is not included in the terms of credit in a bank loan?
(a) The rate of interest
(b) The lender's land
(c) The borrower's land
(d) The time period of the loan

2. Which of the following are not modern forms of money?
(a) Currency notes (b) Gold seals
(c) Metallic coins (d) None of these

3. What is the consequence of a higher cost of borrowing for borrowers?
(a) Increased income for borrowers
(b) Greater savings for borrowers
(c) Less income left for borrowers, leading to a potential debt trap
(d) Easier access to loans for borrowers

4. Why is cheap and affordable credit considered crucial for a country's development?
(a) It allows people to accumulate wealth easily.
(b) It discourages people from borrowing for various needs.
(c) It facilitates growth in agriculture, business and small-scale industries.
(d) It leads to higher interest rates for borrowers.

Subjective Questions (VSA, SA & LA)

1. Mention any two difficulties of Barter system?

2. State any two advantage of SHGs.

3. Mention the sources of informal credit.

4. How do currency notes act as a medium of exchange?

5. 'Interest rate, collateral and documentation requirement and the mode of repayment together comprises are called the terms of credit'. Analyse the statement with examples.

6. Explain loans from cooperatives.

7. 'It is important to have a control over the formal sector loans by the Government of India.' Substantiate this statement with examples.

8. Explain the role of Self Help Groups in empowering women.

9. How does a Self Help Group function? Elucidate with examples.

10. How can rural poor be encouraged to take loans from the formal sector of credit? Explain.

12. Describe four major sources of credit for rural house holds in India.

CHAPTER 4

Globalisation and the Indian Economy

Globalisation is the process of increased connectivity and interdependence among countries, driven by cross-border trade, investment and cultural exchange. MNCs play a key role in increasing the flow of goods, services and capital across borders.

4.1 Production Across Countries

Production was mainly done within countries until the mid-20th century. Countries traded raw materials, food, and finished goods with each other.

For example, India as a colony exported raw materials and food to other countries and received finished goods in return. Trade was the main channel connecting distant countries.

Later, large companies called Multinational Corporations (MNCs) emerged. An MNC is a company that owns or controls production in more than one country.

MNCs set-up offices and factories for production in regions where they can get cheap labour and other resources, to minimise cost and maximise profit.

They sell their finished products globally and also produce the goods and services globally. The production process is divided into small parts and spread out across the globe.

By spreading out production across different countries, the MNCs get the best quality resources at cheap prices. This increases their profit.

4.2 Interlinking Production Across Countries

MNCs usually set up production facilities close to the markets, where they can find cheap labour (skilled and unskilled) and other resources. They also prefer countries with favourable government policies.

The money that is spent to buy assets such as land, building, machines and other equipment is called **investment**. Investment made by MNCs is called **foreign investment**. Investment is made with the hope of earning profits.

MNCs control and spread their production across countries in the following ways

- **Partnerships/Joint Venture** Sometimes MNCs merge with local companies and produce jointly. In this way, MNCs provide money for additional investments like buying new machines for faster production and bring latest technology for production.
- **Merge or Takeover Local Companies** MNCs buy local production units or merge with local companies to expand production. For example, Cargill Foods of USA has taken over Parakh Foods in India and has become the largest producer of edible oil in India.
- **Contracts to Local Companies** MNCs in developed countries also place orders with small producers for production. These small producers make the products, and the big companies sell them with their brand names. The MNC determines the price, quality, delivery and labour conditions for these distant producers, etc.

Thus, MNCs are expanding their production globally by interacting, competing or buying local companies. As a result, production in these widely dispersed locations is getting interlinked.

4.3 Foreign Trade and Integration of Markets

Foreign trade refers to the trade between different countries of the world. It consists of **imports** and **exports**.

Foreign trade helps in the integration (connection) of markets in the following ways

- It creates an opportunity for the producers to reach beyond domestic markets. They can sell their products in markets located in the countries of the world.

- It expands the choices available to the buyers with the import of goods produced in another country.
- Prices of similar goods in the two markets tend to become equal and producers closely compete against each other.

An example of foreign trade in India is that how the cheap and better quality of Chinese toys replaced the Indian toys. Thus, foreign trade results in connecting the markets or integration of markets in different countries.

Try These

1. Give a way of interlinking production across countries.
2. Name the investment which is made by a company based in one country to a company based in other country.
3. What is meant by an MNC?
4. What does the integration between countries through foreign trade and foreign investment known as?

4.4 Globalisation

It is the process of rapid integration or interconnection between countries by greater foreign investment and greater foreign trade.

In the process of globalisation, MNCs are playing major role. More and more goods and services, investments and technology are moving among different countries. Foreign investment by MNCs has been rising. A large part of the foreign trade is also controlled by MNCs.

Besides the movements of goods, services, investments and technology, countries are connected through the movement of people between them, i.e. **migration**[1]. People usually move from one country to another in search of a better life, higher income, better jobs or better education.

Factors that have Enabled Globalisation

Technology

Rapid movement in technology has enabled the globalisation process in the following ways

- Fast improvement in technology during the last 50 years, such as improvements in transportation technology have resulted in much faster delivery of goods across long distances at lower costs.
- Information and Communication Technology has increased the speed of the communication services across the globe.
- Telecommunication facilities (telegraph, telephone, mobile phones, fax) and internet through satellite communication is used to contact one another around the world, to access information instantly and to communicate from remote areas.

An example of this is a news magazine published for readers in London, which is designed and printed in Delhi by using telecommunication facilities and internet.

Liberalisation of Foreign Trade and Foreign Investment Policy

Removal of barriers or restrictions set by the government is known as liberalisation.

Tax on imports is an example of **trade barrier**. Governments uses trade barriers to control foreign trade and to decide the types and quantities of goods allowed into the country.

After Independence, India imposed trade and investment barriers to protect domestic producers from foreign competition.

In 1950s and 1960s, India allowed imports of only essential items like machinery, ferstilisers, and petroleum. Similarly, other developed countries also protected their domestic industries during their early stages of development.

In 1991, Government of India made some major changes in its foreign investment policy. Liberalisation was one such change.

Therefore, the barries to foreign trade and foreign investment were removed to a great extent. Now goods could be easily imported and exported, and foreign companies could also set up factories and offices in India.

Steps to Attract Foreign Investment

In recent years, the central and state governments in India are taking special steps to attract foreign companies to invest in India. These are

- They have set-up industrial zones, called **Special Economic Zones (SEZs)**. SEZs have world class facilities including electricity, water, roads, transport, storage, recreational and educational facilities. Companies who set-up production units in the SEZs do not have to pay taxes for an initial period of five years.
- Government has also allowed flexibility in the labour laws to attract foreign investment.
- The companies in the organised sector have to obey certain rules that aim to protect the workers' rights.
- Instead of hiring workers on a regular basis, companies hire workers for short periods when there is intense pressure of work. This is done to reduce the cost of labour for the company.

1 **Migration** It refers to the movement of a person or people from one country, locality, place of residence, etc to another.

4.5 World Trade Organisation (WTO)

World Trade Organisation (WTO) is an organisation whose aim is to **liberalise international trade**. It was established by the initiative of developed countries.

WTO establishes rules regarding international trade, and ensures that these rules are obeyed. 160 countries of the world are currently members of the WTO.

Even though the World Trade Organisation is meant to allow free trade for all, it is seen that the developed countries still keep some trade barriers.

On the other hand, the WTO forces the developing countries to remove trade barriers. An example of this is the current debate about trade in agricultural products.

4.6 Impact of Globalisation in India

- Globalisation has resulted in more competition among producers (both local and foreign). It gives greater choice of goods to consumers with improved quality at lower prices.
- MNCs have increased their investments in India in industries such as cell phones, automobiles, electronics, soft drinks, fast food or services such as banking in urban areas. In these industries and services, new jobs have been created, and local companies supplying raw materials and services to these industries have prospered.
- Several top Indian companies have been able to benefit from the increased competition. They have invested in newer technology and production methods and raised their production standards.
- Globalisation has enabled some large Indian companies to emerge as multinationals themselves, e.g. Tata Motors (automobiles), Infosys (IT), Ranbaxy (medicines), Asian Paints (paints), Sundaram Fasteners (nuts and bolts), etc.
- Globalisation has also created new opportunities for companies providing services, particularly those involving IT.
- A number of services such as data entry, accounting, administrative tasks, engineering are now being done cheaply in countries such as India and are exported to the developed countries.

Growing Competition and Uncertain Employment

Globalisation and the pressure of competition have changed the lives of workers. With growing competition, most employers these days prefer **flexible employment**[2]. This means that workers jobs are no longer secure.

For example, in the garment export industry. Indian garment exporters try to cut their own costs by reducing labour costs, as raw material costs cannot be reduced. So, they employ workers only on a temporary basis.

Workers get very low wages and forced to do overtime to manage their expenses. Even in the organised sector, workers no longer get the protection and benefits that they were enjoyed earlier.

4.7 The Struggle for a Fair Globalisation

People with education, skill and wealth have made the best use of the new opportunities arised due to globalisation. To make it more 'fair', government can play a major role in the following ways

- It can ensure that policies such as labour laws are strictly implemented and workers get their rights.
- It can support and protect small producers from global competition and to improve their performance.
- It can negotiate with the WTO to ensure fairer rules and concessions for developing countries.
- It can use trade and investment barriers to protect the interest of domestic produce.
- It can align with other developing countries with similar interests to fight against the authority of developed countries in the WTO.

In the past few years, large campaigns and representation by people's organisations have influenced important decisions relating to trade and investments at the WTO. This has demonstrated that people can also play an important role in the struggle for fair globalisation.

Try These

1. **Give an example of foreign investment policy.**
2. **Which economic policy came into existence in 1991?**
3. **Which organisation deals with the global rules of trade between nations?**
4. **This organisation supported liberalisation in India. Identify the organisation.**

2 **Flexible Employment** Employment on a temporary basis, i.e. only as and when required. This is in contrast with permanent employment, which means employment throughout the year along with provident fund, provision for leave etc.

Mind Map

GLOBALISATION AND THE INDIAN ECONOMY

Merge or Takeover Local Companies
MNCs buy local production units or merge with local companies to expand production.

Contracts to Local Companies
MNCs in developed countries place orders with small producers

Partnership/Joint Venture
MNC merge with local producers and produce jointly.

World Trade Organisation
- It aims to liberalise International trade.
- Established rules regarding International Trade and ensures that they are followed.
- About 160 countries of the world are members of WTO.

Production Across Countries
- An MNC is a company that owns or controls production in more than one country.
- MNCs establish offices and factories in regions with low-cost labour and resources to minimise production expenses and maximise profits.

Interlinking Production Across Countries
- Money that is spent to buy assets is called Investment.
- Investments made by MNCs is called foreign Investment.

Foreign Trade and Integration of Markets
- Foreign trade helps sellers to find customers all around the world.
- It results in connecting the markets of integration of markets

Globalisation
Process of rapid integration or interconnection between countries by greater foreign investment and greater foreign trade.

Impact of Globalisation in India
- Globalisation has resulted in more competiton among both local and foreign producers.
- It has enabled some large Indian companies to emerge as multinationals themselves.
- MNCs have increased their investments in various industries in India.

Factors that have Enabled Globalisation

Technology
- Fast improvement in technology.
- Increase in the speed of communication services.
- Telecommunication facilities and internet through satellite communication.

Liberalisation of Foreign trade and Foreign Investment Policy
Removal of barriers or restrictions on foreign trade and foreign investment, set by the government, e.g. Trade barrier.

Struggle for a Fair Globalisation
- Ensure that policies such as labour laws are strictly implemented.
- Can support and protect small producers.
- Can negotiate with the WTO to ensure fairer rules and concessions for developing countries.

NCERT FOLDER

Covering Intext Questions and Exercises of NCERT

INTEXT QUESTIONS

Q.1 Would you say Ford Motors is an MNC? Why?

Ans. Ford motors is an MNC because it owns or controls its production units in many countries, with its headoffice in USA. Their production facilities are very well developed that is well supported by research and newer developments. These companies always look for newer growth opportunities and markets. Also, they have huge money and manpower resources and therefore they do not hesitate from any expansion opportunities.

Q.2 What is foreign investment? How much did Ford Motors invest in India?

Ans. Investment made by an MNC to buy assets like land, building and machinery equipment in a country other than the country of their origin is termed as foreign investment. Ford Motors invested ₹ 1,700 crore in India.

Q.3 By setting up their production plants in India, MNCs such as Ford Motors tap the advantage not only of the large markets that countries such as India provide, but also the lower costs of production. Explain the statement.

Ans. It is true that to reduce their costs and maximise their profits, MNCs generally set-up production plants where they find certain facilities. These are as follows

(i) Location close to markets.
(ii) Skilled / unskilled labour is available at a low cost.
(iii) Availability of other factors of production is there.
(iv) Government policies are favourable.

Ford Motors has done the same by setting up a large plant near Chennai, as all the above conditions were met.

Q.4 Why do you think the company wants to develop India as a base for manufacturing car components for its global operations? Discuss the following factors.
(a) Cost of labour and other resources in India.
(b) The presence of several local manufacturers who supply auto-parts to Ford Motors.
(c) Closeness to a large number of buyers in India and China.

Ans. The company wants to develop India as a base for manufacturing car components for the following reasons

(i) Cost of labour and materials is low in India, which result in more profits for the MNC.
(ii) A number of local manufacturers are supplying car components to their Chennai plant so they get resources at cheap prices.
(iii) India and its neighbour China has large number of buyers for Ford Cars.

Q.5 In what ways will the production of cars by Ford Motors in India lead to interlinking of production?

Ans. Ford Motors has taken the following steps which will lead to interlinking of production

(i) They have set-up a production plant for cars in Chennai in partnership with a local company, Mahindra and Mahindra.
(ii) They are asking the local companies of car parts for supplying parts for their cars manufactured in their production unit and are also planning for supplying these parts to their other car production units around the globe.
(iii) They are closely competing with local companies in the Indian market in selling their cars.

Q.6 In what way is an MNC different from other national companies? CBSE 2012

Ans. In the following ways, an MNC is different from other national companies

Multinational Company	National Company
It owns or controls production in more than one nation.	It owns or controls production within the country.
It sets-up offices and factories for production in regions where they can get cheap labour and other resources.	It has no such option.
Since the cost of production for an MNC is low, it can earn greater profits.	It has no such scope to earn greater profits.

Q.7 Nearly all major multinationals are American, Japanese or European, such as Nike, Coca- Cola, Pepsi, Honda, Nokia. Can you guess why?

Ans. All major multinationals are American, Japanese or European because America, Japan and European countries are developed countries. They have advanced technology, better marketing strategies and continuous product innovations that led to industrial progress. They are in advantageous position to collaborate and expand their business operations across the nations, therefore they turn as MNCs.

Q.8 What was the main channel connecting countries in the past? How is it different now?

Ans. Trade was the main channel connecting the countries in the past. Silk route connected different countries of the world; as a result extensive trade took place through this route.

Now besides trade, capital, technology, people and services are taking place all over the world.

Q.9 Distinguish between foreign trade and foreign investment.

Ans. The trade between two or more countries is termed as foreign trade. It helps in connecting the markets of different countries across the world.

On the other hand, investment made by an MNC or a financial institution in another country is termed as foreign investment.

Q.10 In recent years, China has been importing steel from India. Explain how the import of steel by China will affect.

(a) Steel companies in China.

(b) Steel companies in India.

(c) Industries buying steel for production of other industrial goods in China.

Ans. (a) Steel supply in China will improve. Steel companies in China will face a stiff challenge from Indian companies.

(b) Steel companies in India will expand their production. They will have to improve their quality, reduce the cost of production and try to capture the Chinese market.

(c) Other Chinese industries using steel will be benefitted as they will have a greater choice at competitive prices.

Q.11 How will the import of steel from India into the Chinese markets lead to integration of markets for steel in the two countries? Explain.

Ans. The import of steel from India into the Chinese markets lead to integration of markets for steel in the two countries in the following ways

- Due to imports from India, choice in the Chinese market will increase.
- Producers of steel in India will be able to sell steel not only in India but can also in the Chinese market.
- Prices of similar varieties of steel in the Indian and Chinese markets will fluctuate and tend to become equal after some time.

Q.12 What is the role of MNCs in the globalisation process?

Ans. The role of MNC in the globalisation process is that it rapidly integrates the markets by interlinking production across different countries through various ways.

Q.13 What are the various ways in which countries can be linked?

Ans. Some of the ways in which countries can be linked are

- Movement of goods between countries.
- Services being provided for one country from another country (e.g. call centres).
- Foreign investments being done by one country through companies in another country.
- Immigration of people into one country from another for working there or for study.

Q.14 Choose the correct option.

Globalisation, by connecting countries, shall result in

(a) lesser competition among producers.

(b) greater competition among producers

(c) no change in competition among producers

Ans. (b) greater competition among producers

Q.15 How is Information Technology connected with globalisation? Would globalisation have been possible without expansion of IT?

Ans. Information Technology (IT) has played an important role in globalisation. Telecommunication facilities have helped the people to connect to different corners of the world instantly. Internet has dramatically transformed the way in which business is conducted nowadays.

Except physical movement of products, every other transaction is possible through internet. It has facilitated closer interaction between different countries of the world.

Globalisation would not have been effective and profitable to the participating companies without the expansion of IT. This is because sending information about matters which require quick decision making would not have been possible without IT. In many cases, the decisions would be taken too late to be really effective.

Q.16 What do you understand by liberalisation of foreign trade?

Ans. Liberalisation means lifting up the restrictions on foreign trade. The restrictions on foreign trade is imposed by two ways. One is by imposing taxes that raises the price of imported goods and the other is by restricting the volume of goods. Liberalisation means lifting up both the restrictions so that more foreign trade takes place.

Q.17 Tax on imports is one type of trade barrier. The government could also place a limit on the number of goods that can be imported. This is known as quotas. Can you explain, using the example of Chinese toys, how quotas can be used as trade barriers? Do you think this should be used? Discuss.

Ans. In the case of Chinese toys, quotas should be used as trade barriers to a limited extent only. It should be done so that both Indian and Chinese toys compete on an equal footing in the Indian market so that it leads to a healthy competition and the quality of toys improve.

If Chinese toys were totally restricted, then in the absence of competition, Indian manufacturers will be tempted to lower their quality and increase prices.

On the other hand, if there are no quota restrictions then Indian market will be full of Chinese toys thus reducing the sales of the Indian producer leading to closure of toy industries and rise in unemployment.

Q.18 Fill in the blanks.

WTO was started at the initiative of .... countries. The aim of the WTO is to .... WTO establishes rules regarding .... for all countries and sees that .... In practice, trade between countries is not .... Developing countries like India have ...., whereas developed countries, in many cases, have continued to provide protection to their producers.

Ans. Developed, liberalise international trade, international trade, they are obeyed, free and fair, removed trade barriers.

Q.19 What do you think can be done so that trade between countries is more fair?

Ans. Trade between countries would be more fair if

- both the countries removed trade barriers and allowed the free flow of goods and services.
- both the countries let the market forces of demand and supply to decide the volume of goods that will be transacted between countries.

Q.20 In this chapter, we saw that the US government gives massive sums of money to farmers for production. At times, governments also give support to promote production of certain types of goods, such as those which are environment friendly. Discuss whether these are fair or not.

Ans. These support measures are not justified if they cover those goods which enter international market. These goods are cheaper and more in demand. Due to this, farmers in developing countries suffer as they are not able to sell their products.

Developing countries would be justified in raising trade barriers against such measures that hurt their market.

Q.21 How has competition benefitted people in India?

Ans. Competition from imported goods has benefitted people in India in the following ways

(i) Indian producers have improved their technology and quality to compete with foreign goods.

This has benefitted the buyers of the goods as well as the producers, who can now compete in the world market.

(ii) Prices of Indian goods have reduced to match those of foreign goods and so buyers have more choice of goods now.

(iii) Some Indian companies have entered into collaboration with the foreign companies and some MNCs have invested in Indian companies, thus benefitting both.

Q.22 Should more Indian companies emerge as MNCs? How would it benefit the people in the country?

Ans. Yes, if more Indian MNCs are set-up, this would not only contribute to the Indian economy, but also generate employment in the country, besides helping India to emerge as an economic super power.

Since MNCs produce on a large scale at lower costs, they earn profits. Thus, India would be able to spread its production across the globe and also dominate the international markets.

With Indian MNCs contributing to world trade, India's position will become stronger in the WTO.

Q.23 Why do governments try to attract more foreign investment?

Ans. Governments try to attract more foreign investment for the following reasons

- It helps in improving the financial condition of the people by accelerating growth of the economy.
- Foreign investments create new job opportunities in the country, thereby reducing unemployment.
- The government gains additional taxes by taxing the profits made from foreign investments.

Q.24 In Chapter 1, we saw what may be development for one may be destructive for others. The setting of SEZs has been opposed by some people in India. Find out who are these people and why are they opposing it.

Ans. Two group of people are opposing the setting up of the SEZs. These are

(i) The rural people or the tribals who live where the SEZs are being established.

They are afraid of loosing their livelihoods, that depend on the land that is being acquired for setting up the SEZs.

(ii) The group that is producing goods and services outside the SEZs similar to those proposed inside the SEZs.

They fear that the price of goods produced in the SEZs will be cheaper.

Q.25 Consider the information given below

(a) What are the ways in which Ravi's small production unit was affected by rising competition?

(b) Should producers such as Ravi stop production because their cost of production is higher compared to producers in other countries? What do you think?

Ans. (a) Ravi's small production unit was affected by rising competition in the following ways

- His customers have changed their product, as they are now manufacturing TV sets for the MNC brands, who do not use the capacitors produced by Ravi's unit.
- His production and sales have also reduced due to his capacitors being costlier than the imported variety.
- With such a small amount of production he is running into losses.

(b) Ravi should either improve the technology of his manufacturing process to compete with the imported products or try to manufacture any other product which does not have so much competition from imported products.

In both cases, he will need to make some capital investment, for which he must approach the concerned government agencies or the banks for necessary loans.

Q.26 Recent studies point out that small producers in India need three things to compete better in the market

(a) better roads, power, water, raw materials, marketing and information network.

(b) improvements and modernisation of technology.

(c) timely availability of credit at reasonable interest rates.

(i) Can you explain how these three things would help Indian producers?

(ii) Do you think MNCs will be interested in investing in these? Why?

(iii) Do you think the government has a role in making these facilities available? Why?

(iv) Can you think of any other step that the government could take? Discuss.

Ans. (i) The three things in the following will help the Indian producers to compete better in the market in the following ways

- Better infrastructure will help them to work more efficiently and timely so that they can compete with foreign companies in the market.
- Better technology will help the producers to create better quality products efficiently at cheaper rates.
- Better finance will enable them to run their production smoothly without any delays, thus improving their competitiveness.

(ii) MNCs will not be interested in investing in these because it will develop the infrastructure and will give a chance to the Indian producers to compete.

(iii) Government must make these facilities available, as developing infrastructure is important responsibility of the government.

(iv) Government can take many other steps to better facilitate matters by reducing the procedures and remove the corruption which is rampant in their offices.

Further, they can provide single-window clearance for people wanting to set up production to reduce hassles.

Q.27 How has the pressure of global competition affected the employment practices in the garment industry, particularly in the context of Indian exporters supplying to MNCs in Europe and America?

Ans. The pressure of global competition has led to a shift in employment practices in the garment industry, where employers prefer flexible arrangements. In order to secure orders from large MNCs seeking the cheapest goods, Indian garment exporters attempt to cut costs, especially in labour.

This has resulted in a shift from permanent to temporary employment, with workers facing long hours, night shifts and low wages. While MNCs enjoy substantial profits, workers are often denied fair benefits due to the intense competition driven by globalisation.

Q.28 What can be done by each of the following so that the workers can get a fair share of benefits brought by globalisation?

(a) Government

(b) Employers at the exporting factories

(c) MNCs

(d) Workers

Ans. (a) Government can set rules and regulations implemented for free and fair globalisation.

(b) Employers can invest in new technology which will help them in bringing down their cost of production.

(c) MNCs may offer relief to workers who have lost their jobs due to globalisation, by giving financial aid. This will help them till they find another job.

(d) Workers will have to change their mindset and will have to see themselves as equal partners with the management in pursuit of better productivity.

Q.29 One of the present debates in India is whether companies should have flexible policies for employment. Based on what you have read in the chapter, summarise the point of view of the employers and workers.

Ans. **Point of View of Employers** They prefer to employ workers on flexible basis, i.e. employ them as and when required. This means the workers are employed on temporary basis. In case, extra work is there for a short period, i.e. 'in season', the workers can be asked to do overtime and paid extra wages.

Point of View of Workers They always prefer permanent employment so that they can have a regular income to look after their families. Along with wages, workers want other benefits like medical, PF, etc.

EXERCISE

Q.1 What do you understand by globalisation? Explain in your own words.

Ans. Globalisation is the process of rapid integration or interconnection between countries by foreign investment and foreign trade. In this process, goods and services are produced and marketed throughout the world. More and more goods, services, investments and technology move between countries. Countries also get connected by movement of people, who work in countries other than their own.

Q.2 What were the reasons for putting barriers to foreign trade and foreign investment by the Indian Government? Why did it wish to remove these barriers.

Ans. Barriers to foreign trade and investment were put by the Indian government to protect domestic producers from foreign competition, especially when Indian industries had just begun to come up in the 1950s and 1960s.

The Indian Government wished to remove barriers because

- domestic producers were now ready to compete with foreign industries.
- foreign competition would improve the quality of goods produced by Indian industries.

Q.3 How would flexibility in labour laws help companies?

Ans. Flexibility in labour laws help companies in being competitive in the following ways

- Instead of hiring workers on a regular or permanent basis, companies hire workers flexibly for short periods when there is intense pressure of work.
- The companies negotiate wages and terminate employment, depending on market conditions. This reduces company's cost and increases its profit.

Q.4 What are the various ways in which MNCs set-up or control or produce in other countries?

Ans. The various ways in which MNCs set-up or control or produce in other countries are

- By buying up a local production company.
- By placing orders for production with small producers, i.e. contract manufacturing.
- By setting up a partnership (joint venture) with a local company.
- By setting up their wholly owned subsidiary in the other country.
- By licensing or franchising their brand to a local company.

Q.5 Why do developed countries want developing countries to liberalise their trade and investment? What do you think should the developing countries demand in return?

Ans. Developed countries want developing countries to liberalise their trade and investment so that the MNCs of the developed countries can set-up their manufacturing centres in developing nations. This greatly reduces their manufacturing costs and increases their profits.

In my opinion, the developing countries should demand, in return, strict enforcement of labour laws so that they hire skilled and unskilled people of the developing countries properly thereby reducing unemployment.

Q.6 "The impact of globalisation has not been uniform." Explain this statement.

Ans. The impact of globalisation has not been uniform. Different countries, regions and groups of people have experienced globalisation differently. This can be explained through the following points

- Globalisation has increased the sale of consumer goods which are demanded by only a small section of people in developing countries like cell phone, automobile, soft drinks. Large section is still deprived of basic necessities.
- Globalisation increases the concentration of economic power and leads to inequalities. It is mainly beneficial to large capitalists, industries and large companies like google. The small scale producers and workers have suffered as a result of rising competition.
- Globalisation has changed the nature of employment as now workers are hired on temporary basis and their jobs are no longer secure.

Q.7 How has liberalisation of trade and investment policies helped the globalisation process?

Ans. Liberalisation of trade and investment policies has helped in Globalisation in the following ways

- This has helped in the import and export of goods. This means that goods can be exported and imported easily and also foreign companies could set up factories and offices here.
- Larger foreign investment and larger foreign trade have led to greater integration of production and markets across countries. As a result, more and more companies are coming closer to each other due to MNCs.
- Latest technology such as ICT is spread throughout the world due to liberalisation.

Q.8 How does foreign trade lead to integration of markets across countries? Explain with an example other than those given here.

Or **"Globalisation is the process of rapid integration or interconnection between countries." Explain the statement with example.** **CBSE 2024**

Ans. Foreign trade has led to the integration of markets across the countries as the producers are now able to export their goods to the markets of other countries.

The choices of the buyers have also expanded as now they get to choose products manufactured by not only the domestic companies but also by the foreign companies. Because of the competition, the goods have also become cheaper and of better quality. Producers from different countries now compete with each other.

For example, the Indian markets are flooded with designer imported handbags of famous foreign brands. This has benefitted the consumers as large varieties of handbags are now available in India at competitive prices. It has also encouraged domestic producers to improve their quality.

Q.9 Globalisation will continue in the future. Can you imagine what the world would be like twenty years from now? Give reasons for your answer.

Ans. Globalisation will continue in the future. Twenty years from now, the world would undergo a positive change with the features of healthy competition, improved productive efficiency, increased volume of output, income and employment, better living standards, greater availability of information and modern technology. These are going to happen because

- Human resources, both quantity wise and quality wise will be available globally.
- Countries will have a broad resource and industrial base by the setting up of MNCs.
- Domestic markets of all major countries will experience growth as there be better availability of goods.

Q.10 Supposing you find two people arguing: One is saying globalisation has hurt our country's development. The other is telling, globalisation is helping India develop. How would you respond to these arguments?

Ans. I will say that globalisation has benefitted India in the following ways

- Increase in the volume of trade in goods and services.
- More productive efficiency, less wastage of resources.
- Increased volume of output, income and employment.

Whatever may be the fears of globalisation, I feel that it has now become a process which is irreversible and thus, we must be ready to accept globalisation and maximise our economic gains from the world market.

Q.11 Fill in the blanks.

Indian buyers have a greater choice of goods than they did two decades back. This is closely associated with the process of (i)...... . Markets in India are selling goods produced in many other countries. This means there is increasing (ii) .... with other countries.

Moreover, the rising number of brands that we see in the markets might be produced by MNCs in India. MNCs are investing in India because (iii) .... While consumers have more choices in the market, the effect of rising (iv) .... and (v) .... has meant greater (vi) .... among the producers.

Ans. (i) globalisation (ii) trade

(iii) of the cheaper production costs (iv) demand

(v) purchasing power

(vi) competition

Q.12 Match the following.

(i) MNCs buy at cheap rates from small producers	(a) Automobiles
(ii) Quotas and taxes on imports are used to regulate trade	(b) Garments, footwear, sport items
(iii) Indian companies who have invested abroad	(c) Call centres
(iv) IT has helped in spreading of production of services	(d) Tata Motors, Infosys, Ranbaxy
(v) Several MNCs have invested in setting up factories in India for production	(e) Trade barriers

Ans. (i) (b), (ii) (e), (iii) (d), (iv) (c), (v) (a)

Q.13 Choose the most appropriate option.

(a) **The past two decades of globalisation has seen rapid movements in**

(i) goods, services and people between countries.

(ii) goods,services and investments between countries.

(iii) goods, investments and people between countries.

(b) The most common route for investments by MNCs in countries around the world is to
(i) set-up new factories.
(ii) buy existing local companies.
(iii) form partnerships with local companies.

(c) Globalisation has led to improvement in living conditions
(i) of all the people
(ii) of people in the developed countries
(iii) of workers in the developing countries
(iv) None of the above

Ans. (a) (ii), (b) (ii), (c) (iv)

REVIEW EXERCISE | Including Competency Based Questions

Part I

Multiple Choice Questions (MCQs)

1. The reason due to which multinational companies set up their branches in other countries is
(a) cheap labour and resources
(b) welfare motive
(c) to generate employment
(d) to generate income

2. When an MNC opens its company in India then it can be termed as
(a) Foreign trade (b) Foreign link
(c) Foreign investment (d) Foreign migration

3. Foreign trade gives more number of choices for
(a) producers (b) sellers
(c) buyers (d) government

4. In the competition between Indian and Chinese toys in Indian markets, China proved better because of
(a) low price and variety
(b) good shape
(c) trade relations
(d) high price and quality

5. Which one of the following is a significant aspect of globalisation? CBSE 2024
(a) Uniform Culture (b) Environmental Support
(c) Support Domestic Market (d) Access to New Markets

6. In which one of the following ways has information and communication technology stimulated the 'globalisation' access the most ? CBSE 2023
(a) Access foods across countries.
(b) Access raw material across countries.
(c) Access services across countries.
(d) Access information instantly across countries.

7. A situation in which all the countries get equal benefits of foreign trade equally is known as
(a) Privatisation
(b) Fair globalisation
(c) Liberalisation
(d) Equal globalisation

8. The result of greater foreign investment and greater foreign trade has been .... across countries. Find the correct option from below. CBSE SQP 2024-25
(a) greater bifurcation of production and markets
(b) greater segregation of production and markets
(c) greater differentiation of production and markets
(d) greater integration of production and markets

9. Find the correct option.
(a) Expansion through MNCs – Tata, Ranbaxy
(b) Liberalisation – MNCs free to import
(c) 1991 Policy – Tightening of trade barriers
(d) Spreading out – Design in India, production in China

10. Identify the organisation with the help of given features.
- Its main function is to ensure that trade flows as smoothly, predictably and as freely as possible.
- It supported the liberalisation of foreign trade and investment in India.
- It was started at the initiative of the developed countries.
- Its objective is to liberalise international trade and ensure that its members obey its rules.

Options
(a) WTO (b) WHO
(c) FAO (d) IMF

11. Aparna, an entrepreneur based in Maharashtra, plans to expand her textile business by setting up production units in different countries. She aims to take advantage of cheaper labour and resources available globally to increase her profit margins. She has observed the impact of globalisation on markets and intends to leverage these opportunities.

Which of the following outcomes is most likely to result from Aparna's initiative in setting up production units in multiple countries? **Competency Based**

(a) Creation of new job opportunities and economic growth in the regions of the production units.
(b) Escalation of trade barriers between countries affecting the flow of goods and services.
(c) Decrease in the quality of the products due to outsourcing production to different countries.
(d) Reduction in local production and a decline in the profitability of small-scale textile businesses within India.

12. Despite the challenges posed by globalisation, certain segments of society have benefitted while others have faced adversities. Which of the following strategies aligns most closely with the advocated approach for a fairer globalisation as per the discussion? **Competency Based**

(a) Promoting flexibility in employment to reduce labour costs.
(b) Ensuring strict adherence to labour laws and regulations.
(c) Implementing trade barriers to restrict foreign competition.
(d) Encouraging temporary employment contracts to meet production demands.

13. Read the following statements for stimulating the process of globalisation and choose the correct options: **CBSE 2025**

I. Government reduces trade barriers.
II. Government reduces competition among producers.
III. Government reduces import and export taxes.
IV. Government removes restrictions on foreign investment.

Options

(a) Only I, II and III are correct.
(b) Only II, III and IV are correct.
(c) Only I, III and IV are correct.
(d) Only I, II and IV are correct.

14. Mr X is a small-scale manufacturer of traditional handcrafted items. He has been in business for several years, selling his products locally. However, in recent times, due to globalisation, cheaper machine-made products from other countries have flooded the market. Mr X is finding it increasingly challenging to compete with these cheaper imports.

Which of the following statements best describe the impact of globalisation on Mr X's business? **Competency Based**

(a) Mr X's business has expanded globally due to increased demand for traditional handcrafted items.
(b) Globalisation has helped Mr. X to reduce production costs and improve the quality of his products.
(c) Mr X faces stiff competition from cheaper machine-made imports, impacting his local sales.
(d) Mr X's business has remained unaffected by globalisation as he caters to a niche market.

15. Which of the following factors significantly contribute to the process of globalisation? Select the correct options. **CBSE SQP 2024-25**

(i) Expansion of Multinational Corporations (MNCs).
(ii) Advancements in information and communication technology.
(iii) Nationalisation and trade barriers.
(iv) Cross-border movement of people for jobs and education.

Options

(a) Statements (i) and (ii) are appropriate
(b) Statements (i), (ii) and (iii) are appropriate
(c) Statements (ii), (iii) and (iv) are appropriate
(d) Only statement (iii) is appropriate

16. 35 year old sunil works from 8 AM to 8 PM all seven days of the week in a garment exporter firm. He works as a contract labour. His employer do not give him any other facility. He knows that he is employed just for a few months of the year but he continues to work as he has no other option.

Analyse the above information, considering one of the following correct option.

(a) MNCs creating job opportunities
(b) Workers jobs no longer secure
(c) People denied fair share of benefits
(d) Ill effects of globalisation

17. Identify the reason as to why MNC's would like to collaborate with India in producing goods. Choose from the appropriate statements among the following options: **CBSE Additional SQP 2023-24**

I. India has highly skilled engineers who can understand the technical aspects of production.
II. It also has educated English speaking youth who can provide customer care services. This means 50-60 percent cost savings for the MNC.
III. It's the cheapest manufacturing location.
IV. It's close to the markets in the US and Europe.

Options

(a) Statements I and II are appropriate.
(b) Statements I, II and III are appropriate.
(c) All the statements are appropriate.
(d) Only statement IV is appropriate.

18. Consider the statements given below and choose the correct answer.

Statement I Globalisation primarily involves the integration of countries through foreign trade and foreign investments facilitated by multinational corporations (MNCs).

Statement II Special Economic Zones (SEZs) in India do not offer any tax benefits or incentives to companies establishing production units within their boundaries. **CBSE Additional SQP 2023-24**

Options

(a) Statement I is correct and statement II is incorrect
(b) Statement I is incorrect and statement II is correct
(c) Both statements I and II are incorrect
(d) Both statements I and II are correct

19. Evaluate the impacts of opening foreign trade on the global economy by identifying the appropriate statements among the following options **CBSE Additional SQP 2023-24**

(i) The choice of goods in the markets increase.
(ii) Producers from two countries closely compete against each other despite the distance between their locations.
(iii) Foreign trade thus results in connecting the markets or integration of markets in different countries.
(iv) The quality of the product is always good.

Options

(a) Statements (i) and (ii) are appropriate.
(b) Statements (i), (ii) and (iii) are appropriate.
(c) All the statements are appropriate.
(d) Only statement (iv) is appropriate.

20. The process of integration between different countries is called as .... **CBSE Additional SQP 2023-24**

(a) Privatisation (b) Globalisation
(c) Liberalisation (d) Competition

Answers

1. (a)	2. (c)	3. (c)	4. (a)	5. (d)
6. (d)	7. (b)	8. (d)	9. (d)	10. (a)
11. (a)	12. (b)	13. (c)	14. (c)	15. (b)
16. (d)	17. (b)	18. (a)	19. (b)	20. (b)

Assertion-Reason

1. Assertion (A) Large MNCs in the garment industry look for cheapest goods from India as Indian exporters provide very cheap raw materials.

Reason (R) Since cost of raw materials cannot be reduced, Indian exporters cut labour costs and reduce wages in order to cut down their production cost.

Codes

(a) Both A and R are true and R is the correct explanation of A
(b) Both A and R are true, but R is not the correct explanation of A
(c) A is true, but R is false
(d) A is false, but R is true

2. Assertion (A) Globalisation led to increased competition among producers, providing consumers with a greater choice of goods at improved quality and lower prices.

Reason (R) Multinational Corporations (MNCs) invest in various industries, driving innovation and technological advancements, ultimately benefitting consumers.

Codes

(a) Both A and R are true and R is the correct explanation of A
(b) Both A and R are true, but R is not the correct explanation of A
(c) A is true, but R is false
(d) A is false, but R is true

3. Assertion (A) Liberalisation in India, initiated in 1996, aimed to improve the competitiveness of domestic producers by reducing barriers to foreign trade and investment.

Reason (R) The removal of trade barriers allowed businesses greater freedom in making import and export decisions, enhancing their adaptability to global markets.

Codes

(a) Both A and R are true and R is the correct explanation of A
(b) Both A and R are true, but R is not the correct explanation of A
(c) A is true, but R is false
(d) A is false, but R is true

4. Assertion (A) Foreign investment by Multinational Corporations (MNCs) often leads to increased employment opportunities in underdeveloped countries.

Reason (R) MNCs set up production units in regions with high paid labour and resources, contributing to job creation and economic growth in those areas.

Codes

(a) Both A and R are true and R is the correct explanation of A
(b) Both A and R are true, but R is not the correct explanation of A
(c) A is true, but R is false
(d) A is false, but R is true

5. **Assertion** (A) Globalisation has posed challenges to small-scale producers, affecting their production significantly due to increased competition from larger entities.

Reason (R) The emergence of Multinational Corporations (MNCs) and the liberalisation of trade have disproportionately impacted small-scale industries in India.

Codes

(a) Both A and R are true and R is the correct explanation of A
(b) Both A and R are true, but R is not the correct explanation of A
(c) A is true, but R is false
(d) A is false, but R is true

Ans. 1. (b) Both A and R are true, but R is not the correct explanation of A

2. (a) Both A and R are true and R is the correct explanation of A

3. (d) A is false, but R is true

4. (c) A is true, but R is false

5. (a) Both A and R are true and R is the correct explanation of A

Picture Based Question

1. **The image shows a shipping port with multiple cranes and containers. This is an example of how globalisation has affected the Indian economy by**

CBSE Additional SQP 2023-24

(a) increasing the demand for skilled workers in the port sector
(b) reducing the barriers to trade and facilitating the movement of goods
(c) enhancing the competitiveness of Indian products in the global market
(d) All of the above

Ans. (d) All of the above

Case Based Question

1. **Read the passage given below and answer the questions that follow.**

Tax on imports is an example of trade barrier. It is called a barrier because some restriction has been set up. Governments can use trade barriers to increase or decrease (regulate) foreign trade and to decide what kinds of goods and how much of each, should come into the country. The Indian government, after Independence, had put barriers to foreign trade and foreign investment. This was considered necessary to protect the producers within the country from foreign competition. Industries were just coming up in the 1950s and 1960s, and competition from imports at that stage would not have allowed these industries to come up. Thus, India allowed imports of only essential items such as machinery, fertilisers, petroleum etc. Note that all developed countries, during the early stages of development, have given protection, to domestic producers through a variety of means.

(i) Which of the following is true regarding trade barriers?

(a) Trade barriers encourage unrestricted foreign trade for all types of goods.
(b) Governments implement trade barriers to regulate the inflow and outflow of goods in a country.
(c) Trade barriers are solely intended to promote foreign competition within a nation.
(d) Trade barriers are primarily established to hinder domestic production.

(ii) Why did the Indian government impose barriers to foreign trade and investment after Independence?

(a) To encourage unrestricted competition from foreign markets for local producers.
(b) To safeguard domestic producers from foreign competition during the initial stages of industrial growth.
(c) To limit the production of essential items such as machinery, fertilisers, and petroleum.
(d) To establish trade agreements with developed countries for essential imports.

(iii) What was the primary reason India restricted imports to only essential items like machinery, fertilisers, and petroleum during the 1950s and 1960s?

(a) To promote unrestricted growth of industries within the country.
(b) To prevent any foreign goods from entering the Indian market.
(c) To allow ample space for competition among domestic industries.
(d) To facilitate the development of nascent industries without foreign competition.

(iv) **What was the general approach adopted by most developed countries during their early stages of development concerning domestic producers and foreign competition?**
(a) Providing no protection to domestic producers to encourage global competitiveness.
(b) Employing trade barriers to eliminate foreign competition completely.
(c) Offering complete access to their markets for foreign goods.
(d) Granting protection to domestic producers through various means during initial developmental stages.

Ans. (i) (b) Governments implement trade barriers to regulate the inflow and outflow of goods in a country.
(ii) (b) To safeguard domestic producers from foreign competition during the initial stages of industrial growth.
(iii) (d) To facilitate the development of nascent industries without foreign competition.
(iv) (d) Granting protection to domestic producers through various means during initial developmental stages.

Part II

Very Short Answer Type Questions

1. What are the features of an MNC?

Ans. The features of an MNC are
(i) It owns production units in more than one nation.
(ii) It employs labour from different countries in different production units.

2. What is the benefit of joint production between a local company and an MNC?

Ans. Joint production helps local company in getting the latest technology brought by MNCs, thus improving the value of the product.

3. Why do MNCs set-up their offices and factories in those regions where they get cheap labour and other resources?

Ans. MNCs set-up their offices and factories in regions where they get cheap labour and other resources to minimise cost of production and maximise profit earnings

4. What leads to availability of greater choice of goods in the market for consumers?

Ans. A consumer gets greater choices of goods because of entry of MNCs, increase in foreign trade and free trade regulated by international organisation.

5. Name any two large Indian companies that emerged as multinational companies.

Ans. Infosys and Tata Motors are two large Indian companies that emerged as multinational companies.

6. What is the basic function of foreign trade?

Ans. Foreign trade creates an opportunity for the producers to reach beyond the domestic markets. Producers can sell their produce not only in markets located within the country but can also compete in markets located in other countries of the world.

Similarly, for the buyers, imports of goods produced in another country is one way of expanding the choice of goods beyond what is domestically produced.

7. How foreign investment is differentiated from investment?

Ans. The money that is used to set up industries, buy assets, merge with companies based in foreign land is called foreign investment, while investment is simply the buying of assets, land, building, etc.

8. Who can play a major role in the achievement of fair globalisation?

Ans. Governments of respective countries can play a major role in achieving fair globalisation.

9. What are the impacts of globalisation on India?

Ans. The impacts of globalisation is that, although it has created a lot of jobs but labour laws are not implemented properly, workers are denied their rights and its benefits have not been shared equally.

10. The latest models of a digital camera, a tab or I-pad are available in India now. How is this possible?

Ans. The latest models of a digital camera, a tab or I-pad are available in India. This is possible through globalisation that has made foreign trade of goods and services easier.

11. 'Kashish Garments' bagged a huge order of supplying jute fabric to US based MNC. To reduce its cost of production, it hired workers only on temporary basis. Which aspect of globalisation it shows? Competency Based

Ans. It shows negative aspect of globalisation as the benefits of foreign trade is not equally shared. The workers do not receive any benefit and major profit is shared between the MNC and the exporting company.

12. How did the process of liberalisation initiated in India in the 1990s promote globalisation? Explain. CBSE 2025

Ans. In the 1990s, Indian opened up its economy by removing trade barriers, allowing foreign companies to invest and set up businesses. This led to more imports, exports and foreign investment. Advances in technology made global communication faster, helping India connect more with the world economy.

13. **Analyse the contribution of communication technology on globalisation.**

Or **How did information and communication technology promote the process of globalisation? Explain.** **CBSE 2025**

Ans. Communication technology has provided fast means of communication through which information can be send, received or processed at a very rapid pace. This has linked the world and facilitated globalisation.

14. **What is meant by trade barrier? Give one example.**

Ans. Trade barriers are restrictions imposed on import and export of goods. An example of trade barrier is import duty.

15. **A Japanese company sells mobile phones which is not only cheap but of better quality. What should the Indian government do to protect domestic producers?** **Competency Based**

Ans. The Indian government can impose import taxes on the mobile phones of that country. In this way, the prices will rise making the domestic mobile phones cheaper.

Short Answer Type Questions

1. **Why had the Indian government put barriers to foreign trade and foreign investments after independence? Analyse the reason.**

Ans. Indian government put barriers to foreign trade after independence because of the following reasons

- To protect the domestic producers within the country from foreign competition in the form of imports.
- To encourage more production of goods so that more industries can be started.
- During 1950s and 1960s, Indian industries were just coming up, they were not prepared to face challenges from foreign countries.

2. **How are local companies benefitted by collaborating with multinational companies? Explain with examples.**

Ans. The local companies benefitted by collaborating with multinational companies in the following ways

(i) Local companies get additional investments, to buy new machines for faster production.

(ii) Local companies get the latest technology for production.

(iii) By more production, local companies earn greater profits.

3. **What are the various ways in which MNCs set up or control production in other countries.**

Or **Explain by giving examples that MNCs are spreading their production in different ways.**

Ans. The way in which MNCs control or spread their production are

- **By Buying Local Companies** Large MNCs buy companies that are operating locally. By doing this, they get a good customer base and the local company gets latest technology. For example, Cargill Foods (MNC) merged with Parakh Foods (local).
- **By Joint Ventures** MNCs set-up production units jointly with any company that may be operating in a country. By doing this, MNCs not only increase their production but also get a vast market. For example, Ford Motors set up automobile plant in collaboration with Mahindra and Mahindra.
- **By Placing Orders with Small Producers** MNCs place orders for their products with small producers in developing countries where the resources are cheap. Then the MNCs sell those products under their own brand. Ex Garments, footwear, jeans, footballs, etc.

4. **List the factors that encourage the MNCs to set up their production units at a place.**

Or **Why do multinational corporations set up their offices and factories in certain areas only?**

Ans. The factors that promote the setting up of MNCs or the reason for setting up MNCs at a certain place are as follows

- Availability of skilled and unskilled labour
- Availability of raw materials at cheap prices
- Well developed infrastructure like roads and railways
- Liberalised governmental policies
- Closeness to markets
- Safe environment

5. **What is investment? Name the companies which make foreign investment. Write any two benefits which a local company expects from joint production with a Multinational company.**

Ans. The money that is spent to buy assets such as land, building, machines and other equipments is called investment.

The companies which make foreign investment in India are Ford Motors, Nike, Coca-Cola, Pepsi, Honda, Nokia, Tata Motors, Infosys, Ranbaxy, Asian Paints, etc.

A local company expects the following benefits from joint production with a multinational company

(i) To provide money for additional investments, like buying new machines for faster production.

(ii) To bring with them the latest technology for production.

6. **'Barriers on foreign trade and foreign investment were removed to a large extent in India since 1991; Justify the statement.**

Or **Why did the Indian Government remove barriers to a large extent on foreign trade and foreign investment?**

Ans. In 1991, the Government of India liberalised its policy and felt that Indian producers must compete with producers around the world.

The Government had an opinion that trade competition would improve the performance of the local producers within the country since they will be forced to improve their quality.

Another reason was the economic crises in India in 1990-91 and support of WTO and IMF led the government to remove trade barriers. Thus, Indian Government removed barriers to a large extent on foreign trade and foreign investment.

7. How does Government attract foreign investment? Explain different ways.

Or **Examine the steps taken by the Central and State governments to attract foreign companies to invest in India.** **CBSE Term II 2022**

Ans. Government attracts foreign investment in the followings ways

- Special Economic Zones have been set up to have world-class facilities such as cheap electricity, roads, transport, storage, etc.
- The companies setting their units in SEZs are exempted to pay tax for initial period of five years which increases their profit.
- Labour laws are made flexible in SEZs. This has attracted foreign investment.

8. How our markets been transformed in recent years. Explain with current examples.

Or **Assess any three advantages of globalisation.**

Ans. After the advent of globalisation many changes have occurred in the Indian markets. The various transformation in Indian market in recent years are

- There is availability of wide range of goods and services.
- Products are of better quality.
- Good quality products available at low costs.
- We can easily avail the latest products with advance technology, e.g. digital cameras, mobile phones, etc. These products are affordable as well as accessible.

9. "Technology has stimulated the globalisation process." Support the statement with examples. **Competency Based**

Or How did imporvement in transportation technology stimulate the globalisation process? Explain.

Ans. Rapid improvement in technology has been playing a key role in encouraging the globalisation process in the following ways

- Improvements in transportation technology, e.g. container manufacturing and air transport has made faster delivery of goods across long distances at lower costs.
- There have been rapid developments in information technology, e.g. computer, internet, etc. They have made easy access to information around the world thus stimulating globalisation.
- Rapid development in means of communication are used to contact one another which have established trade links around the world.

Thus, it can be said that technology has stimulated the globalisation process.

10. "The development process of India has experienced transformation due to the significant influence of Information Technology (IT) and Electronic Industry." Explain the statement with examples. **CBSE 2024**

Ans. The development process of India has experienced transformation due to the significant influence of the IT and Electronic industry.

Following examples support the statements

- **Economic Growth** The IT and electronic industry in India has boosted the economy by bringing in lots of money and creating many jobs.
- **Technological Innovation** India's IT industry is a hub for new ideas and inventions in technology. Companies create software, build smartphones, and make apps that help people do things easier and faster.India's UPI system is the fastest and reliable system.
- **Digital Transformation** Services like online shopping, mobile payments and government services have all been made easier and more accessible through technology developed in India.

11. Explain the functions and importance of World Trade Organisation (WTO).

Ans. The following points state functions and importance of WTO

- WTO deals with regulation of trade between participating countries.
- It provides a forum for negotiation and for setting disputes.
- It is also a centre of economic research and analysis.
- It is an organisation that intends to supervise and liberalise international trade.
- It oversees the implementation, administration and operations of the covered agreements.

12. "Globalisation has been advantageous to consumers as well as to producers." Support the statement with suitable examples. **Competency Based**

Ans. Globalisation has benefitted the producers and the consumers in the following ways

- Globalisation has led to an intense increase in industrial competition. As a result, producers are competing over each other to provide better and cheaper services to the consumers. This has also resulted in reduction in the prices.
- With the initiation of globalisation, producers now have relatively free access to international markets, Also, they can now avail more easily of the credit facilities forwarded in terms of capital and technology. This is illustrated by the example of the electronics goods and garments industry.
- Consumers have more choice of goods and services as compared to earlier times specially in modern digital technological equipments like cell phones cameras, etc.

13. What are Special Economic Zones? Why have they been set up?

Or Explain the facilities available in SEZ that are developed by central and state governments to attract foreign Investment.

Ans. SEZs are industrial zones set up by the government to promote the establishment of MNCs.

The facilities available in SEZ are

- SEZ are provided with world class facilities like electricity, water, roads, transport, storage, recreational and educational facilities.
- Companies operating in SEZ do not have to pay taxes for five years.
- Government has allowed flexibility in the labour laws to attract MNCs.

14. "Fair globalisation would create opportunities for all and also ensure that benefits of globalisation are shared better". Support the statement. **Competency Based**

Or How can the government of India play a major role to make globalisation more fair? Explain with examples.

Ans. The statement points to the fact that the government can work for the cause of fair globalisation through the following ways

(i) By framing policies that protect the interests of not only the rich and powerful but also the weaker sections of the society.

(ii) By supporting small producers so that they can compete with large manufacturers.

(iii) By ensuring that labour laws are properly implemented and workers get their rights.

(iv) By using trade and investment barriers and negotiating for fairer rules at the WTO.

15. Read the statements below regarding the impact of Globalisation on the Indian economy:

Statement 1 Since the implementation of liberalisation in 1991, India has witnessed a surge in multinational companies investing in various sectors such as technology, automotive, and services, leading to economic growth and job creation.

Statement 2 Despite its benefits, globalisation has also resulted in increased competition, affecting small-scale industries like local toy manufacturers, leading to a decline in their production and market share.

Explain what these statements, S1 and S2, reflect about the effects of globalisation on India's economy. **Competency Based**

Ans. Statement 1 portrays the positive outcomes of liberalisation post-1991, highlighting increased foreign investments from multinational companies across industries, fostering economic expansion and employment generation.

Conversely, statement 2 emphasises the negative side, referring to increased competition due to globalisation which adversely impacted small-scale sectors like local toy manufacturing, resulting in decreased production and market presence.

Collectively, these statements signify the dual impact of globalisation, showcasing both the growth opportunities and challenges faced by diverse sectors within the Indian economy.

Long Answer Type Questions

1. Why do people generally move from one country to another? Why has there been slow movement of people between countries in the past few decades? Explain.

Ans. Due to following reasons people move from one country to another

- People generally move from one country to another in search of better living standard.
- They move from one country to another in search of better jobs.
- They also move for the purpose of better education.

Due to following reasons there has been slow movement of people during past few decades

- In the past few decades, there has not been much increase in the movement of people between countries due to various trade restrictions.
- Information and communication technology was not so well developed. This restricted movement of information.

2. "MNCs often opt for foreign collaborations to expand and diversify. But their foreign collaborations have given rise to growth of monopolies and concentration of power in few hands". Comment. **Competency Based**

Ans. Foreign collaboration give rise to monopolies that is true and entry of MNCs in a domestic market may prove harmful for small-scale producers who are not able to compete with them. MNCs buy up local companies. The most common route for MNCs investment is to buy up local companies and then to expand production. MNCs with huge wealth can quite easily do so.

The large MNCs have tremendous power to determine price, quality and labour conditions for the small producers of other countries.

The small industries in India employ the largest number of workers in the country next only to agriculture. Several of these units have shut down due to tough competition by MNCs. As a result, many workers became jobless.

These days most employers prefers to employ workers flexibly. So, the workers' jobs are no longer secure.

Thus, it can be concluded that MNCs often opt for foreign collaborations to expand and diversify.

3. Analyse the importance of multinational companies in the globalisation process.

Ans. Importance of MNCs can be analysed through the following points

- MNCs by spreading the production, generate employment opportunities in underdeveloped/less developed countries.
- MNCs bring latest technology of production which is very helpful in the growth of developing countries.
- Due to MNCs, local producers and manufacturers make more quality products which create fair competition in the market.

This competition gives more choices to consumers to opt the best products at reasonable prices.

- Government establishes SEZ to attract MNCs for investment. This results in development of the entire region where SEZ is established.
- MNCs have contributed a lot in the growth of developed countries and both have progressed side by side. This has been an evolutionary development and, therefore, there are now strong institutions, including legislating bodies, regulatory agencies, judicial system, and consumer societies, to check and maintain the balance from within.

4. How do we feel the impact of globalisation on our daily life? Explain with examples.

Or "The impact of globalisation has not been uniform." Explain the statement with suitable examples.

Ans. We can feel the impact of globalisation on our daily life in following ways

- It has provided huge market where we can buy and sell things produced in any part of the world. For example, there are many international brands operating worldwide. These include McDonald's, Nestle, Gillete, Toyota, etc.
- With wide use of internet and other kinds of information technology, it has become much easier and faster to share information worldwide.
- The growth rate of the economy has gone up with the increase in foreign investment and foreign technology in India.
- Globalisation in some ways has provided very high salary benefits to skilled people. However, in other ways, it has made the provision of flexible employment also.
- The quality of certain products and the availability of certain services have improved due to globalisation like electronic goods and customer care service.

5. Examine five factors to promote the process of globalisation. CBSE 2024

Or What stimulated the process of globalisation in India?

Or Explain the factors which facilitate globalisation in India. CBSE Term II 2022

Ans. The factors which have enabled or promoted the process of globalisation in India are

- Improvements in technology and technical innovations have made globalisation possible.
- For example, in transportation technology, containers are now used for the transportation of goods. This has led to huge reduction in cost. Air transport has speed up the transportation of goods.
- Improvements in telecommunication facilities around the world and internet enables us to send instant electronic mail and talk across the world at negligible costs. It is an important factor of globalisation.
- The Government of India has removed barriers or restrictions to trade which were set earlier. This step has enabled goods and services to be exported and imported easily.
- Multinationals have been allowed to set-up factories and offices in India. Due to this, there is greater integration of production and markets across countries.

6. Explain four ways in which 'globalisation' and 'the pressure of competition' have changed the lives of workers substantially.

Or Globalisation has created problems for large number of small producers and workers. Justify the statement.

Ans. The lives of workers have been changed by globalisation in the following ways

(i) Workers have to work long hours in potentially hazardous conditions at low wages as companies always try to save their costs.

(ii) Workers face an uncertain employment. Casual workers are hired on contract when demand is high and laid off when demand is low.

(iii) MNCs are prone to shift their centres of production in accordance with the benefits they receive from the government.
Thus, when a centre shifts, either the workers are transferred or laid off.

(iv) Many Indian companies have closed down due to competition from MNCs, rendering their workers jobless.

(v) Globalisation has created the problem of flexible employment and temporary employment in many countries.

7. In your opinion, is globalisation fair? Give reasons in support of your answer. Can you suggest some measures to make globalisation just and fair? State measures.

Ans. No, globalisation can not be said fair. Although, it has many advantages, still, there are many problems that it faces.

Not everyone has benefits from globalisation. Rather, it has benefitted only well-off consumers and also producers with skill, education and wealth.

It widens economic inequality among people. The rich has become more rich and the population of poor is still on the rise.

Globalisation leads to insecurity of jobs. In the case of policy changes, the MNC closes its offices. Also, at the time of recession, there is generally large-scale retrenchment in MNCs.

Following measures can be suggested to make globalisation just and fair

- The government should ensure that labour laws are properly implemented and the workers get their rights.
- It should protect small domestic producers at their initial stage.
- It should work with other developing countries to negotiate at the WTO for fairer rules.

Case Based Questions

1. Read the sources given below and answer the questions that follow.

Source A Production across countries

India has highly skilled engineers who can understand the technical aspects of production.

It also has educated English speaking youth who can provide customer care services. And all this probably can mean 50-60 per cent cost savings for the MNC!

(i) To what extent do you agree that India is a good destination for the MNCs?

Source B Interlinking production across countries

In general, MNCs set up production where it is close to the markets; where there is skilled and unskilled labour available at low costs; and where the availability of other factors of production is assured. In addition, MNCs might look for government policies that look after their interests.

(ii) How MNC choose a particular place for investment?

Source C Special Economic Zones

In recent years, the Central and State Governments in India are taking special steps to attract foreign companies to invest in India. Industrial zones, called Special Economic Zones (SEZs), are being set up. SEZs have world class facilities: electricity, water, roads, transport, storage, recreational and educational facilities. Companies who set up production units in the SEZs do not have to pay taxes for an initial period of five years.

(iii) To what extent do you agree that SEZs are encouraged by the government?

Ans. (i) India is definitely a good destination for the MNCs as it provides highly skilled, qualified and English speaking youth.

(ii) MNC look for various criterias before investing such as availability of skilled-unskilled labour, closeness to the markets, government policies that look after their interest, etc.

(iii) Government encourage SEZs which is known from the fact that government provides world class facilities like electricity, water, roads, transport, storage, recreational and educational facilities in these industrial zones. SEZs are encouraged so that MNCs set up their factories or offices in SEZs.

2. Read the source given below and answer the questions that follow.

Large MNCs in developed countries place orders for production with small producers. Garments, footwear, sports items are examples of industries where production is carried out by a large number of small producers around the world.

The products are supplied to the MNCs, which then sell these under their own brand names to the customers. These large MNCs have tremendous power to determine price, quality, delivery, and labour conditions for these distant producers.

Thus, we see that there are a variety of ways in which the MNCs are spreading their production and interacting with local producers in various countries across the globe.

By setting up partnerships with local companies, by using the local companies for supplies, by closely competing with the local companies or buying them up, MNCs are exerting a strong influence on production at these distant locations. As a result, production in these widely dispersed locations is getting interlinked.

(i) What do you understand by small producers?

(ii) Why do large MNCs are invited by the government into a country?

(iii) List two ways in which MNCs interlink production.

Ans. (i) Small producers refer to those producers who are producing consumer goods of small value like footwear, garments, sports items, etc.

(ii) Government invites large MNCs for the following reasons

- The large MNCs invest in the country by opening factories, offices which provide employment to people.
- Large MNCs support local producers by giving them bulk orders.

(iii) MNCs interlink production by

- Buying the local companies completely
- Setting up partnership with local companies.

ASSESSMENT EXERCISE

Multiple Choice Questions (MCQs)

1. Which of the following has not helped to give a greater choice of goods in the market for consumers?
(a) Multi-national companies
(b) Increased foreign trade
(c) The World Trade Organisation
(d) Increased foreign investment

2. Which one of the following types of countries has benefitted most from globalisation?
(a) Rich countries
(b) Developed countries
(c) Developing countries
(d) All of the above

3. What is the impact of the Indian government putting a tax on the import of Chinese toys?
(a) Indian toy makers will face no competition
(b) Chinese toys will become more affordable
(c) Buyers will experience a lower price for imported toys
(d) Imports of Chinese toys will reduce due to higher prices

4. What is liberalisation in the context of trade?
(a) Imposing more restrictions on foreign trade
(b) Allowing businesses to make decisions freely about imports and exports
(c) Introducing higher taxes on imported goods
(d) Encouraging government control over domestic producers

Subjective Questions (VSA, SA & LA)

1. What does Cargill Foods India limited produce?

2. Which international organisation looks after the liberalisation of foreign trade?

3. Give one example of MNC in India and an Indian MNC.

4. Name the group of countries which dominates the WTO.

5. Explain any three methods of controlling production across countries by MNCs.

6. How development of communication and IT sector has impacted the world trade?

7. Explain the impact of flexible labour laws on workers.

8. Explain three ways in which pressure of competition due to globalisation has significantly changed the lives of Indian workers.

9. Local companies get two-fold production benefits through MNCs. Explain the statement with examples.

10. Explain the good and bad effects of globalisation on Indian industry.

11. In what ways are MNCs different from national companies? Explain by giving three reasons.

12. For a long time foreign trade has been the main channel connecting countries. How?

13. 'Globalisation is the process of rapid integration or interconnection between countries'. Evaluate the statement and substantiate it with examples.

CHAPTER 5

Consumer Rights*

Market is a place of selling and buying of goods and services in exchange of money. In the market, there are two major components: producer and consumer. The rights of producers are safeguarded by the government through the MRP, fixed prices, subsidies, etc.

There were no awareness and rights for consumers, for a long time. In 2005, the Government of India introduced the right to information through which consumers were able to ask questions about the production and safety of the goods they are purchasing.

5.1 The Consumer in the Marketplace

Consumer is a person who buys and uses a goods or service from the market after making a payment.

A person participates in the market as both producer and consumer. As producer, a person participates by working in sectors like agriculture, industry or services and as a consumer, a person participates by purchasing final goods and services.

There is a need for rules and regulations for the protection of the consumers in the marketplace as they are exploited in various ways such as

- Whenever there is a complaint regarding a good or service that had been bought, the seller tries to shift all the responsibility on to the buyer.
- Sometimes traders indulge in unfair trade practices such weighing less than actual, adding charges that were not mentioned before, or selling adulterated/ defective goods.
- Sometimes large companies pass false information through the media, and other sources to attract consumers.

5.2 Consumer Movement

In India, consumer dissatisfaction with unfair market practices and lack of legal protection led to the rise of the **Consumer Movement**. Earlier, there was no legal system available to consumers to protect them from exploitation.

During 1960s, widespread food shortages, **hoarding**[1], black marketing, adulteration of food and edible oil gave rise to the Consumer Movement in an organised form in India.

Till the 1970s, consumer organisations were largely engaged in writing articles and holding exhibitions. They formed consumer groups to look into the malpractices in ration shops and over crowding in the road passenger transport.

All these efforts succeeded in bringing pressure on business firms as well as government to control unfair practices which are against the interest of consumers.

KNOWLEDGE PLUS In 1985, United Nations adopted the UN Guidelines for Consumer Protection.

Consumer Forums

The consumer movement in India has led to the formation of various organisations locally known as Consumer Forums or **Consumer Protection Councils**[2].

They guide consumers on how to file cases in the Consumer Court. Many times, they also represent individual consumer in the Consumer Courts.

These voluntary organisations receive financial support from the government for creating awareness among people.

1 **Hoarding** It refers to the practice of collecting large amount of goods.

2 **Consumer Protection Councils** The Consumer Protection Act has established Consumer Protection Councils at the central, state and district levels for the purpose of spreading consumer awareness. The objectives of the councils, as per the Act, shall be to promote and protect the rights of the consumers given in the Act.

* This chapter is to be done as Project Work.

Consumer Protection Act, 1986

In 1986, the Indian government enacted the Consumer Protection Act, popularly known as **COPRA.**

Under COPRA, a three-tier semi-judicial machinery at the district, state and national levels has been set-up for redressal of consumer disputes.

The district-level authority called **District Consumer Disputes Redressal Commission** deals with the cases involving claims up to ₹ 1 crore, the state-level authority called State Commission between ₹ 1 crore and ₹ 10 crore, and the national-level authority called **National Commission** deals with cases involving claims exceeding ₹ 10 crore.

If a case is dismissed in district-level commission, the consumer can also appeal in the state and then in national-level commissions.

5.3 Consumer Rights

- **Right to be Protected/Right to Safety** Consumers have the right to be protected against the marketing of goods and delivery of services that are hazardous to life and property.

  Producers and service providers need to strictly follow the required safety rules and regulations.

  There are many goods (like pressure cooker's safety valves, electrical equipments, geysers, iron, etc) which requires special attention to safety. If it is defective, it can cause a serious accident.

  So, in this case manufacturers are required to ensure that safety and quality of products and services are maintained.

- **Right to be Informed** Government has made it mandatory to mention all details of a product like ingredients used, date of manufacture, price, expiry date, direction for use, etc. on the pack of the product.

  If the product proves to be defective in any way, the consumer can complain and ask for compensation or replacement.

  The manufacturers have to display these information because consumers have the right to be informed about the particulars of goods and services that they purchase.

  A consumer can also protest and complain if someone sells a good at more than the MRP (Maximum Retail Price) printed on the packet.

> **Right to Information (RTI) Act**
>
> In October 2005, the Government of India enacted the RTI Act. It ensures all the citizens to provide all information about the functioning of government departments.

- **Right to Choose** Any consumer who receives a service in whatever capacity, regardless of age, gender and nature of service, has the Right to Choose whether to continue to receive the service or not.

  For example, the consumer can choose to continue using the services of the cable operator or opt for a new connection. Similarly, he can also choose to continue buying a particular good or opt for a new brand.

- **Right to Seek Redressal** Consumers have the right to seek redressal against unfair trade practices and exploitation. It means if any damage is done to a consumer, he has the right to get compensation depending on the degree of damage.

  The consumer can file a complaint before the appropriate consumer forum on his/her own with or without the services of lawyers.

- **Right to Represent** The consumers have the right to be represented in Consumer Courts while seeking any redressal.

> **ISI and Agmark**
>
> A logo like **ISI, Agmark** or **Hallmark** on a product helps consumers get assured of quality while purchasing such goods. The organisations that monitor and issue these certificates allow producers to use their logos so that they follow certain quality standards.
>
> These organisations develop quality standards for many products, but it is not compulsory for all the producers to follow such standards.
>
> It is compulsory for producers to get certified by these organisations for some products that affect the health and safety of consumers or products of mass consumption. These include LPG cylinders, food colours and additives, cement, packaged drinking water, etc.

5.4 Taking the Consumer Movement Forward

The National Consumers' Day is celebrated on **24th December.** On this day, the Indian Parliament enacted the Consumers' Protection Act in 1986.

There are more than 2000 consumer groups in India due to consumer movement, out of which about 50-60 are well organised and recognised for their work.

The COPRA was amended in the year 2019 to further strengthen consumers in India and buying through internet is included. If there is any defect in product or deficiency in service, then manufacturer or service provider is held responsible and would be penalised or even imprisoned.

The settlement of disputes with the help of a neutral intermediary outside the Consumer Disputes Redressal Commission, called **mediator**, is encouraged at all the three tiers Consumer Commissions.

However, there are still some problems such as

- The consumer redressal process is difficult, expensive and time consuming.
- Consumer awareness in India is spreading but slowly.
- The enforcement of laws, especially in unorganised sector, is weak.
- Court proceedings for consumer redressal are long.
- Most of the traders do not issue cash memos.
- Rules and regulations for market functioning are not followed.

Try These

1. **In which court a consumer should file a case if he/she is exploited in the market?**
2. **In which year, COPRA came into existence?**
3. **When was RTI (Right to Information) Act enacted by Government of India?**
4. **If any damage is done to a consumer by a trader, under which consumer right one can move to consumer court to get compensation?**
5. **When is National Consumer's Day celebrated?**

Mind Map

CONSUMER RIGHTS

Consumer Rights

Right to be Informed

Manufactures have to display all the information because the consumers have the right to be informed about the particulars of goods and services that they purchase.

Right to Choose

Any consumer who receives a service in whatever capacity regardless of age, gender and nature of service, has the right to choose whether to continue the service or not.

Right to Safety

Consumers have the right to be protected against the marketing of goods and delivery of services that are hazardous to life and property.

Right to Represent

The consumers have the right to be represented in consumer Courts while seeking any redressal.

Right to Seek Redressal

Consumers have the right to seek redressal against unfair trade practices and exploitation.

Consumer Movement

The Consumer in the Market Place

- Consumer buys and uses a goods or service from the market after making a payment.
- There is a need for rules and regulations for the protection of the consumers in the marketplace from being exploited.

Consumer Forums

- The Consumer Movement in India led to the formation of consumers forums.
- These guide consumers on how to file cases in the Consumer Court.

Taking the Consumer Movement Forward

- National Consumers Day is celebrated on 24th December.
- On 24th December the Indian Parliament enacted the Consumers' Protection Act in 1986.
- The COPRA was amended in the year 2019.
- COPRA is a three tier semi-judicial machinery set-up for redressal of consumer disputes.

NCERT FOLDER

Covering Intext Questions and Exercises of NCERT

INTEXT QUESTIONS

Q.1 What are the various ways by which people may be exploited in the market?

Ans. The various ways by which consumers (people) may be exploited in the market are

- Charging high price of the product
- Not giving proper after sale service
- Less measurement
- Under weighing goods
- Selling substandard quality goods
- Adulteration

Q.2 What do you think should be the role of government to protect consumers?

Ans. The government must lay down rules and regulations to protect and safeguard the interests of consumers. The rules and regulations must be supervised on a regular basis by the government.

Q.3 What could have been the steps taken by consumer groups?

Ans. The steps taken by consumer groups are as follows

- Consumer groups should have forced the business organisations or groups to strictly follow rules and regulations laid down by the government.
- They should also have supervised whether these rules and regulations are fully implemented or not.
- On behalf of consumers, they should launch complaints to seek redressals.
- They should organise mock street plays to make the people aware about the consumer's rights and their duties as a good consumer.

Q.4 There may be rules and regulations but they are often not followed. Why? Discuss.

Ans. There are rules and regulations to protect consumers from exploitation, but they are not followed because often consumers do not have enough time to pursue, so they do not want to get into legal hassles.

Q.5 For the following (you can add to the list) products/services discuss what safety rules should be observed by the producer?

(a) LPG Cylinder (b) Cinema theatre
(c) Circus (d) Medicines
(e) Edible oil (f) Marriage pandal
(g) A high-rise building

Ans. The safety rules for producer in each of the given products/services are stated below

(a) **LPG cylinder**

- Ensure that there is no leakage of gas from the cylinder.
- Ensure that cylinders are transported to the godown / customer premises in a safe manner.
- Ensure that the seal on the cylinder is secure.

(b) **Cinema theatre**

- Adequate number of fire extinguishers should be installed in the premises.
- Clearly marked and well illuminated exits should be there in all areas for emergencies like fire.

(c) **Circus**

- The cage for dangerous animals like lions should be secured tightly.
- Safety net should be there for trapeze artists.
- Adequate number of fire extinguishers should be installed in the premises.
- Clearly marked and well illuminated exits should be there in all areas for emergencies like fire.

(d) **Medicines**

- Date of manufacture, date of expiry, batch number and composition, direction of use and risk associated must be printed on the packaging.
- The contents must be sealed with tamper-proof seals.

(e) **Edible oil**

- Date of manufacture, date of expiry, batch number and composition must be printed on the packaging.
- The contents must be sealed with tamper-proof seals.
- Agmark seal should be there.

(f) **Marriage pandal**

- Adequate number of fire extinguishers should be installed in the premises.
- Clearly marked and well illuminated exits should be there in all areas for emergencies like fire.

(g) **A high-rise building**

- Adequate number of fire extinguishers should be installed in the premises.
- Clearly marked and well illuminated exits should be there in all areas for emergencies like fire.
- Lifts should be well maintained periodically and have all safety features.
- Staircases must have handrails.
- Fire escape staircases must be provided at locations away from the main staircases and lifts.

Q.6 When we buy commodities we find that the price charged is sometimes higher or lower than the Maximum Retail Price printed on the pack. Discuss the possible reasons. Should consumer groups do something about this?

Ans. The possible reason for higher price may be overcharging by the retailer from an ignorant customer. The possible reason for a price lower than Maximum Retail Price (MRP) may be due to bargaining by the customer, or a discount being given by the retailer to increase his sale.

Consumer groups should pressurise the dealers to ensure that no dealer charges more than the MRP under any condition. They should in fact put pressure on dealers to reduce their margins and charge lesser than the MRP as far as possible.

Q.7 Pick up a few packaged goods that you want to buy and examine the information given. In what ways are they useful? Is there some information that you think should be given on those packaged goods but is not? Discuss.

Ans. The information given on the package can be useful as follows

(i) **Maximum Retail Price** (MRP) The seller cannot ask you to pay more than this amount.

(ii) **Expiry Date and Date of Manufacture** You can see how much time has passed since the product was manufactured and also whether you can safely use it.

(iii) **Ingredients Used** You should know what is used in making the product so that, in case some ingredient does not suit your health condition, you can avoid it. Examples are sugar for diabetes and salt for high blood pressure patients.

(iv) **Address of Manufacturer** If the product is defective and the seller does not replace it, you can contact the manufacturer for redressal of your complaint.

On all products, especially medicine and food items, additional information regarding safe and proper use should be mentioned.

Q.8 People make complaints about the lack of civic amenities such as bad roads or poor water and health facilities but no one listens. Now the RTI Act gives you the power to question. Do you agree? Discuss.

Ans. Yes, I agree that RTI gives us the power to find out how the government departments work so that we can approach the correct agency which will repair the bad road, ensure adequate and clean water supply or improve the health facilities. The RTI Act helps us to approach the concerned department to get the work done.

Q.9 The following are some of the catchy advertisements of products that we purchase from the market. Which of the following offers would really benefit consumers? Discuss.

(a) 15 gm more in every 500 gm pack ....

(b) Subscribe for a newspaper with a gift at the end of year ......

(c) Scratch and win gifts worth ₹ 10 lakh ....

(d) A milk chocolate inside a 500 gram glucose box ......

(e) Win a gold coin inside a pack ....

(f) Buy shoes worth ₹ 2,000 and get one pair of shoes worth ₹ 500 free ....

Ans. (a) Yes, it will benefit because it is given at the time of purchase.

(b) No, because you have to keep paying every month for one year without any guarantee that you will get the gift at the end of the year.

(c) No, as you can scratch the card only after purchasing and in most cases you will get nothing.

(d) Yes, as it is a usable benefit being provided with the pack.

(e) It may not benefit the consumer as the possibility of being lucky to win a gold coin is very low as only a few coins, may be 5-10 will be placed in about thousands or lakhs of pieces.

(f) It may not benefit the consumer as the shoes may not be of the style and standard required by the consumer. Also, the price of ₹ 2,000 may have been increased to include the cost of the shoe of ₹ 500. So probably the consumer is not benefitted.

Q.10 Arrange the following in the correct order.

(a) Arita files a case in the District Consumer Disputes Redressal Commission.

(b) She engages a professional person.

(c) She realises that the dealer has given her defective material.

(d) She starts attending the commission proceedings.

(e) She goes and complains to the dealer and the Branch office, to no effect.

(f) She is asked to produce the bill and warranty before the commission.

(g) She purchases a wall clock from a retail outlet.

(h) Within a few months, the dealer was ordered by the commission to replace her old wall clock with a brand new one at no extra cost.

Ans. (g), (c), (e), (a), (b), (d), (f), (h)

Q.11 What is the difference between consumer protection council and consumer Disputes Redressal Commission?

Ans. Consumer protection council has got no legal right and is a voluntary organisation. On the other hand, consumer Disputes Redressal Commission are a three tier quasi-judicial machinery set-up for redressal of consumer disputes.

Q.12 The Consumer Protection Act, 1986 ensures the following as rights which every consumer in India should possess.

(i) Right to choice (ii) Right to information
(iii) Right to redressal (iv) Right to representation
(v) Right to safety (vi) Right to consumer education

Categorise the following cases under different heads and mark against each in brackets.

(a) Lata got an electric shock from a newly purchased iron. She complained to the shopkeeper immediately. ( )

(b) John is dissatisfied with the services provided by MTNL/BSNL/TATA Indicom for the past few months. He files a case in the District Level Consumer Forum. ( )

(c) Your friend had been sold a medicine that has crossed the expiry date and you are advising her to lodge a complaint. ( )

(d) Iqbal makes it a point to scan through all the particulars given on the pack of any item that he buys. ( )

(e) You are not satisfied with the services of the cable operator catering to your locality but you are unable to switch over to anybody else. ( )

(f) You realise that you have received a defective camera from a dealer. You are complaining to the head office persistently. ( )

Ans. (a) (v), (b) (iii), (c) (vi), (d) (ii), (e) (i), (f) (iv)

Q.13 If the standardisation ensures the quality of a commodity, why are many goods available in the market without ISI or Agmark certification?

Ans. Standardisation ensures the quality of a product but it is time consuming and expensive to avail it. Millions of small producer cannot afford it. Also it is not compulsory in the case of most products in the market. So, many goods are available in the market without ISI or Agmark certification.

EXERCISE

Q.1 Why are rules and regulations required in the marketplace? Illustrate with a few examples.

Ans. Rules and regulations are required in the marketplace for the following reasons

(i) To protect consumers against exploitation by the producers, sellers and service providers.

(ii) They often indulge in unfair trade practices and also provide false information about a product or service. For example, selling expired medicines by a chemist, defective goods by a supplier or not providing proper choice of channels by the cable operators.

Q.2 What factors gave birth to the Consumer Movement in India? Trace its evolution.

Or **Explain three factors that gave rise to the Consumer Movement in India.**

Ans. The factors that gave birth to the Consumer Movement are listed below

(i) Dissatisfaction of consumers, as many unfair practices were being indulged by the sellers like short weighing, black marketing, adulteration, etc.

(ii) There was no legal system available for consumers to protect them from exploitation in the marketplace. If consumers were not happy with a particular brand, product or shop, they generally avoid buying that brand or product or would stop purchasing from that particular shop.

(iii) It was presumed that it is for the consumers to be careful while buying a commodity or availing of a service.

Evolution of Consumer Movement

- The Consumer Movement in India started as a social force with the need to protect consumers against unfair and unethical trade practices being followed by many retailers and manufacturers.
- These included creating artificial shortages, hoarding cereals and other agricultural products, black marketing of goods and adulteration of cooking oils and food items.
- Till 1986, consumer organisations were highlighting issues by writing articles in newspapers and magazines about unfair practices of merchants. But nowadays, as the consumers have become more aware, the number of consumer groups have grown who have highlighted these malpractices.
- In 1986, the Government of India enacted the Consumer Protection Act, also known as COPRA. This was a major step in the Consumer Movement in India.

Q.3 Explain the need for consumer consciousness by giving two examples.

Ans. Consumer consciousness refers to being aware of your right as a consumer while buying any goods or services.The following two examples state the need of consumer consciousness

(i) The ISI and Agmark logos are quality certifications on certain classes of products. Consumers must look for such certifications while purchasing items.

(ii) Consumers must have an adequate knowledge about the products that they are buying, so that they can make an informed choice of the correct product to buy.

Q.4 Mention a few factors which cause exploitation of consumers.

Ans. Factors which cause exploitation of consumers are as follows

(i) Lack of awareness among consumers.

(ii) Limited competition, leading to consumers being forced to buy a certain product.

(iii) Some consumers are illiterate.

(iv) Limited supply of goods, products or services, leading to shortages and black marketing.

(v) Misleading advertising in the media.

Q.5 What is the rationale behind the enactment of Consumer Protection Act, 1986?

Ans. The rationale behind the enactment of Consumer Protection Act, 1986 was to safeguard the interest of the consumers and protecting them against exploitation. It has led to the formation of the three-tier Consumer Courts at the district, state and national levels.

Q.6 Describe some of your duties as consumers, if you visit a shopping complex in your locality.

Or **Who is a consumer? Explain five duties of a consumer.**

Ans. Some of my duties as a consumer, if I visit a shopping complex are

(i) Ensuring that the product is within the expiry date at the time of purchase.

(ii) Paying no more than the maximum retail price printed on the goods purchased.

(iii) Always asking for a cash memo/receipt for the goods purchased.

(iv) Ensuring that the goods purchased are not spurious or of inferior quality.

(v) In case, it is found later that the goods are defective, getting it exchanged or repaired. In case, the trader refuses or does not refund the amount paid, the consumer's duty is to lodge a complaint with the District Consumer Forum.

Q.7 Suppose you buy a bottle of honey and a biscuit packet. Which logo or mark you will have to look for and why?

Ans. Honey and biscuit is an agricultural product and thus, we have to look for the 'Agmark' logo of its quality certification.

Q.8 What legal measures were taken by the government to empower the consumers in India?

Ans. The legal measures taken by the government to empower the consumers in India were

(i) The Consumer Protection Act (COPRA) enacted in 1986, to protect consumers from exploitation in the marketplace.

(ii) Consumer Courts have been set up to provide justice to consumers who have been treated unfairly in the marketplace.

Q.9 Mention some of the rights of consumers and write a few sentences on each.

Or **Explain the rights of the consumer provided under the Consumer Protection Act (COPRA), 1986.**

Or **Describe any three rights of consumer which help him/ her against unfair trade practices and exploitation?**

Ans. Rights of consumer which protect him/her against unfair practices are as follows

(i) **Right to Safety** The consumer has the right to be protected against goods that are hazardous to life and property.

(ii) **Right to Choose** The consumer can choose the product to be bought and also whether to buy or not to buy a product. He cannot be forced to purchase a product or service not of his choice.

(iii) **Right to be Informed** The consumer has the right to know important facts about the product or service being purchased.

(iv) **Right to Seek Redressal** The consumer has the right to seek redressal if the supplier has exploited him. He has the right to be compensated by the trader/ producer if any damage or loss occurs due to the product or service purchased.

(v) **Right to Representation** In case there is a dispute between the consumer and the seller or service provider which is not settled, the consumer has the right to approach the local Consumer Court for redressal. In case, his representation in the District Level Court is dismissed, he can approach the state level and then at the national level.

Q.10 By what means can the consumers express their solidarity?

Ans. The consumers can express their solidarity by forming the following

(i) Consumer Protection Councils

(ii) Consumer Clubs

(iii) Resident Welfare Associations (RWAs)

Q.11 Critically examine the progress of Consumer Movement in India.

Ans. The Consumer Movement in India has evolved largely since it began. There has been a significant change in consumer awareness in the country. Till the enactment of COPRA in 1986, the Consumer Movement did not bear much force, but ever since its inception, the movement has been empowered substantially.

The setting up of consumer courts and consumer groups has been a progressive move. However, in contemporary India, the consumer redressal process is quite complicated, expensive and time-consuming. Filing cases, attending court proceedings, hiring lawyers, and other procedures make it inconvenient.

In India, there are over 2000 consumer groups of which, unfortunately, only about 50-60 are well-organised and functioning smoothly.

Q.12 Match List I with List II and select the correct alternative accordingly.

List I	List II
A. Availing details of ingredients in a product	1. Right to Safety
B. Agmark	2. Dealing with consumer cases
C. Accident due to faulty engine in a scooter	3. Certification of edible oil and cereals
D. District Consumer commission	4. Agency that develops standards for goods and services
E. Consumers International	5. Right to Information
F. Bureau of Indian Standards	6. Global level institution of consumer welfare organisations

Codes

	A	B	C	D	E	F
(a)	2	6	1	4	5	3
(b)	5	3	1	2	6	4
(c)	5	2	6	3	4	1
(d)	4	3	1	5	2	6

Ans. (b)

Q.13 State true or false.

(i) COPRA applies only to goods.

(ii) India is one of the many countries in the world which has exclusive courts for consumer redressal.

(iii) When a consumer feels that he has been exploited, he must file a case in the District Consumer Court.

(iv) It is worthwhile to move to Consumer Courts only if the damages incurred are of high value.

(v) Hallmark is the certification maintained for standardisation of jewellery.

(vi) The consumer redressal process is very simple and quick.

(vii) A consumer has the right to get compensation depending on the degree of the damage.

Ans. (i) False (ii) True (iii) True (iv) False (v) True (vi) False (vii) True

PROJECTS/ACTIVITIES

Q.1 Mrs Krishna bought a Colour Television (CTV) against six months warranty. The CTV stopped working after three months. When she complained to the dealer/shop where it was purchased, they sent an engineer to set it right.

The CTV continues to give trouble and Mrs Krishna no longer gets any reply to the complaint she made to the dealer/shop. She decides to write to the Consumer Forum in her area.

Write a letter on her behalf. You may discuss with your partner/group members before you write it.

Ans. The format of the letter is given below

House No. 568, Sector 28,
NOIDA - 201303

25th August, 2016

To
The Chairman,
Consumer Forum,
NOIDA (UP)

Subject Defective Colour TV not replaced despite repeated complaints

Sir,

I wish to bring to your notice the following facts, for which you are requested to guide me on further action to be taken in this regard

- I have purchased a 'Standard' make of Colour TV from their dealer M/s Gujral Entertainment with their shop at H-45, Sector 18, NOIDA - 201301 vide their Cash Memo no. GE/134 dated 15th April, 2016. The TV was guaranteed for six months against manufacturing defects, as informed by the dealer.
- The TV became defective (it went dead) on 17th July, 2016. The dealer sent a service engineer to repair it, but it again went defective after one week.
- When I complained the second time, they did not send their engineer for repairs till date.
- I have been complaining regularly to the dealer, but he no longer replies to the complaints.
- I tried to contact the manufacturer, but found that their factory has closed down and that the company no longer exists.

I am now left with a defective colour TV set and the dealer is neither replacing it nor repairing it.

You are requested to kindly guide me on the next course of action.

Sincerely yours,
Sd/-
(Mrs Krishna)

Q.2 Conduct a survey in your locality by supplying the following questionnaire to get an idea as to how alert they are as consumers.

For each question, tick one.

Always	Sometimes	Never
A	B	C

(i) When you buy some item, do you insist on a bill?

(ii) Do you keep the bill carefully?

(iii) If you realise that you have been tricked by the shopkeeper, have you bothered to complain to him?

(iv) Have you been able to convince him that you've been cheated?

(v) Do you simply grumble to yourself reconciling that it is your fate that you are often being victimised so and it is nothing new?

(vi) Do you look for ISI mark, expiry date, etc?

(vii) If the expiry date mentioned is just a month or so away, do you insist on a fresh packet?

(viii) Do you weigh the new gas cylinder/old newspapers yourself before buying/selling?

(ix) Do you raise an objection if a vegetable seller uses stones in place of the exact weight?

(x) Do excessively bright coloured vegetables arouse your suspicion?

(xi) Are you brand-conscious?

(xii) Do you associate high price with good quality (to reassure yourself that after all you have not paid a higher price just like that)?

(xiii) Do you unhesitatingly respond to catchy offers?

(xiv) Do you compare the price paid by you with those of others?

(xv) Do you strongly believe that your shopkeeper never cheats a regular customer like you?

(xvi) Do you favour 'home delivery' of provision items without any doubt regarding weight, etc?

(xvii) Do you insist on 'paying by meter' when you travel by auto?

Note

(i) You are extremely aware as a consumer if your answers for questions 5, 12, 13, 15 and 16 are (c) and for the rest (a).

(ii) If your answers are (a) for questions 5, 12, 13, 15 and 16 and the rest (c), then you have to wake up as consumer.

(iii) If your answer is (b) for all the questions you are somewhat aware.

Ans. (i) A (ii) A (iii) A (iv) A (v) C
(vi) A (vii) A (viii) A (ix) A (x) A
(xi) A (xii) C (xiii) C (xiv) A (xv) C
(xvi) C (xvii) A

REVIEW EXERCISE

Including Competency Based Questions

Part I

Multiple Choice Questions (MCQs)

1. A person purchasing goods and services for self use is referred as

(a) consumer (b) producer (c) investor (d) worker

2. Shopkeepers who sell goods and services to people in small quantities are called

(a) retailers (b) wholesellers
(c) producers (d) shop owners

3. In what ways people can be exploited by traders?

(a) Traders charging more price than listed
(b) Giving less quantity
(c) Not giving complete information about the product
(d) All of the above

4. Large companies also exploit people. They do this by which of the following ways?

(a) Ensuring consumer protection
(b) Listening to consumer complaints
(c) Giving false information through media
(d) Helping in consumer movement

5. The movement that arose due to dissatisfaction of people as many unfair practices done by the shopkeepers is known as

(a) producer movement
(b) protection movement
(c) movement against unfair practice
(d) consumer movement

6. The consumer grievances redressal cell formed by Government of India is

(a) Consumer Forum Council
(b) COPRA
(c) ISI
(d) Consumer Protection Council

7. The Consumer Protection Act, 1986 ensures that every consumer in India should possess .... consumer rights.

(a) four (b) two (c) ten (d) six

8. What does COPRA stands for ?

(a) Consumer Protection Amendment
(b) Consumer Protection Act
(c) Consumer Protection Association
(d) Consumer Protection Assembly

9. Consider the following statements and select the correct option associated with COPRA.

(a) COPRA stands for Consumer Protection Amendment.
(b Under COPRA, three tier quasi-judicial machinery was set up at District, State and National levels.
(c) The district level court deals with the cases involving claims up to 30 Lakh.
(d) COPRA was enacted in 1987, by Government of India.

10. You have bought a packet of biscuits whose advertisement you saw in television. The packet has price, batch number, manufacturing and expiry date but does not mention its ingredients. It is the violation of which of the following rights? Competency Based

(a) Right to Information (b) Right to Safety
(c) Right to Seek Redressal (d) Right to Choice

11. The Bureau of Indian Standards gives a mark of certification to products of the Indian industries for quality assurance which is known as

(a) AGMARK (b) ISO (c) COPRA (d) ISI Mark

12. Find the incorrect option.

(a) The Consumer Protection Act, 1986 is popularly known as COPRA.
(b) The National levels Court deals with cases involving claims exceeding ₹ 3 crores.
(c) In October 2005 RTI Act was enacted by Government of India.
(d) The consumer redressal process is difficult, expensive and time consuming.

13 Find the incorrect option.

(a) Consumers have the Right to seek redressal against unfair trade practices and exploitation.
(b) In India 25th December is celebrated as National Consumer's Day.
(c) Law enforcement in unorganised sector is weak.
(d) While seeking any redress, the consumer have the right to be represented in Consumer Courts.

14. Radha, a resident in Delhi, recently purchased a home appliance labelled with the ISI mark. She noticed that the product didn't meet the safety standards as advertised and was concerned about its potential hazards.

Which of the following consumer rights is most relevant to Radha's situation? Competency Based

(a) Right to be informed (b) Right to seek redressal
(c) Right to choose (d) Right to safety

15. Which of the following statements accurately describes "Consumer Forums" in India's market structure? Competency Based

I. Consumer Forums are government appointed entities to manage consumer grievances and disputes in the marketplace.
II. Consumer Forums, also known as Consumer Protection Councils, are primarily responsible for creating awareness among consumers.
III. Consumer Forums, established under the Consumer Protection Act (COPRA) of 1986, guide consumers on how to file cases in the Consumer Court and represent individual consumers in legal proceedings.
IV. Consumer Forums are voluntary organisations that receive support from the government to promote fair trade practices and maintain market regulations.

Codes

(a) Only I (b) Only III
(c) Only IV (d) Both I and II

16. Mr. Z recently purchased an electronic device. He later found that the product had numerous defects and was not functioning as advertised. He approached the seller to seek compensation for the faulty product. Competency Based

Which of the following rights of consumers would support Mr. Z's claim for compensation?

I. Right to Seek Redressal
II. Right to Choose
III. Right to be Informed
IV. Right to Representation

Codes

(a) Only I (b) III and IV
(c) I and II (d) Only II

17. Why is the Consumer Protection Act of 1986 significant in India and what rights does it provide to consumers? Competency Based

(a) It established consumer councils and redressal authorities, providing rights such as safety, information, choice, redressal and representation.
(b) It initiated consumer awareness programs without granting specific rights to consumers.

(c) It focused solely on regulating market prices without addressing consumer rights.
(d) It centralised governmental control over consumer related issues, limiting consumer influence.

18. Consider the statements given below and choose the correct answer. **Competency Based**

Statement I The Consumer Movement in India began due to the necessity of protecting and promoting the interests of consumers against unethical and unfair trade practices during the 1960s.

Statement II The Consumer Protection Act, 1986, established a three-tier quasi-judicial machinery at the district, state, and national levels for redressal of consumer disputes.

Codes
(a) Statement I is correct and II is incorrect
(b) Statement I is incorrect and II is correct
(c) Both Statements I and II are incorrect
(d) Both Statements I and II are correct

Answers

1. (a)	**2.** (a)	**3.** (d)	**4.** (c)	**5.** (d)
6. (d)	**7.** (d)	**8.** (b)	**9.** (b)	**10.** (a)
11. (d)	**12.** (b)	**13.** (b)	**14.** (d)	**15.** (b)
16. (a)	**17.** (a)	**18.** (d)		

Assertion-Reason

1. Assertion (A) The Consumer Protection Act, 1986 (COPRA) was enacted in India to safeguard consumer interests.

Reason (R) The Consumer Movement in India emerged due to the necessity of protecting consumers against unethical and unfair trade practices.

Codes
(a) Both A and R are true and R is the correct explanation of A
(b) Both A and R are true, but R is not the correct explanation of A
(c) A is true, but R is false
(d) A is false, but R is true

2. Assertion (A) The National Consumers' Day is celebrated on 24th December in India.

Reason (R) The Consumers' Protection Act was enacted by the Indian Parliament on 24th December, 1986.

Codes
(a) Both A and R are true and R is the correct explanation of A
(b) Both A and R are true, but R is not the correct explanation of A
(c) A is true, but R is false
(d) A is false, but R is true

Ans. 1. (a) Both A and R are true and R is the correct explanation of A
2. (a) Both A and R are true, and R is the correct explanation of A

Picture Based Questions

1. Identify the mark in the picture.

(a) ISI (b) Agmark
(c) Hallmark (d) Woolmark

2. Identify the mark in the picture given below.

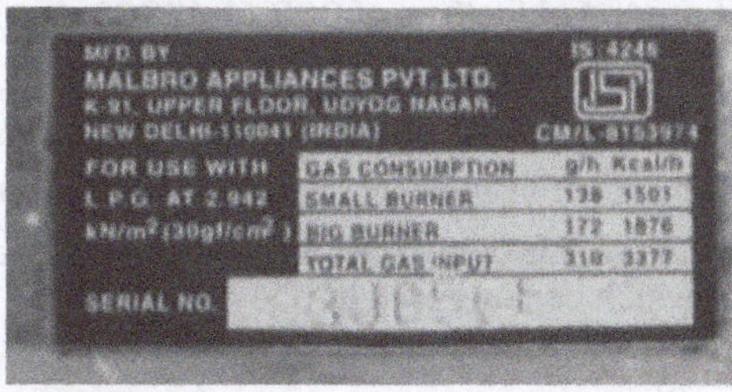

(a) Hallmark (b) Agmark
(c) ISI mark (d) Woolmark

3. The image shows a group of people standing in front of a post office that offers personal loans. Which of the following consumer rights is most relevant for them to exercise before availing the loan service? **Competency Based**

(a) Right to safety (b) Right to be informed
(c) Right to choose (d) Right to privacy

Ans. 1. (c) Hallmark 2. (c) ISI mark
3. (b) Right to be informed

Part II

Very Short Answer Type Questions

1. What are Consumer Forums?

Ans. Consumer Forums are the organisations working for the rights of consumers. They provide assistance and guide the consumers to file cases in consumer courts.

2. What led to the formation of Consumer Protection Councils?

Ans. The Consumer Movement in India has led to the formation of various organisations which are locally known as Consumer Protection Councils.

3. Why was the Consumer Protection Act enacted by the Indian Parliament?

Ans. Consumer Protection Act was enacted by the Indian Parliament to protect consumers against exploitation by the producers, sellers and service providers.

4. What are the objectives of COPRA,1986?

Ans. The objectives of COPRA, 1986 include

(i) To ensure better protection of interests of consumer.

(ii) To protect consumer against unfair trade practices.

5. If any damage is done to a consumer by a trader, under which consumer right one can move to consumer court to get compensation.

Ans. Under Right to safety, one can move to consumer court to get compensation for any damage done to him/her by a trader.

6. You went to a marriage pandal and found that it is beautifully decorated and well illuminated but there is no fire extinguisher installed in the premises. Under which right you can ask the organiser to arrange for fire extinguishers. Competency Based

Ans. Under the right to safety, I can ask the organiser to arrange for fire extinguishers as it is his duty to see the safety of the people inside the pandal.

7. If you are to purchase spices for food from the market, which logo will you like to see to be sure of quality?

Or **Suppose you have to buy a packet bottle of drinking water in your journey. Which logo will you like to see to be sure of its quality?**

Ans. The logo related to certifying the quality product i.e. Agmark, FPO (Food Processing Organisation), etc.

8. Seema purchased a packet of milk powder of which the expiry date had passed. Which of her right is violated and what can she do about it? Competency Based

Ans. Seema's right to information has been violated and she can take the matter to consumer forum.

9. Why is consumer redressal process expensive and cumbersome?

Ans. Consumer redressal process is expensive and cumbersome because consumers often have to engage lawyers and attend court hearings.

10. Which logo would you like to see for purchasing electrical goods?

Or **Suppose you want to purchase a television from market, then which logo of quality should have been marked on the television?**

Ans. We would like to see the ISI mark before purchasing electrical goods such as television from the market.

11. 'Consumer Affairs raids Malda markets to check malpractices, complaints were received that soft drinks were being sold at a higher price.' CBSE Additional SQP 2023-24

Source (edited) Millennium Post

(i) Which consumer right was being violated in the above instance of soft drinks being sold at a higher price?

(ii) Which consumer right was likely invoked in response to the complaints?

Ans. (i) The consumer right being violated in the instance of soft drinks being sold at a higher price is the 'Right to choose' as consumers have the right to decide whether to continue purchasing at the increased price or not.

(ii) In response to the complaints about soft drinks being sold at a higher price, the consumer right that was likely invoked was the right to seek redressal.

12. Amit purchased a newly released electronic gadget from an online store. After a few uses, it malfunctioned and caused minor electric shocks. Discuss the rights violated according to the Consumer Protection Act (COPRA) and the possible actions she can take for redressal. Competency Based

Ans. Amit's right to safety' is violated as per COPRA since the product can lead to a hazard. He can file a complaint in the Consumer Court seeking compensation or replacement. The defective gadget limits his right and he has the authority to seek redressal under consumer protection laws.

Short Answer Type Questions

1. How do we participate in the market as producers and consumers? Explain with three examples.

Ans. We participate in the market as producers and consumer. As a producer of goods and services we could be working in different sector of economy like agriculture, industry or services.

As a consumer we participate in the market when we purchase goods and services that we need.

For example, if we cultivate crops or manufacture cars or run a school we act as producer but when we purchase food grain from market, or buy car or go to a doctor as patient then we act as consumer.

2. How are consumers exploited in the marketplace? Explain with three examples.

Ans. Exploitation in the marketplace happens in various ways.

Some examples are

(i) When traders indulge in unfair trade practices such as when shopkeepers weigh or measure less than what they should. This is usually in materials sold loose like rice, flour, milk, etc.

(ii) When traders add charges that were not mentioned before, like handling charges, packing charges, etc.

(iii) When adulterated/defective goods or expired medicines are sold.

3. Explain the circumstances under which markets do not work in a fair manner.

Ans. The circumstances under which markets do not work in a fair manner occur when producers are few and powerful, whereas consumers purchase in small amounts and are scattered. This happens especially when large companies are producing these goods.

These companies with huge wealth, power and reach can manipulate the market in various ways. At times false information is passed on through the media and other sources to attract consumers. Rules and regulations to protect consumers are needed to prevent this.

4. What are the main factors which cause exploitation of consumers? Explain three factors.

Ans. Exploitation of consumers is a situation in which a consumer is cheated or given false information by the producer. The factors which causes exploitation of consumers are

(i) **Limited Information** Consumers have limited information about their rights and duties. Therefore, they get exploited by dishonest sellers.

(ii) **Low Literacy and Awareness** The lack of knowledge about the quality or prices of various products or illiteracy causes exploitation of consumers.

(iii) **Limited Competition** When producers are few then they start to manipulate the market through various ways. They know that conusmers are scattered and purchase in small amounts so they are helpless.

5. "Rules and Regulations are required for the protection of the consumers in the market place." Justify the statement with arguments.

Ans. The rules and regulations are required for the protection of the consumers in the market for the following reasons

(i) **To Check Adulterations** At times, greedy traders try to play with the health of consumers by indulging in adulteration of edible oils, milk, butter, ghee, etc. So, there is need of rules and regulations in the market.

(ii) **To Check Powerful Producer** Markets do not work in a fair manner if there is monopoly of few and powerful producers and when purchase of consumer is small and they have no single voice. So there is need of rules and regulations in the market.

(iii) **False Information** Most of the time the false information is passed to consumers through media and other sources to attract the consumers.

6. How do Consumer Protection Councils help consumers? Explain three ways.

Ans. Consumer Protection Councils or Consumer Forums help consumers in the following ways

(i) They guide consumers on how to file cases in the Consumer Court.

(ii) On many occasions, they also represent individual consumers in the Consumer Courts.

(iii) They create awareness among the people by conducting consumer melas, conferences, meetings, etc for which they are funded by the government.

7. What are the various courts set up under COPRA?

Or **What are the institutions set up under COPRA for the redressal of grievances? Explain.**

Ans. Under Consumer Protection Act COPRA, a three-tier quasi-judicial machinery at the district, state and national levels has been set up for redressal of consumer disputes.

District Courts deal with cases involving claims up to ₹ 1 Crore, State Level Courts between ₹ 1 Crore and ₹ 10 Crore and the National Level Court deals with cases involving claims exceeding ₹ 10 Crore.

If a case is dismissed in District Level Court, the consumer can also appeal to the State and then to the National Level Court.

8. Assess the impact of COPRA on consumers.

Ans. The impact of COPRA is as follows

(i) By the enactment of COPRA, consumers are aware of their rights that they can exercise while purchasing a good or a service.

(ii) COPRA has empowered the consumers so that they get full value of the money they spend in buying different items.

(iii) The formation of quasi-judicial courts under COPRA has made seeking justice in consumer matters easy and effective.

9. How can the consumer use his Right to Information when he is not satisfied with the service he gets?

Ans. The consumer has the Right to Information about the particulars of goods and services that they purchase. He/she can complain and ask for compensation or replacement of the product, if it is proved to be defective in any manner.

Consumers can complain and ask for compensation in case of wrong information or promises. The consumer can file an application using the RTI Act that keeps us informed about progress of any work and makes the government departments answerable to the consumer.

10. How will an aggrieved person get his or her compensation? Explain with an example.

Ans. An aggrieved person can get his or her compensation in the following ways

(i) Consumers have the right to seek redressal against unfair trade practices and exploitation. If any damage is done to a consumer, he/she has the right to get compensation depending on the degree of damage.

For example Karim realised that the dealer has given him a defective TV and does not bother about his complains. Any aggrieved consumer like Karim can go to the consumer forums or consumer protection councils. They guide consumer on how to file cases in the Consumer Court.

(ii) Under COPRA, a three-tier quasi judicial machinery at the district, state and national levels is set-up for redressal of consumer disputes. The act has enabled the consumer the right to represent in the Consumer Court.

11. Highlight any three problems which a consumer may face in the process of redressal.

Ans. The problems which a consumer may face in the process of redressal are

(i) It may be time-consuming, as the consumer may have to take out time from his daily activities for filing a complaint, engaging a lawyer, attending hearings, etc.

(ii) It may be expensive, as a consumer has to engage a lawyer.

(iii) If cash memos or receipts are not issued, then it makes the collection of evidence difficult.

12. How do the logos and certification on cover help the consumers to buy standardised products?

Ans. The logos and certification on cover help consumers get assured of quality while purchasing the goods and services because these are issued by the government organisations. The organisations that monitor and issue these certificates allow producers to use their logos provided that they follow certain quality standards.

For some products that affect the health and safety of consumers or of products of mass consumption like LPG cylinders, food colours and additives, cement, packaged drinking water, it is mandatory on the part of the producers to get certified by these organisations.

13. Sudha bought a tin of edible oil. After coming home she found that the seal was broken and oil leaked from it. What are the things that she should keep in mind while making such purchases? Competency Based

Ans. Sudha should do the following

(i) Check the manufacturing and expiry date, batch number, composition of oil, price and associated risks (if any).

(ii) She should check that oil packet or tin of oil is sealed and tamper proof.

(iii) In case of edible oil, she should check the logo of Agmark or any other standard certifying seal of quality.

Long Answer Type Questions

1. What are consumer forums? What is their importance?

Or Analyse the functions of consumer protection council or consumer forum.

Ans. The consumer movement in India has led to the formation of various organisations locally known as consumer forums or consumer protection councils.

The importance or functions of consumer forums are

(i) They guide consumers on how to file cases in the consumer court.

(ii) On many occasions, they also represent individual consumers in the consumer courts.

(iii) These voluntary organisations also receive financial support from the government for creating awareness among the people.

(iv) It works for the protection of the consumer rights.

(v) It imparts knowledge about consumer rights by writing articles and getting it published in newspaper.

2. Explain any three strategies adopted by the government to protect the interest of the consumers.

Ans. Following are the strategies adopted by the government to protect the interest of the consumers

(i) **Enactment of COPRA** Under this Act, a three-tier judicial machinery at the district, state and national levels was set up for redressal of consumer disputes. The Act enables the consumers to represent them in consumer courts.

(ii) **RTI Act** In October 2005, the Government of India enacted Right to Information Act (RTI) which ensures the citizens all the information about the functions of government departments and people can ask and make complaints on issues like bad roads, poor water and health facilities, government jobs and their status, etc.

(iii) **Standardisation of the Products** There are organisations like ISI, Agmark or Hallmark which develop quality standards for many products. They provide logos and certificates that help consumers get assured of quality while purchasing the goods and services.

3. Explain the various functions of consumer organisation which protect consumers against exploitation.

Ans. The following functions of consumer organisation protect consumers against exploitation

(i) Consumer organisations create awareness amongst people about their rights. Till the 1970s, consumer organisations were largely engaged in writing articles and holding exhibitions.

(ii) They formed consumer groups to look into the malpractices in ration shops and overcrowding in the road passenger transport.

(iii) The consumer movement in India has led to the formation of various organisations locally known as consumer forums or consumer protection councils. They guide consumers on how to file cases in the consumer courts.

(iv) On many occasions, they also represent individual consumers in the consumer courts.

(v) These voluntary organisations also receive financial support from the government for creating awareness among the people.

4. "Consumer awareness in India faced so many obstacles and had not been an easy growth". Explain. Competency Based

Ans. Consumer awareness in India faced the following obstacles for which it had not been an easy growth

(i) The consumer redressal process is becoming cumbersome, expensive and time consuming.

(ii) Many a time, consumers are required to engage lawyers. These cases require time for filing and attending the court proceedings, etc.

(iii) Evidence is not easy to gather as most of purchases are done without cash memo.

(iv) Most purchases in the market are small retail sales. The enforcement of laws that protect consumers especially in the unorganised sectors is weak.

(v) The existing laws are also not very clear on the issue of compensation to consumer injured by defective products.

ASSESSMENT EXERCISE

Multiple Choice Questions (MCQs)

1. Which one of the following quality certifications should be obtained by fruit processing companies?

(a) ISI (b) Hallmark
(c) ISO (d) FPO

2. At how many levels Consumer Courts have been established?

(a) Four (b) Three
(c) Two (d) One

3. In which year, the United Nations adopted the UN Guidelines for consumer protection?

(a) 1987 (b) 1986
(c) 1985 (d) 1984

4. Consider the following statements and select the correct option associated with market place.

(a) We participate in the market as a producer only.
(b) Consumers participate in the market when they pruchase goods and services that they need.
(c) Rules and regulations are not required for the protection of the consumers in the market place.
(d) In a market place individual consumers often find themselves in a strong position.

Subjective Questions (VSA, SA & LA)

1. Name three voluntary organisations that promote consumer movement in India.

2. When was consumer movement organised for the first time in India?

3. What major step was taken by Indian Government in 1986 for consumer protection?

4. Explain the right to choice with the help of an example.

5. Why is the three-tier quasi-judicial machinery set-up for redressal of consumer disputes?

6. Write about judicial structure of consumer disputes in India.

7. Describe any three legal measures taken by the government to empower the consumer in India.

8. How has the consumer movement evolved in India?

9. Do you agree that RTI serves to redress consumer grievances?

10. While using many goods and services, we as consumers have the right to be protected against the marketing of goods and delivery of services that are hazardous to life and property. Analyse which right of a consumer do you think is most important and why?

DISASTER MANAGEMENT

CHAPTER 1

Introduction... Do You Remember

People have been living with risk ever since they first joined efforts, shared resources and assumed responsibilities in social groups. Social development and human well being have advanced only because people have taken risk. Time and again, we see the terrible toll that natural disasters inflict on vulnerable communities around the world.

Over the recent decades, there has been an alarming increase in the occurrence of natural disasters and the magnitude of their social, economic and environmental impacts. This extensive damage to lives, property and livelihood of the affected communities has turned back the development clock of the areas by decades.

Chapter 2 of the book discusses the devastating killer waves that hit the country disrupting the normal life and ways and measures to prevent oneself from them.

Chapter 3 deals with the survival skills, which would give you an insight into search and rescue measures that need to be taken during an emergency and first aid measures that need to be taken for burns, bleeding, snakebite, poisoning, etc.

Chapter 4 of the book discusses about various alternative communication systems that exist in the world of science and technology today. As this chapter is based on science, do take help from your science teachers. Hope you all will enjoy reading it and relate it to your favorite subject of 'Physics. This case study that you have just read points out how important it is for us to have an understanding of good constructional practices so that you are safe in your schools and at home.

To have a better understanding of safe construction practices, **Chapter 5** of the book discusses about various safe construction practices that needs to be adhered to by people residing in vulnerable pockets like earthquake, landslide, flood and cyclone prone regions of the country.

It is time to take help and support from the government and various agencies like the NCC, NSS, Home Guards, etc and get ourselves prepared.

Chapter 6 discusses the roles that government and various agencies play in managing disasters. You too as an active and responsible citizen of the country can play a major role. You can be a volunteer and also a skilled personnel and save lives of your near and dear country men/women in any disaster scenario.

To have a safer living and a safer tomorrow it is time for us to plan ahead for our community/locality that we live in.

Chapter 7 of the book discusses the components and the process of preparing the disaster management plan for your area. The case study in the chapter shows how proper planning at the community level has saved people of Bangladesh from the devastating cyclones.

Tsunami The Killer Sea Wave

CHAPTER 2

Tsunami is a major natural disaster that frequently hits the Pacific coasts i.e. Eastern Asia, South-Eastern Asia and American coast. The term 'Tsunami' has been coined from the Japanese term **'tsu'** meaning **'harbour** and **nami'** meaning **waves**.

A devastating and killer Tsunami hit the South Eastern countries of Asia on 26th December, 2004. The killer sea wave had affected 11 countries including India killing more than 1.5 lakh precious lives and the toll rose further by the after effects. It was the biggest Tsunami in the world in past 40 years. The emotional, economical and ecological loss cannot be calculated. It can take more than decades to revive the affected countries. This Tsunami was triggered by a massive earthquake in the Indian Ocean.

2.1 Occurrence of Tsunami

In the recorded history, Tsunamis have killed lakhs of people world wide. Tsunamis are waves generated by earthquakes, volcanic eruptions or under water landslides and it can reach upto 15 m or more in height devastating coastal communities.

In the deep sea, due to availability of huge water and depth, the killer waves cannot be noticed and are seen as ripples or small, but broad (high **wavelength**[1]) waves. When waves approaches the coast, the depth reduces and the water that is propelled by oceanic force now emerges as killer waves with slower speed and much heights that can travel hundreds of kilometres on the land with much devastation.

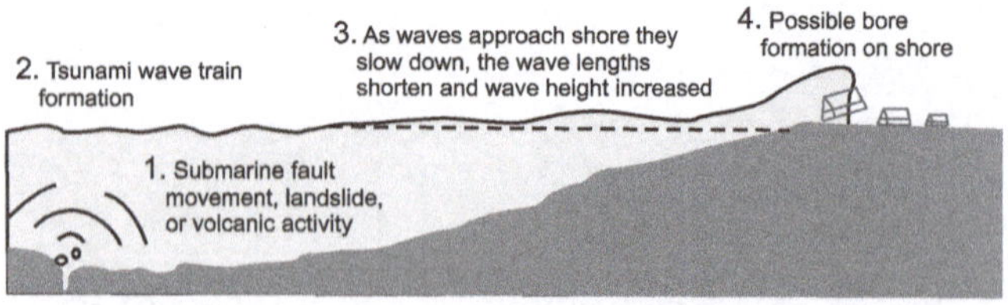

The Tsunami danger period can continue for many hours after a major earthquake. Waves can travel with very high speed of hundreds of kilometres per hour and reach the coast several hours after the earthquake.

Its nature is different from ordinary tides which are short, frequent and at surface level. In comparison, it can be imagined that if a earthquake hits Los Angeles (West Coast of America), a Tsunami can reach Tokyo (East Coast of Asia) less than the time taken by a jet air plane. Some places a myth regarding Tsunami is prevailing that Tsunamis are pulled by Moon which is not a scientific fact.

Krakatoa in Indonesia

In 1883, the violent explosion of famous volcano, Krakatoa in Indonesia, produced Tsunamis measuring 40 metres, which crashed upon Java and Sumatra.
Over 36000 people lost their lives and almost whole of the islands were flooded. This Tsunami was triggered by a huge volcanic explosion. The explosion was so violent that huge amount of debris fall into ocean and triggered this killer Tsunami.

2.2 Important Facts About Tsunamis

- Some Tsunamis can be very large, in coastal areas their height can be as great as 10 m or more (30 m in extreme cases).
- In deep oceans, Tsunamis can travel at speed of upto 800 km/h but appear as small waves.
- All low-lying coastal areas can be struck by Tsunamis and the Tsunami can move inland several hundred kilometres.
- A Tsunami consists of a series of waves, with subsequent waves lasting for several hours after the arrival of the first wave.
- Sometimes, a Tsunami causes the water near the shore to initially recede, exposing the ocean floor. This is a

1 **Wavelength** It is the length of a single wave or technically the distance between two consecutive crest or trough (peaks).

natural warning of an approaching Tsunami and should be understood.

- The forces of some Tsunamis are so high that large rocks weighing several tons, along with boats and other debris, can be moved inland several metres by them.
- Houses and other buildings are destroyed. All floating material and water move with great force and can kill or injure people.
- It can occur in day or night and can move with a speed as fast as 50 km per hour on coastal plain and capture all human being and domestic animals on its path.
- Tsunamis can travel up rivers and streams that lead to the ocean, especially estuaries and can cause massive flood in the **hinterlands**[2].

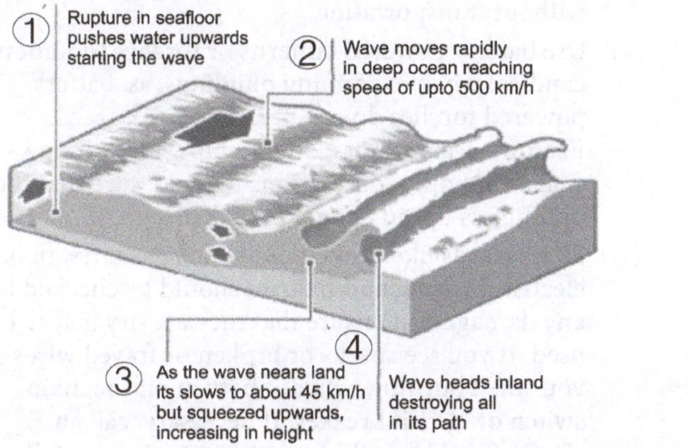

Tsunami wave train formation Seen in the figure is the rupture in the seafloor shunted in the vertical direction. This movement displaces hundreds of cubic kilometres of the overlaying water, generating a massive Tsunami or sea surge.

Detecting Tsunamis

Using satellite technology, nearly immediate warning of potential **Tsuna-migenic earthquakes**[3] can be given. Warning time depends upon the distance of the **epicentre**[4] of the ocean floor earthquake from the coastline. The warning includes predicted times at selected coastal communities.

Coastal tidal gauges can stop Tsunamis close to the shore, but they cannot do so in deep oceans. Tsunami detectors are deployed at depths down to 50 km or more out at sea and are called **Tsunameters**[5]. These Tsunameters transmit acoustic warnings of buoys on the sea surface, which relay it to satellites.

2.3 What to do Before a Tsunami?

(i) Find out the height of the road / lane of your home / school /workplace above sea level and check whether it is a Tsunami hazard prone area.

(ii) Plan evacuation routes from any place where it could be known that Tsunami risk is there. Practice evacuation from these places.

(iii) Have **disaster supplies**[6] like drinking water, food, torches and other essential items on hand.

(iv) Talk with your family members about Tsunamis, so that all are aware about them.

(v) Develop an emergency communication plan for family members getting separated from one another during a Tsunami. Ask an out of state relative or friend to serve as the family contact.

If you are at risk from Tsunamis, you should

- Avoid building or living in buildings near the coast.
- Make a list of items to bring inside the home in case a Tsunami occurs.
- If living near the coast, the home should be at a height where most Tsunami waves do not reach, i.e. more than 10 feet above sea level.
- Take precautions to prevent flooding inside the home.
- Ask a civil engineer to check your home and give suggestions on how to make it more resistant to force of water due to a Tsunami.

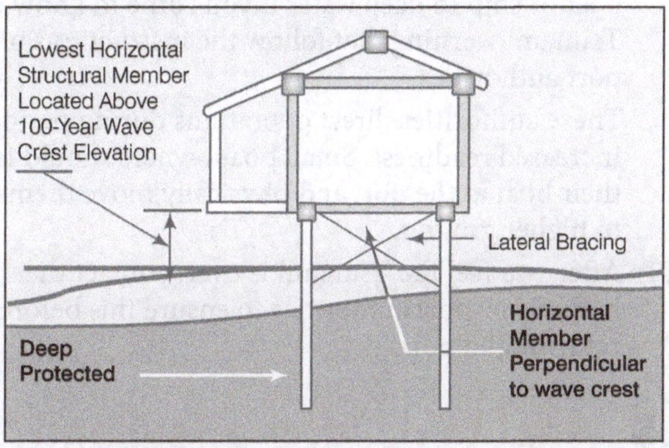

- Listen to local radio or television stations for updated emergency information and adhere to instructions issued by local authorities.

2 **Hinterland** The areas of a country that are away from the coast, from the banks of a large river or from the main cities.

3 **Tsuna-migenic earthquakes** Tsuna-migenic is referring to those earthquakes, which commonly occur along with major subduction-zone (converging plate boundary) i.e. plates bordering the Pacific Oceans, Indo-Burma Plates etc those have potential for creating Tsunamis.

4 **Epicentre** It is the point on the Earth's surface that is directly above the focus (the point of origin) of an earthquake. The epicentre is usually the location where the greatest damage associated with an earthquake occurs.

5 **Tsunameter** It is an equipment used to detect tsunamis, deployed across the open ocean to form a network for the purpose of early warning.

6 **Disaster Supplies** These refer to a collection of basic items your household may need in the event of an emergency. This means having your own food, water and other essentials in sufficient quantity to last for at least 72 hours (3 days). Local authorities and relief workers cannot reach everyone immediately. You could get help in hours or it might take a few days.

2.4 What to do During a Tsunami?

If you are at home

(i) If you get information about a Tsunami warning for your area, inform your entire family. If you live in a Tsunami prone area, you should evacuate the house to a higher safe place, moving in a calm and safe manner to the evacuation site.

(ii) Take your disaster supplies with you to ensure your comfort till the disaster is over. Also take your animals with you.

(iii) If you are at the beach or near the ocean and you feel the earth shake, do not wait for a Tsunami warning, but move immediately to an elevated place. Stay away from rivers and streams that lead to the oceans.

(iv) Upper floors of high multi-storey, reinforced concrete buildings can provide a safe evacuation area. Staying away from low-lying coastal areas is the safest advice when there is a tsunami warning.

(v) Keep updating yourself and others by the radio or television from time to time and find out the latest announcements.

If you are on a boat or ship

(i) Do not return to port if you are at sea and a Tsunami warning has been issued for your area, as Tsunamis create unpredictable and dangerous currents in harbours and ports.

(ii) If you are in the port or on the coastline, move your boat or ship to deep water if you come to know of a Tsunami warning, but follow the instructions of the port authorities.

These authorities direct operations during periods of increased readiness. Small boat owners should leave their boat at the port and physically move themselves to higher ground.

(iii) After you feel the Tsunami is over, contact the harbour or port authorities to ensure this before returning to port.

2.5 What to do After a Tsunami?

After a Tsunami you should

(i) Keep listening to radio or television for current information about damaged roads, bridges or other unsafe areas. Avoid visiting areas where a disaster has occurred, as this may hamper rescue operations and put you at risk from floods, contaminated water, crumbled roads, landslides, etc.

(ii) Use telephones and mobile phones only for emergency calls, so that lines should not get overloaded to ensure people in emergency can get through.

(iii) Stay out of a building if water remains around it. Water can weaken foundations, causing buildings to sink, floors to crack or walls to collapse. When entering buildings after a Tsunami, watch every step you take. Wear long pants, a long-sleeved shirt and good shoes, otherwise you may get cuts on your feet.

(iv) Check yourself for injuries and get first aid if necessary before helping injured or trapped persons. If someone needs to be rescued, call professionals with the right equipment to help. Help people like infants, the elderly, the handicapped and those without transportation.

(v) Use battery powered lanterns or torches (do not use candles) when examining buildings, as battery powered torches do not present a fire hazard. Examine walls, floors, doors, staircases, windows as well as building foundations to make sure that the building is not in danger of collapsing.

(vi) Fire hazards like broken or leaking gas lines, flooded electrical wiring and fixtures should be checked for any damage and ensure that they are dry before being used. If you see sparks or broken or frayed wires or if you smell burning insulation, turn off the main switch or circuit breaker. If necessary, call an electrician. Fire is the most frequent hazard following floods.

(vii) If you smell gas or hear a blowing or hissing noise, open a window and ask all to move outside. Turn off the piped gas from the main valve outside the building, if possible and call the gas company from a neighbour's home.

(viii) Check for damage to sewage and water lines. If damaged, avoid using the toilets and call a plumber. Contact the water supply company if water pipes are damaged. Do not use water from the tap. Use tap water only if the Local Health Department advises that it is safe.

(ix) Watch out for wild animals, especially poisonous snakes, that may have come into buildings with the water. Use a stick to poke through accumulated debris.

(x) Watch for loose plaster and roofs that could fall. Open the windows and doors to help dry the building. Remove mud from inside the building before it solidifies.

REVIEW EXERCISE

Including CBSE Textbook Questions

Q.1 Name three causes of Tsunami and explain its impacts. CBSE Textbook

Ans. Three causes of Tsunami are

(i) Earthquakes

(ii) Volcanic eruptions

(iii) Under water landslides

Impacts

- Tsunamis are waves which can reach upto 18 metres or more in height, devastating coastal communities.
- In recorded history, Tsunamis world wide have killed hundreds of thousands of people.
- Tsunamis caused by nearby earthquakes may reach the coast within minutes. When the waves enter shallow water, they may rise to several metres, striking the coast with devastating force.
- The Tsunami danger period can continue for many hours after a major earthquake.

Q.2 Explain two different ways of detecting Tsunami. CBSE Textbook

Ans. Two ways of detecting Tsunamis now-a-days are

(i) With the use of satellite technology, it is possible to provide nearly immediate warning of potentially Tsuna-migenic earthquakes. 'Tsunameters' transmit warnings of buoys on the sea surface, which relay it to satellites. Warning time depends upon the distance of the epicentre from the coastline. The warning includes predicted times at selected coastal communities where the Tsunami could travel within a few hours.

(ii) Tsunami detectors, linked to land by submarine cables, are deployed at about 50 kms out at sea.

Q.3 State two preparedness measures each in pre, during and post Tsunami scenarios. CBSE Textbook

Ans. The preparedness measures for pre Tsunami are

(i) Know the height of your home / road above sea level and the distance of your home from the coast or other water sources in which Tsunami water can flow.

(ii) Plan evacuation routes from your home, school, workplace or any other place you could be where Tsunamis present a risk.

The preparedness measures during Tsunami are

(i) Your family should evacuate the house if you live in a Tsunami prone area. Evacuate to a safe elevated area and move in an orderly, calm and safe manner to the evacuation site.

(ii) Take your Disaster Supplies Kit. Having supplies will make you more comfortable during the evacuation.

The preparedness measures for post Tsunami are

(i) Continue using a battery operated radio for updated emergency information. The Tsunami may have damaged bridges or other places that may be unsafe.

(ii) Avoid disaster areas, your presence might hamper rescue and other emergency operations and put you at further risk from the residual effects of floods, such as contaminated water, crumbled roads, landslides, mudflows and other hazards.

PROJECTS

Q.1 Choose a Tsunami hit area and study the following in that region.

(i) Extent of damage and location of the epicentre.

(ii) Areas affected.

(iii) How could the damages be minimised?

(iv) What measures should be adopted to save the coastal fishermen, villagers, hoteliers and the tourists?

(v) What guidelines are to be followed by the people so that they can prevent loss of life next time?

Q.2 Suggest operations of a rescue team and disaster management team in a disaster prone area.

(i) How will the rescue team operate to help save maximum people and also resettle them?

(ii) Mention the probabilities of damage and suggest the action plan of the rescue team.

(iii) How should the disaster management team operate before a Tsunami to restrict the extent of damage? You can show the probable areas of damage on a map.

(iv) Make two indexes (a) for a high risk zone and (b) low risk zone.

Hint For both projects, refer to textbook and what you have been taught in earlier classes. Take the help of your teacher where required.

Survival Skills

CHAPTER 3

Mankind has been coping with disasters since time immemorial. India is also not isolated from this phenomena. Modern techniques alongwith indigenous ways of disaster preparedness and management are adopted in India.

In 1999, a devastating super cyclone[1] hit Odisha, causing massive destruction. It struck the Eastern coast of India near Paradip on 29th October, with wind speed of 270 to 300 km/h. This happened just after another cyclone had hit Odisha on 17th October.

The super cyclone affected over 19 million people, including 3.5 million children and caused severe damage in 14 districts and 128 blocks. Many people, including the NCC, civil defence and national and international organisations, worked together for rescue[2] and relief efforts.

This disaster showed how important disaster management is and taught many valuable lessons to prepare for such events in the future.

3.1 Search and Rescue Skills

In emergency situations arising immediately after a disaster, there is a need for a large number of volunteers with good search and rescue[3] skills, as these can help to save many precious lives. The first response for search and rescue is always at the local level. However, it is a daunting task for the locals to rescue the victims due to lack of skill.

We cannot stop hazards from happening, but preparedness can make all the differences between life and death. People living in areas vulnerable to disasters, cope with disasters based on their acumen, accumulated knowledge and skills and resources of the community. After a disaster, search and rescue have always played a major role in disaster management.

3.2 Defining Search and Rescue

Search and rescue is a technical activity rendered by an individual or a group of specially trained personnel, who rescue and attend to the casualties under adverse conditions, where life is at threat. It is done as a team task organised in close cooperation with the community.

Search and rescue activities are performed at two levels

(i) **Community as local rescuers** With adequate safety measures, rescue activities are taken up immediately by the community after any disaster.

(ii) **Outside community resources** Where the situation is grave and the local rescuers do not have required skills and equipment then specialist assistance from outside the community is required.

The major objectives of a search and rescue team are

(i) Rescue the survivors trapped under the debris of damaged buildings or from a cyclonic storm surge.

(ii) Provide first aid[4] services to the trapped survivors and send them for further care to hospitals if required.

(iii) Take other immediate actions like temporary support and protection to endangered or collapsed buildings.

(iv) Recover, handover and dispose off the bodies of the people who have died.

(v) Train, demonstrate and raise awareness of the people on how to use the local materials for rescuing the community people.

1 Super Cyclone It is a rapidly rotating storm system characterised by spiral arrangement of thunderstorms rains, a low-pressure centre and strong wind is known as a super cyclone.

2 Rescue It is the action of evacuating or taking out victims of natural or man-made disasters to a safer place. This is an emergency life saving action.

3 Search and Rescue It is the search for and provision of aid to people who are in distress or imminent danger due to a disaster.

4 First Aid It is the preliminary treatment given to a victim at first approach is called first aid. Normally, necessary equipments or treatment aids are kept in a box called first aid box.

Team Composition

Male and female adults who are able to read and write the local language should be made part of such teams. They should be honest, emotionally sound and professionally decisive, in good physical condition, with a demonstrated capacity and willingness to work in an emergency. Ex-Army and paramilitary persons should be preferred as members of such teams.

The Case of Maggie

Maggie, an 18 years old young girl from Pilloba - one among several small islands in Nicobar,belongs to the fishing community and is an only daughter. On Sunday morning, she was woken up by the roar of the sea.

She felt her home giving way. She quickly clutched on to a large bamboo raft and shoved her ailing parents onto it. She held on to it tight. "So did several others", says Maggie. She did scream at everyone to hold as tight as she was doing. That was the only way to escape the fury of the giant waves.

The Coast Guard commander confirms: "The waves were well above 10 metres high. They sucked in anything in their path." He says 44 persons from Pilloba were found hanging on the rafts on the violent sea when Coast Guard vessels stopped them. Maggie says "I did what I could do for my dear villagers. I knew I would survive this way and if I could, the others would too."

What are the Duties of a Rescuer?

The first job of a rescuer is to assess the area regarding the extent of damage, approach to the damage area, assess particulars of the damage and understand if any further damage is likely to occur.

This information should be collected from the local people.

Follow three key principles during the survey

(i) **Look** See physically the incidents and make a thorough visual inspection.

(ii) **Listen** Listen to all the sources of information from the community, government records and media reports.

(iii) **Feel** Feel convinced regarding the fact, the gravity of the dangers and our own capacity to respond.

Plan

Rescue is a teams effort and for achieving the optimum level of response operation it needs proper coordination and planning amongst the members.

Only after the assessment of damage is done, the rescue team can plan a rescue operation, keeping in mind the following aspects

(i) **Manpower** Use skilled manpower where available and also take help from the local community.

(ii) **Equipment** Bamboos or sticks, stretchers, ropes, ladders, boats, etc are essential. If these are not available at the disaster site, locally available materials like tubes of tyres, barrels and tin cans should be used.

In modern days, some advanced equipments are used in rescue operations like Infra red cameras, Acoustic devices and **Bio radars**[5], etc. These are as follows

- **Infrared cameras** detects the body heat of victims and locate them under the rubble.
- **Acoustic devices** are used to detect faint noises of the victims from the rubble.
- Bio radars can locate marooned victims in flood-affected areas.

(iii) **Method** The correct method of rescue is decided depending on the nature of casualty, the type of injuries and the position in which the casualty is found.

3.3 Precautions

Precautions[6] are necessary to be taken while rescuing victims from affected building.

Before entering a building

- Observe the damaged portion of the building and structural pattern to avoid accident.
- Check the walls and assure support for weak walls.
- Be careful for possible hazards from weak structures.

When entering the damaged buildings

- Use helmets and avoid touching damaged walls or blocked doors in the affected portion.
- Do not move alone.
- Keep calling.
- Keep attention to possible sounds.
- Be aware of naked wires and treat them as live wires.

While moving inside the damaged building

- Do not ignite fire and be careful in all of your movements.

5 **Bio Radar** It is the equipment with sensors able to detect human heartbeats and respiration signals without direct skin contact.
6 **Precaution** It is the necessary action to be taken on wisdom to avoid future disasters or lessen disaster effects.

- Keep close to the walls and do not pull anything projecting out from the collapsed portions.

Keep in Mind During Search and Rescue Operations

Do's	Don'ts
Keep calm.	Do not panic.
Make a thorough assessment prior to rescue.	Do not start rescue work until you get adequate informations and equipment.
Properly examine the casualty and protect the casualty from further harm with applying proper aid.	Do not carelessly move an injured casualty unless the person is in immediate danger.
Be careful in using sharpen tools, avoid naked wires while rescuing casualties.	Do not touch live wire.
Give artificial respiration, if required and control bleeding.	Do not violate safety measures.

3.4 First Aid

First aid means measures taken immediately after an accident to prevent further harm being done, but not with an idea to cure.

It uses the available human and material resources at the site of accident to provide initial care to the victim of injury or sudden illness until proper care can be organised.

The objectives are

(i) To preserve life.

(ii) To prevent the victim's condition from worsening.

(iii) To promote recovery.

The goals of first aid are

(i) To restore and maintain vital functions, the ABC of basic life support (airway, breathing and circulation) are always given the first priority.

This means that

- The airway must be open so that air containing oxygen enters the body.
- Breathing must take place so that oxygen passes through the lungs into the bloodstream.
- The heart must circulate the oxygen carrying blood.

(ii) To prevent further injury or deterioration.

(iii) To reassure the victim and make him or her as comfortable as possible.

Make Your Own First Aid Kit

- Cotton wool
- Crepe bandage
- Triangular bandage
- Scissors
- Soap
- Antacid
- Adhesive tape
- Sterile dressing
- Thermometer
- Gloves
- Pain reliever
- ORS packets

Action Plan

An action plan helps a first aider in assessing whether the victim has any life threatening conditions or if any immediate first aid is necessary. This has five questions to be answered and is given the name '**DRABC**'.

Danger	Is there any danger to the victim, yourself or others?
Response	Is the victim conscious or unconscious?
Airway	Is the airway open and clear of objects?
Breathing	Is the victim's chest rising and falling? Can you hear the breath or feel it on your cheek?
Circulation	Can we feel a pulse or other obvious signs of life?

Based on the kind of problem observed, first aid has to be carried out.

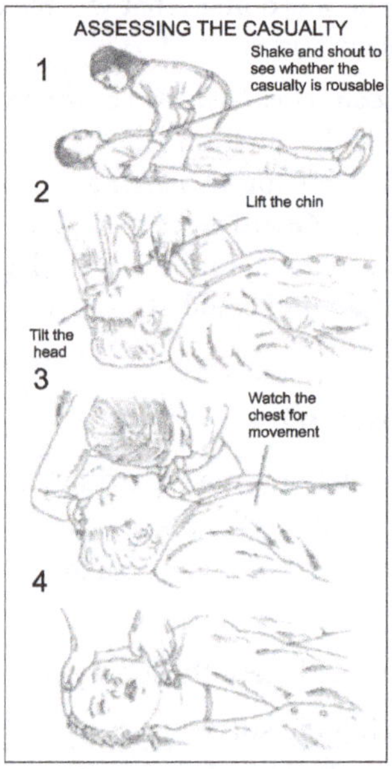

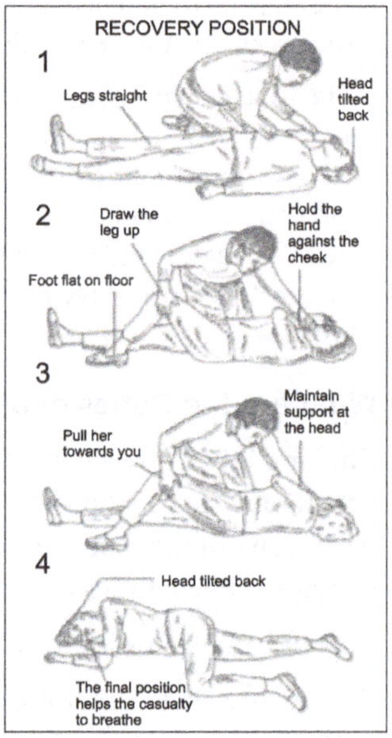

Fainting or Losing Consciousness

Fainting is a brief loss of consciousness that results of any interference with the function of the brain. Common causes are head injury, epilepsy, stroke, poisoning, diabetes and any conditions associated with lack of oxygen.

Procedure for First Aid

- Examine properly the causes of unconsciousness and pinch the victim to test his/her consciousness.
- Right position for the victim to lay would be tilting head back, keeping arms at right angle to body and raising the legs 8 to 12 inches to promote blood flow to the brain.

- Loosen his/her clothes, keep him/her warm and record regularly the condition of the casualty.
- Avoid crowd and do not allow the person to get up unless he/she gains full consciousness and do not give the patient anything to eat or drink.

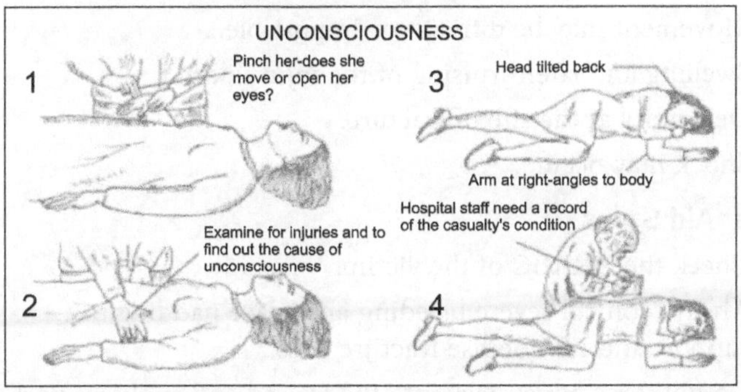

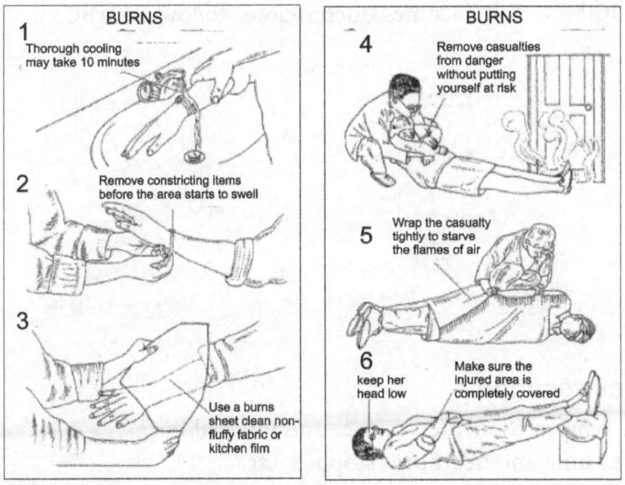

Burns

These are damage to the skin caused by contact with dry heat. They may be caused by fire, flames, steam, hot liquids, hot metal, sunlight, electricity or chemicals. The degree of burn varies

- **First degree** (superficial) burns involves only top layer of skin and generally painful and the area often swells. Most burns are of this type.
- **Second degree** (partial-thickness) burns involve both outer and inner skin layers. The area is red and blisters may open and fluids weep out making skin appear wet. It is severely painful and the area often swells.
- **Third degree** (full thickness) burns destroy both layers of the skin with muscles, bones, blood vessels and nerves and charred the tissues underneath.

Procedure for First Aid

- Immediately immerse the burnt area in cool water, but not extreme water pressure, clothes soaked in cool water may be applied.
- Cover the area with dry, sterile dressing not cotton or other fluffy material, but do not remove the cloth that is stuck to the burnt area.
- Remove jewellery and constrictive clothing before swelling or blisters occur.
- Drop, cover and roll if caught fire, or cover the person with a blanket, but do not apply butter ointment, oil, ice in the area affected.

Frost-Bite

This occurs when body tissues freeze after exposure to below zero temperatures. The signs and symptoms include white, waxy looking skin that is firm to the touch, but the tissue underneath feels soft and pain followed by numbness.

Procedure for First Aid

- Cover frost bitten toes, ears with warm hands.
- Do not apply direct heat as this may rewarm the area too quickly, only the area affected can be warmed by breathing on them or placing the affected area in warm water (40°C).
- Do not rub the body as tiny ice crystals may cause more damage, never rub snow on the area.
- Do not break blisters if any and do not let the patient walk.

Bleeding

Bleeding occurs when blood flows out of the body through a cut, wound, scraps or broken vessel. It could be external bleeding (visible blood flow) or internal bleeding (blood loss inside the body).

Necessary Steps

- To stop bleeding, restore to direct pressure, lie the victim down and raise the injured part above the heart.
- Clotting slows down bleeding and bandage is necessary to stop bleeding and avoid infection of the wound. Change the bandage at least once a day and tetanus injection needs to be taken if required.
- Put on gloves to guard against infection.
- Apply pressure according to the situation of wound.

- If the victim becomes unconscious, follow DRABC.

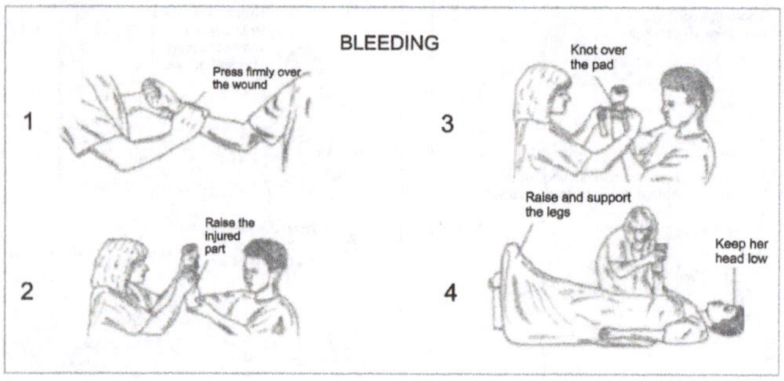

Electrocution

Its symptoms include surface and internal burns, breathing and heart beat stopped, etc.

The best way to treat the victim is first to cut off the power supply (do not touch the victim until this has been done) and remove the victim from the source using non-conductive material.

Carry the DRABC exercise and send him to the hospital immediately.

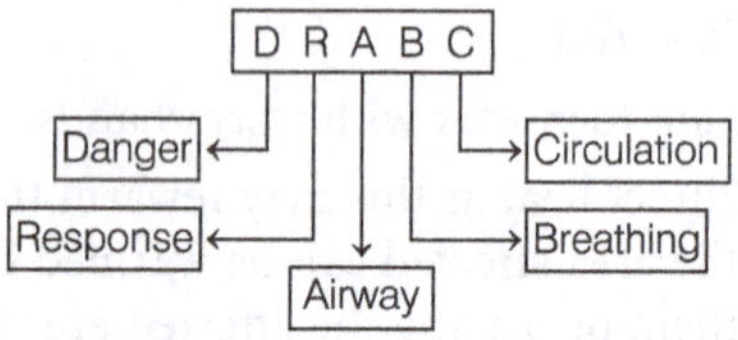

Never approach the casualty in a high-voltage zone, it may cause danger to first aider also.

Snake Bite

This generally occurs on the limbs and most often on the legs.

Necessary Cautions

- It is suggested to assume the bite to be from a venomous snake always and must be treated with a pressure immobilisation bandage.
- Keep the bitten limb below the level of the heart and allow the bleeding freely for 15-30 seconds.
- Wash the affected area with soap or dettol and bandage it.
- Start resuscitation if needed but avoid if there is wound in the mouth. Suck it out but do not swallow and spit the venom out.
- Shift the patient immediately to the hospital.
- Stay calm and instruct the person to avoid all movement on the area affected.

Fractures and Sprains

This is an injury affecting the skeleton and can be caused by the application of direct or indirect force. The general signs and symptoms are

- Pain at or near the site of injury increased by movement.
- Movement may be difficult or impossible.
- Swelling and later bruising of the injury part.
- Deformity at the site of fracture.
- Shock may occur.

First Aid Steps

- Check the DRABC of the victim.
- Always control severe bleeding and place padding to support and immobilise fracture sites.
- Do not force bones back into the wound and apply ice pack on the affected area to reduce pain and control swelling.
- Treat to prevent shock.

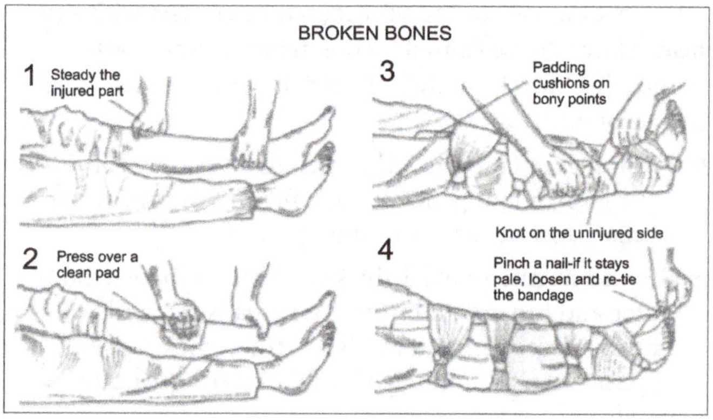

Poisoning

This occurs due to any substance causing injury, illness or death, when introduced into the body. Ingested poisons are introduced through the mouth by eating or drinking poisonous substances.

Inhaled poisons are introduced through the lungs by inhaling industrial gases, fumes from fire, chemical vapours and engine exhaust.

Absorbed poisons are absorbed through the skin *via* contact with poisonous sprays such as pesticides and insecticides.

Necessary Steps

- Check the DRABC of the victim.
- Give milk or water to dilute down the poison.
- Monitor vital signs and observe the amount and colour of vomitus.
- Do not induce him to vomiting and send him to hospital.

Heat Stroke

Heat stroke occurs when the body's cooling system fails, the body temperature rises fast.

Signs and Symptoms In this, the temperature of the body is very high and it feels hot and dry. The skin is red with no sweating and fast pulse rate, dilated pupils, confusion and sometimes victim may be unconscious. Heat strokes[7] strike suddenly when the body's cooling system fails and body temperature rises fast.

Necessary Action Needed

- Lower the body temperature by loosing the clothes or fanning and put ice packs or cold compresses to the neck, under the arm pits and to the groin area.
- Provide more fluid drinks and avoid hotter places.
- During dehydration[8] give the patients Oral Rehydration Solution[9] (ORS).
  It can be prepared in home by dissolving a pinch of salt and a table spoon of sugar to a glass of water. ORS rehydrate the body by restoring back the electrolyte balance.

Dog Bite

Here, the first job is to prevent rabies, to reduce the risk of infection and to get medical aid as soon as possible.

First Aid Actions

- Wipe the saliva away from the wound and wash the wound properly with plenty of soap and water.
- Cover the wound with a dry, sterile dressing and send the patient to hospital as soon as possible.

REVIEW EXERCISE

Including CBSE Textbook Questions

CLASSROOM EXERCISES

Q.1 What is the main objective of a search and rescue team? Define the team composition. CBSE Textbook

Ans. The main objectives of a search and rescue team are

(i) Rescue the survivors trapped under the debris of the damaged buildings.

(ii) Provide first aid services to the trapped survivors and send them for medical care.

(iii) Take immediate and necessary actions like temporary support and protection to endangered or collapsed buildings and structures.

(iv) Recover, handover and dispose off the bodies of the deceased.

(v) Train, demonstrate and raise awareness on how to use the local materials for rescuing community people.

Team Composition

(i) Honest, emotionally sound, professionally decisive volunteers, both male and female, having good physical condition, with demonstrated capacity and willingness to work in an emergency, should be part of a rescue team. They should be above the age of 18 years with a minimum education level (reading and writing the local language).

(ii) Preference should be given to ex-military or army personnel.

Q.2 Identify two indigenous ways to rescue people in case of floods. CBSE Textbook

Ans. The indigenous methods can be

(i) Deploy rescue teams with rowboats or motorboats to evacuate people from flooded areas.

(ii) In case, somebody is already in the flood waters, throw them an inflated tube of a car or truck, by using which they can reach to a safe place.

Q.3 Name three different ways to make a stretcher with the locally available resources. CBSE Textbook

Ans. Three different ways to make a stretcher are

(i) Hand-made stretchers

(ii) Upper garment as stretchers

(iii) Ladder/rope as stretcher

---

7 **Heat Stroke** It is a severe condition caused by impairment of the body's temperature-regulating abilities, resulting from prolonged exposure to excessive heat. The characteristics are no sweating, severe headache, high fever, hot dry skin and in serious cases, collapse and coma situation

8 **Dehydration** It is a condition in which salt and water are lost in the body.

9 **Oral Rehydration Solution** It is a liquid preparation developed by the World Health Organisation (WHO) that can decrease fluid loss in persons with cholera or diarrhoea. It can also be prepared at home using one litre of plain water with half a teaspoon of salt, six level teaspoons of sugar.

Q.4 Explain the goals of first aid. CBSE Textbook

Ans. The goals of first aid are

(i) To restore and maintain vital functions. The ABC of basic life support (Airway, Breathing and Circulation) are always the first priority. Airway must be open so that air containing oxygen enters the body.

Breathing must take place so that oxygen passes through the lungs into the blood stream. The heart must circulate the oxygen carrying blood.

(ii) To prevent further injury or deterioration.

(iii) To reassure the victim and make him or her as comfortable as possible.

Q.5 What are the causes of fainting and what are the measures that need to be taken up if you see someone who has fainted? CBSE Textbook

Ans. Fainting is a brief loss of consciousness and is the result of an interference with the function of the brain. There are many causes of unconsciousness, the most common of which are head injury, epilepsy, stroke, poisoning, diabetes and conditions associated with lack of oxygen.

If you have seen a person fainting, do the following

(i) Catch the person before he/she falls.

(ii) Pinch the person and see if she moves or opens her eyes.

(iii) Examine the injuries and causes of unconsciousness.

(iv) Tilt the person's head back and keep arms at right angle to body.

(v) Raise the legs 8 to 12 inches. This promotes blood flow to the brain.

(vi) Loosen any tight clothing.

(vii) Keep the victim warm if it is cold outside.

(viii) Keep a record of the casualty's condition.

The following points should also be remembered

(i) Do not give the patient anything to eat or drink.

(ii) Do not allow the person who has just fainted to get up until the victim is fully conscious.

(iii) Do not crowd around the victim if the area is warm.

Q.6 Identify two signs and symptoms of sprain and fracture. CBSE Textbook

Ans. The general signs and symptoms of sprain and fracture are

(i) Pain at or near the site of injury increased by movement.

(ii) Movement may be difficult or impossible.

(iii) Swelling and later bruising of the injured part.

(iv) Deformity at the site of the fracture.

(v) Shock may occur.

PROJECT WORK

Q.1 Mention the necessary steps for survival skills to be adopted for the common incidents that take place in a school, prepare a manual as a help guide. (common incidents - heat stroke, fire, fracture, nose bleeding, electrocution, fainting).

Q.2 State the role of a Disaster Management team like 'Red Cross Society' or the like in a post disaster scenario. Relate a disaster to describe their roles.

Q.3 Managing Disasters (The Role of Students) Choose any man-made or natural disaster which your area may be vulnerable to e.g. gas leaks, building collapse, rail or road accidents, laboratory accidents, health hazards due to toxic waste disposal, earthquakes, floods, volcanic eruptions, etc.

(i) Prepare a survey schedule detailing the different areas that are posing threats due to the various natural and man-made disasters in and around your school, e.g. factory/slum/dump yard located nearby.

(ii) Collect the data and prepare a report.

(iii) Develop posters and skits for awareness generation in your school.

(iv) Make a plan to deal with any one of the disasters likely to affect your school.

Q.4 Preparedness for Disasters

(i) Create activities to make people, particularly primary school children and school workers aware of disaster mitigation.

(ii) Write a manual of instructions and make kit lists for use by teachers to manage laboratory, classroom, corridors and school building security, buses, etc.

(iii) Prepare instructions to deal with any accidents in school or in the bus.

Hints

(i) Try to take the help of local people working with the Red Cross, or other aid agencies involved in relief work, who will help you to obtain free literature available on these issues with government agencies.

(ii) Find out anybody who works in a government hospital/private hospital/ nursing home who can help you to get more information about first aid procedures besides the ones given in the textbook.

Alternative Communication Systems... During Disasters

CHAPTER 4

In this chapter, various basic telecommunication facilities, need for alternative communication systems during the large-scale natural disaster/emergency situations and modes of emergency communication systems including satellite based communication systems are explained.

The floods in 2004, submerged telephone exchanges and disrupted telephone communication, and road and rail transportation in Assam and Bihar. As a result, the district headquarters got totally cut-off from the state headquarters and neighbouring districts.

In the severely affected districts, the need for relief and rescue operation could not be communicated to the state headquarters.

Realising these, both the State Governments requested National Disaster Management Division of the Government of India to immediately send the emergency coordination kits containing satellite phones to establish communication links among the severely affected districts and state headquarters. If this step had not been taken, it would have resulted in severe loss of human lives, livestock, property, etc.

Thus, it is very important to have proper communication between government authorities at different levels to help the affected people.

4.1 Public Switched Telephone Network (PSTN)

It is the prime network which is responsible for transmitting and receiving voice, fax and data. These are the landline telephones. All governments and private offices, police stations, fire stations, hospitals, a majority of homes and business places are connected by the PSTN line.

A major natural disaster or emergency situation like earthquake, cyclone, floods and landslides, etc leaves the public wired and wireless mobile telephones infrastructure damaged and non-functional.

The transmission towers may be damaged and power supply to operate telephone exchanges may be disrupted. Any damage to cellular transmission towers also affects the radio communication network of police and civil authorities.

Necessity of PSTN

It is extremely necessary to have the communication links operational at the time of any major disaster or emergency situation.

Proper communications of the critical needs of search and rescue operations, relief and response measures between the authorities of State Government, local administration, voluntary organisations and the affected people should be maintained and this calls for a reliable alternate communication link.

It may also happen that some severely affected areas get completely disconnected from other parts of the world.

In such situations, the urgent needs of the disaster-affected population are not shared with government authorities, voluntary organisations and unaffected populations in the vicinity. This may lead to severe losses in terms of human lives, livestocks and property.

Generally, a perfectly working PSTN system is designed so that no more than 5% of the phones connected to it can be talking at the same time.

During a crisis, there may be too much traffic for it to handle as 'Everyone wants to speak to everyone', and hence the network gets jammed.

Prime Communication Networks

Bharat Sanchar Nigam Limited (BSNL)

The Department of Telephone Operations, Government of India became a Corporation on 1st October, 2000 and was named as Bharat Sanchar Nigam Limited (BSNL)

Today, it is the leading telecommunication company and the largest public sector undertaking of India with a network of over 45 million lines, covering 7330 cities/towns with over 93 million telephone connections.

Expansion of the telecom network and improvement of the quality of telecom services in rural areas and instilling confidence among its customers are some of its major responsibilities.

National Informatics Centre (NIC)

NIC or the National Informatics Centre is a premier science and technology organisation of the Government of India in the field of informatics services and information technology applications and it was established in 1976.

To facilitate information and communication applications in government departments at the Central, State and District levels, it has established a nationwide Information and Communication Technology (ICT) network i.e. **NICNET**. It connects all district headquarters to the state capitals and to the centre with IT services.

4.2 Modes for Emergency Communication

Radio communications and satellite based communication systems are highly reliable and widely used.

Radio Communications

A disaster or emergency situation calls for reliable alternate communication links to ensure that the right resources are provided to the right people at the right time. A radio wave is an electromagnetic wave propagated by an antenna. The first obvious choice regarding this is to establish a wireless radio communication network.

Any such link based on the radio waves either use the terrestrial or satellite systems. Radio waves have different frequencies and by tuning a radio receiver to a specific frequency, you can pick up a specific signal.

Hand held wireless sets (also called 'walky talky') are considered to be more suitable for local communication in case of such emergencies.

Amateur (Ham) **Radio**

It refers to a special set of rules which apply to certain frequencies, as defined by the **International Telecommunications Union (ITU)** and regulated by wireless planning and Coordination Wing (Ministry of Communications) in India.

The rules allow these frequencies which to be used only for research, education and personal purposes.

This is the use of designated radio frequency spectrum for purposes of private recreation, non-commercial exchange of messages, wireless experimentation, self-training and emergency communication.

Amateur Radio as a Career

Its operation does not use ground based infrastructure. It requires a small amount of power to operate, which can easily be met by batteries and generators. Therefore, it has been experienced that Amateur Radio has worked successfully, when no other communication worked.

It is getting popular in India as a creative hobby and there are around 15000 licenced Ham radio operators.

Most of governments expect their amateurs to provide emergency communication support in case of an emergency and amateurs always come forward for such situations.

One of such examples can be taken from Odisha Super Cyclone (1999) and Gujarat Earthquake (2001) where Amateur volunteers provided remarkable services.

In an effort to popularise the Amateur Radio in the country, and to develop a trained force of licenced Amateurs, Department of Information Technology initiated a nationwide programme to establish Amateur Radio stations at various places and provide necessary training for operators.

HAM Operator Helps Families Connect with Tsunami Victims

An inspirational story of an amateur radio operator was published on 28th December, 2004 in 'The Tribune' of New Delhi.

Sandeep Baruah, a licenced HAM operator who works in a government organisation by day and pursues his hobby from home at night, has managed to establish communication links with Port Blair, the capital of Andaman and Nicobar Islands and has helped relay messages between the people stranded on the island and their families back home.

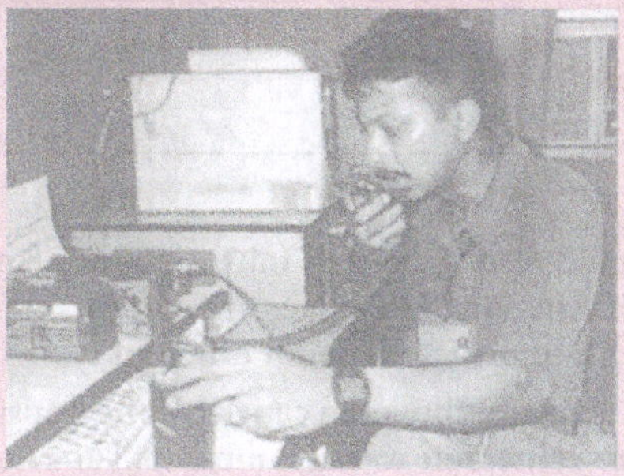

4.3 Satellite Based Communication Systems

Satellite Based Communication Systems refer to communication systems designed for users on the Earth, but have some equipment in space called a Satellite. These satellites perform tasks like taking weather pictures or finding exact locations on Earth, such as latitude and longitude.

When deadly floods struck Central and Southern Texas-USA in mid-October 1998, amateur radio operators from four states volunteered their time. A volunteer is shown helping with communications at a **Red Cross Office**.

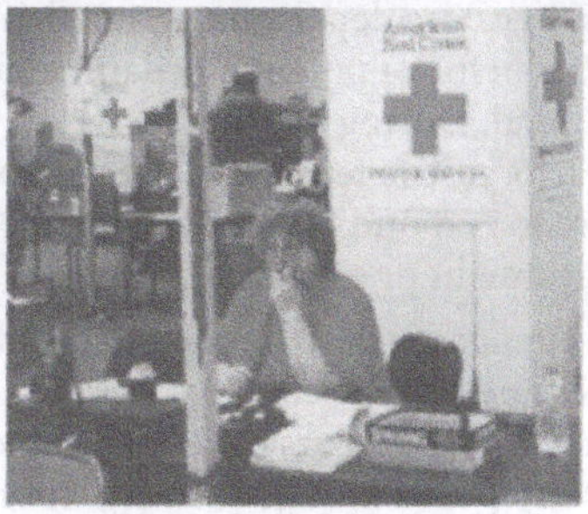

A Ham operator is on the radio, reporting a new flare up during the forest fires that broke out in several countries in Florida-USA during June and July of 1998.

You can also become an amateur at this age by passing the **Amateur Station Operators Licence** (ASOL) examination taken by WPC wing, Ministry of Communication, Government of India.

A young operator enjoys making friends over the radio. Amateur radio is a fascinating hobby for people of all ages and all walks of life irrespective of educational qualifications and status.

Communication Satellites (COMSATs) are essentially radio relay stations in space. The most important feature of these COMSATs is a **transponder**[1]. In other way, it is recognised as SATCOMS for **satellite**[2] communications and SATPHONE for a satellite phone terminal. A satellite contains hundreds or thousands of such transponders.

The satellite-based communication system is more reliable as the radio relay stations and in space communication satellite are not at all vulnerable to any disaster on the Earth. Most widely used means of satellite communications in disaster management is **satellite phone.**

These phones provide very reliable voice and data communication and are very handy and can be transported to any location.

1 **Transponder** A radio that receives conversation at one frequency and then amplifies it and re-transmites it back to the Earth on another frequency.

2 **Satellite** It refers to an artificial body or a machine that is launched into space and moves around Earth or another body in space to collect information for communication.

Government of India is providing such instruments to disaster/emergency managers in multi-hazard prone districts/states with portable satellite phones so that proper communication among the administrations at local and state level can be maintained in case the main communication lines fail.

All India Radio, Doordarshan and Press Trust of India also play a key role in collecting and disseminating information.

Present Operational Indian Space Systems

- **Indian National Satellite** (INSAT) For telecommunication, television broadcasting, meteorology and disaster warning
- **Indian Remote Sensing Satellite** (IRS) For resource monitoring and management

REVIEW EXERCISE

Including CBSE Textbook Questions

ASSIGNMENTS

(i) **In the context of this chapter, what are the suggested ways by which you can enhance life skills?**

(ii) **What are your suggestions to the meteorology department and also the Ministry of Information and Broadcasting in order to organise warning system for flood/cyclone?**

(iii) **How can a vulnerability map help in warning?**

(iv) **How can SMS be a tool to help people at the time of disaster?**

Ans. (i) Life skills, in the context of this chapter, can be enhanced by training to become a Ham (Amateur Radio) operator, as this ability will be useful at the time of a disaster. This training is conducted by the Department of Information Technology, Government of India.

(ii) Suggestions to the meteorology department and the Ministry of Information and Broadcasting can be as follows

(a) Equipment like satellite phones need to be provided to designated government officials in hazard-prone and disaster-prone areas of the country and they should be trained to use them at the time when a disaster strikes.

(b) A list of Ham operators in such areas should be made and known to the district authorities, so that their services can be requisitioned when needed.

(iii) A vulnerability map gives the precise location of sites where people, the natural environment or property are at risk due to a potentially catastrophic event that could result in death, injury, pollution or other destruction. Such maps are made in conjunction with information about different types of risks.

A vulnerability map can show the housing areas that are vulnerable to a chemical spill at a nearby factory. But such a map could also delineate the commercial, tourist and residential zones that would be damaged in case a flood or tsunami strikes.

Vulnerability maps are usually created with the assistance of computer technology called Geographic Information Systems (GIS) and digital land survey equipment designed for use in the field. Vulnerability maps can be used in all phases of disaster management, prevention, mitigation, preparedness, operations, relief and recovery.

In the prevention stage, planners can use vulnerability maps to avoid high risk zones when developing areas for housing, commercial or industrial use.

Technical experts can be alerted about places where the infrastructure can be affected in case of a disaster. Fire departments can plan for rescues before a potentially dangerous event which is at hand. During an exercise with a planned scenario, rescue teams can use a map to decide where to respond first to save lives, protect the environment or safeguard property.

These maps can also be used to decide evacuation routes and test the effectiveness of these routes for saving large numbers of residents and tourists and moving special groups such as senior citizens, children and handicapped persons.

The operation officers can be updated about the disaster situation, the need for relief measures and the location of sensitive areas.

(iv) SMS from a mobile phone when sent to the police will identify the location of a mobile phone, as police are able to trace the location of the phone through the concerned service provider of the mobile services. Thus, they will be able to arrange rescue of the person, who has either been injured or otherwise not able to move after a disaster has struck.

EXERCISE

Q.1 Why should the alternative communication systems be installed? **CBSE Textbook**

Ans. At the time of any major disaster or emergency situation, it is extremely necessary to have the communication links operational between government authorities at various levels and the people/volunteers working in the disaster affected areas to help the affected population.

It becomes imperative to ensure that the critical needs of search and rescue operations, relief and response measures are communicated among the authorities of government, local administration, voluntary organisations and the affected population. This situation calls for reliable alternate communication links, which ensure the rapid movement of the right resources to the right place at the right time.

It may also happen that some severely affected areas get completely disconnected from other parts of the world. In such situations, the urgent needs of the disaster-affected population are not known or communicated to the responsible government authorities, voluntary organisations and unaffected population in the vicinity. This may lead to severe losses in terms of human lives, livestock and property.

Q.2 Name two prime communication networks of Government of India and explain their functions. **CBSE Textbook**

Ans. The two prime communication networks of Government of India are

(a) **NIC** or **National Informatics Centre** It is a premier science and technology organisation of the Government of India in the field of informatics services and information technology applications. It functions through a nationwide Information and Communication Technology (ICT) network called NICNET.

(b) **BSNL** The Department of Telephone Operations, Government of India, became a corporation on 1st October, 2000 and was renamed Bharat Sanchar Nigam Limited (BSNL).

Today, BSNL is a leading telecommunication company and the largest public sector undertaking of India.

It has a network of over 45 million lines covering 7330 cities/towns with over 93 million telephone connections. Its responsibilities include improvement of the quality of telecom services, expansion of telecom networks, introduction of new telecom services in all villages and instilling confidence among its customers.

Q.3 How is Amateur (Ham) Radio different from the common radio communication? **CBSE Textbook**

Ans. Amateur Radio, also known as 'Ham Radio', does not refer to a special kind of radio but to a special set of rules which apply to certain frequencies as defined by the International Telecommunications Union (ITU) and regulated in India by the Wireless Planning and Coordination Wing, Ministry of Communications, Government of India.

The laid down rules allow these frequencies to be used only for research, education and personal purposes. The word 'Amateur' implies the use of radio communications for non-commercial purposes. Amateur Radio operation does not use the ground based infrastructure and has limited power requirements which can be easily met by batteries and generators and thus, works successfully in emergencies.

Q.4 What makes the satellite based communication systems more reliable in case of large-scale natural/man-made emergencies? **CBSE Textbook**

Ans. Satellite based communication systems are more reliable because communication satellites are in space and not at all vulnerable to any natural disaster on the Earth, while global communication link can be established with very small, portable and easy to install satellite antennas.

CHAPTER 5

Safe Construction Practices

The most successful way to mitigate loss of life and property from disaster is to construct buildings that are disaster resistant. This chapter will discuss some of the structural safety measures that need to be taken up for constructing disaster-resistant buildings to four kinds of disasters, namely **earthquakes**, **landslides**, **floods** and **cyclones**, as the cost of natural disasters to live, property, livelihood and infrastructure have increased in last few decades.

5.1 Earthquakes

A powerful earthquake measuring 6.6 at the Richter scale struck South-Eastern Iran on 26th December, 2003 and caused enormous loss of life and near total destruction of physical assets, killing 30,000 people and injured another 30,000. The health and education infrastructure was severely damaged and over 85% houses collapsed. Thus, it is very essential to combat such type of natural hazard.

Earthquake in Nicaragua

On 23rd December, 1972, a series of earthquakes shook the Central American nation of Nicaragua. The largest earthquake registered 6.2 on the Richter scale. The earthquake's epicenter was located precisely at the capital city of Managua. The earthquake resulted in the destruction of the heavily populated central zone and damaged to a total area of about 27 square kilometers (10 square miles).

Subsequent fires blazed throughout the city, compounding the damages. In the wake of the disaster, at least 8,000 of Managua's total population of 4,30,000 had died, 20,000 were injured, over 2,60,000 had fled the city, 50 per cent of the employed were jobless, and 70 per cent were left temporarily homeless.

At least 10 per cent of the nation's industrial capacity, 50 per cent of commercial property, and 70 per cent of government facilities were rendered inoperative. Overall, the damage estimated in US dollars was $845 million.

Ground Movements

An earthquake can cause severe ground movements which can have several types of damaging effects. Some of the major effects are

(i) **Ground shaking** It is back-and-forth motion of the ground, caused by the passing vibratory waves through the ground.

(ii) **Soil failures** Such as liquefaction[1] and landslides, caused by shaking.

(iii) **Surface fault ruptures** Such as cracks, vertical shifts, etc.

(iv) **Tidal waves** (tsunamis) They are large waves on the surface of water bodies due to under sea earthquake. They can cause major damage to shoreline areas.

Effect on Buildings

Each building moves differently in response to the ground movement, depending on its construction. The lower part of a building on the Earth's surface immediately moves with the Earth while the upper portion initially remains at rest. Thus, the building is stretched out of shape.

Gradually, the upper portion tries to catch up with the bottom, but as it does so, the Earth moves in the other direction, causing a 'whiplash' effect[2]. The vibration can cause structural failure in the building itself, or to an adjacent building having different response characteristics. Taller buildings tend to shake longer than short buildings, which can make them relatively more susceptible to damage.

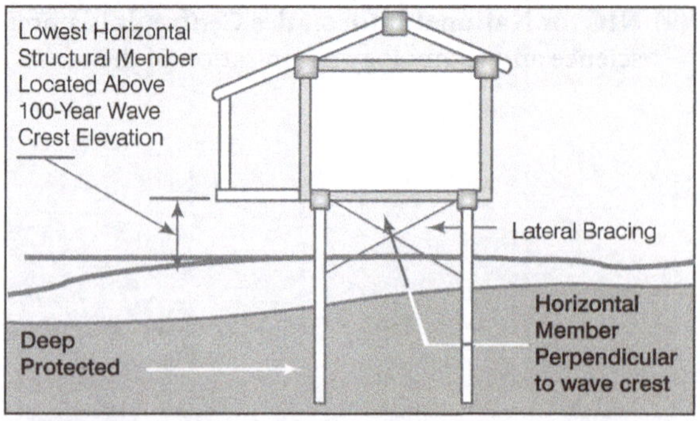

• Shaking of short and tall building due to ground acceleration

1 Liquefaction It is a process by which water-saturated sediment temporarily loses strength and acts like a fluid.

2 Whiplash Effect It is a deformation that occurs in buildings and other structures during an earthquake.

Protection Measures

Certain features must be taken into consideration at the stage of architectural planning and structural design of buildings to improve their performance during earthquakes.

The primary objective is to prevent collapse during earthquakes which led to minimise the risk of death or injury to the people.

To save life, some structural designs of buildings are as follows

Building Configuration

- The building should have a simple rectangular plan, with long walls being supported by Reinforced Concrete Columns (RCC).
- Large buildings with shapes like T, L, U or X should be separated into rectangular blocks by providing gaps in between.

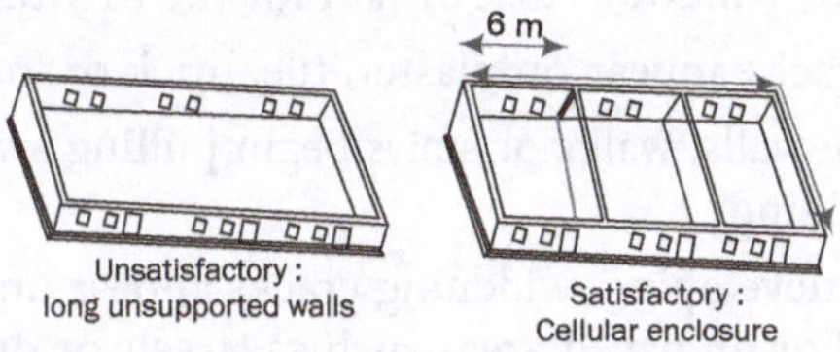

Foundation

Buildings sometimes fail to withstand earthquakes due to inadequate foundation design, which can cause tilting, cracking and failure of the structure due to **soil liquefaction**[3]. It is transformation of the soil from a solid state to a liquid state due to increased pressure. Accordingly, the depth of the foundation should be decided based on the condition of the soil.

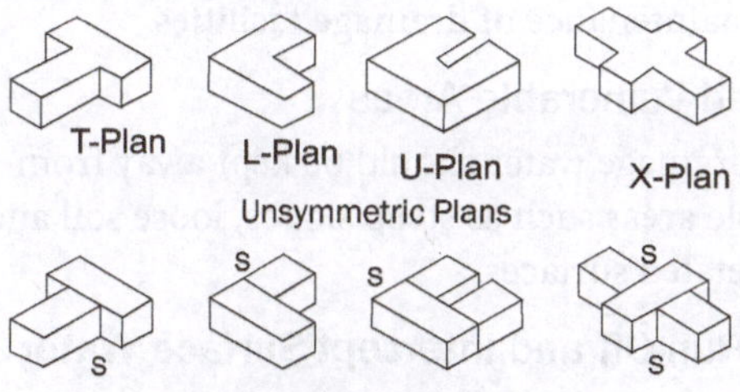

Use of seperation Gaps

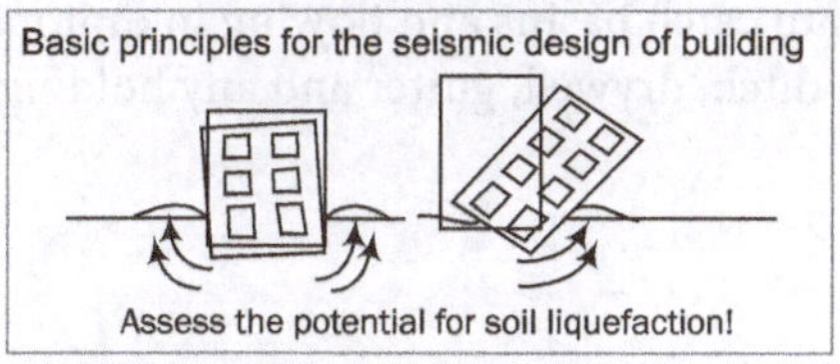

Tilting of building due to liquefaction

Control on Openings in Walls

Door and window openings in walls should preferably be small and more centrally located. Too many or large openings will make the wall vulnerable to collapse during earthquakes. The location of openings should not be too close to the edge of the wall.

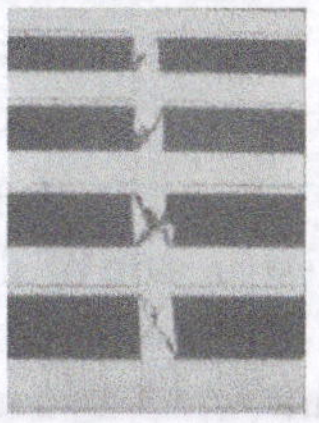

Damage to coloumns due to long openings and windows located at the edge of the coloumn

Reinforced Concrete Bands in Masonry Buildings

Reinforced concrete bands should be provided in masonry buildings which run continuously on all external and internal walls including fixed partition walls. These bands can be at the levels of the plinth, lintel, gable or roof as per the necessity of the building.

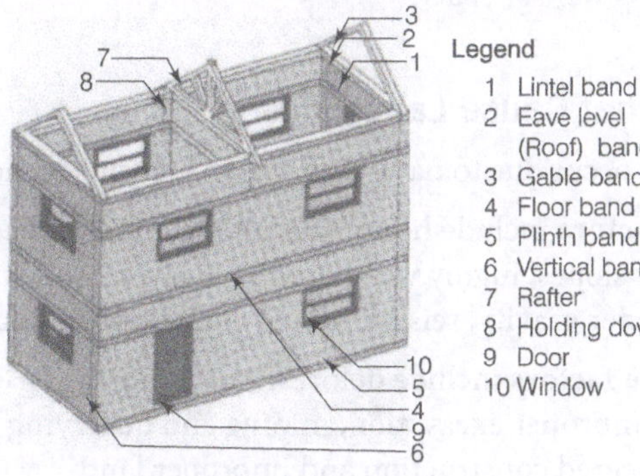

Arrangement of reinforcing

Vertical Reinforcement

It should be provided at corners and junctions of walls, which pass through the lintel bands and floor slabs or floor level bands in all storeys of the building.

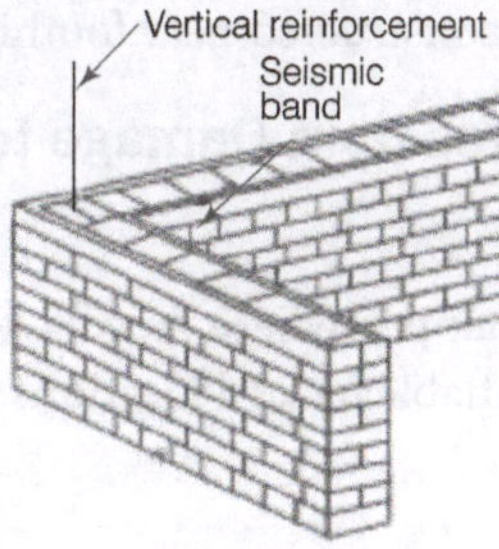

Vertical reinforcement

3 **Soil Liquefaction** This is a phenomenon in which the strength and stiffness of a soil is reduced by earthquake shaking or other rapid loading. This occurs in saturated soils, *i.e.* in which the space between individual soil particles is completely filled with water.

A properly designed building minimises the casualities associated with the disaster, by incorporating the features of earthquake resistance.

5.2 Landslides

Landslides are common natural disasters in hilly areas, causing loss of life, damage to property and great suffering. It also severly affect roads and communication systems.

Landslides also include debris fall, debris slide, debris flow, rock toppling, etc and cause destruction of slope and ground surface initiating the change of uncontrolled erosion in mountainous terrains.

Flash Floods in Nepal

On 21st August, 2002, heavy monsoon in Eastern Nepal triggered landslides and flashfloods which killed 419 people and injured 105 people. More than 53,152 families were affected and about 19,485 houses were destroyed. A total of 47 districts were affected.

Factors that Cause Landslides

Landslides occur due to natural as well as man-made factors.

Natural factors include heavy rainfall, steep hill slopes, stiffness of slopes, highly weathered rock layers, soil layers formed under gravity, seismic activity and poor drainage.

Man-made factors include deforestation (causes soil erosion), improper excavation, mining and quarrying, non-engineered construction and improper land use pattern.

Most Vulnerable Houses

The most vulnerable houses to landslides are those which are situated on existing landslide areas, on a steep natural slopes areas in or at the mouths of drainages (such as canyons) and houses constructed near foothills.

Protection Measures from Damage to Buildings

Site Selection

Landslides generally happen where they have occurred in the past, and in identifiable hazard locations. Areas that are typically considered safe from landslides include areas that have not moved in the past; relatively flat areas away from sudden changes in slope; and areas at the top of or along ridges. However, houses built at the toe of steep slopes are often vulnerable to slides and debris flows.

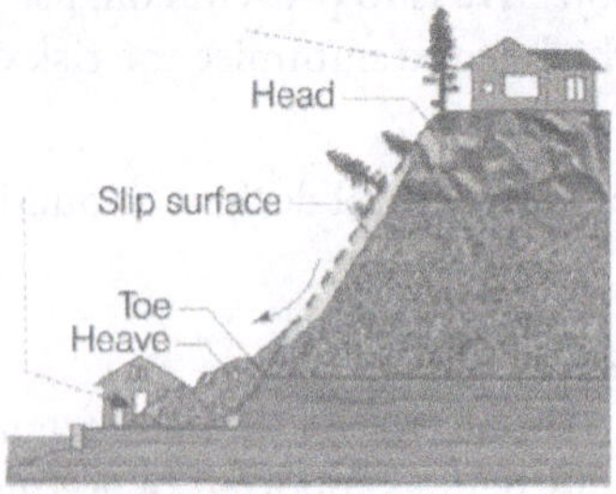

Signs and Warnings

If your house is on a hill, you can detect possible slope failure if you watch for the following signs :

- Doors or windows stick or jam for the first time.
- New cracks appear on plaster, tile, brick or foundations.
- Outside walls, walks or stairs begin pulling away from the building.
- Slowly developing, widening cracks appear on the ground or on paved areas such as streets or driveways.
- Underground utility lines break.
- Fences, retaining walls[4], utility poles or trees tilt or move.
- Water or bulging ground appears at the base of a slope.

Take Preventive Action

The potential for landslides and destructive erosion can be greatly reduced or prevented with proper development, sound construction techniques, seasonal inspections and regular maintenance of drainage facilities.

Protected Vulnerable Areas

Surface drainage water should be kept away from vulnerable areas such as steep slopes, loose soil and non-vegetated surfaces.

Collect Run-Off and Intercept Surface Water

Collecting water from patios, driveways, non-vegetated surfaces, into catch basins and flowing in drainpipe such as a drainage ditch, drywell, gutter and any holding pond.

4 **Retaining Wall** It is a structure that is built to keep soil, rocks and water in place. Normally, retaining walls are built to keep dirt in its proper place, so it doesn't become washed away from rain.

Surface water and run off should be intercepted and diverted away from your building.

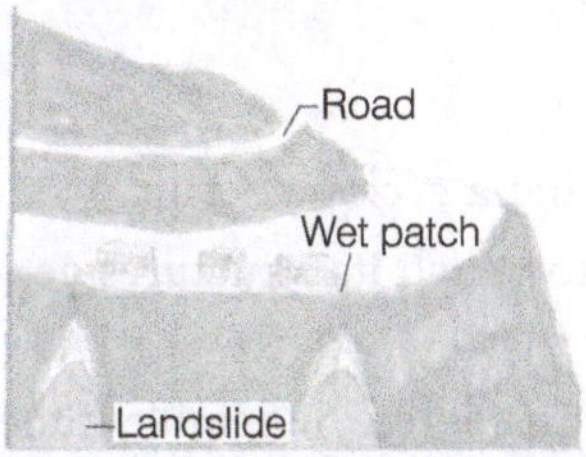

If a discharge point is available near your property, dig a shallow, gently sloping ditch to intercept the water and direct it into a natural water course, vegetated drainage area, street pavement, or road drainage ditch. Your intercepting ditch should be nearly horizontal with a minimum slope, sufficient to allow water to flow slowly which smoothen the sides of the ditch and grow vegetation and also keep all ditches free of debris.

Stabilise Slopes

- Improve your soil's ability to resist erosion by stabilising slopes by increasing vegetation and trees.
- Straw, woodchips or bark applied to a depth of at least one inch are effective in holding soil in place on slopes.

Barriers

At the toe of steep slopes, we can also create barriers or catchments that trap smaller landslides. Such structures must be designed to withstand the volumes and velocities of material in any potential slide.

The barrier design must allow removal of trapped material. Barriers can be of reinforced walls on the side of a building facing the slope.

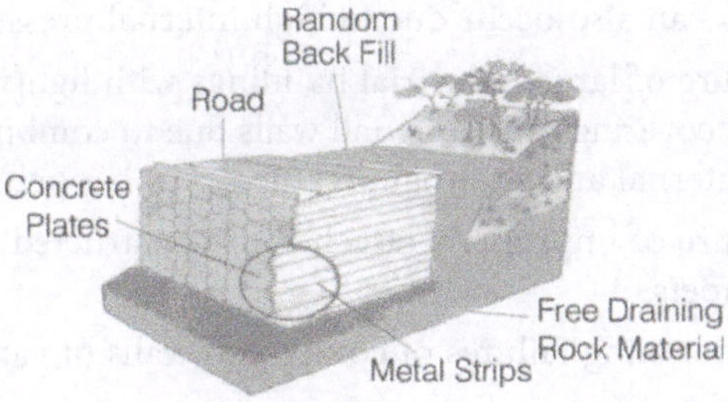

5.3 Floods

Water is a source for all life forms. Without water no life is sustainable. How tragic it is, when water in the form of floods takes away thousand of human and cattle lives. More than one million huts and poor houses are lost every year in floods in India. It is important to prevent this loss.

Flood in Bangladesh

Bangladesh is a riverine country where recurrent flooding is both common and necessary. Every year large areas are submerged during the monsoon season and fertilised by deposits of fresh alluvium, i.e. the soil deposited by moving water. However, if the waters remain stagnant for too long, these beneficial floods become major disasters.

Such was the case in the summer and fall of 1974 when flooding extended over nearly one-half of the country and stagnated for more than a month. At least 1,200 people died in the floods and another 27,500 died from subsequent disease and starvation. Approximately 4,25,000 houses were destroyed or severely damaged. A total of 36 million people suffered severe hardship and losses due to the disaster.

Most Vulnerable Homes

Buildings constructed with Earth-based materials or using stone and brick in mud mortar as well as huts made from biomass materials like bamboo, leaves, thatch or light construction using metal sheets are easily damaged or destroyed in floods and washed away. The occupation of flood plains has increased **vulnerability** especially in areas of high population concentration. Flood plains attract poor people because of inexpensive land values.

Effect on Buildings

(i) Houses may be washed away due to the impact of water flowing swiftly, usually so severely that they cannot be reconstructed.

(ii) Houses constructed out of light materials like wood which will float if they are not anchored properly.

(iii) If a house is inundated, it may remain intact on its foundation, but damage to materials may be severe. Repair may be feasible but may require special procedures to dry out properly.

(iv) Sometimes the speed of water may scour and erode the foundation of the house or the Earth under the foundation. This may result in the collapse of the house or it may require substantial repair. It is called undercutting of houses.

(v) Sometimes massive floating objects like trees, electric poles, etc may also damage houses.

Protection Measures from Damage to Buildings

(i) Avoid residing on river banks and slopes on river sides or sides of gorges.

(ii) Have your house at least 250 meters away from the sea coast/river bank.

(iii) Build a proper drainage system in all flood prone areas, so that the water can be drained off quickly.

(iv) Construct the building with a plinth level higher than the known high flood level.

(v) Construct the whole village or settlement on a raised platform higher than the high flood level.

(vi) Construct buildings on stilts or columns with wall-free space at ground level permitting free flow of water provided that columns are circular and strong. In dry weather condition, the ground area could be fenced and used for cattle, sheep poultry farming or storage, etc.

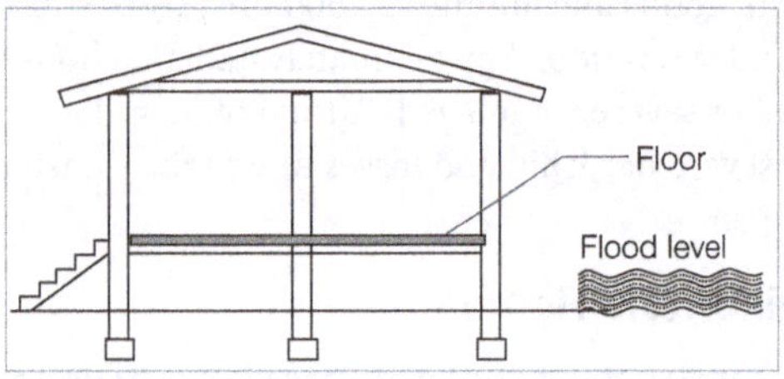

Reckless building in vulnerable areas, poor watershed management and failure to control flooding also help create a disaster condition.

Thus, we must mitigate flood hazards by proper habitat management, watershed management and incorporating flood resistant features in our buildings.

5.4 Cyclones

Cyclones bring widespread devastation to coastlines and islands lying in their erratic paths. A windstorm's destructive work is done by the high wind, flood producing rains and associated storm surges.

Cyclone in Andhra Pradesh

On 19th November, 1977, a cyclone, which had been expected to hit Tamil Nadu, instead struck the central coast of Andhra Pradesh State in the Krishna Godavari Delta. Many people perished because advance warning was either too slowly or too narrowly disseminated. Damage in Andhra Pradesh was caused primarily by a storm surge that devastated some 65 villages, about 21 of which were completely washed away. The storm surge was reported to have been 5.7 meters (19 feet) high, 80 kilometers (50 miles) long, 16 kilometers (10 miles) wide, with a speed of 190 kilometers per hour (120 miles per hour). Many of the victims of the Andhra Pradesh cyclone were migrant labourers. This made identification of the dead difficult.

Most Vulnerable Homes

The vulnerability of home depends upon following factors

- Location
- Probability that a cyclone occur
- The degree to which its structures get damaged by cyclone.

Buildings are considered vulnerable if they cannot withstand the forces of high winds and storm surges. Generally, those most vulnerable to cyclones are lightweight structures with wooden frames, especially older buildings where wood has deteriorated and weakened the walls.

Houses made of poorly constructed concrete blocks are also vulnerable. Urban and rural communities on low islands or in unprotected low-lying coastal areas or river floodplains are vulnerable to cyclones. Also, the degree of exposure of land and buildings will be affected by the velocity of the cyclone wind at ground level.

Effects on Buildings

Due to storm surge and high wind speed, following types of effects on buildings are commonly seen

- Damages due to cyclones can be uprooting of trees, disrupting transportation and relief supply missions.
- Damage to signposts, electric poles and transmission line towers.
- Damage to improperly attached windows or window frames.
- Damage to roof/lintel projections.
- Failure of roofing elements and walls along the gable ends can also occur due to high internal pressures.
- Failure of large industrial buildings with lightweight roof coverings and long/tall walls due to combination of internal and external pressures also happens.
- Failure of improperly attached or constructed parapets.
- Overturning failures of compound walls of various types.
- Brittle failure of asbestos.
- Punching and blowing off of corrugated iron roofing sheets attached to steel trusses.

Protection Measures from Damage to Buildings

Site Selection

Storm tides leading to coastal inundation commonly are generated by cyclonic windstorms. In cyclonic regions, close to the coast, a building site above the likely inundation level should be given preference. In case of non-availability of high elevation natural ground, construction should be done on stilts with no masonry or bracings up to the maximum surge level, or raised Earthen mounds to avoid flooding or inundation.

Platforms and Orientation

The desirable platforms and orientations for cyclone resistant buildings are follows

(i) For individual buildings, a circular or polygonal plan shape is preferred over rectangular or square plans.

(ii) A symmetrical building with a compact-plan form is more stable than an asymmetrical building with a zig-zag plan having empty pockets, as the latter is more prone to wind/cyclone related damage.

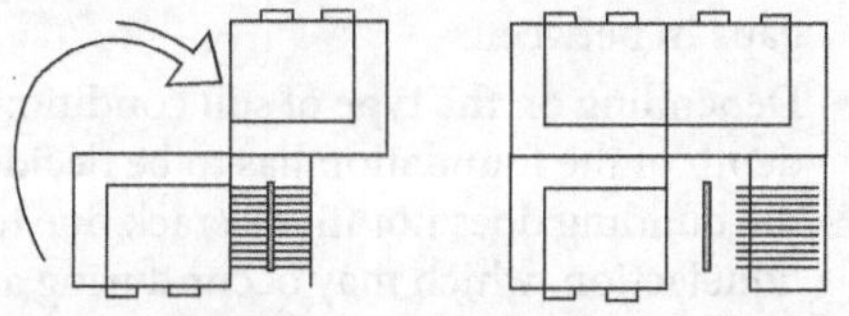

Asymmetric buildings with empty pockets are more vulnerable to damage

Symmetric buildings are more stable

Desirable orientation and plan form for reducing wind damage

Foundations

While constructing buildings in coastal areas, some parameters need to be properly accounted for in the design of foundation.

(i) **Effect of surge or flooding** Torrential rain and tidal surge is always followed by a cyclonic storm which resulting into flooding of low-lying areas. The flurry of tidal surge extend even upto 10-15 km.

(ii) **Building on stilts** While building is constructed on stilts, it is necessary that stilts are braced properly on both the directions.

Wall Openings

Wall openings for protecting buildings are as follow

(i) Opening just below roof level are avoided and two small vents without shutters are provided in opposite walls to prevent suffocation in case room gets filled with water if people try to climb up on lofts.

(ii) Doors and windows should have strong closing/locking arrangements and glass/wooden panels be securely fixed.

Glass Panelling

Uses of glass panels to protect buildings are as follow

(i) One major reason of damaging effects is the extensive breakage of glass panes caused by high wind pressure or impact of flying objects in the air. The larger size of door or window glass panes may shatter because they are too thin to resist the wind pressures.

(ii) Glass panes should be of smaller dimensions.

(iii) Pasting thin plastic film or paper strip can strengthen glass panes.

(iv) Metallic fabric/mesh should be provided outside the panels.

(v) Provide proper locking arrangements of shutters.

Roof Architecture

Effects of wind on roof building given below in these figures

(i) The roof projections should be kept minimum, may not exceeding 500 mm or else are tied down adequately.

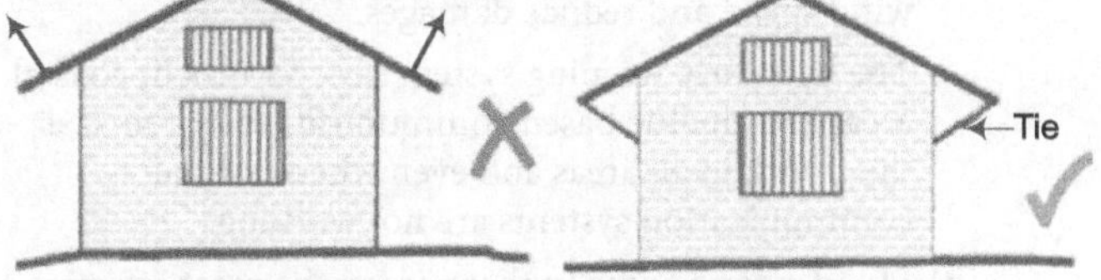

Left: Large overhangs get lifted and broken

Right: Avoid large overhangs and use ties

(ii) For the purpose of reducing wind forces on the roof, a hipped or pyramidal roof is preferable to the gable type roof as shown in the figures given below.

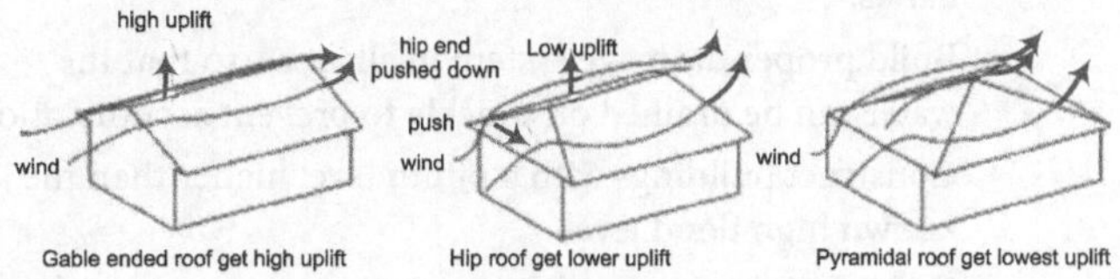

• Effect of roof architecture on uplift force.

By having shelterbelts plantation across the wind direction and by adopting the technologies and procedures mentioned above can check the wind speed and reduce damage caused by storm.

REVIEW EXERCISE

Including CBSE Textbook Questions

ASSIGNMENTS

(A) What kind of infrastructural and structural facilities are required in rural/urban communities living in coastal areas or flood-prone areas or earthquake-prone areas?

(B) What could be the early warning system that could be best used in that given area for that community? Early warning for which hazard?

Ans. (A) For each of these areas, the details of the requirements are given below

(a) **Coastal areas** In these areas, cyclonic windstorms commonly generate storm tides leading to coastal inundation. In cyclonic regions close to the coast, building sites should be above the likely inundation level.

In case of non-availability of high elevation natural ground, construction should be done on stilts with no masonry or bracings upto maximum surge level or raised Earthen mounds to avoid flooding/inundation. We should also have shelter belt plantation across the wind direction in all large establishments to check the wind speed and reduce damages.

The best early warning system for cyclones in coastal areas are satellite based communication systems, as they work in all areas and even when normal communication systems are not working.

(b) **Flood-prone areas** In these areas, the most effective structural measures for prevention against inundation are as follow

- Do not construct buildings on river banks and slopes, on river sides and the sides of gorges.
- Build at least 250 meters away from the sea coast/river banks.
- Build proper drainage system in all areas, so that the water can be drained off quickly to prevent accumulation.
- Construct buildings with a plinth level higher than the known high flood level.
- Construct the whole village or settlement on a raised platform higher than the high flood level.
- Construct buildings on stilts or columns with wall-free space at ground level permitting free flow of water, provided that columns are circular and strong.
- In dry weather condition, the ground area could be fenced and used for cattle, sheep poultry farming or storage, etc. The best early warning system for flood-prone areas are satellite based communication systems, as they work in all areas and even when normal communication systems are not working.

(c) **Earthquake-prone areas**
In these areas, the most effective structural measures are as follow

- To have buildings with earthquake resistant design, which prevents collapse during earthquakes, thus minimising the risk of death or injury to people in or around the buildings.
- For this, the building should have a simple rectangular plan. Long walls should be supported by RC columns. Large buildings having plans with shapes like T, L, U and X should preferably be separated into rectangular blocks by providing gaps in between.
- Depending on the type of soil conditions, the depth of the foundation has to be decided, so that the building does not tilt or crack due to soil liquefaction, which may occur during an earthquake.

Other requirements to prevent building collapse due to earthquake are as follow

(i) Door and window openings in walls should preferably be small and more centrally located.

(ii) Provide horizontal reinforced concrete bands which run continuously on all external and internal walls including fixed partition walls. One or more bands at different levels may be necessary in a building.

(iii) Vertical reinforcement should be provided at corners and junction of walls. It shall be passing through the lintel bands and floor slabs or floor level bands in all storeys.

(B) For earthquake-prone areas it is not possible to provide an early warning system, as we cannot predict when an earthquake will strike.
However, after an earthquake occurs, the best communication systems to use for rescue and relief measures are satellite based communication systems, as they work in all areas and even when normal communication systems are not working.

EXERCISE

Q.1 What should be the configuration of an earthquake resistant building? **CBSE Textbook**

Ans. The configuration of an earthquake resistant building should be

(a) The building should have a simple rectangular plan.

(b) Long walls should be supported by Reinforced Concrete (RC) columns.

(c) Large buildings having plans with shapes like T, L, U and X should preferably be separated into rectangular blocks by providing gaps in between.

Q.2 How should the foundation be constructed in soft and firm soil? **CBSE Textbook**

Ans. Buildings which are structurally strong to withstand earthquakes sometimes fail due to inadequate foundation design. Tilting, cracking and failure of the structure may result from soil liquefaction.

So, the foundation of the building should be strong. Building constructors should ensure that there is no movement of underground soil once the building is built. If the soil is soft the foundation has to be deeper, if the soil is firm the foundation can be moderate.

Q.3 Which homes are the most vulnerable due to flood?

Ans. The most vulnerable homes due to flood are as follow

(a) Buildings which are constructed with earth-based materials or using stone and brick in mud mortar are highly vulnerable to damage in heavy rains and/or floods.

(b) The huts made from biomass materials like bamboo, leaves, thatch or light construction using metal sheets are easily destroyed in floods and washed away.

Q.4 What are the general protection measures for buildings against flood damage?

Ans. The most effective measures for prevention against flood damage are as follow

(a) Avoid constructing buildings on river banks and slopes, on riversides or the sides of gorges.

(b) Build at least 250 metre away from the sea coast/river banks.

(c) Build proper drainage system in all flood-prone areas, so that the water can be drained off quickly to prevent accumulation.

(d) Construct the building with a plinth level higher than the known high flood level.

(e) Construct the whole village or settlement on a raised platform higher than the high flood level.

(f) Construct buildings on stilts or columns with wall-free space at ground level permitting free flow of water (inundation or flowing), provided that the columns are circular and strong. In dry weather condition, the ground area could be fenced and used for cattle, sheep, poultry farming, storage, etc.

Q.5 What are the considerations for selecting the site in areas prone to landslides? **CBSE Textbook**

Ans. Landslides generally happen where they have occurred in the past and in identifiable hazard locations.

Areas that are typically considered safe from landslides include areas that have not moved in the past; relatively flat areas away from sudden changes in slope and areas at the top of or along ridges. Houses built at the toe of steep slopes are often vulnerable to slides and debris flows.

Q.7 What are the desirable plan forms and orientations for cyclone resistant buildings? **CBSE Textbook**

Ans. The desirable plan forms and orientations for cyclone resistant buildings are as follow

(a) For individual buildings, a circular or polygonal plan shape is preferred over rectangular or square plans.

(b) A symmetrical building with a compact plan form is more stable than an asymmetrical building with a zig-zag plan having empty pockets, as the latter is more prone to wind/cyclone related damage.

Q.8 What kind of roof designs should be used in cyclone prone areas and why?

Ans. The following kinds of roof designs should be used in cyclone prone areas

(a) The overall effect of wind on a pitched roof building and the critical locations are shown in the figures given below.

(b) For the purpose of reducing wind forces on the roof, a hipped or pyramidal roof is preferable to the gable type roof as shown in the figure given below.

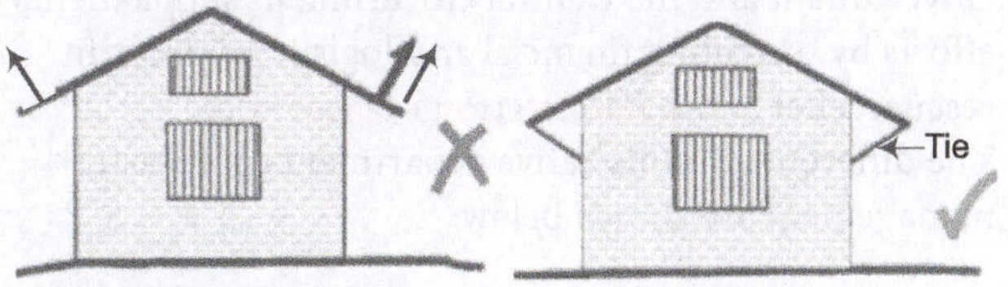

Left: Large overhangs get lifted and broken

Right: Avoid large overhangs and use ties

Therefore, the roof projections should be kept minimum, may not exceeding 500 mm, or else, are tied down adequately.

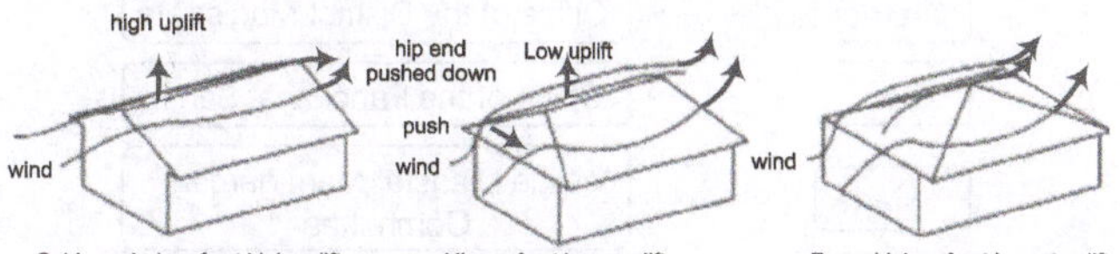

Gable ended roof get high uplift

Hip roof get lower uplift

Pyramidal roof get lowest uplift

CHAPTER 6

Sharing Responsibility
(Role of Local and State Bodies)

When disasters occur, they teach us lessons at a very high cost, usually to life and property. This indicates how important and how crucial planning for a disaster is to be prepared. Various agencies coordinate rescue and relief operations in the disaster prone area.

6.1 Managing Disasters

At the time of disaster, various agencies both government and non-government organisations play a crucial role in preparing the society. Home Guards, Civil Defence, volunteers of National Service Scheme, Nehru Yuva Kendra Sangathan too play a major role at the time of crisis. Proper coordination and effective communication help agencies in management of disaster.

How are Disasters Managed?

India with its federal system of government has specific roles for the Central and the State Governments. The country has an integrated administrative machinery for management of disasters at the National, State, District and Sub-District levels.

The basic responsibility lies with the concerned State Government and the Central Government supplements the efforts by providing financial and logistic support in rescue, relief and **rehabilitation measures**[1].
The different administrative departments of disaster management are shown below

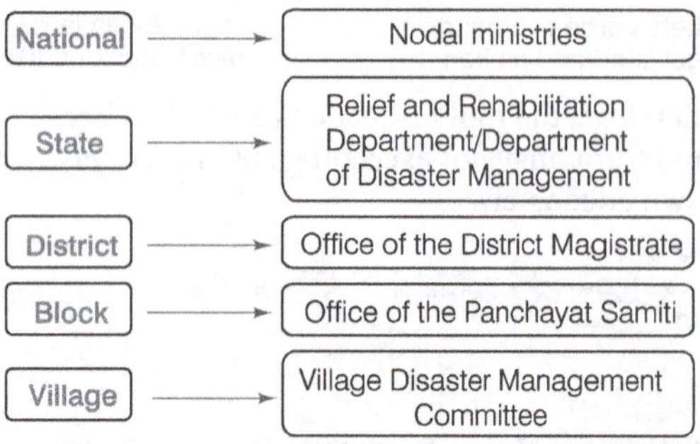

National Level

The response from the Central Government is based on

1. the gravity of the disaster
2. the scale of relief operations
3. the requirements of the central assistance for augmenting financial resources and logistics support at the disposal of the State Government.

The **Ministry of Home Affairs** is the nodal ministry at the centre for coordinating disaster management activities for all natural hazards except drought which is taken care by Ministry of Agriculture under the Department of Agriculture and Cooperation.

Other ministries are assigned the responsibility of providing emergency support in case of disasters that fall within their preview

S. No.	Disasters	Nodal Ministries
1.	Natural disasters (other than drought)	Ministry of Home Affairs
2.	Drought	Ministry of Agriculture
3.	Air accidents	Ministry of Civil Aviation
4.	Railway accidents	Ministry of Railways
5.	Chemical disasters	Ministry of Home Affairs
6.	Biological disasters	Ministry of Home Affairs
7.	Nuclear	Ministry of Home Affairs
8.	Epidemics	Ministry of Health and Family Welfare

1 **Rehabilitation Measures** After providing basic relief, every effort is made to rehabilitate the affected population. This requires a careful examination of their special needs not only for their economic revival (*i.e.* revival of their occupations), but also for their emotional satisfaction.

State Level

It is the responsibility of the State Government to cope up with natural disasters. Central Government plays the role to support in terms of physical and financial resources. The Chief Minister or the Chief Secretary of the State heads a state level committee, which is in overall charge of the relief operations at the state and the Relief Commissioner who is in charge of the relief and rehabilitation measures in the wake of natural disasters.

In some states, the Secretary, Department of Revenue is also incharge of relief operations. To manage disaster scenarios, the states have the relief manual called as the **'State Relief Code'** and the State Contingency Plan.

District Level

The district administration is the focal point for implementation of all governmental plans and activities. The actual day-to-day function of administering relief is the responsibility of the District Magistrate/District Collector/Deputy Commissioner, who exercises coordinating and supervising powers over all the departments at the district level.

The 73rd and the 74th constitutional amendments recognise **Panchayati Raj Institutions** as 'Institutions of Self-government'. These local bodies can be effective instruments in tackling disasters through early warning system, relief distribution, providing shelter to the victims, medical assistance, etc.

Block Level

The Disaster Management Committee at the block/taluka level is headed by the **Nodal Officer**[2], who is the Block Development Officer (BDO) for all the disaster management activities. The other members of the committee are officers from the various departments, like Social Welfare, Health, Rural Water Supply and Sanitation, Police, Fire Services, representatives from youth organisations, community based organisations, Non-Governmental Organisations (NGOs), eminent senior citizens, elected representatives, etc.

The main functions of Block Disaster Management Committee are as follow

- Helping the block administration in preparation of the Block Disaster Management Plan.
- Coordinating training for the members of the Disaster Management Teams.
- Carry out mock drills.

Village Level

At the village level, the Village Disaster Management Committee headed by the Sarpanch/Village Headman is responsible for preparing the Village Disaster Management Plans and also coordinating with various agencies for providing training to the Disaster Management Teams.

The members should ensure that mock drills are carried out by the villagers at regular intervals for various disasters.

6.2 Other Agencies Helping in Disaster Management Activities

Apart from government organisations, various institutions are also involved in disaster management at various levels. This includes the police, para-military forces, Civil Defence and Home Guards, National Cadet Corps (NCC), youth organisations, UN agencies, voluntary groups (national and international) public and private sector enterprises, media, etc.

Functions of some of the above agencies are given below

1. UN Disaster Management Team (UNDMT) - India

UN Office for Coordination of Humanitarian Affairs (UN OCHA) has been made responsible by the UN General Assembly mandate for all international disaster response. This represents various UN agencies to implement disaster preparedness and mitigation efforts and strengthen government's capacities on disaster risk management.

The UNDMT has representation from various UN agencies (FAO, ILO, UNDP, UNFPA, UNICEF, WFP and WHO) which act together whenever there is a disaster. Its primary purpose is to ensure prompt, effective and concerted country level disaster preparedness by the UN system and the response when appropriate.

2. Indian Armed Forces (IAF)

They intervene and take on specific tasks only when the situation is beyond the capacity of civil administration. Due to their ability to organise action in adverse ground circumstances, speed of operational response and the resources and capacities at their disposal, the armed forces have historically played a major role in emergency support functions, especially in the immediate aftermath of a disaster.

---

2 **Nodal Officer** He is the officer responsible for preparing the Sectoral Action Plan/Emergency Support Function Plan for managing disasters in a district.

3. National Cadet Corps (NCC)

The National Cadet Corps, a body formed in 1948 aims at developing qualities of character, courage, comradeship, secular outlook, spirit of adventure and sportsmanship and the ideals of selfless service among the youth to make them useful citizens.

The National Cadet Corps has created a human resource of organised, trained and activated youth. These youth can be used as volunteers to help and manage disasters.

Be a Part of NCC and Serve the Country...

Every Indian school going student can join NCC. The NCC is open to all regular students of schools and colleges on a voluntary basis. The officers and cadets have no liability for active military service. It has been divided into four divisions (they are not similar to the army divisions).

4. Civil Defence

Civil Defence aims at saving life, minimising damage to property and maintaining continuity of industrial production in the event of a hostile attack. They are essential for efficient conduct of relief operations during natural disasters.

Today, there are around 5,00,000 Civil Defence volunteers throughout the country. The two wars (1962 and 1965) compelled the Central Government to reorient its emergency training activities from natural disasters to those concerning protection of life and property against enemy action.

National Civil Defence College

It was founded on 29th April, 1957 at Nagpur as the Central Emergency Relief Training Institute (CERTI) to function as the training wing of Emergency Relief Organisation of Government of India.

It focuses on advanced and specialist training to the leaders of relief services.

5. National Service Scheme (NSS)

On the recommendation of the first Education Commission (1950), the Ministry of Education introduced the National Service Scheme for students on a voluntary basis during 1969-70. Any student enrolled as a NSS volunteer, as per NSS manual should put in at least 240 hours of useful social work in a continuous period of 2 years.

These volunteers have been used regularly in relief operations related to natural disasters and also expected to adopt a nearby village/slum and work for its all round development.

The motto of NSS is **'NOT ME BUT YOU'** and its symbol is **'Rath Wheel'** of Konark Sun temple of Odisha which stands for dynamism and progressive outlook of youth.

6. Nehru Yuva Kendras

These were launched in 1972 as part of Silver Jubilee celebration of India's independence. They function under Ministry of Youth Affairs and Sports.

This was formed on the recommendation of the National Advisory Board on youth with the objective of providing the non-student rural youth avenues to take part in nation building activities and also to provide opportunity for the development of their own personality and skills. As volunteers, the members have helped the community at times of crisis and in disaster management activities.

NYKS is registered society and is governed by a Board of Governors headed by the Minister of Youth Affairs and Sports.

7. Home Guard

It was raised as voluntary force in December 1946, to assist the police in civil disturbance and communal riots. After Chinese Aggression (1962), the centre advised to merge their existing voluntary organisation into one uniform voluntary force known as 'Home Guards'.

The function of Home Guards is to serve as an auxiliary to the police in maintenance of internal security related to disaster management, which helps the community in any kind of emergency such as air raid, fire, cyclone, earthquake, epidemic, etc. They also help in the maintenance of essential services to promote communal harmony and participate in socio-economic and welfare activities and perform civil defence duties.

Mainstreaming Disaster Management in Education

The National Institute of Disaster Management (NIDM) and Indian Institute of Technology (IIT) intend to upgrade the skilled human resources for the country by providing training to various government level functionaries of various departments. Disaster management has also been made a part of the foundation course for All India Services like the Indian Administrative Services (IAS), Indian Police Services (IPS), Indian Forest Services (IFS) and also in engineering by All India Council of Technical Education (AICTE) and architecture courses and urban planning and medical courses.

REVIEW EXERCISE

Including CBSE Textbook Questions

ACTIVITY 1 READ AND ANALYSIS

26th January, 2001, reports of the State Government state that, more than 13,000 people have been declared dead and about 1.67 lakh people have been injured. About 1.97 crore population spread over 21 districts have been affected.

About 3.20 lakh, permanent and semi-permanent (pucca/kucha) houses and 14,000 huts have been fully destroyed and about 7.33 lakh permanent and semi-permanent (pucca/kucha) houses and 31,000 huts have been partially damaged.

28th January, 2001, relief teams started reaching Ahmedabad and Bhuj. Individuals, voluntary organisations, professionals, aid agencies have started approaching materials for providing assistance.

Mr Khan is a driver in the town of Bhuj. Thankfully none in his family was injured during the quake; they lost all their valuables, cash and their house. More than 100 organisations, private, government and non-government, were providing relief materials after the earthquake, but Mr Khan could not get a single tent for his family, who were living on the street.

It is not only Mr Khan a poor driver who was suffering. There were many ill-fated families. When disasters occur they teach us lessons at a very high cost usually to life and property. This indicates how important and how crucial planning for a disaster is.

On the basis of above passage, analyse the following

(a) What went wrong? Did the houses have faulty structural design?

(b) Are we prepared to face another jolt like the Bhuj? Isn't it time for us to learn from our past experiences?

Hint Students can do this exercise with the help of their teacher and parents.

ACTIVITY 2 ASSIGNMENT

Topic

As a District Magistrate of a district of Delhi, which is in seismic zone IV (high risk zone), what are the measures or activities you would have organised to generate awareness among the school children and the communities around your school?

Hint As the District Magistrate of a district of Delhi, I will arrange to conduct awareness sessions in the community and in the schools of the district, based on the measures which are to be taken in case they feel the occurrence of an earthquake.

(i) Protect yourself and your family. Immediately get under a table, desk, etc to protect your head from any falling object when the Earth shakes.

(ii) When the Earth stops shaking, turn off gas and electric heaters to protect against any breakout of fire.

(iii) Avoid rushing out of the house. Carefully check the situation and try to act accordingly.

(iv) Open a window for exit from the building if during the earthquake the doors have been damaged and cannot be opened. Otherwise, open the door quickly to secure a safe exit.

(v) If outside when there is an earthquake, protect your head from falling objects like bricks, concrete, signboards, etc.

(vi) In case you are travelling when you feel an earthquake, stop driving and park the vehicle in a safe area.

Driving on the road may create traffic blockage, causing problems for any rescue operation.

(vii) Avoid being mislead by false alarms and try to obtain the correct information.

ACTIVITY 3 GROUP DISCUSSION

Topic

Recollect and discuss with your friends in the classroom regarding various disaster management teams at the village level—their members and their roles and responsibilities in before, during and after disasters.

Hint At the village level, the Village Disaster Management Committee (VDMC) headed by the Sarpanch/Village Headman is responsible for preparing the Village Disaster Management Plans and also coordinating with various agencies for providing training to the Disaster Management Teams.

The members of the teams should ensure that mock drills are carried out by the villagers at regular intervals for various hazards. It is accepted that the government alone cannot take on the entire responsibility of Disaster Management.

EXERCISES

Q.1 If you were the Relief Commissioner of the State of Assam, which is affected by floods every year, list out five departments that you need to contact. **CBSE Textbook**

Ans. The departments I need to contact will be

(i) Home Affairs (ii) Health
(iii) Environment (iv) Defence
(v) Food and Civil Supplies

Q.2 List out members of the Disaster Management Committee at the district level. **CBSE Textbook**

Ans. Disaster Management Committees have been set-up at the district level headed by the District Magistrate/ Deputy Commissioner and senior officials from the following departments

(i) Health (ii) Irrigation
(iii) Veterinary (iv) Water and Sanitation
(v) Police (vi) Fire Services and others
(vii) NGOs

Q.3 Write the main aim of the National Cadet Corps. **CBSE Textbook**

Ans. The main aim of the National Cadet Corps (NCC) is to develop qualities of character, courage, comradeship, discipline, leadership, secular outlook, spirit of adventure and sportsmanship and the ideals of selfless service among the youth to make them useful citizens.

This is done by creating a human resource of organised, trained and activated youth who will provide leadership in all walks of life including the armed forces and making themselves available for the service of the nation.

Q.4 List the organisations which help the State Government functionaries in responding to disasters. **CBSE Textbook**

Ans. The Disaster Management Committee, which is basically the decision-making body, takes the help of the Disaster Management Teams like the Fire Services, Police, Health Practitioners (doctors), NGOs and other voluntary bodies.

Q.5 Explain the role of the Central Government in responding to disasters. **CBSE Textbook**

Ans. The role of the Central Government is based on keeping in view the following factors

(i) The gravity of the disaster
(ii) The scale of the relief operations.
(iii) The requirements of central assistance for augmenting financial resources and logistics support at the disposal of the State Government.

The Ministry of Home Affairs is the nodal ministry at the centre for coordinating disaster management activities for all natural hazards except drought, which is taken care of by the Ministry of Agriculture under the Department of Agriculture and Cooperation.

Other ministries are assigned the responsibility of providing emergency support in case of disasters that fall within their preview.

Planning Ahead... by the People, for the People

CHAPTER 7

A community plan is a list of activities a neighborhood, community or a group of people agree to follow. It prevents loss of life, livelihoods and property in case of warning or a disaster. The plan identifies, in advances, the action to be taken by individuals.

7.1 Community Planning

Community planning is a forward planning process, which identifies human and material resources and puts in place potential response system. It involves active participation from the people residing in that locality in making decision about the implementation of processes, programmes and projects which affect them.

In other words, a community plan is a list of activities a neighborhood, community or a group of people agree to follow to prevent loss of life, livelihoods and property in case of warning or a disaster.

The plan identifies in advance action to be taken by individuals in the community, so that each one knows what to do when a warning is received or when a disaster strikes. The major thrust is to address possible scenario of an event and focus on the impact the humanitarian operations.

For What do We Need to Plan?

We can plan for any possible critical event. It can vary upon the scale of operations or processes involved as well as the population that could possibly be affected in case of an untoward event. The most common could be natural disasters affecting human operations or industrial disaster.

The primary goal of Community Planning for disasters is to reduce the vulnerability of the concerned community and strengthen its existing capacity to cope up with disasters.

The approach of preparing a Community Based Disaster Management Plan considers people's participation, a necessary pre- requisite for disaster management. By involving the community in the preparedness phase, it increases the likelihood of coordinated action by the communities during emergencies.

Importance of Peoples' Contingency Plan

A contingency plan need not be sophisticated, very scientific, or computer generated model. It need not have a series of flow diagrams showing the process of planning. Use of technology or sophisticated analysis is only useful when it is combined with the people's participation.

Basic information, risk assessment and intelligence analysis is normally adequate to have a functional people contingency plan for various hazards. The task cannot be of a single person in the preparation of a working plan, since accuracy is considerably enhanced through the assimilation of experience, information and skills of widest possible range of sources.

Contingency plans are prepared at different levels such as Neighborhood, Village, Block, District, State and National Levels. It has to be made very specific by involving both government and non-government organisations. The plan should be ideally people-centric and hence the term peoples' contingency plans.

An effective contingency plan is prepared involving people from all areas and different categories using participatory process. The active community members take a lead in facilitating and developing the plan. It is also important that the plan prepared at the lowest level should be in line to the plans prepared at the higher levels for effective coordination during a disaster.

How to Prepare a Plan and What Should a Contingency Plan Consist of?

The Contingency Planning Exercise is a forum and opportunity for all sections of the society to participate. Each has something useful to contribute to the planning. The views of one may differ from others, but this will often be to the advantage of the planning process since it provides a useful forum for all assumptions to be questioned and refined.

The end product is thus more realistic. To start with the plan one individual or a group of people may facilitate the Contingency Planning Exercise. Due importance is given to each individual in the development of the plan. In this part we will look into some detail on the preparation of the Contingency Planning process.

There is no clear demarcation of an exact procedure as situation may vary in terms of geographical spread, the hazard, the location from the hazard, the exposure, vulnerability aspects and processes involved.

A typical Community Contingency Plan will involve following basic steps

- Initial awareness and rapport building
- Outlining the profile of the community
- Analyzing the situation on a participatory basis
- Selection of Task Forces, Indicative Responsibilities and Capacity Building of Task Forces
- Rehearsals/ Mock Drills.

Rapport Building and Initial Awareness

Rapport building with the senior citizens, Village Self Help Groups: youth clubs, elected representatives, etc is the first step in preparation of the Community Contingency Plan.

The main objective is to motivate them and get them involved in the planning process. Usually Government functionaries working at the village level, elected representatives and voluntary organisations help in the preparation of plans at the community level.

Discussing the recent disaster incident and the losses and risks that were involved could generate initial interest. The discussion has to be done through a participatory process.

If the community does not have a recent experience to recollect, but still is a potentially vulnerable area the incidences of nearby areas should be discussed.

Local knowledge to cope up with the disaster should not be overlooked during these discussions. It is essential to tap information and take it forward towards a meaningful process during the next step of analysing situations.

The important task here is to mobilise community participation through awareness generation techniques by various options such as:

- Mass meetings
- Cultural activities
- Street plays
- Audio/visual aids
- Displaying of posters

This awareness campaign will help the people to understand the need for planning,

Formation of a Village Disaster Management Committee (VDMC)

Village Disaster Management Committee (VDMC) is formed in each of the village and it is responsible for initiating disaster preparedness activities. It consists of local elected representatives, grass root level government functionaries, NGOs, CBOS, youth clubs and members from the Mahila samities. Senior citizens too are a part of the committee.

The head of the VDMC takes a lead in mobilising the community for the preparation of the Disaster Management Plan.

Outlining the Profile of the Community

It involves outlining data pertaining to the following namely

- Population
- Local resources (both human like skilled manpower -health practitioners; e.g. servicemen, etc and material like boats, generators, etc)
- Housing pattern in that locality (RCC, tiled, etc).
- Cropping and occupational pattern

Review and Analysis of Past Disasters

It refers to prioritising disasters based on its frequency and analysis of the estimated losses. This can be carried out by taking the help of elderly people of the village.

The villagers analyse the losses that they had incurred during various disasters and learn the best practices carried out. Based on the assessment of the situation actions need to be assigned to the community members.

Seasonality Calendar for Disasters

While analysing the past experiences pertaining to various natural hazards, communities develop the seasonality calendar based on the occurrence of the disaster.

Mapping Exercise

One of the most important activities of preparing the Disaster Management Plan at the village level is the mapping of risk, vulnerabilities and capacities of the village by the community itself as it is a simple and cost effective tool for collecting ground level data. This is done through **Participatory Rural Appraisal (PRA) exercise.**

This mapping exercise aims to provide a pictorial base to the planning process especially to the semi- literate populace and ensures maximum community involvement across gender, caste and other divides. The villagers/community members are encouraged to draw the maps on the ground using locally available resources such as stones, colour powders, etc for different items and indicators.

The type of maps are as follows

- **Social mapping** The village community need to pictorially show the overall layout of the locality. The map shows location of habitat, topography, number of pucca/kuchha houses etc.
- **Resource mapping** It focuses on the locally available resources and assets that can be identified in the map. The resource map is therefore not limited to a map depicting the available resources but also plotting the distribution, access and its use.
- **Vulnerability mapping** In this mapping exercise the members of the community are expected to know the hazards that the village is prone to and the possible areas that are likely to get affected like
  - Household wise valuable groups
  - landslide prone areas etc.
- **Safe and alternate route mapping** In this exercise the members of the community are expected to know the places that are safe. For example, areas which are frequently affected by floods, mounds etc.

Selection of Disaster Management Teams (UMTS)

After analysing the situation and mapping out the resources the next step is to form disaster management teams/task forces from the village/ward/city so as to carry out response activity for facing any crisis situation.

Willing and active men and women folk from the community can be members of the disaster management teams.

The DMTs/task force should also involve experienced and skilled people such as doctors nurses, fire fighting personnel, e.g. service men, police personnel, swimmers, youth with Scout/NCC/NSS background. Civil Defence personnel's, mahila samiti members and others.

It is ideal to have a team of 25 members per task force for a unit of 400-500 households. If the area/community is large, it is advised to increase the number of teams accordingly.

Training of Disaster Management Teams (DMTs)s

The selected team members need to be well trained and efficiently during a given situation of a disaster. The DMTs which need to be well trained, are

1. First Aid Group
2. Rescue and Evacuation Group
3. Water and Sanitation
4. Trauma Counseling

To train the DMTs/task force, members one take the help of the Fire Services, Local health Centre, Red Cross, St. John's Ambulance, etc.)

Rehearsals/Mock Drills and Plan Updating

It is important to conduct live disaster situation drills/rehearsals. Mock drill is an integrated part of the disaster preparedness plan, as it is a preparedness drill to keep the community alert.

The drills are basically a series of actions according to the plan and are usually tried out as a dummy exercise by keeping the people informed of the exercises. If practiced several times the community would be well prepared to respond to the situation.

This is usually done keeping in mind the real time situation. In case of areas prone to cyclone or flood the drills shall be conducted twice a year, one immediately before the cyclone/ flood season and other after 6 months time.

The plans should not just remain on paper rather it should be dynamic and working. The plan should ensure that it addresses the responsibilities of the task force members as well as the families/ individuals living in that area. Over a period of time there could be many changes/ developments in an area for which the contingency plan has been prepared.

Hence, it is very important that the plan is revised every six months or at least once in a year with updated information. The working plan prepared by the community should be aimed towards the development in the region. It is also important to note that there should be an effective convergence of the plan prepared by the community with the lager programmes/development plans of the region.

EXERCISE

Q.1 Define community contingency plan and give two reasons for the need of a plan?

Ans. A community contingency plan is a strategy developed to prepare for and manage potential disasters or emergencies within a community. It outlines steps to reduce risks, ensure safety, and provide resources during a crisis.

Two reasons for needing such a plan are

- **Quick Response** It helps the community react efficiently in emergencies, saving lives.
- **Resource Management** It ensures that resources are available and distributed properly during a disaster.

Q.2 Name four elements of community contingency plans or what should the community contingency plan consist of?

Ans A community contingency plan should consist of the following four elements

- **Initial Awareness and Rapport Building** It is important to create awareness and build trust within the community for better cooperation during emergencies.
- **Outlining the Profile of the Community** Understanding the community's demographics, resources, and vulnerabilities helps in planning effectively.
- **Analysing the Situation on a Participatory Basis** Involving the community in assessing risks ensures that all perspectives are considered.
- **Selection of Task Force, Indicative Responsibilities, and Capacity Building** A task force should be formed with clear responsibilities, and their skills should be developed to handle crisis situations effectively.

Q.3 Identify the components to be present in a Resource map?

Ans. The components to be present in a resource map are

- Individual skills (community leaders/doctors/drivers, swimmers etc)
- Resources around the area (boats, food stock etc)
- Important locations such as open land/low lying and elevated areas
- Protection bunds
- Drainage facilities
- Agriculture area, forest area, mangrove plantations, shelterbelts etc.

Q.4 Identify four different task forces and list out two responsibilities of each of the task forces?

Ans. Four different task forces in a community contingency plan are

Early Warning Team

- Monitor weather and disaster warnings.
- Inform the community about impending threats.

First Aid Team

- Provide basic medical care to injured people.
- Assist in evacuations when necessary.

Rescue and Evacuation Team

- Rescue people from dangerous areas.
- Ensure safe evacuation to shelters.

Water and Sanitation Team

- Ensure clean water supply during a disaster.
- Maintain sanitation facilities to prevent disease outbreaks.

PROJECT REPORT

PROJECT REPORT

Title of the Project: Consumer Rights and Consumer Movement in India

Objective : The objective of the project is to create awareness among consumers about their rights which will minimise the chances of being exploited in the market place.

Name : ....

School : ....

Year : ....

Class : ....

Submitted To : ....

PROJECT REPORT

ACKNOWLEDGEMENT

I would like to express my special thanks of gratitude to my teacher...............as well as our Principal............ who gave me the golden opportunity to do this wonderful project on the topic 'Consumer Rights and Consumer Movement in India.'

This project helped me a lot in gaining adequate knowledge about the topic. I have completed this project after proper analysis and research and I came to know about so many new things.

I am really thankful to all of my friends and co-partners who have devoted their precious time in completing my project. Secondly, I would also like to thank my parents or guardians who helped me a lot in finishing this project within the prescribed time.

I am making this project not only for marks but also to increase my knowledge and intellect development.

Thanks again to all who helped me.

CERTIFICATE

This is to Certify that the project work 'Consumer Rights and Consumer Movement in India' is the bonafide work of .... (Name of the student) who carried out the work under supervision of ....

Name and Signature of
Teacher/Supervisor).

CONTENTS

Who is a Consumer?

Any individual who buys a product or service for his personal use is called a Consumer.

Consumers are the decision makers who decide which product they want to buy, why do they buy and from which store they will make their purchases.

Consumers buy products after being influenced by advertisement and marketing. Every time someone goes to a store and buys a shirt, toy, beverage or anything else, they make a decision as a consumer.

Consumers participate in the market place by purchasing final goods and services as per their requirements. However, consumers are exploited in the market place because they do not insist on their rights.

Thus, being a consumer it is our responsibility to speak out and inform manufacturers and government about our needs and wants and to make complain or inform business alongwith other people about discontentment with a product or service in an honest way. There should be responsibility of being an ethical consumer and be fair and not engage in any kind of malpractices which make all consumers pay.

Malpractices in the Market Place

Being consumers when we buy any product or service from the market place, we expect a certain value for money, i.e., right quality, right quantity, right prices, information about the product, etc. However, in the present day, we end up being harassed and cheated by sellers and manufacturers very often.

There are many ways by which consumers are exploited such as

- Selling at higher prices.
- Adulteration in food products.
- Sub-standard products where quality of products is far below the required standard.
- False claims by some manufacturers in the market place through attractive representations and advertisements about their products in the media which usually mislead the ignorant consumers. e.g. They claim that by using their particular oil will cure baldness, or using a company's fairness cream for a specific period will make one fair, etc, are all typical examples of exaggerated, misleading advertisements.
- There is another common malpractice in the market. e.g. in many cases, though the product will have a warranty or will be under Annual Maintenance Contract (AMC), when a problem arises, the consumer is asked to pay for certain parts or is refused to get maintenance work without paying.
- Creating artificial scarcity through hoarding and black marketing.
- Indulging in unfair trade practices like weighing less than required.

This often happen because of lack of knowledge or ignorance among the customers for the whole variety of goods and services that they buy. Usually most of the consumers do not bother to check the details regarding the date of manufacture, the date of expiry and the MRP. They buy only because of attractive advertisements thus, get exploited by the hands of such sellers or manufacturers.

Need for Protecting the Consumers

There is need for protecting the consumers from the malpractices exercised by the manufacturers or sellers in the market place. It is essential especially in the developing countries like India where most of the consumers just go and buy products on being attracted by the flashy representations or advertisements. Most of the consumers act as herd of sheep that just follow one person who they may like. e.g. if some consumers follow a particular celebrity and who is acting in an advertisement of a particular products like fairness cream, so some followers would blindly buy that product having a belief that it would prove to be a quality product. Thus, to eliminate such practices it is needed to make consumers aware about their rights.

Consumer Movement

In India, the Consumer Movement act as a social force originated with the necessity of protecting and promoting the interests of consumers against immoral and unfair trade practices. Rampant food shortages, hoarding, black marketing, adulteration

PROJECT REPORT

of food and edible oil gave birth to the Consumer Movement in an organised form in the 1960s. Till the 1970s, consumer organisations were largely engaged in writing articles and organising exhibitions.

Ways to Protect Consumers

Many ways have been taken by the government to protect consumers. Some of these ways are as follows

Consumer Forums

The Consumer Movement in India has led to the formation of various organisations locally known as **Consumer Forums** or **Consumer Protection Councils.** They guide consumers on how to file cases in the Consumer Court. Many times, they also represent individual consumer in the Consumer Courts. These voluntary organisations also receive financial support from the government for creating awareness among people.

Consumer Protection Act, 1986

As a result of all efforts since 1960s, the Consumer Movement succeeded in bringing pressure on businesses and firms, as well as government to improve business conduct, which earlier was against the interests of consumers at large. In this regard, a major step taken in 1986 by the Indian Government, was the enactment of the Consumer Protection Act, 1986, popularly known as COPRA. This act was enforced after the formation of Consumers International.

Consumer Protection Act (COPRA), 1986 is an act of Parliament enacted to protect the interests of consumers in India. It makes provision for the establishment of Consumer Councils and other authorities for the settlement of consumers' disputes and connected matters.

Three-tier System

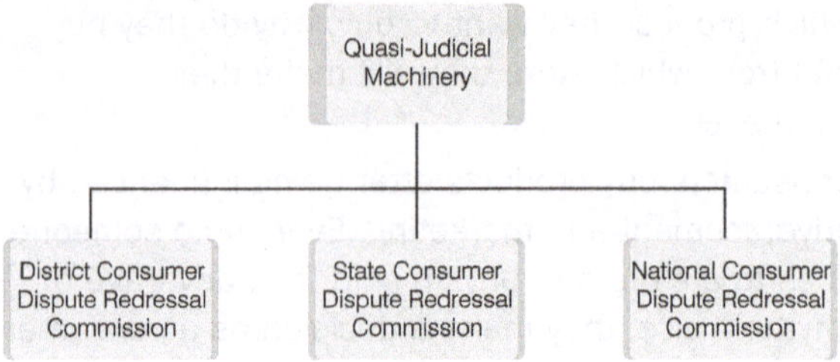

- Diagram (Three-tier System)

Under Consumer Protection Act (COPRA), a three-tier Quasi judicial machinery at the district, state and national levels has been set-up for redressal of consumer disputes. The district level court deals with the cases involving claims upto ₹ 1 crore, the state level courts between ₹ 1 crore and ₹ 10 crore and the national level court deals with cases involving claims exceeding ₹ 10 crore.

If a case is dismissed in district level court, the consumer can also appeal in the state and then in national level court.

Challenges to Consumer Protection

- The consumer redressal process is difficult, expensive and time consuming.
- Existing laws are not very clear on the issue of compensation to consumers.
- Law enforcement in unorganised sector is weak.
- Court proceedings for consumer redressal are long.
- Most of the traders do not issue cash memos.
- Rules and regulations for market functioning are not followed.

Consumer Rights

The right to have information about the quality, potency, quantity, purity, price and standard of goods or services are known as Consumer Rights. It is very essential for the consumers to know their rights. These rights enable consumers to file their complaint in Consumer Court if they find violation of their rights. The rights of consumers are given below

Right to be Protected / Right to Safety

Consumers, have the Right to be Protected against the marketing of goods and delivery of services that are hazardous to their life and property. Producers and service providers need to strictly follow the required safety rules and regulations. There are many goods (like pressure cooker's safety valves, electrical equipments, geysers, iron, etc.) which requires special attention to safety. If it is defective, it can cause a serious accident. So, in this case manufacturers are required to ensure that safety and quality of products and services are to be maintained.

Right to be Informed

Government has made it mandatory to mention all ingredients and safety features, date of manufacture, price, quantity, expiry date, direction for use, etc, on the pack of a product. This information ,is given because it helps the consumer in making' an informed buying decision.

If the product proves to be defective in any way, the consumer can complain and ask for compensation or replacement. The manufacturers have to display these information because consumers have the Right to be Informed about the particular goods and services they purchased.

Use of RTI for Consumers

- In October 2005, the Government of India enacted a law popularly known as RTI (Right to Information) Act, which ensures all the information about the functioning of government departments to its citizens.
- It ensures accountability and transparency of working of public authority.
- This act is applicable to all the states and union territories except the State of Jammu and Kashmir. The reason behind this is that, the State of Jammu and Kashmir has its individual act which is known as Jammu and Kashmir Right to Information Act, 2009.
- As per the RTI Act, any person citizen can request from the public authority, which is then required to furnish the required information within 30 days or expeditiously.

An Example of Using RTI Act

Amrita attended the interview for a government job and did well, but did not receive information about her selection. The officials also refused to answer her queries she then filed an application under the RTI Act, in reply to which she was informed about the reasons for delay in informing her. Later on she got her call letter for appointment also.

Right to Choose

- Any consumer who receives a service in whatever capacity, regardless of age, gender and nature of service, has the Right to Choose whether to continue to receive the service or not. The consumer has a right to choose a good or a service and decide to continue with it like the services of the cable operator or to buy the toothpaste without the toothbrush even if the shopkeeper insists on buying both.
- As per this right, no consumer in India can be trapped in the monopoly of a product in the market. In other words, no consumer can be forced to choose a particular product to consume as no market is allowed to be dominated by a single producer. Thus, each and every consumer has the right to choose according to his/her will across a range of options provide to him.
- This right can be better exercised in a competitive market where a variety of goods are available at competitive prices.

Right to Seek Redressal

- Consumers have the Right to Seek Redressal against unfair trade practices and exploitation. It means if any damage is done to a consumer, he/she has the right to get compensation depending on the degree of damage.
- Thus, it is needed to provide an easy and effective public system by which this can be done.

As the markets are globalising, the direct link between the manufacturer and the final user getting distant, post purchase grievances have to be heard through a strong redressal system. For this, consumer disputes redressal agencies (popularly known as Consumer Forums of Consumer Courts) are set up under the Act at District, State and National level to provide simple and inexpensive quick redressal against consumer complaints.

Right to Represent

This right enables consumers to represent in Consumer Courts. Many Consumers do not know how to file a complaint in Consumer Courts. After considering this, the Consumer Movement in India established various organisations under the name of Consumer Forums or Consumer Protection Councils which guide consumers on how to file their complaints/cases in the Consumer Court. These organisations also help the consumers to represent in the Consumer Courts, where they get compensation depending on the degree of their damage.

Right to Consumer Education

This means every consumer should be aware about the rights that have been provided to him/her so that, he/she could save himself/herself from being exploited at the market place.

Consumer education might refer to formal education through college and school curriculums. Consumer awareness campaigns run by non-governmental and governmental organisations are also a past of consumer education.

Ignorance of consumers, is the root cause of their exploitation. Thus, consumers should know their rights and must exercise them.

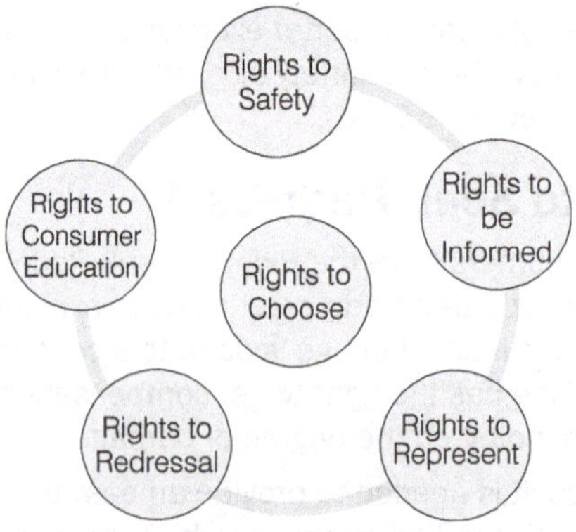

• Consumer Rights in India

Learning to Become Well-informed Consumers

To become well-informed consumer, a person should know his/her responsibilities. The responsibility includes to be more alert and to question about prices, quantity and quality of goods bought and services used. Consumers should buy quality products and for this they should know about the quality standards/marks which have been introduced by the Bureau of Indian Standards (BIS). A quality mark gives consumer a visual and easily identifiable quality assessment tool, originating from a reliable source.

These quality standards marks are as follows

ISI Mark This mark is supposed to be of minimum standard and safe for use by consumers. This mark is both mandatory and voluntary. The ISI certification is mandatory for the products such as LPG cylinder, electrical appliances, batteries, oil pressure stove, automobile accessories, medical equipment, steel products, chemicals, cement, fertilisers, infant foods and packaged drinking water and so on.

Agmark This certification is done of agricultural commodities. There are total 222 products that need AGMARK. e.g. pulses, cereals, essential oils, vegetable oils, fruits and vegetables and semi-processed products and so on. The scheme is legally enforced by Agricultural Produce (Grading and Marking) Act, 1937.

Vegetarian and Non-vegetarian Marks There is provision in India that every packaged food item must be labelled with a mandatory mark in order to be distinguished between lacto-vegetarian and non-lacto-vegetarian. As per Food Safety and Standards (Packaging and Labelling) Regulations, 2011, vegetarian foods should be identified by a green symbol and non-vegetarian foods by brown symbol.

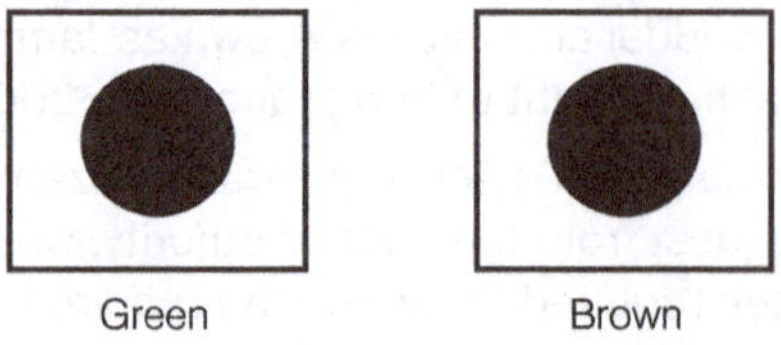

Hallmark The BIS hallmark is a hall marking system began for gold in 2000 and for silver in 2005. It has a wide acceptance among consumers.

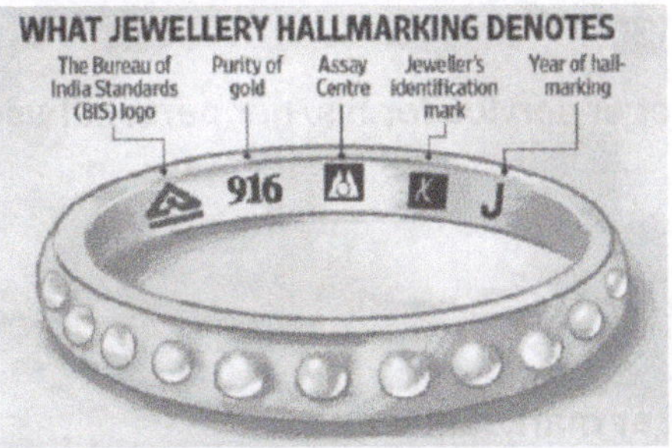

Bee' Star Label Mark This mark was launched by the Bureau of Electrical Efficiency (BEE) of Ministry of Power, Government of India in 2006. This mark gives surety of energy saving and then cost saving on some electrical appliances listed by the government.

These are frost-free (no frost) refrigerators, direct cool refrigerators, room air conditioners, distribution transformers, induction motors, pump sets, tubular fluorescent lamps, ceiling fans, LPG stoves, electric geysers and colour TVs and so on.

Handloom Mark This Mark scheme was launched by the Government of India to promote handloom products in the domestic and international markets. This mark provides assurance to consumers about the genuineness of handloom products. This logo is used for all handloom fabrics and products made thereof.

FSSAI It stands for Food Safety and Standards Authority of India. This certification mark ensures that food is hygienic and meets the approved safety standards set for food items under the Food Safety and Standards (FSS) Act, 2006. The FSSAI has prescribed standards for the food products such as Dairy products, fats, oil, fruits and vegetable products, cereal and cereal products, meat and meat products, fish and fish products, sweets and confectionery, sweetening agents including honey, salt, spices, beverages, proprietary food and so on.

Besides knowing these quality standards, there are other responsibilities of consumers at the market place. Some of these are given below

- Avoid purchase of products or services from a company which do not provide details of the consumer grievance officers to handle consumer grievances.
- Consumer must file a complaint if he/she is not satisfied with the quality of product or services even for a small loss. Consumers should file only a genuine complaint.
- Do not get distracted by advertisements only or believe on the words of the seller.
- Consumer must look market reviews. Similarly give feedback about the product if it is of sub-standard.
- Compare specifications, competition and fair prices of the goods and services before finalising the purchase.
- We should be aware and to understand the environmental consequences of our consumption. Thus, always choose eco-friendly products.
- Being a consumer, it is our responsibility to conserve natural resources and protect the Earth for future generations.

Thus, we can conclude that it is the collective responsibility of both the government and consumers to create awareness about the rights of consumers in the society which will help to minimise the prevalent malpractices in the market place. Thus, as consumers it is our responsibility to come forward and take the Consumer Movement ahead.

VIVA VOCE

1. Which term is used for a person who buys a product or service for his/her personal use from market place?

Ans. Consumer

2. How consumers participate in the market place?

Ans. By purchasing final goods and services.

3. Give an example by which consumers are exploited at market place.

Ans. Selling at higher prices or adulteration in food products.

4. What is the major reason of malpractices in the market place?

Ans. Ignorance by consumers is the major reason of malpractices in the market place.

5. When did Consumer Movement organise?

Ans. During 1960s

6. Till which period consumer organisations were largely engaged in writing articles and holding exhibitions?

Ans. Till the 1970s

7. State any one way to protect consumers.

Ans. Consumer forums

8. Name the organisations which guide consumers on how to file case in the Consumer Court.

Ans. Consumer Forums or Consumer Protections Councils.

9. Consumer Protection Act, (COPRA) was enacted in which year?

Ans. In 1986

10. A three-tier Quasi-judicial machinery, which is under COPRA, is found at which levels?

Ans. District, state and national levels (3 levels).

11. How many consumer rights are there in India?

Ans. 6 consumer rights.

12. Which right enables a consumer to know about all ingredients, safety features, data of manufacture about a product?

Ans. Right to be Informed.

13. What is the aim of RTI Act?

Ans. The aim of the Right to Information or RTI Act is to ensure the citizens of India and provide all the information about the functioning of government departments.

14. Consumer awareness campaigns, run by non-governmental and governmental organisations are part of which right of consumers?

Ans. Right to Consumer Education.

15. Why have you chosen this project?

Ans. It is very essential to know and create awareness among people about the 'Rights of Consumers'. So, I wanted to have a clear vision about the consumer rights and the Consumer Movement in India, hence, I have chosen this project.

Inter-Disciplinary Project
&
Periodic Assessment

INTER-DISCIPLINARY PROJECT

HISTORY

The Making of a Global World

Paragraph Writing

1. Imagine that you are an agricultural worker, who has arrived in America from Ireland. Write a paragraph on why you chose to come and how you are earning your living.

Ans. The potato crop has failed in Ireland last year and I was reduced to poverty. There was no food to eat and I also had no money. The cities were very crowded and many diseases were prevalent.

Also, we Catholics were persecuted by the Englishmen, who were mostly protestants. The English tried to dominate us by imposing the English language on us. That is why, I decided to leave Ireland and emigrate to America, where I was sure, I will have a better future. Here, I am earning my living as an agricultural labourer in a very big wheat farm. I get a regular salary and very happy that I left Ireland.

Project

1. Prepare a flow chart to show how Britain's decision to import food led to increased migration to America and Australia.

Ans. Britain decides to import food items

↓

Russia, America and Australia export food items to Britain

↓

These countries increase their production to supply Britain

↓

America and Australia were newly colonised and did not have enough labour

↓

Thus, many people migrated to these countries to fulfil the demand for labour

Field Trip

Topic

The teacher will organise a visit to a factory, which manufactures goods on 'assembly line' method.

Procedure

(i) Observe the procedure of production.

(ii) Find out the wages of the workers. Talk to them to find out their working conditions.

(iii) Find out from the employer the Labour Act and provisions which they should follow.

(iv) Make field notes.

(v) Write a report on the factory visit.

Learning Outcomes

The students who visit the factory will be able to do the following after the visit.

- Get a first hand experience of the assembly line method.
- Comprehend the procedure of the assembly line method.
- Develop the skill of collating data and reporting.

Related Activities

- The students can prepare a Power Point presentation showing each stage of the method of assembly.
- Some can show the same by means of a flow chart.

After collecting reports from all students, the teacher will discuss the main findings of the visit in the class.

Picture Comprehension

- Migrant agricultural worker's family, homeless and hungry, during the Great Depression, 1936

1. **What was Great Depression? Explain the condition of the family in the picture.**

2. **What was the impact of depression in India?**

Hint The Great Depression was a severe worldwide economic depression in the decade preceding the Second World War. The timing of the Great Depression varied across nations, but in most countries, it started in 1929 and lasted until the mid-1930s. It was the longest and most widespread depression of the 20th century. (Consult your NCERT textbook and Internet)

Learning Outcomes

- This activity will enable the students to learn the importance of the Great Depression.
- Develop critical thinking and analytical skills.

Assessment Criteria

- Wide coverage of the topic.
- Impressive presentation.
- The ability to understand the topic.

Picture Comprehension

- Indentured labourer's photographed for identification for the employers, the numbers and not the names mattered

On the basis of above picture, imagine yourself to be an indentured labour-number 7366.

Write a letter to your friend telling him about your experience in Trinidad as an indentured labour.

Learning Outcomes

- This activity will enable the students to learn the importance of individual identity in one's life.
- Develop creative expression.
- Develop the skill of understanding another person's feelings.

Assessment Criteria

- This activity can be given to all students of the class. The teacher will assess.
- Creative expression of the student.
- The ability to understand the importance of having an individual identity.

Project (Group Activity)

Topic

Globalisation in the 19th Century

Major Points

(i) Flow of trade (Especially goods)
(ii) Flow of labour (Migration)
(iii) Movement of capital (Both short-term and long-term investments across continents)
(iv) Each area could be taken by a group of 5/6 students.

All groups give presentation to the class along with the material they use (say, pictures of goods, maps/sketches, pictures with titles given by them followed by reports about them).

Teacher's Support

- Identifying the areas of work under each head.
- Working with each group in helping them decide the content and helping them procure material through the library.

In cases where the resources in the school are limited, focus on the text and pictures and their interpretation.

This is also to fight the perception among students that collecting more information is more learning.

Besides maximum utilisation of the text and discussion, the student should also be encouraged to explore on individual level and to collect information about any given project.

GEOGRAPHY

Lifelines of National Economy

Report Writing

Topic

Imagine a week without any means of transport or communication.

Learning Outcomes

By doing this activity the students will be able to

- Realise the significance of means of transport and communication.
- Recall the functional linkages of means of transport and communication with other areas.

Procedure

(i) This activity should be undertaken after the lesson is completed.
(ii) Students may be asked to imagine a week without any means of transport or communication. How would your life be influenced by it? Give a detailed description of it.

(iii) After completion of this task, students may be asked to present their write-up in the class.

Assessment Criteria

This is a fun based activity, which need not to be assessed. Students with good imagination may be mentioned by the teacher.

At the end, the teacher may brief the real implications of the absence of means of transport and communications.

Group Visit

Topic

Visit to a Bus Terminal/Railway Station.

Learning Outcomes

By doing this exercise the students will be able to

- Realise how many persons are involved in running a rail or road network.
- Understand the importance of communication linkages in transportation networks.
- Analyse the problems faced by agencies running such networks.

Procedure

The students may be asked to visit a main bus terminal /railway station and prepare a report based on the answers to the questions given below

(i) What is the area of influence of the bus terminal/railway station, *i.e.*, places linked by it?

(ii) Average number of buses/trains operating from the place daily (both incoming and outgoing traffic).

(iii) On an average, how many passengers are benefited by it?

(iv) How much goods are transported on a daily basis from here?

(v) How many employees are working in it?

(vi) Are there any daily wage workers? If yes, how many?

(vii) How much is the annual/monthly/daily collection/income of the unit?

(viii) Which is the longest route terminating here?

(ix) Also mention the name of any special bus or train, if any, operating from here.

(x) Which type of track is mostly used here/which type of roads based on their layout/significance are found in the region?

(xi) Which authority is responsible for its maintenance?

(xii) Problems faced by the people using the facility.

- Is the service adequate for the population of the area?
- How far is the environment maintained?
- How much is the pollution level of the area?
- Any other problems faced.

Assessment Criteria

- Relevance of the content
- Presentation of the report
- Use of graphic / maps / photographs
- Genuineness of the information collected

Make a Brochure

Topic

Preparation of a tourist guide brochure to visit a beach/hill station/desert/any other tourist spot.

Learning Outcomes

On completion of this activity the students will be able to

- Understand the potential of tourism in India.
- Analyse the role of means of transport and communication in enhancing tourism.
- Understand the contribution of tourism to the country's GDP.
- Appreciate the richness of our country.

Procedure

(i) Students may be encouraged to prepare a brochure for a particular tourist spot of their choice. Teacher should explain the requirements of a tourist guide.

(ii) This guide should include the details of the place in terms of its

- Location
- Climate
- Season to visit
- Type of clothes preferred
- Nearest rail/bus/airport
- Map of the area
- How to reach there
- Places to visit
- Any other relevant information
- Based on the features mentioned, students may be guided to create their brochure.
- They may need to explore further for relevant information to include in it.

Assessment Criteria

- Presentation
- Richness of the content
- Placement of facts
- Use of maps, diagrams and pictures
- Neatness

Report Writing

Topic

Pipeline Transport

Learning Outcomes

By preparing the report the students will be able to

- Know about the different ways in which pipelines are used as a means of transport of materials.
- Understand the significance of pipeline transport.

Procedure

(i) The students may be asked to prepare a report on the different kinds of pipelines used for transporting material.

(ii) They may also be asked to prepare a report on the benefits of using pipelines.

Assessment Criteria

- Clarity of ideas
- Presentation of facts
- Originality

Report Making and its Presentation

Topic

Indian Ports

Learning Outcomes

By preparing the report the students will be able to

- Know about the ports of India.
- Understand the significance of ports to the nation.
- Make a comparison of one port on the Eastern coast with one on the Western coast of India.

Procedure

The class may be divided into small groups. Each group may be given two ports, one from the Western and the other from the Eastern coast.

Students will prepare a report based on the following

- Location of the ports on the map.
- Reasons for their development.
- Special features, if any.
- Items handled for export and import
- Hinterland
- Problems, if any
- Significance of the ports
- Members of each group will present their report based on the above mentioned points in the class.

Assessment Criteria

Students work may be assessed based on the following criteria

- Content
- Logical Presentation
- Research work done
- Originality

Follow Up

Teacher may conduct a quick oral test to understand the level of learning. Teachers may encourage students to interject during other team's presentations and the best interjection may be given long applause. Through this, the motivation level will increase and hence enhance learning.

Picture Based

Topic

Interpretation of diagrams on roadways

Learning Outcomes

On interpreting the picture the students will be able to

- Understand the concept of expressways.
- Identify the expressway and its significance.

Procedure

Study the picture showing an expressway and answer the questions based on it.

Students will answer the following questions based on the above figure.

1. Name this expressway connecting Ahmedabad - Vadodara, which is shown in the picture.
2. Name the state in which this expressway is located.
3. Name the agency responsible for its construction.
4. Why is it considered as a major breakthrough in the history of road transportation?

Hints and Answers

1. This expressway is known as National Expressway number 1.
2. Gujarat
3. The National Highways Authority of India (NHAI) is responsible for its construction.
4. It is considered as a major breakthrough because it reduces the travel time and distance between the two main commercial centres of Gujarat to about 1 hour (95 km), from the earlier 2½ hours (113 km).

ECONOMICS

Globalisation and the Indian Economy

Individual Research

Topic

Tracing the origin of a company (finding a logo, relating it to the company and finding its origin).

Learning Outcomes

This activity introduces the concept of liberalisation. Students will become interested in products that they consume and will appreciate liberalised policies of the government that bring a wide range of products to the market.

After this task, students shall be able to

- Identify the logos of many companies whose products are of everyday use.
- Identify some logos of MNC's, Indian companies and institutions.
- Relate the company to its product and logo.
- Research about the company's/institution's origin.
- Appreciate the liberalisation policies of the government on the availability of wide ranging products in India.
- Articulate their ideas interestingly and share them with peers.

Procedure

(i) Each student is given a week's time to bring a picture of the logo, name and information of the company/ institution.

(ii) Some logos can be discussed in class to initiate interest.

(iii) Some students at random can read out their research.

(iv) The information can be displayed on the bulletin board in four groups—MNC, Indian Company, Indian Institution and Foreign Institution.

Time Estimate

One week should be given to the students to research and 40 minutes (1 period) time to present their findings to the class. Each student can't get the opportunity to present, so four groups as given above can be made to display the information.

Assessment Criteria

The activity can be marked considering the research, the correlation between logo, company name and its origin, as found by each student. This activity can also be taken up in groups.

Feedback

A class discussion on the variety of logos displayed on the bulletin board and sources of their research will spark interest among students. A universal participation in the discussion should be encouraged.

Creation and Research

Topic

Disparities of income and opportunity

Learning Outcomes

This activity should be undertaken after a discussion is held on the merits and demerits of globalisation. The activity will enable students to understand that disparities are universally prevalent in the world which lead to unequal opportunities.

After completing the task, students shall be able to

- Identify the inequalities of income and wealth depicted.
- Identify the difference in the opportunities available.
- Relate these disparities to the demerits of globalisation.
- Communicate effectively their ideas through a cartoon or picture along with a slogan.

Procedure

(i) The teacher should make a copy of the representative cartoon/pictures on a Powerpoint/ OHP/ Chart paper which is displayed in the class for all students to observe.

(ii) Ask students to comprehend the pictures.

(iii) Class could be divided into pairs.

(iv) Students have to create a cartoon or picture on their own depicting problems of disparity, its causes and solutions offered.

(v) Teacher will assess each student's write ups.

Time Estimate

One week should be given to the students to research and make their creation. They will be given 40 minutes (1 period) to present their picture / cartoon to the class. Students' work can be displayed on the class notice board afterwards.

Assessment Criteria

This activity can be assessed considering the idea, correlation between its depiction and the slogan. This activity can also be taken up in groups.

Feedback

A class discussion on the variety of cartoons and ideas depicted can reinforce the concept of disparities in income and opportunities.

Remedial Activity

The demonstrations at the various WTO meetings by the members of developing countries can be associated with the topic and discussed.

Article Interpretation

Topic

Demerits of Globalisation

Learning Outcomes

This activity should be undertaken to take children beyond the academic curriculum of discussing the disadvantages of globalisation. It allows students to realise that many MNCs promote their products to the detriment of the host country.

The teacher should encourage substantial discussion on the advantages and disadvantages of MNCs and globalisation through this article.

After completing the task, students shall be able to

- Identify the issues mentioned in the article.
- Understand the reasons for farmer's discontentment.
- Distinguish between subsidy and market price.
- Discuss the role played by the government.
- Have a better understanding of the merits and demerits of MNCs for a host country.

Procedure

(i) The newspaper article given below is read aloud to the students.

(ii) A class discussion follows. The merits and demerits of globalisation are discussed.

(iii) The teacher explains and discusses the issues involved.

(iv) The students discuss the concerned issues with parents or elders at home.

(v) Each student must write a paragraph reflecting their understanding of the situation and suggesting solutions to the problem.

White Gold

(Newspaper article from 'The Hindu')

Paradoxically, the suicides have taken place in some of the best agricultural areas–paddy farmers in Eastern Vidarbha, wheat farmers in Punjab, coffee growers in Kerala. In more marginal areas, farmers continue to lead a life of poverty–but a self-reliant, debt-free or at least debt-manageable poverty.

The suicides started among cotton farmers and remain most prevalent among the producers of what was once called 'white gold'. And it is in the dry cotton country of Vidarbha where the problem is most acute.

In these dusty villages, where poor farming families try to scratch out a living, a group of committed activists maintains a kind of suicide watch, complete with a macabre map covered with labels in the form of skulls.

Nagpur is the capital of the region and it is here I meet Jaideep Hardikar. Hardikar has interviewed hundreds of farmers in his attempt to publicise their plight. He is from Vidarbha and is deeply committed to its 25 million people.

'There is a mass depression that has crept in. Poverty has always been pervasive in this country, but no one committed suicide. It is not the issue of poverty but the issue of indebtedness that affects all spheres of a farmer's life'.

Jaideep's anger and frustration shows through as he talks. 'Last year (in 2005) I reported that there was a suicide every 36 hours. Then it came down to 24. Then down to 12. And now it stands at 8. That is 3 suicides a day.'

Jaideep, who is writing a book on the suicides, is not much puzzled by the cause. As they say, he has 'done the math'. 'In Vidarbha there are 1.8 million households engaged in cotton. In the US, there are 25000 cotton farmers. If the subsidy that they receive, that depresses the world price for cotton, was removed, prices would rise to $ 4500 to $5000 a bushel.

Efficient Indian cotton farmers could easily compete with a price of $ 3500 a bushel. Today the farmers usually get less than $2000 (below the cost of production) and it is impossible to make even ₹ 10000 a year from an eight-hectare plot. That is just $ 200 for your entire family to live on.

As I wandered through the dusty villages of Vidarbha, the reasons for the suicides started to come into focus. I was nervous to approach people at such a tragic time.

But I found that people who would have every reason to tell you to leave them alone and mind your own business always received you with tea and courtesy. It seemed to give them some relief to be able to tell their story.

Certainly this was true of Bravin Vijay Bakamwar's father. The Bakamwars live in Sunna village. The 26-year-old Bravin had been married for just six months. On 25th November, 2006, he got up early and rode his new (but unpaid-for) motorbike out into the fields and hanged himself from an electric pole.

Bravin was deep in debt to both moneylenders and the Cooperative Bank. A loan for a well had come up dry. Cotton prices were what they were.

He was responsible not only for his new wife but also for his parents and siblings. He was caught between the obligations of old rural India and the desires of shiny new consumer India, as represented by his new motorbike.

He must have felt that he could satisfy neither. His father referred to Bravin as a sensitive son who felt that 'all the responsibilities fell on him'.

We sadly agreed that a parent should never outlive their child. I thought of my own son. In the end the father, left in sadness and despair, felt that his only recourse was to follow the example of his son. He shook my hand warmly as I left and I hoped he would find a different way out.

BT cotton is genetically modified cotton containing the gene of the soil bacteria B thuringiensis, which serves as a natural pesticide.

Initially it was developed by the US based Monsanto Corporation as their flagship GM product for sale to farmers in order to reduce chemical pesticides. It is now widely used in the US, India and China.

Much to the dismay of Monsanto, many hybrid copies are currently on the cotton seed market despite distinctly mixed BT results.

Time Estimate

- Classroom time 40 minutes (1 period) can be used to read the article, discuss the issues involved and initiate the paragraph writing by the students.
- Home task–30 minutes to write the home assignment.

Assessment Criteria

- The activity can be assessed considering the participation in class discussion and content of the home assignment.

Feedback

- A class discussion on the talk and inputs given by parents or elders at home.

Remedial Activity

- Meaning of subsidy, MSP and issue price as studied the previous year can be discussed again. The tussle over subsidy at the WTO forum can also be explained again.

PERIODIC ASSESSMENT

PEN PAPER TEST

{TEST 1}

Instructions Chapter covered in this test is Chapter 4 of History.

1. What is proto-industrialisation?

(a) Industry based on heavy factory production
(b) First and early form of Industrialisation
(c) Industry based on modern technology
(d) Rural Industry

2. The earliest factories in England came up by the ....

(a) 1730s (b) 1700s
(c) 1850s (d) 1900s

3. Which among the following industrialists began selling cloth in India with labels on cloth bundles?

(a) Manchester industrialists
(b) Yorkshire industrialists
(c) Lancashire industrialists
(d) Glasgow industrialists

4. .... introduced the cotton mill.

(a) James Watt (b) Mathew Boulton
(c) Henry Patullo (d) Richard Arkwright

5. Before the age of the machine industry, where did the finer varieties of silk and cotton goods come from?

(a) Egypt (b) India
(c) Persia (d) Rome

6. Which of the following was not a problem of Indian weavers at the early 19th century?

(a) Shortage of raw materials
(b) The collapse of the local and foreign market
(c) Setting up of factories
(d) Clashes with Gomasthas

7. First cotton mill of India in Bombay was established in ....

(a) 1854 (b) 1855
(c) 1862 (d) 1885

8. Who established six joint-stock companies in India during 1830-1840?

(a) Seth Hukumchand (b) G D Birla
(c) Jamsedjee Nusserwanjee Tata (d) Dwaraknath Tagore

9. There are two statements marked as Assertion (A) and Reason (R). Mark your answer as per the codes provided below.

Assertion (A) European Managing Agencies were interested in certain kinds of products such as tea and coffee.

Reason (R) They established tea and coffee plantations and invested in mining, indigo and jute.

Codes

(a) Both A and R are true and R is the correct explanation of A
(b) Both A and R are true, but R is not the correct explanation of A
(c) A is true, but R is false
(d) A is false, but R is true

10. Match the following.

List I	List II
A. London underground railway starts operation	1. 1863
B. First jute mill comes up in Bengal	2. 1855
C. James Watt patents the steam engine	3. 1781
D. James Hargrieves invents the Spinning Jenny	4. 1764

Codes

	A	B	C	D
(a)	1	2	3	4
(b)	4	3	2	1
(c)	2	1	4	3
(d)	1	4	3	2

{TEST 2}

Note *See instructions in Test 1*

1. .... is considered to be the first industrial nation of the world.

(a) Germany (b) Russia
(c) Britain (d) Italy

2. Which of the following cities was known as a finishing centre of the cloth at the time of proto-industrialisation?

(a) London (b) Berlin
(c) Paris (d) Rome

3. Which of the following mechanical devices is used for weaving, with rope and pulleys which helps to weave wide pieces of cloth?

(a) Handloom (b) Power loom
(c) Fly cutter (d) Fly shuttle

4. .... was the role of the jobber.

(a) A production manager
(b) A finance manager
(c) Employed by the business house to get new recruits
(d) Sales head

5. The introduction of which technology in England angered women?

(a) The spinning jenny (b) The underground railways
(c) The steam engine (d) None of these

6. Which pre-colonial port connected India to the Gulf countries and red seaports?

(a) Bombay (b) Surat
(c) Hooghly (d) Machhalipattanam

7. Which among the following cities had the trade links with South Asian parts?

(a) Masulipatam and Hooghly
(b) Masulipatam and Surat
(c) Surat and Bombay
(d) Bombay and Hooghly

8. Which industry becomes the largest industry in Britain during the second phase of industrialisation?

(a) Chemical industries (b) Machine industries
(c) Agro-based industries (d) Iron and steel industries

9. There are two statements marked as Assertion (A) and Reason (R). Mark your answer as per the codes provided below.

Assertion (A) European Managing Agencies were interested in certain kinds of products such as tea and coffee.

Reason (R) They established tea and coffee plantations and invested in mining, indigo and jute.

Codes

(a) Both A and R are true and R is the correct explanation of A
(b) Both A and R are true but R is not the correct explanation of A
(c) A is true, but R is false
(d) A is false, but R is true

10. Match the following.

	List I		List II
A.	First iron and steel work started in Jamshedpur	1.	1912
B.	Spinning and weaving mill production started in Madras	2.	1874
C.	First cotton mill in India start productions in Bombay	3.	1856

Codes

	A	B	C		A	B	C
(a)	1	2	3	(b)	3	2	1
(c)	2	1	3	(d)	1	3	2

{TEST 3}

Note *See instructions in Test 1*

1. .... image of the God which was most commonly used to popularise baby products.

(a) Shiva (b) Ram
(c) Krishna (d) Hanuman

2. By which country was yarn mainly exported to?

(a) Burma (b) Britain
(c) China (d) Japan

3. Who among the following set up the Indian jute industry in Calcutta in 1917?

(a) Seth Hukumchand
(b) G D Birla
(c) Jamsedjee Nusserwanjee Tata
(d) Dwarakanath Tagore

4. Which among the following were the most important ports, used for trade?

(a) Surat (b) Masulipatnam
(c) Hooghly (d) All of these

5. The industrial revolution is referred to ....

(a) mass production by factories
(b) collection of raw materials
(c) process of raw materials
(d) None of the above

6. Who improved the steam engine produced by Newcomen and patented the new engine in 1781?

(a) James Watt
(b) Mathew Boulton
(c) Richard Arkwright
(d) Henry Patullo

7. Cost of raw cotton increased in the Indian market during the later nineteenth century because of ....

(a) the civil war in America
(b) the civil war in France
(c) the restriction imposed by the British towards the export of cotton
(d) None of the above

8. Production processes involving carding, twisting, rolling and stapling are associated with ....

(a) Textile industries
(b) Railway industry
(c) Shipping industry
(d) Glass industry

9. There are two statements marked as Assertion (A) and Reason (R). Mark your answer as per the codes provided below.

Assertion (A) The history of trade started from the late eighteenth century when British in India began exporting opium to China and took tea from China to England.

Reason (R) Some of the businessmen who were involved in these trades had visions of developing industrial enterprises in India.

Codes

(a) Both A and R are true and R is the correct explanation of A

(b) Both A and R are true, but R is not the correct explanation of A

(c) A is true, but R is false

(d) A is false, but R is true

10. Match the following.

List I	List II
A. Gomastha	1. An Indian word meaning an agent
B. Sepoy	2. Indian soldier of the British army
C. Guild	3. An association of craftman

Codes

	A	B	C		A	B	C
(a)	3	2	1	(b)	2	1	3
(c)	1	3	2	(d)	1	2	3

{TEST 4}

Note *See instructions in Test 1*

1. How does advertisement help us to create new consumer?

(a) It makes products appear desirable and necessary.

(b) It tries to shape the minds of people and create new needs.

(c) It helps in expanding the markets for products.

(d) All of the above

2. What was the impact on the handloom industry with the invention of the fly shuttle?

(a) It needed too much training

(b) It increased productivity per worker, speeded up production and reduced labour demand

(c) It reduced production

(d) It was not very productive

3. Advertisements became a vehicle of the nationalist message of ....

(a) Swaraj (b) Anti British

(c) Swadeshi (d) Independence of India

4. First Indian Jute mill was set up in Calcutta in ....

(a) 1862 (b) 1855

(c) 1874 (d) 1917

5. Which regions benefitted from the fly shuttle equipment?

(a) Madras

(b) Cochin

(c) Bengal

(d) None of the above

6. Which was a popular mode of advertisement?

(a) Newspapers

(b) Magazines

(c) Radio news

(d) Calendars

7. Growing at a rapid pace, ... was the leading sector in the first phase of industrialisation up to the 1840s.

(a) Shipping

(b) Mineral industry

(c) Cotton

(d) Metals

8. How did the East India Company set up a monopoly over the weaving industry in India?

(a) By openly fighting with the Portugese and other traders

(b) By dominating the weaver through force of action

(c) By bribing the weavers in the favour of the Company

(d) By appointing the gomastha to get direct control over the weavers, providing loans and giving time limits

9. There are two statements marked as Assertion (A) and Reason (R). Mark your answer as per the codes provided below

Assertion (A) In 1772, Henry Patullo said that the demand for Indian textiles could never reduce since no other nation produced goods of the same quality.

Reason (R) But, unfortunately, by the beginning of the nineteenth century, India witnessed a decline in textile exports.

Codes

(a) Both A and R are true and R is the correct explanation of A

(b) Both A and R are true, but R is not the correct explanation of A

(c) A is true, but R is false

(d) A is false, but R is true

10. **Match the following.**

List I	List II
A. Stapler	1. A person who staples or sorts wool according to its fibre.
B. Fuller	2. A person who fulls - gathers cloth by pleating.
C. Carding	3. A process of preparing fibres such as cotton or wool, prior to spinning.
D. Efficacy	4. Effectiveness; power to produce certain effect.

Codes

	A	B	C	D
(a)	4	3	2	1
(b)	2	1	4	3
(c)	1	2	3	4
(d)	1	4	3	2

{TEST 5}

Note *See instructions in Test 1*

1. **Identify the true statement regarding the difficulty faced by workers in a factory in 19th century Britain.**

(a) Employers were looking for only skilled workers and they rejected inexperienced applicants.

(b) The number of jobs were less than the number of job seekers.

(c) Employers did not prefer migrants.

(d) Employers wanted educated workers.

2. **During the late eighteenth-century, British export opium to China and import .... to England.**

(a) Tea (b) Coffee

(c) Gold (d) Silk

3. **What was the rate of technological changes occurring in England at the time?**

(a) Rapid (b) Moderate

(c) Slow (d) No change

4. **Till independence capital goods manufacturing companies are not developed in India because of ....**

(a) low interest of Indian manufacturer

(b) lack of raw materials

(c) mostly capital goods are imported from Europe

(d) None of the above

5. **Where were the Indian large scale industries located around 1911?**

(a) Gujarat

(b) Calcutta

(c) Bombay

(d) Both (b) and (c)

6. **What was the status of the handloom industry in the first half of the 20th century in India?**

(a) Collapsed

(b) Partially survived

(c) Handloom cloth production expanded steadily

(d) British interference was too much

7. **Which two ports grew after the European companies gained power in trade?**

(a) Surat and Hooghly

(b) Madras and Masulipatnam

(c) Bombay and Calcutta

(d) None of the above

8. **Where did the workers come from to work in the Indian Industries that were set up?**

(a) In most industrial regions workers came from the districts around.

(b) They came from different states and regions around.

(c) They were brought in from Burma and Ceylon.

(d) They did not come around due to lack of mobility.

9. **There are two statements marked as Assertion (A) and Reason (R). Mark your answer as per the codes provided below**

Assertion (A) In India, silk and cotton goods dominated the international market in textiles, before the age of machine industries.

Reason (R) A variety of Indian merchants and bankers were involved in this network of export trade - financing production, carrying goods and supplying exporters.

Codes

(a) Both A and R are true and R is the correct explanation of A

(b) Both A and R are true, but R is not the correct explanation of A

(c) A is true, but R is false

(d) A is false, but R is true

10. **Match the following.**

List I	List II
A. Earliest factories start in England	1. 1730
B. Richard Arkwright creates the first cotton mill	2. 1771
C. First jute mill comes up in Bengal	3. 1855

Codes

	A	B	C		A	B	C
(a)	1	2	3	(b)	3	2	1
(c)	2	1	3	(d)	1	3	2

SAMPLE
QUESTION PAPERS (1-5)

Sample Question Paper 1 (Solved)
Social Science

Time : 3 hrs	M.M. : 80

General Instructions

1 Question paper comprises Six Sections – A, B, C, D, E and F. There are 37 questions in the question paper. All questions are compulsory.
2 Section A – From questions 1 to 20 are MCQs of 1 mark each.
3 Section B – Question no. 21 to 24 are Very Short Answer Type Questions, carrying 2 marks each. Answer to each question should not exceed 40 words.
4 Section C – Question no. 25 to 29 are Short Answer Type Questions, carrying 3 marks each. Answer to each question should not exceed 60 words
5 Section D – Question no. 30 to 33 are long answer type questions, carrying 5 marks each. Answer to each question should not exceed 120 words.
6 Section E – Questions no. from 34 to 36 are case based questions with three sub-questions and are of 4 marks each.
7 Section F – Question no. 37 is map based, carrying 5 marks with two parts, 37a from History (2 marks) and 37b from Geography (3 marks).

Section-A (1 × 20 = 20)

(Multiple Choice Questions)

1. Choose the correctly matched pair. **(1)**

(a) Union of India – Prime Minister
(b) State – Sarpanch
(c) Municipal Corporation – Governor
(d) Gram Panchayat – Mayor

2. Match List I and II and select the correct answer using the codes below in the lists.

List I	List II
A. Laterite soil	1. High moisture retention
B. Black soil	2. Intensively cultivated
C. Alluvial soil	3. Source of salt
D. Arid soil	4. Problem of leaching

Codes

	A	B	C	D		A	B	C	D
(a)	1	1	2	3	(b)	2	1	3	4
(c)	4	1	2	3	(d)	1	4	3	2

3. There are two statements marked as Assertion (A) and Reason (R). Mark your answer as per the codes given below. **(1)**

Assertion (A) Sringaverapura near Allahabad had sophisticated water harvesting system channelling the flood water of the river Ganga.

Reason (R) Sophisticated hydraulic structures like Sringaverapura were build in 19th century to fulfill water needs for industrial purposes.

Codes

(a) Both A and R are true and R is the correct explanation of A
(b) Both A and R are true, but R is not the correct explanation of A
(c) A is true, but R is false
(d) A is false, but R is true

4. Find the incorrect option about WTO. **(1)**

(a) World Trade Organisation was the national organisation that varies from country to country.
(b) 160 countries of the world were members of WTO.
(c) WTO is supposed to allow free trade for all.
(d) 164 member countries are the part of WTO in 29th July, 2016.

5. Two statements I and II are given below. Read both the statements carefully and choose the correct option. **(1)**

Statement I The Communist Party of India was formed in 1925.

Statement II It opposed the forces of secessionism and communalism.

Options

(a) Both statements I and II are correct and statement II is the correct explanation of statement I.
(b) Both statements I and II are correct, but statement II is not the correct explanation of statement I.
(c) Statement I is correct, but statement II is incorrect.
(d) Statement I is incorrect, but statement II is correct.

6. Consider the following statements about exhaustion of natural resources. (1)

I. Crude oil resources would last only 50 years more.
II. Oil extraction is undertaken by middle East region at a very fast pace.
III. Non-conventional fuel sources should be encouresed that reduces use of crude oil.

Which of the following statements gives an idea of sustainable development?

(a) Only II (b) Only I and II
(c) Only I (d) Only III

7. Arrange the following sectors in decreasing order as per their share in employment in 1977-78. (1)

I. Primary Sector II. Secondary Sector
III. Tertiary Sector

(a) I, II, III (b) I, III, II (c) III, II, I (d) II, III, I

8. Which of these Indian leaders worked for the elimination of caste system? (1)

(a) Jyotiba Phule (b) Dr BR Ambedkar
(c) Mahatma Gandhi (d) All of these

9. A potter making pots, wants to exchange pots for wheat. Luckily, he meets a farmer who has wheat and is willing to exchange it for the pots. What is this situation known as? (1)

(a) Incidence of wants
(b) Double coincidence of wants
(c) Barter system
(d) None of the above

10. Match List I and II and select the correct answer using the codes below in the lists. (1)

List I		List II
A. Invasion of Italy by Napolean	1.	1814-1815
B. Fall of Napolean	2.	1797
C. Unification of Italy	3.	1866-1871
D. Unification of Germany	4.	1859-1870

Codes

	A	B	C	D		A	B	C	D
(a)	4	3	2	1	(b)	2	1	3	4
(c)	2	1	4	3	(d)	3	4	1	2

11. What this picture signifies during 1824 in France? (1)

(a) Peasant uprising (b) The club of thinkers
(c) The Massacre of Chios (d) None of these

12. Read the given data and find out which state has the highest Infant Mortality Rate. (1)

States	Per Capita Income for 2018-19 (in ₹)	Infant Mortality Rate per 1,000 live births (2018)	Literacy Rate % 2017-18	Net Attendance Ratio (per 100 persons) Secondary Stage (age 14 and 15) years 2017-18
Haryana	2,36,147	30	82	61
Kerala	2,04,105	7	94	83
Bihar	40,982	32	62	43

Sources : Economic Survey 2020-21, P.A 157, National Sample Survey Organisation (Report No. 585), National Statistical Officer, Government of India.

(a) Kerala (b) Bihar
(c) Haryana (d) Both (b) and (c)

13. Nari Shakti Vandan Adhiniyam, 2023 does not provide reservation to women in .... (1)

(a) Lok Sabha
(b) State Legislative Assemblies
(c) Delhi Legislative Assembly
(d) Panchayats

14. Which of the following statements is not correct about the language policy of India? (1)

(a) India did not give the status of national language to any one language.
(b) States too have their own official language.
(c) Besides Hindi, there are 22 other languages recognised as Scheduled Languages by the Constitution.
(d) The use of English was discontinued by the central government in 1965.

15. Arrange the following manganese producing states from highest to lowest production. (1)

I. Odisha **II. Madhya Pradesh**
III. Karnataka **IV. Andhra Pradesh**

Codes

(a) II, I, III, IV (b) I, II, III, IV
(c) III, II, I, IV (d) II, III, IV, I

16. Which language was spoken for purpose of diplomacy in the mid-18th century in Europe? (1)

(a) English (b) French
(c) Spanish (d) German

17. India is a tropical country. It has enormous possibilities of tapping solar energy. Photovoltaic Technology converts sunlight directly into electricity. Solar energy is fast becoming popular in rural and remote areas. Some big solar power plants are being established in different parts of India, which will minimise the dependence of rural households on firewood and dung cakes, and in turn it will contribute to environmental conservation and adequate supply of manure in agriculture.
Which of the following statements is true about solar energy?

(a) India solar energy potential is limited due to its tropical climate.
(b) Photovoltaic technology primarily utilises wind energy.
(c) Rural households in India primarily rely on solar energy for cooking.
(d) Solar energy adoption in rural areas can reduce reliance on traditional biomass fuels and contribute to environmental conservation.

18. What is the sequence of manufacturing steel? (1)

I. Pig iron
II. Shaping metal
III. Blast furnance
IV. Steel making

Codes

(a) I, III, II, IV (b) III, I, IV, II
(c) I, II, III, IV (d) IV, II, III, I

19. Which one of the following is a major linguistic groups of Sri Lanka? (1)

(a) Christian and Tamil (b) Buddhist and Hindu
(c) Sinhali and Tamil (d) Sinhali and Christian

20. Consider the following statements and choose the appropriate option associated with Belgium. (1)

(a) Belgium is a small country in North America.
(b) Belgium has borders with France, the Netherlands, Germany and Luxembourg.
(c) Out of total population of Belgium, 80% lives in the Flemish region and speaks French language.
(d) The total population of Belgium is 10 crore.

Section–B (2×4=8)

(Very Short Answer Type Questions)

21. John was reading the newspaper, he saw some cartoons and caricatures that describe the French Revolution. He didn't understand it and asked his father- what was the role of cartoons and caricatures in French Revolution? **(2)**

22. Mention any two features of arid soil. **(2)**

Or What are determinant factors in the use of land?

23. What is the contribution of Information and Communication Technology? **(2)**

24. How far does economic inequalities exist in democratic countries? **(2)**

Section–C (3×5=15)

(Short Answer Type Questions)

25. "Like Germany, Italy too had a long history of political fragmentation." Justify. **(3)**

26. Which obstacle restricts certain borrowers to get a loan from the banks? State with example. **(3)**

27. Rohan saw that a political party meeting is going on outside his colony. He noticed that the leader is giving his speech about caste and its relation with politics. He got confused and asked his father - beside caste, which other factors do matter in electoral politics? Explain. **(3)**

28. Analyse the meaning of sustainable development. How can sustainable development be achieved? **(3)**

Or "Water scarcity may be an outcome of large and growing population in India." Analyse the statement.

29. Explain how the public sector contributes to the economic development of a nation. **(3)**

Section–D (5 × 4 = 20)

(Long Answer Type Questions)

30. Almost every person has different developmental goals. Explain in brief. **(5)**

Or With the help of an example, show how two groups may have different notions of development.

31. 'Culture played an important role in creating the idea of the nation: art and poetry, stories and music helped express and shape nationalist feelings.' Substantiate the statement.

Or 'The most serious source of nationalist tension in Europe after 1871 was the area called the Balkans.' Analyse the statement.

32. The elder brother of Ravi, got a new job with decent salary in an IT sector, the headquarter of the company is in USA, whereas he also notice that people are not coming to his father local store, as they are preferring to go in malls to get their necessary thing, and that effect his father business. He asked his teacher - what are the advantages and disadvantages of globalisation? Explain 3 points in each case. **(5)**

Or Which factors have enabled globalisation in India? Explain.

33. Describe any three demands of the Sri Lankan Tamils. How did they struggle for their demands? **(5)**

Or What do you mean by homogeneous society? What are its main features?

Section–E (4 × 3 = 12)

(Case Based Questions)

34. Read the source given below and answer the questions that follow. (4)

In 1956, an Act was passed to recognise Sinhala as the only official language, thus disregarding Tamil. The governments followed preferential policies that favoured Sinhala applicants for university positions and government jobs. A new Constitution stipulated that the state shall protect and foster Buddhism.

All these government measures, coming one after the other, gradually increased the feeling of alienation among Sri Lankan Tamils. They felt that none of the major political parties led by the Buddhist Sinhala leaders was sensitive to their language and culture. They felt that the Constitution and government policies denied them equal political rights, discriminated against them in getting jobs and other opportunities and ignored their interests. As a result, the relations between the Sinhala and Tamil communities strained over time.

(i) Evaluate the majoritarian measures taken by the Sinhala Government. (1)

(ii) To what extent you agree the measures by the Sinhala Government increase the feeling of alienation among the Sri Lankan Tamils? (1)

(iii) Is it justified that the denial of more autonomy for provinces led to the dissatisfaction among the Sri Lankan Tamils ? (2)

35. Read the source given below and answer the questions that follow. (4)

Mahatma Gandhi now felt the need to launch a more broad-based movement in India. But he was certain that no such movement could be organised without bringing the Hindus and Muslims closer together. One way of doing this, he felt, was to take up the Khilafat issue.

The First World War had ended with the defeat of Ottoman Turkey. And there were rumours that a harsh peace treaty was going to be imposed on the Ottoman emperor – the spiritual head of the Islamic world (the Khalifa). To defend the Khalifa's temporal powers, a Khilafat Committee was formed in Bombay in March 1919. A young generation of Muslim leaders like the brothers Muhammad Ali and Shaukat Ali, began discussing with Mahatma Gandhi about the possibility of a united mass action on the issue. Gandhiji saw this as an opportunity to bring Muslims under the umbrella of a unified national movement. At the Calcutta session of the Congress in September 1920, he convinced other leaders of the need to start a non-cooperation movement in support of Khilafat as well as for swaraj.

(i) Why did Mahatma Gandhi choose non-cooperation as a method struggle against British rule? (1)

(ii) Many within the Congress were concerned about the proposal of the Non-Cooperation Movement? Why? (1)

(iii) **How did people participate in the Non-Cooperation Movement in cities?** **(2)**

36. Read the source given below and answer the questions that follow. **(4)**

The chemical industry in India is fast growing and diversifying. It comprises both large and small scale manufacturing units. Rapid growth has been recorded in both inorganic and organic sectors. Inorganic chemicals include sulphuric acid (used to manufacture fertilisers, synthetic fibres, plastics, adhesives, paints, dyes stuffs), nitric acid, alkalies, soda ash (used to make glasses, soaps and detergents, papers) and caustic soda. These industries are widely spread over the country.

(i) **For what purpose, organic chemicals are used?**

(ii) **Why chemical industry is known as its own largest consumer?** **(2)**

(iii) **Explain any three characteristics of the Chemical Industry of India.** **(2)**

Section-F (2 + 3 = 5)

(Map Based Questions)

37. (a) Identify the following on the given map of India. **(2)**

(i) The location of Indian National Congress Session of 1927.

(ii) The place where the Civil Disobedience Movement started.

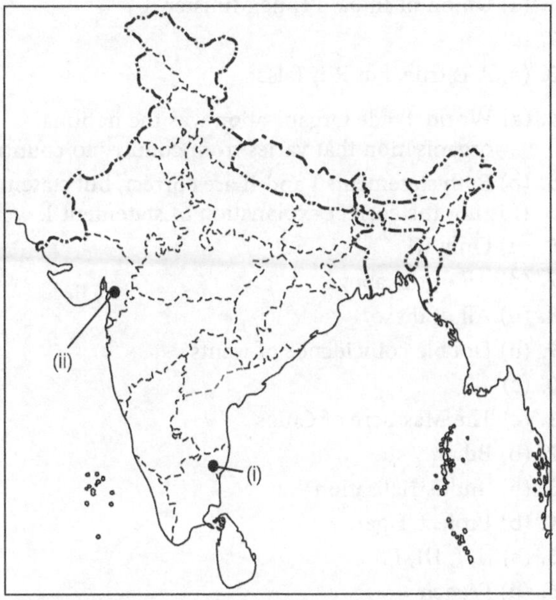

(b) On the same political map of India, locate and label any three of the following. **(3)**

(i) Vijayanagar iron and steel plant

(ii) Kandla port

(iii) Tungabhadra dam

(iv) Singrauli thermal power plant

Answers

1. (a) Union of India–Prime Minister
2. (c)
3. (c) A is true, but R is false
4. (a) World Trade Organisation was the national organisation that varies from country to country.
5. (b) Both statements I and II are correct, but statement II is not the correct explanation of statement I.
6. (d) Only III
7. (d) All of the above
8. (d) All of these
9. (b) Double coincidence of wants
10. (c)
11. (c) The Massacre of Chios
12. (b) Bihar
13. (b) Industrialisation
14. (b) Project Tiger
15. (a) II, I, III, IV
16. (b) French
17. (d) Solar energy adoption in rural areas can reduce reliance on traditional biomass fuels and contribute to environmental conservation.
18. (b) III, I, IV, II
19. (c) Sinhali and Tamil
20. (b) Belgium has borders with France, the Netherlands, Germany and Luxembourg.
21. John's father will tell John that during the French revolution, cartoons and caricatures highlighted the sufferings of ordinary people, peasants and workers. It also highlighted that nobility enjoyed life and oppressed people.
22. The two features of arid soil are
    - The colour of the arid soil ranges from red to brown.
    - Arid soils are generally sandy in texture and saline in nature.

Or The use of land is determined both by physical factors such as topography, climate, soil types as well as human factors such as population density, technological capability and culture and traditions, etc.

23. In recent times, technology in the areas of telecommunication, computers, internet has become important. Telecommunication facilities like telegraph, telephone, mobile, fax, etc., help to communicate in remote areas also.
24. In democratic countries, economic inequalities exist as, a small number of ultra-rich enjoy a highly disproportionate share of wealth and incomes. Not only that, their share in the total income of the country has been increasing. Those at the bottom of the society suffer.
25. "Like Germany, Italy too had a long history of political fragmentation." This can be justified in the following ways
    - Italians were scattered over several dynastic states as well as the multi-national Habsburg empire.
    - It was divided into seven states, of which only one, Sardinia-Piedmont, was ruled by an Italian Princely House.
    - The North of Italy was under Austrian Habsburgs, the Centre was ruled by the Pope and the Southern regions were under the domination of the Bourbon kings of Spain.
    - Even the Italian language had not one specific common form, it had many regional and local variations.
26. The obstacle which restricts certain borrowers to get a loan from the banks is collateral. Having a collateral is a necessity to get a loan from banks. A collateral is an asset that the borrower owns and pledges as a guarantee to the lender until the loan is repaid. A number of borrowers have no collateral to pledge against loans, especially small farmers requiring crop loans.

    Repayment of such a loan is crucially dependent on the income from selling the crop. As there is a risk involved (in case the crop yield is inadequate for any reason), banks are not willing to lend to such borrowers who cannot pledge collateral, which can be sold to recover the loan amount in case of default in paying the loan amount.
27. Rohan's father described that, besides the caste, there are other factors which do matter in electoral politics.

    These are
    - The voters have strong attachment to political parties which is often stronger than their attachment to their caste or community.
    - People within the same community have different interests depending on their economic status. Rich and poor, men and women from the same caste often vote very differently.
    - People's own assessment of the performance of the government vis-a-vis the performance of the candidate for the development of his own constituency are often decisive factors in elections.

28. Sustainable development means that development should take place without damaging the environment. The development in the present should not compromise with the needs of the future generations.

Sustainable development can be achieved by :

- Scientific and proper use of resources.
- Finding out ways to stop environmental pollution.
- Developing renewable sources of energy such as water, wind and solar energy.

Or Water scarcity may be an outcome of large and growing population in India.

It can be analysed through the following points

(i) Post-independent India witnessed intensive industrialisation and urbanisation. This situation increased water demand.

(ii) The growing demand of water by the growing population leads the over-exploitation of water resources for various purposes. For example, for drinking, domestic uses, agriculture, electricity generation and so on.

(iii) Increasing urban centres with large and dense populations and urban lifestyles have not only added to water and energy requirements but have further aggravated the problem of water scarcity.

29. The public sector contributes to the economic development of a nation by

- **Improving Infrastructure** Economic development depends upon the creation of basic infrastructure such as power, transportation, communication, irrigation, education, etc. As only public sector enterprises can arrange the large investment necessary for such infrastructure, they contribute greatly to economic development.
- **Job opportunities** A large number of job and business opportunities are created by the public sector.
- **Reduction in Regional Disparities** The government sets up industries in underdeveloped regions to reduce and overcome regional disparities in development.

30. It is true, that almost every person has different developmental goals besides income. Income is the first priority of people but besides this, there are other important developmental goals. This can be understood through the following points

- For rich farmer, development means higher support price for crops, cheap labour and subsidised inputs.
- For landless rural labourers, development means more days of work, schools for their children and no social discrimination.
- For urban youth, development means opportunity for higher education, availability of an office job and own house.
- For urban girl from rich family, development means freedom to choose her profession or being able to pursue her higher studies abroad.
- For adivasis, development means no social discrimination, year round employment, school education for children and PDS (Public Distribution System) shop in their village.

Or Two groups may have different notions of development. For example, the construction of a dam near a tribal area has different notions for industrialists and tribal people. For tribal people, the construction of the dam will mean loss of access to forest produce, displacement from their own land, and threat to their way of living. People who will live in areas near the constructed dam will always live in fear that they will be submerged.

For industrialists, the dam will mean various opportunities. They can establish factories near the dam. Their factories can use the water supplied by the dam. Urban people will also benefit from a dam if it is used in generating electricity. So, they will not oppose the construction of the dam.

31. Culture played an important role in creating the idea of the nation and poetry, stories and music helped express and shape nationalist feelings. This statement can be substantiated on the basis of following points

- Romanticism, a cultural movement sought to develop a particular form of nationalist sentiment. Romantic artists and poets generally criticised the glorification of reason and science and focused instead on emotions, intuition and mystical feelings. Their effort was to create a sense of a shared collective heritage, a common cultural past, as the basis of a nation.
- Other Romantics such as the German philosopher Johann Gottfried Herder claimed that true German culture was to be discovered among the common people. It was through folk songs, folk poetry and folk dances that the true spirit of the nation (volksgeist) was popularised.
- The emphasis on vernacular language and the collection of local folklore helped to recover an ancient national spirit. It also helped carry the modern nationalist message to large audiences who were mostly illiterate. Language too played an important role in developing nationalist sentiments. People in Poland used Polish language as a weapon of national resistance against Russia.

Or The most serious source of nationalist tension in Europe after 1871 was the area called the Balkans. The Balkans was a region of geographical and ethnic variations. It comprised modern Romania, Balgaria, Albania, Greece, Macedonia, Croatia, Boasnia-Herzegovina, Slovenia, Serbia and Montenegro. The inhabitants of this region were broadly known as the Slavs. The large part of the Balkans was under the control of the Ottoman Empire.

The spread of the ideas of romantic nationalism in the Balkans together with the disintegration of the Ottoman Empire made this region very explosive. One by one, its European subject nationalities broke away from Ottoman's control and declared independence. The Balkan peoples based their claims for independence and used history to prove that they had once been independent. The Balkan states were fiercely jealous of each other and each hoped to gain more territory at the expense of the others. Each power - Russia, Germany, England, AustroHungry-was keen on countering the hold of other powers over the Balkans. This led to a series of wars in the region and finally the First World War.

32. Teacher explained to him that globalisation is the process of rapid integration or interconnection between countries.

The advantages of globalisation are as follows

(i) Globalisation has resulted in greater competition among producers–both local and foreign.

(ii) This has improved the quality of the product and lowered the prices.

(iii) A wide variety of goods is available in the market for consumers.

The disadvantages of globalisation are as follows

(i) For a large number of small producers, globalisation has posed major problems.

(ii) These producers were not able to face the competition from large foreign producers and hence, several such production units had to shut down, rendering workers jobless.

(iii) Workers in MNCs are employed on temporary basis and laid off without any compensation during the slack period.

Or The factors which have enabled globalisation in India are

- Improvements in technology and technical innovations have made globalisation possible. For example, in transportation technology, containers are now used for the transportation of goods. This has led to huge reduction in cost. Air transport has speed up the transportation of goods.
- Improvements in telecommunication facilities around the world and internet enables us to send instant electronic mail and talk across the world at negligible costs. It is an important factor of globalisation.
- The Government of India has removed barriers or restrictions to trade which were set earlier. This step has enabled goods and services to be exported and imported easily.
- Multinationals have been allowed to set-up factories and offices in India. Due to this, there is greater integration of production and markets across countries.
- Joint ventures of MNCs also have resulted in globalisation.

33. Demands of Sri Lankan Tamils The three demands of Sri Lankan Tamils were as follows

(i) They wanted recognition of Tamil as an official language.

(ii) They wanted regional autonomy for their region.

(iii) They wanted equality of opportunity in securing education and jobs.

Struggle for Demands The demands of the Sri Lankan Tamils for more autonomy to provinces populated by the Tamils were repeatedly rejected. By the 1980s, several political organisations were formed demanding an independent Tamil Eelam (state) in Northern and Eastern parts of Sri Lanka.

Sri Lankan Tamils launched their own political party LTTE (Liberation Tigers of Tamil Eelam). The conflict between the Sri Lankan Tamils and the Sinhala government turned into a Civil War.

As a result, thousands of people of both Sinhala and Tamil communities were killed and this caused a terrible setback to the social, cultural and economic life of the country.

Or A homogeneous society is a society that has similar kinds of people, especially where there are no significant ethnic differences. In this society, people share the same type of cultural values, language, ethnicity and religious system. Germany and Sweden were once highly homogeneous, but are now undergoing rapid change with influx of people from other parts of the world.

The main features of homogeneous society are as follows

- A homogeneous society has similar kinds of people.
- It has the same religious beliefs.

- The people in a homogeneous society speak the same language.
- It shares the same cultural aspects and traditions of society.
- In a homogeneous society, there is a strong sense of nationalism.

34. (i) The Sinhala government took various majoritarian measures to establish Sinhala supremacy. These measures were declaring Sinhala as the official language, promoting Buddhism as state religion, and following preferential policies towards Sinhala applicants for university positions and government jobs.

(ii) All the government measures to establish Sinhala supremacy gradually increased the feeling of alienation among the Sri Lankan Tamils. They started to believe that the Buddhist Sinhala leaders were not sensitive to their language and culture. Not only this, the Constitution and government policies denied their social and political rights.

(iii) One of the demands of Sri Lankan Tamil was regional autonomy for provinces where their population is more. But their demand was denied repeatedly by the government. This really annoyed the Sri Lankan Tamils and they formed different political organisation. So their dissatisfaction is justified.

35. (i) Mahatma Gandhi believed that the British rule was established and had survived in India due to the cooperation of Indians. If Indians refuse to cooperate, the British rule in India would collapse within a year. So he chose non-cooperation as a method to struggle against British rule.

(ii) Many within the Congress were concerned about the proposal of Non-Cooperation Movement due to following reasons

- They were reluctant to boycott the council elections scheduled for November 1920.
- They feared that the movement might lead to popular violence.

(iii) People participated in the Non-Cooperation Movement in cities by the following ways

- Thousands of students left government-controlled schools and colleges, headmasters and teachers resigned, and lawyers gave up their legal practices.
- Foreign goods were boycotted, liquor shops picketed, and foreign cloth burnt in huge bonfires.
- Merchants and traders refused to trade in foreign goods or finance foreign trade in many places.

36. (i) Organic chemicals include petrochemicals, which are used for manufacturing of synthetic fibers, synthetic rubbers, plastics, dye-stuffs, drugs and pharmaceuticals.

(ii) Chemical industries are known as its own largest consumers as basic chemicals undergo processing to further produce other chemicals that are used for industrial application, agriculture or directly for consumer markets.

(iii) The characteristics of chemical industries of India are

- Chemical industries in India are fast growing and diversifying.
- It contains both large scale and small scale manufacturing units.
- Inorganic chemical industry is more widespread while organic chemical industry is located near oil refineries or petro-chemical plants.

37.

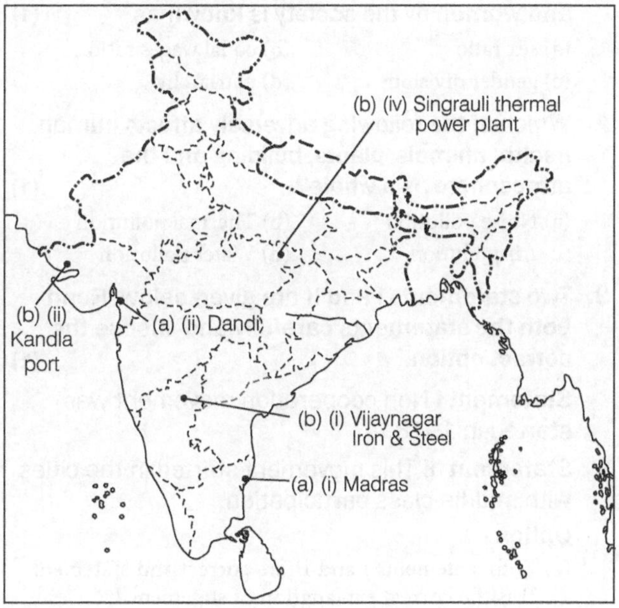

Sample Question Paper 2 (Solved)
Social Science

Time : 3 hrs	M.M. : 80

General Instructions

1 Question paper comprises Six Sections – A, B, C, D, E and F. There are 37 questions in the question paper. All questions are compulsory.
2 Section A – From questions 1 to 20 are MCQs of 1 mark each.
3 Section B – Question no. 21 to 24 are Very Short Answer Type Questions, carrying 2 marks each. Answer to each question should not exceed 40 words.
4 Section C – Question no. 25 to 29 are Short Answer Type Questions, carrying 3 marks each. Answer to each question should not exceed 60 words
5 Section D – Question no. 30 to 33 are long answer type questions, carrying 5 marks each. Answer to each question should not exceed 120 words.
6 Section E – Questions no. from 34 to 36 are case based questions with three sub-questions and are of 4 marks each.
7 Section F – Question no. 37 is map based, carrying 5 marks with two parts, 37a from History (2 marks) and 37b from Geography (3 marks).

Section-A $(1 \times 20 = 20)$

(Multiple Choice Questions)

1. The hierarchical unequal roles assigned to men and women by the society is known as (1)

(a) sex ratio (b) equal wages ratio
(c) gender division (d) patriarchy

2. Which of the following adversely affects human health, animals, plants, building and the atmosphere as a whole? (1)

(a) Noise pollution (b) Thermal pollution
(c) Air pollution (d) Water pollution

3. Two statements I and II are given below. Read both the statements carefully and choose the correct option. (1)

Statement I Non-cooperation movement was started in 1918.

Statement II This movement started in the cities with middle-class participation.

Options

(a) Both statements I and II are correct and statement II is the correct explanation of statement I.
(b) Both statements I and II are correct, but statement II is not the correct explanation of statement I.
(c) Statement I is correct, but statement II is incorrect.
(d) Statement I is incorrect, but statement II is correct.

4. Communal politics is based on the idea of (1)

(a) caste is the basis of social community.
(b) religion and caste are the basis of social community.
(c) religion is the basis of social community.
(d) None of the above

5. Read the following data and select the appropriate option from the following. (1)

Growth Rate of GDP and major sectors (in%) in India

Sector	2013-14	2014-15
Agriculture	4.2	-0.2
Industry	5.0	7.0
Services	7.8	9.8

From the above information, how much increase in the growth rate of GDP under the services sector between 2013-2015?

(a) 4% (b) 2.25%
(c) 2% (d) 1.8%

6. Sarah, an environmental researcher from a coastal region, has been studying the impact of urbanisation on the local ecosystem. She noticed a significant rise in construction activities along the coastline, leading to the destruction of mangrove forests and the natural habitat of several species of fish and birds.
Which of the following consequences is most likely to occur as a result of the described development in the coastal region? **(1)**

(a) Decline in marine biodiversity and disruption of the local ecosystem.
(b) Increased employment opportunities for the local community.
(c) Enhanced recreational activities and tourism influx in the area.
(d) Improved infrastructure leading to better living conditions for residents.

7. Consider the following statements about Mahatma Gandhi. **(1)**

I. Mahatma Gandhi returned to India in January 1915.
II. In 1917, he travelled to Champaran in Bihar to inspire the peasants to struggle against the oppressive plantation system.
III. In 1918, he organised a cotton mill strike in Kheda.

Which of the following statements is/are true?

(a) Only I
(b) I and II
(c) II and III
(d) I and III

8. Identify the correct statements about the theory of Federalism in the Indian Constitution. **(1)**

I. The Constitution declared India as a Union of States.
II. Sharing of power between the Union Government and the State Governments is basic to the structure of the Constitution.
III. It is easy to make changes to this power sharing arrangement.
IV. The Parliament can make changes in this arrangement on its own.

Codes

(a) I and II (b) II and III
(c) I and III (d) II and IV

9. Look at the picture given below and select the correct option which describes it properly. **(1)**

(a) Banks pay an amount as interest on the deposits.
(b) Banks are useful in keeping surplus cash.
(c) Banks mediate between depositors and borrowers.
(d) Banks are very important for the economy.

10. There are two statements marked as Assertion (A) and Reason (R). Mark your answer as per the codes given below. **(1)**

Assertion (A) Borrowers when borrow from informal sources, then they fall into debt traps.

Reason (R) Formal sector institution need to lend more to the borrowers in order to prevent them from falling into debt traps.

Codes

(a) Both A and R are true and R is the correct explanation of A
(b) Both A and R are true, but R is not the correct explanation of A
(c) A is true, but R is false
(d) A is false, but R is true

11. MatchList I and II and select the correct answer using the codes below in the list. **(1)**

	List I		List II
A.	Ferrous minerals	1.	Potash
B.	Non-ferrous minerals	2.	Uranium
C.	Non-metallic minerals	3.	Nickel
D.	Energy minerals	4.	Bauxite

Codes

	A	B	C	D		A	B	C	D
(a)	3	4	1	2	(b)	1	2	3	4
(c)	1	3	2	4	(d)	2	1	4	3

12. Choose the correctly matched pair. **(1)**

(a) Coal mines and railways – Community owned resources
(b) Humans and coal – Biotic resources
(c) Parks and burial grounds – National resources
(d) Water – Renewable resources

13. In the class, how do we compare different students. As they differ in height, health, talents and interests. The healthiest may not be the strongest. (1)

What is the criterion on which comparison depends?

(a) Criterion depends upon the purpose of segregation.
(b) Criterion depends upon the purpose of similarity.
(c) Criterion depends upon the purpose of comparison.
(d) None of the above

14. Arrange the following in the correct sequence. (1)

I. Treaty of Vienna
II. Napoleonic wars began
III. Unification of Italy
IV. French Revolution

Codes

(a) IV, II, I, III (b) III, I, IV, II
(c) I, II, III, IV (d) II, IV, I, III

15. Find the incorrect option. (1)

(a) Democracy promotes equality among citizens.
(b) Democracy enhances the dignity of the individual.
(c) Democracy does not have room to correct mistakes.
(d) Democracy provides a method to resolve conflict.

16. Who among the following gets more number of choices due to foreign trade? (1)

(a) Buyers (b) Sellers
(c) Government (d) Producers

17. MatchList I and II and select the correct answer using the codes below in the list.

	List I (Rainwater Harvesting System)		**List II** (Location)
A.	Kuls	1.	Meghalaya
B.	Johads	2.	Barmer
C.	Tankas	3.	Kaza Village
D.	Bamboo drip	4.	Jaisalmer

Codes (1)

	A	B	C	D		A	B	C	D
(a)	3	4	2	1	(b)	1	4	3	2
(c)	2	3	1	4	(d)	4	2	3	1

18. Which of the following is a foundational challenge to federalism? (1)

(a) Extension of federal principle to all the units of federation.
(b) Greater power to local governments.
(c) Bringing down the existing non-democratic regime.
(d) To increase people's participation.

19. Which of the following statements about Mahatma Gandhi's nationwide satyagraha against the Rowlatt Act is/are correct?

I. The Rowlatt Act allowed the government to detain political prisoners without trial for two years.
II. Mahatma Gandhi called for a nationwide hartal on 6th April, 1919 to protest against the Act.
III. The British administration permitted Mahatma Gandhi to enter Delhi to lead the protests peacefully.
IV. Martial law was imposed in Amritsar after police firing on a peaceful procession.

Codes

(a) Statements I and IV only
(b) Statements I, II, and IV only
(c) Statements II and III only
(d) All statements are correct

20. In which of the following states is Kalpakkam Nuclear Power Plant located? (1)

(a) Gujarat (b) Odisha
(c) Kerala (d) Tamil Nadu

Section-B (2 × 4 = 8)

(Very Short Answer Type Questions)

21. The legacy of the French Revolution is not found in physical monuments, but in the ideals of liberty, equality and justice that still inspire modern democracies. More ambitious than the American revolutionaries of 1776, the French in 1789 were not just fighting for their own national independence: they wanted to establish principles that would lay the basis for freedom for human beings everywhere.

Source (edited): aeon

What happened in the first upheaval of France in July 1830? (2)

Or What were the ideas of romantic artists and poets on nationalism?

22. What do you know about iron-ore deposits of the Maharashtra-Goa belt? (2)

23. What measures were adopted by the Sri Lankan government to establish Sinhala supremacy, and how did they affect the Tamil community? (2)

24. What is the importance of Judiciary in a federal government? (2)

Section–C (3 × 5 = 15)

(Short Answer Type Questions)

25. In Panchayati Raj system, 1/3rd of the seats have been reserved for women. Do you feel that the same should be done for State Legislature and Parliament? Support your answer with arguments. **(3)**

26. How the Salt March was an effective symbol of resistance against colonialism? Discuss **(3)**

Or Why did political leaders differ sharply over the question of separate electorates?

27. Which sector usually provides maximum number of employment opportunities in urban centres? Why is it so? **(3)**

28. Radha wants to open a tea stall near the village bus stand for which she needs ₹ 15000. Briefly explain which is the best credit source for her and why? **(3)**

29. "Forest and wildlife are vital to the quality of life and environment." Justify this statement by giving three reasons. **(3)**

Section–D (5×4=20)

(Long Answer Type Questions)

30. Explain the term 'Conservatism' with special reference to Europe. **(5)**

Or Analyse the measures and practices introduced by the French revolutionaries to create a sense of collective identity amongst the French people.

31. "A group of friends were discussing about 'Railways' and one of them said railways are the lifelines of the country and other agreed with him."

Give your comments about how 'railways are the lifelines of the country'. **(5)**

Or In India, roads are classified in different classes according to their capacity. State different types of roads in brief.

32. Give examples to prove that there are other important developmental goals than income. **(5)**

Or With the help of an example, show how two groups may have different notions of development.

33. What is communal politics? Explain the idea behind the communal politics. **(5)**

Or

Explain the role of caste in Indian politics.

Section–E (4 × 3 = 12)

(Case Based Questions)

34. Read the source given below and answer the questions that follow. (4)

Large MNCs in developed countries place orders for production with small producers. Garments, footwear, sports items are examples of industries where production is carried out by a large number of small producers around the world.

The products are supplied to the MNCs, which then sell these under their own brand names to the customers. These large MNCs have tremendous power to determine price, quality, delivery and labour conditions for these distant producers. Thus, we see that there are a variety of ways in which the MNCs are spreading their production and interacting with local producers in various countries across the globe.

By setting up partnerships with local companies, by using the local companies for supplies, by closely competing with the local companies or buying them up, MNCs are exerting a strong influence on production at these distant locations. As a result, production in these widely dispersed locations is getting interlinked.

(i) What do you understand by small producers? (1)

(ii) Why do large MNCs are invited by the government into a country? (1)

(iii) List two ways in which MNCs interlink production. (2)

35. Read the source given below and answer the questions that follow. (4)

The recent efforts and suggestions in our country to reform political parties and its leaders.

The Constitution was amended to prevent elected MLAs and MPs from changing parties. This was done because many elected representatives were indulging in defection in order to become ministers or for cash rewards. Now the law says that if any MLA or MP changes parties, he or she will lose the seat in the Legislature.

This new law has helped bring defection down. At the same time this has made any dissent even more difficult. MPs and MLAs have to accept whatever the party leaders decide. The Supreme Court passed an order to reduce the influence of money and criminals. Now, it is mandatory for every candidate who contests elections to file an

Affidavit giving details of his property and criminal cases pending against him.

(i) What is defection? (1)

(ii) Infer the importance of an Affidavit given by the candidate during contesting election. (1)

(iii) Suggest any two ways to reform political parties. (2)

36. Read the source given below and answer the following questions.

New forms of popular literature appeared in print, targeting new audiences. Booksellers employed pedlars who roamed around villages, carrying little books for sale. There were almanacs or ritual calendars, along with ballads and folktales. But, other forms of reading matters, largely for entertainment, began to reach ordinary readers as well. In England, penny chapbooks were carried by petty pedlars known as chapmen, and sold for a penny, so that even the poor could buy them.

(i) What were chapbooks? (1)

(ii) How 'Biliotheque Bleue' was different from chapbooks? (1)

(iii) What were the new forms of literature introduced in Europe to attract the new readers? (2)

Section-F (2 + 3 = 5)

(Map Based Questions)

37. (a) On the political map of India, locate the following. (2)

(i) The place associated with the Jallianwala Bagh incident.

(ii) The place where the December 1920 session of the Indian National Congress took place.

(b) On the given political outline map of India, identify and label any three of the following.

(i) The largest tea producing state (3)

(ii) A type of soil

(iii) A dam

(iv) An iron ore mine

Answers

1. (c) gender division
2. (c) Air pollution
3. (d) Statement I is incorrect, but statement II is correct.
4. (c) religion is the basis of social community.
5. (c) 2%
6. (a) I and II
7. (b) I and II
8. (a) Decline in marine biodiversity and disruption of the local ecosystem.
9. (c) Banks mediate between depositors and borrowers.
10. (b) Both A and R are true, but R is not the correct explanation of A
11. (a)
12. (d) Water-Renewable resources.
13. (c) Criterion depends upon the purpose of comparison.
14. (a) IV, II, I, III
15. (c) Democracy does not have room to correct mistakes.
16. (a) Buyers
17. (a)
18. (c) Bringing down the existing non-democratic regime.

19. (b) Statement 1, 2 and 4.

20. (d) Tamil Nadu

21. The first upheaval took place in July 1830. The Bourbon kings, who had been restored to power during the conservative reaction after 1815, were now overthrown by liberal revolutionaries, who installed a constitutional monarchy with Louis Philippe at its head.

Or Romantic artists and poets generally criticised the glorification of reason and science. Instead it focused on emotions, intuition and mystical feelings. Their effort was to create a sense of a shared collective heritage, a common cultural past as the basis of a nation.

22. The iron-ore deposits belt includes the state of Goa and Ratnagiri District of Maharashtra. Though the iron-ores are not of a very high quality, yet they are efficiently exploited and exported through Marmagao port.

23. The Sri Lankan government passed the 1956 Sinhala-only Act, favored Sinhala applicants for jobs and education, and prioritised Buddhism. These measures alienated Tamils, denying them equal rights and opportunities, leading to discrimination and resentment.

24. The importance of judiciary in a federal government is to apply the laws to specific cases and settle disputes. The judiciary has the power to interpret the constitution regarding the division of power. The Supreme Court and High Courts have the power to solve the disputes between the Central and State Government.

25. Yes, 1/3rd seats should be reserved for women in the State Legislature and Parliament like the Panchayati Raj System. The reservation of seats for women can be supported on the basis of following arguments
   - It will increase the representation of women in the state legislature and Parliament.
   - It will lead to better decisions on issues especially related to women.

26. Salt March was an effective symbol or tool of resistance against colonialism because
   (i) All classes could identify with salt as it was an essential food item.
   (ii) Tax on salt and the monopoly over its manufacturing was a sign of the oppression of British rule.

   Gandhiji reached Dandi on 6th April, 1930 and violated Salt law by manufacturing salt from sea water. Breaking the Salt law was an apparent refusal of British authority and was a direct challenge to British rule in India.

   People were not only asked to refuse cooperation with the British, but to break the unjustified colonial laws. Thousands of people from different parts of the country broke the Salt law, manufactured it and demonstrated in front of government salt factories.

Or Political leaders differed sharply over the question of separate electorates because
   (i) The Muslim leaders thought that their interest could only be protected in a Muslim state, and in a Hindu majority state they would be at the mercy of the Hindus. They wanted reserved seats in the Central Assembly and representation in proportion to population in the Muslim- dominated provinces, viz, Bengal and Punjab.
   (ii) Dr BR Ambedkar, the leader of the depressed classes, was in favour of separate electorates for his community but, Gandhiji believed that separate electorate for Dalits would slow down the process of their integration into society. Later, Ambedkar accepted Gandhiji's position and signed 'Poona Pact'.

27. Tertiary sector provides usually maximum number of employment opportunities in urban centres. Reasons for providing such a huge number of employment in this sector are given below
   - The tertiary sector provides essential services like banking, healthcare and education.
   - Developments in agriculture and industry have led the requirement of services like transport, storage, trade, etc.
   - When income levels rise, people start demanding more services like shopping malls, tourism, professional training, etc. This increases the demand for such services, especially in urban centres.
   - Due to Westernisation, the needs of people keep changing from time to time, which increases demands of various goods and services. Thus, to meet these demands, the tertiary sector is continuously expanding its area by providing jobs to people.

28. The best credit source for Radha is to go to Self Help Groups (SHGs). The reasons are as follows
   - The Self Help Groups are organisations of the rural poor people specially for women. They provide small loans on reasonable rates.

- SHGs do not require collateral and documentation.
- SHGs also take up social issues related to women so if Radha becomes a member of SHGs then she will not only get financial assistance but also get support of other women members.
- SHGs make the loan process very easy for poor people.

Thus, we can say that SHGs can be stated as a plan by the people, of the people and for the people, reflecting the real people's participation in the process of development at micro-level.

29. Forest and wildlife are vital components of environment. These contribute a lot to the quality of life in the ecological system. The three reasons are

(i) Forests regulate the rainfall pattern on which agricultural practice depends. The depletion of forests brings natural hazards like flood, landslides, etc.

(ii) Depletion of forests and wildlife affects the food chain and food web. As a result, this depletion would collapse the eco-system in long-term.

(iii) Forests and wildlife are the part of our culture. So, their depletion not only affects the biological aspects, but also the cultural aspects. Women who collect forests products and tribals are affected the most.

30. Conservatism was a political philosophy that stressed the importance of tradition, established institutions and customs and preferred gradual development to quick change. After the defeat of Napoleon in 1815, European governments were driven by conservatism.

Conservatives were people who believed that established traditional institutions of state and society like the monarchy church, social hierarchies, property and the family should be preserved.

But after the rule of Napoleon, the basic ideas of conservatism were changed. Most conservatives did not want to return to the society of pre-revolutionary days. They realised that the changes initiated by Napoleon strengthened the traditional institutions like the monarchy in reality.

They understood that a modern army, an efficient bureaucracy, a dynamic economy, the abolition of feudalism and serfdom could strengthen the autocratic monarchies in Europe. Thus, the conservatives of that time accepted the changes which were in favour of their interests.

Or The measures and practices introduced by the French revolutionaries to create a sense of collective identify among the French people were as follows

- **Union of People** The idea of la patrie (the fatherland) and le citoyen (the citizen) emphasised the idea of united people enjoying equal rights under a Constitution.
- **New Flag** A new French flag, the tricolour, was chosen to replace the former royal standard.
- **National Assembly** The Estates General was elected by the active citizens and renamed as the National Assembly.
- **Patriots Honoured** New hymns were composed, oaths taken and martyrs commemorated in the name of the nation.
- **Centralised Administration** A centralised administrative system was put in place and it formulated uniform laws for all citizens within its territory.
- **Common Language** Regional dialects were discouraged and French, as it was spoken and written in Paris, became the common language of the nation.
- **Uniform Systems Adopted** Internal custom duties were abolished and a uniform system of weights and measures was adopted.

31. It is true that railways are the lifelines of the country. It can be understood through the following points

- **Employment** Railways create many opportunities of employment in India. Lakhs of skilled and unskilled people are employed in operating the railway functions.
- **Encouragement to Tourism** The connectivity of railways to various tourist spots gives encouragement to tourism industry. Thus, it boosts national economy.
- **Cover Long Distance** Railways can carry goods and passengers over very long distance. Thus, cover different parts of India.
- **Helpful during Calamities** During natural calamities railways help the stranded people to reach the relief centres. These are helpful during famines by carrying food grains from surplus to affected areas.
- **Strategic Importance** Railways are useful for internal security of the country and also carry the defence material to various regions during external threat.

Or In India, roads are classified in six classes according to their capacity as given below

(i) **Golden Quadrilateral Super Highways** This super highways links India's four largest metropolitan cities, i.e. Delhi-Kolkata-Chennai-Mumbai by six-lane Super Highways. North-South and East-West corridor are part of this. These highways reduce time and distance between mega cities.

(ii) **National Highways** These are primary road systems that link important parts of the country.

(iii) **State Highways** These roads link a state capital with its district headquarters. These are constructed by State Public Works Department.

(iv) **District Roads** These roads connect the district headquarters with other places of the district.

(v) **Rural Roads** These roads also known as other roads, link rural areas and villages with towns.

(vi) **Border Roads** These roads are constructed along the international border of India by Border Road Organisation. It has improved accessibility in areas of difficult terrain.

32. Besides income, the developmental goals of various categories of people are different from person to person. Some examples of developmental goals other than income are

(i) For rich farmer, development means higher support price for crops, cheap labour and subsidised inputs.

(ii) For landless rural labourer, development means more days of work, schools for their children and no social discrimination.

(iii) For adivasi, development means no social discrimination, year round employment, school education for children and PDS shop in his village.

(iv) For urban youth, development means opportunity for higher education, availability of an office job and own house.

(v) For urban girl from rich family, development means freedom to choose her profession or being able to pursue her higher studies abroad.

Or Two groups may have different notions of development. For example, the local community's notion of development on the case of construction of a dam, the areas in which they live will be submerged and their will be greater environmental degradation.

However, the government's notion of development in this case would be that by raising the height of the dam, they would be able to provide more water to the people of Saurashtra region of Gujarat, which always suffers from water scarcity. In addition, more electricity would be generated with this measure, which would benefit all the people living in that area.

33. The use of religion in politics, where one religion is shown as superior to other religions is called communal politics. Here, one religious group is against the other religious group and the demands of one religious group are against the demands of the other religious group.

The idea behind the communal politics are

(i) Communal politics is based on the idea that religion is the only basis of forming a community. It believes that followers of one religion belong to the same community. Their interests, ideas and opinions are the same.

(ii) Communal politics follows that people belonging to different religions can not be a part of the same community. Their ideas and demands are bound to be different.

(iii) In an extreme case of communalism, communal politics follows that people from different religions are not equal citizens and cannot live together within one nation, which leads to partition of that country.

(iv) Communal politics is a belief that a particular community has same voice is fundamentally wrong. People of one religion do not have the same interests and aspiration in every context. All voices inside a community have a right to be heard.

Or The role of caste in Indian politics is as follows

(i) Castes are ranked in hierarchical order, which determines the behaviour of one member of society over another.

(ii) Caste plays a very important role in election. Political parties select their candidates on the basis of caste composition in the constituency.

(iii) The voting in elections and mobilisation of political support from top to bottom moves on the basis of caste.

(iv) Caste is an important factor, for influencing the selection of candidates in elections, appointment of ministers, transfer and posting of public officials, etc.

(v) Caste functions as a pressure group in politics. Political bargaining is also done on caste lines.

34. (i) Small producers refer to those producers who are producing consumer goods of small value like footwear, garments, sports items, etc.

(ii) Government invites large MNCs for the following reasons
- The large MNCs invest in the country by opening factories, offices which provide employment to people.
- Large MNCs support local producers by giving them bulk orders.

(iii) MNCs interlink production by
- Buying the local companies completely.
- Setting up partnership with local companies.

35. (i) Defection is changing party allegiance (a person's continued support for a political party) from the party on which a person got elected to a legislative body to a different party.

(ii) Due to the Supreme's Court order, candidate has to give the details of his property and criminal case report through an Affidavit. It helps the public to decide the suitable candidate to elect.

(iii) The ways which can be used to reform political parties are as follow
(a) A law should be made to regulate the internal affairs of political parties.
(b) There should be state funding of elections. The government should give parties money to support their election expenses.

36. (i) Chapbooks were the pocket size books that were sold by travelling pedlars called chapmen.

(ii) 'Biliotheque Bleue' were low priced small books printed in France. There were printed on poor quality paper and bound in cheap blue covers.

On the other hand, chapbooks were pocket size book, published in England. These became popular from the time of the 16th century print revolution.

(iii) The new forms of literature introduced in Europe to attract the new readers were
- There were almanaces along with ballads and folktales.
- In England, chapbooks were carried by petty peddlers and sold for penny.
- Biliotheque Bleues were low priced books sold in France.
- There were romances printed for a to six pages and the more substantial 'histories' which were stories about the post.

37.

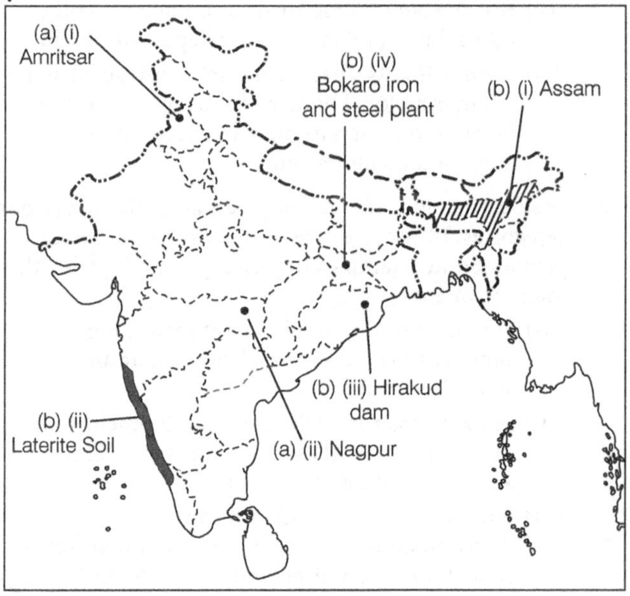

Sample Question Paper 3 (Unsolved)
Social Science

Time : 3 hrs	M.M. : 80

General Instructions

1 Question paper comprises Six Sections – A, B, C, D, E and F. There are 37 questions in the question paper. All questions are compulsory.
2 Section A – From questions 1 to 20 are MCQs of 1 mark each.
3 Section B – Question no. 21 to 24 are Very Short Answer Type Questions, carrying 2 marks each. Answer to each question should not exceed 40 words.
4 Section C – contains Q. 25 to Q. 29 are Short Answer Type Questions, carrying 3 marks each. Answer to each question should not exceed 60 words
5 Section D – Question no. 30 to 33 are long answer type questions, carrying 5 marks each. Answer to each question should not exceed 120 words.
6 Section E – Questions no. from 34 to 36 are case based questions with three sub-questions and are of 4 marks each.
7 Section F – Question no. 37 is map based, carrying 5 marks with two parts, 37a from History (2 marks) and 37b from Geography (3 marks).

Section–A (1 × 20 = 20)

(Multiple Choice Questions)

1. Identify the appropriate reason for the formation of the Swaraj Party from the options given below. (1)

(a) It wanted members of Congress to return to Council Politics.
(b) It wanted members of Congress to spread Non-Cooperation Movement in India.
(c) It wanted members of Congress to oppose Simon Commission.
(d) It wanted members of Congress to ask Dominion State for India.

2. The literacy rate is highest in Kerala while the Infant Mortality Rate is highest in Bihar. In relation to this information which statement is true? (1)

(a) Most of the people in Kerala and Bihar have good living conditions.
(b) Both Bihar and Kerala lack basic necessities of life.
(c) The standard of living in Kerala is better than Bihar.
(d) The standard of living in Bihar is better than Kerala.

3. India stands second as a world producer of sugar but occupies the first place in the production of gur and khandsari. The raw material used in this industry is bulky and in haulage its sucrose content reduces. The mills are located in Uttar Pradesh, Bihar, Maharashtra, Karnataka, Tamil Nadu, Andhra Pradesh, Gujarat, Punjab, Haryana, and Madhya Pradesh. Sixty per cent of the mills are in Uttar Pradesh and Bihar. This industry is seasonal in nature. (1)
Which of the following is a likely consequence of the seasonal nature of the sugar, gur and khandsari industry as described in the passage?

(a) Reduced efficiency in raw material transport during peak production periods.
(b) Decreased availability of sugarcane during off-seasons.
(c) Increased competition among states for sugarcane cultivation.
(d) Fluctuations in sugar prices based on seasonal demand.

4. Match List I and II and select the correct answer using the codes below in the lists. (1)

List I	List II
A. Availing details of ingredients in a product	1. Right to safety
B. AGMARK	2. Dealing with consumer cases
C. Accident due to faulty engine in a scooter	3. Certification of edible oil and coreds.
D. District consumer court	4. Global level institution of consumer welfare organisations

Codes

	A	B	C	D		A	B	C	D
(a)	2	3	1	4	(b)	4	3	1	2
(c)	4	1	2	3	(d)	2	4	3	1

5. The given picture depict which among the following events during British rule? (1)

(a) Boycott of Foreign Cloth
(b) The Dandi March
(c) Khilafat Movement
(d) Kisan Sabha

6. Which of the following pairs given below is incorrectly matched. (1)

(a) Expansion through MNCs – Tata, Ranbaxy
(b) Liberalisation – MNCs free to import
(c) 1991 Policy – Tightening of trade barriers
(d) Spreading out – Design in India, production in China

7. Collateral is an important part of lending operations of Banks and it is the part of terms of Credit because (1)

(a) it is used as a guarantee to a lender.
(b) it is the sale asset of government only.
(c) borrower has no control on collateral even after payment of full loan amount.
(d) no property can be used as a collateral in borrowing operations.

8. Which of the following is the correct reason for the formation of gullies in bad lands? (1)

(a) Formed when running water cuts through soils making deep channels.
(b) When water flows over large areas down a slope.
(c) When moving wind blows away loose soil of flat lands.
(d) Formed when ploughing is done in a wrong way.

9. On which of the following modern aspects did the new Germany place a strong emphasis? (1)

I. Currency
II. Banking
III. Legal system
IV. Demography

Codes

(a) Only I and II are correct
(b) Only II and III are correct
(c) Only III and IV are correct
(d) Only I, II and III are correct

10. Which of the following statements about Frederic Sorrieu's vision and artwork is/are correct? (1)

I. Frederic Sorrieu's series of prints envisioned a world made up of 'democratic and social republics.
II. The first print depicts people from Europe and America paying homage to the Statue of Liberty.
III. The black, red and gold flag carried by the German peoples symbolised their hope for unification under a democratic constitution.

Codes

(a) I and II are correct
(b) I is correct
(c) II is correct
(d) All statements are correct

11. When power is taken from the State governments and is given to Local government, it is called (1)

(a) Decentralisation
(b) Privatisation
(c) Panchayat Samiti
(d) Federalism

12. Which of the following is the essential element of a political party.

(a) Organisation
(b) National interest
(c) Fundamental principles
(d) All of these

13. The early phase of globalisation involved export of raw material from colonial countries such as India and import of finished products from industrially developed European countries and the USA. (1)

Analyse and select the option that leads to the change in the economy in 20th century.

(a) Human Development Index
(b) World Trade Organisation
(c) Multinational Corporation
(d) Information and Communication Technology

14. Arrange the following in the correct sequence. (1)

I. Identification and inventory of resources
II. Planning for resource development
III. Matching the resource

Codes

(a) I, III, II
(b) II, III, I
(c) I, II, III
(d) III, II, I

15. Two statements I and II are given below. Read both the statements carefully and choose the correct option. (1)

Statement I The French Revolution occurred in 1789.

Statement II Napoleonic code was introduced in 1804.

Options

(a) Both statements I and II are correct and statement II is the correct explanation of statement I.
(b) Both statements I and II are correct, but statement II is not the correct explanation of statement 1.
(c) Statement I is correct, but statement II is incorrect.
(d) Statement I is incorrect, but statement II is correct.

16. Which one of the following ethnic communities is in majority in Sri Lanka? **(1)**

(a) Sri Lankan Tamils (b) Indian Tamils
(c) Muslims (d) Sinhalese

17. Read the following data and select the appropriate option from the following. **(1)**

Year	General land use categories 1960-61	General land use categories 2014-2015
Area under non-agricultural uses	4.95%	8.7%
Culturable waste land	6.23%	4.0%
Area under pasture and grazing land	4.71%	3.3%

According to land use pattern in India, what are the changes in percentage of the culturable waste land between 1960 to 2015?

(a) Increased by 2% (b) Decreased by 2.23%
(c) Decreased by 5% (d) Increased by 1%

18. Consider the statements given below and choose the correct answer. **(1)**

Statement I Currency is considered to be important for a country.

Statement II Currency gives nation a purchasing power and facilitates trade.

(a) Statement I is correct and II is incorrect.
(b) Statement I is incorrect and II is correct.
(c) Both I and II are correct.
(d) Both I and II are incorrect.

19. According to the given data, what is the ratio between the Gross National Income per capita (2011 PPP $) of Sri Lanka and India? **(1)**

Some data regarding India and its neighbours for 2019.

Country	Gross National Income (GNI) per capita (2011 PPP $)	Life Expectancy at Birth	Mean Years of Schooling of People Aged 25+ yrs and above	HDI Rank in the World (2018)
Sri Lanka	12,707	77	10.6	73
India	6,681	69.7	6.5	130
Myanmar	4,961	67.1	5.0	148

Source : Human Development Report, 2020, United Nations Development Programme, New York.

(a) Approx 3 (b) Approx 2 (c) Approx 1 (d) Approx 4

20. Which of the following statements about Pradhan Mantri Krishi Sinchai Yojana are correct **(1)**

I. To enhance access to water in household.
II. To increase cultivable area under irrigation.
III. Use of efficient water usage techniques to conserve water.
IV. 'Har ghar ko pani' is the motto of the scheme.

(a) I and II (b) II and III
(c) III and IV (d) I and IV

Section–B **(2 × 4 = 8)**

(Very Short Answer Type Questions)

21. The era of coalition government at the centre has changed the meaning of federalism in India. Justify the statements with suitable examples. **(2)**

22. Analyse the role of 'Peasant leaders' in spreading of the Gandhian movements in India. **(2)**

Or What was Gutenberg's press to slow as compared to present press technology?

23. Traditional communities play a vital role in conserving forest and natural resources in India. Justify this statement with examples. **(2)**

24. Raju read in the newspaper, the rank of India is 132nd, among 191 countries in Human Development Index. Raju Google the topic and learned about it.

What is Human Development Index? **(2)**

Section–C **(3 × 5 = 15)**

(Short Answer Type Questions)

25. The presence of ferrous minerals in India significantly contributes to the development of metallurgical industries. Explain this statement with suitable examples. **(3)**

26. Federalism is a system of government in which the power is divided among sections. Is India a federal country? If yes, then how power is divided in the system of Indian government?

Or In 1947, the boundaries of several old states of India were changed in order to create new states. On which basis new boundaries were decided?

27. Why salt was chosen as a weapon by Gandhiji to fight against the Britishers? **(3)**

28. Shalini insists to her friend to carry jute bags for shopping. How will it help the jute industry and also improve the environment? **(3)**

29. What do you understand by the policy of accommodation? **(3)**

Section-D **(5 × 4 = 20)**

(Long Answer Type Questions)

30. "Advancement of international trade of a country is an index of its economic prosperity." Justify the statement with five arguments. **(5)**

Or Analyse the factor that contributed to the Balkans becoming a source of nationalist tension in Europer after 1871.

31. Sohan learns in the school that there are three sectors in the economy and they are interrelated on each other. He asked his mother - how they are interdependent on each other and explain with suitable examples. **(5)**

Or Explain the distinction among the primary sector and secondary sector in an economy. Highlight their unique characteristics within the aspect of economic development.

32. Liberalisation of economy with rapid technological upgradation has helped in the growth of Globalisation. Justify this statement with suitable examples. **(5)**

Or Globalisation and the pressure of competition have changed the lives of workers substantially. Justify the statement with suitable arguement.

33. The formation of linguistic states and language policy in India has strengthened the values of federalism in India. Justify the statement with suitable arguments. **(5)**

Or There are frequent delays in decision making in democratic states as compared to non-democratic states. Analyse the statement with suitable points.

Section-E **(4 × 3 = 12)**

(Case Based Questions)

34. Read the source given below and answer the questions that follow. (4)

Ever since humans appeared on the Earth, they have used different means of communication. But, the pace of change, has been rapid in modern times. Long distance communication is far easier without physical movement of the communicator or receiver. Personal communication and mass communication including television, radio, press, films, etc, are the major means of communication in the country. The Indian postal network is the largest in the world. It handles parcels as well as personal written communications. Cards and envelopes are considered first-class mail and are airlifted between stations covering both land and air. The second-class mail includes book packets, registered newspapers and periodicals. They are carried by surface mail, covering land and water transport. To facilitate quick delivery of mails in large towns and cities, six mail channels have been introduced recently. They are called Rajdhani Channel, Metro Channel, Green Channel, Business Channel, Bulk Mail Channel and Periodical Channel.

(i) **Examine the role of the Indian postal network. (1)**

(ii) **Differentiate between mass communication and personal communication. (1)**

(iii) **Analyse the significance of communication for a nation. (2)**

35. Read the source given below and answer the questions that follow. (4)

A second test for Indian federation is the language policy. Our Constitution did not give the status of national language to any one language.

Hindi was identified as the official language. But Hindi is the mother tongue of only about 40 per cent of Indians. Therefore, there were many safeguards to protect other languages. Besides Hindi, there are 21 other languages recognised as Scheduled Languages by the Constitution. A candidate in an examination conducted for the Central Government positions may opt to take the examination in any of these languages. States too have their own official languages. Much of the government work takes place in the official language of the concerned state.

Unlike Sri Lanka, the leaders of our country adopted a very cautious attitude in spreading the use of Hindi.

According to the Constitution, the use of English for official purposes was to stop in 1965. However, many non-Hindi speaking states demanded that the use of English continue. In Tamil Nadu, this movement took a violent form. The Central Government responded by agreeing to continue the use of English along with Hindi for official purposes. Many critics think that this solution favoured the

English speaking elite. Promotion of Hindi continues to be the official policy of the Government of India. Promotion does not mean that the Central Government can impose Hindi on states where people speak a different language. The flexibility shown by Indian political leaders helped our country avoid the kind of situation that Sri Lanka finds itself in.

(i) Why our Constitution did not give the status of national language to any one language? (1)

(ii) How our country differs from Sri Lanka in respect of language? (2)

(iii) Infer the importance of continuing English as the official language of India. (1)

36. Read the source given below and answer the questions that follow.

The pre-modern world shrank greatly in the 16th century after European sailors found a sea route to Asia and also successfully crossed the Western Ocean to America. For centuries before, the Indian Ocean had known a bustling trade, with goods, people, knowledge, customs, etc criss-crossing its waters. The Indian sub-continent was central to these flows and a crucial point in their networks. The entry of the Europeans helped expand or redirect some of these flows towards Europe.

Before its 'discovery', America had been cut off from regular contact with the rest of the world for millions of years. But, from the 16th century, its vast lands and abundant crops and minerals began to transform trade and lives everywhere.

(i) Why the pre-modern world shrank greatly in 16th century? (1)

(ii) Name the European countries, who conquest and colonialised the America. (1)

(iii) Why was America cut off regular contact with the rest of the world? (2)

Section–F (2 + 3 = 5)

(Map Based Questions)

37. (a) Mark and locate the following on the map of India. (2)

(i) A place associated with the cotton mill workers' satyagraha.

(ii) The place where an incident occurred due to which Mahatma Gandhi called off the Non-Cooperation Movement.

(b) On the same outline map of India, identify any three features with suitable symbols. (3)

(i) A dam in Rajasthan

(ii) A soil type

(iii) A software technology park

(iv) A sea port

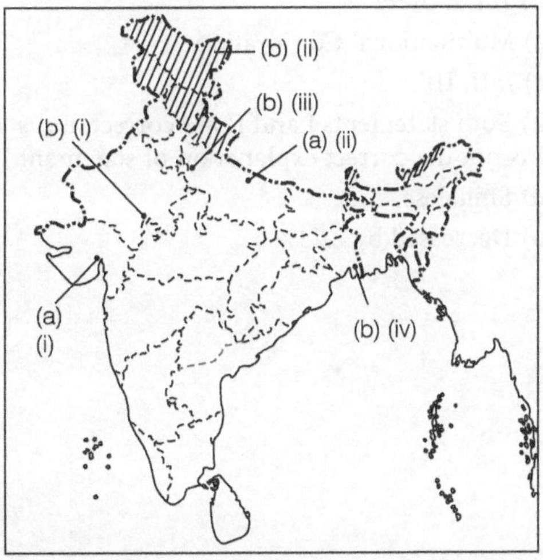

Answers

1. (a) It wanted members of Congress to return to Council Politics.
2. (c) The standard of living in Kerala is better than Bihar.
3. (b) Decreased availability of sugarcane during off-seasons.
4. (b)
5. (b) The Dandi March
6. (c)
7. (a) It is used as a guarantee to a lender.
8. (a) Formed when running water cuts through soils making deep channels.
9. (d) Only I, II and III are correct
10. (b) I is correct.
11. (a) Decentralisation
12. (d) All of these
13. (c) Multinational Corporation
14. (c) I, II, III
15. (b) Both statements I and II are correct, but statement II is not the correct explanation of statement I.
16. (d) Sinhalese
17. (b) Decreased by 2.23%
18. (c) Both I and II are correct.
19. (b) Approx 2
20. (b) II and III.

37.

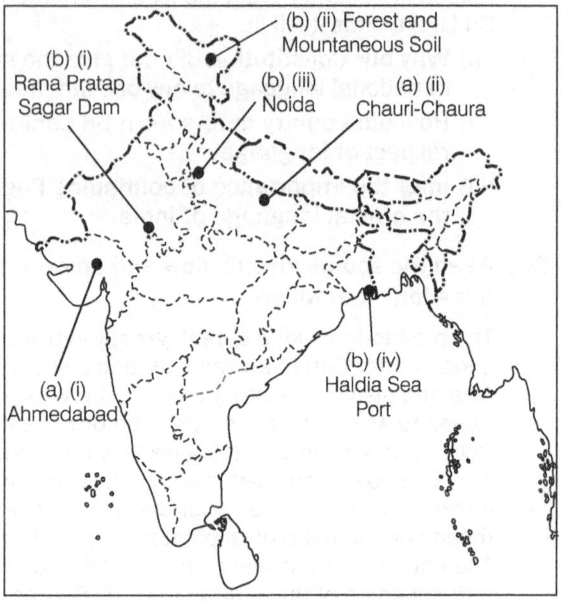

Sample Question Paper 4 (Unsolved)

Social Science

Time : 3 hrs M.M. : 80

General Instructions

1 Question paper comprises Six Sections – A, B, C, D, E and F. There are 37 questions in the question paper. All questions are compulsory.

2 Section A – From questions 1 to 20 are MCQs of 1 mark each.

3 Section B – Question no. 21 to 24 are Very Short Answer Type Questions, carrying 2 marks each. Answer to each question should not exceed 40 words.

4 Section C – Question no. 25 to 29 are Short Answer Type Questions, carrying 3 marks each. Answer to each question should not exceed 60 words

5 Section D – Question no. 30 to 33 are long answer type questions, carrying 5 marks each. Answer to each question should not exceed 120 words.

6 Section E – Questions no. from 34 to 36 are case based questions with three sub-questions and are of 4 marks each.

7 Section F – Question no. 37 is map based, carrying 5 marks with two parts, 37a from History (2 marks) and 37b from Geography (3 marks).

Section–A (1 × 20 = 20)

(Multiple Choice Questions)

1. The high interest rates charged by the money lender, exemplify the concept of ...., where the cost of borrowing is disproportionately high. (1)

(a) usury (b) inflation
(c) deflation (d) credit crunch

2. A situation in which all the countries reap equally the benefits of foreign trades equally is known as (1)

(a) Internationalisation
(b) Fair globalisation
(c) Liberalisation
(d) Equal globalisation

3. Least expectation from democracy is that (1)

(a) it cannot accommodate various social life.
(b) it should produce a harmonious social life.
(c) it develops procedure to conduct competition.
(d) it reduces the possibility of violent tensions.

4. Paper, pulp, chemical, textile and dyeing, petroleum refineries and tanneries are agents of causing which type of pollution? (1)

(a) Air pollution (b) Water pollution
(c) Noise pollution (d) None of these

5. Which of the following activity is part of the secondary sector? (1)

(a) Sugar from sugarcane
(b) Transportation by trucks
(c) Borrow money from bank
(d) Cultivation of cotton

6. Which one of the following is an incorrect match. (1)

(a) Sugarcane – Tropical as well as sub-tropical crop
(b) Cotton – In 2015, India was largest producer
(c) Pulses – India is the largest producer
(d) Maize – Both food and fodder crop

7. Select the option which is incorrect to say that Human Development Report depends upon the following criteria. (1)

(a) Living standard (b) Health status
(c) Religious background
(d) Educational level of the people

8. Match List I and II and select the correct answer using the codes below in the lists. (1)

	Political Party		Year of Formation
A.	Indian National Congress	1.	1925
B.	Communist Party of India	2.	1885
C.	Bharatiya Janata Party	3.	1984
D.	Bahujan Samaj Party	4.	1980

	A	B	C	D		A	B	C	D
(a)	1	2	3	4	(b)	2	1	4	3
(c)	4	2	1	3	(d)	4	3	2	1

9. In 1831, an armed rebellion against which country rule took place which was ultimately crushed? (1)

(a) Prussia (b) Russia
(b) Austria (d) Germany

10. Arrange the following in the correct sequence. (1)

I. Civil Code was introduced
II. Piedmont and France defeated Austria
III. Unification of Italy
IV. Unification of Germany

Codes

(a) I, II, III, IV (b) IV, III, II, I
(c) I, II, IV, III (d) II, IV, I, III

11. Which of the following statements are correct in context to rice production? (1)

I. India is the 2nd major producer in world.
II. It is a rabi crop, requires low temperature with less humidity.
III. It is grown with the help of tubewell in the areas of less rainfall.

Codes

(a) I and II only (b) II and III only
(c) I and III only (d) All of these

12. Identify the techniques of water conservation shown in the given picture. (1)

(a) Rainwater harvesting
(b) Hydraulic structures
(c) Plant vegetation
(d) None of these

13. Democracy attain people happiness by (1)

(a) government function to represent general view
(b) equal distribution of resources
(c) better governance
(d) All of the above

14. Consider the statements given below and choose the correct answer. (1)

Statement I Tax on import is an example of trade barrier.

Statement II Liberalisation leads to rise in foreign investment.

Options

(a) Statement I is correct and II is incorrect.
(b) Statement I is incorrect and II is correct.
(c) Both I and II are correct.
(d) Both I and II are incorrect.

15. Two statements are given below. They are Assertion (A) and Reason (R). Read both the statements carefully and choose the correct options. (1)

Assertion (A) Power sharing increases the chances of conflict and disrupts the social harmony.

Reason (R) In power sharing, power is shared among different organs of the government (*e.g.*, legislative, executive and judiciary).

Options

(a) Both A and R are true and R is the correct expanation of A
(b) Both A and R are true, but R is not the correct explanation of A
(c) A is true, but R is false
(d) A is false, but R is true

16. Read the following data and select the appropriate option from the following. (1)

Educational Achievement of Rural Population of Uttar Pradesh

Category	Male	Female
Literacy rate for rural population	76%	54%
Literacy rate for rural children in age group of 10-14 years	90%	87%
Percentage of rural children in age group of 10-14 years Attending school	85%	82%

How much percentage of female is illiterate in rural population?

(a) 36% (b) 46% (c) 56% (d) 52%

17. Emboldened with this success, Gandhiji in 1919 decided to launch a nationwide Satyagraha against the proposed Rowlatt Act (1919). This Act had been hurriedly passed through the Imperial Legislative Council despite the united opposition of the Indian members. It gave the government enormous powers to repress political

activities and allowed detention of political prisoners without trial for two years.

Which of the following is the primary reason behind Mahatma Gandhi's decision to launch a nationwide Satyagraha against the Rowlatt Act (1919)?

(a) The Act granted significant powers to repress political activities.

(b) The Act allowed detention of political prisoners without trial for two years.

(c) The Act was passed despite the opposition of Indian members.

(d) All of the above

18. Which of the following statements is correct definition of the word 'Plebscite'? (1)

(a) A direct vote of the government the will of people.

(b) A direct vote by which all the people of a country are asked to accept or reject the will.

(c) It is related to the 'Napolean code of 1804'.

(d) A condition when freedom of markets is established and state based restrictions are removed.

19. Match List I with II and select the correct answer using the codes given below in the list. (1)

List I (Years)	List II (Events)
A. 1448	1. Gutenberg invented the printing press
B. 1517	2. Martin Luther wrote 'Ninety Five Theses'
C. 1812	3. Fairy Tales printed by the Grimm Brothers
D. 1878	4. Vernacular Press Act Passed

Codes

	A	B	C	D		A	B	C	D
(a)	1	2	3	4	(b)	4	3	2	1
(c)	3	1	4	2	(d)	2	4	1	3

20. Read the data given in the table, find out the difference in the HDI Ranks of Pakistan and Bangladesh. (1)

Some data regarding India and its neighbours for 2019.

Country	Gross National Income (GNI) per capita (2011 PPP $)	Life Expectancy at Birth	Mean Years of Schooling of People Aged 25+ yrs and above	HDI Rank in the World (2018)
Pakistan	5,005	67.3	5.2	154
Nepal	3,457	70.8	5.0	143
Bangladesh	4,976	72.6	6.2	134

(a) 21 (b) 20 (c) 22 (d) 23

Section–B (2 × 4 = 8)

(Very Short Answer Type Questions)

21. 'Reserved constituencies ensures representation for marginalised communities within the democratic structure'. Justify the statement. **(2)**

22. Identify the key objective of the swadeshi movement and historical events that led to its beginning. **(2)**

23. How people harvest water in the semi-arid and arid regions of Rajasthan? **(2)**

Or Raju told his friends that his uncle is using some new water harvesting system to renew the groundwater. Name any two states where rooftop rainwater harvesting is common.

24. "The tertiary sector or service sector plays an important role in the development of primary and secondary sectors of the economy'. Justify your answer with examples. **(2)**

Section–C (3 × 5 = 15)

(Short Answer Type Questions)

25. Explain the difference between red soil and laterite soil in terms of their formation and suitability for farming. **(3)**

Or Why is it important to have a planned strategy for the development of resources in India?

26. Analyse the importance of rainwater harvesting in India. **(3)**

27. "Deposits in the banks are beneficial to both depositors as well as the nation." Examine the statement. **(3)**

28. Why did Civil War breakout in Sri Lanka? Explain the results of it. **(3)**

29. Shyam and Sunder are two friends, discussing about the benefits of different political parties gaining in India. Ravi joins the discussion and told them the challenges face by the political parties. Explain in any three challenges faced by the political parties. **(3)**

Section–D (5 × 4 = 20)

(Long Answer Type Questions)

30. Why and when was the 'Poona Pact' signed? Give five points. **(5)**

Or Discuss about the role of women in the Civil Disobedience Movement.

31. Identify how caste based politics and communalism pose a threat to Indian democracy. Give some examples. **(5)**

Or How is communalism a hindrance in the functioning of Indian democracy?

32. Shankar is a landless labourer who works in the farmland of the rich farmer in his village, while Deepak is a teacher. Describe the sectors and the conditions in which they are engaged. **(5)**

Or The workers in unorganised sector need protection on the issues of wages, safety and health. Explain.

33. Highlight the differences between primitive subsistence farming and commercial farming. Give some names of the states where primitive subsistence farming is practiced. **(5)**

Or 'Sustained uses of land without compatible techno-institutional changes have hindered the pace of agricultural development.' Analyse the statement with relevant points.

Section-E **(4 × 3 = 12)**

(Case Based Questions)

34. Read the source given below and answer the questions that follow.

What we know today as Germany, Italy and Switzerland were divided into kingdoms, Duchies and Cantons whose ruler had their autonomous territories. Eastern and Central Europe were under autocratic monarchies within the territories of which lived diverse peoples. They did not see themselves as sharing a collective identity or a common culture. Often, they even spoke different languages and belonged to different ethnic groups. The Habsburg empire that ruled over Austria-Hungary, for example, was a patchwork of many different regions and peoples.

In Hungary, half of the population spoke Magyar, while the other half spoke a variety of dialects. In Galicia, the aristocracy spoke Polish. Besides these three dominant groups, there also lived within the boundaries of the empire, a mass of subject peasant peoples-Bohemians and Slovaks to the North, Slovenes in Carniola, Croasts to the South and Roumans to the East in Transylvania.

Such differences did not easily promote a sense of political unity. The only tie binding these diverse groups together was a common allegiance to the emperor.

(i) Why were Germany, Italy and Switzerland not nation-states till the mid-18th century? (1)

(ii) Were there any nations-states in Europe till the mid-18th century? How? (1)

(iii) Describe the Habsburg empire. (2)

35. Read the source given below and answer the questions that follow. (4)

Communalism becomes more acute when religion is expressed in politics in exclusive and partisan terms, when one religion and its followers are pitted against another. This happens when beliefs of one religion are presented as superior to those of other religions, when the demands of one religious group are formed in opposition to another and when state power is used to establish domination of one religious group over the rest. This manner of using religion in politics is communal politics.

The followers of different religion have some commonalities, these are superficial and immaterial. Their interests are bound to be different and involve a conflict. In its extreme form, communalism leads to the belief that people belonging to different religions cannot live as equal citizens within one nation. Either, one of them has to dominate the rest or they have to form different nations.

This belief is fundamentally flawed. People of one religion do not have the same interests and aspirations in every context. Everyone has several other roles, positions and identities. There are many voices inside every community. All these voices have a right to be heard. Therefore, any attempt to bring all followers of one religion together in context other than religion is bound to suppress many voices within that community.

(i) When does communalism happen in our society? (1)

(ii) What will happen if the followers of different religions have some commonalities? (1)

(iii) How does communal politics suppress many voices within same community? (2)

36. Read the source given below and answer the questions that follow. (4)

In general, MNCs set up production where it is close to the markets; where there is skilled and unskilled labour available at low costs; and where the availability of other factors of production is assured. In addition, MNCs might look for government policies that look after their interests. You will read more about the policies later in the chapter. Having assured themselves of these conditions, MNCs set up factories and offices for production. The money that is spent to buy assets such as land, building, machines and other equipment is called investment. Investment made by MNCs is called foreign investment. Any investment is made with the hope that these assets will earn profits.

At times, MNCs set up production jointly with some of the local companies of these countries. The benefit to the local company of such joint production is two-fold. First, MNCs can provide money for additional investments, like buying new machines for faster production. Second, MNCs might bring with them the latest technology for production.

(i) **Why do MNCs often prefer to set up production in locations with low-cost skilled and unskilled labour? (1)**

(ii) **What are the two main benefits that a local company can gain from entering into a joint production venture with an MNC? (1)**

(iii) **The text states that "Any investment is made with the hope that these assets will earn profits." Explain how this statement applies to the concept of foreign investment by MNCs. (2)**

Section–F (2 + 3 = 5)

(Map Based Questions)

37. (a) On the outline map of India, mark and locate the following (2)

(i) The location of Indian National Congress Session of 1927.

(ii) A place where Gandhiji ceremonially violated the Salt Law and manufactured salt by boiling sea water.

(b) On the same outline map of India, identify any three of the following with suitable symbols. (3)

(i) A major port on the East coast of India.

(ii) A major sugarcane producing state.

(iii) A cotton cultivation state.

(iv) Famous coalmine in Tamil Nadu.

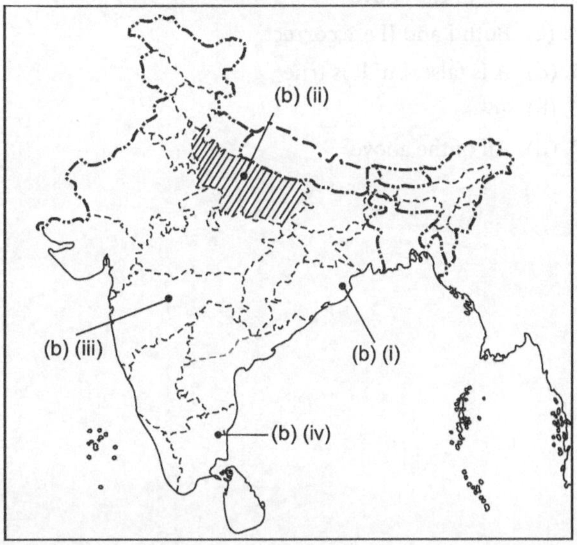

Answers

1. (d) credit crunch
2. (b) Fair globalisation
3. (a) it cannot accommodate various social life.
4. (b) Water pollution
5. (a) Sugar from sugarcane
6. (b) Cotton – In 2015, India was largest producer
7. (c) Religious background
8. (b) 2 1 4 3
9. (b) Russia
10. (a) I, II, III, IV
11. (c) I and III only
12. (a) Rainwater harvesting
13. (d) All of the above
14. (c) Both I and II are correct.
15. (d) A is false, but R is true
16. (b) 46%
17. (d) All of the above
18. (b) A direct vote by which all the people of a country are asked to accept or reject the will.
19. (a) 1 2 3 4
20. (b) 20
37.

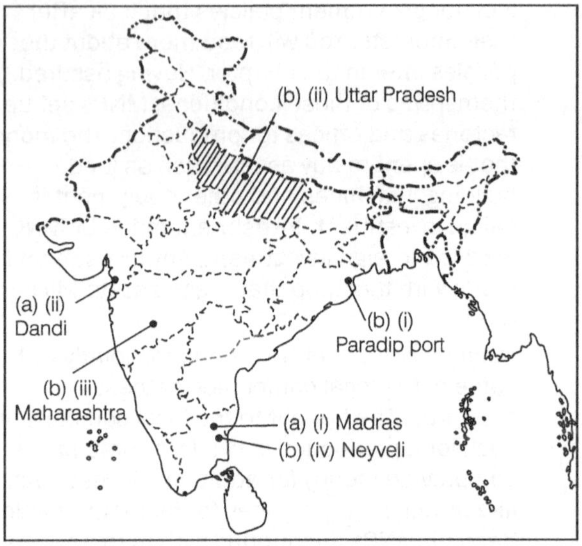

Sample Question Paper 5 (Unsolved)
Social Science

Time : 3 hrs	M.M. : 80

General Instructions

1 Question paper comprises Six Sections – A, B, C, D, E and F. There are 37 questions in the question paper. All questions are compulsory.
2 Section A – From questions 1 to 20 are MCQs of 1 mark each.
3 Section B – Question no. 21 to 24 are Very Short Answer Type Questions, carrying 2 marks each. Answer to each question should not exceed 40 words.
4 Section C – Question no. 25 to 29 are Short Answer Type Questions, carrying 3 marks each. Answer to each question should not exceed 60 words
5 Section D – Question no. 30 to 33 are long answer type questions, carrying 5 marks each. Answer to each question should not exceed 120 words.
6 Section E – Questions no. from 34 to 36 are case based questions with three sub-questions and are of 4 marks each.
7 Section F – Question no. 37 is map based, carrying 5 marks with two parts, 37a from History (2 marks) and 37b from Geography (3 marks).

Section–A $(1 \times 20 = 20)$

(Multiple Choice Questions)

1. Disguised unemployment refers to a situation in which people are **(1)**

(a) employed but getting less salary.
(b) unemployed for a temporary period.
(c) employed but are less productive.
(d) unemployed.

2. Which of the following is a regional party? **(1)**

(a) Bharatiya Janata Party (BJP)
(b) Bahujan Samaj Party (BSP)
(c) Dravida Munnetra Kazhagam (DMK)
(d) Communist Party of India (Marxist) CPI (M)

3. Consider the following statements regarding jute and select the correct options. **(1)**

I. It is one of the major fibre crops grown in India.
II. It is used in making gunny bags.
III. It is grown majorly in West Bengal, Assam, Odisha and Meghalaya.

Codes

(a) Statements I and II are appropriate
(b) Statements I, II and III are appropriate
(c) Statements II and III are appropriate
(d) Only Statement III is appropriate

4. Identify the crop with the help of given features.

- It is known as the golden fibre.
- It grows well on well-drained fertile soil in the flood plains.
- It require high temperature during the growing period.
- This fibre is very strong. **(1)**

Options

(a) Cotton (b) Wheat (c) Jute (d) Bajra

5. Which of the following comes under the 'tertiary sector' in the economy? **(1)**

(a) Agriculture and Dairy
(b) Mining
(c) Manufacturing and Industries
(d) Banking and Ed-Tech

6. Read the following data and select the appropriate option from the following. **(1)**

Land use pattern in India

Year	General land use categories 1960-61	General land use categories 2014-15
Forest	18.11%	23.3%
Barren and unculturable waste land	12.01%	5.5%
Area under non-agricultural use	4.95%	8.7%

How much percentage of forest area under general land use category increased from 1960 to 2015?

(a) 5% (b) 5.19% (c) 8.7% (d) 4.9%

7. Which countries follow the unitary system of government? **(1)**

(a) Belgium, Spain and India
(b) USA, Japan and Belgium
(c) United Arab Emirates, China and Sri Lanka
(d) France, Germany and India

8. Read the data given in the table and find out the difference in Gross National Income (GNI) per capita (2011 PPP $) between countries India and Myanmar. **(1)**

Some data regarding India and its neighbours for 2019.

Country	Gross National Income (GNI) per capita (2011 PPP $)	Life Expectancy at Birth	Mean Years of Schooling of People Aged 25+ yrs and above	HDI Rank in the World (2018)
India	6,681	69.7	6.5	130
Myanmar	4,961	67.1	5.0	148
Nepal	3,457	70.8	5.0	143

(a) 1735 (b) 1720 (c) 1580 (d) 1650

9. Which type of government does the Belgium have?

(a) Federal (b) Communist
(c) Central (d) Victory

10. What is the primary purpose of the loans provided by the Self-Help Groups (SHGs)? **(1)**

(a) To pay off personal debts of the members.
(b) To provide financial assistance to non-members.
(c) To support members in educational expenses.
(d) To generate self-employment opportunities for the members.

11. Consider the following statements about unclassed forests. **(1)**

I. Unclassed forests are mostly managed by both private communities and the government.
II. All human activities are allowed in these forests.
III. Northern-Eastern states and parts of Gujarat have mostly unclassed forests.

Which of the following statement given above are correct?

(a) I and II (b) II and III
(c) I and III (d) All of these

12. Arrange the following in chronological sequence.

I. Giuseppe Mazzini sent into exile
II. Treaty of Constantinople
III. Napolean invades Italy
IV. Unification of Germany

Codes

(a) I, II, III, IV (b) II, I, IV, III
(c) III, I, II, IV (d) III, II, IV, I

13. This cartoon drawn during the presidency of George Bush in USA suggest that **(1)**

(a) Two party system is ignored.
(b) Republican Party is the only party.
(c) Corporate American dictates all majors institutions of the country.
(d) Republican Party faces many problems.

14. Why did the Indian Government restricted foreign trade after independence? **(1)**

(a) To protect domestic producers
(b) To increase competition
(c) To know the international level of quality
(d) All of the above

15. Match List I with II and select the correct answer using the codes below in the lists **(1)**

	List I (Year)		List II (Events)
A.	1821	1.	Greek struggle for Independence began
B.	1797	2.	Napoleon Wars began
C.	1815	3.	Treaty of Vienna
D.	1804	4.	Civil Code

Codes

	A	B	C	D		A	B	C	D
(a)	1	2	3	4	(b)	4	3	2	1
(c)	1	3	2	4	(d)	4	2	1	3

16. Match List I with II and select the correct answer using the codes below in the lists

List I	List II
A. Alluvial Soil	1. Rajasthan
B. Black Soil	2. Uttar Pradesh
C. Laterite Soil	3. Odisha
D. Arid Soil	4. Maharashtra

Codes

	A	B	C	D		A	B	C	D
(a)	2	4	3	1	(b)	3	4	1	2
(c)	1	2	3	4	(d)	2	4	1	3

17. Raghav has surplus money so he opens a bank account and deposits in it. Whenever he needs money, he can go to his bank and withdraw from there. This kind of deposit with the banks are known as **(1)**

(a) demand deposit (b) term deposit
(c) fixed deposit (d) surplus deposit

18. Match List I with II and select the correct answer using the codes below in the lists

List I	List II
A. Jallianwala Bagh Massacre	1. 1930
B. Salt March	2. 1919
C. Second Round Table Conference	3. 1920
D. Non-Cooperation Movement	4. 1931

Codes

	A	B	C	D		A	B	C	D
(a)	4	1	3	2	(b)	2	1	4	3
(c)	3	2	1	4	(d)	1	2	3	4

19. Consider the following statements and choose the correct answer. **(1)**

Statement I In 1947, the boundaries of several old states of India were changed in order to create new states.

Statement II States like Jharkhand and Uttrakhand were created on the basis of culture, ethnicity or geography and not on the basis of language.

Codes

(a) Statement I is correct and II is incorrect
(b) Statement I is incorrect and II is correct
(c) Both I and II are incorrect
(d) Both I and II are correct

20. Two statements are given below. They are Assertion (A) and Reason (R). Read both the statements carefully and choose the correct option. **(1)**

Assertion (A) Following the defeat of Napoleon in 1815, European governments were driven by a spirit of conservatism.

Reason (R) Conservatives believed that the established, traditional institutions of the society should not be preserved.

Option

(a) Both A and R are true and R is the correct explanation of A
(b) Both A and R are true, but R is not the correct explanation of A
(c) A is true but R is false
(d) A is false but R is true

Section–B **(2 × 4 = 8)**

(Very Short Answer Type Questions)

21. 'Religion can never be separated from politics'. Justify the statement. **(2)**

Or Mention any two provisions of Indian Constitution which makes India a secular state.

22. Ravi's mother gave him a story book "India's Independence in 1947" on his 13th birthday. In the book, he learned about various incidents that occur in protest of British rules. There he learned that the kheda farmers also protested against the British but the reason was not mentioned.

Write an answer to explain to Ravi why did kheda farmers protested against Britishers? **(2)**

23. 'The big dams have mostly been unsuccessful in controlling floods at the time of excessive rainfall'. Justify the statement with examples. **(2)**

24. 'Average income is an important criterion for development.' Justify this statement. **(2)**

Section–C **(3 × 5 = 15)**

(Short Answer Type Questions)

25. Modern currency is accepted as a medium of exchange without any use of its own. Why? **(3)**

26. There are a number of factors which are responsible for the location of jute mills in the Hugli basin. State these factors. **(3)**

Or State any three reasons which are responsible for shifting of sugar industry from North to South India.

27. Resource planning is essential in countries like India. Analyse the statement. **(3)**

28. Suggest any three economic effects of the Non-Cooperation Movement. **(3)**

29. Raju read in the newspaper about the ethnic conflict which resulted in civil war in Sri Lanka and many people are moving out of the country. He asked his teacher what were the results of the ethnic conflict in Sri Lanka? **(3)**

Section–D (5 × 4 = 20)

(Long Answer Type Questions)

30. "Communalism should not be seen as a threat to some people in India. It threatens the very idea of India." Justify the statement with suitable arguments. **(5)**

Or

Gender division is an example that some form of social division needs to be expressed in politics. This shows that disadvantaged groups to benefit when social divisions become a political issue. Do you think that women could have made the gains, if their unequal treatment was not raised in the political domain? Analyse the statement.

31. Besides Non-Cooperation Movement, some other movements also took place in different regions of country. Describe them. **(5)**

Or

The Rowlatt Act, 1919 gave the government enormous power to repress the political activities. Elucidate.

32. Sita noticed that some people of the municipal corporation and some workers were working in an open area, outside their colony near the slum. She learned that they are planning to build a public toilet for the people living in the slum area as it is an important public facility. She asked her mother. What do you mean by public facilities? Explain two public facilities given by the government.

Or

'We have not inherited the world from our forefathers. We have borrowed it from our children'. Justify the statement with examples.

33. Salim obtains credit to meet the working capital needs of production. The credit helps him to meet the ongoing expenses of production and thereby increase his earnings.

Analyse how can access to credit contribute to the overall success and growth of a small-scale producer like Salim? Provide examples to support your answer. **(5)**

Or 'A large number of transactions in our day to day activities involve credit in some form or the other. Explain the statement by analysing the positive and negative role of the credit.

Section–E (4 × 3 = 12)

(Case Based Questions)

34. Read the source given below and answer the questions that follow. (4)

Deposits with Banks

The other form in which people hold money is as deposits with banks. At a point of time, people need only some currency for their day-to-day needs. For instance, workers who receive their salaries at the end of each month have extra cash at the beginning of the month. What do people do with this extra cash? They deposit it with the banks by opening a bank account in their name. People also have the provision to withdraw the money as and when they require. Since the deposits in the bank accounts can be withdrawn on demand, these deposits are called demand deposits.

(i) **Why do people deposit their extra cash in banks instead of keeping it at home? (1)**

(ii) **Why are demand deposits considered as money? (2)**

(iii) **How does the banks benefit from accepting individual deposits? (1)**

35. Read the source given below and answer the questions that follow. (4)

The Movement in the Towns

The movement started with middle-class participation in the cities. Thousands of students left government- controlled schools and colleges, headmasters and teachers resigned and lawyers gave up their legal practices. The council elections were boycotted in most provinces except Madras, where the Justice Party, the party of the non-Brahmans, felt-that entering the council was one way of gaining some power-something that usually only Brahmans had access to.

The effects of non-cooperation on the economic front were more dramatic. The import of foreign cloth halved between 1921 and 1922, its value dropping from ₹ 102 crore to ₹ 57 crore. In many places merchants and traders refused to trade in foreign goods or finance foreign trade.

(i) Explain the role of 'Justice Party' in boycotting of Council elections. (1)

(ii) How was the effects of 'non-cooperation on the economic front' dramatic? (1)

(iii) Explain the effect of 'Boycott' movement on 'foreign textile trade.' (2)

36. Read the source given below and answer the questions that follow.

Sustained uses of land without compatible techno-institutional changes have hindered the pace of agricultural development. Inspite of development of sources of irrigation most of the farmers in large part of the country still depend upon monsoon and natural fertility in order to carry on their agriculture. For a growing population, this poses a serious challenge. Agriculture which provides livelihood for more than 60 percent of its population, needs some serious technical and institutional reforms.

(i) Why do many farmers still rely on monsoon despite irrigation development? (1)

(ii) Discuss some steps and schemes initiated by the government of India for the benefit of farmers. (1)

(iii) What technological and institutional reforms are needed to support agriculture for a growing population? (2)

Section–F (2 + 3 = 5)

37. (a) On the given map of India, two locations are marked. Identify and label them. (2)

(i) The place where the Indian National Congress Session was held in December 1920.

(ii) The place where the Cotton Mill Workers Satyagraha was conducted.

(b) On the same outline map of India, locate any three features of the following with suitable symbols (3)

(i) A major cotton producing state

(ii) A copper mine in Madhya Pradesh.

(iii) An oilfield in Gujarat.

(iv) A nuclear power plant in Uttar Pradesh.

Answers

1. (c) Employed but are less productive.
2. (c) Dravida Munnetra Kazhagam (DMK)
3. (b) Statements I, Ì I and III are appropriate
4. (c) Jute
5. (d) Banking and Ed-Tech.
6. (b) 5.19%
7. (c) United Arab Emirates, China and Sri Lanka
8. (b) 1720
9. (a) Federal
10. (d) To generate self employment opportunities for the members.
11. (d) All of these
12. (c) III, I, II, IV
13. (c) Corporate American dictates all majors institutions of the country.
14. (a) To protect domestic producers
15. (a) 1 2 3 4
16. (a) 2 4 3 1
17. (a) demand deposit
18. (b) 2 1 4 3
19. (d) Both I and II are correct.
20. (c) A is true but R is false

37.

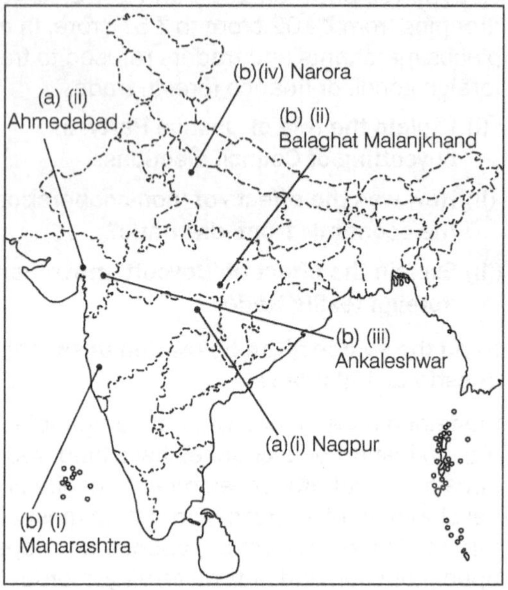

CBSE
EXAMINATION PAPER 2025

CBSE Examination Paper 2025
Social Science

Time : 3 hrs	M.M. : 80

General Instructions

1 Question paper comprises Six Sections – A, B, C, D, E and F. There are 37 questions in the question paper. All questions are compulsory.
2 Section A – From question 1 to 20 are MCQs of 1 mark each.
3 Section B – Question no. 21 to 24 are Very Short Answer Type Questions, carrying 2 marks each. Answer to each question should not exceed 40 words.
4 Section C – Question no. 25 to 29 are Short Answer Type Questions, carrying 3 marks each. Answer to each question should not exceed 60 words
5 Section D – Question no. 30 to 33 are long answer type questions, carrying 5 marks each. Answer to each question should not exceed 120 words.
6 Section E – Questions no from 34 to 36 are case based questions with three sub-questions and are of 4 marks each.
7 Section F – Question no. 37 is map based, carrying 5 marks with two parts, 37a from History (2 marks) and 37b from Geography (3 marks).

Set 1 (32/1/1)

Section – A
(Multiple Choice Questions)

1. Which one of the following regions became a part of unified Italy in 1866? (1)

(a) Sardinia-Piedmont (b) Venetia
(c) Sicily (d) Papal State

2. Read the following reasons of migration of people from Europe to America till the 19th century and choose the correct option. (1)

I. Poverty and hunger
II. Slaves for sale
III. Wide spread of diseases
IV. Religious conflicts and persecution

Options

(a) Only I, II and III are correct.
(b) Only II, III and IV are correct.
(c) Only I, III and IV are correct.
(d) Only I, II and IV are correct.

3. The author of 'Book of Marvels' is (1)

(a) Marco Polo (b) Columbus
(c) Vasco da Gama (d) Alfred Crosby

4. Assume you are doing research on 15th century print culture. Which of the following would be the most significant advantage for your research? (1)

(a) Easier access to rare manuscripts
(b) Reduced need for libraries
(c) Increase in the ability to copy text by hand
(d) Increased speed and accuracy of print

5. Arrange the following categories of forests in India from the largest to the smallest in terms of area and choose the correct option. (1)

I. Reserved II. Protected
III. Unclassed

Options

(a) III, 11, 1 (b) 1, II, III
(c) II, III, I (d) III, I, II

6. 'Sariska Tiger Reserve' is located in which one of the following states? (1)

(a) Madhya Pradesh (b) Rajasthan
(c) Uttar Pradesh (d) Maharashtra

7. Match Column I with Column II and choose the correct option (1)

Column I (Dam)	Column II (River)
A. Hirakud	1. Chambal
B. Gandhi Sagar	2. Krishna
C. Nagarjuna Sagar	3. Kaveri
D. Mettur	4. Mahanadi

Options

	A	B	C	D
(a)	4	1	3	2
(b)	1	2	4	3
(c)	4	1	2	3
(d)	1	2	3	4

8. **Choose the correct option regarding major states involved in the Krishna - Godavari issue.** (1)

(a) Karnataka, Kerala and Tamil Nadu
(b) Maharashtra, Karnataka and Andhra Pradesh
(c) Gujarat, Maharashtra and Madhya Pradesh
(d) Jharkhand, Andhra Pradesh and Odisha

9. **Imagine you are travelling from Delhi to Chandigarh to attend a wedding, by road in January. Which of the following crops will you notice prominently in the fields during the journey?** (1)

(a) Paddy (b) Maize
(c) Wheat (d) Jowar

10. **Two statements are given below. They are Assertion (A) and Reason (R). Read both the statements carefully and choose the correct option.** (1)

Assertion (A) Minerals are an indispensable part of our lives.

Reason (R) All living things need minerals.

Options

(a) Both A and R are true and R is the correct explanation of A.
(b) Both A and R are true, but R is not the correct explanation of (A).
(c) A is true, but R is false.
(d) A is false, but R is true.

11. **Match Column I with Column II and choose the correct option.** (1)

	Column I (Minerals)		Column II (Major Mines)
A.	Iron ore	1.	Gaya
B.	Mica	2.	Singarauli
C.	Bauxite	3.	Chandrapur
D.	Coal	4.	Maikala

Codes

	A	B	C	D		A	B	C	D
(a)	3	1	4	2	(b)	3	1	2	4
(c)	2	3	1	4	(d)	2	3	4	1

12. **Belgium solved its problem of majoritarianism by strengthening which of the following types of government?** (1)

(a) Unitary (b) Presidential
(c) Federal (d) Parliamentary

13. **Choose the correctly matched pair from the following.** (1)

	(Country)	(System)
(a)	Canada	Unitary
(b)	Bolivia	Federal
(c)	Australia	Unitary
(d)	Spain	Federal

14. **Which of the following are the main components of a political party?** (1)

Choose the correct option

I. Leaders II. Active members
III. Followers IV. Pressure groups

Options

(a) Only I, II and III are correct.
(b) Only II, III and IV are correct.
(c) Only I, III and IV are correct.
(d) Only I, II and IV are correct.

15. **Study the following table related to 'World Human Development Index' and answer the questions given below.** (1)

S.No.	Country	HDI Rank in the world
1.	India	130
2.	Myanmar	148
3.	Nepal	149
4.	Pakistan	150

Amongst the given countries, which one of the following countries has the highest rank in 'Human Development Index'?

(a) Pakistan (b) India (c) Nepal (d) Myanmar

16. **'X' lives in a town. He cultivates flowers along with animal husbandry. The work of 'X' will fall under which sector of the economy?** (1)

(a) Primary (b) Secondary (c) Tertiary (d) Quaternary

17. **Look at the given picture and answer the question that follow** (1)

The work being done in the picture falls under which sector of the economy?

(a) Primary (b) Quaternary (c) Secondary (d) Tertiary

18. **Why does it become difficult for farmers in rural areas to take loans from government banks ? Read the following reasons and choose the most appropriate option.** (1)

I. Lack of collateral II. Complicated procedure
III. Higher cost of borrowing IV. Lack of awareness

Options

(a) Only I, II and III are correct.
(b) Only II, III and IV are correct.
(c) Only I, II and IV are correct.
(d) Only I, III and IV are correct.

19. **Which of the following groups in urban India depend on informal sources to meet their credit needs ?** (1)

(a) Poor households
(b) Households with few assets
(c) Both poor households and households with few assets
(d) Both well-off households and households with few assets

20. **Two statements I and II are given below. Read both the statements carefully and choose the correct option.** (1)

Statement I Rapid improvement in technology has been one major factor to stimulate the globalisation process.

Statement II This has made much faster delivery of goods across long distances possible at lower costs.

Options

(a) Both statements I and II are correct and statement II is the correct explanation of statement I.
(b) Both statements I and II are correct, but statement II is not the correct explanation of statement I.
(c) Statement I is correct, but statement II is incorrect.
(d) Statement I is incorrect, but statement II is correct.

Section - B

(Very Short Answer Type Questions)

21. Explain the role of anti-colonial movement in the rise of modern nationalism in India. (2)

Or Why Gandhiji say 'Satyagraha is pure soul-force? Explain by giving two arguments.

22. Explain any two problems of the global indiscriminate use of resources. (2)

23. Suggest any two measures to remove gender inequality. (2)

24. How did the process of liberalisation initiated in India in the 1960s promote globalisation? Explain. (2)

Section - C

(Short Answer Type Questions)

25. "Tribal peasants interpreted the message of Mahatma Gandhi and the idea of 'Swaraj' in yet another way." Explain the statement in the context of Non-Cooperation Movement. (3)

26. Read the story of Rinjha and answer the question that follows (3)

Story of Rinjha

Rinjha lived with her family in a small village at the outskirts of Diphu in Assam. She enjoys watching her family members clearing, slashing and burning a patch of land for cultivation. She often helps them in irrigating the fields with water running through a bamboo canal from the nearby spring. She loves the surroundings and wants to stay here as long as she can, but this little girl has no idea about the declining of the soil and her family's search for a fresh patch of land in the next season.

What type of farming is Rinjha's family doing describe any tow of its characteristics.

27. "That democratic system of government is considered good in which maximum number of citizens are made stakeholders in political power." Explain the statement with suitable arguments. (3)

28. Explain the importance of political parties in democracy.

Or Why did India adopt the multiparty system ? Explain with suitable arguments.

29. Explain the difference between public and private sector of Indian economy with example. (3)

Section - D

(Long Answer Type Questions)

30. Analyse the significance of the 'Napoleonic Code' in making the administrative system rational and efficient. (5)

Or How was liberalism allied to national unity in Europe in the early decades of the 19th century? Analyse.

31. "Manufacturing industries are considered the backbone of the economic development of a country". Justify the statement. (5)

Or "Agriculture and industries complement each other". Justify the statement.

32. Explain any five bases for assessing the outcomes of democracy. (5)

Or Explain any five values of democracy.

33. "Recent evidence suggests that overuse of groundwater is becoming a serious threat in many parts of the country". Evaluate the statement in the context of sustainability of development. (5)

Or "The development goals of different categories of people may differ". Evaluate the statement.

Section - E

(Case Based Questions)

34. **Read the given source and answer the questions that follow.**

Print and Censorship

The power of the printed word is most often seen in the way governments seek to regulate and suppress print. The colonial government kept continuous track of all books and newspapers published in India and passed numerous laws to control the press.

During the First World War, under the Defence of India Rules 22 newspapers had to furnish securities. Of these, 18 shut down rather than comply with government orders. The Sedition Committee Report under Rowlatt in 1919 further strengthened controls that led to imposition of penalties on various newspapers. At the outbreak of the Second World War, the Defence of India Act was passed, allowing censoring of reports of war-related topics. All reports about the Quit India movement came under its purview. In August 1942, about 90 newspapers were suppressed.

(i) **Explain the meaning of 'censor'.** (1)

(ii) **Why did the colonial administration keep an eye on books and newspapers?** (1)

(iii) **Why did Gandhiji start a nationwide Satyagraha against the Rowlatt Act? Explain any two reasons.** (2)

35. Read the given source and answer the questions that follow

An Experiment in Brazil

A city called Porto Alegre in Brazil has carried out an extraordinary experiment in combining decentralisation with participative democracy. The city has set up a parallel organisation operating alongside the municipal council, enabling local inhabitants to take real decisions for their city. The nearly 13 lakh people in this city get to participate in making the budget for their own city. The city is divided into many sectors or what we call wards. Each sector has a meeting, like that of the gram sabha, in which anyone living in that area can participate. There are some meetings to discuss issues that affect the entire city. Any citizen of the city can participate in those meetings. The budget of the city is discussed in these meetings. The proposals are put to the municipality that takes a final decision about it.

(i) **Explain the meaning of 'participatory democracy'.** (1)

(ii) **In the context of separation of powers, the given example define which type of government?** (1)

(iii) **Describe the structure of the system in India which is almost similar to the above example of Brazil.** (2)

36. Read the given source and answer the questions that follow

Loans From Cooperatives

Besides banks, the other major source of cheap credit in rural areas are the cooperative societies (or cooperatives). Members of a cooperative pool their resources for cooperation in certain areas. There are several types of cooperatives possible such as farmers cooperatives, weavers cooperatives, industrial workers cooperatives, etc. Krishak Cooperative functions in a village not very far away from Sonpur. It has 2300 farmers as members. It accepts deposits from its members. With these deposits as collateral, the Cooperative has obtained a large loan from the bank. These funds are used to provide loans to members. Once these loans are repaid, another round of lending can take place. Krishak Cooperative provides loans for the purchase of agricultural implements, loans for cultivation and agricultural trade, fishery loans, loans for construction of houses and for a variety of other expenses.

(i) **Cooperative societies come under which source of credit?** (1)

(ii) **Mention any two sources of capital of cooperative societies.** (1)

(iii) **Explain the role of cooperative societies in increasing the income of farmers.** (2)

Section - F

(Map Based Questions)

37. (a) Two places 'A' and 'B' have been marked on the given political outline map of India. Identify them with the help of the following information and write their correct names on the lines drawn near them. (2)

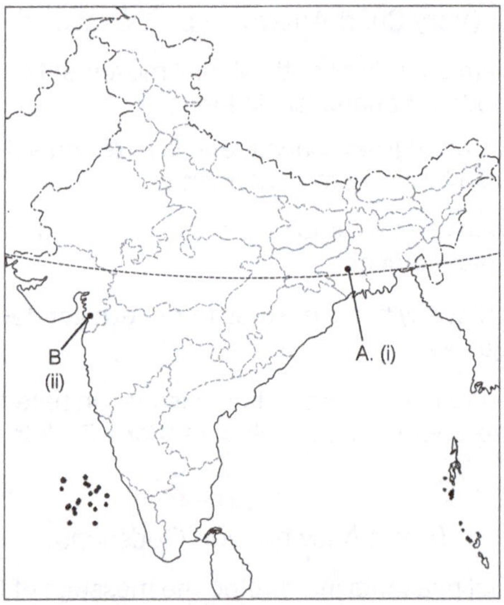

(i) The place where the session of Indian National Congress was held in 1920.

(ii) The place where Gandhiji started Dandi March.

(b) On the same political outline map of India, locate and label any three of the following with suitable symbols. (3)

(i) Leading state in production of Jute

(ii) Atomic Power Plant located in Gujarat

(iii) Iron and Steel Plant located in Jharkhand

(iv) Sri Guru Ram Das Jee International Airport

Set 2 (32/1/2)

(Uncommon Questions from Set 1)

Section – B (Very Short Answer Type Question)

22. Explain any two measures to solve the problem of land degradation. (2)

23. Suggest any two measures to increase the number of women in legislatures of India. (2)

Section – C (Short Answer Type Questions)

25. "Workers too had their own understanding of Mahatma Gandhi and the notion of Swaraj". Support the statement in context of plantation workers of Assam. (3)

27. "Power sharing is the very spirit of democracy". Support the statement by giving suitable arguments. (3)

29. Explain the difference between organised and unorganised sector of economy with example. (3)

Section – D (Long Answer Type Questions)

30. Analyse the role of Giuseppe Mazzini in the unification of Italy. (5)

Or "The 1830s were considered the beginning of great difficulties in Europe". Analyse the statement.

31. Explain the role of industries in increasing air pollution and suggest any three measures to reduce air pollution. (5)

Or Explain the role of industries in increasing water pollution and suggest any three measures to reduce water pollution.

Set 3 (32/1/3)

(Uncommon Questions from Set 1 & Set 2)

Section – B (Very Short Answer Type Questions)

22. Explain two important characteristics of Black soil.

24. How did improvement in transportation technology stimulate the globalisation process? Explain.

Section – C (Short Answer Type Questions)

25. "The ideas of nationalism developed, through a movement to revive Indian folklore". Explain the statement in the context of the national movement.

27. "Political power cannot be divided". Analyse suitable arguments against the statement.

29. Evaluate the contribution of the tertiary sector in Gross Domestic Product (GDP) in India.

Section – D (Long Answer Type Questions)

30. "Culture played an important role in creating the idea of the nation in 19th century Europe". Evaluate the statement in the context of romanticism.

Or "The most serious source of nationalist tension in Europe after 1871 was the area called the Balkans." Evaluate the statement in context of Slavic Movement.

32. "One distinct feature of democracy is that its scrutiny never ends". Explain the statement with appropriate arguments.

Or "Democratic system is better than other systems". Explain the statement with appropriate arguments.

ANSWERS

1. (b) Venetia
2. (c) only I, III and IV are correct
3. (a) Marco polo
4. (d) increased speed and accuracy of print
5. (a) III, II, I
6. (b) Rajasthan
7. (c) a-iv, b-i, c-ii, d-iii
8. (b) Maharashtra, Karnataka and Andhra Pradesh
9. (c) Wheat
10. (a) both A and R are true and R is the correct explanation of A
11. (a)
12. (c) Federal
13. (d) Spain-Federal
14. (a) Only I, II and III are correct
15. (b) India
16. (a) Primary
17. (c) Secondary
18. (c) Only I, II and IV are correct
19. (c) Both poor households and households with few assets
20. (a) Both statements I and II are correct and statement II is the correct explanation of statement I.
21. The growth of nationalism in the colonies is closely linked to the anti-colonial movement because in places like India, people united in their struggle against colonial rule. The shared experience of being oppressed by colonial

powers created a sense of unity across different groups. However, each group experienced colonialism in different ways and had different ideas of freedom. Leaders like Mahatma Gandhi and the Congress worked to bring these groups together in a single movement, but this unity was not achieved easily and involved conflicts.

Or For answer, refer to History ch-2, page no. 53, Q.2(i) (Or).

22. For answer, refer to Geography ch-1, page no. 137, Q.7 (Or).

23. For answer, refer to Polity ch-3, page no.310, Q.4 of Very Short Answer Type Questions.

24. For answer, refer to Economy ch-4, page no.429, Q.12 of Very Short Answer Type Questions.

25. The tribal peasants interpreted the message of Mahatma Gandhi and the idea of Swaraj in different manner and participated in the Non-Cooperation Movement differently. For example, in the Gudem Hills of Andhra Pradesh, a militant guerrilla movement spread in the early 1920s. It is not a form of struggle that the Congress could approve. They were against the colonial rule and policies because it affected their livelihood as well as their traditional rights were also denied.

The leader of the guerilla movement, Alluri Sitaram Raju talked about the greatness of Mahatma Gandhi and said he was inspired by the Non-Cooperation Movement and Swaraj. He persuaded people to wear khadi and give up drinking. But at the same time, he asserted that India could be liberated only by the use of force, not non-violence. The Gudem rebels attacked police stations, attempted to kill British officials and carried on guerrilla warfare for achieving Swaraj.

26. Rinjha's family is performing shifting cultivation. Two of its characteristics are

- **Temporary Cultivation of Land** In shifting cultivation, a piece of land is cleared, cultivated for a few years, and then abandoned once the soil fertility decreases. The land is left to regenerate naturally through fallow periods before it is used again.
- **Use of Traditional Farming Techniques** The farming techniques in shifting cultivation often involve simple tools and methods. The focus is on subsistence farming, and the system relies on the natural regeneration of the land.

27. Suitable arguments for the above statement are as follows

- **Ensures Representation** When more citizens are stakeholders, diverse interests are represented, making policies more inclusive and reflective of society's needs.
- **Promoting Accountability** Shared political power ensures that leaders are accountable to the people, reducing corruption and abuse of power.
- **Increased Legitimacy** Broad participation in decision-making boosts the legitimacy of the government, making it more accepted and fair to the public.

28. For answer, refer to Polity ch-4, page no.334, Q.7 of Long Answer Type Questions.

Or India adopted multi-party system for the following reasons

- India being a vast and diverse country, the multi-party system was needed to accommodate the vast population.
- The social and geographical diversity of India could not be represented by two or three parties.
- The multi-party system in India evolved over a long time, depending on the nature of society, its social, regional division, its history of politics and its system of elections.
- Multi-party system ensures a healthy competition between different parties and prevents dictatorship of a single party. Indian Constitution declares India as a democratic country. Multi-party system fulfils this criteria and provides chance for proper growth of the nation.

29. For answer, refer to Economy ch-2, page no.384, Q.18 (Or).

30. The 'Napoleonic code' made the administrative system rational and efficient in the following ways

- **Abolition of Privileges** The Napoleonic Code abolished privileges based on birth, ensuring equality before the law for all citizens.
- **Property Rights** It secured property rights, fostering a stable economic environment and encouraging trade and investment.
- **Simplification of Administrative Divisions** Napoleon simplified administrative structures, reducing complexity and strengthening central authority across regions.
- **Abolition of Feudalism** He abolished feudal systems, freeing peasants from serfdom and manorial dues, promoting social and economic mobility.
- **Standardisation of Laws and Economy** Introduced uniform laws, standardized weights and measures, and a common national currency, facilitating trade and economic integration.
- **Improvements in Transportation and Communication** Enhanced transportation systems and postal services, improving efficiency in governance and commerce.

Or The ideas of national unity in early nineteenth century Europe allied to the ideology of liberalism in the following ways

- For the liberal middle classes, the ideas of national unity means the abolition of aristocratic privileges.

Liberalism stood for freedom for the individual and equality of all before the law.

- Liberalism emphasised the concept of government. It urged for a Constitution and representative government through Parliament. National unity can be maintained by the proper governance of the Parliament.
- In the economic sphere, liberalism is in favour of the freedom of markets and the abolition of state-imposed restrictions on the movement of goods and capital. During the nineteenth century, this was a strong demand of the middle class which was in favour of national unity.

31. Manufacturing sector is considered as the backbone of economic development of a country because

- Manufacturing industries help in modernising agriculture which forms an important part of our economy.
- Manufacturing also reduces the heavy dependence of people on agricultural income by providing them jobs in secondary and tertiary sectors.
- Industrial development helps in removal of unemployment and poverty as it creates jobs and more income. It also aims at reducing regional differences by establishing industries in tribal and backward areas.
- Export of manufactured goods increases trade and commerce, and brings foreign exchange.
- Countries that transform their raw material into a wide variety of value finished goods of higher value, are prosperous. Thus, India's prosperity lies in increasing and diversifying its manufacturing industries.

Or For answer, refer to Geography ch-6, page no.231, of Q.3 Short Answer Type Questions.

32. Assessing democracy's outcomes involves evaluating whether it fulfills the expectations associated with democratic governance. This assessment can be done through following criteria

- **Promotion of Equality** Evaluate the extent to which democracy promotes equality among citizens, both in terms of political rights and socio-economic opportunities. This involves examining indicators such as income distribution, social mobility and access to education and healthcare.
- **Enhancement of Individual Dignity** Assess whether democracy upholds the dignity of individuals by safeguarding their fundamental rights and freedoms. This includes evaluating the protection of civil liberties, freedom of expression and the rule of law.
- **Quality of Decision-making** Evaluate the effectiveness and transparency of decision-making processes within democratic institutions. This involves assessing the extent to which decisions are made through open debate, public participation and adherence to democratic norms and principles.
- **Conflict Resolution** Examine democracy's ability to peacefully resolve conflicts and manage societal tensions through democratic means, such as dialogue, negotiation and compromise.
- **Capacity for Course Correction** Assess whether democracy provides mechanisms for accountability and responsiveness to address mistakes and address societal challenges.

Or The five values of democracy are as follows

- **Equality** Democracy ensures that all citizens, regardless of their caste, creed, religion, or gender, are treated equally before the law. This value of equality is fundamental in ensuring that no one is discriminated against and everyone has the same rights and opportunities in society.
- **Freedom** In a democracy, individuals are granted freedom of expression, speech, assembly, and association. Citizens have the right to express their opinions, form associations, and participate freely in political processes, without fear of oppression.
- **Justice** A democratic system strives to provide justice to all its citizens by ensuring that laws are applied fairly, and individuals have access to justice through courts and legal mechanisms. It promotes both social and economic justice by addressing inequalities and upholding human rights.
- **Dignity of the Individual** Democracy emphasises the dignity of every individual. It protects the rights and freedoms of individuals, ensuring that their personal dignity and autonomy are respected by others and the state. This includes the right to live without fear or discrimination.
- **Majority Rule with Minority Rights** While democracy is based on the rule of the majority, it also protects the rights of minorities. It ensures that the majority's decisions do not infringe on the basic rights of minority groups, thus maintaining a balance between the will of the majority and the protection of minority interests.

33. The overuse of groundwater, as mentioned above, can pose a serious threat to long-term sustainability. The evaluation of the statement is as follows

- **Groundwater as a Renewable Resource** Groundwater is considered a renewable resource because it is replenished naturally through rainfall and infiltration into the ground. However, like other renewable resources, it can still be overused if consumption exceeds its natural rate of replenishment.
- **Overuse and Its Impact** The overuse of groundwater, especially in agriculturally rich regions like Punjab and Western Uttar Pradesh, can lead to severe depletion of water reserves. This depletion not only affects water availability for future generations but also results in land degradation, reduced agricultural productivity, and the loss of biodiversity.

- **Long-term Sustainability Concerns** Unsustainable water extraction leads to the salinisation of groundwater, lowering of water tables, and reduced access to clean water, which are all major barriers to sustainable development.

Or For answer, refer to Economy ch-1, page no.369, Q.2 (Or) Long Answer Type Questions.

34. (i) Censor means to remove the parts of a book, film, etc. that might offend people or that are considered politically dangerous.

(ii) The colonial administration closely monitored books and newspapers in India because they recognised the power of the press to spread nationalist ideas and mobilise resistance against British rule.

(iii) Gandhiji started a nationwide satyagraha against the Rowlatt Act because of the following reasons

- **Unjust Nature of the Act** The Act gave the British government oppressive powers, allowing detention without trial for up to two years, which Gandhi viewed as a violation of civil rights.
- **Non-Violent Resistance** Gandhi advocated for non-violent civil disobedience and called for a nationwide hartal on 6th April, 1919, to peacefully protest the Act and unite Indians against British rule.

35. (i) Participatory democracy refers to a system in which citizens actively participate in decision-making processes, particularly in matters that directly affect them.

(ii) In the context of separation of powers, the given example of Porto Alegre in Brazil represents a participative democracy combined with a decentralised government.

(iii) In India, a system that is most similar to the example of Porto Alegre in Brazil is the structure of local self-government, specifically through Panchayats and Urban Local Bodies (ULBs). The Panchayati Raj system and municipalities in India provide a decentralised governance structure where local residents can actively participate in decision-making processes, similar to Porto Alegre's participatory democracy model.

36. (i) Cooperative societies come under the category of informal sources of credit.

(ii) Two sources of capital for cooperative societies are member deposits and bank loans.

(iii) Cooperative societies help in increasing farmers' income by

- **Providing Affordable Loans** They offer low-interest loans for purchasing agricultural tools, cultivation, and trade, boosting productivity.
- **Access to Resources** Farmers can pool resources to access funds they may not get individually, improving their economic situation.

37. (a) (i) 1920-Calcutta, Nagpur

(ii) (ii) Dandi (Gujarat)

(b)

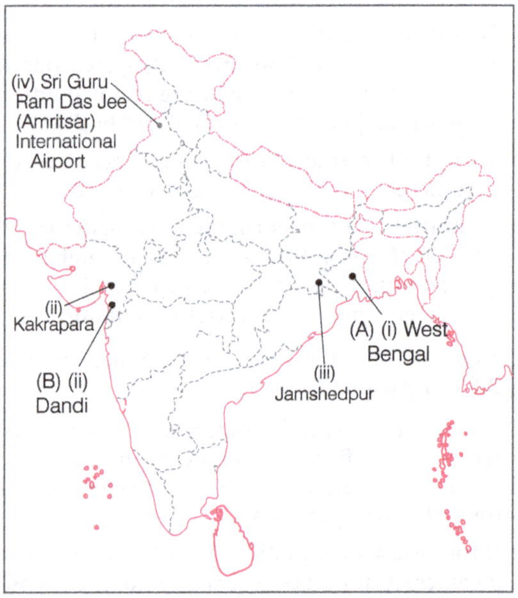

Set 2

22. For answer, refer to Geography ch-1, page no.137, Q.8 of Short Answer Type Questions.

23. Two measures to increase the number of women in legislatures in India are as follows

(i) **Reservation of Seats** Reserve 33% of seats in the Lok Sabha and State Assemblies for women, ensuring greater political representation.

(ii) **Encourage Political Participation** Provide training, support, and opportunities for women to participate in politics and take leadership roles.

25. The plantation workers in Assam understood Swaraj as the freedom to move freely and return to their villages, which was restricted under the Inland Emigration Act of 1859. When they heard about the Non-Cooperation Movement, they believed Gandhi Raj would grant them land and the right to go home. However, they were stopped by a strike, caught by the police, and beaten. Their idea of Swaraj focused on freedom of movement and dignity in their communities.

27. Power sharing is the very spirit of democracy because of the following reasons

- **Ensures Representation of All** In a democracy, power sharing allows diverse groups, such as different regions, communities, or social groups, to have a voice in governance. This prevents any one group from dominating and ensures that decisions are made in the best interest of all.
- **Promotes Inclusivity and Fairness** When power is shared, it ensures that all citizens, regardless of their background or status, are included in the decision-making process. This leads to more equitable and just policies that cater to the needs of various segments of society.
- **Strengthens Legitimacy** A legitimate government is one where citizens are actively involved in decisions that affect their lives. Power sharing through participation makes people feel that they have a stake in the system, which strengthens the government's authority and legitimacy.

29. Differences between organised and unorganised sector are as follows

Basis	Organised Sector	Unorganised Sector
Job security	In organised sector workers have job security.	In unorganised sector workers do not have any job security. There jobs can be terminated anytime.
Rules and regulations	The organised sector follows all the rules and regulations and they are registered.	Unorganised sector do not follow any rules and regulations as they are not registered.
Wages	Workers in organised sector are paid regularly.	Workers in unorganised sector are not paid regularly.
Other benefits	Organised sector pays other benefits like medical leaves, provident funds, paid leaves apart from wages.	Unorganised sector do not pay anything other than salary.
Number of hours	There are fixed number of hours in organised sector.	In unorganised sector the number of hours increases or decreases as per the work.

30. For answer, refer to History ch-1, page no.24, Q.6 of Long Answer Type Questions.

Or The 1830s were considered the beginning of great difficulties in Europe due to the following reasons

- **Economic Hardship** The 1830s saw significant economic struggles across Europe. A sharp increase in population led to a surplus of job seekers, causing high unemployment rates. Many rural people migrated to cities, resulting in overcrowded slums and poor living conditions.
- **Competition and Industrialisation** Small producers, especially in towns, faced intense competition from cheap, machine-made goods imported from industrialised England. The textile industry, which was still largely manual or semi-mechanised in Europe, was hit particularly hard by this competition.
- **Feudal Burdens** In regions where the aristocracy retained power, peasants continued to suffer under feudal dues and obligations. They faced financial difficulties due to high taxes and lack of land reforms, exacerbating their economic struggles.
- **Agricultural Crisis** A rise in food prices or bad harvests in the 1830s led to widespread poverty, both in towns and rural areas. Many people were pushed into pauperism, unable to afford basic necessities.

31. Role of industries in increasing air pollution is as follows

- **Emissions from Factories** Industrial activities release a significant amount of harmful gases such as sulfur dioxide (SO_2), nitrogen oxides (NO_2), carbon monoxide (CO), and particulate matter into the air. These emissions contribute to smog, acid rain, and poor air quality.
- **Burning of Fossil Fuels** Industries that rely on the burning of fossil fuels, such as coal, oil, and natural gas, release large quantities of carbon dioxide (CO_2), a major greenhouse gas, into the atmosphere, contributing to global warming and climate change.
- **Chemical and Smoke Emissions** Certain industries, like chemical plants and cement factories, emit volatile organic compounds (VOCs) and smoke, which pollute the air, negatively impacting both human health and the environment.

Measures to reduce air pollution are as follows

- **Adopting Cleaner Technologies** Industries should switch to cleaner, greener technologies that produce fewer emissions, such as using renewable energy sources or adopting cleaner industrial processes.
- **Strict Emission Standards** Governments should enforce strict emission standards for industries and ensure regular monitoring to limit the amount of harmful gases and particulate matter released into the atmosphere.
- **Promoting Use of Filters and Scrubbers** Industries should install air filters and scrubbers to capture harmful pollutants before they are released into the air, reducing industrial air pollution.

Or Role of industries in increasing water pollution is as follows

- **Discharge of Industrial Waste** Industries often discharge untreated or inadequately treated waste into rivers, lakes, or other water bodies. This waste may contain harmful chemicals, heavy metals, and toxic substances, which pollute water and make it unsafe for both humans and aquatic life.

- **Chemical Contamination** Many industries, such as chemical factories, textile mills, and paper mills, use harmful chemicals in their processes. These chemicals are sometimes released directly into water sources, causing chemical contamination. This leads to changes in the water's pH levels and disrupts the aquatic ecosystem.
- **Effluents and Sewage** In addition to industrial waste, the sewage generated from industrial activities also contributes significantly to water pollution. Large quantities of effluents and untreated sewage often make their way into nearby rivers, polluting the water and harming the environment.

Measures to reduce water pollution are as follows

- **Treatment of Industrial Wastewater** Industries should install proper wastewater treatment plants to treat and filter out harmful chemicals and contaminants before discharging water into natural water bodies. This will help in reducing the harmful effects of industrial waste on water quality.
- **Strict Regulations and Enforcement** Governments should enforce stricter regulations to ensure industries follow proper disposal guidelines for waste. Pollution control boards should monitor industrial discharge and impose penalties on violators to discourage negligent practices.
- **Promotion of Eco-friendly Technologies** Encouraging the use of green technologies and cleaner production methods can help reduce the generation of harmful waste. Industries can switch to non-toxic raw materials and adopt sustainable practices to minimize environmental harm.

Set 3

22. Two important characteristics of black soil are as follows

(i) It is made up of fine clayey material with a high moisture retention capacity.

(ii) It is rich in soil nutrients like calcium carbonate, magnesium carbonate, potash and lime, but poor in phosphoric content.

(iii) It develops deep crack during hot weather which helping in proper aeration of the soil.

24. Rapid improvement in technology has been playing a key role in encouraging the globalisation process in the following ways

- Improvements in transportation technology, e.g. container manufacturing and air transport has made faster delivery of goods across long distances at lower costs.
- There have been rapid developments in information technology, e.g. computer, internet, etc. They have made easy access to information around the world thus stimulating globalisation.
- Rapid development in means of communication are used to contact one another which have established trade links around the world.

25. There were a variety of cultural processes through which nationalism spread in people. History and fiction, folklore and songs, popular prints and symbols played a significant role in making of nationalism in the following ways

- Nationalist historians urged the readers to take pride in India's great achievements in the past and inspired them to struggle to change their miserable condition under British rule. Novels like 'Anandamath' written by Bankim Chandra Chattopadhayay inspired the revolutionaries in our country.
- Ideas of nationalism also developed through a movement to revive Indian folklore. In late 19th century, Indian, nationalists, like Rabindranath Tagore and Natesa Sastri collected folk tales, folk songs, ballads, nursery rhymes, myths.
- They wanted to give a true picture of traditional culture that had damaged by colonisers. Because folklore was the most trust worthy manifestation of people's real thoughts and characteristics.
- In the 20th century, with the growth of nationalism, the identity of India came to be visually associated with the image of Bharat Mata.
- Abanindranath Tagore and many more artists painted Bharat Mata and the devotion to this mother figure came to be seen as evidence of one's nationalism. Further, Gandhiji designed the Swaraj flag (red, green, white). Carrying this flag, holding it aloft during marches became a symbol of defiance.

27. The argument against the statement 'Political power cannot be divided' is based on the principles of democracy and governance. In democratic systems, power is often divided among different branches of government to prevent any single entity from becoming too powerful. This division is essential for maintaining checks and balances, ensuring that power is exercised responsibly and that citizens' rights are protected. Furthermore, the separation of powers allows for a more equitable distribution of authority, fostering accountability and transparency in governance.

29. Contribution of the Tertiary Sector to GDP in India is discussed below

- **Largest Contributor** The tertiary sector (also known as the service sector) is the largest contributor to India's GDP. It includes industries such as transportation, communication, banking, education, health services, tourism and information technology (IT).

- **Growth in Services** Over the years, the service sector in India has grown rapidly. It has become the dominant sector, contributing more than 50% of the total GDP, reflecting a shift from an agrarian-based economy to a service-oriented one.
- **Employment Generation** The tertiary sector also provides significant employment opportunities, particularly in sectors like IT, tourism, retail, and financial services. This has helped reduce unemployment and underemployment in the country.

30. The nationalism developed through culture in Europe in the following ways

- Art, poetry, stories and music helped express and shape nationalist feelings in Europe.
- Romanticism, a cultural movement in Europe developed a particular form of nationalist sentiment. Romantic artists and poets criticised the glorification of science and reason. They tried to create a sense of a shared collective heritage as the basis of a nation. They gave importance on emotions, intuitions and mystical feelings.
- German philosopher Johann Gottfried Herder claimed that true German culture was to be discovered among the common people (*das volk*) in their folk song, folk poetry and folk dances.
- Vernacular languages and folklores strengthen the national spirit.
- In Poland, Karol Kurpinski celebrated the national struggle through opera and music.
- Allegory of Germania and Marianne developed national feelings among citizens.

Or The most serious source of nationalist tention in Europe after 1871 in Europe were

- The Balkans was a region of geographical and ethnic variation comprising modern-day Romania, Bulgaria, Albania, Greece, Macedonia, Croatia, Bosnia-Herzegovina, Slovenia, Serbia and Montenegro whose inhabitants were broadly known as the Slavs.
- A large part of the Balkans was under the control of the Ottoman Empire. The spread of the ideas of romantic nationalism in the Balkans together with the disintegration of the Ottoman Empire made this region very explosive.
- All through the nineteenth century the Ottoman Empire had sought to strengthen itself through modernisation and internal reforms but with very little success. One by one, its European subject nationalities broke away from its control and declared independence.
- The Balkans people based their claims for independence or political rights on nationality and used history to prove that they had once been independent but had subsequently been subjugated by foreign powers. Hence, the rebellious nationalities in the Balkans thought of their struggles as attempts to win back their long-lost independence.

32. In a democracy, scrutiny of the government and its policies never stops. The explanation of the above statements with arguments is as follows

- **Elections and Public Participation** In a democracy, elections are held regularly, providing citizens with the opportunity to assess the performance of their representatives and hold them accountable. People have the power to vote for new representatives if the current ones fail to meet expectations. This cycle of periodic elections ensures that scrutiny of the government is continuous.
- **Freedom of Expression** Democracy allows citizens, media, and civil society to freely express their opinions, criticize policies, and raise issues. This creates an environment where the government's actions are always under public scrutiny. Criticism and debates ensure that decisions are not made in isolation but are subjected to public discussion and reflection.
- **Role of Institutions** In a democracy, there are independent institutions like the judiciary, media, and election commissions that continuously scrutinise government actions. For example, the judiciary can review laws, while the media plays a key role in highlighting issues of public concern, ensuring the government remains answerable.
- **Civil Rights and Activism** Civil society organisations and activists play a crucial role in monitoring government policies and advocating for the rights of citizens. The presence of a vigilant public ensures that governments cannot take unchecked actions, as they are always being observed and evaluated.

Or Democracy is a better form of government when compared with any other form of government because of the following reasons

- Democracy promotes equality among citizens. Every citizen of the country has equal rights before the law. All individuals have equal rights in electing their representatives.
- Democracy enhances the dignity of the individual. By giving its citizens equal rights, it enhances dignity and freedom of the individual. Democracy gives equal treatment and respect to women, disadvantaged and discriminated castes in our society.
- Democracy improves the quality of decision-making. As there is open debate in major issues in democracy thus, quality of decisions is improved.
- Democracy provides a method to resolve conflicts. Democracy reduces the possibility of social tension which leads to peaceful social life. It allows room to correct mistakes.
- Democracy is a legitimate government. Democracy gets the popular support of the people by regular, free and fair elections.